Praise for
GUN AND SWORD

"Chris D. has done it again. This dense reference guide is a valuable source of information for Japanese film novices as well as savvy genre fans eager to learn more about the fascinating word of Japanese crime cinema."

– **Kimberly Lindbergs**, writer at CINEBEATS.COM
and MOVIE MORLOCKS at TCM.COM

"An epic achievement! Chris D. is the Japanese film obsessive nonpareil as this massive tome attests. GUN AND SWORD is simply the last word in yakuza film reference."

– **Patrick Galloway**, author of WARRING CLANS, FLASHING BLADES:
A SAMURAI FILM COMPANION
and STRAY DOGS & LONE WOLVES:
THE SAMURAI FILM HANDBOOK

"Chris D's exhaustive research and dry wit gives us the sense of a dark city detective leading us through the dangerous terrain of an exotic mystery...packed with rare stills and essential, new information on the genre...it is an awesome tome in the true sense of the word."

– **Kier-La Janisse**, author of HOUSE OF PSYCHOTIC WOMEN
and A VIOLENT PROFESSIONAL: THE FILMS OF LUCIANO ROSSI

Praise for Chris D.'s
OUTLAW MASTERS OF JAPANESE FILM

"Legends have a basis in both a perceived 'virtual' reality and in a 'true life' reality. Chris D.'s book shows both sides, which is essential in understanding how filmmaking legends are born."

– **Takashi Miike** director of AUDITION, DEAD OR ALIVE,
ICHI THE KILLER and 13 ASSASSINS

"...a must for anyone who has ever wanted to explore the fringes of Japanese film and beyond."

– **Patrick Macias**, author of TOKYOSCOPE:
THE JAPANESE CULT FILM COMPANION

"Highly recommended for anyone with an interest in Japanese cinema."

– **Stuart Galbraith IV**, author of
THE EMPEROR AND THE WOLF:
THE LIVES OF AKIRA KUROSAWA AND TOSHIRO MIFUNE

GUN
AND
SWORD

An Encyclopedia
of
Japanese Gangster
Films

1955-1980

ALSO BY CHRIS D.

Double Snake Bourbon
Outlaw Masters of Japanese Film
A Minute to Pray, A Second to Die
No Evil Star
Dragon Wheel Splendor and Other Love Stories of Violence and Dread
Shallow Water
Mother's Worry

GUN
AND
SWORD

An Encyclopedia
of
Japanese Gangster
Films

1955-1980

by

CHRIS D.

A POISON FANG BOOK

If you enjoy this book, tell someone about it.

A very small fraction of the individual film write-ups originally appeared in much different, rougher form in the publications Cult Movies Magazine *and* Asian Cult Cinema *(then known as* Asian Trash Cinema*) in the early 1990s. The one-page introductions to the six studios sections originally appeared in slightly different form as part of an appendix in my book* Outlaw Masters of Japanese Film.

Copyright of illustrations reproduced in these pages is the property of the production or distribution companies concerned. These illustrations are reproduced here in the spirit of publicity, and while every effort has been made to trace the copyright owners, the author and publishers apologize for any omissions and will undertake to make any appropriate changes in future editions of this book if necessary.

**Publication of this book was aided by a grant from
The Japan Foundation.**

A Poison Fang Book

Front and back cover designs by C. D.

ISBN: 978-0615798806

First Poison Fang Edition May 2013

Printed in the United States

10 9 8 7 6 5 4 3 2 1

FOR
YOSHIKI HAYASHI,
ISAO TSUJIMOTO
AND
DENNIS BARTOK,
WITH GRATITUDE

Acknlowledgements

There are a couple of people I must thank right from the top, two persons without whom this book would probably not exist – at least in the form you now see before you: **Isao Tsujimoto**, who was head of the Los Angeles office of The Japan Foundation in the mid-1990s to the early 2000s, who enthusiastically encouraged me to not become frustrated, and who suggested I apply for a research grant to the Foundation; and **Yoshiki Hayashi**, a Japanese journalist, editor and film buff who became a pen pal after he had read an article on samurai cinema I had written for the now defunct *Cult Movies* magazine. His help was invaluable, for a number of years supplying me with impossible-to-see-on-VHS-or-DVD yakuza movies recorded off of Japanese cable and satellite television, sans subtitles, movies from all eras and subgenres. He was also an invaluable guide to poster and book shops, cinemas, lodgings, etc., as well as the prime instigator of my interviews with directors Kazuo Ikehiro and Teruo Ishii, when I spent my two months grant stay in Tokyo in the autumn of 1997. I owe them big time.

I also must thank **Dr. Akiko Agishi** and the late director **Kinji Fukasaku** for their enormous help in setting up 80% of the interviews I did while I was in Tokyo (including Shinichi "Sonny" Chiba, Meiko Kaji and directors Eiichi Kudo and Junya Sato.)

I am grateful, as well, to **Toshiko Adilman** (who was a long-time friend of Mr. Fukasaku and acted as his translator/interpreter on many occasions) and her late husband **Sid Adilman**. Toshiko and Sid provided the gentle prodding to Kinji to remember to write the foreword for this book, an amazing feat of patience and kindness as Kinji was then entering the last six months of his life and had many more important things on his mind, including trying to complete the sequel to *Battle Royale* with the help of his son, Kenta, before cancer could snuff out the lights. Sid, especially, was instrumental in making this foreword happen.

Also huge thanks to **Dennis Bartok** who I had met in the early-1990s when he was starting work as head programmer at The American Cinematheque in Los Angeles. His confidence and trust in my judgment led to many happy collaborations co-programming various film series in the mid-to-late 1990s, including the original *Outlaw Masters of Japanese Film* screenings. Dennis was the one to introduce me to Isao Tsujimoto and also, with the approval of **Barbara Smith** (more thanks) brought me on board as part of the Cinematheque staff in 1999. He also made my initial interviews/Q&As with directors Kinji Fukasaku, Takashi Miike, Kiyoshi Kurosawa and Kihachi Okamoto possible when they traveled to Los Angeles. Thanks to **Mark Rance** of Film Forum, who set up my interview with director Seijun Suzuki and also thanks to **Christian Storms** who set up and acted as my proxy in interviews with directors Koji Wakamatsu and Yasuharu Hasebe; thanks to **David Shultz** for having me write all those DVD liner notes as well as setting up the interview with director Masahiro Shinoda. A Special Thanks to **Donna Lethal**, for her support, her perverse, anarchic sense of humor, her love and friendship.

More thanks to: Ai Aota, Shoko Ishiyama, Kurando Mitsutake; Naoko Watanabe, Rie Takauchi & Masako Miwa of the Japan Foundation; Kazuo Nawada; Toshinobe Mogami; Yoshihiro Ishimatsu; **Stuart Galbraith IV**; **Quentin Tarantino; Jules McLean; Jerry Martinez;** Andres Chavez ; Takashi Miike; Akiko Funatsu; Hiromi Aihara; Kenta Fukasaku; Linda Hoaglund; **Marc Walkow;** Kyoko Hirano; **Harvey Fenton**; Mitch Davis; Eiichi Ito; Daniel Savitt; Patrick Macias; Carl Morano; Mona Nagai; **Merlin David;** Anthony and Matthew Timpson; Lydia Lunch; Gene Gregorits; RJ Gallentine; Sarah Finklea & Susan Arosteguy at Janus Films/Criterion Collection; Animeigo; Michael Copner and Buddy Barnett of Cult Movies Magazine; Thomas Weisser; Mark Schilling; Satoko Ishida & Masaki Koga of Shochiku; Yasue Nobusawa of Nikkatsu; Takayuki Yuhara & Tomoko Suzuki of Kadokawa-Daiei; Masaharu Ina of Toho; Hideyuki Baba & Yasuhiko Nakajima of Toei; **my family, including my brother, Vincent and sister, Mary, and my late mother and father, Rosemary and Paul;** Philippa Brewster and Sheila Whitaker of IB Tauris; Shepherd Stevenson, Byron Coley, Eddie Muller; Alan K. Rode; Kier-La Janisse; Patrick Galloway; Peter Maravelis of City Lights; Liz Garo, Claudia Colodro and Alex Maslansky of Stories Books, Dan Kusunoki of Skylight Books; Tosh Berman of TamTam Books (formerly of Book Soup); Billy Shire of La Luz de Jesus Gallery/Wacko; **Diane Baker, Denah Johnston and Jesse Hawthorne Ficks** of AAU; and Eve Golden.

TABLE OF CONTENTS

PREFACE

I originally started working on this book in late 1989, and the material has changed, grown, mutated, been added to, chopped-up, mutilated (in a gentle, constructive way) and otherwise transformed into the monstrous behemoth you now hold. There are times when I never thought it would ever see the light of day, for a variety of reasons.

Initially, I received interest from Rolling Thunder books, one of the mid-1990s divisions of Quentin Tarantino's still-expanding empire. One of his then-main colleagues behind the scenes, Jerry Martinez (a co-worker from that fabled Torrance video store where Quentin worked before his filmmaking career), was in charge of the publishing arm and, with Andres Chavez, had authored and laid out the excellent book on blaxploitation movies, *What It Is, What It Was*. Along with the help of Jerry, Andres and Jules McLean, I worked on getting the book ready to be a future release for their company. It should be noted that Jerry came up with the splendid idea of dividing up the film listings in this book by studio, something that had not occurred to me, but was certainly necessary to help make the book more reader-friendly. Jerry also just as importantly came up with the book title *Gun and Sword*.

In the meantime, I received a Japan Foundation grant to develop the book. I headed for Japan to live for approximately two months (from the end of September 1997 until the end of November 1997), collecting all manner of illustrations and research materials, and conducting interviews with various film-makers and two performers (interviews largely made possible by director Kinji Fukasaku, Dr. Akiko Agishi and Yoshiki Hayashi).

Not too far into 1998, if I remember correctly, Quentin and company decided not to do any more books. Quentin's main big time partner, Miramax, was sold off by owners, the Weinstein brothers, to Disney, and everyone moved out of the Miramax building on Beverly Boulevard, including not just Miramax, but also Quentin's Bande Apart, Rolling Thunder, et al.

I began working at the American Cinematheque, headquartered at the Egyptian Theatre in Hollywood, as a film traffic coordinator and assistant programmer in January 1999. Shortly after, I began writing DVD liner notes on the side, at first for a smattering of vintage Japanese genre pictures (such as FEMALE CONVICT SCORPION-JAILHOUSE 41, BLACK TIGHT KILLERS and Koji Wakamatsu's ECSTASY OF THE ANGELS and GO, GO SECOND TIUME VIRGIN) for David Shultz who was releasing them in association with his Vitagraph Films distribution company and the Cinematheque. The liner notes were read by Sheila Whitaker in the UK, and she and her associate, Philippa Brewster (who worked for UK publisher, IB Tauris) asked me if I had any book projects in mind. From the beginning, this encyclopedia seemed to be too gargantuan for them as far as word count, and I had already been toying with the idea of doing another much shorter book which would make use of the interviews I had done while in Japan. This became *Outlaw Masters of Japanese Film*, which was published in the summer of 2005 by IB Tauris.

A year or so later, Philippa asked me if I would be interested in revisiting the idea of trying to do the encyclopedia in a more abbreviated form for IB Tauris (which would have resulted in cutting at least half of the material here). Frustrated, I told her I would think about it and, for a while, it seemed to represent a compromised but viable alternative.

Enter Harvey Fenton and Fab Press sometime – I think – in 2006; they were also headquartered in the UK. Harvey was a gentleman I knew through Outcast Cinema's Marc Walkow and Mitch Davis, the programmer of Montreal's Fantasia Film Festival. I loved Fab Press' books. Their artistic presentation and layouts of massive coffee-table size tomes on directors like Mario Bava and Lucio Fulci were right up my alley and were on exactly the kind of simpatico wavelength that I had been searching for. Harvey and I had many long email conversations about *Gun and Sword* and agreed to do it – unexpurgated – though because of several other big projects that were ahead of mine, it would probably not be until 2008 before he could start work on the layout.

Lo and behold, like so many other frustrating things that happened for people all over the world due to the global recession, Harvey contacted me in 2008 and explained he was taking on a part-time, outside job with a newspaper, and he was curtailng any huge projects for the foreseeable future. He would be concentrating on small books (such as Mark Schilling's excellent study of Nikkatsu Studios action cinema, *No Borders, No Limits*), and it could be several years, if not more, before he could feasibly see *Gun and Sword* back on the drawing boards.

Enter New Texture. Already writing poetry for Wyatt Doyle's literary website, he had long been after me to do an update of *Double Snake Bourbon* from 1989, a collection of poetry and song lyrics (from my days with my bands The Flesh Eaters and Divine Horsemen). This update became the 500 page collection *A Minute to Pray, A Second to Die* which was published in December 2009. It was around this same time he and I decided to release *Gun and Sword* through New Texture. Along with completing three novels and a short story collection (all out now through New Texture), I have spent the last three years editing, revising and laying out the volume you now hold.

Ultimately, at the 11th hour – actually the 11th hour, 59 minute mark – this connection with New Texture proved problematic as well. Down to the final proofs, and serious irreconcilable differences reared their unruly heads, hence *Gun and Sword* appears now under yet another imprint, Poison Fang Books. Poison Fang was already on the radar, set to release my two newest novels *Volcano Girls* and *Tightrope on Fire* in the Fall of 2013.

A few notes about the text: Multiple English titles exist for many of these Japanese productions. I have used varying criteria to gauge which title comes first in any specific entry, thus affecting where it will fall in alphabetical order within the respective studios' sections. Sometimes I have used what title I think would be most familiar to the reader; other times I have used the English title I feel aesthetically or viscerally best characterizes the movie in question. I have done my best to correctly romanize the Japanese language titles. This can be a daunting task (more about that in a few sentences) because occasionally studios were using unorthodox readings/pronunciations on the *kanji*-spelled titles as a marketing ploy or publicity stunt, something one might not necessarily be aware of unless translating the title from an actual movie poster (that often had pronunciation keys in tiny *hiragana* letters above the *kanji* symbols). Likewise, Japanese names of crew and performers can be even more problematic. As anyone even vaguely familiar with the Japanese language knows, names, especially given names, can have a wide variety of readings. Many times even Japanese natives who have not heard a name spoken aloud may not know the correct pronunciation/reading. I have done my best, based partly on English references when available or, if not, using my best guess what seems to be the most common reading for the given name in question. Sometimes I will come across a person that I have seen consistently referenced in both film credits and reference books with a 50/50 split reading on their name (e.g., sometimes cinematographer Himeda – who worked mostly at Nikkatsu Studios – was referenced with given name Shinsaku and other times, Masahisa; and director Mori – who worked predominantly at Daiei Studios – with given name Kazuo, other times, Issei. There are many other examples).

I have used a simplified romanization of names and movie titles, omitting any accents over vowels or consonants; I have also written proper names in the English style: given name first, family or surname second.

Regards the number of films included here: I am certain that as soon as this book becomes set in stone, more movie titles will come to light that I have missed. Except for the appendices (i.e., the final MATATABI/PERIOD YAKUZA and ATG/INDEPENDENT/PINK sections), I have tried to make the film listings as complete as possible. Some readers and fans of Japanese cinema, particularly those who are rabid purists, may think I have cast too wide a net. But I would rather do that than the opposite.

– Chris D.
April, 2013
Highland Park, CA

FOREWORD

I smiled but said nothing when I met Chris D. for the first time in the spring of 1997 in Los Angeles, and he told me – through an interpreter, of course – that he was planning to write an encyclopedia of yakuza films. But I thought to myself how could a Westerner who did not understand the Japanese language, who did not come from Japanese culture and who would have enormous problems seeing enough yakuza films, how could such a person be able to write an all-encompassing encyclopedia? No one had done one in English to my knowledge, so, I wonder, how could a westerner with such limitations be able to achieve what I thought would be impossible?

He obviously knew something about the subject because he had been instrumental in proposing the American Cinematheque retrospective series, *Outlaw Masters of Japanese Film*, which included some films of mine and which then brought me to Los Angeles.

What I had not counted on, because I barely knew him, was Chris's persistence. Many yakuza and samurai films, I found out later, were available on video without English subtitles, and as I also learned later he must have watched each of them hundreds of times and picked up not just the plots but their underlying layers.

In the late 1990s, Chris D. and I met again in Tokyo because the Japan Foundation had given him a grant to work on the encyclopedia. During his visit he bought so many posters and relevant materials of the old films that I didn't know how he would have enough room to store them all when he got home.

I marveled at his diligence and the way he kept burrowing along and the information he was gathering. By this time, also through an interpreter, he was able to talk to me about some of the films he had seen, and I discovered that he knew much more than the plots. He knew who the actors were. He knew who the screenwriters and directors, my contemporaries, were and how one of their films linked to the next one they made and what studios were specializing in what kind of films and not only that, but why.

Along with most of my contemporaries, I directed many films from 1955 to 1980, the years Chris D. mainly centers on in this book and, frankly, I hadn't seen many of them for 10 or 20 years. Chris D. spoke to me about them with such precision that I could see them all again, almost frame by frame, in my mind.

Chris D. and I did not meet often since 1997, but each time we did meet I was more and more impressed that this film buff really was getting to the heart of what he calls Japanese gangster films. I would say that these films are about Japanese society and the way some people organize a parallel existence and codes of behavior that directly challenge the rule of law and what we often think of as the forces of good. To me this parallel conduct of behavior has been fascinating whether it be the modern-day yakuza or the olden times samurai. This criminal element existed and still exists feeding on the innocent and the vulnerable, but it does so by following a rigid code of organization and fellowship. It is not unlike the way we are told the mafia operates.

Now after what seems to be a few short years, Chris D. has produced this remarkable book of scholarship and general interest. I have read *Gun and Sword: An Encyclopedia of Japanese Gangster Films* page by page, and I am flabbergasted. He's got it all and he's got it right. I am amazed at all the details he gathered.

Those of us who made the films and those of you who are fans are in his debt.

– Kinji Fukasaku
2002, Tokyo, Japan

Last Days of the Underworld (listed in Toei Studios section, M-Z, Underworld series)
Tetsuro Tanba on left, Hiroki Matsukata on right (IMAGE © TOEI)

INTRODUCTION

YAKUZA EIGA: Losers On Parade

The yakuza, or Japanese gangster, exists, as does the samurai, in a different and separate reality in film, TV and literature in much the same way that the cowboy, the gunfighter and the private eye do in American culture. If you look for too many correlations to "real life" in yakuza films, you will come up short. You will be doing the actors, directors and writers as much a disservice as yourself. It is best to look at these pictures as you would the spaghetti western – violent, sometimes ultraviolent, tall tales with romantic and/or nihilistic protagonists caught up in conflicts where very often the only way out is Death.

Obviously, the yakuza are, and have been, a very real part of Japanese life. In one of my Japanese dictionaries, the word, yakuza, is defined as: "useless; worthless; good-for-nothing; scrubby; trashy; a good-for-nothing fellow; a ne'er-do-well; a bad egg; coarse things; trash; wretched stuff." No mention, though, of: "gangsters, hoodlums, gamblers or organized crime" Why? Perhaps the 1933 copyright date of the dictionary provides a feasible explanation. At the time the Japanese government was reveling in a militaristic nationalist fervor. The powers-that-be would not have been keen on seeing references to any kind of loosely united

alliance of criminal gangs, even in a dictionary. The term yakuza has been around
for scores of decades. But the closest this dictionary comes to the popular usage
are "a good-for-nothing fellow; a bad egg; a ne'er-do-well." Strangely enough,
the United States was also extremely reluctant to acknowledge the existence of
its own brand of organized crime, the mafia or Cosa Nostra, during the same
time period. FBI director J. Edgar Hoover openly ridiculed the idea of a criminal
underworld alliance until the likes of such crusading politicians as Senator Estes
Kefauver forced his hand in the 1950s with a series of committees investigating
the mob.

There is an undeniable, seemingly innate duality of feeling, a hate/love/hate
relationship, an attitude almost of "you scratch our back and we'll scratch yours"
that the Japanese have for and about the yakuza. Euphemisms rule, or rather, as in
this case, abstractions.

Perhaps one of the most explicit examples of the contradictions underground
yakuza society elicits in Japanese law and cultural traditions is the following
testimony of symbiosis. Although the police stage intermittent crackdowns on
various yakuza rackets: prostitution, drugs, gambling, loan-sharking/debt
collection, etc., it barely makes a dent in their revenues. In fact, there is what
amounts to an unspoken, undocumented treaty of sorts between Japanese law
enforcement and the yakuza. Ever since the gangs' descent from comparatively
small aggregations of gamblers in the 1700s, there has been tolerance and tacit
cooperation to varying degrees from the established legal powers. One of the
reasons the yakuza have been able to not just survive but flourish is that they
act as a virtual underworld police force. That is the reason blue collar, or street,
crime is, compared to the USA, virtually non-existent in Japan. Quite often the
anti-social or violent teenagers of a district will be absorbed into the local gang
as soon as they begin upsetting the delicate balance of the applecart. Their unruly
behavior and outcast feelings will be channeled and directed into "constructive"
gang activities, giving many of them a family they have never had.

The yakuza began as small conglomerates or affiliated mobs and have
grown into multi-million dollar criminal enterprises. From these affiliated
consolidations of gangs, the yakuza has branched out from their illegal businesses
into legitimate commerce such as construction, nightclubs, the television and
motion picture industry, etc. The late 1980s' genesis then abrupt 1997 deflation
of Japan's bubble economy can also be seen as a direct result of tacit societal
approval of many yakuza practices as well as the yakuza significantly penetrating
legitimate banking and the stock exchange (i.e. billions of yen worth of
unsecured bad loans – sound familiar?).

For decades, yakuza groups have hung out their shingles, so to speak, proud
signs on their building headquarters and tiny lapel pins on their suits delineating their clan ideogram (one or two *kanji* symbols that make up their "group's"
name.) Such in-the-open, at times arrogant, exhibitionism on the part of yakuza

gangs has no corresponding correlation in American organized crime. The very idea of a mafia family or subgroup advertising its criminal presence in a New York, New Jersey, New Orleans or Las Vegas neighborhood is not just unthinkable, it is absurdly surreal. That is just one of the differences between Japanese organized crime known as the yakuza and their American counterparts.[1]

There are three different types of yakuza : *bakuto* – gamblers; *tekiya* – street peddlers; and *gurentai* – your normal everyday hoodlums. The yakuza were originally made up primarily of *bakuto* – and despite their somewhat shady reputation and sometimes violent temperment, they were supposedly ruled by feudal codes of chivalry and *giri* (obligation) – in *oyabun/kobun* (master/ apprentice or father/son relationships that were cemented with ties of fanatical loyalty. The term yakuza actually is made up of the numbers YA-8-KU-9-SA(ZA)-3 which, when added together, forms the worst score in the popular game of *hana fuda* (flower cards): a 20, which equals zero. So, a loser. A self-conscious and supposedly gallant, chivalrous loser. That there is a vaguely discernible, yet still definite, lineage traceable to the samurai class of yore[2] is without question. Masterless samurai, or *ronin*, made unemployable by the gradual onslaught of peace and the slow-as-molasses dissolving of the feudal system took to the road as roving, independent spirits. More often than not, *ronin* were reduced to starving, disenchanted and disillusioned swords-for-hire willing to do work as *yojinbos* (bodyguards) or, if such was not available, anything from armed robbery to paid assassinations to helping some wealthy merchant build their own private army of brigands. Of course, good and bad *ronin*, both in the fantasy of films and literature and in real-life, were given to gambling in their spare time. That these gamblers would form bands, either out of deep fraternal bonds of friendship or out of realistic necessity to protect themselves

Samurai Wolf - Hell Cut (see Matatabi)
(IMAGE © TOEI)

---

and their financial interests was inevitable. Thus, the initial clans of yakuza were born. Some of the gangs were noble, ex-samurai gamblers who pledged to not prey on the weak or common people, and there were some looked up to as Robin Hood-types,[3] while others were little better than shrewd, cutthroat con men hungry for wealth, power and hedonistic pleasures and not particular about how they achieved these materialistic goals. There are some who even relegate the yakuza Robin Hoods, Chuji and Jirocho, to this latter description.

Since the turn of the century, various real-life yakuza personalities have allied themselves with, at best, right-wing, at worst, fascist causes. Powerful men like ex-samurai, Mitsuru Toyama, founded in 1881 one of the first of many rightist/fascist secret societies to come: Genyosha, or The Dark Ocean Society. These yakuza were self-described patriots, fanatical devotees of the Emperor and a feudal system of government. Their methods were rooted in blackmail, terrorism and assassination of leftist ideologues if they grew too powerful. These "political" yakuza thought of themselves as different from the *bakuto* (gamblers) and *tekiya* (street peddlers), persons who were often blue collar and from a different, lower strata of society.[4] As time went on, *bakuto* and *tekiya* gangs would frequently meld with rightist-political activists, forging an impressive ultra-nationalist front that held sway over labor unions in not only Japan, but Japanese colonies like Manchuria and Korea as well. Yakuza/rightist bigwigs that only briefly lost their power post-WW2 (some who were actually originally classified as war criminals, but finagled their way out of such a category with assistance from rightist U.S. militarists) were Yoshio Kodama, Kazuo Toaka (head of the famed, far-reaching yakuza mob, Yamaguchi-gumi), and Ryoichi Sasakawa (who apparently liked to call himself "the world's wealthiest fascist".)[5]

In any case, I am pursuing too much of the reality. What we are concerned with in this volume is a life and a world that exists only on celluloid. And, as you will no doubt become fatigued of hearing, there are some aspects of even this fantasy life and fantasy world that no longer exist – even on film.

Romanticized in story and song for at least a good two hundred years, it was not until the 1960s that the demythologizing of the wandering, samurai had impact,

---

3   Two real-life personalties: Chuji Kunisada, whose character has appeared in over a dozen different films since the silent movie era; and Jirocho of Shimizu, his persona showcased in scores of films since 1920, and especially during the 1950s.

4   There were many other secret societies between the 1880s and the outbreak of WW2, groups with names like the Blood Pledge Corps, the Farmers' Death-Defying Corps, Association for Heavenly Action, the Amur River Society (aka the Black Dragon Society), and the Great Japan National Essence Society.

5   For an excellent book on the subject of the "real" yakuza , see the volume simply titled YAKUZA by David Kaplan and Alec Dubro, Addison-Wesley Publishing Co.; however, when it comes to their knowledge and understanding of the yakuza film genre (at least in their first edition), it is pretty much haven't-got-a-clue time.

first in Akira Kurosawa's pair of Samurai-With-No-Name films YOJINBO (BODYGUARD) and SANJURO (TSUBAKI SANJURO)[6]. As early as the 1920s–1930s, Japanese films depicted existentialist/nihilist swordsmen[7]. Reasons why it was not until YOJINBO that this image had impact are partly self-evident. There is neither the time nor the space to go into the more esoteric whys and wherefores of the disillusionment, cynicism and yearning for a more realistic picture of what the world was really like – but, just for starters, WW2 (the only time in modern history that the Japanese have been defeated), the subsequent U.S. Occupation (which, despite its contradictory liberating and oppressive elements, gave the Japanese a radically different way-of-life[8]), the Vietnam war, and the worldwide student unrest of the sixties (which possibly had an even greater impact in Japan than it did in the USA and France).

*(left) Shintaro Katsu & Jiro Tamiya in **Bad Reputation (#3)** (see Daiei Studios); (right)*
***Black River** (see Shochiku Studios)* (LEFT IMAGE © KADOKAWA) (RIGHT IMAGE © SHOCHIKU)

---

6   then more prolifically in the films of directors Hideo Gosha, Tai Kato, Kihachi Okamoto, Kenji Misumi, Tokuzo Tanaka, Kazuo Ikehiro, Kimiyoshi Yasuda, Kazuo Mori, Daisuke Ito, Teiji Matsuda, Tomu Uchida, Shigehiro Ozawa, Kiyoshi Saeki, Yasuo Furuhata, et.al.

7   In such films as Daisuke Ito's three part CHUJI'S TRAVEL DIARY (CHUJI TABI NIKKI) (1927) and MAN-SLASHING, HORSE-PIERCING SWORD (ZANJIN ZAMBA KEN) (1930); Sadao Yamanaka's catalogue of real people not cardboard heroes in such explosive fare as SLEEPING WITH A LONG SWORD (DAKINE NO NAGADOSU) (1932), THE VILLAGE TATTOOED-MAN (MACHI NO IREZUMI MONO) (1935), ISHIMATSU OF THE FOREST (MORI NO ISHIMATSU) (1936) and what many believe to be his greatest (and his last before dying as a common foot soldier in Manchuria) HUMANITY AND PAPER BALLOONS (NINJO KAMI-FUSEN) (1937); Buntaro Futagawa's awesome bloodfest BLOOD AND MAN'S BACKBONE (O RO CHI) (1925) and even Hiroshi Inagaki's original version of the story of Ryunosuke Tsukue, the psycho-sociopath swordsman, THE GREAT BODDHISATVA PASS (DAIBOSATSU TOGE) (1935) (remade many times, most recently and famously as SWORD OF DOOM by Kihachi Okamoto with Tatsuya Nakadai in 1966.)

8   The schizophrenia of at first leftist, pro-labor union, then right-wing, anti-union, anti-communist factions predominating in the Occupation bureaucracy left a bitter aftertaste in the mouths of many filmmakers including Akira Kurosawa, Tadashi Imai, Satsuo Yamamoto, Hideo Sekigawa, Nagisa Oshima, Yoshishige Yoshida, Kinji Fukasaku, Junya Sato, Koji Wakamatsu, et. al. Many of the yakuza films of Fukasaku and Sato display the radically angry vision of an ultra-violent microcosm of a larger amoral society bent on nothing but material gain, bereft of human and spiritual values and consequently toppling into chaos.

In many ways, Japan was going through a cultural/artistic fit of existential self-awareness in the late 1950s through the mid-1970s that helped to spawn the great yakuza *eiga* of that period. A similar wave of dark malaise had hatched the amazing film noir boom in 1945–1960 postwar America, then again in the brutal, unsentimental crime films[9] and radical social consciousness/exploitation pictures[10] of late 1960s/early 1970s Hollywood (as well as all the attendant sub-genres such as black action and biker pictures). There was a strange synchronicity in the film genres of many nations from the early 1950s through the 1970s: Italy's postwar neo-realist movement, their grotesquely romantic and downbeat Gothic horror films of the 1960s that metamorphosed first into delirious *giallo* movies (sexy mystery/suspense thrillers) then, by the late 1970s, gory, cynically contemporary bloodfests. Not to mention Italy's gangster pictures[11] and phenomenally gritty reinvention of the western as operatic tall-tale,[12] France's noir/crime film explosion headed by such giants as Henri-Georges Clouzot, Jacques Becker, Jean-Pierre Melville[13], Georges Franju, Jacques Deray and Rene Clement that helped give birth – or at least stoke the fires – of the French New Wave; such uncompromisingly great gangster pictures as Roy Boulting's BRIGHTON ROCK (1947), Basil Dearden's THE BLUE LAMP (1950) and Joseph Losey's THE SLEEPING TIGER (1954) that helped create a climate for Britain's "angry young man" genre in the late 1950s/early 1960s (by such directors as Tony Richardson, Lindsay Anderson, Karel Reisz, Sidney Furie) that further evolved into stinging portraits of urban dysfunction, madness and decay in the late 1960s/through the 1970s and beyond by such uncompromising

---

9   Such as POINT BLANK (1967) directed by John Boorman, BULLITT (1968) and FRIENDS OF EDDIE COYLE (1973) directed by Peter Yates, BONNIE AND CLYDE (1967) directed by Arthur Penn, THE BROTHERHOOD (1968) directed by Martin Ritt, THE FRENCH CONNECTION (1971) directed by William Friedkin, DIRTY HARRY (1971) directed by Don Siegel, HICKEY & BOGGS (1972) directed by Robert Culp, THE GODFATHER I and II (1972, 1974) directed by Francis Ford Coppola, MEAN STREETS (1973) directed by Martin Scorcese

10   Such as CISCO PIKE (1972) directed by Bill Norton, WALKING TALL (1973) directed by Phil Karlson, WHITE LINE FEVER (1975) directed by Jonathan Kaplan, CAGED HEAT (1974) and FIGHTING MAD (1976) directed by Jonathan Demme, JACKSON COUNTY JAIL (1976) directed by Michael Miller, MOVING VIOLATION (1976) directed by Charles S. Dubin to name but a few.

11   Such as SALVATORE GIULIANO (1972), LUCKY LUCIANO (1973) and ILLUSTRI-OUS CORPSES (1975) directed by Francesco Rosi; WAKE UP AND KILL (1966), BANDITS IN MILAN (1968), CRAZY JOE (1973) and TEENAGE PROSTITUTION RACKET (1975) directed by Carlo Lizzani; ALMOST HUMAN (1974), ROME: ARMED TO THE TEETH (aka ASSAULT WITH A DEADLY WEAPON) (1976) and THE CYNIC, THE RAT AND THE FIST (1977) directed by Umberto Lenzi; MILAN CALIBER 9 (1972), MANHUNT (1972), THE BOSS (1973) directed by Fernando di Leo, DAY OF THE OWL (aka MAFIA) (1968), CONFESSIONS OF A POLICE CAPTAIN (1971), HOW TO KILL A JUDGE (1974), I AM SCARED (1977) directed by Damiano Damiani; I AM THE LAW (1977) directed by Pasquale Squitieri, once again to name but a select few.

12   Primary "spaghetti" western practitioners being the legendary Sergio Leone and Sergio Corbucci

13   Especially Melville's LE DOULOS (1962), SECOND BREATH (LE DEUXIEME SOUFFLE) (1966), LE SAMOURAI (1967)

filmmakers as Mike Hodges[14], Ken Loach, Donald Cammell/Nicholas Roeg[15] and Alan Clarke.

Frequently, the lead character in a yakuza film will be a quiet, strong man of principle – a role usually played by Ken Takakura, Koji Tsuruta, Yujiro Ishihara, Hideki Takahashi, Ryo Ikebe – forced into untenable situations because of either loyalty to friends, obligation (*giri*) to the gang or something as nebulous as responsibility to themselves. Just as often you will find the lead characters to be amoral, barely-in-control homicidal maniacs – usually played by the likes of Bunta Sugawara and Noboru Ando (an actual former yakuza himself) who, nevertheless, end up being gutsy individualists, beautiful losers bravely facing certain Death by going up against the faceless corporate gangs that have branded them hotheaded outcasts. Akira Kobayashi, Tetsuya Watari, Joe Shishido, Hiroki Matsukata[16] and Tatsuo Umemiya are actors whose careers seem to have been evenly divided between both types.

*(left) Testsuya Watari in **Tokyo Streetfighting**, (center) Hideki Takahashi in A **Man's Crest** series (both, see Nikkatsu Studios); (right) Junko Fuji and Bunta Sugawara in **Chivalrous Woman (#2)** (see Toei Studios)* (LEFT AND CENTER IMAGES © NIKKATSU) (RIGHT IMAGE © TOEI)

---

14   GET CARTER (1971)

15   PERFORMANCE (1970)

16   son of famous *chanbara* samurai film star, Jushiro Konoe

Another actor who appears in countless yakuza pictures, though rarely in the lead role, is someone fairly familiar to American audiences, Tetsuro Tanba[17] . Shinichi "Sonny" Chiba, although featured in many yakuza films since the early 1960s, would have undoubtedly been even more of a prime contender in the leading-man-stakes had his rise in international popularity (via the STREET-FIGHTER films) not seemed to have coincided with the waning of the genre. The great Tomisaburo Wakayama, both pre-and-post-LONE WOLF AND CUB (KOZURE OKAMI) also appeared in innumerable character and secondary-lead roles. Performers such as Saburo Kitajima and Hideo Murata came into limited yakuza stardom from having successful singing careers.

Meiko Kaji in **Stray Cat Rock (#1)**   *Tomisaburo Wakayama in the* **Evil Priest** *series*
(see Nikkatsu Studios) (IMAGE © NIKKATSU)   *(see Toei Studios)* (IMAGE © TOEI)

The legendary Raizo Ichikawa and Shintaro Katsu both appeared in numerous yakuza pictures, even to the point of having their own series: Ichikawa in the eight film YOUNG BOSS (WAKA OYABUN) series and Shintaro Katsu in the 16 film BAD REPUTATION (AKUMYO) series and the nine picture HOODLUM SOLDIER (HEITAI YAKUZA)[18]. However, both Ichikawa and

---

17   In such English-language movies as THE 7TH DAWN (1964), YOU ONLY LIVE TWICE (1967) and FIVE MAN ARMY (1970)

18   Technically not really yakuza films but immensely entertaining B&W war movies - included here because of Katsu's character, a drafted, small-time yakuza gambler who constantly rubs against the grain of the Japanese army's sadistic discipline.

Katsu are known predominantly for their samurai genre output which outnumbers their yakuza efforts two-to-one – Ichikawa for his roles in the 12 film KYOSHIRO NEMURI – SON OF THE BLACK MASS (aka SLEEPY EYES OF DEATH) series and the eight film NINJA, BAND OF ASSASSINS (SHINOBI NO MONO) series; Katsu for his portrayal of the wandering, blind swordsman/masseur and yakuza gambler ZATOICHI in 1860s Japan in 26 motion pictures and over 100 televsion episodes.[19]

Last but not least are the Japanese actresses who appeared in yakuza *eiga* in their own unique and tradition-busting brand of action picture. Foremost

(left) Christina Lindberg and Reiko Ike in a salacious publicity still for **Elder Sister (#1)** *aka* **Sex and Fury;** *(right) Junko Fuji in* **Red Peony Gambler (#2)** (IMAGES © TOEI)

amongst female stars who actually became the focus of their own series were Junko Fuji, Meiko Kaji, Junko Miyazono, Reiko Ike, Reiko Oshida, Etsuko "Sue" Shiomi, Miki Sugimoto at Toei Studios; Yumiko Nogawa, Hiroko Ogi, Meiko Kaji, Junko Natsu at Nikkatsu; Michiyo Yasuda, Kyoko Enami, Mari Atsumi, Eiko Yatsunami at Daiei; Yoko Matsuyama, Chizuko Arai at Shochiku; Meiko Kaji (yet again) at Toho; and in the beginning, Naoko Kubo and Yoko Mihara at Shintoho. These were female performers who actually got to stand toe-to-toe with male heroes and villains and, for the most part, emerge as equals. However, these same actresses also had to appear in many severely limited suffering wife/girlfriend roles in countless male-dominated yakuza *eiga*. Other

---

19   See APPENDIX 1: MATATABI/PERIOD YAKUZA FILMS.

noteworthy, talented actresses who appeared in yakuza pictures (virtually never as equals or gun/knife wielding protagonists and frequently with not much to do): Mayumi Nagisa[20], Hiroko Sakuramachi, Akiko Kudo, Eiko Nakamura[21], Yumi Takigawa[22] , Hiroko Fuji, Ruriko Asaoka, Chieko Matsubara, Kayo Matsuo[23], Mari Shiraki, Shiho Fujimura, Machiko Yashiro[24], Masako Izumi, Masayo Banri, Masumi Tachibana, Yoshiko Mita plus many more.

Yumiko Nogawa in **Cat Girl Gambling (#1)** *(see Nikkatsu Studios)* (IMAGE © NIKKATSU)   *Mayumi Nagisa in* **Modern Yakuza (#6) aka Street Mobster** *(see Toei Studios)* (IMAGE © TOEI)

In the book's main section, I will be covering not only yakuza cinema made during the heyday of the genre – 1960 through 1976 – but also films produced a few years either side of the boom. Thus the 1955 through 1980 span. You may ask yourself "Why such a time limit at all, whatever it may be?" To answer: Toei Studios alone (the main producer of yakuza films) made over 300 yakuza *eiga* in a 12-year-period, from 1962 through 1974. The Japanese film industry told

20   Nagisa's role in Toei Studio's MODERN YAKUZA #6 – OUTLAW KILLER (aka STREET MOBSTER) is a notable exception

21   She did appear in a fighting role in one-off THE RED SILK GAMBLER (HICHIRIMEN BAKUTO) (1972) which initially seemed as if it might turn into a series

22   Takigawa took over Meiko Kaji's FEMALE CONVICT SCORPION role for the fifth film in the series, NEW FEMALE CONVICT SCORPION (SHIN JOSHUU SASORI) (1976) but proved miscast in a hardboiled action role. She also had the lead in the notoriously surreal, over-the-top, mainstream pink film SCHOOL OF THE HOLY BEASTS (SEIJU GAKUEN) (1974)

23   Matsuo later appeared as an impressively ruthless villain in LONE WOLF AND CUB #2 – BABY CART AT THE RIVER STYX (KOZURE OKAMI series) (1972) and Hideo Gosha's HUNTER IN THE DARK (YAMI NO KARIUDO) (1979)

24   Yashiro did get to be a bit aggressive as THE MINI SKIRT GAMBLER (GENDAI ONNA DOSHI), a one-off at Toei Studios in 1970

yakuza stories pre-1960s[25] But this was before the genre had really developed. In some ways, since no rules, no traditions had been set forth, this occasionally resulted in more original stories. Just as often the 1950s yakuza film could be moronically formulaic and slavishly western in flavor. Some cynical critics in the West might scoff at the assertion that any originality existed or could exist, especially in Japanese genre *eiga* of the 1950s. There were also directors – Kurosawa is a case in point – who were noted detractors of the explosion of yakuza films in the 1960s. Kurosawa refused to even consider a yakuza scenario as a possible project after his borderline yakuza film THE BAD SLEEP WELL (1960) and his famous in-period yakuza picture YOJINBO (1961). I am a great admirer of Kurosawa's pictures, but to me that kind of moral superiority, cultural snobbery and genre elitism, is incomprehensible except on a level of egocentric meanness and pretentious ostentation. But one can understand the frustration of Kurosawa and many of his filmmaking colleagues. The yakuza were becoming an ever-burgeoning problem in Japanese society, and Kurosawa felt that way too many of the yakuza films glorified/romanticized the life style. Some of the studios had a huge percentage of their output devoted to gangster films, thus squeezing out space for movies with other subject matter. Yakuza *eiga* in the 1960s and early 1970s were truly using up most of the oxygen in the room.

*still and frame grab from Akira Kurosawa's **Drunken Angel** (1948) with Toshiro Mifune and Takashi Shimura (both left); sci-fi and gangsters: Ishiro Honda's **The H-Man** (1958) (below) (both films are not covered in listings in this book)*

(ALL THREE IMAGES © TOHO)

---

25   Kurosawa's DRUNKEN ANGEL (YOIDORE TENSHI) (1948) and STRAY DOG (NORA INU)(1949) (albeit atypical ones), Nobuo Nakagawa's LYNCH LAW (RINCHI) (1949), Kajiro Yamamoto's THE MERCILESS BOSS (OTOKO #1 SEI) (1955) and UNDERWORLD (ANKOKUGAI) (1956), Shigehiro Ozawa's GUN VS. GUN (KENJU TAI KENJU) (1956), Seijun Suzuki's SATAN'S TOWN (AKUMA NO MACHI) (1956), THE NUDE AND THE GUN (RAJO TO KENJU (1957) and UNDERWORLD BEAUTY (ANKOKUGAI NO BIJO) (1958) to name but a few disparate examples.

My point about any yakuza films made before roughly 1960, is that they just do not have the look, the feel – no matter the originating studio – that blossomed, as if by spontaneous combustion, when the genre exploded in the 1960s.

1979 seems to be the last year any yakuza films in the 1960s-style were produced. These films preceding 1980 had a definite visual signature, an optical simplicity and directness, usually determined, though not constricted, by budget, that is unmistakable. All of the yakuza movies since 1980 – even from the likes of Toei Studios – look and feel different. Since the number of yakuza *eiga* dropped precipitously after 1980, the ones that were made had more money behind them.

*Yoshishige Yoshida's **Good-For-Nothing** (see Shochiku Studios)* (IMAGE © SHOCHIKU)

That additional money meant higher production values which quite often meant less setbound ambience. Due to the partial disintegration of the studios and production line systems, production design became more problematic and some of the great stylized sets disappeared. The use of real locations opened things up, and any director without a personal style or without the strength to keep a tight rein, lost control of atmospherics to the outside world. Often, too, more money spent meant more actors or guest stars in small roles – which would hopefully mean more folks lured in to buy a ticket. This newfound, semi-epic status did not necessarily serve the story-to-be-told well. Since 1990, the number of yakuza films being made has once again steadily increased – most of the films being shot for direct-to-video/DVD release. Lamentably, the level of quality and consistency nowhere approaches what it did in the 1960s and early 1970s. There have been exceptions, most notably in atypical efforts by newer filmmakers like Takashi Miike, Yoichi Sai and Kiyoshi Kurosawa and even some 1990s efforts by veterans like Sadao Nakajima and Eiichi Kudo.

What is the attraction of the yakuza film, the Japanese gangster movie, to a Westerner, as opposed to a regular American/Euro-style gangster movie? Since we are talking about Japan, a whole strata of codified behavior (as already mentioned) enters the equation which is just not applicable to an American or Euro counterpart genre. *Bushido* is a code of the samurai, the individual bound by duty and justice to his clan, his master and the nation. One must sacrifice one's personal feelings to duty no matter what – no matter whether the action one must commit is inhuman or "evil." The arrogant pride of the ruling class is at stake. However, the code of the yakuza – *ninkyodo* (the path of chivalry) or *jingi* (honor and humanity, also known as the Gambler's Code) – is a different kind of chivalric value system diametrically opposed to *bushido* because it balances one's obligation and duty with humaneness, or *ninjo*. Usually those that subscribe to *ninkyodo* are commoners or *ronin* who have had their "status" reduced. Quite often yakuza *eiga* – even some of the *jitsuroku* (modern true document) variety – deal with inner moral conflicts in their main protagonists that the viewer is less likely to find in gangster films from the West. Many *ninkyo eiga* almost perversely engineer the most unbearable psychological situations to put their heroes through, creating mind-snapping, soul-warping tension between the equations of humanity and duty. This sensation of witnessing a film's protagonist being nearly pulled apart by a conflicted conscience is rare in Western gangster cinema, with few exceptions. Toei Studios was the most rigidly formulaic in their *ninkyo* films, creating virtual sado-masochistic emotional torture fests for their anti-heroes. When handled well, by such directors as Tai Kato, Kosaku Yamashita or Sadao Nakajima (the latter of which directed mainly modern *jitsuroku* yakuza films, once he had paid his dues as a novice), they can be nightmarishly existentialist action movies; when handled in a production-line-by-rote manner by competent but less subtle directors such as Shigehiro Ozawa or Kiyoshi Saeki, the *ninkyo* subgenre film can often teeter over into a histrionic, cornball display of macho bluster and sentiment, sometimes with unspoken socio-political subtexts bordering on xenophobic nationalism and vigilantism. Outside the Toei Studios *ninkyo* yakuza universe, *ninkyo eiga* may not have always carried the same webs of obligation, but they often picked up other more subtle characteristics. Studios like Nikkatsu (with filmmakers Toshio Masuda and Akinori Matsuo) and Daiei (with directors Kazuo Ikehiro and Kimiyoshi Yasuda) brought more dynamic, less generic production design to their *ninkyo* films, sometimes more clearly defined characters and far less kow-towing to formula. Daiei's *ninkyo* pictures, in particular, were often diametrically opposed to the Toei ethos (director Ikehiro is on record as hating Toei's *ninkyo* yakuza *eiga*.) Then again, that individuality and rejection of the slavishly formulaic was comparatively relative and came at a price.

Ken Takakura (left, kneeling) and Koji Tsuruta (right), visit the grave of their boss in **Gambling Den (#10)** *(see Toei)* (IMAGE © TOEI)

Nikkatsu and Daiei's *ninkyo* yakuza films did okay at the box office, but Toei's went through the roof in ticket sales – they were phenomenally, ridiculously popular.

Paul Schrader has written that yakuza *eiga* is one of the most restricted genres yet created. In a 1974 Film Comment article[26], he describes the inherent unoriginal quality of genre films, whether western, horror or yakuza films, and that this rigidity of form is necessary for genres to exist. *"Genres are not free flights of the imagination. The art of the genre occurs within its strictures. Only when one understands that icons are supposed to be two-dimensional does the study of their shape and form become interesting."*

*Traditional gambling scene in **The Greatest Post-War Gambler** (see Toei Studios)* (IMAGE © TOEI)

The *ninkyo* (chivalrous) yakuza film (in vogue from roughly 1962–1973) is often more one dimensional when compared to the more *gendai* (modern picture (in vogue from approximately 1969–1979.) The *jitsuroku* film quite often has no chivalrous characters; everyone is guilty of some less-than-honorable behavior – it is only a matter of degree. The anti-hero protagonists are usually equipped with some slight redeeming quality, despite their cruelty or violent personalities, while the villains are totally beyond control, beyond all redemption.

In real life, yakuza may have been gamblers, thieves, possibly even murderers – shady characters without redeeming attributes of a *ninkyodo*-bound spirit. But in films, literature and song the yakuza became outcast heroes pressed into their outlaw state by the cruel machinations of an avaricious ruling class. That they never sacrifice their compassion, never give up their kinship with the weak and the poor to make their life easier is their most endearing trait. *Ninkyodo* (chivalrous path) and *jingi* (honor and humanity, often described as "the gambler's code") – as you will be able to discern from the terms used *ad infinitum* in yakuza film titles – is the lynchpin of their moral universe, their *raison d'etre*. *Ninkyodo* translated well to the big screen adventures of yakuza anti-heroes and proved a great part of the magnetizing influence on the Japanese domestic audience.

---

26   "Yakuza-Eiga: A Primer" by Paul Schrader, Film Comment, January 1974

Bunta Sugawara (center, standing), Toshio Kurosawa (extreme lower right, sitting) in
Battles Without Honor and Humanity (#4) aka The Yakuza Papers – Police Tactics
(see Toei Studios) (IMAGE © TOEI)

With the advent of television into an ever-increasing number of Japanese homes
in the 1960s and a burgeoning industry supplying the programming, many families stopped visiting their neighborhood cinemas as often as they did in the movie
production boom of the 1950s. This trend worsened attendance until a nadir of
ticket sales was reached in 1975. Movie audience demographics shifted. By the
mid-sixties, studios were catering more to the huge population of lonely bach-
elors cast adrift in the big cities, an audience that, as Japanese critic Tadao Sato,
observed: *"...empathized with the yakuza hero, an orphan in the universe, and
longed for the desperate friendship of a yakuza gang. Thus the modern yakuza
movie offered a kind of utopia for the lonely young men. The more unreal it was,
the more beautiful the ideal became, which was none other than the dream of
the lost home floating before the eyes of an audience of loners... "*. The desire
to be an integral part of such a closely-knit group *"...transcends all social
distinctions, and if an age of control by computers does arrive, it will become
all the more precious."*[27]

Sato's comments potently illustrate why the yakuza films that came to define
the genre in the 1960s through the late 1970s are so unique. What is unfortunate
is the fact that the genre lost that magic, that intoxicating headiness – something
even a Westerner can recognize, enjoy and identify with – as the 1980s
approached.

---

27   From CURRENTS IN JAPANESE CINEMA: Essays by Tadao Sato, translated by
Gregory Barrett, Kodansha International, 1982

In his Film Comment article, Paul Schrader also wrote about the then-starting-to-wane yakuza film genre. He asserted that what is important to realize about *"...strict genre forms like yakuza eiga is that these films are not necessarily individual works of art but instead variations on a complex social metaphor, a secret agreement between the artists and the audiences of a certain period. When massive social forces are in flux, rigid genre forms arise to help individuals make the transition. ...The yakuza eiga is a popular social contract between the artists and audiences of Japan to reevaluate and restructure these traditional virtues..."*

Kojiro Hongo (left), Jun Fujimaki (right) in **Wind God, Thunder God** *(see Daiei Studios)* (IMAGE © KADOKAWA)

From a strictly Western point of view, I have to testify that all of this sociological theorizing on the attraction of the yakuza film does not have to be as restricted to a Japanese sensibility as one might expect. Anyone brought up in a system of values, whether it be tradition-bound Japanese virtue or a Judeo-Christian philosophy of "love thy neighbor as thyself" or the "what goes around, comes around" idea of karma (something that all religions seem to have loosely in common), anyone with a conscience, with scruples trying to survive in the modern profit-and-material-wealth-as-priority-over-spirituality-and-humanity-world we all live in (seemingly more relevant in 2013 than ever), can very easily identify with the desperation of the principled lone wolf up against impossible odds. There is a unique 3 o'clock-in-the-morning ambience testifying to the dark night of the soul, the spiritual hunger of outcasts and outsiders who cannot even fit into their outcast society. Subtle unspoken nuances of friendship and loyalty, a chivalrous generosity of spirit, even amongst strangers, that is dying-out, ebbing into glowing embers even as we watch the frames unspool. Something which metamorphoses until only the vaguest hint is left, then savagely torn apart amidst the rabid wolfpack of the grittiest *jitsuroku* (true document) pictures.

Many yakuza films that have appeared on video and DVD (in Japan), have NOT been dubbed-in nor subtitled-in-English. Obvious? That is because 75% of the yakuza *eiga* that have found their way onto the older VHS or analog laser video mediums, and now on DVD and streaming-online, have done so *mostly* as domestic Japanese releases (when I originally wrote this sentence in the late 1990s, I had the figure at 90%, so there *has* been progress in visibility to Western audiences over the last decade). Action and other genre films made in Hong Kong were, and still are, subtitled in English because, for decades, Hong Kong was a British colony and English the official second-language. Unfortunately for the non-Japanese-speaking fan of

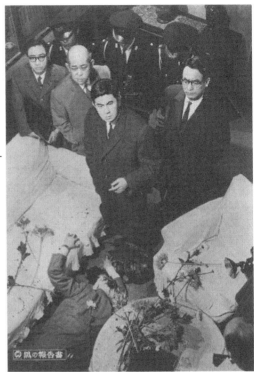

*Ken Utsui (center) in **Blackness (#2),** Daiei Studios-suspense-yakuza series about big business corruption and homicide* (IMAGE © KADOKAWA)

Japanese genre films there was no similar past twist of fate to somehow give impetus to the English-subtitling of videos. If one is diligent, lucky and knows friends or relatives in Hawaii (which has a large Japanese-speaking population), one might come across English-subtitled films recorded off of local Hawaiian television. But even that recourse offers generally slim pickings. So, what are the alternatives for the hapless buff of Japanese genre films? Learn to watch the films without the English? You will need patience and concentration. A small knowledge of Japanese would definitely be helpful. If you run into a film without much action, a scenario composed largely of "talking-heads" scenes, even patience, concentration and a bit of Japanese will not help. Then again, since I wrote the first draft of this introduction in the late 1990s, there has been a mushrooming of "grey market" websites offering DVDs with fan-generated subtitles (many of them well-done). Major, as well as smaller boutique, DVD labels such as Criterion, Home Vision, Media Blasters/Tokyo Shock, Synapse, Diskotek and Animeigo have put out legitimate releases. There have also been many Region 2 British and French DVD releases, as well as subtitled movies exclusively streaming on the internet.

One of the reasons I have gone into as much detail as I have on story/plot descriptions in some of this book's film listings' is because, for many of you readers out there, figuring it out on your own, especially during the first ten or fifteen films viewed, can be a daunting and frustrating experience. And I, myself, still do not know enough Japanese to deduce the finer details and subtleties of character development/storyline without subtitles. Another reason I have gone into so much detail on selected movies' plots is that one of the most fascinating aspects of the genre is the seemingly countless variations on *ninkyo* and/or *jitsuroku* formula – the variations on a theme. It boggles the mind. And it truly proves the old axiom that there are only three or four basic story plots, and everything else – the differences, what makes the story special (or not) – is in the details.

Japanese video and DVD boxes for yakuza *eiga* – the 1960s–1970s variety and from Toei Studios' especially – are covered with collages made up of lurid pop art, garish colors, stylized representations of Japanese characters (the *kanji* alphabet delineating the titles/credits) and still photos and/or original poster art from the movies. On initial exposure, the best description I can give of my first impression was: overwhelming sensory overload. That is another reason I love these movies. They are different in style and content from the more glossy, action-choked Hong Kong crime thrillers they heavily influenced – more mood, often better-developed characters, more introspective in tone.[28]

They are also – depending on the individual film – amongst the most warped, nihilistic and/or romantic motion pictures I have ever seen.

ONE LAST WORD OF CAUTION BEFORE YOU PROCEED. AS THIS IS AN ENCYCLOPEDIA, AND I FIRMLY BELIEVE A DESCRIPTION OF A MOVIE'S STORYLINE, INCLUDING THE ENDING, IS ESSENTIAL, THERE ARE WHAT MANY READERS MIGHT CONSIDER SPOILERS AHEAD. DO NOT SAY YOU WERE NOT WARNED.

---

28   Although there are many later Hong Kong films that compare very favorably with the best of yakuza *eiga*: DANGEROUS ENCOUNTERS OF THE FIRST KIND (aka DON'T PLAY WITH FIRE) (1980) and BETTER TOMORROW 3 (aka LOVE AND DEATH IN SAIGON) (1989) directed by Tsui Hark; BETTER TOMORROW (1986), BETTER TOMORROW 2 (1987), THE KILLER (1989), JUST HEROES (1989), BULLET IN THE HEAD (1990), and HARDBOILED (1992) directed by John Woo; CITY ON FIRE (1987), PRISON ON FIRE (1987), PRISON ON FIRE 2 (1988), WILD SEARCH (1989) and FULL CONTACT (1992) directed by Ringo Lam; MY HEART'S THAT ETERNAL ROSE (1987) directed by Patrick Tam; THE BIG HEAT (1988) directed by Andrew Kam/Johnny To; CASINO RAIDERS 2 (1991) directed by Johnny To; et. al.

GLOSSARY OF JAPANESE TERMS

abare – rampage, rampaging, violent
abarenbo – thunder, thundering
Abashiri – notorious prison on Japan's northern island of Hokkaido
akai – red
aku – evil, bad
akuma – devil, demon
akumyo – bad reputation, bad name
akuto – villain, scoundrel
ankoku gai – the criminal underworld, organized crime; literal translation: "dark street"
ansatsu – assassin(s)
arashi – storm, anger
asobi – games, sometimes gambling

baka – fool, jerk, idiot, moron
bakudan – bomb
bakuto – gambler
bakuchi, bakuchiuchi – gambling den
bangaichi – native turf, home ground
bokyo – nostalgic, homesick
boryoku – violent
boryokudan – violent gang
boso – violent
bosozoku – violent tribe (slang used to describe gangs of teenage hooligans also known as "hot-rod gangs" though their transport is more likely motorcycles; many *bosozoku* gangs serve as apprenticeship/training for the big-time yakuza
botan – peony flower
burai – hoodlum, villain

chi – blood
chizome(no) – bloodstained
chi kemuri – blood spray
chimatsuri – blood offering; offering to war god; slang for bloodbath
chi(no)ame – bloodshed; literal translation: "rain of blood"

dai kanbu – leading members (as in leading mobsters or *capos*)
datsu goku – escape
datsu goku sha – escape artist
-den – suffix meaning "story(ies)," "tale(s)," "account of," "record of." "report"
deka – slang for detective, cop
do – road, path, highway
dosu – sword

eiga – film(s), cinema

furyo – depraved, bad, delinquent

gaiden – authentic account, true story
gendai – current, modern, contemporary
gokudo – scoundrel, yakuza member
gorotsuki – rogue, scoundrel
gumi – gang, group
gurentai – hoodlums, hooligans
gyangu – gang

hada – flesh
hakaba – burial, graveyard
hamonjo – act of expulsion, excommunication, to exile
hana – flower(s)
hana fuda – flower cards (one of the most popular forms of gambling in Japan; unique to Japanese culture, composed of small picture cards – mainly featuring flowers and abstract patterns/designs of color; about the size of one's thumb)
hanzai – crime
hatashijo – challenge to a fight, usually issued from one clan to another
heitai – soldier
hen – story, saga
hissatsu – killer(s), assassin(s), hit man(men)
hitokiri – killer

ichiban – first; the best; foremost; number one; person at the forefront; top grade
ikka – clan, gang
inochi – life
inu – dog
ippiki okami – lone wolf
irezumi (shisei) – tattoo

jigoku – hell; inferno
jingi – gambling code; honor and humanity
jinginaki – without a code; without honor and/or humanity
jitsuroku – true or authentic account
joshuu – female prisoner
joro – whore
ju – beast

kaoyaku – boss, leader
karajishi – lion; sometimes slang for courage
katana – sword, blade
kaze – wind
keiji – cop, detective

keisatsu – police
kemono(kedamono) – beast, animal, monster
ken – sword
kenju – gun
kenka – violent; fight
kenka jo – invitation/challenge to a gangfight
kessen – bloody battle
kessho – written in blood
ketsu – blood
ketto – duel, feud, fight, confrontation
kirikomi – attack
kirikomi tai – counterattack
kobun – apprentice
kogarashi – cold wind
koroshi – murder
koroshi ya – hit man (men), killer(s), assassin(s)
koso – feud, duel, battle
kumicho – boss, leader
kurenai – red, crimson
kuro, kuroi – dark, black, darkness
kyodai – brother(s)
kyoden – brotherhood
kyojotabi – fugitive
kyokaku – chivalrous, chivalry
kyokatsu – blackmail, threat, extortion

ma – devil
machi – town, quarters; district
maka – evil
mamushi – viper(s), snake(s)
matatabi – wanderer (as in wandering gambler/wandering gambler-swordsmen)
mesu – woman
mesu inu – bitch
michi – road, path, highway, street
minagoroshi – massacre
mon – gate
mori – forest
mure – band of, group of
mushuku, mushuku mono, mushuku nin – wanderer

nagaremono – drifter
nagurikomi – killing
narazu mono – rogue, scoundrel, outlaw
neko – cat
ningen – person, human being
ninkyo, ninkyoshi – chivalrous, chivalry

ninkyodo – path of chivalry
nora – stray, wild

okami – wolf
okite – law, code
onna – woman
otoko – man
oyabun – leader, boss; more of an old-fashioned term used to affectionately delineate the almost fatherly figure of the boss; used profusely in *ninkyo* (chivalrous) yakuza films; used somewhat in the *jitsuroku gendai* (more modern "true" accounts) but in these films you just as often hear the less affectionate (but no less respectful) term for boss: *kumicho, kaoyaku, shacho, socho,* etc.,.

retsuden – biography(ies), life story (ies)
roku denashi – good-for-nothing(s)
ronin – masterless samurai
ryo – gold coin
ryu – dragon
ryuketsu – bloodshed

sakazuki – loyalty offering ceremony with sake cup exchange; usually a ceremony to induct a new initiate into the gang, to cement ties between gangs, or patch up differences between rivals or enemies; in the latter case, where tensions may be high, the ceremony is officiated by a respected neutral third party of rank
sakura – cherry tree/cherry blossoms
sakusen – strategy, tactics, operations
satsu – killing, murder
satsujin – killer(s)
seishun – youth, young people
sengo – post-war
senso – war
shi, shin – death
shin – new (different *kanji* from previous)
shikaku – killer(s), assassin(s)
shobu – showdown, victory, game of chance/skill
socho – leader, boss
soshiki – system, organization, organism, i.e. *soshiki boryoku* = organized crime

tabi – travels, trip, journey
taiketsu – duel, feud, fight
tatakai – war, battle
tekiya – street peddler(s)
tengu – goblin
teppo – gun

toba – gambling, gambler(s)
tobaku – gambling, gambling den
tobakushi – gambling expert
tosei – life, living, livelihood, profession; chivalrous
toseinin – chivalrous man, yakuza member
totsu geki – sudden attack, ambush

uta – song

warui – bad, evil
wataridori – wanderer; literal trans.: "bird-of-passage"

yaburi – broken, breaking; break-out (as in jailbreak)
yadonashi – homeless, vagrant, poor trash
yaju – wild beast
yakuza – aside from being the word literally representing the numbers *ya*-8-*ku*-9-*sa(za)*-3 which, when added together is 20, the worst score in *hana-fuda* (flower cards), has come to symbolize the collectives of gangsters in Japan; the Japanese equivalent of the Italian mafia. In reference to the term as far as the lowest *hana-fuda* score coming to represent groups of gamblers (now mostly gangsters), the term is meant as both bitter irony and symbol of surviving and/or transcending the worst life has to offer.
yojinbo – bodyguard
yota mono – shameless young man; outlaw
yugi – games

zankyo – last; only remaining
zankoku – cruel, cruelty
zenka mono – ex-convict

FILM LISTINGS CREDIT KEY:

DIR. = DIRECTOR   SCR. = SCREENWRITER
PHOTO COLOR (OR B&W) 'SCOPE = CINEMATOGRAPHER (ALL JAPANESE FILMS SHOT BEFORE 1958 WERE IN STANDARD ACADEMY RATIO OF 1:33; AFTER 1958, 90% OF MAJOR STUDIO FILMS WERE SHOT IN 2:35 SCOPE ASPECT RATIO. HOWEVER, THERE WERE A SMALL NUMBER OF SHINTOHO STUDIOS FILMS THAT WERE STILL BEING PHOTOGRAPHED IN ACADEMY RATIO AS LATE AS MID-1958)
MUSIC = MUSIC

I HAVE GIVEN RATINGS TO THE FILMS I HAVE SEEN WITH A NUMBER OF STARS (OR RATHER * ASTERISKS), * BEING POOR TO * * * * BEING EXCELLENT. IF THERE IS A SYNOPSIS BUT NO RATING, I HAVE NOT SEEN THE MOVIE, AND THE PLOT HAS BEEN PARAPHRASED FROM A THEN-CONTEMPORARY UNI-JAPAN FILM MONTHLY PAMPHLET.

SHINTOHO STUDIOS

Female Beast

INTRODUCTION

Shintoho Studios came to be after several years of contentious labor disputes at Toho
Studios in the turbulent post-WW2 period (the late 1940s). At the time, the Communist
Party had a huge following amongst many cast and crew at Toho, as well as at other
studios, and were instrumental in helping to unionize the industry. Which was a good
thing. However, things got so ridiculous in matters of political correctness, there was an
enormous backlash, not just from a more right-wing quarter but also from leftist as well as
apolitical performers and filmmakers who were devoted to cinema as an art rather than as
simply a business or political platform. A great deal of proletariat propaganda forcefed by
the infant unions was starting to show up in some Toho productions as well as crippling
demands that had the unfortunate effect of making the pendulum swing the other way.

    A number of big names, mostly star actors such as Denjiro Okochi and Kazuo
Hasegawa split off with various producers and crew to help form a new company, which
became known as Shintoho. In its early years, Shintoho was owned by Toho. Eventually
Shintoho became an independent, although their films were still distributed by Toho, and
they were often subjected to unfair economic constraints due to Toho's massive post-war
labor problems and consequent mismanagement. Directors working at Toho such as Akira
Kurosawa would often make films at Shintoho, superior genre efforts such as STRAY
DOG (1949). Kon Ichikawa also made his debut film at Shintoho and later turned out such
hard-to-now-see genre efforts as HEAT AND MUD (1950), NIGHTSHADE FLOWER
(1951) and POLICE VS. VIOLENT MOB (1959).

    Older, bigger Toho's distribution of Shintoho product would become an increas-
ingly bitter bone of contention as the decade of the fifties progressed. By 1951, many
of the big stars that had helped to start Shintoho had left for better deals at Daiei and
Shochiku. Since Shintoho never had too many heavyweight directors in their stable –
despite the occasional movies by Daisuke Ito, Nobuo Nakagawa and Kunio Watanabe –
and often had to scramble to keep their doors open, there was a constant struggle to keep
heads above water.

    In 1956, former carnival showman Mitsugu Okura came on board at Shintoho as
executive producer. Okura's manner and taste was laid on with a trowel and was perceived
by many as being vulgar and catering to the lowest-common denominator. Okura shifted
the emphasis from a selection of quickly produced prestige dramas as well as genre films,
to almost exclusively genre "outlaw" cinema. He amped up the sex and violence – as
much as he could get away with – and began producing scores of ever more lurid melodramas, sexy gangster thrillers, samurai films chockfull of swordfights, period horror and
ghost chillers and disturbingly right-wing, nationalist war movies. The formula worked
for a while. Indeed, there were films by directors like Teruo Ishii with his sleaze noir
LINE (aka ZONE) series and Nobuo Nakagawa with his horror and samurai sagas (such
as HELL (JIGOKU, 1960), GHOST OF YOTSUYA (TOKAIDO YOTSUYA KAIDAN,
1959), SHADOW PRIEST'S CRIME CASEBOOK (1959), BLACK CAT MANSION
(BOREI KAIBYO YASHIKI,1958), WICKED WOMAN ODEN TAKAHASHI (1958),
MILITARY COP AND THE GHOST (KENPEI TO YUREI, 1958), THE DEPTHS (KAI-
DAN KASANEGAFUCHI, 1957), et. al.,) that are now looked on as touchstone classics
of their respective genres.

    Unfortunately, the distribution issue with Toho became so acrimonious, Shintoho
attempted to split off from their symbiotic stronger twin as the decade came to a close.
Bankruptcy and studio closure resulted in 1961. Long unavailable, the mid-nineties finally
saw more and more video and DVD releases in Japan of old Shintoho titles, particularly
their horror titles and films directed by Ishii and Nakagawa.

In The Beginning...

SHINTOHO Studios

BAD BOYS aka FURYO SHO-
NEN 1961 **DIR./SCR.** Susumu Hani
PHOTO B&W: Mitsushi Kinu **MUSIC:**
Toru Takemitsu **w/** Tatsuo Yamada,
Hirokazu Yoshitake   A devastating
pseudo-documentary with real-life
reform school veterans portraying
themselves. Hani researched, then
shot a faithful scenario on the streets
and in the institutions where these
boys ended up. A fascinating depiction
of their day-to-day routine of commu-
nal labor, camaraderie and brutality in
reform school which, for many, serves
as a breeding ground for filling the
rosters of future yakuza. * * *

Beast's Flesh

BEAST GANG aka YAJU GUN
aka HERD OF BEASTS 1958 **DIR.**
Tatsuo Asano **SCR.** Tatsuo Asano/
Osamu Nishizawa **PHOTO 'SCOPE:**
Tamotsu Inoue **MUSIC:** Tatsuya
Yoshino   **w/** Hiroshi Kondo,
Kazutoyo Nakajima

BEAST'S FLESH aka NIKUTAI
NO YAJU aka NAKED BEAST
1960 **DIR.** Keinosuke Doi   **w/** Yoko
Mihara, Ryuji Oki

**BROTHERS OF THE ANGRY
WAVES** aka DOTO NO KYODAI
1957 **DIR.** Toshio Shimura **w/** Asao
Matsumoto, Kikuko Hanaoka

**CONDEMNED CRIMINAL'S
VICTORY** aka SHIKEISHU NO
SHORI 1957 **DIR.** Toshio Shimura
SCR. Junichi Nakamura
w/ Ryutaro Amagi, Asao Matsumoto,
Michiko Maeda

Condemned Criminal's Victory

**A CONDEMNED WOMAN
ESCAPES** aka ONNA SHI KEISHU

NO DATSUGOKU aka DEATH
ROW WOMAN 1960 78 min. **DIR.**
Nobuo Nakagawa **SCR.** Yoshihiro
Ishikawa **PHOTO B&W 'SCOPE:**
Shigenari Yoshida **MUSIC:** Teizo
Matsumura   **w/** Miyuki Takakura,
Keinosuke Wada, Ayako Miyata,
Kan Hayashi, Yasuko Mita, Tatsuo
Terashima, Yoichi Numata
A somewhat cliche-ridden but evocative and refreshingly straightforward
action/suspense picture about a
wrongly accused woman escaping
from prison to find evidence on those
who framed her for murder. This has
virtually no yakuza trappings what-
soever except for the heroine's brief
sojourn in the penitentiary. There are
also some slightly shocking (for the
time period) lesbian overtones to these
prison inmate sequences. Directed by
the great Nakagawa.   * * 1/2

Cordon at Dawn

CORDON AT DAWN aka
AKATSUKI NO CHOSEN aka

SUNRISE ROADBLOCK 1957
76 min. **DIR.** Kiyoshi Komori
SCR. Mitsuo Kaneda **PHOTO B&W:**
Yoshitomi Okado **MUSIC:** Sadao
Hase   **w/** Shigeru Amachi, Utako
Mitsuya, Yoichi Numata, Takashi
Wada, Gen Funabashi
Yakuza Amachi snaps, suffering a
psychotic break and kills his boss,
woman and comrades in the process.
He kidnaps his dead boss's daughter
as hostage but is finally shot-to-death
on board a freighter in Yokohama
harbor.

Cordon at Dawn

DARK BREASTS aka KUROI
CHIBUSA aka BRUTAL WOMAN
1960 **DIR.** Michiyoshi Doi **SCR.**
Akira Sugimoto **PHOTO B&W**
'SCOPE: Mamoru Morita **MUSIC:**
Teizo Matsumura   **w/** Bunta
Sugawara, Kinuko Obata, Keiji
Takamiya, Junko Ikeuchi, Kazuko
Wakasugi, Yuji Kawakita   A twisted
noir with Obata as a cynical prosti-
tute exploited by her yakuza pimp
Takamiya. She has also got a nice

younger sister Ikeuchi, who is a nurse. Their longsuffering mom is killed in a crosswalk by a speeding truck, and Obata soon after gets the guts to call in an anonymous tip on her brothel, something which results in Takamiya and gang's arrest. This makes for a great first ten minutes. Doi then takes seemingly forever to set up her gold-digging attempt to wed an ailing millionaire with the clandestine assistance of one of his less-than-honest assistants. At this point, Sugawara enters the picture in a thankless role of token pretty boy, the millionaire's honest assistant who falls in love with the old man's nurse – who just happens to coincidentally be Obata's sister Ikeuchi. Once more Takamiya appears on the scene, released from prison and ready to become the third unwanted partner in Obata's get-rich scheme. Things finally kick into high gear again during the last third of the tale when Takamiya kills Obata's wimpy crime partner then forces her to accompany him to dispose of the body in a remote canyon. Obata takes the opportunity to push Takamiya over the cliff, too, something she hopes will leave her with a clear path to the old man's money. However, fierce wind and lightning during a rainstorm spooks her into haunted flashbacks. Several days later, her apparently paranoid fears suddenly turn out to be well-founded when the scarred, gimpy still-alive Takamiya returns from the grave to stab her to death in her wedding dress! This definitely puts a crimp in her happily-ever-after plans and supplies a poignant denouement with sis Ikeuchi and Sugawara cradling the dying villainess in their arms as she breathes her last. Unusual in that Takamiya's wild part is just the type of macho lunatic role Sugawara later came to portray in many seventies Toei Studios productions. Except for the one already-mentioned slow patch, director Doi shows a real flair for evocative, atmospheric visuals. He also has the ability to get inside lead actress Obata's head, providing her with several voice-over interior monologues that stay just this side of unbridled delirium and keep her from being totally unsympathetic. Doi not only made many other thrillers at Shintoho such as the even crazier SHINING HORIZON, but also went on to helm crime pictures at Shochiku in the mid-sixties. But Shochiku's films from that period remain even more difficult to see than these earlier Shintoho movies. * * *

Dark Breasts

DEADLY PURSUER aka SHI NO TSUISEKISHA 1960 **DIR.** Hiroyuki Nomura **w/** Shuji Sano, Susumu Fujita, Akemi Tsukushi, Keinsouke Wada

Deadly Pursuer

ERA OF VICTORY OR DEFEAT
aka SEIKI NO SHOHAI 1956 **DIR.**
Kyotaro Namiki **w/** Ken Utsui,
Yoichi Numata, Junko Ikeuchi,
Tetsuro Tanba

FEMALE BEAST aka MEJU aka
VICIOUS FEMALE DETECTIVE
1960 77 min. **DIR.** Morihei Magatani
SCR. Kozo Hayama/Hiroshi Shibara
PHOTO B&W 'SCOPE: Yoshitomi
Hirano **MUSIC:** Keitaro Miho
w/ Kinuko Obata, Bunta Sugawara,
Namiji Matsuura, Toshio Hosokawa,
Shuntaro Emi
A fairly fast-moving potboiler about
policewoman Matsuura going undercover to discover various prostitutes'
and female thieves' connections with
a drug gang. Obata is a victimized
female criminal, who is also an addict,
who eventually gets persecuted by
her male cohorts for betrayal at the
climax. Sugawara is another cop who
acts as liaison for Matsuura. There is a
welcome, uninhibitedly trashy nightclub and gang milieu – at least for the
rather conservative time period. Obata
not only shoots up heroin a couple of
times, but also must endure a rather
grueling bondage and water torture
scene near the end before being rescued by Matsuura and Sugawara. Per
usual, to maximize box office returns,
executive producer Ogura made sure
that the audience would be fed rawer
thrills than they would get from the
fare of competing studios. Although at
the time Nikkatsu and Toei did often
come close to the envelope-pushing
in this regard, Shintoho still won the
sleaze-stakes by a narrow margin.
* * *

**FEMALE THIEF AND THE
BOMB** aka BAKUDAN ODAKU
ONNA KAITO aka FEMALE
THIEF'S EXPLOSIVE EMBRACE
1960 77 min. **DIR.** Michiyoshi Doi
SCR. Michiyoshi Doi/Masayoshi
Otsura **PHOTO B&W 'SCOPE:**
Mamoru Morita **MUSIC:** Chumei
Watanabe **w/** Bunta Sugawara,
Miyuki Takakura. Yoko Mihara,
Yoichi Numata, Teruo Yoshida, Mako
Sanjo   Although director Doi
has some genre near-masterpieces
to his credit, this particular outing is
too hamstrung with hackneyed plot
conventions to really transcend into
that territory. Which is not to say it
isn't watchable. It *is* an entertaining
potboiler, and Doi keeps the story
moving with plenty of action, often
quite violent for the time period. Then
again, going the extra mile with sleaze
and violence was underdog Shintoho
Studios stock-in-trade. Supplying the
former is alluring Yoko Mihara as
mustachioed villain Numata's main
squeeze. Miyuki Takakura is the head

of a gang of thieves pursuing uncut diamonds, but we learn by the end that she is only trying to get back what was rightfully family property. Her father had been killed during the war in Manchuria, and dad's originally loyal right hand man (Numata) had taken over. A very young Sugawara is a cop hoodwinked by Takakura in the opening scene on a train. He meets her days later and claims to have been sacked for his incompetence, but in reality he has gone undercover trying to penetrate her gang. One of Takakura's own smitten men teeters off the deep end with jealousy as Sugawara becomes the favored henchman, and he tries to rip off Numata alone. Captured, he is repeatedly tortured (with a blowtorch! – ah, the joys of Shintoho!) then strapped to a broad crucifix. Young Teruo Yoshida, the only conscientious one of Numata's gang, is forced by Numata to shoot the man to death to make his bones. Numata actually has to clasp Yoshida's hand and help pull the trigger to get him to comply. Meanwhile Yoshida's girl (and Numata's secretary) played by Sanjo is in reality Takakura's niece and an informant to what is going on in the villain gang. Needless to say, by the end everything is resolved happily, with Numata and villains arrested, and Sugawara saving bound Takakura and Sanjo from a bomb on a speeding boat. The film's real saving grace is Doi's orchestration of tough-guy action, which is never less than involving. * * *

FOLLOW THE CRIME MAP aka HANZAI CHIZU O SAGASE 1958 **DIR.** Tadashi Morizono **SCR.** Keiichi Abe   w/ Jiro Takano, Masatoshi Yasuda, Kazuhiko Tanaka

(SHINTOHO/NTV)

GEISHA'S VIOLENCE aka BORYOKU NO GEISHA aka VIOLENT GEISHA 1956 **DIR.** Seiichiro Uchikawa   w/ Shoji Nakayama, Ken Utsui, Masayo Banri

Girls Without Return Tickets

GIRLS WITHOUT RETURN TICKETS aka JOTAI UZUMAKI-TO aka WOMEN OF WHIRLPOOL ISLAND 1960 72 min. **DIR.** Teruo Ishii **SCR.** Toshiaki Okado/ Teruo Ishii **PHOTO COLOR 'SCOPE:** Hiroshi Suzuki **MUSIC:** Chumei Watanabe w/ Teruo Yoshida, Yoko Mihara, Masayo Banri, Kimi Hoshi, Shigeru Amachi, Miho Shiro, Masayo Yoshida, Kiyoko Wakamizu, Reiko Sedo
A sexploitive epic of brash young hero Yoshida trying to save his girl Mihara from a drug/prostitute/slavery ring run by penicil-mustachioed gangster Amachi on one of the Japanese islands. We actually do not even get

to see villain Amachi until the last third of the saga when he gets fed up enough with his underboss to step in for harsher measures. The one catch in the narrative is that Mihara is hooked on the drugs the gang smuggles, has gotten more than used-to the whole set-up and is now the head madam. This plays havoc with her conflicted feelings for Yoshida, but she redeems herself by stopping a bullet met for him at the climax. There are quite a few evocative scenes, some shocking for the time. One in particular has a crew of just-arrived women taking off their stockings, garters and high heels to turn over smuggled packets of heroin to the gangsters. It is a surprisingly strong sequence with the girls immediately exchanging their cash pay for doses of the drug. The close-ups of the girls cramming tobacco cigarettes full of the smack, then "chasing the dragon" bathed in red light burns itself into the memory. Likewise, a scene where Mihara, haunted by her own addiction and unrequited love for Yoshida, drunkenly dances to her club's rock 'n roll singer (with a skull-and-crossbones on his silver shirt), with her, all the while, swirling into evermore hellish surroundings, is extremely well done. Ishii develops the scene so the dancers around her, lit from below, take on an increasingly demonic appearance. There is also a great romantic, noirish ambience augmented by weirdly surreal-day-for-night sequences on the quay and sea cliffs as well as Watanabe's plaintive guitar-and-harmonica-heavy score. This is similar to Shintoho's LINE (CHITAI aka ZONE, 1958-1961) series, which were mostly helmed by Ishii, chronicling the fictional illicit goings-on in prostitu

tion districts in Japan's seedier urban population centers. There is alot of well-integrated action here, softcore (for the time) sex, and an uncommonly strange, almost subtle image of a S&M netherworld, a simultaneously dreamy/nightmarish subtext. Ishii, though not always consistent, often manages to create a fearfully medieval, nocturnal vale of cinematic tears – tongue-in-cheek or not doesn't matter. His sometimes subtle, sometimes obvious *grand guignol* clockwork of Man's existence laden with humorous delusions of romance and ambition, all futilely aimed at the final leveler, the grave, is, without a doubt, his main theme. GIRLS WITHOUT RETURN TICKETS, though fairly devoid of character development and rife with cliches, is nevertheless so watchable, so full of fresh energy and a willingness to go the distance, it emerges as a just-about-perfect fifties exploitation film. * * * 1/2

Gun and Escape

GUN AND ESCAPE aka KENJU TO BAKUSO 1960 **DIR.** Go (Satoru) Kobayashi **SCR.** Mitsuo

Kaneda w/ Teruo Yoshida, Hiroshi
Aikawa, Yoko Mihara

KAABISHI GUN TERROR aka
KYOFU KAABISHIJU 1954 **Dir.**
Tetsu Taguchi **Scr.** Tatsuo Asano
Photo B&W: Kan Inoue **Music:**
Senji Ito w/ Shigeru Amachi, Yoko
Mihara, Hiroshi Kondo, Kiyoshi
Murayama

Kaabishi Gun Terror

KILLER AND GUN aka
SATSUJIN TO KENJU 1958
Dir. Tatsuo Asano **Scr.** Tatsuo
Asano/Osamu Nishizawa w/ Hiroshi
Kondo, Shinsuke Ashida, Michiko
Kyo

KILL THE TOP MAN aka TOPPU
YA O KOROSE 1960 **Dir.** Tsukasa
Takahashi **Scr.** Shintaro Ishihara
w/ Shigeru Amachi, Jun Otomi,
Tomoo Nagai, Junko Nozumi,
Yoshiko Mita

Kill the Top Man

KING OF THE HARBOR aka
HATOBA NO OJA   1956
Dir. Seiichiro Uchikawa
w/ Michiko Maeda, Tetsuro Tanba

King of the Naked District

KING OF THE NAKED DISTRICT aka AZARASHI NO KINGU 1959 **DIR.** Akira Miwa w/ Ken Utsui, Yoko Mihara

KING OF VIOLENCE aka BORYOKU NO OJA 1956 DIR. Seiichiro Uchikawa **SCR.** Yoshihiro Ishikawa/Michiyoshi Doi w/ Ken Utsui, Shoji Nakayama, Naoko Kubo, Utako Mitsuya, Tetsuro Tanba

KING OF THE WOMEN'S GROTTO aka ONNA GANKUTSU O aka KING OF THE GIRL CAVE 1960 **DIR.** Yoshikazu (Yoshiki) Onoda **PHOTO COLOR 'SCOPE:** Yamanaka w/ Teruo Yoshida, Masayo Banri. Yoko Mihara, Keiji Takamiya

LIFE AND DEATH STRUGGLE IN THE SNOWSTORM aka MO FUBUKI NO SHITO 1959 76 min. **DIR./SCR.** Teruo Ishii w/ Ken Utsui, Akiko Futami, Yoko Mihara, Bunta Sugawara

LINE aka ZONE aka CHITAI series

Secret White Line Zone (#1)

SECRET WHITE LINE ZONE aka HAKUSEN HIMITSU CHITAI aka CALL-GIRL TERRITORY

1958 71 min. **DIR.** Teruo Ishii **SCR.** Kozo Uchida **PHOTO B&W:** Shigenori Yoshida **MUSIC:** Chumei Watanabe w/ Ken Utsui, Yoko Mihara, Shigeru Amachi, Toshiaki Konoe, Teruo Wakatsuki, Satsuki Arakawa, Mitsuhiko Oe, Bunta Sugawara   A "quasi-documentary" series on crime and the rackets of prostitution and white slavery. When I saw the stills from these five films, all but one directed by a very maniacal Ishii, what came to my mind was sexploitative, violent trash – fifties style. The whole time of Shintoho's existence (about 1948 to 1961), they teetered on the brink of financial extinction. From 1957 onwards, you can tell from many of the movies that there was a hunger and desperation behind the scenes that made the powers-that-be pull out all the stops. This was a time – 1957-1961 – when their most visceral films were conjured up out of collective fever dreams. The series is built on stories of denizens of the red-light districts – good-hearted whores; bitter, evil whores; intrepid reporters; diligent, no-nonsense cops; lonely, misunderstood hitmen; arrogant yakuza; slick, manipulating pimps; exotic dancers/ strippers/hostesses; exploited, obsessed salarymen pushed over the edge into violence. This first in the series appears to have been on the verge of being a lost film. A video off of Japanese cable shows considerable wear-and-tear to the negative as well as apparent gaps in the narrative (missing footage?). While the original running time of record is an economical 71 minutes, this currently available version runs an even-shorter 56 fast-moving minutes. Police detective Utsui investigates a murder of a Turkish bath girl and finds the killer has been snuffed, too, by gangsters (one of them an extremely young, baby-faced Bunta Sugawara.) Ishii is on top of his game here with considerable energy and imagination put into his set-ups, his editing and pacing. #1 of 5 films   * * *

Black Line Zone (#2)

BLACK LINE ZONE aka KURO-SEN CHITAI aka INVISIBLE BLACK HANDS 1960 79 min. **DIR.** Teruo Ishii **SCR.** Ichiro Miyagawa/Teruo Ishii **PHOTO B&W 'SCOPE:** Shigenori Yoshida **MUSIC:** Chumei Watanabe **w/** Shigeru Amachi, Yoko Mihara, Toshio Hosokawa, Utako Mitsuya, Jun Otomi, Masayo Yoshida, Ryuji Moriyama, Reiko Sedo, Daijiro Kikugawa, Kuniko Yamamura, Masaru Kodaka   At times, a visual *tour-de-force* with some amazingly chiaroscuro nocturnal 'scope compositions. Ishii keeps the offbeat, sometimes nightmarishly surreal imagery coming as Amachi, a freelance reporter on the trail of a dope gang, is drugged and framed for murder. From the time he encounters a fortuneteller on a Shinjuku backstreet through waking up next to a necktie-strangled hooker to traversing a jungle of strippers, drag queens, cops, addicts and gangsters, Ishii keeps interest, sidestepping the hackneyed plot contrivances with a relentlessly frenetic momentum. The film climaxes with a bravura fight sequence, Amachi tracking one of the killers over rooftops then onto a moving train, each beating the bloody pulp out of the other. The cops pick the villain up at the end. It looks as if we'll get the usual pat happy denouement when Ishii suddenly stands the formula on its head, heart-of-gold hooker Mihara walking away from Amachi, apparently to do time for her part in the drug ring. #2 of 5 films   * * * 1/2

TIGER TRACK ZONE aka IERO – RAIN aka OSEN CHITAI aka YELLOW ZONE 1960 80 min. **DIR./SCR.** Teruo Ishii **PHOTO COLOR 'SCOPE:** Hiroshi Suzuki **MUSIC:** Chumei Watanabe   **w/** Teruo Yoshida, Shigeru Amachi, Yoko Mihara, Mako Sanjo, Jun Otomi, Yoichi Numata, Masayo Yoshida, Katsuko Wakasugi Reporter Yoshida's gal Mihara is snatched by hitman/white slaver Amachi, after Amachi completes a nocturnal murder contract, and the chase is on. Fugitive and hostage catch a train to a harbor town, what looks like an Osaka ghetto by way of the Parisian slums. Ishii creates a strangely twisted ambience of hot-house depravity as Yoshida follows them through back alley districts similar to those in the previous BLACK LINE film. A bit short on the action compared to that saga until Amachi shoots it out with the cops on a sunset-dappled beach at the appropriately nihilistic, bittersweet climax. #3 of 5 films * * *

SEXY ZONE aka SEKUSHI – RAIN aka SEKUSHI CHITAI aka GIRLS OF THE SECRET CLUB 1961 83 min. **DIR./SCR.** Teruo Ishii **PHOTO B&W 'SCOPE:** Noboru Sudo **MUSIC:** Seiji Hiraoka   w/ Teruo Yoshida, Yoko Mihara, Mako Sanjo, Junko Ikeuchi, Toshio Hosokawa, Ryuji Oki, Koko Sasaki, Yoji Naruto, Masayo Yoshida, Kazuo Harada Yoshida is waylaid by pickpocket Mihara, who slips a stolen wallet in his coat while flirting with him. Subsequently, he is the one who gets arrested. He manages to clear things up. Both angry and fascinated, he searches for Mihara only to learn that she has been shanghaied by a yakuza gang for their sex club. Using a phony "artist's model studio" setup, they attract salarymen and other shady types to sketch nude models. For an added price, the models must sleep with the libidinous clients. Yoshida affects a somewhat exaggerated rockabilly conk hairdo (!) and pinstriped suit to go undercover and rescue Mihara. Sadly, this is extremely action-deficient as well as skimpy on the sleaze. Ishii does generate some suspense and arresting visuals near the end when Yoshida and Mihara flee, are caught and bound, then once again escape through a labyrinth of shadowy, decrepit corridors and cellars. Not only Ishii's last film directed for the series, but his last film for Shintoho as well. His next film was the old-fashioned, Rat Pack-inspired yakuza/heist thriller, FLOWERS, THE STORM

AND THE GANG (1961) at Toei. #4 of 5 films * * 1/2

Firing Line Zone (#6)

FIRING LINE ZONE aka KASEN CHITAI 1961 **DIR.** Hiromichi Takebe **SCR.** Teruo Ishii/Hiromichi Takebe **PHOTO COLOR 'SCOPE:** Noboru Sudo **MUSIC:** Rinichiro Manabe w/ Teruo Yoshida, Yoko Mihara, Shigeru Amachi, Jun Tazaki, Ryuji Wakamiya   A very fast-moving, gritty, occasionally in-your-face romp with con men Yoshida and his younger pal posing as bookies lurking outside the horse races who then abscond with the bets. Not only do they run afoul of the local yakuza run by Tazaki but also lone wolf/tough guy gambler Amachi. Amachi and Yoshida eventually establish an uneasy rapport since they are both larcenous but not in the same bloodthirsty mold as Tazaki's henchmen. Tazaki's mistress Mihara falls-in-love with Yoshida. The story bogs down a bit in the middle but recovers nicely in the last third with a chaotic harbor district shoot-out. There are some exhilarating tracking shots with fatally wounded Mihara making a run for it alongside Yoshida and Amachi, then Tazaki's gang being cut down in a hail of bullets from a rival mob. Mihara dies in Yoshida's arms amidst the grimy, slick pilings while an embarrassed Amachi looks on. There is quite a bit of location work on the streets of Tokyo, Osaka and Yokohama in the whole LINE series, and this final entry achieves an ambience similar to some of Seijun Suzuki's late fifties Nikkatsu pictures (such as UNDERWORLD BEAUTY). Newcomer director Takebe shows talent, but I'm not aware of anything else he did after this. If he stayed in the business, he most likely found his way into television (or went back to being an assistant director). #5 and final in series   * * *

NUDE ACTRESS MURDER – FIVE CRIMINALS aka NIKUTAI JOYU GOROSHI – GONIN NO HANZAI-SHA 1957 74 min. **Dir.** Teruo Ishii **Scr.** Isamu Nakata/Akira Miwa **Photo B&W:** Hiroshi Suzuki **Music:** Raymond Hattori w/ Ken Utsui, Utako Mitsuya, Shigeru Amachi, Reiko Kita, Yoko Mihara, Shigeru Ogura, Kan Hayashi
One can discern a perversely culti-vated imagination already at work in Ishii as far back as this early sexploit-ive crime/action potboiler. Utsui is the classic investigative reporter in hat and trenchcoat on the scent of a wave of strip club murders, threatened by gangsters, deceitful strippers and a psycho killer. Considering Ishii's in-volvement, though, this is not as wild as it should be.   * * 1/2

POLICE AND THE VIOLENT MOB aka KEISATSU TO BORY-OKUDAN 1959 **Dir.** Kon Ichikawa w/ Ryo Ikebe, Jun Tazaki Apparently one of the low budget films Ichikawa did at Shintoho to help put bread on the table. But even in Japanese film reference books there is an appalling dearth of information on this seem-ingly lost film. Ichikawa did two other crime films at Shintoho, HEAT AND MUD (1950) and NIGHTSHADE FLOWER (1951) which are also impossible to see.

POLICE OFFICER aka KEISAT-SU KAN 1957 **Dir.** Kyotaro Namiki w/ Ken Utsui, Ayako Ebata, Saburo Sawai

Poison Fang Oran

POISON FANG ORAN aka DO-KUJA NO ORAN 1958 73 min. **Dir.** Goro Kadono w/ Kinuko Obata, Shigeru Amachi, Ryuzaburo

Nakamura, Kazuko Wakasugi, Kotaro Bando Oran (Obata) is an innocent girl who falls in love with a reformer samurai (Nakamura) right before the Shogunate's downfall. They become separated after his cohorts are massacred by the infamous Shogunate support-group of assassins, the Shinsengumi. A number of years later, after the beginning of the Meiji Restoration, and still pining for Nakamura, Obata goes on a pilgrimage with her female friend. Along the way, she is shanghaied into prostitution by villainous yakuza Amachi. Gradually, she becomes accustomed to their debauched lifestyle in Edo, now renamed Tokyo, and helps Amachi with his crimes, which include gambling, extortion and con games. When the cops get wise, they assault Amachi's headquarters at the climax. Both Amachi and Obata wound or kill scores of policemen with their revolvers and knives before being captured. Lo and behold, Nakamura is the chief of police. There is a tearful reunion between the two at the police office, but there is little Nakamura can do for her. At the close, he watches her through his window, being led away in shackles in the falling snow. A reasonably entertaining potboiler somewhat similar to Nobuo Nakagawa's 1958 Shintoho film WICKED WOMAN ODEN TAKAHASHI, but with more violence. It is also sometimes reminiscent of a Mizoguchi female tragedy film but without the deeper resonances and inflections. The storyline prefigures Yasuzo Masumura's THE SPIDER TATTOO as well as numerous efforts at Toei in the later 1960s. Kadono is not a particularly accomplished director, but he keeps things moving along at a relatively fast pace

and is able to orchestrate a few vigorous action scenes, particularly at the climax. Despite being made in 1958, it was apparently lensed before Shintoho switched over to CinemaScope lenses that year – it is shot in standard aspect ratio. * * *

QUEEN BEE aka JO BACHI series

Queen Bee (#1)

QUEEN BEE aka JO BACHI 1958 76 min. **DIR.** Tetsu Taguchi **SCR.** Kozo Uchida **PHOTO B&W:** Tadashi Nishimoto **MUSIC:** Senji Ito w/ Naoko Kubo, Shoji Nakayama, Shigeru Amachi, Yoko Mihara, Tomihiko Otani, Kazuhei Yokoyama, Masaru Kodaka Kubo is the daughter of a stern, yet benevolent *tekiya* boss. She takes over the reins of the gang when he is mortally injured in a brawl and a fire instigated by nightclub owner/gang boss Amachi, who wants to take over the street peddlers and their waterfront properties. Nakayama is the chivalrous seaman in love with Kubo. Strangely old-fashioned through a great deal of the film, with Shintoho's trademark, gratuitous sleaze factor in the form of voluptuous, scantily-clad strippers doing their thing at Amachi's watering hole. There is also too much talk and sentiment. The film miraculously boils over and comes to life in the last fifteen minutes with an incredibly savage, rolling gang-fight in the district alleys and clubs culminating in a lonely western-style shootout between Kubo and Amachi on the deserted pier. They both fatally wound each other, and Kubo dies in Nakayama's arms. The picture ends with Kubo receiving a reverent burial in the cemetery adjoining the Catholic mission overlooking the harbor. Seaman Nakayama, Kubo's Christian kid-sister and the chain-smoking Japanese priest/doctor at graveside create a strangely surreal, moving denouement. This undoubtedly became a series after the fact, since Kubo returns in a similar role in the next installment. These were probably the closest Shintoho came to "real" yakuza films that were more in the mid-1960s Toei/Nikkatsu mold. #1 of 4 films * * 1/2

QUEEN BEE'S ANGER aka JO BACHI NO IKARI 1958 75 min. DIR. Teruo Ishii SCR. Kozo Uchida PHOTO COLOR 'SCOPE: Shigenori Yoshida MUSIC: Chumei Watanabe w/ Naoko Kubo, Ken Utsui, Shoji Nakayama, Shigeru Amachi, Miyuki Takakura, Tadao Takashima, Yoko Mihara, Bunta Sugawara, Takamaru Sasaki
A very enjoyable melodrama with Kubo up against various villains.

Ishii unfurls a surreal beauty pageant production number in the middle of a street under the opening titles and from then on the eyes are pretty much kept occupied to "The End" unscrolls. This has a similar kind of visual imagination in regards to use of color and movement as Seijun Suzuki but in a more scattershot, "let's-see-what-sticks-to-the-wall" fashion. Despite the effect being uneven compared to Suzuki, otherwise the comparison is apt, and Ishii deserves more attention from critics, buffs and archivists of Japanese genre films than he has been given. #2 of 4 films * * 1/2

Queen Bee (#3)

QUEEN BEE AND THE SCHOOL FOR DRAGONS aka JO BACHI TO DAIGAKU NO RYU aka RETURN OF THE QUEEN BEE 1960 81 min. DIR. Teruo Ishii SCR. Teruo Ishii/Kozo Uchida PHOTO COLOR 'SCOPE: Kinnao Okada MUSIC: Yoshi Eguchi w/ Kanjuro Arashi, Yoko Mihara, Teruo Yoshida, Shigeru

Amachi, Ryuji Oki, Masayo Banri, Hiroshi Asami, Kazuhiko Saeki An entertaining, fast-moving tall tale with virtually non-stop action. Lone wolf navy veteran Yoshida helps Mihara and gang boss father Arashi, ward off rival Japanese and Chinese gangs in the Kanto district (although it looks more like Okinawa) then starts a small gang of outcasts himself. Mihara also has a girl gang on the side very much in the mold of such later films as Toei's GIRL BOSS series and Nikkatsu's STRAY CAT ROCK films. In fact, this picture seems like the prototype for many late sixties yakuza *eiga* but with even more vitality. One exhilarating sequence has scantily-clad Mihara parading on her gang's altar palanquin to challenge the rival gang's scantily-clad girl on a palanquin during festival. Father Arashi can't handle this uninhibited lusty behavior and tries in vain to get Mihara to stop. Everyone ignores him, and he is surrounded by a harassing bunch wearing festival masks who chase him out onto a deserted thoroughfare. They turn out to be rival yakuza who take out a roll of barbed wire and actually begin to tie Arashi up with it before he is rescued by Mihara, Yoshida and friends. Then there is the broad daylight, spectacular all-out, pitched gun/sword battle between the gangs at the climax – a mindblowing setpiece with an intoxicating exuberance. Nothing profound nor original, but a vibrant piece of cinema overflowing with life. One of Ishii's best films. #3 of 4 films * * * *

QUEEN BEE'S COUNTER-ATTACK aka JO BACHI NO GYAKUSHU 1961 82 min. **DIR.** Yoshikazu (Yoshiki?) Onoda **SCR.**

Kozo Uchida **PHOTO COLOR 'SCOPE:** Kinnao Okada **MUSIC:** Chumei Watanabe **w/** Yoko Mihara, Shigeru Amachi, Ryuji Oki, Shinsuke Mikimoto, Terumi Hoshi Despite gorgeous rustic mountain locations and almost as much action as the previous film, this falls far short of its anarchic spirit and perverse humor. Too often the vitality here just degenerates into silliness. Director Onoda seems a bit inept at sustaining tone or suspense as Mihara, aided and abetted by a bratty pair of teenage sidekicks (the girl constantly brandishes a slingshot), helps a friend's clan resist the bad boss's gang. Cowboy hat-wearing Amachi is a fake lone hitman who turns out to be a government agent whom Mihara falls for as the story wraps. #4 and final in series * * 1/2

Roar of the Bullets

ROAR OF THE BULLETS aka DOGO SURU KYODAN 1960 **DIR.** Yoshihiro Ishikawa **w/** Shigeru Amachi, Ken Utsui

RULE OF THE ROSE AND THE GUNWOMAN aka BARA TO ONNA KENJU O 1958 **DIR.** Kiyoshi Komori **SCR.** Toshiaki Okado **w/** Kinuko Obata, Akemi Tsukushi, Tetsuro Tanba

Rule of the Rose and the Gunwoman

SEAGOING G-MEN aka KAI JO
G-MEN 1959 **DIR.** Toshio Shimura
w/ Susumu Fujita, Yumeji Tsukioka

*The Shining Horizon aka The Horizon
Glitters*

THE SHINING HORIZON aka
CHIHEISEN GA GIRAGIRA 1961
86 min. **DIR.** Michiyoshi Doi **SCR.**
Kozo Uchida/Michiyoshi Doi **PHOTO**
B&W 'SCOPE: Mamoru Morita
w/ Jerry Fujio, Jun Tatara, Shigeru
Amachi, Kimi Hoshi, Masayo Banri

A demented action thriller-cum-black-
comedy energized with an intoxicatingly primitive vitality. Six very different cellmates break out of prison to
retrieve buried diamonds in the countryside. Hated, belligerent bigmouth
Fujio – giving a volcanic performance – becomes de facto boss of the
bunch. On the last leg of the convicts'
journey they hijack an empty, clown
tour bus, put the unconscious driver in
a box and bury him alive in the forest!
Two of the most bumbling, funny
fugitives don clown outfits and end up
perpetrating their shocking violence
as Pierrot and Charlie Chaplin. Along
the way, they also kidnap a girl who
actually becomes enamored of the
less vicious Fujio. All six wind up
shot, snakebit, stabbed or bludgeoned
to death by the time they reach the
location of the loot – a strikingly lone,
denuded tree on an otherwise barren
rocky hill. Black leather-jacketed
Fujio exudes considerable charisma
and went on to become a mostly
comic supporting player at Toho and
Toei in the sixties. * * * 1/2

SPEED AGERS aka ONNA TO
INOCHI KAKETE BUTTOBASE
1960 **DIR.** Morihei Magatani **PHOTO**
B&W 'SCOPE: Yoshihiro Okado
w/ Ken Utsui, Mako Sanjo
Gamblers, teenage delinquents and
speedboat racing don't mix.

**STREETCORNER OF TEEN-
AGERS** aka JUDAI NO MAGARI
KADO 1959 **DIR.** Go (Satoru)
Kobayashi **PHOTO B&W 'SCOPE:**
Hidemitsu Iwahashi **w/** Mayumi
Ozora, Tadao Takashima, Ayame
Hanazono, Yumiko Matsubara
Teen girls are forced into
prostitution by young hoods.

THE STRIPPER AND THE BLIND ALLEY OF KILLERS aka RAJO TO SATSUJIN-MEIRO 1959 79 min. DIR. Yoshikazu (Yoshiki?) Onoda SCR. Yusuke Watanabe/ Shigeru Kawakami PHOTO B&W: Susamu Yamanaka MUSIC: Koji Eguchi w/ Keinosuke Wada, Utako Mitsuya, Masao Shimizu, Tetsuro Tanba, Kazuko Wakasugi, Masayo Banri   This begins with brutal hood Tanba coercing his mentally challenged accomplice to shoot a scantily-clad girl in a dirty alley. Tanba then kicks the girl's corpse into an adjacent canal. The foregoing brutality occurs pre-titles, and director Onoda delivers similar periodic jolts throughout this squalid saga's compact running time. But, although it is an occasionally violent programmer, Onoda and writers Watanabe and Kawakami let the events mushroom out of the depths of the characters rather than from a pro-scribed set of contrived events. It is all rather surprisingly good, especially considering the seemingly meager budget and limited access to sets. Bitter Shimizu is the much older leader of a very small gang who plan to heist the take from a baseball stadium's big game. Wada is the decent kid involved who works as a guard at the ballpark. Mitsuya is his sweet, but no-nonsense girl who improbably works as a stripper at a nearby club. There are a few slow, talky patches, but the film keeps interest and has a particularly riveting last fifteen minutes as the thieves fall out when the cops close in, leading to violent death. Shot in standard aspect ratio for some reason, even though 90% of Shintoho's output from 1958 on was shot in anamorphic 'scope.
* * *

Tears of a Tokyo Night

TEARS OF A TOKYO NIGHT aka TOKYO NO YORU WA NAITEIRU 1961 DIR. Morihei Magatani w/ Ken Utsui, Kazuko Matsuo

This is a Man's World

THIS IS A MAN'S WORLD aka OTOKO NO SEKAI DA 1960 80 min. DIR. Michiyoshi Doi SCR. Kozo Hayama PHOTO B&W 'SCOPE: Mamoru Morita MUSIC: Keitaro Miho w/ Teruo Yoshida, Mayumi Ozora, Bunta Sugawara, Keiji

Takamiya, Tatsuo Terajima, Masayo Banri, Toshio Hosokawa A two-fisted action tale of student boxing champion Yoshida being informed by friend Sugawara that their comrade has been murdered by a yakuza gang trying to take control of the dock-workers in a busy harbor district. Yoshida plunges into a fight against the gang and is occasionally aided by lone wolf killer Takamiya a conflicted anti-hero employed by evil, behind-the-scenes string-puller Hosokawa. Good girl Ozora has little to do. But second-billed female lead Banri makes a great impression as the bar hostess sweetheart of Takamiya, a gutsy gal who ends up sacrificing her life for her beau. Not as downright crazy as director Doi's other notable Shintoho efforts, DARK BREASTS and THE SHINING HORIZON, but still overflowing with vitality. It is a shame that Doi's later crime action films at Shochiku during the 1960s seem to be unavailable for viewing. * * 1/2

Three Female Thieves

THREE FEMALE THIEVES aka SANNIN NO GOTO 1960 **DIR.** Go (Satoru) Kobayashi **w/** Masayo Banri

TIME OF A MAN'S BLOODSHED aka OTOKO GA CHI O MITAJI 1960 **DIR.** Akira Miwa **w/** Utako Mitsuya, Rokuro Matsubara, Hisashi Asami

Time of a Man's Bloodshed

Traitor

TRAITOR aka HANGYAKUJI aka CONSPIRATOR 1960 **DIR.** Go (Satoru) Kobayashi **w/** Hisashi Asami, Ken Utsui, Sumiko Abe

UNDERGROUND EMPIRE'S DEATH CHAMBER aka CHIKA TEIKOKU NO SHIKEISHITSU 1960 **DIR.** Kyotaro Namiki **PHOTO B&W 'SCOPE:** Tadashi Nishimoto **w/** Ken Utsui, Junko Ikeuchi, Keinosuke Wada, Tadao Takashima, Keiji Takamiya, Mako Sanjo

VENGEANCE OF THE FEMALE PEARL'S RULE 1956 Dir. Toshio Shimura w/ Susumu Fujita, Michiko Maeda, Tetsuro Tanba

WHERE'S PARADISE? aka TENGOKU WA DOKO DA 1956 Dir. Muneyoshi Matsubayashi Scr. Masahiro (Shoji) Segawa w/ Isao Kimura, Yoichi Numata, Keiko Tsushima

WHORE GANG'S ZERO LINE aka ZERO SEN NO JORO GUN aka FURY OF SEDUCED WOMEN 1960 73 min. Dir. Akira Miwa Scr. Akira Miwa/Kiyoshi Oda Photo B&W 'scope: Kinnao Okada Music: Chumei Watanabe w/ Kinuko Obata, Tatsuo Terajima, Tetsuro Tanba, Jun Otomi, Rokuro Matsubara   Lonely decent girl Obata comes to the big city to find work but is ensnared by a gang of jive-talking, sadistic yakuza. Before long she is forced to turn tricks along with other indentured girls. Tanba is the slick, cruel boss of the sex-slave mob, a bunch who also make porno movies on the side. Good guy Terajima – who Obata had met at the train station on her arrival – returns to town and tries to help when he finds out what's going on. When there is a police raid on their brothel, Obata and another girl use the distraction to make a run for it. But the gang tracks the other girl to her mother's house, murdering her in the woods behind her home. After Obata and the other girls hear about it, they go on the rampage, turning the tables on the hoods. Tanba tries to escape along a building ledge, the women stone him, and he falls on power lines to his death. Director Miwa, who helped direct some of the SUPERGIANT (aka STAR-

MAN) installments with Teruo Ishii, turns in a respectable effort here with a surplus of credibly sleazy atmosphere. It is unfortunate that he didn't seem to have much of a movie career after Shintoho went bankrupt. * * *

Whore Gang's Zero Line

WICKED WOMAN ODEN TAKAHASHI aka DOKUFU TAKAHASHI ODEN 1958 74 min. Dir. Nobuo Nakagawa Scr. Katsuyoshi Nakatsu/Makoto Nakazawa w/ Kazuko Wakasugi, Juzaburo Akechi, Tetsuro Tanba, Asao Matsumoto, Ko (Akira) Nishimura, Keiko Oma, Gen Funabashi In 1870s Tokyo, Oden Takahashi steals to support her consumptive second husband and her daughter from her first marriage. She falls in love with a young policeman, but is coerced into becoming the mistress of and procurer for a vice boss. After the deaths of her second husband and daughter, Oden moves to Yokohama. There she runs a casino for the vice boss. Her remorseful first husband and the disgraced policeman follow her. Oden kills her former husband and the vice boss, but when she tries to escape with the casino takings, she is arrested and returned to Tokyo to stand trial. Atmospheric and full of great performances. * * *

Wicked Woman Oden Takahashi

A WOMAN'S BODY AND THE WHARF aka JOTAI SAMBASHI 1958 73 min. DIR. Teruo Ishii SCR. Akira Sagawa PHOTO B&W: Yoshitomi Hirano MUSIC: Chumei Watanabe   w/ Ken Utsui, Akemi Tsukushi, Yoko Mihara, Shigeru Ogura, Hiroshi Asami, Masao Takamatsu, Sachio (Yukio?) Sayama Something of a precursor to GIRLS WITHOUT RETURN TICKETS. Shot in standard 1:33 aspect in B&W mere months before Shintoho switched to anamorphic 'scope, this has a great gritty, lurid first ten minutes with Utsui as a plainclothes undercover cop investigating a pros-

titution slave ring who finds two of his informants, a pimp and a stripper, brutally murdered. He discovers his ex-girl Mihara is involved with a gangster allied to the American boss of the sex racket. Regrettably, until the ocean liner-at-dock shootout climax, the middle fifty minutes of this short feature is somewhat talky and plodding, without director Ishii's customary over-the-top images and shenanigans. * *

A Woman's Body and the Wharf

A WOMAN'S CHALLENGE AT DAWN aka ONNA KANCHO AKATSUKI NO CHOSEN 1959 DIR. Michiyoshi Doi SCR. Akira Sugimoto   w/ Shigeru Amachi, Miyuki Takakura, Yoko Mihara

WORTHLESS POLICE aka MU KEISATSU aka LAWLESS 1957 83 min. DIR. Kiyoshi Komori SCR. Mitsuo Kaneda PHOTO B&W: Yoshitomi Okado MUSIC: Hideo Ozawa   w/ Shigeru Amachi, Kinuko

Obata, Tetsuro Tanba, Saburo Sawai, Keiji Takamiya   A routine, but nevertheless brutally fast-moving, noirish action thriller with Amachi going up against Tanba's yakuza gang who killed his sweetheart's father. Lone wolf gangster Takamiya complicates matters and gets murdered. Amachi ends up getting help from Tanba's unhappy, alcoholic mistress Obata as well as an undercover cop. However, Tanba gets wise and captures Amachi, Obata and the cop. Obata frees herself from her bonds and rescues Amachi before he is fried-to-death on an electric metal bed! The story wraps up with a shootout in the cellar, Amachi and Obata against the gang, then the undercover cop's reinforcements saving the day. Unhappily, Obata is mortally wounded. Very entertaining.
* * *

YOUNG GIRL WIFE – TERRIBLE SIXTEEN ABILITIES aka SHOJO TSUMA – OSORERU BEKI JUUROKU SAI 1960 **DIR.** Yusuke Watanabe **SCR.** Yusuke Watanabe/ Mitsuo Iida   **w/** Kimi Hoshi, Keiko Hashi, Mako Sanjo, Shigeru Amachi, Ken Utsui, Kinuko Obata

TOEI STUDIOS A-L

Chivalrous Man's Life Story aka *Life Stories (#3)* (ALL IMAGES THIS SECTION © TOEI)

INTRODUCTION

Toei was born at the start of the 1950s, financed by railroad and trucking magnate Hiroshi Okawa, who also owned many other businesses, including baseball teams. By 1953, Toei had inaugurated an extremely successful policy of double bills, one longer 'A' picture, one shorter 'B' picture that revolutionized film exhibition in Japan. Previously, theatres had shown double bills, but the bills would be split between the output of any two studios. When Toei started supplying both features on double bills, the staid, more conservative studios like Toho and Daiei had a hard time matching the competition.

Toei's output through most of the fifties was almost exclusively samurai and crime genre movies. Although there were occasionally prestige efforts by directors such as Tomu Uchida, Tadashi Imai or Daisuke Ito, they were usually in the guise of samurai sword fests or war films. As the sixties progressed, the fare gradually became more violent and gritty.

Toei was the earliest to jump with both feet on the yakuza film bandwagon, continuing with their contemporary urban crime movies and almost singlehandedly creating, circa 1963, the *ninkyo* or chivalrous yakuza film. *Ninkyo* gangster films were usually set in the 1890 – 1940 time period and invariably featured complex webs of obligation and moral quandaries for the conflicted anti-heroes played by the likes of Koji Tsuruta and Ken Takakura. Swordfighting rather than gunplay was the norm. Gradually, as the sixties came to a close, the contemporary urban yakuza films once more came to take precedence. By the mid-1970s, *ninkyo* yakuza pictures had virtually disappeared from not just Toei's line-up but most other studios' as well. The early seventies saw the rise of the *jitsuroku*, or true account, yakuza film as best personified in the films of directors Kinji Fukasaku, Junya Sato and Sadao Nakajima. Toei also struck paydirt with their GIRL BOSS (SUKEBAN) series in the mid-seventies.

The late sixties and seventies saw an increasingly sleazy, sometimes shocking proliferation of nudity, softcore sex and violent bloodshed in many of Toei's efforts. Toei, through pandering to the basest of human nature – albeit in an incredibly entertaining, sometimes transcendentally beautiful, anarchic way – were offering what the dwindling numbers of moviegoers seemed to want. In other words, elements too strong to be found on television, the burgeoning boom of which was helping to destroy the Japanese motion picture industry.

Home of the
Big Guns and Swords...

TOEI Studios

ABASHIRI PRISON aka
ABASHIRI BANGAICHI series:

Abashiri Prison (#1)

ABASHIRI PRISON aka ABA-
SHIRI BANGAICHI aka ABA-
SHIRI NATIVE GROUND 1965
92 min. **DIR.** Teruo Ishii **ORIG STORY**:
Hajime Ito **SCR.** Teruo Ishii **PHOTO**
B&W 'SCOPE: Yoshikazu (Giichi)
Yamazawa **Music:** Masao Yagi
w/ Ken Takakura, Tetsuro Tanba,
Koji Nanbara, Kanjuro Arashi, Kunie
Tanaka, Toru Abe
The first in probably the most well-
known and successful yakuza film
series in Japan. Takakura plays his
most common character: a lone wolf/
outcast who moves easily through
the underworld but, because he is

basically a decent and honorable
fellow, he gets little peace. He is
constantly running afoul of either bad
guys or hypocritical cops, or a rowdy,
irresponsible friend leads him into
trouble. This one begins with him
entering prison. As usual, personal
feuds erupt, and, before too long, he
is put in solitary. A sympathetic cop
(Tanba) is favorably disposed towards
Takakura, but things are spoiled when
Takakura and a homicidal maniac
(Nanbara) he is handcuffed to make
a break, jumping off the work-detail
transport into the snow. At least half
to the last third of our tale is the conflict between Takakura and Nanbara
and how Tanba eventually catches up
to them. #1 of 18 films * * *

ANOTHER ABASHIRI PRISON
STORY aka ZOKU ABASHIRI
BANGAICHI 1965 87 min. **DIR./**
SCR. Teruo Ishii **ORIG. STORY:**
Hajime Ito **PHOTO COLOR 'SCOPE:**
Yoshikazu (Giichi) Yamazawa
MUSIC: Masao Yagi   w/ Ken
Takakura, Michiko Saga, Toru Abe,
Kunie Tanaka, Kanjuro Arashi, Joji
Ai, Ichiro Nakatani, Hideo Murota,
Yoko Mihara, Shiro Osaka
Takakura gets out of prison and
involved with a sockfull of stolen diamonds, a drunk stripper (Mihara), her
baby and her house-husband (Osaka),
a goony sidekick (Tanaka) and an
elderly mentor (Arashi), both from
prison, a devoted girlfriend (Saga),
and a gang boss (Abe) who ends up
throwing Takakura in a sauna box to
extract diamond info from him. The
climax was shot on location at an
authentic fire festival. The first entry
in color. #2 of 18 films * * 1/2

Abashiri Prison (#2)

Yagi   **w/** Ken Takakura, Naoki Sugiura, Kunie Tanaka, Margaret Hayashida, Kyosuke Machida, Kanjuro Arashi, Ichiro Nakatani, Hiroko Sakuramachi, Toru Abe, Hideo Sunazuka, Renji Ishibashi One of my favorites in the series despite the first appearance of one of the sentimental contrivances that occasionally mar the saga – a little kid. Even though the tyke in this one is coal-black and Japanese (and in blackface (!) – undoubtedly an American GI for a father?). Sugiura deserves special mention for his charismatic portrayal of the tubercular, sunglasses-and-white-suit-wearing number one killer for the villain clan. His ominous off-screen whistling prelude to his every appearance marks one of the all-time great signature motifs for a cinematic bad guy. A short-but-sweet, stupendously choreographed sword duel between Takakura and Sugiura occurs at the climax.   #3 of 18 films   *   *   *

ABASHIRI PRISON – SAGA OF HOMESICKNESS aka ABASHIRI BANGAICHI – BOKYO HEN 1965 88 min. **DIR./SCR.** Teruo Ishii **ORIG. STORY:** Hajime Ito **PHOTO COLOR 'SCOPE:** Kiichi Inada **MUSIC:** Masao

Abashiri Prison (#3)

ABASHIRI PRISON – NORTHERN SEACOAST STORY aka ABASHIRI BANGAICHI – HOKKAI HEN aka MAN FROM ABASHIRI JAIL 1966 90 min. DIR./SCR. Teruo Ishii ORIG. STORY: Hajime Ito PHOTO COLOR 'SCOPE: Kiichi Inada MUSIC: Masao Yagi w/ Ken Takakura, Shinichi "Sonny" Chiba, Naoki Sugiura, Eitaro Ozawa, Reiko Ohara, Takashi Fujiki, Kanjuro Arashi, Kunie Tanaka, Toru Abe Our hero ends up with the usual assortment of weirdos running illicit goods in a decrepit truck in the snowy north. An idiot pal accidentally lets his foot off the brake when they are trying to ease the wheel out of a rut, and Chiba has his chest crushed. The other tough guy (Abe) brutalizes the cast off-and-on until Takakura gets the upper hand. There is a great scene when Takakura stops off at a rural yakuza clan's HQ enroute to avenge some past offense. After coercing the boss to cut off his pinkie in atonement – while holding off the villainous leader's men – he feeds the amputated finger joint to the chickens! #4 of 18 films * * 1/2

Abashiri Prison (#5)

Abashiri Prison (#6)

ABASHIRI PRISON – DUEL IN THE WILDERNESS aka ABASHIRI BANGAICHI – KOYA NO TAIKETSU aka BULLET AND THE HORSE 1966 89 min. DIR./SCR. Teruo Ishii ORIG. STORY: Hajime Ito PHOTO COLOR 'SCOPE: Kiichi Inada MUSIC: Masao Yagi w/ Ken Takakura, Yoko Mihara, Jun Tazaki, Naoki Sugiura, Seizaburo Kawazu, Kyosuke Machida, Toru Yuri, Kanjuro Arashi, Kunie Tanaka A strange episode with Takakura involved with horsebreeders and, at one point, getting revenge on the guy who killed his Shetland pony! It has its moments, though. #5 of 18 films * *

ABASHIRI PRISON – DUEL IN THE SOUTH aka ABASHIRI BANGAICHI – NANGOKU NO TAIKETSU 1966 88 min. DIR./

Abashiri Prison - Duel in the Blizzard (#10)

SCR. Teruo Ishii ORIG. STORY: Hajime Ito PHOTO COLOR 'SCOPE: Kiichi Inada MUSIC: Masao Yagi w/ Ken Takakura, Shinichi "Sonny" Chiba, Teruo Yoshida, Reiko Ohara, Yoko Mihara, Kunie Tanaka, Kanjuro Arashi, Toru Yuri, Hayato Tani, Seizaburo Kawazu Takakura gets a crewcut and heads down to the semi-tropical environs of Japan's south coast. Entertaining when detailing the small-time smuggling/piracy story. An annoying subplot with a kid whose mom is a whore with a penchant for white lipstick brings this down half-a-notch. There is an atmospheric sunset swordfight at the close. #6 of 18 films * * 1/2

ABASHIRI PRISON – DUEL IN THE SNOW COUNTRY aka ABASHIRI BANGAICHI – DAI SETSUGEN NO TAIKETSU 1966 90 min. DIR. Teruo Ishii ORIG.STORY: Hajime Ito SCR. Hiro Matsuda/ Norio Konami/Teruo Ishii PHOTO COLOR 'SCOPE: Kiichi Inada MUSIC: Masao Yagi w/ Ken Takakura, Reiko Ohara, Teruo Yoshida, Kunie Tanaka, Kichijiro Ueda, Kanjuro Arashi, Hideo Sunazuka, Ryohei Uchida, Toru Yuri, Hosei Komatsu #7 of 18 films

ABASHIRI PRISON – DUEL AT THIRTY BELOW ZERO aka ABASHIRI BANGAICHI – KETTO REIKA SAN JU DO 1967 88 min. DIR./SCR. Teruo Ishii PHOTO COLOR 'SCOPE: Yoshio Nakajima MUSIC: Masao Yagi w/ Ken Takakura, Tetsuro Tanba, Kunie Tanaka, Reiko Ohara, Kanjuro Arashi, Teruo Yoshida, Yoko Mihara, Toru Yuri, Toru Abe, Jun Tazaki Takakura is back in the snow, hanging out with

miners and running afoul of a creepy protection/extortion crew victimizing the workers and their families. Tanba runs a local saloon. #8 of 18 films
* * *

ABASHIRI PRISON – CHALLENGING THE WICKED aka ABASHIRI BANGAICHI – AKU E NO CHOSEN 1967 90 min. DIR./ SCR. Teruo Ishii ORIG. STORY: Hajime Ito PHOTO COLOR 'SCOPE: Kiichi Inada MUSIC: Masao Yagi w/ Ken Takakura, Kunie Tanaka, Kanjuro Arashi, Jun Tazaki, Yoko Mihara, Harumi Sone, Yusuke Kawazu, Hayato Tani, Hiroko Kuni, Hosei Komatsu #9 of 18 films

ABASHIRI PRISON – DUEL IN THE BLIZZARD aka ABASHIRI BANGAICHI – FUBUKI NO TOSO aka SNOWSTORM COMBAT 1967 87 min. DIR. Teruo Ishii ORIG. STORY: Hajime Ito PHOTO COLOR 'SCOPE: Yoshio Nakajima MUSIC: Masao Yagi w/ Ken Takakura, Noboru Ando, Tatsuo Umemiya, Rinichi Yamamoto, Junko Miyazono, Ichiro Nakatani, Bunta Sugawara, Renji Ishibashi, Jotaro Togami, Hayato Tani A bizarre and thoroughly enjoyable entry with Takakura escaping a solitary cell through a tunnel, then in an elderly, deceased prisoner's coffin. Ando and Umemiya are co-leaders of a brutal bandit quartet that end up helping Takakura kidnap his ex-girlfriend (Miyazono) and torch her villainous hubby Nakatani's ski-lodge (he just happens to be the man who framed Takakura's father as a spy many years before, resulting in the patriarch's suicide and Nakatani taking over the family business) Plenty of bigger-than-life tall tale details and violent dynamics. This was Ishii's last ABASHIRI film. As of #11 he was reportedly sick of it and turned the directorial reins over to directors Makino, Saeki and Furuhata, for the remaining eight. And he not only has two other Toei Studios leading men (Ando, Umemiya; actually three if you count a cameo by Sugawara) to join Takakura, he also treats the whole saga as a sort of series climax. Exciting all the way through in an almost old-fashioned cliffhanger tradition with some of Ishii's subversively surreal visual flourishes. One of the best in the series. #10 of 18 films * * * 1/2

NEW ABASHIRI PRISON STORY aka SHIN ABISHIRI BANGA-ICHI aka MAN FROM ABASHIRI STRIKES AGAIN 1968 94 min. **DIR.** Masahiro Makino **SCR.** Akira Murao **PHOTO COLOR 'SCOPE:** Makoto Tsuboi **MUSIC:** Masao Yagi **w/** Ken Takakura, Tatsuya Mihashi, Takashi Shimura, Michitaro Mizushima, Kayo Matsuo, Nobuo Kaneko, Hiroyuki Nagato
A new take on the ABASHIRI saga. Takakura is just back from World War 2 when he spots some U.S. GIs trying to rape a Japanese woman. He beats the bejesus out of them and gets hauled off to an integrated (American/Japanese) military prison up north in Hokkaido. About a third of the way through, he is once again a free man and befriends numerous folks earning a living as *tekiya* – street peddlers. Of course, there is a local gang of bad guys trying to monopolize the street trade. One of Takakura's pals (Mizushima), who is also one of the most respected men in the community, gets murdered in a drive-by shooting. His

other best friend (Mihashi) goes to avenge the death singlehandedly and is ventilated, too. Which obviously necessitates Takakura heading over to bad guy HQ for some mass slaughter. #11 of 18 films * * *

NEW ABASHIRI PRISON STORY – HARBOR DUEL aka SHIN ABASHIRI BANGAICHI – RYUJIN MISAKI NO KETTO aka CONFLICT OF WANDERERS 1969 109 min. **DIR.** Yasuo Furuhata **SCR.** Akira Murao **PHOTO COLOR 'SCOPE:** Shichiro Hayashi **MUSIC:** Masao Yagi **w/** Ken Takakura, Takashi Shimura, Kaneko Iwasaki, Minoru Oki, Sanae Tsuchida, Kenji Sugawara, Shingo Yamashiro   Takakura and fellow inmates get transferred down to the sunny environs on a low-security beach community. They live in a prison dorm, work loading on the docks, and have more freedom than usual. Familiar Takashi Shimura (IKIRU, SEVEN SAMURAI, etc.,.) plays the crusty but liberal warden who engenders a great deal of loyalty and love from the prisoners. Too talky and occasionally too sentimental through 75% of the film – until Takakura has to perpetrate the usual radical surgical removal of evil yakuza clan by massacre – this time at a bizarre Op Art eyesore of a nightclub. #12 of 18 films * * 1/2

NEW ABASHIRI PRISON STORY – VAGRANT COMES TO A PORT TOWN aka SHIN ABASHIRI BANGAICHI – SAI HATE NO NAGARE MONO 1969 93 min. **DIR.** Kiyoshi Saeki **SCR.** Akira Murao **PHOTO COLOR 'SCOPE:** Masahiko Iimura **MUSIC:** Masao Yagi **w/** Ken Takakura, Yuriko

Hoshi, Michitaro Mizushima, Hayato Tani, Rinichi Yamamoto, Kenji Imai, Hiroyuki Shimozawa, Toshiaki Minami, Fujio Suga, Hideo Sunazuka Again just out of stir, Takakura tries to play it straight, working as a fisherman so he can help the crippled son of his ex-lover. However, he soon sees that the port is being fought over by two rival gangs. He joins the more decent of the two and eventually is put in the position of wiping out the villains, including evil boss Suga. As he is led away by the cops, he leaves the young boy with widow Hoshi. The parting shot of arrested Takakura bidding farewell to Hoshi as she tries to return the gold band he has given her to help pay for wrecking her place is very bittersweet without being sentimental. He refuses to take it back, and she puts it back on her finger. There is a nice touch, too, with Yamamoto, one of Suga's brutal henchmen, being transformed by having his life saved by Takakura and crew while at sea then being murdered by his boss and gang for his conflicted loyalties. But this is probably one of the most by-the-numbers films in the series with little else to make it stand out. #13 of 18 films * * 1/2

NEW ABASHIRI PRISON STORY – DUEL IN THE FOREST aka SHIN ABASHIRI BANGAICHI – DAI SHINRIN NO KETTO 1970 105 min. **DIR.** Yasuo Furuhata **SCR.** Akira Murao/Akikazu Kitamura **PHOTO COLOR 'SCOPE:** Shichiro Hayashi **MUSIC:** Masao Yagi w/ Ken Takakura, Joe Shishido, Shunji Imai, Yuriko Hoshi, Rinichi Yamamoto, Fujio Suga, Yuriko Mishima, Shingo Yamashiro, Hideo

Murota   #14 of 18 films**NEW NEW**

New Abashiri Prison - Duel in the Forest (#14)

NEW ABASHIRI PRISON STORY – A WOLF IN THE BLIZZARD aka SHIN ABASHIRI BANGAICHI – FUBUKI NO HAGURE OKAMI 1970 107 min. **DIR.** Yasuo Furuhata **SCR.** Akira Murao **PHOTO. COLOR 'SCOPE:** Shichiro Hayashi **MUSIC:** Masao Yagi w/ Ken Takakura, Tomisaburo Wakayama, Masumi Okada, June Adams, Hayato Tani, Toshiaki Minami, Rinichi Yamamoto, Kenji Imai, Atsushi Watanabe Here is one that comes totally out of left field. Takakura has his life saved by a missionary visiting the prison and, once released, feels so indebted he goes to work for him at the local mission where there is an althetic camp for ex-cons. Okada is nothing less than amazing as the good-natured priest from the West. Takakura finds a retired boss, now shopowner, whom he convinces to perform an impromptu *sakazuki* ceremony with Okada, and thereafter calls the priest, *oyabun*. The first hour or so of this is more a comedy than anything else with the expected fish-out-of-water antics for Takakura encountering a religious environment. Astonishingly enough, director Furuhata and writer Murao really make the humor work. Performances are good without much of the mugging and silly shtick that too often passes for comedy in Japanese genre films. Takakura goes through many trials learning how to turn the other cheek when confronted by bullies from the local village gang. He is also confounded when he develops a painful crush on a beautiful young nun (June Adams – despite the Western name, she looks Japanese) in the neighboring convent. Hayato Tani is an up-and-coming boxer at the mission who is obligated to wicked boss Yamamoto. Wakayama has little to do as Takakura's friend from jail who turns out to also be obligated to Yamamoto but is instrumental in helping Takakura when he comes to the gang's brothel to retrieve Tani's held-hostage girlfriend. There is a beautiful sequence while Tani is being pummeled in his decisive bout in the ring as he deliriously recalls images of his girl embracing him by the sea, her handing him a seashell and the raging waves in the background. He is about to cave in with despair when Takakura shows up ringside with the rescued girl, and Tani manages to turn the tide, knocking out his opponent. Yamamoto and cronies are very angry, and Tani is shot dead as he is victoriously hoisted up on everyone's shoulders. As everyone clusters around his corpse in the ring, another gangster stabs the priest Okada. The

missionary dies in Takakura's arms, and we know instinctively Takakura's never going to be able to turn the other cheek on this. He apologizes in advance at the church altar to his dead *"oyabun"* then heads over to the bad guys' HQ. Wakayama is accidentally shot by corrupt, in-cahoots prison guard Imai while fighting Takakura. Takakura explodes with new anger and wipes out all the hoodlums, finally dispatching the too-tough-to-die Yamamoto in the back alley outside. Upon completion of the carnage, Takakura's anguished call of *"oyabun!"* to the heavens above is genuinely moving. A very strange, atypical entry with skillfull, patient handling of the narrative. One really comes away with the feeling that Furuhata wanted to get things right rather than succumb to the usual breakneck pace of most Japanese genre production schedules. If you are looking for an action-packed narrative you might want to turn elsewhere. But if you have the patience and desire for a very different kind of yakuza *eiga*, you will be amply rewarded. One of the best in the series. #15 of 18 films * * * 1/2

NEW ABASHIRI PRISON STORY – STORM AT CAPE SHIRETOKO aka SHIN ABASHIRI BANGAICHI – ARASHI O YOBU SHIRETOKO MISAKI aka DUEL AT CAPE SHIRETOKO 1971 105 min. **DIR.** Yasuo Furuhata **SCR.** Akira Murao **PHOTO COLOR 'SCOPE:** Ichiro Hoshijima **MUSIC:** Masao Yagi w/ Ken Takakura, Tatsuya Mihashi, Noboru Ando, Rinichi Yamamoto, Susumu Fujita, Hitomi Nozoe, Kenji Imai, Hayato Tani, Haruo Tanaka As usual, Takakura is just out of the slammer, and all he has got to dress in is a spectacularly ugly red suitjacket, white slacks and a T-shirt with two-finger-peace/ U.S.-stars-'n-stripes design. That the picture has its tongue-in-cheek is emphasized when Takakura does a double-take upon spotting himself in an ad poster for Asahi beer. He gets into a fight with some *bosozoku* (Japanese slang expression literally translates as "violent tribe" – which certainly conveys the general idea even in contempo times – but here refers more to delinquent bikers) in a bar. The owners, appreciative of his help, haul his unconscious form out to their horsebreeding ranch, and we learn they are all reformed yakuza. It seems there is also a decidedly unreformed yakuza clan nearby headed up by a sadist in white flowing, frilly shirt, leather vest, toreador hat (!) and horsewhip (Yamamoto). His lover (Imai), a barely-in-control psycho (who here looks like WELCOME BACK, KOTTER's Gabe Kaplan), lords it over the *bosozoku* bikers, using them as muscle when his boys are outnumbered. Until about halfway through, this entry seemed a poor specimen. Then suddenly the feud between the good guys and the bad guys really erupts. Things get even stranger starting with the drug-injected killing of one of the good clan's thoroughbreds and the vendetta blooms finally into full flower. #16 of 18 films   * * *

NEW ABASHIRI PRISON STORY – ESCAPE IN THE BLIZZARD aka SHIN ABASHIRI BANGAICHI – FUBUKI NO DAI DASSO 1971 110 min. **DIR.** Yasuo Furuhata **SCR.** Kusumasa Yamato **PHOTO COLOR 'SCOPE:** Shichiro Hayashi **MUSIC:** Masao Yagi **w/** Ken Takakura, Kunie Tanaka, Noboru Ando, Toshio Kurosawa, Yuriko Hoshi, Kazuko Maki, Susumu Fujita, Rinichi Yamamoto, Michitaro Mizushima, Toshiaki Minami, Ryoichi Tamagawa #17 of 18 films

NEW ABASHIRI PRISON STORY – HONOR AND HUMANITY, AMMUNITION THAT ATTRACTS THE STORM aka SHIN ABASHIRI BANGAICHI – ARASHI YOBU DANPU JINGI 1972 105 min. **DIR.** Yasuo Furuhata **SCR.** Akira Murao **PHOTO COLOR 'SCOPE:** Masahiko Iimura **MUSIC:** Masao Yagi **w/** Ken Takakura, Joe Shishido, Kunie Tanaka, Tetsuro Tanba, Akiko Kudo, Rinichi Yamamoto, Etsuko Ikuta, Toshiaki Minami, Nobuo Kaneko, Michitaro Mizushima #18 and last of series

ACCOUNT OF THE ANDO GANG – KILLER YOUNGER BROTHER aka ANDO GUMI GAIDEN – HITOKIRI SHATEI 1974 94 min. **DIR.** Sadao Nakajima **ORIG. STORY:** Noboru Ando **SCR.** Hiro Matsuda **PHOTO COLOR 'SCOPE:** Hanjiro Nakazawa **MUSIC:** Kenjiro Hirose **w/** Bunta Sugawara, Noboru Ando, Tatsuo Umemiya, Tsunehiko Watase, Yuko Katagiri, Kyoko Okada, Hiroshi Nawa, Kenji Imai, Mikio Narita, Hosei Komatsu Ando, a local ganglord who oversees several gangs run by his blood brothers, does a voiceover narration at certain points, relating the sadistic foibles of his maniacal underlings. Noboru Ando was a real-life yakuza before he went into movies; he achieved notoriety being involved in a non-fatal shooting of a famous shady entrepeneur. After emerging from prison, he sold his story to the press and became a celebrity. He started off making a few films at Shochiku Studios, then at Toei where he became one of their major yakuza *eiga* superstars. He wrote original stories for several of his films.

Account of the Ando Gang - Killer Younger Brother

This story begins with lone Sugawara being beaten to a bloody pulp by Umemiya and cohorts and coming back for more. Sugawara and Watase are both too arrogant for their own good, and, before long, Watase gets his arm cut off in a bloody fight in the rain. Sugawara avenges, killing the male/female couple responsible. We get to see Watase in one more scene where, despite his one-arm, feeling humiliated, he rapes his girl after she tries to help him tie his tie! Well, as Sugawara grows more powerful under Ando, the feud worsens between

Sugawara and Umemiya. At one point Sugawara is shot, gets stitched up by a doctor, then goes to the bar where he had last been. He pulls out his bloody stitches and some guts (?), plunks 'em on the bar and rubs Umemiya's barmaid girlfriend's face in it! Whew! Well, before long all get busted together. Once out, Sugawara takes a kinder, gentler view of life, tracks down his abandoned girlfriend and seems to be settling down when he is stabbed by four guys. A swaggering, anarchic tale of brutality and chaos. Nakajima bathes almost a third of the interiors in a flickering, unnatural blue light that adds to the unreality of the proceedings. Ando revived ACCOUNT OF THE ANDO GANG writing the stories for a pair of 1998 yakuza films (under that series title), both directed by master filmmaker, Eiichi Kudo (helmsman of Ando's late sixties series, JAPAN'S UNDERWORLD HISTORY). * * *

ACCOUNT OF A SHOWA ERA SCOUNDREL aka SHOWA GOKUDO SHI 1972 87 min. DIR. Kiyoshi Saeki SCR. Isao Matsumoto/ Hideaki Yamamoto PHOTO COLOR 'SCOPE: Masahiko Iimura MUSIC: Harumi Ibe w/ Tatsuo Umemiya, Tsunehiko Watase, Kyosuke Machida, Mariko Kaga, Nobuo Kaneko, Fumio Watanabe, Tetsuro Tanba

AGENT OF WAR OF THE NORTH aka HOKURIKU DAIRI SENSO aka HOKURIKU PROXY WAR 1977 98 min. DIR. Kinji Fukasaku SCR. Koji Takada PHOTO COLOR 'SCOPE: Nobuaki Nakajima MUSIC: Toshiaki Tsushima w/ Hiroki Matsukata, Yumiko Nogawa, Shinichi "Sonny" Chiba,

Mikio Narita, Ko Nishimura, Yoko
Takahashi, Takeo Chii, Goro Ibuki,
Hajime Hana, Sanae Nakahara,
Tatsuo Endo, Ichiro Nakatani
An insane tale of Matsukata, an indie
yakuza boss in a far northern coastal
town, bent on gaining wider control
of the rackets in his territory. Chiba is
slickly venal as a smooth-talking, oily
gangster and Nishimura convincing
as always as an elder boss obstinately
sticking to his guns. The splendid
Yumiko Nogawa unfortunately does
not have much to do. Filmed on
actual northern locations, the stormy
winter atmosphere is spectacularly
savage and palpably chilling, giving
the coldblooded brutality on display a
suitably teeth-chattering edge.

*Agent of War of the North aka Hokuriku
Proxy War*

Scenes where Matsukata's enemies
are buried up to their necks in the
snow, then jeeps aimed at their heads
are so shockingly well done that they
are a bit hard to take. Violent and

unrepentant, with Fukasaku's own
brand of intoxicating vitality that he
seemed to reserve solely for direction
of his yakuza pictures. Most of his
samurai/ *chanbara,* even his science-
fiction (such as THE GREEN SLIME,
MESSAGE FROM SPACE, etc.,. for
which he is most famous internation-
ally), though always entertaining,
are nevertheless missing that certain
indefinable something that make
his yakuza pictures so vicariously
rewarding. * * *

Angel from Hell - Red Explosion

**ANGEL FROM HELL – RED
EXPLOSION** aka JIGOKU NO
TENSHI – AKAI BAKU ON 1977
77 min. **Dir.** Makoto Naito **Scr.**
Akinari Tanaka /Teruhiko Arai
Photo color 'scope: Yoshio
Nakajima **Music:** Chuji Kinoshita
w/ Hiroshi Tate, Hiroko Iruka, Aiko
Morishita, Yasuko Naito, Shinji Kono
The tale of a misfit teen girl who
inadvertently provokes a gangfight
with rival female hooligans that re-

sults in her guitarist boyfriend getting his most valuable fingers cut off. The band – who are such bad actors they must be a real band outside the film – don't like the anti-heroine. She is just too moody, sitting around staring into space and playing with her switch-blade. This particular gal (unfortunately I don't know which actress is who – the only person I recognize is Tate) has such an awkward demeanor, genuinely depressed expression and plainjane looks, she actually is quite effective in the role. *Bosozoku* gangs pull her in, and the usual romantic tragedy results. Amateurish, low-budget (even for Toei) and poorly-acted except for one or two of the more seasoned professionals. Still, all this works to its advantage. It is a strangely haunting film and one of the best from director Naito.   * * *

ASAKUSA CHIVALRY aka ASAKUSA NO KYOKAKU 1963 **Dir.** Kiyoshi Saeki **Scr.** Toshio Matsuura **Photo 'scope:** Akira Mimura **Music:** Hideo Ozawa w/ Hideo Murata, Naoki Sugiura, Shinichi "Sonny" Chiba, Yoshiko Fujita, Junko Miyazono, Miyoko Kuroiwa, Hisako Tsukuba

ASSASSIN WOMAN'S FIST aka LADY KARATE aka HISSATSU ONNA KENSHI 1976 81 min. **Dir.** Yu Kohira **Scr.** Hiro Matsuda **Photo color 'scope:** Hanjiro Nakazawa **Music:** Shunsuke Kikuchi w/ Etsuko "Sue" Shiomi, Yasuaki Kurata, Shinichi "Sonny" Chiba, Bin Amatsu, Keiichi Sato, Masashi "Milton" Ishibashi, Yoshi Kato, Jiro Chiba   This seems to be a follow-up to the SISTER STREET-FIGHTER series (1974-'76) also with

Shiomi. However, it makes those films look like examples of sophisti-cated narrative by comparison. There is virtually non-stop fighting with Shiomi going against the nefari-ous Bin Amatsu and his killers who crippled her father (Shinichi "Sonny" Chiba) in the pre-titles sequence. Chiba only makes it to the half hour mark before being mortally wounded by accident while he puts Shiomi through grueling karate paces. Still in mourning, she journeys to Tokyo where she stays with priest Kato. Not only does she find Amatsu running a training school for brutal martial arts assassins there, she also runs afoul of a gang who are harassing the neigh-borhood. Her battle in the forest with the hoodlums' pack of dobermans is pretty wild. Before long, Amatsu learns of her existence and plans her demise. He sends his men to the temple, but one of his prize students (real-life martial arts expert Yasuaki Kurata), switches sides when he realizes how treacherous Amatsu is. Priest Kato is killed, and shortly after there is a wild fatal free-for-all in a field. The sequence where white-haired, blind killer Ishibashi is so traumatized by Shiomi's placement of little bells tied to the reeds, it causes him to undergo psychedelic hallucina-tions (!) has to be seen to be believed. Is it any surprise that Shiomi and Kurata triumph?   * * 1/2

AUTHENTIC TRUE ACCOUNT – OSAKA SHOCK TACTICS aka JITSUROKU GAIDEN – OSAKA DENGEKI SAKUSEN 1976 95 min. **Dir.** Sadao Nakajima **Scr.** Koji Takada **Photo color 'scope:** Umio Masuda **Music:** Toshiaki Tsushima   w/ Hiroki

Matsukata, Akira Kobayashi, Tsunehiko Watase, Tatsuo Umemiya, Tetsuro Tanba, Mikio Narita, Sanae Nakahara, Renji Ishibashi, Hideo Murota, Takuzo Kawatani When Watase and Umemiya's boss capitulates to big boss Kobayashi and enforcer Narita, absorbing their gang, hothead Watase breaks away, allying himself with former mortal enemy and fellow hellion Matsukata. Before long, Kobayashi's minions are rubbing out any strays that fail to come into the fold. When Watase is captured after a clumsy assassination attempt, he is tortured. Matsukata and pals stage a trap, kidnapping Umemiya who is now Kobayashi's man. They arrange for an exchange in a wrecking yard, but things go wrong, and Watase is killed. Guys get cooked to death in oil drums, fires erupt and cars explode – just a usual night in Osaka. Matsukata at last feigns subservience to Kobayashi and Narita.

He then tries to kill them but is foiled in a chaotic, bloody melee. There is almost non-stop action and violent brutality here with some especially nice touches: the dead Matsukata left still standing poised to strike in an opening elevator, freaking out the waiting-to-attack yakuza who, for a split second, believe he is unkillable; the closing shot of Kobayashi holding court with cowed former indie bosses Murota, et. al., each kneeling before him with their cut-off pinkies and Matsukata's empty place filled only by his pickled finger in a jar. The only problem with OSAKA SHOCK TACTICS is that character development and nuance is nil.

* * *

Bad Angel (#1)

BAD ANGEL aka ZUBEKO TENSHI series

BAD ANGEL aka ZUBEKO TENSHI aka DELINQUENT ANGEL 1960 **DIR.** Shigehiro Ozawa **SCR.** Toshio Matsuura **PHOTO B&W**

Authentic True Account - Osaka Shock Tactics

'SCOPE: Noboru Takanashi MUSIC: Kuharu Kutsuki w/ Ken Takakura, Mitsue Komiya, Michiko Hoshi, Eijiro Yanagi One of the earliest of *sukeban*/girl boss type *eiga*. #1 of 2

BAD ANGEL RETURNS – A BRIDE'S SEVEN CHARMS aka ZOKU ZUBEKO TENSHI – NANA IRO NO HANAYOME 1960 DIR. Eiichi Koishi SCR. Toshio Matsuura PHOTO B&W 'SCOPE: Noboru Takanashi MUSIC: Akira Ishimatsu w/ Mitsue Komiya, Akiko Yamato, Shinjiro Ebara, Shinji Yamada, Michiko Hoshi, Naoko Kubo, Kazuko Namiki, Nijiko Kiyokawa #2 of 2 films

BAKAMASA-HORAMASA-TOPPAMASA 1976 DIR. Sadao Nakajima SCR. Kazuo Kasahara/ Motohiro Torii/Sadao Nakajima MUSIC: Kenjiro Hirose w/ Bunta Sugawara, Jin Nakayama, Keshi Takamine, Mitsuko Baisho, Toru (formerly Ryunosuke) Minegishi, Mikio Narita, Tadao Nakamaru, Tatsuo Endo, Junzaburo Ban

In case the Japanese-ignorant reader does not realize it, the film title represents the names of the three crazy main characters, incorrigible lone wolf ruffians up against corporate gangs. There is a nicely atmospheric nightclub milieu in the first third of our tale, but then the story descends into subpar *jitsuroku* (true account) posturing. Not terrible by any means – just not very good either. * *

BALLAD OF DEATH aka HITOKIRI KANNON UTA aka KILLER'S SONG OF MERCY aka BLIND WHIPMASTER aka SONG OF THE GODDESS OF MERCY

KILLER 1970 88 min. DIR. Takashi Harada SCR. Koji Takada PHOTO COLOR 'SCOPE: Umeo Masuda MUSIC: Takeo Yamashita w/ Bunta Sugawara, Minoru Oki, Akiko Kudo, Tomisaburo Wakayama, Norihiko Umeji, Meicho Soganoya, Utako Kyo, Bin Amatsu, Takuzo Kawatani

Ballad of Death

A wild, wild ultraviolent film with Sugawara as Ryototsu, the blind, renegade gambler priest who has a whip with a dagger in its handle and a lethal knowledge of judo/karate. He also has a blind orphan boy in tow throughout the tale. Sugawara's Ryototsu also appears in virtually all of the THE EVIL PRIEST movie series, starring Tomisaburo Wakayama as Shinkai. Nemesis Shinkai had been the one to blind Ryototsu in one of the early films. Even though Wakayama appears in this film, it is not as Shinkai but as an aging and eccentric, gambling doctor who believes that there may be hope for the young boy's eyesight. * * * 1/2

Battles Without Honor and Humanity

**BATTLES WITHOUT HONOR
AND HUMANITY aka JIN-
GINAKI TATAKAI aka THE
YAKUZA PAPERS aka GANG
WAR WITHOUT THE GAM-
BLING CODE aka COMBAT
WITHOUT A CODE series**

**BATTLES WITHOUT HONOR
AND HUMANITY** aka JINGI-
NAKI TATAKAI aka GANG WAR
WITHOUT THE GAMBLING
CODE aka THE YAKUZA PAPERS
aka TARNISHED CODE OF THE
YAKUZA aka COMBAT WITH-
OUT A CODE 1973 99 min. **DIR.**
Kinji Fukasaku **SCR.** Kazuo
Kasahara **PHOTO COLOR 'SCOPE:**
Sadatsugu Yoshida **MUSIC:**
Toshiaki Tsushima **w/** Bunta
Sugawara, Tatsuo Umemiya, Hiroki
Matsukata, Nobuo Kaneko, Kunie
Tanaka, Tamio Kawaji, Tsunehiko
Watase, Goro Ibuki, Eiko Nakamura,
Mayumi Nagisa   This is the yakuza
film that Fukasaku did that got the
most raves (not the somewhat better
GRAVEYARD OF HONOR) and is
probably the most critically acclaim-
ed yakuza movie ever produced in
Japan. It is certainly excellent – in
1990, Japanese KINEMA JUNPO
magazine tied it with Kurosawa's
HIGH AND LOW (TENGOKU TO
JIGOKU) for #11 spot in the best 20
Japanese films ever produced (not
just crime films, *any* films). Sugawara
plays his usual homicidal self. However, he is quite a bit more restrained
and wise in the ways of the despicable clans than the characters he usually plays. He becomes member of a
mob led by the sneaky, venal and sap-
pily sentimental Kaneko. Umemiya is
Kaneko's underboss and Sugawara's
blood brother from stir. He is killed
midway through in a shootout with
the cops at his mother-in-law's house.
Matsukata is another young comrade
who eventually becomes a greedy,
murderously ambitious mover upon
his disillusionment with Kaneko.
There is a great scene where
Sugawara shows up after being

released from another prison stay.
Matsukata is so freaked-out when
Sugawara goes for his smokes – he
thinks Sugawara's going to blow him
away – that he goes into a total fit
clawing at the window, trying to escape and babbling incoherently before
he shamefacedly realizes Sugawara's
calmly blowing smoke rings. Great!
At the end, Sugawara goes to
Matsukata's funeral – a situation
notorious for being one of the times
most used for vendetta massacres -
and when everyone sees him, folks
go for their swords, knives and revolvers. They panic even more when
he pulls out his pistol. But amazingly
enough, he shoots up the photos,
banners and flowers on the dead
man's altar – symbolically killing the
idea of *jingi* (honorable ethics of the
gambler's code), exposing it for the
lie it is. After all, a couple hypocritical, backstabbing bosses attending the
memorial in *faux* grief are the ones
who had had Matsukata snuffed. #1
of 9 films   * * * *

**BATTLES WITHOUT HONOR
AND HUMANITY – HIROSHIMA
DEATH MATCH** aka JINGINAKI
TATAKAI – HIROSHIMA SHITO
HEN 1973 100 min. **DIR.** Kinji
Fukasaku **SCR.** Kazuo Kasahara
PHOTO COLOR 'SCOPE: Sadatsugu
Yoshida **MUSIC:** Toshiaki Tsushima
w/ Bunta Sugawara, Kinya Kitaoji,
Shinichi "Sonny" Chiba, Meiko Kaji,
Asao Koike, Mikio Narita, Hiroshi
Nawa, Nobuo Kaneko, Takuzo
Kawatani   The first sequel and
establishes what would be the M.O.
for the rest of the series: Sugawara,
off-and-on is a more or less stoic
observer of younger guys getting
caught in the whole "honorable

gangster" bullshit. He watches them
get exploited by their bosses and then
discarded or killed.

Battles Without Honor & Humanity (#2)

Set in the 1950s, a young fellow
(Kitaoji) anxious to get ahead, is willing to make hits and ends up, because
of his misplaced loyalty and terrible
self-esteem, a despondent hulk hiding
in the wreckage of an abandoned

restaurant. He blows his brains out. Grimmest of all 9 films. Chiba is great as a hair-trigger, sadistic bully who becomes one of Kitaoji's main tormentors. In this film, action icon Kaji's chaacter has to be completely submissive to her outcast, low-self-esteem lover Kitaoji and her cruel, avaricious father Nawa. It would be a difficult role for any woman – a gentle, beautiful soul completely crushed by the fucked-up psyches of the selfish men in her life. Kaji plays it straight and very effectively. She certainly emerges as the most sympathetic character in the movie. Although not true in this series entry, the rest of the films, for the most part, are disappointingly devoid of strong women's roles. A real shame since this series is otherwise an unique effort. #2 of 9 films * * *

BATTLES WITHOUT HONOR AND HUMANITY – AGENT OF WAR aka JINGINAKI TATAKAI – DAIRI SENSO 1973 102 min. **Dir.** Kinji Fukasaku **Scr.** Kazuo Kasahara **Photo color 'scope:** Sadatsugu Yoshida **Music:** Toshiaki Tsushima w/ Bunta Sugawara, Akira Kobayashi, Tsunehiko Watase, Mikio Narita, Nobuo Kaneko, Takeshi Kato, Tatsuo Umemiya, Reiko Ike, Tetsuro Tamba, Eiko Nakamura, Tatsuo Endo, Rinichi Yamamoto, Shingo Yamashiro, Kunie Tanaka, Hideo Murota A very good entry with Sugawara actually becoming the boss of his own gang. There is a great scene near the end where Sugawara and *kobuns* are with the family of a very young deceased comrade. They are carrying away his ashes when attacked in a drive-by shooting. The container of

ashes is crushed under the wheels of the attackers' car adding insult to injury and poignant emotional weight to Sugawara's self-entrapment in yakuza life. #3 of 9 films * * *

Battles Without Honor & Humanity (#4)

BATTLES WITHOUT HONOR AND HUMANITY – SUMMIT OF OPERATIONS aka JINGINAKI TATAKAI – CHOJO SAKUSEN aka OPERATION: SUMMIT aka POLICE TACTICS 1974 101 min. **Dir.** Kinji Fukasaku **Scr.** Kazuo Kasahara **Photo color 'scope:** Sadatsugu Yoshida **Music:** Toshiaki Tsushima w/ Bunta Sugawara, Akira Kobayashi, Tatsuo Umemiya, Toshio Kurosawa, Kunie Tanaka, Nobuo Kaneko, Takeshi Kato, Asao Koike Set in the early 1960s, the upcoming Olympics leads to a police crackdown on the yakuza.

Kurosawa, a weapons expert, joins Sugawara's gang. Umemiya, Kobayashi, Kaneko, Uchida are other bosses, with Kato as the most greedy. His intractability and grudges throw a spanner in the works, causing factional infighting. Kato is eventually taken hostage by Kobayashi and Kaneko. Sugawara and Kurosawa are arrested in police crackdowns following spiralling-out-of-control reprisals. Underbosses Koike and Matsukata are assassinated. By the close of this entry, Sugawara and Kobayashi have established a strategic alliance. #4 of 9 films   * * *

BATTLES WITHOUT HONOR AND HUMANITY – SAGA CONCLUSION JINGINAKI TATAKAI – KANKETSU HEN 1974 98 min.

Dir. Kinji Fukasaku **Scr.** Kazuo Kasahara **Photo color 'scope:** Sadatsugu Yoshia **Music:** Toshiaki Tsushima   w/ Bunta Sugawara, Yumiko Nogawa, Kinya Kitaoji, Hiroki Matsukata, Akira Kobayashi, Joe Shishido, Goro Ibuki, Kunie Tanaka, Asao Uchida, Sanae Nakahara, Bin Amatsu, Takuzo Kawatani   Set between 1965-1970, Kitaoji is one of Kobayashi's more level-headed underbosses. He is tries to avert gang warfare, even after lover Nogawa's father is killed by upstart Matsukata's gang. Shishido is a short-tempered loudmouth associated with Kobayashi who wants to wipe out Matsukata. Sugawara is in Abashiri Prison through the first two thirds of the tale. Eventually Matsukata and Tanaka are assassinated. Shishido is more of a drunken maniac than ever and is jailed along with Kitaoji. Kitaoji becomes more powerful upon his release. Sugawara finally gets out

and has a serious meeting with Kobayashi. Tension develops between Sugawara and Kitaoji. Shishido's former sidekicks attempt to murder Kitaoji, but he survives. One of the most memorable sequences has more young tinhorns trying to make a hit, this time on Ibuki outside a theater showing a Junko Fuji *ninkyo* yakuza picture. One of the violent youngsters is killed and collapses on her overturned poster display. Asked in an interview if this was perhaps his comment on the possible harmful effects on youth of the romanticized *ninkyo* yakuza films, Fukasaku said he was not positive he had that in mind at the time, but it could be looked at that way. Sugawara visits the kid's family's home in the closing scenes and looks on unobserved as the boy's mother tenderly slips funeral booties on the deceased young fellow's feet. He cannot bring himself to enter, so leaves a wad of cash on the counter and splits. #5 of 9 films   * * *

NEW BATTLES WITHOUT HONOR AND HUMANITY aka SHIN JINGINAKI TATAKAI aka NEW GANG WAR WITHOUT THE GAMBLING CODE 1974 98 min.

Dir. Kinji Fukasaku **Scr.** Fumio Konami/Yoshikazu Arai **Photo color 'scope:** Sadatsugu Yoshida **Music:** Toshiaki Tsushima w/ Bunta Sugawara, Hiroki Matsukata, Tomisaburo Wakayama, Tsunehiko Watase, Joe Shishido, Noboru Ando, Kunie Tanaka, Sanae Nakahara, Reiko Ike, Nobuo Kaneko, Hiroshi Nawa   Sugawara is presented as a new, different character in each of the next three pictures (#'s 6,7,8) (that is what the word *"shin"* in the Japanese title means – "new").

The time frame is once again immediately post-war, and Sugawara, disguised as a crippled soldier, gets the snowball rolling with a hit on an opposing boss. He then has to hide out in a deserted, freezing warehouse and passes his time shooting methedrine. He is in-and-out of prison during the titles.

New Battles Without Honor &
Humanity (#6)

Wakayama is a cold-blooded opportunistic boor who starts murdering his way to the top. His extended assassination by Sugawara and Watase's men at the climax of the film where he is repeatedly shot stumbling down a street in broad daylight, finally ending up headfirst in a trash can, has to be seen to be believed. There is a funny denouement where betrayer Tanaka's phony display of blubbering histrionics at Wakayama's wake leaves Sugawara in open-mouthed disbelief. #6 of 9 films   * * * 1/2

NEW BATTLES WITHOUT HONOR AND HUMANITY – THE BOSS'S HEAD aka   SHIN JINGI-NAKI TATAKAI – KUMICHO NO KUBI aka BOSS OF BOSSES 1975 94 min. **Dir.** Kinji Fukasaku **Scr.** Susumu Saji/Koji Takada/ Harumi Tanaka **Photo color** 'scope: Tetsu Nakajima **Music:** Toshiaki Tsushima   w/ Bunta Sugawara, Tsutomu Yamazaki, Tsunehiko Watase, Meiko Kaji, Mikio Narita, Ko Nishimura, Hideo Murota, Asao Uchida, Takuzo Kawatani, Sanae Nakahara   This time, set in the 1960s, Sugawara and dope addict cohort Yamazaki make a hit at the beginning which Yamazaki nearly botches when his gun fails to go off.

New Battles Without Honor &
Humanity - The Boss's Head (#7)

Sugawara succeeds and consequently goes to prison for a short stretch. When he is released, he goes to work for more traditional boss Nishimura.

Narita is a Machivellian underboss gradually murdering those that would thwart his rise to the top. Eventually Yamazaki is coerced into killing Nishimura whom he hates anyway because he is also his father-in-law (!). When Yamazaki barges in – in front of his wife Kaji – and shoots her father Nishimura to death it is quite shocking. Sugawara is upset but fatalistically accepts the turn of events. It is not until Narita's men make an attempt on *his* life that he becomes obsessed with destroying Narita. There are a couple of failed attempts, one involving a prolonged chaotic car chase before Sugawara's doomed sidekick succeeds in killing Narita in a crowded nightclub. Rather than continue to wipe out Narita's minions, Sugawara cynically consolidates his power by becoming Narita's replacement, inducted and blessed by craven head boss Uchida in a *sakazuki* ceremony as the end credits unspool. #7 of 9 films   * * *

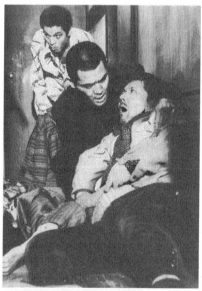

New Battles Without Honor & Humanity - Boss's Last Days (#8)

NEW BATTLES WITHOUT HONOR AND HUMANITY – BOSS'S LAST DAYS aka SHIN JINGINAKI TATAKAI – KUMICHO SAIGO NO HI 1976 91 min. **DIR.** Kinji Fukasaku **SCR.** Koji Takada **PHOTO COLOR 'SCOPE:** Tetsu Nakajima **MUSIC:** Toshiaki Tsushima w/ Bunta Sugawara, Chieko Matsubara, Koji Wada, Isao Bito, Takuya Fujioka, Hiroshi Nawa, Jun Tatara, Mikio Narita, Sanae Nakahara, Takeo Chii, Eitaro Ozawa, Takuzo Kawatani Sugawara is an underboss in charge of a construction gang under old-fashioned *oyabun* Tatara. Soon Tatara is stabbed-to-death by a masseuse while he and good-ole-boy comrade bosses, Nawa, Fujioka et. al. frolic at a resort/yakuza conference. Comic Fujioka is amusing as an underboss addicted to Benzedrine nasal inhalers whom Sugawara first targets in his revenge attempts. These go for naught with Fujioka ending up in police protection. Matsubara is Sugawara's little sister who is married to ne'er'do-well smooth-talker-in-hiding Wada. Tragedy looms when a visit Sugawara pays to the couple culminates in Wada trying to kill Sugawara before being accidentally mangled-to-death under the wheels of a speeding dump truck. Sugawara and cohorts, aided by Matsubara, target ailing head boss Ozawa, infiltrating the cop-protected hospital and finally realizing their objective. As Sugawara is led away by the police, angry rival yakuza taunt him from behind barricades, then cheer when a young hothead breaks through to stab him several times. The severely wounded Sugawara is whisked away by the police with sirens blaring.

In a near state-of-shock, Sugawara stares at his handcuffed bloody hands as the end freeze-frames. Just a side-note: Chieko Matsubara, maturing here into an accomplished actress, was never lovelier nor more effective in her 1960s Nikkatsu Studios star days than in this. #8 of 9 films
* * * 1/2

AFTERMATH OF BATTLES WITHOUT HONOR AND HU-MANITY aka SONOGONO JIN-GINAKI TATAKAI 1979 128 min. Dɪʀ. Eiichi Kudo Sᴄʀ. Fumio Konami/Hiro Matsuda Pʜᴏᴛᴏ ᴄᴏʟᴏʀ 'sᴄᴏᴘᴇ: Tetsu Nakajima Mᴜsɪᴄ: Rudo Uzaki   w/ Hiroki Matsukata, Jinpachi Nezu, Rudo Uzaki, Mikio Narita, Mieko Harada, Shigeru Matsuzaki, Kenichi Hagiwara, Tsutomu Yamazaki, Hosei Komatsu, Asao Koike, Nobuo Kaneko, Kayo Matsuo, Shingo Yamashiro

Aftermath of Battles Without Honor & Humanity (#9)

Matsukata is the only main star returning from the series, with new blood being purposely introduced, principally Jinpachi Nezu and Mieko Harada (both later to star with Tatsuya Nakadai in Kurosawa's RAN) and pop musician Rudo Uzaki. The plan seemed to be to have Kudo,

director of such excellent realistic samurai *jidai geki* as THIRTEEN ASSASSINS (JUSANNIN NO SHIKAKU) (1963), THE GREAT KILLING (DAI SATSUJIN) (1964) and ELEVEN SAMURAI (JUICHIN-IN NO SAMURAI) (1967), on board to bring the same grittiness to this entry as Fukasaku brought to the rest of the series. Although it has its effective moments and an interesting subplot of one of the main characters (ironically not Uzaki) becoming a corrupt popstar, the film does not quite cohere as a story or action film, nor are the young leads at this point in their careers quite charismatic enough to bring it off. #9 of 9 films   * * 1/2

THE BEAST MUST DIE aka YAJU SHISUBESHI 1980 119 min. Dɪʀ. Toru Murakawa Sᴄʀ. Shoichi Maruyama Pʜᴏᴛᴏ ᴄᴏʟᴏʀ 'sᴄᴏᴘᴇ: Seizo Norimoto Mᴜsɪᴄ: Akihiko Takashima   w/ Yusaku Matsuda, Hideo Murota, Asami Kobayashi, Takechi Kaga, Sukinue Negishi
The psychopathology of the lone gun-man/thief is played up in this radically retooled version, with the late, charismatic Matsuda giving a suitably disturbing performance. The story was remade yet again in 1997. For the majority of the earlier versions, see the Toho Studios section.   * * *

Beast's Path

BEAST'S PATH aka KEDAMONO NO TORU MICHI aka BEAST'S PASSAGE 1959 DIR. Hideo Sekigawa SCR. Susumu Saji PHOTO 'SCOPE: Hanjiro Nakazawa MUSIC: Chuji Kinoshita w/ Ken Takakura, Katsuo Nakamura, Mitsue Komiya, Isao Kimura, Takashi Shimura, Yoshiko Sakuma, Rinichi Yamamoto

BEHIND JAPAN'S BLACK CURTAIN aka NIHON NO FUIKUSAICHI (this last word is usually romanized "Kuromaku") aka JAPAN'S WIREPULLER 1979 131 min. DIR. Yasuo Furuhata SCR. Koji Takada PHOTO COLOR 'SCOPE: Tetsu Nakajima MUSIC: Hajime Kaburagi w/ Shin Saburi, Masakazu Tamura, Kyoko Enami, Kayo Matsuo, Tatsuo Umemiya, Kunie Tanaka
One of director Furuhata's few misfires. It is a strangely convoluted narrative of a shadowy bigwig who straddles politics and the yakuza to manipulate government, finance and other interests. The occasionally pretentious approach does not help matters. A very good cast is bogged down with strained seriousness. The term *kuromaku* literally means "black curtain" and is a term coined mid-20th century to refer to corrupt fatcats behind the scenes who pull the puppet strings that make fortunes for some while ruining thousands of lives for the majority – all without conscience. Sound familiar?　*　*

THE BIG BOSS'S SILK HAT aka SHIRUKU HATTO NO OO OYABUN series

THE BIG BOSS'S SILK HAT aka SHIRUKU HATTO NO OO OY-ABUN aka A BOSS WITH A SILK HAT 1970 89 min. DIR. Norifumi Suzuki SCR. Koji Takada PHOTO COLOR 'SCOPE: Motoya Washio MUSIC: Toshiaki Tsushima w/ Tomisaburo Wakayama, Junko Fuji, Goro Ibuki, Nijiko Kiyokawa, Ichiro Sugai, Tatsuo Endo
An apparent spin-off – in a humorous vein judging from the titles and posters – from the RED PEONY GAMBLER series with Fuji appearing in guest mode as her Oryu character. I have not seen these two but Wakayama seems to be playing his rowdy bumpkin boss character with the Chaplin moustache from the RED PEONY series. #1 of 2 films

A BOSS WITH A MOUSTACHE aka SHIRUKU HATTO NO OO OYABUN – CHOBI HIGE NO KUMA 1970 89 min. DIR. Norifumi Suzuki SCR. Koji Takada PHOTO COLOR 'SCOPE: Kenji Tsukagoe MUSIC: Toshiaki Tsushima w/ Tomisaburo Wakayama, Goro Ibuki, Junko Fuji, Asao Koike, Ryuji Kita, Masumi Tachibana, Kenjiro Ishiyama, Fujio Suga, Hiroshi Nawa, Mari Shiraki #2 of 2 films

BLACKMAIL aka KYOKATSU aka THREAT 1963 DIR. Yusuke Watanabe SCR. Kei Tasaka PHOTO 'SCOPE: Makoto Tsuboi MUSIC: Hajime Kaburagi w/ Ken Takakura, Shoji Yasui, Yoshiko Mita, Yoshi Kato, Yoko Mihara, Isao Yamagata, Kei Sato

BLOODSTAINED CLAN HONOR aka CHIZOME NO DAIMON aka BLOODY GAMBLES 1970 87 min. DIR. Kinji Fukasaku SCR.

Makoto Naito/Kinji Fukasaku
PHOTO COLOR 'SCOPE: Hanjiro
Nakazawa **MUSIC:** Chuji Kinoshita
w/ Bunta Sugawara, Tatsuo
Umemiya, Koji Tsuruta, Junko
Miyazono, Kyosuke Machida, Fumio
Watanabe, Isamu Nagato, Asao Uchida, Hosei Komatsu, Hideo Murota
Sugawara is a young, decent *oyabun*
of a small gang and a native of a poor
local shantytown. He is given the
task of evicting the slumdwellers and
clearing the junkyard by underhanded
godfather Uchida. Watanabe is a rival
boss who will do anything to get his
hands on the land to build a new harbor. Umemiya is a cynical shantytown
leader with his own agenda. Brutal
exploitation and sabotage by Watanabe's unprincipled rival yakuza clan
causes the usual ranting and raving
that results in prodigious bloodshed.
Somewhat uninvolving, despite
Fukasaku's energetic direction. But
the customary bloodbath at the climax
rejuvenates the jaded viewer. When
Sugawara and Umemiya, who are
also coincidentally childhood friends,
end up on the same defeated side at
the end, they singlehandedly attack
the groundbreaking ceremony with all
the local politicians. Bosses Uchida
and Watanabe are stabbed to death,
but so are Sugawara and Umemiya.
Yes, everyone dies! * * *

**BODYGUARD KIBA aka BO-
DEE GADO KIBA aka KARATE
KIBA series**

BODYGUARD KIBA aka BODEE
GADO KIBA aka THE BODY-
GUARD aka KARATE KIBA 1973
87 min. **DIR.** Ryuichi (Tatsuichi?)
Takamori **SCR.** Ryuzo Nakanishi

PHOTO COLOR 'SCOPE: Yoshio
Nakajima **MUSIC:** Toshiaki Tsushima
w/ Shinichi "Sonny" Chiba, Mari
Atsumi, Yayoi Watanabe, Ryohei
Uchida, Eiji Go , Rinichi Yamamoto
This first BODYGUARD picture is
one of Chiba's worst films. Of course,
I have only seen the atrociously-
dubbed American video release, so
perhaps I should reserve judgement.
One point in its favor: it co-stars
Daiei Studios' former resident sex-
star, the charismatic Atsumi. Chiba is
a modern, karate-fightng vigilante
obsessed with wiping out the scourge
of drug dealers. Known for his
fighting prowess after finishing off
a number of assassins aboard an in-
flight jetliner (!), he goes on television to offer his services as bodyguard to anyone who has information
on drug dealers and wishes to be of
help. He is approached by Atsumi
who, it turns out, does not have the
purest of motives. Chiba soon learns
she is the former lover of a just-
murdered New York Cosa Nostra
druglord and has her own agenda of
retrieving an enormous amount of
heroin. Chiba is not pleased about
this but is tempted by the idea of
ripping off both the pursuing yakuza
and American mafia for a tremendous
amount of money. So he continues
to help Atsumi and her in-cahoots
yakuza lover Uchida. There are also a
couple of crazy nightclub owners (Go
and Yamamoto) who have been dealing drugs to American soldiers who
try to muscle their way in. Mayhem
ensues in a series of fairly boring
action setpieces. #1 of 2 films * *

BODYGUARD KIBA 2 aka
BODEE GADO KIBA – HISSATSU
SAN KAKUTOBI 1973 88 min.

DIR. Ryuichi (Tatsuichi?) Takamori
SCR. Ryuzo Nakanishi PHOTO COLOR
'SCOPE:Yoshikazu (Giichi) Yamazawa
MUSIC: Toshiaki Tsushima
w/ Shinichi "Sonny" Chiba,
Tsunehiko Watase, Etsuko "Sue"
Shiomi, Eiji Go   #2 of 2 films

THE BOSS aka KAOYAKU aka
THE BIG FIGURE 1965 91 min.
DIR. Teruo Ishii SCR. Kazuo
Kasahara/Kinji Fukasaku/Teruo
Ishii PHOTO COLOR 'SCOPE: Ichiro
Hoshijima MUSIC: Masao Yagi
w/ Koji Tsuruta, Ken Takakura,
Shigeru Amachi, Harumi Sone,
Kyosuke Machida, Yoshiko Mita,
Yoshiko Sakuma, Shinjiro Ebara,
Junko Fuji, Hiroyuki Nagato,
Takamaru Sasaki, Minoru Oki   As
you can discern from the all-star cast
and writing team, this was one of
Toei's biggest efforts of 1965. It has
an atmospheric jazzy score by Yagi.

The Boss

One of the last of the more old-fash-

ioned Toei gangster pictures, re. the
GANG and UNDERWORLD series.
These films were – especially when
helmed by Ishii or Fukasaku – stick-
ing-their-toe-in-the-water predecessors of the *jitsuroku* (true document)
sagas that completely took over the
genre by the early-1970s.   * * 1/2

Boss in Jail

BOSS IN JAIL aka GOKUCHU
NO KAOYAKU 1968 90 min.
DIR. Yasuo Furuhata SCR. Kazuo
Kasahara/Koji Takada/Motohiro Torii
PHOTO COLOR 'SCOPE: Ichiro
Hoshijima MUSIC: Harumi Ibe
w/ Ken Takakura, Junko Fuji, Ryo
Ikebe, Shogo Shimada, Shingo
Yamashiro, Hideo Murota, Ichiro
Ryuzaki, Bin Amatsu, Tatsuo Endo,
Harumi Sone, Takashi Fujiki
Set in the then contemporary sixties,
we are immediately plunged into a
knifefight in the rain when Takakura

is challenged by a rival gangster. Seriously wounded, he stumbles back to gang HQ after fatally stabbing the man. He does a stretch in prison, then is released. However, he barely gets to catch his breath, enjoying a brief tryst with his *oyabun's* daughter, Fuji, before going back in for killing a number of evil boss Amatsu's yakuza who have shot blood brother Murota to death. Once in jail, he meets up with long lost lone wolf Ikebe, who is now obligated to newly incarcerated Endo, an associate of Amatsu. Soon Ikebe challenges Takakura but their fight ends in a stalemate when both go to help suicidal tubercular inmate Fujiki. Once released, Ikebe is informed by Endo that he must assassinate Takakura's boss to fulfill his obligation. Ikebe reluctantly carries out the contract, only to be stabbed to death himself by Endo and Amatsu's men after he has done the deed. Takakura reads about all this from a smuggled news clipping. He is on the verge of getting out himself when he is set upon by two of Endo's men in the prison boiler room. Elderly mentor, tough guy Shimada (who keeps a pet squirrel in a cage in his cell!) comes to his aid, locking Takakura out of the room and facing the two killers alone. All three end up dead as a result. Released, Takakura goes to see Fuji, meeting her at her dad's grave. Then, despite her pleas, he treks to the bicycle racetrack Amatsu and Endo wrested from her father's control. Takakura finds them upstairs in their special glassed-in box seats and launches a stabbing binge, wiping out both evil bosses. He is led away by the police as frantic, tearful Fuji arrives on the scene. For the most part, this is an assured, even-handed account of Takakura's trials as a principled yakuza but, as is all too common in films of this period, there is a bit too much humor in the middle third of the picture. With BOSS IN JAIL, Furuhata continued to prove himself a director of consistent quality and sensitivity, although not always as exciting as some of his colleagues. He wound up being star Takakura's main partner behind the camera in many of the actor's most popular '80s and '90s pictures. * * *

THE BOSS'S HEAD aka SOCHO NO KUBI aka THE BOSSES' BOSS 1979 136 min. **DIR.** Sadao Nakajima **SCR.** Sadao Nakajima/ Fumio Konami **PHOTO COLOR** 'SCOPE: Umeo Masuda **MUSIC:** Tomokazu Morita w/ Bunta Sugawara, Noboru Ando, Koji Tsuruta, Kentaro Shimizu, Ichiro Ogura, Junko Natsu, Asao Koike, Hideko Matsuda, Jonni Ogura, Yoichi Miura, Aiko Morishita
One of the earliest of the metamorphosing big budget epic Toei yakuza films – okay films but not nearly as good as the production-line, budget quickies they had been turning out since 1961 – films that had one thing going for them that the later epics did not: energy, conviction (at least a hint of it) and heart. This was one of the first "starring" screen appearances of Kentaro Shimizu, an actor who went on to become one of the reigning yakuza superstars from the mid-eighties into the late nineties.   * * 1/2

BOSS'S RUIN aka BOSU O TOSE 1963 **DIR./SCR.** Teruo Ishii **PHOTO B&W** 'SCOPE: Shoe Nishikawa **MUSIC:** Masao Yagi w/ Ken Takakura, Yoshiko Mita,

Naoki Sugiura, Tadao Sawamoto,
Ryuji Oki, Akemi Negishi, Koreya
Senda, Nobuo Kaneko, Mikijiro Hira,
Kyosuke Machida

BROTHERHOOD'S HONOR AND HUMANITY aka KYODAI JINGI aka FAMILY OBLIGA-TIONS series

Brotherhood's Honor & Humanity (#1)

BROTHERHOOD'S HONOR AND HUMANITY aka KYODAI JINGI aka FAMILY OBLIGATIONS 1966 87 min. **DIR.** Kosaku Yamashita **SCR.** Akira Murao/Norifumi Suzuki **PHOTO** B&W 'SCOPE: Motoya Washio **MUSIC:** Shunsuke Kikuchi **w/** Hiroki Matsukata, Koji Tsuruta, Saburo Kitajima, Hideo Murata, Junko Miyazono, Toru Abe, Kyosuke Machida, Kyoshi Hitomi

Set predominantly at a mountain hot springs resort town during the Taisho era (turn of the 20th century), this ini-tial entry has a bit more grittiness and less formula than some of the films that followed in the series. There are some stirring action setpieces and also some very atmospheric quiet scenes – such as when ne'er-do-well lone wolf Kitajima, having been ostracized for cheating at dice, finds out his long lost mother is dead and silently weeps while leaning against a telephone pole with a train speed-ing by in the background. There is also a nice balance where the plethora of main characters – young hothead Matsukata, wise lone wolf Tsuruta, ultimately loyal and fatally heroic Kitajima, stalwart boss Murata, and villains Abe and Machida (the lat-ter has no lines at all but projects astonishing menace just by his stare, facial scar and perpetually chewed matchstick) – all get their due without the usual confusing potpourri effect of many of Toei's *ninkyo* yakuza pic-tures. #1 of 9 films * * *

BROTHERHOOD'S HONOR AND HUMANITY 2 aka ZOKU KYODAI JINGI aka FAMILY OB-LIGATIONS 2 1966 89 min. **DIR.** Kosaku Yamashita **SCR.** Akira Murao **PHOTO COLOR 'SCOPE:** Motoya Washio **MUSIC:** Shunsuke Kikuchi **w/** Saburo Kitajima, Koji Tsuruta, Hideo Murata, Minoru Oki, Kotaro Satomi, Hosei Komatsu, Junko Miyazono, Tatsuo Endo Oki and his loyal clan are up against evil rival *oyabun* Komatsu. Kitajima is a strange, but good leading man. Famous primarily for his spectacular singing prowess, his short stature and intense personality make him a natural for blending humor with the usual tragic fate of a yakuza anti-hero. It was a custom at most studios for the leading performer to sing the

title song during the opening credits of *chanbara* and yakuza cinema, especially at Toei and Nikkatsu. This always produced entertaining results – from the traditionally-trained Kitajima and Hideo Murata to the pop-star stylings of Akira Kobayashi and Tetsuya Watari to the romantic, effective monotone of Ken Takakura and Shintaro Katsu to the inept but nevertheless charming non-voices of Bunta Sugawara and Tomisaburo Wakayama. #2 of 9 films   * * *

BROTHERHOOD'S HONOR AND HUMANITY – THREE BROTHERS FROM THE KANTO DISTRICT aka KYODAI JINGI – KANTO SAN KYODAI aka BROTHER'S VOW 1966 89 min. **Dir.** Kosaku Yamashita **Scr.** Akira Murao **Photo color 'scope:** Nagaki Yamagishi **Music:** Shunsuke Kikuchi   w/ Saburo Kitajima, Hideo Murata, Koji Tsuruta, Junko Fuji, Tomisaburo Wakayama, Kotaro Satomi, Kenji Sugawara, Junko Miyazono, Shingo Yamashiro Another *ninkyo* piece focusing on a clan protecting and working with the fishermen and dockworkers. It starts slow but by mid-film has picked up steam. It also bears Yamashita's trademark excellence of more complex characters and relationships than usual. Wakayama does one of his awesome turns as a manic, egocentric villain. #3 of 9 films   * * * 1/2

BROTHERHOOD'S HONOR AND HUMANITY – RETURN OF THE THREE BROTHERS FROM THE KANTO DISTRICT aka KYODAI JINGI – ZOKU KANTO SAN KYODAI 1967 88 min.

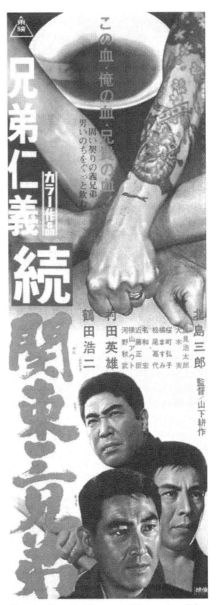

Brotherhood's Honor & Humanity (#4)

Dir. Kosaku Yamashita **Scr.** Akira Murao **Photo color 'scope:** Nagaki Yamagishi **Music:** Shunsuke Kikuchi   w/ Saburo Kitajima, Hideo Murata, Koji Tsuruta, Kotaro Satomi, Hiroko Sakuramachi, Minoru Oki, Kayo Matsuo, Masumi Tachibana,

Hiroshi Nawa   Tsuruta has TB in this one and barely makes it through to the climactic swordfight massacre. Suspenseful and once again filled with director Yamashita and writer Murao's more realistic characters. This was one of my earliest experiences viewing a *ninkyo* yakuza film, and it not only created a love of the subgenre, but also made me a fan of Koji Tsuruta's melancholic persona. #4 of 9 films * * *

BROTHERHOOD'S HONOR AND HUMANITY – THE TRUTH ABOUT KANTO LIFE aka KYODAI JINGI – KANTO INOCHI SHIRAZU 1967 88 min. DIR. Kosaku Yamashita SCR. Akira Murao PHOTO COLOR 'SCOPE: Shigeru Akatsuka MUSIC: Takeo Watanabe w/ Saburo Kitajima, Koji Tsuruta, Hideo Murata, Kyosuke Machida, Naoko Kubo, Ryosuke Kagawa, Tatsuo Endo, Masaomi Kondo, Bin Amatsu, Itaro Kuni Not too promising to begin with as Kitajima falls in with a bunch of con-men (Endo et.al.) who fleece restaurants for meals and brothels for sex. When Kitajima gives all his money to a tubercular geisha (Kubo) in a brothel run by Amatsu's gang, the ball of yarn begins to unravel and things begin to get interesting. Initially, he is indebted to boss Amatsu. He also has an antagonistic flare-up everytime he runs into Machida, one of the decent clan's right hand men. Machida's boss, a ne'er-do-well addicted to Amatsu's crooked dice games, signs over the gang's territory on the Yokohama dockside then dies. Kagawa is the big *oyabun* of the area, a senior boss who holds sway over many groups. When Amatsu

tries to take over the dead boss's turf, Kagawa and other bosses veto the move. Subsequently, Amatsu calls in Kitajima's debt ordering him to assassinate Kagawa. A refreshing change from the usual Toei formula is that Kitajima actually makes the attempt. But Kagawa's larger-than-life personality and Machida's patience after the botched attack convince Kitajima he is in the wrong gang. He is inducted into Kagawa's clan with a full *sakazuki* ceremony. Subsequently, visiting tough guy Tsuruta saves Kitajima and Machida from Amatsu's HQ. Consumptive Kubo is Tsuruta's long lost love, and he rescues her from the brothel with the help of his new comrades. She opts to die in peace in Kagawa's compound. Shortly thereafter, Kagawa is murdered by Amatsu's men. Kitajima, Tsuruta and Machida do the vengeance thing with a strategically-choreographed attack on Amatsu's HQ, dispatching the villains. * * * #5 of 9 films

BROTHERHOOD'S HONOR AND HUMANITY – KANTO BIG BROTHER aka KYODAI JINGI – KANTO ANIKI BUN aka PLEDGE OF BROTHERS – KANTO AFFAIR 1967 87 min. DIR. Sadao Nakajima SCR. Akira Murao/Norifumi Suzuki PHOTO COLOR 'SCOPE: Shigeru Akatsuka MUSIC: Shunsuke Kikuchi w/ Saburo Kitajima, Hideo Murata, Koji Tsuruta, Bin Amatsu, Masaomi Kondo, Sanae Kitabayashi, Sachiko (Yukiko?) Kuwabara, Shotaro Hayashi   A stunningly beautful *ninkyo eiga* saturated with a poetic, melancholic atmosphere, largely due to the extensive on-location work at an old fashioned village on the coast. In addition, the script by Murao and Suzuki draws from formula but remains amazingly fresh and cliche-free. Nakajima's muscular direction is resolutely determined to avoid the often inappropriate comedy relief that even great directors like Yamashita and good ones like Ozawa felt compelled to put in their films. Kondo is a hot-headed bad boy escaping from a village with geisha Kuwabara in tow. Lone wolf Tsuruta is instrumental in deflecting their pursuers – including Kitajima. The two lovers end up at the aforementioned coastal village, landing at Murata and Kitabayashi's inn. However, Murata knows Kondo is trouble and won't allow him to stay. They end up employing Kuwabara, and Kondo rebelliously joins ruthless Amatsu's gang who are intent on shanghaiing girls from poor families into prostitution. Kitajima appears on the scene, stays at Murata's and runs into Kuwabara whom he knows from his past. Soon Tsuruta shows up, too, and lo and behold, Murata's wife, Kitabayashi, is his ex-girlfriend he had left behind years previous, and there are some poignant moments between the two. Confusing? Not if you pay rapt, obsessive attention. Eventually Kondo realizes how horrible the monsters are he is hooked up with, but is killed when he tries to rescue Kuwabara. Murata gets murdered, too, and Tsuruta and Kitajima go on a sword-swinging rampage at Amatsu's HQ to decimate the evil gang. Director Nakajima constantly avoids many of the corny pitfalls that other Toei *ninkyo* directors were sometimes prone to, affecting a beautfully realized story with a wistful romantic feel that is nevertheless fairly unsentimental considering some of the plot develop-

ments. This compares very favorably to the best of directors Hideo Gosha and Tai Kato. #6 of 9 films * * * *

BROTHERHOOD'S HONOR AND HUMANITY – LOYALTY OFFERING ON BRINK OF ADVERSITY aka KYODAI JINGI – GYAKU EN NO SAKAZUKI aka BROTHERS' CODE – THE BACK RELATION 1968 90 min. **Dir.** Norifumi Suzuki **Scr.** Kazuo Kasahara/Kikusei Umebayashi **Photo color 'scope:** Sadatsugu Yoshida **Music:** Shunsuke Kikuchi w/ Saburo Kitajima, Tomisaburo Wakayama, Bunta Sugawara, Nobuo Kaneko, Minoru Oki, Hiroko Sakuramachi, Tatsuo Endo
A not bad but not particularly distinctive yarn of Kitajima attacking an evil gang, then returning to his distant hometown until the heat is off. Once there, he becomes embroiled in a feud between decent Oki's gang and evil Kaneko's bunch. He is doubly chagrined to see that not only Wakayama, a new friend made on the ferry home, is suspected to be the hired killer of boss Oki (Oki barely has a cameo here), but that his own restaurant-managing mom (!) is also one of villain Kaneko's cohorts. Things come to a head when Wakayama sees the error of his ways and is then assassinated by Kaneko's men. To make matters worse, Kaneko has kidnapped decent Sakuramachi into prostitution out of town then attempts the same with Kitajima's sister. Kitajima and new boss Sugawara head over to rescue sis and dispatch Kaneko's mob. The usual sword melee follows. Kitajima and Sugawara emerge relatively unscathed, but Kitajima's mom dies in a hail of bullets when

she shields her son from Kaneko's aim. Kitajima then applies blade tip to Kaneko's jugular before cradling the dying parent in his arms. Considering Suzuki's other great forays into *ninkyo* territory, the storytelling here gets a bit perfunctory. Also Miyazono is wasted as Oki's widow. Excellent actress Sakuramachi is given a bit more to do but, as usual when featured as a female "co-star" she is criminally underused, only hinting at the breadth of character of which she is capable. A subplot at the beginning with Tatsuo Endo as a drunken, crusading scientist attempting to blow the whistle on Kaneko's pollution-spewing factory is an interesting, welcome departure from the formulaic narrative conventions, but this minor subplot goes nowhere and seems tacked on. #7 of 9 films * * 1/2

NEW BROTHERHOOD'S HONOR AND HUMANITY aka SHIN KYODAI JINGI aka NEW FAMILY OBLIGATIONS aka CODE OF THE GAMBLERS 1970 85 min. **Dir.** Kiyoshi Saeki **Scr.** Morimasa Owaku **Photo color 'scope:** Ichiro Hoshijima **Music:** Shunsuke Kikuchi **w/** Saburo Kitajima, Bunta Sugawara, Toru Abe, Ryoji Hayama, Akiko Kudo, Kenji Imai, Ichiro Sugai, Hiroku Nakata, Sonosuke Sawamura
Toei Studios was more likely to use the prefix "Shin" (meaning "New") on their movie titles when trying to pump fresh box-office life into a long-running series than any of the other Japanese production companies. Then again, except for Daiei with their ZATOICHI films and Nikkatsu with their A MAN'S CREST pictures, most of the other studios' film series

New Brotherhood's Honor & Humanity (#8)

seldom generated the box office legs to go beyond three or four installments. This is a by-the-numbers *ninkyo* tale with Sugawara going to jail for a time to take the rap for his gang's decimation of a rival, evil boss's mob. Kudo, in another thankless longsuffering wife role, is given little to do. Kitajima and Imai, Sugawara's blood brothers become estranged as elder boss Sugai's son takes over the clan, enlisting craven Abe as his partner in greed. When Sugawara is released, he takes a decidedly lower profile to cultivate a family life. Eventually their former comrade Imai, who has become Abe and the young boss's righthand man, can no longer stomach their unethical deeds and cruelty and goes against them. This leads to Imai being murdered which in turn leads to Kitajima and Sugawara going on the obligatory vengeance quest. They destroy Abe and his cohorts, but Sugawara is mortally wounded and Kitajima left near death himself. Unfortunately, despite decent veteran director Saeki at the reins, there isn't much to grab onto here that would distinguish it from many other average *ninkyo* yakuza pictures. It is a welcome change of pace, though, to see usually typecast villain actor Imai playing a heroic role. #8 of 9 films * * 1/2

KANTO BROTHERHOOD'S HONOR AND HUMANITY – CHIVALRY aka KANTO KYODAI JINGI – NINKYO aka KANTO FAMILY OBLIGATIONS – CHIVALRY 1971 89 min. **Dir.** Buichi Saito **Scr.** Koji Takada **Photo color 'scope:** Shigeru Akatsuka **Music:** Taiichiro Kosugi w/ Saburo Kitajima, Kyosuke Machida, Goro Ibuki, Hideo Murata, Hiroko Sakuramachi, Bunta Sugawara, Nobuo Kaneko, Hiroshi Nawa, Ryoji Hayama A worthy final entry to the series with restaurant owner Kitajima at odds with cheating card dealer Machida.

Brotherhood's Honor & Humanity (#9)

But he soon realizes that the reason tormented Machida is pulling fast ones for villains Nawa and Hayama is to earn money for indentured geisha Sakuramachi. Machida had caught her husband cheating years before, then fought and killed the man,

realizing too late the horror he had unleashed on widow Sakuramachi and her young child. Kitajima and Machida gradually become friends, but things spiral out-of-control as both men go to bat for Sakuramachi against boss Kaneko and henchmen Nawa and Hayama. Machida is nearly beaten to death when he tries to help the tormented geisha escape with her boy. Only Kitajima's intervention saves him. He sacrifices himself and his loyalty to good, young boss Ibuki to save Machida and help release Sakuramachi from her slavery. He is wedged in a classic rock-and-a-hard-place situation, finally compelled by evil Kaneko to assassinate his friend Ibuki. Machida is accidentally killed when he tries to intervene between the two former friends, and this causes Kitajima and Ibuki to reunite. Shortly thereafter, Ibuki is killed by Hayama, and Kitajima and another decent boss (Sugawara) go into massacre mode to wipe out Kaneko, Nawa et. al. Okay, now repeat all that back to me! #9 and last of series
* * *

BULLETS OF SLACKER STREET aka YUMINGAI NO JUDAN aka OPERATION DIA-MOND 1962 85 min. DIR. Masuichi (Koichi?) Iizuka SCR. Susumu Saji PHOTO B&W 'SCOPE: Ichiro Hoshijima MUSIC: Tomokazu Kawabe w/ Ken Takakura, Tetsuro Tanba, Yoshiko Sakuma, Hisako Tsukuba, Harumi Sone, Danny Yuma, Mike Daneen, Isaac Saxon Supposedly a fairly close copy of Fukasaku's 1961 HIGH NOON FOR GANGSTERS. Not too big a stretch when you realize the writer, cinema-tographer and five of the actors also worked on Fukasaku's picture. This time, the gang steals a shipment of diamonds from a U.S. Army base with the gems secreted in a torpedo. The catch is that once it is in their possession and they yank out the stones, the torpedo blows them all up.

CAPONE'S YOUNGER BROTHER aka KAPONE NO SHATEI series

IMPORTED GAMBLING CODE – CAPONE'S YOUNGER BROTHER aka HAKURAI JINGI – KAPONE NO SHATEI aka BOSS FROM CHICAGO 1970 88 min. DIR./SCR. Takashi Harada PHOTO COLOR 'SCOPE: Sadatsugu Yoshida MUSIC: Masao Yagi w/ Tomisaburo Wakayama, Minoru Oki, Fumio Watanabe, Shingo Yamashiro, Gurashira, Kenji Kusumoto, Jerii Ito, Toru Abe, Hiroshi Minami, Yoichi Numata Another violent crime-comedy series with Wakayama, although it is not-as-good and consid-erably more shortlived in comparison to his SCOUNDREL (GOKUDO) series. #1 of 2 films * 1/2

CAPONE'S YOUNGER BROTHER – HEART AND SPECULATION aka KAPONE NO SHATEI – YAMATO DAMASHI aka BOSS WITH THE SAMURAI SPIRIT 1971 90 min. DIR. Takashi Harada SCR. Tatsuo Nogami PHOTO COLOR 'SCOPE: Umio Masuda MUSIC: Takeo Yamashita w/ Tomisaburo Wakayama, Minoru Oki, Seizaburo Kawazu, Tomoko Mayama, Toru Yuri, Kikue Mori, Daian Koonin (Diane Konan?), Tatsuo Endo

Bullets of Slacker Street

Capone's Younger Brother (#2) (with a poster heavily promoting star Wakayama in huge kanji much, much bigger than the movie title)

Wakayama is a Japanese-American boss arriving from Chicago for the opening of a chemical plant owned by his mob. However, he encounters opposition from a local Japanese boss and has the man killed. Then he is shocked to discover that his own grandmother (also a boss in her neighborhood!) opposes the chemical plant on similar ecological/ community grounds. His conscience is finally awakened when she is murdered by a member of his Chicago gang. He joins forces with the Japanese mob to protect the environment from foreign exploiters. #2 of 2 films

CEREMONY OF DISBANDING
aka KAISANSHIKI 1967 93 min. **DIR.** Kinji Fukasaku **SCR.** Isao Matsumoto/ Hideaki Yamamoto/ Kinji Fukasaku **PHOTO COLOR**

Ceremony of Disbanding

'SCOPE: Ichiro Hoshijima **MUSIC:** Isao Tomita w/ Koji Tsuruta, Tetsuro Tanba, Junko Miyazono, Fumio Watanabe, Misako Watanabe, Hosei Komatsu, Asao Uchida, Yasuhiro Komiya, Nobuo Kaneko, Minoru Uezu A kind of combination *ninkyo/ jitsuroku* yakuza saga, and it is unusually grim, even for a downbeat specimen of the genre. When a subgang is disbanded. Tsuruta and several others are not absorbed into the larger mobs but remain only tangentially affiliated. Traditional Tsuruta gradually loses respect for his friend, Watanabe, who has become head of an up-and-coming gang. His former comrade is fast evolving into being just as unscrupulous as rival mob boss Komatsu. The two are vying for contracts in construction of what are basically gross-polluting factories in a lower class neighborhood already surrounded by a variety of environmentally unsafe plants. Not only does Tsuruta identify with the poor folk who have had enough, but his old flame, her son and several other comrades live there. One other associate, also no longer a yakuza, has a junkie wife who is forced into porno films by Watanabe's mob to procure her dope. The irate spouse is killed as is a crusading doctor trying to reason with the craven gangs. Tanba portrays a former enemy who lost his arm to Tsuruta when Tsuruta assassinated his boss. They develop an uneasy friendship when a duel they fight ends in a draw. Tensions between Watanabe's and Komatsu's groups reach the breaking point. Tsuruta is arguing with Watanabe when Watanabe is suddenly stabbed to death by an ambitious teenage boy loyal to boss Komatsu. Peace-loving Tsuruta finally goes over the edge, killing Komatsu and his manipulating politician higher-ups (Uchida and Kaneko). Mortally wounded, he then expires in their compound. * * *

Chase After Opium Smugglers

CHASE AFTER OPIUM SMUG-GLERS aka SHIROI KONA NO KYOFU aka WHITE POWDER TERROR 1960 88 min. **DIR.** Shinji Murayama **SCR.** Kazuo Funabashi **PHOTO B&W 'SCOPE:** Ichiro Hoshijima **w/** Rentaro Mikuni, Kaneko Iwasaki, Hitomi Nakahara A hybrid detective/gangster yarn with

Mikuni as a G-man on the trail of a narcotics gang. He falls for an addict whore (Iwasaki) who is later given a fatal hotshot by the villains. From all accounts, a supposedly gritty, atmospheric rendering of a standard program story.

Cherry Blossom Gang

CHERRY BLOSSOM FIRE GANG aka KANTO HIZAKURA IKKA 1972 102 min. **DIR.** Masahiro Makino **SCR.** Kazuo Kasahara **PHOTO COLOR 'SCOPE:** Motoya Washio **MUSIC:** Chuji Kinoshita **w/** Junko Fuji, Ken Takakura, Koji Tsuruta, Tomisaburo Wakayama, Bunta Sugawara, Chiezo Kataoka, Kyosuke Machida, Goro Ibuki, Shingo Yamashiro, Michiyo Kogure, Kanjuro Arashi, Akiko Kudo, Yoko Minamida, Hiroyuki Nagato, Michitaro Mizushima, Nobuo Kaneko, Kenjiro Ishiyama, Bin Amatsu, Tatsuo Endo, Hiromi Fujiyama   Fuji is a geisha/gambler in 1920s Japan who not only sings traditional songs but presides over *hana-fuda* (flower cards) games for the "good" yakuza clan. When she is provoked, then insulted by a couple of visiting head bad guys, a test of skill involving her hairpin/blade against the villain's sword causes the bad guys to lose face. Soon after, one of the heads (Mizushima) of her clan, who had been present, is murdered. Thus the dominoes start to fall. Fuji's beau Takakura is walking with her the night after the funeral when they are set upon by the bad clan's toughs. He fights them off and accidentally kills one. We don't see him again for a while because he goes into hiding. Relations between the two clans continue to deteriorate. Fuji's clan also carries the fire brigade franchise in town (hence the English release title), and the villains try to discredit them by starting a huge fire. Eventually Tsuruta, Takakura, and Fuji head over to the bad guys' HQ to get satisfaction. Tsuruta dies, but Fuji and Takakura finish off the whole rotten bunch in a protracted battle that pretty much sums up the pattern for other *ninkyo* (chivalrous) film series of this ilk such as TALES OF THE LAST SHOWA YAKUZA, TALES OF JAPANESE CHIVALRY and RED PEONY GAMBLER – the more traditional type of yakuza picture. Program filler elevated to blood-ritual status, performed in such a relentlessly ritualistic genre style, as opposed to mere formula, that they become intoxicating. Fuji's character seems like the prototype for her Oryu/RED PEONY GAMBLER persona, except this was produced after the last film in that series. In fact, this was Fuji's swan song. She retired immediately after, even

though at the height of her popularity, to marry a kabuki stage actor. She has since reappeared in several films (non-yakuza), most notably in Kinji Fukasaku's THE GEISHA HOUSE (1998). Another unique element of this film is that Fuji and Takakura's characters are given a victorious send-off by their clan as they emerge, tired and bloody, from their battle/ massacre. It is almost unheard of for a *ninkyo* or *jitsuroku* yakuza film to have an even halfway happy ending, and Fuji's and Takakura's characters leaving town to be married, with their clan's approval, is something virtually unseen in *ninkyo* films. Needless to say, the ending intentionally mirrors Toei Studios' lavish sendoff of Fuji to retire into real-life wedded bliss. Yakuza film buffs will also notice that the cast is jampacked with a surfeit of Toei *ninkyo* stars. This may be a partial remake of WOMAN BOSS aka GEISHA FIREFIGHTER that Makino directed at Daiei in 1970 with Kyoko Enami. This would be up another half-notch if not for a glut of comic relief in the first third of the film. * * *

CHIVALROUS ISHIMATSU OF THE FISH MARKET aka KYOKAKU UOGASHI NO ISHIMATSU aka WATERFRONT ISHIMATSU 1967 **DIR.** Norifumi Suzuki **SCR.** Koji Takada **PHOTO COLOR 'SCOPE:** Motoya Washio **MUSIC:** Masao Yagi **w/** Saburo Kitajima, Hideo Murata, Teruo Yoshida, Masumi Tachibana, Tomiko Ishii, Bin Amatsu, Shingo Yamashiro, Asao Uchida, Yuriko Mishima

CHIVALROUS LIFE IN THE BONE

aka KYOKOTSU ICHIDAI aka SKELETON OF A CHIVAL-ROUS LIFE aka THE CHIVAL-ROUS LIFE 1967 92 min.
DIR. Masahiro Makino SCR. Akira Murao/Isao Matsumoto/ Hideaki Yamamoto PHOTO COLOR 'SCOPE: Ichiro Hoshijima MUSIC: Masao Yagi w/ Ken Takakura Junko Fuji, Minoru Oki, Kenjiro Ishiyama, Junko Miyazono, Takashi Shimura, Rinichi Yamamoto, Kenji Imai, Tatsuo Endo, Koji Nanbara, Yoichi Numata   Takakura and Oki are pals abused by their Japanese military superiors in early 1930's Manchuria. Takakura, in particuliar, is singled-out for punishment for seemingly no other reason than he is a sensitive misfit haunted by separation from his mother as a young boy. He often ends up in the stockade for strik-ing back at his attackers. Just before he gets kicked-out, he brandishes a machine gun at his commanding officers. Returning to the port town of his youth, he visits his mother's grave then makes a pathetic attempt at drowning himself only to find the canal he has chosen is only a couple of feet deep. He subsequently rescues two itinerant beggar musicians from a gang of bullying yakuza. Recovering from a good thrashing, he is invited to the tramps' shantytown for a meal. Beggar Yamamoto decides to leave with him. Soon they are recruited into decent boss Shimura's clan of coal loaders and dockworkers. Shortly thereafter Takakura becomes obsessed with a beautiful whore (Fuji) who is a dead ringer for his mom. This could actually have been a much better film had Makino and the writers been able to develop this facet more naturally

instead of slavishly kowtowing to *ninkyo eiga* formula. Certainly the most emotionally resonant scenes are played between Takakura and Fuji. Takakura's psyche struggles confusedly between the nostalgic, embryonic ache of childhood longing for a lost mother and the fighting-to-emerge sexual urge for a beautiful woman. Fuji is mystified to find her sexy ways ineffectual. This is yet another *ninkyo* yakuza film that seems to be (unconsciously?) trying to deal with issues of repressed homosexu-ality. In any case, long-lost friend Oki returns but is in debt to the evil bosses Amatsu and Nawa. Miyazono is boss Shimura's daughter who has an unrequited yen for Takakura. In the end, she realizes she will never have him and decides to enlighten Fuji on why Takakura is not responding to her. Fuji despairingly gives up, leav-ing town. Takakura discovers this too late and is left only with his duty to avenge the shooting of boss Shimura as solace. He is joined by his yakuza brethren as well as his beggar friends in wiping out Amatsu and Nawa in a deserted lumberyard.   * * *

CHIVALROUS MAN aka TOSEININ series

CHIVALROUS MAN

aka TOSEININ aka GAMBLER'S WORLD 1967 89 min. DIR. Kiyoshi Saeki SCR. Goro Tanada PHOTO COLOR 'SCOPE: Masahiko Iimura MUSIC: Chuji Kinoshita w/ Tatsuo Umemiya, Koji Tsuruta, Tomisaburo Wakayama, Masako Ichikawa, Hiromi Fujiyama, Nobuo Kaneko, Hiroshi Nawa, Michitaro Mizushima

Chivalrous Man (#1)

Toei's primary *ninkyo* yakuza vehicle
for matinee hearthrob Umemiya.
Brutal tough Wakayama and his compromised best friend Tsuruta make a
hit on Umemiya's godfather and underboss (Mizushima) at the behest of
evil Nanbara and allied villains Kaneko and Nawa. Soon Umemiya has to
go on the run after he kills an attacker
in self-defense, leaving his wife and
son alone. Before long, the wife and
little boy encounter basically decent
Tsuruta who begins to look out for
them. Soon Kaneko and Nanbara get
wind that Umemiya is still around.
Their strongarm mainman, Wakayama, cajoles his obligated comrade,
Tsuruta – who is also an expert
marksman – to assassinate Umemiya.
Tsuruta cannot bring himself to kill
Umemiya, though, and only wings
him. Coincidentally, Umemiya's wife
encounters her wounded and once
again on-the-run hubby later that
night, spiriting him away to nurse

him back to health. Tsuruta finally
realizes who Umemiya is and ends
up helping him in the final revenge-
binge slaughter on Kaneko, Nanbara,
Nawa and their gang of cutthroats.
Unhappily, chivalrous Tsuruta perishes in the bloodbath. Alhough Saeki
is an expert director of this kind of
ninkyo film, and he lenses almost the
entire picture on evocative locations
– as opposed to Toei's usual setbound
films from the period – this still
emerges as a bit halfbaked despite its
strengths and a savage final sword
melee. #1 of 2 films   * * 1/2

**RETURN OF A CHIVALROUS
MAN** aka ZOKU TOSEININ aka
GAMBLER'S WORLD 2 1967 87
min. **DIR.** Kiyoshi Saeki **SCR.** Goro
Tanada/Yukio Shiraishi **PHOTO
COLOR 'SCOPE:** Masahiko Iimura
MUSIC: Shunsuke Kikuchi **w/** Tatsuo
Umemiya, Koji Tsuruta, Masayo
Banri, Tomisaburo Wakayama,
Takehiro Nakamura, Michitaro
Mizushima, Tatsuo Endo, Koji
Nanbara   This has a very similar
story to the preceding film and
emerges as more a variation on
a theme than a bonafide sequel.
Wakayama and Tsuruta play similar
parts, but this time around Tsuruta
opts out when bad boss Endo requests he and Wakayama make a hit
on the good gang's Mizushima.
However, Wakayama follows through
and Tsuruta is still implicated as
well as getting into trouble with
Endo's bunch. He goes on the run,
leaving his tubercular wife (Masayo
Banri) and their son with benevolent godfather Nakamura. Saeki and
screenwriters Tanada and Shiraishi
actually relax a little with the material here, digging much deeper into

the relationship between Tsuruta and Wakayama, a welcome development.

Chivalrous Man (#2)

There is also a great deal of skillful tension-building on display with some squirm-inducing encounters, especially between chivalrous Umemiya and corrupt military officer Nanbara, who is secretly allied with Endo. Eventually, Tsuruta returns to repay kindhearted Nakamura and reunite with wife Banri – only to find both dead – Nakamura assassinated by Endo's bunch and Banri dead from consumption. To Wakayama's chagrin, Tsuruta teams up with Umemiya to get justice. The pair attack Endo and his gang as well as militarist Nanbara in a spectacular nocturnal sword battle on the seashore. Wakayama perishes saving his friend Tsuruta. Once Tsuruta and Umemiya have de-cimated the villains, Tsuruta opts to wander, leaving his son in the care of Umemiya and Umemiya's girl. #2 of 2 films   * * *

CHIVALROUS THIRD GENERA-TION aka YUKYO SANDAI 1966 DIR. Shinji Murayama SCR. Hajime Takaiwa PHOTO COLOR 'SCOPE: Masahiko Iimura MUSIC: Minoru Miki w/ Tatsuo Umemiya, Koji Tsuruta, Ryutaro Tatsumi, Chikage Ogi, Kenjiro Ishiyama, Yuki Jono, Meicho Soganoya, Koji Nanbara, Takashi Kanda

CHIVALROUS WOMAN aka ONNA TOSEININ aka OKOMA, THE ORPHAN GAMBLER series

CHIVALROUS WOMAN aka ONNA TOSEININ aka OKOMA, THE ORPHAN GAMBLER 1971 90 min. DIR. Shigehiro Ozawa SCR. Tatsuo Honda PHOTO COLOR 'SCOPE: Shin Furuya MUSIC: Takeo Watanabe w/ Junko Fuji, Koji Tsuruta, Ganosuke Ashiya, Michiyo Kogure, Tatsuo Endo, Eizo Kitamura, Shizue Natsukawa, Minoru Shiraki,

Shoji Arikawa, Takuzo Kawatani
Unlike the RED PEONY GAMBLER
films, Fuji plays Okoma, a bit of a
struggling neophyte, fighting her way
through a male-dominated world of
gamblers. The film starts with her
challenging a gang on a precipitous
mountain road and almost immediately cutting off the boss's arm. Later
Fuji crosses paths with and watches
over a little girl. Soon the angry villain gang catches up, taking Fuji into
the mountains to kill her only to have
traveling Tsuruta intervene and fight
them off. It turns out Tsuruta is the
little girl's dad, and he asks Fuji to
shepherd the tyke to her uncle who
owns a hot springs inn in a nearby village. Meanwhile he goes on the attack
at the bad guys' HQ. After arriving
and delivering the girl, Fuji encounters the mistress (Kogure) of greedy
village boss Endo. Before long she
realizes Kogure is her own long lost
mother who had abandoned her as a
child. Kogure first denies everything
but, tortured by guilt, finally admits
her true identity. Craven *oyabun* Endo
wants to monopolize the hotel trade
and kidnaps Tsuruta's daughter, hoping to extort the inn from the uncle
as ransom. Kogure tries to sneak the
tiny girl out of the storeroom but is
caught and beaten mercilessly by
Endo and his cronies. Fuji breaks into
where Endo holds Kogure and the girl
at his lumberyard. The villains are
alerted, and Kogure steps in front of
a bullet to shield Fuji. They get away,
but Kogure's wound is fatal. Fuji and
her friends cremate Kogure's body at
dawn on a cliff overlooking a waterfall. Endo angrily sets fire to the hot
springs inn that night, and the uncle
is seriously wounded. As a result,
Fuji and the returning Tsuruta take up

arms to wipe out the gangsters.
Tsuruta is fatally shot, but Fuji manages to at last slay Endo, a geyser of
his blood festooning the newly falling
snow. Fuji returns through the woods
at dawn, crossing the snow covered
ground. This is an enormously romantic, beautiful piece nicely paced
with action, grown out of standard
cliche programmer elements. Ozawa
and cinematographer Furuya manage
to achieve an almost fairy tale quality
at times through the judicious use of
the gorgeous rural locations. One of
director Ozawa's best films. #1 of 2
films   * * * 1/2

**CHIVALROUS WOMAN – I
REQUEST SHELTER** aka ONNA
TOSEININ – OTA NO MOSHI-
MASU 1971 103 min. **DIR.** Kosaku
Yamashita **SCR.** Kazuo Kasahara
PHOTO COLOR 'SCOPE: Nagaki
Yamagishi **MUSIC:** Takeo Watanabe
w/ Junko Fuji, Bunta Sugawara,
Shogo Shimada, Kyosuke Machida,
Tatsuo Endo, Aiko Mimasu, Nobuo
Kaneko, Yoko Mihara, Toshiaki
Minami, Shotaro Hayashi
The phrase *"Ota No Moshimasu"* is
a colloquial expression usually said
by a person approaching a house for
admittance – for either visiting or
lodging purposes. It is used in the
straight world, too, but it is one of the
most famous yakuza expressions (at
least in the world of Japanese yakuza
cinema). It generally precedes the,
at times, lengthy formal introduction
delivered by the traditonally-minded
yakuza when arriving at his/her host's
domicile. Director Yamashita makes
it resonate even more profoundly
than usual in this second installment
as Fuji's status of a decent wandering gambler is called into question

人を斬ったという噂
賭場を割ったという噂
女だてらに日陰に咲いたこぼれ花
ながれる先は
なぜ、なぜ、いつもドス修羅場

カラー作品
監督・山下耕作

藤 純子
〈艶豪華配役〉

Chivalrous Woman (#2)

not only by the thuggish yakuza she encounters but also the excessively provincial townfolk who resent her even after she has stood up for them. Unlike the RED PEONY GAMBLER films with Fuji where it takes little to engender loyalty from the common people, here she is a true outcast except to a very few close friends. Fuji arrives in the port town of Ueno, presenting her letter of introduction to inn owner/ sewing shop manager Shimada and his blind wife. The first instance Fuji sees of evil boss Kaneko and his wife exerting their influence is when a bunch of bullying yakuza throw their weight around at the sewing factory. Shimada drives them out. But things worsen when an indentured couple Shimada helps to escape are captured by Kaneko's gang. This escalates into a riot at the sweatshop when the villains crack down. Fuji sends the hoodlums packing with her judo but the female workers are more alienated by her and her abilities than impressed. The gang later tries to attack her at the seashore, but former gambling acquaintance Machida intervenes. An incident with the male of the indentured couple managing to once again flee to Shimada's house enables Machida to further ingratiate himself with Fuji. The pair converse over drinks, and Machida starts to detail some scam when Fuji's shipboard companion Sugawara materializes. Brandishing a knife, he drags Machida outside and exposes his subterfuge. The pair fight with their blades in the driving rain, and it is only Fuji stepping into the fray that prevents Sugawara from slaying Machida. Soon afterwards Kaneko's men set the sweatshop ablaze, and Fuji is the only one who rushes into

the burning building to rescue a baby. However, the women are as ungrateful as ever, resentfully grabbing the child away from Fuji and not even thanking her. This sends Fuji into a deep depression. While Sugawara commiserates with her, Shimada goes to Kaneko's HQ to forcefully coerce concessions from the wicked boss. Underhanded Machida sneaks up from behind and stabs him in the back. The rest of the craven gang finish him off. Fuji goes to retaliate, ready to draw her knife on the villains when her former boss (Endo) suddenly appears, berating her and ordering her to apologize to Kaneko and Machida! Fuji, believing she must be wrong about everything, especially with her former *oyabun* taking Kaneko's part, is so deflated and demoralized, she actually cuts off a pinkie joint in atonement! Later that night she sits alone in her room, lit only by the moonlight. Sugawara comes to talk and quickly convinces her that they have both been right about Kaneko's gang all along. They unsheath their swords and go on the attack, staging a bloody massacre, decimating scores of villains including Endo. Sugawara and Machida stab each other to death. Fuji, bleeding from a slashed arm, pursues Kaneko to the quay and finally manages to dispatch him. She rushes back to Sugawara, who dies in her embrace. At Shimada's wake, the cops lead Fuji away. Initially Shimada's blind widow refuses to talk to her, then suddenly has a change of heart. She tries to reach Fuji but the still jealous townswomen bar her way, keeping her back. It is hard to think of another *ninkyo* yakuza film that leaves the main protagonist – a chivalrous female at that – in so much pain and sorrow, such an emotional abyss of desolation at the climax. Perhaps RED PEONY GAMBLER #7 – DEATH TO THE WICKED comes close. Yamashita and writer Kasahara have fashioned a bleak, haunting, exciting and beautiful film. #2 of 2 films * * * *

CHIVALRY OF JUDO LIFE aka NINKYO YAWARA ICHIDAI 1966 88 min. **DIR.** Sadao Nakajima **SCR.** Sadao Nakajima/Takeo Kaneko **PHOTO COLOR 'SCOPE:** Shigeru Akatsuka **MUSIC:** Chuji Kinoshita w/ Hideo Murata, Hiroki Matsukata, Kayo Matsuo, Tomisaburo Wakayama, Kanjuro Arashi, Saburo Kitajima, Kenji Sugawara, Hosei Komatsu   A surprisingly invigorating hybrid of martial arts and *ninkyo* yakuza elements. Tortured soul Murata is stabbed when he tries to assassinate evil boss Komatsu. Young judo hothead Matsukata rescues him and helps to nurse him back to health with assistance from a very young Kayo Matsuo and her dad, boss Arashi. Lone wolf and wandering judo expert Kitajima complicates matters with his grudge against Matsukata. Kitajima, though, hates Komatsu and Komatsu's right hand man/judo killer Wakayama even more. Matsukata and Kitajima patch things up, but their new friendship is shortlived. Kitajima is challenged and throttled-to-death by Wakayama in an expertly choreographed, grueling nocturnal judo match in a windswept graveyard. Boss Arashi loses his temper at Matsukata for getting involved at the tail end of the fight, and a rift occurs. However, Arashi is predict-

ably the next one on boss Komatsu's hit list. At the climax, Murata grabs his sword and, with Matsukata, wipes out Komatsu, Wakayama and gang. Matsukata then watches forlorn Murata stumble off alone in the distance down a darkened lane. * * *

Chivalry of One Lone Flower

CHIVALRY OF ONE LONE FLOWER aka NINKYO HANA ICHIRIN 1974 **DIR.** Atsushi Mibori **SCR.** Akira Murao **PHOTO COLOR 'SCOPE:** Masahiko Iimura **MUSIC:** Shunsuke Kikuchi w/ Tatsuya Fuji, Yumi Takigawa, Junko Miyazono, Tatsuo Umemiya, Bin Amatsu   Though he had already appeared in a few DELINQUENT BOSS efforts, this was former Nikkatsu star Tatsuya Fuji's first film as a leading man at Toei.

CHIVALRY OF THREE PRO-VINCES – DUEL ON SATOKE ISLAND aka KYOKAKU SAN

GOKUSHI – SATOKE SHIMA NO TAIKETSU 1966 **DIR.** Kiyoshi Saeki **SCR.** Akira Murao **PHOTO COLOR 'SCOPE:** Ichiro Hoshijima **MUSIC:** Shunsuke Kikuchi w/ Koji Tsuruta, Minoru Oki, Kenji Sugawara, Naoko Kubo, Seizaburo Kawazu, Ryutaro Tatsumi, Rinichi Yamamoto, Nako Tamura, Takashi Kanda, Jiro Takagi

Chivalry of Three Provinces - Duel on Satoke Island

COCKROACH CORPS aka GOKKIBURI BUTAI 1966 **DIR.** Mikio Koyama **SCR.** Susumu Saji/ Michio Suzuki/Mikio Koyama **PHOTO COLOR 'SCOPE:** Makoto Tsuboi **MUSIC:** Shinsuke Kikuchi w/ Tatsuo Umemiya, Eitaro Shindo, Ryohei Uchida, Tetsuro Tanba, Ryoichi Tamagawa, Akemi Kita, Yuki Jono One of those "gangsters-drafted-into-the-military-do-the-craziest-things" films probably influenced by the success of Shintaro Katsu's HOODLUM SOLDIER series at Daiei Studios.

Code of Chivalry

CODE OF CHIVALRY aka KY-OKAKU NO OKITE 1967 89 min. **DIR.** Motohiro Torii **SCR.** Ichiro Miyagawa/Akira Murao/Motohiro Torii **PHOTO COLOR 'SCOPE:** Sadatsugu Yoshida **MUSIC:** Ichiro Saito w/ Tatsuo Umemiya, Kyosuke Machida, Ken Takakura, Yumiko Nogawa, Kenji Imai, Kenjiro Ishiyama, Shingo Yamashiro, Tatsuo Endo, Kazuko Takasugi

CONTINENTAL DRIFTER aka DAI RIKU NAGAREMONO 1966 92 min. **DIR.** Kosaku Yamashita **SCR.** Akira Murao **PHOTO COLOR 'SCOPE:** Ichiro Hoshijima **MUSIC:** Chuji Kinoshita **w/** Koji Tsuruta, Junko Fuji, Tetsuro Tanba, Minoru Oki, Kenji Imai, Asao Uchida, Isa Shu, Rinichi Yamamoto, Tatsuo Endo

CRUEL HIGH SCHOOL BAD BOY aka HIJO GAKUEN WARU series

CRUEL HIGH SCHOOL – BAD BOY aka HIJO GAKUEN – WARU 1973 **DIR.** Atsushi Mibori **SCR.** Isao Matsumoto/Hideaki Yamamoto **PHOTO COLOR 'SCOPE:** Masahiko Iimura **MUSIC:** Toshiaki Tsushima **w/** Hayato Tani, Mari Atsumi, Kunie Tanaka, Teresa Noda, Rikiya "Ricky" Yasuoka, Tetsuro Tanba, Misuzu Ota, Rokko Toura, Hiroshi Oizumi, Kenji Imai, Toru Abe A *manga*-based series on the sexy, violent adventures of a rebellious, misanthropic student (Tani) – who also just happens to be a *kendo* expert! – his encounters with girls, gangs and other delinquents. This was Mibori's debut as director, and he brings an almost spaghetti western visual dynamic to the proceedings that makes his picture never less than diverting. However, as per its comic book origins, it remains pretty shallow unlike other *manga*-inspired films such as the LADY SNOWBLOOD and LONE WOLF AND CUB series. At times, such as when a quiet girl, who is smitten with our violent, pouty anti-hero, commits suicide by jumping from the roof in front of him and the whole student body, the film takes on an added dimension. Refreshingly, Tani's reaction is the exact opposite of what we expect. Instead of the girl's death finally making him come to grips with his isolation, he flips out, invading her quiet funeral to smash the altar and intimidate the mourners. There are amusing supporting roles by Kunie Tanaka as the bespectacled nerd instructor who is constantly tormented and Mari Atsumi (THE HOT LITTLE GIRL, PLAY IT COOL) as a sexy teacher given to flirting with the boys in her charge. She gets more than she bargains for when she comes up against the abusive Tani. After he rips open the front of her dress three separate times, Atsumi decides teaching is perhaps not her vocation and becomes a bar hostess at the club he frequents! There is also a new student with a rich father who enrolls in the anarchic school after living in America. He is an expert in judo and karate and gives Tani a run for his money in the thrashing-department before Tani finally manages to bludgeon him to death at the film's climactic duel. Veteran cult performer Tanba has what amounts to little more than a cameo as a bemused police official. #1 of 3 * * *

CRUEL HIGH SCHOOL BAD BOY – TEACHER HUNT aka HIJO GAKUEN WARU – KYOSHI GARI 1973 83 min. **DIR.** Atsushi Mibori **SCR.** Isao Matsumoto/Hideaki Yamamoto **PHOTO COLOR 'SCOPE:** Yoshio Nakajima **MUSIC:** Toshiaki Tsushima **w/** Hayato Tani, Mari Atsumi, Makoto Sato, Isao Bito, Gajiro Sato, Rikiya "Ricky" Yasuoka, Michitaro Mizushima, Toru Abe Sulky bad boy Tani's continuing misanthropic misadventures.

Cruel High School Bad Boy -
Teacher Hunt (#2)

He goes up against rival student
gangs as well as a judo proficient
teacher (Makoto Sato), encounters
which culminate when one of the
main school officials challenges him
one-on-one to a nocturnal *kendo*
match on a back street. The official
is accidentally killed when he is
impaled on a protruding pipe. The
official's father, elderly *kendo* master
Abe, one of Tani's nemesises from
the first entry, commits suicide, and
Tani is captured by the cops when he
sets fire to the altar and Abe's body
at the wake. When Tani is sent to
juvenile prison, his former teacher/bar
girl sweetheart Atsumi (also returning from the first film) arranges his
escape. Previously abusive, once he
is out from behind bars, Tani actually
exhibits affection towards her – a bit
of a character development and his
only show of human warmth in the
first two films. He abandons her to

kidnap the school principal and, with
his fellow delinquent cronies, intimi-
dates the man into revealing in front
of the PTA (!) that he and supertin-
dent Mizushima had pressured Abe's
son into attacking him, thus causing
the man's accidental death. Teacher
Sato confronts Tani in a massive,
bloody brawl in the school halls with
Sato eventually mortally wounded.
Tani leaves the school to confront the
waiting police cars. Once again director Mibori moves things along at a
brutally brisk pace, always managing
to keep interest. But, unfortunately,
once again there is little depth or il-
lumination in any of the one dimensional characters.   #2 of 3   * * *

**CRUEL HIGH SCHOOL BAD
BOY – IRON BOUND CLASS-
MATE** aka HIJO GAKUEN WARU
– NERIKAN DOKISEI 1974
DIR. Atsushi Mibori **SCR.** Isao
Matsumoto/Hideaki Yamamoto
PHOTO COLOR 'SCOPE: Giichi Inada
w/ Hayato Tani, Koji Wada, Mihoko
Nakagawa, Noboru Ando, Rikiya
"Ricky" Yasuoka, Hiroshi Kubo,
Hideo Murota, Shoki Fukae, Tadao
Nakamaru, Sammi Suzuki
There is an incredible first five minutes to this last entry with a gang of
rowdy teen bikers forcing a car off a
winding mountain road. Of course,
inside the car are two prison guards
and on-his-way-to-reform-school
anti-hero Tani. The guards die, and
the gaping, open-mouthed cyclists
are astonished to see bloodied Tani
climbing from the wreckage, shoot
off his handcuffs and steal one of
their bikes. Tani immediately heads
back to the prison and, surprisingly
enough, turns himself in. He is victimized by also-jailed former school

pals (including stocky Yasuoka) and is soon fighting for his life against older inmate kingpin Wada. He finally manages to poke out one of Wada's eyes in a savage brawl, but this act doesn't seem to keep Tani from getting released on parole a year later. Tani runs into mute, teen girl thief Nakagawa, and discovers his also-paroled chums have been recruited by nationalist politician/scam artist Nakamaru. Soon after, Tani is involved with the politician, too, but not for long. He and pals have their eyes opened when they see Nakamaru deep in partnership with a monstrously brutal yakuza gang. Ando has a thankless, office-bound cameo as one of the head yakuza. And guess who else is working for the gang as a contract enforcer? Tani's one-eyed nemesis Wada. Before the film is over, Tani has an opportunity to blind the vengeful Wada in the other eye. Midway through the saga, Tani also gets to actually have a teen girl wet dream sequence where he and mute Nakagawa cavort idyllically on a sun-dappled beach. Near the story's end, Nakagawa is captured by the sexually abusive yakuza who are intent on rape. Against the backdrop of a fierce rainstorm, she jumps out a fourth story window to her death mere seconds before her protector Tani breaks down the door. Tani subsequently goes on a rampage, carrying the girl's broken body to Nakamaru's political rally. He challenges martial arts expert Nakamaru to a *kendo* match on the dais before the politician's shocked supporters then, after a brutal match, bludgeons the venal hypocrite to death. The cops arrive on the scene after it is all over. Although not a truly great film, it is nice to see Tani

go through some character development here after the two previous, entertaining, but shallower entries. #3 of 3   * * *

DANGEROUS G-MEN – BEAST OF THE UNDERWORLD aka AYAUSHI G-MEN – ANKOKU GAI NO YAJU 1960 DIR. Masamitsu Igayama SCR. Kenji Watanabe PHOTO 'SCOPE: Hiroshi Fukushima MUSIC: Hajime Kaburagi w/ Shinji Hata, Susumu Namishima, Akitake Kawano, Junji Watanabe, Mitsuru Hagiwara

DEAD DRIFTER aka HYORYU SHITAI 1959 DIR. Hideo Sekigawa SCR. Kozo Shiraishi MUSIC: Isao Tomita w/ Ken Takakura, Rentaro Mikuni, Takashi Kanda, Mitsue Komiya, Akitake Kono, Eitaro Ozawa, Yoshi Kato There is a chance this may be more of a mystery/suspense thriller than a yakuza film. Director Sekigawa made the acclaimed 1953 picture, HIROSHIMA. But he had to eat, so ended up as a second string director of B programmers. He still goes unacknowledged, even today, for turning out consistently good genre pieces, often with much more character development than similar fare then being released; the ones this writer has seen – his films are almost impossible to see.

DELINQUENT BOSS aka **FURYO BANCHO** aka **WOLVES OF THE CITY series**

DELINQUENT BOSS aka FURYO BANCHO aka WOLVES OF THE

CITY 1968 89 min. DIR. Yukio
Noda SCR. Isao Matsumoto/Hideaki
Yamamoto PHOTO COLOR 'SCOPE:
Yoshikazu (Giichi?) Yamazawa
MUSIC: Masao Yagi w/ Tatsuo
Umemiya, Hayato Tani, Tamami
Natsu, Koji Nanbara, Reiko Ohara,
Fumio Watanabe, Tetsuro Tanba,
Tamaki Sawa   Toei's most successful, longest-running *bosozoku*
film series. It lasted from 1968 till
1972 through sixteen films (seven-
teen if you count THE SCOUNDREL
VS. WOLVES OF THE CITY (1974)
(#10 in the SCOUNDREL series
and a revival of the DELINQUENT
BOSS characters who had already bit-
ten the dust two years previous). The
series has much more humor than the
far better and shorter-lived DETO-
NATION! (1975-'76), Toei's other
bosozoku series. As it stands – at
least judging by the five or so I have
viewed – the DELINQUENT BOSS
pictures are very uneven; uneven as
competently-made individual movies,
uneven of quality from-entry-to-
entry-as-a-series. A couple are quite
entertaining (see individual listings),
others are nearly worthless even as
"fun" timewasters. The aforementioned humor is, more often than
not, crude, stupid and occasionally
scatological. The action and/or violence, as well as the sixties fashions –
sometimes cool-looking black leather,
other times tasteless polyester plaids
and plastics – are on the level of stylized cartoons. There are descriptions
of the series in Japanese that say this
depraved wolfpack call themselves
Kapone Dan, or the Capone Gang.
Ninety percent of the time, their nemesises are dyed-in-the-wool yakuza.
In this initial outing, Umemiya and
pals are hired by the yakuza to find
the blackmailers who are screwing up
their construction business monopoly.
#1 of 16 films

Delinquent Boss (#2) (Japanese VHS art)

DELINQUENT BOSS – OCHO, THE SHE WOLF aka WOLVES OF THE CITY – THE HUSSY AND THE HOOLIGANS aka FURYO BANCHO – INOSHIKA OCHO

1969 90 min. DIR. Yukio Noda SCR.
Hideaki Yamamoto/Isao Matsumoto
w/ Tatsuo Umemiya, Shinichi
"Sonny" Chiba, Shigeru Katsumi,
Junko Mitazono
Ocho, the sexy con artist and swordswoman from the two ELDER
SISTER/OCHO films (set at the turn
of the 20th century in the Taisho era)
becomes a guest star character in this
second entry of the 1960s contemporary delinquent gang crime comedy

series. This is apparently where her character originated, as the two ELDER SISTER/OCHO (SEX AND FURY) pictures were not released until 1973. The character is played here by Junko Miyazono since Reiko Ike had not been discovered yet by Toei and would have been too young anyway. #2 of 16 films

WOLVES OF THE CITY – BLUES IN PRISON aka FURYO BANCHO – NERIKAN BURUUSU 1969 90 min. **Dir.** Yukio Noda **Scr.** Hideaki Yamamoto/Isao Matsumoto **Photo color 'scope:** Ichiro Hoshijima **Music:** Masao Yagi w/ Tatsuo Umemiya, Hayato Tani, Iwao (Izuo?) Dan, Keiko Natsu, Ichiro Chakawa, Tamami Natsu, Bunta Sugawara, Chota Tamagawa, Asao Uchida, Fumio Watanabe   Our lovable delinquents fight hordes of gangsters over rights to a casino.

DELINQUENT BOSS – DIS-PATCHING THE WOLF aka FURYO BANCHO – OKURI OKA-MI aka WOLVES OF THE CITY – WOLF ESCORT 1969 90 min. **Dir.** Makoto Naito **Scr.** Isao Matsumoto/Hideaki Yamamoto **Photo color 'scope:** Ichiro Hoshijima **Music:** Masao Yagi w/ Tatsuo Umemiya, Hayato Tani, Bunta Sugawara, Miyoko Akaza, Kiyoko Tange, Toru Abe, Masao Komatsu, Shingo Yamashiro, Yoichi Numata #4 of 16 films

DELINQUENT BOSS – RAT THIEF'S STRATEGY aka FURYO BANCHO – DOBU NE-ZUMI SAKUSEN aka WOLVES OF THE CITY – OPERATION RAT 1969 88 min. **Dir.** Yukio Noda **Scr.**

Hideaki Yamamoto/ Isao Matsumoto w/ Tatsuo Umemiya   #5 of 16 films

WOLVES OF THE CITY – CHECKMATE aka FURYO BANCHO – OTE HISHA 1970 87 min. **Dir.** Makoto Naito **Scr.** Isao Matsumoto/Hideaki Yamamoto **Photo color 'scope:** Ichiro Hoshijima **Music:** Masao Yagi w/ Tatsuo Umemiya, Hayato Tani, Bunta Sugawara, Toru Abe, Noriko Sakakibara, Fumio Watanabe   Delinquent *bosozoku* Umemiya and cohorts are arrested for fraud. After a prison stay, they renew their con man exploits as efficiency experts and run into former partner, yakuza Sugawara who is now head of a construction company. Abe is an unscrupulous businessman who contracts with Sugawara. Umemiya and comrades help Sugawara oust reluctant tenants from a site they need to tear down and build on, but Umemiya falls for defiant girl Sakakibara who refuses to close down her print shop. He becomes temporarily at odds with Sugawara. Things reach a head when vicious yakuza boss Watanabe black-mails Abe into getting the building contract. Umemiya and his pals help Sakakibara by creating porno prints which they sell to raise funds to fight off Watanabe. Things get nasty when Watanabe destroys Sugawara's offices and the print shop, killing innocent people. Discovering that Abe, Watanabe and his mob are play-ing golf in the hinterlands, Umemiya, Sugawara and the rest attack them at the base of Mount Fuji for the cus-tomary over-the-top, tongue-in-cheek violent free-for-all. Only Umemiya and right hand sidekick Tani survive. #6 of 16 films   * *

**WOLVES OF THE CITY –
MONEY HUNTERS** aka FURYO
BANCHO – IKKAKU SEN KIN
1970 88 min. **DIR.** Yukio Noda **SCR.**
Hideaki Yamamoto/ Isao Matsumoto
PHOTO COLOR 'SCOPE: Masahiko
Iimura **MUSIC:** Masao Yagi
w/ Tatsuo Umemiya, Hayato Tani,
Shingo Yamashiro, Bunta Sugawara,
Yasushi Suzuki, Reiko Oshida, Akiko
Wada, Machiko Yashiro, Haruo
Tanaka #7 of 16 films

**WOLVES OF THE CITY – TAKE
YOUR CHANCE** aka FURYO
BANCHO – DETA TO KO SHOBU
1970 87 min. **DIR.** Makoto Naito
SCR. Hideaki Yamamoto/Isao
Matsumoto **PHOTO COLOR 'SCOPE:**
Yoshio Nakajima **MUSIC:** Masao
Yagi w/ Tatsuo Umemiya, Hayato
Tani, Shingo Yamashiro, Kyosuke
Machida, Reiko Oshida, Yasushi
Suzuki, Tsunehiko Watase, Toru Abe
#8 of 16 films

**WOLVES OF THE CITY -
HOOLIGANS ON BUGGIES** aka
FURYO BANCHO - BOSO BAGI
ICHI DAN 1970 87 min. **DIR.**
Makoto Naito **SCR.** Isao Matsumoto/
Hideaki Yamamoto **PHOTO COLOR
'SCOPE:** Yoshikazu (Giichi)
Yamazawa **MUSIC:** Tomikazu
Kawabe w/ Tatsuo Umemiya,
Hayato Tani, Yasushi Suzuki, Shingo
Yamashiro, Bunta Sugawara, Akemi
Negishi, Hideo Sunazuka, Kichijiro
Ueda, Bin Amatsu #9 of 16 films

**WOLVES OF THE CITY - THE
SWINDLERS** aka FURYO BAN-
CHO - KUCHI KARA DEMAKASE
1970 87 min. **DIR.** Yukio Noda **SCR.**
Hideaki Yamamoto/ Isao Matsumoto
PHOTO COLOR 'SCOPE: Kiichi Inada

MUSIC: Masao Yagi w/ Tatsuo
Umemiya, Bunta Sugawara, Shingo
Yamashiro, Tsunehiko Watase, Reiko
Oshida, Rikiya Yasuoka, Shinichi
Ruukii, Harumi Sone, Hiroshi Date,
Keijiro Morokado The guys begin
on a raft in the ocean flying their
familiar skull 'n' crossbones colors,
come to an island solely inhabited by
women, and that is only the first ten
minutes. Silly, but intermittently entertaining. #10 of 16 films * * 1/2

**FURYO BANCHO – YARAZU
BUTTA KURI** 1971 89 min.
DIR. Yukio Noda **SCR.** Hideaki
Yamamoto/Isao Matsumoto **PHOTO
COLOR 'SCOPE:** Kiichi Inada **Music:**
Masao Yagi w/ Tatsuo Umemiya,
Tsunehiko Watase, Shingo
Yamashiro, Bunta Sugawara
#11 of 16 films * *

Delinquent Boss (# 12)

**FURYO BANCHO – TE HAACHO
KUCHI HAACHO** 1971 87 min.
DIR. Makoto Naito **SCR.** Isao

Matsumoto /Hideaki Yamamoto
PHOTO COLOR 'SCOPE: Yoshikazu
(Giichi?) Yamazawa MUSIC:
Hiroki Tamaki w/ Tatsuo Umemiya,
Kyosuke Machida, Yasushi Suzuki,
Reiko Ohara, Hideo Murota, Shingo
Yamashiro, Peter
Pirate-biker apocalypse! The funny
blackmail/extortion plot of a lower
yakuza boss – his passion pit bed is a
funky miniature roman galleon/gon-
dola floating in an oversize Japanese
bath – backfires, leading the guys
into open war with the yakuza gang
(including mortars, grenades, etc..,).
Featuring one of the strangest female-
impersonators-by-way-of-lip-synch-
ing-popstars (Peter) you will ever see.
#12 of 16 films * * 1/2

Masao Yagi   w/ Tatsuo Umemiya,
Shingo Yamashiro, Yasushi Suzuki,
Rikiya (Ricky) Yasuoka, Takeo Chii,
Tsunehiko Watase, Junko Natsu,
Kamatari Fujiwara #13 of 16 films

**DELINQUENT BOSS – MOV-
ING AGAINST THE STRAY DOG**
aka FURYO BANCHO – NORA
INU KIDO TAI 1972 DIR. Yukio
Noda SCR. Isao Matsumoto/ Hideaki
Yamamoto PHOTO COLOR 'SCOPE:
Kiichi Inada MUSIC: Masao Yagi
w/ Tatsuo Umemiya, Tatsuya Fuji,
Ryunosuke Minegishi, Toru Okazaki,
Rikiya (Ricky) Yasuoka, Eiko
Yatsunami, Reiko Ike, Toru Abe,
Ryohei Uchida, Shoki Fukae #14
of 16 films

Delinquent Boss (# 13)

Delinquent Boss (# 14)

**DELINQUENT BOSS - FIRST TO
FIGHT** aka FURYO BANCHO -
TOTSU GEKI ICHI BAN   1971
DIR. Yukio Noda SCR. Hideaki
Yamamoto/Isao Matsumoto PHOTO
COLOR 'SCOPE: Kiichi Inada MUSIC:

**FURYO BANCHO - ICHI MODA-
JIN** 1972 88 min. DIR. Yukio
Noda SCR. Hideaki Yamamoto/Isao
Matsumoto PHOTO COLOR 'SCOPE:
Yoshikazu (Giichi?) Yamazawa
MUSIC: Masao Yagi   w/ Tatsuo

Umemiya, Shingo Yamashiro, Rikiya (Ricky) Yasuoka, Tatsuya Fuji, Asao Uchida, Annu Mari #15 of 16 films

DELINQUENT BOSS – PIERCED TO THE BONE AND SUCKED DRY aka FURYO BANCHO – HONEMADE SHABURA 1972 DIR. Yukio Noda SCR. Hideaki Yamamoto/Isao Matsumoto w/ Tatsuo Umemiya, Shingo Yamashiro The pirate-biker guys ditch a pursuing yakuza gang in a porno theater. Eventually, with the help of an interracial trio of trashy chicks – whose tits keep falling out of their dresses – they steal the gang's already twice-stolen diamonds. Regrettably, they hide out in a tourist resort. and it is downhill with bad situation comedy from there. Last of the series and, of the ones I have seen, certainly the worst. #16 and final in series * 1/2

DELINQUENT GIRL BOSS aka **ZUBEKO BANCHO** aka **TOKYO BAD GIRLS** series

DELINQUENT GIRL BOSS – BLOSSOMING NIGHT DREAMS aka ZUBEKO BANCHO – YUME WA YORU HIRAKU aka TOKYO BAD GIRLS 1970 87 min. DIR. Kazuhiko Yamaguchi SCR. Norio Miyashita/Kazuhiko Yamaguchi PHOTO COLOR 'SCOPE: Hanjiro Nakazawa MUSIC: Toshiaki Tsushima w/ Junko Miyazono, Reiko Oshida, Tatsuo Umemiya, Nobuo Kaneko, Masumi Tachibana, Yukie Kagawa, Mieko Tsudoi, Hayato Tani, Junko Natsu One of Toei's earliest forays into girl gang territory. It is unfortunate it is so silly

because the cast and beautiful color cinematography/production design are reminiscent of Nikkatsu Studios – late sixties eye candy – and are wonderful. The humor is so poorly done, obvious and all pervasive – this is really an action comedy with dramatic moments (such as Umemiya's death while fighting for Miyazono) – it makes Toei's later GIRL BOSS (SUKEBAN) series look like Chekhov by comparison. The girls' reform school gang alumni are led by bar hostess/owner Miyazono, her yakuza lover Umemiya and the wild, unusually charismatic Oshida in an all-out war against Shinjuku's head drug dealer Kaneko. #1 of 4 films * *

DELINQUENT GIRL BOSS – TOKYO DRIFTERS aka ZUBEKO BANCHO – TOKYO NAGAREMONO aka GIRL VAGRANTS OF TOKYO 1970 86 min. DIR. Kazuhiko Yamaguchi SCR. Norio Miyashita/Kazuhiko Yamaguchi PHOTO COLOR 'SCOPE: Yoshio Nakajima MUSIC: Toshiaki Tsushima w/ Reiko Oshida, Tsunehiko Watase, Masumi Tachibana, Yukie Kagawa, Koji Nanbara, Mieko Tsudoi, Kichijiro Ueda, Tonbei Hidari, Chikako Miyagi Even more humor this time around, if that is possible. The difference is this time it works with a spontaneity and lusty good spirit that generally transcends mere shtick. Unfortunately, the middle third bogs down with the incessant banter amongst *tekiya* at a nightime festival, going from funny to tiresome. Also the abrupt shift to tragedy in the last third – in what is basically a teen delinquent action comedy – strikes an incredibly jarring note, with the lovable female *oyabun* who has taken in Oshida and her mates being murdered by the weak-willed beau of one of the girls. He in turn is offed just as he is about to leave town with his gal. Watase is a lone wolf *tekiya* and estranged son of the murdered lady boss who sparks romance with Oshida. He joins the girls when they go on their vengeance binge against slimy mob boss Nanbara.

Delinquent Girl Boss (#2)

Once more there is some imaginative production design ala Nikkatsu materialized out of meager resources in what is, even for the early seventies, an extremely low-budget Toei film. Oshida is again incredibly charsimatic with a streetwise gleam in her eye, a sexy voluptuousness and an almost klutzy charm. Likewise, Watase is fine as are all the girls. Nanbara is stupendous as always, a sideburned, wolfish gangster who is forever obsessively polishing his putting iron everytime he is on-

screen. He even uses it as a weapon in the closing free-for-all. In what is a very entertaining climax, director Yamaguchi dresses the girls up in red leather cowboy hats and dusters and has them ceremonially pop sticks of gum in their mouths to chew while solemnly walking the blocks to Nanbara's HQ. Once there, they discard their coats and hats to reveal bellbottoms and paisley tops, each clutching a sword. Probably the most incongruously preposterous note is struck at the denouement when the cops arrive and cart away only Watase (!) even though all the girls have been equally guilty of decimating the gangsters. #2 of 4 films   * * *

DELINQUENT GIRL BOSS – BALLAD OF YOKOHAMA HOODS aka ZUBEKO BAN-CHO – HAMAGURE KAZOE UTA 1971 **Dir.** Kazuhiko Yamaguchi **Scr.** Norio Miyashita/ Kazuhiko Yamaguchi **Photo color 'scope:** Masahiko Iimura **Music:** Toshiaki Tsushima   w/ Reiko Oshida, Yukie Kagawa, Asao Koike, Yoko Mihara, Nijiko Kiyokawa, Hayato Tani, Meicho Soganoya, Harumi Sone, Mieko Tsudoi, Toru Yuri   Oshida and Tsudoi are released from reform school at the beginning of the story and are soon camping out at the western style saloon of surrogate parents Soganoya and Kiyokawa. Menacing the neighborhood and local rock nightclub is a girl biker gang who dress in red leather. Kagawa, Oshida's former nemesis from the reformatory, is the biker boss and quite fetching in a black leather outfit and cowboy hat. Kagawa's gang run interference for the down-and-dirty yakuza mob led by Koike and Sone.

Delinquent Girl Boss (# 3)

Eventually Kagawa comes around to Oshida's antipathy towards Koike et. al. when Koike tries to turn in a deserting black American GI for the reward, then resorts to shanghaiing girls into prostitution. It is too bad that the humor in this third film once again slips into annoying terrain with very little that isn't shtick or poorly executed slapstick. Silly Yuri has one or two amusing moments as a *tekiya* helping his buddy and Yoko Mihara sell sex toys. However, there are several worthwhile dramatic sequences that make one wish the whole film had been as good: Oshida returning with paternal Soganoya from visiting the grave of her real father only to have him shot-to-death by a hit man targeting her; mortally wounded Kagawa, having escaped the gangsters, challenging Oshida to a final knifefight but succumbing to her injuries and then dying in Oshida's arms as both girl gangs gather round, reconciled; wounded Oshida carted away by the sympathetic police inspector at the end and being chivalrously offered his handkerchief to wipe the blood from her face. These are small bits, but they are done well. But the climactic battle where Oshida dons Kagawa's leathers and leads all the girls on a motorbike assault on the gangsters at the seaside is not very well-staged and seems to have been shot in a hurried, haphazard manner. All the more frustrating when the closing violent moments – Oshida chasing Koike and Sone down the pier with a sword between her teeth then facing their bullets as she cuts them down – being so monumentally great, so iconographically perfect, I am almost tempted to rate this up another notch. #3 of 4 films   * * *

DELINQUENT GIRL BOSS – WORTHLESS TO CONFESS aka ZUBEKO BANCHO – ZANGE NO NEUCHI MONAI aka NO ESCAPE FROM REMORSE 1971 **DIR.** Kazuhiko Yamaguchi **SCR.** Norio Miyashita/Kazuhiko Yamaguchi **PHOTO COLOR 'SCOPE:** Hanjiro Nakazawa **MUSIC:** Toshiaki Tsushima w/ Reiko Oshida, Yumiko Katayama, Tsunehiko Watase, Junzaburo Ban, Yukie Kagawa, Ichiro Nakatani, Nobuo Kaneko, Masumi Tachibana, Mirei Kitahara, Mieko Tsudoi
It was a pleasant surprise to find this last entry to be the best in the series. Oshida does time in a reformatory before and during the credits. There is a very funny initial scene with all the inmates rioting when the uptight prison officials shut down the movie they are screening, one of the ABASHIRI PRISON series, because it is too violent. A year later, Oshida's out of stir, drifting, and visits the widower mechanic father (Ban) of angry, ungrateful spitfire Katayama. Ban had tried to establish contact with his out-of-control daughter in the reform school, but she had refused his overtures. Sweet-natured Oshida, herself longing for a decent parental figure, stays on at Ban's garage, hired as an apprentice grease monkey. Tubercular, ex-gambler Nakatani, and devoted, just-miscarried Kagawa are genuinely touching as an impoverished, loving couple pushed to the edge to make ends meet. Watase is Nakatani's boisterous comrade who develops a crush on Oshida. Of course, there is a neighborhood yakuza mob making life miserable, shaking down Ban, Nakatani and the

nightclub where Oshida, Kagawa, Tsudoi and Tachibana work as go-go dancers. Oshida visits slimy boss Kaneko in his lair to plead for leniency on Ban but is humiliated when the gang forces her to strip. Outraged, eavesdropping Katayama intervenes but is shouted down by her spineless, mod hoodlum beau. The villains tie up the girls and phone Ban demanding ransom. But Ban, an ex-yakuza himself, refuses to kowtow this time, instead terrorizing Kaneko and his minions with a razor and liberating the girls. Formerly embittered Katayama has a change of heart and accepts the good will of her friend Oshida and dad Ban. Nevertheless, the happy reunion is shortlived. Kaneko and men offer Nakatani an outrageous amount of money to kill Ban. Principled but in-love Nakatani flashes back to walking happily in a field of yellow wildflowers with pregnant wife Kagawa and accepts for her sake. He attempts to stab the drunken Ban who is making his way home through a tunnel but is too weak from his illness to complete the task. The gangsters are standing by and run down both Ban and Nakatani to tie up the loose ends. Oshida, Katayama, Kagawa et. al erupt in righteous anger and are asskicking comrades once more. Back at the garage, they break out their crimson dusters and swords and bid a poetic, elegiac farewell to Ban's corpse. The carnage that subsequently takes place at Kaneko's nightclub is really the only major action setpiece in the film, but the rest of the tale has been so skillfully wrought, so poignantly done it doesn't matter. This climactic swordfighting binge is without question the best in the series and only suffers from the girls

obviously killing four or five times as many hoodlums as we know to be in Kaneko's brood. But, considering the over-the-top tall tale vibe dominating throughout, such quibbling is beside the point.

Delinquent Girl Boss (# 4)

Watase joins the fray towards the end, at which point the deathdealing reaches an orgiastic pop art crescendo, gangster Kaneko being gorily run through by Oshida and filmed from beneath a glass floor ala director Seijun Suzuki! The hoods vanquished and the cop sirens wailing in the distance, we realize the coughing, widowed Kagawa has the TB now, too. Her loyal friends hide her. She weeps with futility as she sees Watase, Oshida and the girls being hauled off to jail. Judging from the three previous films, you would not have guessed WORTHLESS TO CONFESS would turn out to be such a *tour de force*. If not for a bit too much silly humor in the first third of the picture I would say this was excellent. #4 and final in series   * * * 1/2

DELINQUENT STREET aka FURYO GAI 1972 **DIR.** Yukio Noda **SCR.** Isao Matsumoto/ Hideaki Yamamoto **PHOTO COLOR** 'SCOPE: Yoshikazu Ozawa w/ Hiroki Matsukata, Bunta Sugawara, Shingo Yamashiro, Hayato Tani, Mari Tsutsui, Zeko Nakamura, Asao Koike, Masahiko Tanimura, Bin Amatsu, Michitaro Mizushima   It is surprising, considering the cast and the time period in which this movie was released, that this movie seeems impossible to track down.

DETECTIVE MORGAN AND A MAN OF MYSTERY aka MOGAN KEIBU TO NAZO NO OTOKO 1961 80 min. **DIR.** Hideo Sekigawa **SCR.** Hajime Takaiwa **PHOTO COLOR** 'SCOPE: Shizuka Fuji w/ Koji Tsuruta, John Bromfield, Naoko Kubo, James Griffith, Shoji Nakayama   A bizarre hybrid with

Tsuruta as an undercover cop and Bromfield as an American sheriff tracking a drug-smuggling mob. The action shifts from Arizona to Hong Kong to Tokyo, Bromfield's casting undoubtedly the result of his then current, syndicated-American TV show, SHERIFF OF COCHISE.

Delinquent Street

DETONATION! aka
BAKUHATSU! series

DETONATION! VIOLENT TRIBE
aka BAKUHATSU! BOSO ZOKU
1975 86 min. DIR. Teruo Ishii SCR.
Isao Matsumoto/Teruo Ishii PHOTO
COLOR 'SCOPE: Yoshikazu (Giichi)
Yamazawa MUSIC: Keitaro Miho
w/ Shinichi "Sonny" Chiba, Koichi
Iwaki, Junko Matsuhei, Susumu
Toyooka, Akihiko Yokoo, Hiroshi
Nawa

Detonation! - Violent Tribe (#1)

The first entry in a series of *bosozoku*
or "hot rod gang" movies similar to
but a bit more serious, a little less
silly than the DELINQUENT BOSS
series, also from Toei. *Bosozoku* literally translates "violent tribe" which
is considerably more evocative and
accurate. The *bosozoku* gangs are
much younger than yakuza and seem
to often serve as apprenticeships
for the yakuza rackets. Basically,
they are loosely-organized juvenile
delinquents, with the amount and balance of organization depending upon
the nature of each individual gang.
By their very nature, the *bosozoku*
are more mercurial, impulsive and
anarchic than their elder yakuza
cousins. Despite the occasional "hot
rod gang" appelation, they seem to
be, nine-times-out-of-ten, equipped
with motorcycles or scooters (!) as
opposed to four-wheel vehicles. However, anything fast and dangerous
will do. Sometimes the gang majority
will be mounted on motorcycles with
a souped-up, customized auto in the
center as a kind of command vehicle.
This particular series features Koichi
Iwaki as a sullen, surly, magnetically-
attractive-to-females stud who ends
up pitted against delinquents even
more cruel and savage than himself
(he is not the same character in each
film – he gets killed at the end of at
least two of them). Sonny Chiba stars
only in this initial piece, portraying a
wiser, more seasoned biker who owns
his own repair shop. Considering
Chiba and director Ishii were working
together here, this should have been
better. Many of the action sequences,
especially towards the end, are very
poorly staged. I neglected to ask
Ishii about this film when I interviewed him, so I don't know if there
were some severe production woes
involved. Considering his otherwise
consummate professionalism, I
couldn't imagine it was anything else.
This string of films is violent, funny
and has some frequently stupendous
rock music numbers. Preferable,
hands-down, to the DELINQUENT
GANG BOSS series. #1 of 3 films
* *

DETONATION! VIOLENT GAMES aka BAKUHATSU! BOSO YUGI 1976 86 min. **DIR.** Teruo Ishii **SCR.** Teruo Ishii/Shinichi Hashimoto **PHOTO COLOR 'SCOPE:** Tetsuya Dezaki **MUSIC:** Hajime Kaburagi **w/** Koichi Iwaki, Yutaka Nakajima, Yumi Takigawa, Masami Kuwajima, Masando Hoshi, Akira Oda, Susumu Toyooka   Garage mechanic Iwaki and seamstress girl-friend Nakajima lead a cycle-riding pack of leatherclad, blue collar kids.

Kuwajima arrives late, with Takigawa and Iwaki's girl Nakajima. He tries to stop the gangfight, but ends up in a knife duel with Iwaki where both mortally wound each other. They die in their respective girls' arms, Kuwa-jima with Takigawa (who is clad in a white lace wedding dress!) and Iwaki with Nakajima. Although uneven with lazily put-together action setpieces nearly as shoddy as the first entry, this is still quite entertaining. There are several long stretches of finger-

Detonation! - Violent Games (#2)

They are constantly running afoul of a rival gang of rich, spoiled brats. Famous Japanese race car driver Kuwajima portrays a racing champion loner prone to hanging out with the smarmy upscale kids. However, he doesn't go in for their sadistic pranks and decadent orgies. A romance gradually blooms between Kuwajima and Iwaki's kid sister, seamstress Takigawa. The violence escalates when Takigawa's former beau Hoshi begins spraypainting the rich kids' classic cars with graffiti. Things end tragically when Iwaki leads a seashore attack on their hedonistic enemies after Hoshi is killed.

snapping/WEST SIDE STORY-style (a la The Sharks) rock'n' roll cho-reography that are extremely well done, exhilaratingly gratuitous and a reminder to the viewer not to take what they are seeing on the screen too seriously.   #2 of 3 films   * * *

SEASON OF VIOLENCE aka BOSO NO KISETSU 1976 86 min. **DIR./SCR.** Teruo Ishii **PHOTO COLOR 'SCOPE:** Tetsuya Dezaki **MUSIC:** Hajime Kaburagi **w/** Koichi Iwaki, Yutaka Nakajima, Yayoi Watanabe, Kentaro Shimizu, Taro Shukaki Iwaki displays his usual sulky bad boy charsima as a lower class teenag-er working as helmsman on yachts for various rich, decadent young people. He develops a strange love/hate relationship with spoilt rich bitch Nakajima. Her sensitive young housemaid Watanabe also has a soft spot for Iwaki, and he ends up forcing himself on her, too. Iwaki and his motorcycle riding comrades soon run afoul of gay sadist Shimizu who is *de facto* leader of the sex-crazed, upper middle class teens in the area. Gradually, hostilities escalate until Nakajima's romance with Iwaki inspires actual attempts on his life.

Nakajima and Watanabe arrive too late. Nakajima takes the gold medallion Iwaki had left with her, wraps it in some wildflowers and throws it into the water after him. This entry is also reminiscent of the controversial *taiyozoku* (sun tribe) films CRAZED FRUIT, SEASONS IN THE SUN, THE WARPED ONES, EVERYTHING GOES WRONG and AGE OF NUDITY from 1950s Nikkatsu. #3 of series　* * *

Detonation! - 750cc Tribe (#4)

Detonation! - Season of Violence (#3)

There is a chaotic ending where Shimizu, accompanied by his hoodlum lover and another rich girl whom Iwaki raped, chase him relentlessly up a winding road. Finally Iwaki aims his cycle back down the road at them, breaking their windshield with the flying bike. The souped-up car bursts into flames as Iwaki shoots through the air and over the cliff to his death in the icy sea. Heartthrobs

DETONATION! 750cc TRIBE aka BAKUHATSU! NANAHAN ZOKU 1976 85 min. **DIR.** Yu Kohira **SCR.** Ryunosuke Kono **PHOTO COLOR 'SCOPE:** Tetsuya Dezaki **MUSIC:** Masao Yagi　w/ Koichi Iwaki, Takako Kitagawa, Janet Hatta, Kentaro Shimizu
For those of you not mechanically-inclined, 750cc refers to the motor-size/capacity of their cycles. Once again, Iwaki is a rebellious garage mechanic and *de facto* leader of a blue collar

bosozoku gang. He runs afoul of a bunch of richer youths led by the gangsterish son of a very wealthy prominent businessman. Along the way, Hatta, a prosperous clothing business manager and friend of the villain, falls for Iwaki. The mayhem escalates until Iwaki's sister Kitagawa is gang-raped and his best friend severely beaten. Iwaki, already jailed once for having threatened his young nemesis's father, now kidnaps the boy and demands ransom from the dad. The cops are waiting, but Iwaki escapes with the loot on his cycle, leading the law on a frenzied chase that takes up the last third of the film. Several *bosozoku* gangs see the pursuit on TV and join the fracas, causing distraction, battling with the cops, even supplying Iwaki with food and drink as he drives to demonstrate their solidarity. Hatta sees the chase on TV and makes her way to a checkpoint, only to die crashing into the police blockade. The cops are fighting a losing battle and enlist two of their best, craziest drivers to go after Iwaki. This serves to furnish some of the most gonzo footage of the manhunt with the two cop cars finally exploding in flames. It appears as if Iwaki has made it as he rides along a deserted shoreline, tossing the loot into the sea and crying "Fools!" to assert his independence. But there is a faceless sniper – hired by the cops or boy's father, we never know – zeroing in on Iwaki. Several shots ring out, and the dead Iwaki ends up being tossed by the waves much like Michael Caine at the close of the original GET CARTER. This also has some plot similarities to INSANE SEX TRIBE, another Toei *bosozoku* film. #4 and final in series   *   * 1/2

DOBERMAN DETECTIVE aka DOOBERMAN DEKA 1977 **DIR.** Kinji Fukasaku **SCR.** Koji Takada **PHOTO COLOR 'SCOPE:** Toru Nakajima **MUSIC:** Kenjiro Hirose w/ Shinichi "Sonny" Chiba, Hiroki Matsukata, Janet Hatta, Koichi Iwaki, Eiko Matsuda, Hideo Murota, Takuzo Kawatani   Action with Chiba an aggressive detective from Okinawa in Tokyo to battle the yakuza over the fate of a female pop singer.

DRAGON'S LIFE aka RYU KO ICHIDAI 1964 **DIR.** Tsuneo Kobayashi **SCR.** Akira Murao **PHOTO COLOR 'SCOPE:** Shichiro Hayashi **MUSIC:** Chuji Kinoshita w/ Koji Tsuruta, Shigeru Amachi, Yoshiko Sakuma, Junko Fuji, Shinichi "Sonny" Chiba   Another obscure, early entry in the just-beginning *ninkyo* cycle.

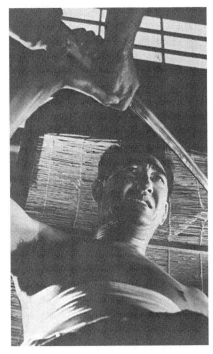

Dragon's Life

DRIFTER'S HONOR AND HUMANITY aka NAGAREMONO JINGI 1965 **DIR.** Hideo Sekigawa

Drifter's Honor and Humanity

SCR. Akira Murao /Hideaki Yamamoto/Isao Matsumoto
PHOTO B&W 'SCOPE: Masahiko

Iimura **MUSIC:** Masao Yagi
w/ Tatsuo Umemiya, Keiji Takagi, Minoru Oki, Jiro Okazaki, Hiroko Sakuramachi, Kyosuke Machida, Akiko Koyama   Umemiya is a police detective concerned about the declining revenues of his future wife's family's diamond business. When he investigates, he unearthes the schemes of a smuggling gang headed by his future brother-in-law Takagi.

THE DUPE aka KAMO 1965 **DIR.** Hideo Sekigawa **SCR.** Masashige Narusawa **PHOTO 'SCOPE:** Hanjiro Nakazawa **MUSIC:** Kazumi Naito w/ Tatsuo Umemiya, Mako Midori, Reiko Ohara, Chisako Hara, Hiroko Kuno, Mako Sanjo

EIGHTEEN YEAR JAIL TERM aka CHOEKI JUNHACHI NEN series

Eighteen Year Jail Term

EIGHTEEN YEAR JAIL TERM
aka CHOEKI JUNHACHI NEN
1967 91 min. **Dir.** Tai Kato **SCR.**
Kazuo Kasahara/Shin Morita **PHOTO**
COLOR 'SCOPE: Shin Furuya **MUSIC:**
Hajime Kaburagi w/ Noboru Ando,
Asao Koike, Hiroko Sakuramachi,
Tomisaburo Wakayama, Shinobu
Chihara, Masaomi Kondo   Ando
and Koike are just returning soldiers
in post-WW2 Japan who, because of
the poverty, food shortages, disillu-
sionment-turned-to-nihilism, form
the routine criminal enterprises. They
come in conflict with the already
established yakuza black marketeers
and the blood starts spilling. Although
marked by Kato's tasteful, kinetically
violent direction, it is not one of his
best. Still, Ando, a former yakuza
himself, and Koike are their usual excellent selves, and writer Kasahara's
uncompromising intelligence shines
through. Ando's first film for Toei
after doing a string of yakuza films at
Shochiku Studios.   #1 of 2 films
* * *

DISCHARGE FROM PRISON
AFTER EIGHTEEN YEAR TERM
aka CHOEKI JUNHACHI NEN –
KARI SHUTSUGOKU
aka PAROLE 1967 89 min.
DIR. Yasuo Furuhata **SCR.** Yoshihiro
Ishimatsu/Yasuo Furuhata **PHOTO**
COLOR 'SCOPE: Hanjiro Nakazawa
MUSIC: Takeo Watanabe w/ Noboru
Ando, Tomisaburo Wakayama, Kayo
Matsuo, Juzo Itami, Junzaburo Ban
Ando gets out of jail and, with his
deaf/mute pal Itami and the boister-
ous Wakayama, plans a nefarious
caper involving the U.S. Occupation
Forces. Note future director Juzo
Itami's appearance in the cast.
#2 of 2 films   * * 1/2

ELDER SISTER aka OCHO aka
SEX AND FURY series

Elder Sister (#1) aka *Sex and Fury*

STORY OF A DEPRAVED ELDER
SISTER – OCHO, A DEER
AMONGST WILD BOARS
aka **SEX AND FURY** aka FURYO
ANEGO DEN – CHO NO ROKU
OCHO 1973 88 min. **DIR.**
Norifumi Suzuki **SCR.** Masahiro
Kakefuda/Norifumi Suzuki **PHOTO**
COLOR 'SCOPE: Motoya Washio
MUSIC: Ichiro Araki w/ Reiko Ike,
Seizaburo Kawazu, Christina
Lindberg, Hiroshi Nawa, Akemi
Negishi, Yoko Hori, Chiomi Oka,
Masataka Naruse, Yoko Mihara,
Tatsuo Endo   Apparently Toei's
third (and last?) attempt to strike
paydirt ala the RED PEONY
GAMBLER style of in-period (1900
-1930s) female yakuza films, albeit
this time with heavy doses of sex
and S&M. The two efforts preced-
ing ELDER SISTER were SHOWA

WOMAN GAMBLER (1972)
with Kyoko Enami and THE RED
SILK GAMBLER (1972) with Eiko
Nakamura. The pink film was coming
into its own as a genre in Japan, and
it was perfectly natural, if not a bit
cynical, to insert the softcore S&M/
sex ingredients into the period-action
recipe. Perhaps it was fortuitous that
yakuza superstar Junko Fuji did retire
in 1972, because it is impossible to
imagine her indulging in the antics
of gratuitous nudity that proved
to be just around the corner. The
groundbreaking, pioneering aspect
of Junko Fuji as an invincible female
protagonist undoubtedly played a part
in nudging the Toei brass into taking
a chance with even more brutal-
heroine-scenarios. Toei was already
undergoing considerable success with
their contemporary GIRL BOSS series, also starring Reiko Ike. Another
series that was certainly spawned by
Fuji's action-heroine success was the
LEGENDS OF THE POISONOUS
SEDUCTRESS aka QUICK DRAW
OKATSU trilogy (see section on
period-yakuza films). The first of this
ELDER SISTER/OCHO duo has got
to be one of the loopiest, most gonzo,
most entertaining, most violent
Japanese sexploitation pictures ever
made. Orphaned as a child when her
gambler undercover cop father is
murdered by three unknown assailants, Ike is Ocho, a pickpocket and
card sharp in 1905 Tokyo. She
encounters and helps wounded
anarchist Naruse, who is in love with
foreign spy Lindberg. Lindberg is
being coerced by her sexually abusive
superior – who is bent on engineering another opium war, this time with
Japan – to steal a set of secret documents from political bigwig Kawazu.

Kawazu is, coincidentally, the man
Naruse is bent on assassinating and,
lo and behold (!) one of Ike's father's
killers. Also thrown into the mix is
Simon Legree-ish satyr and evil gang
boss Nawa. Nawa happens to be the
lover of Kawazu's wife (Mihara), as
well as one more of the trio who murdered Ike's father. Ike dispatches him
when he unknowingly licks up the
poisoned perfume she has spread all
over her naked body! Ike then helps
Naruse in his assassination attempt
but is captured in the process and
whipped by Lindberg (who is undercover pretending to do Kawazu's bidding) in Kawazu's bizarre cellar with
Christ-crucified as an S&M motif!
Later, Mihara tries to rescue Ike, but
is stopped by Kawazu who reveals
that Mihara is not only Ike's mother,
she is also the third in the trio of her
father's killers! He then strangles
Mihara. Meanwhile, Lindberg and
Naruse rendezvous but are ambushed
by her superior. A gunfight/sword-
fight ensues leaving everyone dead
or dying. Lindberg and Naruse expire
in each other's arms. In the riproaring conclusion, Ike escapes into the
main part of Kawazu's HQ with her
sword, wiping out all of his minions and finally Kawazu. She is so
slashed and shot up by this time it's
a wonder she survives to the second
film. As usual with Suzuki there are
some incredible setpieces: Ike's early
massacre of a betraying yakuza gang
performed with her completely in the
nude (they had ambushed her in her
bath); the meeting of Kawazu, Nawa
and cohorts in a magic lantern show
presented as psychedelic happening;
Ike's stumbling away from the final
slaughter in a night of (real) falling
snow that slowly becomes a fluttering

Story of a Wild Elder Sister - Widespread Lynch Law aka Female Yakuza Tale (#2)

rain of *hana fuda* cards. Suzuki uses his customary arsenal of surreal and tongue-in-cheek humor foreshadowing his later non-yakuza SCHOOL OF THE HOLY BEASTS. He and fellow screenwriter Kakefuda also seem to have been influenced by the LADY SNOWBLOOD films with Meiko Kaji, albeit with much, much more sex. One wishes that Suzuki had been as faithful to period detail as he is to letting his imagination have free rein. There are some jarring inconsistencies such as Lindberg wearing panties of obviously sixties vintage and later a buckskin fringe top and miniskirt! Still, this transcends into a pop culture realm of genuinely anarchic art just as director Russ Meyer transcends. #1 of 2 films * * * *

STORY OF A WILD ELDER SISTER – WIDESPREAD LYNCH LAW aka FEMALE YAKUZA TALE – INQUISITION AND TORTURE aka YASAGURE ANEGO DEN – SOKATSU RINCHI 1973 **Dir.** Teruo Ishii **Scr.** Teruo Ishii/ Masahiro Kakefuda/Ikuo Sekimoto **Photo color 'scope:** Motoya Washio **Music:** Hajime Kaburagi **w/** Reiko Ike, Akemi Negishi, Tatsuo Endo, Ryohei Uchida, Kanjuro Arashi, Toru Abe, Hiroshi Nawa, Makoto Aikawa This is resolutely absurd, uneven and nowhere near as rewarding as the first entry. That said, this still manages to be fairly entertaining as Ike is helped by lone wolf Uchida in going up against bad boss Endo (clad in some hard-to-look-at striped suits) who runs drugs and girls. There are some deliriously beautiful, borderline psychedelic tableau as well as some incredibly stupid, gratuitous sex scenes and poorly excecuted slapstick

and scatalogical humor. The last third of the film is nearly incoherent with Ishii throwing everything but the kitchen sink into the mix, including an out-of-left field asylum sequence that seems to be a parody of his initial scenes in 1969's HORROR OF MALFORMED MEN. The final protracted showdown, too, with numerous shanghaied prostitutes disrobing, clasping their swords, then decimating the mobsters while led by Ike and Uchida is so ludicrous, so threadbare, one wonders how Ishii got away with it. It veers crazily from exhilarating mayhem to poorly staged *kabuki*-cum-striptease antics. For a perfect example of when Ishii could take the same kind of scenario a bit more seriously and turn out near-masterpieces, see THE RED SILK GAMBLER or BOHACHI BUSHIDO. #2 of 2 films * * 1/2

ESCAPE GAME aka DASSO YUGI 1976 93 min. **Dir.** Kosaku Yamashita **Orig. story:** Koji Takada **Scr.** Ikuo Sekimoto **Photo color 'scope:** Umio Masuda **Music:** Masao Yagi **w/** Shinichi "Sonny" Chiba, Haruko Wanibuchi, Eiji Go, Kazumasa Negishi

EVIL BODYGUARD TROOPS aka AKU NO SHIN-EITAI 1971 **Dir./Scr.** Kazuhiko Yamaguchi **Photo color 'scope:** Yoshio Nakajima **Music:** Toshiaki Tsushima **w/** Tsunehiko Watase, Jerry Fujio, Tatsuo Umemiya, Tsune Kawaguchi,Tetsuro Tanba, Ichiro Sugai, Bunsaku Han, Machiko Yashiro, Fumio Watanabe, Hosei Komatsu

Evil Boss vs. Henchmen

Evil Priest (#1)

EVIL BOSS VS. HENCHMEN
aka AKU OYABUN TAI DAIGASHI
1971 Dir. Buichi Saito Scr. Koji
Takada Photo. color 'scope:
Nagaki Yamagishi w/ Tomisaburo
Wakayama, Bunta Sugawara, Hiroshi
Nawa, Kanjuro Arashi, Toru Abe,
Yukari Wakayama, Machiko Yashiro,
Tatsuo Endo, Ryoichi Tamagawa

EVIL CHARMS aka IRO MA
1973 Dir. Yasuo Furuhata Scr. Isao
Matsumoto Photo color 'scope:
Kiichi Inada Music: Hiroshi Fujita
w/ Tatsuo Umemiya, Jun Fujimaki,
Misuzu Ota, Tetsuro Tanba, Yayoi
Watanabe, Fumio Watanabe, Bontaro
Miake, Rokko Toura, Hiroshi Kondo

**THE EVIL PRIEST aka GOKU-
AKU BOZU aka THE PRIEST
KILLER aka THE SCOUNDREL
PRIEST aka KARATE KILLER
PRIEST series**

THE EVIL PRIEST aka
GOKUAKU BOZU aka
KARATE KILLER PRIEST aka
THE SCOUNDREL PRIEST
1968 90 min. Dir. Kiyoshi Saeki
Scr. Akira Murao/Hideaki Yamamoto
Photo color 'scope: Nagaki
Yamagishi Music: Shunsuke
Kikuchi w/ Tomisaburo Wakayama,
Kenjiro Ishiyama, Tsu Ishiyama,
Hosei Komatsu, Masumi Tachibana,
Mari Shiraki, Bunta Sugawara,
Hiroshi Nawa Wakayama plays
Shinkai, a rambunctious, wandering gambler priest at the turn of the
century who is as proficient in martial
arts (judo/karate/swordplay) as he is
grifting (con-artistry) as he is sincere
as a cleric. I have not seen the first
two in the series, but sometimes the
excessively broad comedy overstays
its welcome.When I had initially
heard of these films, I had high hopes
since these were shot immediately
before and perhaps simultaneously to

Wakayama's excellent Toho Studios samurai series LONE WOLF & CUB (KOZURE OKAMI) (1972 -'74). But the lower budgets, meandering, near non-existent storylines and sometimes excessive comic relief keep the EVIL PRIEST movies from excellence. Don't get me wrong – Wakayama as Shinkai and Bunta Sugawara as blind Ryototsu (who does not appear nearly enough) are enormously entertaining, as are the bloody, extended action setpieces. Strange that Wakayama's brother, Shintaro Katsu, did a nearly identical pair of pictures (HOOD-LUM PRIEST), set, I think, in the 1860s-1870s for Daiei Studios (re-leased 1967-'68). #1 of 5 films

THE EVIL PRIEST – BALLAD OF MURDER aka GOKUAKU BOZU – HITOKIRI KAZOE UTA 1968 90 min. **DIR.** Takashi Harada **SCR.** Akira Murao/Hideaki Yamamoto **PHOTO COLOR 'SCOPE:** Nagaki Yamagishi **MUSIC:** Isao Tomita w/ Tomisaburo Wakayama, Asao Koike, Bunta Sugawara, Eitaro Ozawa, Masumi Tachibana, Toru Abe, Eiko Takehara, Bin Amatsu, Katsu Shiga, Hosei Komatsu Rumored to be the best of the series. For some strange reason these first two entries are harder to see. #2 of 5 films

THE EVIL PRIEST – KILL-ER'S TRAVEL PRAYER aka GOKUAKU BOZU – NENBUTSU HITOKIRI TABI aka THE PRIEST KILLER 1969 92 min. **DIR.** Takashi Harada **SCR.** Akira Murao/Hideaki Yamamoto **PHOTO COLOR 'SCOPE:** Umeo Masuda **MUSIC:** Isao Tomita w/ Tomisaburo Wakayama, Minoru Oki, Bunta Sugawara, Hiroko

Sakuramachi, Tatsuo Terajima, Tomoko Mayama, Shigeko Ito, Shigeyoshi Fujioka, Tatsuo Endo, Takuzo Kawatani

Evil Priest (#3)

Shinkai (Wakayama) comes to the aid of a coastal village being held hostage by a yakuza clan. My favorite of the three that I have seen, with an astonishingly beautiful sunrise sword-battle-on-the-beach climax. Sugawara also shines as vengeful, blind, rival priest, Ryototsu who shows up briefly for his requisite fight scene with Wakayama. The film's only liability is Harada's haphazard direction which nullifies any suspense with poorly in-tegrated humor and inept transitions. #3 of 5 films   * * *

THE EVIL PRIEST – PRAYER OF THE TRIPLE-CUT STYLE aka GOKUAKU BOZU – NENBUTSU SANDAN GIRI aka THE PRIEST KILLER COMES BACK 1970 94 min. **DIR.** Takashi Harada **SCR.**

Akira Murao/Koji Takada **PHOTO COLOR 'SCOPE:** Nagaki Yamagishi **MUSIC:** Toshiaki Tsushima w/ Tomisaburo Wakayama, Bunta Sugawara, Ichiro Nakatani, Yuki Jono, Yuriko Mishima, Eizo Kitamura, Shinichiro Mikami

Evil Priest (#4)

Nakatani is a cheating gambler given to carrying a sawed-off scattergun who turns out to be an old childhood pal of Wakayama. Wakayama saves him from a beating when he is caught in the act of slipping in doctored dice. However, Nakatani is far from grateful and harbors a resentment which leads him to going after a bounty on Wakayama's head set by survivors of a gang decimated in the opening scene by our hero. Meanwhile, Wakayama has journeyed to his wintry hometown of Nogata to not only erect a memorial to his own mother but also to visit Nakatani's still-living elderly mom. Of course, there are two different yakuza clans

exploiting the river workers of the town, and Wakayama goes to bat for them, something that does not win him any friends in the bad guy camp. Wakayama is temporarily blinded about two thirds of the way through, and a larcenous gambling, judo-throwing nun who had fleeced him earlier in the saga, softens and helps him train to fight the villains with his new affliction. Simultaneously, Sugawara as blind priest Ryototsu appears and is initially disposed to taking advantage of his old nemesis' situation. However, he soon realizes Wakayama is trying to help the townsfolk. He relents, lending a hand in the final battle while Wakayama makes like Zatoichi (he is obviously having a royal time aping his real-life brother Shintaro Katsu's film antics here). Even bitter Nakatani changes horses in midstream, turning on the villains to help his old friend but paying for it in the process with his life. Once again, Harada's direction is fairly lackluster, failing to set fire to the convoluted proceedings. As usual, the most enjoyable moments are Wakayama's interactions with Sugawara. #4 of 5 films * * 1/2

THE EVIL PRIEST – CAST A NET OF DRUNKEN ANGER aka GOKUAKU BOZU – NOMU UTSU KAU aka THE BLOODY PRIEST 1971 89 min. **DIR.** Buichi Saito **SCR.** Tatsuo Honda/Masahiro Shimura **PHOTO COLOR 'SCOPE:** Juhei Suzuki **MUSIC:** Taiichiro Kosugi w/ Tomisaburo Wakayama, Bunta Sugawara, Takashi Shimura, Toru Abe, Kyosuke Machida, Sanae Kitabayashi, Fumio Watanabe, Yuriko Mishima, Takuzo Kawatani Of the entries I have seen, this one

has the most comedy relief – unfortunately. But director Saito keeps things moving at a nice clip, despite the usual convoluted storyline. Once again there is a great judo battle between Wakayama and a larcenous nun. Also the final, spectacular karate/judo duel between Wakayama and blind Ryototsu (Sugawara) in the sand dunes keeps this from being just average. See the excellent BALLAD OF DEATH (HITOKIRI KANNON UTA), Sugawara's sole solo outing as Ryototsu. #5 and final in series
* * 1/2

Evil Priest (#5)

EX-CONVICT aka KUROI YUBI NO OTOKO aka A MAN'S DARK FINGER 1959 **DIR.** Masuichi Iizuka **SCR.** Katsundo Inomata/Eisaburo Shiba **PHOTO 'SCOPE:** Akira Mimura **MUSIC:** Isao Tomita **w/** Ken Takakura, Eijiro Yanagi, Yoshiko Sakuma, Yoshi Kato, Hiroshi Nihonyanagi

EX-CONVICT aka ZENKA MONO series

EX-CONVICT aka ZENKA MONO aka THE MARKED MAN 1968 89 min. **DIR.** Kosaku Yamashita **SCR.** Motohiro Torii/Isao Matsumoto **PHOTO COLOR 'SCOPE:** Juhei Suzuki **MUSIC:** Isao Tomita **w/** Tomisaburo Wakayama, Kyosuke Machida, Junko Miyazono, Minoru Oki, Bunta Sugawara, Kanjuro Arashi, Masumi Harukawa, Rinichi Yamamoto, Tatsuo Endo, Hosei Komatsu, Toru Abe An action yakuza series leavened with humor starring Wakayama as a pipe-smoking ex-con. #1 of 3 films

Desperate Hoodlum aka Ex-Convict (#2)

DESPERATE HOODLUM aka YOKOGAMI YABURI NO ZENKA MONO 1968 90 min. **DIR.** Shigehiro Ozawa **SCR.** Kazuo Kasahara **PHOTO COLOR 'SCOPE:** Sadatsugu Yoshida **MUSIC:** Takeo Watanabe **w/** Tomisaburo Wakayama, Kyosuke Machida, Tamao Nakamura,

Masumi Harukawa, Toru Abe, Bin
Amatsu   #2 of 3 films

Ex-Convict (#3)

Ex-Convict Women - Murder Song aka
Criminal Women, Killing Melody

EX-CONVICT – TURF WAR aka
ZENKA MONO – SHIMA ARASHI
1969 90 min. **DIR.** Shigehiro Ozawa
SCR. Kazuo Kasahara/Ryunosuke
Kono **PHOTO COLOR 'SCOPE:**
Sadatsugu Yoshida w/ Tomisaburo
Wakayama, Tatsuo Umemiya, Junko
Miyazono, Shogo Shimada   #3 and
final in series

EX-CONVICT WOMEN –
MURDER SONG aka ZENKA
ONNA – KOROSHI BUSHI aka
CRIMINAL WOMEN, KILLING
MELODY 1973 86 min. **DIR.**
Atsushi Mibori **SCR.** Fumio Konami/
Hiro Matsuda **PHOTO COLOR 'SCOPE:**
Masahiko Iimura **MUSIC:** Masao
Yagi w/ Reiko Ike, Miki Sugimoto,
Ryoji Hayama, Hosei Komatsu,
Yumiko Katayama, Chiyoko Kazama,
Bontaro Miake, Takeo Chii, Shinzo
Hotta

Mixing elements from both the
FEMALE CONVICT SCORPION
and GIRL BOSS series, this is a
ferociously entertaining tall tale of
Ike's attempts at violent retribution on
Hayama and men, the yakuza responsible for her gang rape and her father's ruin and death. Her first knife-
slashing attack on them in a nightclub
lands her in prison where she is
soon befriended by Katayama at. al
and becomes rivals with Sugimoto,
Hayama's tattooed mistress. There are
some wild flashbacks depicting how
the girls landed in stir, the standout
being one drunken, motorcycle-riding
gal's tossed beer bottle causing a cop
to crash his bike when it conks him
on the head. When the girls are released midway through the saga, they
decide to help Ike on her vendetta and
are soon engineering a Machivellian
gang war between drunken ruffian,
Chii's bunch and Hayama's. Eventu-

ally Sugimoto, even though she is once more in her comfortable niche as the only woman in Hayama's mob, offers her help in sabotaging the gang from the inside. The climax sees every single male yakuza dead. But when the smoke clears, all the women have miraculously survived, triumphant and comparatively liberated. Ike and Sugimoto immediately feel free to renew their feud, first with knives then their fists on the corpse-strewn battlefield until both are so exhausted they collapse. Rising up with their hostilities spent, they leave together as friends. Visually intoxicating, the violent action is exciting and the humor generally amusing as opposed to the sophomoric idiocy that often mars the middle thirds of the GIRL BOSS pictures (a series which also stars Ike and Sugimoto).
* * *

EXPELLED BY A MAN'S RIVALS aka OTOKO NAMIDA NO HAMONJO aka THE EXPULSION 1967 89 min. **DIR.** Kosaku Yamashita **SCR.** Akira Murao **PHOTO COLOR 'SCOPE:** Motoya Washio **MUSIC:** Takeo Watanabe w/ Koji Tsuruta, Minoru Oki, Kyosuke Machida, Kanjuro Arashi, Masumi Tachibana, Hiroko Sakuramachi, Hiroshi Murai, Kenjiro Ishjiyama   Machida is driven from his clan when his pal Murai steals a substantial bunch of money from their boss Arashi. Tsuruta, Machida's best friend, is astonished by this when he is released from prison. A letter arrives from Arashi's daughter Tachibana at Tsuruta's *shusso iwai* (prison release celebration) that explains she is running off with Machida, and all hell breaks loose. Machida goes in search

of his renegade friend Murai and, in the process, gets a job in another village with a coal mine. When Machida confronts Murai, he finds his former comrade allied with evil rural *oyabun* Amatsu. Tsuruta coincidentally visits coal mine gang boss Ishiyama and not only discovers rage-filled Machida and longsuffering Tachibana, but that boss Amatsu has it in for Ishiyama's clan. Soon Murai turns over a new leaf, partly due to his sister Sakuramachi, who is smitten with Tsuruta. With Murai's help, they foil Amatsu's plot to assassinate Ishiyama, but Murai is brutally stabbed-to-death soon afterwards. More complications ensue when Oki, one of Tsuruta's old rivals, turns up allied with Amatsu. Things come to a head with Oki getting killed, Amatsu's dynamiting of the mine which traps Ishiyama and causes Machida's death by falling timbers when he rescues his new boss. Tsuruta ends up tracking down Amatsu and henchmen, dispatching them on a mountain of slag. He returns with old boss Arashi to the site of the cave-in to gather at dying Machida's side. The cycle of falling-from-grace and subsequent chivalrous redemption is completed with Tsuruta and Sakuramachi taking Machida's ashes back home by boat. As usual, expert *ninkyo* director Yamashita makes the most of screenwriter, Murao's heartbreakingly ironic juxtapositions, stripping away quite a bit of the old-fashioned baggage inherent in the genre. While a good example of *ninkyo eiga*, this still isn't focused enough to wring the maximum potential from the proceedings, undoubtedly due to the usual breakneck writing and shooting schedule.   * * *

FANCY MAN aka DANI 1965 83 min. **DIR.** Hideo Sekigawa **SCR.** Kikuma Shimoizaka **PHOTO 'SCOPE:** Hanjiro Nakazawa **MUSIC:** Kazumi Naito w/ Tatsuo Umemiya, Reiko Ohara, Naoki Sugiura, Junko Miyazono, Akemi Kita, Renji Ishibashi, Minako Katsuki, Akitake Kimura   Umemiya plays one of his stock-in-trade roles of the lates sixties and early seventies: the handsome heel who is a hoodlum exploiter of women and a blackmailer of men. However, here his greed and avarice backfire when he is injured by one of the more headstrong vengeful women. Thereafter he finds himself impotent, and all meaning in his shallow life is destroyed.

FEARLESS MAN'S BLOODY WOUNDS aka KIZU DARAKE NO FUTEKI NA MONO 1963 **DIR.** Setsuya Kondo **SCR.** Ryuta Akimoto **PHOTO 'SCOPE:** Ichiro Hoshijima **MUSIC:** Masuo Furukawa w/ Joji Ai, Tetsuro Tanba, Tatsuo Umemiya, Yoshiko Mita, Mihoko Inagaki

FEMALE CONVICT SCORPION aka JOSHUU SASORI aka LADY SCORPION series

FEMALE CONVICT #701 – SCORPION aka JOSHUU 701 GO – SASORI aka LADY SCORPION 1972 87 min. **DIR.** Shunya Ito **SCR.** Fumio Konami/Hiro Matsuda **PHOTO COLOR 'SCOPE:** Hanjiro Nakazawa **MUSIC:** Shunsuke Kikuchi w/ Meiko Kaji, Hiroko Ogi, Fumio Watanabe, Yayoi Watanabe, Isao Natsuyagi, Rie Yokoyama, Nori Rinari
A very satisfying and strikingly photographed women's prison picture. Our heroine is beautiful, strong, principled and basically honorable and decent – at least when compared to her fellow inmates.

Female Convict #701 - Scorpion (#1)

The basic premise of the tale – and of the series – is Meiko Kaji as Matsu nicknamed Sasori (meaning Scorpion) wronged woman/fanatical avenger raining wrath down on the heads of various yakuza cruds, betraying lovers, corrupt politicians, vindictive fellow prisoners and sadistic prison officers. Here in the first entry, from Kaji and fellow prisoner (Yayoi Watanabe) being pursued through a marshy shoreline by dogs to the gonzo prison riot to Kaji's escape and subsequent killing of her enemies, specfically ex-lover and corrupt cop Natsuyagi, the narrative never lets up. Director Ito conjures up psychedelic, erotic/grotesque madness in not only Kaji's flashback to her gang rape by Natsuyagi's cronies but also when a crazy prisoner (Yoko Mihara) attempts to attack Kaji in the bathhouse but accidentally gouges out an eye of the cruel warden played by Fumio Watanabe. This episode also contains Kaji's virtually sole sex scene in the series when she seduces a female undercover cop (Yumiko Katayama) who has been planted in her cell to wheedle damning evidence out of our anti-heroine.

Female Convict #701 - Scorpion (#1)

These first four films with Kaji are reportedly an improvement over their *manga* source. When Kaji had balked at continually spewing obscenities, she and director Ito had decided to make the character more mysteriously elemental. Sasori is no longer a foul-mouthed ruffian but a virtually silent, deadly force uttering only a few cryptic sentences in each film. This series possesses all the traditional exploitation elements, including grueling violence but with

a socio-political subtext and a surreal, comic book use of color as well as a succession of mythical/ archetypal images that leave a haunting, eerie shiver when the last frame unspools. #1 of 6 films * * * 1/2

Female Convict Scorpion - Jailhouse 41 (#2)

FEMALE CONVICT SCORPION – JAILHOUSE #41 aka JOSHUU SASORI – DAI 41 ZAKKYOBO 1972 93 min. **DIR.** Shunya Ito **SCR.** Shunya Ito/Hiro Matsuda/Fumio Konami **PHOTO COLOR 'SCOPE:** Masao Shimizu **MUSIC:** Shunsuke Kikuchi w/ Meiko Kaji, Kayoko Shiraishi, Hiroko Isayama, Fumio Watanabe, Yuki Arasuna, Eiko Yatsunami, Yuki Kagawa, Hideo Murota   An absolutely phenomenal surrealist cum exploitation picture with Kaji and other even more hardened female convicts breaking out of stir, then mutilating and killing their brutal, rapist guards. They traverse a desolate, blasted landscape, entering a deserted village half-buried in volcanic ash (this scene was actually filmed in a real town abandoned after a nearby volcanic eruption). When they hide out in a dilapidated hut, we learn the history of Kaji's main nemesis, bitter, sadistic battleaxe, Shiraishi. An impoverished, already abused middle-aged woman, she had murdered her children in suicidal despair then been nearly beaten-to-death by her native fishing village. This is depicted in a dreamlike, slow-motion *kabuki* sequence that is disturbingly heartbreaking. Leaving the ghost town, the fugitives encounter a senile old woman who may be a witch or perhaps a ghost, continue to flee through melancholic autumnal woods and finally reach a barren, mountainous area of stone. When one of the more vulnearable girls goes off on her own, she is raped, killed then tossed into a river by bestial, vacationing salarymen. Her blood taints the whole river, transforming a waterfall completely crimson. When the others find her corpse, Kaji and cohorts capture the guilty parties, taking a whole busload of the vulgar, selfish men hostage as the police close in. The closing fantasy image of Kaji and all the women from the prison running liberated through the deserted streets of Tokyo as the sun rises has to be one of the most transcendental, exhilarating and bittersweet images in any exploitation film, Japanese or otherwise. One of the truly genuine masterpieces of violent 1970s cinema and, in its own way, as subversive as Donald Cammell/ Nicolas Roeg's PERFORMANCE, John Boorman's POINT BLANK and Jean-Luc Godard's WEEKEND. #2 of 6 films * * * *

FEMALE CONVICT, SCORPION – DEPARTMENT OF BEASTS
aka JOSHUU SASORI – KEMONO BEYA aka BEAST STABLE 1973 87 min. **Dir.** Shunya Ito **Scr.** Hiro Matsuda **Photo color 'scope:** Masao Shimizu **Music:** Shunsuke Kikuchi **w/** Meiko Kaji, Mikio Narita, Yayoi Watanabe, Reisen Lee, Koji Nanbara, Takashi Fujiki

Kaji is collared on the subway by plainclothes cop, Narita. He handcuffs her, and a fight ensues. Kaji jumps off the train just as the doors close. Narita's arm is caught, then torn off! Still handcuffed to Kaji, she trails the bloody appendage behind her as she runs amongst shocked passersby on the street. Eventually she takes refuge in a primitive cottage in the ghetto inhabited by a decent, beautiful young woman (Watanabe) who has sex with her extremely retarded brother to keep him from becoming violent. Kaji is soon captured by yakuza Nanbara and his mistress Lee (a nemesis from prison). Twisted female ex-con Lee dresses in black feathers and cages Kaji in a barred cell full of vicious ravens. When Kaji finally escapes, she hides in a maze of underground storm drains, aided and abetted by benevolent Watanabe who had sheltered her. Kaji avenges herself on all concerned with Nanbara thrown out a third story window. Narita, though, is still in pursuit and finally manages to snare her. In the end he's strangled between the bars of her jail cell doors for his trouble.   #3 of 6 films   * * * 1/2

Female Convict, Scorpion - Department of Beasts (#3)

Female Convict, Scorpion - Department of Beasts (#3)

FEMALE CONVICT, SCORPION – #701'S SONG OF HATE

aka JOSHUU SASORI – 701 GO URAMI BUSHI 1973 89 min. **DIR.** Yasuharu Hasebe **SCR.** Yasuharu Hasebe/Fumio Konami/Hiro Matsuda **PHOTO COLOR** 'scope: Hanjiro Nakazawa **MUSIC:** Hajime Kaburagi w/ Meiko Kaji, Masakazu Tamura, Yayoi Watanabe, Toshiyuki Hosokawa   Tamura is a former student radical who has been crippled and made impotent by torture at the hands of fascist police detective Hosokawa. He now works as a lighting man in a sleazy strip club. He falls in love with escapee Kaji, helping her in her flight. The cops are in hot pursuit, but they only capture Tamura. They bring in his mother who guilt trips him for wasting his life as a student radical and sheltering a known murderess. She convinces him that the police will let him go if he gives up his lover. Inwardly tortured, he nevertheless gives in and Kaji is captured. Before long, she exerts her near superhuman will to avenge herself on Tamura. The climax has her lynch evil Hosokawa at sunset on the very scaffold on which she was to be executed the following morning. This was the last of the SCORPION pictures with Kaji. At the time, she felt the premise had been exhausted and that Toei was engineering more gratuitously grotesque scenarios with every installment. Also the budget was being successively slashed on each new film, despite the incredible popularity of the series. Original director Ito had gone way over schedule on the first two. Having to cut corners on the preceding third picture was undoubtedly part of the reason he was replaced by able, yet ultimately hamstrung Nikkatsu veteran Hasebe for this fourth episode. #4 of 6 films
* * *

NEW FEMALE CONVICT, SCORPION – NUMBER 701

aka SHIN JOSHUU SASORI – 701 GO 1976 88 min. **DIR.** Yu Kohira **SCR.** Tatsuhiko Kamoi **PHOTO COLOR** 'SCOPE: Masahiko Iimura **MUSIC:** Masaaki Hirao w/ Yumi Takigawa, Yusuke Natsu, Yaku Hanbun, Ichiro Nakatani, Toshie Negishi, Bunsaku Han, Rinichi Yamamoto, Nobuo Kaneko, Yoshiko Maki, Runa Takamura   Takigawa, star of such surreal sexploitation pictures as SCHOOL OF THE HOLY BEASTS, takes over Kaji's role. For the most part, a severe letdown. This is a partial remake of the first film, and it just does not live up to any of its predecessors despite the occasional decent moment. Takigawa is a competent actress, but she is miscast and unimpressive in the Sasori role. One of the very few scenes worth mentioning is Takigawa's nightmarish meeting with corrupt politician Nakatani. Kohira uses a strangely shimmering white water reflection alternating with a hellish red backlight in the set design for this encounter that equals some of the imagery in Kaji's films. Otherwise the picture is a washout with the lowest budget yet. Doubly frustrating in that writer Kamoi helped to pen some masterpieces such as GRAVEYARD OF HONOR and Nikkatsu Studio's KANTO SOCIETY OF LEADING MOBSTERS. #5 of 6 films   * *

NEW FEMALE CONVICT, SCORPION – SPECIAL CELL

BLOCK X aka SHIN JOSHUU
SASORI – TOKUSHUBO X
1977 84 min. DIR. Yu Kohira
SCR. Tatsuhiko Kamoi PHOTO COLOR
'SCOPE: Yoshio Nakajima MUSIC:
Tomokazu Kawabe w/ Yoko
Natsuki, Takeo Chii, Kaori Ono,
Hiroshi Tate, Masashi "Milton"
Ishibashi   For some reason,
Takigawa only starred in one entry
before being replaced by Natsuki.
Not to disparage Takigawa, but this
was a step back in the right direction. Natsuki is able to convey some
vulnerability while still assuming a
tough-as-nails persona. Regrettably,
the budget is still impossibly low.
Director Kohira does some starkly
minimal things with basic primary
colors in some effective nightmare
flashbacks, but was obviously con-
strained by time and money. Ishibashi
is the cowardly warden who gets
head guard Chii to do his dirty work
for him. However, when Chii rebels
against new sharpshooter enforcer
Tate, he is thrown into confinement
himself. He and Scorpion Natsuki
escape from jail, chained together ala
THE DEFIANT ONES. The scenario
is fairly fast-moving and packed with
action, but there is little of the surreal, macabre flavor of Kaji's films.
Ultimately it amounts to little more
than programmer status. This was the
last film in the series until the 1991
revival FEMALE CONVICT, SCOR-
PION – DEATH THREAT (JOSHUU
SASORI – SATSUJIN YOKOKU)
with Mineko Nishikawa directed
by Toshiharu Ikeda (EVIL DEAD
TRAP). Yet another SCORPION
film appeared in 1997, SASORI IN
THE U.S.A. (aka THE SCORPION'S
REVENGE) and two more in the year
2000. #6 and last of series * * 1/2

FEMALE YAKUZA CONVICT
aka SUKE YAKUZA aka YOUNG
GIRL YAKUZA 1974 DIR.
Masahide Shinozuka SCR. Isao
Matsumoto PHOTO COLOR 'SCOPE:
Kunio Kunisada MUSIC: Masao
Yagi w/ Yoko Horikoshi, Reiko
Ike, Tsunehiko Watase, Momoko
Naito, Yuriko Mishima, Harumi
Sone, Shotaro Hayashi, Ryuko
Azuma, Shoji Arikawa
The Japanese title would traditionally
be romanized JOSHUU YAKUZA,
but the marketplace was so full of
"SUKE"-this and "SUKEBAN"-that
(most of it from Toei Studios themselves), the marketing strategy, I
suppose, was to add one more to the
pack. The thing is the *kanji* connotes
the aspect of "female-prisoner",
something you do not get when just
seeing the romanized *"SUKE,"* which
usually translates as "girl" or "young
girl". As it is, lead star Horikoshi is
only in stir for a brief time after being
captured for helping her co-ed pals,
handsome Watase and goofy couple
Naito and Nagahama rob various
banks and moneylenders. While
behind bars, she becomes friends with
tough girl Ike, who joins their gang
once they have escaped. The last half
of the rather humdrum story revolves
around the group's efforts to rip off
small time yakuza boss Sone's mob.
They accomplish their task only to
pay dearly. Nagahama is shot to
death and Watase is mortally wounded in a shoot out with Sone's men.
Horikoshi and Ike end up holding off
the cops from dying Watase's second
story hospital room. When they run
out of ammunition, the two women
toss their stolen yakuza loot out the
window, and it is blown on the wind,
swirling about the neighborhood.

Only simple Naito, who had left earlier, gets away free with a small portion of the cash. FEMALE YAKUZA CONVICT is not particularly memorable, and it certainly pales next to many of Toei's other female action films. The budget is extremely low and the action is meager. Horikoshi, whom I do not recall in any other lead roles, is merely adequate. However, the cast does have some chemistry, especially Ike and Watase, and there is a certain welcome sincerity in evidence in the performances and direction that is all too often missing from Toei's formula programmers from this period. * * 1/2

FESTIVAL OUTLAW – BROTHER APPRENTICES OF THE RIVERSIDE FISH MARKET aka OMATSURI YARO – UOGASHI NO KYODAI BUN 1976 94 min. DIR. Norifumi Suzuki SCR. Masahiro Kakefuda/Norifumi Suzuki PHOTO COLOR 'SCOPE: Masahiko Iimura MUSIC: Shunsuke Kikuchi w/ Hiroki Matsukata, Junko Natsu, Koichi Iwaki, Jiro Sakagami, Etsuko "Sue" Shiomi, Hideo Murota, Ichiro Ogura, Yayoi Watanabe, Yoko Mihara

FLOWER AND DRAGON aka HANA TO RYU 1954 DIR. Kiyoshi Saeki w/ Susumu Fujita

FLOWER AND DRAGON aka HANA TO RYU series

FLOWER AND DRAGON aka HANA TO RYU aka CHRYSANTHEMUM AND THE DRAGON 1965 97 min. DIR. Kosaku Yamashita SCR. Kei Tasaka PHOTO

COLOR 'SCOPE: Shin Furuya MUSIC: Minoru Miki w/ Kinnosuke Nakamura, Ryunosuke Tsukigata, Yoshiko Sakuma, Takahiro Tamura, Keiko Awaji, Asao Uchida, Junko Miyazono, Kei Sato, Yuriko Mishima, Sonosuke Sawamura

Another version of the popular novel. Nakamura plays the lead as much more of a naive bumpkin who becomes the object of sophisticated card dealer Awaji's affections. He wins big at her dice game and, since he has also just gotten a knife that day, he decides to become a wandering yakuza, much to his buddy's consternation. A year later he meets Sakuma while working for a coal carter's clan on the coast. He begins to fall-in-love with her when she helps him out in a brawl with another rival clan while loading a ship. Shortly thereafter, his clan is hit by a cholera epidemic, and they are soon burying their mates (something not gone into in the later two part TALES OF JAPANESE CHIVALRY version or in the 1972 epic Shochiku film directed by Tai Kato). Nakamura's best pal Tamura is beaten up while defending Sakuma from rival yakuza, and Nakamura goes to complain to boss Tsukigata. Even though his daughter had been the one to start the whole mess, Tsukigata surprisingly takes Nakamura's side. Subordinate Kei Sato is not amused. The tension isn't over as Nakamura and Sakuma have to help Tamura and his girl escape a villainous yakuza search party. Once the crisis has passed, Nakamura and Sakuma realize how much they love each other, then pack up their stuff and leave town. Two years later, he is an underboss of a clan at another port and married to Sakuma. Fate intervenes when he runs into Awaji again. At first, she does not recognize him, and it is he that is excited to see her. He gets drunk, falls asleep and, when he awakens, discovers that she has given him a huge tattoo of a dragon. She has fallen in love with him, and he has to tell her that he is married. There is added poignance to the situation since she is a bit older and in, what polite society considers, a sleazy occupation. Complications ensue when Tsukigata's second-in-command Sato re-enters the picture, hoodwinking Nakamura's boss Kagawa with the aid of a traitor and making it look like Nakamura's doing. Singlehandedly, Nakamura ventures out to where Sato has taken over a shiploading job to challenge his authority. After a brutal fistfight with the betrayer, Nakamura wins back the respect of boss Kagawa, who sets him up with a gang of his own. This is an entertaining take on this

oft-lensed tale but is curiously lacking in emotional resonance, especially when compared to Makino and Yamashita's later two-part version with Ken Takakura and Tai Kato's picture at Shochiku Studios with Tetsuya Watari. #1 of 2 films * * *

Flower and Dragon (#2)

FLOWER AND DRAGON – DUEL OF THE SEA CAVES aka HANA TO RYU – DO KAIWAN NO KETTO 1966 90 min. **DIR.** Kosaku Yamashita **SCR.** Kei Tasaka/Sadao Nakajima **PHOTO COLOR 'SCOPE:** Shin Furuya **MUSIC:** Minoru Miki **w/** Kinnosuke Nakamura, Kei Sato, Ryunosuke Tsukigata, Yoshiko Sakuma, Takahiro Tamura, Keiko Awaji, Kenji Egi, Toshio Sugawara, Junko Miyazono, Hosei Komatsu, Jun Hamamura

Nakamura is now a respected boss in his own right but is caught up in a three way power struggle with bosses Sato and Hamamura. Elder boss Tsukigata is still around but does not do much except occasionally scold Sato and Hamamura when things get too rambunctious. Sato also seems to have farmed out his more violent machinations to Hamamura's hotheaded ruffians, something that ultimately backfires. Cruel Komatsu, one of Nakamura's mortal enemies from the first film, helps to orchestrate an ambush on the unarmed Nakamura at the climax of the picture. This attack

Flower and Dragon (#1)

where Nakamura defends himself with his parasol against Komatsu and cronies on a deserted, raindrenched wharf, is the action setpiece of the film. It is so expertly choreographed and performed by all concerned, one is certain Nakamura is a true goner. A loyal sidekick happens on the scene, chases off the attackers and, in the process, beats Komatsu to death. In fact, Nakamura just barely survives, hanging on in the hospital for weeks before he is finally able to get to his feet and present a petition to every member of the three gangs to unite into a true coal carter/dockworker labor union. The denouement finds him finally coercing the reluctant holdout Sato to sign. This is not bad at all. But it is still curiously uninvolving in much the same way as the first film. It is bewildering because director Yamashita and star Nakamura made some geuinely affecting masterpieces together, such as YATAPPE OF SEKI (see Matatabi/Period Yakuza Section). And there is also excellent writer Kei Tasaka, a frequent collaborator of master director Hideo Gosha, helming both of the screenplays here. It is really a mystery why the films don't go beyond from the merely good to the excellent. Part of the problem is undoubtedly the lack of emphasis placed on the sensitive, yet worldly, female gambler Awaji. Her character is certainly one of the most compelling in the entire saga. This misstep was rectified when Masahiro Makino and Yamashita remade the story as two consecutive entries in the TALES OF JAPANESE CHIVALRY series (with Junko Fuji playing the tragic woman yakuza). #2 of 2 films * * *

FLOWER CARDS CHIVALRY
aka HANA FUDA TOSEI 1967
DIR./SCR. Masashige Narusawa
PHOTO B&W 'SCOPE: Masahiko Iimura **MUSIC:** Takeo Watanabe
w/ Tatsuo Umemiya, Haruko Wanibuchi, Ko Nishimura, Junzaburo Ban, Tatsuo Endo, Chitose Kobayashi

Flower Cards Gambling Diary

**FLOWER CARDS GAMBLING
DIARY – DUEL TO THE DEATH
OF THE BEST THREE** aka
HANA FUDA TOBAKU – INO SHI
KA SANBAN SHOBU aka THE
FINAL GAMBLE 1970 89 min.
DIR. Ryuichi (Tatsuichi) Takamori
SCR. Masashige Narusawa **PHOTO
COLOR 'SCOPE:** Kiichi Inada **MUSIC:**
Toshiaki Tsushima
w/ Yumiko Nogawa, Tatsuo
Umemiya, Masumi Tachibana,
Junzaburo Ban, Yasuko Sanjo,
Ema Sugimoto, Hayato Tani, Junko
Miyazono, Asao Koike, Keiji Takagi
This may be a follow-up to FLOWER
CARDS CHIVALRY above.

GAMBLER aka BAKUTO series

GAMBLER aka BAKUTO 1964
93 min. **DIR.** Shigehiro Ozawa
SCR. Shigehiro Ozawa/Akira Murao
PHOTO COLOR 'SCOPE: Nagaki
Yamagishi **MUSIC:** Toshiaki
Tsushima   w/ Koji Tsuruta, Hiroki
Matsukata, Shigeru Amachi, Junko
Fuji, Kotaro Satomi, Yoko Minamida,
Ryunosuke Tsukigata
Generally agreed to be, along with
the three film THEATER OF LIFE –
HISHAKAKU series (1963-'64) the
start of the modern *ninkyo* yakuza
film – in spite of the fact that all were
set in the pre-WW2 period. The first
five films in the series are of the
ninkyo (chivalrous) variety. With director Fukasaku's and Sato's particpa-
tion (starting with film #6) the series
became more of a cross between the
jitsuroku (true account) film – which
tended to be even more downbeat
and cynical – and the *ninkyo* type.
This first entry is jampacked with
Toei stars, old and new, depicting a

tapestry of gangs and their shifting
alliances and rivalries. Tsuruta is an
honorable yakuza shepherding younger mischief-makers like Matsukata
in the right direction. The ambience
here is a bit more realistic than some
of Toei's later *ninkyo eiga*, with
emphasis on no one, even the heroes,
being too angelic. There are decent
gangs allied with corrupt gangs, and
a society of gamblers having to all
swim in the same pool. Amachi is a
greedy young boss given to western
ways and intent on maximizing his
real estate revenue by indiscriminately pulling buildings down in his
district, something which results in an
accidental death and tenant riots.
Tsuruta, Matsukata and Satomi are
stalemated in their opposition.
Tsuruta is severely beaten and must
recuperate. Satomi goes to prison for
killing his drunken, cowardly boss.
Matsukata has contnual run-ins with
evil boss Endo over the fate of his

Gambler (#1)

girl, geisha Fuji. Eventually, Tsuruta is successful in discrediting Endo in front of elder head boss Tsukigata, who forces Endo to do the pinkie-cutting routine. Soon Endo is conspiring with Amachi who has numerous police and politicians in his pocket to crack down on rival gambling dens. Tsuruta, Matsukata and newly-released Satomi band together to open a gambling den with such prominent patrons that Amachi does not dare engineer a roust. Endo kidnaps Fuji to provoke Matsukata, and the young hothead is shot to death in the process of rescuing her. Tsuruta does his best to protect Fuji. Endo subsequently murders head boss Tsukigata, and Tsuruta formally challenges Amachi and Endo to a gangfight. Frightened Amachi responds by calling the cops. Tsuruta executes Endo then, with Satomi, stampedes a horse-drawn wagon through a police phalanx into Amachi's HQ for a violent sword binge. Although seriously wounded, the two heroes are successful in killing Amachi, and the cops rush in to arrest them. The music is not as obtrusive as it would later become in some Toei *ninkyo eiga*. The formula was relatively fresh here, and there is action galore as well as authentic atmosphere and period production design. That said, the dramatic tension of duty/obligation versus humanity/decency is not as much in evidence as it would be in later *ninkyo* yakuza *eiga*. #1 of 10 films * * *

PRISON GAMBLER aka KANGOKU BAKUTO 1964 **Dir.** Shigehiro Ozawa **Scr.** Shigehiro Ozawa/Akira Murao **Photo color** 'scope: Nagaki Yamagishi w/ Koji Tsuruta, Minoru Oki, Yoko

Minamida, Kotaro Satomi, Hizuru Takachiho, Kikuko Hojo, Yuriko Mishima, Bin Amatsu, Shingo Yamashiro   #2 of 10 films

Prison Gambler (#2)

Gambler vs. Street Peddler (#3)

GAMBLER VS. STREET PEDDLER aka BAKUTO TAI TEKIYA 1964 **Dir.** Shigehiro Ozawa **Scr.** Akira Murao/ Shigehiro Ozawa **Photo color** 'scope: Shin Furuya **Music:** Ichiro Saito w/ Koji Tsuruta, Tetsuro Tanba, Hiroki Matsukata, Chiyoko Shimakura, Chiezo Kataoka, Junko Fuji, Minoru Oki, Jushiro Konoe, Bin Amatsu, Kusuo Abe

A routine *ninkyo* potboiler with lone wolf Tsuruta becoming allied with little brother Matsukata's boss Kataoka against greedy, indiscriminately homicidal *tekiya* boss Konoe (actor Matsukata's real-life father). Per usual, Kataoka's character is just a trifle too saintly, and Konoe's a bit too Simon Legree-ish. There are also way too many talking-heads pieces of exposition. The film does have its attributes, namely a much more realistic-than-usual leading lady in Shimokura. She portrays Tsuruta's longsuffering, plain-jane whore lover with the air of truth. There is also a spectacular, climactic sword-duel-on-the-rooftops between Tsuruta and Konoe which results in both falling to their death (!) before a crowd of townspeople including Matsukata, Shimokura and compassionate police detective, Tanba. #3 of 10 films
* * 1/2

SEVEN GAMBLERS aka BAKUTO SHICHININ 1966 DIR. Shigehiro Ozawa   SCR. Kazuo Kasahara/ Shigehiro Ozawa   PHOTO COLOR 'SCOPE: Juhei Suzuki   MUSIC: Ichiro Saito   w/ Koji Tsuruta, Minoru Oki, Rinichi Yamamoto, Kyosuke Machida, Hiroko Sakuramachi, Shingo Yamashiro, Hosei Komatsu, Hiromi Fujiyama, Kayo Matsuo, Nobuo Kaneko, Ko Nishimura
A very loosely-related cousin (more in marketing promotion of movie titles than anything else) to another Tsuruta-starring Toei *ninkyo* opus, SEVEN FUGITIVES from 1966. #4 of 10 films

THREE GAMBLERS aka SANNIN NO BAKUTO 1967 85 min. DIR. Shigehiro Ozawa SCR.

Shigehiro Ozawa/Akira Murao PHOTO COLOR 'SCOPE: Juhei Suzuki MUSIC: Toshiaki Tsushima w/ Koji Tsuruta, Ryo Ikebe, Kyosuke Machida, Toru Abe, Yoshiko Mita, Sanae Kitabayashi, Shigeyoshi

Seven Gamblers (#4)

Fujioka, Akitake Kono, Tatsuo Endo, Hosei Komatsu   Tsuruta goes to prison after assassinating a rival yakuza boss. Lo and behold, he finds opposite number Machida – who assassinated *his* boss – also in stir. At first, they are mortal enemies, but, by the end of their term they wind up comrades. Unhappily, evil Abe, who had taken over Tsuruta's gang, has moved operations to Macao and shanghaied Tsuruta's girl into whoredom in the process, after forcibly addicting her to heroin. Tsuruta and Machida accidentally figure this out after being released, and try to redeem her. Machida's old comrade Ikebe, wracked with consumption, turns up, indebted and employed by Abe as a killer. This complicates matters because Ikebe is smitten with Tsuruta's former paramour. Loyalties get divided, especially after the woman's little boy also enters the picture. Although there is a setbound feel for at least half of the scenes, there is also some occasional nice location work in old Macao. Nevertheless, it can't really make up for what is a more formulaic-than-usual, by-the-numbers approach to this *ninkyo* programmer. Things get pushed over into absurdity with Abe and his gang running around the streets blowing people away with their cumbersome, antique machine gun, seemingly with impunity without a single policeman ever in sight.   #5 of 10 films * * 1/2

GAMBLER - CEREMONY OF DISBANDING aka BAKUTO - KAISANSHIKI 1968 90 min. DIR. Kinji Fukasaku SCR. Fumio Konami/ Kibu Nagata PHOTO.COLOR 'SCOPE: Ichiro Hoshijima MUSIC: Isao Tomita   w/ Koji Tsuruta, Masayo

Banri, Eiji Okada, Tetsuro Tanba, Fumio Watanabe, Seizaburo Kawazu, Rinichi Yamamoto, Hosei Komatsu, Harumi Sone, Hideo Murota
In the first modern, more *jitsuroku* (true account) series entry, Tsuruta returns after a jail term to assume control of a dockworker's union. Kawazu, for once playing a good boss, is on the verge of retiring. Tanba plays a dissolute ne'er-do-well junkie out of the new boss (Watanabe)'s past. Tsuruta would like to chuck all the aggravation that begins with the death of Kawazu (the new guy Watanabe is a greedy, two-faced bastard) and take off with his gal Banri. He had rescued her from raping U.S. soldiers in postwar times. Anyway, things are a bit talky, but Fukasaku keeps interest. One of the most violent scenes in the film turns out to be one of emotional rather than physical abuse with villain Watanabe and cronies mercilessly haranguing Kawazu to sign some crucial documents on his hospital deathbed. At the end, Tsuruta goes to Watanabe's office, casually locks all the doors, tosses him a knife and challenges him to a death duel. They fight in silence. Tsuruta wins, but his victory is bittersweet. He has just missed the boat on which his gal has set sail. For some reason, Fukasaku has all the flashbacks in a bright lime-green.   #6 of 10 films * * *

GAMBLER CLAN aka BAKUTO IKKA aka THE TERRITORY 1970 116 min. DIR. Shigehiro Ozawa SCR. Akira Murao PHOTO COLOR 'SCOPE: Sadatsugu Yoshida MUSIC: Toshiaki Tsushima w/ Ken Takakura, Tomisaburo Wakayama, Minoru Oki, Koji Tsuruta, Junko Fuji, Hiroko

Sakuramachi, Takashi Shimura, Fumio Watanabe, Asao Uchida, Tatsuo Endo   This and Ozawa's next entry in the series below, GAMBLER MONEY, were a return to the *ninkyo* variety of yakuza *eiga*. Fukasaku and Sato (director of the final GAMBLER COUNTERATTACK entry) were not particularly enamored of *ninkyo* yakuza stories and, if they had the choice, would opt for the more modern, *jitsuroku* (true document) type. The longer running time here is actually to the story's advantage as there is much more attention to character detail as well as a more realistic approach to passing time and story development. Takakura is a *hana fuda* card dealer for elder *oyabun* Takashi Shimura's clan who attacks boss Watanabe's gang HQ after several of his ruffians cause a melee at their gambling den. It is unusual to have a ferocious sword battle this early in a *ninkyo* film, but it is cut short when the police arrive to cart Takakura away to prison. While gone, Shimura decides to retire, splitting up the territory between Takakura's other senior comrades Oki and Wakayama (the latter actually acting as surrogate until Takakura is released). There is also an uneasy peace made with Watanabe. He immediately takes advantage of the situation, engineering obligations from Oki who, in a pinch, has asked his assistance. This does not sit well with uncompromising Wakayama, and the rift between the blood brothers worsens when Takakura finally gets out. Although it sticks in his craw, newly made boss Takakura agrees with Oki that it is better to try to co-exist with Watanabe. He bends over backwards to get along despite Watanabe's ever more devious

behavior. One standout sequence has Takakura volunteer to go to Watanabe's to do a pinkie-cutting apology routine despite Wakayama's vociferous protests. Watanabe reluctantly accepts this token and actually prevents one of his men from killing Takakura. However he does let his minions then beat Takakura to a pulp. Respected lone wolf pal Tsuruta helps Takakura home. Soon Oki demands that something be done about hothead Wakayama, and Takakura is half-prepared to kill his close friend.

Gambler Clan (#7)

But hyped-up Wakayama, brandishing a gun, accidentally shoots himself (!) and dies in Takakura's arms. Oki is the next to bite the dust with Watanabe doing the deed himself by sword. His deathbed scene is another tearful coming together with Takakura, patching up their differences as they both repeatedly call each other *"kyodai"* (brother). Takakura and

Tsuruta then wipe out Watanabe's stronghold with their swords. It is an especially well choreographed fight with some actual fencing depicted. This as opposed to the ease with which *ninkyo* heroes usually slash through the villainous ranks. Takakura and Watanabe's final prolonged duel is particularly well done with both protagonists evenly matched. Slightly wounded Takakura finishes off the evil boss while loyal friend Tsuruta is dying from numerous bullet and sword wounds. This installment emerges with probably the most pronounced homo-erotic subtext of any *ninkyo eiga,* the heroes repeatedly holding dying comrades in their arms while murmuring testaments of undying loyalty and friendship. All the while Takakura suffers the presence of devoted love interest Fuji. He seems almost resentful he has to deal with her, only at the climax finally making a concession as he treks to his revenge mission, draping his cloak around her shoulders when she follows him out into the snow. #7 of 10 films * * * 1/2

GAMBLER MONEY aka SATSUTABA BAKUTO aka NOTORIOUS GAMBLER 1970 93 min. Dir. Shigehiro Ozawa Scr. Kazuo Kasahara/ Masahiro Shimura Photo color 'scope: Kenji Tsukagoe Music: Toshiaki Tsushima w/ Koji Tsuruta, Minoru Oki, Hiroko Sakuramachi, Akiko Kudo, Asao Koike, Kyosuke Machida, Rinichi Yamamoto, Bin Amatsu, Asao Uchida, Yuriko Mishima #8 of 10 films

Gambler - Foreign Opposition (#9) aka Sympathy for the Underdog

GAMBLER – FOREIGN OPPOSITION aka BAKUTO – GAIJIN BUTAI aka **SYMPATHY FOR THE UNDERDOG** aka GAMBLERS IN OKINAWA aka YAKUZA COMBAT FORCES 1971 93 min. Dir. Kinji Fukasaku Scr. Fumio Konami/Kinji Fukasaku/Hiro Matsuda Photo color 'scope: Hanjiro Nakazawa Music: Takeo Watanabe w/ Koji Tsuruta, Noboru Ando, Tomisaburo Wakayama, Akiko Kudo, Tadao Nakamaru, Asao Uchida, Tsunehiko Watase, Rinichi Yamamoto, Kenji Imai, Asao Koike, Hideo Murota, Harumi Sone Tsuruta is banished by the mainland yakuza to Okinawa and ends up allied with Ando and young Watase going head-to-head with not only the local rival gang led by scarred Wakayama and one-armed psycho Imai, but American gangsters as well. Brutal, unsentimental, but with a subtle sense of humor (Tsuruta keeps his sunglasses on almost all the way through the picture – even in bed with his gal Kudo). The climax sees Tsuruta, Ando and what is left of their motley crew make a suicidal attack on big mainland boss Uchida when he arrives at the pier with his gangster army. A bit better than Fukasaku's other *jitsuroku* GAMBLER install-ment (CEREMONY OF DISBAND-ING) (see above). #9 of 10 films * * * 1/2

GAMBLER – COUNTERAT-TACK aka BAKUTO – KIRIKOMI TAI 1971 97 min. **DIR.** Junya Sato **SCR.** Junya Sato/Yoshihiro Ishimatsu **PHOTO COLOR 'SCOPE:** Masahiko Iimura **MUSIC:** Masanobu Higurashi w/ Koji Tsuruta, Tomisaburo Wakayama, Fumio Watanabe, Tetsuro Tanba, Seizaburo Kawazu, Akiko Kudo, Tsunehiko Watase, Takeo Chii, Hideo Murota, Hiroshi Kondo Director Sato brings his acidic nihil-ism, anti-captalist-excess sentiments and searingly downbeat perspective to climax the series with one of the most individualistic, unflinching de-pictions ever of a Japanese gangster. It is the saga of one man's unrepent-ant though ethical outlaw life. This is probably the film Tsuruta was com-plaining about when he claimed the newer yakuza films "have no heart." He had been discussing one of his roles without specifying the title (it was not mentioned in Paul Schrader's piece in the 1974 *Film Comment* where the story was repeated), and as-serted that it was completely against the grain of his character to shoot a policeman in the back. At the time I remember feeling sympathetic to his attitude. Then I saw this film, the picture he was undoubtedly referring

to. If there was one circumstance where his character would not only be justified, but morally required to shoot someone in the back, it would be at the climax of this final GAMBLER entry. Tanba, as the op-portunistic, cold-blooded, politically

Gambler - Counterattack (#10)

ambitious, nearly reptilian police inspector has set up the two gangs, manipulating them not out of some YOJINBO-ish moral twilight, but a murderous will to destroy those in the outlaw gangs, good or bad, and thus circumvent the justice system and the laws he is sworn to uphold. Tsuruta is lying, near death, in the driveway of the rival gang's mansion. He haas just ambushed Kawazu and his henchmen who had been forewarned through Tanba's machinations. Tanba had then ordered his policemen to open fire on the few remaining of Kawazu's men whom Tsuruta had missed. Surveying the scene of carnage as he breathes his last, Tsuruta tries to raise his head as Tanba greets him with a cynical smile. Tanba makes a wisecrack and it is the last straw. As Tanba turns, Tsuruta summons all of his strength and fires in between Tanba's shoulder blades. The shot freeze-frames. #10 and last of series * * * *

GAMBLER NUN aka AMADERA BAKUTO aka NUN AT THE CASINO 1971 85 min. **Dir.** Shinji Murayama **Scr.** Morimasa Owaku **Photo color 'scope:** Yoshio Nakajima **Music:** Toshiaki Tsushima w/ Yumiko Nogwa, Haruko Kato, Mari Shiraki, Hideko Aki, Masumi Tachibana, Yayoi Watanabe, Fumio Watanabe, Meicho Soganoya, Junzaburo Ban, Goro Ibuki, Toru Abe Toei blends their yakuza and nun-sploitation genres in this inventive, occasionally sleazy scenario (after all, what is a convent in a Japanese exploitation film without a bout of nude lesbian love-making?) Female gambler Nogawa, thrown into an emotional crossroads when her gam-

bling partner dad (Ban) is wounded then jailed after a knifefight with yakuza, enters the convent to become a Buddhist nun. However, she finds she cannot escape the secular world even inside a religious community as the convent's male temple official (Watanabe) develops a serious gambling problem which leads to his blackmail by Toru Abe's gang. This results in his suicide, something that causes a further chain of death and betrayal, with Nogawa and former beau Ibuki finally having to unsheath their knives and slaughter Abe's heartless mob. Absurdly ridiculous as only Toei exploitation could be but, consequently, never less than entertaining. * * 1/2

Gambler Nun

GAMBLER'S CODE – LOYALTY OFFERING aka BAKUTO JINGI – SAKAZUKI 1970 87 min. **Dir.** Kiyoshi Saeki **Scr.** Morimasa Owaku

PHOTO COLOR 'SCOPE: Umeo Masuda MUSIC: Toshiaki Tsushima w/ Bunta Sugawara, Tomisaburo Wakayama, Goro Ibuki, Akiko Kudo, Kanjuro Arashi, Kyosuke Machida, Kenji Ushio A fairly entertaining yarn told in somewhat broad strokes with Wakayama playing against type as a reformed-gambler-turned-Christian minister. Of course, before the tale is finished he is forced by the utterly nefarious, heinous villains to once again pick up a sword and join fellow anti-hero Sugawara in wiping out Evil. * * 1/2

GAMBLING CODE AND FEUDS aka JINGI TO KOSO 1977 90 min. DIR. Akinori Matsuo SCR. Koji Takada/ Hiro Matsuda PHOTO COLOR 'SCOPE: Tetsu Nakajima MUSIC: Hiroaki Tamamoto w/ Hiroki Matsukata, Atsuo Nakamura, Hiroyuki Nagato, Rumi Matsumoto, Joe Shishido, Kenichi Sakuragi, Asao Koike, Kunio Naito, Hiroshi Kondo, Katsu Shiga, Saburo Date
A bizarre tall tale with Matsukata a schizo lone wolf killer/yakuza hustler who is totally merciless to his enemies but is domesticated to the point he scrupulously helps his beloved, longsuffering wife run their tiny restaurant. One of the few later yakuza films helmed by director Matsuo, an esteemed and accomplished veteran of many yakuza *eiga* at Nikkatsu Studios all through the sixties. * * *

GAMBLING CODE OF JAPAN aka NIHON NO JINGI aka HONOR AND HUMANITY OF JAPAN 1977 106 min. DIR. Sadao Nakajima SCR. Sadao Nakajima/ Fumio Konami/ Hiro Matsuda PHOTO COLOR 'SCOPE:

Umeo Masuda MUSIC: Hachiro Aoyama w/ Bunta Sugawara, Shinichi "Sonny" Chiba, Koji Tsuruta, Mariko Okada, Frankie Sakai, Susumu Fujita, Eiji Okada Rinichi Yamamoto, Takeo Chii, Takuzo Kawatani, Mikio Narita, Kei Sato, Hiroshi Nawa, Renji Ishibashi, Kyosuke Machida
The crazy story of a powerful Japanese gang headed by meth-addicted Sugawara. Loads of violence, ironic confrontations and juxtapositions as well as the usual perversion pepper the narrative. Comic actor Sakai does an unusual dramatic turn as Tsuruta's right-hand man who looks after Tsuruta's little boy. Sakai also happens to be in love with Tsuruta's wife Okada. Midway through, sickened by the machinations of the gang and his unrequited love, he goes bonkers, firing on folks from a second story window until brought down by the police. Another intriguing development is at the climax when Chiba is so angered by Sugawara's callous, insulting treatment, he puts out a contract on him. Only to have the contrite Sugawara humbly apologize at a restaurant the next evening. Moments later the hired killer bursts in and does his deed, despite the regretful Chiba trying to now stop him. One of director Nakajima's best films. * * * 1/2

GAMBLING DEN aka BAKUCHIUCHI series:

GAMBLING DEN aka BAKU-CHIUCHI 1967 90 min. DIR. Shigehiro Ozawa SCR. Akira Murao/ Koji Takada/Shigehiro Ozawa PHOTO COLOR 'SCOPE: Juhei Suzuki MUSIC: Toshiaki Tsushima w/ Koji Tsuruta, Tomisaburo Wakayama,

Kyosuke Machida, Seizaburo Kawazu, Asao Koike, Hiromi Fujiyama, Shingo Yamashiro, Hiroko Sakuramachi, Masumi Tachibana, Hiroshi Nawa

A bit more natural *ninkyo* yakuza piece with a decided emphasis on a seedy milieu. Tsuruta is a respected dealer occasionally working for his gang boss father along with cohorts Machida and Yamashiro. Unscrupulous boss Kawazu and right-hand man Wakayama make their presence known by first taking over the local brothel where Yamashiro's woman is the anxiety-ridden madam. She commits suicide shortly after the takeover. Courtesans Sakuramachi and Tachibana, who are friends of Tsuruta and Machida. get into trouble when they sneak out to go to her wake. Things gradually escalate with sadistic Wakayama throwing his weight around, trying to provoke cool, calm Tsuruta. A nice touch has Machida and Yamashiro get caught cheating at cards by Wakayama in Kawazu's casino, instigating pinkie finger-cutting by Tsuruta to redeem them back from captivity. Tsuruta is appalled because his comrades have helped to undermine their gang's credibility as honorable yakuza. He ends up returning to Kawazu's gambling den and winning big, nearly breaking the bank. While still playing, he gives some money to Machida and instructs him to go to ransom Sakuramachi and Tachibana by buying up their contracts/debts. However, Wakayama refuses to let them go, throwing the money in Machida's face. Machida goes ballistic, drawing his knife but is killed before he can do much. Yamashiro goes for Tsuruta but meanwhile the two women are spirited away, sold

to a dealer who hurries them onto a train never to return. Tsuruta belatedly arrives, kills Wakayama and his men, then returns to the casino to kill Kawazu. Rival card dealer and friend Koike, obligated to his boss, tries to defend Kawazu as the melee spills

Gambling Den (#1)

out into the nocturnal landscape. Tsuruta reluctantly ends up killing Koike as well as villain Kawazu. Downbeat, focused and a much more realistic *ninkyo* yakuza picture than usual. Ozawa approaches the story with taste and restraint, entering into Gosha and Yamashita territory. One of his best films as director. #1 of 10 films * * * 1/2

GAMBLING DEN – ONE LONE DRAGON aka BAKUCHIUCHI – IPPIKI RYU 1967 **DIR.** Shigehiro Ozawa **SCR.** Shigehiro Ozawa/ Koji Takada **PHOTO COLOR 'SCOPE:** Motoya Washio **MUSIC:** Toshiaki Tsushima **w/** Koji Tsuruta, Tetsuro Tanba, Kyosuke Machida, Kayo Matsuo, Bin Amatsu, Tatsuo Endo, Shingo Yamashiro, Hosei Komatsu, Takehiro Nakamura One of the looniest, most overtly sentimental *ninkyo eiga* you are ever likely to see. Unbelievably, despite its obvious flaws, it is quite entertaining, mostly due to the extremely atypical story. Tsuruta is a respected yakuza tattoo artist working with comrades Machida and Yamashiro. His former boss, who also just happens to be the master who had tattooed the magnificent dragon on Tsuruta's back, is now a dissolute, bitter drunk living with his son-in-law and sickly grandson. His daughter, the boy's mom, is indentured at the brothel run by boss Nakamura and daughter Matsuo. They are basically as decent as you can be and still run a whorehouse. However, Nakamura's two-faced second-in-command Amatsu is as dastardly sadistic and underhanded as Toei villains come. He hates Tsuruta with a passion and throwing roadblocks in his way to prevent him helping the mother from

seeing her ailing child. Matsuo, who is falling in love with Tsuruta because of his concern for others, allows the woman out to see the boy on the condition she returns by midnight. Amatsu and his evil henchmen kidnap her and sell her to boss Tanba's

Gambling Den - One Lone Dragon (#2)

gang in a remote village, all the while blaming her disappearance on Tsuruta and Machida, Tsuruta goes to retrieve her, explaining the situation to even-handed Tanba, offering to let Tanba cut off his arm as proof of his sincerity. Tanba pretends to take him up on the proposition to see if Tsuruta is really serious, then stops at the last second when convinced. He tears up the woman's contract and hands her over to Tsuruta. Machida goes down to the quay early on the morning they are due to return, lured by Amatsu's bogus message. Amatsu and men are waiting for him in the mist. A brief knife fight ensues in one of the film's best and only action sequences. Machida valiantly holds his own but is soon too ventilated by their blades to continue. Amatsu delivers the final fatal blow, and Machida's corpse goes into the bay. When Tsuruta and the woman return that afternoon, it looks like they are in for the same since Amatsu and cronies are waiting. However, Tanba appears off the next boat with several of his *kobun*, arriving to act as one of the judges on a tattoo competition. Foiled, Amatsu and hooligans skulk away. Alarmed at Machida's disappearance, Tsuruta has fellow comrades drag the bay. Matsuo is with him and faints when they find Machida's corpse. Next Amatsu sends two of his killers to waylay Tsuruta on his way to the tattoo competition. It turns out that he feels Tsuruta is a sure winner, and he knows his own elaborate tattoo won't stand a chance if Tsuruta shows up. It looks like Amatsu is a shoo-in until Tsuruta stumbles in, bloody and disoriented, but still able to showcase his full body art. Already favorably disposed to Tsuruta, bosses Tanba, Nakamura,

et. al. give the first prize to him. Amatsu feels supremely snubbed and explodes when boss Nakamura kicks him out of the gang for his nefarious shenanigans. Amatsu and Tsuruta then duel with knives before the rapt attention of an audience of gang members and townspeople while a corny song about yakuza chivalry sung by Tsuruta plays on the soundtrack. The fight spills out onto the street, then into a canal where Amatsu grabs Matsuo as a hostage. Tsuruta distracts him by beaning him with a rock. Matsuo escapes, and Tsuruta rushes in to plunge his blade home. Everyone is jubilant at our selfless hero's victory. Extremely old-fashioned in tone without even the moderate restraint of some of director Ozawa's other *ninkyo* films, let alone more subtle masters like Yamashita, Kato and Gosha. Nevertheless, it is a fascinating peek into what amounts to a bizarrely arcane alternate universe, especially for any Western viewer. #2 of 10 films * * 1/2

GAMBLING DEN – SHOWDOWN OF INVULNERABILITY aka BAKUCHIUCHI – FUJIMI NO SHOBU 1967 89 min. DIR. Shigehiro Ozawa SCR. Shigehiro Ozawa/Koji Takada PHOTO COLOR 'SCOPE: Nagaki Yamagishi MUSIC: ChumeiWatanabe w/ Koji Tsuruta, Tomisaburo Wakayama, Kyosuke Machida, Kenjiro Ishiyama, Michiyo Kogure, Masumi Tachibana, Hosei Komatsu, Shingo Yamashiro, Hiromi Fujiyama Wakayama is the villainous leader of a clan of construction workers/gamblers. He constantly vies with decent *oyabun* Ishiyama, Ishiyama's loyal second Tsuruta, and their gang for jobs. He quite often wins out since he also finagles all kinds of graft, etc., something old-fashioned Ishiyama won't do. Wakayama also organizes the gambling for all workers in the area. There is actually quite a bit more gambling in this tale than in many other yakuza gambler films. Highlighted is a strange, complicated dice game that is the catalyst/means of showdown between Wakayama and Ishiyama, then Wakayama and Tsuruta. Entertaining, but also has its histrionic moments, something that keeps the film from excellence. Ozawa, one of Toei's most prodigious directors, was an unpretentious and a skillful storyteller. But he also seemed occasionally less willing to rein in actors or trim a scene to achieve maximum effectiveness. These traits usually keep his always enjoyable films from attaining the heights of excellence often reached by his close colleagues, Yamashita and Kato. Heady heights reached, in fact, on the very next entry in the series. #3 of 10 films   * * *

GAMBLING DEN – GAMBLING BOSS aka BAKUCHIUCHI – SO-CHO TOBAKU aka THE GREAT CASINO aka BIG-TIME GAMBLING BOSS aka PRESIDENTIAL GAMBLING 1968 95 min. **DIR.** Kosaku Yamashita **SCR.** Kazuo Kasahara **PHOTO COLOR 'SCOPE:** Nagaki Yamagishi **MUSIC:** Toshiaki Tsushima   **W/** Koji Tsuruta, Tomisaburo Wakayama, Junko Fuji, Nobuo Kaneko, Hiroshi Nawa, Hiroko Sakuramachi, Shinichiro Mikami, Harumi Sone, Yoichi Numata, Ryosuke Kagawa According to most Japanese and American critics alike, this is one of the preeminent classics of *ninkyo* yakuza cinema. Director Yamashita purposely subverts audience expectations while still satisfying them, somehow still managing to stay just this side of genre conventions. Nevertheless, the film is slightly overrated. Overrated is not the best term. How can an excellent film be overrated? It can't. But there can be other yakuza films just as fine that are underrated. What is worse, excellent films in the genre that have been, and still are being, ignored. GAMBLING BOSS's script and direction are a symbiotic marriage of deceptive simplicity. Tsuruta and Wakayama belong to the same clan and are very close blood brothers. When their *oyabun* succumbs to a heart attack and is left a mute, bedridden and dying man, the machinations begin to subvert his choice of successor. Tsuruta, the first choice, declines, and Wakayama, just out of prison, is passed over as a result of efforts by a venal, outside manipulator. A "puppet" *oyabun* (Nawa) ends up being chosen. Tsuruta does his best to go along with something that clearly goes against his intuition and principles. Wakayama, however, publicly resists. Before long it is open warfare, the *oyabun* stabbed by Wakayama but only wounded. The manipulator (Kaneko) has one of his henchmen sneak in to finish off the recuperating boss. Since there are no witnesses to this, Wakayama is blamed for his death. Kaneko publicly accuses Tsuruta of shielding a murderer and demands a display of clan loyalty. Tsuruta kills Wakayama, who cannot believe that he is being betrayed by his best friend. Tsuruta then returns to clan HQ to kill Kaneko who demanded such a

Gambling Den (#4) - Gambling Boss aka Big Time Gambling Boss

warped test of loyalty. The wildly violent mise-en-scene usually in evidence in Toei's yakuza pictures is toned-down here, and part of the problem with this otherwise excellent film is having to sit through quite a few "talking heads" scenes. #4 of 10 films * * * 1/2

GAMBLING DEN KILLING aka BAKUCHIUCHI NAGURIKOMI aka THE RAID 1968 **DIR.** Shigehiro Ozawa **SCR.** Kazuo Kasahara **PHOTO COLOR 'SCOPE:** Shigeru Akatsuka **MUSIC:** Toshiaki Tsushima **w/** Koji Tsuruta, Daisuke Kato, Kayo Matsuo, Kenjiro Ishiyama, Hiroshi Nawa, Ryuichi Tamagawa, Tatsuo Endo, Rinichi Yamamoto, Kyosuke Machida, Seizaburo Kawazu #5 of 10 films

GAMBLING DEN'S MASTER CLAN aka IKKA SAMA BAKU-CHI aka THE FAKE GAME 1968 92 min. **DIR.** Shigehiro Ozawa **SCR.** Akira Murao/ Koji Takada **PHOTO COLOR 'SCOPE:** Nagaki Yamagishi **MUSIC:** Shunsuke Kikuchi **w/** Koji Tsuruta, Tomisaburo Wakayama, Tamao Nakamura, Tatsuo Endo, Bin Amatsu, Masumi Tachibana, Kichijiro Ueda, Takuzo Kawatani This saga has the most gambling scenes of any yakuza film. Tsuruta spends almost the entire story trying to outwit gambling hall owner Amatsu and his master gambler/sharpie Wakayama at *hana fuda* (flower cards). Even without subtitles, the tale keeps attention riveted to the screen. Most of the credit goes to the exciting, fairly restrained performances of Tsuruta and Wakayama, but Ozawa's direction and Murao/Takada's script also deserve mention. Tatsuo Endo,

virtually always a Toei villain, gets a rare chance to play a good guy. As Tsuruta's mischievious but loyal sidekick, he nevertheless gets killed. #6 of 10 films * * * 1/2

Gambling Den's Master Clan (#6)

GAMBLING DEN ASSASSINS aka HISSATSU BAKUCHIUCHI aka A GAMBLER'S PLACE TO DIE 1969 93 min. **DIR.** Kiyoshi Saeki **SCR.** Goro Tanada **PHOTO COLOR 'SCOPE:** Shigeru Akatsuka **MUSIC:** Masanobu Higurashi **w/** Koji Tsuruta, Isamu Nagato, Yuko Hama, Shogo Shimada, Rinichi Yamamoto, Tatsuo Endo, Kinzo Shin A serious yakuza gambling saga with a consistent tone, unafflicted by the jarring humor that frequently intrudes in the first half of too many Toei *ninkyo eiga*. However, the tale of wandering *hana fuda* dealer Tsuruta and impetuous sidekick Yamamoto settling in with benevolent elder boss Shimada's clan is inordinately talky.

Gambling Den Assassins (#7)

The conflict that occurs is much more realistic than most formula *ninkyo* programmers, detailing the rivalry that erupts when Tsuruta realizes unscrupulous Endo's gang is perpetually fleecing a retired businessman and the man's wife, Hama, in horse race action and card games. Tsuruta and Yamamoto tactfully try to put a stop to it, to no avail. Eventually the man dies, and wife Hama is shanghaied into prostitution by Endo in lieu of the deceased's unpaid debt. Tsuruta plays a game with Endo's likable crooked dealer, the always charismatic Nagato, to decide her freedom. Nagato purposely does not cheat, much to Endo's displeasure, and Tsuruta wins Hama's release. This causes obligated Nagato more grief when Endo calls him to task and forces him into killing Tsuruta's benefactor, boss Shimada. Tsuruta then goes on the requisite rampage, wiping out Endo and gang as well as resigned-to-his-fate rival comrade

Nagato. If only the film was not so rife with long patches of expository dialogue, director Saeki could have spun a much more moving, exciting tale. #7 of 10 films   * * *

GAMBLING DEN – DRIFTER aka BAKUCHIUCHI – NAGAREMONO aka THE DRIFTING GAMBLER 1970 100 min. **DIR.** Kosaku Yamashita **SCR.** Motohiro Torii/Masanora Shimura **PHOTO COLOR 'SCOPE:** Juhei Suzuki **MUSIC:** Takeo Watanabe **w/** Koji Tsuruta, Junko Fuji, Tomisaburo Wakayama, Kyosuke Machida, Asao Uchida, Michitaro Mizushima, Bin Amatsu, Sanae Kitabayashi, Fujio Suga, Ryuji Kita

Gambling Den - Drifter (#8)

Wandering Tsuruta tries to find the daughter (Fuji) of an elder comrade. He not only discovers her working as a geisha in a snowy northern town, but also his blood brother Mizushima in her care. Tsuruta runs into Amatsu, too, a former blood brother who betrayed his clan by cowardly running from a gangfight five years earlier, now a powerful boss. This is the same fight that left their old boss mortally stabbed, Mizushima embittered and scarred and Tsuruta a drifter. Things heat up as Tsuruta and pal Wakayama are faced with having to prevent Amatsu from selling Kitabayashi, widow of a despondent gambler, to a sleazy rich man. Old pals Mizushima and Machida, conflicted by loyalty to evil Amatsu, finally decide to go against him and are killed for their decision. The murder of benevolent boss Uchida is the final straw, and Tsuruta and Wakayama wipe out Amatsu's stronghold in a bloody sword battle. Wounded, they wistfully part company afterwards. But as Tsuruta saunters away alone down the moonlit beach we see he is probably mortally injured. Fuji, his sweetheart who he has stood up at dinner, has a psychic flash of her favorite comb breaking against a blood red background. The sudden symbolic image is inexplicably moving and serves only to make the viewer wish that once again a little more time was spent on the love back story. #8 of 10 films * * * 1/2

GAMBLING DEN – A LIFE OF CARDS aka BAKUCHIUCHI – INOCHI FUDA aka GAMBLER'S LAST GAMBLE 1971 DIR. Kosaku Yamashita SCR. Kazuo Kasahara PHOTO COLOR 'SCOPE: Sadatsugu Yoshida MUSIC: Chuji Kinoshita w/ Koji Tsuruta, Tomisaburo Wakayama, Michiyo Yasuda, Tsunehiko Watase, Michitaro Mizushima, Asao Uchida, Tatsuo Endo, Bin Amatsu, Eisei Amamoto, Takuzo Kawatani   This represents

something of a rarity as one of the few very romantic (as in a love story) *ninkyo* yakuza *eiga*. Quite often the main protagonist – hero or anti-hero – has a romantic attachment with a woman that, because of conflicting obligations and duty, can never be fulfilled.

Gambling Den - A Life of Cards (#9)

However, LIFE OF CARDS starts with Tsuruta and Yasuda already embroiled in a passionate love affair on the snowy northern coast. Tsuruta is gone for quite a while in prison and, while he is away, Yasuda is persuad-ed to marry Tsuruta's *oyabun* Mizushima. Soon Mizushima is murdered by rival Amatsu's hired gun. One of Toho Studios' preeminent villain actors, Eisei Amamoto, is on hand as the degenerate, demonic killer. Yasuda takes over the clan aided by loyal second Wakayama. When Tsuruta returns, he acts as Yasuda's acting *oyabun* . But, to the unspoken frustration of both, they curtail their love affair. To complicate matters, Yasuda's sister is Amatsu's woman, and this ends up compromising Yasuda in the eyes of some of her men. At the climax, Tsuruta avenges Mizushima and Wakayama's deaths when Amatsu's gang attacks their HQ. But Yasuda is shot in the process while trying to protect Tsuruta. As he props up her dying form with one arm and slashes away at bad guys with his sword, his clan's meeting room/altar becomes a surreal interior landscape. He and Yasuda stumble down a white strip of cloth separating two pools of blood while the remaining bad guys (some of whom he has already killed) attack from all sides. Before long, they are all covered in the red stuff. Abruptly, Tsuruta sees the real, empty room. Suddenly overcome with the spiraling-out-of-control-cycle of vengeance, he lashes out with his blade, cracking the *sakazuki* cups on the altar. #9 of 10 films * * * 1/2

TRUE ACCOUNT OF A GAM-BLING DEN aka BAKUCHIUCHI GAIDEN 1972 **Dir.** Kosaku Yamashita **Scr.** Tatsuo Nogami **Photo color 'scope:** Shin Furuya **Music:** Chuji Kinoshita w/ Koji Tsuruta, Tomisaburo Wakayama, Ken Takakura, Hiroki Matsukata, Bunta Sugawara, Ryutaro Tatsumi, Goro Ibuki, Nobuo Kaneko, Junko Matsuhei, Tomiko Ishii, Asao Uchida, Takuzo Kawatani   A sublime final entry in the series with Tsuruta and Wakayama heading up rival clans. Totally warped-in-mind-and-crippled-in-body Matsukata, Wakayama's second-in-command, keeps engineering situations that will pit the two clans against each other. Each time, Tsuruta and Wakayama manage to

work things out. Finally, the paranoid Matsukata convinces Wakayama that Tsuruta and Wakayama's mutual mentor/father figure, the retired *oyabun* Tatsumi, is against them. He then reveals to Wakayama that he has just had Tatsumi assassinated.

True Account of a Gambling Den (#10)

SinceSugawara, Takakura and Ibuki have also just been murdered by Matsukata's pals, Tsuruta comes by himself to fight Wakayama. He ends up killing both Matsukata and Wakayama in a devastating climax. #10 and last of series   * * * 1/2

GAMBLING DEN HEIST aka PLUNDERING THE SOURCE OF CAPITAL aka SHIKINGEN GO-DATSU 1975 92 min. **DIR.** Kinji Fukasaku **SCR.** Koji Takada **PHOTO COLOR 'SCOPE:** Shigeru Akatsuka **MUSIC:** Toshiaki Tsushima
w/ Kinya Kitaoji, Tatsuo Umemiya, Kiwako Taichi, Yayoi Watanabe, Hiroki Matsukata, Takuzo Kawatani, Toru Abe, Hideo Murota, Hiroshi Nawa, Kenji Imai, Yoko Koizumi, Bin Amatsu, Shingo Yamashiro
Dapper, self-obsessed Kitaoji decides to betray boss Abe by recruiting the two bumbling, yet capable lone wolf ne'er-do-wells he occasionally robs banks with (Kawatani and Murota) to help heist his gang's huge gambling take. Abe does not initially suspect Kitaoji but sicks his maddog killer Imai on the trail to find the culprit. He also hires suave, buffoonish private eye Umemiya, who ironically turns out to be a doggedly intrepid, intuitive detective. There are a lot of *de rigeur* yet still nicely-executed twists, and director Fukasaku balances the bloody violence and sudden death with some pungent humor that does not resort to silliness. Most of the characters are sharply drawn, although the female roles – Taichi as Kitaoji's submissive, traditional-minded girl and Watanabe as Umemi-ya's cherished, airheaded bimbo – could have been more developed.

Gambling Den Heist

There is a nice bit at the denouement when Kitaoji's one act of kindness from earlier in the film pays off un-expectedly, enabling him to get away scot-free at the airport. * * *

GAMES aka YUGI series

GAMES OF MAXIMUM RISK aka MOTTOMO KIKEN NA YUGI aka MOST DANGEROUS GAME 1978 89 min. **DIR.** Toru Murakawa **SCR.** Shuichi Nagahara **PHOTO COLOR 'SCOPE:** Seizo Norimoto **MUSIC:** Yuji Ono   w/ Yusaku Matsuda, Keiko Tasaka, Asao Uchida, Ichiro Araki, Daigo Kusano, Hiroshi Nawa
Another lonely hitman series (see the Nikkatsu Studios section for the majority of these), this time with the late Matsuda, an actor who enjoyed tremendous popularity during the late 1970s/early 1980s, and again in the 1990s. He seems to be a part of the

Games of Maximum Risk (#1)

same phenomenon that practically
deifies deceased movie stars in Japan
(especially if they are male like Raizo
Ichikawa, Yujiro Ishihara, Keiichiro
Akagi, Shintaro Katsu etc.,). Nevertheless, it is a disappointment that
this is not better. Low key, low budget
and a depressingly dismal, shallow
account of eccentric, counterculture
lone wolf Matsuda, who does hits and
troubleshooting for various corporations and gangs. He is hired by
corporate honcho Uchida to kidnap
back a bigwig who is being held for
ransom by the mob. He begins the
assignment by abducting yakuza
Nawa's gal Tasaka and imprison-
ing her in his apartment. He then
strikes in a nocturnal raid, rescuing
the bigshot. Unfortunately, the man
is killed in the ensuing bloodbath,
and Matsuda is so seriously wounded
he barely makes it back to his pad.
Miraculously, Tasaka falls in love
with him and tries to nurse him back

to health, only to receive his sullen petulance and drunken abuse as
thanks. Matsuda attempts to patch
things up with employer Uchida but
is now in trouble with both sides.
Uchida, using corrupt cop Araki,
shakes Matsuda down to assassinate
a mob boss. Matsuda acquiesces but
as soon as he has shot the boss from
a building rooftop, squads of police
snipers open fire on him from higher
buildings. He narrowly escapes death.
Subsequently, Araki and goons snatch
Tasaka from Matsuda's place mere
seconds before he returns. An absurd
chase follows where Matsuda actually keeps up with their car on foot
(!) for scores of blocks until the road
dead ends at the harbor. You really
need to suspend your disbelief here
since not only have we been led to
believe Matsuda's ambivalent about
Tasaka, but we have also seen no
evidence he could possibly have such
superhuman capabilities. He ends up
triumphant in a shootout with Araki
and cohorts, kisses Tasaka goodbye,
then goes off to massacre Uchida and
another elderly mob boss. Although
director Murakawa is obviously
going for minimalism, too often we
get shallowness instead of a judiciously economic narrative. Character
development is nonexistent, despite
Matsuda's charismatic abilities. Also
the same kind of jazz rock fusion that
nearly ruined many of Lalo Schifrin
and Dave Grusin's otherwise good
1970s American crime film scores
goes way overboard here, in several
places distracting rather than punctuating.   #1 of 3 films   * * 1/2

KILLER'S GAMES aka SATSU-
JIN YUGI 1978 92 min. DIR. Toru
Murakawa SCR. Koji Harima/

Susumu Saji PHOTO COLOR 'SCOPE:
Seizo Norimoto **Music:** Yuji Ono
w/ Yusaku Matsuda, Kei Sato, Yutaka
Nakajima, Kojiro Kusanagi   #2 of 3
films

EXECUTION GAMES aka
SHOKEI YUGI 1979 100 min.
DIR. Toru Murakawa SCR. Shoichi
Maruyama PHOTO COLOR 'SCOPE:
Seizo Norimoto MUSIC: Yuji Ono
w/ Yusaku Matsuda, Yoshiro Aoki,
Kei Sato, RiRie, Aiko Morishita
#3 and final in series

GANG aka GYANGU series

**FLOWERS, THE STORM AND
THE GANG** aka HANA TO AR-
ASHI TO GYANGU 1961 83 min.
DIR. Teruo Ishii SCR. Susumu Saji
PHOTO B&W 'SCOPE: Ichiro
Hoshijima MUSIC: Keitaro Miho
w/ Ken Takakura, Koji Tsuruta,
Shinjiro Ebara, Mitsue Komiya,
Harumi Sone, Mamoru Ogawa,
Takamaru Sasaki, Nijiko Kiyokawa,
Rinichi Yamamoto   Basically
a heist film, as were several of the
other early entries in this series. Ishii
uses much seemingly "rat pack"
imagery in the *mise en scene*, as well
as too much tension-diffusing humor.
At times, he seems to be riffing on
the original OCEAN'S 11 as well
as more serious American pictures
like THE KILLING and ASPHALT
JUNGLE. Not too much yakuza-type
imagery appears until much later in
the series. #1 of 12 films   * * 1/2

*Japanese DVD art for **Flowers, The
Storm and The Gang** (#1)*

**LOVE, THE SUN AND THE
GANG** aka KOI TO TAIYO TO
GYANGU aka ALL RASCALS
1962 87 min. DIR. Teruo Ishii SCR.
Teruo Ishii /Susumu Saji PHOTO
B&W 'SCOPE: Yoshikazu (Giichi)
Yamazawa MUSIC: Masao Yagi
w/ Ken Takakura, Tetsuro Tanba,
Mitsue Komiya, Shinjiro Ebara,
Harumi Sone, Shinichi "Sonny"
Chiba, Nijiko Kiyokawa, Yoko
Mihara, Masao Mishima, Chiyoko
Honma   Takakura, Tanba and
mother-daughter duo Kiyokawa
and Komiya plan to knock over a
gambling den owned by Chinese
mobsters. They get together a crew
made up of several hard luck lone
wolves, among them untrustworthy
mechanic Ebara and backstabbing
hood Sone. There is a nice opening
scene under the titles where Takakura
rescues Komiya from the casino in
question, then engages in a running

gunfight through streets and back alleys with their pursuers. After that it is pretty talky until the midway point, although the conversations occur in some atmospheric nightclubs. There is also one sequence of Tanba and lover Mihara bandying about in a playground that is shot with such a relentlessly-in-motion camera it gradually becomes so disorienting it induces vertigo in the viewer. The heist is imaginatively staged but curiously lacking in suspense, perhaps because the tone from the outset has been too tongue-in-cheek. However, there is a nice sequence where Ebara dodges his partners, catches up to Mihara who has one of the money bags in a makeup case and tries to con it out of her possesion. This leads into a spiralling out-of-control greed scenario as Sone backtracks, finds them and helps Ebara corner her in a taxi. All the while they are being tracked unobserved by Tanba and Takakura in a Jaguar. Clever Mihara holds her own until they are then caught in a fight with another gang led by Mishima that is bent on grabbing the loot. A gunfight erupts, and Sone and Mishima bite the dust. Tanba, Takakura, Ebara and Mihara escape. Simultaneously, Kiyokawa and Komiya traveling separately are stopped and captured when some intrepid cops spot numerous bullet-holes in their car's chassis. The gang luckily makes it to the beach cabin hideout set up by black leather-clad helicopter pilot Chiba. His blind sister has tagged along, unaware of the illegal shenanigans. The next morning Chiba and sis hike over the hills to warm up the 'copter engine.

Love, The Sun and The Gang (#2)

Regrettably, as soon as they have left, a huge contingent of gangsters stage a raid on the secluded cove. Takakura, Tanba et.al. hold them off, but the odds are against them. Hearing the gunshots, Chiba decides to take off with the rest of the loot. But his blind sister, thinking the bag of money is yet another bunch of flyers she usually helps her brother drop, inadvertently tosses the money out at high altitude, scattering it over the ocean. This is a bit of an improvement over the initial film. It is quite enjoyable, with many small pleasures, but ultimately does not add up to much, perhaps because the narrative seems somewhat lazily strung together. However, as with many of Ishii's pictures, individual *tour-de-force* setpieces linger pleasantly in the memory. #2 of 11 films * * *

GANG VS. GANG aka GYANGU TAI GYANGU 1962 88 min. **DIR./ SCR.** Teruo Ishii **PHOTO B&W 'SCOPE:** Yoshikazu (Giichi) Yamazawa **MUSIC:** Shunsuke Kikuchi **w/** Koji Tsuruta, Tetsuro Tanba, Tatsuo Umemiya, Hideo Taka, Ko Nishimura, Yoshiko Mita, Masahiko Naruse, Koji Mitsui, Harumi Sone, Kazuko Matsuo After serving time for a comrade,

Tsuruta is wounded in a driveby as soon as he gets out of prison. His *oyabun* has capitulated to such craven interests as drug dealing and wholesale murder and does not think Tsuruta will go along. Tsuruta confronts his boss at gang HQ, wounding him in the arm. Immediately after Tsuruta splits, glib opportunist underboss Tanba finishes off the injured leader. In no time, Tanba steps up heroin production, floods the nightclub districts, and an epidemic of addiction mushrooms. Tsuruta is enlisted by another boss and young proteges, Tatsuo Umemiya and Yoshiko Mita, to foil the drug traffic. Disguised as propane gas deliverymen, they steal the gang's dummy, dope-filled propane tank only to have Tanba and cronies roar after them in hot pursuit. A pitched gun battle erupts on a winding mountain road. Tsuruta and comrades roll real gas tanks off the back of the truck, an action that eventually causes Tanba's car to explode in a ball of flame. Severely wounded, Tsuruta leaves his dead chums and is picked up in a car by young Mita. Not wishing to burden her with his corpse, the dying Tsuruta tries to jump out. Distracted, Mita grabs for him which sends the car over the cliff. Down on the rocky ledge below, the two attempt to crawl to each other but expire mere inches before their fingertips can touch. Decidedly more bleak in tone than the earlier two films in the series, this has a noirish fatalism enhanced by a strong, downbeat ending. Unfortunately, nothing that earthshaking happens through most of the movie. The scenes of addicts in turmoil are evocative, but director Ishii created stronger similar tableaus in his earlier crime sleaze epics at Shintoho

Studios in the late fifties (see GIRLS WITHOUT RETURN TICKETS). #3 of 11 films   * * 1/2

Gang vs. Gang (#3)

GANG VS. G-MEN aka GYANGU TAI G-MEN 1962 83 min. **DIR.** Kinji Fukasaku **SCR.** Sakae (Shigeru?) Hokijima **PHOTO COLOR 'SCOPE:** Yoshikazu (Giichi) Yamazawa **MUSIC:** Tomikazu Kawabe **w/** Koji Tsuruta, Tetsuro Tanba, Yoshiko Sakuma, Yoshi Kato, Shinichi "Sonny" Chiba, Tatsuo Umemiya, Harumi Sone, Hideo Sunazuka, Tamaki Sawa   Tsuruta is a former yakuza now running a garage with his wife (Sakuma) and younger brother (Chiba). He is approached by police detectives to do undercover work to expose villain Tanba's gang. He ends up drafting several of his shady lone wolf buddies to help. Most perish in the ensuing carnage. Despite Fukasaku trying to inject some of the brutal realism later to be found in his BATTLES WITHOUT HONOR... series this ends up being pretty much

Gang vs. G-Men (#4)

standard programmer material. #4 of
11 films   * * 1/2

Underworld Boss - Eleven Gangsters (#5)

**UNDERWORLD BOSS – ELEVEN
GANGSTERS** aka ANKOKU GAI
NO KAOYAKU – JUICHININ NO
GYANGU aka ELEVEN GANG-
STERS 1963 91 min. DIR. /SCR.
Teruo Ishii PHOTO COLOR 'SCOPE:
Shoe Nishikawa MUSIC: Masao
Yagi   w/ Koji Tsuruta, Naoki
Sugiura, Ken Takakura, Yoko
Mihara, Shinjiro Ebara, Tetsuro
Tanba, Michiyo Kogure, Kyosuke
Machida, Reiko Hitomi, Toru Abe,
Joji Ai   Tsuruta and Sugiura recruit
truck driver Takakura and other lone
wolf hoods to go after a company
payroll. In the climactic nocturnal
car chase involving Toru Abe's rival
mob, there is an accident on a rural
road, and the haul nearly burns in
the wreckage. Sugiura manages to
salvage it but, along with Tsuruta and
the rest of both gangs, is killed in the
fierce gun battle Long on style and

once again riffing on the OCEANS
11 fashion sense, this starts out a bit
talky, but it slowly and steadily builds
into a more than competent heist
picture. There is much less humor and
more suspense than Ishii's first two
films in the series. The middle third,
though short on action, is drenched
in the noirish atmosphere of rainsoaked streets and cozy apartments
where love is made and schemes
are hatched. Yet another fresh and
welcome change is the nearly equal
part the gangsters' women have to
play in the robbery. The couples' relationships are keenly observed and
more complex than one usually finds
in this kind of picture. Tanba and
Kogure are particularly good as the
shady, decadent rich pair that Tsuruta
convinces to fund the operation, and
seem to have stepped right out of a
Jean-Pierre Melville movie. #5 of
11 films   * * *

**GANG VS. G-MEN – SAFE-
CRACKER GANG** aka GYANGU
TAI G-MEN – SHUDAN KINKO
YABURI 1963 86 min. DIR. Teruo
Ishii SCR. Akira Murao/Teruo Ishii
PHOTO COLOR 'SCOPE: Yoshikazu
(Giichi) Yamazawa MUSIC: Masao
Yagi   w/ Koji Tsuruta, Tetsuro
Tanba, Naoki Sugiura, Yoshiko
Sakuma, Shinjiro Ebara, Haruo
Tanaka, Harumi Sone, Tatsuo
Umemiya, Akemi Tsukushi, Yoshi
Kato   A claustrophobic, familiar
tale of an undercover cop (Tsuruta)
infiltrating a gang of safecrackers led
by ruthless Sugiura. Nevertheless,
despite the cliches, this admirably
strays from old-fashioned potboiler
territory into the realm of Melville,
Don Siegel and Sam Fuller. Ishii's
compositions via cinematograher

Yamazawa's framing are concise and dynamic, with enough close-ups to truly do justice to the fine array of performances, especially Tanba, a tubercular safe expert who ends up helping Tsuruta. Sakuma is also fine as the one female of the group, a lock expert who falls for Tsuruta and saves his life at the climax before being poignantly led away to jail. There are also some surprising scenes such as when Tsuruta must stand idly by to keep his cover while his undercover cop contact is murdered before his very eyes.   #6 of 11 films * * *

Gang vs. G-Men - Safecracker Gang (#6)

LEAGUE OF GANGSTERS aka GYANGU DOMEI aka GANG LIFE 1963 80 min. **Dir.** Kinji Fukasaku **Scr.** Kinji Fukasaku/ Susumu Saji/ Ryuta Akimoto **Photo color 'scope:** Yoshikazu (Giichi) Yamazawa **Music:** Rinichiro Manabe   w/ Ryohei Uchida, Yoshiko Mita, Kei Sato, Joji Ai,

Rinichi Yamamoto, Rokko Toura, Harumi Sone, Mikijiro Hira, Kenji Susukida, Minoru Sawada
Another critically-appreciated early film from the helmsman of the BATTLES WITHOUT HONOR... series.

League of Gangsters (#7) dvd cover art

Uchida leaves jail to find that his gang's territory has been taken over by the rival elder yakuza Susukida and dapper killer Hira. Abetted by his gang of Sato, Yamamoto, et. al., Uchida kidnaps Susukida's daughter Mita who, by the end, becomes his lover. Miraculously, the two are the sole survivors of the resulting mass slaughter. Fukasaku employs a similar in-your-face energy prowling the slums of Tokyo, ending in a deserted shantytown for the concluding massacre, that he used to such awesome effect in WOLVES, PIGS AND PEOPLE and HIGH NOON FOR GANGSTERS.   #7 of 11 films * * *

THE LOYAL 47 GANGSTERS
aka GYANGU CHUSHINGURA
aka THE GANG'S LOYAL 47
MEMBERS 1963 93 min. DIR.
Shigehiro Ozawa SCR. Toshio
Matsuura PHOTO COLOR 'SCOPE:
Shoe Nishikawa MUSIC: Taiichiro
Kosugi   w/ Chiezo Kataoka,
Ryunosuke Tsukigata, So Yamamura,
Ken Takakura, Koji Tsuruta, Yoshiko
Mita, Yoshiko Sakuma, Tatsuo
Umemiya, Shinichi "Sonny" Chiba,
Tetsuro Tanba, Eitaro Shindo,
Shinjiro Ebara, Ryohei Uchida
A strictly-by-the-numbers formula
adapting the most-filmed Japanese
saga – an old *kabuki* samurai melo-
drama called CHUSHINGURA (THE
LOYAL 47 RONIN) – to a modern
gangster milieu. If you are at all
familiar with the story elements
(Hiroshi Inagaki lensed the most
world-famous version called simply
CHUSHINGURA in 1962; other
directors with versions: Kenji
Mizoguchi, Masahiro Makino,
Sadatsugu (Teiji) Matsuda, Kunio
Watanabe, Kinji Fukasaku (twice),
and many, many more), there is the
novelty of matching up the original
samurai characters to their modern
counterparts. Occasionally moving
(before Takakura, in the Asano part,
knocks himself off), occasionally
imaginative, but frequently absurd.
At the shoot-'em-up climax, the tale
dissolves into a live-action car-
toon. Much more successful as an
adaptation into a yakuza subgenre
is Daiei Studios' *matatabi*/period
yakuza version, THE LOYAL 47
LONG SWORDS (1962), with Raizo
Ichikawa, which is set in the mid-
1860s during the downfall of the
Tokugawa Shogunate, approximately
150 years after the original tale's

time frame (1700-1705) (see the
MATATABI/PERIOD YAKUZA film
section elsewhere in book). NOTE:
THE LOYAL 47 GANGSTERS has
the words "Part One" over "The End"
title which leads me to believe that,
especially since the chronological
events of the story were only halfway
through, there was supposed to be a
Part Two. But LOYAL 47 GANG-
STERS Part Two never appeared
– neither in the GANG series nor
independent of the series. One can
only conjecture that sometime after
Part One's answer print was struck, a
financial decision was made by Toei
brass that a Part Two would not be a
fortuitously auspicious occasion at
the box-office. #8 of 11 films
* * 1/2

Tokyo Gang vs. Hong Kong Gang (#9)

**TOKYO GANG VS. HONG KONG
GANG** aka TOKYO GYANGU
TAI HONG KONG GYANGU aka
TOKYO – HONG KONG GANG-
STERS 1964 86 min. DIR. Teruo
Ishii SCR. Akira Murao/Teruo Ishii
PHOTO COLOR 'SCOPE: Shichiro Hay-
ashi MUSIC: Masao Yagi
w/ Koji Tsuruta, Tetsuro Tanba, Ken
Takakura, Toru Abe, Minoru Oki,
Ryohei Uchida, Kyosuke Machida,
Yoshiko Mita, Kenjiro Ishiyama,
Chiyoko Honma, Hideo Murota
An unusually perverse and sleazy

movie for the time period (even for Toei) with Ishii foreshadowing some of his later much more explicit celluloid descents into human criminality (SHOGUN'S JOYS OF TORTURE, etc.,.). Not that the degenerate reader should become too excited. What it amounts to is some fascinating location work in Hong Kong exteriors, a peculiarly frank and acrobatic striptease chronicled by a roving, intimate camera, and one of the main characters (Tsuruta, of all people) being an unredeemed drug addict whose addiction temporarily incapacitates him. And the usual emerging cinematic brutality. Evidence was steadily mounting, even in 1964, that Ishii was someone to watch. While not as consistently imaginative or forceful as Hideo Gosha or Seijun Suzuki, while often cynically pandering to the lowest common denominator (which made most of his films enormously popular as well as sometimes mediocre), Ishii still remains a remarkably disturbing, entertaining filmmaker. It is fortunate that his extensive reportoire at Shintoho Studios in the 1950s, when he was just beginning, is largely available on Japanese dvd. #9 of 11 films   * * *

GANG'S UPWARD STRATEGY
aka GYANGU CHOJO SAKUSEN
aka DICE OF GOLD 1965 **Dir.**
Umeji Inoue **Scr.** Umeji Inoue/
Ichiro Miyagawa **Photo color
'scope:** Shoe Nishikawa **Music:**
Kenjiro Hirose **w/** Tatsuo Umemiya,
Keiji Takagi, Kyosuke Machida,
Mako Midori, Kikuko Hojo, Asao
Koike, Toru Abe, Rinichi Yamamoto
Two rival yakuza gangs clash over a
gold shipment. #10 of 11 films

King of Gangsters (#11)

KING OF GANGSTERS
aka GYANGU NO TEIO aka
EMPEROR OF THE GANG 1967
Dir. Yasuo Furuhata **Scr.** Yoshihiro
Ishimatsu **Photo B&W 'scope:**
Hanjiro Nakazawa **Music:** Ichiro
Saito **w/** Noboru Ando, Shinichi

"Sonny" Chiba, Hideo Murota, Hiroshi Kondo, Takashi Shimura, Tetsuro Tanba, Shingo Yamashiro, Asao Uchida Masumi Tachibana Set immediately post-WW2, still-in-uniform Ando battles the U.S. Occupation forces as well as rival yakuza. #11 of 11 films

GANG VS. GANG – RED & BLACK BLUES aka GYANGU TAI GYANGU – AKA TO KURO NO BURUUSU 1972 88 min. DIR./SCR. Junya Sato PHOTO COLOR 'SCOPE: Masahiko Iimura MUSIC: Masanobu Higurashi w/ Koji Tsuruta, Hiroko Fuji, Noboru Ando, Hideaki Nitani, Fumio Watanabe, Kei Sato, Tsunehiko Watase, Rokko Toura, Michitaro Mizushima, Koji Fujiyama If this didn't come five years after the last installment of the GANG series, one could consider it a climax to the bunch. After all, there was a different set of characters in each opus anyway. Here Tsuruta is an ex-con and crack shot recruited by Mizushima's mob. He is soon embroiled in the machinations of Mizushima's three murderously ambitious *dai kanbu*, or capos, who wish to usurp their boss. More of the resigned anti-heroic fatalism, the honorable lone wolf facing no one else with any values, no one he can trust. A brooding, melancholic disenchantment with the fixed game of the rat's maze of Life – similar emotional ambience also to be found in the JAPAN'S VIOLENT GANGS series and the last couple of the GAMBLER series.

GANG OF MEN aka OTOKO GUMI 1975 78 min. DIR. Makoto Naito SCR. Masachika Hata/ Katsuhiko Taguchi PHOTO COLOR 'SCOPE: Tetsuya Dezaki w/ Masato Hoshi, Satoko Yamaguchi, Masao Tsumori, Toru Okazaki, Hideo Murota, Asao Uchida, Mayumi Oka A borderline yakuza story with erupting youth gang violence.

Gang of Men - Delinquent Prison

GANG OF MEN – DELINQUENT PRISON aka OTOKO GUMI – SHONEN KEIMUSHO 1976 84 min. DIR. Akihisa Okamoto SCR. Nobuaki Nakajima/ Satoru Kariya PHOTO COLOR 'SCOPE: Yoshio Nakajima MUSIC: Hajime Kaburagi w/ Hiroshi Tate, Yusuke Kami, Midori Takei, Hayato Tani, Masako Ozeki, Rinichi Yamamoto Teenage apprentice gangsters in prison, with sexy teen heartthrob Tate.

GINJO aka SILVER BUTTERFLY series

GINJO WANDERER aka GINJO WATARIDORI aka WANDERING GINZA BUTTERFLY aka SILVER

BUTTERFLY WANDERER 1972
86 min. DIR. Kazuhiko Yamaguchi
SCR. Kazuhiko Yamaguchi/Isao
Matsumoto PHOTO COLOR 'SCOPE:
Hanjiro Nakazawa MUSIC: Toshiaki
Tsushima
w/ Meiko Kaji, Tatsuo Umemiya,
Tsunehiko Watase, Akiko Koyama,
Tomiko Ishii, Koji Nanbara, Yayoi
Watanabe, Mari Mochida, Mieko
Aoyagi, Matasaburo Tanba
The wonderful Kaji in her first two
films for Toei Studios after leaving
Nikkatsu. Director Yamaguchi also
helmed the majority of the SISTER
STREETFIGHTER and DELIN-
QUENT GIRL BOSS film series. Kaji
is an ex-con just released from prison
after participating with her girl gang
in the killing of a prominent mobster.
They had accidentally done the deed
in front of his wife and son, and her
capture was due to her hesitancy in
leaving the scene after spotting the
distraught young boy. Once she gets
out of stir, she heads to a billiard
parlor run by her uncle and meets
lone wolf dandy Watase, a freelance
bodyguard for Koyama's hostess bar.
Watase hooks her up with a hostess
job, but the usual aggravation develops when slimeball boss Nanbara
attempts to take over Koyama's club.
Most of the last third of the film is
filled by Kaji playing billiards against
Nanbara's junkie hoodlum champion
(Matasaburo Tanba) for the deed to
the bar. This whole sequence is done
in a most entertaining fashion with
the tensions escalating straight into
tall tale territory. At one point, the
junkie gangster starts to go through
withdrawals. Director Yamaguchi
uses hot orange lights from below to
suggest the acute distress Tanba is
going through. Finally, when he has

the shakes so bad he can't take it any-
more, he flips his lid, runs to the adjacent wetbar, grabs a loaded syringe
lying there and plunges it into his
arm right through his black silk shirt!
Despite Tanba's nerve-steadying

Ginjo Wanderer (#1) aka **Wandering
Ginza Butterfly**

second wind, Kaji wins. When Nanbara reneges on his promise to hand over the deed, Watase gets boisterous but is subdued by Nanbara's men. Suddenly, lone wolf con man Umemiya, who is also friend to Koyama, bursts in, breaks the stalemate and gets hold of the deed. Needless to say, evil Nanbara is not inclined to take this lying down. A short time later Umemiya is shot to death in a driveby while talking to a little girl flower seller on the street. This pushes Kaji and Watase over the edge. Kaji dresses up in traditional kimono and, with her sword, joins Watase in storming Nanbara's HQ. They break in while Nanbara, girlfriend and gang are watching porno movies and proceed to wipe out the whole bunch in a very violent, very exciting no-holds-barred bloodbath. Kaji and Watase, covered in the red stuff, walk casually down the deserted main street at dawn. They stop when a police car careens up to them, and they offer no resistance as they are arrested. This is very low budget with an unusually meager, lackluster production design. It is also noticeably short on action until the last ten minutes or so. Even still, it is an unpretentious, extremely entertaining vehicle for Kaji, putting a unique spin on the usual programmer elements. Director Yamaguchi has a better handle on character development and story pacing than he usually does, and the whole cast, especially Kaji and Watase, are overflowing with charismatic chemistry. #1 of 2 films * * * 1/2

GINJO DRIFTER – CAT GIRL GAMBLING aka GINJO NAGAREMONO – MESU NEKO BAKUCHI

aka WANDERING GINZA BUTTERFLY – SHE-CAT GAMBLER aka SILVER BUTTERFLY DRIFTER 1972 **DIR.** Kazuhiko Yamaguchi **SCR.** Kazuhiko Yamaguchi/Isao Matsumoto **PHOTO COLOR 'SCOPE:** Yoshio Nakajima **MUSIC:** Toshiaki Tsushima w/ Meiko Kaji, Shinichi "Sonny" Chiba, Shingo Yamashiro, Fujio Suga, Junzaburo Ban, Tamase Mitsukawa, Toru Yuri, Yukie Kagawa, Hideo Murota, Hiroshi Tate

Ginjo Drifter - Cat Girl Gambling aka Wandering Ginza Butterfly (#2) - She-Cat Gambler

After the first great installment, this comes as a bit of a letdown with a story quite often played too much for laughs. Kaji saves a girl from sexually abusive gangsters in the hot springs hinterlands, then helps her get a job as a club hostess in Tokyo. Of course, the very same gangsters like to hang out at that club. Kaji runs into goofy, stammering gambler Chiba who eventually joins her in her fight against the hoodlums when their friends, Yamashiro and Ban (the hostess's dad) bite the dust. Kaji finally recognizes bad boss Suga as the man who had murdered her father in front of her as a child during a particularly contentious card game. The saga finally jump starts to vibrant life during the last fifteen minutes when Kaji and Chiba grab their swords and attack Suga's gang HQ, resulting in a jarringly brutal, well-choreographed slaughter. #2 of 2 films * * 1/2

GINZA OUTLAW aka GINZA YARO series

GINZA OUTLAW aka GINZA YARO 1961 **Dir.** Atsundo Wada **Scr.** Junji Tashiro **Photo 'scope:** Ichiro Hoshijima **Music:** Masao Yoneyama w/ Toru Ono, Noriko Haruoka #1 of 2 films

THUNDER OF THE SEA OF NEON aka NEON NO UMI NO ABARENBO 1961 **Dir.** Atsundo Wada **Scr.** Junji Tashiro **Photo 'scope:** Ichiro Hoshijima **Music:** Masao Yoneyama w/ Toru Ono, Noriko Haruoka, Midori Urano, Saburo Otsuji #2 of 2 films

GIRL BOSS aka SUKEBAN series

GIRL BOSS BLUES – QUEEN BEE'S COUNTERATTACK aka SUKEBAN BURUUSU – MESU-BACHI NO GYAKUSHU aka 1971 **Dir.** Norifumi Suzuki **Scr.** Norifumi Suzuki/ Takashi Minagawa **Photo color 'scope:** Shin Furuya w/ Reiko Ike, Yukie Kagawa, Miki

Sugimoto, Shigeru Amachi, Kenjiro Nagare, Shunsuke Taki, Yayoi Watanabe, Toru Abe, Rena Inchinose, Ichiko Kawasaki

Girl Boss Blues - Counterattack (#1)

This series clearly owes a debt to its similar predecessors Toei's DELIN-QUENT GIRL BOSS films as well as Nikkatsu Studios' STRAY CAT ROCK and GIRL SCHOOL pictures, all from the 1969-1971 period. The DELINQUENT GIRL BOSS scenarios were full of often annoying humor and, no matter the violence, possessed a sweetness at their core. One did not really feel the apocalypse might be just around the corner. However, in little over a year, Toei's world of delinquent anti-heroines had evolved into a cynical dog-eat-dog maelstrom of sexual chaos and sadistic mayhem, an imploding universe of disintegrating affection and rampant amorality. The steely-eyed lethal vamps of the GIRL BOSS stories and its sister series, TERRIFYING GIRLS HIGH SCHOOL, may survive at the end of the majority of the tales but just barely. And whatever microscopic shred of humanity they still possess is hanging by a thread. The poster art speaks for itself. In this first entry, what starts out as a run-of-the-mill action potboiler with comedy relief gradually becomes a genuinely heartfelt tableau of Ike and her female cohort outcasts, their scams, betrayals and heartbreaks. Particularly affecting is Ike's friendship with a young recruit who ends up sleeping with Ike's yakuza beau, Nagare. The two girls' confrontation and subsequent poignant reconciliation is done in a lyrical, unsentimental way. There is also additional pathos with Amachi as a world-weary hitman. A sweet, no-frills scene with him and his daughter on a carousel is another of this film's small pleasures. But director Suzuki does not skimp on the insanity. One sequence features Ike and gang participating in a game with their *bosozoku* buddies, being laid back across motorcycle handlebars while the guys simultaneously fuck them while they race. The rule is whenever a driver

comes, he has to stop. Of course, Ike and her other beau, *bosozoku* Taki, emerge as the winners. Another evocative scene features Kagawa, Ike's newly returned rival who challenges Ike, claiming she has abused her responsibility to the girls and then proceeds to drag her behind a motorboat. Later they have a knockdown dragout brawl in concrete ruins that spills into a vacant lot full of wildflowers bathed by a golden sunset. When Kagawa is defeated, she valiantly acknowledges she must be the one to leave and bids one of the girls sing a sad song as she splits. One of the gang lip-synchs a very emotional ballad of farewell that is quite moving despite its artificiality and sentimental manipulation. From there it returns to potboiler territory with Taki taken hostage by a yakuza gang led by the typecast Abe who demands ransom from Taki's rich father. Renegade yakuza Nagare, Ike and newly released Taki then attempt to steal back the loot. Well-meaning Amachi, under obligation to Abe, is betrayed and mortally stabbed by his yakuza comrades. Strength failing, he fights alongside the three youths as they attack. But both he and Nagare succumb to their wounds. Abe, all his men wiped out, follows Ike and Taki in a crazy car chase down a winding mountain road that results in everyone's death, except for lone Ike who manages to jump clear. #1 of 7 films
* * *

GIRL BOSS BLUES – QUEEN BEE'S CHALLENGE aka SUKEBAN BURUUSU – MESUBACHI NO CHOSEN 1972 **DIR.** Norifumi Suzuki **SCR.** Norifumi Suzuki/Takashi Minagawa **PHOTO COLOR 'SCOPE:** Shin Furuya **MUSIC:**

Hajime Kaburagi   w/ Reiko Ike,
Chiyoko Kazama, Asao Koike, Miki
Sugimoto, Akiko Koyama, Tatsuo
Umemiya, Hiroshi Miyauchi, Ichiro
Araki, Yayoi Watanabe, Midori
Yamada, Shingo Yamashiro
Ike of Kyoto and Kazama of Osaka
are feuding rival gang bosses. Things
heat up to fever-pitch when they
both fall for the same hoodlum stud,
Miyauchi. Craven *oyabun* Koike
takes advantage of the women's
enmity to ensnare the two for a
round of sexual abuse. Occasionally
gritty, credibly streetwise but saddled with bits of clumsily-inserted
comedy relief. Just as often it is
baldly sexploitive. Yet many of the
gratuitous sex and violence scenes
Suzuki accomplishes with such wild
imagination and bravura style that
the kinkiest torture rises above trash
boundaries into the heady, if still
unapologetically decadent, world of
genuine erotic art. Suzuki and his
writers often transcend cliche into
the realm of archetype, forging an
urban mythology of female warriors
composed of society's outcasts. The
film abounds with what amounts to
the series' trademark sequences: Ike
and rival Kazama's rumble; Ike's encounter with her bar hostess mother;
Ike and Kazama playing chicken by
having a truck continually drive over
them lengthwise until one of them
passes out from fright; Ike making
love to her beau Miyauchi in a forest
blanketed with autumn leaves;
Kazama sacrificing herself to save
newly befriended Ike's life. At the
end, Ike manages to finally turn the
tables and dispatch their tormentor
Koike, shooting him after trapping
him in a revolving door.   #2 of 7
films   * * *

GIRL BOSS GUERILLA aka
SUKEBAN GERIRA 1972 **Dir.**
Norifumi Suzuki **Scr.** Norifumi
Suzuki/Takashi Minagawa **Photo
color 'scope:** Shigeru Akatsuka
Music: Toshiaki Tsushima **w/** Miki
Sugimoto, Reiko Ike, Emi Shiro, Chie

*Girl Boss Blues - Queen Bee's Challenge
(#2)*

Girl Boss Guerilla (#3)

Girl Boss - Escape from Reform School (#5)

Kobayashi, Ringu Kimoto, Chiomi
Oka, Midori Hiro, Kyoko Tsukasa,
Michitaro Mizushima, Natsuko Miura
Sugimoto is the leader of a motor-
bike-riding gang who becomes allied
with former rival, lone wolf boss Ike.
They find themselves increasingly
at odds with the established yakuza
gang led by – who else? – Toru Abe.
Sugimoto becomes lovers with an
anti-social boxer who had rescued her
from Abe's men. Unhappily, the middle section of the picture is punctuated with stupid episodes of the girls
seducing, then blackmailing lecherous Buddhist monks and Catholic
priests. Once this "comic" relief is out
of the way, Sugimoto et. al. go wandering on their bikes down the coast
to Katsuragawa where her guy is in
training. Of course, more grief from
Abe and his goons is not far off. They
show up to put the heat on the boxer
and his trainer Mizushima. A huge
battle ensues in a warehouse with Ike,
Sugimoto and followers arriving like
the cavalry to save the two men. At
this point, Abe's minions actually pull
a Perils-of-Pauline routine, attempting to slice off Sugimoto's arm with a
buzzsaw. Her boxer beau intervenes,
saving her but is stabbed to death in
the process. The escaping thugs leave
the grieving Sugimoto and her gals to
hold an impromptu wake on the sunset-dappled beach for her lover and
the other casualties. The boxer's hippie minstrel buddy sings a sad song
on his guitar. Needless to say, from
then on the girls are bent on a path of
vengeance and return to their home
turf. Sugimoto is caught when she
sneaks into the yakuza HQ through
a heating duct and is subsequently
bound and beaten. She is about to
have her pussy burnt with a lighter

when Ike brazens her way in with a
rifle, liberating her but then getting
captured herself. Tied-up, raped by
Abe, she is then left alone only to be
abruptly freed by Abe's number two
man who is smitten with her. At the
climax, Sugimoto and Ike finally trick
Abe into stealing their bomb-rigged
car and blast him to kingdom come.
Our cozy tale ends with Ike bidding
adieu then Sugimoto's gang roaring
off down the highway in pursuit of
new adventures. 3 of 7 films * * ½

Girl Boss (#4)

GIRL BOSS aka SUKEBAN 1973
86 min. DIR. Norifumi Suzuki SCR.
Norifumi Suzuki/Takashi Minagawa/
Kiyohide Ohara PHOTO COLOR
'SCOPE: Umeo Masuda MUSIC:
Masao Yagi w/ Miki Sugimoto,
Reiko Ike, Ichiro Araki, Hiroshi
Miyauchi, Bin Amatsu, Yoko Mihara,
Misuzu Ota, Akira Shioji, Tatsuo
Endo, Hiroshi Nawa As usual with
director Suzuki, this sports some
flamboyantly inventive, intoxicating

visuals mingled inextricably with the unabashedly, gratuitously sexploitive. Also as customary, the heady brew is tinged with an earthy, amusing but more often annoying sense of humor. This time out, Sugimoto and cohorts take advantage of the situation when another pair of bad girls stage a break from the reform school van in which they are riding. They quickly hightail it to Tokyo where they set up grifting and thieving. They run afoul of first a gang of delinquent schoolgirls then a yakuza group led by Amatsu. Amatsu and cronies run a sex slave operation, shanghaiing young girls into their brothel of kinky perversions. Sugimoto is captured after helping sleazy hipster Araki blackmail a gang associate (Endo) and his nympho spouse (Mihara). Sugimoto is chained, repeatedly beaten and sexually harassed. One of the younger gangsters (Miyauchi) softens and helps her to escape. They make love in a cluttered alleyway only for Sugimoto to learn that he is the ex of her lone wolf rival Ike. Boss Amatsu promises to give Miyauchi a break for helping Sugimoto if he snares ex-heartthrob Ike. Several years previously, volcanic schoolgirl Ike had stabbed Amatsu when Amatsu was beating up beau Miyauchi. Miyauchi is torn but perversely more loyal to stern Amatsu! So he delivers Ike up to his gang for a round of torture. Appalled Sugimoto helps her nemesis Ike make a break for it. Ike then arranges to meet Miyauchi in a deserted baseball stadium where she plans to kill him for his betrayal. However, she cannot complete the task and only wounds him. They surrender themselves to a bout of obsessive sexual delirium, kissing and fondling each other until Miyauchi spots a sniper in the distance and places himself in the line of fire to shield Ike. Shot, he stumbles toward the assassin with his knife. More bullets pierce his body, but he manages to throw the blade and kill his killer from at least a hundred yards away! Incensed Ike and Sugimoto then lead their girls on the usual climactic raid of the yakuza den, freeing the sex slaves and massacring Amatsu and gang. As is often the case with this series, the imaginative imagery, the exuberance and sheer vitality lend this the extra impetus to go beyond mere programmer status. #4 of 7 films * * *

GIRL BOSS – ESCAPE FROM REFORM SCHOOL aka SUKE-BAN – KANKAIN DASSO 1973 DIR. Sadao Nakajima SCR. Tatsuhiko Kamoi/ Sadao Nakajima PHOTO COLOR 'SCOPE: Shin Furuya MUSIC: Ichiro Araki   w/ Miki Sugimoto, Tsunehiko Watase, Yuko Kano,Hiroko Isayama, Rika Sudo, Misuzu Ota, Nobuo Kaneko, Hideo Murota, Takuzo Kawatani, Hiroshi Nawa Nakajima directs for the first time in the series and, although not possessed of as much over-the-top flamboyant imagery, this entry is the most impressive as far as consistency of tone and a relentless building of momentum. There is less humor and what there is is much better integrated into the overall narrative than in Suzuki's films. Sugimoto and mates make a break for it after setting their reform school dorm ablaze but, unlike the last film, this hews closer to reality with the girls all going their separate ways for the time being. One particularly disturbed girl returns to the "father" who had been bedding her only to find "dad" doing it with sis (both girls call Hiroshi Nawa "papa" so I assume they are blood relations and he is not just a sugar daddy). There is a flashback to Nawa selling the now-returned girl to a slick yakuza and her stabbing of the gangster, the crime that landed her in reformatory. Back in the present, Nawa refuses to take her back which spurs her to stab him, too. Meanwhile tough-as-nails Sugimoto has hooked up with drifter thief Watase, and they proceeed to hide out in a rural cabin. While Watase sleeps, Sugimoto steals his money. A confrontation ensues when he awakens, but before long their passion for each other overwhelms financial concerns. They make love in one of the steamiest scenes in the series. Eventually Sugimoto, Watase and the other fugitive girls converge to camp out in an abandoned boathouse on the deserted seashore. One of them has been followed by the cops, and the next morning the police launch their assault – only to be repelled by Watase's shotgun and the girls molotov cocktails. They make a break for Watase's truck, racing off only to be blockaded a short distance away. Watase is killed by a bullet to the head, the truck bursts into flames and the girls are yanked out by the cops. Sugimoto continues to rail against them, scratching, kicking, spitting and screaming her lover Watase's name until the picture freeze-frames to the end. Even though there is Nakajima's trademark lack of character development, he still achieves a blisteringly intense, often more serious, less tongue-in-cheek narrative than earlier entries. #5 of 7 films * * * *

Girl Boss - Diamond Showdown (#6)

GIRL BOSS – DIAMOND SHOW-DOWN aka SUKEBAN – TAIMAN SHOBU aka MANO a MANO 1974 87 min. **DIR.** Ikuo Sekimoto **SCR.** Tatsuhiko Kamoi/Masahiro Shimura **PHOTO COLOR 'SCOPE:** Shin Furuya **MUSIC:** Kenjiro Hirose **w/** Reiko Ike, Ryoko Kinuma, Tsunehiko Watase, Rika Sudo, Rena Ichinose, Midori Shirakawa, Tsuko Fujiyama, Toru Abe   Ike is a lonely, easily bullied girl in stir for wounding her brutal gang boss pimp (Abe) with a knife. During the prologue and titles we see the tide gradually turn until Ike has usurped dominance from the reigning girl boss in prison. After release, Ike shacks up with her other newly released mates and pursues various scams including purse-snatching, extorting money from lecherous salarymen and selling dogmeat from wild canines they have captured on the city outskirts. One of her girls is shanghaiied back into sex service by Abe and his mama-san to pay off her accumulated debt. Ike confronts Abe about the matter and is mercilessly beaten in the sex club backroom as a consequence. The gang is on the verge of raping her when she is rescued by principled lone wolf mobster Watase. Watase is a high-powered mover whom Abe wants to deal with, so there is an uneasy truce. He is also the estranged brother of one of Abe's main girls (Kinuma), an emotionally disturbed wretch who detests Ike for having had the guts and self-confidence to liberate herself from Abe's pimpish clutches. Watase, a lonely drinker tormented by his sister's plight, forms a bond with Ike. Ike soon crosses paths with her just-released former nemesis, who is now vulnerable-and-transformed-by-love for her crippled mechanic/ ex-race car driver beau. Ike thrashes the girl and is threatening her with a welding torch when the mechanic intervenes, diffusing the powderkeg. The mechanic is also in thrall to Abe, under pressure to deliver an armored car he is building. He dies at the hands of Abe's gang, and Abe cynically uses a bloody thumbprint from his corpse as a seal on the contract (in Japan a seal or thumbprint in red ink is often used in lieu of a signature). Ike consoles her former rival, and they both lead their girls to confront the gangsters. Brandishing a shotgun, Ike bursts in to find Watase making a payment to Abe. However, it is news to Watase that Abe's gang had killed the mechanic, and he immediately reneges on the deal. Once more at the garage, Ike and the girls hold a wake for the dead youth. Watase slips quietly into the background. Back at gang HQ, Abe persuades Watase's estranged

sibling Kinuma to murder her brother. She then shows up at the wake, wings Watase only to have Ike shield him with her body. Both Watase and Ike try to talk sense to her. They seem to have reached an impasse when Watase abruptly walks out. His sister chases him into the parking lot but both of them are cut down by a hail of drive-by bullets from Abe's henchmen. That night, grieving Ike and girls burn the corpses of Watase, his sister and the mechanic in the junkyard, then stage an all-out assault on Abe's HQ, obliterating the villains. This could have been as good as the last film, ESCAPE FROM REFORM SCHOOL, if not for a pat ending that has Ike and the girls happy-go-lucky again the very next morning, absconding with a truck formerly belonging to the dead mobsters. #6 of 7 films * * * 1/2

GIRL BOSS – CRAZY BALL GAME aka SUKEBAN – GYOKU TOTSUKI ASOBI 1974 **DIR.** Ikuo Sekimoto **SCR.** Isao Matsumoto **PHOTO COLOR 'SCOPE:** Juhei Suzuki/ Shin Furuya **MUSIC:** Kawachi Kuni w/ Yuko Kano, Noboru Shiraishi, Noriko Fujiyama, Harumi Tajima, Rie Saotome, Junko Miwa, Nobuo Kaneko, Hiroshi Nawa, Hiroshi Oizumi   Director Sekimoto turns out another decent entry that could have been one of the best of the series if not for a few basic missteps. Although not as versatile as Reiko Ike or Miki Sugimoto, new lead Yuko Kano does exhibit a rough hewn charisma that grows on you as the film progresses. Kano and cohorts are released from reform school and go up against a rival girl mob allied to wicked yakuza Abe's gang. Things go haywire for Kano's bunch when they team up with her lone wolf/thief lover Shiraishi to hijack Abe's diamond transport. Various of Kano's gals get whacked when Abe's men catch up.

Girl Boss - Crazy Ball Game (#7)

Ultimately, Abe gets his goods back, leaving Kano and survivors barely alive. Armed with spearguns, they perpetrate a ludicrous hang-gliding-by-motorboat attack on Abe's island stronghold that pushes credibility past the breaking point. It all culminates in doom for the villains. However, there is a wonderful shootout between Kano's beau Shiraishi and Abe's main hitman (who is the rival girl boss's man) that is very spaghetti western-esque and results in both their deaths. Despite Kano and her girls getting the loot back, there is no pat happy ending. and we are left with the decidedly bittersweet feeling that all the carnage was not worth it. #7 and final in series   * * *

GLOWING RED VERMIN aka AKAI YAKOCHU 1966 **DIR.** Shinji Murayama **SCR.** Masashige Narusawa **w/** Tatsuo Umemiya Needless to say, one of the more evocative titles in this book.

G-MEN OF THE PACIFIC aka TAIHEIYO NO G-MEN 1962 86 min. **DIR./SCR.** Teruo Ishii **PHOTO COLOR 'SCOPE:** Shoe Nishikawa **w/** Chiezo Kataoka, Shinjiro Ebara, Tetsuro Tanba, Ryuji Oki, Yoshiko Sakuma, Tatsuo Umemiya, Nobuo Yana   Per aging *chanbara* star Katoaka's involvement, this leans more to the old-fashioned gangster film style/formula spilling over from Toei's 1950s heyday.

Golgo 13

GOLGO 13 aka GORUGO 13 1973 104 min. **DIR.** Junya Sato **SCR.** Takao Saito/ Motomitsu (Genmitsu?) K. **PHOTO COLOR 'SCOPE:** Masahiko Iimura **MUSIC:** Chuji Kinoshita **w/** Ken Takakura, Banai Puri, Sorabi Moseime   The first live-action picture from the extremely popular comic about the stoic hitman. It may be a stretch calling GOLGO 13 films "yakuza". This one was shot in location in Iran. At first, I found it somewhat surprising that GOLGO 13 did not become an ongoing film or TV series as it was one of the longest running *mangas*. However, director Sato in an interview supplied insight into the reason: as the character is constantly roaming the world on his assignments, the international elements involved (in other words, expensive location filming) precluded too many GOLGO 13 pictures. The difficulties of shooting in the still-Shah-dominated-Iran may also explain why the film is so disappointing considering the people involved. There is also a decided paucity of ideas and imagination in GOLGO creator Takao Saito's script. Usually director Junya Sato works on the screenplays he directs (often collaborating with such excellent writers as Yoshihiro Ishimatsu). Unfortunately, that is not the case here. Too little action, a static rhythm and a shortage of enthusiasm from the performers further subtracts from the mix. * *

GOLGO 13 – NINE HEADED DRAGON aka GORUGO 13 – KURYU NO KUBI aka GOLGO 13 – KOWLOON ASSIGNMENT 1977 93 min. **DIR.** Yukio Noda **SCR.** Nobuaki (Shigeaki?) Nakajima/Tsutomu (Isao?) Sugimoto **PHOTO COLOR 'SCOPE:** Shigeru Akatsuka **MUSIC:** Harumi Ibe **w/** Shinichi "Sonny" Chiba, Etsuko "Sue" Shiomi, Koji Tsuruta, Jerry Ito, Ellen Sung, Callan   Judging between the Japanese and English language versions of this, the Japanese one has even worse dubbing, if that is possible (there are many non-Japanese as well as non-English speaking folks in the cast). The production values are very lackluster with a general sloppiness to the proceedings, something totally uncharacteristic of the usually at least competent Toei

films from this period. The story is totally predictable, but then so are the majority of the GOLGO 13 comics. However, this entry does surpass the previous Takakura film in a noticeably higher energy level with much mayhem punctuating the scenario of Golgo aka Duke Togo pursuing contracts on high-level druglords throughout Hong Kong and Southeast Asia. That said, this still is nothing to write home about. The always great Koji Tsuruta is completely wasted in what amounts to no more than a few minutes cameo screentime as an eyepatch-wearing weapons expert. This would be down another half notch if not for the fact Golgo 13/Duke Togo is a role Chiba was obviously born to play, and he is charsimatically bigger-than-life in the outlandish role. NOTE: For those of you into the GOLGO 13 comics, there have also been two anime films, GOLGO 13, THE PROFESSIONAL (1983) and GOLGO 13: QUEEN BEE (1998). * *

GRAVEYARD OF HONOR AND HUMANITY aka JINGI NO HAKABA aka BURIAL OF THE GAMBLING CODE aka DEATH OF HONOR 1975 94 min. **DIR.** Kinji Fukasaku **ORIG. STORY:** Goro Fujita **SCR.** Tatsuhiko Kamoi/Fumio Konami/Kinji Fukasaku **PHOTO COLOR 'SCOPE:** Hanjiro Nakazawa **MUSIC:** Toshiaki Tsushima **w/** Tetsuya Watari, Tatsuo Umemiya, Yumi Takigawa, Reiko Ike, Kunie Tanaka, Noboru Ando, Mikio Narita, Hajime Hana, Eiji Go, Kenji Imai, Meika Seri, Harumi Sone   An amazing saga set in post-war Japan of boisterous sociopath Rikio Ishikawa, a loser who cannot even get

Graveyard of Honor and Humanity

to clear. Something about her draws him back, and he falls in love. But he is a dysfunctional kind of guy (that is an understatement), and his love and ways of showing it are constantly at odds with the innocent girl's experience. She does, however, gradually start to care for him. Watari, in deeper and deeper trouble with the clan he belongs to, gets slapped around by his *oyabun* (Hana), and he comes back later for a freeform-stabbing melee. Soon he is an outcast with a contract on his life. He does the pinkie-trimming scene to try to beat the heat, and it brings an uneasy truce (no one died from his knife attack). He remains an outcast, though, exiled from Tokyo, and he begins hanging out with a junkie (Tanaka) after being introduced to the dubious pleasures of heroin by a more-degenerate-than-usual whore (Seri). His addiction sinks him deeper and deeper into a pit of self-pity and resentment that, before long, has him assassinating best friend Umemiya over an imagined slight. Meanwhile, his gal Takigawa has contracted tuberculosis from him. She constantly coughs up blood and, despairing of Watari's insanity, decides to bid adieu to this cruel world. Watari wakes up one morning to find she has slit her wrists. This really pushes him over the edge. After cremation, he takes the jar of her ashes and few remaining bones and heads over to his former boss's pad. Everyone is alarmed at his deeply depressed state and, when he takes out his girl's bones and begins to eat them, they explode. Soon after, Watari and junkie buddy Tanaka have a shootout with the cops. In a scene near the end, he is stabbed repeatedly by his old yakuza comrades.

along with his loser buddies. While fleeing a gambling den that he and his pals have just knocked over, Watari ducks into an innocent woman's (Takigawa) apartment. He ends up raping her while waiting for the coast

He had just been returning from the tombstone engraver – trying in a very pathetic way to make amends to the dead Takigawa and Umemiya by getting them headstones – when attacked and left for dead. Weeping in blood-and-mud-drenched agony, writhing on the ground, he looks up into the sky and his gaze fixes on a child's balloon ascending into heaven. With Tsushima's lyrical score and Fukasaku's non-manipulative, matter-of-fact imagery, this emerges as one of the most heartbreakingly memorable moments in any gangster film, let alone *yakuza eiga*. And Watari still does not die! Finally, he jumps from the prison hospital roof to his death. Thrilling and emotionally exhausting. Fukasaku has stated that Watari's character was based on a real-life yakuza renegade who railed against everything and everyone, and had a similar end. It is a testament to Fukasaku and screenwriters Konami and Kamoi's skills and compassion as storytellers that they manage, without cheap sentimentality or obvious manipulation of audience emotion, to make us really care about a fucked-up, degenerate loser – someone who has never recognized love when he has seen it nor knows how to give it. Certainly Fukasaku's best film. It is almost as if he decided to let all the insanity bubbling under the surface in his other movies, all the perversities only hinted at, come to the surface in full poisonous flower. Not that he has not made some excellent films before and after this, but GRAVEYARD OF HONOR... is devastating. Going back to the original Goro Fujita-penned source novel, *enfant terrible wunderkind* Takashi Miike remade the film in 2002. * * * *

The Great Escape

THE GREAT ESCAPE aka DAI DATSU GOKU 1975 91 min. **Dir./ Scr.** Teruo Ishii **Photo color 'scope:** Tetsuya Dezaki **Music:** Hachiro Aoyama **w/** Ken Takakura, Bunta Sugawara, Nana Kinomi, Eiji Go, Tatsuo Ito, Hideo Murota, Yoshi Kato, Rinichi Yamamoto, Kunie Tanaka, Asao Koike   There are not too many yakuza trappings as we follow Takakura and Sugawara escaping from prison death row in an action-packed saga set in the snow country. Two of their maniacal companions are so nuts, they kill each other right away. Three more die of exposure in the fierce climate. Once they reach an abandoned cabin, Takakura knocks out the antagonistic Sugawara so he can continue on alone. He runs across a sick woman (Kinomi) outside a snowbound village and brings her with him to a nearby inn. Slowly, he nurses her back to health while trying to keep a low profile around town.

We learn in flashback that Tanaka, his partner in a heist gone wrong, was the one guilty of the security guard killing that resulted in his conviction and death sentence. Not only had Tanaka, boss Suga and the rest of his gang stood idly by in court, but his girlfriend had also testified against him. So he is intent on evening the score. Takakura then discovers that the woman he has helped is a stranded stripper and, despite her falling-in-love with him, he splits. Back in the city, he finds his betraying ex and simultaneously runs into Sugawara. Coincidentally, fellow fugitive Sugawara has an axe to grind against the same gang. Soon there is an escalating tide of violence as Takakura and Sugawara tail Tanaka and fellow hoods onto a train. The villains are carrying a huge suitcase full of cash which has ended up attracting another unscrupulous bunch out for easy plunder. Full scale carnage erupts culminating with a train derailment. Severely wounded Takakura, the sole survivor, somehow makes it back to the city but collapses as he nears an intersection where the stripper waits for a bus with her co-workers. Both of them are completely unaware of the other's proximity. Despite a somewhat slow middle, this is an exceptionally well-crafted, well-written thriller with genuine mounting suspense, nuanced characters, excellent performances and incredible on-location atmosphere. In its best moments, it has a similar flavor and attitude to director Jean-Pierre Melville's most downbeat noirs, especially SECOND BREATH and THE RED CIRCLE. One of maverick director Ishii's best pictures.
* * * 1/2

THE GREATEST BOSS aka SAIGO NO KAOYAKU 1963 Dir. Ko (Yasushi) Sasaki Scr. Akira Murao Photo B&W 'scope: Shoe Nishikawa Music: Tadashi Makime w/ Ken Takakura, Chiezo Kataoka, Tatsuo Umemiya, Tatsuo Matsumura, Shinjiro Ebara, Isao Yamagata, Naoko Kubo, Chiyoko Honma

Greatest Boss of the Showa Era

GREATEST BOSS OF THE SHOWA ERA aka SHOWA SAIDAI NO KAOYAKU 1966 90 min. **Dir.** Kiyoshi Saeki **Scr.** Akira Murao **Photo color 'scope:** Ichiro Hoshijima **Music:** Chuji Kinoshita w/ Koji Tsuruta, Tatsuo Umemiya, Tetsuro Tanba, Yunosuke Ito, Takashi Shimura, Reiko Ohara, Hiroshi Nawa, Michitaro Mizushima, Naoko Kubo, Asao Uchida, Joji Ai
Set in the mid-1950s, Mizushima is a benevolent boss assassinated aboard a train. Struggle for control of the gang and the gang's survival in the face of villain Ito's clan are the main

ingredients here. Fairly ho-hum until a strolling guitar minstrel (Joji Ai) is intimidated by the bad yakuza guys into making a hit on good yakuza guy Tsuruta. When Ai cannot go through with it, Tsuruta gives him money and sends him off. The villains blow the sensitive musician away as soon as he walks out of Tsuruta's house with the deed obviously undone. Next, Umemiya takes his overdosed gal out of the evil clan's clutches only to be followed and shot at. Fatally hit, he steers his car off a freeway overpass, and it explodes into a fireball. Tsuruta and comrades decide to try the revenge-binge-massacre shtick but are persuaded to postpone the attack by very traditional-minded Tanba who wants a solo crack at offing opposition boss Ito. He gets ventilated by bullet and blade for his trouble and only manages to take a few underlings along with him. Finally, Tsuruta rounds up the guys, and they head out for a death-dance with knife and gun. Mass slaughter results as usual with Tsuruta challenging scumbag Ito in the decadent fellow's garden. Both fatally wound each other with their blades. Fin. Somewhat unique as it appears to be one of the very rare appearances of master thespian Ito in a yakuza role. 　* * *

GREATEST POST-WAR GAM-BLER aka SENGO SAIDAI NO TOBA 1969 109 min. **DIR.** Kosaku Yamashita **SCR.** Akira Murao **PHOTO COLOR 'SCOPE:** Nagaki Yamagishi Music: Ichiro Saito w/ Koji Tsuruta, Ken Takakura, Yoshiko Mita, Rinichi Yamamoto, Akiko Koyama, Toru Abe, Nobuo Kaneko, Hiroshi Nawa, Gen Shimizu, Itaro Kuni One of the most sublime, perfectly-constructed

modern *ninkyo* yakuza pictures. If one needed a textbook example of all the situations, the ensnaring webs of obligation, friendship, loyalty and deceit that make up a successful yakuza film, this would be the one. The death of loyal comrade Yamamoto early on, then Takakura's brave "going-down-in-a-blaze-of-glory" retaliation, followed by best friend Tsuruta's quiet and specific vengeance mission are handled with subtle, graceful buildups, understated performances (comparatively speaking), and the effect is shattering. Very moving, despite its slow start. Supposedly an updating and remake of BIG TIME GAMBLING BOSS also directed by Yamashita. 　* * * 1/2

Greatest Post-War Gambler

GREAT OKINAWA YAKUZA WAR aka OKINAWA YAKUZA DAI SENSO 1976 96 min. **DIR.** Sadao Nakajima **SCR.** Koji Takada/ Fumio Konami **PHOTO COLOR 'SCOPE:** Shigeru Akatsuka **Music:** Kenjiro

Hirose w/ Hiroki Matsukata, Shinichi "Sonny" Chiba, Mikio Narita, Tatsuo Umemiya, Tsunehiko Watase, Hideo Murota, Isao Bito, Takeo Chii, Yoshihiro Igarashi, Katsu Shiga   Another contender for most violent yakuza film. Chiba does what amounts to a super-exaggerated caricature (if that is possible) of his Terry Tsurugi (STREETFIGHTER) role, playing a slightly-disfigured, over-the-top psycho karate expert-cum-veteran who runs around in sweat-stained khakis bullying everyone in sight, extorting money from various merchants as well as gangster Matsukata's guys. At one point, Chiba and pals take a pair of industrial pliers to a guy's crotch (carefully obscured by the protruding corner of a box). In another psychotic episode, Chiba's men in a big American car run back-and-forth over a rival yakuza who had scoffed at one of Chiba's karate demonstrations. We get a gutter's-eye-view and, although it is obviously fake, it is still pretty disgusting. The fact that Chiba is dispatched in one of the most outrageously overacted death scenes ever two thirds of the way through our story doesn't cause the mayhem to cease. Chiba's loyal comrades hunt Matsukata's gang until everyone is dead and Matsukata barely left alive. * * *

THE GREAT TRAIN RAID aka RESSHA DAI SHUGEKI 1964 **DIR.** Miki Wakabayashi **SCR.** Ichiro Ikeda **PHOTO 'SCOPE:** Yoshikazu (Giichi) Yamazawa **MUSIC:** Minoru Yoshino w/ Tatsuo Umemiya, Yusuke Kawazu, Ryohei Uchida, Shoji Nakayama, Mayumi Fujisato, Kenji Imai, Harumi Sone, Toru Abe, Tetsuko Kobayashi, Rinichi Yamamoto

GUN VS. GUN aka KENJU TAI KENJU 1955 **DIR.** Shigehiro Ozawa **SCR.** Shinji Dezaki   **PHOTO B&W:** Ichiro Hoshijima **MUSIC:** Eiichi Yamada   w/ Eiji Okada, Harumi Urasato, Ichiro Ryuzaki, Hisaya Ito, Takamaru Sasaki, Miki Sanjo, Ushio Akashi, Hisao Toake

THE HAPPY SCOUNDREL aka YUKAI NA GOKUDO 1976 86 min. **DIR.** Kosaku Yamashita   **SCR.** Koji Takada/ Isao Matsumoto/ Shoji Shimura **PHOTO COLOR 'SCOPE:** Shigeru Akatsuka **MUSIC:** Hachiro Aoyama   w/ Tomisaburo Wakayama, Yoshiko Mita, Saburo Kitajima, Tomoko Kihi, Tonbei Hidari, Masumi Harukawa   In all likelihood, a one-off revival of Wakayama's 11 film SCOUNDREL (GOKUDO) series, which originally called it a day in 1974.

HELL aka JIGOKU series

VENGEANCE AT CAPE HELL aka JIGOKU MISAKI NO FUKU-SHU aka DUEL AT DEVIL'S CAPE 1957 **DIR.** Tsuneo Kobayashi **SCR.** Hajime Takaiwa/Shin Morita **PHOTO B&W:** Shoe Nishikawa w/ Chiezo Kataoka, Shinjiro Ebara, Isao Yamagata, Mitsue Komiya, Eijiro Yanagi, Eitaro Shindo There was a whole group of gangster/yakuza movies starring Kataoka with the word HELL in the title that Toei released starting in the late fifties and on into the early sixties. A case can be made that they are all part of a loosely-linked series. But they have never been called that in any of their separate entries nor have they been grouped together in Japanese film reference books (the rare volume that even mentions them). This is one of the earliest HELL films. Most were directed by Shigehiro Ozawa, and written by Toshio Matsuura. For some reason, they make a thing of romanizing the *kanji* characters for gun in the title as *"hajiki"* instead of the usual *"kenju"*. The visual style and dramatics are definitely old-fashioned.

HELL OF A GUN SLAVE aka DO NO HAJIKI WA JIGOKU DAZE 1958 DIR. Sadatsugu (Teiji) Matsuda SCR. Yoshitake Hisa PHOTO 'SCOPE: Shintaro Kawazaki MUSIC: Shiro Fukai w/ Chiezo Kataoka, Ken Takakura, So Yamamura, Mitsuko Miura, Isao Yamagata, Eitaro Shindo, Shinjiro Ebara, Eijiro Kataoka, Eijiro Yanagi, Kan Yanagiya

HELL'S COMPANION aka JIGOKU NO SOKO MADE TSUKI AUZE 1959 DIR. Shigehiro Ozawa SCR. Toshio Matsuura PHOTO 'SCOPE: Shoe Nishikawa MUSIC: Eiichi (Hidekazu?) Yamada w/ Chiezo Kataoka, Ken Takakura, So Yamamura, Yoshiko Sakuma, Miki Sanjo, Eitaro Shindo, Shinjiro Ebara, Eijiro Yanagi, Isao Yamagata, Hitomi Nakahara
Takakura is a boxer in with gangsters.

THE SECOND BULLET aka NIHATSU ME WA JIGOKU YUKI DAZE aka EXPERIENCE OF TWO DISPATCHED ON A TRIP TO HELL 1960 90 min. DIR. Shigehiro Ozawa SCR. Toshio Matsuura PHOTO 'SCOPE: Shoe Nishikawa MUSIC: Eiichi Yamada w/ Chiezo Kataoka, Ken Takakura, Yoshiko Sakuma,

Eitaro Shindo, Shinjiro Ebara, Isao Yamagata, Hitomi Nakahara, Naoko Kubo, Mitsue Komiya One of the promo photos from this depicts Takakura and Shindo in a bathhouse, both sporting full-upper-body tattoos, something not that common in pre-1963 yakuza films.

HELL'S JUGGLERS aka ORE GA JIGOKU NO TEJINASHI DA aka I'M THE MAGICIAN OF HELL 1961 89 min. DIR. Shigehiro Ozawa SCR. Toshio Matsuura PHOTO 'scope: Shoe Nishikawa MUSIC: Chumei Watanabe w/ Chiezo Kataoka, Koji Tsuruta, Ken Takakura, Shinjiro Ebara, Hiroki Matsukata, Eitaro Shindo, Katsuo Nakamura, Takashi Kanda, Mitsue Komiya, Yoshiko Sakuma, Yunosuke Ito, Naoko Kubo, So Yamamura
Big lug nebbish Shindo escapes from Abashiri Prison. He had taken the blame for a murder committed by his *oyabun*. Dapper undercover cop/super-magician (!) Kataoka, suave young fellow fugitive Nakamura and police detective Tsuruta help him. The errant boss is in the process of playing two other gangs off against each other, and he ends by paying dearly for his Machievellian shenanigans. This is an irredeemably silly gangster adventure comedy which really doesn't pretend to be anything else. Entertaining on its own for some of the hoary, old-fashioned cliches trotted out as well as some outlandish dueling magician antics between Kataoka and villainous rival conjurer Ito. Takakura and Ebara are members of the dead boss's gang who assist Shindo and Kataoka in overthrowing the "evil" gang. Reminiscent of some of the throwaway comedies the

Hell's Jugglers

Hollywood studios' B-movie units were churning out in the late forties.
* *

**BREAK OUT FROM THE
DEPTHS OF HELL** aka JIGOKU
NO SOKO O BUCHI YABURE
1962 **DIR.** Ko (Yasushi) Sasaki
SCR. Toshio Matsuura **PHOTO**
'SCOPE: Shoe Nishikawa **w/** Chiezo
Kataoka, Shinjiro Ebara, Chikage
Awajima, Kotaro Satomi, Yoshiko
Mita, Naoko Kubo, Hiroshi Minami,
Shigemi Kitahara, Nakajiro Tomita

TRAITORS GO TO HELL
aka URAGIRI MONO WA JIGOKU
DAZE aka HELL IS FOR TRAI-
TORS 1962 **DIR.** Shigehiro Ozawa
SCR. Toshio Matsuura **PHOTO** 'SCOPE:
Shoe Nishikawa **MUSIC:** Seiichi
Suzuki **w/** Ken Takakura, Chiezo
Kataoka, Koji Tsuruta, Yoshiko Mita,
Tatsuo Umemiya, Shinjiro Ebara,

Yoshiko Sakuma, Eitaro Shindo,
Tetsuro Tanba, Shinobu Chihara,
Hisako Tsukuba

DECREE FROM HELL aka
JIGOKU MEIREI 1964 **DIR.**
Shigehiro Ozawa **SCR.** Toshio
Matsuura/Akira Murao **PHOTO COLOR**
'SCOPE: Shoe Nishikawa **MUSIC:**
Satoshi Suzuki **w/** Chiezo Kataoka,
Michiyo Kogure, Tatsuo Umemiya,
Shinjiro Ebara, Shinichi "Sonny"
Chiba, Koji Nanbara, Yoshiko
Sakuma, Eitaro Shindo

JUDGE OF THE UNDERWORLD
aka JIGOKU NO SABAKI WA ORE
GA SURU 1967 94 min. **DIR.**
Shigehiro Ozawa **SCR.** Toshio
Matsuura **PHOTO COLOR** 'SCOPE:
Shoe Nishikawa **MUSIC:** Seiichi
Suzuki **w/** Chiezo Kataoka, Koji
Tsuruta, Shinjiro Ebara, Hiroki Mat-
sukata, Eijiro Yanagi, Eitaro Shindo,
Chiyoko Honma, Yumiko Hasega
Final in the series?

HELL ON THE WHARF aka
FUTO NO NAWABARI 1959 **DIR.**
Kiyoshi Saeki **w/** Shinjiro Ebara,
Yoshiko Sakuma

HENCHMEN aka DAIGASHI aka
MERCENARY GENERATION aka
THREE CHIVALROUS MEN 1968
89 min. **DIR.** Kiyoshi Saeki **SCR.**
Goro Tanada **PHOTO COLOR** 'SCOPE:
Kiichi Inada **MUSIC:** Kanyo Ogawa
w/ Tatsuo Umemiya, Koji Tsuruta,
Tomisaburo Wakayama, Minoru Oki,
Ryutaro Tatsumi, Yuki Jono, Mari
Shiraki, Shingo Yamashiro, Yoko
Mihara, Bin Amatsu, Kenji Imai
In the early 1930s, discharged soldier
Umemiya returns to his hometown,

meeting burly lone wolf yakuza
Wakayama in the process. The two go
back and forth being friends/enemies
until they hook up again with returning mutual pal and revered yakuza
Tsuruta in the last half hour. At that
point, their bond is cemented, and the
three storm bad boss Oki's stronghold
after one too many transgressions by
Oki's brutal cohorts. Director Saeki
and writer Tanada take a fairly routine
plot and, by refusing to resort to the
usual extremes of character (which
often become caricatures in many
Toei *ninkyo* productions), manage to imbue this effort with some
occasional glimpses of recogniz-
able humanity. Although Umemiya
and Tsuruta (sporting a black metal
hand!) are not particularly interesting
characters, Wakayama gets to stretch
a bit more than usual, offering some
tender moments towards Umemiya's
persecuted sister Jono and giving in
to an emotional outburst upon being
reunited with Tsuruta. Likewise bad
guys Oki and Mihara (playing Oki's
mistress) achieve a fuller dimension than villains usually do in Toei
ninkyo efforts. Make no mistake, they
are unscrupulous bastards, but they
are also people with a wide range of
emotions. Although Shiraki, portraying Tsuruta's longsuffering wife, and
Jono don't get to do that much, their
characters nevertheless rise above
cardboard level. It is especially nice
to see Shiraki in a decent role. She
is certainly one of the more underrated actresses in 1960s Japanese
genre cinema. After she had earned
minor stardom for a couple of years
in the late 1950s as one of Nikkatsu's
leading ladies (especially in Seijun
Suzuki's UNDERWORLD BEAU-
TY), she soon became relegated to

very minor supporting roles at Toei
in the following decade. But for all of
HENCHMEN's virtues, the fact that
violent action stems naturally from
real conflicts and is not artificially
inserted, the fighting is not that much
in evidence till the end, saddles the
film with occasional, boring talking
heads sequences. * * *

HERO GAMPEKI aka HOERO
GAMPEKI 1960 **DIR.** Eijiro
Wakabayashi **SCR.** Morimasa Owaku
PHOTO 'SCOPE: Shizuka Fujii **MUSIC:**
Hideo Ozawa w/ Shinjiro Ebara,
Yoshiko Sakuma, Mitsuo Komiya,
Kenji Imai, Rinichi Yamamoto,
Nakajiro Tomita

HIGH NOON FOR GANGSTERS
aka HAKUCHU NO BURAIKAN
aka VILLAINS IN BROAD DAY-
LIGHT 1961 82 min **DIR.** Kinji
Fukasaku **SCR.** Susumu Saji **PHOTO**
B&W 'SCOPE: Ichiro Hoshijima
MUSIC: Tomokazu Kawabe
w/ Tetsuro Tanba, Naoko Kubo, Isaac
Saxon, Danny Yuma, Harumi Sone,
Hitomi Nakahara, Mitsuo Ando
Tanba assembles a motley crew
including a Korean, two American
men (one black, one white) and three
women. They engineer a hold-up of a
U.S. Army base payroll but are nearly
thwarted when another gang has the
same idea. Escaping with the loot,
things go further awry when they
begin squabbling amongst themselves. Dying Kubo, Tanba's jilted
mistress, blows him up after the rest
of the gang is decimated. The only
one to survive is the innocent mulatto
Japanese-American woman. This was
Fukasaku's earliest full-length feature
(as opposed to the short WANDER-
ING DETECTIVE second features

stills from **High Noon for Gangsters**

Fukasaku initially did with then-newcomer Shinichi "Sonny" Chiba). There are many wild ideas and daringly offbeat juxtapositions. One that is still as timely now as it was in 1961 shows cynical manipulator Tanba using the racist tension generated by southern cracker played by Danny Yuma, who is jealous of his nympho wife's attention to black rapist/G.I. deserter Isaac Saxon, to keep the whole gang slightly off-kilter and under his thumb. Believed lost until very recently, HIGH NOON... elements were found in early 2000. The mushrooming interest in Fukasaku's films around the world subsequently caused new prints to be struck and begin circulating . * * *

HIROSHIMA HONOR AND HUMANITY – STRATEGY FOR RECAPTURING THE HOSTAGE aka HIROSHIMA JINGI – HITO-JICHI DAKKAI SAKUSEN aka HIROSHIMA GAMBLING

CODE 1976 90 min. **DIR.** Yuji Makiguchi   **SCR.** Isao Matsumoto/ Ichiro Otsu **PHOTO COLOR 'SCOPE:** Shigeru Akatsuka **MUSIC:** Takeo Watanabe   **w/** Hiroki Matsukata, Akira Kobayashi, Yutaka Nakajima, Hideo Murota, Tomomi Sato, Ryuji Katagiri, Isao Natsuyagi, Takuzo Kawatani, Kenji Imai, Takeo Chii Kobayashi cuts down everyone in his path, finally betraying his best friend Matsukata, despite his misgivings, to stay top man in Hiroshima. Director Makiguchi is best known for following in Teruo Ishii's footsteps, continuing an *ero/guro* series of sadistic films featuring historical samurai torture vignettes, also for Toei, in the late 1970s/early 1980s. Here he proves himself adept at helming a relatively decent, uncompromising *jitsuroku* picture, which is unfortunately his only effort in that subgenre. * * *

HISTORY OF THE RISE AND FALL OF CHIVALRY – BOSS AND HENCHMEN aka NIN-KYO KOBOSHI – KUMICHO TO DAIGASHI aka BORN CHIVAL-ROUS 1970 96 min. **DIR.** Yasuo Furuhata **SCR.** Kazuo Kasahara/ Kibu Nagata **PHOTO COLOR 'SCOPE:** Ichiro Hoshijima **MUSIC:** Shunsuke Kikuchi **w/** Koji Tsuruta, Kyosuke Machida, Makoto Sato, Akiko Kudo, Tadashi Sawamura, Minoru Oki, Ichiro Sugai, Rinichi Yamamoto, Nobuo Yana, Hideo Murota   Nightclub owner and former bigwig yakuza Tsuruta goes up against greedy boss Yamamoto in a drugs dispute. Compromised Oki is caught in the middle. Tsuruta's comrades, hotheaded Sato and tubercular Machida and girlfriend Kudo help him, but all is for naught. Machida is taken prisoner, and both

*History of the Rise and Fall of
Chivalry - Boss and Henchmen*

Sato and he are killed when they try
to do a drug-for-hostage swap. Although Tsuruta eventually triumphs
over Yamamoto, he is overrun and
killed by the dead man's henchmen.
A diverting but not particularly
distinctive programmer full of gritty
action. Yet another *ninkyo/jitsuroku*
hybrid made as the genre was mu-
tating into more realistic accounts of
the Japanese underworld. * * *

**IMPACT! PROSTITUTION
CAPITAL** aka SHOGEKI!
BAISHUN TO 1974 **DIR.** Makoto
Naito **SCR.** Masahiro Kakefuda/
Nobuharu Nakajima **PHOTO COLOR**
'SCOPE: Masao Shimizu **MUSIC:**
Toshiaki Tsushima **w/** Tatsuo
Umemiya, Noboru Shiraishi, Yutaka
Nakajima, Sami Suzuki, Asao
Uchida, Hosei Komatsu, Hiroshi
Nawa, Fumio Watanabe, Chie
Kobayashi   G-men vs. yakuza
prostitution rackets with, judging

from the production date, undoubtedly prodigious sexploitation elements.

IMPUDENT VIXEN aka
ABAZURE 1966 **DIR.** Yusuke
Watanabe **SCR.** Yusuke Watanabe/
Fumio Konami **w/** Mako Midori

INSANE BEAST aka KURUTTA
YAJU 1976 **DIR.** Sadao Nakajima
SCR. Sadao Nakajima/Kiyohide
Ohara/ Ikuo Sekimoto **PHOTO COLOR**
'SCOPE: Kenji Tsukagoe **MUSIC:**
Kenjiro Hirose **w/** Tsunehiko
Watase, Jun Hoshino, Takuzo
Kawatani, Ryuji Katagiri, Kojiro
Shirakawa   More of a suspense film
with some yakuza trappings as a
group of wacked-out punk hoodlums
take bus passengers hostage.

INSANE SEX TRIBE aka KYO
SO SEKKUSU ZOKU 1973 **DIR.**
Takashi Minagawa **SCR.** Takashi
Minagawa/Norifumi Suzuki **PHOTO**
COLOR 'SCOPE: Umeo Masuda
w/ Tsunehiko Watase, Takashi Shirai,
Miki Sugimoto, Hiroko Isayama,
Hiroshi Nawa, Yoko Mihara, Rokko
Toura   A decent premise but unhappily a bit threadbare in execution.
Motorcycle cop Watase has it in for
upper middle class bad boy Shirai, the
leader of a small *bosozoku* biker pack
given to rape, mayhem and general
unsafe driving practices. Shirai perpetually dresses all in white with an
American flag on hs helmet. I am not
sure if this is supposed to symbolize
his individuality or his callous dis-
regard for others – possibly both. Or
then again, perhaps it just means he
is trendy. The feud between Shirai
and Watase escalates after several
arrests, and Shirai retaliates by raping Isayama, Watase's moody, rock

groupie (!) girlfriend. Watase gradually oversteps his bounds and is sus-
pended from the force. Meanwhile,
Shirai finds true love with sports car-
driving, cool cat loner Sugimoto. He
also has a falling out with his three
violent partners when they try to rape
Sugimoto in the woods. There are
many so-so motorcycle chases in the
film, culminating in Watase's mam-
moth unauthorized pursuit of Shirai
at the end, something which climaxes
in Shirai's death. Watase's superiors
catch up after it is all over and arrest
the out-of-control ex-cop. Shirai's
lonely corpse is left on the asphalt in
a pool of blood with only Sugimoto to
mourn him. Though lacking in originality, the story has potential, which
newcomer director Minagawa only
occasionally realizes. Also, though
lacking in the usual stupid humor so
often found in most other *bosozoku*
films, this does start with a hilarious,
out-of-left-field encounter between
Shirai's lusty pack and four sexy
young ladies riding around on their
motorcycles in the nude! The lead bad
girl of the nudist bikers also seduces
Shirai's father Nawa, but then she
disappears from the tale after the first
fifteen minutes and is regrettably
never heard from again.   * * 1/2

**ISHIMATSU OF THE STREET
PEDDLERS** aka TEKIYA NO
ISHIMATSU 1976 DIR. Shigehiro
Ozawa SCR. Akira Murao/Isao
Matsumoto/ Shigehiro Ozawa PHOTO
COLOR 'SCOPE: Umeo Masuda
MUSIC: Hachiro Aoyama w/ Hiroki
Matsukata, Bunsaku Han, Linda
Yamamoto, Asao Koike   An updat-
ing of the Ishimatsu character, a usu-
ally found in the period yakuza film,
done as a boisterous action/comedy.

**JAPAN'S DON aka NIHON NO
DON series**

**JAPAN'S DON – GREAT YAKU-
ZA WAR** aka NIHON NO DON –
YAKUZA DAI SENSO 1977 132
min. DIR. Sadao Nakajima SCR.
Koji Takada PHOTO COLOR 'SCOPE:
Umeo Masuda MUSIC: Harumi Ibe/
Toshiro Mayuzumi w/ Shin Saburi,
Koji Tsuruta, Hiroki Matsukata, Ko
Nishimura, Etsushi Takahashi, Asao
Uchida, Bunta Sugawara, Shinichi
"Sonny" Chiba, Asao Koike, Mikio
Narita, Shotaro Hayashi, Tsunehiko
Watase, Tatsuo Umemiya
A supposedly true-to-life story of
one of the biggest rightists/yakuza
bosses in 1950s-'60s Japan (Yoshio
Kodama?) played by Saburi. By this
time, many of Toei's yakuza films
were starting to acquire a slick,
overly-professional sheen that robbed
them of much of their vitality. Also,
gradually diminishing attendance,
even for yakuza *eiga* , were forcing
companies like Toei to go for the
all-star cast epics – something which
accomplished nothing. The films were
in danger of becoming big-budget
snorefests. The story is continued in
two subsequent films. #1 of 3 films
* * 1/2

**JAPAN'S DON – SAGA OF
AMBITION** aka NIHON NO DON
– YABO HEN 1977 141 min.
DIR. Sadao Nakajima SCR. Koji
Takada PHOTO COLOR 'SCOPE:
Umeo Masuda MUSIC: Toshiro
Mayuzumi w/ Shin Saburi, Toshio
Mifune, Hiroki Matsukata, Bunta
Sugawara, Kyoko Kishida, Naoko
Otani, Etsushi Takahashi, Sayoko

Nimiya, Mikio Narita, Takuyo Fujioka, Eitaro Ozawa, Kanjuro Arashi   One of Mifune's very few yakuza film appearances, and he does not look too enthusiastic about it. He all but walks through the role in a wooden, leaden state. #2 of 3 films * * 1/2

JAPAN'S DON – SAGA CONCLUSION aka NIHON NO DON – KANKETSU HEN 1978 131 min. DIR. Sadao Nakajima SCR. Koji Takada PHOTO COLOR 'SCOPE: Umeo Masuda MUSIC: Toshiro Mayuzumi w/ Shin Saburi, Toshiro Mifune, Chiezo Kataoka, Bunta Sugawara, Naoko Otani, Ko Nishimura #3 and last of series * * 1/2

JAPAN'S G-MEN – SKYSCRAPER WOLVES aka NIPPON G-MEN – MATENRO NO OKAMI 1960 DIR. Masamitsu Igayama SCR. Junji Tashiro/ Susumu Takahisa PHOTO 'SCOPE: Hiroshi Fukujima MUSIC: Hajime Kaburagi w/ Tatsuo Umemiya, Yoshiko Mita

JAPAN'S G-MEN – SPECIAL ARMS SQUAD GOING OUT aka NIPPON G-MEN – TOKUBETSU BUSO HAN SHUTSU DO 1956 DIR. Eiichi Koishi SCR. Mansaku Haru PHOTO: Ichiro Hoshijima MUSIC: Saburo Iida w/ Katsuhei Matsumoto, Ken Takakura, Fusataro Ishijima, Ken Sudo

JAPAN'S MOST CHIVALROUS aka NIHON DAI KYOKAKU 1966 95 min. DIR. Masahiro Makino SCR. Kazuo Kasahara PHOTO COLOR 'SCOPE: Nagaki Yamagishi MUSIC: Shunsuke Kikuchi w/ Koji Tsuruta,

Junko Fuji, Minoru Oki, Jushiro Konoe, Eiji Okada, Michiyo Kogure, Takehiro Nakamura, Yuriko Mishima, Asao Uchida, Bin Amatsu   Set in early 1890s Osaka, Tsuruta portrays a less complex, more extroverted character than usual. Fireworks ignite from the outset, with Tsuruta taking money from a gang who refuse to pay after he has won their cockfight. Fuji is stupendous in the atypical role of a smart-aleck geisha in madam Kogure's inn who, along with Tsuruta, holds off the bad guys with sword and gun. Another welcome variation has typecast Amatsu getting to play a good guy, an old pal of Tsuruta. Complications set in for Tsuruta when Kogure dies of illness, and he is forced into becoming guardian to her daughter Mishima. Since Tsuruta is also active in good bosses Nakamura and Ryuji Shinagawa's coal-carters' clan, villain boss Uchida and his deceptively good-natured *yojinbo* Konoe, have it in for him. Okada, in a rare yakuza role, delivers an impressive, understated performace as Oki's old friend, a tubercular assassin hired by Konoe to kill Tsuruta. However, once he has challenged Tsuruta, he begins coughing up so much blood he cannot continue, and Tsuruta and Oki take him to the hospital. Frustrated in her feelings for lover Tsuruta, depressed Fuji gets drunk and raises a ruckus at the geisha inn with a sword. When Tsuruta goes to calm her, she is so distraught she tries to run him through. Oki restrains her, and she tearfully flees. Konoe et. al. make their move to take over the ethical coal carting interests. This results in Tsuruta and Oki attempting to negotiate with political bigwigs that have been brought in.

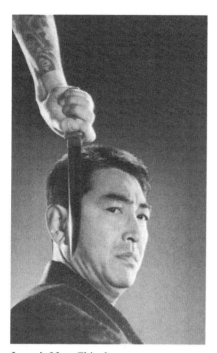

Japan's Most Chivalrous

One of the ostentatious politicians arrives with the missing Fuji in tow, now in westernized dress and a kept woman. This only adds to Tsuruta's shock and disapointment when Uchida and Konoe's gang comes out on top. Fuji agrees to rendezvous with Tsuruta at their old meeting place under the pier, and she is bitter. Okada returns to warn Tsuruta's clan, then assists them in a running gun and sword battle through the streets that ends at bad guy HQ. Okada perishes killing greedy boss Uchida. But when Tsuruta and Oki close in on Konoe, he commits impromptu *hara-kiri*. Once the battle is over, Fuji shoots herself in the heart in the middle of the street! This is an extremely fast-moving, emotionally draining saga and is the best version of this familiar tale. Director Makino remade it with Shintaro Katsu, Machiko Kyo and

Michiyo Yasuda as TALE OF DARK OCEAN CHIVALRY – WITH THE COURAGE OF DESPERATION at Daiei in 1970. This version is the better of the two. * * * *

JAPAN'S UNDERWORLD HISTORY aka NIHON ANKOKUSHI series

JAPAN'S UNDERWORLD HISTORY – BLOOD FEUD aka NIHON ANKOKUSHI – CHI NO KOSO aka A HISTORY OF THE JAPANESE UNDERWORLD – THE BLOODY RESISTANCE 1967 90 min. **DIR.** Eiichi Kudo **SCR.** Susumu Saji **PHOTO COLOR 'SCOPE:** Juhei Suzuki **MUSIC:** Masao Yagi w/ Noboru Ando, Asao Koike, Ryohei Uchida, Junzaburo Ban, Michiko Saga, Toru Abe, Shingo Yamashiro Ando gets nailed after attacking U.S. Occupation soldiers with a shovel when they rape some Japanese home girls. How many yakuza films have opened this very same way? A local Japanese police detective (Ban, in an unusual dramatic role) takes him into custody but refuses to turn him over to the U.S. Army for imprisonment without a hearing. Thus a bond is established that we will see more of throughout the story. Starting at the bottom, Ando and pals start a gang and, of course, achieve success selling black market items, intimidating folks, strikebreaking, pimping, etc.,. This has one of the funniest pinkie-cutting scenes in any yakuza picture with a wild guy who had botched an assassination attempt, jumping up and down, screaming and crying under a blanket. Also a great scene where Ando, going stir-crazy in jail during

Japan's Underworld History (#1) - Blood Feud

questioning, tears off a jagged piece of his tin meal plate and swallows it. He succeeds in getting transferred to a hospital ward where all his loyal pals and underlings congregate. At one point, they kill a squealer there in Ando's room, roll him up in a sheet and then sneak the body out. Next, they sneak Ando out right past the guards. The whole mob heads over to the rival gang HQ and, in broad daylight, start a firefight. Of course, the cops soon arrive. Ando's gang holds up in a building, and it is open warfare. Ando is pale, having lost a lot of blood and supposedly still bleeding internally. When the cops finally storm the bastion, and Ando is led away, he suddenly breaks from his captors, grabs a pistol and annihilates the opposition's gang boss (who is also being arrested). Ando's cop rival Ban – the guy who had stood up for him so many years before and had an emotional stake in his welfare – flips out and has to be pulled off as he shouts and pummels the barely surviving Ando with his fists. Exhausting and mindblowing, though it does have some slow patches. #1 of 2 films * * * 1/2

JAPAN'S UNDERWORLD HISTORY – FUTILE COMPASSION aka NIHON ANKOKUSHI – NASAKE MUYO aka HISTORY OF JAPANESE UNDERWORLD 1968 90 min. **DIR.** Eiichi Kudo **SCR.** Susumu Saji/ Ryonosuke Kono **PHOTO COLOR 'SCOPE:** Shin Furuya **MUSIC:** Hajime Kaburagi **w/** Noboru Ando, Fumio Watanabe, Hiroko Sakuramachi, Asao Koike, Toru Abe

Ando, under the patronage of godfather Abe, cultivates a gang by recruiting members from the various l

Japan's Underworld History (#2)

anti-social young males in the loca community. Sakuramachi is a delight to watch in the atypical role of Abe's evervescent daughter who is not only Ando's bookkeeper but also his good natured, opinionated wife. Former Osaka associate boss Watanabe slyly plays up an accidental misunderstanding between Ando's bunch and allied boss Koike's gang, something that leads to escalating violence. One of Ando's resentful men, doing Watanabe's bidding, assassinates Koike. This brings things to a boil with in-law/godfather Abe who nearly kills Ando. His temper is diffused when his daughter Sakuramachi tearfully shields her husband. But Ando's troubles are not over. The cops stage a raid on his HQ, arresting everyone. Ando and Sakuramachi escape by the skin of their teeth and, the next day, drive to where Watanabe is breaking ground for his shoreline project. Ando shoots Watanabe to death, then has a running gun battle with his minions along the muddy shore. As Ando is felled by bullets, Sakuramachi runs to his side. She, too, is cut down, and the two lie dead in a pool of bloody mud. Director Kudo expertly steers this early, prototypical *jitsuroku* picture, eschewing much of the silly humor and overly exploitive sex that sometimes mars similar films.   #2 of 2 films * * *

JAPAN'S VIOLENT GANGS aka NIHON BORYOKUDAN series

JAPAN'S VIOLENT GANGS – BOSS aka NIHON BORYOKUDAN – KUMICHO aka THE BOSS aka JAPAN ORGANIZED CRIME BOSS 1969 96 min. **DIR.** Kinji Fukasaku **SCR.** Kinji Fukasaku/Fumio Konami/ Kibu Nagata **PHOTO COLOR 'SCOPE:** Hanjiro Nakazawa **MUSIC:** Masanobu Higurashi **w/** Koji Tsuruta, Tomisaburo Wakayama, Bunta Sugawara, Noboru Ando, Michitaro Mizushima, Ryohei

Uchida, Sanae Nakahara, Seizaburo Kawazu, Asao Uchida, Rinichi Yamamoto

Japan's Violent Gangs (#1) - Boss

A detailed story with believable characters that is one of the several transitional preludes from *ninkyo* to *jitsuroku* (true account) yakuza *eiga*. A greedy older boss (Asao Uchida) begins to whittle away bosses of allied opposition gangs, assimilating the surviving mobsters into his corporate hoodlum monolith, until only avenging Tsuruta is left. Wakayama's character, a bullyingly childish, drug-addicted boor, slaps boss Tsuruta around when Tsuruta comes to collect one of the homeboys who has been beaten up by Wakayama's gang. When stoic Tsuruta stands his ground and does not strike back, he wins Wakayama's respect – even though immediately after Tsuruta leaves, Wakayama takes it out on his own men, beating the shit out of anyone in his path. When it is Wakayama's turn to be cut down, he calls Tsuruta in the middle of the night from where he is hiding alone in a deserted nightclub. An incredible scene ensues where Wakayama spills his guts trying to make emotional contact with the only person he knows he can trust. Tsuruta listens sympathetically and is moved to impotent rage as he hears over the receiver the doors being broken down and Wakayama executed. Part of this film's success is the use of Tsuruta, a traditional actor with a stoic, melancholy persona most often associated with chivalrous roles, as a protagonist coming up against the unprincipled rabid wolfpacks of the postwar modern gangster. His roles in the more realistic yakuza films of the very late sixties/early seventies were rumored to be not always to his liking. Directors such as Fukasaku and Junya Sato used this dichotomy to create a real dynamic tension that can be palpably felt on the screen. Also of note, Ryohei Uchida is his usual excellent self as a chivalrous friend of Tsuruta (perpetually clad in a white suit) duty-bound to the rival corporate gang, something which helps to cement his, as well as Tsuruta's, demise. #1 of 4 films   * * * 1/2

JAPAN'S VIOLENT GANGS – THE BOSS AND THE KILLERS aka NIHON BORYOKUDAN – KUMICHO TO SHIKAKU 1969 92 min. DIR. Junya Sato SCR. Junya Sato/Fumio Konami PHOTO COLOR 'SCOPE: Hanjiro Nakazawa MUSIC: Masanobu Higurashi w/ Koji Tsuruta, Takashi Shimura, Ryohei Uchida, Tetsuro Tamba, Hitomi Nozoe, Tadao Nakamaru, Asao Uchida, Fumio Watanabe, Ichiro Sugai, Michitaro Mizushima

Tsuruta is ambushed in broad daylight by a rival gang while walking beside a parade route during festival. He escapes them, dodging into the back room of a small, deserted shop in a back alley. The woman owner helps, finding him medical attention. While recuperating, flashbacks waft through his mind, and we see the events that led up to the violence. As per usual, there is an emotionally draining, nihilistic ending. #2 of 4 films * * *

JAPAN'S VIOLENT GANGS – DEGENERATE BOSS aka NIHON BORYOKUDAN – KUMICHO KUZURE aka EPITAPH FOR AN UNKNOWN GANGSTER 1970 93 min. DIR. Shin Takakuwa SCR. Shin Takakuwa/Fumio Konami PHOTO COLOR "SCOPE: Hanjiro Nakazawa MUSIC: Toshiaki Tsushima w/ Koji Tsuruta, Ryo Ikebe, Tomisaburo Wakayama, Akiko Kudo, Fumio Watanabe, Ryoji Hayama, Rinichi Yamamoto, Kyosuke Machida
This starts with Tsuruta coming out of the fog, entering a house and assassinating a rival boss right in front of his terrified wife. Cut to a stripper as the titles unspool while a terrifically sleazy jazz/R'n'B score plays. When Tsuruta gets out of jail he takes over a nightclub aided by loyal Yamamoto and best friend Ikebe. Of course, there are folks out to get Tsuruta for his past sins. This entry includes some of the series' most brutal violence, especially the bad guys' torture of Tsuruta's girlfriend Kudo. #3 of 4 films * * *

JAPAN'S VIOLENT GANGS – LOYALTY OFFERING MURDER aka NIHON BORYOKUDAN – KOROSHI NO SAKAZUKI

Japan's Violent Gangs (#2) - The Boss and the Killers

Japan's Violent Gangs (#3)- Degenerate Boss

1972 98 min. **DIR.** Yasuo Furuhata
SCR. Kazuo Kasahara **PHOTO COLOR**
'SCOPE: Shigeru Akatsuka **MUSIC:**
Takeo Yamashita **w/** Koji Tsuruta,
Tetsuro Tanba, Akiko Kudo, Rinichi
Yamamoto, Hiroyuki Nagato,
Kyosuke Machida, Seizaburo
Kawazu, Bin Amatsu, Hosei
Komatsu, Hiroshi Nawa   One of
my favorite yakuza films. Tsuruta is
leaving a friend's upstairs gambling
den when it is robbed, and he has to
shoot-to-death the attackers. Due to
the heat, he goes to another town to
lay low and is the guest of yakuza
boss Tanba. Tanba's clan is small
but successful; the guys are not any
saints, but they are also not murderously greedy nor overly ambitious.
The other gangs in town *are,* and
Tsuruta finds himself drawn into the
feud out of obligation to Tanba.
To complicate matters, one of Tanba's
henchmen, a not particularly bright
fellow, played by Rinichi Yamamoto
in a devastatingly neurotic performance, resents Tsuruta's help and intru-
sion. Before long, Tsuruta, in defending himself, makes this guy lose face.
Gradually, out of *jingi* and *giri* –
loyalty code and obligation – to
Tanba, Yamamoto comes unraveled.
He is wrapped so tight he cannot
tolerate Tsuruta's friendship/counsel
with Tanba, and before long he is
plotting to kill Tsuruta. He is foiled,
but loses even further face when
Tsuruta intervenes to save his life
from a very angry Tanba. Plus don't
forget, meanwhile, we have the
vicious rival usurpers waiting in the
wings for a false move.

*Japan's Violent Gangs (#4) - Loyalty
Offering Murder*

Tsuruta is squeezed between the bad
guys, Tanba's clan, the psycho-obses-
sive Yamamoto (who has been thrown
out of the gang) and loyal, adoring
girlfriend Kudo. Kudo is one of
several unsung heroines of the yakuza

film genre. Some of these actresses, such as Junko Fuji, Meiko Kaji, Hiroko Ogi, Yumiko Nogawa, Reiko Ike, Michiyo Yasuda, Kyoko Enami, Junko Miyazono, Eiko Nakamura et.al., were lucky enough to have several motion pictures or even a film series built around their personas. But they, too, along with such great talents as Kudo, Mayumi Nagisa, Sanae Nakahara, Sanae Kitabayashi, Kayo Matsuo, Yoshiko Sakuma, Yukiji Asaoka, Shiho Fujimura (and others too numerous to mention) often had to put up with skimpy, stereotypical, occasionally sexist parts. It is a testament to their fortitude and professionalism that they managed to make their roles come alive with an empathy for character, a sensual vitality, all the time drawing on their personal arsenals of subtle body language, nuanced inflection and uninhibited intelligence. Akiko Kudo's performance here, where her love and loyalty to Tsuruta's character drive her to help him complete his vendetta when he is mortally wounded, is a case in point. #4 and last of the series * * * *

JAPAN'S VIOLENT ISLANDS – MURDER IN THE CAPITAL BY AN ARMY OF KILLERS aka NIHON BORYOKU RETTO – KEI HANSHIN KOROSHI NO GUNDAN 1975 93 min. DIR. Kosaku Yamashita SCR. Isao Matsumoto/Tatsuo Nogami PHOTO COLOR 'SCOPE: Nagaki Yamagishi MUSIC: Masao Yagi w/ Akira Kobayashi, Tatsuo Umemiya, Mikio Narita, Yutaka Nakajima, Goro Ibuki, Nobuo Káneko, Yoko Koizumi, Tatsuo Endo, Toru Abe, Kenji Imai Lower echelon but powerful yakuza

comrades Kobayashi and Umemiya are eventually betrayed by the icy, white-collar Narita. Umemiya is murdered, but Kobayashi achieves retribution on Narita at the film's denouement. * * *

Japan's Violent Islands - Murder in the Capital by an Army of Killers

JEAN'S BLUES – VILLAINS WITHOUT A TOMORROW aka JIINZU BURUUSU – ASU NAKI BURAI HA 1974 91 min. DIR. Sadao Nakajima SCR. Sadao Nakajima/ Takeo Kaneko PHOTO COLOR 'SCOPE: Umeo Masuda MUSIC: Tadao Inoue w/ Meiko Kaji, Tsunehiko Watase, Ryohei Uchida, Hideo Murota, Takuzo Kawatani When asked about this film in an interview, Kaji explained it was a project she had felt she had owed Toei's Kyoto branch at the time and advised me not to see it as she felt it was not up to par. Although proud of her work, she did not seem overly-enamored of any of her action/

yakuza films as they ended up helping to unfairly pigeonhole her as a mere action star. Something resoundingly disproved if you ever see her in any of director Yasuzo Masumura's masterworks from the late 1970s.

Jean's Blues - Villains Without a Tomorrow

JEAN'S BLUES is fairly uneven, but better than Kaji's description. Her character here is an excessively bored *mama-san* at a weird hostess/sex bar who takes off to wander, falling in with well-meaning ne'er-do-well Watase, who has just absconded with a huge wad of cash from sadistic killer thieves Uchida, Murota and Kawatani. The couple's odyssey leads them through a strange gauntlet of car crashes, beatings and shootouts, the violence escalating in what amounts to a modern Japanese take on Bonnie and Clyde. Watase accidentally drops the money along the way while Kaji loses her distaste for men, growing fond of her hard-luck companion.

Although the two try to avoid violence, once they are confronted with resistance they have no compunctions about killing the obstinate party. Their murders and the robbery of a gambling den lead the sadistic trio as well as the cops to their whereabouts, the rural village dwelling of Watase's delinquent sister. The film really comes alive in the last twenty minutes as leather-clad Kaji and her shotgun come to Watase's rescue in the mountains just a little too late. She kills stammering psychopath Kawatani and Uchida's treacherous girl while Uchida and Murota escape, only they then get picked off by the cops. Watase has already been beaten and stabbed, and dies a prolonged, difficult-to-watch death, all the time begging Kaji to finish him off. Which she reluctantly does, despite his sister's protests. Kaji lets the sister go as the cops surround the area. She decides to go down in a hail of gunfire and manages to take many cops out before being plugged between the eyes. The potential was certainly there for a minor classic, but muddled story construction and a thoroughly banal, soft rock score by Inoue suck the tension and energy out at key moments in the saga. Watase turns in a natural, relaxed performance while Kaji is appropriately stoic, undoubtedly using her own distaste for the script to embody her character's inability to feel much emotion about anyone or anything. Uchida and Murota are appropriately menacing but Kawatani is the standout of the three, hilarious as the pathetic nut so handicapped by stuttering he never ever finishes one of his lines. * * 1/2

JUDO LIFE aka JUDO ICHIDAI series

JUDO LIFE aka JUDO ICHIDAI 1963 **DIR.** Kiyoshi Saeki **SCR.** Toshio Matsuura **PHOTO 'SCOPE:** Shichiro Hayashi **MUSIC:** Taiichiro Kosugi w/ Shinichi "Sonny" Chiba, Naoki Sugiura, Takashi Kanda, Hideo Murata, Tetsu Saeki, Hisako Tsukuba, Harumi Sone, Apparently a *ninkyo* yakuza pair of films where *jujitsu* is the form of fighting. Also probably Chiba's first martial arts pictures. #1 of 2 films

JUDO LIFE – JUDO HALL DEMON aka JUDO ICHIDAI – KODOKAN NO ONI 1964 **DIR.** Kiyoshi Saeki **SCR.** Shinji Dezaki **PHOTO 'SCOPE:** Ichiro Hoshijima **MUSIC:** Hideo Ozawa w/ Shinichi "Sonny" Chiba, Hiroko Sakuramachi, Ryohei Uchida, Fukitake Omura, Chihoko Honma, Takashi Kanda, Rinichi Yamamoto #2 of 2 films

KAMIKAZE MAN – SHOW-DOWN AT NOON aka KAMIKA-ZE YARO – MAHIRU NO KETTO aka KAMIKAZE GUY 1966 90 min. **DIR./SCR.** Kinji Fukasaku **PHOTO COLOR 'SCOPE:** Yoshikazu (Giichi) Yamazawa **MUSIC:** Masao Yagi w/ Shinichi "Sonny" Chiba, Ken Takakura, Minoru Oki, Pailan, Hiroko Kuni, Ririko Sawa Three former soldiers who stole 20 billion yen worth of diamonds in Formosa during World War 2 then murdered their commander who wanted to return them, suddenly resurface. Takakura, the dead man's son, has been searching far and wide for the culprits. But footloose adventurer pilot Chiba has the same name and is, at first, mistaken by the bad guys for Takakura. Chiba becomes embroiled, along with his Taiwanese photographer sweetheart in the escalating death rate. A fairly innocuous timewaster with its tongue-firmly-in-cheek. Fukasaku keeps the action at full throttle so you don't really have time to think about the cliche plot. In fact, at some points, the choreography of mayhem becomes truly inspired. Chiba is in his action star element here, but for some reason Takakura is given little to do. His guest star status was undoubtedly intended to boost the box office. * * 1/2

Kamikaze Man - Showdown at Noon

KANSEI UNDERWORLD GANG aka KANSEI CHIKA SOSHIKI 1964 **DIR.** Masuichi Iizuka **SCR.** Kimiyuki Hasegawa w/ Minoru Oki, Shinichi "Sonny" Chiba

KANTO DRIFTER aka KANTO NAGAREMONO series

KANTO DRIFTER aka KANTO NAGAREMONO aka A VAGRANT FROM KANTO 1965 92 min. **DIR./ SCR.** Shigehiro Ozawa **PHOTO COLOR 'SCOPE:** Nagaki Yamagishi **MUSIC:** Shunsuke Kikuchi **w/** Koji Tsuruta, Junko Fuji, Minoru Oki, Akiko Koyama, Hideo Murata, Saburo Kitajima, Rinichi Yamamoto, Asao Uchida, Shingo Yamashiro, Tatsuo Endo The first entry in one of Toei's earliest *ninkyo* yakuza series. In the late Meiji era (early 1890s), Tsuruta is a respected wandering yakuza who makes enemies when he defeats rival Oki in a *kendo* match. After Oki and pals Yamamoto and Sone try to kill Tsuruta, boss Murata intervenes and the two men become comrades. Before long, Tsuruta and Oki go on a pilgrimage to Tsuruta's home village, which results in Tsuruta forming his own gang to run a local mining operation. This has boss Murata's blessing but does not sit well with Uchida, a rival boss. Koyama is a tormented geisha and former flame of Tsuruta's who gets together with Oki when he rescues her from gangsters. It is a measure of Tsuruta's chivalry that he wishes both of them well when they decide to marry. Feisty young Fuji is a woman activist who develops unrequited love for Tsuruta and, to complicate matters, is the daughter of greedy boss Uchida. Uchida decides to horn in on the mining interests and takes violent action, causing Koyama's death in a bombing and the killing of bullheaded Oki by ambush. This is the straw that breaks the camel's back, sending Tsuruta on a vendetta that decimates Uchida's

Kanto Drifter (#1)

whole mob. A tearful Fuji, placed between a rock and a hard place, shields her dad, causing Tsuruta to finally relent and spare the craven elder *oyabun*. Murata and other "good" yakuza arrive after it is all over, with the cops hot on their heels intent on

arresting Tsuruta.   #1 of 5 films
* * *

LONE KANTO YAKUZA aka
KANTO YAKUZA MONO aka
THE GAMBLER 1965 DIR./SCR.
Shigehiro Ozawa PHOTO COLOR
'SCOPE: Nagaki Yamagishi MUSIC:
Shunsuke Kikuchi w/ Koji Tsuruta,
Junko Fuji, Hideo Murata, Tetsuro
Tanba, Rinichi Yamamoto, Minoru
Oki, Saburo Kitajima, Kyosuke
Machida, Yuriko Mishima   Two opposing gangs, one led by Tsuruta and
Murata, the other by dapper, western-
ized Tanba and his doting mother,
run shipping businesses vying for
control of the early 1920s Tokyo
harbor. Thanks to Tanba's understated
performance, his villainous role is
not as one-dimensionally evil as is
usually the case in *ninkyo eiga*. He is
ruthless, but not totally without honor.
When he confronts Murata in a nocturnal showdown, he doesn't ambush
the opposing boss but hands him a
sword, forcing him into a fair duel.
When Murata is seriusly wounded,
Tanba doesn't finish him off. But his
honorable side is tempered by callous
practicality. When one of Tsuruta
and Murata's loyal men, terminally
tubercular Machida, singlehandedly
raids Tanba's HQ to kill him but is
unable to accomplish the task because
of a fit of bloody coughing, Tanba
restrains his men. Knowing Machida
is suffering a fatal hemmorhage, he
wants him to be unmarked when they
return his body to Tsuruta. Realizing
from his profiteering partners that the
recuperating Murata is still opposing
him, Tanba also decides to assassinate
Murata as he leaves the hospital.
Murata's death causes Tsuruta to
finally go over the edge. He attacks

Tanba's HQ, wiping out many of his
men and finally fighting a protracted
duel with Tanba. Since Tanba also
had a lot of experience in *chanbara*
samurai films, he and Tsuruta get to
actually do a bit more fencing than
is usually seen in a yakuza film's climactic battle. #2 of 5 films * * *

**EXPELLED FROM THE KANTO
MOB** aka KANTO HAMONJO
1965 DIR./ SCR. Shigehiro Ozawa
PHOTO COLOR 'SCOPE: Sadatsugu
Yoshida MUSIC: Shunsuke Kikuchi
w/ Koji Tsuruta, Hideo Murata,
Takahiro Tamura, Junko Fuji,
Takashi Shimura, Minoru Oki, Yuriko
Mishima, Nobuo Kaneko, Kazuko
Takamori   An unpretentious, fast-
moving tale of Tsuruta sticking up to
slimy boss Kaneko for comrade
Tamura, then getting mercilessly
beaten for his trouble. When Kaneko
is about to knife defiant pal Tamura,
Tsuruta grabs Kaneko's blade and
slashes the villain's arm off. Despite
being in the right, Tsuruta is expelled
from the clan by his boss, Shimura, to
avoid a gang war. Shimura's daughter, Fuji, is in love with Tsuruta and
mortified to see her beloved depart.
Tsuruta takes up residence in a small
town called Mishima, helping a female boss who runs a theatre troupe.
He soon becomes friends with Oki, a
misguided ruffian who has tried to kill
him twice for boss Kaneko. Meanwhile, back on Tsuruta's home turf,
Kaneko's evil influence mushrooms.
Tamura tries to singlehandedly raid
Kaneko's HQ to kill the boss but is
shot to death by Kaneko. Kaneko uses
Tamura's attack as a pretext to attack
Shimura's gang. They stage a nocturnal roust on Shimura's compound,
brutally killing him and many of his

men in front of powerless daughter Fuji. When Tsuruta learns of the tragedy, he and Oki travel to Shimura's funeral, confer with Fuji, then attack Kaneko's gang. The fighting spills out into the surrounding back alleys for a nicely choreographed string of action sequences. Both heroes are bloodied, but Tsuruta succeeds in finally eliminating one-armed monster Kaneko. A nicely balanced *ninkyo eiga* with a perfect orchestration of elements setting up the inevitable clash of "good-and-evil" with plenty of action. Tamura was son to famous silent *chanbara* star Tsumasaburo Bando and had previously appeared in many low budget Shochiku crime films as well as co-starring with Shintaro Katsu in Daiei Studio's mid-sixties HOODLUM SOLDIER series. He and Kurosawa film veteran Shimura get to actually sink their teeth into their roles a bit, something which doesn't always happen with the multitude of talented supporting players in most *ninkyo eiga*. #3 of 5 films
* * * 1/2

KANTO FIGHT CHALLENGE
aka KANTO HATASHIJO 1966
DIR. Shigehiro Ozawa SCR.
Shigehiro Ozawa/ Akira Murao
PHOTO COLOR 'SCOPE: Nagaki Yamagishi MUSIC: Toshiaki Tsushima w/ Koji Tsuruta, Minoru Oki, Rinichi Yamamoto, Junko Fuji, Hiromi Fujiyama, Seizaburo Kawazu, Hiroyuki Nagato, Hideo Murata, Hiroshi Nawa, Kusuo Abe After the brutally straightforward previous entry, this seems a bit more old-fashioned with some occasional sentimental contrivances as well as a dated score. It seems especially strange in regards to the music as the composer

was Toshiaki Tsushima who had just done some excellent, unusual scores for Hideo Gosha's THREE OUTLAW SAMURAI (1964) and SWORD OF THE BEAST (1965) and would go on to do Fukasaku's BATTLES WITHOUT HONOR & HUMANITY series in the 1970s. Only one bit of music sounds like Tsushima with the rest of the corny music resembling lifted cues from old fifties *chanbara* films.

Kanto Fight Challenge (#4)

Kawazu's gang begins causing havoc early on, trying to drive Murata's gang from the territory. Young Fuji is blinded when some villains throw dynamite at underboss Tsuruta, and there is much bittersweet interaction between the two as she tries to recover. However, Fuji inexplicably disappears for almost an hour in the middle of the film. Midway through the story, Kawazu catches Tsuruta's henchmen Fujiyama and Yamamoto cheating at *hana fuda* cards, and the film achieves its one superior

sequence as the carefree Fujiyama
is tortured to death, being dunked
headfirst into freezing well-water.
Yamamoto returns with Tsuruta,
and the two men are presented with
Fujiyama's corpse. There is a tense
standoff in the geisha house's snowy
courtyard with Tsuruta's pal Nagato –
one of Kawazu's men – taking sides
against him. Murata intervenes and a
bloodbath is averted. Kawazu finally
forces Nagato to betray Tsuruta,
ordering him to kill Murata. Nagato
sneaks into a meeting where Murata
is, then tries to stab him. When he
fails, Murata's men fatally stab Nagato before Tsuruta even knows what
is happening. One of Kawazu's other
men is stationed outside and shoots
Murata through the window, winging him. Tsuruta issues a challenge to
Kawazu's gang, and they rendezvous
at dawn on the banks of the river. The
film falters a bit here, straining for
epic status with a full-blown battle. It
is not until Tsuruta finally confronts
Kawazu and dispatches him that the
film finally gets back on track. #4 of
5 films * * 1/2

KANTO YAKUZA STORM aka
KANTO YAKUZA ARASHI 1966
DIR. Shigehiro Ozawa **SCR.** Shigehiro
Ozawa/ Ichiro Miyagawa **PHOTO
COLOR 'SCOPE:** Juhei Suzuki **MUSIC:**
Chuji Kinoshita **w/** Koji Tsuruta,
Rinichi Yamamoto, Shigeru Amachi,
Hiroko Sakuramachi, Junko
Miyazono, Hideo Murata, Yoshi
Kato, Hiromi Fujiyama, Bin Am-
atsu, Asao Uchida   A brawling,
two-fisted tall tale with a straightfor-
ward, no-nonsense narrative flow that
doesn't skimp on either story details
or action. Exceptionally violent for

Kanto Yakuza Storm (#5)

a *ninkyo* yakuza film in that it is not
just the climactic swordfight but
the whole picture that is punctuated
with mayhem. Cruelty and chaos
are constantly interrupting tender
romantic moments and more constructive human endeavors. Tsuruta
assassinates the boss father of his
beloved Sakuramachi after his own
boss Kato is seriously stabbed. After
a few years prison stay, Tsuruta is
released to discover his *oyabun* Kato
is still bedridden and the gang now
under the thumb of craven Amachi.
Amachi banishes Tsuruta, and Kato
supplies him with an introduction
to boss Murata's canal construction
gang. Yamamoto is the hard-drinking,
put-up-your-dukes Victor McClaglen-
type foreman who, at first, has it in
for Tsuruta. Following an extended
endurance challenge then fistfight,
they become pals. Meanwhile, old
flame Sakuramachi even though she
still carries a torch for Tsuruta, is
forced to become Amachi's mistress.

For his part, Tsuruta is still haunted with the image of her repeatedly calling him a fool while cradling her just-killed father in her arms. Miyazono is Yamamoto's kid sister who is also in love with Tsuruta and, in fact, saves his life by fatally stepping in front of a bullet for him when a full-scale gang war ignites. Tsuruta and Yamamoto retaliate, attacking Amachi's HQ for a protracted gun and sword fight that culminates with everyone dead. Mortally wounded Tsuruta is helped from the wreckage by Sakuramachi and Murata as the cops arrive. Very entertaining and unpretentious with a story somewhat varied from what would prove to be a strict formula in later sixties *ninkyo eiga*. The best of the series. Note: The more famous TALES OF JAPANESE CHIVALRY and TALES OF THE LAST SHOWA YAKUZA pictures were still to come, but this comparatively lesser known, excellent KANTO YAKUZA string of films set the template. #5 and last of the series * * * *

KANTO STREET PEDDLERS CLAN aka KANTO TEKIYA IKKA series

KANTO STREET PEDDLERS CLAN aka KANTO TEKIYA IKKA aka CODE OF RACKETEERS 1969 92 min. **DIR.** Norifumi Suzuki **SCR.** Akira Murao **PHOTO COLOR 'SCOPE:** Nagaki Yamagishi **MUSIC:** Shunsuke Kikuchi **w/** Bunta Sugawara, Minoru Oki, Hiroko Sakuramachi, Sanae Tsuchida, Tatsuo Terajima, Tomiko Ishii, Fumio Watanabe, Kanjuro Arashi, Bin Amatsu, Seizaburo Kawazu

A series relating the adventures of a major yakuza contingent that does not always receive as much of the spotlight as the *bakuto* (gamblers) and *gurentai* (hoodlums): *tekiya* or street peddlers – a collective of small merchants, entrepeneurs and "medicine show" types (some honest/on the up-and-up, some not) who have, historically, had a similar background to *bakuto* /gamblers.

Kanto Street Peddlers Clan (#1)

This background is a well-documented record of *tekiya* (just like *bakuto*) having had to band together into clans, despite their differences and territorial squabbles, to protect themselves from the samurai (in the past) and straight society/government (in the present) as well as unscrupulous gangsters. Sugawara portrays a comparatively ethical *tekiya* (a different character in each film) up against the usual cruelly unprincipled yakuza opposition. Sometimes, as in other series, Sugawara will be a lone wolf who does not even have much use for his own clan until his blood brothers are threatened or killed by the forces of evil yakuza. Then, reluctantly drawn into a spiralling-out-of-control-conflict, he becomes either the clan's savior or avenger (depending on the film) at the climax. In this first picture, Sugawara is a hardheaded, hot tempered member of elderly Arashi's gang of merchants. They come in conflict with the unholy alliance of evil bosses Watanabe, Amatsu and Kawazu. Family man Terajima is one of the few principled members in Watanabe's ranks, and he and Sugawara develop a mutual respect, then friendship. Tiring of Sugawara flying off the handle, boss Arashi makes a point of muzzling him by asking for his knife then taping it shut in its sheath. Subsequently, Sugawara's clan journeys to a neighboring town's festival and, in a ridiculous subplot, pick up mischievous Ishii and her female wrestling team who are stranded on the highway. Once at the festival, Sugawara pow-wows with liaison female boss Sakuramachi. Eventually decent Terajima is coerced into making an assassination attempt on Arashi, but Sugawara fends him off. When Terashima sees that his friends knife is still taped shut, he hesitates, only to have Sugawara's overzealous mates abruptly burst in and stab him to death. A picture of Terajima's wife and child falls to the floor and is soon covered in blood. Depressed, angry Sugawara begins to walk to bad guy HQ for revenge when best friend Machida knocks him out so he can wreak vengeance himself. This all resonates with extra poignance as Sugawara has long carried a torch for

tekiya Tsuchida, but she is in love with Machida. There is a wonderful moment when Machida, on his way to fight, goes to meet Tsuchida and her mom but only watches them from a distance, knowing he may never see them again. He then raids the gang HQ where Kawazu and Watanabe are playing mah jong. A wild knifefight erupts that quickly spills into a darkened pachinko parlor. To bring Machida down, the villains finally shoot him then stab him to death. Boss Arashi is simultaneously being murdered in a brutal drive-by. Sakuramachi and good guy Oki come to pay their respects. Upstairs alone in his room, bathed in the red neon light from outside, Sugawara decides to seek revenge. First he stops off to leave Terajima's widow some money, then walks through the rain to bad guy HQ. Sakuramachi and Oki join him once the fight has already started. Much blood is spilled, and the villains are destroyed. There is a stupendous closing image of wounded Sugawara walking silhouetted in a rainy alley, his knife falling in a puddle that swiftly turns blood red. Although a bit all over the place with story – undoubtedly partly due to accomodating the customary large supporting cast – director Suzuki manages to grab the viewer by the lapels. Nice, too, in that actress Sakuramachi gets to do a bit of fighting, a rare occurence in her yakuza roles. #1 of 5 films   * * *

KANTO STREET PEDDLERS CLAN – VIOLENT LOYALTY aka KANTO TEKIYA IKKA – GOROMENTSU aka VOW OF RACKETEERS 1970 94 min. **DIR.** Norifumi Suzuki **SCR.** Akira Murao/

Masahiro Shimura **PHOTO COLOR** '**SCOPE**: Umeo Masuda **MUSIC**: Shunsuke Kikuchi **w/** Bunta Sugawara, Ryoji Hayama, Isamu Nagato, Tatsuo Umemiya, Hiroko Sakuramachi, Yoshi Kato, Bin Amatsu, Kenji Imai   Sugawara and Hayama try to protect elderly *oyabun* Kato from evil new guys on the block Amatsu, Imai and their ruffians. Nagato is excellent as an idiosyncratic boss with a dark sense of humor and a no-nonsense attitude. He steps in to keep the peace but is soon siding exclusively with the good guys. Hayama has a kid brother whom he had accidentally blinded in one eye as a child, and the bitter sibling belongs to Amatsu's gang. He helps steal a briefcase of cash from Hayama which puts Kato's clan in debt to Amatsu. Kato dies. Nagato, Sugawara and Hayama try to hold things together. However, things start to unravel when Sugawara's old flame Sakuramachi is coerced into being Amatsu's woman. Unable to get away on her own, Hayama's little brother and sweetheart engineer her escape only to get in dutch with Amatsu and Imai themselves. Hayama sacrifices his life to rescue them. Next Nagato is mortally stabbed in the chaos of a boisterous festival. Old acquaintance Umemiya sees Nagato fall and helps him back to HQ. When Sugawara runs into old rival Umemiya at Nagato's deathbed, they bury the hatchet and join forces. They furiously attack Amatsu's gang, resulting in Umemiya' death and Sugawara being severely wounded. Waiting lover Sakuramachi embraces Sugawara as he emerges from the bloodbath, but he is so drained and disoriented he stumbles off alone. #2 of 5 films   * * *

KANTO STREET PEDDLERS CLAN – ROYAL TEMPLE DUEL aka KANTO TEKIYA IKKA – TENNO USHI NO KETTO aka BLOODY FESTIVAL 1970 90 min. **DIR.** Norifumi Suzuki **SCR.** Koji Takada **PHOTO COLOR** '**SCOPE**: Shigeru Akatsuka **MUSIC**: Shunsuke Kikuchi **w/** Bunta Sugawara, Goro Ibuki, Ryoji Hayama, Sanae Tsuchida, Nijiko Kiyokawa, Shingo Yamashiro, Eiko Takehara, Masando Nagawa, Asao Koike, Tatsuo Endo   Sugawara travels to Osaka to go to bat for ne'er-do-well Yamashiro's blind peddler sister Takehara and ends up joining female boss Kiyokawa's gang. Ibuki is Kiyokawa's estranged, rebellious son who, at first, takes sides against her with slick pimp/ construction magnates Koike and Endo. It is not long before Ibuki's abrasive, still decent personality rubs his new friends the wrong way, and Sugawara offers himself as hostage if Koike will release the beaten-to-a-pulp Ibuki. Eventually, Koike and Endo have the local peddlers' market bulldozed, and blind girl Takehara is killed in the melee. Ibuki publicly confronts Koike and Endo but is shot to death for his brazen affrontery. Big boss Soganoya holds a meeting where the evil pair are reprimanded. As a result, that night Kiyokawa is stabbed to death and right hand man Hayama wounded. Daughter Tsuchida assumes the leadership reins. This, of course. inspires Sugawara to break out his sword, and he delivers the chastizing, killing blow to Koike, Endo and their gang. Director Suzuki conjures some truly astounding sequences, especially the hypnotic camerwwork during Sugawara's torture, Ibuki's shooting, and Kiyokawa's assassination beneath a night sky virtually full of cherry blossoms. The denouement is especially jawdropping when Sugawara, having sustained incredible damage in a particularly savage final massacre, actually manages to stumble away. Unfortunately, the story elements don't coalesce as well as they should and there is way too much coarse humor in the first half, a common problem in many of Suzuki's pictures. #3 of 5 films * * *

Kanto Street Peddlers Clan - Violent Fire Festival (#4)

KANTO STREET PEDDLERS CLAN – VIOLENT FIRE FESTI-VAL aka KANTO TEKIYA IKKA – GOROMENTSU HIMATSURI aka FIGHT AT THE FIRE FESTIVAL 1971 87 min. **DIR.** Noriumi Suzuki **SCR.** Masahiro Shimura/Norifumi Suzuki **PHOTO COLOR 'SCOPE:** Motoya Washio **MUSIC:** Shunsuke Kikuchi **w/** Bunta Sugawara, Yumiko Nogawa, Tsunehiko Watase, Tatsuo Umemiya, Hiroshi Nawa,

Yukie Kagawa, Toshiaki Minami, Yoko Koyama, Tatsuo Endo, Keiji Takagi One of the most disorienting series entries and certainly one of Suzuki's most schizophrenic pictures. Virtually the entire first hour is an only occasionally amusing yakuza comedy with Sugawara and bumbling sidekick Minami trying to keep female boss Nogawa's merchant clan from being victimized by unscrupulous gangsters. Beginning with the last half hour, the film suddenly transforms into a *ninkyo* tragedy with director Suzuki pulling out all the stops in his stylized use of color, slow-motion and strange juxtapositions. Standout scenes include Nogawa's shooting as she whirls in a slow-motion dance against a background that turns blood red and her death scene where, cradled in Sugawara's arms as her gang clusters around her bed, festival fireworks reflect on her angelic face through the open doors. These sequences, as well as several others, show Suzuki can be a great filmmaker when he wants to be. However, one gets the feeling that he doe not really give a damn. He does not seem to be interested in "art," only in having a few laughs and an undisciplined good time while occasionally throwing in startling, mind-blowing visual pyrotechnics just to show us he could be great if he wanted. What do we then make of his consistent, truly great films such as RED PEONY GAMBLER #2 with Junko Fuji, ELDER SISTER #1 (aka SEX AND FURY), PATH OF CHIVALRY starring Noboru Ando, and even the non-yakuza SCHOOL OF THE HOLY BEASTS? #4 of 5 films * * 1/2

KANTO STREET PEDDLERS CLAN – SHALLOW CLAN HONOR aka KANTO TEKIYA IKKA – ENKO NO DAIMON 1971 90 min. **DIR.** Takashi Harada **SCR.** Motohiro Torii **PHOTO COLOR 'SCOPE:** Juhei Suzuki **MUSIC:** Toshiaki Tsushima **w/** Bunta Sugawara, Noboru Ando, Hiroki Matsukata, Fumio Watanabe, Yoichi Numata, Eizo Kitamura, Toshiaki Minami
A fairly ho-hum entry until about the halfway point where it begins to pay off. Sugawara and Minami come across a clan whose decent boss is married to Sugawara's ex. She and Sugawara are still in love, but both are too "honorable" to do anything about it. Ando is a yakuza with a wife and small child who eventually goes up against the villain gang led by Numata and bigwig Watanabe. Matsukata, a seemingly unprincipled lone wolf, whose sassy sister has a crush on Sugawara, is doing dirty deeds for Watanabe. When Ando tries to off Numata and Watanabe but only snuffs a few henchmen, he is pumped full of lead. Matsukata, sitting idly in the next roon, suddenly realizes the unfair odds and jumps into the fray to try to save Ando. Later Ando dies at the good gang's HQ. Matsukata is then slashed at a car park that night but escapes when Sugawara and pals belatedly arrive to help. Their benevolent boss's efforts to sway the bigger *oyabuns* on ostracizing the villains are in vain because Watanabe still has too much clout. As the meeting breaks up, Sugawara and heavily bandaged Matsukata confront the boss of bosses, spilling the beans firsthand about Watanabe's nefarious doings. A hidden assassin shoots Matsukata. This is the straw that breaks the camel's back, and the big boss immediately divests Watanabe of his new marketing contract. At dawn Sugawara wipes out the villain's clan but is so ventilated by blades and bullets it is inconceivable he could possibly survive. There is a freeze-frame on his anguished face as he leans against a tree. Another uneven entry with a few great moments   #5 and last of the series   * * 1/2

KILLER'S HIT LIST aka KOROSHI YA NINBETSU CHO aka KILLER'S BLACK LIST aka 1970 93 min. **DIR.** Teruo Ishii **SCR.** Teruo Ishii/Masahiro Kakefuda **PHOTO COLOR 'SCOPE:** Shin Furuya **MUSIC:** Hajime Kaburagi **w/** Tsunehiko Watase, Teruo Yoshida, Yoshiko Fujita, Makoto Sato, Ichiro Nakatani, Yukie Kagawa, Goro Ibuki
A companion piece to another Ishii-directed picture from 1970, also starring Watase, Yoshida and Sato called PRISONERS' BLACK LIST.

Killers' Hit List

KILLERS IN BROAD DAYLIGHT
aka HAKUCHU NO SHIKAKU
1979 154 min. **Dir.** Toru Murakawa
Scr. Fumio Konami **Photo color**
'scope: Seizo Norimoto **Music:**
Rudou Uzaki **w/** Tsutomu Natsuki,
Katsu Ryuzaki, Akira Nakao, Yoko
Shimada, Mitsuko Oka, Shinichi
"Sonny" Chiba, Shin Kishida, Kei
Sato, Shigeru Amachi, Hideo Murota,
Another one of those films on the
subgenre borderline. There is a slight
possibility it is not a yakuza film.

KILLING FIST AND CHILD aka
KOZURE SATSUJINKEN aka
KARATE WARRIORS 1976 88
min. **Dir.** Kazuhiko Yamaguchi **Scr.**
Tatsuhiko Kamoi/Shinji Nakajima
Photo color 'scope: Yoshio
Nakajima **Music:** Taiichiro Kosugi
w/ Shinichi "Sonny" Chiba, Isao
Natsuyagi, Akiko Koyama, Akane
Kawasaki, Hideo Murota, Eiji Go,
Bin Amatsu, Yayoi Watanabe, Tatsuo
Umemiya   Resolutely unredeemable
trash that is nevertheless supremely
entertaining by the sheer nature of
its runaway locomotive approach
to action and narrative. Chiba is a
cigar-chomping lone wolf who plays
off Go's gang against rival Murota's.
Natsuyagi is a ruthless swordmaster
yojinbo for Murota. His one saving
grace is his devotion to his small
son. Just about any excuse is used to
plunge the characters into wholesale
carnage, and this features some absolutely phenomenal swordplay as well
as some of Chiba's most astonishing
hand-to-hand fighting. Natsuyagi
bites the dust two thirds of the way
through, then Go's and Murota's
gangs, only to have head boss,
super-evil, one-eyed Amatsu released
from prison to cut a swath through
whomever is left, all to retrieve a
cache of dope that had been secreted
under a dead gangster's tombstone.
Of course, Chiba's already one step
ahead spiriting it away with him in
Natsuyagi's ashes. Another full scale
massacre erupts on a lonely seashore
with Chiba emerging victorious. Too
bad Natsuyagi's son has walked out
on a jetty to scatter his dad's ashes –
and the dope! – across the breaking
waves. Despite the virtual vacuum in
character development, screenwriters
Kamoi (GRAVEYARD OF HONOR
& HUMANITY) and Nakajima
jack the violence with many bizarre,
grotesque *grand guignol* touches as
well as an over-the-top go-for-broke
attitude of which director Yamaguchi
takes full advantage.   * * * 1/2

KING aka TEIO series

KINGPIN OF FAIR LADIES aka
ONNA TARASHI NO TEIO aka
EMPEROR OF THE LADYKILL-
ERS 1970 **Dir.** Buichi Saito **Scr.**
Ryunosuke Kono **Photo color**
'scope: Ichiro Hoshijima **Music:**
Taiichiro Kosugi   **w/** Tatsuo
Umemiya, Hiromi Hanazono, Shingo
Yamashiro, Manami Fuji, Akemi
Negishi, Yukie Kagawa, Kunie Tanaka, Chikako Miyagi, Nobuo Kaneko,
Hiroshi Kondo   Another one of
those sexploitive potboiler series with
Umemiya as the handsome bastard
rescuing or screwing over the many
females (prostitutes, bar hostesses, independently wealthy society women,
etc.,) – his hero/villain status dependent upon which movie we are discussing. Some are more yakuza-oriented
than others. This particular entry
relates the career of loyal, fast-talking

son Umemiya determined to make his fortune and send money home to mom and siblings by seducing and fleecing various vulnerable ladies with the help of his hammy sidekick Yamashiro. But two thirds of the way through, his new bar comes under the scrutiny of Kaneko and Kondo's gang. Umemiya, Yamashiro and telephone repairman pal Tanaka are also looking after the daughter of a victimized geisha, which further jeopardizes their operation. The film abruptly shifts tone to tragedy when inexperienced-at-fighting Tanaka goes on his own to confront the geisha's violent ex-beau. Director Saito shoots this in tight close-ups, as well as overhead long shots in what amounts to the most effective, riveting scene in the movie. Tanaka is stabbed by the bad guy in a back alley, then shoots his attacker to death as the man calmly walks away. Frantic Umemiya arrives seconds later to cradle his dying comrade in his arms. However, the tone changes back to silliness when Umemiya and Yamashiro go to confront Kaneko and Kondo at their HQ, threatening to blow up their offices. When the gangsters realize the two are bluffing, the pair are almost killed before a police siren blares outside, thus allowing the "heroes" to escape the alarmed villains. Once they are safe, we see that one of Yamashiro's buddies is waiting for them with a portable crank siren, and the conmen have a good laugh as they make their way home. Things end happily with the geisha reunited with her daughter, and the lovable rascals seeing off the mother/daughter at the airport. One of several films in the loosely-linked KING (TEIO) series. I am not sure how many there are or if I have listed

them in the order of release. * *

KING OF THE NIGHT LIFE aka YORU ASOBI NO TEIO aka KING OF NIGHT GAMES 1970 Dɪʀ. Buichi Saito Sᴄʀ. Ryunosuke Kono Pʜᴏᴛᴏ ᴄᴏʟᴏʀ 'sᴄᴏᴘᴇ: Ichiro Hoshijima Mᴜsɪᴄ: Taiichiro Kosugi w/ Tatsuo Umemiya, Shingo Yamashiro, Manami Fuji, Fujio Suga, Mami Yamamoto, Yukie Kagawa, Nobuo Kaneko, Kyosuke Machida, Yoko Mihara, Ryohei Uchida
There are also scores of moody Toei crime films with *yoru* (night) in the title with Tatsuo Umemiya starring (see the NIGHT/YORU series). Most of them are about whores or bar hostesses and their protectors/victimizers (yakuza hoods, barmen, cops, private eyes, or hired security). It has been difficult to figure out which of these films should be included here as *yakuza eiga*. Most of the time I have had to use my intuition – which, admittedly, is not always the most accurate of criteria. Many films are on that thin, sometimes almost invisible borderline separating the yakuza from the action or sex film. This is perhaps one of the most strangely schizophrenic with Umemiya once again leaving his poor mom and younger siblings in the boondocks to make his fortune in the big city. Even more of a bumpkin than in the previous entry, he runs into tattooed Yamashiro who advises him to become a gigolo once he spies Umemiya's well-endowed manhood at the bathhouse. Nothing much happens except for some very tame sex comedy (not even really any nudity) for a full hour before their sisterly girlfriend's coerced yakuza brother tries to kill Umemiya. Yamashiro comes to his comrade's

aid, chasing the flustered young gangster off. The boy jumps in a waiting getaway car only to be pushed out onto the freeway once they are speeding along by bad boss Suga and henchmen. They then back over him, crushing him repeatedly under their wheels. Soon after, Umemiya and Yamashiro head over to Suga's HQ for vengeful satisfaction. * 1/2

KING OF THE WIDOW-KILL-ERS aka MIBOJIN GOROSHI NO TEIO 1971 **DIR.** Makoto Naito **SCR.** Ryunosuke Kono **w/** Tatsuo Umemiya, Shingo Yamashiro

KING OF PORNO aka PORUNO NO TEIO 1971 **DIR.** Makoto Naito **SCR.** Ryunosuke Kono **PHOTO COLOR 'SCOPE:** Masakazu Shimizu **MUSIC:** Taiichiro Kosugi **w/** Tatsuo Umemiya, Shingo Yamashiro, Tomoko Mayama, Naoko Fujiyama, Tetsuro Tanba, Chiharu Kuri, Fumio Watanabe Part of the ongoing KING (TEIO) film series (which you would never know unless you read it in a Japanese review, as I did). Also the first of two films with Umemiya as the underworld's "King of Porno". Umemiya stars as a sexist son-of-a-bitch yakuza involved with the sex business.

KING OF PORNO – RED GOD OF THE TURKISH BATH aka PORUNO NO TEIO – SHU JIN TORUKO FURO 1972 **DIR.** Makoto Naito **SCR.** Ryunosuke Kono **PHOTO COLOR 'SCOPE:** Yoshio Nakajima **MUSIC:** Taiichiro Kosugi **w/** Tatsuo Umemiya, Shingo Yamashiro, Hiromi Hanazono, Chiharu Kuri, Hitomi Ariyoshi, Yoko Mihara, Fumio Watanabe, Hideo Murota, Yumiko

Katayama, Mieko Tsudoi Last of the KING series?

King of Porno

KOBE INTERNATIONAL GANG aka KOBE KOKUSAI GYANGU 1975 99 min. **DIR.** Noboru Tanaka **SCR.** Isao Matsumoto/ Hideaki Yamamoto **PHOTO COLOR 'SCOPE:**

Shigeru Akatsuka **MUSIC:** Hachiro
Aoyama **w/** Ken Takakura, Bunta
Sugawara, Tetsuro Tanba, Koji Wada,
Yoko Maki, Kunie Tanaka, Isao
Natsuyagi, Renji Ishibashi, Shuji
Otaki, Kenji Imai, Rokko Toura

Kobe International Gang

Director Tanaka was a veteran of
Nikkatsu Studio's thriving roman
porno scene with such films as a
WOMAN CALLED SADA ABE and
WATCHER IN THE ATTIC, but he
also occasionally directed more mainstream pictures. This is a wild saga of
two friends (Takakura and Sugawara)
who run a local gang of black market
freebooters feuding with Korean and
Chinese emigre gangs in post-WW2
Kobe. There is a multitude of great
characters, subplots and over-the-top
mayhem. Eventually, Takakura and
Sugawara grow apart. When Takakura
returns from a short prison term,
Sugawara's envy spills over, and
the gang splinters into rival factions.
Takakura's is the more honorable
and "decent", Sugawara's is the
more ruthless and brutal. Finally, it
is all-out war with the U.S. Occupation Forces also involved. Everybody
dies! Great. And Sugawara's butch
outfit with crimson ascot, kneeboots
and flattop crewcut has to be seen to
be believed. * * * 1/2

THE LAST RAMPAGING FLESH
aka ZANKYO ABARE HADA
1967 **DIR.** Kiyoshi Saeki **SCR.**
Hideaki Yamamoto/Isao Matsumoto
PHOTO COLOR 'SCOPE: Masahiko
Iimura **MUSIC:** Chuji Kinoshita
w/ Ryo Ikebe, Tatsuo Umemiya,
Miyuki Kuwano, Seizaburo Kawazu,
Hiroshi Nawa, Michitaro Mizushima

LEATHER JOHN'S REBEL-
LIOUS TRIBE aka KAWA JAN
HANKO ZOKU 1978 82 min.
DIR. Yasuharu Hasebe **SCR.** Yoshio
Shirasaka **PHOTO COLOR'SCOPE:**
Toshiro Yamazaki **MUSIC:** Daiko
Nagato **w/** Hiroshi Tate, Yoko
Natsuki, Aiko Morishita, Yuri
Yamashina, Kazuko Shirakawa, Ryuji
Kataoka, Yuya Uchida, Jun Aki,
Natsuko Yashiro An offbeat chronicle of loner garage mechanic Tate
who dresses in black leather and enjoys tooling around on his motorcycle when he's not aping John Travolta
on the disco dance floor. There are
a couple of incredibly absurd disco
setpieces, including one certifiably
over-the-top interlude with Tate dancing with trashy one-night stand
Natsuki in a fountain soon to be
joined by all their friends from the
club. The rowdy DJ supplies the
sounds with a boom box blasting
"Funky, Funky Disco..." (for the
gazillionth time). Tate is idolized
by a teenage boy living next to the
garage with his single mother. One
day he finds Tate upstairs with mom
and, even though she is only sewing
Tate's garage tunic, he misunder-
stands, thinking his surrogate big
brother is having sex with mom.
Jealously flying off the handle, he
steals Tate's cycle, and Tate follows
with his tow truck in hot pursuit. It

is too bad because the inexperienced boy drives too fast along a cliff and plummets to a fiery death. The thing is Tate, a romantic at heart, is fighting against his own jaded personality – one of the only things that makes this film interesting. He soon rebuffs Natsuki whose cruel rich boyfriend is already looking for an excuse to humiliate Tate. Tate is in love with sweet, supermarket check-out girl Morishita, periodically bringing her a white rose without uttering a word. He is finally able to help her when he sees her stumbling along the street in tears. It seems she is pregnant by one of the local hoods, a handsome tough in a red jacket with whom Tate has already fought. Tate takes her to a clinic and remains with her through her abortion. Later on, when she offers herself to him at her apartment, he is disappointed at her easy morals, slaps her and splits. Soon after, one of the gals from the neighborhood girl gang – who he has also had a run-in with – tells the boy with the red jacket that Tate has been with Morishita. Coincidentally, Tate has just gone to get another white rose to take to Morishita to make up. But he is waylaid by the jealous hood who fatally stabs him. As Tate expires, he reaches out with the white rose towards the camera, and we see that it is covered in blood. Peculiarly low-key and subdued, this is pretty tame compared to other comparable films like Makoto Naito's ANGEL FROM HELL–RED EXPLOSION (also starring Tate) and the superlative RANKING BOSS ROCK, as well as director Hasebe's own STRAY CAT ROCK pictures at Nikkatsu. It is basically a prototype for a teenage girl's wet dream, spotlighting Tate's vulnerably

romantic hooliganism. I am strangely conflicted by this movie, because it *does* have its great moments. But if it was not for the real-life on-location ambience, the tragic ending and a few striking images this would be rated down one more notch.   * * 1/2

LEGENDARY LULLABY aka ROKYOKU KOMORI UTA series

LEGENDARY LULLABY aka ROKYOKU KOMORI UTA 1966 DIR. Ryuichi (Tatsuichi) Takemori SCR. Yuichi Ikeda PHOTO COLOR 'SCOPE: Shoe Nishikawa MUSIC: Shunsuke Kikuchi w/ Shinichi "Sonny" Chiba, Michiko Saga, Toru Abe, Reiko Ohara, Jun Negami, Kenji Imai, Hiroyuki Sanada
Future action star and Chiba protege Sanada, leading man in the original Japanese version of RING (1997), portrays Chiba's young son in this *ninkyo* yakuza series.   #1 of 3 films

LEGENDARY LULLABY 2 aka ZOKU ROKYOKU KOMORI UTA 1967 DIR. Ryuichi (Tatsuichi) Takemori SCR. Yuichi Ikeda PHOTO COLOR 'SCOPE: Shoe Nishikawa MUSIC: Shunsuke Kikuchi w/ Shinichi "Sonny" Chiba, Akiko Koyama, Kanjuro Arashi, Kunie Tanaka, Reiko Ohara, Hiroyuki Sanada, Seizaburo Kawazu, Jiro Okazaki #2 of 3 films

LULLABY FOR MY SON aka SHUSSE KOMORI UTA 1967 88 min. DIR. Ryuichi (Tatsuichi) Takemori SCR. Yuichi Ikeda PHOTO COLOR 'SCOPE: Shoe Nishikawa MUSIC: Shunsuke Kikuchi w/ Shinichi "Sonny" Chiba, Tetsuro

Lullaby to My Son *aka Legendary Lullaby (#3)*

Tanba, Kinuko Obata, Hiroyuki
Sanada, Kenjiro Ishiyama, Yoko
Mihara, Tatsuo Endo   #3 and final
in series

LIFE OF BLACKMAIL
aka WAGA KYOKATSU NO
JINSEI 1963 DIR. Kiyoshi Saeki
SCR. Masaharu (Shoji) Segawa/Hisao
Ogawa PHOTO B&W 'SCOPE: Ichiro
Hoshijima MUSIC: Harumi Ibe
w/ Tatsuo Umemiya, Shinichi
"Sonny" Chiba, Ryuko Mizugami,
Shoji Nakayama, Akitake Kimura,
Shigemi Kitahara, Masao Mishima,
Takashi Kanda

Life of Blackmail

LIFE OF A CHIVALROUS WOM-
AN aka NOREN ICHIDAI – JO-
KYO 1966 DIR. Tadashi Sawashima
SCR. Tatsuo Nogami/ Norifumi
Suzuki PHOTO COLOR 'SCOPE:
Sadatsugu Yoshida MUSIC: Makoto
Saeki w/ Hibari Misora, Yoichi

Hayashi, Takashi Shimura, Kayo
Matsuo, Tatsuo Endo, Seizaburo
Kawazu, Yoshiko Nakamura, Haruo
Tanaka, Takehiko Kayama
An above-average yakuza *ninkyo*
story, especially considering Misora's
involvement. Not that she is a bad
actress – she isn't. However, her
singer's reputation has ruined more
than one melodrama with the clumsy
insertion of musical numbers in the
most unlikely places. Although, if I
remember correctly, she does sing
here, it is integrated skillfully into the
narrative; something Sawashima had
a lot of practice at. He was director
of the Misora pictures that came off
best.   * * 1/2

LIFE'S BLOODY WOUNDS aka
KIZU DARAKE NO JINSEI series

LIFE'S BLOODY WOUNDS
aka KIZU DARAKE NO JINSEI
aka A SCARRED LIFE 1971
96 min. DIR. Shigehiro Ozawa SCR.
Akira Murao PHOTO COLOR 'SCOPE:
Sadatsugu Yoshida MUSIC: Chumei
Watanabe w/ Koji Tsuruta,
Tomisaburo Wakayama, Akiko
Kudo, Tatsuo Endo, Bin Amatsu,
Eizo Kitamura, Kyosuke Machida,
Machiko Yashiro, Sanae Kitabayashi,
Shoji Arikawa, Keijiro Morokado,
Hiromi Fujiyama A well-written,
labyrinthine saga of two gang bosses,
Tsuruta and Wakayama, and their
clash with unprincipled blood brother
bosses, Endo and Amatsu. The complex emotional network between the
bosses and gangs is particularly well
delineated, although once again the
pure selfishness and vicious arrogance of the story's villains tends to
be a bit one dimensional. It actually

Life's Bloody Wounds aka *A Scarred Life*

seems like maybe we might get more complexity with Amatsu deep in unbridled lust with the daughter of the late boss of Tsuruta and Wakayama, a young woman who herself is not of the highest moral caliber. But this ends up a fairly superficial subplot. The film's real strengths are in the Tsuruta, Wakayama and Machida characters, men devoted to each other who scrupulously tolerate transgressions from their allied gang brethren Endo, Amatsu et. al. because they are bound by a *sakazuki* bond of loyalty. Transgressions which begin with Endo's gang running crooked *hana fuda* games escalating to Amatsu's unwelcome attentions to the revered dead *oyabun's* daughter culminating finally in a near rape that Wakayama intrudes upon, causing him to severely wound Amatsu. Things mushroom further when Machida's vulnerable girlfriend is raped and murdered by Endo's

sadistic henchmen, then returning Wakayama is wounded and his small son murdered in broad daylight. That Tsuruta is willing to go to war with Endo's mob several times but stopped by either boss of bosses Ishiyama or his own tattoo artist father is the ironic, tension-building dynamic that milks the suspense for all it is worth. Finally, Wakayama goes solo to get satisfaction, barely managing to kill Amatsu and a few others. When Tsuruta and Machida learn Wakayama has gone alone, they quickly move to join him only to find him and a loyal follower dead. That night the two attack Endo's gaudy gambling boat party in an elaborate action setpiece that reaches a crescendo of bloody carnage when it moves to Endo's nearby land HQ. Tsuruta and Machida are both shot and slashed several times, but the literally-bloodsoaked Tsuruta at last kills Endo. Tsuruta and Machida assist each other, stumbling out to their waiting gang and scores of police. One of the subtly rewarding things about this film is the contrast of the comparatively normal married life of boss Tsuruta and wife Kudo, boss Wakayama and his wife and son, and their extended gang families with the wholly selfish, macho-oriented lifestyle of Endo's bunch where women are regarded as objects to be defiled and humiliated. Director Ozawa acquits himself well here, exhibiting more complex shadings than in some of his other *ninkyo eiga*.   #1 of 2 films   * * *

LIFE'S BLOODY WOUNDS – A MAN OF OLD-FASHIONED VALUES aka SLAVE TO OBSOLETE IDEAS aka KIZU DAR-

AKE NO JINSEI – FURUI DO DE
GOZANSU 1972 92 min. **Dir.**
Shigehiro Ozawa **Scr.** Akira
Murao/Shigehiro Ozawa **Photo**
color 'scope: Sadatsugu Yoshida
Music: Chumei Watanabe w/ Koji
Tsuruta, Tomisaburo Wakayama,
Hiroyuki Nagato, Yuko Hama,
Shigeru Amachi, Minoru Oki,
Kyosuke Machida, Eizo Kitamura,
Yuriko Mishima, Bin Amatsu, Takuzo
Kawatani, Fumio Watanabe
Another quite good *ninkyo* saga with
Tsuruta and Wakayama as brothers
who find themselves bosses of op-
posing gangs. Despite the influence
of his own decent right hand man
Amachi and wise, upright Tsuruta,
Wakayama is motivated by fear of
his gang falling apart. So he relentlessly follows the lead of greedy elder
boss Endo, who is in thrall to right
wing military policeman Amatsu
and Manchurian profiteer Watanabe.
Amatsu and Watanabe, among other
things, are bent on shipping all the
geishas from a local brothel to Manchuria to act as joy girls for soldiers
at the battlefront. This does not sit
well with Tsuruta, fellow boss Oki,
or elder boss Kitamura. It eventually results in Machida, Nagato and
Kitamura's deaths – something that
pushes tolerant Tsuruta over the edge
to retaliation. Ironically enough,
Amatsu and Watanabe betray their
own yakuza partners, Endo's men,
which in turn causes Wakayama to simultaneously rebel, joining his brother Tsuruta in an all-out bloodbath
where Amatsu, Watanabe, Endo and
the military police squad are wiped
out. The end titles seee bleeding-to-
death Tsuruta and Wakayama writhe
in agony on the courtyard grounds
while Hama, a geisha friend to both

men, watches helplesssly from behind
a locked gate. This could have been
an even better film if director Ozawa
had been willing to rein in Tsuruta's
and Wakayama's histrionics in the
final battle sequence – over-the-top
performances that, at certain moments, attain new heights of scenery-
chewing absurdity. #2 of 2 films
* * *

LIFE STORIES aka BIOGRA-
PHIES aka RETSUDEN series

CHIVALROUS LIFE STORY
aka KYOKAKU RETSUDEN
aka HISTORIES OF THE
CHIVALROUS 1968 106 min.
Dir. Masahiro Makino **Scr.** Goro
Tanada **Photo color 'scope:** Juhei
Suzuki **Music:** Chuji Kinoshita
w/ Ken Takakura, Tomisaburo
Wakayama, Koji Tsuruta, Minoru
Oki, Junko Fuji, Hiroyuki Nagato,
Hiroko Sakuramachi, Hiromi
Fujiyama, Takehiro Nakamura, Kenji
Sugawara, Junko Miyazono, Bunta
Sugawara   Kenji Sugawara is a
waka oyabun (young boss) who is
manipulated into a horrible "between-
a-rock-and-a-hard-place" situation
that results in his demise. Chivalrous
stalwarts Takakura and Wakayama,
amongst others, are thrown into battle to avenge not only Sugawara but
several additional loyal persons dispatched by the nefarious villain clan.
At one juncture, there is a beautifully
straightforward, lyrical interpretation
of what is one of the myriad standard
setpieces in about half of all *ninkyo*
yakuza pictures: Takakura has to fight
a duel with Oki, a chivalrous and
decent fellow who just happens to belong to the opposing gang. Tradition

dictates and, though they both may personally tend to inner "lone wolf" emotions, their intense loyalty, their inescapable *giri* (obligation) to their respective groups make them raise their swords in combat. The duel basically ends in a draw, immediate fur-

Chivalrous Life Story (#1)

ther bloodshed is momentarily postponed and, however implausible the cliche situation may seem, the subtle performaces and Makino's direction make it very moving. Wakayama does a brief takeoff – when he returns to clan HQ after a long absence – on his EVIL PRIEST series role. There is a very nice poetic ending where, after a massive massacre at the villain compound, Wakayama slowly expires in wounded Takakura's arms. There is an extreme close-up on Takakura's blood-streaked face then a slow dissolve to O-Bon Festival (summer Festival of the Dead) paper lanterns, symbolizing dead souls, floating down river into the oblivion of the night.   #1 of 5 films   * * *

GAMBLER LIFE STORIES aka BAKUTO RETSUDEN aka GAMBLER BIOGRAPHY 1968 98 min. **DIR.** Shigehiro Ozawa **SCR.** Kazuo Kasahara **PHOTO COLOR** 'SCOPE: Juhei Suzuki **MUSIC:** Takeo Watanabe **w/** Koji Tsuruta, Junko Fuji, Tomisaburo Wakayama, Ken Takakura, Bunta Sugawara, Saburo Kitajima, Kyosuke Machida, Bin Amatsu, Minoru Oki, Hiroshi Nawa, Seizaburo Kawazu   Tsuruta and Oki are blood brother bosses who drift apart when Oki becomes allied with elder corrupt boss Kawazu, an *oyabun* who constantly looks the other way when underbosses Amatsu, Nawa and their motley crews perpetrate all kinds of violent extortion and mischief. Oki and Tsuruta finally come to a parting of the ways with Tsuruta expelled and his gang dissolved. Former friendly rival boss Takakura is appalled by this turn of events and becomes closer to Tsuruta. Wakayama is an honorable lone wolf obligated to elder Kawazu. Smitten with Fuji, he realizes she is really in love with Tsuruta. Oki establishes a formal relationship with underhanded Kawazu in a *sakazuki* ceremony but comes to regret it immediately when Kawazu springs some unpleasant revelations on him. Oki reacts by breaking his sake cup, thus shattering their alliance, and Kawazu has him murdered on the way home by Amatsu and Nawa. Tsuruta's new restaurant is torched, and good friend, *tekiya* Kitajima, is mortally wounded in the subsequent fight. Love interest Fuji reveals Kitajima has died when she meets Tsuruta at reconciled pal Oki's deathbed. Tsuruta, Machida and the rest of his former gang storm Kawazu's HQ, killing Amatsu and Nawa. However, guest Wakayama is obligated to Kawazu and protects the evil elder. Tsuruta seriously wounds Wakayama and dispatches Kawazu. Meanwhile new comrade Takakura is at the crossroads, singlehandedly holding off a gang allied to Kawazu. When it is all over, Tsuruta helps Wakayama and, with Takakura, et. al they make the trek back home, every one of them stumbling and bleeding profusely. This is an example of *ninkyo eiga* pumped up to ludicrous extremes – the all-star vehicle lurching out-of-control as the expert director and scriptwriter jump through hoops to give all the major performers a role important to story progression. They make a good stab at it but, as is too often the case with these sixties Toei mega-star showcases, there are still people like Junko Fuji and Bunta Sugawara with virtually nothing to do. It still remains a ridiculously entertaining potpourri of *ninkyo* elements.   #2 of 5 films   * * *

CHIVALROUS MAN'S LIFE STORY aka TOSEININ RETSUDEN aka A BIOGRAPHY OF RAMBLERS 1969 99 min. **DIR.** Shigehiro Ozawa **SCR.** Motohiro Torii/Masahiro Shimura **PHOTO COLOR 'SCOPE:** Sadatsugu Yoshida **MUSIC:** Toshiaki Tsushima **w/** Koji Tsuruta, Ken Takakura, Tomisaburo Wakayama, Junko Fuji, Ryo Ikebe, Michiyo Kogure, Minoru Oki, Tatsuo Terajima, Asao Uchida, Asao Koike, Takuzo Kawatani, Bin Amatsu   Tsuruta's boss, Uchida, is murdered by Ikebe at boss Endo's instigation. Just released from prison and bent on tracking Ikebe, Tsuruta leaves behind sweetheart Fuji and finds himself a laborer in a mining camp on the side of a volcano. The mine is lorded over by disfigured boss Amatsu and his sadistic sidekicks. Tsuruta discovers that Ikebe is also living there with his woman

Chivalrous Man's Life Story (#3)

and challenges him to a duel. But consumptive Ikebe starts coughing up so much blood Tsuruta can't, in good conscience, dispatch him. Times are hard, and Ikebe's lover, desperate to make ends meet, agrees to sell herself to Amatsu. However, Ikebe finds out and fights off Amatsu's thugs. Tsuruta and Koike help them escape, but Koike is killed in the process. Tsuruta deposits the couple at his former gang's HQ and ends up attending Ikebe on his tubercular deathbed along with Ikebe's woman and wandering comrade, Takakura. Amatsu's gang arrives, Takakura fights them and, as a result, Tsuruta's blood brother underboss Oki is murdered by boss Endo's man Nawa. Tsuruta and Takakura pair up to attack the now allied Endo and Amatsu, slaughtering the whole gang in a protracted battle in the falling snow. Mortally stabbed Takakura and severely wounded Tsuruta stumble away from the scene of the massacre. There are some beautifully shot setpieces here, particularly the long, poetic swordfight climax. Unfortunately. as is so often the case with not only Ozawa's films but many *ninkyo eiga*, the villains are completely one-dimensional Simon Legree types – something which keeps the film from emotionally resonating into greatness. #3 of 5 films   * * *

BIOGRAPHY OF A CHIVAL-ROUS MAN aka YUKYO RETSU-DEN aka THE BLOODY GAM-BLER 1970 96 min. **Dir.** Shigehiro Ozawa **Scr.** Morimasa Owaku **Photo color 'scope:** Nagaki Yamagishi **Music:** Takeo Watanabe w/ Ken Takakura, Junko Fuji, Watako Hamaki, Bin Amatsu, Kanjuro

Arashi, Tatsuo Endo, Masahiko Tanimura, Toru Yuri, Hiromi Fujiyama   We're talking another pre-WW2 *ninkyo* scenario, this one probably a bit more romantic than most. Takakura and Fuji are on their way to an early morning train ride when stopped in the dawn mist by Fuji's elder brother Amatsu, who tries to forcibly restrain them. Takakura knocks the hothead out, and the two lovers are on their way. It transpires they still have quite a struggle to go through. Takakura makes good with the local *tekiya* (street peddler) yakuza clan in their new environs. Soon, however, what appeared to be only Fuji's bronchitis turns into coughing-up-blood-all-the-time-TB. She gives birth and starts to raise their little boy, but before three years have passed she is on her consumptive deathbed. After Fuji is gone, a young neighbor woman (Hamaki) helps heartstricken Takakura with the child. Then Fuji's brother Amatsu, finds Takakura, challenging him in the street. They go at it but are interrupted by the evil rival clan who have it in for Takakura. The fight mushrooms. Enter the boy. One of the bad guys grabs the kid, holding a knife to his throat. Amatsu is as upset as Takakura, seeing his nephew in mortal danger. He does the heroic thing, snatching the boy away but is stabbed in the process. The villains freak since they had not meant to go so far. The noble elder brother dies reconciled in Takakura's arms, gazing at his nephew. This is notable as one of the very rare times Amatsu portrays something other than a sadistic villain. Takakura's anger boils over. That night he takes up his sword and goes looking for blood at the local bad guys' den. Need I say that he finds it in spades? During this time period, Ozawa was probably Toei's most prolific director. He was also a prolific screenwriter. The majority of his films are good, solid entertainments (he directed all three STREETFIGHTER films with Sonny Chiba as well as samurai and yakuza movies). But he rarely approached the excellence of stablemates, Yamashita or Kato. BIOGRAPHY OF A CHIVALROUS MAN, along with SWORD – the last film in the TALES OF JAPANESE CHIVALRY series, are probably the closest. #4 of 5 films * * *

CHIVALROUS BIOGRAPHY – A MAN aka NINKYO RETSU-DEN – OTOKO 1971 97 min. **DIR.** Kosaku Yamashita **SCR.** Kazuo Kasahara **PHOTO COLOR 'SCOPE:** Motoya Washio **MUSIC:** Chuji Kinoshita   w/ Koji Tsuruta, Ken Takakura, Junko Fuji, Kenji

Biography of a Chivalrous Man (#4)

Sugawara, Hiroyuki Nagato, Goro Ibuki, Sanae Kitabayashi, Michitaro Mizushima, Hiroko Sakuramachi, Hiromi Fujiyama, Tatsuo Endo, Bin Amatsu   One striking feature of this series is that all the film titles could be virtually translated identically. The Toei marketing department was certainly determined to give the viewing public exactly what they wanted: more and more of the same. This time out, Tsuruta is a respected underboss who goes to prison at the end of the Taisho era after assassinating an opposition boss. When he is released at the beginning of the Showa era, he slowly realizes the morale and principles of his gang have diminished due to new second generation boss Sugawara who is married to Sakuramachi, daughter of the late boss. Sugawara is overly concerned about his clan's survival and, not being particularly smart or immune to influence, he falls under the sway of evil boss Endo and his sadistic assistant Amatsu. There are also subplots involving Tsuruta's growing love for restaurant manager Fuji and the tubercular decline of Fuji's colleague Kitabayashi, who is Ibuki's girl and Takakura's estranged sister. Although the story components here are all too familiar to any fan of *ninkyo* yakuza films, what diverges from the norm is perhaps one of Kasahara's (BATTLES WITHOUT HONOR AND HUMANITY) most exceptionally well written *ninkyo* scripts. It is full of detailed character development and nuances even in lesser characters. We are presented with a labyrinthine web of shifting loyalties and obligations manifested and threatened by deceptively quiet talks and snatches of overheard conversations. The overall effect, despite a lack of action until the final ten or fifteen minutes when Tsuruta and Takakura raid Endo and Amatsu HQ, is cumulatively devastating. Takakura perishes and Tsuruta, almost certainly fatally slashed, does his best to stumble away at the end. It is strange, especially since it was directed by expert Yamashita, that it isn't even more moving. #5 and final in series

* * *

LION ENFORCER aka KARAJI-SHI KEISATSU aka LION POLICE 1974 90 min. **DIR.** Sadao Nakajima **SCR.** Tatsuo Nogami **PHOTO COLOR** 'SCOPE: Shigeru Akatsuka **MUSIC:** Kenjiro Hirose **w/** Akira Kobayashi, Noboru Ando, Tsunehiko Watase, Fumio Watanabe, Takashi Shimura, Yukie Kagawa, Hiroko Fuji, Shoji Arikawa, Takuzo Kawatani, Seizaburo Kawazu
Kobayashi gets out of prison and hooks up with his old established gang. However, his younger *chinpira* brother Watase gets underfoot with his brutal, hotheaded antics. Watase allies his own up-and-coming gang with old school gangster Ando's mob and gang war erupts. When Watase steps over the line once too often, Ando balks, settles with elder boss Shimura, and bosses Watanabe and Kawazu. This sends Watase flying off the deep end. He assassinates Ando and Watanabe, then hightails it back to his hometown village. Kobayashi follows, knowing he is going to off his sociopath sibling in order to maintain equilibrium in the yakuza heirarchy. The last ten minutes of the film really come alive with their final

Lion Enforcer

gunfight, then knife duel. Watase dies in the same stagnant shallows where his father expired. Fatally wounded Kobayashi manages to climb back in his car and head down the mountain, only to have it plummet backwards off the cliff road when he passes out. Gritty and nihilistic, but curiously unmoving.   * * *

TOEI STUDIOS M-Z

Modern Yakuza - Outlaw's Honor and Humanity (#2) (ALL IMAGES THIS SECTION © TOEI)

HOME OF THE BIG GUNS AND SWORDS (CONTINUED)

A Man's Family Crest

A MAN'S FAMILY CREST aka
OTOKO NO DAIMON aka
A MAN'S CLAN HONOR 1972
91 min. **DIR.** Kosaku Yamashita
SCR. Akira Murao **PHOTO COLOR**
'SCOPE: Juhei Suzuki **MUSIC:** Hajime
Kaburagi **w/** Hideki Takahashi,
Kyosuke Machida, Minoru Oki,
Bin Amatsu, Utako Mitsuya, Shogo
Shimada, Asao Uchida, Michitaro
Mizushima, Tatsuo Endo
Takahashi does his first (and seem-
ingly only) yakuza film at Toei. The
title is meant to capitalize on his most
popular Nikkatsu yakuza films, the
MAN'S CREST (OTOKO NO MON-
SHO) series. A decent but predictable
ninkyo effort. * * 1/2

A MAN'S INVULNERABLILITY
aka FUJIMI NO OTOKO aka A

MAN'S IMMORTALITY aka GUN
AND YOUTH 1960 **DIR.** Satoru
Ainoda **SCR.** Makoto Nishizawa
PHOTO 'SCOPE: Saburo Sato **MUSIC:**
Akira Ishimatsu **w/**Tatsuo
Umemiya, Isamu Yamaguchi,
Yoshiko Mita, Mitsuo Ando, Harumi
Sone, Eijiro Yanagi, Yoshio Inaba

**A MAN'S SHOWDOWN aka
OTOKO NO SHOBU series**

A MAN'S SHOWDOWN aka
OTOKO NO SHOBU aka GUYS
FIGHT 1966 91 min. **DIR.** Sadao
Nakajima **SCR.** Sadao Nakajima/
Motohiro Torii **PHOTO COLOR**
'SCOPE: Nagaki Yamagishi **MUSIC:**
Shunsuke Kikuchi **w/** Hideo
Murata, Shigeru Amachi, Ken
Takakura, Saburo Kitajima, Bin
Amatsu, Junko Fuji, Hiroyuki
Nagato, Yoko Minamida, Takehiro
Nakamura, Kayo Matsuo   Amachi
and Murata are blood brother bosses
of two comparatively decent gangs in
the late Meiji era (1890s). Amatsu is
the usual scheming villainous boss of
an unscrupulous gang who, through
various machinations, manages to set
the two comrades against each other.
Takakura is a lone wolf who arrives
with tubercular wife Fuji and is sheltered by Amachi. Kitajima is a side-
show *tekiya* at odds with his sister's
resentful ex-beau, now a member
of Amatsu's bunch. Before the last
frame unspools, Amachi and Murata
have re-established their friendship
to raid evil Amatsu's den only to
discover fatally wounded Takakura
alread cutting a swath through the
villainous ranks. This was one of
director Nakajima's first films, and it
was shot under the supervising mantle

of veteran *ninkyo* expert Masahiro Makino. There are many classic moments as well as plenty of action.

A Man's Showdown (#1)

The picture also has a freshness, undoubtedly due in part to the relative newness of the *ninkyo* genre formula. But there is also a welcome lessening

of sentimentality, something that certainly comes from gritty Nakajima, later known for his over-the-top *jitsuroku* (true account) films, being at the helm. There are nice touches with regards to character, especially Amachi as a conflicted family man and boss who has to really work at being courageous and staying true to his principles. #1 of 4 films * * * 1/2

A MAN'S SHOWDOWN – TATTOO OF TWO KINGS aka OTOKO NO SHOBU – NIO NO IREZUMI 1967 DIR. Norifumi Suzuki SCR. Koji Takada/Akira Murao PHOTO COLOR 'SCOPE: Nagaki Yamagishi MUSIC: Ichiro Saito w/ Hideo Murata, Shigeru Amachi, Junko Fuji, Saburo Kitajima, Koji Tsuruta, Bin Amatsu, Hiroshi Nawa, Shoji Nakayama, Masao Hori, Ushio Akashi, Tatsuo Endo   Murata gets kicked out of his clan and banished to Osaka after losing his temper and thrashing some drunken revelers who had heckled him at a traditional song performance. Feisty Junko Fuji carries a torch for Murata and follows him. When fugitive Tsuruta leaves a baby in Murata's care, Murata and Fuji finally end up tying the knot to give the tyke a home. Murata becomes de facto boss of the benevolent waterfront clan he is hooked up with when the elder *oyabun* becomes too infirm, and he is soon butting heads with stern, no-nonsense rival boss Amachi. However, Murata's bullheadedness and courage impress Amachi, and the pair end up devoted comrades with the two gangs establishing an alliance. Things go well for a time, then suddenly Fuji is stricken with a severe illness and expires.

Meanwhile, senior boss Amatsu of a much more mercenary gang foments trouble. Amachi goes to kill Amatsu, manages to dispatch several underlings but is stabbed to death before he can reach the head villain. Unfortunately, fugitive Tsuruta is obligated to villain Amatsu and is coerced into

A Man's Showdown - Tattoo of 2 Kings

making an assassination attempt on Murata, a man to whom he is also obligated. When Amatsu tries to hedge his bets by having a sniper also shoot Murata, Tsuruta steps into the bullet's path and is wounded. Murata and Tsuruta's bond re-established, the two go to Amatsu's HQ to get satisfaction. With the help of ally Kitajima, they destroy Amatsu and his gang in a particularly well-choreographed, exciting swordfight. Although not introducing any new or outrageous elements into the mix, director Suzuki, aided by a good script penned by Takada and Murao, manages to make familiar situations seem fresh. He also elicits superior performances from everyone involved. Fuji, especially, reveals how underrated she is as a versatile actress. She is headstrong and funny here, with an at times achingly melancholic reserve and longing. She radiates genuine warmth without pretentious actorly pyrotechnics. She may have been the boss's daughter (her dad was Koji Shundo, one of the most powerful producers at Toei from the sixties until his death at the turn of the millenium) but her rise to stardom on late 1960s Japanese movie screens was entirely deserved. Even Murata, who could be prone to overacting, comes off well, playing a boisterous character that is equal parts Wallace Beery, Anthony Quinn and Ken Takakura in the charisma department. #2 of 4 films * * *

A MAN'S SHOWDOWN – KANTO STORM aka OTOKO NO SHOBU – KANTO ARASHI aka MEN'S FIGHTING - KANTO AFFAIR 1967 90 min. DIR. Kosaku Yamashita SCR. Koji Takada PHOTO COLOR 'SCOPE: Shin Furuya MUSIC:

Shunsuke Kikuchi w/ Hideo Murata, Saburo Kitajima, Ryo Ikebe, Kyosuke Machida, Ichiro Sugai, Masaomi Kondo, Hiroko Sakuramachi, Masumi Tachibana, Midori Komatsu, Jun Tazaki   Once more Murata's character is a bit of a blustery, hard-headed regular guy, highly principled and unwilling to take offenses lying down. He impresses elder boss Sugai and is soon working for the benevo-lent leader in his timber business. An altercation with very young Masaomi Kondo leads to Sugai's flashback explanation of how Kondo's dad (Kyosuke Machida) was assassinated by evil Endo at the behest of villain-ous boss Tazaki. The scenes where Machida is repeatedly stabbed, falling atop his young son are grueling. This tale of woe gets to Murata who be-gins to look out for the occasionally drunken, angry teenager. He soon has to intervene to rescue Kondo when the impetuous youth beans underboss Endo on the head with a sake bottle. This results in a fractured skull for Murata when he is punished by the evil yakuza. A gun-toting restaurant owner – feisty, tattooed ex-gambler Hiroko Sakuramachi – nurses him back to health in her rear parlor. Romance blossoms between the two. There is another squirm-inducing encounter when Endo and his men wrench Kondo's inexperienced geisha girlfriend from his grasp, then proceed to torment and playfully stab at him until he is seriously wounded. Once more Murata and Sakuramachi come to the rescue. Sugai, Kondo's surrogate dad, is enormously grateful but is soon laid low when injured in the great Kanto earthquake (the film's one drawback is the anemia of these scenes, undoubtedly due to the low

budget). Murata becomes de facto boss. Head villain Tazaki and Endo appear one day when Murata and men are out and proceed to extort business documents out of an ailing Sugai. After Sugai has signed over the deeds, Tazaki takes one of his men's knives and stabs to death the elder boss as well as his teen daughter. Kitajima, one of Tazaki's lone wolf henchmen, balks at this cowardly display and is about to turn the tables when he is ambushed from behind by one of his now former comrades. Murata arrives shortly thereafter, gets the scoop from the dy-ing Kitajima and is soon headed over to Tazaki's HQ with principled lone wolf Ikebe, another blood brother of Tazaki and Endo, who feels betrayed by their despicable, cruel behavior. Murata and Ikebe are slightly wound-ed but succeed in decimating Tazaki, Endo and minions in a harrowingly violent sword melee. The cops arrive to lead the two anti-heroes away to jail with Murata's men on the sidelines, including grateful young Kondo, tearfully bidding farewell. Forlorn Sakuramachi watches from afar and despondedntly lets her pistol drop into the canal as the police pro-cession disappears into the distance. Yet one more great riveting, hard-boiled little action gem from expert director Yamashita. Also notable for a very strong role for Sakuramachi, an exceptionally talented actress not always so well-served by the genre. #3 of 4 films * * * 1/2

A MAN'S SHOWDOWN – TETSU, THE WHITE TIGER aka OTOKO NO SHOBU – BYAKKO NO TETSU aka MEN'S FIGHT-ING – WHITE TIGER, TETSU

1968 89 min. **DIR.** Kosaku
Yamashita **SCR.** Koji Takada **PHOTO**
COLOR 'SCOPE: Shin Furuya **MUSIC:**
Shunsuke Kikuchi **w/** Hideo Murata,
Tomisaburo Wakayama, Kyosuke
Machida, Saburo Kitajima, Junko
Fuji, Masumi Tachibana, Toru Abe,
Bin Amatsu, Hiroshi Nawa, Tatsuo
Endo   Murata is Tetsu, a decent
yakuza who gets thrown out of
his clan by boss Kagawa when he defends a young lady beset by drunken
rival gangsters, in the process scarring the face of evil *oyabun* Abe's
hotheaded right hand, Amatsu.
Murata sets out wandering, much to
the consternation of sweetheart
Fuji, who also happens to be boss
Kagawa's daughter. Several years
later, Kagawa on his deathbed bestows absolution, and Murata returns
to become acting boss. Wakayama is
an honorable, tough yakuza staying
with Abe and Amatsu's gang and thus
obligated to them. But he admires
Murata, going so far as to curtail
a beating after Murata offers himself
up as a substitute for comrade
Machida, who tried to kill Amatsu.
In the closing fight, Wakayama stays
clear, waiting until Murata has wiped
out the villains before challenging
him outside in the falling snow, something he must do to fulfill his debt
to the late Abe who had given him
shelter. Director Yamashita handles
this closing duel very simply as the
two bullish men collide with their
blades. Wakayama is fatally stabbed,
and Murata is severely wounded, only
able to stumble off with Fuji's assistance. #4 and final in series * * *

Meiji Underworld - Yakuza G-Men

**MEIJI UNDERWORLD – YAKU-
ZA G-MEN** aka MEIJI ANKOKU-
GAI – YAKUZA G-MEN 1965
DIR. Eiichi Kudo **SCR.** Akira Murao/
Norifumi Suzuki **PHOTO B&W**
'SCOPE: Juhei Suzuki **MUSIC:**
Toshiaki Tsushima

w/ Hiroki Matsukata, Ryunosuke Tsukigata, Tomoko Ogawa, Shinichi "Sonny" Chiba, Jushiro Konoe, Shingo Yamashiro, Naoko Kubo, Kunie Tanaka, Bin Amatsu, Jiro Okazaki   Since director Kudo already had two of his excellent, very gritty *jitsuroku* samurai trilogy (13 ASSASSINS (1963), THE GREAT KILLING and 11 SAMURAI) behind him – and the viewer thus knows his capabilities – one can only lament that his program pictures like this have such low visibility.

MEI KARETEMO 1968
Dir. Ryuichi (Tatsuichi?) Takemori
w/ Tatsuo Umemiya (No Video)

MINI-SKIRT GAMBLER aka GENDAI ONNA DOSHI 1970 89 min. Dir. Shin Takakuwa Scr. Shigehiro Ozawa/Hideaki Yamamoto Photo color 'scope: Hanjiro Nakazawa Music: Chuji Kinoshita w/ Machiko Yashiro, Kyosuke Machida, Junko Miyazono, Michitaro Mizushima, Kanjuro Arashi, Junzaburo Ban, Ryutaro Tatsumi, Tatsuo Terashima, Rinichi Yamamoto, Kinuko Obata   Yashiro, daughter of veteran card dealer Ban, is a decidedly mod gambler in the violent, late sixties yakuza gaming circuit, despite her dad's opposition. She runs into old school chum Miyazono, who has a huge gambling debt, and decides to help her unlucky friend. Yashiro goes to the gambling hall where Machida is a dealer and, knowing he likes her, manages to win because she fixes the game. But Miyazono's hard luck fiancé isn't so fortunate and is soon in hock to the tune of 25,000,000 yen. Ban's boss backs the man's debt hoping to antagonize the greedy rival

gamblers. But they turn the tables, causing a fatal accident to occur at the fiancé's construction company site. They then set up Ban's gang to be busted by the cops for gambling. Ban challenges the evil boss to a game for the huge debt and wins. However the villain won't return the IOU and wounds Ban. A boss of bosses commands that things be settled by a game between Yashiro and Machida. This, of course, causes massive psychological upheaval for Machida because on the one hand he digs Yashiro and on the other he is obligated to his boss. To my knowledge, this was Yashiro's only starring role. She was limited to mainly meager supporting roles in the late sixties through the seventies.

Modern Chivalry

MODERN CHIVALRY aka GENDAI NINKYOSHI aka ACCOUNT OF MODERN CHIVALRY 1973 96 min. Dir. Teruo Ishii Scr. Shinobu Hashimoto Photo color 'scope:

Mini-Skiri Gambler

Shin Furuya Music: Chuji Kinoshita
w/ Ken Takakura, Meiko Kaji, Asao
Koike, Noboru Ando, Kunie Tanaka,
Ryutaro Tatsumi, Isao Natsuyagi,
Eiji Go, Asao Uchida, Mikio
Narita   Takakura returns to his
home environs and, intent on reform-
ing his wayward outlaw life, gets
a job as a chef at a sushi bar. He
becomes romantically involved with
Kaji who is also employed there.
Needless to say, he is drawn back in
by various yakuza – both good and
bad – from his past. This marks one of
the very few yakuza efforts by screenwriter Hashimoto, who is known
primarily for contributing to such
jidai-geki masterpieces as SEVEN
SAMURAI and TENCHU (HI-
TOKIRI). According to director Ishii,
he was not particularly enamored of
Hashimoto's scenario and did some
rewriting of his own. This apparently
resulted in no one being that happy
with the end product. So, despite
Hashimoto's involvement, despite
wild maverick Ishii's direction and
an exceptional cast, this falls short of
masterpiece status. * * 1/2

Modern Porno Story - Hereditary Whore

**MODERN PORNO STORY –
HEREDITARY WHORE** aka
GENDAI PORUNO DEN – SEN-
TENSEI IMPU 1972 Dir. Norifumi
Suzuki Scr. Masahiro Kakefuda/
Norifumi Suzuki Photo color

'scope: Shigeru Akatsuka Music:
Hajime Kaburagi   w/ Reiko Ike,
Yoko Mihara, Hiroshi Miyauchi,
Takashi Fujiki, Asao Koike, Yayoi
Watanabe, Eizo Kitamura, Tatsuo
Endo, Fumio Watanabe, Takuzo
Kawatani The yakuza and prostitu-
tion/porno rackets.

**MODERN YAKUZA aka
GENDAI YAKUZA series**

**MODERN YAKUZA – OUTLAW'S
CODE** aka GENDAI YAKUZA –
YOTA MONO NO OKITE aka 1969
92 min. Dir. Yasuo Furuhata Scr.
Akira Murao Photo color 'scope:
Ichiro Hoshijima Music: Shunsuke
Kikuchi w/ Bunta Sugawara,
Kyosuke Machida, Tomisaburo
Wakayama, Junko Fuji, Takashi
Shimura The first series Sugawara
starred in as a Toei leading player.
Ironic in that during the late fifties,
while still very young, Shintoho
was featuring him in many gangster,
action and horror pictures as a leading man. Once they went bankrupt,
he had to basically start all over
again from scratch, paying his dues
as a character and bit player, first
at Shochiku, then at Toei, before
regaining lost ground and finally
once again being rewarded with lead
roles circa 1968 –'69 (largely thanks
to director Kinji Fukasaku). These
films are mostly slanted in the gritty,
unsentimental *jitsuroku* (true document) mold, usually leavened with
a bit of crude humor in the first half
of each saga. This first entry sees
Sugawara released from prison and
almost immediately getting in trouble
on the subway when he can't pay. He
had chivalrously given up his seat

to a young mom with kids and had had his pocket picked by a bogus minister. Gangster Machida offers to cover his fare then disappears before Sugawara can thank him. Later that day at a pachinko parlor, Sugawara makes friends with elderly ex-boss Shimura, who decides to temporarily put him up. Sugawara soon discovers that subway benefactor Machida is associated with bad yakuza bosses Abe and Nawa. At first, this doesn't cause too much friction, with Sugawara actually helping Machida attack a rival gang then patching him up when he is wounded in the arm. A band of inept hoods – Ishibashi, Yamashiro, Sunazuka and even the fake holy man – all of whom Sugawara has had occasion to thrash for their bad behavior – begin following him around various psychedelic nightspots begging him to act as their boss. Since Sugawara sees they have actually gotten their act together with a smalltime bookie business and various grifting scams, he agrees to shepherd them. This doesn't sit well with Abe and Nawa, and things deteriorate further when Sugawara and chums con one of Abe's business associates out of a large chunk of cash. Sugawara runs into lone wolf Wakayama at a nightclub, and the two bond over drinks and sentimental songs. Before long Machida is caught between a rock and a hard place, obligated to evil boss Abe, but also feeling loyalty to new bro Sugawara. Violence escalates with Yamashiro killed when he goes to pick up the con job loot from a locker. This causes Sugawara and Machida to clash, with Machida purposely letting his pal fatally stab him. Wakayama subsequently goes to villain HQ, breaks his blood brother

sake cup with Abe and attempts to kill him. Abe's minions pump Wakayama full of lead as he chases Abe through their office building's corridors. Mortally wounded, Wakayama expires. Sugawara gets wind of his new friend's demise and begins his vengeance walk to Abe's. On the way he glimpses Fuji, the keyboard player who he had violently defended from brutal toughs long past, the act that had sent him briefly to jail. Once again he can only longingly look at her for a brief instant before continuing on his fated path. When Sugawara finally arrives, Abe thinks it is funny as he has many men armed with guns. But Sugawara has a gun as well as a knife and commences the bloodbath without hesitation. He takes out many henchmen, is shot several times but manages to jump on Abe's car as Abe and cronies speed away. The car crashes, and Sugawara pursues them on foot. He is shot again but at last kills both Abe and Nawa. Covered in blood, he is handcuffed by the just arriving police and carried away on a stretcher. This is an entertaining, involving story with very nice interplay between characters, especially Sugawara and Machida. Also the realistic, poignant situations seem to arise naturally out of the story elements rather than as manipulative pasted-on contrivances. If only there was a little less clumsy comic relief with the goofier members of Sugawara's gang. #1 of 6 films   * * *

MODERN YAKUZA – OUTLAW'S HONOR AND HUMANITY aka GENDAI YAKUZA – YOTA MONO JINGI aka OUTLAW'S CODE 1969 92 min. DIR. Yasuo Furuhata SCR. Akira Murao/Kibu Nagata

PHOTO COLOR 'SCOPE: Yoshikazu (Giichi) Yamazawa **MUSIC:** Masao Yagi   **w/** Bunta Sugawara, Ryo Ikebe, Masakazu Tamura, Yoshie Mizutani , Reiko Aso, Fumio Watanabe, Seizaburo Kawazu, Tadao Nakamaru, Keiji Takagi, Asao Uchida Sugawara and Nakamaru try to help driver Tamura, who is on the run after he cowardly abandoned the shooter of boss Kawazu in a heavy traffic jam. Boss Watanabe and second-in-command Ikebe are not happy with the situation. Things are not helped by the fact that Ikebe is an old friend/rival of Sugawara now living with Sugawara's ex, Mizutani. Sugawara, Nakamaru and Tamura try to even the score by breaking into a safe at Ikebe's jazzy nightclub to obtain incriminating documents they can use as leverage. Nakamaru and Tamura escape with the papers, but Sugawara is caught by Ikebe's men when he tries to divert their attention. He is mercilessly beaten and tortured by Ikebe and cronies in the club cellar but won't break. Meanwhile back at their riverfront hideout, Tamura decides to do something to help Sugawara. Nakamaru thinks it is hopeless but agrees to tag along. Tamura's girl is convinced there will be a tragic outcome. Down in the cellar, Sugawara is left alone to ponder his fate when former flame Mizutani suddenly materializes and frees him. Unfortunately, Ikebe picks that moment to return, and Mizutani just manages to hide in the nick of time. Sugawara pretends that he is still chained until Ikebe gets ready to kill him, then shows he is free and armed with a knife. Mizutani jumps between them as they fight only to be fatally stabbed by Ikebe. Both men

are horrified. Across town, Nakamaru and Tamura have been sidetracked, chased along the polluted shoreline and finally shot by Watanabe's hoods. The cops are taking away their bodies when Sugawara returns. He immediately turns around and heads back to the club, bent on vengeance. The nightspot is actually divided into two parts, and he wafts through a maze of nightmarish psychedelia looking for the bigwigs. When he finds boss Watanabe in the jazzier upscale lounge, he proceeds to whittle away the cowardly boss's henchmen in a ferocious knifefight where chaos reigns. He follows Watanabe and the remaining hoods into the depths of the building only to run across Ikebe who has decided to change sides to aid him. Ikebe shoots several former comrades before being stabbed to death. His demise amps Sugawara up the extra notch into homicidal overdrive. He battles Watanabe on the roof against a flashing checkerboard of lights. Watanabe finally dispatched, severely bleeding Sugawara stumbles back through the psychedelic club as go-go dancers frug. As the film ends, he throws his knife, and it sticks in an abstract op art painting. This is one of director Furuhata's best early films, rich with emotional resonance, story elements cut to the bone and a continually arresting visual scheme. #2 of 6 films   * * * 1/2

MODERN YAKUZA – OUTLAW OF SHINJUKU aka GENDAI YAKUZA – SHINJUKU NO YOTA MONO aka HOODLUM OF DOWNTOWN 1970 87 min. **DIR.** Shin Takakuwa **SCR.** Akira Murao **PHOTO COLOR 'SCOPE:** Ichiro Hoshijima **MUSIC:** Toshiaki

Tsushima w/ Bunta Sugawara, Makoto Sato, Ryoji Hayama, Nobuo Kaneko, Shingo Yamashiro, Fumio Watanabe, Shinichi Ruukii, Koji Sekiyama, Chie Kobayashi
Sugawara gets out of stir only to be immediately snubbed by stammering fellow jailbird Yamashiro's mom. He goes his own way, confusedly observing strange changes in society such as shorter skirts, guys' long hair and psychedelic art. He jumps into a fight over a hostess at a bar with lone wolf Sato, who soon becomes his best pal and co-conspirator. They are hired by a local gang to roust pachinko parlors and mahjong games but are reprimanded when they hit a steam bath patronized by boss Hayama. Big boss Kaneko, unhappy with the shenanigans, pays them off but instructs them to stop their extortion. Sugawara, Sato and buddies take revenge by raiding the gang's liquor storehouse, polluting the booze, then putting the bottles back as if nothing happened. Suddenly, fights are breaking out all over Shinjuku from clientele disgruntled by the bad hooch. The outcast bunch start their own protection racket but do not have the muscle to back it up. At one point, the boys come out of a Toei theater showing TALES OF THE LAST SHOWA YAKUZA and see a poster for the very film in which they are appearing as the second feature! – which is pretty funny. They go back and forth in their fortunes, getting beaten up, then winning for brief periods before Sato decides to finally sell out to Kaneko and Hayama. Something which backfires shortly thereafter when Sugawara's gang decides to help a businessman who is being victimized by the bigger yakuza. Sato is held responsible

by his new playmates and held in exchange for the businessman. The swap is made, only to have Sato assassinated on the street a few days later while he is Christmas shopping with his girl. Sugawara returns from the hospital to find the rest of his gang decimated and newly returned partner Yamashiro also breathing his last. Sugawara stalks Kaneko and Hayama on a busy Shinjuku street, finally stabbing them to death in broad daylight before hordes of horrified onlookers. He is then snared and led away by the cops. This entry is fairly entertaining but afflicted with bouts of idiotic humor, something which pulls it down a half notch. #3 of 6 films * * 1/2

Modern Yakuza - Outlaw of Shinjuku (#3)

MODERN YAKUZA – LOYALTY OFFERING BREAKDOWN aka GENDAI YAKUZA – SAKAZUKI KAE SHIMASU 1971 86 min. Dir. Kiyoshi Saeki Scr. Morimasa

Modern Yakuza (#4)   *Modern Yakuza (#5)*

Modern Yakuza - Outlaw Killer (#6) aka Street Mobster

Owaku **PHOTO COLOR 'SCOPE:**
Ichiro Hoshijima **MUSIC:** Shunsuke
Kikuchi **w/** Bunta Sugawara, Hiroki
Matsukata, Yumiko Nogawa, Akiko
Kudo, Asao Koike, Michitaro
Mizushima, Goro Ibuki
This is probably the most *ninkyo*-
oriented of the series, undoubtedly
because of director Saeki's involvement. Evil boss Koike, hoping to
speed up his plans for airport expan-
sion, bids Sugawara kill opposing
boss Mizushima. Sugawara stabs him
but cannot finish the job and is fought
off by valiant Ibuki. Mizushima's
daughter Kudo and Matsukata cart the
severely wounded boss to the hospital. Mizushima instructs that there be
no reprisals. Meanwhile Sugawara
has landed in prison, and old flame
Nogawa goes to visit him. Two years
later, he is released and is once more
given instructions by Koike, this
time to kill young boss Matsukata.
Sugawara tries with his knife, but
Matsukata draws a pistol to defend
himself and forces Sugawara to hear
his side of the story. Sugawara returns
to Koike, explains that he cannot do
it and leaves to revisit Nogawa in her
hometown. Koike engineers another
attempt. This one succeeds with the
killer pretending to be Sugawara.
After Sugawara and Nogawa get to
spend an idyllic night, a friend arrives
to tell Sugawara about Matsukata
being offed by someone using his
name. Sugawara is horrified and saddened, and he returns to kill Koike.
He takes most of the villains out,
dispatches Koike, but not before he
himself is fatally wounded. The last
shot is of Nogawa returning with
Sugawara's ashes to their home
village. Lyrical, soulful and a nice
counterbalance to some of the more
cynical mayhem in other entries in
the series. #4 of 6 films * * * 1/2

**MODERN YAKUZA – THREE
CHERRY BLOSSOM BLOOD
BROTHERS** aka GENDAI YAKU-
ZA – CHI SAKURA SAN KYODAI
1971 92 min. **DIR.** Sadao Nakajima
SCR. Tatsuo Nogami **PHOTO COLOR
'SCOPE:** Umeo Masuda **MUSIC:** Takeo
Yamashita **w/** Bunta Sugawara,
Tsunehiko Watase, Goro Ibuki, Asao
Koike, Ichiro Araki, Seizaburo
Kawazu, Hiroshi Nawa, Kin Omae
Sugawara, Watase and Ibuki are three
best friends operating independently
in a nightclub district. Araki is their
shy, nerdish buddy given to perpetually masturbating at the various strip
bars in the hood. Koike, as a heavily
tattooed, womanizing lone wolf hitman, is stupendous as always. Soon
Sugawara and his two blood brothers
run afoul of boss Kawazu's yakuza
clan operating in the district, and it is
all-out war. #5 of 6 films * * *

**MODERN YAKUZA – OUT-
LAW KILLER** aka GENDAI
YAKUZA – HITOKIRI YOTA aka
SHAMELESS HUMAN SACRI-
FICE aka **STREET MOBSTER**
aka BLOODTHIRSTY MAN 1972
90 min. **DIR.** Kinji Fukasaku **SCR.**
Yoshihiro Ishimatsu **PHOTO COLOR
'SCOPE:** Hanjiro Nakazawa **MUSIC:**
Toshiaki Tsushima **w/** Bunta
Sugawara, Mayumi Nagisa, Noboru
Ando, Asao Koike, Noboru Mitani,
Mayumi Fujisato, Takeo Chii, Hideo
Murota, Kyosuke Machida, Keijiro
Morokado An astonishing tale of
Sugawara doing his arrogant thing,
trying to barnstorm into the rackets
with his few loyal but inept and not-
vicious-enough henchmen. He contin-

ues to mess up and is scolded, beaten and constantly screwed-over by the bigger gangs. Ando, who remembers what it was like to be a down-at-the-heels lone wolf, is fond of Sugawara despite his big mouth. One night out at a gambling den, Sugawara's gal (Nagisa) takes a razor to the face of one of his one-night stands, and the mayhem escalates. Before long the other gangs have had enough. Sugawara, Nagisa and buddies are holed-up in an abandoned building. The gangs track them down. In a last-ditch effort, Sugawara and hench-men all chop off their little fingers in venerable yakuza-style apology. Not good enough. Ando, who is trying to keep the others from killing Sugawara, cannot terminate the death-dealing. Nagisa, returning with groceries, sees Sugawara in the va-cant lot in the midst of bad guys, pulls her knife and charges, only to be fatally stabbed. Sugawara finally loses his cool, stabs those nearest him, including Ando, then is gunned down by the rest of the gang. Helped to his car, Ando stoically surveys the carnage. A devastating piece of cellu-loid, and, along with GRAVEYARD OF HONOR AND HUMANITY (1975) and BATTLES WITHOUT HONOR AND HUMANITY (1973), one of Fukasaku's best pictures. Also noteworthy for the strong female role by Nagisa, a real contrast to the usu-ally thankless and disposable girl-friend parts too many good actresses have had to endure in this genre. #6 and last of the series   * * * *

MUD DOG aka DORO INU 1964 **Dir.** Satoji Saeki **Scr.** Ichiro Ikeda **Photo 'scope:** Masahiko Iimura

Music: Masaru Sato **w/** Minoru Oki, Yoshiko Harachi, Keiji Takagi, Takashi Kanda, Shoji Nakayama, Ko Nishimura, Kunie Tanaka, Hideo Murota, Masaya Takahashi, Akitake Kimura

NARCOTICS/PROSTITUTION G-MEN aka MAYAKU BAISHUN G-MEN series

NARCOTICS/PROSTITUTION G-MEN aka MAYAKU BAISHUN G-MEN 1972 **Dir.** Shin Takakuwa **Scr.** Takeo Kaneko/ Shin Takakuwa **Photo color 'scope:** Ichiro Hoshijima **Music:** Toshiaki Tsushima **w/** Shinichi "Sonny" Chiba, Eiko Takehara, Hiroshi Miyauchi, Atsuo Nakamura, Fumio Watanabe, Yayoi Watanabe, Rokko Toura, Takashi Oizumi   #1 of 2 films

Narcotics/Prostitution G-Men - Terrifying Flesh Hell (#2)

NARCOTICS/PROSTITUTION G-MEN – TERRIFYING FLESH HELL aka MAYAKU BAISHUN G-MEN – KYOFU NO NIKU JIGOKU 1972 DIR. Shin Takakuwa SCR. Takeo Kaneko/ Shin Takakuwa PHOTO COLOR 'SCOPE: Ichiro Hoshijima MUSIC: Toshiaki Tsushima w/ Shinichi "Sonny" Chiba, Tsunehiko Watase, Mitsuko Aoi, Rie Yokoyama, Akiko Mori, Michitaro Mizushima, Eiji Go, Rokko Toura #2 of 2 films

NAVAL PRISON – HORIZONTAL BY ANY MEANS NECESSARY aka KAIGUN O SHU GA KEIMUSHYO 1973 DIR. Kosaku Yamashhita SCR. Teruo Ishii PHOTO COLOR 'SCOPE: Hanjiro Nakazawa w/ Shintaro Katsu, Bunta Sugawara, Hiroki Matsukata, Akio Hasegawa This was a hard one. The only place I found it mentioned, even in Japanese references, was in a posthumous photo book commemorating Katsu's career. It is startling that it was so hard to find just the bare bone credits above, let alone anything else about this film, such as a synopsis or whether it is a serious or humorous picture. Considering not only the people in front of, but also behind, the camera, you would think it would have higher visibility. Judging from the very rough translation of the title, it seems that this is pitched in an action comedy vein. Katsu's only movie at Toei Studios.

NEON JELLYFISH – SHINJUKU FLOWER STREETCAR aka NEON KURAGE – SHINJUKU HANA DENSHA 1973 71 min. DIR. Kazuhiko Yamaguchi SCR.

Takeo Kaneko/Kazuhiko Yamaguchi PHOTO COLOR 'SCOPE: Masahiko Iimura MUSIC: Kan Mikami w/ Emiko Yamauchi, Seiji Sawada, Takeo Chii, Mitsuru Mori A surprisingly effective, matter-of-fact chronicle of streetwalker Yamauchi and her exploits in Tokyo's Shinjuku district. The tale starts pre-credits with Yamauchi, a naive, pigtailed teenager, conned, then gang-raped by a mob of supposedly harmless hippies. After the titles, time has already passed and Yamauchi is a seasoned whore operating out of a tiny bar that is lorded over by crippled, sadistic pimp Chii. Soon she rebels, taking up with a yakuza-persecuted street urchin, and the two fall-in-love. Before you know it, they are stagng live sex shows in their cramped one room flat for money. Chii finds out and attempts to muscle his way into their action. Eventually Yamauchi gets pregnant by her new beau. The two intend to start a family, but the twisted Chii intervenes once more in a back alley, this time thrashing Yamauchi's beau with his cane. The boy retaliates with a piece of concrete to the gimpy one's bad leg, Chii unsheathes his cane into a sword, and stabs him. The boy dies just as Yamauchi appears on the scene with a wad of cash. She drops it, and Chii writhes in the pile of money, reaching out in vain to Yamauchi as she walks away in shock. The closing scene depicts her trying to turn tricks on the street but being rebuffed by one potential patron when he notices she is pregnant. This barely phases her, and she continues hawking her wares without remorse. Poignant and hard-hitting without being sentimental, the film runs the perfect length

– just a bit over an hour. It is punctuated throughout by Mikami's music, a score composed of melancholic street ballads and atonal, sparse percussion-oriented pieces. Also refreshingly free of the incongruous, sophomoric humor that detracts from some of director Yamaguchi's other efforts. * * *

NIGHT aka YORU series

NOTE: As with actor Umemiya's KING (TEIO) pictures, this is a loosely-linked series where it is unclear how many installments there were and in what order (beyond intuiting from relesse dates). Umemiya appears in sleazy roles involving nightclubbing, prostitution and gambling rackets, often as a gigolo or pimp. (see the related series, SONG OF THE NIGHT)

BAD WOMEN OF THE NIGHT aka YORU NO AKUJO 1965 **Dir.** Shinji Murayama **Scr.** Masashige Narusawa **Photo B&W 'scope:** Hanjiro Nakazawa **Music:** Naozumi Yamamoto **w/** Tatsuo Umemiya, Mako Midori, Chiharu Kuri, Yuki Jono, Chieko Seki, Reiko Ohara, Ryohei Uchida, Shiro Osaka, Bokuzen Hidari The emphasis here is mostly comic, Midori coming off best. Otherwise pretty weak. * *

BITCHES OF THE NIGHT aka YORU NO MESU INU 1966 **Dir.** Shinji Murayama **Scr.** Masashige Narusawa **Photo B&W 'scope:** Hanjiro Nakazawa **Music:** Masao Yagi **w/** Tatsuo Umemiya, Mako Midori, Shinichi "Sonny" Chiba, Monmu Omura, Atsushi Nagasawa,

Kikuko Hojo, Reiko Ohara, Eitaro Ozawa, Sadako Sawamura   This entry starts off light, with Umemiya feigning a gay persona as a bartender, but who goes to bed with women. It turns out he is a manipulstor, although the ladies love him. By the end, things get tragic, with a shy, sickly wallflower girl stabbing Umemiya's older lover who owns a sushi bar. Other prime girlfriend Midori tries to kill both herself and Umemiya as they drive in his sports car. A super-downbeat climax, followed by strange interior monologues by dying Umemiya and injured Midori, as well as the wallflower girl on a prison transport, elevate this half a notch. * * *

Bitches of the Night

NIGHT GUY aka YORU NO TEIHAISHI 1968 87 min. **Dir.** Shinji Murayama **Scr.** Kikuma Shimoizaka **Photo B&W 'scope:** Hanjiro Nakazawa **Music:** Masao Yagi **w/** Tatsuo Umemiya, Mihoko Inagaki, Mari Shiraki, Yuki Jono,

Rogue of the Night   *Hunting Night Women*

Tamaki Sawa, Annu Mari, Koji Nanbara, Takashi Fujiki Umemiya gets beaten and kicked out of his gang after sleeping with his boss's girl. He becomes a pimp procuring girls as hostesses and whores. He helps one girlfriend, who has just started managing a bar, raid another girlfriend's stable of hostesses. Then, when the raided girlfriend offers him a huge sum, he turns the tables on the original girl. He tries to put together enough cash so the woman he really loves will marry him and join him in managing a restaurant. But a former gang associate sees his goal, seduces his true love and marries her. When Umemiya gives his sweetheart the restaurant he has bought, he is shocked when her new husband steps up to accept it as a wedding gift.

**MASTER NIGHT MANIPULA-
TOR – 1,000 WOMEN KILLER**
aka YORU NO TEKUBARI SHI – SUKE CHI HITOKIRI 1971 DIR. Makoto Naito SCR. Ryunosuke Kono PHOTO COLOR 'SCOPE: Ichiro Hoshijima MUSIC: Kenjiro Hirose w/ Tatsuo Umemiya, Hiroshi Kawaguchi, Yukie Kagawa, Tomiko Ishii

ROGUE OF THE NIGHT aka YORU NO NARAZU MONO 1972 DIR. Makoto Naito SCR. Ryunosuke Kono PHOTO COLOR 'SCOPE: Ichiro Hoshijima MUSIC: Tomokazu Kawabe w/ Tatsuo Umemiya, Tomoko Mayama, Rinichi Yamamoto, Tamase Mitsukawa

HUNTING NIGHT WOMEN
aka YORU NO SUKE GARI aka THE NIGHT'S WOMEN HUNT 1972 DIR. Makoto Naito SCR.

Ryunosuke Kono PHOTO COLOR 'SCOPE: Masao Shimizu MUSIC: Hachiro Aoyama w/ Tatsuo Umemiya, Akiko Kudo, Tamase Mitsukawa, Rinichi Yamamoto, Nijiko Kiyokawa, Shoji Nakayama

Noboru Ando's Filthy Escape into Sex

NOBORU ANDO'S ACCOUNT OF FILTHY ESCAPE INTO SEX aka ANDO NOBORU NO WAGA TOBO TO SEKKUSU NO KIROKU aka NOBORU ANDO'S CHRONICLE OF FUGITIVE DAYS AND SEX 1976 85 min. DIR. Noboru Tanaka SCR. Jun Takada PHOTO. COLOR 'SCOPE: Yasuo (?) Hanazawa MUSIC: Shigeru Izumiya w/ Noboru Ando, Asao Koike, Renji Ishibashi, Mayumi Hagino, Jun Kosugi, Reika Maki, Katsumasa Uchida, Hiroshi Kondo, Hosei Komatsu A trashy, sleazy perspective on real life former yakuza Ando's and gang's last criminal forays and capture, with real newsreel footage of Ando at the close of the picture. Ando, after leaving a two-timing executive severely wounded in a shooting, goes on the run, sexing several mistresses (basically groupies) all over the city, some of whom keep press clippings of his crimes. When one girl feels betrayed, she rats him out, and he holes up in a hillside mansion. A shootout ensues, and he is captured. On the way to the slammer, he masturbates beneath his shirttails, much to the consternation of his cop captors. Bizarre and, to some degree, fairly divergent from the facts (surprise!), at least as told in the previous version, TRUE ACCOUNT OF THE ANDO GANG #3 – STORY OF THE ATTACK. Supposedly Ando's sexual exploits were embellished *just a wee bit* for this update. * * 1/2

FOR US 1979 131 min. **Dir.** Yukihiro Sawada **Scr.** Yohiro (Takahiro) Tanaka **Photo color** **'scope:** Hidenobu Nimura **Music:** Yoshihiko Takeda w/ Yusaku Matsuda, Koichi Iwaki, Katsu Shiga, Kahori Takeda, Renji Ishibashi Lone wolf Matsuda, Iwaki and others plan a heist. Director Sawada made several very good yakuza films at Nikkatsu before the company devolved into *pinku eiga*. Too bad that this does not live up to any of them, despite late cult star Matsuda and DETONATION! actor Iwaki. One more example of the strange phenomenon of charismatic Matsuda becoming such a huge star after appearing in largely mediocre movies. It is too bad he never did anything with some of the better directors at Toei.   * *

No Release from Our Graves

Nostalgic Lullaby

NO RELEASE FROM OUR GRAVES aka ORETACHI NI HAKA HANAI aka NO EPITAPHS

NOSTALGIC LULLABY aka BOKYO KOMORI UTA 1972 94 min. **Dir.** Shigehiro Ozawa **Scr.** Tatsuo Nogami **Photo color**

'SCOPE: Sadatsugu Yoshida MUSIC:
Takeo Watanabe   w/ Ken Takakura,
Ryo Ikebe, Susumu Fujita, Junko
Matsuhei, Goro Ibuki, Yuriko Hoshi,
Rinichi Yamamoto, Shingo
Yamashiro, Bin Amatsu

OFFICIAL'S GUNMAN aka
KENJU YARO NI GOYOJIN 1961
DIR. Masaharu (Shoji) Segawa SCR.
Masando Ide PHOTO 'SCOPE:
Shizuka Fujii MUSIC: Rinichiro
Manabe w/ Katsuo Nakamura,
Yoshiko Sakuma, Isao Kimura,
Naoko Kubo

Okinawa Ten Year War

OKINAWA TEN YEAR WAR aka
OKINAWA 10 NEN SENSO 1978
102 min. DIR. Akinori Matsuo
SCR. Isao Matsumoto/Ichiro Otsu/
Masahiro Shimura PHOTO COLOR
'SCOPE: Shigeru Akatsuka
MUSIC: Hajime Kaburagi w/ Hiroki
Matsukata, Shinichi "Sonny" Chiba,
Makoto Sato, Yumiko Nogawa,
Makoto Fujita   The story of three

guys, all in the yakuza, who as children lived together in an Okinawan
cave during WW2. Matsukata has
made it into the bigger, richer gang,
while Chiba and Sato are still stuck
in the local blue collar gang. When
Chiba's mob starts stepping on the
wrong toes, he and Sato become
expendable. Suddenly, it is all-out
war, with Matsukata following Chiba
to the hideout bomb war shelter/tomb
where Chiba's dad still lives. The rest
of Chiba's gang is wiped out. Then
Chiba kills everyone who has come
for him but Matsukata. Wounded, he
makes a run for his boat, all the time
in Matsukata's rifle sights. Finally
Matsukata lowers the gun, unable to
kill his childhood pal.   * * *

One Hundred Unfashionable Men

**ONE HUNDRED UNFASHION-
ABLE MEN** aka KINAGASHI
HYAKUNIN 1972 DIR. Shigehiro
Ozawa SCR. Toshio Matsuura PHOTO
COLOR 'SCOPE: Sadatsugu Yoshida
MUSIC: Kenjiro Hirose   w/ Koji

One Man's Chivalry

Organized Crime - Loyalty Offering Brothers (#3)

Tsuruta, Akiko Mori, Tomisaburo
Wakayama, Tamio Kawaji, Saburo
Kitajima, Tatsuo Endo, Tetsuro
Tanba, Michitaro Mizushima,
Yukari Wakayama, Toshiaki
Minami

ONE MAN'S CHIVALRY aka
NINKYO OTOKO IPPIKI
1965 DIR. Masahiro Makino SCR.
Toshio Matsuura PHOTO B&W
'SCOPE: Makoto Tsuboi MUSIC:
Ichiro Saito w/ Hideo Murata,
Koji Tsuruta, Hiroko Sakuramachi,
Michitaro Mizushima, Hiroyuki
Nagato, Saburo Kitajima, Rinichi
Yamamoto, Jun Negami

**ORGANIZED CRIME aka
SOSHIKI BORYOKU aka
VIOLENT MOB series**

ORGANIZED CRIME aka
SOSHIKI BORYOKU aka
ORGANIZED VIOLENCE 1967
90 min. DIR. Junya Sato SCR.
Susumu Saji/Michio Suzuhashi
PHOTO COLOR 'SCOPE: Hanjiro
Nakazawa MUSIC: Masaru Sato
w/ Tetsuro Tanba, Koji Tsuruta,
Ryohei Uchida, Shinichi "Sonny"
Chiba, Fumio Watanabe, Junko
Miyazono, Ryunosuke Tsukigata,
Keiji Takagi, Hosei Komatsu,
Hideo Murota
A fast-moving, insightful series
with a pared-to-the-bone economic
structure that is emblematic of
Sato's painfully truthful direc-
tion. Sato, along with Fukasaku
and Yamashita, is one of the most
intelligent and perceptive of Toei's
second generation of yakuza film
directors that started helming their
own films in the sixties (Makino,

Kato, Saeki, and Ozawa are among the
first generation). There is a constant
undercurrent of perversely unrestrained
sadism in Sato's films. even though
the cruel violence is meant to illustrate
capitalist excess taken to its logical
extremes. It is not as pronounced in this
initial series' outing, but #3, LOYALTY
OFFERING BROTHERS (1969)
and his separate GAMBLER COUN-
TERATTACK (1971) and TRUE
ACCOUNT OF GINZA SECRET
ENFORCERS (1973) are akin to fetish
textbooks of modern gangster cruelty.
All are fascinating and disturbingly
unforgettable as a result of this intensity. With Sato's ruthless intelligence,
unabashedly leftist social sensibilities, the cast's gleefully over-the-top
performances, the uncompromising
nihilism (firmly rooted in just how low
humans can sink), the comic strip vivid-
ness ironically makes it all the more
entertaining. It is the excessive scenery-
chewing as far as acting and the lurid
pulp presentation that make it tolerable
to watch. Otherwise, in a more neo-
realistic, documentary milieu it would
be unbearable for most western viewers to stomach. Sato has an underlying
radical social conscience at work as a
subtext in his films – even more so than
the uncompromising Fukasaku – and it
is at the service of this sensibility that
his cinematic violence functions. A
couple of his later yakuza films such as
TRUE ACCOUNT OF GINZA SE-
CRET ENFORCERS are every bit as
disturbing as many of Koji Wakamatsu's
more radical pictures. Back to ORGAN-
IZED CRIME, a film which is actually
quite tame and old-fashioned, not just
when compared to Sato's other movies
but when juxtaposed against most other
mid-sixties Japanese yakuza fare.
Tsukigata plays a right-wing Shinjuku

oyabun engineering a gunrunning scheme from the Phillipines to arm his subordinates. Hard-as-nails cop Tanba foils the arms shipment but because the villain's go-between has diplomatic status, most of the guilty are immune and go free for lack-of-evidence. What makes it intriguing is not just Tanba's sympathetic police inspector, but Chiba's portrayal (despite his youthful overacting) of one of the smaller fish, a guy from the lowest echelon caught up in events beyond his control that will eventually climax with his melodramatic demise. #1 of 3 films   * * 1/2

ORGANIZED CRIME 2 aka ZOKU SOSHIKI BORYOKU aka ORGANIZED VIOLENCE 2 1967 90 min. **DIR.** Junya Sato **SCR.** Yoshihiro Ishimatsu **PHOTO COLOR 'SCOPE:** Hanjiro Nakazawa **MUSIC:** Masaru Sato **w/** Tetsuro Tanba, Noboru Ando, Kyosuke Machida, Fumio Watanabe, Seizaburo Kawazu, Ryohei Uchida, Hayato Tani   Tanba is once again the intrepid, super-diligent cop out to get the gangs. By the end of this second film he is beginning to be a bit world-weary, frustrated at the violence, the reasons why people are driven to such insanity and his own inability to touch the poisonous old men who run the rackets, dispassionately dealing out suffering and death to everyone they touch. This has a surprising climax with one of the underbosses being assassinated as he is led away by Tanba from a meeting of gangs, an incident that triggers bodyguards and hitmen into having a shootout in the driveway of the head bigwig's house. That this old, benign-appearing syndicate head looks on with stoic indifference, even con-

tempt, at what his underlings are perpetrating in his name speaks volumes about the cycle of exploitation that is core root of the modern gangs' evil. What we see in Tanba's face as he watches the elderly gangster's display of arrogant invulnerability is an emotion most policemen must have felt – the desire to take a gun and shoot an inhuman monster to death. That he restrains himself, instead turning his attention to a couple of young men he has just had to kill, then wearily gets in the rear seat of his car and lays his head back in momentary resignation, makes the ending painfully real to watch. Alongside his score for Kihachi Okamoto's samurai/*chanbara* masterpiece KILL!, this has one of Masaru Sato's most memorable, identifiable sixties scores. #2 of 3 films   * * *

ORGANIZED CRIME – LOYALTY OFFERING BROTHERS aka SOSHIKI BORYOKU – KYODAI SAKAZUKI aka PRIVATE POLICE aka CRUEL BROTHERS aka THE NOTHINGNESS BROTHERS 1969 93 min. **DIR.** Junya Sato **SCR.** Yoshihiro Ishimatsu **PHOTO COLOR 'SCOPE:** Masahiko Iimura **MUSIC:** Shunsuke Kikuchi **w/** Bunta Sugawara, Noboru Ando, Kyosuke Machida, Fumio Watanabe, Kanjuro Arashi, Tetsuro Tanba, Hitomi Nozoe, Mina Isshiki This really has nothing to do with the previous two films as far as storyline – the inclusion in the series seems a bit arbitrary, perhaps based more on film promotion than cinematic dramaturgy. Anyway, it starts with Sugawara and Ando getting back from WW2, meeting and almost immediately saving a gal from raping U.S. Occupation soldiers (as we know from scores of yakuza pictures, those American soldiers just can't get enough of sexual coercion). Joining forces, Sugawara and Ando build their gang, selling black market goods and stealing back Japanese women from U.S. Occupation whorehouses to pimp themselves (except for Sugawara's woman, the one they rescued in the beginning). Sugawara seems the more idealistic of the two. Though he is still not the kind of guy who would readily sit still for injustice, it doesn't take him long to harden his heart to the savage brutality that the cold-blooded Ando brings to the gang – Ando has even outfitted a torture chamber in the gang's offices for extorting money from reluctant businessmen, and we see it in use through most of the middle third of the story. After all, the stated purpose of their gang business is "debt collection." At the end, a gang war erupts because both Ando and Sugawara just don't know when to stop. Everyone dies in all-out annihilation, and Sugawara's car and corpse burn under the end titles. #3 and final in series * * * 1/2

OSAKA BAD TEMPER STORY – MANSERVANT aka OSAKA DOKONJO MONOGATARI - DOERAI DO 1965 **DIR.** Norifumi Suzuki **SCR.** Sadao Nakajima/Norifumi Suzuki **w/** Makoto Fujita
In Fujita's early career, he usually appeared in comedies, especially if he was the top-billed performer. This leans heavily in a comic direction.

OUR BOSS'S GUN aka BOSU WA ORE NO KENJU DE 1966 **DIR.** Shinji Murayama **SCR.** Hidekazu

(Eiji?) Yamamura **PHOTO 'SCOPE:** Hanjiro Nakazawa **MUSIC:** Masao Yagi **w/** Tatsuo Umemiya, Eiji Okada, Susumu Fujita, Shinjiro Ebara, Reiko Ohara, Shunji Imai, Hayato Tani, Hiroshi Kondo

Outcast Man

OUTCAST MAN aka HIKAGE MONO 1972 96 min. **DIR.** Kosaku Yamashita **SCR.** Goro Tanada **PHOTO COLOR 'SCOPE:** Shin Furuya **MUSIC:** Chumei Watanabe **w/** Koji Tsuruta, Ryo Ikebe, Kyosuke Machida, Mariko Kaga, Rinichi Yamamoto, Kayo Matsuo, Ryoji Hayama, Asao Uchida, Ryuko Azuma, Bin Amatsu

OUTLAW CORPS aka GOROTSUKI BUTAI 1969 94 min. **DIR.** Shigehiro Ozawa **SCR.** Isao Matsumoto **w/** Tomisaburo Wakayama, Bunta Sugawara, Junko Fuji, Minoru Oki, Hiroko Sakuramachi   Yakuza prisoners are trained-for, then sent on a special mission during wartime.

Undoubtedly at least partly influenced by the success of Daiei Studios' HOODLUM SOLDIER series with Wakayama's real-life brother, Shintaro Katsu.

Outlaw Corps

OUTLAW KILLER – THREE MADDOG BROTHERS aka

HITOKIRI YOTA – KYOKEN SAN KYODAI 1972 86 min. DIR. Kinji Fukasaku SCR. Hiro Matsuda/ Fumio Konami PHOTO COLOR 'SCOPE: Hanjiro Nakazawa MUSIC: Toshiaki Tsushima w/ Bunta Sugawara, Kunie Tanaka, Mayumi Nagisa, Yoko Mihara, Noboru Mitani, Fumio Watanabe, Kenji Imai, Asao Uchida, Fujio Suga A fast-moving travelogue of chaos and depravity led by gonzo Sugawara through a nocturnal urban jungle. Sugawara and schlep Tanaka begin by hitting boss Suga. Only Sugawara goes to prison, and Tanaka is waiting for him upon his release. Boss Uchida welcomes him back, but Sugawara and Tanaka

are childish screw-ups who constantly antagonize the new rival boss Watanabe and his lieutenant Imai, who was slashed by Sugawara in the earlier assassination. Soon Sugawara and Tanaka are on the outs with their own gang and take over a local hostess bar, forcing innocent Nagisa into prostitution. They later team up with oddball snake fetish freak (!) Mitani in ripping off various Watanabe interests. Mitani is caught, beaten and stabbed to death so Sugawara kills Imai in revenge. Fed-up boss Uchida sanctions Sugawara's death and coerces Tanaka into being the assassin. However, Tanaka can't go through with it. Later, trying to extort money from his mother, Tanaka is beaten to death by his straight-laced brother. Sugawara arrives right after this occurs and is dumbfounded to find the deceased Tanaka being wept over by his family. He leaves quietly in the rain. Shortly thereafter, Watanabe's gang attacks Sugawara's bar, shooting him to death. Surprisingly enough, sex slave Nagisa, the only character in the film with any trace of humanity, mourns his death. A bit of a loosely-linked variation on director Fukasaku's last film in the MODERN YAKUZA series, OUTLAW KILLER (aka STREET MOBSTER) but not quite as good. * * *

Outlaw Killer - Three Mad Dog Brothers

OUTLAW – LIST OF DUPES 1956
Dir. Tsuneo Kobayashi **Scr.** Hajime
Takaiwa **Photo:** Shoe Nishikawa
Music: Yoshio Nikita **w/** Chiezo
Kataoka, Mieko Takamine, Michiko
Hoshi, Isao Yamagata, Jun Tatara

Outlaws of Lawless Street

**OUTLAWS OF LAWLESS
STREET** aka MUHO GAI NO
YARO DOMO aka THE GANG-
STERS 1959 **Dir.** Shigehiro Ozawa
Scr. Toshio Matsuura **Photo**
'scope: Shoe Nishikawa **Music:**
Eiichi Yamada **w/** Ken Takakura,
Chiezo Kataoka, Chizue Kitagawa,
Yoshiko Sakuma, Erin Higgins,
So Yamamura, Eitaro Shindo,
Takamaru Sasaki, Eijiro Yanagi,
Masao Mishima   A story dealing
with underworld factions feuding
over rights to a red-light district.

PATH OF CHIVALRY aka
KYOKAKUDO 1967 90 min.
Dir. Norifumi Suzuki **Scr.** Kazuo
Kasahara/ Ichiro Miyagawa **Photo**

color 'scope: Sadatsugu Yoshida
Music: Shunsuke Kikuchi
w/ Noboru Ando, Shigeru Amachi,
Kinuko Obata, Junko Miyazono,
Kenjiro Ishiyama, Asao Koike,
Shotaro Hayashi   This fast-moving
picture is a bit of a hybrid between
the *ninkyo* and the emerging *jitsuroku* subgenres. By its unpretentious, uncompromising execution,
it transcends its programmer status
and shows what Suzuki was capable
of as a director when disciplined and
focused.

Path of Chivalry

There are many nice touches: bitter
police official Amachi, a former student who had been in love with boss
Ishiyama's daughter (Obata) and had
to pay for it with his pinkie cut off
by Ishiyama's men; Ishiyama making
peace with estranged daughter Obata,
who is now married to Amachi;
Ishiyama perishing when he tries to
kill villain boss Watanabe, with neurotic, conflicted traitor Koike deliver-

ing the final blows; the moral fiber of several gang members deteriorating after Ishiyama's death under Koike's deleterious influence; Koike, kicked out of the gang, torturing Ando's brave barmaid girlfriend (Miyazono) at her club before shooting her to death. Ando's assault on Koike's *sakazuki* ceremony where he dispatches Watanabe and finally Koike, is especially well-choreographed with real mounting tension, all culminating in old friend cop Amachi compassionately taking Ando into custody after the slaughter. * * * 1/2

Path of Japanese Chivalry - Story of All-Out Attack

PATH OF JAPANESE CHIVALRY – STORY OF ALL-OUT ATTACK

aka NIHON NINKYODO – GEKI TOTSU HEN 1975 95 min. **Dir.** Kosaku Yamashita **Scr.** Koji Takada **Photo color 'scope:** Shin Furuya **Music:** Masao Yagi w/ Ken Takakura, Joe Shishido, Fumio Watanabe, Kinya Kitaoji,

Naoko Otani, Hiroko Takeshita, Tsunehiko Watase, Ryutaro Tatsumi, Hiromi Fujiyama, Kyosuke Machida, Kunie Tanaka, Hosei Komatsu One of Toei's last *ninkyo* yakuza pictures of the 1970s. The number of film productions were dwindling at all studios, and the few yakuza movies Toei made in the later seventies proved to be more in the contemporary, cynical *jitsuroku* (true account) vein. Takeshita is a teenage girl orphaned after her *oyabun* father is assassinated. She is taken under the wing of benevolent *oyabun* Takakura and his wife Otani. Takeshita falls in love with a young member of Takakura's gang. A third of the way into the tale, she is raped by two rival yakuza and, after the fact, her lover arrives on the scene, killing one of the men. For this Takakura reluctantly must banish him since the two offenders had belonged to his brother-in-law Watanabe's gang, an unruly bunch with whom he has a truce. More conflicts arise with animalistic, drunken ruffian Shishido being one of the prime kindlers of hostilities. When evil boss Komatsu forms an alliance with the cynical Watanabe, the die is cast. Watanabe gradually sacrifices his few remaining ideals. A number of Takakura's loyal henchmen bite the dust, including lone wolf Kitaoji and right hand man Watase. The scene where Watase jumps on a bomb thrown at a restaurant to protect Takakura and Otani is especially grueling. Finally, after elder boss Tatsumi is cut down, then Takeshita is killed protecting Otani, Takakura slashes Shishido to death. Traumatized Otani commits suicide beside Takeshita's lying-in-state body, thus freeing the grief-stricken Takakura to lead his gang in an everyone-dies-attack on Komatsu and brother-in-law Watanabe's HQ. In the end, fatally wounded Takakura weaves his way amongst the corpses. One of them is Takeshita's banished young lover who had run to Takakura's aid at the last minute. When Takakura comes upon an empty room, he suddenly sees the whole floor awash in blood, and he stumbles into freeze-frame. This is a concluding motif director Yamashita previously used in his GAMBLING DEN – LIFE OF CARDS with Koji Tsuruta. Curiously, though this film is good and resolutely unsentimental, it still lacks the magic of many of Toei's earlier *ninkyo* efforts, perhaps a symptom the *ninkyo* formula had been tapped once too often. * * *

PATH OF MODERN CHIVALRY – BROTHER APPRENTICES aka GENDAI NINKYODO – KYODAI BUN aka ONE-WAY PASSAGE TO DEATH 1970 88 min. **DIR.** Shinji Murayama **SCR.** Akira Murao **PHOTO COLOR 'SCOPE:** Kiichi Inada **MUSIC:** Chuji Kinoshita w/ Bunta Sugawara, Kyosuke Machida, Koji Tsuruta, Keijiro Morokado, Hiroshi Kondo, Fumio Watanabe, Hideo Sunazuka, Kazuko Yoshiyuki
One of the more soulful and senti-mental of the early 1970s modern day yakuza films from Toei. And when I say "sentimental," I don't mean corny but genuinely touching and lyrical. Sugawara is his usual hair-trigger-temper self, but his disposition is decidedly honorable, even sensitive, especially with his on-screen wife (a big contrast to the asshole characters he usually portrays). Machida is his almost exact double as far as being an honorable but insolent member of the opposing clan (which is a largely dishonorable bunch) led by cowardly, sex-maniac *oyabun* Watanabe. The scene where Machida tries to kill Watanabe after learning he had raped Sugawara's wife (thus causing her su-icide) and is thwarted, stabbed by the guys who had, only minutes before, been his blood brothers, is devastat-ing. His death scene has to be one of the most hard-to-watch bloodbaths in any yakuza film. Machida's body is repeatedly pierced with deafening flesh-ripping sound effects and the contrast with the soulful lyricism that has come before, although nakedly manipulative, is truly gut-wrenching. Tsuruta appears more than halfway through the picture as Machida's old pal and a would-be peacekeeper. However, with Machida slain and Sugawara's bearded, bohemian *oyabun* subsequently murdered in a driveby shooting, Tsuruta joins Sugawara in an attack on Watanabe's HQ to bloodily avenge all the past wrongs. * * * 1/2

PIER OF HELL aka JIGOKU NO HATOBA aka WHARF INFERNO 1965 **DIR./SCR.** Masaharu Segawa **PHOTO 'SCOPE:** Yoshikazu (Giichi) Yamazawa **MUSIC:** Rinichiro Manabe w/ Tatsuo Umemiya, Jiro Okazaki, Sanae Nakahara, Takashi Shimura, Reiko Ohara, Kyosuke Machida

PIRANHA CORPS aka PIRANIYA GUNDAN series

PIRANHA CORPS aka PIRANIYA GUNDAN 1976 **DIR.** Sadao Nakajima w/ Takuzo Kawatani, Tsunehiko Watase, Ryuji Katagiri,

Hideo Murota, Katsu Shiga
The first of a duo of violent action
comedy yakuza films. This first one
has small cameo parts for three of
Toei's most prolific yakuza *eiga*
directors – Sadao Nakajima, Kinji
Fukasaku and Kosaku Yamashita.
When I mentioned these obscure
films to Fukasaku in an interview
with him, he jokingly remarked, "I
hate people like you," implying he
was hoping these goofy timewasters
had been forgotten, even by obsessive
buffs like me. #1 of 2

PIRANHA CORPS 2 aka PIRANI-
YA GUNDAN – DABOSHATSU NO
TEN 1977 **Dir.** Kosaku Yamashita
Scr. Isao Matsumoto **Photo color**
'**scope:** Umeo Masuda **Music:** Takeo
Watanabe w/ Takuzo Kawatani, Isao
Natsuyagi, Hideo Murota #2 of 2

PLEASURE RESORT BLUES
aka SAKARIBA BURUSSU 1968
Dir. Michio Onishi **Scr.** Kazuo
Funabashi **Photo 'scope:** Masahiko
Iimura **Music:** Harumi Tomobe
w/ Tatsuo Umemiya, Yumiko
Nogawa, Shinichi Mori, Nobuo
Kaneko, Mari Shiraki, Ryohei
Uchida, Ruriko Ito, Hosei Komatsu
Judging by lead stars Umemiya and
Nogawa, as well as singer Mori in the
cast, this may be related to the SONG
OF THE NIGHT series.

PRETTY DEVIL YOKO aka
HIKO SHOJO YOKO aka YOUNG
DELINQUENT GIRL YOKO 1966
Dir. Yasuo Furuhata **Scr.** Fumio
Konami/Ryunosuke Kono **Photo**
B&W 'scope: Hanjiro Nakazawa
Music: Masao Yagi w/ Mako
Midori, Hayato Tani, Renji Ishibashi,

Eiji Okada, Yuki Jono, Reiko Ohara,
Ichiro Araki   This appears to be the
first film by Furuhata as a full-fledged
director. Although not a yakuza film,
this does have tangential genre links,
embodying many motifs that would
become commonplace in Toei's later
delinquent girl and *bosozoku* films.
Midori is a bored, disillusioned teen
at loose ends who briefly works as a
waitress in a café until her roommate,
short order cook Araki, tries to rape
her. Thrown onto the street, she falls
in with smooth-talking, middle-aged
Okada, a guy who seems to be a gentleman and interested in her welfare.
All too soon, she finds he has shady
connections and, worst of all, is even
more brutal than her previous male
companions. He rapes her and has another debauched woman friend come
over to induct Midori into call girl
status. Midori blows the scene, eventually falling into a loose-knit gang
of middle class kids who congregate
at a jazz club. Drinking and drugging
drag several of them down, including
Midori. For a time, things seem to
get better with decent teen art student
Tani becoming her beau. When he
briefly leaves town, things go to hell,
with her best friend OD'ing and a
chance encounter with Araki (now a
yakuza) culminating in another rape.
She attempts suicide, but luckily Tani
returns. Although the film ends on a
happy note, the two given blessings
to marry by Tani's rich dad, director
Furuhata's treatment is so matter-of-
fact, it comes off as a fairly realistic
ending. * * *

PRISON aka MUSHYO series

**MASTER KILLER'S ESCAPE
FROM HIROSHIMA** aka DATSU

GOKU HIROSHIMA SATSUJIN
SHU aka ESCAPED MURDERER
FROM HIROSHIMA PRISON
1974 97 min. **DIR.** Sadao Nakajima
SCR. Tatsuo Nogami **PHOTO COLOR**
'**SCOPE:** Shigeru Akatsuka **MUSIC:**
Kenjiro Hirose

Master Killer's Escape from
Hiroshima aka Prison (#1)

w/ Hiroki Matsukata, Tomisaburo
Wakayama, Naoko Otani, Tsunehiko
Watase, Tatsuo Umemiya, Goro
Ibuki, Ko Nishimura, Hosei Komatsu,
Tatsuo Endo, Nobuo Kaneko
A loosely-linked trio of violently
anarchic films with as much boisterously crude/black humor as well as
drama about unrepentant yakuza in-
and-out of prison. This first follows
the exploits of black marketeer
Matsukata who kills over an argument in the marketplace. He is
arrested, sentenced, then escapes.
Soon recaptured, it is not long before
he tries again with fellow killer
Umemiya and rapist Wakayama. For

a while, he takes over a gang dealing in beef and black market food
who have been victimizing his sister.
Once more he is captured with a
correspondingly escalated jail term.
When his pal Umemiya is nearly
killed in prison, Matsukata goes on
the rampage, dispatching the whole
prison gang responsible. Up on more
charges, Matsukata escapes from the
courthouse and is still at large at the
close of the film, although his sister
has been implicated for helping him.
#1 of 3

PRISON ISLAND RIOT aka
BODO SHIMA NE MUSHYO
1975 95 min. **DIR.** Sadao Nakajima
SCR. Tatsuo Nogami **PHOTO COLOR**
'**SCOPE:** Umeo Masuda **MUSIC:**
Kenjiro Hirose w/ Hiroki Matsukata,
Kunie Tanaka, Nobuo Kaneko, Kinya
Kitaoji, Tamio Kawaji, Yukie
Kagawa, Goro Ibuki, Kei Sato,
Rokko Toura, Hideo Murota #2
of 3 films

Robbery, Arson and Killer Convicts aka
Prison (#3)

**ROBBERY, ARSON AND KILLER
CONVICTS** aka GOTO HOKA
SATSUJIN SHU 1975 91 min. **DIR.**
Kosaku Yamashita **SCR.** Koji Takada
PHOTO COLOR 'SCOPE: Shigeru
Akatsuka **MUSIC:** Hachiro Aoyama
w/ Hiroki Matsukata, Tomisaburo
Wakayama, Renji Ishibashi, Yoichi

Numata, Janeeto (Janet) Hata, Ko Nishimura   An occasionally entertaining and violent comedy/drama with Matsukata and chums taking it on the lam from the slammer. Director Yamashita is capable of creating masterpieces, but this is not one of them.   #3 of 3 films   * * 1/2

Prisoners' Black List

PRISONERS' BLACK LIST aka KANGOKU NINBETSU CHO aka PRISON CENSUS LIST 1970 96 min. **DIR.** Teruo Ishii **SCR.** Teruo Ishii/Masahiro Kakefuda **PHOTO COLOR 'SCOPE:** Shin Furuya **MUSIC:** Hajime Kaburagi **w/** Tsunehiko Watase, Makoto Sato, Goro Ibuki, Kanjuro Arashi, Nijiko Kiyokawa, Yukie Kagawa, Ryohei Uchida, Ichiro Sugai   A loosely-linked companion piece to Teruo Ishii's other then-current film with Watase, Ibuki and Sato, KILLERS' HIT LIST.

Profit from Violence

PROFIT FROM VIOLENCE aka BORYOKU KIN MYAKU 1976 95 min. **DIR.** Sadao Nakajima **SCR.** Tatsuo Nogami/Kazuo Kasahara **PHOTO COLOR 'SCOPE:** Umeo Masuda **MUSIC:** Toshiaki Tsushima **w/** Hiroki Matsukata, Tatsuo Umemiya, Tetsuro Tanba, Tomisaburo Wakayama, Reiko Ike, Eitaro Ozawa, Kunie Tanaka, Torahiko Hamada, Hideo Murota, Goro Ibuki

Ranking Boss Rock

Matsukata is an ex-boxer reduced to skinning cats with his pals to make fake fur. He also goes around with old drunken mentor Ozawa, extorting large sums of money by creating noisy disturbances at corporation offices or shareholders' meetings and refusing to leave unless paid. There are actually yakuza thugs called *sokaiya* who have been doing this off-and-on for decades in real-life Japan. This was one of the first high profile films made about this gangster subgroup. Matsukata and Ozawa, as well as pal Umemiya, get in trouble with a more established gang. There is lots of boisterous humor punctuating the first half, then midway the drama is tinged with pathos. There is a weird cameo by Wakayama as a lecherous mob boss whom our heroes' set up in a blackmail/sex plot. Matsukata, in turn, gets set up when Wakayama's wife seduces him. The saga turns bleak and ironic by the end. * * 1/2

Rampaging Dragon of the North

RAMPAGING DRAGON OF THE NORTH aka HOKKAI NO ABARE RYU 1966 85 min. **DIR.** Kinji Fukasaku **SCR.** Susumu Saji/ Fumio Konami **PHOTO COLOR 'SCOPE:** Yoshikazu (Giichi) Yamazawa **MUSIC:** Isao Tomita **w/** Tatsuo Umemiya, Susumu Fujita,

Nijiko Kiyokawa, Yoko Mihara, Shingo Yamashiro, Hayato Tani, Michitaro Mizushima, Toru Yuri, Jiro Okazaki, Toru Abe   Umemiya returns home to his fishing village and must soon do battle with a cruel gang that is trying to usurp financial control of the industry. This exhibits Fukasaku's vitality and impatience with extraneous sentiment and contrivance, but still remains one of his lesser efforts, hampered a bit by the formulaic, programmer script-boilerplate often imposed at mid-sixties Toei. * * 1/2

RANKING BOSS ROCK aka BANKAKU ROKKU 1973 **DIR.** Makoto Naito **SCR.** Hideaki Yamamoto/Atsushi Yamatoya **PHOTO COLOR 'SCOPE:** Giichi Inada **MUSIC:** Masao Yagi **w/** Emiko Yamauchi, Naoya Masashi,Takashi Shikauchi, Etsuko Shibata, Maya Poruneo, Akemi Yamaguchi, Yumiko Katayama, Hideo Murota, Carol (rock band)   Since it isn't as flamboyant or garishly over-the-top as the GIRL BOSS films, this initially does not seem as impressive. But director Naito is taking a bit different tack, similar to his ANGEL FROM HELL – RED EXPLOSION picture. This has a somewhat documentary or CRUEL STORY OF YOUTH-feel to it, coupled with the standard violent female delinquent Toei formula. Yamauchi (Yumi Takigawa's bad girl ally in SCHOOL OF THE HOLY BEASTS) is the quiet, stoic leader of a bunch of gang girls who, nevertheless, is prone to outbursts of brutal violence if crossed. There is the usual rivalry with another girl mob as well as Yamauchi's slavish emotional dependence on her weak-

willed yakuza beau. Unhappily, her boyfriend is in thrall to a slightly older mentor, a facially-scarred man who has deep feelings of inadequacy as well as a psychopathic hatred of women. In fact, he is really a serial killer who has murdered a girl or two from each gang in nocturnal fits of impotent rage. Of course, the girls conclude the deaths were at the hands of their female enemies, thus escalating the internecine warfare. Rival girl boss Shibata is a talented artist given to obsessively sketching then destroying portraits of Yamauchi (!) before being defeated by her nemesis in a vacant lot duel. She is then shanghaied by Yamauchi's beau and his scarred mentor, forcibly addicted to drugs then set up in a brothel. When Yamauchi realizes this at the climax, coming upon the unawares Shibata shooting up in her anonymous, antiseptic sex booth, she takes decisive action against both of their male exploiters by shooting them to death with the macho pair's own high-powered rifle. Despite occasional slow patches and some amateurish acting, this has a welcome absence of the usual comic relief and a catchy, though innocuous, batch of pop songs supplied by black leather-clad rock band Carol. An unassuming and strangely powerful little film that is undoubtedly helped by co-screenwriter Atsushi Yamatoya, a great, unsung scenarist who also co-wrote BRANDED TO KILL and STRAY CAT ROCK – SEX HUNTER as well as several of Koji Wakamatsu's transgressive sixties masterpieces.
* * * 1/2

RECORD OF YAKUZA PUNISHMENT – LYNCH LAW!

aka YAKUZA KEIBATSUSHI – RINCHI! aka YAKUZA LAW 1969 96 min. **DIR.** Teruo Ishii **SCR.** Teruo Ishii/ Masahiro Kakefuda **PHOTO COLOR 'SCOPE:** Shin Furuya **MUSIC:** Masao Yagi **w/** Ryutaro Otomo, Bunta Sugawara, Minoru Oki, Teruo Yoshida, Renji Ishibashi, Yukie Kagawa, Yoko Koyama, Shinichiro Hayashi, Takashi Fujiki, Ichiro Sugai, Yoshiko Fujita, Masumi Tachibana
A trilogy of tales starting in samurai times with two different clans engaged in a gory gangfight. The boss of the winning clan is a cruel and unforgiving individual. One of the younger clan members has been stealing a gold coin from the gambling den's take every now and then to give to his sister and sick father.

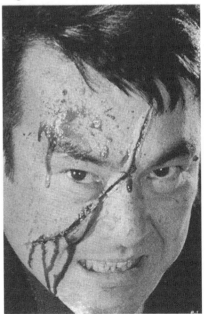

Record of Yakuza Punishment - Lynch Law!

A sneaky colleague (Ishibashi) threatens him with exposure, then says he was only joking. But then he rapes the fellow's sister. The brother catches him in the act, stabs him in the stomach, then, as he lays dying, cuts his tongue out. The boss has both the killer and killer's friend (Sugawara) who tried to hide him, punished. First, he has the ear of the girl's brother sliced-off. Then he has one of Sugawara's eyes plucked-out – all in loving close-up detail. Fair-minded second-in-command Otomo, who is also a friend to the two men, intervenes as the boss is about to re-move Sugawara's other eye. The boss is outraged and orders his men to attack Otomo. Sugawara, the brother and Otomo try to fight off the huge contingent of swordsmen. The brother ends up dying to protect Sugawara. Otomo and Sugawara make their way to the crossroads where the dead man's sister waits. However, the clan gets there first. Luckily, Otomo is able to repel them. He pries the girl from their grasp and sends her and Sugawara on their way while he holds off the villains. The boss approaches. Otomo takes his sword, cuts out one of his own eyes, throws it, and it splats in the surprised boss's face. Wow. Let me say that again…wow. Otomo then kills the boss. The second story, set in the Taisho era (1912 – 1926), has Oki released from prison. He makes a beeline for the rival clan HQ, confronts the head boss and cuts off the man's arm. As he holds off the hysterical clan members, he wraps the arm in a piece of cloth and runs out. He delivers the grisly package to his own boss as a token of obligated vengeance. Later, a young man from the opposing clan tries to kill Oki in the street. Just as he is about ready to strike with his sword, he falters and coughs up prodigious gouts of blood.

Oki, moved to pity for the tubercular fellow, helps him home. They run into Oki's old flame who is now this young man's girlfriend! Anyway, the two try to hide the young man, but Oki's clan is now after him. The climax has Oki fight off his own clan brothers to defend his new ill friend. Everyone dies except for Oki and the girl. The last story concerns a comparatively decent hitman (Yoshida) who does not torture people before he kills them (unlike most of his cohorts) and always makes the sign of the cross when he witnesses a death. As you can probably im-agine, he is crossing himself every other minute. This episode, which takes place in the sixties, is much more tongue-in-cheek than the other two tales. However, people still get their faces burnt-off with cigarette lighters, are crushed in junkyard car compacters, etc.,. This was one of several gory "cinema-of-cruelty" pictures Toei cranked out in the late sixties. Ishii helmed the majority and the best of them SHOGUN'S JOY OF TORTURE (TOKUGAWA ONNA KEIBATSUSHI) (1968), OR-GIES OF EDO (GENROKU ONNA KEIZU) (1969) HELL'S TATTOO-ERS (1969), LOVE AND CRIME (MEIJI-TAISHO-SHOWA – RYOKI ONNA HANZAI SHI) (1969). Most of these were trilogies, and they all feature extreme gore, fairly explicit but still softcore sex and excessive violence. They are also probably some of Ishii's best and most imagi-native pictures. * * *

RED FLOWERS OF THE HAR-BOR MIST aka KIRI NO MINATO NO AKAI HANA aka LOVE AT THE FOGGY HARBOR 1962 94

min. **DIR.** Shinji Murayama **SCR.**
Shin Morita **PHOTO B&W 'SCOPE:**
Ichiro Hoshijima **MUSIC:** Minoru
Miki **w/** Koji Tsuruta, Kyoko
Kagawa, Kyoko Kishida, Hiroshi
Takada, Mitsue Komiya, Sumiko Kaji

RED FLOWERS OF HELL aka
JIGOKU NI MAKKANA HANA
GA SAKU 1961 98 min. **DIR.**
Kiyoshi Saeki **SCR.** Yasunori
Kawachi **PHOTO COLOR 'SCOPE:**
Shizuka Fujii **w/** Koji Tsuruta,
Yoshiko Sakuma, Tetsuro Tamba,
Naoko Kubo, Keiko Ogawa, Peggy
Hayama   A disapponting trifle with
the "humorous" element of Tsuruta
playing a dual role.   * *

RED PEONY GAMBLER aka
HIBOTAN BAKUTO aka
WOMAN GAMBLER series

RED PEONY GAMBLER aka
HIBOTAN BAKUTO aka WOMAN
GAMBLER 1968 98 min. **DIR.**
Kosaku Yamashita **SCR.** Norifumi
Suzuki **PHOTO COLOR 'SCOPE:** Shin
Furuya **MUSIC:** Takeo Watanabe
w/ Junko Fuji, Ken Takakura,
Tomisaburo Wakayama, Kyosuke
Machida, Minoru Oki, Rinichi
Yamamoto, Nobuo Kaneko, Nijiko
Kiyokawa, Shingo Yamashiro
First in a series with Junko Fuji as
Oryu – aka Hibotan or Red Peony be-
cause of a tattoo of that flower on her
right shoulder – a beautiful woman
gambler in 1920s Japan. In this
initial outing, her father, a benevolent
yakuza boss is killed by Oki's clan,
and she gives up much of what is traditionally feminine so she can avenge
his death. Fuji 's Oryu character falls
in love with lone wolf Takakura who

goes with her on her sword raid
to dispatch evil Oki's gang. But
Takakura is mortally wounded and
dies in her arms at the end.

Red Peony Gambler (#1)

Once her mission is accomplished,
Fuji's Oryu finds the die is cast. She
continues to wander as a respected

Red Peony Gambler - Flower Cards Match (#3)

independent boss from adventure to adventure in the next seven films. An amazing piece of cinematic evolution when you consider this was the most popular of all sword/knife-wielding heroine series in Japan, with a graceful, feminine, yet strong, independent female protagonist capable of killing scores of villains to achieve justice/ revenge. There had been very little output from any Japanese studio with a strong, aggressive female lead, let alone one who wielded a sword. Shintoho had produced quite a few samurai films with Misako Uji as a sword-slashing heroine in the late fifties. They were a definte exception. A few of Hibari Misora's period films at Toei had her sporting a sword in *matatabi* drag. But these were odd musical/action/comedy/drama potpourris. A pioneering three film effort in the yakuza genre with Yumiko Nogawa, CAT GIRL GAMBLING, had blazed a trail in 1965-1966 at Nikkatsu. The RED PEONY series was also undoubtedly influenced by Daiei Studiio's WOMAN GAMBLING EXPERT series with the great Kyoko Enami. It had started in 1966 and ran for 17 films until 1971. However, Enami hardly ever did any fighting, leaving the knife/ sword-swinging and fisticuffs to the male co-stars 90% of the time. #1 of 8 films   * * *

Red Peony Gambler (#2)

RED PEONY GAMBLER – MEAL AND A NIGHT'S LODGING aka HIBOTAN BAKUTO – ISSHUKU IPPAN aka WOMAN GAMBLER – KANTO AFFAIR 1968 95 min. DIR. Norifumi Suzuki SCR. Norifumi Suzuki/Tatsuo Nogami PHOTO COLOR 'SCOPE: Shin Furuya MUSIC: Takeo Watanabe w/ Junko Fuji, Koji Tsuruta, Tomisaburo Wakayama, Kyosuke Machida, Bin Amatsu, Tatsuo Endo, Bunta Sugawara, Michitaro Mizushima, Ko Nishimura, Mari Shiraki   Oryu (Fuji), with Tsuruta's help, tries to break the hold of an evil clan headed by Endo and Amatsu who have enslaved many women villagers in their cloth manufacturing sweatshop. Sugawara has an uncharacteristically small, wordless role as Endo and Amatsu's sword killer. Director Suzuki is Fuji's real-life uncle and also served as contributing screenwriter to most of the series' entries.   #2 of 8 films * * * 1/2

RED PEONY GAMBLER – FLOWER CARDS MATCH aka HIBOTAN BAKUTO – HANA FUDA SHOBU 1969 98 min. DIR. Tai Kato SCR. Motohiro Torii/ Norifumi Suzuki PHOTO COLOR 'SCOPE: Shin Furuya MUSIC: Takeo Watanabe w/ Junko Fuji, Ken Takakura, Tomisaburo Wakayama, Kanjuro Arashi, Kyosuke Machida, Asao Koike, Miyoko Shibata Hiromi Fujiyama, Nijiko Kiyokawa, Rinichi Yamamoto, Asao Uchida   Regarded by most Japanese critics as not just the best of the series, but one of the best yakuza films ever made. The story begins with Oryu (Fuji) saving a blind girl from the path of an onrushing train. Subsequently, she discovers the girl's mother (Shibata) is also a gambler impersonating her, Oryu. and she ends up rescuing the imposter from villain Koike's clan's gambling den. A lone wolf (Takakura) obligated to the bad guys shows up and is made an offer he can't refuse – challenge the elderly *oyabun* (Arashi) of the clan Oryu is staying with to a death match. This effectively ends up being a fatal duel. Arashi is mortally wounded, although he does not die for a few days, and still insists on carrying on clan functions as usual. The injustices pile up, and when Oryu, at last, goes to Koike's HQ for satisfaction, Takakura, who has had as much as a just man can take, fights by her side. They cut down the villains with knife and sword. The unspoken love between the two that might have been, is, as always, chaste, awkwardly romantic in a poetically minamalist way, and, because of their differing obligations, will never be consummated.   #3 of 9 films * * * 1/2

Red Peony Gambler (#4)

RED PEONY GAMBLER – SECOND HEIR IN SUCCESSION aka HIBOTAN BAKUTO – NI-DAIME SHUMEI 1969 95 min. **DIR.** Shigehiro Ozawa **SCR.** Norifumi Suzuki **PHOTO COLOR 'SCOPE:** Sadatsugu Yoshida **MUSIC:** Takeo Watanabe   **w/** Junko Fuji, Ken Takakura, Kanjuro Arashi, Kenjiro Ishiyama, Kyosuke Machida, Hiroyuki Nagato, Nijiko Kiyokawa, Bin Amatsu, Hosei Komatsu, Tatsuo Endo, Shoji Nakayama, Ryosuke Kagawa   Fuji visits her rural hometown with friend Machida, encountering bowler hatted, goateed weirdo Nagato along the way. Arriving, she finds that her uncle Arashi, who is boss of the gang laying track for the railroad, has received a head injury

in a fight with an opposing gang. It is somewhat amusing that his injuries eventually prove fatal because he keeps getting worked up about things and jumping around when he is not supposed to. Fuji is then formally ushered in as the new boss. Ishiyama is excellent as the boisterous, hot-tempered *oyabun* of a mob of brutal ruffians who also believe they should be able to work on the rail line. Amatsu, the Machivellian boss of a third gang, is sitting on the sidelines, engineeering situations to pit the two other gangs against each other. Lone wolf Takakura, who is friends with Ishiyama, negotiates with Fuji and brings the two gangs together into an alliance that angers Amatsu. Once the railroad is finished, he sets about trying to sabotage it. After several folks heroically bite the dust, including Nagato and Ishiyama, Fuji challenges Amatsu's bunch to a duel at night by the misty river. This is a nice change

Red Peony Gambler - Oryu's Visit (#6)

from the usual climactic swordfights with some atmospheric, suitably savage setpieces. Of course, Takakura is fatally wounded and, once Fuji has slaughtered Amatsu, he dies in tearful Fuji's arms. #4 of 8 films * * *

RED PEONY GAMBLER – GAMBLING DEN BIOGRAPHY aka HIBOTAN BAKUTO – TEKKABA RETSUDEN aka ORYU, THE BEAUTIFUL WOMAN GAMBLER 1969 110 min. **DIR.** Kosaku Yamashita **SCR.** Kazuo Kasahara/ Norifumi Suzuki **PHOTO COLOR 'SCOPE:** Shin Furuya **MUSIC:** Takeo Watanabe w/ Junko Fuji, Koji Tsuruta, Tetsuro Tanba, Tomisaburo Wakayama, Seizaburo Kawazu, Kotaro Satomi, Bin Amatsu   Oryu (Fuji) hooks up with a clan loading produce at a river dock. Of course, as usual, they are beset by harassment from a craven, more powerful gang. Tsuruta is a prole lone wolf yakuza and single father with a very young daughter in tow. Before the halfway point, he is mortally wounded by the villains. Oryu attends him at his death bed, setting up the portable altar of his deceased wife he carries with him and bringing in his little girl. This is one of the main catalysts for Oryu's eventual violent confrontation of bad guy Amatsu, et. al. Tanba plays another roving, independent boss clad in a white, western Euro-style suit. He and Oryu engage in a duel on a sunny river bank until they realize they are kindred spirits and become friends. Wakayama, though portraying his same country cousin persona, is not as much of a buffoon as in the other series' installments. Both he and Tanba come to Oryu's aid in the closing fight. #5 of 8 films * * * 1/2

Red Peony Gambler (#6)

RED PEONY GAMBLER – ORYU'S VISIT aka HIBOTAN BAKUTO – ORYU SANJO aka THIS IS ORYU 1970 99 min. **DIR.** Tai Kato **SCR.** Tai Kato/Norifumi Suzuki **PHOTO COLOR 'SCOPE:** Shigeru Akatsuka **MUSIC:** Ichiro Saito w/ Junko Fuji, Bunta Sugawara, Tomisaburo Wakayama, Kanjuro Arashi, Akio Hasegawa, Shingo Yamashiro, Toru Abe, Bin Amatsu, Yoichi Numata   Oryu (Fuji) vists Asakusa, staying with a theatrical troupe run by decent boss Arashi. Abe and Nawa are the villains trying to take over the theater (which is very popular, thus profitable). They trick a bitter actress who has been sacked into luring Arashi to a deserted square. The whole gang of bad guys then ventilates him with their swords. This is about halfway through the story, and from then on the action barely lets up. At the *sakazuki* ceremony of yakuza bosses being held to decide on who will take over Arashi's territory, Oryu gets in a confrontation with Abe and his men. They actually come at her with their swords. She manages to hold them off with her judo. Suddenly, Wakayama appears in one of the most bizarre entrances of any film. He is clad in black tie and tails, top hat, Charlie

Chaplin-moustache and is basically akin to Oryu's country cousin, a comical bumpkin who, nevertheless, is a judo expert as well as proficient at gun and swordplay. He terrorizes Abe and cohorts and even coerces Abe to cut off his pinkie to apologize to Oryu. While Oryu sees Wakayama off out in the countryside, young hothead Hasegawa has gone to Abe's HQ to retrieve the young actress who has been kidnapped. Abe is hoping to thus extort possession of the theater from the weakwilled owner. However, Oryu unexpectedly arrives. She is too late to save Hasegawa, who has been stabbed to death, but she hustles the girl and owner out while holding the villains at bay. Making a run for it herself, she bumps into Sugawara, a quiet and honorable friend of hers who likewise has a beef with the bad guys. They return to villain HQ together and proceed to engage in one of the most brutal swordfights in any Toei yakuza film. The fact that it takes place in the tower of the scoundrels' compound visually augments the strife, plying a feverishly hypnotic spell on the viewer as the two slash their way up from floor-to-floor. There is an unusual highlight when Nawa is about to draw his gun on Oryu, and she beats him to it, drawing her pistol from behind her back and killing him. Finally, with all bad men dead and both Oryu and Sugawara wounded, him seriously so, they pause in bloody reverie on the roof of the tower.   #6 of 8 films * * * *

RED PEONY GAMBLER – DEATH TO THE WICKED aka HIBOTAN BAKUTO – O INOCHI ITADAKIMASU 1971 93 min.
DIR. Tai Kato SCR. Morimasa

Owaku/Norifumi Suzuki PHOTO COLOR 'SCOPE: Motoya Washio MUSIC: Chuji Kinoshita w/ Junko Fuji, Koji Tsuruta, Tomisaburo Wakayama, Kyosuke Machida, Kanjuro Arashi, Minoru Oki, Seizaburo Kawazu, Hiroshi Nawa, Kenjiro Ishiyama, Asao Uchida Visiting another rural village brings Oryu (Fuji) into contact with boss Tsuruta's clan, a group allied closely to the common people – farmers and factory workers. When Oryu arrives at the clan house, no one is at home. She has inadvertently picked the date of a labor dispute with the local factory management, a factory that is also emptying its pollution run-off on fertile land.

Red Peony Gambler (#7)

Tsuruta finally arrives home but only with the help of his friends. He has been savagely beaten in the corporate office by a military martinet (Oki) abusing his power, helping factory management and another evil yakuza clan to arrest demonstrators. Before you can blink, boss Tsuruta has been assassinated. Oryu returns from a gambling sojourn in a nearby town to attend the funeral and avenge the wrongs being done by military man Oki and villainous yakuza boss Kawazu. The final fight between Fuji and Kawazu, after she and friend Machida have obliterated the whole nefarious clan, is an occasion to see Oryu at her most vulnerable. Her hair is down, her kimono ripped to reveal her tattoo, her arm bleeding. Once she has run Kawazu through with her knife, the sky darkens with clouds, then goes white with lightning, She pauses in the polluted creek where she has dispatched the villain, then reels in shame as Tsuruta's tiny son runs up with a picture of her that he has drawn. She is mortally ashamed of her unabashed bloody and criminal appearance – she puts one hand over her arm to hide her bloodstained, tattooed flesh and tells the boy to go back. He refuses, running to her, and she is forced to embrace him to keep him from looking at her. You don't think much else can happen, then Kato inserts an emotionally-draining scene like this that lays bare the duality of his character, the hell that Oryu lives in as a woman destined, because of her gambler's life, to never have children of her own and to always see the kindest men she meets cut down by the evil, less principled monsters of the yakuza underworld.   #7 of 8 films * * * *

RED PEONY GAMBLER – ON THE ETERNAL JUST PATH aka HIBOTAN BAKUTO – JINGI TO OSHIMASU aka TO SIDE WITH DUTY 1972 95 min.

DIR. Buichi Saito **SCR.** Koji Takada **PHOTO COLOR 'SCOPE:** Nagaki Yamagishi **MUSIC:** Taiichiro Kosugi w/ Junko Fuji, Bunta Sugawara, Chiezo Kataoka, Tomisaburo Wakayama, Hiroki Matsukata, Kyosuke Machida, Hiroyuki Nagato, Seizaburo Kawazu, Nijiko Kiyokawa, Hiroshi Nawa, Yuriko Mishima
Oryu (Fuji) travels to Osaka, soon becoming a temporary boss, along with young Matsukata, of female *oyabun* Kiyokawa's clan when the ailing woman dies after a protracted illness. Bitter Machida, a hardworking senior member, feels slighted and is pushed to the point he eventually joins the camp of evil gangsters Kawazu and Nawa. Sugawara is a lone wolf obligated to the decent gang who seems to turn up whenever he is needed.

Red Peony Gambler (#8)

Matsukata is killed about two thirds of the way through the tale when the villains stage a dynamite-throwing raid on the small boat he, Fuji and

Red Silk Gambler

Nagato are using to cross the river. Concussed Fuji, nursed by Sugawara, is unaware that decent married man Nagato has gone by himself to stage a raid on the villain HQ. After he is out-numbered and killed, there is then a cut to Nagato's spouse Mishima lying dead from a self-inflicted wound back at home. Sugawara and Fuji proceed with newly-arrived country cousin Wakayama (in top-hat-and-tails again) to avenge all the past nefarious doings. Before the trio wipe everyone out, Fuji has her arm slashed and Sugawara is fatally stabbed. The elder godfather of the area, Kataoka, arrives as they finish, and his men respectfully light their way home, Wakayama carrying Sugawara's corpse and Fuji stumbling along as best she can. Director Saito acquits himself reasonably well here in this last entry. There are some nice poetic scenes, especially with a nicely re-strained Nagato (who can sometimes get carried away with too much mug-ging in his comic roles), but the story is often too convoluted and talky for its own good. One also wishes to know a bit more about Sugawara's character. #8 and last of the series
* * *

THE RED SILK GAMBLER aka HICHIRIMEN BAKUTO aka THE SILK GAMBLER aka TIGER LILY 1972 86 min. **DIR.** Teruo Ishii **SCR.** Koji Takada **PHOTO COLOR 'SCOPE:** Shigeru Akatsuka **MUSIC:** Hajime Kaburagi **w/** Eiko Nakamura, Bunta Sugawara, Sanae Tsuchida, Reiko Ike, Minoru Oki, Shingo Yamashiro, Asao Koike, Hiroshi Nawa, Hiroko Fuji, Junko Matsuhei, Midori Hoshino Just after the demise of the RED PEONY GAMBLER series with Junko Fuji, who had retired to marry (see her last film, CHERRY BLOSSOM FIRE GANG), Toei had released the very good SHOWA WOMAN GAMBLER. But it ap-parently did not do very well and was not turned into a series. Toei's next bid to strike lightning ala RED PEONY GAMBLER was this picture with newcomer Eiko Nakamura, an actress who had already been paying her dues in numerous throwaway sup-port roles, usually as a yakuza moll. Toei seemed to initially push this with two full-page ads in successive issues of bi-weekly Kinema Junpo maga-zine. However, except for a mention by Jessica Amanda Salmonson in an article on Japanese swordswomen in the long defunct American *Martial Arts Movies* magazine, RED SILK GAMBLER (aka TIGER LILY) ap-pears to have sunk without a trace. Too bad, especially with one ad's multiple swordswomen imagery and director Ishii's sure-to-be-perverse involvement. I had gotten the impres-sion that this was to be the first of a prospective series – but no more were forthcoming. Set in the Meiji era (the late 1870s), the film begins with lone wolf, gambling swordswoman Nakamura assassinating a yakuza boss and accidentally scarring the man's mistress (Reiko Ike) across her back. Nakamura ends up in prison, is released five years later and hooks up with pal Yamashiro's gang when she gets out. Before long, she becomes the nemesis then friend of a blind swordswoman who has it in for boss Oki, as well as yakuza sex slav-ers Koike and Nawa. Complicating matters, Ike materializes and tries to avenge herself on Nakamura several

times, to no avail. Nakamura, already feeling guilty, refuses to harm her. Sugawara, a bitter ex-samurai who had rescued Nakamura during a riot after the Shogunate's downfall, reappears as boss Oki's bodyguard. This, along with Ike becoming Sugawara's lover, causes conflicts. Things come to a head after one of Nakamura's swordwielding girlfriends kills Oki and then Sugawara kills her. Eventually, though, Sugawara joins Nakamura when she reaches her breaking point and assaults Koike and Nawa's compound where they are keeping many young girls captive. There is really not much of a plot to speak of, other than that. But it is a perfect excuse for *grand guignol/* erotic-grotesque director Ishii and excellent cinematographer Akatsuka to create some beautifully lit, color-coordinated tableaus of poetic, bloody carnage. Then there is a surplus of gratuitous nudity, especially by very sexy Ike, all through the tale. Despite the lack of deep emotional resonance at the bloody climax, it does not really matter. Strangely satisfying.
* * *

RENOUNCE THE GUN aka KENJU O SUTERU 1956 **DIR.** Eiichi Koishi **SCR.** Keinosuke Uekusa **PHOTO:** Shizuka Fujii **w/** Ken Takakura, Yuriko Tashiro, Yukiko Sono, Harumi Urasato, Jiro Takagi, Yoshi Kato

RETURN FOR THE BOSS'S MEMORIAL aka BOSU OMOTE HE DERO 1960 **DIR.** Masamitsu Igayama **SCR.** Shin Morita **PHOTO 'SCOPE:** Hiroshi Fukujima **MUSIC:** Hajime Kaburagi **w/** Tatsuo Umemiya, Yoshiko Mita, Takashi

Kanda, Masao Mishima, Hideo Murota

ROARING FIRE aka HOERO TEKKEN aka HERO'S RAGING FIST 1980 95 min. **DIR.** Norifumi Suzuki **SCR.** Norifumi Suzuki/ Shinsuke Inoue/Masahiro Shimura **PHOTO COLOR 'SCOPE:** Kiyoshi Kitazawa **MUSIC:** Kentaro Haneda **w/** Hiroyuki "Henry" Sanada, Shinichi "Sonny" Chiba, Mikio Narita, Etsuko "Sue" Shiomi Sanada finds out his dad (Chiba) is really a foster father who adopted him when his real father was murdered by the mob (his foster dad was one of them). Chiba reveals all this on his deathbed. Sanada then must go up against his murderous gangster uncle Narita in order to stay alive. In the late 1990s, Sanada portrayed the male lead character in the original Japanese version of horror hit RINGU and, in the early 2000s, Yoji Yamada's award-winning TWILIGHT SAMURAI.

ROGUE aka GOROTSUKI aka KICKBOXER 1968 92 min. **DIR.** Masahiro Makino **SCR.** Yoshihiro Ishimatsu **PHOTO COLOR 'SCOPE:** Masahiko Iimura **MUSIC:** Takeo Watanabe **w/** Ken Takakura, Bunta Sugawara, Minoru Oki, Nobuo Kaneko, Saneko Yoshimura, Kenjiro Ishiyama, Nijiko Kiyokawa As you can discern from the release date, this came way before the fad/ wave of martial arts kickboxing movies (most of them terrible, banal American dreck) that inundated both the video and cable-TV marketplace in the early nineties. Too bad this is not any great shakes either. The kickboxing sequences are much less convincing than Toei's usually well-choreographed yakuza fist and sword fights. Coal miner Takakura is forced to quit his village and leave his mother and siblings behind. Mining buddy Sugawara accompanies him to Tokyo, and the pair enjoy several annoyingly predictable "fish-out-of-water" sequences before finding employment at a boxing gym with trainer Oki and his spunky sister Yoshimura. The boys also find part time night jobs as roving minstrels in the club district courtesy of benevolent gang boss Ishiyama. Of course, they run afoul of boss Watanabe's cruel gang. Watanabe also has it in for Ishiyama, and this indirectly throws a spanner into the works as far as Takakura's burgeoning success as a kickboxer. When Ishiyama's HQ is burned to the ground by Watanabe's men, Ishiyama tries to kill Watanabe – which, of course, leads to his own gruesome death. Takakura goes on the rampage with his sword, wiping out Watanabe and men. Disappointingly by-the-numbers, especially considering the involvement of excellent writer Ishimatsu. * *

THE ROGUES aka NARAZU MONO aka OUTLAW aka THE RASCALS 1964 98 min. **Dir./Scr.** Teruo Ishii **Photo color 'scope:** Shichiro Hayashi **Music:** Masao Yagi **w/** Ken Takakura, Tetsuro Tanba, Mariko Kaga, Naoki Sugiura, Shinjiro Ebara, Yoko Minamida, Yoko Mihara, Toru Abe, Shunji Imai, Keiji Takagi, Takashi Shikauchi Various hitmen, crooks, and assorted hoods in Macao chase down a doll full of heroin. A truly disposable plot is made visually exciting by Ishii's continually imaginative touches.

Double-crossed killer Takakura and fellow hood Tanba develop a friendship, and one can see why director John Woo cites this film, along with Jean-Pierre Melville's LE SAMOUR-AI, as one of his major inspirations for THE KILLER. Actor Shikauchi should be given credit, too, as he does an effective turn as a scary villain – his glee while strangling an innocent woman who is in possession of the dope doll is frightening. To top things off, there is a grueling climactic fist/gun/knife melee between Takakura and head villain Abe and Abe's bodyguard that leaves the bad guys dead and Takakura mortally wounded.
* * *

ROGUE'S SELF-SACRIFICE aka SUTEMI NO NARAZU MONO aka A HOODLUM AT THE RISK OF HIS LIFE 1970 97 min. **Dir.** Yasuo Furuhata **Scr.** Yoshihiro Ishimatsu/Shinichiro Sawai **Photo color 'scope:** Masahiko Iimura **Music:** Masao Yagi **w/** Ken Takakura, Joe Shishido, Mie Hama, Rinichi Yamamoto, Michitaro Mizushima, Jotaro Togami, Hosei Komatsu, Shunji Imai, Hideo Murota, Nakajiro Tomita   This deserves points for breaking from the usual slavish yakuza formula, but it is still a bit lackluster. Takakura is a two-fisted tabloid journalist who gets framed for murder by Mizushima's gang. Corrupt cop Murota makes sure he is put in prison. After a three year stay, Takakura gets paroled but almost immediately becomes involved with beautiful, quiet Hama, Mizushima's runaway daughter. So, of course, Takakura gets snatched, tortured, escapes, all the while attempting to help Hama get away and find out

The Rogues aka **Outlaw**

more dirt on Mizushima and the new split-off mob led by even more brutal Yamamoto. Joe Shishido has little to do as Takakura's newspaper editor friend who tries to lend a hand.

Rogue's Self-Sacrifice

There is a big confrontation at the end where Yamamoto and cronies as well as corrupt Murota bite the dust. The standoff ends when Takakura is forced to kill Mizushima in front of traumatized daughter Hama. * * 1/2

ROGUE WANDERER aka GOROTSUKI MUSHUKU 1971 110 min. **DIR.** Yasuo Furuhata **SCR.** Shunya Ito/Shinichiro Sawai **PHOTO COLOR 'SCOPE:** Shichiro Hayashi **MUSIC:** Takeo Watanabe **w/** Ken Takakura, Takashi Shimura, Rinichi Yamamoto, Yoshi Kato, Tanie Kitabayashi, Etsuko Nami, Toshiaki Minami, Yoko Hayama, Hiroshi Kondo, Fumio Watanabe Once again, a disappointing outing with another bumpkin-goes-to-the-big-city tale bogging down in sludgy sentimentality. It starts off well with miner Takakura losing his job and leaving mom behind when dad (Kato) is killed in a cave-in. Arriving in the teeming metropolis, Takakura gets a job as a strongarm construction work-er for heartless boss Watanabe's gang. Before you can say "little orphan boy," Takakura bridles at his yakuza supervisors' cruelty towards the local fishermen and street peddlers led by Shimura. He leaves the gang, intent on making himself a useful part of the community and making friends with a little boy whose father was killed in a freak accident. Eventually, Shimura is murdered as well as strong good guy Yamamoto. Takakura suddenly real-izes he is in a yakuza movie, takes up a sword and massacres evil Watanabe and cronies. ROGUE WANDERER is not really sure what it wants to be with director Furuhata and screen-writers obviously following dictates from the Toei brass to toe-the-line regarding successful Takakura *ninkyo* formula. It does not add up to much more than yakuza-lite. * *

SATSU RARETE TAMA RUKA

1960 DIR. Eijiro Wakabayashi
SCR. Toshio Matsuura PHOTO
'SCOPE: Shunichiro Nakao MUSIC:
Kanoki Ogawa w/ Tatsuo Umemiya,
Hisaku Inoue, Tokubei Hanazawa,
Yoshiko Mita, Minoru Chiaki, Naoko
Kubo, Yoshi Kato

SCOUNDREL aka GOKUDO series

Scoundrel

SCOUNDREL aka GOKUDO

aka THE FAST LIVER 1968
92 min. DIR. Kosaku Yamashita
SCR. Motohiro Torii/Isao Matsumoto
PHOTO COLOR 'SCOPE: Nagaki
Yamagishi MUSIC: Masao Yagi
w/ Tomisaburo Wakayama, Koji
Tsuruta, Minoru Oki, Nijiko
Kiyokawa, Kyosuke Machida,
Sanae Kitabayashi, Yoshiko Fujita,
Nobuo Kaneko, Shingo Yamashiro,

Bin Amatsu, Asao Uchida, Hosei
Komatsu, Bunta Sugawara
The late, great Wakayama – Itto
Ogami in the LONE WOLF AND
CUB (KOZURE OKAMI) film series
(1972-'74) and Shintaro "Zatoichi"
Katsu's real-life brother – plays a
bumbling, small-time yakuza boss in
this eleven film action/comedy series.
It is a tad peculiar that this turned
into a series since "Gokudo" gets
shot about twenty times – a couple
of times in the head! – while taking
revenge on a betraying clan boss, then
seems to blow himself up with a gre-
nade as the cops close in. Purposely,
absurdly over-the-top. #1 of 11 films
* * *

RETURN OF THE SCOUNDREL

aka KAETTE KITA GOKUDO aka
RETURN OF THE OUTLAW 1968
93 min. DIR. Kosaku Yamashita
SCR. Motohiro Torii/Isao Matsumoto
PHOTO COLOR 'SCOPE: Motoya Washio
MUSIC: Isao Tomita w/ Tomisaburo
Wakayama, Minoru Oki, Nijiko
Kiyokawa, Kyosuke Machida, Reiko
Oshida, Shingo Yamashiro, Seizaburo
Kawazu, Takuzo Kawatani, Tatsuo
Endo, Mitsuo Nagata   Once again,
despite the absurdity of Wakayama's
good-hearted, bad-tempered and resolutely goofy gang boss, director
Yamashita keeps the humor from
getting too silly and undisciplined.
There are some actual laughs here
with Wakayama quite funny as he
goes to prison, at first feuding with
fashion plate rival Oki, then bonding
in friendship with him when their
gangs are victimized by some corrupt
guards. Once out, Wakayama and
Oki pool their resources, establishing a bigger gang and developing a
showplace for the theatrical group of

song-and-dance performers they're sponsoring. Kiyokawa returns as Wakayama's battleaxe spouse who has to constantly keep her man's roving eye for young ladies in check.

全身45発のタマ傷くらって
それでも死なないミスター極道！
バズーカと装甲車で大暴れ

カラー作品

待望！極道シリーズ第2弾

若山富三郎

監督 山下耕作

Return of the Scoundrel (#2)

Evil bosses Kawazu and Endo try to horn in on the theatre action, and soon a gang war erupts. Oki's girl, the beautiful, charming Reiko Oshida, is murdered with her girlfriend, packed into giant gift boxes and then delivered to Wakayama and Oki's HQ. Stalwart sidekick Machida also dies violently, so Wakayama, Oki et. al. go on a rampage with machine guns in their war surplus armored vehicle, decimating Kawazu and his mob. At the close, our "heroes" are greeted warmly as they return to the slammer. #2 of 11 films   * * *

SCOUNDREL SOLDIER aka HEITAI GOKUDO aka A PROFLIGATE SOLDIER 1968 91 min. DIR. Kiyoshi Saeki SCR. Isao Matsumoto/ Motohiro Torii PHOTO COLOR 'SCOPE: Juhei Suzuki MUSIC: Isao Tomita w/ Tomisaburo Wakayama, Hiroshi Nawa, Junko Miyazono, Kotaro Satomi, Reiko Oshida, Shingo Yamashiro, Bunta Sugawara
The Scoundrel gets drafted. Occasionally entertaining but often afflicted with a strained silliness, this entry was obviously inspired by the HOODLUM SOLDIER series at Daiei Studios starring Wakayama's brother, Shintaro Katsu. #3 of 11 films   * *

THE SCOUNDREL LIVES FOR THE STAGE aka MATTEI ITA GOKUDO aka THE DESPERATE GANG 1969 91 min. DIR. Kosaku Yamashita SCR. Isao Matsumoto/ Motohiro Torii PHOTO COLOR 'SCOPE: Motoya Washio MUSIC: Shunsuke Kikuchi w/ Tomisaburo Wakayama, Minoru Oki, Nijiko Kiyokawa, Keiko Yuge, Masumi Tachibana, Shingo Yamashiro
A by-the-numbers installment with Wakayama doing his lovable, blustery

gang boss thing, becoming involved with oppressed construction workers being persecuted by an unprincipled yakuza mob. Kiyokawa returns again as his wandering jealous spouse with her giant Chinese manservant always by her side. Pretty anonymous, although the villain gang's several arbitrary machne gun drive-bys of Wakayama's gang and workers is fairly jarring for its brutality and body count. Coming from director Yamashita, this should have been better.   #4 of 11 films   * * 1/2

THE SCOUNDREL TAKES A TRIP aka TABI NI DETA GOKU-DO   aka DESPERADO IN HONG KONG 1969 95 min. DIR. Junya Sato SCR. Motohiro Torii/Isao Matsumoto PHOTO COLOR 'SCOPE: Shigeru Akatsuka MUSIC: Isao Tomita w/ Tomisaburo Wakayama, Nijiko Kiyokawa, Minoru Oki, Shingo Yamashiro, Bunta Sugawara, Reiko Oshida   Wakayama winds up in Hong Kong fighting a Chinese mobster and American gangsters who are selling aphrodisiacs to common laborers. #5 of 11 films   * *

THE SCOUNDREL RETURNS FROM KAMAGASKI aka GOKUDO KAMAGASAKI NI KAERU aka RETURN OF THE DESPERADO 1970 100 min. DIR. Kosaku Yamashita SCR. Motohiro Torii/Isao Matsumoto PHOTO COLOR 'SCOPE: Motoya Washio MUSIC: Takeo Watanabe w/ Tomisaburo Wakayama, Minoru Oki, Nijiko Kiyokawa, Tomoko Mayama, Shingo Yamashiro, Bin Amatsu   Wakayama returns to his hometown to find it taken over by Chinese (Kaneko) and Japanese-

American gangsters. He is assisted by Yamashiro and Oki in routing the interlopers.   #6 of 11 films   * *

Scoundrel (#6)

FUGITIVE SCOUNDREL aka GOKUDO KYOJOTABI aka DESPERATE JOURNEY 1970 89 min. DIR. Kosaku Yamashita SCR. Takashi Harada PHOTO COLOR 'SCOPE: Shigeru Akatsuka MUSIC: Masao Yagi w/ Tomisaburo Wakayama, Nijiko Kiyokawa, Shingo Yamashiro, Miyoko Akaza, Bin Amatsu, Bunta Sugawara #7 of 11 films   * * 1/2

GOKUDO MAKARITORU 1972 94 min. DIR. Shigehiro Ozawa SCR. Koji Takada PHOTO COLOR 'SCOPE: Sadatsugu Yoshida MUSIC: Chumei Watanabe w/ Tomisaburo Wakayama, Bunta Sugawara, Nijiko Kiyokawa, Takashi Shimura, Junko Matsuhei #8 of 11 films

Fugitive Scoundrel (#7)

**SCOUNDREL FROM KAMA-
GASAKI** aka KAMAGASAKI
GOKUDO 1973 91 min. **DIR.** Kosaku
Yamashita **SCR.** Motohiro Torii/Isao
Matsumoto **PHOTO COLOR 'SCOPE:**
Nagaki Yamagishi **MUSIC:** Yukiaki
Sone w/ Tomisaburo Wakayama,
Nijiko Kiyokawa, Mariko Kaga,
Shingo Yamashiro, Minoru Oki,
Michi Azuma #9 of 11 films

**THE SCOUNDREL VS.
THE DELINQUENT BOSS**
aka GOKUDO TAI FURYO BAN-
CHO 1974 94 min. **DIR.** Kosaku
Yamashita **SCR.** Koji Takada/ Shoji
Shimura **PHOTO COLOR 'SCOPE:** Shin
Furuya **MUSIC:** Masao Yagi
w/ Tomisaburo Wakayama, Tatsuo
Umemiya, Tsunehiko Watase, Shingo
Yamashiro, Minoru Oki, Judi Ongu,
Makoto Arashi, Katsuhiko
Kobayashi, Asao Uchida, Hiroshi
Nawa, Takuzo Kawatani #10 of 11
films

*The Scoundrel vs. The Viper Brothers
(#11)*

**THE SCOUNDREL VS. THE
VIPER BROTHERS** aka GOKU-
DO TAI MAMUSHI 1974 89 min.
DIR. Sadao Nakajima **SCR.** Sadao

Nakajima/Isao Matsumoto/Hideaki
Yamamoto PHOTO COLOR 'SCOPE:
Motoya Washio MUSIC: Kenjiro
Hirose w/ Tomisaburo Wakayama,
Bunta Sugawara, Tamio Kawaji,
Nijiko Kiyokawa, Yuriko Mishima,
Takuzo Kawatani, Hosei Komatsu,
Rokko Toura   Toei Studios was
obviously seeing diminishing returns
from all three of their violent crime/
comedy series, thus the hybridization
here and the preceding title. Never-
theless, Wakayama, Sugawara and
Kawaji are an entertaining team-up,
regardless of how ridiculous this gets.
#11 and last of the series   * * *

SCOUNDREL BOSS aka
GOKUDO SHACHO 1975 82 min.
DIR. Sadao Nakajima SCR. Sadao
Nakajima/Isao Matsumoto/Hideaki
Yamamoto PHOTO COLOR 'SCOPE:
Umeo Masuda Music: Kenjiro
Hirose w/ Tatsuo Umemiya, Takuzo
Kawatani, Shingo Yamashiro, Hideo
Murota   A silly comedy hybrid of
salaryman and yakuza genres.

SECRET INFORMATION aka
TAREKOMI 1968 90 min.
DIR. Masaharu (Shoji) Segawa SCR.
Masaharu Segawa /Moto Nagai
PHOTO COLOR 'SCOPE: Masahiko
Iimura MUSIC: Chuji Kinoshita
w/ Noboru Ando, Isao Kimura, Eiji
Okada, Tamaki Sawa, Toru Abe,
Sanae Kitabayashi, Hideo Takamatsu,
Tokuhiko Umeji, Hiroshi Minami,
Machiko Yashiro   Ando plays a
hitman in hiding, relying on an old
comrade (Kimura). The friend is a
normal guy with a kid, but he gets
compromised and ends up very reluc-
tantly betraying Ando to keep sonny
safe. When Ando finds out after

escaping the massive forces unleashed to snare him, he decides to
kill his old buddy. But, however much
he tries, he can't bring himself to do
it. Because Ando has gotten away, the
bad guys end up kidnapping the little
boy, and Kimura and Ando go on a
bloody rescue mission to the boss's
forest mansion hideaway. The story
has a comparatively upbeat ending
with Ando still alive and free at the
end.   * * 1/2

Secret Information

**SECRET REPORT ON YAKUZA
CRUELTY – ARM AMPUTATION**
aka YAKUZA ZANKOKU HIROKU
– KATAU DESTSUDAN 1976
65 min. SUPERVISING PRODUCER:
Noboru Ando   Looks and smells
like a documentary. Gritty handheld
black-and-white photography spies on
gangsters/hoodlums as they gamble,
shoot-up, get tattooed, beat each other
as well as innocents. And these are
not rich mobsters or higher-echelon
criminals. These guys look like cruel

losers, for the most part, and they seem about one robbery or gambling score away from the poverty-stricken gutter. There are several small-time bosses and an old-time tattooist interviewed. We see the ancient, primitive tattooing method favored by the yakuza where the artist uses a manual needle (on the end of a wooden stick) that he pricks into the epidermis over and over and over until the work is done. It is said to be much more painful than an electric needle and takes much longer. Also spotlighted: a fellow doing the pinkie-finger-cutting-apology-number (real). There is also footage of a guy getting stabbed in the stomach and another gentleman getting his hand whacked-off – both of which look decidedly realistic in black-'n'-white. But these last two items were undoubtedly faked if only because of the editing and number of set-ups – something that real-life frantic behaviour would have definitely precluded. Ando's motivation for coming out with this documentary, other than I suppose money, is a mystery. The video I saw did not have English subtitles, and my Japanese is not good enough to understand much of what was said, especially with the low-tech, poor fidelity sound recording that was employed. As the reader undoubtedly recalls – having read this far – Ando was a yakuza himself. He went to jail for several years after shooting (not fatally) a shady entrepeneur who supposedly double-crossed him. There was a piece in a 1995 issue of Vanity Fair magazine about the big-time multimillionaire who was shot by Ando in the late 1950s. In the early 1990s, it is alleged that this millionaire and his daughter purchased the Empire State build-

ing under the aegis of a third party, and his ownership was being hotly contested by American "national landmark"-types touchy about a Japanese corporate pirate with yakuza connections owning such a famous and expensive piece of American history – but that is another story). Once Ando was released from prison, he sold his story in serialized form to the Japanese newspapers and became an overnight sensation. He was subsequently recruited by first Shochiku, then Toei and Nikkatsu to star in a number of films in a genre of ever-increasing popularity: the yakuza film. * * 1/2

SECRET STORY – PLUNDERING THE JEWEL aka SENGO HIWA – HOSEKI RYAKU DATSU aka THE UNDERGROUND SYNDICATE 1970 100 min. **Dir.** Sadao Nakajima **Scr.** Sadao Nakajima/ Takeo Kaneko **Photo color 'scope:** Yoshikazu (Giichi) Yamazawa **Music:** Isao Tomita **w/** Bunta Sugawara, Chiezo Kataoka, Tetsuro Tanba, Tomisaburo Wakayama, Asao Koike, Nobuo Kaneko, Hosei Komatsu, Yukie Kagawa, Masumi Tachibana, Rokko Toura, Hideo Murota, Yasuko Matsui
Only tangentially a yakuza story as the saga relates the violently sadistic machinations of various underworld characters trying to lay their hands on a rare jewel plucked from the Japan National Bank as the U.S. Occupation Forces took over immediately post-WW2. There is an incredible sequence at the end with Sugawara dying, driving frantically down a dark road and hallucinating various folks in the way of his car, then pools of blood and fire. Finally, his car plunges

into a lake of burning blood. Too bad that the rest of the film is not as visually brilliant. * * *

SECRETS OF JAPANESE ASSASSINATIONS aka NIPPON ANSATSU HIROKU aka MEMOIR OF JAPANESE ASSASSINATIONS 1969 142 min. **DIR.** Sadao Nakajima **SCR.** Sadao Nakajima/Kazuo Kasahara **PHOTO COLOR 'SCOPE:** Sadatsugu Yoshida **MUSIC:** Isao Tomita **w/** Shinichi "Sonny" Chiba, Chiezo Kataoka, Koji Tsuruta, Ken Takakura, Tomisaburo Wakayama, Junko Fuji, Yukie Kagawa, Jiro Tamiya, Masao Hori, Teruo Yoshida, Bunta Sugawara, Toshio Chiba
An epic in an episodic/anthology framework of stories detailing political assassinations from the samurai era down through the turbulence of right wing yakuza influences pre-WW2. One of the longer stories focuses on Chiba – admirably acquitting himself quite well amidst more seasoned thespians – a common worker, who comes under the sway of radical Buddhist leader Kataoka and military man Tamiya. * * *

SETTLEMENT aka OTOSHI-MAE series

SETTLEMENT aka OTOSHIMAE aka THREE GAMBLERS 1967 89 min. **DIR.** Teruo Ishii **SCR.** Kozo Uchida/Teruo Ishii **PHOTO COLOR 'SCOPE:** Kiichi Inada **MUSIC:** Masao Yagi **w/** Tatsuo Umemiya, Teruo Yoshida, Kanjuro Arashi, Minoru Oki, Tetsuro Tanba, Hayato Tani, Hideo Sunazuka, Seizaburo Kawazu, Rinichi Yamamoto, Renji Ishibashi
An energized, entertaining, though not particularly memorable pot-

boiler with director Ishi's trademark irreverent approach. Umemiya and Yoshida are young comrades in elder Arashi's gang. When ruthless new rival boss Yamamoto, backed by elder villain Kawazu, starts whittling away Arashi's territory, Arashi tries to keep the peace. Umemiya makes ends meet working as lighting guy at a strip club while Yoshida has a job as a mechanic. Both men have to endure harassment from Yamamoto's hoods. Things get complicated when teen protégé Tani is murdered in a back alley, then feisty old Arashi also meets his death.

Settlement (#1)

Finally, aided by elder lone wolf Oki, Umemiya and Yoshida decimate the bad guys' ranks. Tanba does an unforgettable turn as an ambivalent, smart aleck gunman in a pork pie hat. His hitman character is employed by Yamamoto, but his sympathies obviously lie with the underdogs, and he shows his true colors before the final frames unspool. Also of some note is Masao Yagi's very cool, jazz-inflected score as well as the fiery interaction between Umemiya and his lover, a stripper who works part time as a Turkish bath hostess. Also interesting is a still photo montage of the Hiroshima bomb blast and post-war black market in a pre-title sequence – an opening that bears striking similarities (though comparatively truncated and without the detailed context) to Fukasaku's first BATTLES WITHOUT HONOR & HUMANITY film in 1973. Evidence that other Toei filmmakers were thinking along similar lines. #1 of 2 films * * 1/2

THE SETTLEMENT 2 aka ZOKU OTOSHMAE aka THE FINAL DECISION 1968 80 min. **Dir.** Teruo Ishii **Scr.** Kozo Uchida/ Teruo Ishii **Photo color 'scope:** Yoshio Nakajima **Music:** Masao Yagi **w/**Tatsuo Umemiya, Teruo Yoshida, Koji Nanbara, Takuya (Takushi?) Shiro, Jun Tazaki, Kanjuro Arashi, Junko Miyazono, Toru Yuri, Reiko Ohara, Hideo Sunazuka, Toru Abe, Hayato Tani #2 of 2 films

SEVEN COLORFUL DAUGHTERS OF THE FLOWER aka HANA ZAKARI NANA 1961 **Dir.** Shigeaki Hidaka **Scr.** Morimasa Owaku **Photo 'scope:** Noboru Takanashi **Music:** Akira Ishimatsu **w/** Naoko Kubo, Mitsue Komiya, Akiko Yamato, Midori Urano, Kazuko Namiki, Nijiko Kiyokawa, Michiko Hoshi, Eijiro Yanagi From the promo photos, it seems this is an action/comedy about females fighting with each other in a yakuza gang.

SEVEN FUGITIVES aka **OTAZUNE MONO SHICHININ series**

SEVEN FUGITIVES aka OTAZUNE MONO SHICHININ 1966 **Dir.** Shigehiro Ozawa **Scr.** Kazuo Kasahara/ Shigehiro Ozawa **Photo color 'scope:** Juhei Suzuki **Music:** Toshiaki Tsushima **w/** Koji Tsuruta, Hiromi Fujiyama, Kyosuke Machida, Tomisaburo Wakayama, Junko Fuji, Rinichi Yamamoto, Bin Amatsu, Yuriko Mishima, Tatsuo Endo, Tomoko Ogawa, Haruo Tanaka #1 of 2

Osaka Chivalry - Courage of Slain Seven

OSAKA CHIVALRY – COURAGE OF SLAIN SEVEN aka NANIWA KYOKAKU – DOKYO SHICHININ GIRI 1967 **Dir.** Shigehiro Ozawa **Scr.** Norifumi Suzuki/Motohiro Torii **Photo color 'scope:** Juhei Suzuki **Music:** Ichiro Saito **w/** Koji Tsuruta, Kayo Matsuo, Sanae Kitabayashi, Bin Amatsu, Minoru Oki, Takashi

Shimura, Auto Yokoyama, Nobuo Kaneko, Masumi Tachibana, Asao Uchida   A bizarrely schizophrenic *ninkyo eiga* composed of several different storylines that gradually come together by the end. But Ozawa's inability or unwillingness to integrate the radical shifts in tone amongst all the subplots seriously undermines the film. A pity, because there are certain scenes, especially between Tsuruta and Shimura and then Tsuruta and Matsuo that are superbly performed and actually moving. Then there are interludes with a childishly tempermental buffoon/yakuza wannabe (Auto Yokoyama) that are annoying in the extreme. Obviously played for comic relief, these scenes have the unintended effect of showing any man who is not masculine and tough enough to be a yakuza to be a worthless, immature troublemaker (all of Yokoyama's non-yakuza drinking buddies are cut from the same moronic cloth). This seriously undermines the whole saga. Matsuo is superb in the not-unfamiliar role of a tubercular whore down on her luck rescued from suicide by the hero (in this case, Tsuruta). She truly takes the character out of cliché territory because of her great skill as an actress. There were many, many actresses in 1950s and 1960s Japanese cinema who played consumptive heroines who die in agonizingly slow death scenes. Matsuo certainly takes top honors hands down for two of the most convincing (the other being in the second entry of Tetsuya Watari's modern yakuza series, HOODLUM, at Nikkatsu Studios). Likewise, Takashi Shimura excels playing Tsuruta's elderly *oyabun* in poor health. Shimura played many a benevolent, elderly gang boss in Toei yakuza potboilers, but few allowed his talent to rise to its maximum potential. This film is one of the exceptions, especially in the scene where he delivers a moving monologue to his gang after the return of formerly banished Tsuruta. At the climax, Tsuruta assaults bad guy HQ during a fierce rainstorm, dispatching ex-comrade-turned-traitor Amatsu and spineless, evil rival boss Kaneko. Fine actress Kitabayashi is largely wasted as Tsuruta's longsuffering, sushi waitress girfriend. All in all, the film has its moments, but it is disappointingly inconsistent. It may or may not actually be related to the 1966 SEVEN FUGITIVES release above (but it *was* as far as Toei's marketing division was concerned – also see the entry for SEVEN GAMBLERS under Toei's GAMBLER series). * * 1/2   #2 of 2

SEX DIARY aka SHIJIKO TORU-KO NIKKI 1974 **DIR.** Kazuhiko Yamaguchi **SCR.** Masahiro Kakefuda **PHOTO COLOR 'SCOPE:** Yoshio Nakajima **MUSIC:** Tomokazu Kawabe **w/** Tatsuo Umemiya, Sami Suzuki, Chie Kobayashi, Harumi Sone, Miyoko Tanimoto, Keiko Ito, Saburo Date, Sharon Kelly

THE SEX PEDDLERS aka HIMO aka THE PROCURER 1965 86 min. **DIR.** Hideo Sekigawa **SCR.** Masashige Narusawa/Ryunosuke Ono **PHOTO B&W 'SCOPE:** Shichiro Hayashi **MUSIC:** Kazumi Naito **w/** Tatsuo Umemiya, Mako Midori, Sanae Nakahara, Romi Yamada, Koji Nanbara, Rinichi Yamamoto, Tatsuzo Ishibashi, Toshiro (?) Otsuji, Kazuo Kitamura, Kenji Ushio

Midori is a teenager living on the streets who is exploited by pimp Umemiya. Before long she becomes streetwise and uses her gangster associations to break away and eventually become a madam. Umemiya subsequently kills her patron with his boss's okay in an attempt to show off his power. But Midori decides to rat Umemiya out to the cops rather than once again fall into his clutches.

SHINJUKU'S NUMBER ONE DRUNK – KILLER TETSU aka SHINJUKU YOIDORE BANCHI – HITOKIRI TETSU 1977 87 min. Dir. Yu Kohira Scr. Hiro Matsuda/ Masahiro Kakefuda Photo color 'scope: Yoshio Nakajima Music: Hajime Kaburagi w/ Bunta Sugawara, Makoto Sato, Etsuko Ikuta, Akira Nishikino, Hiroshi Tate, Yoshiro Aoki, Joji Takano, Mikio Narita, Tamio Kawaji, Nobuo Yana Sugawara portrays an alcoholic yakuza killer.

Showa Woman Gambler

SHOWA WOMAN GAMBLER aka SHOWA ONNA BAKUTO 1972 91 min. Dir. Tai Kato Scr. Motohiro Torii/Tatsuo Honda Photo color 'scope: Shin Furuya Music: Chuji Kinoshita w/ Kyoko Enami, Hiroki Matsukata, Shigeru Amachi, Kanjuro Arashi, Michitaro Mizushima, Junko Matsuhei, Fumio Watanabe, Rinichi Yamamoto, Tatsuo Endo, Masazumi Okabe, Shoji Arikawa, Mieko Hoshino
Junko (RED PEONY GAMBLER) Fuji had just retired, and Daiei, Kyoko (WOMAN GAMBLING EXPERT) Enami's contract studio, had just gone under financially. So Toei, testing the waters, teamed-up excellent yakuza director Kato with Enami hoping to hit paydirt with another female yakuza series. It actually announces this as the first of a series in the film's trailer. But this appears to be the only one Enami made with Toei, so I surmise things did not turn out that well at the box-office. Not surprising, as this is, in some ways, even grimmer, more downbeat and more minimalist than even the most uncompromising of Kato's other *ninkyo* yakuza fare at Toei – most of which were extremely popular. Enami's character is almost diametrically opposed to Fuji's Red Peony Gambler, not seeming to have a similar inner wellspring of courage and fortitude to draw on. Neither does she possess the unsullied virginal persona of Fuji's character. Enami's character is crippled by inner torment. Every bit of courage she musters is in direct proportion to the feelings of loyalty she has for those she loves, and she struggles to remain upright in a cruel man's world. She also is capable of total lustful abandon with the man

she truly loves. Matsukata, a decent underboss to ailing elder Mizushima, rescues Enami after a botched suicide attempt in a freezing river.

Showa Woman Gambler

Thereafter, she becomes more and more devoted to him. Things take a turn for the worse when Mizushima passes over degenerate, resentful underboss Watanabe and bestows the successor's mantle instead on Matsukata. Almost immediately, Watanabe plots easygoing Matsukata's death. Numerous botched attempts on his life finally give way to a successful one, mere days after Enami's and Matsukata's heated consummation of their love. From then on, Enami is an unstoppable engine of destruction, first seducing and cutting the throat of bad boss Watanabe (in a very bloody, hard-to-watch scene) then wiping out political boss and yakuza string-puller Yamamoto and his henchmen. She is aided in the final massacre by former enemy Amachi, someone else who has also lost a mate to the villains' homicidal attacks. Although possessed of standard *ninkyo* formula, Kato's bare bones approach, from shot compositions to sparse use of Kinoshita's effective score to his expert direction of actors, raises this far above many similar Toei *ninkyo* efforts. Memorable, moving and an unfairly neglected gem. Toei tried two more times after this to start another female gambler film series, with Teruo Ishii helming RED SILK GAMBLER (1972) with Eiko Nakamura, then Norifumi Suzuki and Teruo Ishii turning out two entries in the OCHO aka ELDER SISTER series (1973) with Reiko Ike. Unfortunately, despite their high entertainment value, none of these ever matched the popularity of Junko Fuji in her RED PEONY role. On a side note, it is fascinating to see the different approaches from Toei marketing in their posters: in the long narrow "speed" poster, they emphasize a more violent, aggressive pose as in

Junko Fuji's previous Red Peony character, and in the one-sheet, an image more reminiscent of the posters for Enami's role in the long-running-WOMAN GAMBLING EXPERT series that she had just completed at Daiei Studios. * * * *

Sister Streetfighter (#1)

SISTER STREETFIGHTER aka WOMAN KILLER'S FIST aka ONNA HISSATSU KEN series

SISTER STREETFIGHTER aka ONNA HISSATSU KEN aka WOMAN KILLER'S FIST 1974 86 min. **DIR.** Kazuhiko Yamaguchi **SCR.** Norifumi Suzuki/Masahiro Kakefuda **PHOTO COLOR 'SCOPE:** Yoshio Nakajima **MUSIC:** Shunsuke Kikuchi **w/** Etsuko "Sue " Shiomi, Shinichi "Sonny" Chiba, Asao Uchida, Bin Amatsu, Hiroshi Kondo, Emi Hayakawa   Shiomi is, as they say in the movie, a "karate woman" whose undercover cop brother has been fatally victimized by a drug ring. She goes undercover, too, with the

help of her *"sensei"* Chiba (comparatively benevolent compared to his Terry Tsurugi STREETFIGHTER persona). Amatsu is the over-the-top flamboyant gangster whose island mansion's underground HQ is strictly dimestore James Bond. There are some marvelously bad, yet still entertaining scenes with Amatsu barechested and in ugly striped (!) pants doing hand-to-hand combat with Shiomi. Their fighting space is a subterranean tunnel of papier-mache rocks glutted with fluttering-and-flopping fake bats. All of these Toei martial arts/yakuza/action hybrids are just a shade less professional than their other yakuza and samurai fare. For some reason, probably partly due to seeing them in their horrendously-dubbed New Line Cinema versions, I always find them a minute-eyebrow-hair short of competence. Everything else is... well, great pacing; slambang editing; anonymous, conspicuous, sometimes evocative music score; fairly acceptable, rough-'n-tumble fighting; mindless stories and dialogue; dutifully ambitious performances. What I'm getting at is that these are strictly nothing-profound action movies. But the American versions (original U.S. distributors tinkered with the STREETFIGHTER aka SATSUJINKEN films also and even worse butchered a yakuza masterpiece, TRUE ACCOUNT OF THE YAMAGUCHI GANG – LIFE AND DEATH OPERATIONS ON KYUSHU gutting it of twenty minutes and releasing it here as THE TATTOOED HITMAN) are blatantly coated with condescending attitude. The SISTER STREETFIGHTER and STREETFIGHTER movies are not any highbrow entertainments or pieces of multilevel storytelling. My convoluted point is that these movies are nowhere near as stupid in their original Japanese versions as their American manifestations. In fact, many were not stupid at all until they got released in dubbed-English. Many of the folks who imported the Chinese kung-fu pictures thought they were idiotic, some distributors might have even hated them. But I am sure there were also many film industry people working on the post-production of the American versions who loved these films on a certain level. However, their affection and enjoyment was/is steeped in that old familiar attitude of American superiority. In some cases, such as here and the STREETFIGHTER series, the movies in question were only knocked down a peg or two. In some other cases, such as the most mediocre Chinese kung fu and the lamest of the GODZILLA (GOJIRA) movies, the dubbing perhaps even helped make them more entertaining. Tragically, many of these distributors of Asian genre pictures, the ones who actually did the language-dubbing and even reworking of the edit, looked on all their "product" as just that: "product" that could maybe be transformed into "so bad it's good" pieces. Of course, sometimes, as in the case of some misguided Asians pioneering on their own and unfamiliar with the English language, the aural and visual mangling was accidental. The most annoying thing is that even many fans of Japanese and Chinese genre films, people who otherwise may have good taste, do not get it. Many otherwise intelligent people do not even know the difference between Japanese and Chinese film – as if it is all been produced by some United States of Asia and not different countries with profoundly different cultures and approaches to moviemaking. Many have the "so bad it's good" attitude about even acknowledged classics. One could go on, but this is supposed to be about the SISTER STREET-FIGHTER films. As an afterthought: I believe this first SISTER STREET-FIGHTER was the only one released by New Line in America – unlike the STREETFIGHTER series which were all released stateside but heavily gutted of their original violence (more the Motion Picture Ratings Board's fault than NEW LINE's). This first SISTER STREETFIGHT-ER film and all the STREETFIGHT-ER movies have had their original, over-the-top cartoon-style brutality completely restored in their most recent U.S. video/laser/dvd editions. #1 of 4 films   * * 1/2

WOMAN KILLER'S FIST – THE CRITICAL MOMENT aka ONNA HISSATSU KEN – KIKI IPPATSU 1974 85 min. **DIR** Kazuhiko Yamaguchi **SCR.** Norifumi Suzuki/Masahiro Kakefuda **PHOTO COLOR 'SCOPE:** Yoshio Nakajima **MUSIC:** Shunsuke Kikuchi w/ Etsuko "Sue" Shiomi, Tamase (Tamayo?) Mitsukawa, Hideo Murota, Michiyo Bando, Yasuaki Kurata #2 of 4 films

RETURN OF THE WOMAN KILLER'S FIST aka KAETTE KITA ONNA HISSATSU KEN 1975 77 min. **DIR.** Kazuhiko Yamaguchi **SCR.** Takeo Kaneko/ Masahiro Kakefuda **PHOTO COLOR 'SCOPE:** Masahiko Iimura **MUSIC:** Shunsuke Kikuchi w/ Etsuko "Sue"

Shiomi, Yasuaki Kurata, Akane
Kawazaki, Miwa Cho, Rinichi
Yamamoto #3 of 4 films

**WOMAN KILLER'S FIFTH
RANKING FIST** aka ONNA HIS-
SATSU GODAN KEN 1976 77
min. DIR. Shigehiro Ozawa SCR.
Motohiro Torii/Isao Matsumoto/
Masahiro Shimura PHOTO COLOR
'SCOPE: Sakushi Shiomi MUSIC:
Hajime Ueshiba (Kamishiba?)
w/ Etsuko "Sue" Shiomi, Rabu
Micchii (Robert Michee), Tsunehiko
Watase, Ken Uorusu
There was a follow-up of sorts to
this series the same year, KILLER
WOMAN'S FIST (HISSATSU
ONNA KEN) directed by Yu Kohira,
also starring Shiomi but, for some
reason, it is not considered part of
the series #4 and final in series

SONG OF THE NIGHT aka
YORU NO KAYO series

**SONG OF THE NIGHT – EVEN
IF I DIE** aka YORU NO KAYO –
INOCHI KARETOMO 1968 DIR.
Ryuichi Takamori SCR. Masashige
Narusawa w/ Tatsuo Umemiya,
Sanae Nakahara, Junzaburo Ban,
Kikko Matsuoka
In this prolific series of programmers,
Umemiya reprises his suave, smooth-
talking pimp role that he had essayed
in a few grittier, slightly more serious
films circa 1965 directed by the likes
of Hideo Sekigawa. The series focuses on comic and tragic stories about
nightclub hostess life with alternating
romantic and sexual overtones. Once
again, to paraphrase my comments
on Tatsuo Umemiya's other NIGHT
(YORU) films, these are only border-

line yakuza pictures. It is not clear the
order of this series since many were
released the same year. So they are
listed here in the same order that they
were reviewed in different issues of
Kinema Junpo magazine. Umemiya,
with few exceptions, appears as the
male lead in the majority of the films.
This first one is strictly a program
potboiler loaded down with offensive
comedy about conning middle-aged
johns – most prominently, Junzaburo
Ban – out of their money and
Umemiya's many conquests with
the vulnerable bar girls he dallies
with behind spouse and bar co-owner
Nakahara's back. It is even more disappointing since the script was by
Narusawa who wrote many worthwhile films. His sole signature of
originality is to have repeated voice-
overs from all the characters indicat-
ing their true thoughts, obviously to
ironically humorous effect. There
are affecting moments, such as when
Umemiya awakens to find his bed
partner, sad girl Matsuoka, to have
committed suicide during the night,
and near the end of the film when he,
after doublecrossing his lover Nakahara, gets run over by her. But by the
closing scene, Narusawa and director
Takamori are once again going for
cheap laughs as flush john Ban lays
some money on wheelchair-bound
Umemiya to get him a girl.   * *

**SONG OF THE NIGHT –
NAGASAKI BLUES** aka YORU
NO KAYO – NAGASAKI BURU-
USU 1969 89 min. DIR. Ryuichi
Takamori SCR. Kazuo Funabashi
PHOTO COLOR 'SCOPE: Ichiro
Hoshijima MUSIC: Harumi Ibe
w/ Hiroki Matsukata, Junko
Miyazono, Tatsuo Umemiya, Hayato

Tani, Reiko Ohara, Arihiko Fujimura, Mari Shiraki, Keiji Takagi, Harumi Sone, Yaeko Wakamizu

Song of the Night - Nagasaki Blues

Matsukata is a bar manager of a Tokyo male escort nightclub that caters to rich women of all ages. He helps shy, down-on-his-luck Tani out with a new suit and makeover, then a job. Tani's beautiful, old-fashioned sister Miyazono visits from Nagasaki and is unhappy to see her brother working as a glorified gigolo. Happy-go-lucky womanizer Matsukata tries to win her over, to no avail. Finally, he forces himself on her, but before things go too far, Tani walks in. Miyazono leaves in shame and heads back to Nagasaki. Matsukata, his macho ego bruised but also genuinely smitten, follows her only to find Miyazono hooking up again with her just-released-from-stir small-time yakuza fiancé Umemiya. Complicating matters is Matsukata's former girl Ohara who is so angry

at being dumped, she tries to kill him. Matsukata deflects her tirade and doesn't miss a beat, engineering a meeting with Umemiya whom he promptly fills up with lies about Miyazono's loyalty. Fathead Umemiya actually believes him and breaks it off, relegating Miyazono to a despair that ends in a suicide attempt. Matsukata luckily happens by and saves her from the gassed apartment. At first she is unresponsive but soon warms to him as he nurses her back to health. However, Umemiya's friends have it in for Matsukata for disrespecting their boss, and they knife him one night on a busy downtown street. He miraculously makes it back to Miyazono's pad. This time it is her turn to save his life, riding with him in the ambulance as he professes his love to her. The melodrama ends here so we don't know for sure if he survives, somehing that would definitely affect my enjoyment of the film. His death would seem somewhat appropriate after all his self-willed manipulation of other people's emotions. Even still, this stands out as an exceptional and, at times, deliriously romantic entry in what is too often a lackluster series. This is due as much to the incredible, nuanced performance by the underrated Miyazono, one of Toei's stalwart standby leading ladies who never ever achieved real stardom, as it is to the script by writer Funabashi (a veteran of numerous films at Daiei Studios, including several for maestro Yasuzo Masumura). * * *

SONG OF THE NIGHT – HARBOR-TOWN BLUES aka YORU NO KAYO – MINATO MACHI BURUUSU 1969 85 min. **DIR.** Ryuichi

Takamori SCR. Masashige Narusawa
PHOTO COLOR 'SCOPE: Yoshio
Nakajima **MUSIC:** Masao Yagi
w/ Yumiko Nogawa, Kyosuke
Machida, Tatsuo Umemiya,
Hayato Tani, Yukie Kagawa, Hisao
Toake, Chie Kobayashi, Makiko
Kitashiro, Sayoko Tanimoto, Kanako
Yamaguchi   The always versatile, brilliant Nogawa is amazingly
authentic as a happy-go-lucky bar
hostess/whore who has some doubts
about her freewheeling, don't-give-
damn lifestyle after meeting handsome, womanizing sailor Umemiya.
Machida is the longsuffering playboy
son of one of Nogawa's clients, an
old guy who basically likes to just
take naps at her place and cook her
breakfast. Machida is a good friend to
Nogawa and genuinely in love with
her, but Nogawa doesn't like him as a
lover. However, midway through the
saga she goes on an alcoholic binge
that sparks a demoralizing episode
where she bites the tongue of a *gaijin*
flirt, is subsequently thrashed by his
less than chivalrous friends, *then*
beaten by her own hostess comrades
who do not like her ungrateful, supposedly "unprofessional" attitude.
Left pummeled and bleeding in a
back street, she makes the decision
to marry Machida. The Christian
wedding ceremony offers some of
the strangest juxtapositions when
a bit player known exclusively for
playing brutal toughs in all of Toei's
other genre films pops up as the priest
presiding at the marriage! Nogawa
has second thoughts right when she
is supposed to kiss groom Machida
and runs out of the church and down
the street in her wedding dress. She
hightails it to her club only to find
the police roping off a crime scene. A

sweet young guy who was introduced
to her by Umemiya and whom she
deflowered has been killed in a knifefight. At the end of the saga, Nogawa
comes to friendly terms again with
both Umemiya and Machida and
takes off for another port town, resolute in her independence. Although
this is one of the SONG OF THE
NIGHT series that cannot be considered a yakuza film, it still has all the
ambience of underworld nightlife and
characters living on the periphery
of society. Nogawa is a luminous,
go-for-broke presence in all her roles,
and her gutwrenching performance
here is no exception. * * *

**SONG OF THE NIGHT –
VILLAIN BLUES** aka YORU
NO KAYO – AKUTO BURUUSU
1969 **DIR.** Ryuichi Takamori **SCR.**
Masashige Narusawa **w/** Tatsuo
Umemiya, Junko Miyazono, Masumi
Tachibana, Hayato Tani, Harumi
Sone, Ryohei Uchida, Machiko
Yashiro, Nobuo Kaneko
A really excruciatingly bad action
comedy of womanizer Umemiya trying to win back lost love Miyazono,
even as he periodically beds smitten
Tachibana and other bar girls. Tani is
his younger comrade who gets into
trouble falling in love with the wrong
girls. Tani gets stabbed by sleazy
assistant pimp Sone. Even though
Tani survives, Umemiya goes on a
rampage to kill Sone and nearsighted
villain Uchida. However, at the end
of their duel, Uchida gets the upper
hand and is about to kill Umemiya
when Tachibana stabs the villain from
behind. Kaneko is a slimy business-
man/pimp who likes to torture his
sexy mistress Yashiro with ice cubes
when he is not pulling the strings on

Uchida and Sone. Embarassing for all performers involved – most of whom are exceptionally talented – but especially shameful for screenwriter Narusawa. He co-wrote the screenplay for Kinji Fukasaku's version of BLACK LIZARD (1968), but more importantly he collaborated with Kenji Mizoguchi on some of the master's last films, including STREET OF SHAME, PRINCESS YANG KWEI FEI and NEW TALES OF THE TAIRA CLAN. * 1/2

Song of the Night - Isezaki District Blues

SONG OF THE NIGHT – ISEZA-KI DISTRICT BLUES aka YORU NO KAYO – ISEZAKICH BURU-USU 1969 **DIR.** Shinji Murayama **SCR.** Kazuo Funabashi **PHOTO COLOR 'SCOPE:** Ichiro Hoshijima **MUSIC:** Minoru Miki   **w/** Tatsuo Umemiya, Junko Miyazono, Junzaburo Ban, Teruo Yoshida, Mayumi Shimizu, Koji Nanbara, Hosei Komatsu

This entry is a bit annoying at first, handicapped with the usual banal TV-level comedy of Umemiya and bar partner mama-san Miyazono trying to separate lecherous Ban from his money. However, a third of the way through Miyazono's estranged-spouse, yakuza Yoshida, is released from prison. This throws a monkey-wrench into not only Umemiya's con game but also his love life. Suddenly, Miyazono is reunited with her true love, and she gradually disassociates herself from her happy-go-lucky, cad lover. The idiotic, carefree humor in the beginning actually works to the story's advantage serving as weird counterpoint to the "when-it-rains-it-pours" spiral of bad luck that dogs Umemiya once ambivalent Yoshida appears on the scene. Umemiya ends up thrashed by hooligans hired by angry mark Ban, and soon after he is stabbed during an argument with Yoshida. Miyazono and Yoshida then blow town, leaving Umemiya severely depressed. Devoted bar girl-on-the-sidelines, sweet Shimizu, is there to help pick up the pieces, and there is a nice moody scene where they walk along the pier together at night as the saga winds to its denouement. * * *

SONG OF THE NIGHT – WOMAN aka YORU NO KAYO – ONNA 1969 86 min. **DIR.** Ryuichi Takamori **SCR.** Masashige Narusawa w/ Yumiko Nogawa, Tatsuo Umemiya, Masumi Tachibana, Tatsuo Endo, Shinichi Mori

One rainy night, tearful, jilted Nogawa confronts her former beau, bar manager Umemiya with a knife. Things flashback to their original meeting when Umemiya had rescued her from yakuza abductors. Nogawa is not the usual devil-may-care bar girl and emerges as a sweet-natured, sensitive individual caught up in the maelstrom of Tokyo nightlife. At first, Umemiya could not care less, attracted to her and abusing her simultaneously. As the story progresses, we realize much of his anger towards Nogawa stems from his own self-hatred at being too weak to leave the employ of his dominating bar madam boss/mistress. This mama-san is one cruel, vindictive creature and devises her own sadistic traps for Nogawa. Coinicidentally, Nogawa's roommate and sister Tachibana is just the opposite – a nympho, do-anything-for-fun party girl who works for the mama-san. Eventually, Tachibana's fast, hard living catch up with her, and Umemiya and Nogawa are both chagrined when she is consigned to the hospital to die from her debauched lifestyle. At the close, Umemiya admits his craven ways and, despairing of ever having the guts to take up with Nogawa, he grabs her knife hand and guides the blade into his stomach. She is horrified and saddened as she holds her dying lover in her arms. This could have been a real little masterpiece. The first third is nearly perfect, a melancholic, atmospheric paen to bar nightlife and a neon milieu of ne'er-do-well losers. However, the saga bogs down a bit in the second act as it concentrates more on sibling Tachibana's decadent lifestyle before rebounding at the climax. Another liability is that the story fails to really capture the essence of why Nogawa keeps subjecting herself to horrible abuse at the hands of Umemiya, the cruel mama-san and her salaryman molester clients. Nogawa, as usual, profoundly elevates the proceedings,

emerging as soulful and nakedly honest in her portrayal – a performance that has few equals in bravely enduring gross humiliation and abuse. Although this is one of director Takamori's better films, one can't help but wonder what screenwriter Narusawa's frequent collaborator-from-the-past director Mizoguchi would have done with the same material. * * *

SONG OF THE NIGHT SERIES – STREET WOMAN aka YORU NO KAYO SHIIRIIZU – ONNA NO MICHI 1973 80 min. **DIR.** Kazuhiko Yamaguchi **SCR.** Masashige Narusawa **PHOTO COLOR 'SCOPE:** Masao Shimizu **MUSIC:** Toshiaki Tsushima **w/** Tatsuo Umemiya, Yutaka Nakajima, Yukie Kagawa, Yayoi Watanabe, Fujio Suga, Shiro Miya, Goro Miya, Hiroshi Namiki, Ichiro Araki A lackluster, lazy narrative of seducer/pimp/barfly Umemiya and his enabling girlfriend Nakajima. There are no yakuza trappings whatever in this outing, and one wishes for even some formulaic-bad-guy-mobsters-harassing-the-mama-san subplot to enliven the dire proceedings. Miraculously, the film does threaten to get interesting at the 2/3 point when the innately charismatic Nakajima flashes back to when she first hooked up with Umemiya before his jaded, oily back alley denizen phase when he was a champion race car driver. She is rudely interrupted from her melancholic reverie by sleazeball salaryman Suga who tries to rape her. She manages to bite off the tip of his tongue then escape by jumping out the window into a handy canal. Unfortunately, the cab she hails is helmed by another scummy sex maniac who drives her out to the forest and rapes her! The next time she sees Umemiya, she is mortified to see him seducing yet another naive waif. When she is driving with him later, she suddenly loses her cool and fights him for control of the steering wheel. He manages to push her clear of the car just as they hit a huge billboard showcasing a gigantic pair of red lips. Consequently, Nakajima is guilt-wracked when Umemiya is laid up in hospital. Ultimately, she makes the dubious spiritually-uplifting decision to accept wastrel Umemiya as he is rather than lose him. Despite the occasional memorable image (i.e. the car crash through the billboard lips), this is another disappointing effort from writer Narusawa. Hard to believe that this is the same Narusawa who collaborated with Mizoguchi on some of his most revered masterpieces. To make matters even worse, the musically-talented Pinkara Trio provide some of the most unfunny comedy I have ever seen in Japanese cinema. * *

SONG OF THE NIGHT – TEARFUL LOVE aka YORU NO KAYO – NAMIDA GOI 1973 74 min. **DIR.** Buichi Saito **SCR.** Masashige Narusawa **PHOTO COLOR 'SCOPE:** Giichi Yamazawa **MUSIC:** Taiichiro Kosugi w/ Yutaka Nakajima, Hayato Tani, Akemi Namiro, Isao Sasaki, Chitose Kobayashi, Yumiko Katayama, Fujio Suga   Nakajima is a bored, romantic bargirl sick of helping her bar mama-san mother recruit females off the street to turn tricks with the sleazy salaryman customers that frequent their establishment. Her mom's lover is the lecherous bartender who has an

even stronger yen for Nakajima. Too bad that Nakajima has a barely concealed disgust for most males – that is until she falls hard for a wounded young gangster (Tani) who slips his gun in her purse – (a little phallic foreshadowing) – when he is pursued by cops in a neighboring back alley. She helps nurse him back to health, but he disappears for the middle third of the saga. Soon after she awakens in the middle of the night to find a young man raping her. At first, both she and the audience are fooled into thinking it is yakuza Tani. But it turns out to be the bartender. Nakajima's mother has a heart attack and dies when she finds out her slutty, bartender beau has gone behind her back to screw her daughter. The death of mom as well as Nakajima's association with Tani causes her to be hauled in for questioning by the cops. The rest of the bargirl whores turn on Nakajima, blaming her for mama-san's death as well as being sick-to-death of what they perceive as her snobbish avoidance of the freewheeling prostitute lifestyle. After some particularly cruel abuse at the hands of the girls, the bartender briefly steps in as her protector, but we soon realize he only wants to make Nakajima his lover and cares little for her true feelings. Finally, the impatient, witless bartender tries to rape Nakajima again, but this time she won't give in and ends up stabbing him-to-death. Immediately after doing the deed, her true love Tani reappears, and the two leave to enjoy an idyllic tryst in a flower-covered field and an empty baseball stadium (!) before he splits for good. It is implied he will take the blame for the dead lecher bartender's murder. The last shot is of Nakajima

tending the bar she has inherited,
finally a mature woman who is able to
transcend the sordid goings-on in the
neighborhood and keep her dignity
intact. This is a modest, low key,
unusually good entry in the series that
shows how good writer Narusawa
could be when he wanted. Veteran
director Saito establishes just the
right tone, keeping a delicate balance
between melancholy urban romance
and teen girl's wet dream without
resorting to either cheap sentiment or
too much goofball, sleazy humor.
A great example of this series at its
best. * * *

SONG OF OSSAN OF KAWACHI
aka KAWACHI NO OSSAN NO
UTA 1977 **Dir.** Buichi Saito **Scr.**
Ikuo Sekimoto/ Jun Takada **Photo**
color 'scope: Yoshio Nakajima
Music: Hajime Kaburagi w/ Takuzo
Kawatani, Junko Natsu, Keiko Hara,
Kagari Asagawa, Shunji Imai, Koichi
Iwaki, Tamio Kawaji, Mayumi
Shimizu A slapstick comedy yakuza
picture with manic buffoon (and often
funny) Kawatani getting the star treat-
ment. *Followed by one sequel.*

**STATE POLICE VS. ORGAN-
IZED CRIME**   aka KENKEI TAI
SOSHIKI BORYOKU aka COPS
VS. THUGS 1975 101 min.
Dir. Kinji Fukasaku **Scr.** Kazuo
Kasahara **Photo color 'scope:**
Shigeru Akatsuka **Music:** Toshiaki
Tsushima   w/ Bunta Sugawara,
Hiroki Matsukata, Tatsuo Umemiya,
Nobuo Kaneko, Mikio Narita, Asao
Sano, Shingo Yamashiro, Shoji
Arikawa, Reiko Ike, Kunie Tanaka,
Hideo Murota   Police detective
Sugawara is already moderately on
the take when the applecart is upset

*stills from **State Police vs. Organized
Crime** aka **Cops vs. Thugs***

by internecine yakuza warfare. His
higher-ups order a crackdown, and
Sugawara comes under new strict,
straight arrow supervisor Umemiya.
Umemiya proceeds to clean house
and raid yakuza HQs. Young gang
boss Matsukata, who also happens
to be Sugawara's drinking buddy, is
not pleased. Before long the crackdown becomes so severe Matsukata's
gang vindictively kidnaps a former

cop who was fired for corruption. Sugawara rescues the man by stealing into Matsukata's armed stronghold, forcing Matsukata, Murota, et. al. to surrender. Matsukata convinces his former pal Sugawara to not handcuff him then, once outside, promptly grabs a gun and takes Umemiya hostage. Sugawara takes a chance and shoots Matsukata, killing him. Free, Umemiya tries to shake Sugawara's hand. But Sugawara ignores him, kneeling over his dead friend Matsukata. Busted down to police box duty in the styx, Sugawara is subsequently set up and fatally run down by a truck one night in a rainy, deserted street. This is a very good film, but similar subject matter was handled even more dramatically by Fukasaku in the emotionally explosive YAKUZA BURIAL – JASMINE FLOWER with Tetsuya Watari, Meiko Kaji and Umemiya. * * *

Story of Japanese Bad Men (#1)

STORY OF JAPANESE BAD MEN aka NIHON AKU NIN DEN series
STORY OF JAPANESE BAD MEN aka NIHON AKU NIN DEN 1971 DIR. Shinji Murayama SCR. Fumio Konami PHOTO COLOR 'SCOPE: Juhei Suzuki MUSIC: Toshiaki Tsushima w/ Tomisaburo Wakayama, Machiko Yashiro, Fumio Watanabe, Minoru Oki, Hiroko Ebata, Hiroshi Fuji, Tatsuo Endo, Hosei Komatsu, Nobuo Kaneko, Kenji Kusumoto #1 of 2 films

STORY OF JAPANESE BAD MEN – TRAVELING COMPANIONS TO HELL aka NIHON AKU NIN DEN – JIGOKU NO MICHIZURE 1972 90 min. DIR. Shinji Murayama SCR. Takayuki Yamada PHOTO COLOR 'SCOPE: Shigeru Akatsuka MUSIC: Toshiaki Tsushima w/ Tomisaburo Wakayama, Asao Koike, Tomoko Mayama, Nobuo Kaneko, Asao Uchida, Fumio Watanabe, Eizo Kitamura, Hosei Komatsu, Akiko Mori, Harumi Sone Very entertaining trash about outlaw Wakayama and the colorful gang he builds up (Koike and Mayama are especially wonderful) to fight the forces of corruption that would deprive them of their score. Kaneko plays a rich, but sexually inadequate district political boss wielding government power, with Watanabe as a nearsighted, sadistically vindictive policeman. The only liabilities are Toei's usual skimping on sets, costumes, and time, something that grew common in the early-to-mid-1970s. #2 of 2 films
* * *

Story of Japanese Bad Men (#2)

STRAY DOG'S HELL aka JIG-
OKU NO NORA INU 1966 **DIR.**
Ryuichi Takemori **SCR.** Masaharu
(Shoji) Segawa **PHOTO 'SCOPE:**
Shoe Nishikawa **MUSIC:** Shunsuke
Kikuchi **W/** Tatsuo Umemiya, Naoki

Sugiura, Yuki Jono, Haruo Tanaka,
Jun Tazaki, Ryohei Uchida, Keiko
Yuge, Akitake Kono, Tetsu Furutani
(Furuya?), Zeko Nakamura
Judging from the poster and photos,
this seems to be about a reformed
tough guy victimized by gangsters
while he coaches a kids' baseball
team.

THE STREETFIGHTER aka
SATSUJINKEN aka
THE KILLING FIST series

The Streetfighter (#1)

THE STREETFIGHTER aka
GEKI TOTSU! SATSUJINKEN aka
SUDDEN ATTACK! KILLING FIST
1974 91 min. **DIR.** Shigehiro Ozawa
SCR. Koji Takada/Motohiro Torii
PHOTO COLOR 'SCOPE: Kanji
Horikoshi **MUSIC:** Toshiaki
Tsushima **W/** Shinichi "Sonny"
Chiba, Etsuko "Sue" Shiomi,
Fumio Watanabe, Masaichi "Milton"

Ishibashi, Rinichi Yamamoto, Yutaka Nakajima, Bin Amatsu, Masafumi Suzuki, Reiko Ike, Eizo Kitamura A perfect example of Toei finding a way to exploit the yakuza film style outside Japan, capitalizing on the Bruce Lee/martial arts phenomenon in the process. These actually are not that different from the studio's more genuine yakuza films. They have been dumbed-down, but still there is the same flat but strikingly functional cinematography, many of the same performers, a veteran yakuza film director, yakuza villains and, most of all – in keeping with the *jitsuroku* (true document) subgenre – an ultra-violent, amoral anti-hero in the form of Chiba. It is nice to see this with its total violence/brutality quotient intact pre-American rating board's scissors (it may not have been the Motion Picture Rating Board, but they are certainly the ones who intimidated New Line Cinema at the time into trimming the picture to get an R rating in the U.S., in effect emasculating it). Without the outlandish, cartoonish/comic book ultra-violence and theater of cruelty/*grand guignol* approach to the action, the film might as well not exist. The funny thing is, now that the whole world can be treated to the uncut version – maybe I am jaded – I just do not see what was so X-rated about the violence. Well, maybe the scene where Chiba rips off the big black bodyguard's genitalia after the villain has raped Nakajima. But other than that – ? Oh, well, I suppose in the eyes of some folks, there is no hope for people like me. But the latest dvd editions of these three films (as I mentioned in the SISTER STREET-FIGHTER/ONNA HISSATSU KEN piece) still contain the condescending, dumbed-down in-joke dubbing of English dialogue. #1 of 3 films
* * *

RETURN OF THE STREET-FIGHTER aka SATSUJINKEN 2 aka KILLING FIST 2 1974 83 min. **Dir.** Shigehiro Ozawa **Scr.** Shigehiro Ozawa/Hajime Takaiwa **Photo color 'scope:** Sadatsugu Yoshida **Music:** Toshiaki Tsushima **w/** Shinichi "Sonny" Chiba, Masafumi Suzuki, Yoko Ichiji, Masachi "Milton" Ishibashi, Hiroshi Tanaka, Shingo Yamashiro More absurd yet strangely entertaining antics featuring Terry Tsurugi (Chiba) against a conglomeration of organized crime. The team-up of the mafia and yakuza is especially ludicrous. By the way, in all three of these films, the American versions' dialogue misrepresents the yakuza – even the unreal, film-based-reality yakuza – as being a wimpy extension of the Italian mafia and the Hong Kong triads!   #2 of 3 films * * *

THE STREETFIGHTER'S LAST REVENGE aka GYAKUSHU! SATSUJINKEN aka COUNTERATTACK! THE KILLING FIST 1974 **Dir.** Shigehiro Ozawa **Scr.** Koji Takada/Masahiro Shimura/Shigehiro Ozawa **w/** Shinichi "Sonny" Chiba, Reiko Ike, Etsuko "Sue" Shiomi, Yutaka Nakajima   Various yakuza and big business factions vie for possession of a formula to manufacture synthetic heroin. For some strange reason, many western-based writers still often mistakenly credit this film's direction to Teruo Ishii, not Ozawa.
* * 1/2   #3 and final in series

TALE OF A CHIVALROUS RICK-SHAW MAN – FIGHTING TATSU

aka SHAFU YUKYODEN – KENKA TATSU aka FIGHTING TATSU, THE RICKSHAW MAN 1964 99 min. **DIR.** Tai Kato **SCR.** Norifumi Suzuki/Tai Kato **PHOTO COLOR** 'SCOPE: Shintaro Kawazaki **MUSIC:** Ban Takahashi **w/** Ryohei Uchida, Jushiro Konoe, Hiroko Sakuramachi, Meicho Soganoya, Junko Fuji, Minoru Oki, Choichiro Kawarazaki A simultaneously very moving and very funny yakuza action/romance/comedy. It is nothing less than amazing that Kato was able to create such a delicate balance between all the elements. This rivals Kurosawa's YOJINBO for that peculiar totality of grittiness, earthy humor and effortless narrative flow. A hothead lone wolf rickshaw man, Uchida, comes to turn-of-the century Osaka, mixes it up with the local yakuza clan of rickshaw pullers before falling-in-love with the equally-strongwilled mistress (Sakuramachi) of the gruff, but softhearted boss (Soganoya). Oki is a resentful, frustrated judo master who hates rival Konoe (Soganoya's brother-in-law). Konoe has a judo dojo adjoining the yakuza clan HQ. After his defeat at Konoe's hands, Oki puts together his own gang of toughs in an attempt to seize power in the town. Kawarazaki, a poor, quiet youth studying to be a lawyer and his girl, geisha Fuji, become tragically enmeshed in the machinations. This description of plot elements can't hope to do justice to what is truly a masterpiece. Kato blends bone-crunching action, bawdy humor and a genuinely heartwrenching, unsentimental lyricism seamlessly together.
* * * *

Tale of a Chivalrous Rickshaw Man - Fighting Tatsu

TALE OF HOKKAI YAKUZA

aka HOKKAI YUKYODEN aka CHIVALROUS TALES OF THE NORTH 1967 90 min. **DIR.** Ryuichi Takemori **SCR.** Isao Matsumoto/Hideaki Yamamoto

Tale of Kawachi Chivalry

Tale of Meiji Era Chivalry - Third Generation Boss aka *Blood of Revenge*

Photo color 'scope: Shoe Nishikawa **Music:** Shunsuke Kikuchi **w/** Hideo Murata, Saburo Kitajima, Shinichi "Sonny" Chiba, Tomisaburo Wakayama, Kanjuro Arashi, Minoru Oki, Reiko Ohara, Hideo Murota, Akira Oizumi, Hiroshi Nawa

Tale of Hokkai Yakuza

TALE OF JAPANESE YAKUZA – A LEADER'S PATH aka NIHON YAKUZADEN – SOCHO HE NO MICHI aka PATH OF A BIG BOSS 1971 96 min. **Dir.** Masahiro Makino **Scr.** Koji Takada **Photo color 'scope:** Shigeru Akatsuka **Music:** Chuji Kinoshita **w/** Ken Takakura, Tomisaburo Wakayama, Koji Tsuruta, Yumiko Nogawa, Hiroki Matsukata, Jushiro Konoe. Michiyo Kogure, Kanjuro Arashi, Minoru Oki, Rinichi Yamamoto, Tatsuo Endo, Bin Amatsu Another beautifully done, violent period piece (1920s) with Makino's trademark masterwork atmospherics of doomed heroics/romanticism.

Wakayama especially shines this time out as Takakura's boisterous friend who dies in his arms in the aftermath of the last massacre. This seems to have been the first entry of another *ninkyo* series, but no more entries followed. Chivalrous yakuza stories were starting to fade in popularity in the 1971 – 1972 time period, with the more ultra-cruel *jitsuroku* (true document) films set in a more contemporary period gradually taking over.
* * *

TALE OF KAWACHI CHIVALRY aka KAWACHI YUKYODEN aka TALE OF KAWACHI YAKUZA aka THE ROUGHS OF KAWACHI 1967 88 min. **Dir.** Ryuichi Takamori **Scr.** Yuichi Ikeda **Photo color 'scope:** Ichiro Hoshijima **Music:** Toshiaki Tsushima **w/** Shinichi "Sonny" Chiba, Mako Midori, Junzaburo Ban, Reiko Ohara, Sadako Sawamura, Yoshiro (?) Ichikawa, Bin Amatsu, Hideo Murota, Tatsuo Endo I know nothing about this film, but it has one of the truly great yakuza/action film posters of the 1960s.

TALE OF MEIJI ERA CHIVALRY – THIRD GENERATION BOSS aka MEIJI KYOKAKUDEN – SANDAIME SHUMEI aka THIRD GENERATION'S RISE TO FAME aka BLOOD OF REVENGE 1965 91 min. **Dir.** Tai Kato **Scr.** Norifumi Suzuki/Akira Murao **Photo color 'scope:** Motoya Washio **Music:** Shunsuke Kikuchi **w/** Koji Tsuruta, Junko Fuji, Tetsuro Tanba, Toru Abe, Hiromi Fujiyama, Minoru Oki, Masahiko Tsugawa, Kanjuro Arashi, Shingo Yamashiro   Again a tale set in the late Meiji era – circa 1880s – 1890s as opposed to early Meiji (which began in the1860s with the Tokugawa Shogunate's overthrow). One of Tai Kato's best "middle period" films – films he did between 1964 – 1971. He began at Shintoho in the very early 1950s, directing almost exclusively *chanbara* (samurai swordplay pictures). Sometime in the mid-fifties he started making films for Toei, also mostly *chanbara*. He made one more movie, mid-fifties at Shintoho before they went belly-up in 1961. His first movies to achieve acclaim were both at Toei: WIND, WOMEN AND RAVEN TRAVELS (1958) with Kinnosuke Nakamura and GHOST OF OIWA (1961) with Tomisaburo Wakayama. He alternated between *chanbara* and *ninkyo/ jitsuroku* yakuza films all through the 1960s,with TOKIJIRO KUTSU- KAKE – LONE YAKUZA (1966), HISTORY OF A MAN'S FACE (1966) with Noboru Ando (this one at Shochiku Studios), three of the RED PEONY GAMBLER films being perhaps the best of many outstanding achievements. In 1972, with films he directed for Shochiku and Toho, he seemed to begin his "epic" period. Most of these more recent pictures ran somewhere between 130 – 140 minutes. One of the three films from this time, MUSASHI MIYAMOTO aka the two-part SWORD OF FURY (1973) is just fair. The second, third and fourth films,THEATER OF LIFE (1972), FLOWER AND DRAGON (1973), and BLOSSOM AND THE SWORD (1973), epic *ninkyo* yakuza sagas, are all extremely good. These early seventies opuses are apparently the films Paul Schrader had in mind when he compared Kato to Sergio Leone in his 1974 Film Comment article. Getting back to TALE OF

MEIJI CHIVALRY, it has all the standard necessary elements for a dramatically successful *ninkyo* picture but, with its passionate conviction, minimal sentimentality, complex characters, one of Tsuruta's most heartfelt performances, with the integration of period detail and the choreography of violence and movement, it moves to another plateau occupied by very few action films. The brutally violent climax when Tsuruta jumps from a moving train through the window of the "evil" clan's HQ, immediately running villain Oki through with his sword is one of the most intense, economically pared-to-the-bone action sequences in any yakuza film. The camera follows Tsuruta as he eludes the panicking cops, pursuing Abe, his other nemesis. Abe heads straight for Fuji's house – Tsuruta and he had been rivals for her affections – and when Tsuruta catches up he kills Abe right in front of terrified Fuji. The police immediately arrive to haul him away. Fuji runs after them, embracing Tsuruta's chained form, rubbing her face against his bare tattooed and bloodstained chest. This is one of the most cathartic moments in any of Kato's films. The romance had, up until this moment, been very suppressed for various period social conventions. Fuji's explosion of sensual affection is incredibly liberating and much more true-to-life than many other such scenes in similar films. Like his Toei colleague, Kosaku Yamashita, Kato restrains certain histrionic elements and accentuates others – he has the taste, the visual and dramatic intuition to create sublimely transcendent cinematic ritual out of the most commonplace elements. He also has a way of creating a nostalgic mood for a bygone era with a minimal amount of exposition and only the most economic of atmospheric, emotional visual triggers. By the way, this movie bears no relation in either story or character to director Shigehiro Ozawa's THIRD GENERATION BOSS (1974) with Ken Takakura. * * * *

Tale of Showa Era Chivalry

TALE OF SHOWA ERA CHIVALRY aka SHOWA KYOKAKUDEN 1963 90 min. **DIR./SCR.** Teruo Ishii **PHOTO COLOR 'SCOPE:** Yoshikazu (Giichi) Yamazawa **MUSIC:** Shunsuke Kikuchi w/ Koji Tsuruta, Minoru Oki, Kanjuro Arashi, Tatsuo Umemiya, Kyosuke Machida, Yoshiko Mita, Koji Mitsui, Mikijiro Hira, Ryohei Uchida, Hideo Murota   This begins with an elder boss (Arashi), walking with his daughter and a young *kobun*, being attacked. Arashi is actually quite spry and manages to almost fend off his attackers. Distracted for a second out of concern for his daughter, he is stabbed. Back at the clan house everyone is in a state over the critical condition of the boss. But, surprise! he pulls through, something that usually does not happen in these films. Tsuruta's character, although honorable, is not held in high regard by Arashi for some reason. However, when he exposes cheating going on in Oki's gambling den, his guts/virtue inspire younger fellows Machida and Umemiya, who virtually become his disciples. There is a disturbing, emotion-wringing scene where Umemiya and Machida are jumped by Oki and his henchmen; Machida dodges them, runs the few blocks back to his place and then returns with his knife. Unfortunately, Umemiya is being held helpless in the dark street, totally at their mercy. Oki taunts Machida, then orders his men to kill Umemiya. Machida stands there, horror-stricken as his friend is repeatedly stabbed. Ishii shows close-ups on the different characters' faces – the attackers cruel, sadistic eyes darting back and forth between their prey Umemiya and paralyzed pal Machida; Machida sweating profusely, pleading, on the verge of tears; Oki laughing coldbloodedly. Suddenly, Umemiya's girl appears on the scene begging for mercy. We next see Umemiya in bed with his friends gathered around. Tsuruta has appeared, and he is about at the end of his rope. Umemiya dies, and recovered Arashi bids the clan to ready for an attack on Oki's HQ. Unknown to everyone else, Tsuruta heads over there first, intent on killing Oki and his underboss. Once again, Ishii handles things a bit differently as Tsuruta ends up attacking only Oki. Tsuruta is stabbed repeatedly but holds on until he has killed his target,

---

then turns his attention to the other head villain, once more weathering numerous slashings and piercings until this guy is dead, too. The whole scene is played with dissonant, spare music that accentuates the tension and horror of violent death. Tsuruta passes out and reawakens, dying, his head in Arashi's lap, his other friends surrounding him as they sail across the river in a small boat. Reaching the other side, Arashi's daughter runs up, weeping. Koji dies and everyone cries. Manipulative, but so well done and unpretentious, the viewer does not mind. * * * 1/2

TALES OF JAPANESE CHIVAL-RY aka NIHON KYOKAKUDEN series

TALES OF JAPANESE CHIVAL-RY aka NIHON KYOKAKUDEN 1964 98 min. **DIR** Masahiro Makino **SCR** Kazuo Kasahara/Akira Murao/Tatsuo Nogami **PHOTO COLOR 'SCOPE:** Shigeto Miki **MUSIC:** Ichiro Saito **w/** Kinnosuke Nakamura, Ken Takakura, Hiroki Matsukata, Masahiko Tsugawa, Takahiro Tamura, Minoru Oki, Hiroyuki Nagato, Yoshiko Mita, Junko Fuji, Yoko Minamida, Ryuji Shinagawa, Toru Abe, Bin Amatsu, Asao Uchida The elderly boss of Nagato, Oki, Matsukata and Tamura dies of a stroke shortly after confronting evil, unprincipled bosses Abe and Amatsu. Nakamura is a semi-retired member of the clan living with his wife and tiny daughter. About mid-story, Takakura returns from military duty in Manchuria to become the new *oyabun*. Nagato is killed when he and his geisha gal try to abscond on

her debt to the evil clan. Probably the most moving scene in the film has Nakamura's last moments with his wife and child at sunset before going singlehandedly, suicidally to avenge Nagato. Takakura and blood brothers, finally pushed to the limit, retaliate with only Takakura surviving.

Tales of Japanese Chivalry (#1)

A very young Junko Fuji provides the love interest for Takakura. She is so sweet and gentle here, it is hard to believe she would be a sword-wielding heroine a mere four years later in the RED PEONY GAMBLER pictures. This first film of the TALES OF JAPANESE CHIVALRY series sets the pattern for at least the next few entries, with much more of a general ensemble of characters/ performers sharing the spotlight. This as opposed to only two or three central characters from #5 or 6 on and nearly all the entries in the similar TALES OF THE LAST SHOWA ERA YAKUZA series. The TALES OF JAPANESE

CHIVALRY series time frame is 1900 – 1939 except for SEVERED RELATIONS which takes place in the 1960s. #1 of 11 films * * *

TALES OF JAPANESE CHIVAL-RY – OSAKA STORY aka NIHON KYOKAKUDEN – NANIWA HEN 1965 98 min. **DIR.** Masahiro Makino **SCR.** Tatsuo Nogami/Kazuo Kasahara/ Akira Murao **PHOTO COLOR 'SCOPE:** Shigeto Miki **MUSIC:** Ichiro Saito w/ Ken Takakura, Koji Tsuruta, Hideo Murata, Ryutaro Otomo, Kotaro Satomi, Hiroyuki Nagato, Yoko Minamida, Wakaba Irie, Kaoru Yachigusa, Hiromi Fujiyama, Bin Amatsu   Although there is the same basic plot in almost all *ninkyo* yakuza *eiga*, this differs somewhat in that the action formula is broken up a bit. It is also strange that top-billed Tsuruta does not appear until the last thirty minutes of the saga. Takakura is a newly arrived worker who quickly becomes a champion of the coal cart-ers in Osaka's port. He is adopted into the benevolent clan headed by no-nonsense, gruff Murata, then helps the young Satomi take over when Murata is murdered by Otomo and Amatsu's thugs. Nagato is killed when attempt-ing to escape with his geisha girl-friend in a subplot virtually identical to his part in the series' first film. Tsuruta's returning estranged geisha lover is also killed trying to defend Nagato. Her affections had been forcibly co-opted by Otomo – coinci-dentally an old associate of Tsuruta's. Tsuruta is a bit more ruthless as a hero than most of his other *ninkyo* portrayals, killing bad guys without too much provocation. Takakura also helps in the vengeance activities, but there is not the extensive massacre

that usually climaxes a *ninkyo* yakuza film. This entry has a similar ambi-ence to the oft-filmed FLOWER AND DRAGON saga (see series films #9 & #10 for one version) and the Makino-directed Daiei Studios feature TALE OF DARK OCEAN CHIVALRY aka THE BORN FIGHTER with Shintaro Katsu (both dealing with coal carters in early 1900s Osaka). #2 of 11 films * * *

TALES OF JAPANESE CHIVAL-RY – KANTO STORY aka NIHON KYOKAKUDEN – KANTO HEN 1965 98 min. **DIR.** Masahiro Makino **SCR.** Akira Murao/Kazuo Kasahara/Tatsuo Nogami **PHOTO COLOR 'SCOPE:** Sadatsugu Yoshida **MUSIC:** Ichiro Saito w/ Ken Takakura, Junko Fuji, Tetsuro Tanba, Koji Tsuruta, Hiroyuki Nagato, Yoko Minamida, Kyosuke Machida, Matasaburo Tanba, Minoru Oki, Saburo Kitajima   Minamida is a prominent dealer at the fish market suffering under gang boss Amatsu's attempts to take over her business. Takakura portrays a good-natured ex-navy man who goes to bat for her as well as other honest fishmongers whose stalls are at risk. Lone yakuza Tsuruta, Minamida's former flame, returns and also helps out. Kitajima is a sushi chef who gets killed when he makes a solo raid on Amatsu's HQ, something which prompts Takakura to go to fishing fleet captain Tanba to enlist his men. They arrive near the end for a full scale riot between the fish merchants and evil yakuza. Meanwhile Tsuruta has followed vengeance-bent Nagato to Amatsu's HQ to keep him from getting killed by the remaining gangsters. But his efforts are in vain, so he lets it rip, cutting a bloody swath through the villains. The denouement finds the police leading Takakura and Tsuruta off to jail as Minamida and the triumphant fishomongers look on. Although it is not particularly moving, this is one of the most seamlessly put together of the earlier entries in the series, skillfully blending the formula *ninkyo* elements, something that could not always be said for other *ninkyo eiga* or even for other of director Makino's films in the sixties. #3 of 11 films * * *

TALES OF JAPANESE CHIVALRY – DUEL AT KANDA FESTIVAL aka NIHON KYOKAKUDEN – KETTO KANDA MATSURI aka BLOODY FESTIVAL AT KANDA 1966 95 min. DIR. Masahiro Makino SCR. Kazuo Kasahara PHOTO COLOR 'SCOPE: Motoya Washio MUSIC: Ichiro Saito w/ Ken Takakura, Koji Tsuruta, Minoru Oki, Junko Fuji, Hiromi Fujiyama, Rinichi Yamamoto, Kotaro Satomi, Hiroyuki Nagato, Seizaburo Kawazu, Ryuko Azuma, Katsuhiko Kobayashi   One of the most highly-regarded-of-the-series by Japanese critics. But frankly it is hard to see why, especially with its surfeit of Fujiyama's ham-fisted comic relief in the first half. Not bad, but nothing special, particularly in relation to some of the later better entries. #4 of 11 films * * 1/2

TALES OF JAPANESE CHIVALRY – DUEL AT THUNDER GATE aka NIHON KYOKAKUDEN – KAMINARI MON NO KETTO 1966 93 min. DIR. Masahiro Makino SCR. Tatsuo Nogami/Kazuo Kasahara PHOTO COLOR 'SCOPE: Nagaki Yamagishi MUSIC: Ichiro Saito w/ Ken Takakura, Kyosuke Machida, Junko Fuji, Hiromi Fujiyama, Akifumi Inoue, Asao Uchida, Shogo Shimada, Bin Amatsu, Hideo Murata, Michitaro Mizushima Rival theatrical troupe/yakuza clans (one decent, one unscrupulous, of course) clash. Shimada is a general patriarch of the benevolent gang. It was hard to distinguish if his character really is anyone's father (everyone calls him *"ototo-san"*). But he does actually prove to be papa to Fuji's character. Uchida is a decent, though harassed elder in the community driven to suicide by Mizushima/ Amatsu's bunch, and from then on Shimada's troupe is pushed into progressively worse confrontations. Takakura returns from naval duty (the Manchurian conflict?) and reunites with heartthrob Fuji. One bone of contention between the two gangs is who will showcase a popular traditional singer (played by Murata, who actually was a famous Japanese singer from the fifties/sixties as well as being a yakuza *eiga* star). Murata's sympathies are with Shimada's contingent. However, their show with him is disrupted by the bad guys. A couple of Shimada's loyal men are subsequently murdered, and then Shimada, too, is killed in a solo attack on Mizushima's gang. For once, though, an elderly *oyabun* acquits himself well, dispatching several bad guys, including underboss Amatsu, before his own demise. The climax has Takakura and cohort Machida attack Mizushima's gang in their theater. The two survive the carnage and are led away by the police at the end. #5 of 11 films * * 1/2

Tales of Japanese Chivalry - Duel at Thunder Gate (#5)

**TALES OF JAPANESE CHIV-
ALRY – LOYALTY OFFERING
SUICIDE** aka NIHON KYOKAKU-
DEN – SHIRAHA NO SAKAZUKI
1967 95 min. **DIR.** Masahiro Makino
SCR. Sadao Nakajima/Norifumi
Suzuki **PHOTO COLOR 'SCOPE:**
Motoya Washio **MUSIC:** Ichiro Saito
w/ Ken Takakura, Junko Fuji, Minoru
Oki, Kenji Sugawara, Kayo Matsuo,
Hiroyuki Nagato, Yuriko Mishima,
Katsuhiko Kobayashi, Hideo
Sunazuka, Junzaburo Ban, Bin
Amatsu, Kenji Kusumoto, Junko
Miyazono, Asao Uchida
Takakura and tubercular spouse
Fuji hitch a ride with drivers for
Sugawara's clan/trucking company.
The locale is the snowy north, and as
soon as the couple reach civilization,
Fuji is hospitalized. Although second-
billed, she has very little to do here
– she remains in bed for the entire
film! Matsuo, a mother of a small boy
waiting for her husband Oki to return
from jail, and Nagato's barmaid gal
Miyazono, both have much more
screen-time. Takakura joins Kenji
Sugawara's clan. Before you know it,
bad guy Amatsu's gang is fomenting
chaos and ill will. He rapes servant
Matsuo, who opts to drown herself in
the ocean out of shame when hubby
Oki returns. Nagato for once has a
role worthy of his talent. Although
stuck in his customary part of the
hero's doomed sidekick, writers
Nakajima and Suzuki have given him
a more developed character than the
usual stereotype. He and Miyazono
have a nice chemistry together. When
Nagato is knifed by several villains
mere paces from his beloved, we
genuinely care about his demise.
Needless to say, Takakura discour-
ages Sugawara from seeking redress,

then, as soon as things calm down,
makes the vengeance trek solo. This
has what amounts to one of the most
frantic, kinetic and explosively angry
swordfights in not just this series
but also many of Toei's other *ninkyo
eiga*. There are moments when the
rambunctious action actually jars the
camera. #6 of 11 films   * * *

**TALES OF JAPANESE CHIVAL-
RY – ATTACK** aka NIHON
KYOKAKUDEN – KIRIKOMI
aka THE STORM 1967 93 min.
DIR. Masahiro Makino **SCR.** Kazuo
Kasahara **PHOTO COLOR 'SCOPE:**
Nagaki Yamagishi **MUSIC:** Ichiro
Saito w/ Ken Takakura, Junko Fuji,
Minoru Oki, Fumio Watanabe, Yoko
Minamida, Nobuo Kaneko, Hiroyuki
Nagato, Kenjiro Ishiyama, Bin
Amatsu, Kensaku Hara
A somewhat slow-moving saga of
single father Takakura, on the run
with his son after killing a boss in an
outlying village. He receives kindness
from boss Ishiyama and his daughter
Fuji, who ends up falling in love with
him. Ishiyama sets Takakura up with
a quantity of children's books (!) to
sell in the newly developing district
of Shinjuku in Tokyo. Watanabe and
Amatsu's gang have a stranglehold
on the area, exploiting the local
tekiya. Oki is another gang boss
devoted to fair play. He stands up for
Takakura who has become de facto
leader of the *tekiya*. Before long,
with Oki's help, Takakura founds his
own clan. Fuji has moved in to help
with Takakura's son, and soon they
are keeping house as husband and
wife. When Oki is shot and critically
wounded for his support of
Takakura's bunch, Takakura goes on
the rampage. He is aided by pals

Nagato et.al.. Although a bit ho-hum, the film does have its pleasures. Fuji is postively luminous and the final massacre/swordfight is a bit more exciting than some of the other films. This has a very unusual happy ending with Takakura and Fuji strolling happily down a sunny Shinjuku thoroughfare at the denouement. #7 of 11 films   * * 1/2

TALES OF JAPANESE CHIV-ALRY – STATE OF SEVERED RELATIONS aka NIHON KY-OKAKUDEN – ZETSU ENJO 1968 95 min. DIR. Masahiro Makino SCR. Goro Tanada PHOTO COLOR 'SCOPE: Motoya Washio MUSIC: Chuji Kinoshita w/ Ken Takakura, Kayo Matsuo, Kyosuke Machida, Fumio Watanabe, Kenji Sugawara, Hiromi Fujiyama, Harumi Sone, Tatsuo Endo, Junya Usami, Yukiko Kuwabara Peculiar, as this is one of the only entries in the series set in a then contemporary time period (the 1960s), with Takakura a benevolent, traditional and married (to Matsuo) underboss acting as *oyabun*, since the elderly godfather is in prison. His clan is trying to break into legitimate construction with honest business and company owners paving the way. But some of the affiliated shadier gangs headed by Endo and Amatsu are also trying to slice an inordinately big piece of the pie. Takakura also has his own *dojo* where he practices his swordmanship. Yakuza film buffs Paul and Leonard Schrader must have seen this, as their character for Takakura in the American co-production THE YAKUZA, co-starring Robert Mitchum, has a very similar set-up. Fujiyama, a comical sidekick, also wants to go straight and starts

a sushi restuarant with a local gal and her dad. But, before too long, the bad guys kill Fujiyama and other good guy Machida. Takakura's blood brother and best friend Sugawara who is another underboss, is also murdered when he tries to warn Takakura of the evil afoot. Takakura sacrifices everything to assassinate Amatsu and Endo at the climactic clan meeting. This is especially poignant as his wife Matsuo is pregnant with their first child. #8 of 11 films * * *

TALES OF JAPANESE CHIV-ALRY – FLOWER AND DRAGON aka NIHON KYOKAKUDEN – HANA TO RYU aka CHIVAL-ROUS DRAGON aka TATTOO OF A DRAGON 1969 112 min. DIR. Masahiro Makino SCR. Goro Tanada PHOTO COLOR 'SCOPE: Masahiko Iimura MUSIC: Chuji Kinoshita w/ Ken Takakura, Yuriko Hoshi, Junko Fuji, Hideaki Nitani, Tomisaburo Wakayama, Michitaro Mizushima, Rinichi Yamamoto, Yuriko Mishima, Masahiko Tsugawa, Tatsuo Endo   Another one of the numerous versions of this popular set-in-turn-of-the-20th-century yakuza novel, this time as an installment of this ongoing series. It had already been remade by Toei just a few years previous – FLOWER AND DRAG-ON (1965) and a sequel, FLOWER AND DRAGON – DUEL IN THE SEA CAVES (1966) both directed by Kosaku Yamashita and both starring Kinnosuke (Yorozuya) Nakamura. However, the card dealer/tattoo artist character Fuji portrays has a bit more to do here, especially at the climax. Takakura plays the humble, decent, though strong guy who comes to a village on the coast and becomes involved with a clan of coal-loaders, dockworkers and fishermen. He meets Fuji – she deals *hana fuda* at the "bad" clan's gambling den – and they immediately establish a silent bond of "platonic" friendship, despite Takakura's eventual marriage to a female dockworker (Hoshi).

Tales of Japanese Chivalry - Flower and Dragon (#9)

His interest in Fuji never really seems to develop beyond a spiritual affin-

ity. But when Takakura attacks the gambling den at the end on a mission of revenge, Fuji takes his side and backs him up, helping him stand even after he has received a crippling stab in the back. In a very moving finale, Hoshi and Takakura's other comrades frantically arrive to collect him and, with a smile and a few kind words, Fuji gallantly turns over the guy she is in love with to wife Hoshi – which surprises the hell out of Hoshi. #9 of 11 films   * * * 1/2

TALES OF JAPANESE CHIVAL-RY – RISING DRAGON aka NI-HON KYOKAKUDEN – NOBORI RYU aka MAN WITH THE RISING DRAGON TATTOO 1970 117 min. **Dir.** Kosaku Yamashita **Scr.** Kazuo Kasahara **Photo color 'scope:** Sadatsugu Yoshida **Music:** Ichiro Saito **w/** Ken Takakura, Junko Fuji, Tamao Nakamura, Koji Tsuruta, Chiezo Kataoka, Goro Ibuki, Michiko Araki, Bin Amatsu, Tatsuo Endo, Kunio Kaga   A continuation of the FLOWER AND DRAGON saga focusing on Fuji and Takakura with the primary emphasis on Fuji's unrequited love. This is, of Fuji's films that I have seen, her most versatile and challenging role. She really gets to show her range without any cornball theatrics. Yamashita's setups and payoffs with scene dynamics and editing are brilliantly realized, with Fuji's subtle nuances of expression and voice inflection adding emotional weight. Screenwriter Kasahara jettisons many subplots and goes for broke with the most intriguing relationship in the saga. It is a daring approach in many ways because the piece ends up being more of a woman's film than many of Fuji's

Tales of Japanese Chivalry - Rising Dragon (#10)

RED PEONY GAMBLER pictures.
Nakamura excels (replacing Hoshi
from the last film) as Takakura's
strong, not-a-jealous-bone-in-her-
body spouse. Oddly, though Takakura
has considerable screen time, his
character comes off as a cypher – so
stoic, so faithful, so repressed that he
seems a bit too good to be true. We
never really get to know him as well
as we did in Makino's first installment (#9). A more realistic depiction of the character can be seen in
Tai Kato's 1972 epic version with
Tetsuya Watari as a more lusty, human and flawed hero. Undoubtedly
the chaste nature of Takakura and
Fuji's love scenes at the start, where
she tattoos him while nursing him
back to health, helps set the stage for
the painful longing and spiritual ache
experienced by her throughout the
remainder of the tale. The denouement where Takakura is summoned to
Fuji's consumptive deathbed is one of
the most sublime love scenes I can recall seeing on film. It constantly veers
close to sentimental cliche but never
crosses over. Takakura and Fuji's performances are so sincere and devoid
of histrionics, Kasahara's dialogue so
awkwardly perfect and Yamashita's
direction so judiciously restrained,
it wrings genuine emotion from the
most jaded viewer. Fuji's dying wish
is to fill in a part of the tattoo on
Takakuura's shoulder where she had
signed her name, thus obliterating her
ties to him. Once done, she lets go
of her needle and ink brush, pauses
savoring the odor of Takakura's flesh,
then collapses, dying in his arms.
There has been no nudity, no heavy
breathing, no passionate kiss nor love
talk. Yet this emerges as a very erotic
scene. That the spiritual bond is also

made so resoundingly manifest is a
tribute to director Yamashita, writer
Kasahara and the two performers.
This would be up another half notch
if not for the overly-talky middle
third of the film. #10 of 11 films
* * * 1/2

Tales of Japanese Chivalry - Sword (#11)

**TALES OF JAPANESE CHIV-
ALRY – SWORD** aka NIHON
KYOKAKUDEN – DOSU 1971
97 min. **DIR.** Shigehiro Ozawa
SCR. Kazuo Kasahara **PHOTO COLOR**
'SCOPE: Sadatsugu Yoshida **MUSIC:**
Toshiaki Tsushima   **w/** Ken
Takakura, Ryo Ikebe, Yukiyo Toake,
Minoru Oki, Ryutaro Tatsumi, Fumio
Watanabe, Ryoichi Tanagawa, Rinichi
Yamamoto   Takakura is an im-
poverished, humble yet nevertheless
hotheaded ne'er-do-well who is taken
in by Tatsumi's transport company
in the late 1880s. He is in love with
Toake, a kindhearted geisha who had
helped him after he had been beaten
by the police. Oki is a progressive re-

form candidate and friend of Tatsumi. When Toake's brother is forced by his boss, Watanabe, to attempt to kill Oki, Takakura intervenes. Later, he helps the oppressed brother to escape and delivers him to the grateful Toake. However, he has compromised his position with Tatsumi's bunch and goes wandering. When he returns several years later, Toake is married to Oki. Takakura is now a more mature person, no longer given to temper tantrums, Watanabe has only gained more power and Tatsumi's company has floundered. Oki is attacked and nearly killed. Takakura goes into Watanabe's compound on the heels of friendly independent boss Ikebe, and finds he has already been severely slashed. Takakura finishes the job, but not before he is also mortally wounded. Toake receives word of Takakura and Ikebe's attack and runs through the deserted streets trying to reach her devoted friends. The last few minutes of the film cut between Toake rushing to their aid and the dying Takakura trying to help the dying Ikebe walk. Both men collapse several times and finally are not able to rise again. Certainly one of the more downbeat of the series and one of Ozawa's best films. In addition, this starts out much differently from other *ninkyo eiga*, a very welcome change from the customary formula. And, if RISING DRAGON was a vehicle for Fuji's versatility, SWORD is a definite showcase for Takakura's acting range. He actually gets to cry in the first fifteen minutes of the story as well as mature significantly as a character during the time frame of the narrative.   #11 and final in series * * *

TALES OF JAPAN'S CHIVALROUS WOMEN aka NIHON JOKYODEN series

TALES OF JAPAN'S CHIVALROUS WOMEN – CHIVALROUS GEISHA aka NIHON JOKYODEN – KYOKAKU GEISHA 1969 99 min. Dir. Kosaku Yamashita Scr. Tatsuo Nogami Photo color 'scope: Juhei Suzuki Music: Chuji Kinoshita w/ Junko Fuji, Ken Takakura, Tomisaburo Wakayama, Hiroko Sakuramachi, Yuriko Mishima, Nobuo Kaneko, Hiromi Fujiyama   After RED PEONY GAMBLER, Junko Fuji's next longest-running series. Too bad that it still only amounts to five films. Of course, this might not have been the case had she not retired in 1972. She plays a different character in each film, and they hopscotch around a bit as far as period – two seem to be set in the 1920s, another two in the contemporary 1960s and one in the immediately post-war 1940s. In the first, Junko is a geisha fighting a gang trying to exploit coal miners. She does a bit of judo and stands up to some of the villains, but her beau Takakura does the revenge-binge swordfight at the climax all by his lonesome. When she arrives in the aftermath, it is only to watch Takakura's corpse being carried away from a scene of total devastation. #1 of 5 films * * *

TALES OF JAPAN'S CHIVALROUS WOMEN – BRAVE RED FLOWER aka NIHON JOKYODEN – MAKKANA DOKYO BANA aka RED FLOWER OF THE NORTH 1970 94 min. Dir. Yasuo Furuhata Scr. Kazuo Kasahara

PHOTO COLOR 'SCOPE: Shin Furuya **MUSIC:** Masao Yagi   **w/** Junko Fuji, Ken Takakura, Masumi Tachibana, Rinichi Yamamoto, Bin Amatsu, Eitaro Ozawa, Shingo Yamashiro, Kenjiro Ishiyama, Yuriko Mishima, Hosei Komatsu   Educated Fuji returns to her rural Hokkaido hometown only to find her father Ozawa, boss of the local horse traders, murdered by Amatsu's gang.

Tales of Japan's Chivalrous Women - Brave Red Flower (#2)

She takes over the business, trying to keep war from breaking out between the horse traders and yakuza, but to no avail. Embittered lone wolf Takakura, who actually had had a bone to pick with her late father, despises the local yakuza even more. After several innocent horse traders are murdered, including Yamashiro's wife – a very bizarre sequence where we see a veritable geyser of blood bloom from the bullethole in her throat – Fuji and Takakura stage a

huge gun battle with the villains. Fuji finally shoots Amatsu in his office, and we are treated to a similar slow motion scene where blood blossoms flower-like from Amatsu's neck. Strange in that there is very little blood in evidence throughout the rest of the film, despite the wholesale carnage. With the frontier Hokkaido locale, the early 20th century time frame, the horse trader angle, composer Yagi's occasional Morricone-style flourish, there is more than just a bit of spaghetti western ambience. #2 of 5 films   * * *

Tales of Japan's Chivalrous Women - Iron Geisha (#3)

TALES OF JAPAN'S CHIVALROUS WOMEN – IRON GEISHA

aka NIHON JOKYODEN – TEKKA GEISHA aka GEISHA'S SWORD aka A LIVELY GEISHA 1970 100 min. **DIR.** Kosaku Yamashita **SCR.** Kazuo Kasahara **PHOTO COLOR 'SCOPE:** Shin Furuya **MUSIC:** Chuji Kinoshita   w/ Junko Fuji, Bunta

Sugawara, Keiko Yuge, Junzaburo Ban, Hiromi Fujiyama, Meicho Soganoya, Keiji Takagi, Toru Abe, Keiko Oshima, Ryoichi Tamagawa One of Yamashita's most visually beautiful movies. There are moments when his direction and Kasahara's script meld into genuine poetry. Fuji is a turn-of-the-century geisha bound by tradition but not above defying any boorish or brutal men she encounters at their inn, often raising the hackles of her just-want-to-get-along geisha rivals. Fuji also looks out for more vulnerable girl Yuge, whose radical activist beau Takagi is leading action against controlling yakuza labor boss Abe. Benevolent boss Soganoya and second-in-command Sugawara run a rice business that employ many of the village workers. Gradually, through Soganoya's friendship, Fuji comes in contact with Sugawara, and they develop a subtly intense, platonic relationship that evolves into full blown love by the film's end. Soon Soganoya has been assassinated, the rice warehouse razed to the ground and Yuge and Takagi mortally wounded. However, the saintly Yuge on her deathbead manages to unite Fuji in friendship with her spiteful geisha rival. At the end, Sugawara leaves Fuji's kabuki performance in a packed house to raid Abe's HQ. There he expires after decimating the gang, vainly reaching out for Fuji's keepsake that was split in two by Abe's blade. Though not as deep as some of Hideo Gosha's similarly-themed films, the attempt to penetrate into the life of a principled, giving, yet strong woman in a world dominated by men, strikes a deep resonance by the final frame. The flashback within a flashback where Fuji recalls refusing to have sex with a customer and then running out into the snowy moonlit night, crying and reflecting on how she came to be placed in training as a geisha as a prepubescent girl, is especially moving and sublime. #3 of 5 films * * * 1/2

TALES OF JAPAN'S CHIVALROUS WOMEN – DUEL OF SWIRLING FLOWERS aka NIHON JOKYODEN – KETTO MIDARE BANA 1971 107 min. **DIR.** Kosaku Yamashita **SCR.** Tatsuo Nogami **PHOTO COLOR 'SCOPE:** Nagaki Yamagishi **MUSIC:** Takeo Watanabe **w/** Junko Fuji, Ken Takakura, Minoru Oki, Bin Amatsu, Masahiko Tsugawa, Michitaro Mizushima, Rinichi Yamamoto Fuji is a young woman in the late 1890s who follows her beau Tsugawa to a rural coastal area where he is fruitlessly trying to mine coal with his comrade Yamamoto. He dies in a cave-in, and Fuji joins Yamamoto in attempting to make the mine pay off. In the process, she runs up against other mining concerns run by three allied yakuza bosses – Oki, Endo and Amatsu. To protect her interests, she becomes partners with crusty old Mizushima, underboss Takakura and their clan. After a couple of arduous years, the mine begins to produce. One night in the moonlit fields, Endo's men try to kill Takakura, but he manages to slay them instead. He then disappears for several years. Meanwhile, Fuji and Mizushima stand in stalemate against the yakuza now headed by Oki. Amatsu, virtually always limited to villain parts, gets to play a character with a bit more dimension, a bitter old man fueled by resentment and fear rather than greed. Shortly after Takakura returns, Fuji goes to Amatsu and manages to convince him to break his gang away from Endo and Oki. When he tries to go through with the split, he is savagely beaten by Endo's men then shot in the back by Oki. Mizushima and several other workers are later killed when the mine is dynamited. This spurs Takakura to hit the Oki/Endo HQ, destroying them all, but getting himself mortally wounded in the fray. He ends up crawling down an alley overgrown with weeds and expires with Fuji's image materializing before him. This is even more of a saga than the last film, and there is little action in the overly-long narrative. Fuji also doesn't get to do much, although the film is ostensibly about her and her refusal to give up in the face of overwhelming odds. Also, as is usually the case, her and Takakura's love is never consummated. Along with writer Nogami, Yamashita does manage to balance things out, creating a different narrative than usual and just barely staying in the confines of the genre. #4 of 5 films * * *

**TALES OF JAPAN'S CHIVAL-
ROUS WOMEN – BATTLE AT
CAPE HIMEYURI** aka NIHON
JOKYODEN – GEKI TO HIME
YURI MISAKI aka TRIALS OF AN
OKINAWAN VILLAGE 1971 96
min. **DIR.** Shigehiro Ozawa **SCR.**
Kazuo Kasahara **PHOTO COLOR**
'SCOPE: Sadatsugu Yoshida **MUSIC:**
Toshiaki Tsushima w/ Junko Fuji,
Bunta Sugawara, Minoru Oki,
Kyosuke Machida, Michitaro
Mizushima, Bin Amatsu, Eizo
Kitamura   In immediately post-
WW2 Okinawa, Fuji and Oki run a
salvage business and occasionally

sell pigs and other items on the black market. Enter Amatsu and villains intent on excavating a cavern where they believe a cache of wartime munitions is stored. However, Fuji had been a nurse in the war's final days and has recurring traumatic visions of the last battle when the U.S. bombarded the area. One of the only survivors, she and the villagers hold the cave sacred. Another survivor was soldier Sugawara, who had given Fuji a watch that fateful day and kept her from a despairing suicide. Now he returns as a fugitive lone wolf yakuza bent on cutting a deal with Amatsu. But he is unprepared for Amatsu's cruel, eventually homicidal behavior towards the villagers – forced labor and murder of dissenters. He eventually joins forces with Fuji, and together the two decimate Amatsu's gang with sword and gun in a nocturnal battle outside the cavern. The U.S. military police arrive just as the two are stumbling away and arrest them. The arrogant U.S. commander lets Fuji off with a reprimand but sends wanted man Sugawara to the firing squad. Fuji tearfully watches through the fence as he is executed in the driving rain. Her character clad through most of the picture in army fatigues, the final shot at sunset depicts Fuji in a kimono as she performs a mournful dance beside Sugawara's grave on his favorite piece of rocky shoreline. Though this goes a long way from the usual *ninkyo* formula and was penned by future BATTLES WITHOUT HONOR... writer Kasahara, the film still does not quite live up to expectations. Despite Fuji and Sugawara's emotional scars shown in effective flashbacks, there is little more of their inner emotional lives in evidence.

Tales of Japan's Chivalrous Women - Battle at Cape Himeyuri (#5)

mated. In stories set pre-WW2 this might be understandable, but in a tale set after the war, what with inhibitions swept aside and widespread disillusion, it seems painfully unrealistic. Fuji is presented as a mass of contradictions, being tradition-bound but liberated and spunky enough to kill villains. But the prudish, non-eventful depiction of her and Sugawara's mutual attraction saps this of the fire that could have made it a truly great film. #5 and final in series * * *

TALES OF THE LAST SHOWA ERA YAKUZA aka SHOWA ZAN KYODEN aka BRUTAL TALES OF CHIVALRY aka LEGENDS OF THE LAST YAKUZA series

TALES OF THE LAST SHOWA YAKUZA aka SHOWA ZAN KYO-DEN aka LEGEND OF THE LAST YAKUZA 1965 90 min. **Dir.** Kiyoshi Saeki **Scr.** Akira Murao/Hideaki Yamamoto/Isao Matsumoto **Photo color 'scope:** Ichiro Hoshijima **Music:** Shunsuke Kikuchi w/ Ken Takakura, Ryo Ikebe, Tatsuo Umemiya, Shinjiro Ebara, Yoshiko Mita, Hiroki Matsukata, Kenji Sugawara, Michitaro Mizushima Takakura in what is his best film series and what is probably, along with RED PEONY GAMBLER, Toei's best *ninkyo* yakuza series. Per usual, Takakura does his principled lone wolf routine, tempering his tough-minded and occasionally violent character with soft-spoken spiritual strength and decency while still not above operating in an underworld/outlaw milieu. Beautiful and atmospheric, though at times a bit too obviously setbound. Also, oddly

Another liability is that, although the two are obviously in love with each other, Kasahara and director Ozawa remain slavish to the most extreme *ninkyo* conventions by keeping the relationship chaste and never consum-

enough, this is probably one of the most rigidly formulaic of any *ninkyo* yakuza film series. There are many poetic scenes at the close of each story as Takakura and friend Ikebe walk together through the falling snow or fluttering cherry blossoms bathed in eerie moonlight, their swords in hand, headed for a date with revenge/justice and perhaps a painful, violent death. Of course, as in 90% of all *ninkyo* yakuza films, each saga climaxes in a brawl of utter carnage and massive bloodshed. This first entry has Takakura welcomed back into the fold of his clan after returning from WW2, then embroiled in all kinds of

Wanderer Ikebe, who had previously been obligated to the bad guys for sheltering him, joins old pal Takakura, on a climactic attack on the evil clan. #1 of 9 films * * *

TALES OF THE LAST SHOWA YAKUZA – LION PEONY aka SHOWA ZAN KYODEN – KARAJISHI BOTAN 1966 90 min. DIR. Kiyoshi Saeki SCR. Hideaki Yamamoto/Isao Matsumoto PHOTO COLOR 'SCOPE: Shichiro Hayashi MUSIC: Shunsuke Kikuchi w/ Ken Takakura, Ryo Ikebe, Yoshiko Mita, Kenji Sugawara, Michitaro Mizushima, Shinsuke Ashida, Masahiko Tsugawa, Yuriko Mishima

Tales of the Last Showa Yakuza (#1)

problems with villain Mizushima. Before long, folks start dying. Umemiya bites the dust, ambushed on his way home after having beaten up a rival clan guy extorting cash from his prostitute girlfriend.

With this entry the series went back into the early Showa era of the late 1920s and 1930s, pre-WW2. This is one of the most entertaining and action-packed of the series, with plenty of nefarious villainy (though painted in broad strokes). There are several showdown setpieces between Takakura and the villain clan, climaxing in a dynamite-dodging, sword-fighting bash in a moonlit stone quarry. Mizushima is once again the evil *oyabun*, but here goes way over-the-top, sporting grey hair, a constantly unshaven visage and perpetually drunk demeanor. In fact, his performance is just this side of ludicrous. However, one can tell he is having so much fun in the role, it becomes infectious. A well-constructed tall-tale. #2 of 9 films   * * *

Tales of the Last Showa Yakuza - Lone Wolf aka Brutal Tales of Chivalry (#3)

TALES OF THE LAST SHOWA YAKUZA – LONE WOLF

aka SHOWA ZAN KYODEN – IPPIKI OKAMI aka BRUTAL TALES OF CHIVALRY #3 1966 90 min. DIR. Kiyoshi Saeki SCR. Hideaki Yamamoto/Isao Matsumoto PHOTO COLOR 'SCOPE: Shichiro Hayashi MUSIC: Shunsuke Kikuchi w/ Ken Takakura, Ryo Ikebe, Junko Fuji, Shogo Shimada, Chikage (Chikei?) Ogi, Seizaburo Kawazu, Takehiro Nakamura   Another extremely entertaining entry, this time set in a harbor town. It opens with Takakura assassinating an evil *oyabun* in a bar under the title credits, going to jail then released to have to cope with the new evil boss Kawazu. There is a stupendous nocturnal duel on the beach at the climax where Takakura emerges victorious over Kawazu, only to end up cradling dying comrade Ikebe in his arms as he expires. #3 of 9 films   * * *

TALES OF THE LAST SHOWA YAKUZA – BLOODSTAINED LION

aka SHOWA ZAN KYODEN – CHIZOME NO KARAJISHI 1967 90 min. DIR. Masahiro Makino SCR. Norifumi Suzuki/Motohiro Torii PHOTO COLOR 'SCOPE: Ichiro Hoshijima MUSIC: Shunsuke Kikuchi w/ Ken Takakura, Ryo Ikebe, Junko Fuji, Masahiko Tsugawa, Seizaburo Kawazu, Michitaro Mizushima, Bin Amatsu, Nobuo Kaneko, Shingo Yamashiro, Katsuhiko Kobayashi, Yoshi Kato Takakura is discharged from the Navy and returns to his yakuza clan headquarters. Although not bad, this entry is subpar in comparison to others in the series. It has way too many talking heads scenes – without the often attendant emotional impact – until the last twenty minutes, when it pretty much redeems itself with the usual spectacularly choreographed carnage. #4 of 9 films   * * 1/2

*Tales of the Last Showa Yakuza -
Bloodstained Lion (#4)*

TALES OF THE LAST SHOWA YAKUZA – LION'S HONOR AND HUMANITY aka SHOWA ZAN KYODEN – KARAJISHI JINGI aka MAN WITH THE DRAGON TATTOO aka A LION'S GAMBLING CODE aka BRUTAL TALES OF CHIVALRY #5 1969 90 min.

DIR. Masahiro Makino SCR. Hideaki Yamamoto/Isao Matsumoto PHOTO COLOR 'SCOPE: Makoto Tsuboi MUSIC: Shunsuke Kikuchi w/ Ken Takakura, Ryo Ikebe, Junko Fuji, Kyosuke Machida, Takashi Shimura, Seizaburo Kawazu

A great *ninkyo* tall tale with a beautifully straightforward, to-the-point, poetic opening. Takakura and Ikebe meet by the side of a lake in moonlight amidst autumnal falling leaves for a death duel with swords. Ikebe is wounded and Takakura leaves it at that. He is arrested anyway, endures a prison term and is released

to take a train ride home under the opening titles. Once on board, he is befriended by benevolent *oyabun* Shimura. Arriving at the village, we see that the evil yakuza clan has it in for lone wolf Takakura, and try to stir up bad feelings between him and Ikebe. However, Ikebe has no desire for vengeance and thwarts their efforts at manipulation. Of course, by the climax Takakura and Ikebe are close friends and attack bad guy HQ together. Ikebe once again expires in a very convincing and emotion-wringing death scene. #5 of 9 films * * * 1/2

Tales of the Last Showa Yakuza - Lion's Honor and Humanity aka Brutal Tales of Chivalry (#5)

TALES OF THE LAST SHOWA YAKUZA – KILLER LION aka SHOWA ZAN KYODEN – HITOKIRI KARAJISHI aka MURDER OF COURAGE aka RETURN OF THE MAN WITH THE DRAGON TATTOO 1969 109 min. DIR. Kosaku

Yamashita Scr. Fumio Konami/ Kibu Nagata Photo color 'scope: Shichiro Hayashi Music: Shunsuke Kikuchi w/ Ken Takakura, Ryo Ikebe, Chiezo Kataoka, Minoru Oki, Ryoji Hayama, Akiko Koyama, Akio Hasegawa   Another superlative effort in this series. Kataoka is the good elder *oyabun* up against the usual vicious opposing clan. Takakura is a lone wolf obligated to Kataoka's brotherhood. This time there is a fanatically over-principled young guy (Hasegawa – he played a similar unbending character in Nikkatsu Studios' YAKUZA NATIVE GROUND) who has a terminal grudge against Takakura. He is uninterested in Takakura's background, his loyal nature and wise, patient character. He knows one apparent affront, and his unswerving devotion to his vengeance-soaked ethics, his fragile young ego that repeatedly causes him to act before he thinks make him just as dangerous as the unprincipled villains. As is customary in the best of Yamashita's pictures, the lone wolf hero/antihero must constantly traverse a moral minefield with moral/ethical quandaries that keep him from barely a night's rest, let alone peace of mind. Yamashita, along with Tai Kato, seems to be one of the most skilled directors in creating the "between- a-rock-and-a-hard-place" dynamic that is the struggle between the character's feeling of *giri* (duty and obligation to gang) and *ninjo* (responsibility to one's fellow man or, in a word, humanity). It is a tightrope act that is usually impossible to accomplish safely, even for the most conscientious, wisdom-filled yakuza veteran. Of course, that is the *raison de etre* of the *ninkyo* (chivalrous) yakuza picture. Without that tortuous inner struggle there is only the simple equivalent of an American or Euro gangster film.   #6 of 9 films * * * 1/2

TALES OF THE LAST SHOWA YAKUZA – I SINCERELY WANT TO KILL YOU aka SHOWA ZAN KYODEN – SHIN DE MORAI-MASU aka HELL IS A MAN'S DESTINY aka THE BROTHER-HOOD'S CRUEL GIFT 1970 93 min. Dir. Masahiro Makino Scr. Morimasa Owaku Photo color 'scope: Shichiro Hayashi Music: Shunsuke Kikuchi w/ Ken Takakura, Ryo Ikebe, Junko Fuji, Rinichi Yamamoto, Yoshi Kato, Takehiro Nakamura, Hiroyuki Nagato, Haruko Uemura, Tomiko Ishii, Michiko Araki, Shinji Takano   The most critically acclaimed of the series (in Japan). It is certainly good, but I personally feel #5, A LION'S HONOR & HUMANITY, #6, KILLER LION and #8, HERO LION are more deserving of praise. Takakura is working in a restaurant and falls in love with Fuji. There is a young child involved – something that happens in a couple of the other entries – and this "tugging-at-the-heartstrings" kind of manipulation occurs way too much in the *ninkyo* strata of the genre. Fortunately, here and elsewhere in the series, it is handled fairly well, without schmaltzing it up to any sickening degree. Per routine, equally alienated lone wolf comrade Ikebe takes a sword-in-the-hand walk with Takakura to bad-guy HQ at the blood-soaked climax. #7 of 9 films   * * *

TALES OF THE LAST SHOWA YAKUZA – HERO LION aka SHOWA ZAN KYODEN – HOERO KARAJISHI 1971 91 min. **DIR.** Kiyoshi Saeki **SCR.** Akira Murao **PHOTO COLOR 'SCOPE:** Ichiro Hoshijima **MUSIC:** Chuji Kinoshita w/ Ken Takakura, Koji Tsuruta, Ryo Ikebe, Chieko Matsubara, Hiroki Matsukata, Ryoji Hayama, Yoichi Numata   One of the best entries in the series, this follows Takakura in a gradually growing crisis of conscience as he must follow the dictates of his boss, Hayama, a man he comes to realize is not worthy of his loyalty. One of the impressive things about the narrative is just how long Takakura takes to break away from a gang that becomes less and less human as each day passes. The catalyst is young comrade Matsukata learning his runaway tubercular sister has been sexually abused by boss Hayama. This sets in motion a search for the sister with Matsukata keeping barely ahead of Takakura, sadistic Numata et. al.   The tale turns on Takakura acting as a voice of reason and humanity when confronted with the selfishness, false pride and cruelty espoused by his comrades. He is continually presented with other marginal outlaw characters such as old flame and boss's spouse Matsubara, retired boss Ikebe, and ethical yakuza Tsuruta, who are more humane and honorable than he is, individuals willing to sacrifice themselves to help Matsukata and his sister. The tension of Takakura's obligation to a callous, bestial *oyabun* reaches closer to the breaking point with each new broken promise and dishonorable act by Hayama. It is rather shocking that, even after Takakura has told

Matsukata that he will be forgiven if he cuts off his finger and then sees Numata murder Matsukata at his sister's deathbed, he is still ready to fight honorable Tsuruta on Hayama's orders. It is only after Hayama's men interfere, wounding Tsuruta with a gun as they fight, that Takakura blows his stack. He finally dissolves his ties with the villains, joins Ikebe in visiting Matsukata and sister's graves, then indulges in an incredibly bloody massacre at Hayama's HQ, a melee that leaves Ikebe dying and Takakura severely wounded. Despite some occasional slow patches, this is one of the most perfect distillations of the Toei *ninkyo* formula.   #8 of 9 films
* * * *

TALES OF THE LAST SHOWA YAKUZA – TORN PARASOL aka SHOWA ZAN KYODEN – YABURE GASA 1972 95 min. **DIR.** Kiyoshi Saeki **SCR.** Akira Murao **PHOTO COLOR 'SCOPE:** Masahiko Iimura **MUSIC:** Chuji Kinoshita   w/ Ken Takakura, Koji Tsuruta, Ryo Ikebe, Noboru Ando, Yuriko Hoshi, Saburo Kitajima, Rinichi Yamamoto, Fumi Dan   This last entry gets a bit too formulaic, even for the most formulaic of all genres. You can tell that the writer was trying to create juicy parts for all the major yakuza stars the producers wanted to cram into the big finale. This often happens in the last of a Japanese film series from this time period, particularly at Toei – drafting all the studio's main guns so the saga can go out with a big bang/ blaze of glory. Which I actually do not mind. Because the cast could not be much better. There is also plenty of action and some very nice moments. Of special note, the poetically-staged

Tales of the Last Showa Yakuza - Torn Parasol (#9)

duel by the river between Takakura and Ikebe which accidentally causes the death of the woman with whom they are both in-love. Another is the ambush of Tsuruta beside a long wall in the falling night snow, the act that precipitates the final revenge-binge massacre. #9 and final in series
* * *

Tattooed Ambush

TATTOOED AMBUSH aka IREZUMI TOTSU GEKI aka SHOCK TROOP OF OUTLAWS aka TATTOOED SUDDEN ATTACK 1964 91 min. **DIR./SCR.** Teruo Ishii **PHOTO B&W 'SCOPE:** Yoshikazu (Giichi) Yamazawa **MUSIC:** Masao Yagi **w/** Ken Takakura, Naoki Sugiura, Yukiji Asaoka, Masahiko Tsugawa, Toru Abe, Hideo Sunazuka, Kin Omae, Mamoru Ogawa, Rinichi Yamamoto   This is a noirish war film set in late 1930s Manchuria with Takakura and his outfit composed of former yakuza. Takakura is antago-

nistic to his higher-ranking officer Sugiura, even challenging him to a private nocturnal fistfight in the mud. When he discovers that Sugiura is an okay fellow and also a respected yakuza, they become friends. Too bad that Takakura's sadistic immediate superior Abe has it in for him, especially after Takakura and the object of Abe's affection, prostitute/joy girl Asaoka develop a yen for each other. Before this enmity can reach crisis stage, serious hostilities with the Chinese escalate and battles ensue. When Takakura is put in charge of transporting some of the comfort girls to the front as nurses, Asaoka follows him into the field. Abe chases her on horseback, and she is caught in the crossfire when Abe tries to kill the rescuing Takakura. Abe is killed by Chinese snipers, and Takakura has to make a run for it with Asaoka slung across his saddle. She dies in a hut at the front with Takakura and tearful fellow whore Mihara at her side. All perish in the final battle with Mihara helping Takakura at the end by feeding bullets into his machine gun. The only one left, Takakura strips to his loincloth revealing his tattoo, grabs the dead Sugiura's sword and, with a live bomb attached to his waist, wades suicidally into the morass of Chinese. A downbeat, nihilistic picture leavened with just the right amount of bawdy humor, this is another one of Ishii's better films. Not particularly deep, but Ishii's irreverent, perverse tone and the great chemistry between Takakura and Asaoka make it work. * * *

TERRIFYING GIRLS' HIGH SCHOOL aka KYOFU JOSHI KOKOSEI series

Terrifying Girls' High School - Women's Violent Classroom (#1)

TERRIFYING GIRLS' HIGH SCHOOL – WOMEN'S VIOLENT CLASSROOM aka KYOFU JOSHI KOKOSEI – ONNA BORYOKU KYOSHITSU 1972 78 min.

DIR. Norifumi Suzuki SCR. Masahiro Kakefuda/Ikuo Sekimoto/Norifumi Suzuki PHOTO COLOR 'SCOPE: Juhei Suzuki MUSIC: Masao Yagi
w/ Miki Sugimoto, Reiko Ike, Natsuko Miura, Rika Sudo, Nobuo Kaneko, Hiroshi Nawa, Eiko Azuma, Chiomi Oka, Hiroshi Oizumi
These pictures are very similar to Toei's GIRL BOSS series (also starring Reiko Ike and Miki Sugimoto), the only difference being that these girls are still stuck in high school. Unfortunately, this first entry is so relentlessly mean-spirited, with little of director Suzuki's trademark outlandishness until late in the film, it is a bit hard to warm up to. Even usually supercharged Miki Sugimoto as the thoroughly nasty delinquent boss fails to register much on the jolt meter. I have actually rated this film up a notch due to Reiko Ike's charismatic presence. Her portrayal of a super-intelligent teen orphaned by a familial murder/suicide is an astonishingly matter-of-fact performance that truly embodies the essence of cool without flashy pyrotechnics. Her character is schizophrenically given to playing classical piano as well as introducing herself as an "I-Can-Take-Care-Of-Myself" yakuza lone wolf. Her refusal to knuckle under to a lecherous guardian/school official (Nawa) or her bullying rival Sugimoto raises the film up out of its programmer status. If only the rest of the picture had been as good. #1 of 4 films   * * 1/2

TERRIFYING GIRLS' HIGH SCHOOL – LYNCH LAW CLASSROOM aka KYOFU JOSHI KOKOSEI – BOKO RINCHI KYOSHITSU 1973 88 min.

DIR. Norifumi Suzuki SCR. Tatsuhiko Kamoi PHOTO COLOR 'SCOPE: Juhei Suzuki MUSIC: Masao Yagi
w/ Miki Sugimoto, Reiko Ike, Tsunehiko Watase, Nobuo Kaneko, Yoko Mihara, Shunji Imai, Misuzu Ota, Rika Sudo, Hiroshi Kondo
A lunatic erotic/grotesque sleaze fest with director Suzuki, aided by writer Kamoi, back up to full speed on the outlandish comic book violence scene. Sugimoto is the leader of a trio of underdog loner delinquents at a super strict girls' school. Independent yakuza biker chick and all-around

free spirit Ike arrives midway to help
Sugimoto and others fight a homicid-
ally fascist band of schoolgirls that
principal Imai has recruited to keep
the rowdier misfits cowed. These
neo-nazi types are merciless sadists
who love to drain their victims of
blood, burn them with hot lightbulbs
and generally make their lives miserable enough that they will commit
suicide. Ike is in turn assisted by her
lone wolf yakuza pal, the suave but
somewhat klutzy Watase. Watase
engineers blackmail scenarios trapping various school staff and a corrupt member of the Diet (Kaneko),
a bunch that are unable to curtail
their appetite for underage poontang.
The climax sees a full scale riot at
the school with the girls keeping the
hordes of cops at bay with rocks and
firehoses. Supremely anarchic entertainment. #2 of 4 films * * * 1/2

*Terrifying Girls' High School -
Delinquent Convulsion Group (#3)*

**TERRIFYING GIRLS' HIGH
SCHOOL – DELINQUENT
CONVULSION GROUP** aka
KYOFU JOSHI KOKOSEI – FU-
RYO MONZETSU SURU GURU-
UPU 1973 86 min. **DIR.** Masahiro
Shimura **SCR.** Ikuo Sekimoto/
Norifumi Suzuki/Masahiro Shimura
PHOTO COLOR 'SCOPE: Shigeru
Akatsuka **MUSIC:** Ichiro Araki
w/ Reiko Ike, Yuko Kano, Vera
Shima, Rena Ichinose, Misuzu Ota,
Sachi Suzuki, Tatsuo Endo, Hiroshi
Oizumi, Yoko Mihara, Hiroshi Nawa
Ike is a tough schoolgirl butting heads
with her more ruthless, amoral rival
whose father is Nawa, the school
principal. Soon after Ike wins a vote
of the girls as the unofficial defacto
student *bancho* (boss), her trucking
transport company owner dad is murdered in a fake car accident. Ike's
mom (Mihara) is not only conned
into signing over dad's business but
is also rudely seduced into becoming
the new American gangster owner's
mistress. Principal Nawa turns out
to have been in on the plot to kill
Ike's dad and is in cahoots with the
American gangsters to smuggle in
heroin. Ike is toppled from her place
of prestige at the school. Too make
matters worse, she has to watch
her mom degenerate into a drunken
whore when she is jilted by the
sleazy American mob boss. Ike makes
friends with a handsome halfbreed
guy (his pop was an American GI).
Her new beau, though given to wearing white hiphuggers (!), is something
of a closet anarchist actually plotting to wipe out the gangsters who
have also ruined his life. There is a
simultaneously funny/erotic scene
where the boyfriend allows Ike to
fondle the new machine gun he keeps

stashed under his bed, something which gets her so excited they have to immediately hit the floor and fuck their brains out. Too bad he gets murdered by the gang when they find him snooping around their heroin warehouse. To get revenge, Ike and pals kidnap Nawa's daughter, drug her then substitute her in the bed of singer Misuzu Ota – who is a comrade of Ike – when Nawa comes to court the singer. Once they catch Nawa in bed with his pants down, Ike and the girls snap pictures as he discovers his nude daughter lying beside him. Seconds later, the cops burst in, and slimy Nawa is arrested for molesting his own daughter. Ike then heads over to her dead beau's pad, grabs his machine gun and makes her way to bad guy HQ. There in the driving rain, she proceeds to ventilate the whole gang with a hail of lead. A nicely constructed tall tale with action and humor well integrated with the more "serious" elements. The pacing is great and the ending is stark, violent and particularly satisfying. #3 of 4 films   * * * 1/2

TERRIFYING GIRLS' HIGH SCHOOL – ANIMAL COURAGE aka KYOFU JOSHI KOKOSEI – ANIMARU DOKYOSEI 1973 86 min DIR. Masahiro Shimura SCR. Masahiro Kakefuda/Nobuaki Nakajima PHOTO COLOR 'SCOPE: Umeo Masuda MUSIC: Hajime Kaburagi w/ Reiko Ike, Haruko (Ryoko?) Kinuo, Miki Nakai, Junko Miwa, Nobuo Kaneko, Rena Ichinose, Hiroshi Oizumi An uneven but entertaining final entry to the series as tough Reiko Ike as well as her rivals have to eventually band together to overthrow their

private Catholic school administration where institutionalized sexual abuse is endemic. Tables are turned eventually on lay principal Kaneko as well as the evil *gaijin* priest (who drives a virgin to suicide when he deflowers her!) and other hypocritical teachers. Ike also teams up with a lone wolf yakuza beau who is employed by Kaneko for setting up blackmail schemes. He wholeheartedly comes over to Ike and the girls' side when Ike saves his life from Kaneko's whip-wielding dominatrix assassin! Per usual, the climax sees Kaneko and other villainous parties publicly humiliated and exposed before the entire student body. #4 and last of series   * * *

Terrifying Girls' High School - Animal Courage (#4)

TEST OF A MAN'S COURAGE aka OTOKO DOKYO DE SHOBU 1966 DIR. Shinji Murayama SCR. Hideaki Yamamoto/ Isao Matsumoto PHOTO COLOR 'SCOPE:

Hanjiro Nakazawa **MUSIC:** Minoru
Miki **w/** Tatsuo Umemiya, Ryutaro
Tatsumi, Ryo Ikebe, Misa Kanchai,
Michiyo Kogure, Naoki Sugiura, Yuki
Jono, Manami Fuji, Hideo Murota

Test of a Man's Courage

**THEATER OF LIFE – PART ONE/
PART TWO** aka JINSEI GEKIJO –
DAI ICHI BU/DAI NI BU 1952
105 min./111 min. **DIR.** Shin Saburi
SCR. Yasutaro Yagi /Goro Tanada
PHOTO B&W STANDARD: Shizuka
Fujii **MUSIC:** Fumio Hayazawa
w/ Shin Saburi, Hajime (Gen?)
Funabashi, Tanie Kitabayashi, Mieko
Takamine, Ryunosuke Tsukigata,
Chiezo Kataoka, Daisuke Kato

**THEATER OF LIFE –
HISHAKAKU aka JINSEI
GEKIJO – HISHAKAKU series**

**THEATER OF LIFE –
HISHAKAKU** aka JINSEI GEKIJO
– HISHAKAKU aka A GAMBLER

STORY 1963 95 min. **DIR.** Tadashi
Sawashima **SCR.** Kinya Naoi
PHOTO COLOR 'SCOPE: Shizuka Fujii
MUSIC: Masaru Sato
w/ Koji Tsuruta, Yoshiko Sakuma,
Ken Takakura, Tatsuo Umemiya,
Ryunosuke Tsukigata, Hideo Murata,
Haruo Tanaka, Yoshi Kato, Michitaro
Mizushima   Another adaptation of
the popular THEATER OF LIFE novel. The first two thirds of this trilogy
are a couple of the most beautiful,
atmospheric, romantic *ninkyo* yakuza
films, fairly devoid of the by-the-
numbers formula which would soon
become *de rigeur* in Toei *ninkyo eiga*.
They also give, more than most other
yakuza films, an idea of the horrible
paradoxical anachronism that is a
woman's existence in a love relationship with a yakuza clan member – a
hell of damned-if-you-do, damned-
if-you-don't, and we are talking the
heroine's relationship with the hero.
There are so many affecting setpieces,
many of which occur as Tsuruta sits
in his solitary jail cell staring out at
the stars or at the falling snow and
flashing back on his love for geisha
Sakuma; his killing of the rival boss
that landed him in stir; his friendship
with elderly, scholarly ex-boss
Tsukigata. Sakuma is placed by
Tsuruta in boss Mizushima's place
to be looked after while he is in stir.
While Tsuruta's inside, Sakuma goes
walking with Mizushima during
festival. They watch the fireworks as
they stroll along, and suddenly they
are witnessing Tsuruta's former boss
Kato being stabbed to death. Sakuma
is horrified and turns to Mizushima
only to find him smiling at the scene.
Takakura later rescues her from
Mizushima's men not knowing who
she is. He nurses her back to health

and falls in love with her. One night he cannot control himself and forces his attentions on her.

Theater of Life - Hishakaku (#1)

When he discovers she is his best friend Tsuruta's wife, he is mortified and goes mad with grief. The scene where Sakuma and Takakura confront the newly-released Tsuruta to ask his forgiveness, kneeling before him on a desolate beach at sunset is gut-wrenchingly perfect. Takakura goes to avenge Kato's death but is killed. The film ends in cliffhanger style with Tsuruta heading off to avenge Takakura. #1 of 4 films * * * 1/2

THEATER OF LIFE – RETURN OF HISHAKAKU aka JINSEI GEKIJO – ZOKU HISHAKAKU 1963 96 min. **Dir.** Tadashi Sawashima **Scr.** Ko Aii (Sagai?) **Photo color 'scope:** Shizuka Fujii **Music:** Masaru Sato w/ Koji Tsuruta, Yoshiko Sakuma, Tatsuo Umemiya, Hiroyuki Nagato, Mikijiro Hira, Rinichi Yamamoto, Hideo Murata, Ryunosuke Tsukigata, Eijiro Tono   This does not begin, as one would expect, with where we left off in the previous film with Tsuruta attacking the evil gang. Instead time has passed, and this installment begins by following the lost, despairing Sakuma wandering by herself at night through village streets while, elsewhere, friends Tsukigata and Umemiya reminisce about Hishakaku (Tsuruta). Apparently after Tsuruta's raid on the wicked gang's den, he had had to go on the run to another town. Nagato is a knockabout bigmouth *tekiya* who is aided by Tsuruta in his fight to sell goods in another clan's territory. Midway through the saga, after learning that true love Sakuma has been sold into prostitution in Manchuria, Tsuruta tries to arrange passage. But in order to make any headway, he must deal with some greedy yakuza funneling arms to the Chinese and an unscrupulous warlord (Hira). The scene where he finally tracks

down the dying tubercular Sakuma in a remote Manchurian village and maintains vigil at her bedside is the emotional core of the film. Director Sawashima wisely accomplishes this in one long take, Tsuruta waiting until Sakuma has finally breathed her last to completely lose it and break down. This is an astonishing performance, all the more so since it is coming from the usually stoic and emotionally conservative Tsuruta. It is profoundly beautiful, resonating a deep reservoir of repressed feeling rare in even the best *ninkyo eiga*. One of the few comparable sequences would be the end of Tai Kato's TALE OF MEIJI ERA CHIVALRY – THIRD GENERATION BOSS, also with Tsuruta. A few years pass following Tsuruta's return to Japan. He eventually marries again and becomes an influential boss. However, since he continues to be opposed to imperialist yakuzas as well as warlord Hira, he is assassinated in the snow at the film's conclusion. #2 of 4 films
* * * 1/2

THEATER OF LIFE – NEW HISHAKAKU STORY aka JINSEI GEKIJO – SHIN HISHAKAKU 1964 DIR. Tadashi Sawashima SCR. Kazuo Kasahara PHOTO COLOR 'SCOPE: Hanjiro Nakazawa MUSIC: Masaru Sato w/ Koji Tsuruta, Yoshiko Sakuma, Minoru Oki, Jun Usami, Hiroyuki Nagato, Yoshi Kato, Takashi Shimura, Kei Sato, Rinichi Yamamoto, Masumi Harukawa Somewhat confusing as the viewer, at first, takes this for a prequel to the first two films, then realizes due to this saga's time frame that that is impossible. Since most of the action takes place not just after the war with Manchuria but also after WW2, since Sakuma is never sold into prostitution, one can only assume Tsuruta portrays a different character. The story begins with Sakuma waiting at a train station for Tsuruta's return from the war. She flashes back to how he had belonged to a gang led by decent boss Kato, and how they had met when he had rescued her from a bunch of harassing hooligans. Subsequently they had been married. However they miss each other at the station. Tsuruta returns to his clan's house to find the elderly Kato ailing and new opportunist Sato in control. Everything has been westernized, members sporting Hawaiian shirts and running whores. Tsuruta becomes more and more disgusted with the postwar conditions. At one point in the black market, he is offered flowers by a young girl. Touched by her sweetness, he buys a bunch and is then horrified when she propositions him. Everything around him starts to get to him: hunger, drug addiction, prostitution and basic desperation. This leads to a fight with Sato and his men. Boss Kato is simultaneously shot to death when he stabs a drunken American GI raping one of the gang's girls. Blasted on drink, Tsuruta has a nervous breakdown. He awakens in transit in the back of a motor-tricycle wagon his pal Nagato is using to transport strippers from village to village. While on his travels with Nagato and the girls, Tsuruta runs into Nishimura, a cowardly ex-soldier who had protected Sakuma during the war then forced her to be his lover. He also encounters benevolent gang boss Shimura who is on the verge of a mob war with rambunctious Yamamoto. Tsuruta's old friend Oki turns up, enlisted by Yamamoto to kill Shimura. But Oki is himself stabbed to death when he cannot bring himself to go through with it. Tsuruta is briefly reunited with Sakuma who had left her traveling theater troupe to find him. Unfortunately, he cannot get beyond her having been sicko-obsessive Nishimura's forced mistress. Leech Nishimura turns up again and harangues despairing Sakuma into leaving with him. At the same time, Tsuruta is engaged in a knockdown dragout gangfight with Yamamoto's bunch at their black market warehouse. When Sakuma and Nishimura pass the beach at sunrise, she makes him stop the car, hoping against hope to catch a glimpse of Tsuruta on his favorite piece of coastline. But she sees only sand and crashing waves, and they depart. Unbeknownst to her, we then see the bleeding, severely wounded Tsuruta crawling along the edge of the dune after them, just out of sight. Another heartrending, beautifully shot *ninkyo* saga by underrated master Sawashima. To place it in context, as the events here don't take place in any of the other THEATER OF LIFE film adaptations, this seems to be a very liberal, loosely-linked remake of some of the elements from the other films. #3 of 4 films * * * 1/2

THEATER OF LIFE – HISHAKAKU AND KIRAT-SUNE aka JINSEI GEKIJO – HISHAKAKU TO KIRATSUNE

1968 109 min. DIR. Tomu Uchida SCR. Goro Tanada PHOTO COLOR 'SCOPE: Hanjiro Nakazawa MUSIC: Masaru Sato w/ Koji Tsuruta, Ken Takakura, Junko Fuji, Tomisaburo Wakayama, Hiroki Matsukata, Takehiro Nakamura, Ryutaro Tatsumi, Minoru Oki, Hiroshi Nawa, Rinichi Yamamoto, Kinzo Shin, Bin Amatsu

Theater of Life - Hishakaku and Kiratsune

A remake of Sawashima's first HISHAKAKU film, this emerges as an even more elegiac saga, if that is possible. But director Uchida, too, brings a slightly more objective, omniscient tone to the proceedings, something that occasionally leeches out the heartrending emotional pull of the story. Tatsumi returns to his home village and reminisces by a huge, ancient tree about his former *oyabun* Nakamura, who committed suicide there. He also hooks up with young Matsukata, Takakura (repeating his role of Kiratsune) and former teacher-turned-dissolute-reprobate, Shin, after they have been released from jail for being drunk and disorderly. Tsuruta (once again as Hishakaku) lives with tubercular love Fuji in an impoverished state, and the couple, holed up in their ramshackle, empty rooms while the wind howls outside, supply some of the most evocative moments in the first half of the film. After Tsuruta, along with Takakura, Oki and boss Wakayama emerge triumphant from a rainy, nocturnal swordfight with an opposing gang, Tsuruta is given money so he can leave safely with Fuji. But slimy pimp Nawa has already spirited her away, hoping to sell her. Fuji manages to escape out a window and over the rooftops just as Tsuruta arrives and fatally stabs Nawa. Tsuruta then turns himself in. Tatsumi visits him in stir, but does not disclose that Fuji is having to work as a whore. The upshot has Takakura and Fuji, not knowing each other's identities, become involved. Once they discover through Tatsumi who is who, Takakura offers the just-released Tsuruta his amputated pinkie in atonement. Tatsumi later takes Tsuruta to the geisha house to find Fuji. Tsuruta's character here is somewhat more forgiving than he was in director Sawashima's version. But when Tsuruta and Fuji go to the windswept beach to talk, despairing Fuji tries to drown herself. Her yakuza masters simultaneously materialize, but Tatsumi intervenes and, with eloquent words, curtails the attack. The strain is too much, though, and he is stricken with a heart attack. Tsuruta nurses him while Takakura surreptitiously raids boss Yamamoto's gang HQ, only to die a bloody death. Tsuruta, now joined by Matsukata and Shin at Tatsumi's deathbed, receives word of Takakura's demise. Tsuruta goes to avenge Takakura with the desperate Fuji vainly trying to restrain him. The entire sequence where the inconsolable Tsuruta destroys Yamamoto's gang is presented totally in black-and-white. It changes back to color only after the life-affirming entity that is Fuji appears to help Tsuruta stumble away from the carnage. #4 and final in series * * *

THIRD CLASS SOLDIER BOSS aka SANTO HEI OYABUN series

THIRD CLASS SOLDIER BOSS aka SANTO HEI OYABUN aka THIRD CLASS SOLDIER OYABUN 1966 **Dir.** Masaharu (Shoji) Segawa **Scr.** Goro Tanada **Photo 'scope:** Makoto Tsuboi **Music:** Chuji Kinoshita **w/** Shinjiro Ebara, Shingo Yamashiro, Tatsuo Endo, Tetsu Yuri, Kunie Tanaka, Haruo Tanaka, Yuriko Mishima This seems to be a "yakuza-gets-drafted-into-the-military" action/comedy, yet another fish-out-of-water-type film modeled on Daiei Studios' very popular HOODLUM SOLDIER series with Shintaro Katsu, which started almost simultaneously to this. #1 of 2 (?) films

THIRD CLASS SOLDIER BOSS'S DEPARTURE TO THE FRONT aka SANTO HEI OYABUN SHUTSU JIN 1966 **Dir.** Mikio Koyama **Scr.** Goro Tanada **Photo 'scope:** Makoto Tsudoi **Music:** Chuji Kinoshita **w/** Shinjiro Ebara, Akira Oizumi, Tatsuo Endo, Haruo Tanaka, Shingo Yamashiro, Hosei Komatsu, Shiro Osaka #2 of 2 (?) films

THIRD GENERATION series

THIRD GENERATION YAMAGUCHI GANG aka YAMAGUCHI GUMI SANDAI ME 1973 108 min. **Dir.** Kosaku

Yamashita **SCR.** Akira Murao
PHOTO COLOR 'SCOPE: Nagaki
Yamagishi **MUSIC:** Chuji Kinoshita
w/ Ken Takakura, Kayo Matsuo,
Bunta Sugawara, Tetsuro Tanba,
Michitaro Mizushima From what
I understand, this is a "fact-based"
yakuza/action drama based on the
biography of one of the prime movers
and latter-day founders of the modern
Yamaguchi-gumi, or Yamaguchi
gang. The Yamaguchi-gumi, for a
very long time post-WW2, was one
of the largest yakuza groups in the
Japanese nation, a feat mainly accomplished by the consolidation of
many smaller gangs. The scores of
families within the Yamaguchi family
were tightly controlled but with just
the right amount of autonomy so they
could be shrewdly manipulated into
a symbiotic, "goose-that-lays-the-
golden-egg" organism. Before I stray
too much off the track, let me assure
the reader/potential viewer that these
organizational diagrams of gang/
brotherhood structure are nowhere to
be seen on the screen. Hopefully this
supplies a minute crumb of background to the uninitiated amongst
you. What this film amounts to is a
ninkyo yakuza saga set in a pre-WW2
time frame. Takakura's character first
comes on the scene as a small boy
cruelly abused by poor parents and,
in particular, a drunken father. For
all intents and purposes an orphan
from puberty onward, he is eventually taken-in at the Yamaguchi clan's
HQ. As a fairly naive, goodhearted
young man, he starts at the bottom of
the *kobun* (apprentice) ladder. Boss
Tanba is fair but can sometimes be a
stern, even cruel taskmaster. Takakura
is devoted to the whole gang as if it
were his original, one true family,
and Tanba as an elder brother/father-
figure type. Sugawara is another
member of the gang to whom he is
close. But, by the climax, Sugawara
has defected and bears a grudge. He
comes to the clan HQ on a snowy
winter night to kill Tanba. Takakura
volunteers strenuously to act as surrogate for Tanba. Needless to say, he
is wedged into that famous rock-and-
a-hard-place situation so beloved in
the *ninkyo* yakuza genre. He knows a
profound brotherly love for Sugawara
but also is possessed by obligation,
duty and an undying loyalty to his
boss. The bonfire of tragic loss is
once again set ablaze. Director
Yamashita's touch keeps this from
being a sentimental "vanity" production for the Yamaguchi-gumi
personality, a character whose real
name it is probably just a well I do
not remember. Yamashita is a director
of subtlety, taste and integrity, and,
although this is not one of his greatest
pictures, it is still decent. * * 1/2

Third Generation Yamaguchi Gang

THIRD GENERATION BOSS
aka SANDAIME SHUMEI aka
THIRD GENERATION SUCCES-
SOR 1974 96 min. **DIR.** Shigehiro
Ozawa **SCR.** Koji Takada **PHOTO**
COLOR 'SCOPE: Hanjiro Nakazawa
MUSIC: Chumei Watanabe
w/ Ken Takakura, Tetsuro Tanba,
Kayo Matsuo, Minoru Oki, Toshiaki
Minami, Kyosuke Machida, Noboru
Ando, Rinichi Yamamoto, Tsunehiko
Watase, Kunie Tanaka, Fumio
Watanabe   Takakura once again
plays the same based-on-real-life
gangster from the pre-WW2 period
– the man who spearheaded what,
even today, is still one of the largest
yakuza clans. Despite the great cast,
at this point the formula of Toei's
mid-seventies *ninkyo eiga*, even
when supposedly based on fact, had
become so predictable, so going-
through-the-motions, the effect was
usually rather lifeless (as here). One
gets the feeling that there was some
behind-the-scenes input, or at least
tacit blessing, regards the depiction of
this then still-living real-life boss. So,
despite Toei Studios already having
committed to the new *jitsuroku* (true
account) style pioneered by directors
Kinji Fukasaku, Sadao Nakajima and
Junya Sato at this point in time, one
senses there was a limit to just how
truthful these two Yamaguchi-gumi
films could be.   * * 1/2

THE THREAT aka ODOSHI 1966
84 min. **DIR.** Kinji Fukasaku **SCR.**
Ichiro Miyagawa/Kinji Fukasaku
PHOTO B&W 'SCOPE: Yoshikazu
Yamazawa **MUSIC:** Isao Tomita
w/ Rentaro Mikuni, Ko Nishimura,
Masumi Harukawa, Sanae Nakahara,
Hideo Murota, Ken Mitsuda, Ryohei
Uchida   More of a suspense thriller

than yakuza film with Mikuni's son
kidnapped by ex-convict Nishimura
and accomplices, hoping for ransom
from the boy's wealthy grandfather.
Gritty and noirish. * * *

Three Brothers' Identical Dice

THREE BROTHERS' IDENTI-
CAL DICE aka ZORO ME NO
SAN KYODAI 1972 86 min.

DIR. Kosaku Yamashita SCR. Koji Takada PHOTO COLOR 'SCOPE: Nagaki Yamagishi MUSIC: Masao Yagi w/ Akira Kobayashi, Tsunehiko Watase, Kunie Tanaka, Seizaburo Kawazu, Yoko Mihara, Bin Amatsu, Sanae Tsuchida, Tatsuo Endo

THREE EX-CON BROTHERS aka CHOEKI SAN KYODAI 1969 96 min. DIR. Kiyoshi Saeki SCR. Yoshihiro Ishimatsu PHOTO COLOR 'SCOPE: Juhei Suzuki MUSIC: Hiroki Ogawa w/ Bunta Sugawara, Ken Takakura, Kyosuke Machida, Tomisaburo Wakayama, Ryoji Hayama, Michitaro Mizushima, Machiko Yashiro, Bin Amatsu, Yoko Koyama, Tatsuo Endo Sugawara, Machida and, later, Takakura are first rivals then loyal pals with ties cemented during their boisterously humorous prison term. Of course, things start getting progressively more serious once the boys leave confinement until they are forced into the always-just-around-the-corner-bloodshed. Machida and several other decent folks are killed by the evil yakuza. Sugawara and Takakura do the vengeance thing. At the bittersweet denouement, Takakura is the only one left alive. * * 1/2

THREE LAKES PRISON – WIDE-SPREAD BRUTALITY aka SAN IKE KANGOKU – KYO AKU HAN 1973 89 min. DIR. Shigehiro Ozawa SCR. Koji Takada PHOTO COLOR 'SCOPE: Shin Furuya MUSIC: Chumei Watanabe w/ Koji Tsuruta, Joe Shishido, Goro Ibuki, Minoru Oki, Shiro Kuno, Yuriko Hishimi, Nobuo Kaneko, Eizo Kitamura, Bin Amatsu, Rinichi Yamamoto

THREE PRETTY SHE-DEVILS aka SANBIKI NO MESUBACHI aka THREE FEMALE HORNETS 1970 DIR. Motohiro Torii SCR. Sadao Nakajima/Masahiro Kakefuda PHOTO COLOR 'SCOPE: Umeo Masuda MUSIC: Masao Yagi w/ Reiko Ohara, Junko Natsu, Tsunehiko Watase, Asao Koike, Yuriko Mishima An extremely lightweight trifle even for a sexy action comedy. All the more disappointing when you look at the writers: two pros who have – even at their worst – done much better than this. Ohara and Natsu are hustler hostesses who run up against evil Koike, a sadistic yakuza putting the squeeze on the bar where they work. Talented and sensually charismatic waif Natsu is especially wasted. Watase is Koike's righthand man who falls in love with Ohara and eventually is killed when he stands up for her. This also features one of composer Yagi's worst scores. There are very short stretches where he almost approaches the type of surreal pop fluff his Italian colleagues Ennio Morricone, Bruno Nicolai and Riz Ortolani would insert in their late sixties Italian *giallo* soundtracks. But unhappily more often than not the music is reminiscent of the Tijuana Brass on a particularly lame day. * 1/2

TOKYO KILLERS' GROUP aka TOKYO SHINSENGUMI 1961 DIR. Masuichi Iizuka SCR. Makio Tsutabara/ Susumu Takahisa PHOTO 'SCOPE: Hiroshi Fukujima MUSIC: Tomokazu Kawabe w/ Hiroki Matsukata, Naoko Kubo, Rinichi Yamamoto, Harumi Sone, Eitaro Ozawa, Takamaru Sasaki

**TOKYO UNTOUCHABLE aka
TOKYO AANTACHIBIRU series**

TOKYO UNTOUCHABLE aka
TOKYO AANTACHIBIRU 1963
DIR. Shinji Murayama **SCR.**
Kimiyuki Hasegawa **MUSIC:** Ma-
sayoshi Ikeda **w/** Rentaro Mikuni,
Ken Takakura, Tetsuro Tanba, Misako
Watanabe #1 of 3 films

Tokyo Untouchable (#1)

**TOKYO UNTOUCHABLE
– ESCAPE** aka TOKYO AAN-
TACHIBIRU – DASSO 1963 **DIR.**
Hideo Sekigawa **SCR.** Kimiyuki
Hasegawa **w/** Ken Takakura,
Rentaro Mikuni, Tetsuro Tanba,
Yoshiko Mita #2 of 3 films

**TOKYO UNTOUCHABLE –
ORGANIZED FASHION MODEL
PROSTITUTES** aka TOKYO AAN-
TACHIBIRU – BAISHUN CHIKA
SOSHIKI 1963 **DIR.** Masaichi
Iizuka **SCR.** Kimiyuki Hasegawa

PHOTO B&W 'SCOPE: Ichiro
Hoshijima w/ Minoru Oki,
Tetsuro Tanba, Yoshiko Mita,
Shinichi "Sonny" Chiba, Mako
Midori, Mikijiro Hira #3 of 3
films

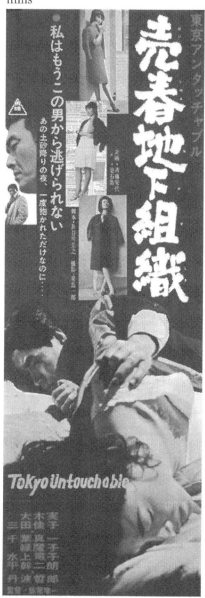

Tokyo Untouchable (#3)

Tomorrow There Will Be No Release from the Law of Hell

TOMORROW THERE WILL BE NO RELEASE FROM THE LAW OF HELL aka JIGOKU NO OKITE NI ASU HANAI 1966 91 min.
DIR. Yasuo Furuhata SCR. Hajime Takaiwa/Kibu Nagata PHOTO COLOR 'SCOPE: Shichiro Hayashi MUSIC: Masao Yagi w/ Ken Takakura, Rentaro Mikuni, Kei Sato, Yukiyo Toake, Yoko Minamida, Seizaburo Kawazu, Shunji Imai, Hiroko Kuni, Kazumi Nakata, Renji Ishibashi The story of Takakura's alienation from his boss and fellow henchmen set against the background of motorboat racing/gambling. More credible (and noirish) than many other of the transitional *ninkyo/jitsuroku* hybrids.
* * *

TRAIL OF A TEENAGE HOOD aka JUDAI NO ASHIDORI 1963
DIR. Hajime Sato SCR. Kimiyuki Hasegawa PHOTO 'SCOPE: Hanjiro Nakazawa MUSIC: Shunsuke Kikumura w/ Takashi Kanda, Yuji Hori, Tokubei Hanazawa, Hiroshi Minami, Rinichi Yamamoto, Ken Sudo

TRUE ACCOUNT OF THE ANDO GANG aka JITSUROKU ANDO GUMI series

The Yakuza and Feuds - True Account of the Ando Gang (#1)

THE YAKUZA AND FEUDS – TRUE ACCOUNT OF THE ANDO GANG aka YAKUZA TO KOSO – JITSUROKU ANDO GUMI 1972 93 min.
DIR. Junya Sato ORIG. STORY: Noboru Ando SCR. Yoshihiro Ishimatsu/Junya Sato PHOTO COLOR 'SCOPE: Kiichi Inada MUSIC: Masanobu Higurashi w/ Noboru Ando, Bunta Sugawara, Tsunehiko Watase, Shinzo Hotta, Bin Amatsu, Fumio Watanabe, Tatsuya Fuji, Hiroko Fuji, Hiroshi Kondo, Hideo Murota It is a bit hard to believe this is a "true" account of the Ando gang, at least Noboru's involvement (don't forget, he *is* a former yakuza.) His character dies at the end, so he would not have been able to ever become an actor! Clan member Ando becomes friendly with a local doctor and daughter who run a clinic for the poor. A spoilsport rival clan starts making these altruistic folks' lives

miserable which acts as a catalyst for Ando's involvement in massive, spiralling-out-of-control bloodshed. Sugawara is a member of the opposition who is basically decent and drawn to Ando because he is another honorable guy. Still, bound by duty to his gang, he kills the doc. But feeling compassion in his heart and shame for what he has done, he allows Ando to kill him in a knifefight.   #1 of 3 films   * * *

TRUE ACCOUNT OF THE ANDO GANG – THE YAKUZA AND FEUDS aka JITSUROKU ANDO-GUMI – YAKUZA TO KOSO 1973 94 min. Dir. Junya Sato Scr. Yoshihiro Ishimatsu Photo color 'scope: Hanjiro Nakazawa Music: Masanobu Higurashi w/ Noboru Ando, Tetsuro Tamba, Hiroko Fuji, Eiji Go, Asao Uchida, Hideo Murota, Rinichi Yamamoto, Fumio Watanabe, Shunji Imai, Shoki Fukae
Ando starts from scratch with school chums and army buddies and builds a business and yakuza clan at the same time. There is loads of violence and labyrinthine plot twists, all apparently detailing Ando's real life rise to prominence as a lower echelon gang boss. This is good but nothing special until Ando goes to the hospital where his wife is having their baby. The power goes out because of a windstorm, and the hospital is pitched into darkness. The wife gives birth in an amazing candlelit scene. There is some moving stuff here where rough, tough, formally emotionally-introverted Ando smiles down at his wife, picks up his baby and cradles it in the flickering orange light. The next morning, he heads to his business in the midst of oil derricks, tanks and refining equip-

ment. He joins his comrades as they barricade, dig out the weapons and prepare to wait for an attack from a giant force of yakuza opposition bent on swallowing up their enterprise. As the trucks full of creeps come over the hill, Ando, poised on the roof, fires the first suicidal shot, and the film ends in freeze-frame.   #2 of 3 films   * * *

True Account of the Ando Gang - Story of the Attack (#3)

TRUE ACCOUNT OF THE ANDO GANG – STORY OF THE ATTACK aka JITSUROKU ANDO GUMI – SHUGEKI HEN 1973 95 min. Dir. Junya Sato Orig. story: Noboru Ando Scr. Yoshihiro Ishimatsu Photo color 'scope: Hanjiro Nakazawa Music: Masanobu Higurashi w/ Noboru Ando, Tatsuo Umemiya, Tetsuro Tanba, Tadao Nakamaru, Rikiya Yasuoka, Eiji Go, Hiroko Fuji, Koji Fujiyama
Based on Ando's memoirs, as are

supposedly the previous two films, this final entry is not always as entertaining, but it does seem the most realistic and matter-of-fact. It details the events leading up to and following the non-fatal shooting of a tour steamship magnate that sent boss Ando and gang to prison for several years. This prison term was the impetus for his memoirs which were initially serialized in newspapers upon his release and served to launch him into notoriety and subsequent screen stardom. These memoirs are also supposedly the basis for some of the material in Ando's first yakuza pictures, the LAW (OKITE aka CODE) series at Shochiku Studios in the mid-sixties. Director Sato rigorously puts Ando and cronies through their paces, utilizing a strict, nearly hour-by-hour chronology spelling out the spiralling-out-of-control shady business antics that culminated in the shooting of the arrogant businessman (Nakamaru). The truly amazing thing about the picture is that, due to adhering fairly close to the facts, there is nowhere near the customary surplus of ultra-violence that is usually on display in Toei's and director Sato's other yakuza *eiga*. There are a few beatings, a couple of shootings and an, at times, police procedural approach to the capture of each member of the gang. Ando, with best friend Umemiya's help, eludes police the longest, finally being apprehended while calmly playing chess with Umemiya on a sun-dappled afternoon. The film's one major liability is an extremely low budget. It is circa 1958, but there are several period detail inconsistencies, especially in regards to automobile vintages. Otherwise, this is an occasionally

fascinating, non-sensationalized account of the mundane microcosm that was the late 1950s Japanese underworld. For a bizarre, sexed-up remake see director Noboru Tanaka's pink NOBORU ANDO'S ACCOUNT OF FILTHY ESCAPE INTO SEX. #3 and last of the series * * * 1/2

True Account of Ginza Secret Enforcers

TRUE ACCOUNT OF GINZA SECRET ENFORCERS aka TRUE ACCOUNT OF GINZA PRIVATE POLICE aka JITSUROKU SHISETSU GINZA KEISATSU aka TRUE ACCOUNT OF GINZA DISTRICT TORTURES 1973 94 min. DIR. Junya Sato SCR. Fumio Konami/ Hiro Matsuda PHOTO COLOR 'SCOPE: Hanjiro Nakazawa MUSIC: Masanobu Higurashi w/ Noboru Ando, Ryoji Hayama, Tsunehiko

Watase, Tatsuo Umemiya, Kyosuke Machida, Eiji Go, Hideo Murota, Eiko Nakamura, Hiroko Fuji, Asao Uchida A saga of returning soldiers set in the immediate post-WW2 period, their cynical-bestial-do-anything-to-survive savagery in building up a dog-eat-dog, grassroots capitalistic society where the only ethics are stab-the-next-guy-in-the-back-before-he-does-it-to-you. Watase plays a soldier returning-gone-mad who has killed his wife and her mulatto baby (from a U.S. soldier) and then is used by an evil methedrine/smack pusher to knock off various folks in the dealer's way. This has some of the sickest imagery I have seen in any commercial film. But this indictment by way of allegory condemning capitalist Japan's lack of human values contains searingly potent and appropriate visual juxtapositions: a corrupt businessman kidnapped by the gang is tortured with boiling grease from a frying pan (as well as other pleasantries) and accidentally killed. In panic, the lovable protagonists dump his corpse in a pigpen, and we witness the hogs dining on pieces of his meaty corpse. Later, when Umemiya and the rest are cavorting in an orgy at a high-priced Ginza area whorehouse, throwing their ransom money all around the room, pasting bills on the sweaty, fornicating bodies, the completely insane Watase – a hollow-eyed, barely-in-control killing machine – retires to the bathroom to shoot-up. He has gone too long without a fix and is shaking so badly he can barely get it together. Suddenly, he starts vomiting prodigious amounts of blood, literally geysers of the stuff until his body is left drained, pale white and lifeless on the bathroom floor. Disturbing. The closest thing to compare it to would be one of James Ellroy's more recent underworld-tablod-from-hell opuses. * * * 1/2

TRUE ACCOUNT OF HISHAKAKU – A WOLF'S HONOR AND HUMANITY aka JITSUROKU HISHAKAKU – OKAMI DOMU NO JINGI 1974 93 min. **DIR.** Shinji Murayama **SCR.** Susumu Saji **PHOTO COLOR 'SCOPE:** Shigeru Akatsuka **MUSIC:** Taiichiro Kosugi **w/** Bunta Sugawara, Kyosuke Machida, Akira Kobayashi, Renji Ishibashi, Nashie Nakagawa, Tsunehiko Watase, Harumi Sone, Ryohei Uchida, Hideo Murota, Takuzo Kawatani   A fast-moving though overall disappointing take on de-romanticizing the *Hishakaku/Theater of Life* saga. In fact, this bears only the slightest resemblance to the *Theater of Life* story with which I am familiar. Sugawara plays Hishakaku as a drunken, selfish Yokohama brutalizer/thief not reluctant to kill if someone crosses him. His sole redeeming qualities are a limited loyalty to his friends, Machida and Watase. Even though he himself has sold girls into prostitution with one-time associate pimp Ishibashi, he falls in love with whore Nakagawa, and steals her from the high-priced, westernized brothel he frequents. They set up house in a remote district and are happy for a while. When gang war erupts, Sugawara is called in to help his former comrades. Shortly thereafter Ishibashi kidnaps Nakagawa and sells her back to her former whorehouse. Rather than rescue her again, fatalistic Sugawara decides instead to knife backstabber Ishibashi to death –

something which sends him promptly to prison. Nakagawa is shipped off to Manchuria while he is inside (seemingly the only concession to the original novel). Sometimes enemy, sometimes friend lone wolf Kobayashi is totally wasted in his role as Sugawara's opposite number allied to the rival gang. There is no character development and no insights – disappointing in light of some of Murayama's better films, such as PATH OF MODERN CHIVALRY – BROTHER APPRENTICES. * * 1/2

TRUE STORY OF THE YAMAGUCHI GANG – LIFE-AND-DEATH OPERATIONS ON KYUSHU aka YAMAGUCHI GUMI GAIDEN – KYUSHU SHIN KO SAKUSEN aka **THE TATTOOED HITMAN** 1974 106 min. (Japanese version)/87 min. (American version) **DIR.** Kosaku Yamashita **SCR.** Koji Takada **PHOTO COLOR 'SCOPE:** Nagaki Yamagishi **MUSIC:** Masao Yagi   w/ Bunta Sugawara, Tsunehiko Watase, Mayumi Nagisa, Tatsuo Umemiya, Masahiko Tsugawa, Tetsuro Tanba, Hiroki Matsukata, Tatsuo Endo, Bin Amatsu, Takuzo Kawatani, Shunji Imai, Kei Sato, Goro Ibuki, Hideo Murota, Fumio Watanabe, Asao Uchida   One of the only pre-1980s yakuza films besides the STREET-FIGHTER pictures and GOLGO 13 – KOWLOON ASSIGNMENT to be dubbed-into-English. Then again, those movies are not really "pure" yakuza *eiga*. The American version of this, known as THE TATTOOED HITMAN, is not a bad job as far as the dubbing. Be forewarned, though, that this story of Ginji, "the tattooed hitman," who gets executed by

order of one of his own bosses while he lies in bed at the end, is quite a bit shorter in its dubbed American release than the Japanese version. The American version ends with Ginji's bloodbath-in-bed while the uncut Japanese film continues to show the demise of the gang when they are raided by the police and indicted by the courts. There is also a substantial bit of character development missing – mainly the friendships between Sugawara and Watase and Sugawara and Umemiya – which makes the violence that much more effective and disturbing. Beginning in the mid-1950s, Ginji (Sugawara) gives blood in a transfusion when his best friend and boss, Umemiya, is riddled with bullets at one of the gang's construction sites. This act is instrumental in saving Umemiya's life. While he is still recuperating, Sugawara and the rest of the clan attack the HQ of the group responsible for the attempted hit on their *oyabun*. After which Sugawara is sent away for a while until things cool off. He will act as enforcer – what he has always done best – helping another gang collect debts. Umemiya gives him a walletful of money to make his trip comfortable. He meets both Nagisa, an innocent beauty working in a pachinko parlor and Watase, a methedrine junkie and petty thief, on his sojourn in the hinterlands. Nagisa basically becomes his common-law wife and Watase soon replaces Umemiya as Sugawara's best friend. When he meets Watase, the young man is being thrown in the river by bouncers who have caught him using a hand magnet to manipulate the metal ball in the pachinko machines. Sugawara helps him out, offers a

True Account of the Yamaguchi Gang - Life-and-Death Operations on Kyushu
aka **The Tattooed Hitman**

sympathetic, bemused ear and lets him stay at Nagisa's already cramped micro-flat. Once Sugawara is called back to Umemiya, things have visibly changed. Though Umemiya still has deep feeling for him, it is obvious that he is uncomfortable with Sugawara's "lone gunslinger" mentality. Umemiya is trying to legitimize parts of the gang's business and explains to Sugawara that there just is not much room for the violent ways of yore. Sugawara does not take kindly to these facts of life. Though fiercely loyal to friends and highly moral in his own twisted way, he is also a tad psychopathic. His revolver is a fetish object from which he gets an almost sexual pleasure when cleaning and polishing it. When he learns that Umemiya wants him to start performing other tasks besides violent enforcement and killing, he is very indignant. When he returns to his haunts in Kyushu, he learns Watase has badly beaten a hooligan who had insulted him. The man was one of another boss (Endo)'s minions, and there is a definite need to square things. Sugawara feels that since he introduced Watase to the rackets in that area, it is he that must bear the responsibility. When he goes to pick up Watase, whom Endo has taken hostage and beaten, he apologizes for Watase's actions. Endo is a weasel and grumbles, despite the fact he has gotten to see punishment inflicted to a much greater degree than anything Watase dished-out to his man. Sugawara boils over, visibly quaking with wounded pride, and draws his pistol. Endo and cohorts are about ready to faint. Sugawara looks at them, points the gun at Watase and suddenly shoots him in the side.

Watase is wide-eyed with dumbfounded shock and pain. Sugawara asks Endo if that is "good enough?" Endo feebly mutters his acquiesence. Sugawara hoists the pale, shivering Watase up and hauls him outside onto the crowded sidewalk. Miraculously, he survives. When this incident is reported back to Umemiya, Endo explaining that Sugawara is nuts and should be killed before he jeopardizes business, Umemiya resists. When his personal advisor – Tsugawa in a sleazy, nearly unrecognizable role – advises him to get rid of Sugawara, he again refuses to consider it. Meanwhile, another upstart gang of brutal hooligans is trying to muscle-in and take over territory from the established gangs. The leader, Amatsu, cools things down but is forced to send his craziest, most vile men (Imai, in particular) into hiding. Umemiya calls Sugawara back to head up a squad of hitmen to find Imai and several others who roughed-up a local boss. Sugawara is resentful that he has to work with anyone at all – he considers himself a lone wolf. The other killers, Matsukata in particular, have no affection for Sugawara either. This whole episode, Sugawara's attitude and angry outbursts, are the final nails in his coffin. Once the hooligans have been dispatched, Sugawara returns to Kyushu. The Kyushu bosses decide to go ahead and have Sugawara killed whether Umemiya is agreeable or not. They wait until Umemiya is away, then give the order. Umemiya accidentally finds out and tries to get to Sugawara in time. But he is too late. Ironically, this renewed spate of violence embodied by Sugawara's death is what brings the wrath of the

police down on their heads. A massive crackdown follows his bloody demise. Yamashita is best known for his *ninkyo* yakuza pictures, especially the critically popular GAMBLING DEN – GAMBLING BOSS, but here he proves he can create a *gendai jitsuroku* (modern true account) yakuza movie that equals anything by Fukasaku or Sato. In fact, in some ways, TRUE ACCOUNT OF THE YAMAGUCHI GANG surpasses the BATTLES WITHOUT HONOR AND HUMANITY series. Unfortunately, now-defunct New Line Cinema own the American rights as THE TAT-TOOED HITMAN and seem uninterested in releasing an uncut English-subtitled version.
Japanese version: * * * *
American version: * * *

Two Bitches

TWO BITCHES aka NIHIKI NO MESU INU aka NIGHT LADIES 1964 DIR. Yusuke Watanabe SCR. Yusuke Watanabe/ Kikuma Shimoizaka PHOTO 'SCOPE: Shoe Nishikawa MUSIC: Chumei Watanabe w/ Mayumi Ogawa, Naoki Sugiura, Mako Midori, Sadako Sawamura, Seiji Miyaguchi, Yaeko Wakamizu, Junko Miyazono

UNDERWORLD aka ANKOKU GAI series

(These films were never delineated in numbered arrangement – they are only loosely-linked, once again through Toei's marketing department, and are listed here in what seems to be chronological order.)

MAIN STREET OF THE UNDERWORLD aka ANKOKU GAI O DORI 1962 103 min. DIR./SCR. Umeji Inoue PHOTO COLOR 'SCOPE: Shoe Nishikawa MUSIC: Hajime Kaburagi w/ Ken Takakura, Tatsuo Umemiya, Kyosuke Machida, Minoru Oki, Yoshiko Mita, Yoko Mihara A so-so tale of woe in gangsterland. It begins with Takakura getting shot drive-by style under the title credits, then flashes back to the how-and-why of it happening.   * * 1/2

LAST DAYS OF THE UNDER-WORLD aka ANKOKU GAI SAI-GO NO HI aka HELL'S KITCHEN 1962 104 min. DIR. Umeji Inoue SCR. Umeji Inoue/ Yoshifumi Oga PHOTO COLOR 'SCOPE: Shoe Nishikawa MUSIC: Hajime Kaburagi w/ Koji Tsuruta, Rentaro Mikuni, Tetsuro Tanba, Ken Takakura, Naoko Kubo, Tatsuo Umemiya, Yoshiko Sakuma, Harumi Sone   Rival gangs vie for control of liquor sales to nightclubs. Mikuni made a few action films at Toei in the early sixties before moving onto more serious films. It is actually a shame he did not do more yakuza *eiga* because his personality, as evidenced in many later roles, was well-suited to portraying characters with a neurotic or paranoid edge. Although there is plenty of action here in stretches, Inoue's approach comes off as a bit old-fashioned. Still, aside from director Kinji Fukasaku's pioneering sixties crime pictures, Inoue's early modern gangster films are the closest at the time to Toei's later *jitsuroku* yakuza films. There is an exciting, old-fashioned nightclub shootout at the climax where numerous main characters bite the dust except Takakura and Mikuni.   * * 1/2

met on the flight turns out to be point man for the mafia who, along with a Chinese gangster, invests substantial amounts with gambling boss Oki in establishing numerous clandestine western style casinos all over Japan. Takakura is the son of a just deceased elderly yakuza boss who assumes the leadership mantle and also inherits the feud with Oki in regards to gambling turf.

Last Days of the Underworld

Duel of the Underworld's Greatest

DUEL OF THE UNDERWORLD'S GREATEST aka ANKOKU GAI SAIDAI NO KETTO aka CRUEL STREET 1963 101 min. DIR./SCR. Umeji Inoue PHOTO COLOR 'SCOPE: Ichiro Hoshijima MUSIC: Hajime Kaburagi w/ Koji Tsuruta, Ken Takakura, Minoru Oki, Naoko Kubo, Tatsuo Umemiya, Yoshiko Sakuma, Toru Abe, Harumi Sone   Tsuruta is a dapper card dealer who returns to Japan from New York at the behest of old pal Oki. A fat, garrulous bespectacled American priest that Tsuruta had

Abe is another rival boss supposedly friendly with Oki but in truth engineering friction between Oki and Takakura's gang. Complicating matters further is the fact Tsuruta is a former clan comrade of Takakura and Umemiya and has affection and loyalty towards them. Things end with a huge battle between the three gangs after Abe has wrested control of Oki's interests. Of course, the cops who have been investigating and accumulating evidence on the gambling action all during the film arrive too late to prevent the massive carnage. Tsuruta and Takakura survive, but Abe's gang and American allies perish in the gunfight. Fatally-wounded Oki and gal Kubo die when Oki blows their nightclub skyhigh with dynamite taped to his waist. Despite the constantly-in-motion storyline and a fair degree of action, the plot is overly contrived, and director Inoue doesn't really spark much interest in the individual characters. Tsuruta probably comes off best at the poignant denouement as he dejectedly pulls out a deck of cards and flips four aces into the massive crater that once was his pal Oki's nightspot.   * * 1/2

UNDERWORLD CODE aka ANKOKU GAI JINGI aka UNDERWORLD HONOR AND HUMANITY 1965 98 min. **DIR.** Yusuke Watanabe **SCR.** Akira Murao/Kazuo Kasahara/Yusuke Watanabe **PHOTO COLOR 'SCOPE:** Ichiro Hoshijima **MUSIC:** Harumi Ibe **w/** Koji Tsuruta, Tetsuro Tanba, Shigeru Amachi, Joji Ai, Ryohei Uchida, Asao Uchida, Yoko Minamida, Kyosuke Machida, Mako Midori, Ichiro Araki
A more intelligent and realistic portrayal of the underworld than was usual in mid-sixties yakuza cinema. Although it is a bit talky until the last fifteen, bullets-flying minutes, director Watanabe and the screenwriters (one of whom, Kasahara, would go on to pen the first five BATTLES WITHOUT HONOR & HUMANITY series) deliver well-drawn characters subject to constantly-shifting loyalties and double-crosses. Tsuruta, just returned from America with a big deal in the works, finds himself at odds with old comrade and neophyte gang

boss Tanba when he does business with ambitious rival mover Amachi. Complicating things are Tsuruta's past relationship with sensitive, artistic Minamida, who is now Tanba's mate. Tsuruta also has a purely platonic friendship with teenage street vendor Midori. Nothing special, but entertaining and well-done on meager sets and a low budget.   * * *

JAPAN'S UNDERWORLD aka NIHON ANKOKUGAI aka RUB OUT THE PAST 1966 **DIR.** Masaharu (Shoji) Segawa **SCR.** Tatsuo Nogami/ Kei Tasaka **PHOTO COLOR 'SCOPE:** Sadatsugu Yoshida **MUSIC:** Chuji Kinoshita **w/** Koji Tsuruta, Ko Nishimura, Susumu Fujita, Kyosuke Machida, Ichiro Nakatani, Rinichi Yamamoto, Toru Abe, Yuriko Mishima, Nobuo Kaneko, Shingo Yamashiro

Japan's Underworld

Pardon My Violent Ways

PARDON MY VIOLENT WAYS – UNDERWORLD Series aka ARAPPOI NO HA GOMEN DAZE – ANKOKU GAI Shiriizu aka THE KILLER COMES BACK 1967

91 min. **DIR.** Masaharu (Shoji) Segawa **SCR.** Masando Ide/ Tatsuo Nogami **PHOTO COLOR 'SCOPE:** Ichiro Hoshijima **MUSIC:** Chuji Kinoshita w/ Koji Tsuruta, Naoko Kubo, Takashi Shimura, Hiroyuki Nagato, Kazuko Takamori, Asao Uchida, Bin Amatsu, Yuriko Mishima, Kyosuke Machida, Minoru Oki

Tsuruta is a hitman released from jail who promptly murders the fellow who ratted him out. A boy witnesses the killing. However, when Tsuruta discovers they have a shared love of trains (!), they become pals. Tsuruta receives a contract on a rival gang leader but learns that his own father has been paid-off to foil his attempt. Then the boy is kidnapped to force Tsuruta to put the brakes on. Apparently it has the opposite effect because he goes wild, wiping out the entire mob. As he dies from his wounds, Tsuruta watches the young boy raptly studying his favorite locomotive.

UNDERWORLD BETRAYAL

aka URA GIRI NO ANKOKU GAI aka THE CHEATING UNDERWORLD 1968 90 min. **DIR.** Yasuo Furuhata **SCR.** Yoshihiro Ishimatsu **PHOTO COLOR 'SCOPE:** Hanjiro Nakazawa **MUSIC:** Masao Yagi w/ Koji Tsuruta, Rinichi Yamamoto, Kyosuke Machida, Yoshiko Kayama, Isamu Nagato, Fumio Watanabe, Michitaro Mizushima, Ken Sanders, Keiji Takagi, Bin Amatsu

VILLAIN'S HONOR AND HUMANITY aka BURAIKAN JINGI aka VILLAIN'S CODE 1965

DIR. Yusuke Watanabe **SCR.** Tatsuo Nogami/Kikuma Shimiozaka **PHOTO 'SCOPE:** Ichiro Hoshijima **MUSIC:** Chuji Kinoshita w/ Koji Tsuruta, Shinichi "Sonny" Chiba, Junko Fuji, Hideo Takamatsu,

Akemi Negishi, Hiroyuki Nagato, Takashi Shimura, Rinichi Yamamoto, Isao Yamagata, Joji Ai

A VILLAIN TAKES AIM aka NERAI UCHI NO BURAIKAN 1962 **DIR.** Shoichi Shimazu **SCR.** Kinya Naoi/Nobuo Yokoyama/ Motoshige Wakai **PHOTO 'SCOPE:** Shichiro Hayashi **MUSIC:** Shunsuke Kikuchi **w/** Tatsuo Umemiya, Yoshiko Mita, Harumi Sone, Shoji Yasui, Fusataro Ishijima, Hideo Taka, Machiko Yashiro, Hideo Murota

VIOLENCE WITHOUT FORM aka SUGATA NAKI BORYOKU 1960 **DIR.** Masuichi Iizuka **w/** Hiroko Kobayashi, Jo Mizuki

Violent Classroom

VIOLENT CLASSROOM aka BORYOKU KYOSHITSU 1976 85 min. **DIR.** Akihisa Okamoto **SCR.** Akihisa Okamoto/Fumio Konami/ Sadayuki Okuyama/Michio

Fukushima **PHOTO COLOR 'SCOPE:** Yoshio Nakajima **MUSIC:** Shunsuke Kikuchi **w/** Yusaku Matsuda, Hiroshi Tate, Maria Anzai, Yukari Yamamoto, Kozo Nanjo, Hiroshi Nawa, Toru Abe, Hideo Murota, Tetsuro Tanba

The violent tale of teacher Matsuda, an ex-boxer who had resigned from the ring after accidentally killing his last opponent, now mixing it up with headstrong, confused delinquent Tate, whose hardline father Tanba slaps his son around. Things escalate as Matsuda emerges as the only teacher refusing to bow to Tate's biker gang hoodlums. Matsuda's student sister (Yamamoto) is raped by Tate, and Matsuda promptly has a knockdown dragout fight with the boy the next day in front of the whole school. He ends up getting sacked by hypocritical Nawa and Abe. Principal Nawa then secretly enlists some of the more athletic boys to act as school vigilantes replete with an arsenal of wooden swords. But Nawa's forces go too far when, disguised as deliquent bikers with ski masks, they stage a nocturnal sexual assault on a female teacher (Anzai) and Matsuda's sibling that results in the sister's hit-and-run death. Tate, already remorseful about the previous rape and in the process of falling-in-love with the girl, is ironically just as broken up about her demise. When he shows up at the hospital, Matsuda nearly beats him to death. Tate and gang torture the truth out of one of Nawa's syncophants, reveal the truth to Matsuda then all of them stage a raid on the high school. Mayhem results with panicking Nawa resorting to his vintage samurai sword in an attempt to kill Tate. The school nearly burns down, the vigilante kids are thrashed, and Nawa is killed. As the cops close in, the badly slashed Matsuda and Tate rise from the ashes with a grudging camraderie. A more serious *bosozoku* picture than the usual Toei fare. * * *

Violent Gang

VIOLENT GANG aka BORYOKUDAN 1963 86 min. **DIR.** Shigehiro Ozawa **SCR.** Akira Murao **PHOTO B&W 'SCOPE:** Hanjiro Nakazawa **MUSIC:** Taiichiro Kosugi w/ Koji Tsuruta, Takashi Shimura, Tatsuo Umemiya, Jun Tatara, Hizuru Takachiho, Chiyoko Honma   A gritty, noirish gangster saga – especially for 1963 – more in the *jitsuroku* (true account) vein before there were many yakuza films like that being made. This one takes place in Okinawa. Tsuruta, Umemiya and Tatara are something of a team, with Shimura being the local doctor in a role similar to the one he played in Akira Kurosawa's DRUNKEN ANGEL. Tatara bites the dust early on, then young Umemiya near the climax. Tsuruta ends up having a wild shootout with the opposing gang. After pretty much decimating them, he then faces the police. However, they regard him as nothing more than just another "mad dog killer" and, before the final credits unspool, Tsuruta's been cut down as well. * * *

Violent Gang Re-Arms

VIOLENT GANG RE-ARMS
aka BORYOKUDAN SAI BUSO
1971 99 min. **DIR.** Junya Sato **SCR.**
Akira Murao **PHOTO. COLOR 'SCOPE:**
Masahiko Iimura **MUSIC:** Masanobu
Higurashi **w/** Koji Tsuruta, Tetsuro
Tanba, Tomisaburo Wakayama,
Jushiro Konoe, Fumio Watanabe,
Tsunehiko Watase, Hideo Murota
Tsuruta is the leader of a dockworkers' union, Wakayama is boss of the
workers, and Tanba, one of several
yakuza underbosses who makes everyone's life hell. This would be down
another half-notch if it wasn't for
the terrific cast and the super-violent
downbeat ending. After Wakayama's
been murdered, Tsuruta confronts
Tanba and the big boss Watanabe in
a shootout. The workers back him
up until he is the only one left, then
start stoning him, too. They are stupid
ingrates because Tsuruta truly gives
a damn and ends up committing
hara-kiri on the dockside to prove it.
*   *   *

VIOLENT PANIC – THE BIG CRASH
aka BOSO PANIKKU –
DAI GEKI TOTSU 1976 85 min.
DIR. Kinji Fukasaku **SCR.** Kinji
Fukasaku/Fumio Konami/Yasuzo
Tanaka **PHOTO COLOR 'SCOPE:**
Nobuaki Nakajima **MUSIC:** Toshiaki
Tsushima **w/** Tsunehiko Watase,
Miki Sugimoto, Yayoi Watanabe,
Hideo Murota, Takuzo Kawatani
Watase is a young rebellious bartender who, along with a couple of
friends, robs banks and outsmarts the
police. The spool of yarn starts un-
raveling when Watase's best friend is
run over by a truck when they have to
flee one scene on foot. Watase steals a
car and the chase is on. Involved with
devoted, simple-minded whore
Sugimoto, he is also being blackmailed by brutal tough Murota.
Kawatani is a frustrated, put-upon
cop on the beat who sees Watase as
his ticket up the ranks. The increased
heat spooks Watase, and he flees to
his coastal hometown up north, laying
a huge pile of cash on his large, desti-
tute family. A band of local hooligans
try to catch him, but he and Sugimoto
manage to barely escape. The hotel
where they then land is also the scene
of a sadistic, gay mobster's murder by
a victimized young mechanic. Watase
steals the slain hood's car, and when
Sugimoto wakes to find him gone,
she believes herself abandoned. She
angrily absconds with his passport
but leaves it for him at a bar where
he used to work. Murota has followed her and then Watase, assaulting him at the airport, attracting cops
which causes him to lose his bag of
cash. Watase flees, once more finds
Sugimoto and saves her from a drug
overdose. Moved by her misery, he
burns his passport for her. He decides
to rob another bank. Kawatani and
Murota both end up in pursuit which
results in a horrible accident. The
victimized mechanic, running after
Murota on foot, is hit and killed
by Kawatani who is subsequently
hounded by irate citizens. The madness escalates when a TV crew doing
a special on *bosozoku* bikers is run
into by Murota, and a biker is fatally
crushed. The pissed-off bikers join
the fray. Finally, there is a huge pile
up with cars careening back and forth
off each other like billiard balls. Yet
again the interminable chase shifts
into high gear. Watase is now minus
a door, and many pursuing citizens
are seriously injured. A TV reporter
goes mad, rams a police car and is

then arrested by a horde of frantic cops. Frenzied Kawatani and Murota both dump their vehicles in the lake, and Watase and Sugimoto escape by stealing a convenient speedboat. An epilogue informs us that they have gotten away free and clear to Rio de Janiero. VIOLENT PANIC is a thoroughly bizarre action comedy/drama that thankfully never descends into the silliness that might have occurred under other Toei directors. Fukasaku holds onto a gritty edginess and keeps a nice balance between the dark humor and breakneck action. He also elicits some poignant character interplay between Watase and Sugimoto, two performers who had already evidenced chemistry together in the GIRL BOSS series of films. * * *

VIOLENT PATH aka KENKA MICHI aka FIGHT STREET 1979 **Dir.** Yu Kohira **w/** Shimatoshi Oda

VIOLENT STREET aka BORYOKU GAI 1963 **Dir.** Tsuneo Kobayashi **Scr.** Kinya Naoi/Yasuro Yokoyama **Photo 'scope:** Shoe Nishikawa **Music:** Chuji Kinoshita **w/** Ken Takakura, Yoshiko Mita, Shinjiro Ebara, Ichiro Sugai, Shinichi "Sonny" Chiba, Kei Sato, Chiyoko Honma, Masao Mishima Apparently unrelated to director Hideo Gosha's 1974 film below.

VIOLENT STREET aka BORYOKU GAI aka VIOLENT CITY 1974 96 min. **Dir.** Hideo Gosha **Scr.** Masahiro Kakefuda/ Nobuaki Nakajima **Photo color 'scope:** Yoshikazu (Giichi) Yamazawa **Music:** Masaru Sato **w/** Noboru Ando, Akira Kobayashi, Isao Natsuyagi, Bunta Sugawara,

Tetsuro Tanba, Asao Koike, Hideo Murota, Miyoko Akaza, Ryoji Hayama, Rikiya (Ricky)Yasuoka One of the most perverse, bloody and just plain strange yakuza films (along with TRUE ACCOUNT OF GINZA SECRET ENFORCERS). Ando plays the owner of a Spanish-motif nightclub called Madrid – with spectacularly authentic flamenco dancers – and the retired underboss of a group of shady friends (Natsuyagi, Murota, et al.) still devoted to him. Ando's club is threatened from all sides, both by his own previous, now corporate yakuza boss as well as rival boss Tanba from Kansai. Unbeknownst to Ando, his pals perpetrate a kidnap-for-ransom of a TV popstar managed by their former gang, hoping for not only money but for a war to erupt between the two rival mobs that will destroy them both. But the poor popstar is accidentally strangled when she pulls off one of her captor's gorilla masks, resisting his advances. When the rest of the guys get back, they are angry but decide to go through with the ransom anyway. The guy designated to pick up the loot dons a Frankenstein mask and cape and pretends to be promoting the local showing of a horror film while he is actually making good his escape. When Ando's ex-comrade, yakuza Kobayashi and chums find the girl's body, all hell breaks loose. Since Ando wasn't actually in on the kidnapping, no one can connect him up with what happened. However, a few of the culprits are obvious, and retaliation is swift. Kobayashi's boss hires a duo of weirdo hitmen – a baldheaded, blackclad maniac with a parrot on his shoulder and a beautiful transexual who uses a straight

Violent Street

razor to slit her victims' throats. That is where the fun really begins. An insane catalogue of killings unspools. Before long, reluctant Kobayashi is forced by his boss to consider Ando involved, and Ando has no choice but to desert his club to start some clandestine slayings of his own. Ando dispatches his greedy former superior while the decadent villain is watching porno with two whores in his heavily guarded mansion. The aftermath sees ruthless second-in-command Koike take over, then establish an alliance with ex-enemy, Kansai *oyabun* Tanba. At the climax, Kobayashi confronts Ando in an almost western-style face-off at deceased pal Natsuyagi's rural chicken farm. But Koike and Tanba's strongarm men – seen only in silhouette – cut both men down, in effect eliminating the last two individual outlaws standing in the way of mega-corporate domination. Once again director Gosha – working with Teruo Ishii-cinema-of-cruelty-screenwriter Kakefuda – unleashes a masterpiece. They create a scarily chaotic universe where no one is safe and anything can happen. Gosha made at least ten excellent samurai films such as HUNTER IN THE DARK (1979), GOYOKIN (1969); THREE OUTLAW SAMURAI (1964); and excellent yakuza picture, THE WOLVES (1971). He was still making films until his death in 1992. His next-to-last is 1991's set-in-Taisho-era yakuza epic, HEAT WAVE aka KAGERO with Tatsuya Nakadai and Kaneko Higuchi as a woman gambler (to which there have already been three sequels as of 2003).
* * * *

VIOLENT WARRIOR aka BORYOKU SENSHI 1979 86 min. DIR. Teruo Ishii SCR. Shinsho Nakajima PHOTO COLOR 'SCOPE: Shinji Dezaki (Izuzaki) MUSIC: Hajime Kaburagi w/ Ken Tanaka, Masanori Machida, Nana Okada, Kinya Sugi, Hisashi Imai

THE VIPER BROTHERS aka **MAMUSHI NO KYODAI series**

JUST OUT OF JAIL – THE VIPER BROTHERS aka CHOEKI TARO – MAMUSHI NO KYODAI 1971 81 min. DIR. Sadao Nakajima SCR. Koji Takada/Keiichi Hashimoto PHOTO COLOR 'SCOPE: Shigeru Akatsuka MUSIC: Shunsuke Kikuchi w/ Bunta Sugawara, Tamio Kawaji, Noboru Ando, Tomomi Sato, Ryoji Hayama, Bin Amatsu, Miwako Onaya, Yuriko Mishima, Keiko Yamada, Keijiro Morokado, Akitake Kono   Sugawara is picked up at the prison release gate by best pal Kawaji and, at Kawaji's instigation, they immediately change into identical black pajama outfits with matching hats while swilling Courvoisier in the back of a delivery truck. They promptly make asses out of themselves at an expensive restaurant, get involved with a beautiful woman who turns out to be a cop, have several brawls in the same gambling den, are left for dead floating in the bay (after trying to rob the game), are saved by fishermen, play Robin Hood to a poor young mother who runs a two-seat noodle stand, etc.,. When the boys see that Ando knows the woman, they decide to bump him off. Since he seems such a hardcore yakuza he, of course, could only bring her grief.

The Viper Brothers - Just Out of Jail (#1)

After seeing Ando getting out of a bath at a remote mountain hot springs resort, they are so freaked-out by his elaborate tattoo, they cannot go through with it. Both end up going to get tattoos in emulation, and the scene is priceless as the traditional, old-fashioned tattooist performs the grueling, primitive ritual without a modern electric needle. They grimace and groan and make all kinds of faces. When their innocent woman friend trips in the street and is helped up by a yakuza card dealer in-jeopardy, she is also gunned-down (though not killed). The boys head over to bad guy HQ and discover Ando already inside, covering the boss and underlings with a gun and about ready to initiate bloody revenge festivities. The violence erupts as Sugawara and Kawaji attack with not only guns and knives but dynamite as well. They regret their misjudging Ando as they see him riddled with lead. The mayhem gravitates out back into the driving rain, down slippery metal stairs and a small hill of coal. As the guys triumph, killing all, the parts of their tattoos that have been just drawn-on in design ink and not yet pricked into their epidermis, wash off in the downpour. This is a violent crime /comedy/melodrama series. Each movie has slapstick overtones – sometimes surprisingly funny (even when there are no subtitles), sometimes just clumsy and dumb – that spiral through gradually more serious situations (most often poorly-contrived bespeaking the haste in Toei's productions) until the films have metamorphosed into bleak, brutally downbeat tales by the final gang massacres. One thing that is quite amusing and helps the series work as a series, is how our two "heroes" immediately snap out of their fighting/killing-the-bad-guys mode as soon as the last villain has been dispatched. Instantly they become re-immersed in their egocentric dreamworld. Covered in blood and often sporting serious wounds, they once more begin their casual banter about anything and everything, completely oblivious to the carnage around them, the police sirens growing ever louder. They wander off into the darkness, loving to hear each other blow hot air. Both Sugawara and Kawaji's characters are amoral, violent, though not hard-hearted bumpkins who idolize the yakuza idyll but always end up getting screwed by their naivete, incompetence or just-plain blindness to the betraying ways of their yakuza brethern. #1 of 8 films * * *

THE VIPER BROTHERS – CRUEL GRATITUDE aka MAMUSHI NO KYODAI – OREI MAIRI 1971 89 min. **DIR.** Tatsuo Honda **SCR.** Koji Takada/Motohiro Torii **PHOTO COLOR 'SCOPE:** Shigeru Akatsuka **MUSIC:** Shunsuke Kikuchi w/ Bunta Sugawara, Tamio Kawaji, Noboru Ando, Yuriko Mishima, Akiko Kudo, Akira Kubo, Miwako Onaya   This one begins in prison just before release – at least a third of both *ninkyo* and *jitsuroku* yakuza pictures begin in jail or just as the hero/anti-hero is getting out – and before two minutes are up some poor schmoe has had his face pissed on by a half-asleep Sugawara. Ando is a suave lone wolf allied to a yakuza clan run by a beautiful woman and proves a reluctant, though loyal friend to the boys. He gets murdered for his loyalty, and the Mamushi boys go on the customary mass slaughter revenge-binge. #2 of 8 films * * *

THE VIPER BROTHERS – PRISON GANG 13 aka

MAMUSHI NO KYODAI – CHOEKI 13 KAI   1972   94 min. **DIR.** Sadao Nakajima **SCR.** Koji Takada/Sadao Nakajima **PHOTO COLOR 'SCOPE:** Umeo Masuda **MUSIC:** Kenjiro Hirose **w/** Bunta Sugawara, Tamio Kawaji, Shigeru Amachi, Asao Koike, Kanjuro Arashi, Bin Amatsu, Tamase (Kanse?) Mitsukawa, Yuriko Mishima, Toyo Takahashi, Ichiro Araki   Here we go again – just out of jail, our boys check out the Japanese version of Folies Bergere. Sugawara and Kawaji start hanging out at a brothel that is adjunct to an unscrupulous yakuza clan. Sugawara pulls a fast one in the gambling den and once more is left for dead in the drink. Of course, he is rescued. Before long, he is playing nursemaid to a little babe-in-arms – the mom is an exiled ex-whore and also ex-girlfriend to the creepy yakuza boss. She ends up getting kidnapped for ransom. Sugawara and Kawaji mount a rescue operation ending in carnage. How unusual. #3 of 8 films * * 1/2

THE VIPER BROTHERS – 18 EXTORTION THREATS

aka MAMUSHI NO KYODAI – SHOGAI KYOKATSU JUHAPPAN 1972 88 min. **DIR.** Sadao Nakajima **SCR.** Susumu Saji/Michio Sotake **PHOTO COLOR 'SCOPE:** Nagaki Yamagishi **MUSIC:** Kenjiro Hirose **w/** Bunta Sugawara, Tamio Kawaji, Tsunehiko Watase, Kyosuke Machida, Sanae Kitabayashi, Keiji Takagi, Bin Amatsu #4 of 8 films   * * 1/2

THE VIPER BROTHERS – JAIL-LIVING FOR 4 1/2 YEARS aka

MAMUSHI NO KYODAI – MUSH-YO GURASHI YONEN HAN 1973 90 min. **DIR.** Kosaku Yamashita **SCR.** Tatsuo Nogami **PHOTO COLOR 'SCOPE:** Nagaki Yamagishi **MUSIC:** Kenjiro Hirose **w/** Bunta Sugawara, Tamio Kawaji, Kyosuke Machida, Tsunehiko Watase, Aiko Mimasu, Keiji Takagi, Hosei Komatsu, Yuriko Mishima, Harumi Sone, Tatsuo Endo #5 of 8 films   * * 1/2

The Viper Brothers (#6)

THE VIPER BROTHERS – EXTORTION PLOT FOR 3,000,000 YEN aka MAMUSHI

NO KYODAI – KYOKATSU SAN OKU-EN 1973 88 min. **DIR.** Norifumi Suzuki **SCR.** Norifumi Suzuki/Koji Takada **PHOTO COLOR 'SCOPE:** Juhei Suzuki **MUSIC:** Kenjiro Hirose **w/** Bunta Sugawara, Tamio Kawaji, Hiroki Matsukata, Yuriko Mishima, Seizaburo Kawazu, Fumio Watanabe   #6 of 8 films * *

**THE VIPER BROTHERS – UP
ON 30 CHARGES** aka MAMUSHI
NO KYODAI – FUTARI AWA SETE
SAN JUPPAN 1974 93 min. DIR.
Eiichi Kudo SCR. Tatsuhiko Kamoi
PHOTO COLOR 'SCOPE: Motoya Washio
MUSIC: Kenjiro Hirose w/ Bunta
Sugawara, Tamio Kawaji, Michi
Azuma, Yuriko Mishima, Fumio
Watanabe, Mikio Narita   A bit of a
surprise as pro veteran director Kudo
helms what is probably the best in the
series. We do get the usual silly antics
of our two heroes. But Michi Azuma
(the tattooed swordswoman in LONE
WOLF AND CUB #4 aka BABY
CART IN PERIL) is a tomboy in
army fatigues who eventually falls in-
love with Sugawara during the course
of their adventures together. When
she transforms herself into a beautiful
feminine woman near the end and is
subsequently killed by the bad guys,
the effect is quite moving. Kudo has
set up the situation with an absolute
minimum of sentimentality, so when
the boys place her in a coffin/shrine
filled with flowers, the jaded viewer
actually feels the eyes getting moist.
Of course, Sugawara and Kawaji end
things with the usual bloody vendetta
against the craven gangsters. #7 of 8
films   * * *

**THE VIPER BROTHERS AND
THE YOUNG GENERAL** aka
MAMUSHI TO AODAISHO 1975
91 min. DIR. Sadao Nakajima SCR.
Koji Takada PHOTO COLOR 'SCOPE:
Shigeru Akatsuka MUSIC: Kenjiro
Hirose w/ Bunta Sugawara, Tamio
Kawaji, Mako Midori, Ichiro Araki,
Yuriko Mishima, Takuzo Kawatani,
Hideo Murota   The final entry (with
co-star Kawaji not featured promi-
nently on the poster – what's up with

The Viper Brothers (#8)

that?). See one of the last pictures in
the SCOUNDREL series with
Tomisaburo Wakayama for a crossover entry called THE SCOUNDREL
VS. THE VIPER BROTHERS
#8 and last of series   * * 1/2

WAR OF ROSES aka BARA
KETSU SHOBU aka HOODLUM
MATCH 1965 DIR. Sadatsugu (Teiji)
Matsuda SCR. Yoshitake Hisa
PHOTO COLOR 'SCOPE: Shintaro
Kawazaki MUSIC: Toshiaki Tsushima
w/ Hashizo Okawa, Minoru Oki,
Takashi Shimura, Ryohei Uchida,
Hiroko Sakuramachi, Junko Fuji,
Naoko Kubo, Shingo Yamashiro,
Tatsuo Endo, Asao Uchida
A good set-in-pre-WW2 *ninkyo* type
film with outstanding performances,
especially from Okawa as a kind of
informal slum gang leader, Fuji as
the headstrong girl who loves him
and Shimura as a tormented police
detective. This has some unexpected
twists such as top-billed female lead

Sakuramachi getting murdered about halfway through, along with most of the rest of her brothel sister comrades when the rival gang tries to frame a passed-out, drunken Okawa for murder. But detective Shimura stumbles on the scene right after Okawa's awakened and fled, and gets blamed instead. Director Matsuda was a renowned *jidai-geki*/samurai film veteran, helming many movies starring Okawa, in particular the multi-picture TEN DUELS OF YOUNG SHINGO series, but this was virtually his only foray into *ninkyo eiga* (except for a few set-in-mid-19th century *matatabi* pictures). * * *

WATERFRONT OUTLAW aka HATOBA YARO 1960 **Dir.** Eiichi Koishi **Scr.** Morimasa Owaku **Photo 'scope:** Noboru Takanashi **Music:** Masao Yoneyama w/ Toru Ono, Shigemi Kitahara, Yuji Hori, Naoko Kubo, Takashi Kanda, Harumi Sone

Wolves, Pigs and People

WOLVES, PIGS AND PEOPLE aka OKAMI TO BUTA TO NINGEN aka HUMAN WOLVES aka WOLVES, PIGS AND MEN 1964 95 min. **Dir.** Kinji Fukasaku **Scr.** Kinji Fukasaku/Junya Sato **Photo B&W 'scope:** Ichiro Hoshijima **Music:** Isao Tomita w/ Ken Takakura, Kinya Kitaoji,

Rentaro Mikuni, Shinjiro Ebara, Renji Ishibashi, Sanae Nakahara, Hideo Murota, Jiro Okazaki Fukasaku's critically acclaimed third feature film. His first to receive accolades was THE PROUD CHALLENGE (HOKORI TAKAKI CHOSEN), a non-yakuza film about a reporter sacked for being a Communist who discovers the CIA and Japan are secretly collaborating in funneling arms to Vietnam. Here in WOLVES..., Takakura is a lone wolf who convinces his younger brother Kitaoji to help rob their elder brother Mikuni's fatcat yakuza outfit of enough money and drugs to enable them to retire to Hong Kong. Kitaoji's gang of delinquents (Okazaki, Ishibashi et. al.) create a diversion by rumbling at an airport terminal long enough for Takakura and Ebara to get a drop on the couriers. Kitaoji then makes off with the swag while the couriers are held at gunpoint. Takakura, girlfriend Nakahara and weaselly Ebara arrive back in Kitaoji's slum shack just a little late. Kitaoji had opened the bag to find millions of yen and had realized brother Takakura had lied to him. Kitaoji had then hidden the money. He and his cohorts are tortured by Takakura and the even more craven Ebara. But they stand firm in the face of brutal beatings and hands being mangled in a vise. One dies from being beaten too savagely by Ebara. To get a break from the relentless punishment, one of the weaker boys lies, saying the money is hidden in a nearby coffee house. When Takakura goes to look, he is spotted by Mikuni's colleagues. Enraged at being fooled, Takakura and Ebara continue the torture. After dark, the

Wolves, Pigs and People

elder brother Mikuni's vengeful gang surrounds the rickety warehouse. Weak sob sister Mikuni tries to soft-soap Takakura and the rest to divulge the money's whereabouts with promises of no repercussions. Ebara gets desperate enough to kill Kitaoji. Takakura is beset by a fit of sibling loyalty and intervenes, shooting it out with Ebara. Ebara dies and Takakura suffers a wounded shoulder. Kitaoji and Takakura re-establish their bond and attempt to get older brother Mikuni to join them in solidarity, to no avail. The deflated Mikuni watches in stunned disbelief as a barrage of gunfire erupts. Within minutes, his brothers and their friends are all dead, riddled with bullets. The other gangsters leave him behind when they split. He is pelted with stones by the neighboring slumdwellers as he saunters pathetically down the rutted dirt road. This has to be one of the angriest, gutsiest, most radically as-tute yakuza films ever made in Japan. That Fukasaku made it in the early sixties when the majority of modern milieu gangster sagas were still con-trived, old-fashioned potboilers (at least in comparison to this) is all the more amazing. As potent as any of his later mid-seventies films, its only deficiency is it doesn't quite get far enough under the skin of its main protagonists. Topped off with Tomita's awe-inspiring hybrid score of lounge jazz, Coltranesque sax squawk and distorted surf guitar. * * * 1/2

WOMAN BOSS – CHIVALROUS FIGHT aka ONNA OYABUN – KENKA TOSEI 1969 93 min. **DIR.** Takashi Harada **SCR.** Motohiro Torii/ Isao Matsumoto **w/** Nijiko

Kiyokawa, Minoru Oki, Shingo Yamashiro   Middle-aged female boss Kiyokawa makes a pilgrimage on behalf of a dead outlaw she had befriended.

WOMEN'S NATIVE GROUND aka ONNA BANGAICHI series

Woman's Native Ground - Bitches' Chains

WOMEN'S NATIVE GROUND – BITCHES' CHAINS aka ONNA BANGAICHI – KUSARI NO MESU INU 1965 **DIR.** Shinji Murayama **SCR.** Kazuo Funabashi **PHOTO B&W 'SCOPE:** Shichiro Hayashi **MUSIC:** Isao Tomita **w/** Mako Midori, Tatsuo Umemiya, Masumi Harukawa, Yuki Jono, Choko Urabe, Wasako Hara, Tamae Kiyokawa, Junko (Sumiko?) Miura, Yuriko Anjo
The poster art suggests this is another of the mid-1960s films with Umemiya as a gangster pimp and Midori a vic-timized woman who turns the tables,

perhaps with a lesbian love affair subplot. #1 of 2 films

RETURN TO WOMEN'S NATIVE GROUND aka ZOKU ONNA BANGAICHI 1966 **Dir.** Michio Konishi **Scr.** Kazuo Funabashi **Photo 'scope:** Ichiro Hoshijima **Music:** Isao Tomita w/ Mako Midori, Yaeko Wakamizu, Yuki Jono, Tamae Kiyokawa, Choko Urabe, Masumi Harukawa, Keiko Yuge, Shunji Imai, Toyo Takahashi #2 of 2 films

Ya-Ku-Za - Hoodlums

YA-KU-ZA – HOODLUMS aka 8-9-3 – GURENTAI aka DREAMY HOODLUMS 1966 89 min. **Dir./ Scr.** Sadao Nakajima **Photo B&W 'scope:** Shigeru Akatsuka **Music:** Kenjiro Hirose w/ Hiroki Matsukata, Shigeru Amachi, Yuriko Mishima, Hideo Takamatsu, Junko Miyazono, Ichiro Araki, Kyosuke Machida, Kunio Kaga
Note the A HARD DAY'S NIGHT

Ya-Ku-Za - Hoodlums

vibe/approach to the poster art. One of his first and best pictures, director Nakajima goes for a noir-ish, cinema verite effect in this gritty, slice-of-life piece on a group of young, amoral hoodlums (Matsukata, Araki, Kondo, mixed-race Sanders, et.al), their relationship with a slightly older, more principled lone wolf (Amachi) and their run-ins with the organized yakuza gang led by ruthless Takamatsu. Almost totally character-driven with vignettes illustrating the various scams and hustles the boys get up to as well as their occasionally abusive behavior towards women. Sweet-faced lady killer Kondo's victimization of a young housewife who has fallen for him is particularly disturbing as is the scene where he delivers her into his buddies' clutches for some "fun." Half-black Sanders is appropriately horrified but doesn't have the guts to try to stop the gang rape and leaves to weep outside. One guesses that that is apparently how he was conceived when his Japanese mom had hooked up with an American GI. Equally disturbing is when Amachi stumbles on the same scene, recoils but also doesn't have the *cojones* to intervene. Notable for its deglamorization and pioneering *jitsuroku* treatment of hoodlum life, this would make a perfect double bill with Fukasaku's even grimmer WOLVES, PIGS AND PEOPLE. Also fascinating for its underworld – a seemingly real-life location tour of pachinko parlors, hostess bars, back alleys and dingy one-room flats. Noteworthy, too, is Nakajima's handling of Amachi's death by Takamatsu's gang after he is betrayed by Kondo (who has switched sides) as well as the climax where the remaining youths rip off Takamatsu. A car chase culminates with the rival gang plunging off an unfinished freeway overpass then the feisty anti-heroes' loot being burned to ashes when they fail to set the brake on their own car and it rolls backwards, crashing in the opposite direction. * * *

YAKUZA BURIAL – JASMINE FLOWER aka YAKUZA NO HAKABA – KUCHINASHI NO HANA aka YAKUZA GRAVE-YARD 1976 96 min. **DIR.** Kinji Fukasaku **SCR.** Kazuo Kasahara **PHOTO COLOR 'SCOPE:** Nobuaki Nakajima **MUSIC:** Toshiaki Tsushima w/ Tetsuya Watari, Tatsuo Umemiya, Meiko Kaji, Mayumi Nagisa, Kenji Imai, Hideo Murota, Nobuo Yana, Mikio Narita, Nobuo Kaneko, Takuzo Kawatani, Kei Sato   A totally over-the-top vehicle for Watari as a maverick cop (somewhat akin to his WILD COP series for Toho) who does not have any patience for the niceties of bureaucratic red tape. He is not above planting evidence to convict a guilty party but will not accept bribes. To his chagrin, he gradually realizes he has more in common with Kaji, a jailed gang boss's Korean wife and Umemiya, his yakuza nemesis. This goes off into an altogether

different direction than the usual vigilante cop film with Watari's brooding loner character. Whether lying despondent on the floor of his cramped flat listening to deafening rock music so loud that the neighbors threaten to call his superiors or rolling around drunk on the beach with Kaji, he is inwardly tortured, lonely, disillusioned and spiritually starved.

Yakuza Burial - Jasmine Flower

He eventually becomes friends with Umemiya, sharing alcohol and whores. At first, he thinks his new found kinship with Kaji and Umemiya is the reason higher-ranking cops Narita et. al. are coming down so hard on him, but it gradually becomes clear they have established an expedient alliance with Umemiya's main rival, boss Sato to help control crime. When a gang war erupts and Umemiya is wounded, Watari helps him hide out. Sato's gang kidnaps Watari, forcibly addicting him to drugs. Soon after, Kaji's father-in-law

is arrested. His underboss Umemiya is subsequently captured then set up to be killed in an escape attempt. Some of Umemiya's comrades think that it is Watari who had sold him out. Lover Kaji is so confused, she tries to shoot Watari in his apartment, but he deflects her aim and is wounded in the arm. Deeply despairing, she takes Watari's drugs, shoots up and we learn that she has been a closet junkie all along to deal with not only the sordid criminal insanity around her but her dispossessed Korean identity. Watari has her drive him to police HQ. He goes upstairs where yakuza Sato is in conference with cop bigwigs and shoots him to death in front of his astonished superiors, then calmly walks out. His former partner Murota follows him outside and across the street, shooting him to death in front of Kaji. He dies in her arms. Fascinating, exciting and an emotionally exhausting flipside to the DIRTY HARRY archetype.
* * * *

YAKUZA COP aka YAKUZA DEKA aka YAKUZA DETEC-TIVE aka GAMBLER COP aka KAMIKAZE COP series

YAKUZA COP aka YAKUZA DEKA aka YAKUZA DETEC-TIVE aka GAMBLER COP aka KAMIKAZE COP 1970 89 min. **DIR.** Yukio Noda **SCR.** Fumio Konami/Yukio Noda **PHOTO COLOR 'SCOPE:** Yoshio Nakajima **MUSIC:** Masao Yagi **w/** Shinichi "Sonny" Chiba, Ryohei Uchida, Machiko Yashiro, Ryoji Hayama, Asao Uchida, Bin Amatsu, Keiji Takagi, Yoko Nogiwa, Nakajiro Tomita

After his partner Hayama is murdered, undercover cop Chiba storms through Amatsu and Asao Uchida's drug gang who have a pipeline to the American mob.

Yakuza Cop (#1)

Despite the always entertaining antics of the incredibly-energized Chiba, this is an imminently forgettable timewaster sloppily put together in what looks like a great hurry. It does move along, and there are a few pleasurable moments. The sardonic charisma of Chiba's outlaw pal/rival Ryohei Uchida and the sensual, yet dignified persona of Yashiro (who ends up sacrificing her life to save Chiba) in particular stand out. It is too bad that YAKUZA COP's storyline is altogether too pedestrian and pat, even for an unpretentious action film. Virtually none of the inspired lunacy of Chiba's KILLING FIST AND CHILD or the STREETFIGHTER and YAKUZA WOLF films is in evidence. #1 of 4 films   * *

YAKUZA COP – MARIJUANA GANG aka YAKUZA DEKA – MARIHANA MITSUBAI SOSHIKI aka KAMIKAZE COP – THE MARIJUANA SYNDICATE aka THE ASSASSIN 1970 87 min. **DIR.** Ryuichi Takamori **SCR.** Fumio Konami/Yukio Noda **PHOTO COLOR** 'SCOPE: Kiichi Inada **MUSIC:** Masao Yagi **w/** Shinichi "Sonny" Chiba, Ryohei Uchida, Fumio Watanabe, Toshiaki Minami, Harumi Kojima, Kaoru Hama, Koji Sekiyama
A fairly incoherent comedy/thriller with Chiba as the devil-may-care rogue cop. He is up against friendly nemesis Uchida – amusing as always – who is involved in smuggling a gigantic shipment of grass. Not so much directed as casually slapped together from what looks like nearly unsupervised footage. It is fun in a very lightheaded, non-discriminating way. Don't go in expecting high quality and you may be able to enjoy it.
* *   #2 of 4 films

YAKUZA COP – POISON GAS TERROR aka YAKUZA DEKA – KYOFU NO DOKU GAS aka KAMIKAZE COP – POISON-GAS AFFAIR 1971 **DIR.** Ryuichi Takamori **SCR.** Fumio Konami/ Ryuichi Takamori **w/** Shinichi "Sonny" Chiba #3 of 4 films

YAKUZA COP – NO EPITAPHS FOR US aka YAKUZA DEKA – ORETACHI NI HAKAWANAI 1971 **DIR.** Ryuichi Takamori **SCR.** Fumio Konami/Ryuichi Takamori **PHOTO COLOR** 'SCOPE: Hanjiro Nakazawa **MUSIC:** Masao Yagi **w/** Shinichi "Sonny" Chiba, Isao Natsuyagi, Ryohei Uchida, Michitaro Mizushima, Hideo Murota, Akira

Hitomi, Sanae Obori, Hitomi Ariyoshi, Hiroshi Tate   #4 of 4 films

Yakuza Mounted Bandits

YAKUZA MOUNTED BANDITS aka BAZOKU YAKUZA aka THE BANDITS 1968 91 min. **DIR.** Shigehiro Ozawa **SCR.** Kazuo Kasahara/Koji Takada **PHOTO COLOR**

'SCOPE: Nagaki Yamagishi MUSIC: Isao Tomita w/ Koji Tsuruta, Hiroki Matsukata, Kyosuke Machida, Tatsuo Endo, Jushiro Konoe, Hiroko Sakuramachi, Sachiko (Yukiko?) Kuwabara, Shigeyoshi Fujioka, Bin Amatsu, Rinichi Yamamoto, Hosei Komatsu Set in 1930s Manchuria, Tsuruta tries to stop opium and gun smuggling by a ruthless businessman shielded by the occupying Japanese military. At the close, victorious Tsuruta joins a Chinese girl and the indigenous mounted bandits to fight the imperialist exploiters.

YAKUZA'S SONG aka YAKUZA NO UTA 1963 DIR. Miki Wakabayashi SCR. Yuichi Ikeda PHOTO 'SCOPE: Noboru Takanashi MUSIC: Tetsu Funamura w/ Shinichi "Sonny" Chiba, Saburo Kitajima, Hideo Murata, Chiyoko Honma, Takamaru Sasaki, Junko Miyazono, Ryuji Kita, Hisao Toake

YAKUZA STUDENT aka SEIGAKU YAKUZA aka HOOD-LUM STUDENT 1974 84 min. DIR. Akira Shimizu SCR. Takayuki Minagawa/Koichi Futsuna PHOTO COLOR 'SCOPE: Motoya Washio MUSIC: Hajime Kaburagi w/ Tsunehiko Watase, Bunta Sugawara, Ryunosuke Minegishi, Rika Aoki, Sammi Suzuki, Ryuji Hayami, Eijiro Sekine, Yoko Horikoshi, Kenji Imai, Takuzo Kawatani The SEIGAKU in the title is the juvenile delinquent/yakuza slang for disrespectfully referring to students and the idea of formal education. The correct romanized spelling is GAKUSEI.

Yakuza Student

YAKUZA VS. G-MEN – DECOY aka YAKUZA TAI G-MEN – OTORI 1973 93 min. DIR. Eiichi Kudo SCR. Koji Takada PHOTO COLOR 'SCOPE: Shigeru Akatsuka MUSIC: Sohei Matsubara w/ Tatsuo Umemiya, Hiroki Matsukata, Bunta Sugawara, Nobuo Kaneko, Fumio Watanabe, Yuriko Mishima, Hiroshi Nawa, Mitsue Horikoshi Umemiya is an undercover agent who gains the ruthless Matsukata's trust and friend-ship, sharing prostitutes and drinking binges, while engineering his down-fall. That it takes a toll on Umemiya's emotional health and moral stamina goes without saying. An interesting attempt by Kudo to create an exis-tential cinematic dilemma. However, the two lead characters are extremely repellent and the treatment somewhat superficial. There is also not enough action, especially when considering the other deficiencies in the dramatic structure. * *

YAKUZA WOLF aka OKAMI YAKUZA series

Yakuza Wolf - I Perform Murder (#1)

YAKUZA WOLF – I PERFORM MURDER aka OKAMI YAKUZA – KOROSHI HA ORE GA YARU aka THE LONE ASSASSIN
1972 **Dir.** Ryuichi Takemori
Scr. Fumio Konami **Photo color 'scope:** Yoshio Nakajima **Music:** Toshiaki Tsushima w/ Shinichi "Sonny" Chiba, Koji Nanbara, Makoto Sato, Ryoji Hayama, Rokko Toura, Yayoi Watanabe, Hideo Murota, Tomoko Mayama, Toru Yuri
An outlandish action-packed tall tale with Chiba as an unshaven lone wolf killer avenging the death of his boss and the drugged sex slavery of his sister. There is a completely gonzo yet effective melange of spaghetti western (Chiba wears a long black duster and wide-brimmed black hat) and surreal comic book imagery that is all the more surprising when direc-tor Takemori is taken into consid-

eration. Most of his films, including others with Chiba, are modest, mildly entertaining action programmers with no indication he had such an intoxi-cating picture in him. A strange film. The character development is nil and most emerge little more than cyphers. However, there are some memorably disturbing, even beautiful setpieces – Chiba's assassination of past evil comrades (one is impaled along with a whore in bed beneath him in the style of Italian director Bava's TWIST OF THE DEATH NERVE); Chiba allowing villainous boss Nanbara's disillusioned, drunken *yojinbo* Hayama to crush one of his hands, then later submitting to the breaking of his other one by betrayed rival mob boss Sato (resulting in the bizarre climax where Chiba lashes a sawed-off shotgun to a dismembered steering wheel with his bandaged appendages and wields it DJANGO-style to decimate Nanbara's gang); Chiba's rescue of his deranged sister from the private mob-owned sex club that is a nightmare of writhing nudes against a yellow and lavender color scheme; Chiba having a climactic showdown with deliciously slimy villain Nanbara in an elaborate rose garden. One of Chiba's most enjoy-able films. #1 of 2 films * * * 1/2

YAKUZA WOLF – EXTEND MY CONDOLENCES aka OKAMI YAKUZA – TOMURA IWA ORE GA DESU 1972 **Dir.** Buichi Saito
Scr. Ryuzo Nakanishi **Photo color 'scope:** Yoshikazu (Giichi) Yamazawa **Music:** Taiichiro Kosugi w/ Shinichi "Sonny" Chiba, Tsunehiko Watase, Reiko Ike, Tatsuya Fuji, Mikio Narita, Asao Uchida, Ryohei Uchida, Shinzo Hotta,

Shoki Fukae, Keijiro Morokado, Rikiya Yasuoka   Another wild and wooly yarn only slightly less worthy than its predecessor. It is somewhat confusing since Chiba's character and image (clean-shaven and suit-wearing) is diametrically opposed to his persona in the first film. Chiba, still a lone wolf operator, is sent to prison after his gun-dealing shipment is hijacked by underboss Fukae. Fukae himself is betrayed by associates Asao Uchida and Hotta moments later. Chiba hooks up with pal and boisterous rival Fuji behind bars, and there is a bit too much goofy humor before they finally get released on parole (the cops are hoping they will infiltrate the gun-running, drug-dealing gang). The boys hook up with inn owner liaison Ryohei Uchida, and before long they have also recruited speargun-toting Watase and burly Morokado to their team. Ike is Chiba's ex-girlfriend, a nightclub chanteuse now unwillingly paired with corrupt, super-sadistic ex-cop Narita. Narita also just happens to be Hotta's new *yojinbo* and crime strategist. There is plenty of action, much of it martial arts-oriented with Chiba frequently getting beaten to a pulp by straight-out-of-a-*manga* killer Yasuoka and his two partners. Pal Fuji and chivalrous Ike bite the dust, all the more to rile Chiba's hair-trigger temper and fuel the climax which finds Chiba and team, now abetted by back-from-the-dead, eyepatch-wearing, hook-armed Fukae, assaulting Asao Uchida's isolated, clifftop mansion in a no-holds barred massacre. #2 of 2 films * * *

Yakuza Wolf - Extend My Condolences (#2)

YANAGASE DISTRICT BLUES
aka YANAGASE BURUUSU 1967 88 min. DIR. Shinji Murayama SCR. Masashige Narusawa w/ Tatsuo Umemiya, Yumiko Nogawa, Reiko

Ohara, Masumi Harukawa, Junzaburo
Ban, Fumio Watanabe
Judging from the title, cast, director
and writer, I would say this might
be another film in either the NIGHT
(YORU) or SONG (KAYO) series
mold.

YOKOHAMA UNDERWORLD – DRAGON'S MACHINE-GUN
aka YOKOHAMA ANKOKUGAI –
MASHINGAN NO RYU 1976 94
min. **DIR** Akihisa Okamoto **SCR**
Hiro Matsuda **PHOTO COLOR 'SCOPE:**
Masahiko Iimura **MUSIC:** Hachiro
Aoyama   w/ Bunta Sugawara,
Shinichi "Sonny" Chiba, Yutaka
Nakajima, Kunie Tanaka, Asao
Koike, Hideji Nakano, Kyoko Enami,
Hideo Murota, Jiro Chiba, Koichi
Iwaki   Cody Jarrett/ WHITE
HEAT-type mama's boy Sugawara
apes Bogart/Cagney in thirties-style
gangster gear while ripping off dope
from a rival gang, all the while aided
by his clinging mother. Mom is soon
incensed to learn Sugawara has a
girl his own age in the form of svelte
Nakajima. Pissed-off rivals join up
with visiting New York mafia, and
Sugawara's ranks are soon drastically
thinned out. Sugawara is jailed, and
mama gets picked up by the cops
for questioning. She dies from the
intense interrogation, and mourning son Sugawara escapes with the
help of weaselly Tanaka. Meanwhile
the yakuza and mafia are amassing
forces, lying in wait for Sugawara and
Nakajima when they try to leave the
country by boat. Tragic carnage is the
result.

YOUNG MEN IN THE STORM'S MIDST
aka ARASHI NO NAKA
NO WAKAMONO TACHI 1960

DIR Masamitsu Igayama **SCR**
Kuniaki Oshikawa **PHOTO 'SCOPE:**
Hiroshi Fukushima **MUSIC:** Masao
Yoneyama   w/ Toru Kono, Naoko
Kubo, Shinji Yamada, Shoji
Nakayama, Shigemi Kitahara,
Hiroshi Mine

YOUNG NOBILITY – MAKI'S 13 STEPS
aka WAKAI KIZOKU
TACHI – 13 KAI DAN NO MAKI
1975 78 min. **DIR** Makoto Naito
SCR Makoto Naito /Takeo Kaneko
PHOTO COLOR 'SCOPE: Yoshikazu
(Giichi) Yamazawa **MUSIC:**
Shunsuke Kikuchi w/ Etsuko "Sue"
Shiomi, Misa Ohara, Hiroshi Nawa,
Tatsuya Nanjo, Hiroshi Kondo,
Shinichi "Sonny" Chiba, Koji
Fujiyama, Hideo Murota, Etsuko
Shibata, Yuko Kano, Meiko Seri

Young Nobility - Maki's 13 Steps

A weirdly brilliant, intoxicating
blend of Toei's girl gang, karate and
yakuza genres with even a nod to the
FEMALE CONVICT SCORPION

series. Shiomi is Maki, the ass-kicking leader of a bunch of karate-savvy vigilante girls she trains in the bottom of a giant, empty swimming pool. They are constantly running up against the local mob run by greasy, pencil-moustached Hiroshi Nawa. There is an amazing scene in the first few minutes where Shiomi and pals raid the gangster's strip club lair, actually breaking through the fake wall onto the stage where they continue beating the hoods, much to the enthusiastic applause of the inebriated patrons. Shiomi also enjoys an intense rivalry with spoiled beauty Ohara, the bratty daughter of Nawa's legitimate wealthy business partner Kondo. At one point, Ohara is kidnapped by Shiomi's gals and forcibly tattooed. This results in several turnabout's-fair-play incidents that escalate into Shiomi being set up for arrest by Nawa and Ohara. Nanjo, Nawa's karate-proficient *yojinbo* and Ohara's beau, is upset at this since he had been on the verge of legitimately defeating Shiomi when the police had burst in. Once behind bars, Shiomi has to deal with not only the sadistic prison guards but also a savagely cruel prison gang led by the criminal-ly-under-used Etsuko Shibata (Emiko Yamauchi's rival in RANKING BOSS ROCK). There is a shocking scene where one of Shibata's henchgirls, using her long hair, attempts to stran-gle Shiomi in her sleep only to have Shiomi get the upper hand, tossing the attacker across the dorm and thusly pulling out the offending hair strands by the roots. Next day, when the girl goes to answer to her boss, she finds Shibata in the greenhouse calmly snipping blooms off rosebushes. Sud-denly Shibata turns and cuts off one

of the inept girl's ears! Meanwhile, on the outside, Ohara realizes she is on the wrong side when not only does Nawa try to rape her, then cripple and imprison defending beau Nanjo, he also murders her father and shanghais all of Shiomi's girls, forcibly addict-ing them to drugs. Suitably contrite Ohara visits Shiomi in stir. Shiomi goes ballistic when she hears about her girls. Before long she defeats jailhouse rival Shibata, gaining her respect and help in an escape attempt. Shiomi then attacks Nawa's gang HQ, interrupting his forced marriage to Ohara. Freed Nanjo dies coura-geously fighting by her side. Shiomi erupts, a furious human tornado decimating the mobster ranks and at last Nawa. Despite the extremely convoluted story, director Naito once again acquits himself well, setting up a tightly wound, drumhead-taut, firmly packed seventy-eight minutes of perverse and inventively choreo-graphed mayhem. In short, YOUNG NOBILITY packs an astonishing wallop. Naito also elicits surprising vulnerability along with the volcanic rage from not only Shiomi, but Ohara, Nanjo and Shibata. One of Shiomi's best (and her only *sukeban*-type film) and superior to many of her SISTER STREETFIGHTER pictures. Just a note: Chiba's part amounts to a two minute flashback cameo as Shiomi's *sensei* training her in the freezing snow.   * * * 1/2

ZERO WOMAN – RED HAND-CUFFS aka ZERO KA NO ONNA – AKAI WAPA 1974 84 min. DIR. Yukio Noda SCR. Hiro Matsuda/Fumio Konami PHOTO COLOR 'SCOPE: Yoshio Nakajima MUSIC: Shunsuke Kikuchi

Zero Woman - Red Handcuffs

w/ Miki Sugimoto, Eiji Go, Tetsuro Tanba, Yoko Mihara, Ichiro Araki, Hideo Murota, Rokko Toura

An unbelievably violent, non-stop ode to carnage with Sugimoto as an undercover cop specializing in sex crime who is jailed after ventilating a *gaijin* serial killer. Because of her expertise at getting the guilty party, she is reluctantly released by cop Murota, when bigwig official Tanba's daughter is raped and kidnapped by psycho Go and his gang of maladjusted delinquents. This emerges as certainly the best picture by Noda, a director renowned for his sloppy-looking action movies. ZERO WOMAN is a live-action, *grand guignol*, pop art mural that sports some new act of blood-gushing brutality every five minutes or so. The wildness and expertly orchestrated build-up of the yarn is undoubtedly due to the nearly always enjoyable screenwriting team of Matsuda and Konami, a pair that can be relied on for more than their share of perverse excess. The atmospheric climax in a windswept junkyard where Sugimoto has to outwit double-crossing cop Murota, as well as maniac Go, delivers the exploitation goods in spades. There are no redeeming qualities here except for nihilistically dignified Sugimoto emerging triumphant at the close. But it is so phenomenally entertaining one just does not mind the incredibly gratuitous nature of the violence. Based on a popular *manga* at the time, the ZERO WOMAN franchise was revived during the nineties in straight-to-video features. * * * 1/2

NIKKATSU STUDIOS

Rising Dragon #3 aka Blind Woman's Curse (ALL IMAGES THIS SECTION © NIKKATSU)

INTRODUCTION

Japan's oldest film studio, Nikkatsu was founded in 1912. They were successful for a time with the pioneering Shozo Makino, and then his son, Masahiro, among the filmmakers working. Akira Kurosawa also got his start as an assistant director at Nikkatsu in the 1930s.

However, the wartime government in 1941, wanting to merge the number of film companies that had mushroomed during the thirties, ordered the ten existing to devolve into two. Former Nikkatsu employee and founder of Dai-Ichi Eiga (soon to become Daiei Studios), Masaichi Nagata, counterproposed a new plan where the companies would form into four rather than two. The government approved. All the companies were happy about this except for Nikkatsu who were forced to connect up with the two weakest studios, Shinko and Daito. Not taking kindly to dissent, the committee establishing value for each firm retaliated by purposely undervaluing Nikkatsu, making the third piece of the pie previously known as Shinko the dominant head of production. This effectively put Nikkatsu out of commission as a film production company (although they were allowed to retain their lucrative theater holdings).

Kyusaku Hori, Nikkatsu's owner, noticing from 1951 onward that there was an expanding growth potential, decided to build new studios and resumed making movies in 1954. Many assistant directors at other studios like Shochiku and Toho, tired of waiting in long lines for their chance to direct, jumped at the chance to work for the new player, knowing they would be helming their own features within a year or two. Two prime examples of this phenomenon were *enfants terribles*, Shohei Imamura and Seijun Suzuki.

Although Nikkatsu made a handful of samurai films in the ensuing years, by 1960 they had all but halted production on historical swordplay films, deciding to concentrate largely on urban youth dramas, comedies, and especially action and gangster films. From the late 1950s through 1971, Nikkatsu became renowned for their easily identifiable style of action movie: a sleek, colorful and economic visual signature abetted by the collaborations between directors, cinematographers and production designers. Nikkatsu cultivated a youthful audience with a succession of young superstars including Yujiro Ishihara, Akira Kobayashi, Joe Shishido, Tetsuya Watari, Hideki Takahashi, Ruriko Asaoka, Chieko Matsubara and, in the studios' waning days, Meiko Kaji and Tatsuya Fuji. Nikkatsu's primary genre action films during the mid-to-late sixties were a combination of contemporary gangster and *ninkyo* yakuza pictures, and they produced the second largest number of those films after reigning outlaw cinema king, Toei Studios. Nikkatsu also gave birth to the career of pantheon prestige director, Shohei Imamura, who directed at least eight features produced or distributed by the studio between 1958 and 1966, amongst them the astonishing *Endless Desire* (1958), *Pigs And Battleships* (1961), *The Insect Woman* (1963) and *The Pornographers* (1966), before migrating to more independent pastures.

By 1971, television had taken its toll in a profound way. Nikkatsu, like the other studios, was struggling to make ends meet. Although there was a microscopic number of mainstream productions throughout the 1970s, Nikkatsu effectively curtailed their conventional output in 1971 and opted for the *pinku* film market, productions that would spotlight softcore, often violent sex blended with S&M and romance. A few talented directors such as Yasuharu Hasebe, Keiichi Ozawa and Shugoro Nishimura decided to stay on while also directing for TV. The new order also witnessed the emergence of talented assistant directors like Tatsumi Kumashiro, Masaru Konuma and Chusei Sone into credible, full blown directorhood.

Akushon Eiga = Action Movie

NIKKATSU Studios

ABASHIRI PRISON aka
ABASHIRI BANGAICHI aka
ABASHIRI NATIVE GROUND
1959 92 min. **DIR.** Akinori
Matsuo **SCR.** Akinori Matsuo/
Kazuhiko Kayaki **PHOTO B&W**
'SCOPE: Kazue Nagatsuka **MUSIC:**
Rinichiro Manabe **w/** Yuji Kodaka,
Ruriko Asaoka, Shiro Osaka,
Shinsuke Ashida, Shoki Fukae
The first adaptation of Hajime Ito's
stories. Most people familiar with
yakuza films are surprised to find out
that this exists. This is much different from Teruo Ishii's later adaptations at Toei Studios, and is a love
story between gangster Kodaka and
nurse Asaoka who helps him regain
his health after he is wounded in a
fight with other yakuza. Soon after
he recovers, he is convicted and sent
to snowy Hokkaido's Abashiri Prison
where he undergoes hardships. Director Matsuo steered many very good
yakuza pictures at Nikkatsu Studios,
including entries in the MAN'S
CREST series with Hideki Takahashi.
Unfortunately, the story here is pretty
threadbare and the budget very low.
One of the only extensive sets Matsuo
seems to have had at his disposal was
the prison location of which he makes
good use. He also manages to do
some nice expressionist things with
one main minimal set featuring nothing but a fountain, a bench and shadows. In addition, Matsuo does not try
to hide the overt phoniness of various
photographed exterior backdrops,
attaining a near surrealistic result. But
despite Matsuo's valiant efforts, the
humdrum aspects of the narrative,
the lack of action-and-significantly-
profound-conflict end up sabotaging
the final result.   * *

**ACCOUNT OF THE GREATEST
JAPANESE ASSASSIN** aka DAI
NIPPON KOROSHI YA DEN 1965
85 min. **DIR.** Hiroshi Noguchi **SCR.**
Akira Saika/Kyo Hanato **PHOTO**
'SCOPE: Kazue Nagatsuka **MUSIC:**
Keitaro Miho **w/** Hiroshi Hijikata,
Joe Shishido, Kon Omura, Kiyoshi
Hitomi, Taro Hiratsune, Juro Sacho,
Minoru Shiraki   A broad comedy
spoofing the hitman genre at Nikkat-
su.

AGE OF NUDITY aka
SUPPADAKA NO NENREI 1959
54 min. **DIR.** Seijun Suzuki **SCR.**
Seijun Suzuki/Nobuyoshi Terada
PHOTO B&W 'SCOPE: Jonobu Fujioka
MUSIC: Chumei Watanabe
w/ Keiichiro Akagi, Uyako Hori,
Bokuzen Hidari, Saburo Fujimaki,
Saneko Ozawa, Toshio Takahara
A kinetic saga full of vitality concerning a gang of street urchin juvenile
delinquents riding around on scooters and motorbikes in a coastal resort
town. They are led by reckless Akagi,
and, though most are in their teens, a
couple of the goonier boys don't look
as if they have quite achieved the
golden mantle of puberty. They are
constantly in trouble for everything
from disturbing the peace to stealing
motorcycles. Hidari plays a kind of
hobo/clown Greek chorus in much
the same way Kamatari Fujiwara
portrayed the strange, mute beggar that Warren Beatty kept running
into everywhere in Arthur Penn's
MICKEY ONE (1965). Of course,

Suzuki's film came first and was such an obscure bottom-half-of-a-double-bill programmer, it is doubtful director Penn ever saw it. At the climax, Akagi ends up challenging his rival to a race down a twisting mountain road – what amounts to a game of chicken that ends in his death as he plummets over a cliff to the rocks of the beach below. An ending that pre-echoes his own real-life death in a go-kart accident on the studio lot in February, 1961 (after just turning 21). Of course, that effectively ended his career as one of Nikkatsu's rising young leading men. Strangely enough, the dozen or so films he made before his death are fairly easy to see in Japan (his most popular, the four film HOODLUM GUN DIARY series, all 1960), testifying to his posthumous ongoing popularity.

Age of Nudity

It is much the same phenomenon that is enjoyed by the late Raizo Ichikawa (star of Daiei's SLEEPY EYES OF DEATH and YOUNG BOSS film series, et.al.) a type of James Dean-worship (although Ichikawa is quite a bit more popular than Akagi). Also – just a note: the title is a total misnomer – there is not even any partial nudity in the film. * * *

ANGEL AND THE OUTLAW aka TENSHI TO YARO DOMO 1962 80 min. **DIR.** Akinori Matsuo **SCR.** Hiroshi Kaneko/Yasushi Inotani **PHOTO COLOR 'SCOPE:** Izumi Hagiwara **MUSIC:** Hajime Kaburagi w/ Ryoji Hayama, Koji Wada, Reiko Sassamori, Kinzo Shin, Akifumi Inoue, Shinsuke Ashida

Annihilate Whomever's in the Way

ANNIHILATE WHOMEVER'S IN THE WAY aka JAMA MONO WA KESE aka KILL THE OUTSIDER 1960 83 min. **DIR.** Yoichi Ushihara **SCR.** Kei Kumai **PHOTO COLOR 'SCOPE:** Shinsaku Himeda **MUSIC:** Taiichiro Kosugi w/ Keiichiro Akagi, Ryohei Uchida,

Ryoji Hayama, Misako Watanabe, Takanobu Hozumi, Toshio Sugiyama, Mayumi Shimizu, Nobuo Kaneko, Kaku Takashina, Keisuke Noro   Heartthrob Akagi portrays an undercover G-man up against an assortment of drug-dealing gangsters and doublecrossers led by Uchida, Takashina and Kaneko. Hayama is an intrepid cop also on the drug dealers' trail. There is some off-kilter, everything-but-the-kitchen-sink touches with Sugiyama as Akagi's upstart rock singer sidekick who is coerced into helping the gangsters and a climactic soccer ball full of heroin that is really a bomb. However, if writer Kumai's scenario is supposed to be satiric, you would be hard pressed to know it with the uneven tone in evidence. Kumai went on to direct some prestigious pictures such as sociological police procedural THE JAPANESE ARCHIPELAGO (NIHON RETTO) but, except for a couple of scenes, this is strictly programmer stuff. One memorably haunting sequence has coerced addict/dealer Hozumi flashing back to when he was busted by the cops in front of all his neighbors in broad daylight. This had so traumatized his beloved wife she had done a nosedive from their outside fourth floor landing as he had been led away. If only the rest of the film had been as riveting as this short scene (which actually is so good, so gutwrenching, it seems as if it is from a different film). Director Ushihara's most memorable film is CRIMSON GUN, also starring Akagi (who died in 1961). * * 1/2

ATTACK aka KIRIKOMI aka SHOWDOWN IN GANGLAND
1970 89 min. **DIR.** Yukihiro Sawada

SCR. Shuichi Nagahara **PHOTO COLOR 'SCOPE:** Kurataro Takamura **MUSIC:** Taichiro Kosugi **w/** Tetsuya Watari, Tatsuya Fuji, Eiji Go, Yoshiro Aoki, Hiroko Ogi, Takehiro Nakamura, Tsuneya Oki, Jiro Okazaki, Harumi Sone
Even though Watari is top-billed, he appears for only a minute or two during the entire first part of the film, not becoming a major character until the halfway point. Until then the picture is more of a starring vehicle for Fuji who, along with his four pals, are the primary focus. The five are in a bar after a hard day of covering horse and boat race bets. They are minding their own business when a rowdy quartet from an opposing gang disrupt the relaxed atmosphere, throwing drinks and boorishly pawing hostesses. One of these boisterous asses spots Fuji giving them a look, and he stumbles over to pick a fight. This leads to mayhem. The assholes draw their knives. One who has been temporarily blinded after having a bottle broken over his head, charges, fatally stabbing his own pal, the guy who had started the brawl. This opposing clan uses the fellow's death as an opportunity to put the squeeze on Fuji's wishy-washy boss. They are not satisfied with financial compensation nor even the *oyabun's* own little finger being chopped-off. Instead, the opposition boss (Aoki) coerces Fuji and his buddies into killing a third boss (Nakamura) of a very minor clan. Boss Nakamura is into trimming his bonsai trees, performing the ancient tea-drinking ceremony, etc., – in other words, he is deeply immersed in the most traditional of Japan's spiritual values. I'm not quite clear why the bad guy's want

Attack

him dead. Fuji and pals, all of them virgins as far as killing, are dramatically changed by committing the murder. One still feeds his rabbit (!), another still plays the guitar, but all of them are paranoid, guilty wrecks. Watari, the dead *oyabun* Nakamura's loyal second-in-command, enters the picture and, after just one confrontation with these sorry amateurs, knows they are Aoki's patsies. Three of these "innocents" are dispatched by Sone, Aoki's hitman. Watari, Fuji and the other remaining survivor head over to where Aoki's gang are having a *sakazuki* shindig with Fuji's now former clan. Watari, Fuji, et.al. dive in, and it is massacre time once more. One of the special things about ATTACK as opposed to many other yakuza pictures, is director Sawada's concentration on the youthful innocence of Fuji and friends. Even the gang rape of a teenage girl they have gotten drunk at a rock club is shown in context of macho gang peer pressure – once they have got the girl in a room, each one is noticeably uncomfortable about the situation. If they weren't drunk and together, if they weren't trying to prove something to each other about their "manhood," trying to live up to some imagined badass macho image, their common individual decency wouldn't let them perpetrate such cruelty. Indeed, one of the guys does back out, disgusted with the whole idea, and he ends up being the one the girl gravitates to later. Another poignant scene detailing the corruption of youth has the guitar player, a poor kid who lives with his ragpicker mother bordering a dump, swinging on a children's swing set when Sone stabs him to death. This was Sawada's first film and, along with his later KANTO

SOCIETY OF LEADING MOBSTERS, it is one of his best.
* * * *

BACK SOUTH TO TOSA aka NAN-GOKU TOSA O ATONI SHITE 1959 78 min. **DIR.** Buichi Saito **SCR.** Yasunori Kawachi **PHOTO COLOR 'SCOPE:** Kurataro Takamura **MUSIC:** Taiichiro Kosugi w/ Akira Kobayashi, Ruriko Asaoka, Ryohei Uchida, Yoko Minamimida, Peggy Hayama, Nobuo Kaneko, Sanae Nakahara, Ko Nishimura
Kobayashi returns to Tosa from prison only to find sweetheart Asaoka taken by tough guy Uchida. Redeemed somewhat by the location shooting and the always great Uchida, this is fairly typical of much of Nikkatsu's late fifties/early sixties action programmers. * * 1/2

BADGE OF A MAN aka OTOKO NO MONSHO series (see A MAN'S CREST)

BADGE OF THE NIGHT aka YORU NO KUNSHO 1963 101 min. **DIR.** Akinori Matsuo **SCR.** Takashi Kanbara/Hiroshi Chino **PHOTO COLOR 'SCOPE:** Kazumi Iwasa **MUSIC:** Masayoshi Ikeda w/ Akira Kobayashi, Naomi Hoshi, Noriko Matsumoto, Ryohei Uchida, Shoichi Ozawa, Shiro Osaka, Yuko Niki, Akifumi Inoue
A noir action whodunit with Kobayashi his usual jaunty self as the smart aleck private eye whose missing person search soon becomes a murder case. Director Matsuo's sober tone is frequently at odds with the convoluted scenario. A feeling of unevenness and inconsistent tone was a problem with many genre films in

the late fifties, early sixties at not just Nikkatsu but most of the Japanese studios. Nightclub-managing, drug-dealing gangster Uchida is the prime suspect in the case until he commits suicide (!). Kobayashi then discovers evidence that points to the doctor sibling of an innocent girl. The climax in a rural snowy locale is suspenseful and well-staged.   * * 1/2

BAD GIRL MAKO aka FURYO SHOJO MAKO 1971 83 min. **DIR.** Koretsugu Kurahara **SCR.** Takashi Fujii/ Saburo Kuroki **PHOTO COLOR 'SCOPE:** Yoshihiro Yamazaki **MUSIC:** Hajime Kaburagi   **w/** Junko Natsu, Tatsuya Fuji, Jiro Okazaki, Tako Tobe, Chieko Harada, Setsuko Miha (Minami?), Joe Shishido, Misuzu Ota, Keiko Aikawa, Shoki Fukae

Bad Girl Mako

Despite the exploitation angle (evidenced clearly in title), this was one of the last regular, "legitimate" films done at Nikkatsu before they

switched over almost completely to a pink/roman porno production schedule. Mako (the charismatic Natsu) is the unofficial leader of a loose gang of wild girls who like to set up businessmen, flirting with them then demanding payment so they won't call the cops. They also like to pick fights with various good-looking arrogant guys at their local rock nightclub. Which leads eventually to a spiralling out-of-control, anarchic mess/grudge fight. Mako and girls want to curtail the revenge, but surrogate big brother Fuji – a yakuza tough – and his gang led by thoroughly craven Shishido, push things beyond the point of no return. As do the rowdy but basically decent teenage guys. Unfortunately, Mako has fallen-in-love with one of the boys (Okazaki). Before long, despite Fuji's restraint, the rest of his gang are also thrashing the girls for changing sides. Which leads to violence, death and a climactic knifing by Mako of one of the teen boys who had betrayed the rest of them and joined the yakuza gang. A partial remake of STRAY CAT ROCK – SEX HUNTER (Natsu even has the same character name as actress Kaji in that film – Nikkatsu really should have given the STRAY CAT ROCK co-writer, Atsushi Yamatoya some of the screenplay credit). Director Koretsugu Kurahara is the younger brother of filmmaker Koreyoshi Kurahara (something that causes plenty of confusion).   * * *

BALLAD OF A LONELY GUN-MAN aka GAN WA SAMUSHO OTOKO NO UTASA 1962 85 min. **DIR.** Tokijiro Yamazaki **SCR.** Toshio Matsuura/ Ryuma Takemori **PHOTO COLOR 'SCOPE:** Shigeyoshi Mine

MUSIC: Hajime Kaburagi w/ Hideaki Nitani, Koji Wada, Sanae Nakahara, Reiko Sassamori, Kiyoji Aoyama, Eiji Go, Nobuo Kaneko

BEAST OF THE RED LIGHT DISTRICT aka KEMONO NO IRU MACHI 1958 95 min. DIR. Takumi Furukawa SCR. Teruaki Miyata PHOTO B&W 'SCOPE: Umeo Matsubayashi MUSIC: Taiichiro Kosugi w/ Ryoji Hayama, Shinsuke Ashida, Minako Katsuki, Taishi Umeno, Hiroshi Nihonyanagi

THE BIG BOSS WHO NEEDS NO GUN aka MUTEPPO TAISHO aka THE RECKLESS BOY BOSS 1961 82 min. DIR. Seijun Suzuki SCR. Toshio Matsuura/Ryuzo Nakanishi PHOTO COLOR 'SCOPE: Kazue Nagatsuka MUSIC: Hajime Kaburagi w/ Koji Wada, Mitsuo Sagawa, Mayumi Shimizu, Izumi Ashikawa, Ryoji Hayama, Ichiro Sugai A freewheeling adolescent fantasy about employed-at-a-roller-rink karate student Wada coming to the aid of bar owner Ashikawa and Sugai, her drunken doctor father, when they are victimized by neighborhood mobsters. What could have been routine programmer material is transformed by inventive Suzuki into the perfect Saturday afternoon matinee for adolescent boys itching for adventure and some escape from their humdrum existence. Suzuki achieves much of the fun, boisterous tone in the film by alternating between poles of irony and its complete absence, refusing to resort to condescension. Much of the joy of Suzuki's pictures also comes from his ability to create a fluid perspective of depth and a constantly engaging visual landscape

no matter how lame the storyline (as it is here). Wada is adequate as the young hero, but the film could have benefited from a stronger presence in the lead. * * 1/2

Biographies of Killers

BIOGRAPHIES OF KILLERS aka SHIKAKU RETSUDEN aka KILLERS' LIFE STORIES 1969 87 min. DIR. Shugoro Nishimura SCR. Ichiro Miyagawa PHOTO COLOR 'SCOPE: Shinsaku Himeda MUSIC: Masayoshi Ikeda w/ Hideki Takahashi, Joe Shishido, Tamio Kawaji, Chieko Matsubara, Eiji Go

BLACK DICE aka KUROI DAISU 1962 70 min. DIR. Yoichi Ushihara SCR. Ichiro Ikeda/Tadaaki Yamazaki w/ Hideaki Nitani, Reiko Sassamori, Koji Wada, Ryoji Hayama

BLACK PANTHER BITCH M. aka KUROI MEHYO EMU 1974 74 min. DIR. Koretsugu Kurahara SCR. Norio Miyashita/Koichi

Black Panther Bitch M

Nakajima **PHOTO COLOR 'SCOPE:**
Teruo Hatanaka **MUSIC:** Tsuneji
Ozawa **w/** Reiko Ike, Mikio Narita,
Chiako Mori, Shunji Imai, Ichiro
Kijima, Milton Ishibashi
Ike, star of Toei Studios' GIRL BOSS,
TERRIFYING GIRLS SCHOOL and
ELDER SISTER/OCHO film series
lends her services to Nikkatsu for this
low-key action film. It is hitwoman-
time aided and abetted with karate
antics at *the* biggest pink film studio
(as of mid-1971). However, despite a
small glimpse of nudity, this is not a
pink film but one of their infrequent
(for the 1970s), comparatively more
mainstream movies. Ike portrays a
ninja-trained assassin ordered by
never-seen shadowy higher ups to
kill ruthless maverick businessman
Narita. He is protected by sadistic
Imai and his large gang of bodyguards. Several of Ike's murder attempts fail and midway through she
suffers in a fall running from Narita's
men. Ironically, she is taken in by
Narita's estranged wife and daughter
who nurse her back to health. There
are several slow patches as well as
some boring scenes of Imai's men
chasing Ike on foot. But there are
also some exhilarating setpieces such
as Ike dodging bullets in a darkened
warehouse as well as deeper-than-
usual character development, especially from Narita and Mori as his
wife. Ike has very little dialogue herself, going the Meiko Kaji-FEMALE
CONVICT SCORPION route of
quiet-but-deadly, entering a realm at
certain times of silent movie emoting
that testifies to just how underrated
she is as an actress. Sultry, intelligent
Ike also possesses the ability – as can
be seen even more blatantly in her
sometimes sexist Toei pictures – to
retain her dignity in even the most
demeaning situations. * * *

BLACK SUN aka KUROI TAIYO
1964 95 min. **DIR.** Koreyoshi
Kurahara **SCR.** Nobuo Yamada
PHOTO B&W 'SCOPE: Mitsuji Kanau
MUSIC: Toshiro Mayuzumi (performed by the Max Roach Quartet,
with Abbey Lincoln) **w/** Tamio
Kawaji, Chico Roland, Yuko
Chishiro, Hideji Otaki
A homeless delinquent (Kawaji)
– that some critics have suggested
may be an older version of Kawaji's
character from Kurahara's 1960's
THE WARPED ONES (since they are
both jazz fanatics and hang out at the
same jazz bar) – lives in the attic of a
ruined church, which he miraculously
has furnished with electricity to play
his jazz records. A wounded black GI
with a machine gun, on the run after
an unspecified violent incident, hides

in Kawaji's loft. Unable to understand each other because of the language barrier, they alternately hold each other hostage. At one point, when Kawaji has the upper hand, he paints the GI's face with whitewash and his own in black face, decorating his wreck of a car with clownish *tekiya* marketing slogans in an attempt to get by MP roadblocks. They manage to do so, but Kawaji's anger over the GI killing his dog (named Monk after Thelonius) and general frustration at the fugitive's perpetual fear and anger, leads him to humiliate the GI in front of his friends at the jazz bar. They are interrupted by a yakuza gang, who think they really are *tekiya* poaching on their turf, and a fight erupts. The two escape, heading to the sea, the GI's idealistic dream. But reaching the water, they find only a polluted inlet and garbage-strewn sand dunes, a wasteland mirroring the hell of both homeless men. When the GI finally breaks down, weeping uncontrollably, Kawaji softens and decides to help him. At dawn, the police and American soldiers close in, and the two run to a nearby neighborhood, climbing to the roof of a building where a large balloon is moored. Strapping himself to the rigging, the GI begs Kawaji to cut him loose. The MPs reach the roof, and the fugitive, crying for his mother, wafts adrift upwards towards the setting sun as Kawaji is snared by the authorities. Bleak, anarchic, exhilarating but, at times, exasperating, partly due to too long a middle third (which could have easily been trimmed of ten minutes). Nevertheless, startling and memorable, despite not always firing on all cylinders. * * *

BLACK TIGHT KILLERS aka ORE NI SAWARU TO ABU NAIZE aka DON'T TOUCH ME, I'M DANGEROUS 1966 87 min. **DIR.** Yasuharu Hasebe **SCR.** Ryuzo Nakanishi/Michio Tsuzuki **PHOTO COLOR 'SCOPE:** Kazue Nagatsuka **MUSIC:** Naozumi Yamamoto w/ Akira Kobayashi, Chieko Matsubara, Akemi Kita, Mieko Nishio, Tomoko Hamakawa, Eiji Go, Bokuzen Hidari
A wild tongue-in-cheek gangster/spy spoof with Kobayashi a just-returned-from-Nam combat photographer up against both Japanese yakuza and American gangsters trying to find a hidden cache of war-time gold.

Black Tight Killers

He is aided and abetted by a weird band of girl assassins throughout the picture while trying to rescue sweetheart, stewardess Matsubara. There seems to be a heavy Seijun Suzuki influence here with the group of girl killers using razor-sharp 45 rpm records as weapons and pieces of thrown, chewed bubble gum to momentarily blind Kobayashi. Each time one of the female assassins bites the dust, the expiring gal has a sentimental death scene with Kobayashi that is very funny. I mentioned a Suzuki influence – this is actually the equal of some of Suzuki's films. The first feature directed by Hasebe, one of Nikkatsu's most talented directors in the late 1960s. A true pop art classic. * * * 1/2

BLIND WOMAN'S CURSE, see RISING DRAGON series (RISING DRAGON GHOST STORY)

BLOOD RED WATER IN THE CHANNEL aka KAIKYO CHI NI SOMETE aka THE STRAITS AWASH IN BLOOD 1961 84 min. Dɪʀ. Seijun Suzuki Scʀ. Goro Tanada Pʜᴏᴛᴏ ᴄᴏʟᴏʀ 'ꜱᴄᴏᴘᴇ: Shigeyoshi Mine Mᴜꜱɪᴄ: Seitaro Omori w/ Koji Wada, Ryoji Hayama, Yuriko Hanabusa, Mayumi Shimizu, Torahiko Hamada, Eiji Go
Nikkatsu, Daiei, Toei, Shintoho and Toho Studios all made plenty of sea-going crime action films in the late fifties and early sixties, many of them dealing with coast guard or fishermen heroes in bloody battle with smugglers and pirates. Most were fairly innocuous, Saturday afternoon timewasters for adolescent boys. It should not surprise anyone familar with director Suzuki during this period that he would be responsible for one of the better ones. Koji Wada is an enthusiastic greenhorn member of the coast guard whose big brother Hayama is a prime mover in an extremely brutal immigrant smuggling gang. The film mostly

deals with Wada's attempts to bond with his embittered older sibling, efforts to little effect until the end of the movie when Wada is caught on board the villain's boat, undercover as an immigrant. The acting is quite good, especially Wada, Hayama, villain Go and Shimizu, Hayama's defiant prostitute girlfriend who stops a bullet for him at the climax. Once again programmer material becomes something more in Suzuki's already expert hands. * * *

BLOOD VENDETTA aka GYA-KEN NITSU SAKAZUKI 1971 89 min. Dɪʀ. Takashi Nomura Scʀ. Takashi Nomura/Susumu Shindo Pʜᴏᴛᴏ ᴄᴏʟᴏʀ 'ꜱᴄᴏᴘᴇ: Shigeyoshi Mine Mᴜꜱɪᴄ: Taichiro Kosugi w/ Hideki Takahashi, Masako Izumi, Yoshi Kato, Mikio Narita, Asao Uchida, Tatsuya Fuji, Toru Abe, Miyoko Akaza

Blood Vendetta

BLOODY BREAKWATER
aka CHI NO GAMPEKI 1958
97 min. Dir. Takumi Furukawa
Scr. Toshio Matsuura/Kiichi Ishii/
Yoshishige Matsubara Photo B&W
'scope: Umeo Matsubayashi
Music: Taiichiro Kosugi
w/ Michitaro Mizushima, Sachiko
Hidari, Mari Shiraki, Masumi Okada

Bloody Feud

BLOODY FEUD aka RYUKE-
TSU NO KOSO aka BLOOD FOR
BLOOD 1971 86 min. Dir.
Yasuharu Hasebe Scr. Shuichi
Nagahara Photo color 'scope:
Yoshihiro Yamazaki Music: Hajime
Kaburagi w/ Joe Shishido,
Makoto Sato, Meiko Kaji, Tatsuya
Fuji, Ryohei Uchida, Eiji Go, Gen
Mitamura, Jotaro Togami, Tsuneya
Oki, Yoshi Kato A uniformly excel-
lent, no-nonsense, straightforward
yakuza saga with Shishido return-
ing to his gang after a prison stay,
joining up with lone wolf pals Sato
and Fuji for vengeance after first his

young, married pal Oki, then his boss
is murdered by evil Togami's men.
Noteworthy for Hasebe's attention
to character detail in Shishido and
Fuji's last hours together alive, both
before and immediately after the
climactic, bloody revenge massacre.
This also has one of underrated and
comparatively-unknown-in-the-west
composer Kaburagi's most exciting
and memorable scores, a testament
to just how much music can add to a
story's already intoxicating momentum and suspense. * * * *

Bloody Territories

BLOODY TERRITORIES aka
KOIKI BORYOKU – RYUKETSU
NO SHIMA 1969 87 min. Dir.
Yasuharu Hasebe Scr. Kazuo Aoki
Photo color 'scope: Muneo Ueda
Music: Hajime Kaburagi w/ Akira
Kobayashi, Tatsuya Fuji, Tadao
Nakamaru, Ryoji Hayama, Yuriko
Hime, Hiroshi Nawa, Jiro Okazaki,
Yoshi Kato A stubborn boss refus-
es to go along with a squeezeplay

consolidation decision made by the majority of bosses in the wake of police crackdowns. At this "good" clan's HQ, head *kobuns* (apprentices) Nakamaru and Kobayashi confer with their comrades about the potential for violence. A kitten frolicking in the arms of Fuji shows the gang has its decent side. All one has to do is imagine a member of rival Hayama's mob enjoying the same childlike play, and their uniqueness becomes apparent. Hasebe then subverts our expectations by showing Kobayashi and Fuji torturing an opposing clan member to get info by twisting a knife in the guy's arm – these fellows may be capable of sensitive feelings, but they are also capable of brutality. Hasebe further turns things on their head by having honorable Hayama continuing to serve the evil rival *oyabun*, killing other honorable fellows just because they are in a different clan. His part in trying to stop the killing of rival underboss Nakamaru (who has just met with them under a truce) then, when he is unsuccessful, being the one to deliver the *coup de grace* stab to the heart, is a case in point. This death scene where Nakamaru is ambushed as he descends a shadowy highrise stairway is a notably realistic death scene. After Nakamaru's been pierced numerous times, Hayama pushes through his heartless *kobuns* to reach his former comrade. Nakamaru is so drained of blood, he is unable to speak. His struggling-for-breath as he gestures to Hayama to finish him off, had me believing he was actually at death's door. As Hayama tearfully cradles the succumbing Nakamaru, he reluctantly bestows the last deadly blow. The story abounds with unexpected

contradictions. Villainous nightclub manager Nawa, a wife-beating lone wolf whose woman has nursed Kobayashi back to health after he was attacked, ends up coming to Kobayashi's aid in the climactic massacre, thus insuring his own death. Kobayashi manages to survive long enough to kill off everyone else, then expires himself. A grim, perversely satisfying film. * * *

The Boss's Wife

THE BOSS'S WIFE aka ANEGO aka FUJITA GORO NO ANEGO aka YOUNGER SISTER aka THE WOMAN GAMBLER 1969 88 min. **DIR.** Buichi Saito **ORIG. STORY:** Goro Fujita **SCR.** Takeshi Aoyama **PHOTO COLOR 'SCOPE:** Kenji Hagiwara **MUSIC:** Taiichiro Kosugi **w/** Hiroko Ogi, Akira Kobayashi, Shinjiro Ebara, Ryohei Uchida, Jiro Okazaki, Ryoji Hayama   Disappointing when you consider that the two main stars and the director have made much superior films. Ogi is wife to boss Ebara. One

Branded to Kill

of the strongest scenes comes right near the top when Ogi grabs the razor sharp blade of an assassin's knife after her husband has been attacked, preventing the killer from making another lunge. She saves her spouse's life – at least for awhile – and the panicked attacker flees. But Ebara ain't long for this world. Kobayashi is a lone wolf who helps Ogi get vengeance. It is unfortunate that this is a bit anemic on the action. Also, considering that 90% of the films made from ex-yakuza Goro Fujita's stories are very good, there is no excuse for this relatively lackluster outing.   * * 1/2

BOSS WITHOUT FORM aka SUGATA NAKI KAOYAKU 1958 60 min. **DIR.** Mitsuo Wakasugi **SCR.** Keiichi Abe **PHOTO B&W 'SCOPE:** Kan Inoue **MUSIC:** Seiichiro Ueno w/ Toshie Takada, Tetsuji Hattori

stills from **Branded to Kill**

BRANDED TO KILL aka KOROSHI NO RAKUIN 1967 91 min. **DIR.** Seijun Suzuki **SCR.** Hachiro Guryu/Takeo Kimura/ Atsushi Yamatoya/Chusei Sone **PHOTO B&W 'SCOPE:** Kazue Nagatsuka **MUSIC:** Naozumi Yamamoto w/ Joe Shishido, Koji Nanbara, Annu Mari, Mariko Ogawa, Isao Tamagawa

A *tour-de-force* masterpiece that has to be seen to be believed. Not a traditional yakuza film per se, although probably the closest to some kind of genre. Extreme violence as well as dreamlike surrealism envelopes hitman, Shishido, who we can only deduce is going insane. One particular scene where he shoots up a drainpipe, hitting an eye doctor in the eye who has just removed a patient's glass eye, is simultaneously funny and shocking. Through no fault of his own, he bungles his next job when a butterfly settles on the sight of his high-powered rifle. A stoic hitwoman (Mari) driving a sportscar, a dead bird with a nail through its throat hanging from the dash rearview, has a strange affinity with Shishido. Despite the fact she has been assigned to kill him for his foul-up, Shishido develops an attraction for her. They make love in a shadowy room filled with dead butterflies. There are many other images of like strangeness, and this is one film I can recommend without reservation whether there are English subtitles or not. A cross between ERASERHEAD-era Lynch, Sam Fuller, Jean-Pierre Melville, Luis Bunuel, Fellini and ? . Suzuki is a true original. He had made scores of yakuza, action and exploitation films at Nikkatsu starting in the mid-fifties. BRANDED TO KILL was the straw that broke the Nikkatsu president's proverbial back. Suzuki had already been warned about his eccentric visual touches in such films as TATTOOED LIFE (1965) and TOKYO DRIFTER (1966). After BRANDED TO KILL, he was fired. Luckily, the film was still released, though lowermost on a double bill. Surprisingly enough, there was a genuine outcry at his dismissal. His films had been steadily develop-ing cult status amongst students and intellectuals as well as others in the film community. However, even their protests and demonstrations could not get Suzuki reinstated at Nikkatsu. He ended up suing them. The case dragged on for years before he finally won. Nikkatsu was basically produc-ing nothing but *pink* sex films by then and the industry joined together in blackballing Suzuki. In the meantime, Suzuki survived the years between 1967 – 1977 (when his next under-rated feature, TALE OF SORROW AND SADNESS aka HISHU MO-NOGATARI was finally released) by directing commercials. * * * *

BURNING FLESH aka MOERU NIKUTAI 1957 81 min. **Dir.** Isamu Kosugi **Scr.** Tetsu Sueyama **Photo B&W:** Toshitaro Nakao **Music:** Taiichiro Kosugi w/ Michitaro Mizushima, Hisako Tsukuba, Joe Shishido   Actress Tsukuba was Nikkatsu's resident sex bomb in the late 1950s. Most of her pictures, in-cluding BURNING FLESH and the next BREASTS AND BULLETS, had sleaze-noir/adults only status. Still the content of these pictures was fairly innocent considerng what came later.

BREASTS AND BULLETS aka CHIBUSA TO JUDAN 1958 80 min. **Dir.** Hiroshi Noguchi **Scr.** Iwao Yamazaki **Photo color 'scope:** Kazue Nagatsuka **Music:** Naozumi Yamamoto w/ Hisako Tsukuba, Hideaki Nitani, Joe Shishido, Minako Katsuki, Ko Nishimura

Callous Gamblers

CALLOUS GAMBLERS aka BAKUTO MUJO aka THE GAMBLER'S LADY 1969 89 min. **Dir.** Buichi Saito **Scr.** Seiji Hoshikawa **Photo color 'scope:** Kenji Hagiwara **Music:** Taiichiro Kosugi w/ Chieko Matsubara, Tetsuya Watari, Shigeru Tsuyuguchi, Hiroko Ogi, Hiroyuki Nagato, Shoki Fukae, Hiroshi Kondo, Kaku Takashina   An atypical *ninkyo* yakuza saga focusing on Matsubara who becomes a geisha after her beau Watari goes up the river following his attack on a yakuza boss he believes ordered the death of his *oyabun*. She undergoes much anguish as she is subjected to abuse from the wife and child of a man (Kondo) who had his arm chopped off by Watari. The villain gang also harasses her. However, badass Tsuyuguchi gradually develops a respect and affection for Matsubara, something that gradually awakens his conscience. This leads to an estrangement from his clan, but cannot keep Watari from seeking vengeance on him once he gets released. It is only through Matsubara's intervention in their one-on-one duel in a sun-dappled field that the two agree to a truce, and Tsuyuguchi decides to leave town. Tragedy still mushrooms when Watari cannot leave his vendetta alone and decides to wipe out bad boss Takashina and his henchmen in a protracted swordfight. The story climaxes on a downbeat, bittersweet note. Writer Hoshikawa can always be counted on to deliver a decent script, and this is one of his best with memorable, fleshed-out characters. Matsubara and Tsuyuguchi are especially good, and Nagato is amusing as a strange, one-eyed tattoo artist. Taiichiro Kosugi is generally known for anonymous-sounding scores. But here he provides some excellent music, subtly augmenting the impact of the film. * * *

CAT GIRL GAMBLING aka TOBA NO MESU NEKO series

CAT GIRL GAMBLING aka TOBA NO MESU NEKO aka SHE-CAT GAMBLING 1965 88 mn. Dir. Hiroshi Noguchi Scr. Kenzo Asada/Jun Ueda Photo B&W 'scope: Toshitaro Nakao Music: Tomokazu Kawabe

Cat Girl Gambling (#1)

w/ Yumiko Nogawa, Hideaki Nitani, Ichiro Sugai, Tatsuya Fuji, Keisuke Yukioka, Eiji Go, Hiroshi Kono, Kaku Takashina   An unpretentious film with a gritty noirish flavor detailing novice dice gambler Nogawa's initiation into back room yakuza gambling in the mid-sixties urban jungle. Nitani is a worldweary lone wolf who takes her under his wing, training her in the art of crooked dice games and tattooing her to give her street credibility with the more macho hoodlums. Sugai is her vice cop uncle who, along with his young sidekick detective Fuji, is investigating gambling – rigged dice games in particular – but is unaware Nogawa is part of it. In a flashback, we learn that Nogawa's ne'er-do-well dad was an expert at manufacturing loaded dice. There is plenty of backstreet ambience as well as well-staged gambling scenes with Nogawa learning her trade. It all culminates in a game for various bosses and their crooked

Cat Girl Gambling (#2)

businessmen clients. Nogawa gets caught in the middle between Nitani's benefactor and her old employers Takashina and Go. The last big game escalates until violence erupts bringing on a police raid led by Sugai. The climax finds Takashina fighting Nitani and quaking-in-her-boots Nogawa who is brandishing a knife for the first time. Nitani dies, Takashina is arrested and Nogawa somehow remains free to employ her newfound wisdom to survive in the criminal demimonde. Although noticeably short on action until the last ten minutes, this still seems to be the first of the knife/sword-wielding female yakuza series – a bit of a groundbreaker! Noguchi's direction is low-key and, along with the street-savvy script by Asada/Ueda, elicits some genuine *jitsuroku* credibility. Much credit must also be given to the performers, especially Nogawa, Nitani and Sugai. Nogawa is an excellent actress and is probably best known by film buffs for her portray-als in Seijun Suzuki's GATE OF FLESH (1964), STORY OF A PROS-TITUTE (SHUNPU DEN) (1965) and CARMEN OF KAWACHI (KAWACHI KARUMEN) (1966). She also did many yakuza and samurai films. Much of CAT GIRL GAMBLING's emotional resonance and impact stems from Nogawa's seemingly effortless but gutwrench-ing ability to coax empathy from the viewer. #1 of 3 films   * * * 1/2

CAT GIRL GAMBLING – NAKED FLESH PAID INTO THE POT aka TOBA NO MESU NEKO – SU HADA NO TSUBO FURI aka DEBT PAID WITH NAKED FLESH 1965   86 MIN.   DIR. Hiroshi Noguchi

SCR. Kenzo Asada/Kazuo Nishida PHOTO B&W 'SCOPE: Kazue Nagatsuka   MUSIC: Tomokazu Kawabe   w/ Yumiko Nogawa, Hideaki Nitani, Tatsuya Fuji, Ryuji Kita, Fujio Suga   #2 of 3 films

CAT GIRL GAMBLING – GAME OF SHARPENED FANGS aka TOBA NO MESU NEKO – SHA KIBA NO SHOBU 1966 80 min. DIR. Hiroshi Noguchi   SCR. Kenzo Asada/Kazuo Nishida   PHOTO B&W 'SCOPE: Toshitaro Nakao   MUSIC: Tomokazu Kawabe   w/ Yumiko Nogawa, Eiji Go, Joe Shishido, Yoko Yamamoto, Daisaburo Hirata #3 and final in series

Cat Girl Gambling (#3)

CHERRY BLOSSOM LOYALTY OFFERING aka SAKURA SAKAZUKI series

CHERRY BLOSSOM LOYALTY OFFERING – CHIVALROUS BROTHERS aka SAKURA SAKA-

ZUKI – GI KYODAI 1969 83 min.
DIR. Nobuo Nakagawa **SCR.** Tokubei
Wakao/Kazuo Nishida **PHOTO COLOR**
'SCOPE: Toshitaro Nakao **MUSIC:**
Hideo Ozawa w/ Hideki Takahashi,
Hideo Murata, Saburo Kitajima,
Sanae Kitabayashi, Kichijiro Ueda,
Harumi Matsukaze, Midori Komatsu,
Kunio Kaga   Nobuo Nakagawa is
another candidate for most under-
rated Japanese director, mainly due
to the fact his career was relegated
almost entirely to genre films: *kaidan*
(horror/ghost story), samurai and
yakuza films in the fifties and sixties.
However, even the predominantly
snobbish Japanese critical establishment *did* sit up and take notice of two
of his most stunning achievements:
GHOST OF YOTSUYA (1959) and
HELL (JIGOKU) (1961) for Shintoho
Studios. Many of his later films for
Toei and Nikkatsu, though amounting
to only a handful in number compared to more prolific directors, are
stunningly original entertainments
more than worthy of rediscovery.
#1 of 2 films

**CHERRY BLOSSOM LOYALTY
OFFERING – GAMBLING CODE**
aka SAKURA SAKAZUKI – JINGI
aka HONOR AND HUMANITY
aka THE SAKURA CODE 1969
83 min. **DIR.** Seiichiro Uchikawa
SCR. Iwao Yamazaki **PHOTO COLOR**
'SCOPE: Izumi Hagiwara w/ Hideki
Takahashi, Saburo Kitajima, Hideo
Murata, Meiko Kaji, Takashi Kanda,
Kinzo Shin, Sanae Kitabayashi
Like the above CHIVALROUS
BROTHERS, GAMBLING CODE
is directed by another old master of
chanbara almost exclusively of the
jidai geki samurai variety. Although
like Nakagawa a veteran of Shintoho

in the fifties, Uchikawa is probably
best known for SAMURAI FROM
NOWHERE (DOJO YABURI) and
ONE-ARMED SWORDSMAN
(TANGE SAZEN), both starring
Tetsuro Tanba, both from 1964 and
Shochiku Studios.

*still and admat for **Cherry Blossom
Loyalty Offering #2 (top and below)***

In 1969, those kinds of films were on
the wane. Many good directors were

finding themselves high-and-dry, even when it came to bread-and-butter assignments. Uchikawa found most of his later work in TV as his movie career faded. #2 of 2 films

CHIVALROUS LIFE aka TOSEI ICHIDAI 1965 85 min. DIR. Buichi Saito SCR. Tatsuo Asano/Goro Tanabe PHOTO COLOR 'SCOPE: Kenji Hagiwara MUSIC: Taiichiro Kosugi w/ Hideki Takahashi, Kayo Matsuo, Masako Izumi, Shinsuke Ashida, Nobuo Kaneko

Chivalrous Life

CHIVALROUS MAN – JUNK-YARD OF LIFE aka TOSEININ – INOCHI NO SUTEBA 1971 86 min. DIR. Akinori Matsuo SCR. Kinya Naoi PHOTO COLOR 'SCOPE: Kazumi Iwasa MUSIC: Hajime Kaburagi w/ Hideki Takahashi, Tadao Nakamaru, Etsuko Nami, Toru Abe, Kanjuro Arashi, Shiro Otsuji, Shinsuke Ashida, Shiro Yanase, Shoki Fukae, Machiko Yashiro

CHIVALROUS RAMPAGE aka ABARE KISHIDO 1965 95 min. DIR. Isamu Kosugi SCR. Ryuzo Nakanishi/Kazuo Nishida PHOTO B&W 'SCOPE: Shigeyoshi Mine MUSIC: Taiichiro Kosugi w/ Joe Shishido, Tetsuya Watari, Yoshie Mizutani, Chieko Matsubara, Yuji Kodaka, Hiroshi Nihonyanagi, Eiji Go Disappointing action-cum-farce with Shishido and sidekick as hustlers back from America dotting their spiels and come-ons with English slang. Watari, in his first major role, is pretty much wasted as a champion motorcycle racer who teams up with his biker buddies and Shishido to do battle with the international gangsters/smugglers Nihonyanagi and Go, who are menacing everyone in sight. Female leads Matsubara and the extremely charismatic Mizutani are, as usual, criminally underused, emerging as not much more than window-dressing. But Shishido and Mizutani are great to watch in even the more mundane moments. If only the film had a more potent delivery in the action department.   * *

CHIVALROUS THREE PROVINCES – FLOWER-COVERED PATH OF SWORDS aka YUKYO SAN GOKUSHI – TEKKA NO HANAMICHI aka THE SWORD GAMBLERS 1968 90 min. DIR. Akinori Matsuo SCR. Seiji Hoshikawa/ Akinori Matsuo PHOTO COLOR 'SCOPE: Kazumi Iwasa MUSIC: Masayoshi Ikeno w/ Yujiro Ishihara, Akira Kobayashi, Hideki Takahashi, Yuji Kodaka, Ruriko Asaoka, Ryoji Hayama, Eijiro Yanagi, Shiro Osaka, Masao Mishima Machiko Yashiro Despite the potent writing team of

Hoshikawa and director Matsuo, this is no more than a just decent, not particularly memorable *ninkyo* yakuza programmer. However, there are several potently choreographed swordfight setpieces. One of Nikkatsu's bigger efforts for 1968, with three of its most popular male stars (Ishihara, Kobayashi and Takahashi) and probably its biggest female performer (Asaoka) on board as the headliners. Perhaps its greatest liability is a somewhat more contrived and convoluted story than usual. Ishihara and Takahashi are young friends in Mishima's gang who are disillusioned with their boss when he begins to kowtow to his unprincipled rivals. Enter smart aleck lone wolf killer, the one-eyed Kobayashi.

Chivalrous Three Provinces

The three change back and forth between being friends or enemies in several combinations before the final protracted battle where the trio unite in common cause. Takahashi bites the dust, and Kobayashi bids sad farewell to wander.   * * 1/2

CHIVALROUS OUTLAW
aka YUKYO BURAI 1963 78 min.
DIR. Hiroshi Noguchi **SCR.** Iwao Yamazaki/Ei Ogawa **PHOTO B&W** **'SCOPE:** Yasuichiro Yamazaki **MUSIC:** Hajime Kaburagi w/ Joe Shishido, Hideaki Nitani, Hideo Murata, Chieko Matsubara, Mari Shiraki, Minako Kazuki, Eiji Go, Hiroshi Sugie, Daisaburo Hirata, Shoki Fukae

CHIVALRY BROKEN FROM ALL SIDES aka NINKYO HAPPO YABURE 1966 76 min. **DIR.** Motomu (Tan) Iida **SCR.** Yoshi Hattori **PHOTO B&W 'SCOPE:** Kazue Nagatsuka **MUSIC:** Seitaro Omori w/ Hideki Takahashi, Yumiko Nogawa, Shinsuke Ashida, Minoru Oki, Ichiro Sugai, Yoko Yamamoto

CLANDESTINE ZERO LINE aka MIKKO ZERO RAIN aka SECRET ZERO ZONE 1960 83 min. **DIR.** Seijun Suzuki **SCR.** Yasuo Yokoyama **PHOTO B&W 'SCOPE:** Shigeyoshi Mine/Toshitaro Nakao **MUSIC:** Taiichiro Kosugi w/ Hiroyuki Nagato, Yuji Kodaka, Sanae Nakahara, Mayumi Shimizu, Tomoo Nagai, Kaku Takashina A fast-moving noirish action picture with Nagato and Kodaka newspaper reporters on a crime beat. Nagato, however, is driven by some inner demon and resorts to anything that will get the job done, including bribing a sleazy drug dealer for tips on underworld action, then reporting his special knowledge to the police so he can get great photos of the ensuing busts. This practice, as well as other

Chivalrous Villain

Chivalry Broken from All Sides

unethical, unscrupulous behavior, puts him at odds with straight arrow Kodaka. Events spiral out-of-control when he crosses violent, sexy dragon lady Nakahara on not only a professional but personal level.

Clandestine Zero Line

Nakahara is behind a foreign freighter that in reality is an extremely trashy sin den of illicit drugs and prostitution. The scenes on board the ship depict a lived-in hellish ambience of sordid sex and vice that makes the soon to follow wild violence all the more thrilling. In the end, Nagato and Kodaka are captured in the coal pit of the boat. They barely escape with their lives when the police bust in at the climax. Nagato, in fact, is shot in the leg by villainess Nakahara, and, even after the gang has been arrested, he refuses help from Kodaka and good girl Shimizu, limping away down the wharf, leaving a trail of blood. Suzuki turns what would have been cliche programmer stuff

in lesser hands, into a truly gritty, sometimes gut-wrenching thrill-ride through an atmospheric underworld of real characters. * * * 1/2

CLASSROOM RENEGADES aka HIKO SHONEN aka DELINQUENT YOUNG BOYS 1965 86 min. **DIR.** Kazuo Kawabe **SCR.** Susumu Saji/Kazuo Kawabe **PHOTO B&W 'SCOPE:** Kanji Inoue w/ Kazumasa Negishi, Teppei Nagahama, Hiroshi Miyao, Joji Nakamura, Masaki Koike
Although I have not seen it, this seems to be a more serious film about the cycle of juvenile delinquency that was starting to rear its head in the turbulent early sixties. A gang of five rebellious students are largely ignored by the school faculty who bury their heads in the sand. The boys' activities escalate from stealing food and fighting to extorting money from couples out alone at night to selling false school papers to fellow students – all with the moral support of a local yakuza gang. Finally things come to a head, the boys are split up and permanently separated with the ringleader becoming a ward of the family court. The faculty bicker about who is to blame. At the end, one of the teachers observes a new youth gang shoplifting at a local store.

THE CLEAN-UP aka ARASHI NO YOSHATACHI 1969 100 min. **DIR.** Toshio Masuda **SCR.** Shuichi Nagahara **PHOTO COLOR 'SCOPE:** Yoshihiro Yamazaki **MUSIC:** Harumi Ibe w/ Yujiro Ishihara, Joe Shishido, Tetsuya Watari, Meiko Kaji, Koji Wada, Mitsuo Hamada, Tatsuya Fuji, Eiji Go, Jiro Okazaki, Mie Hama, Sayuri Yoshinaga, Hideaki Nitani,

Yoko Yamamoto, Shoki Fukae, Yoshiro Aoki, Eijiro Yanagi, Ryohei Uchida   A real all-star cast turns out for this modern yakuza yarn. Ishihara and Watari are heads of two different groups trying to one-up an all consuming syndicate. Hama is a high-paid fashion model engaged to the big boss. Watari's bunch kidnap her from a black-tie formal hoping to snag her 100 million yen diamonds. But Ishihara has already made off with the jewels. Soon the syndicate is after both bands of the feuding renegades, and the mayhem begins.

COCKED SANSHIRO aka NUKI UCHI SANSHIRO aka QUICK DRAW SANSHIRO 1962 71 min. DIR. Tokijiro Yamazaki SCR. Akira Saiga PHOTO B&W 'SCOPE: Shigeyoshi Mine MUSIC: Hajime Kaburagi w/ Koji Wada, Ryoji Hayama, Reiko Sassamori, Akira Yamanouchi, Asao Sano, Masahiko Shimazu, Akio Tanaka, Eiji Go

COCKED THUNDER aka NUKI UCHI ABARENBO aka QUICK DRAW THUNDER 1962 94 min. DIR. Isamu Kosugi SCR. Iwao Yamazaki PHOTO COLOR 'SCOPE: Shigeyoshi Mine MUSIC: Taiichiro Kosugi w/ Joe Shishido, Chieko Matsubara, Shoki Fukae, Daisaburo Hirata, Nobuo Kaneko

CRAZED FRUIT aka KURUTTA KAJITSU 1956 86 min. DIR. Ko Nakahira SCR. Shintaro Ishihara PHOTO B&W: Shigeyoshi Mine MUSIC: Toru Takemitsu/Masaru Sato w/ Yujiro Ishihara, Masahiko Tsugawa, Mie Kitahara, Masumi Okada, Shinsuke Ashida, Shintaro Ishihara   The explosive break-out film about *taiyozoku* (sun tribe) kids, bored, middle class youth with no morals and too much time on their hands that, along with Kon Ichikawa's PUNISHMENT ROOM at Daiei Studios (also based on a Shintaro Ishihara story), fomented a *cause celebre* scandal amongst parents and school officials. Vacationing teenage Ishihara and friends have group sex with Kitahara, something that spurs violence and an accidental death. * * *

Crimson Gun

CRIMSON GUN aka KURENAI NO KENJU aka KILLER WITH-OUT A GRAVE 1961 87 min. DIR. Yoichi Ushihara SCR. Toshio Matsuura PHOTO COLOR 'SCOPE: Shinsaku Himeda MUSIC: Taiichiro Kosugi w/ Keiichiro Akagi, Reiko Sassamori, Mari Shiraki, Kazuko Yoshiyuki, Goro Mutsumi, Eitaro Ozawa, Shinsuke Ashida, Shoichi Ozawa   A violent and bizarre action picture, employing some accidental as well as intentional surreal use of color with one of Nikkatsu's subject-matter specialties in the sixties – the lonely, misunderstood hitman. This was Akagi's last film before being killed on February 14, 1961 in a go-kart accident. They must have just literally wrapped a matter of days before the fatal mishap. * * *

Cruel Gun Story

CRUEL GUN STORY aka KENJU ZANKOKU MONOGATARI 1964 86 min. **DIR.** Takumi Furukawa **SCR.** Hisatoshi Kai **PHOTO B&W** 'SCOPE: Saburo Isayama **MUSIC:** Masayoshi Ikeda **w/** Joe Shishido, Akifumi Inoue, Tamio Kawaji, Chieko Matsubara, Yuji Kodaka, Saburo Hiromatsu, Kojiro Kusanagi, Hiroshi Nihonyanagi, Minako Katsuki   A gutsy, noirish extremely atmospheric and violent heist film which shows obvious influences from such pictures as Kubrick's THE KILLING, not to mention Fukasaku's HIGH NOON FOR GANGSTERS.

There are also some striking similarities to Don Siegel's version of THE KILLERS, which was probably being filmed simultaneously to this in California, and Melville's SECOND BREATH (LE DEUXIEME SOUFFLE), which came two years later. Shishido is a sullen, tortured, sunglasses-wearing lone wolf whose kid sister was crippled in a hit-and-run and now resides at a Christian hospital school. He takes on the assignment from a craven gang to hijack a transport carrying racetrack receipts. With brutal friend Kodaka in tow, he recruits spineless hoods Hiromatsu and Inoue, much against their wills. So it is really not a big shock when they attempt a double-cross. Surprisingly caustic in the violence department, undoubtedly to live up to the word CRUEL in the title. There were several Toei Studios pictures around the same time, TALE OF BUSHIDO CRUELTY (1963), MILITARY SPY SCHOOL CRUELTY (1963) and CRUELTY OF THE SHOGUNATE'S DOWNFALL (1964), and it must have crossed the minds of the guys in Nikkatsu marketing to jump on the bandwagon. There is a great noctunal warehouse shootout with Shishido and Kodaka battling the triple-crossing gang who hired them, then escaping through the sewer with the aid of old pal Kawaji and tough chick Katsuki. But Kodaka doesn't survive. Shishido, abetted by another rival gang, kidnaps one of the traitorous boss's loved ones to ransom the return of their left-behind loot. However, in appropriate downbeat fashion, both the hostage and rival gang are killed in an ambush. So it is fortunate that Shishido is simultaneously cornering the treacherous boss at his home, something which ends with a shootout and Shishido absconding with the swag. The greedy second-in-command underboss – who had hired Shishido in the first place – gets ahead and arrives before him at the bar hideout. He promptly wounds Kawaji, then, surprised by a noise, kills Katsuki whom he mistakes for Shishido. Shishido returns and blasts the traitor to death. In turn, Kawaji mistakes Shishido for the underboss and shoots him! Mortally wounded, Shishido topples over a can of kerosene which ignites against a floor heater, giving birth to the climactic inferno. It is unfortunate most of director Furukawa's other films are so hard to see. * * * 1/2

DAI SHIN RIN NI MUKATTI TATSU 1961 85 min. **DIR.** Takashi Nomura **SCR.** Iwao Yamazaki/Kenji Yoshida **PHOTO 'SCOPE:** Minoru Yokoyama **MUSIC:** Seitaro Omori w/ Akira Kobayashi, Tetsuro Tanba, Ruriko Asaoka, Nobuo Kaneko

DANGER PAWS aka YABA IKO TO NARA ZENI NI NARU 1962 82 min. **DIR.** Ko Nakahira **SCR.** Ichiro Ikeda/Tadaki Yamazaki **PHOTO COLOR 'SCOPE:** Shinsaku Himeda w/ Joe Shishido, Ruriko Asaoka, Hiroyuki Nagato, Bokuzen Hidari, Kojiro Kusanagi A comedy/ action/yakuza picture about counterfeiters with probably one of the most bizarre English-language release titles in this book.

DARK STRAITS aka KUROI KAIKYO 1964 103 min. **DIR.** Mio Ezaki **SCR.** Hisatoshi Kai/Iwao Yamazaki **PHOTO COLOR 'SCOPE:** Minoru Yokoyama **MUSIC:** Harumi

Ibe   w/ Yujiro Ishihara, Yukiyo Toake, Ichiro Nakatani, Tatsuya Fuji, Isao Yamagata, Kazuko Yoshiyuki, Yuji Kodaka, Shoki Fukae, Eiji Go Ishihara made quite a few *"moodo/ akushon"* (Japanese pronunciation of phrase "mood/action") pictures at Nikkatsu Studios during the sixties (they were actually called that in the ads and posters), usually teamed with popular leading actress Ruriko Asaoka. These were full of noirish romantic images as well as action. Most of them, though, were not yakuza sagas but more westernized cop or adventure scenarios. This film plus SUNSET HILL, HAWK OF THE HARBOR and several others were exceptions, straying more heavily into yakuza territory, melding romantic melodrama with gangster hijinks.

Dark Straits

DESPERATION aka YABURE KABURE aka WITH THE COURAGE OF DESPERATION 1961 68 min. **DIR.** Koreyoshi

NIKKATSU STUDIOS 409

Kurahara **Scr.** Nobuo Yamada/
Keiichi Abe **Photo B&W 'scope:**
Yoshio Mamiya **w/** Tamio Kawaji,
Misako Watanabe, Taketoshi Naito

DETECTIVE OFFICE 2-3 aka
TANTEI JIMUSHO NIJUSAN
series

DETECTIVE OFFICE 2-3 –
GO TO HELL, BASTARDS!
aka TANTEI JIMUSHO NIJUSAN –
KUTABARE AKUTODOMO
1963 92 min. **Dir.** Seijun Suzuki
Scr. Iwao Yamazaki **Photo color**
'scope: Shigeyoshi Mine **Music:**
Harumi Ibe **w/** Joe Shishido, Tamio
Kawaji, Reiko Sassamori, Nobuo
Kaneko, Kinzo Shin, Naomi Hoshi,
Asao Sano   Bizarre nuttiness
with hep cool cat Shishido in an
Austin Healey working for a detective
bureau to break up a band of hoods
that have stolen weapons from a U.S.
Army base. Much more conventional
than Suzuki's other Shishido thriller
in 1963, YOUTH OF THE BEAST,
but you can still see the irreverent
visual humor straining to be set free,
especially in some hilarious nightclub
scenes, great 1960s rock/R&B/ Dixie-
land (!) hybrid score and, last but not
least, a flaming gas jet finale down
in the villain (Shin)'s cellar. #1 of 2
films * * *

Detective Office 2-3 - Go to Hell,
Bastards! (#1)

DETECTIVE OFFICE 2-3 –
A MAN INTO WOMEN AND
MONEY aka TANTEI JIMUSHO
NIJUSAN – ZENI TO ONNA NI
OTOKO 1963 98 min. **Dir.** Kan
Hanase **Scr.** Tatsuo Asano/Koto
Yamanaka **Photo B&W 'scope:**
Kumenobu Fujioka **Music:**
Masayoshi Ikeda **w/** Joe Shishido,
Ryoji Hayama, Reiko Sassamori,
Naomi Hoshi, Nobuo Kaneko, Asao
Koike, Daisaburo Hirata, Eiji Go,
Hiroshi Nihonyanagi   Although
shot in black-and-white with prob-
ably an even lower budget, director
Hanase's sequel compares favorably
with – and in some ways surpasses –
Suzuki's initial outing. Once again,
the plot is programmer-type stuff,
but Hanase's shot compositions,
orchestration of action and Shishido's

Detective Office 2-3 - Go to Hell,
Bastards! (#1)

charismatic persona carry the day. The saga begins as murder witness, detective Shishido, is assigned by police detective Kaneko to find the killer. Shishido infiltrates a jewel-smuggling mob of Chinese mobsters led by sadistic Koike and somewhat sympathetic Hayama. A bit shocking in that it starts out as a fairly innocu-ous tongue-in-cheek crime caper but by the halfway point turns amazingly violent with plenty of folks biting the dust. The most out-of-left-field killing occurs when a nervous gun-man misses our hero and accidentally shoots gang moll Hoshi who is enjoy-ing a nocturnal tryst with Shishido on a rocky beach. The climactic shootout in a dilapidated mansion in the forest is a standout, with all dying except Shishido. #2 of 2 films * * * 1/2

Detective Office 2-3 - A Man into Women and Money (#2)

DEVILISH WOMAN aka MASHO NO ONNA 1968 83 min. **DIR.** Kan Hanase **SCR.** Kenzo Asada **PHOTO B&W 'SCOPE:** Muneo Ueda **MUSIC:** Akikazu (Koichi?) Sakata w/ Kaoru Oran, Joe Shishido, Ichiro Sugai, Seizaburo Kawazu, Kenji Sugawara, Shoki Fukae

DIAMOND OF THE ANDES aka SEKIDO O KAKERU OTOKO 1968 103 min. **DIR.** Buichi Saito **SCR.** Akira Saiga/Buichi Saito **PHOTO COLOR 'SCOPE:** Yoshihiro Yamazaki **MUSIC:** Naozumi Yamamoto w/ Akira Kobayashi, Akiko Wakabayashi, Tetsuro Tanba, Ryohei Uchida, Nobuo Kaneko, Celia Paul, Eiji Go
Kobayashi is a smuggler with bad luck. Managing to stay alive, he emi-grates to Rio de Janiero (which has a large Japanese population) in search of his parents. He discovers that they have committed suicide. Realizing Rio is as good as anyplace else, he changes his name and finds work. Once again misfortune finds him. His former smuggling partners are there in Rio. What is worse, he sees his girlfriend Wakabayashi with the gang boss and learns that the man coerced her into marrying him. Kobayashi decides to stay calm and not act im-mediately. However, two of the boss's subordinates (Go, Uchida) spot him and decide he should be eliminated. Meanwhile, a detective (Tanba) ar-rives from Japan to arrest Kobayashi. Kobayashi manages to convince Tanba to give him a couple of days to tie up loose ends. He then tries to thwart a smuggling operation in progress but fails. It turns out that the boss's two lieutenants have killed the headman. Kobayashi snatches away

his girl Wakabayashi and is battling the last villain (Uchida) beside the famous Amazon waterfalls when cop Tanba intervenes.

Document of Blood

DOCUMENT OF BLOOD aka SENKETSU NO KIROKU aka RECORDS OF BLOODSHED 1970 93 min. **DIR.** Takashi Nomura **SCR.** Seiichiro Yamaguchi/Iwao Yamazaki **PHOTO COLOR 'SCOPE:** Shigeyoshi Mine **MUSIC:** Taiichiro Kosugi w/ Akira Kobayashi, Takahiro Tamura, Eiji Okada, Kumi Mizuno, Jiro Okazaki, Takehiro Nakamura, Yoshiro Aoki, Eiji Go A very good saga of Kobayashi, Tamura and Okazaki coming into contact with their former commanding officer (Okada) who had massacred a group of his own men when caught in a tight spot in nocturnal combat. He is now a yakuza bigwig with political connections and will do anything to keep this secret from coming to light. Sparks fly from the thespian pyrotechnics amongst Kobayashi, Tamura and Okada. Another of many candidates for most downbeat yakuza picture – everyone dies, even Kumi Mizuno. * * *

DOWNHILL YOUTH aka WAKAI KEISHA 1959 78 min. **DIR.** Katsumi Nishikawa **SCR.** Ichiro Ikeda/Ei Ogawa **PHOTO B&W** **'SCOPE:** Saburo Isayama **MUSIC:** Masayoshi Ikeda w/ Tamio Kawaji, Ruriko Asaoka, Keiichiro Akagi

DRIFTER aka NAGAREMONO aka THE RAMBLER series

THE DRIFTER RETURNS FROM THE SEA aka UMI KARA KITA NAGAREMONO 1960 82 min. **DIR.** Tokujiro Yamazaki **SCR.** Iwao Yamazaki/Hisao Ogawa **PHOTO COLOR 'SCOPE:** Shinsaku Himeda **MUSIC:** Seitaro Omori w/ Akira Kobayashi, Ruriko Asaoka, Hisako Tsukuba, Joe Shishido, Tamio Kawaji, Ryoji Hayama An almost carbon copy of Kobayashi's antics in his better known action series, THE WANDERING GUITARIST, from the same time frame. That series only occasionally shined through its formula, largely thanks to director Buichi Saito. Here, though, director Yamazaki paints by the numbers with Kobayashi an ex-cop who likes to play the guitar – what a surprise! – and journeys to a village in a volcanic region to crack a gang of smugglers who are also strong-arming wildcat oil drillers led by Asaoka's father. Kobayashi never loses a fight, never seems in true jeopardy. Everything is on the level of a Saturday afternoon western serial which, I guess, to be fair, is all this was ever meant to be anyway. Charismatic Shishido does a nice turn as a smiling villain, and it is fun to see Kobayashi and Asaoka barely out of their teens. Otherwise... #1 of 5 films * *

Duel aka *Endless Duel*

SEA TRIP, HARBOR WIND
aka UMI O WATARU HATOBA
NO KAZE aka VOLCANO WIND
1960 78 min. DIR. Tokujiro
Yamazaki SCR. Iwao Yamazaki/
Hisao Ogawa PHOTO COLOR 'SCOPE:
Shinsaku Himeda MUSIC: Seitaro
Omori w/ Akira Kobayashi, Ruriko
Asaoka, Joe Shishido, Mari Shiraki,
Akira Yamanouchi #2 of 5 films

A SOUTHERN BEACON aka
NANKAI NO NOROSHI aka
THE RAMBLER ON A PEARL
FARM 1960 81 min. DIR. Tokujiro
Yamazaki SCR. Iwao Yamazaki
PHOTO COLOR 'SCOPE: Kurataro
Takamura MUSIC: Seitaro Omori
w/ Akira Kobayashi, Joe Shishido,
Ruriko Asaoka, Uyako Hori, Mari
Shiraki, Ichiro Sugai #3 of 5 films

RAMPAGING DRIFTER aka O
ABARE FURAIBO aka ANGRY
RAMBLER 1960 79 min. DIR.
Tokujiro Yamazaki SCR. Nobunari
Nakakubo/ Satoshi Ichikawa MUSIC:
Seitaro Omori w/ Akira Kobayashi,
Joe Shishido, Ruriko Asaoka, Kaku
Takashina, Mari Shiraki, Yoko
Minamida #4 of 5 films

RAMBLING IN THE WIND
aka KAZE NI SAKARAU
NAGAREMONO 1961 81 min.
DIR. Tokujiro Yamazaki SCR. Iwao
Yamazaki PHOTO COLOR 'SCOPE:
Minoru Yokoyama MUSIC: Seitaro
Omori w/ Akira Kobayashi, Ruriko
Asaoka, Akira Yamanouchi, Mari
Shiraki #5 and final in series

DUEL aka KETTO aka ENDLESS
DUEL 1967 93 min. DIR. Toshio
Masuda SCR. Toshio Masuda/Kaneo

Ikegami PHOTO COLOR 'SCOPE:
Kurataro Takamura MUSIC: Harumi
Ibe w/ Hideki Takahashi, Akira
Kobayashi, Kayo Matsuo, Toru Abe,
Koji Kawamura, Torahiko Hamada,
Sanae Kitabayashi, Yoshiro Aoki, Yuji
Kodaka, Eiji Go One of a duo
of *ninkyo* films dealing with violent
yakuza clan conflict, both starring
Takahashi and Kobayashi. The other
is called FIGHT aka FRIENDLY
ENEMIES. Judging from the uneven
quality, this seems to be the second
film, with less money and less time
available in the shooting schedule.
There are many similar elements,
especially in the relationship between
upright Takahashi and smart-aleck
lone wolf Kobayashi. This time out,
things are much bigger-than-life, with
some exceedingly broad characterizations as far as the villains are
concerned. Abe gives one of his most
over-the-top performances as the hick
boss, aided not only by his henchmen,
but also his sons (among them, Aoki,
Kodaka and Go giving ridiculously
exaggerated performances). Matsuo
plays the main love interest for
Takahashi, the daughter of the "good"
boss who has been murdered by Abe's
sons. She, too – like Kitabayashi in
FIGHT – is forced into prostitution
while Takahashi is away, and she also
dies in a whorehouse swordfight, this
time by shielding Takahashi from
a swinging blade. Composer Ibe
supplies a very spaghetti western-
influenced soundtrack, with passages
heavily-inspired by Morricone's THE
GOOD, THE BAD AND THE UGLY
theme. Likewise, director Masuda
tailors a couple of the showdowns
between Takahashi and the brothers
along the lines of Sergio Leone, as far
as editing and camera placement. The

film is not bad, but it is less inspired
and less well-paced than FIGHT, with
one truly glaring goof in continuity.
* * *

Duel in the Storm

Eight Hours of Terror

DUEL IN THE STORM aka
ARASHI NO HATASHIJO aka
CHALLENGE OF THE STORM
1968 94 min. DIR. Akinori
Matsuo SCR. Seiji Hoshikawa
PHOTO COLOR 'SCOPE: Kazumi Iwasa
MUSIC: Taiichiro Kosugi   w/ Akira
Kobayashi, Hideki Takahashi, Tamaki
Sawa, Yoko Yamamoto, Yumiko
Nogawa, Ryotaro Sugi, Ichiro Sugai
Kobayashi seeks a chivalrous lifestyle
but is disillusioned when his gang
frames him for murder. Once out
of jail, he goes after the real killer,
which causes open war with his
former mob. Friends Sawa and
Takahashi perish while trying to help.
He is then joined by fellow good guy
Sugi on a revenge binge. This has its
moments, particularly with tubercular
lone wolf Takahashi, but ultimately
cannot transcend much beyond the
usual *ninkyo* formula. * * 1/2

EIGHT HOURS OF TERROR aka
HACHIJIKAN NO KYOFU 1957
78 min. DIR. Seijun Suzuki SCR.
Goro Tanada/Rokuro Tsukiji PHOTO
B&W: Kazue Nagatsuka MUSIC:
Yoshio Nikita   w/ Keiko Shima,
Nobuo Kaneko, Kan Yanagiya,
Hiroshi Kondo, Hideaki Nitani
A cross section of Japanese stereotypes is packed into a bus making
its way through the mountains when
they are hijacked by Yanagiya and
Kondo, sadistic gangsters with a bag
full of loot. Kaneko, a forlorn condemned murderer being transported
and Shima, an intelligent, independent whore, turn out to be the saviors
of the trip. The first third of the film
is taken up with pathetically bad
comedy and cute bits before shifting into high gear with the villains'
arrival. But, except for a few patches,
it is still fairly routine. Shima luring
Kondo into the forest while others try
to free the bus from a muddy rut, then

rolling down the hill with him in a lusty embrace so he will tumble into a bear trap is genuinely suspenseful and delivers bona fide jolts. Later, when the group is temporarily free of the surviving Yanagiya, their bourgeois pettiness is perfectly illustrated as they pass around, in scandalized awe, whore Shima's photo of her black American GI boyfriend. She stands at the head of the bus, her feelings hurt as she watches them, but unashamed. This emerges as one of the film's few touchstones with reality. Finally the band of stalwarts is rescued by the cops while Yanagiya, now commandeering the bus by himself in fevered flight, inadvertently runs over a cliff, ala WAGES OF FEAR.. * * 1/2

ELDER BROTHER aka ANIKI 1962 79 min. **Dir.** Tokujiro Yamazaki w/ Hideaki Nitani, Toshio Sugiyama, Sanae Nakahara, Mayumi Shimizu

END THE DAY WITH DYNA-MITE aka DAINOMAITO NI HI O TSUKERO 1959 92 min. **Dir.** Koreyoshi Kurahara **Scr.** Ichiro Ikeda/Keiichi Abe **Photo B&W** 'scope: Kazumi Iwasa **Music:** Taiichiro Kosugi w/ Akira Kobayashi, Mari Shiraki, Shoji Yasui, Masumi Okada, Ko Nishimura

ESCAPE BETWEEN MIDNIGHT AND DAWN aka GOSEN REIJI NO SHUTSUGOKU 1963 91 min. **Dir.** Tokujiro Yamazaki **Scr.** Ei Ogawa w/ Hideaki Nitani, Tamio Kaswaji, Chieko Matsubara, Mari Shiraki, Eiji Go, Eitaro Ozawa

ESCAPE FROM THE WALL OF DEATH aka SHI NO KABE NO DASSHUTSU 1958 98 min. **Dir.**

Eisuke Takizawa **Scr.** Shintaro Ishihara/Hiroshi Nishijima **Photo B&W** 'scope: Minoru Yokoyama **Music:** Masaru Sato w/ Ryoji Hayama, Akitake Kono, Yoko Minamida, Hisako Tsukuba, Hideaki Nitani, Joe Shishido, Ko Nishimura

Escape from the Wall of Death

ESCAPE IN THE FOG aka YOGIRI NO DASSHUTSU aka 1965 91 min. **Dir.** Isamu Kosugi **Scr.** Ryuzo Nakanishi/Yoshihiro Ishimatsu **Photo B&W** 'scope: Toshitaro Nakeo **Music:** Taiichiro Kosugi w/ Hideaki Nitani, Ryoji Hayama, Yoko Yamamoto

ESCAPED MAN aka TOBOSHA 1959 86 min. **Dir.** Takumi Furukawa **Scr.** Seiji Hoshikawa **Photo B&W** 'scope: Umeo Matsubayashi **Music:** Taiichiro Kosugi w/ Hiroyuki Nagato, Mieko Inagaki, Shigeru Tsuyuguchi

Endless Desire

ENDLESS DESIRE aka HATESHI NAKI YOKUBO 1958 101 min. **DIR.** Shohei Imamura **SCR.** Toshiro Suzuki/Shohei Imamura **PHOTO B&W 'SCOPE:** Shinsaku Himeda **MUSIC:** Toshiro Mayuzumi w/ Hiroyuki Nagato, Misako Watanabe, Ko Nishimura, Sanae Nakahara, Taiji Tonoyama, Takeshi Kato, Ichiro Sugai Despite dismassal by some critics, an early, very dark crime comedy by the master in need of wider rediscovery. A pharmacist (Nishimura), ramen shop owner (Tonoyama), brutal yakuza (Kato), a teacher (Shoichi Ozawa) – all WW2 comrades – and supposedly the sister (Watanabe) of their dead lieutenant, tunnel their way from a vacant storefront to an old air raid shelter now concealed under a butcher shop across the street, all to retrieve a cache of buried military morphine. The humor comes as the hardass landlord (Sugai), believing them to be real estate developers, forces them to hire his slacker teenage son (Nagato) who is in love with Nakahara, the feisty daughter of the butcher shop owner. The greedy five's fortunes go from bad to worse as demolition of the slum is announced by the city, and they suddenly have only a few days left to complete their task. A couple of the five are not who they pretend to be, and events spin into a dominoes-falling spiral of homicides. Then the demolition begins as the area is lashed by a tropical storm. A real gem from Imamura, easily equal to some of his other character-driven tragi-comedies like PIGS AND BATTLESHIPS and THE PORNOGRAPHERS. * * * 1/2

Escape in the Fog** aka **Escape in the Night Mist

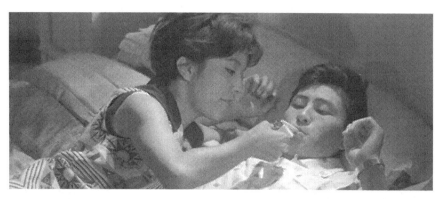

Everything Goes Wrong

EVERYTHING GOES WRONG
aka SUBETE GA KURUTTERU
aka EVERYTHING'S CRAZY 1960
72 min. DIR. Seijun Suzuki   SCR.
Seiji Hoshikawa   PHOTO B&W
'SCOPE: Izumi Hagiwara   MUSIC:
Keitaro Miho   w/ Tamio Kawaji,
Yoshiko Nezu, Shinsuke Ashida,
Tomoko Kataoka, Sayuri Yoshinaga,
Shiro Yanase
An exhilarating over-the-top restless-
youth-goes-wild saga with Kawaji a
frustrated, angry young man with a
chip on his shoulder towards his decent single mom Kataoka and surrogate father figure Ashida. Suzuki has
cinematographer Hagiwara 's camera
swooping, prowling, slithering
through the streets and back alleys
of Tokyo as we follow Kawaji and
his rambunctious footloose friends in
search of thrills. Kawaji knows there
is something more to life but doesn't
know what it is or how to find it.
Nezu is absolutely electrifying as the
pretty little spitfire tomboy in love
with him. In some ways, it is almost
more her film. Suzuki spends a nearly
equal amount of time on her (as well
as a generous amount on some of the
other kids) and it is a mystery why
this incredibly talented actress

did not have a higher profile in Japanese films in the sixties. She is the
spitting image of another Nikkatsu
actress Masako Izumi who also
starred in later Suzuki films such as
THE BASTARD (AKUTARO) and
TATTOOED LIFE as well as the
A MAN'S CREST series. Did she
change her name after only a few
films to Izumi? – otherwise she seems
to have completely dropped off the
radar. Kawaji gets into a spiralling
cycle of more serious scrapes as he
gives into one violent impulse after
another, stealing several cars and
getting into trouble with Yanase's
threadbare yakuza gang. Finally after
Ashida follows him to a tryst with
Nezu, Kawaji explodes and caves in
Ashida's head with a blunt object.
Miraculously Ashida survives in hospital. However, due to the excessive
amount of blood, Kawaji and Nezu
believe him dead, panic and take off
in a stolen car, careening hysterically through the nocturnal streets
until they plow headon into a huge
oncoming truck. In many ways this
echoes the *taiyozoku* (sun tribe) films
CRAZED FRUIT and SEASONS IN
THE SUN as well as Kon Ichikawa's
PUNISHMENT ROOM, all from
the late fifties. It also has elements in

common with Nagisa Oshima's great CRUEL STORY OF YOUTH, though noticeably less pretentious. Unfortunately, of all those films, it is the least well known. It also has a similar ambience and delirious aesthetic to the best of Sam Fuller's and Nicholas Ray's fifties pictures. A real find and further evidence that master Suzuki was operating on all cylinders way before commonly acknowledged by most critics. * * * *

Everything Goes Wrong

EX-CONVICT aka ZENKA series

EX-CONVICT – BAIL aka ZEN-KA – KARI SHAKU 1969 86 min. DIR. Keiichi Ozawa SCR. Kaneo Ikegami PHOTO COLOR 'SCOPE: Kurataro Takamura MUSIC: Hajime Kaburagi w/ Tetsuya Watari, Chieko Matsubara, Minoru Oki, Tsuneya Oki, Minako Osanai, Yoshiro Aoki, Shunji Imai, Jotaro Togami, Taketoshi Naito, Ema Sugimoto
Painfully derivative even for the yakuza genre, but director Ozawa and

writer Ikegami throw in so much off-kilter stuff that it works. Watari is a young, fashion-conscious tough who gets slapped in the slammer for accidentally killing an opposition boss in a bar knifefight (the other side started it). His *senpai* (senior), played by Minoru Oki, is stabbed in the leg and crippled. Shortly thereafter, their boss (Togami) is killed by a drunken assassin-for-hire (Imai). Imai adds immeasurably to the proceedings, emerging as one of the most depraved, degraded killers in the genre. Out of jail again, Watari falls for younger comrade Tsuneya Oki's sister (Matsubara). She is a very taditional young lady – she studies *ikebana* and wears only kimonos – who is nevertheless independent enough to have become a dentist!

Ex-Convict (#1)

She is kidnapped midway through by Imai. Imai has the contract for Watari's life from Imura (Naito), the sleazeball club owner who had Togami killed as well as took over his gang. During a savage rainstorm, Watari rescues Matsubara from the leaky lean-to where she is being held. *Senpai* Oki kills Aoki, the most obvious, in-your-face baddie and the head of the other gang. Subsequently both Okis are murdered by Naito's men. Imai is dispatched by Watari. The climax finds Watari and Naito sparring with long knives in the early morning light between two monolith sculptures until Watari gets the upper hand.   #1 of 2 films   * * *

EX-CONVICT – SWORD STORM aka ZENKA – DOSU ARASHI aka THE KNIFE JUNGLE 1969 89 min. **DIR.** Keiichi Ozawa **SCR.** Seiji Hoshikawa **PHOTO COLOR 'SCOPE:** Kurataro Takamura **MUSIC:** Hajime Kaburagi **w/** Tetsuya Watari, Makoto Sato, Reiko Aso, Joe Shishido, Takehiro Nakamura, Mitsuko Mori, Yoshiro Aoki, Shunji Imai, Tsuneya Oki, Shoki Fukae, Tomoko Aki   Watari gets out of prison after serving a term for killing an opposition boss. But his former colleagues consider him a liability. A craven friend (Fukae) now heads the gang. They have a truce with the rival gang whose boss was killed by Watari. So Watari's presence builds tension to the boiling point. Evil manipulator boss Aoki and his psycho killer Imai bear a heavy grudge. Watari had also cut off Imai's leg in the past attack. Sato is a comparatively honorable member of Aoki's mob and a friend of Watari's who tries to keep the peace. Shishido has a cameo at the beginning as Watari's partner who was killed in the assassination assault. Shishido's former girl (Aso) becomes Watari's. Watari takes to hanging out with a retired *oyabun*, the

benevolent and traditional Nakamura who ends up getting killed for his obstinancy. Sato tries to defend Aso after she is raped and held hostage at Aoki's HQ, but is stabbed to death for his tardy chivalry. Watari busts in a few seconds later, slaughtering Imai and Aoki in one of the most protracted swordfights in Nikkatsu yakuza *eiga*. #2 of 2 films   * * *

Ex-Convict (#2)

EXILED TO HELL aka JIGOKU NO HAMONJO 1969 89 min. **DIR.** Toshio Masuda **SCR.** Iwao Yamazaki/Toshio Masuda **PHOTO COLOR 'SCOPE:** Minoru Yokoyama **MUSIC:** Rinichiro Manabe **w/** Hideki Takahashi, Akira Kobayashi, Ruriko Asaoka, Joe Shishido, Tetsuya Watari, Michitaro Mizushima, Isamu Kosugi, Shoki Fukae, Eiji Go   A real all-star bash including just about all of Nikkatsu's major players except Yujiro Ishihara – four-out-of-five of the reigning superstars of chivalrous mayhem. Although many of the usual *ninkyo* yakuza saga elements are here, the major situation involving Kobayashi is a bit more original. Kobayashi is one of the senior members of a clan who run a traditional theater in 1920s Japan.

Exiled to Hell

They perform songs, music, and plays handed down from many generations past. Kobayashi is one of their star vocal attractions (his performance in his own voice of this classical Japanese material is awesome). Of course, there is a rival clan envious of their financial as well as artistic success. There are a couple of minor violent outbreaks, but a truce is maintained. At a dinner/mediation meeting, things seem to be getting patched-up. Cementing their agreement with drinks, Kobayashi tosses his down. Too late he realizes it is some kind of mildly caustic concoction that immediately burns his larynx. Outnumbered and somewhat incapacitated, he

leaves the dinner. He decides to leave town without even seeing Asaoka, his girl. Takahashi takes over. Anyway, without going into too much detail, Kobayashi eventually returns and, with Takahashi's help, settles the score with the villainous clan. Shishido, a wandering fiddle player/ killer (!), straddles back-and-forth between the clans before finally siding with the good guys and helping to win the climactic gangfight. Nikkatsu made many very good *ninkyo* (chivalrous)-type films, most of them the equal of Toei Studios' (if not better), and this is one of the best. Unfortunately, a great many of Nikkatsu's *ninkyo* output – literally scores of films – have still yet to appear on even Japanese DVD.
* * * 1/2

Exterminate the Wild Beasts

EXTERMINATE THE WILD BEASTS aka YAJU O KESE aka SAVAGE WOLFPACK 1969 84 min. DIR. Yasuharu Hasebe SCR. Shuichi Nagahara/Ryuzo Nakanishi PHOTO

COLOR 'SCOPE: Shinsaku Himeda
MUSIC: Koichi Sakata **w/** Tetsuya
Watari, Tatsuya Fuji, Tamio Kawaji,
Yuri Yoshioka, Mieko Fujimoto, Isao
Bito, Mieko Tsudoi, Toshiya Yamano
Watari returns home at the death of
his sister. She had been found outside
town beside the U.S. Air Force base
in a weed-choked field – a suicide
with a-broken-pop-bottle-to-wrists after being savagely gangraped. Fuji (in
a part similar to the villains he plays
in the STRAY CAT ROCK series)
and Kawaji run a delinquent gang of
black marketeers who buy illicit, stolen goods from American servicemen.
The gang had run into Watari's sister
and decided to have some "fun."
Watari tracks them down and refuses
to rest until he has killed every member of the gang.   * * 1/2

**FAMILY CREST aka DAIMON
series**

Family Crest (#1)

**FAMILY CREST – MAN
AGAINST DEATH** aka DAI-
MON – OTOKO DE SHI NI TAI
aka DIE LIKE A MAN 1969 86
min. **DIR.** Akinori Matsuo **SCR.** Seiji
Hoshikawa **PHOTO COLOR 'SCOPE:**
Kazumi Iwasa Music: Hajime
Kaburagi w/ Hideki Takahashi,
Yoshiro Aoki, Yumiko Nogawa, Yoko

Machida, Shigeru Tsuyuguchi, Shoki
Fukae, Ichiro Sugai, Toru Abe,
Ryohei Uchida #1 of 2 films

**FAMILY CREST – LOYALTY
OFFERING HELL** aka DAIMON
– JIGOKU NO SAKAZUKI aka
HELL'S JUNGLE 1969 86 min.
DIR. Akinori Matsuo **SCR.** Seiji
Hoshikawa **PHOTO COLOR 'SCOPE:**
Kazumi Iwasa **MUSIC:** Hajime
Kaburagi w/ Hideki Takahashi,
Akira Kobayashi, Yumiko Nogawa,
Hiroko Kiku, Ryohei Uchida, Asao
Uchida, Mitsuo Hamada, Ichiro
Sugai, Eiji Go #2 of 2 films

Family Crest (#2)

FANGS OF THE NIGHT aka
YORU NO KIBA 1958 102 min.
DIR. Umeji Inoue **SCR.** Umeji Inoue/
Kenji Watanabe **PHOTO COLOR
'SCOPE:** Kazumi Iwasa **MUSIC:**
Seitaro Omori w/ Yujiro Ishihara,
Yumeji Tsukioka, Ruriko Asaoka,
Mari Shiraki, Masumi Okada, Shoji
Yasui, Ko Nishimura

**FAST DRAW RYUJI – SONG OF
THE GUN** aka NUKI UCHI NO
RYUJI – KENJU NO UTA 1964
92 min. **Dir.** Hiroshi Noguchi **Scr.**
Iwao Yamazaki/Michio Sato **Photo
color 'scope:** Kazue Nagatsuka
Music: Naozumi Yamamoto
w/ Hideki Takahashi, Joe Shishido,
Yoko Yamamoto, Minako Kazuki,
Nobuo Kaneko, Shoki Fukae
I'm not absolutely positive but, judg-
ing from the first part of the title,
I would say this may be a remake
of the first film in the four picture
HOODLUM GUN DIARY series.
That entire set was also directed by
Noguchi in 1960 with the late
Keiichiro Akagi in the lead role of
misunderstood hitman Ryuji.

**FEARLESS BROTHERHOOD –
KANTO DUET** aka KANTO GI
KYODAI aka LOYAL KANTO
BROTHERS 1970 83 min.
Dir. Seiichiro Uchikawa **Scr.**
Seiichiro Uchikawa/Shimobe Yasu
Photo color 'scope: Izumi
Hagiwara **Music:** Seitaro Omori
w/ Hideo Murata, Saburo Kitajima,
Kotaro Satomi, Meiko Kaji, Ryutaro
Tatsumi

FEARLESS GAMBLER aka
ABARE CHO HAN aka ODD/
EVEN GAMBLING RAMPAGE
1970 88 min. **Dir.** Mio Ezaki **Scr.**
Norio Miyashita **Photo color
'scope:** Shohei Ando **Music:** Koichi
(Teruichi?) Sakata w/ Hideki
Takahashi, Masako Izumi, Ryohei
Uchida, Tamio Kawaji, Asao Sano,
Ryoichi Tamagawa

Fearless Gambler

FEMALE CONVICT 101 aka
JOSHUU 101 series

**FEMALE CONVICT 101 – HELL
OF SEXUAL EMOTION** aka
JOSHUU 101 – SEIKAN JIGOKU
1976 **Dir.** Isao Hayashi **Scr.** Keishi
Kubota/Bun (Yutaka?) Ohara **Photo
color 'scope:** Toshiro Yamazaki
w/ Rumi Tama, Naomi Oka, Reika
Maki, Yuri Yamashina, Midori Mori,
Ichiro Kijima   An obvious pink
film knock-off of the FEMALE CON-
VICT SCORPION series with much
more emphasis on the sex. #1 of 2

FEMALE CONVICT 101 – SUCKS
aka JOSHUU 101 – SHABURU
1977 **Dir.** Kosuke Ohara **Scr.** Seiji
Matsuoka **Photo color 'scope:**
Nobumasa Nagano **Music:** Noboru
Seta   w/ Naomi Tani, Tokuko
Watanabe, Michio Murakami, Jun
Aki, Midori Mori, Hirokazu Inoue
#2 of 2

**FEMALE PANTHER AND THE
ROGUE** aka MEHYU TO NARA-
ZU MONO 1957 89 min. **DIR.**
Hiroshi Noguchi **SCR.** Motonari
Wakai/Hideji Toki/Susumu Saji
PHOTO B&W: Umio Matsubayashi
Music: Naozumi Yamamoto
w/ Michitaro Mizushima, Ryoji
Hayama, Sachiko Hidari, Mieko
Hirooka, Akitake Kono

FIGHT aka TAIKETSU aka
DUEL aka FRIENDLY ENEMIES
1967 95 min. **DIR.** Toshio Masuda
SCR. Kaneo Ikegami/Toshio Masuda
PHOTO COLOR 'SCOPE: Kenji
Hagiwara **MUSIC:** Rinichiro Manabe
w/ Akira Kobayashi, Hideki
Takahashi, Yoshiro Aoki, Ichiro
Nakatani, Masako Izumi, Sanae
Kitabayashi, Ryoji Hayama, Isao
Tamagawa, Toru Abe, Hiroko Sanjo
A companion piece to DUEL aka
ENDLESS DUEL, also directed by
Masuda, with a nearly identical cast.
Refreshingly well-written, with some
notable, welcome variations on the
standard *ninkyo* yakuza formula. The
tale begins with a clan run by paternal
Toru Abe (for once playing a comparatively decent boss) readying for
an all-out battle with another gang.
Kobayashi is a rough-and-tumble,
worldly young man in contrast to his
friend Takahashi, a naïve neophyte.
Their gang succeeds in wiping out
most of their enemy, but the rival boss
and a few of his men escape. Later,
during a celebration, the vengeful
fugitives attack, slaying Abe before
they themselves are slain. Second-
in-commands Aoki and Nakatani
convince Takahashi to turn himself in,
as police inspector Hayama will need
a token guilty party. Takahashi reluctantly agrees. When he returns from

prison several years later, he finds
Nakatani a hopeless drunk and Aoki a
domineering boss who has ruined the
community. Aoki has also forced the
love of Takahashi's life, Kitabayashi,
into prostitution. Even worse, Aoki
is guilty of having engineered the
initial feud which killed both bosses,
and is now working with the other
former, rival second-in-command,
Tamagawa. Soon former comrades
are out to get Takahashi. There is
a great scene midway through in
a brothel where Takahashi, having
confronted now-tubercular
Kitabayashi, is set upon by scores
of swordsmen. A massive fight ensues. Takahashi is kept busy trying to
protect Kitabayashi, as well. Startlingly enough, consumptive
Kitabayashi stabs herself in the heart
to free Takahashi to save himself. The
rest of the yarn involves Takahashi
being captured, tortured, saved by
lone wolf Kobayashi, then having
to undergo more tribulations. With
Kobayashi's and Nakatani's help,
he prevails in the end, but then is
challenged to a duel by Kobayashi
after the bad guys are eliminated.
This duel on sun-drenched temple
grounds is awe-inspiring. The whole
film is grueling, occasionally talky
but eloquent, with an expert pacing of
action. The swordfights are very well
choreographed, amazing and plenti-
ful. This compares favorably with the
best *ninkyo* efforts of Tai Kato and
Kosaku Yamashita at Toei Studios.
Co-writer Ikegami penned director Eiichi Kudo's excellent, loosely
linked Toei Studios samurai trilogy,
13 ASSASSINS, THE GREAT KILL-
ING and ELEVEN SAMURAI.
* * * 1/2

Fearless Brotherhood - Kanto Duet

Fight aka *Friendly Enemies*

FIGHTING DELINQUENTS
aka KUTABARE GURENTAI aka DAMN HOODLUMS! 1960 80 min. **DIR.** Seijun Suzuki **SCR.** Iwao Yamazaki **PHOTO COLOR 'SCOPE:** Kazue Nagatsuka **MUSIC:** Seitaro Mori w/ Koji Wada, Mayumi Shimizu, Eitaro Ozawa, Hiroshi Kondo, Yoshiko Nezu, Kaku Takashina   Suzuki's first color film. Also his assistant director was Shugoro Nishimura, a talented director in his own right in the late sixties and through the seventies. In fact, Nishimura remade Suzuki's GATE OF FLESH in a more pink version in 1977. FIGHTING DELINQUENTS concerns Wada, one of several rambunctious orphan teenagers living together, who is discovered to be heir to property on Awaji, one of the smaller Japanese islands. Fast talking lawyer Ozawa brings him back to the family matriarch on the isle, a crusty grandmother who frowns on Wada's outspoken ways and rock'n roll antics. Lo and behold, gang boss Kondo – the same craven individual who accidentally killed Wada's foster dad in a traffic accident – wants the prime seacoast property and pulls ever more wicked, violent subterfuges to get it. Kondo's secretary/mistress, who has long been fond of Wada, turns out to be Wada's long lost mother! Kondo's plotting culminates in kidnapping grandma during festival. But Wada and his mom, realizing where her true loyalties lie, foil the plan. Kondo nearly makes a successful getaway by boat as the cops arrive. This is mainly a youth comedy with plenty of action, romance and silly bits thrown into the mix. It is fairly lightweight, without the subversive humor of Suzuki's other pictures. However, the initial sequence where Kondo, driving a big American car with fuzzy animals in the back, gets amorously carried away with a girl and runs into a ladder holding Wada's surrogate pop is very funny. Other inventive interludes include a drunken party where Suzuki rotates the anamorphic lense back and forth to suggest an inebriated, rocking motion, and the final scene where Kondo perishes when his boat is sucked into one of the many whirlpools that dot the treacherous coast. * * 1/2

FLOOD PLAIN aka OMIZU
HARA 1962 **DIR.** Buichi Saito **SCR.** Ryuta Akimoto **PHOTO 'SCOPE:** Kurataro Takamura **MUSIC:** Taiichiro Kosugi w/ Joe Shishido, Masako Izumi, Yuji Kodaka, Tadao Sawamoto, Shiro Osaka, Chikako Hosokawa, Sanae Nakahara

FLOWER AND THE ANGRY WAVES aka HANA TO DOTO
1964 92 min. **DIR.** Seijun Suzuki **SCR.** Keiichi Abe/Kazuo Funabashi/ Takeo Omura **PHOTO COLOR 'SCOPE:** Kazue Nagatsuka **MUSIC:** Hajime Okumura w/ Akira Kobayashi, Chieko Matsubara, Naoko Kubo, Tamio Kawaji, Akira Yamanouchi, Osamu Takizawa, Shoki Fukae, Isao Tamagawa, Kaku Takashina, Shiro Yanase   Kobayashi is a young anti-hero in a coal carters clan/union in the turn-of-the-century Taisho era up against a rival evil gang. He is also caught between the virginal Matsubara and the more worldly Kubo. Midway through, his face gets slightly disfigured, something which must have wreaked havoc with the sensibilities of the actor's younger female fanbase – Kobayashi was a

kind of crossover matinee-idol/pop-star. Another subversion of audience expectations has Kobayashi acting somewhat cowardly in the snow-bound final showdown, an unheard-of trait in a *ninkyo* yakuza hero. Also with Tamio Kawaji as a sword-wielding assassin in Zorro-cape-and-hat(!). * * *

Flower and the Angry Waves

FLOWER AND DRAGON aka HANA TO RYU aka MAN WITH THE DRAGON TATTOO 1962 109 min. **DIR.** Toshio Masuda **SCR.** Masando Ide **PHOTO COLOR 'SCOPE:** Yoshihiro Yamazaki **MUSIC:** Harumi Ibe **w/** Yujiro Ishihara, Ruriko Asaoka, Ryoji Hayama, Kaneko Iwasaki, Mari Shiraki
Based on a popular novel, there have been numerous film versions. Ishihara portrays a fellow in a yakuza/coal carters clan. He eventually marries one of his co-workers (Iwasaki) but also becomes amorously entangled with a female yakuza card dealer (Asaoka). At the snowy climax, Ishihara fights off swords with his bare hands. * * 1/2

FLOWER OF CHIVALRY'S LIFE STORY – GAMBLING HEIR aka KYOKA RETSUDEN – SHUMEI TOBA aka GAMBLER'S DILEMNA 1969 93 min. **DIR.** Keiichi Ozawa **SCR.** Seiji Hoshikawa **PHOTO COLOR 'SCOPE:** Minoru Yokoyama **MUSIC:** Taiichiro Kosugi **w/** Chieko Matsubara, Meiko Kaji, Hideki Takahashi, Tatsuya Fuji, Shinjiro Ebara, Chikako Hosokawa, Bontaro Miake, Shoki Fukae
A *ninkyo* saga featuring Matsubara, who inadvertently becomes *oyabun* of her clan after her father's death. Regrettably, she herself doesn't do any fighting. She *does* help Fuji, a maverick in dutch with the bad clan. Kaji is Fuji's tattooed, knife-wielding, card sharp girlfriend. The film would have actually been better if they had concentrated on Fuji and Kaji's characters. Fuji has a great scene where he has just put Kaji aboard an outbound train from their rural village. As the train pulls away, Kaji watches in frustration as Fuji is set upon by a gang of knife-swinging toughs. There is some great tracking camera as Fuji, his knife drawn, flees through the overgrown fields alongside the train. Kaji is powerless to help and stares in consternation as this tense scene recedes into the distance. Another memorable sequence has Kaji cornered in a hot springs cave by a couple of villains. She nonchalantly dispatches both of them with her blade. Takahashi has almost nothing to do, although he does go to bat for Matsubara and perishes, slaying evil boss Fukae in a nasty climactic rainstorm. * * *

Flower and Dragon

Flower of Chivalry's Life Story - Gambling Heir

**FLOWER STEM TATTOO – RIP-
ENING IN THE POT** aka HANA
SHIN NO IREZUMI – URETA
TSUBO 1976 **DIR.** Masaru Konuma
PHOTO COLOR 'SCOPE: Katsu Mori
w/ Naomi Hoshi, Tanako Kitagawa,
Shin Nakamaru   Roman porno/
yakuza *eiga.*

**FRONTLINE OF THE NIGHT
aka   YORU NO SAIZENSEN
series**

**FRONTLINE OF THE NIGHT –
WOMEN HUNTING** aka YORU
NO SAIZENSEN – SUKE GARI
1969 83 min. **DIR.** Motomu (Tan) Ida
SCR. Ryuzo Nakanishi **PHOTO COLOR**
'SCOPE: Izumi Hagiwara **MUSIC:**
Seitaro Omori   w/ Koji Wada,
Tatsuya Fuji, Satoko Sato, Jiro
Okazaki   #1 of 3 films

**FRONTLINE OF THE NIGHT –
TOKYO WOMEN MAP** aka
YORU NO SAIZENSEN – TOKYO
ONNA CHIZU aka PRISONER OF
LUST 1969 81 min. **DIR.** Motomu
(Tan) Ida **SCR.** Ryuzo Nakanishi
PHOTO B&W 'SCOPE: Izumi
Hagiwara **MUSIC:** Seitaro Omori
w/ Koji Wada, Tatsuya Fuji, Jiro
Okazaki, Satoko Sato, Mieko Tsudoi,
Kyoko Mine, Shoji Nakadai, Saburo
Hiromatsu, Tomoko Aki, Hiroshi
Kono   Wada is a cook out with his
sister (Sato) on her birthday when
she is hit by a car then abducted by
the drivers. Wada and the cops try to
find her, with no luck. After getting thrashed by some hoodlums, he
is befriended by down-on-his-luck
gangster Fuji. Wada becomes a bartender through Fuji's help. Soon he
discovers his sister is being forced to
work in a secret, perverse, sex/torture
club run by Fuji's evil boss Nakadai.
Fuji hates Nakadai who has taken
over his territory. Wada makes several
friends through Fuji, including Tsudoi
who admits to them she is Nakadai's
daughter. She helps Wada rescue
Sato. #2 of 3 films

**FRONTLINE OF THE NIGHT –
SECRET ZONE OF TOKYO** aka
YORU NO SAIZENSEN – TOKYO
MARUHI CHITAI 1971 83 min.
DIR. Motomu (Tan) Ida **SCR.** Ei
Ogawa/Iwao Yamazaki **PHOTO COLOR**
'SCOPE: Izumi Hagiwara **MUSIC:**
Yutaka Makino   w/ Jiro Okazaki,
Eiji Go, Yaeko Wakamizu, Masami
Maki, Sachiko Kuwabara, Keiko
Aikawa, Shoki Fukae, Koji Sawada,
Toru Yuri, Akira Oizumi
Go is a flashy dresser from the styx
who runs into Kuwabara, an old
friend, on the train. He gets her a job

in the club where he works. Loan shark Fukae causes distress when he demands Kuwabara work for him as a hostess to pay off a debt incurred as a result of her father's accident. Go and Okazaki try to open up their own strip club in a garage but are shut down by Fukae's gang. Go and Okazaki then try their hand at moneylending but are forced out of business when Fukae informs the law they are a front for prostitution. After they are released from jail, Okazaki is killed trying to take back the indentured Kuwabara. Go is finally enraged enough at Fukae to set the vengeance wheels in motion. #3 of 3 films

GAMBLER aka GYANBURAA series

ROVING GAMBLER aka SA-SURAI NO GYANBURAA aka GAMBLER'S WANDERLUST 1964 100 min. **DIR.** Yoichi Ushihara **SCR.** Iwao Yamazaki **PHOTO B&W 'SCOPE:** Kazumi Iwasa **MUSIC:** Taiichiro Kosugi w/ Akira Kobayashi, Reiko Sassamori, Asao Koike, Isao Yamagata, Kayo Matsuo, Kojiro Kusanagi The gambler type here really does not have as much relation to the yakuza *bakuto*-type of gambler, although there are various shady casino operators, mobsters and yakuza gamblers in the mix of this action series. Kobayashi seems to be a suave, intercontinental card-sharp/con man – not the Japanese gambler bound by *giri, jingi*, etc., but an adventurer living by his wits ala James Bond (without the secret service/spy mission attachments). Too bad only one of these has been released on Japanese DVD. #1 of 8 films

CALL MY BLACK DICE aka KUROI DAISU GA ORE O YOBU 1964 81 min. **DIR.** Motomu (Tan) Ida **SCR.** Iwao Yamazaki/Motomu Ida **PHOTO B&W 'SCOPE:** Izumi Hagiwara **MUSIC:** Seitaro Omori w/ Akira Kobayashi, Reiko Sassamori, Koji Wada, Eijiro Tono, Mieko Nishio #2 of 8 films

OUTCAST AND GUITAR ON A SOLITARY JOURNEY aka GITAA KAKAETA HITORI TABI 1964 87 min. **DIR.** Tokujiro Yamazaki **SCR.** Iwao Yamazaki/Yasuo Sakata **PHOTO B&W 'SCOPE:** Kumenobu Fujioka **MUSIC:** Seitaro Omori w/ Akira Kobayashi, Chieko Matsubara, Yuji Kodaka, Shinsuke Ashida, Sachiko Kamitsuki, Toshie Takada #3 of 8 films

TOMORROW CALL THE DICE THROW aka NAGETA DAISU GA ASU O YOBU 1965 86 min. **DIR.** Yoichi Ushihara **SCR.** Hisatoshi Kai **PHOTO COLOR 'SCOPE:** Kazumi Iwasa **MUSIC:** Taiichiro Kosugi w/ Akira Kobayashi, Chieko Matsubara, Nobuo Kaneko, Nobuo Hamada, Shoki Fukae #4 of 8 films

MY FATE IS TO WANDER aka SASURAI HA ORE NO UNMEI 1965 86 min. **DIR.** Motomu (Tan) Ida **SCR.** Iwao Yamazaki/ Motomu Ida **PHOTO COLOR 'SCOPE:** Toshitaro Nakao **MUSIC:** Seitaro Omori w/ Akira Kobayashi, Ruriko Ito, Tamio Kawaji, Asao Sano, Masao Shimizu, Sachiko Kamitsuki, Isao Tamagawa #5 of 8 films

THE BLACK GAMBLER aka
KUROI TOBAKUSHI 1965 86
min. **DIR.** Ko Nakahira **SCR.** Ei
Ogawa/Ryuzo Nakanishi **PHOTO
COLOR 'SCOPE:** Yoshihiro Yamazaki
MUSIC: Harumi Ibe
w/ Akira Kobayashi, Manami Fuji,
Asao Koike, Michiyo Yokoyama,
Masaya Takahashi, Kiiton Masuda
#6 of 8 films

**BLACK GAMBLER – MURDER-
OUS DICE** aka KUROI TOBA-
KUSHI – DAISU DE KOROSE aka
DEADLY DICE 1965 86 min.
DIR. Mio Ezaki **SCR.** Ei Ogawa/
Ryuzo Nakanishi **PHOTO COLOR
'SCOPE:** Minoru Yokoyama **MUSIC:**
Harumi Ibe **w/** Akira Kobayashi,
Hideaki Nitani, Keiko Yuge,
Masahiko Tanimura, Eiji Go
#7 of 8 films

Gambler (#8)

**BLACK GAMBLER – LEFT
HAND OF THE DEVIL** aka
KUROI TOBAKUSHI – AKUMA

NO HIDARI TE 1966 93 min.
DIR. Ko Nakahira **SCR.** Ei Ogawa/
Tadaaki (Chusho?) Yamazaki **MUSIC:**
Harumi Ibe **w/** Akira Kobayashi,
Hideaki Nitani, Misa Hirose, Michiyo
Yokoyama, Eiji Go, Akira Oizumi,
Judy Ongu #8 and final in the series

GAMBLERS AT SEA aka UMI
NO SHOBU SHI 1961 91 min. **DIR.**
Koreyoshi Kurahara **SCR.** Nobuo
Yamada **PHOTO COLOR 'SCOPE:**
Yoshio Mamiya **MUSIC:** Masaru
Sato **w/** Joe Shishido, Takeshi Kato,
Sanae Nakahara, Reiko Sassamori,
Kenji Arikawa, Zeko Nakamura,
Arihiro Fujimura

GAMBLING DEN BREAKDOWN
aka TEKKABA YABURI 1964
106 min. **DIR.** Buichi Saito **SCR.**
Hisatoshi Kai **PHOTO COLOR 'SCOPE:**
Kenji Hagiwara **MUSIC:** Taiichiro
Kosugi **w/** Yujiro Ishihara, Izumi
Ashikawa, Shoichi Ozawa, Akifumi
Inoue, Jukichi Ueno, Kaku Takashina,
Hanaku Yamasa, Akira Nagoya,
Shoki Fukae
A saga-type *ninkyo* yakuza picture
with former gambling rickshawman
Jukichi Ueno's son, Ishihara, growing up to be master dicer in the 1890s
yakuza gambling world. Director
Saito paints a detailed picture of a
bygone era using Nikkatsu's prime
ninkyo screenwriter Kai's scenario as
pallette. After a while, two parallel stories develop – the saga of
Ishihara's redeemed geisha wife
Ashikawa, shanghaied back by her
sleazy pimp and his gang of cheating
gamblers runs side-by-side with
Ishihara's ongoing encounters with
the wandering master dice-cheater
who ruined his dad's life. Ishihara

finally gets revenge on the pimp but is alienated from spouse Ashikawa. Finally at the end he confronts the master dice-cheater, giving his dad Ueno a chance to redeem himself. Ueno wins, then cuts off his own dice-throwing hand – apparently to atone for his past inclination to gamble! Then the master cheater is murdered by Nihonyanagi and Fukae's gang. The film ends with Ishihara slaying the attacking Fukae and his henchmen.   * * *

GAMBLING DEN CODE aka TEKKABA JINGI aka GAMBLING DEN HONOR AND HUMANITY 1966 84 min. **DIR.** Motomu (Tan) Ida **SCR.** Hisatoshi Kai **PHOTO COLOR 'SCOPE:** Izumi Hagiwara **MUSIC:** Seitaro Omori w/ Hideki Takahashi, Shinsuke Ashida, Masako Izumi, Osamu Takezawa, Yoshio Yoshida, Yoko Yamamoto, Kayo Matsuo

Gambling Den Desire

GAMBLING DEN DESIRE aka TEKKABA BOJO aka LOVE IN GANGLAND 1970 95 min. **DIR.** Keiichi Ozawa **SCR.** Goro Tanada **PHOTO COLOR 'SCOPE:** Minoru Yokoyama **MUSIC:** Taiichiro Kosugi w/ Chieko Matsubara, Takahiro Tamura, Meiko Kaji, Ryohei Uchida, Yoshi Kato, Yoshiro Aoki, Yuji Hori, Tomi Yamamoto, Tomoko Naraoka, Shoki Fukae
Saga of a man in love with a gang boss's daughter and the suffering entailed in their tortured relationship.

GAMBLING DEN WIND aka TEKKABA NO KAZE aka THE CARDS WILL TELL 1960 89 min. **DIR.** Yoichi Ushihara **SCR.** Kei Kumai **PHOTO COLOR 'SCOPE:** Shinsaku Himeda **MUSIC:** Taiichiro Kosugi w/ Yujiro Ishihara, Mie Kitahara, Keiichiro Akagi, Shinsuke Ashida, Mayumi Shimizu, Joe Shishido, Eijiro Tono
Set in contemporary time period, this is, for the most part, a well-written tale of lone wolf gambler Ishihara's constant run-ins with craven, treacherous nightclub owner Ashida. Akagi is a resentful delinquent gunman employed by Ashida who eventually softens under Ishihara's decent treatment of him. There are a few nice setpieces such as the marathon dice game between Ishihara and Ashida's cheating diceman Shishido, all played out to the sounds of a nocturnal windstorm outside. Once Ishihara exposes the cheating at the end of the night, things escalate until Ashida kidnaps Ishihara a few days later, torturing him in his underground garage. However, henchman Akagi cannot bring himself to shoot Ishihara and finish him off, no matter how he is goaded

by Ashida. Finally, Ashida's more practical partner intervenes, saving Ishihara's life. The film climaxes with a baseball stadium heist by Ashida, Akagi, et. al. When Akagi is wounded and cannot keep up with the others, cruel Ashida shoots him in the stomach to tie up loose ends. But Akagi lives long enough to make it back to the malt shop (!) where Ishihara hangs out. Ishihara goes after the robbers with Ashida's mistress Kitahara in tow. Finally, the villains are captured by the cops after a shootout outside a U.S. airbase. Not earthshakingly great, but a respectable color noir for the time period at Nikkatsu. Kitahara – sporting a Juliette Greco chanteuse look – is affecting as the gangster's sad, beautiful mistress who would rather be with Ishihara, and Akagi stands out as a brooding, dynamic presence in his supporting role. Kitahara became Mrs. Ishihara in real life the same year. * * *

Gambling Lifeblood

GAMBLING LIFEBLOOD aka SENKETSU NO TOBA aka THE BROKEN VOW 1968 85 min. DIR. Takashi Nomura SCR. Seiji Hoshikawa/Ryozo Nakanishi PHOTO COLOR 'SCOPE: Shigeyoshi Mine MUSIC: Goichi Sakata w/ Hideki Takahashi, Hiroshi Nihonyanagi, Kuroemon Onoe, Yoko Yamamoto, Hiroshi Nawa, Toru Abe, Tatsu-ya Fuji, Rokko Toura, Eiji Go

GANG OF WOLVES STREET aka MURE OKAMI NO GAI 1962 77 min. DIR. Isamu Kosugi SCR. Tatsuo Miyata/Saburo Okado PHOTO B&W 'SCOPE: Umeo Matsubayashi MUSIC: Taiichiro Kosugi w/ Kyoji Aoyama, Hitoshi Miyazaki, Minosuke Nakao, Ryohei Uchida, Minako Kazuki, Etsuko Wada

GANG OF YOUNG PANTHERS aka WAKAI HYO NO MURE 1959 84 min. DIR. Akinori Matsuo SCR. Katsumi Miki PHOTO B&W 'SCOPE: Kurataro Takamura MUSIC: Hajime Kaburagi w/ Akira Kobayashi, Misako Watanabe, Tadao Sawamoto, Kyoji Aoyama, Kyosuke Machida, Mieko Inagaki, Shiro Osaka, Mari Shiraki, Ryohei Uchida, Shinsuke Ashida

A GANGSTER'S MORALS aka SAKARIBA JINGI aka PLEASURE RESORT GAMBLING CODE 1970 87 min. DIR. Yasuharu Hasebe SCR. Takashi Fujii/Yoshi Yokota/Michio Suzuki PHOTO COLOR 'SCOPE: Muneo Ueda MUSIC: Hajime Kaburagi w/ Saburo Kitajima, Shinsuke Minami, Kotaro Satomi, Tamio Kawaji, Meiko Kaji, Tatsuya Fuji, Tsuneya Oki, Mitsuko Oka, Jiro Okazaki, Mari Shiraki, Tomoko Aki

A Gangster's Morals

Gate of Flesh (1964)

GANGSTER VIP, see HOODLUM aka BURAI series

GATE OF FLESH aka NIKUTAI NO MON 1964 90 min. **DIR.** Seijun Suzuki **ORIG. STORY:** Taijiro Tamura **SCR.** Goro Tanada **PHOTO COLOR 'SCOPE:** Shigeyoshi Mine **MUSIC:** Naozumi Yamamoto **w/** Joe Shishido, Yumiko Nogawa, Misako Tominaga, Kayo Matsuo, Koji Wada, Tomiko Ishii An annihilating tale of four prostitutes in post-WW2 Japan and the reversion of three of them to subhuman savagery. Nogawa plays the innocent orphan from the countryside given a crash-course in what it takes to survive in the dog-eat-dog world of a conquered nation. Shishido is a veteran/thief who likes to kill American GIs. There are some strong and disturbing scenes including the actual slaughter of a cow, the whip-lash punishment by the three whores of any other whore who commits

the unpardonable sin of falling-in-love, the humiliating seduction of a basically decent black American Catholic military chaplain. Shishido, because he falls-in-love with Nogawa (and vice-versa) is betrayed by the three jealous whores to the local yakuza clan who are in league with the U.S. Occupation Forces. He is shot and killed. The last scene of the film has Nogawa discovering his bloody knapsack in the dirty canal water where he died. Remade by Hideo Gosha as NIKUTAI NO MON in 1988, but titled CARMEN 1945 in English-speaking territories (his version is almost as good). * * * *

GATE OF FLESH aka NIKUTAI NO MON 1977 **DIR.** Shugoro Nishimura **SCR.** Yozo (Kiyozo?) Tanaka **w/** Suko Miyashita, Reiko (Yoshiko?) Kayama
It would be fascinating to see this, despite the fact Nikkatsu undoubtedly

juiced-up the sex and S&M to the nth degree compared to Suzuki's version. In 1977, the roman porno/pink film genre that Nikkatsu pioneered as far back as 1964 with Suzuki's GATE... (that version is raw – explosive, hallucinatory, shocking even today, let alone 1964, and without hardcore explicitness) was peaking or just about to peak. The rewarding attribute about many of Nikkatsu's pink S&M porno pictures is that they, frequently, were good films.

Gate of Flesh (1977)

Directors of hypnotically direct, superreal visual acuity such as Tatsumi Kumashiro, Masaru Konuma and Chusei Sone emerged. Other filmmakers with established mainstream and/or genre reputations such as Noboru Tanaka (KOBE KOKUSAI GANG), Yasuharu Hasebe (BLACK TIGHT KILLERS, BLOODY TERRITORIES, BLOODY FEUD), Keiichi Ozawa (various of the HOODLUM series) and Shugoro

Nishimura (MIDNIGHT VIRGIN, TOKYO STREETFIGFHTING and the excellent YAKUZA NATIVE GROUND), continued on at Nikkatsu to try their hand at the emerging new genre. Some of these gentlemen would rather have continued on with the yakuza and action genres. Some welcomed, at least for a time, the "throwing-open-the- doors" sensation that came with this cinematic "liberation." Undoubtedly at least a few were frustrated that the Japanese film industry was so poverty-stricken, so abandoned by audiences that they basically had no choice if they wanted to keep up the car and the house payments but to make S&M-tinged, occasionally-romantic, softcore porno. For a while, in the 1990s, there was a popular misconception in some American film buff quarters that the "roman" in roman porn refers to the adjectival modifier as used to describe Rome, Italy, and its inhabitants, particularly its ancient, decadent inhabitants and sex culture. Wrong! Believe it or not – and this is the last of my digressions – the roman in roman porn is used to indicate – yes, you heard right – romance, as in "romantic." That is why, when you run across one of these pink films that have decided to emphasize the "romance," your jaw may very likely drop to the floor when you hear glossy mood music as the masculine lover whips, then repeatedly rapes – sometimes generously sharing with a friend – the love of his life. Not all of them were so sexist. Nishimura, Ozawa, Hasebe undoubtedly produced some rewarding results – despite the disparate pop culture standards of what is acceptable in Japan as opposed to in the West. Nishimura is a perfect example:

he is not a truly great director, but he has directed several great films. There is a good chance, judging by his emotional jackhammer of a movie, YAKUZA NATIVE GROUND, that his version of GATE OF FLESH is every bit as good as Gosha's 1988 version and, maybe, who knows? maybe it is as good as Suzuki's masterpiece. The potential was/is certainly there.

GATE OF THE BEAST aka YAJU NO MON 1961 81min. DIR. Takumi Furukawa SCR. Ei Ogawa PHOTO COLOR 'SCOPE: Saburo Isayama MUSIC: Masaru Sato w/ Hideaki Nitani, Sanae Nakahara, Toshio Sugiyama, Hiroshi Nihonyanagi, Toru Abe, Chieko Matsubara, Shinsuke Ashida A run-of-the-mill programmer relating the adventures of lone wolf undercover cop Nitani out to foil two gangs run by rival bosses Nihonyanagi and Abe. Sugiyama is a young delinquent gangster with whom Nitani establishes a half-baked bond. Disappointing in that the opening sequence of three gangland killings has great hardboiled action, eerie noir ambience and a thrillingly violent mise-en-scene. But the picture falters as soon as the plot begins to unfold, never to rise above mere potboiler status. Another liability, which should have let the producers in for charges of misrepresentation at the time, is that actress Matsubara, though third-billed on posters and in the opening credits, receives less than a minute's screen time as an extorted businessman's daughter.   * *

GET THE KILLER aka KOROSHI TA NO WA DARE DA 1957 91 min. DIR. Ko Nakahira SCR. Kaneto Shindo PHOTO B&W: Shinsaku Himeda MUSIC: Akira Ifukube w/ Ichiro Sugai, Hideko Yamane, Akira Kobayashi, Ko Nishimura, Kyoji Aoyama, Misako Watanabe

GINZA WHIRLWIND aka GINZA SENBUJI aka MAITO-GAI or MIGHTY GUY series

GINZA WHIRLWIND aka GINZA SENBUJI aka GINZA MAITOGAI or the *katakana* phonetic play on words: GINZA MIGHTY GUY 1959 83 min. DIR. Hiroshi Noguchi SCR. Yasunori Kawachi PHOTO COLOR 'SCOPE: Kazue Nagatsuka MUSIC: Kanoku (Hiroku?) Ogawa w/ Akira Kobayashi, Ruriko Asaoka, Joe Shishido, Misako Watanabe, Shinsuke Ashida Kobayashi and Shishido are a couple of scrappy troubleshooters/detectives who fight organized crime and are headquartered in the Ginza district of Tokyo. Note: Nikkatsu had a set of promotional slogans to tout their male leading men in the late 1950s/early 1960s: the entire bunch was known as the DIAMOND LINE consisting of Yujiro Ishihara, Akira Kobayashi, Keiichiro Akagi and Koji Wada. Upon Akagi's death in 1961, Joe Shishido and Hideaki Nitani took his place in the pantheon. They also had pet names for Ishihara and Kobayashi: Yujiro was called "TAFU GAI" (or TOUGH GUY) and Akira, "MAITO GAI" (or MIGHTY GUY). According to CINEMA CLUB 1994, the "MAITO" refers not to the English word "mighty" but the "maito" in the Japanese *katakana* spelling of *"dainomaito"* (dynamite). Strange enough a reference for you? #1 of 6 films

GINZA WHIRLWIND – WHO IS THE BEHIND-THE-SCENES WIRE-PULLER? aka GINZA SENBUJI – KUROMAKU WA DARETA 1959 75 min. Dir. Hiroshi Noguchi Scr. Yasunori Kawachi Photo color 'scope: Kazue Nagatsuka Music: Kanoku (Hiroku?) Ogawa w/ Akira Kobayashi, Ruriko Asaoka, Joe Shishido, Toru Abe, Kyoji Aoyama, Tako Minamikaze, Ichiro Sugai, Keisuke Yukioka   Some supposedly respectable businessmen turn out to be behind a notorious counterfeit ring. Kobayashi puts the kibosh on the villains with the help of waitress Asaoka. #2 of 6 films

GINZA WHIRLWIND – THAT GUY'S THE EYEWITNESS! aka GINZA SENBUJI – MOKU GEKI-SHA WA KYATSUTA 1960 82 min Dir. Hiroshi Noguchi Scr. Kiyoshi Oda Photo color 'scope: Kazue Nagatsuka Music: Takasu Saito w/ Akira Kobayashi, Ruriko Asaoka, Shoichi Ozawa, Kyoji Aoyama, Mari Shiraki, Jun Hamamura, Somemasu Matsumoto #3 of 6 films

GINZA WHIRLWIND – CALL OF THE STORM aka GINZA SEN-BUJI – ARASHI GA ORE O YON-DEIRU 1961 Dir. Hiroshi Noguchi w/ Akira Kobayashi, Kyoji Aoyama, Akira Yamanouchi, Kayo Matsuo, Hiroshi Kondo, Jun Hamamura A whistleblower on corruption is murdered, so private eye Kobayashi and intrepid reporter Aoyama go after the killers. Mindless, non-stop serial action, postcard images and many songs abound. #4 of 6 films * *

RETURN OF THE GINZA WHIRLWIND aka KAETTE KITA GINZA SENBUJI 1962 Dir. Hiroshi Noguchi Scr. Kiyoshi Oda Photo color 'scope: Kazue Nagatsuka Music: Naozumi Yamamoto w/ Akira Kobayashi, Chieko Matsubara, Kyoji Aoyama, Arihiro Fujimura, Sachiko Uetsuki #5 of 6 films

WHIRLWIND CALLS THE STORM – GINZA HOODLUM'S DIARY aka KAZE GA YONDEI-RU SENBUJI – GINZA BURAICHO 1963 Dir. Hiroshi Noguchi   Scr. Kiyoshi Oda/Kiyoshi Nobusawa Photo color 'scope: Kazue Nagatsuka Music: Naozumi Yamamoto w/ Akira Kobayashi, Chieko Matsubara, Kaku Takashina, Yumi Takano, Kayo Matsuo, Shoki Fukae #6 and final in the series

Girl Boss - Broken Honor & Humanity

GIRL BOSS – BROKEN HONOR & HUMANITY aka ONNA

BANCHO – JINGI YABURI 1969
82 min. **DIR.** Mio Ezaki **SCR.** Iwao
Yamazaki **PHOTO B&W 'SCOPE:**
Muneo Ueda w/ Teruko Hasegawa,
Setsuko Minami, Jiro Okazaki, Kaku
Takashina *Sukeban* sleaze action.

**GIRLS' SCHOOL aka JOSHI
GAKUEN series**

GIRLS' SCHOOL – EVIL GAMES
aka JOSHI GAKUEN – WARUI
ASOBI aka DANGEROUS GAMES
1970 84 min. **DIR.** Mio Ezaki
SCR. Iwao Yamazaki **PHOTO COLOR**
'SCOPE: Shinsaku Himeda **MUSIC:**
Koichi (Akikazu?) Sakata
w/ Junko Natsu, Jiro Okazaki,
Chieko Matsubara, Yoshiko Ikedo,
Kazuko Kikuchi, Rumi Goto, Itoko
Inagaki, Hosei Komatsu, Tatsuya
Fuji, Chikako Miyagi   At first, this
would seem to be a counterpart of
Toei Studios violent girl gang pictures, series like their TERRIFYING
GIRLS' SCHOOL. But it actually is
a bit more rooted in reality, despite its
occasional concessions to lowbrow
humor and nowhere near the violence
quotient. Natsu is a maladjusted newcomer at school who runs afoul of the
other bad girls as well as a handsome
young teacher. She and the other girls
attempt to discredit him by accusing
him of making inappropriate advances, something which eventually
ends in his dismissal. Natsu becomes
friends with wacky yakuza Okazaki
who runs a strip club with his friends.
Unfortunately, the film is pretty much
a trifle. If not for the super-charismat-
ic Natsu, an actress who should have
enjoyed even greater success than she
did, this would be down another half
notch.   #1 of 3 films   * * 1/2

*admat for **Girls' School** (#1)*

**GIRLS' SCHOOL – WILD GRAD-
UATION SONG** aka JOSHI
GAKUEN – YABAI SOTSU GYO
aka WILD GRADUATION
CELEBRATION 1970 83 min.
DIR. Yukihiro Sawada **SCR.** Goro
Tanada **PHOTO COLOR 'SCOPE:**
Shohei Ando **MUSIC:** Hiroki Tamaki

w/ Junko Natsu, Jiro Okazaki, Seizaburo Kawazu, Isao Tamagawa, Yoshiko Ikedo, Ichiro Sugai, Yuki Jono, Yumiko Arizaki   #2 of 3 films

Girls' School (#2)

Girls' School (#3)

GIRLS' SCHOOL – I DEMAND GAMES aka JOSHI GAKUEN – OTONA NO ASOBI 1971 82 min. **DIR.** Akira Kato **SCR.** Iwao Yamazaki **PHOTO COLOR 'SCOPE:** Minoru Yokoyama **MUSIC:** Hiroko Tamaki **w/** Junko Natsu, Rumi Goto, Jiro Okazaki, Akiko Yamato, Yoshiko Ikedo, Hosei Komatsu, Akemi E   #3 and last of series

GLASS JOHNNY – LOOKS LIKE A BEAST aka GARASU NO JONI – YAJU NO YO NI MIETE aka GLASS-HEARTED JOHNNY 1962 108 min. **DIR.** Koreyoshi Kurahara **SCR.** Nobuo Yamada **PHOTO B&W 'SCOPE:** Yoshio Mamiya **MUSIC:** Toshiro Mayuzumi w/ Joe Shishido, Izumi Ashikawa, Joji Ai, Daisaburo Hirata, Yoko Minamida, Etsuko Wada   Shishido is an ambitious, bike racetrack tout who becomes inadvertently involved in a triangle with a vulnerable prostitute (Izumi Ashikawa) and her brutal yakuza pimp (Joji Ai). Director Kurahara reportedly used Fellini's LA STRADA as a template, taking a decidedly Italian neo-realist approach to this gritty tale of low-lifes scrambling to survive on the ragged edge of nowhere. Shishido projects a bigger-than-life charisma here, a boorish charm and macho swagger comparable in scope to early Jean-Paul Belmondo and Alain Delon. Astonishingly good and evidence Kurahara, who also helmed I AM WAITING, THE WARPED ONES and BLACK SUN, is yet another of the great Japanese directors unsung because they mostly worked in genre pictures. * * * 1/2

Glass Johnny - Looks Like a Beast

GLOOMY FAREWELL aka
YUSHI NA GARA NO WAKARE
1964 **DIR.** Mio Ezaki **SCR.** Takeo
Kunihiro **PHOTO 'SCOPE:** Kazue
Nagatsuka **MUSIC:** Akira Ifukube
w/ Mitsuo Hamada, Masako Izumi,
Satoshi Yamauchi, Hiroshi Kondo,
Toru Abe

GLORY'S CHALLENGE aka
EIKO E NO CHOSEN 1966 101 min.
DIR. Toshio Masuda **SCR.** Kaneo
Ikegami/Toshio Masuda **PHOTO**
COLOR 'SCOPE: Yoshihiro Yamazaki
MUSIC: Harumi Ibe w/ Yujiro
Ishihara, Ruriko Asaoka, Keiju
Kobayashi, Tamio Kawaji
A tale of boxing and gangland interaction. Ex-boxer Ishihara has become
a successful businessman. His partner, a friend who he had accidentally
injured in the ring, is found murdered,
and Ishihara discovers the yakuza are
behind it. They try to frame him for
the murder of his dead pal's girl, but
Ishihara resorts to a violent shootout with the gangsters and emerges
triumphant.

**GOOD-FOR-NOTHING aka
ROKU DENASHI series**

**PRECIOUS BAD REPUTATION
OF A GOOD-FOR-NOTHING** aka
AKUMYO TAKAKI ROKU DE-
NASHI 1963 82 min. **DIR.** Buichi
Saito **SCR.** Motonari Wakai **PHOTO**
COLOR 'SCOPE: Shigeyoshi Mine
MUSIC: Taiichiro Kosugi w/ Joe
Shishido, Midori Asakaza, Chiharu
Kuri, Toru Yuri, Arihiko Fujimura,
Toshiaki Minami, Keisuke Noro
#1 of 3 films

Red Shoes and a Good-for-Nothing

**RED SHOES AND A GOOD-
FOR-NOTHING** aka AKAI
KA TO ROKU DENASHI 1963
88 min. **DIR.** Yoichi Ushihara/
Ko Nakahira **SCR.** Hisatoshi Kai/

Ryoichi Yamauchi/Seiji Hoshikawa
PHOTO COLOR 'SCOPE: Shigeyoshi
Mine **MUSIC:** Harumi Ibe   w/ Joe
Shishido, Yoshie Mizutani, Akifumi
Inoue, Asao Koike, Reiko Sassamori,
Kaku Takashina   #2 of 3 films

**TRUE LIFE OF A GOOD-FOR-
NOTHING** aka INOCHI SHIRA-
ZU NO ROKU DENASHI 1965
87 min. **DIR.** Mio Ezaki **SCR.**
Motonari Wakai/Hiroaki Hayashi
PHOTO COLOR 'SCOPE: Kurataro
Takamura **MUSIC:** Harumi Ibe
w/ Joe Shishido, Keiko Yuge, Yuji
Kodaka, Nanako Ohama, Masahiko
Tanimura, Kaku Takashina, Hiroshi
Kondo   #3 and final in series

**GOOD-FOR-NOTHINGS'
BUSINESS aka ROKU DENASHI
KAGYO aka JOE OF ACES
series**

**GOOD-FOR-NOTHINGS'
BUSINESS** aka ROKU DENASHI
KAGYO aka JOE OF ACES –
GAMBLING FOR A LIVING 1961
83 min. **DIR.** Buichi Saito **SCR.**
Ryoichi Yamauchi/Hisagohei Maki(?)
PHOTO COLOR 'SCOPE: Kurataro
Takamura **MUSIC:** Taiichiro Kosugi
w/ Joe Shishido, Nobuo Kaneko,
Hideaki Nitani, Yoko Minamida,
Sayuri Yoshinaga, Reiko Sassamori,
Tadao Sawamoto   Shishido's
humorous action/yakuza series with
his Joe-of-Aces persona. Actually
QUICK-DRAW OUTLAW (HAY-
AUCHI YARO) (1960), a western (!)
directed by Takashi Nomura, could be
considered the very loosely-connect-
ed first film in this bunch as it also
features Shishido as Joe-of-Aces.
#1 of 5 films

BODYGUARD BUSINESS aka
YOJINBO KAGYO aka JOE OF
ACES – BODYGUARD 1961 78
min. **DIR.** Toshio Masuda **SCR.**
Ryozo Nakanishi **PHOTO COLOR
'SCOPE:** Shinsaku Himeda **MUSIC:**
Harumi Ibe   w/ Joe Shishido,
Hideaki Nitani, Nobuo Kaneko, Yoko
Minamida, Reiko Sassamori, Yoko
Minamikaze   #2 of 5 films

RESCUE BUSINESS aka SUKE-
TTO KAGYO aka JOE OF ACES
– GIVE AND TAKE 1961 79 min.
DIR. Buichi Saito **SCR.** Yuji Tanno/
Ryochi Yamauchi **PHOTO COLOR
'SCOPE:** Kurataro Takamura **MUSIC:**
Taiichiro Kosugi   w/ Joe Shishido,
Hiroyuki Nagato, Reiko Sassamori,
Nobuo Kaneko, Sanae Nakahara,
Ryohei Uchida, Hiroshi Kondo,
Arihiko Fujimura   #3 of 5 films

*Rescue Business aka Good-for-Nothing
(#3)*

CRIMSON PLAINS aka AKAI KOYA 1961 86 min. **DIR.** Hiroshi Noguchi **SCR.** Iwao Yamazaki/ Norio Ando **PHOTO COLOR 'SCOPE:** Kazue Nagatsuka **MUSIC:** Taiiichiro Kosugi **w/** Joe Shishido, Yuji Kodaka, Ryohei Uchida, Reiko Sassamori, Yoko Minamida
Joe-of-Aces returns to a rural ranch where he used to live many years before. His ex-girlfriend and pal have since been married and have a son. The couple are on the verge of being forced-out of their spread by the local gang. To complicate matters, a bitter, resentful killer hailing from Joe and his buddy's former gang arrives and makes everyone's life miserable. Eventually, Joe routs the bad guys but is cornered by the killer. His old pal rescues him.   #4 of 5 films

Good-for-Nothing - Loner's Travels

LONER'S TRAVELS aka HITORI TABI 1962 85 min. **DIR.** Buichi Saito **SCR.** Iwao Yamazaki/Ryuzo Nakanishi **PHOTO COLOR 'SCOPE:**

Kurataro Nakamura **MUSIC:** Taiichiro Kosugi **w/** Joe Shishido, Ruriko Asaoka, Mari Shiraki, Kojiro Kusanagi, Ryohei Uchida, Toru Abe #5 of 6 films

SAND DUNE DUEL – QUICK-DRAW JOE aka SAKYU NO KETTO – HAYAUCHI JO 1964 **DIR.** Kan Hanase **SCR.** Kan Hanase/ Koto Yamanaka **w/** Joe Shishido, Ryoji Hayama   A one-off revival of the "Joe-of-Aces" series starring Shishido. #6 and final in series

Sand Dune Duel - Quick-Draw Joe

GREATEST BOSS OF JAPAN aka NIHON SAIDAI NO KAOYAKU aka NUMBER ONE GANGSTER BOSS IN JAPAN 1970 88 min. **DIR.** Akinori Matsuo **SCR.** Susumu Saji/Akira Nakano **PHOTO COLOR 'SCOPE:** Kazumi Iwasa **MUSIC:** Hidehiko Kawano
w/ Akira Kobayashi, Joe Shishido, Meiko Kaji, Toru Abe, Jerry Fujio, Tatsuya Fuji, Eiji Go, Akifumi

Inoue, Shoki Fukae, Hyoe Enoki
Seemingly based on fact, this is a
lackluster, episodic account of the
career of a gang boss (Kobayashi)
in post-war Japan, following him
from Kobe to Tokyo to Fukuoka to
snowbound Hokkaido and back again.
There are some evocative images
reminiscent of the same territory covered a short time later by Fukasaku's
Toei Studios BATTLES WITHOUT
HONOR AND HUMANITY series.
However, Kobayashi's character is
too idealized to bear much resemblance to any real character. Kaji is
the traditional singer daughter of a
benevolent boss who is murdered
while Kobayashi is visiting comrade
Tatsuya Fuji in Hokkaido. Kaji is
given virtually nothing to do, although we do actually get to hear her
sing. The most memorable characters
are serio-comic Jerry Fujio and
Akifumi Inoue. In one of the more realistic subplots, the latter dies with his
addict/whore wife (Yoshiko Machida)
when they try to flee her evil, impris-
oning gang.   * *

GUN DEMON WITHOUT FORM
aka SUGATA NAKI KENJU MA
1964 **DIR.** Isamu Kosugi **SCR.** Hisao
Okawa **PHOTO 'SCOPE:** Toshitaro
Nakao **MUSIC:** Taiichiro Kosugi
w/ Ryoji Hayama, Kazuko Yoshiyuki,
Fumi Omachi, Asao Sano, Mizuho
Suzuki, Mari Shiraki

GUNMAN aka KENJU YARO aka
ROGUE GUN 1965 80 min. **DIR.**
Motomu (Tan) Ida **SCR.** Koichi
Saito/Akira Nakano **PHOTO COLOR**
'SCOPE: Izumi Hagiwara **MUSIC:**
Joharu Yamamoto   w/ Hideki
Takahashi, Yukiyo Toake, Yunosuke
Ito, Osamu Takizawa, Akira Nagoya,

Takeshi Yoshida, Ruriko Ito, Jun
Hamamura, Eiji Go   The feeling
given off by the movie poster leans
towards the tongue-in-cheek.

GUNMAN'S ALLEY aka KENJU
YOKO CHO aka KILLER WITH-
OUT A GRAVE 1961 77 min. **DIR.**
Tokujiro Yamazaki **SCR.** Kimiyuki
Hasegawa/ Tatsuo Miyata **PHOTO**
COLOR 'SCOPE: Kazumi Iwasa
MUSIC: Keitaro Miho   w/ Hideaki
Nitani, Yuji Kodaka, Minako Kazuki,
Eitaro Ozawa, Sumiko Minami, Toru
Abe, Jun Hamamura
Nitani is an undercover narc in Kobe
who not only busts two rival drug
gangs but also helps one of the more
decent hoodlums find the killer of the
hood's brother.

Gunman's Alley

GUN NUMBER ZERO aka
KENJU ZERO GO 1959 53 min.
DIR. Tokujiro Yamazaki **SCR.**
Nobuyoshi Terada/Junichi Yoneya/
Masuo Maeda **PHOTO B&W 'SCOPE:**

Umeo Matsubayashi **MUSIC:**
Keitaro Miho **w/** Tamio Kawaji,
Yoshiko Okano, Mihoko Inagaki,
Keiichiro Akagi, Joe Shishido,
Shoichi Ozawa, Toru Abe, Kyosuke
Machida, Jun Hamamura
A short second support feature told
from the point-of-view of a handgun
– that occasionally narrates! – that is
accidentally thrown away in a hotel,
then inadvertently changes hands
many times, going from a ragpicker
to a yakuza gang to a concert violinist
to a thrill-seeking couple to a couple
contemplating double suicide. The
episodic nature dictates an unevenness in the narration. The best seg-
ment by far features Shishido as a
hood in service to cruel boss Abe. He
beats up the true love (Machida) of
Abe's mistress then brings him to the
cellar of the gang's nightclub. There,
in front of his mistress and flunkies, Abe shoots Machida to death.
Barely keeping her composure, the
mistress bides her time till later that
night when she is in bed with Abe.
While he sleeps, she gets the gun,
puts a pillow over it and shoots Abe
in the head. This scene is actually
quite shocking, despite the absence
of blood-and-guts. It is too bad that
this is the only sequence where some
genuine emotion seems to be involved. The conclusion of the film,
with the star-crossed couple nearly
shuffling off the mortal coil in their
suicide pact, doesn't quite realize its
potential. Neverttheless, this is pretty
gutsy material for director Yamazaki
who seemed to be mostly relegated to
helming some of Akira Kobayashi's
more lightweight material (i.e., THE
DRIFTER series).   * * 1/2

THE GUYS WHO BET ON ME
aka ORE NI KAKETA YATSURA
1962 90 min. **DIR.** Seijun Suzuki
SCR. Ei Ogawa/Akira Nakano **PHOTO
COLOR 'SCOPE:** Shigeyoshi Mine
MUSIC: Seitaro Omori w/ Koji Wada,
Yoko Minamida, Ryoji Hayama,
Tamio Kawaji, Kaku Takashina, Mari
Shiraki, Mayumi Shimizu
Wada is a boisterous truckdriving
youth who has ambition for the ring.
He follows his dream and becomes
a hugely successful fighter under the
tutelage of gym owner Hayama and
trainer Takashina. A gang of yakuza
who had already been harassing
Hayama, zero in on Wada as the
perfect property and go through all
kinds of scams to land him under
contract. To complicate matters,
Hayama's wife Shiraki is a raging
nymphomaniac having an affair with
Takashina. When she tries to seduce
Wada and he rebuffs her, she screams
rape and Hayama believes her.
Wada already has his own romantic
problems, having thrown over simple
shop girl Shimizu for sophisticated
nightclub chanteuse Minamida. The
crazy lifestyle pushes Wada closer to
the gang's reach, and they let loose
gimpy fashionplate killer Kawaji on
him to finally snare Wada's services.
Wada seriously injures a bartender
in a fight with Kawaji's men, and the
gang holds the man's supposed brain
damage over Wada's head hoping
to extort a contract from him. These
scenes where the supposedly blither-
ing idiot is used to torment Wada are
milked by director Suzuki for the
maximum macabre effect. Eventually,
Hayama realizes his spouse Shiraki's
perfidy, reconciles with Wada and
Takashina and the boys ready for
the climactic big fight. Wada is put

through grueling paces in the final
match with a huge contingent of
gangsters in the audience on the verge
of a near riot if he wins. Meanwhile,
we learn that the injured bartender
is really in the gang's employ and is
faking his brain damage to put the
pressure on Wada. Lone wolf
yakuza cripple Kawaji, having
developed a grudging respect for
Wada, decides to suicidally shoot it
out with his cronies when the whole
bunch bids to hightail it to the boxing
stadium and kill Wada. Suzuki goes
for broke in this sequence, exag-
gerating the gun battle to the point
of a ridiculously surreal comic book
delirium. All perish. Back at the
stadium, Wada wins, reuniting with
old heartthrob Shimizu, and the cops
apprehend the leftover gangsters.
Suzuki delivers an incredible palette
of primary colors that sear the eyeball
while employing juxtapositions and
editing rhythms that would make later
pioneers like Godard look tame. Despite the happy ending, it is obvious
that Wada's ego-driven youth, living
in such a chaotic universe, will not
be happy for long. Another perfect
example of a good, consistently
entertaining film being spun out of
comparatively hackneyed elements.
* * *

HARBOR'S BRUTAL DENIZENS
aka KYO AKU NO HATOBA 1961
Dir. Takumi Furukawa   Scr. Ryuzo
Nakanishi Photo 'scope: Kenji
Hagiwara Music: Taiichiro Kosugi
w/ Kyoji Aoyama, Minako Kazuki,
Ichiro Sugai, Hiroshi Nihonyanagi

HARBOR OF NO RETURN aka
KAERAZARU HATOBA 1966 89
min. Dir. Mio Ezaki Scr. Nobuo

Yamada/Ryuzo Nakanishi Photo
color 'scope: Minoru Yokoyama
w/ Yujiro Ishihara, Ruriko Asaoka,
Takashi Shimura, Eiji Go
Jazz musician Ishihara finds his gal in
bed with another man and accidentally kills her in an angry confrontation.
It turns out that her lover is part of a
dope ring who had set up Ishihara as
an unwitting mule to bring their stuff
into Japan. After a three year prison
term, Ishihara is used as bait by
detective Shimura to track the drug
gang. Ishihara also finds time to fall-
in-love with Asaoka in this "mood/
action" yakuza film.

HAWK OF THE HARBOR aka
HATOBA NO TAKA 1967 80 min.
Dir. Shugoro Nishimura   Scr. Ei
Ogawa/ Ryuzo Nakanishi Photo
color 'scope: Shinsaku Himeda
Music: Rinichiro Manabe
w/ Yujiro Ishihara, Tetsuro Tanba,
Ruriko Asaoka, Toru Abe, Eitaro
Ozawa, Fujio Suga, Eiji Go
A surprisingly good "mood/action"
opus with Ishihara as the persecuted-
by-yakuza owner of a harbor shipping business. When Ishihara's
refusal to sign with the unscrupulous
gang ends with him putting boss
Suga's head through a TV (!), his car
is sabotaged. He and his kid sister
then suffer a serious accident which
leaves her dead and him limping
through the middle third of the saga.
Per usual, violence escalates. Police
inspector Tanba attempts to help
Ishihara thwart the villains – but to
minimal effect. Finally Ishihara's
partner Abe has his little son kidnapped by the mobsters. Although he
does dispatch ruffian Go, Abe dies in
his attempt to get the boy back. Even
more unhappily, Ishihara is conflicted

because his new nightclub hostess heartthrob Asaoka is the daughter of elder-boss-behind-the-scenes Ozawa. After the big shootout at the factory climax, Ozawa flees from pursuing Ishihara with resisting Asaoka in tow. He steals a fast boat, but Ishihara manages to get on board. Things end tragically with Asaoka stopping a bullet from dad's gun meant for her lover. Cowardly Ozawa is shot dead, and Asaoka dies in Ishihara's arms. Ishihara is left with Abe's traumatized son to raise as his own. Despite the routine elements in the scenario, director Nishimura admirably stirs clear of excessive sentimentality, supplying a very welcome gritty and noirishly bittersweet tone. Yet one more reason to grant Nishimura – maker of such good pictures as YAKUZA NATIVE GROUND, MIDNIGHT VIRGIN, TOKYO STREETFIGHTING, et. al. – status as most neglected, underrated Nikkatsu director of the late sixties. Also of note: the only time I can recall ever seeing mainstay villain actor Abe (who usually portrayed a slimy mob boss) as a good guy. * * *

HEART OF STONE aka ZANKYO MUJO aka LAST OF THE UNFEELING aka ALL THAT REMAINS IS CRUELTY 1968 86 min. **DIR.** Motomu (Tan) Ida **SCR.** Hisatoshi Kai **PHOTO COLOR 'SCOPE:** Shigeyoshi Mine **MUSIC:** Seitaro Omori **w/** Hideki Takahashi, Sanae Kitabayashi, Daisaburo Hirata, Hiroshi Nawa, Koei Hatsui, Asao Koike, Yasuko Sanjo, Yoko Yamamoto, Asao Sano, Saburo Hiromatsu

Heart of Stone

HELL FESTIVAL aka JIGOKU NO SAITEN 1963 94 min. **DIR.** Yoichi Ushihara **SCR.** Ei Ogawa **PHOTO COLOR 'SCOPE:** Kenji Hagiwara **MUSIC:** Taiichiro Kosugi **w/** Joe Shishido, Kunie Tanaka, Reiko Sassamori, Mari Shiraki, Yuji Kodaka, Eiji Go, Akio (Teruo? Meio?) Tanaka, Torahiko Hamada, Shoki Fukae   Shishido is a primitive, virtual caveman devoted to fishing and hunting in the icy seas of northern Hokkaido. He stows away in a freighter bound for Yokohama. Almost as soon as he is off the boat, he crosses paths with Kodaka's gang while rescuing Sassamori. The best moments in the film are in the first third when Shishido is still conflicted with the gangsters and casually keeping them at bay in their nightclub with a rifle. Eventually, he is recruited into the gang as an enforcer and becomes involved in Kodaka's fanatical efforts in trying to retrieve a cache of heroin that has been smuggled in, then stolen. The mobsters clean Shishido up, shaving and otherwise grooming him until he is nearly unrecognizable. It is too bad that the middle third of the picture drags, picking up only at the end with a wild nocturnal gun battle in a graveyard of old ships. By this time Shishido has once again turned on Kodaka and his villains and succeeds in wiping them out. He then opts to return to his simple, primitive existence in northern Hokkaido. As the story would suggest, there is quite a bit of humor on display. Some of it is mildly funny, but more often than not the forced comedy falls flat. Except for a few bright spots, HELL FESTIVAL is a little disappointing. But love the title. * * 1/2

Hell Festival

HELL MONEY aka JIGOKU NO SATSUTABA 1956 80 min. DIR. Hiroshi Noguchi SCR. Yoshihisa Aoki/Kiyomi Kawagami PHOTO B&W: Kazue Nagatsuka MUSIC: Naozumi Yamamoto w/ Michitaro Mizushima, Ichiro Sugai, Mieko Hirooka, Seizaburo Kawazu

HELL'S STREET CORNER aka JIGOKU NO MAGARIKADO 1959 92 min. DIR. Koreyoshi Kurahara SCR. Tae (Ataru?) Baba/Nobuo Yamada PHOTO B&W 'SCOPE: Yoshio Mamiya MUSIC: Rinichiro Manabe w/ Ryoji Hayama, Yoko Minamida, Mieko Inagaki, Hiroshi Oizumi, Kaku Takashina

HIGH-TEEN YAKUZA aka HAI TEIIN YAKUZA 1962 72 min. DIR. Seijun Suzuki SCR. Nozomu Yoshimura/Mamoru Okusono PHOTO B&W 'SCOPE: Kenji Hagiwara MUSIC: Harumi Ibe w/ Tamio Kawaji, Noriko Matsumoto, Toshio Sugiyama, Kayo Matsuo, Keiko Hara, Sazo Kiura, Asao Sano, Midori Tashiro

HIRED GUN aka KENJU KASHIMASU series

HIRED GUN aka KENJU KASHI-MASU 1962 66 min. DIR. Tokujiro Yamazaki SCR. Junichiro Yamaguchi PHOTO 'SCOPE: Kenji Hagiwara MUSIC: Keitaro Miho w/ Tomoo Nagai, Tadao Sawamoto, Yoshio Omori, Keisuke Sonoi #1 of 2

INVADER WITHOUT A SHADOW aka KAGENAKI SHINNYUSHA 1962 62 min. DIR. Tokujiro Yamazaki SCR. Junichiro

Yamaguchi/Hiroshi Nishijima **PHOTO** **'SCOPE:** Kenji Hagiwara Music: Keitaro Miho **w/** Tomoo Nagai, Tadao Sawamoto, Yoshio Omori, Keisuke Sonoi #2 of 2

HOODLUM aka OUTLAW aka BURAI series

HOODLUM - LEADING MOBSTERS aka BURAI YORI - DAI KANBU aka GANGSTER VIP 1968 93 min. **DIR.** Toshio Masuda **ORIG. STORY:** "Hoodlum" ("Burai"): Goro Fujita **SCR.** Kaneo Ikegami/Reiji Kubota **PHOTO COLOR** **'SCOPE:** Kurataro Takamura **MUSIC:** Naozumi Yamamoto
w/ Tetsuya Watari, Kyosuke Machida, Chieko Matsubara, Kayo Matsuo, Yoshiro Aoki, Tamio Kawaji, Tatsuya Fuji, Michitaro Mizushima, Mitsuo Hamada, Sanae Kitabayashi, Kaku Takashina, Shoki Fukae

Hoodlum (#1) aka Gangster VIP

This series is a bit of a rare bird in that it strikes a balance between the modern ultra-cruel, ultra-violent *jitsuroku* (true account) yakuza films that were evolving at Toei in 1969-1976 timeframe and the more romantic, traditional "doomed hero" *ninkyo* (chivalrous) genre best exemplified by Toei's TALES OF THE LAST SHOWA ERA YAKUZA series. HOODLUM #1 begins with a nearly monochromatic prologue showing Goro (Watari) as a child basically going through hell – his mother being rudely seduced by a yakuza hoodlum, his little sister dying of illness while he runs around the neighborhood in the midst of a storm vainly seeking help, stealing food from a peddler in post-war chaos, escaping from a reform school camp only to be roughly abandoned by his older companion as soon as they are a few meters outside the barbed wire. Dissolve into the present where he confronts the same older friend (Machida) who had abandoned him who is now shooting up Watari's *oyabun* (Mizushima)'s bar, Watari reluctantly wounding Machida with a knife and being carted off to prison. The scene where the cops haul him away is a classic: Watari's gal crying softly as she promises to wait for him, then his stabbed buddy Machida's girl (Matsuo) getting in his face. Once Watari is out of prison, the usual downward spiral of unlucky chance encounters and hoodlum companions begins to take its toll in some poignant sequences – he reconciles with the now tubercular Machida, and Machida, to protect Watari's whereabouts, ends up dying at the hands of evil Aoki's gang – as well as ultra-violent knifefights (our anti-hero looking

Hoodlum (#2)

very cool in black leather). The end gangfight is, in particular, a *tour-de-force* with Watari attacking Aoki and his men at a nightclub while all that can be heard on the soundtrack is a woman singing a slightly uptempo but very sad song about life-and-love's sorrows. Supposedly this series is composed of the slightly disguised autobiography of writer Goro Fujita, a former yakuza and the prodigious poet laureate of the Japanese underworld.   #1 of 6 films   * * * 1/2

LEADING MOBSTERS – HOODLUM aka DAI KANBU – BURAI aka OUTLAW SWORD 1968 97 min. **DIR.** Keiichi Ozawa **ORIG. STORY:** Goro Fujita **SCR.** Kaneo Ikegami/ Reiji Kubota **PHOTO COLOR 'SCOPE:** Kurataro Takamura **MUSIC:** Harumi Ibe **w/** Tetsuya Watari, Chieko Matsubara, Hideaki Nitani, Kayo Matsuo, Ryohei Uchida, Kunie Tanaka, Izumi Ashikawa, Masako Ota, Akira Yamanouchi, Jiro Okazaki, Junko Maya   Yes, you aren't seeing things; the only way the title of this film differs from the previous first one is they just reversed the words! Watari continues as Goro, traveling by train to the snowbound north to rejoin his girl (Matsubara). He becomes involved with a nefarious gang led by sadistic Uchida. Nitani plays a middle-aged yakuza trying to raise a family. He is stabbed to death for his trouble. Matsuo's character – she had been Watari's tubercular buddy Kyosuke Machida's girl in the previous film – had traveled north with Matsubara upon Machida's violent death. It turns out she has got the dreaded consumption, too, and she dies a lonely death midway through the film. There are plenty of

extremely well-choreographed black leather knifefights, especially the long, drawn-out climax in a storm drain where the evil Uchida and many of his henchmen meet their demise at Goro's hand.   #2 of 6 films
* * * *

HOODLUM – SAD FEELING aka BURAI – HIBOJO 1968 92 min. **DIR.** Mio Ezaki **ORIG. STORY:** Goro Fujita **SCR.** Iwao Yamazaki/Mio Ezaki **PHOTO COLOR 'SCOPE:** Yoshihiro Yamazaki **MUSIC:** Harumi Ibe **w/** Tetsuya Watari, Chieko Matsubara, Ryohei Uchida, Koji Wada, Chikage Ogi, Eiji Go, Ryoji Hayama, Hiroshi Nawa, Asao Uchida, Fumio Watanabe
Obligated to an evil boss, Watari and friend Go accompany the boss's right-hand Nawa to go roust the boss's enemy Hayama. Hayama and his wife Ogi are packing to split when Watari turns up out of a violent rainstorm. Hayama, who seems honest, explains the situation. Watari realizes, too, that Ogi is not well. He is going to let them go when evil Nawa intervenes, mortally wounding Hayama. Watari is very angry at having been deceived. He and Go attack the bad guy HQ/ gambling den and getaway with the cash box. Watari subsequently tries to look after the sick widow Ogi despite her protestations. Before long, Wada shows up, a boisterous hothead who is related to Hayama (or Ogi, I'm not sure which). The bad guys steer him to Watari as the killer of Hayama. Ryohei Uchida is a good guy this time around, one of Watari's friends. His girlfriend works for Watanabe, one of the bad bosses. The customary violent massacre finale showcases Watari wiping out the despicable opposition

in a paint warehouse. The climactic struggle between Watari and Watanabe is a messy swirl of blood and riotous colors.   #3 of 6 films
* * *

HOODLUM – KILLER GORO
aka BURAI – HITOKIRI GORO
1968 88 min. DIR. Keiichi Ozawa
ORIG. STORY: Goro Fujita
SCR. Kaneo Ikegami/Keiichi Ozawa
PHOTO COLOR 'SCOPE: Kurataro
Takamura MUSIC: Harumi Ibe
w/ Tetsuya Watari, Chieko
Matsubara, Kei Sato, Chitose
Kobayashi, Koji Nanbara, Jiro
Okazaki, Tatsuya Fuji, Shoki Fukae,
Asao Koike, Shuji Otaki
This begins with Watari killing boss
Otaki in the rain while Nanbara looks
on. One of Otaki's men tries to stab
Watari but is deflected by pal Fuji
who ends up seriously ventilated by
the blade. Fuji dies in prison shortly
thereafter from the wounds. The
main thrust of the story is Watari
trying to live-and-let-live after the
carnage but instead being hounded
by the minions of Otaki's successor,
Nanbara. He loses his job with new
heartthrob Matsubara at a resort hotel
when vengeful hoodlums show up,
take him around back, literally nail
his hands to a wall and then beat the
hell out of him. He is on the next bus
out as is Matsubara. When Matsubara
strays into a pool hall where underboss Fukae and other Nanbara goons
have enslaved, drugged prostitutes
stashed, she is prevented from leaving. Watari comes to her rescue,
crossing blades with Fukae and men.
Watari's old friend, underboss Sato
intervenes and achieves a stalemate.
Thereafter Nanbara tries to bribe,
cajole or intimidate various friends of

Watari into selling him out. Okazaki,
Koike and Sato all end up feigning
acquiescence – something that even
convinces Watari for a while. All
three end up dying chivalrous, self-
sacrificing and poetic deaths. Watari
and Matsubara appear destined to
leave town on a ferry when Watari
suddenly jumps ship at the last second, leaving his girl whom he knows
will only suffer if he remains with
her. He then returns to fight Nanbara
and henchmen in one of the most
spectacular knife battles in the series
with action spanning the waterfront.
He finally kills Nanbara, then, lying
on the ground, sees a reflection in
the villain's discarded sunglasses.
He looks up at the crest of a hill and
spots sweetheart Matsubara staring
at him as the end title comes on. This
has a beautiful noirish atmosphere,
excellent performances from a cast
playing well-written characters, a
surplus of well-balanced and fluidly
choreographed action and all the
necessary genre elements to create
a credible hybrid of the *ninkyo* and
jitsuroku yakuza subgenres. Drenched
in romantic emotion, it nevertheless
remains aloof and gritty enough to
avoid any phony sentiment. One of
the best in the series.   #4 of 6 films
* * * *

HOODLUM – DARK SWORD
aka BURAI – KURO DOSU 1968
86 min. DIR. Keiichi Ozawa ORIG.
STORY: Goro Fujita SCR. Kaneo
Ikegami PHOTO COLOR 'SCOPE:
Kurataro Takamura MUSIC: Koichi
Sakata w/ Tetsuya Watari, Chieko
Matsubara, Tamio Kawaji, Shigeru
Tsuyuguchi, Yoshiro Aoki, Ichiro
Nakatani, Kaku Takashina
This starts off well with a moody

opening, a lonely street cluttered with gangsters' bodies sprawled in the street and hanging out of car windows. There is evocative music as Goro (Watari) narrates. Kawaji and other enemies watch from the shadows. Kawaji makes a run at Watari with his knife, but suddenly Watari's gal (Matsubara) appears out of nowhere and is the one who is fatally stabbed. Later Watari meets and falls in love with a nurse who is a dead ringer for Matsubara. You see that kind of "twist" once in a while in samurai *chanbara* films. Somehow such a contrivance is more tolerable in a period film. But here it falls flat as a bit of calculated hokum. Of course, Watari and Kawaji meet up again, too, and there are the inevitable tragically bloody consequences. #5 of 6 films * * 1/2

Ozawa ORIG. STORY: Goro Fujita SCR. Shuichi Nagahara/Kaneo Ikegami PHOTO COLOR 'SCOPE: Kurataro Takamura MUSIC: Koichi Sakata w/ Tetsuya Watari, Chieko Matsubara, Shinjiro Ebara, Michitaro Mizushima, Koji Wada, Asao Koike, Shunji Imai, Hitomi Nozoe
A bit more on track once again with a smashing, somewhat psychedelic finale in the plush basement orgy pad of the head boss's nightclub. Blasting rock music drowns out the sound of the knifefight as Watari battles the villains beneath the two-way mirror dance floor (apparently used solely for looking up women's skirts!). #6 and last of series * * *

HOODLUM'S GUN DIARY aka KENJU BURAICHO series

Hoodlum (#6)

Hoodlum's Gun Diary (#1)

HOODLUM – HOMICIDAL aka BURAI – BARASE aka KILLER GORO 1969 86 min. DIR. Keiichi

HOODLUM'S GUN DIARY – RYUJI'S FAST DRAW aka KENJU BURAICHO – NUKI UCHI

NO RYUJI aka RYUJI, THE
GUNSLINGER 1960 86 min.
DIR. Hiroshi Noguchi **SCR.** Iwao
Yamazaki **PHOTO COLOR 'SCOPE:**
Kazue Nagatsuka **MUSIC:** Naozumi
Yamamoto w/ Keiichiro Akagi, Joe
Shishido, Ruriko Asaoka, Minako
Kazuki, Kojiro Kusanagi, Tadao
Sawamoto, Hiroshi Nihonyanagi,
Ko Nishimura, Arihiro Fujimura,
Ichiro Sugai   Noguchi was one
of Nikkatsu's prime bread 'n' butter
directors all through the fifties until
his untimely death from a heart attack in the mid-sixties. Despite his
unabashedly commercial status, he
nevertheless turned out some consistently fast-moving, violent entertainments. Not as imaginative nor as
don't-give-a-damn-what-the-front-
office-thinks-subversive as Seijun
Suzuki, he did occasionally have moments of a genuinely distilled visual
brilliance. Suzuki, who labored under
him as assistant director for a while,
has also credited him as something of
a mentor. There are sequences in each
of these four films, particularly the
bizarre, nihilistic hitman-from-hell-
undergoing-drug-withdrawals title
sequence in this premiere picture,
that rival anything in Suzuki's
YOUTH OF THE BEAST or
TOKYO DRIFTER. The whole idea
of the misunderstood hitman movie –
basically a strange, tall-tale subgenre
of the fifties Japanese action film that
carried well-over into yakuza pictures
made in the sixties and seventies – is
so wonderfully, surreally over-the-top
absurd to begin with. Unhappily, the
problem with this series as well as
many other program pictures made
at Nikkatsu (and other studios) is the
breakneck scriptwritng and shooting schedule. While a few bravura

sequences stand out, other sections
of the narrative are so bogged down
with stereotypical characters and
cliched formula, the films usually balance out into nothing more than just
above-average-entertainments. Akagi
plays a killer somehow in thrall to
various shady interests. He always
seems to be struggling to break
free from the corruption and craven
yakuza enterprises surrounding him.
And by the end of each installment,
he seems to have not only temporarily
broken free, but also to have gotten
the girl. If only the series had been a
little darker, a little more nihilistic.
At 21, Akagi made only a handful
of films at Nikkatsu before dying a
James Dean car crash (really go-kart)
death in February, 1961. Like fellow
matinee icons, Raizo Ichikawa and
Yusaku Matsuda, his brooding good
looks and tragic demise assured him a
prominent place in the motion picture
pantheon of Japanese pop culture
heaven. #1 of 4 films   * * *

Hoodlum's Gun Diary (#2)

HOODLUM'S GUN DIARY – A MAN ABLAZE WITH LIGHTNING aka KENJU BURAICHO – DENKO SEKKA NO OTOKO aka A GUN LIKE LIGHTNING 1960 85 min. **DIR.** Hiroshi Noguchi **SCR.** Toshio Matsuura **PHOTO COLOR** 'SCOPE: Kazue Nagatsuka **MUSIC:** Naozumi Yamamoto **w/** Keiichiro Akagi, Ruriko Asaoka, Joe Shishido, Hideaki Nitani, Mari Shiraki, Sayuri Yoshinaga, Kaku Takashina, Toshio Sugiyama   Once again, there is a great first ten minutes or so. Shishido, especially, embodies all the cocky, freewheeling, witty arrogance of the prototypical Nikkatsu bad boy. His and Akagi's gun-fondling/gunplay unintentionally amounts to a ludicrously weird panorama of sublimated visual phallic and homo-erotic fetishes. #2 of 4 films   * * *

Hoodlum's Gun Diary (#3)

HOODLUM'S GUN DIARY – FEARLESS BAD MAN aka KENJU BURAICHO – FUTEKI NI WARAU OTOKO aka MAN WITH

THE SINISTER SMILE 1960 84 min. **DIR.** Hiroshi Noguchi **SCR.** Iwao Yamazaki **PHOTO COLOR** 'SCOPE: Minoru Yokoyama **MUSIC:** Naozumi Yamamoto **w/** Keiichiro Akagi, Joe Shishido, Reiko Sassamori, Sayuri Yoshinaga, Kyoji Aoyama, Shoki Fukae, Hiroshi Kono, Chiomi Hoshi Akagi gets out of prison determined to go straight but finds that his girlfriend was murdered the year before. His former gang has now joined up with their rivals. A friendly police detective advises Akagi to leave town. But his former boss approaches him to act as a bodyguard in a forty million yen diamond transaction between the two gangs. Of course, there are all kinds of double-crosses in the works. Shishido, a gunman from the rival gang, becomes friends with Akagi. The two manage to ferret out the scumbags, including the killer of Akagi's gal, before the end credits. #3 of 4 films   * * 1/2

Hoodlum's Gun Diary (#4)

**HOODLUM'S GUN DIARY –
MAN WITH NO TOMORROW**
aka KENJU BURAICHO – ASU
NAKI OTOKO 1960 85 min.
DIR. Hiroshi Noguchi SCR. Toshio
Matsuura/ Yasunosuke Asajima
PHOTO COLOR 'SCOPE: Kumenobu
Fujioka MUSIC: Naozumi Yamamoto
w/ Keiichiro Akagi, Joe Shishido,
Reiko Sassamori, Yoko Minamida,
Michitaro Mizushima, Arihiro
Fujimura #4 and final in series
* * 1/2

**HOODLUM'S GUN DIARY –
BAND OF DRIFTERS** aka KENJU
BURAICHO – NAGAREMONO NO
MURE aka THE DRIFTERS 1965
93 min. DIR. Hiroshi Noguchi SCR.
Toshio Matsuura/Michio Sato
PHOTO COLOR 'SCOPE: Shinsaku
Himeda MUSIC: Hajime Kaburagi
w/ Akira Kobayashi, Joe Shishido,
Ryoji Hayama, Yuko Kusunoki,
Chieko Matsubara, Shoki Fukae, Eiji
Go A one-off follow-up/revival in
name only to the four film HOOD-
LUM'S GUN DIARY (1960) series
that starred the late Keiichiro Akagi.
There is no Ryuji character. Three
members of a gang take off with
the mob's money when a fight goes
badly. Their boss hires a hitman who,
instead of killing them, decides to
join them. The quartet is then joined
by a mysterious man in a vengeance
plot against their former boss, but the
fellow turns out to be an undercover
cop. Rumored to be in a humorous,
tongue-in-cheek vein.

**HURRICANE KID aka SHIPPU
KOZO series**

AMAZING BOY aka
SUTTOBI KOZO 1960 DIR.
Katsumi Nishikawa w/ Koji Wada,
Mayumi Shimizu #1 of 3 films

HURRICANE KID aka
SHIPPU KOZO aka QUICK DRAW
KID 1960 89 min. DIR. Katsumi
Nishikawa SCR. Ryozo Nakanishi
PHOTO COLOR 'SCOPE: Kazumi Iwasa
MUSIC: Masayoshi Ikeda
w/ Koji Wada, Shiro Osaka, Sayuri
Yoshinaga, Ryoji Hayama, Mayumi
Shimizu, Hiroshi Moriya, Masao
Shimizu This supposedly is second
in the series, but I have been unable
so far to find out much info on any of
the films. This one does have yakuza
elements, but it may be that these are
more straight action films. #2 of 3
films

WHIRLWIND KID aka
TATSUMAKI KOZO aka THE
YOUNG HURRICANE 1960 DIR.
Katsumi Nishikawa SCR. Toshio
Matsuura/ Ryozo Nakanishi PHOTO
'SCOPE: Kumenobu Fujioka MUSIC:
Masayoshi Ikeda w/ Koji Wada,
Mayumi Shimizu, Yuji Kodaka, Yumi
Takano, Hiroshi Nihonyanagi, Jerri
Fujio, Toru Abe #3 and final in
series

I Am Waiting

I AM WAITING aka ORE WA
MATTERU ZE 1957 91 min.
DIR. Koreyoshi Kurahara SCR.

Shintaro Ishihara PHOTO B&W: Kurataro Takamura MUSIC: Masaru Sato w/ Yujiro Ishihara, Mie Kitahara, Isamu Kosugi, Kenjiro Uemura, Hideaki Nitani   Ishihara, a former boxer working as a restaurant manager, saves a beautiful, suicidal club hostess (Kitahara) who is trying to escape the clutches of her gangster employer (Nitani). Doing so, Ishihara discovers Nitani is the hood who killed his brother. Generally effective but occasionally old-fashioned in style, with worthy influences from French directors like Marcel Carne (PORT OF SHADOWS). Newcomer director Kurahara diligently keeps the execution of the story more realistic than it has any right to be. Very atmospheric, with Kitahara radiant and Ishihara a convincing tough guy, despite his youth. * * *

IMPERFECT GAME aka KANZEN NA ASOBI aka THE PERFECT GAME 1958 93 min. DIR. Toshio Masuda SCR. Yoshio Shirasaka PHOTO B&W 'SCOPE: Minoru Yokoyama MUSIC: Rinichiro Manabe/Tomikazu Kawabe w/ Akira Kobayashi, Izumi Ashikawa, Ryoji Hayama, Masumi Okada, Mari Shiraki A fairly under-the-radar film by director Masuda that is better than some of his more famous pictures of the time like RUSTY KNIFE and RED HARBOR. Yet another variation on the cruel middle class delinquent *taiyozoku* (sun tribe) subgenre. Kobayashi and student pals figure out a complicated scheme for winning at the bike race track, something that takes up the first third or so of the story, but then have trouble collecting the money from the down-on-his-luck yakuza bookie (Hayama). When Hayama had jokingly told them – before thay had won – he would put up his straight-laced department store worker sister (Ashikawa) as collateral, he never dreamt it would come to that. The callous boys, anxious to get every bit of their loot, kidnap her by subterfuge, with Kobayashi charming her into a date. Okada and the others feign a fight and a beat-down with him while he is out with her (so she won't think he is involved). Meanwhile, the brother learns of the kidnap-and-ransom demand and goes on the run, finally stealing the money from a poor courier delivering a company payroll. Kobayashi keeps clear of the house where his friends are holding Ashikawa. Meanwhile, the sick mother of Hayama and Ashikawa takes a turn for the worse. By this time, Kobayashi is starting to become concerned for the girl's safety and is alarmed to find out Okada has raped her. The boys pick up the money and celebrate. But the sick mother dies, and when Ashikawa, who had fallen-in-love with Kobayashi discovers his complicity, she commits suicide by her dead mother's side. Hayama goes wild when he finds out, knifing to death the cold, brainy ringleader of the bunch as he leaves school. Kobayashi becomes so appalled at what they have done, the consequences and sociopathic coldbloodedness of his comrades, he makes a phone call to a newspaper, giving all their names as the guilty parties behind the three deaths. * * *

I NEVER CHEAT aka ORE WA DAMA SARE NAI 1960 77 min. DIR. Takumi Furukawa SCR. Hajime Takaiwa PHOTO B&W 'SCOPE: Saburo Isayama MUSIC: Taiichiro

Kosugi w/ Yuji Kodaka, Mari Shiraki, Sanae Nakahara, Shiro Osaka

INN OF FLOATING WEEDS aka UKIGUSA NO YADO 1957 74 min. **DIR.** Seijun Suzuki **SCR.** Iwao Yamazaki **PHOTO B&W:** Toshitaro Nakao **MUSIC:** Yoshi Eguchi w/ Hideaki Nitani, Kuno Yamaoka, Hachiro Kasuga, Ikuko Omuro, Toru Abe, Kaku Takashina   A deliriously romantic, atmospheric tale of gangster Nitani killing an adversary in a rain-drenched fight on a Yokohama wharf then, nearly dead himself, disappearing for five years – much to the consternation of his barmaid sweetheart Yamaoka. He returns masquerading as a Chinese seaman aboard a shady American vessel. His former gal is now the mistress of sadistic boss/clubowner Abe. Abe and underlings are unhappy to see Nitani back, and they revel in harassing him. A roving minstrel (Kasuga) takes him in after a beating, and the musician's kid sister Omuro immediately falls head over heels. One of the most visually fluid, imaginative sequences features the young sister bantering with Nitani on a waterfront railroad trestle bridge. Suzuki manages to make Omuro's act of dropping one shoe into the water far below a heart-breaking moment signifying her unrequited love and youthful frustrations. The next shot of her wearing men's shoes as Nitani walks her home in his stocking feet is poignantly sweet, and is more evocative of 1950s French New Wave cinema than Japanese. Finally things come to a head with Abe gradually running amok, accidentally strangling a whore then having his gang go on the rampage against Nitani in a trucking yard. This climactic fight where trucks are trying to run Nitani over while bullets fly is once again, like Suzuki's SATAN'S TOWN, its predecessor the year before, shockingly violent for the time period. Former paramour Yamaoka is killed saving Nitani's life. Wounded, he dispatches every gang member and at last is arrested by roving minstrel Kasuga – in reality an undercover cop! The last montage – Nitani sitting smoking in a sundappled cell and smitten kid sister Omuro mooning over him on the jetty below while her now uniformed sibling Kasuga strolls further down the wharf crooning a plaintive ode to lost love – is classically, absurdly surreal.   * * *

INTIMIDATION aka ARU KYOHAKU 1960 65 min. **DIR.** Koreyoshi Kurahara **SCR.** Osamu Kawase **PHOTO B&W 'SCOPE:** Yoshihiro Yamazaki **MUSIC:** Masaru Sato w/ Ko Nishimura, Noburo Kaneko, Mari Shiraki It is a stretch including this here. But not only is it a superior crime film, it illustrates the hybrid Japanese business culture that has evolved from native feudal roots and American-style capitalism that provides fertile, unfettered free market soil for the yakuza. It also throws up a distorted reflection of the legitimate business world at its most inhuman, where getting-ahead excuses all behavior, whatever side of the tracks on which one finds themself. A self-effacing bank clerk (Nishimura) throws a wrench into the plans of his superior (Kaneko) who has long used him as a rung on his ladder to success. Blackmail, a robbery and a murder enter into the mix, as well as several twists before the ironic climax.   * * *

Kanto Drifter (#1)

Expelled from the Kanto Mob (#3)

Kanto Society of Leading Mobsters (#2)

THE JUDGEMENT OF YOUTH
aka SEISHUN NO SABAKI 1965
DIR. Isamu Kosugi SCR. Eisaburo
Shiba PHOTO COLOR 'SCOPE: Jonobu
(?) Fujioka MUSIC: Taiichiro Kosugi
w/ Tetsuya Watari, Tatsuya Fuji,
Etsuhei Matsumoto, Yumi Takano

**KANTO DRIFTER aka KANTO
NAGAREMONO series**

KANTO DRIFTER aka KANTO
NAGAREMONO aka KANTO
OUTLAW 1971 86 min. DIR. Keiichi
Ozawa SCR. Goro Tanada/Masahiko
Ogura PHOTO COLOR 'SCOPE: Shohei
Ando MUSIC: Taiichiro Kosugi
w/ Tetsuya Watari, Mitsuko Oka,
Koji Nanbara, Tsuneya Oki, Ryohei
Uchida, Yoshiro Aoki, Shunji Imai,
Yoshio Harada, Michitaro
Mizushima Watari saves his boss
from a hotheaded assassin (Harada)
in the opening scenes. Much against
his desire, he ends up killing the
fellow. During the titles, we see him
serving a prison sentence. Soon after,
Mizushima is assassinated, and villainous Nanbara takes over. Watari
also has a naive, but ambitious kid
brother (Oki) whom he tries to keep
from getting involved in the gangster business. Eventually, his brother
proves a liability. The climax shows
Watari single-handedly rescuing his
brother from Nanbara's clutches.
Watari's gal (Oka) lends an unexpected hand and saves his life. Just before
he can reach Nanbara, the police cars
race into the rail/shipyard. As he is
led away, the handcuffed Watari grabs
a sword and manages to fatally slash
Nanbara. Fast-moving, with plenty
of knife-fighting action. #1 of 3 films
* * *

**KANTO SOCIETY OF LEADING
MOBSTERS** aka KANTO KAN-
BUKAI aka LINE-UP OF YAKUZA
BIG SHOTS 1971 86 min. DIR.
Yukihiro Sawada SCR. Tatsuhiko
Kamoi/Saburo Kurusu/Chikei Iji
PHOTO COLOR 'SCOPE: Yoshihiro
Yamazaki MUSIC: Hiroki Tamaki
w/ Tetsuya Watari, Isamu Nagato,
Mitsuko Oka, Yoshio Harada, Yoshiro
Aoki, Eiji Go, Gen Mitamura, Shunji
Imai An excellent yakuza film
which straddles the border between
ninkyo (chivalrous) and *jitsuroku*
(true document) type (as do the other
two films). In the opening, Watari
leaves prison and takes over the
management of a miniscule bar/cof-
fee house with his small, loyal gang.
Nagato is a bit older blood brother
caught in the machinations of the
bigger mob (led by Harada and Aoki)
that is trying to obliterate the obstinate Watari. A beautifully evocative,
wistful score played on harmonica
punctuates the intense performances,
moody nihilistic romanticism and
gut-wrenching brutality. 2 of 3 films
* * * 1/2

**EXPELLED FROM THE KANTO
MOB** aka KANTO HAMONJO
1971 87 min. DIR. Keiichi Ozawa
SCR. Tatsuhiko Kamoi PHOTO COLOR
'SCOPE: Shohei Ando MUSIC: Hajime
Kaburagi w/ Tetsuya Watari, Mitsuko
Oka, Kei Sato, Tatsuya Fuji, Eiji Go,
Takamaru Sasaki, Harumi Sone,
Rinichi Yamamoto #3 and last of
series * * *

**KANTO GOVERNMENT
KILLING SPREE** aka
NAGURIKOMI KANTO MASA
1965 DIR. Hiroshi Noguchi SCR.

Hisatoshi Kai PHOTO COLOR 'SCOPE: Toshitaro Nakao MUSIC: Seitaro Omori w/ Hideki Takahashi, Hideaki Nitani, Yoko Maki, Tatsuya Fuji

KANTO MOKO GOZANSU 1967 87 min. DIR. Hiroshi Noguchi/ Kazushige Takeda SCR. Hisatoshi Kai PHOTO COLOR 'SCOPE: Toshio Ueda MUSIC: (Stock) w/ Hideki Takahashi, Tamio Kawaji, Ryoji Hayama, Kusako Namino, Daisaburo Hirata   Since workaholic director Noguchi died suddenly in 1967, this may explain the co-direction credit with Takeda, who had been only an assistant director until this picture.

KANTO PRISON RETURN TRIP aka KANTO MUSHYO GAERI aka TO KILL A KILLER 1967 87 min. DIR. Kazushige Takeda SCR. Hisatoshi Kai PHOTO COLOR 'SCOPE: Minoru Yokoyama MUSIC: Taiichiro Kosugi   w/ Hideki Takahashi, Yoko Yamamoto, Koji Wada, Ryoji Hayama, Jiro Okazaki

Kanto Prison Return Trip

Kanto Sex Corps

KANTO SEX CORPS aka KANTO SEX GUNDAN 1973 DIR. Keiichi Ozawa SCR. Michio Sotake PHOTO COLOR 'SCOPE: Yoshihiro Yamazaki w/ Noriko Igarashi, Reiko Maki, Masumi Sakae A softcore pink sex film with *sukeban* and yakuza story elements.

KANTO WANDERER aka KANTO MUSHUKU 1963 93 min. DIR. Seijun Suzuki SCR. Yasutaro Yagi PHOTO COLOR 'SCOPE: Shigeyoshi Mine MUSIC: Masayoshi Ikeda w/ Akira Kobayashi, Hiroko Ito, Chieko Matsubara, Yunosuke Ito, Daisaburo Hirata, Sanae Nakahara, Toru Abe   Another one of Suzuki's unique yakuza films which critic Tadao Sato described as having "...strikingly unorthodox use of color and theatrical histrionics that blend humor with pathos..." Considering his build-up as well as the still photos Nikksatsu used for publicity, it is surprising this was not a bit better.

Still, it is quite good, but not as visually stimulating as some of Suzuki's other films. It opens with Suzuki poking fun at Kobayashi's matinee idol popularity, following several schoolgirls just out of class who are mooning over his photo. All the more ridiculous because he doesn't play a movie star in the film – his sex appeal is based on his status (or infamy) in the neighborhood as yakuza gambling den denizen. As it transpires, he never does get involved with any of the schoolgirls (Matsubara, et. al.). He is in-love with a crooked, married *hana fuda* cards dealer (Hiroko Ito). Much of the bizarre humor/pathos involves the battle-of-the-sexes – what men are willing to do or not do to attract a woman (such as kill somebody) and vice-versa. His hotheaded, younger brother (Hirata) plays right into this by becoming smitten with a rival mob boss's daughter. Some famous beautiful scenes such as when Kobayashi gets in a swordfight near the end, and the swish of the blade, just before the walls collapse and fall away, bathes the gambling den in a blood-red light. Unfortunately, there are not as many of those moments as some critics would lead you to believe.   * * *

KAWACHI JOKERS aka KAWACHI ZORO series

KAWACHI JOKERS aka KA-WACHI ZORO – DOKE CHICHU 1964 103 min. **DIR.** Toshio Masuda **SCR.** Ryozo Kasahara **PHOTO B&W 'SCOPE:** Kenji Hagiwara **MUSIC:** Harumi Ibe **w/** Joe Shishido, Tamio Kawaji, Satoshi Yamauchi, Yunosuke Ito, Yuji Kodaka, Kichijiro Ueda, Masahiko Tanimura, Zeko Nakamura,

Michiyo Yasuda, Yoko Minamida A rambunctious, rough-and-tumble tale of a rowdy trio (Shishido, Kawaji, Yamauchi) of gambling bumpkins belonging to a rural yakuza clan. Much humor – some of it funny, some of it lame – enlivens the proceedings. As far as gambling goes, our antiheroes are mostly into cockfighting. There is lots of action but of the saloon-brawl/fistfight variety. Even though plenty of people are beaten to a bloody pulp, no one seems to get killed. Similar in tone to Shintaro Katsu's BAD REPUTATION (AKUMYO) series at Daiei Studios during the same time period. #1 of 3 films   * * 1/2

KAWACHI JOKERS – COCKFIGHT SOLDIERS aka KAWACHI ZORO – KENKA JAMO 1964 100 min. **DIR.** Toshio Masuda **SCR.** Toshio Masuda/Hisatoshi Kai **PHOTO B&W 'SCOPE:** Kenji Hagiwara **MUSIC:** Harumi Ibe **w/** Joe Shishido, Tamio Kawaji, Satoshi Yamauchi, Yoko Minamida, Chiharu Kuri, Michiyo Yasuda, Masahiko Tanimura, Yuji Kodaka, Shigeru Tsuyuguchi, Asao Sano #2 of 3 films

KAWACHI JOKERS – GAMING RAMPAGE aka KAWACHI ZORO – ABARE CHO 1965 96 min. **DIR.** Mio Ezaki **SCR.** Ryozo Kasahara **PHOTO B&W 'SCOPE:** Yoshihiro Yamazaki **MUSIC:** Harumi Ibe **w/** Joe Shishido, Tamio Kawaji, Satoshi Yamauchi, Chieko Matsubara, Michiyo Yasuda, Yoko Minamida #3 and last of the series

KILLER OF NARCOTICS STREET aka MAYAKU GAI NO SATSUJIN 1957 **DIR.** Tatsuo Asano

SCR. Tatsuo Asano/Osamu Nishizawa/ Tatsuo Nogami PHOTO: Yasuo Uchida w/ Shigeru Akabane, Ichiro Kijima, Hiroshi Kondo

KILLER'S FINAL PLANS aka SATSUJIN KEIKAKU KANRYO 1956 88 min. DIR. Hiroshi Noguchi SCR. Tetsu Sueyama PHOTO B&W: Kumenobu Fujioka MUSIC: Rokuro Hara w/ Tatsuya Mihashi, Sumiko Hidaka, Shiro Osaka, Keiko Tama

KILL THE NIGHT ROSE aka YORU NO BARA O KESE 1966 95 min DIR. Toshio Masuda ORIG. STORY: Renzaburo Shibata SCR. Kikuma Shimoizaka PHOTO COLOR 'SCOPE: Yoshihiro Yamazaki MUSIC: Harumi Ibe w/ Yujiro Ishihara, Izumi Ashikawa, Kaoru Yumi, Mieko Nishio, Tatsuya Fuji, Masao Shimizu, Chigako Miyagi, Eijiro Tono, Mari Shiraki
Am entertaining but silly and fairly forgettable action film with much tongue-in-cheek James Bond influence, including the Ishihara-sung theme that has more than a passing resemblance to Tom Jones' "Thunderball." Ishihara is a lone wolf operative-for-hire who gets involved with a greedy clutch of gangsters trying to get their hands on a liquid explosive that detonates when heated to a certain temperature. Ishihara's diminutive barely-out-of-her-teens girl Friday, played by newcomer Kaoru Yumi, supplies some of the most exhilarating moments. There is one sequence that is especially enjoyable where Yumi, clad in Ann-Margaret-style dance tights, high-kicks at candles on the wall while she dances around the room, demonstrating to Ishihara her abil-ity to snuff flames with her balletic martial arts skill. Scenes such as this show there was the potential for a pop art classic ala BLACK TIGHTS KILLERS. Regrettably, it was not to be. Director Masuda tries hard, but despite such occasional *frissons*, this is a pretty humdrum affair. Cruel Tono, Ishihara's employer, turns out to be the main villain of the piece, and his submissive, abused mistress Ashikawa unexpectedly saves the day at the finale when she literally stabs him in the back as the gloating baddie is about to kill Ishihara and Yumi.
* * 1/2

KILL THE KILLER aka SATSUJIN SHA O KESE 1964 94 min. DIR. Toshio Masuda SCR. Ichiro Ikeda PHOTO COLOR 'SCOPE: Kurataro Takamura MUSIC: Harumi Ibe w/ Yujiro Ishihara, Yukiyo Toake, Asao Koike, Yuji Kodaka, Hideo Takamatsu, Kazuko Inano

THE LAW'S BLOODY WOUNDS aka KIZU DARAKE NO OKITE 1960 79 min. DIR. Yutaka Abe SCR. Iwao Yamazaki/Takashi Nomura PHOTO 'SCOPE: Yasuichiro Yamazaki MUSIC: Rinichiro Manabe w/ Ryoji Hayama, Hiroyuki Nagato, Yoko Minamida, Sanae Nakahara, Nobuo Kaneko, Hideaki Nitani, Ryohei Uchida, Asao Sano

THE LAW'S SCARRED FOOT-PRINTS aka KIZU ATO NO OKITE 1959 70 min. DIR. Tadashi Morizono SCR. Keiichi Abe/Tamio Aoyama PHOTO B&W 'SCOPE: Kan Inoue MUSIC: Tadashi Yamauchi w/ Shoji Yasui, Shinsuke Maki, Misako Watanabe, Yuko Minamikaze

LEADING MOBSTERS aka DAI KANBU series

LEADING MOBSTERS – KILLING SPREE aka DAI KANBU – NAGURIKOMI aka THE FATAL RAID 1969 95 min. **DIR.** Toshio Masuda **SCR.** Goro Tanada **PHOTO COLOR 'SCOPE:** Kurataro Takamura **MUSIC:** Harumi Ibe **w/** Tetsuya Watari, Kaneko Iwasaki, Yoshiro Aoki, Tatsuya Fuji, Mitsuo Hamada, Toru Abe, Nobuo Kaneko, Rie Yokoyama, Shoki Fukae Watari, Aoki, and Fuji pay a visit to an evil *oyabun's* private business meeting with assassination in mind. At the last second, Aoki the eldest, grabs the gun from Watari and pulls the trigger. Returning fire, Watari wounds the dead *oyabun's* bodyguard (Fukae) so seriously he later has to have his arm amputated. All three are caught and sentenced to prison. Watari and Fuji get out first since they were only accessories. Flash forward a couple of years later – Watari and Fuji hanging out at a coffee bar run by Aoki's wife. It is a real young folks' joint and serves as an excuse for Watari to sing a poorly-lip-synched (but okay) pop song. Another Japanese pop star (in an anonymous cameo) sings a couple of rowdy sing-a-longs. The partying is interrupted by clan members whose boss had coerced Watari et al. to kill the *oyabun*. Before long everyone at the coffee bar is brutalized on a regular basis. Finally the bar is trashed to coincide with Aoki's release. Everyone is distressed to see that Aoki has caught TB while behind bars. Toughs from the dead boss's clan (now run by Abe and Kaneko) start trying to kill Watari and Aoki. At one point, Fuji, who is now working for Kaneko, is extorted to kill his pal, Aoki. He lures his *senpai* (elder) to a secluded tunnel and draws his knife. Aoki tries to talk sense. Suddenly, four of the bad guys show up, all with blades. The excitement is too much for Aoki. He hemmorhages, coughing up blood, unable to defend himself. Fuji, realizing where his true loyalties lie and despising these men who would attack a defenseless person, rallies to Aoki's defense. He manages to hold them off, but is fatally wounded in the process. Just as the four descend on Aoki, Watari appears, and they flee. Aoki has only been winged. Fuji dies in Watari's arms. Skirmishes develop between the youth/coffee bar contingent and Abe/Kaneko's boys. Finally one of their youngest fellows, a naive garage mechanic is beaten and kidnapped. Having just been released from hospital, Aoki is summoned to the bad guys' stronghold to retrieve the boy. He humbly requests the fellow's return from the tittering bosses. They bring the boy out, dead. Naturally, Aoki explodes. His wife, who has followed, tries to intervene. Aoki acquits himself reasonably well with his knife, but he is no match for the large number of underlings, and four or five gang up on him, plunging in their blades. Abruptly, one-arm Fukae butts in with a drawn luger, appalled at his clan's behavior. Also feeling obligated to Watari who had compassionately spared him in the last gangfight, he accompanies the dying Aoki and his wife back to the coffee bar. The wife's little sis, who is Watari's gal, begs Watari not to do his revenge-binge. When she is unsuccessful, she bids Watari adieu and splits town with her grieving

Leading Mobsters (#2)

sister. However, at the first bus stop, she does an about-face and returns to be with him. Meanwhile, he is in the midst of carnage at a building dedication/bosses convention.Though repeatedly stabbed, he manages to off the evil *oyabuns* (Abe and Kaneko). Everyone that hasn't fallen under Watari's knife, flees. Watari is left tottering amongst the corpses, and he catches sight of his gal tearfully watching him from an alley-vantage-point as we freeze-frame to The End. #1 of 2 films * * *

Leading Mobsters (#2)

LEADING MOBSTERS – A PREDICTABLE DEMISE aka DAI KANBU – KERI O TSUKERO aka END OF THE HUNT aka PAY OFF YOUR DEBT 1970 83 min. DIR. Keiichi Ozawa SCR. Masayasu Daikuhara/Ryuzo Nakanishi PHOTO COLOR 'SCOPE: Minoru Yokoyama MUSIC: Taiichiro Kosugi w/ Tetsuya Watari, Ryohei Uchida, Reiko Ohara, Yoshiro Aoki, Bunsaku Han
Our tale begins with Watari making love to a young lady, then getting dressed, picking up his knife and jumping out the window to keep his appointment with destiny. First thing in the morning – vendetta time. He meets his pal, and they rendez-vous with some bigwigs in a remote vacant lot. A knifefight ensues, then

a prison term. When Watari gets out, he plots a vengeance caper to rob the clan who wronged him. He uses his buddies and gal to assist. It goes off okay, but the bad yakuza find out who is who and start picking up his friends one-by-one, torturing them, then killing them. Uchida is the over-sexed big boss with Aoki his imme-diate second-in-command who has it in for Watari. He had had his arm amputated due to that initial knife-fight. Nihilist violence ends things for everyone except the loyal girlfriend. Watari, dying, stumbles away to meet her on a sunny thoroughfare. #2 of 2 films * * * 1/2

LIFE OF A MAN'S FACE aka OTOKO NO KAO WA JINSEI aka A MAN'S LIFE IS HIS FACE 1971 DIR. Mio Ezaki SCR. Mio Ezaki/ Hiroshi Maegawa PHOTO COLOR 'SCOPE: Kurataro Takamura MUSIC: Akihiko Takashima w/ Shinsuke Minami, Ryohei Uchida, Hideo Inuzuka, Junko Natsu, Rika Fujie
A yakuza comedy.

LIVING AS A STRAY DOG aka IKI TE ITA NORA INU aka HOT-BED OF CRIME 1961 76 min. DIR./SCR. Toshio Masuda PHOTO COLOR 'SCOPE: Shinsaku Himeda MUSIC: Harumi Ibe w/ Hideaki Nitani, Ryoji Hayama, Reiko Sassamori, Shinsuke Ashida, Tamio Kawaji, Mari Shiraki, Shoki Fukae
A comparatively modern crime melo-drama for the time period, something one can certainly attribute to pioneer-ing director Masuda. Even still – much as they would plague colleague filmmaker Fukasaku at Toei Studios – run-of-the-mill programmer elements

occasionally rear their heads. Angry-as-hell Nitani gets out of prison intent on finding out why slimy Ashida has taken over his former gang. There is an elevated brutality quotient unusual for the early sixties, as well as deeper characterizations than usual – Fukae as one of Ashida's number two men and, especially, the great Shiraki as a girl with no illusions who falls for Nitani. * * *

Living as a Stray Dog

LIVING AS A WOLF aka IKI TEIRU OKAMI 1964 83 min. **Dir.** Motomu (Tan) Iida **Scr.** Tadashiro (Takaaki?) Oyamazaki/ Tan Ida **Photo B&W 'scope:** Toshitaro Nakao **Music:** Isao Tomita **w/** Akira Kobayashi, Reiko Sassamori, Eiji Go, Shinsuke Ashida

LONE WOLF aka IPPIKI OKAMI 1960 85 min. **Dir.** Yoichi Ushihara **Scr.** Hayato Takiguchi **Photo B&W 'scope:** Shigeyoshi Mine **Music:** Teizo Matsumura **w/** Yuji Kodaka,

Izumi Ashikawa, Tadao Sawamoto, Hideaki Nitani, Yoko Minamida, Shinsuke Ashida, Kyosuke Machida

THE LOST DIAMOND aka OTOKO NO IKARI O BUCHIMA-KERO 1960 80 min. **Dir.** Akinori Matsuo **Scr.** Tatsume Takemori/ Ryuzo Nakanishi **Photo color 'scope:** Kazumi Iwasa **Music:** Hajime Kaburagi **w/** Keiichiro Akagi, Ruriko Asaoka, Hideaki Nitani, Misako Watanabe, Nobuo Kaneko, Ryohei Uchida

The Lost Diamond

LOST OF THE SUN aka TAIYO WA KURUTTERU 1961 91 min. **Dir.** Toshio Masuda **Scr.** Nobuo Yamada **Photo color 'scope:** Shinsaku Himeda **Music:** Harumi Ibe **w/** Mitsuo Hamada, Tamio Kawaji, Sayuri Yoshinaga, Goro Mutsumi, Shinsuke Ashida, Yatsuko Tanami   Student Hamada, hanging out with youthful hoods, becomes intoxicated by gang life and is expelled from school. Hoodlum Kawaji is Hamada's pal who gets in over his head with debt. He involves Hamada in a blackmail scheme of Hamada's girlfriend's father. Her dad is accidentally hurt in the confrontation, and Hamada then tries to break off his friendship with Kawaji. His life now threatened by one of the gangs, Kawaji accepts a murder contract to earn safe passage to Hong Kong. He convinces Hamada to help, but Hamada balks when he recognizes the victim as his single mother's betrothed. He is stabbed in the process.

LOVE AND DESIRE IN THE NIGHT MIST aka YOGIRI NO BOJO 1966 92 min. **DIR.** Akinori Matsuo **SCR.** Tatsuo Nogami **PHOTO COLOR 'SCOPE:** Kazumi Iwasa Music: Sei Ikeno **w/** Yujiro Ishihara, Joe Shishido, Miyuki Kuwano, Tatsuya Fuji, Shinsuke Ashida, Masako Ota A film from Nikkatsu's *"moodo akushon"* (mood /action) subgenre.

MAKI KARUSARU – WET AFFAIRS OF THE NIGHT aka KARUSARU MAKI – YORU WA SHI O NURASU 1974 **DIR.** Shugoro Nishimura **SCR.** Masahiro Daikuhara **PHOTO COLOR 'SCOPE:** Yoshihiro Yamazaki **MUSIC:** Sansaku Okuzawa **w/** Maki Karusaru, Tsunosuke Koizumi Roman porno with yakuza elements.

A MAN EXPLODES aka OTOKO GA BAKUHATSU SURU 1959 96 min. **DIR.** Toshio Masuda **SCR.** Iwao Yamazaki/Mio Ezaki **PHOTO COLOR 'SCOPE:** Shinsaku Himeda **MUSIC:** Masaru Sato **w/** Yujiro Ishihara, Mie Kitahara, Ruriko Asaoka, Hideaki Nitani, Yuji Kodaka, Mari Shiraki

MANHUNT aka TSUISEKI 1961 Dir. Katsumi Nishikawa **w/** Hideaki Nitani, Chieko Matsubara, Yuji Kodaka, Eiji Go, Toshio Sugiyama, Shoki Fukae, Kaku Takashina

MAN IN THE MIST aka KIRI NO NAKA NO OTOKO 1958 92 min. **DIR.** Koreyoshi Kurahara **SCR.** Shintaro Ishihara **PHOTO B&W 'SCOPE:** Minoru Yokoyama **MUSIC:** Masaru Sato **w/** Ryoji Hayama, Sachiko Hidari, Hiroshi Kondo, Akira Kobayashi, Mari Shiraki

MAN OF THE PACIFIC PLAIN aka TAIHEI HARA NO OTOKO 1961 **DIR.** Hiroshi Noguchi **SCR.** Kan Hanase **PHOTO 'SCOPE:** Kazue Nagatsuka **MUSIC:** Taiichiro Kosugi **w/** Joe Shishido, Ryohei Uchida, Chieko Matsubara, Eijiro Tono

A MAN'S CREST aka OTOKO NO MONSHO aka EMBLEM OF A MAN series

A MAN'S CREST aka OTOKO NO MONSHO aka BADGE OF A MAN aka EMBLEM OF A MAN aka SYMBOL OF A MAN 1963 96 min. **DIR.** Akinori Matsuo **SCR.** Hisatoshi Kai **PHOTO COLOR 'SCOPE:** Kazumi Iwasa **MUSIC:** Hajime Kaburagi **w/** Hideki Takahashi, Masako Izumi, Kenjiro Ishiyama, Yukiko Todoroki, Asao Koike, Akifumi Inoue, Shiro Osaka, Nakajiro Tomita, Hiroshi Kondo A more original story than usual for a *ninkyo* yakuza film. Takahashi plays a boy brought up in a yakuza clan's household in the 1920s. His father (Ishiyama), the clan leader, pays for his education, and we see him making it through medical school and becoming a doctor under title credits. Because of a deranged oaf (Inoue) barely connected to their clan knifing one of the opposition gang, a vendetta is set in motion that leads to the death of Takahashi's father. On his deathbed, his father had forbidden revenge, guessing correctly that unless the violence stopped there, it would never end. Takahashi's left with a horrible choice: knowing he is the only one who can keep the peace, he must either take over leadership to perpetuate the truce or continue his medical career knowing that scores of "honorable" men are likely to die. He eventually finds out that the *oyabun* of one of the opposing clans is his mother (Todoroki), and this, of course, leads to further complications. At the end, backed into a corner where violence is the only way out, he goes up against Boss Kijima's gang, kills one man and cuts off Kijima's hand.

A Man's Crest (#1)

Despite a very low body count compared to most *ninkyo* yakuza climactic massacres, this still traumatizes Takahashi, and he wanders away in mental anguish with mother Todoroki and gal Izumi helplessly watching. Set in the early Showa pre-WW2 period, this has a similar feel to the TALES OF THE LAST SHOWA ERA YAKUZA series at Toei Studios. A very good yakuza film. It is a shame that this has still not been released on DVD in English-subtitles. #1 of 11 films * * * 1/2

A MAN'S CREST 2 aka ZOKU OTOKO NO MONSHO aka BADGE OF A MAN 2 aka EMBLEM OF A MAN 2 1963 102 min. DIR. Akinori Matsuo SCR. Hisatoshi Kai PHOTO COLOR 'SCOPE: Kazumi Iwasa MUSIC: Hajime Kaburagi w/ Hideki Takahashi, Masako Izumi, Ichiro Nakatani, Yukiko Todoroki, Asao Koike, Yoshi Kato, Kichijiro Ueda, Akifumi Inoue, Toshio Sugiyama, Kaku Takashina, Noriko Matsumoto, Hiroshi Kondo, Shiro Yanase, Ichiro Kijima
An amazingly satisfying followup that surpasses the first film in some ways (more action with a better balance of its pace) and is jampacked with enough story elements for three or four sequels – shooting its wad a bit when one considers the paucity of narrative in some of the later middle entries in the series. Takahashi is released after a short prison term for slaying the man at the climax of the initial saga and is met by loyal second-in-command Kondo and heartthrob Izumi. Koike returns as the rowdy, mischievous and hotheaded layabout who is totally devoted to Takahashi and ready to plunge into a

vendetta at the drop of a hat. Almost immediately, Takahashi is tormented by the widow of the slain man who is now a drunken geisha. More guilt and bittersweet memories are spurred by the woman's young son when Takahashi plays taiko drums with the boy, something that reminds him of his own father who also met a violent death. Complicating matters are the geisha widow's growing crush on Takahashi, then his construction business placed in jeopardy when they are cheated out of a contract and his feelings of obligation to aging boss Kato, who is having trouble with unprincipled rival Nakatani. Neglected girlfriend Izumi tries to help by appealing to Takahashi's estranged mom, boss Todoroki. However, the older woman, though very sympathetic and worried about her son, knows he must stand on his own without her help. Izumi still longs for a normal loving life with tormented Takahashi. Unfortunately for her, he strives for an almost priestlike celibacy, a conscientious avoidance of dragging her further into yakuza life. Izumi's role is somewhat thankless but, in her few scenes, she perfectly conveys the frustratingly claustrophobic experience of living in a macho underworld, overwhelmed by the onrush of events in a masculine universe that is driven by ego, honor, tradition and misguided ambition. Things come to a head when one of Kato's men is killed in a nocturnal rainy swordfight with Nakatani's men. One-armed boss Kijima, Takahashi's nemesis from the first film. is also dogging Takahashi's trail, manipulating Nakatani for revenge purposes. Mother Todoroki tries to broker peace by moderating a *sakazuki* ceremony between Nakatani

and son Takahashi. But Nakatani's *yojinbo* attempts to kill our hero. Humanist Takahashi seriously wounds his attacker then immediately rushes the villain to the hospital, something which spurs tortuous memories of his own botched, rejected career as a surgeon. This leads to a drinking binge and finally a confrontation with Nakatani who is holding buddy Koike hostage. Takahashi turns the tables, taking Nakatani captive and freeing his friend. The end sees Takahashi on a deserted, windswept autumnal backstreet. Atmosphere builds as he's confronted in a western-style showdown by boss Kijima. Takahashi rushes toward his one-armed challenger, knocking aside the man's gun then fatally slashing the villain with his sword. #2 of 11 films   * * * 1/2

A Man's Crest (#2)

A MAN'S CREST – WINDS OF CHANGE FOR TWO DRAGONS aka OTOKO NO MONSHO – FUUN FUTATSU RYU aka FIGHT

OF THE GAMBLERS 1963 91 min.
DIR. Akinori Matsuo **SCR.** Hisatoshi
Kai **PHOTO COLOR 'SCOPE:** Kazumi
Iwasa **MUSIC:** Hajime Kaburagi
w/ Hideki Takahashi, Masako Izumi,
Asao Koike, Yoshi Kato, Yukiko
Todoroki, Eijiro Tono, Ichiro
Nakatani, Akifumi Inoue, Toshio
Sugiyama, Shoki Fukae, Hiroshi
Kondo, Isao Fujita   Despairing
of outlaw life, Takahashi leaves his
clan and goes to stay at a temple with
priest Tono. Koike appears, discovers
a tubercular geisha in the rain outside
the temple and, with Takahashi's
help, they take her inside. She dies
almost immediately, and the yakuza
gang who run her brothel materialize
demanding satisfaction. They are
rebuffed at the temple gates. Soon
they are joining forces with boss
Nakatani, Takahashi's enemy from
the second film, and both the gangs
begin harassing Takahashi's mom's
clan. Before it is all over, mom
Todoroki is shot by the villains, and
Takahashi singlehandedly confronts
Nakatani's minions. He uses a fake
fire alarm to divert most of the gang
– they are the fire brigade in town
– and he forces Nakatani to sign a
document relinquishing the gangs'
conflicting interests. A fight ensues
in the rural countryside, Takahashi
chivalrously trying to avoid bloodshed by using the blunt edge of his
sword. Astonishingly, the bad guys
are thwarted by military intervention!
It turns out that one of Takahashi's
former enemies had been so taken
with his chivalrous courage that he
had gone to one of Takahashi's old
school chums in the army for help.
This unlikely development gives way
to even more melodramatic antics as
Takahashi then makes a beeline for
the hospital where mother Todoroki
is being prepped for surgery. He requests that he be allowed to perform
the operation – remember that he is a
former doctor – and under his caring
hands she comes through the ordeal
okay. It is too bad that the last five or
six minutes descend into such unrealistic, forced coincidence because
otherwise the film is not bad. #3 of
11 films * * 1/2

**NEW A MAN'S CREST –
COURAGE FIRST** aka SHIN
OTOKO NO MONSHO – DOKYO
ICHIBAN aka THE GREATEST
COURAGE 1964 101 min. **DIR.**
Eisuke Takizawa **SCR.** Hisatoshi
Kai **PHOTO COLOR'SCOPE:** Kurataro
Takamura **MUSIC:** Taiichiro Kosugi
w/ Hideki Takahashi, Masako Izumi,
Yukiko Todoroki, Toru Abe, Yoko
Yamamoto   The opening sequence
finds Takahashi doing time as a military medical officer in Manchuraia.
One of his friends dies. Upon returning from service, Takahashi goes
to visit the young man's father, a
decent gang boss played by Kinzo
Shin. Takahashi is also reunited with
sidekicks Koike and Kondo and love
interest Izumi. Before long, evil *oyabun* Abe rears his greedy head in the
vicinity, and Takahashi realizes that
the man is somehow tied to his mom,
boss Todoroki. Abe starts orchestrating sneak attacks on Takahashi and
clan, as well as attempting to extort
favors through bribery from local military officers and usurp boss
Shin's construction projects. Abe
is in league with Chinese interests
who eventually assassinate Shin.
The film climaxes with Abe and
gang challenging Takahashi to a
nocturnal duel in a deserted railyard.

A Man's Crest (#5)

Takahashi, per usual, resorts to using the sword's blunt edge to incapacitate his enemies. Takahashi, though wounded, has gained the upper hand when his mother arrives on the scene distracting him. Abe uses this as an opportunity to regain his sword and slashes out at our hero. Takahashi reflexively lashes out with his sword, cutting Abe's face and sending him backwards into the path of an onrushing train. Somber and grateful to be together, Takahashi and mom Todoroki walk away from the scene. Not particularly original or earthshaking, this entry does have a consistency of tone and a balance of action and story elements that is consistently engrossing. It should be noted that director Takizawa was a prominent *chanbara* director in the 1950s, and his MAN'S CREST films represent some of his final efforts. #4 of 11 films * * *

A MAN'S CREST – FLOWER AND THE LONG SWORD aka OTOKO NO MONSHO – HANA TO NAGADOSU 1964 103 min. DIR. Eisuke Takizawa SCR. Hisatoshi Kai/ Ryuzo Nakanishi PHOTO COLOR 'SCOPE: Kurataro Takamura MUSIC: Taiichiro Kosugi
w/ Hideki Takahashi, Masako Izumi, Nobuo Kaneko, Yukiko Todoroki, Yuji Kodaka, Asao Koike, Ichiro Nakatani, Isao Yamagata, Hiroshi Kondo, Eiji Go, Kaku Takashina
A fairly decent entry with Takahashi's mother, boss Todoroki, nearly assassinated in broad daylight at the beginning while being chauffeured in a rickshaw. Her loyal bodyguard (Go) slays the killer but also expires himself. Villainous boss Kaneko, resentful of both Takahashi and his mom, is constantly sabotaging their clan's businesses, construction and gambling. He hires scarred killer Kodaka and has him stage gambling den robberies, Kodaka bragging all the while to be in Takahashi's employ. Takahashi's mom should know better but believes it is true. This serves to help drive a wedge between mother and son, one of Kaneko's goals. Eventually Takahashi's loyal second-in-commands, Kondo and Koike, capture Kodaka redhanded, delivering him back to boss Kaneko. This spurs an amplification of hostilities with Takahashi attacked and an elder friend killed. Takahashi is finally pushed beyond endurance. They infiltrate Kaneko's forest compound, and the climactic fight erupts. Although there has been a fairly decent amount of well-balanced action setpieces in the film, the choreography of this last setquence is not that great and is over in a flash. Kodaka dies after inadvertently spearing himself. #5 of 11 films * * 1/2

A MAN'S CREST – FIGHT CHALLENGE aka OTOKO NO MONSHO – KENKA JO aka THE CHALLENGE 1964 85 min. DIR. Motomu (Tan) Iida SCR. Hisatoshi Kai PHOTO COLOR 'SCOPE: Izumi Hagiwara MUSIC: Joharu Yamamoto
w/ Hideki Takahashi, Masako Izumi, Yukiko Todoroki, Asao Koike, Koji Wada, Hiroshi Nihonyanagi, Mizuho Suzuki, Asao Sano, Kaku Takashina, Hiroshi Kondo
Takahashi encounters new trials and tribulations not only from bad *oyabun* Nihonyanagi, but also in-cahoots corrupt cop Sano. Matters complicate as Takahashi rescues young yakuza Wada as well as takes the part of

victimized merchants. Unfortunately, things are interrupted too often for the comic relief of Takahashi's bumbling hotheaded sidekicks, Koike et.al. There are a couple of nicely choreographed swordfights. But there is not much that is different or imaginative here to separate this entry from the the usual *ninkyo* programmer elements. Izumi is even held hostage in exchange for Wada. Once again the battle at the end where Takahashi and friends are attacked by both evil yakuza and corrupt cops is unrealistically interrupted by benevolent authority figures, this time a bunch of decent police. Things seem to be resolved, only to have Takahashi attacked one more time in the snowy night, this time by escaped cop Sano and several yakuza. Need I say Takahashi survives?   #6 of 11 films * * 1/2

A MAN'S CREST – VIOLENT PATH aka OTOKO NO MONSHO – KENKA KAIDO 1965 95 min.

DIR. Eisuke Takizawa **SCR.** Hisatoshi Kai **PHOTO COLOR 'SCOPE:** Kurataro Takamura **MUSIC:** Hajime Kaburagi w/ Hideki Takahashi, Masako Izumi, Reiko Sassamori, Tatsuya Fuji, Akira Yamanouchi, Yukiko Todoroki, Yoshi Kato, Akiyoshi Fukae, Hiroshi Kondo, Masahiko Tanimura Takahashi presides over a *sakazuki* ceremony, finally creating a formal alliance between his clan and that of his mother Todoroki. He then decides, since things are relatively peaceful, to go on a *matatabi*. He breaks the news to heartthrob Izumi on the banks of a river after telling his gang. But they are interrupted when vengeful Yamanouchi, a friend of dead *oyabun* Abe killed at the end of film #4,

attacks him. Takahashi does not have a sword with him, and the contnually intervening, distraught Izumi convinces the somewhat chivalrous Yamanouchi to stop. However, he promises that they will meet again soon. Takahashi then takes off on his wandering, much to Izumi's chagrin. Yamanouchi, Fukae and another vengeful comrade from rival boss Tamagawa's HQ follow Takahashi at a distance. In his travels, Takahashi helps negotiate a peace between two gangs at odds over the rights to a farmers' market. He then makes his way to another village to visit Kato, an old friend of his late father. Kato explains that his daughter, Sassamori, is indentured as a geisha at a brothel, and Takahashi takes it upon himself to go redeem her. Of course, it isn't easy, and he faces resistance from the brothel's pimp boss. Meanwhile, Yamanouchi and cohorts, linked up with another gang, visit Kato's to coerce Takahashi's whereabouts. Kato draws a sword and is killed. When Takahashi and Sassamori return to find his body, Izumi arrives almost simultaneously to announce one of their clan has been taken hostage by Tamagawa's gang. Takahashi returns, frees the man but is ambushed by the revenge trio. He slaughters all three in a short but nicely choreographed swordfight before going off to wander again.   #7 of 11 films   * * 1/2

A MAN'S CREST – WANDER-ER'S CODE aka OTOKO NO MONSHO – RUTEN NO OKITE aka RULE OF A WANDERING MAN aka LAW OF CONSTANT CHANGE 1965 88 min.

DIR. Eisuke Takizawa **SCR.** Hisatoshi Kai **PHOTO COLOR 'SCOPE:** Kurataro

Takamura **MUSIC:** Hajime Kaburagi w/ Hideki Takahashi, Masako Izumi, Tamio Kawaji, Yukiko Todoroki, Hiroshi Kondo, Nakajiro Tomita, Masako Ota (aka Meiko Kaji), Masahiko Tanimura, Saburo Hiromatsu, Shiro Yanase, Akifumi Inoue   Takahashi goes wandering to a village where Yamanouchi, the expert swordsman he killed at the end of the previous film, is buried. He runs into not only a gang that wants payback, but also Yamanouchi's loved ones, Kawaji and Tanimura, both bent on a vendetta. However, Takahashi proves so relentlessly decent and honorable, helping the two against the evil gang, that the three of them bond. Takahashi's mother, boss Todoroki, is kidnapped and, per usual, he does his "I can't kill anyone unless absolutely necessary" routine. He disables scores of bad guys by attacking them with the blunt edge of his sword. Finally, he kills the evil boss, Kawaji materializes with a rifle to help and the two free mom. Just so-so, this entry has little to elevate it from programmer status.   #8 of 11 films   * * 1/2

A MAN'S CREST – WE KILL aka OTOKO NO MONSHO – ORE WA KIRU 1965 84 min. **DIR.** Motomi (Tan) Iida **SCR.** Hisatoshi Kai **PHOTO COLOR 'SCOPE:** Izumi Hagiwara **MUSIC:** Hajime Kaburagi w/ Hideki Takahashi, Masako Izumi, Koji Wada, Shogo Shimada, Asao Koike, Yukiko Todoroki, Kaku Takashina, Akira Oizumi, Eiji Go, Saburo Hiromatsu, Ichiro Sugai Regrettably, most of the first third of this film is wasted in unfunny comic relief from Takahashi's bothersome sidekicks. The episode starts with more wandering, Takahashi first having to deal with someone impersonating him in a small backwater village, then our hero taking up residence with a clan who do mountain logging but are under assault from a rival gang. Takahashi also reunites aging yakuza Sugai with estranged son Wada. Luckily, the movie keeps getting better as it goes along, with the last third being extremely good. Surprisingly enough, this entry sees the assassination of Takahashi's mother, boss Todoroki. The scenes in mourning beside her body that give way to his frenzied *taiko* drumming, then finally culminate with him giving into a revenge attack (his succumbing to bloodlust made all the more powerful by his having strenuously avoided killing for much of the series), and his scenes with girlfriend Izumi at the end, after the killing is done, recall the poignance and grittiness of the first two films. In fact, the scenes with Izumi are the best in the film. There is real emotion as Izumi tearfully watches Takahashi drumming after his mother's death, then brings him his sandals after the final battle. The very final scene where she kneels to put on his footgear, Takahashi resembling a bewildered boy, both communicating without words, linked by the mutual fate of two friends from childhood who never wanted to be part of the yakuza world but were never given a choice, are truly heartwrenching. Although it takes a while to get there, this last third of the picture more than redeems the film. #9 of 11 films * * *

A MAN'S CREST – CRUEL TIGER AND DRAGON aka OTOKO NO MONSHO – RYUKO

A Man's Crest (#10)

MUJO aka DRAGON AND TIGER
1966 87 min. **DIR.** Akinori
Matsuo **SCR.** Hisatoshi Kai **PHOTO
COLOR 'SCOPE:** Izumi Hagiwara
MUSIC: Hajime Kaburagi w/ Hideki
Takahashi, Joe Shishido, Masako
Izumi, Asao Koike, Takamaru Sasaki,
Masahiko Tanimura A great return
to form for the series with what is
basically the last film (the next one,
#11 is a partial remake of the first
picture with Takahashi as a different
character). Here Takahashi returns
from prison to find his gang scattered except for Koike, gal Izumi and
one other man. For once heartthrob
Izumi has a bit more to do than her
usual thankless look-wistful-and-
heartbroken role. The first part of the
film before Takahashi's return finds
her being badgered by the local gang
boss's madam to join the neighborhood brothel. Shishido is also in
excellent shape as a ruthless lone
wolf gambler and expert swordsman
who initially befriends Takahashi
then defects to the enemy gang to
act as their *yojinbo*. There is a lot of
conflict involving the villains' extortion of decent businesses, exacerbated
by the kidnapping of a shopowner
as well as Izumi. Shishido ends up
killing the bad boss then framing
Takahashi for the act so he can usurp
power. However, a gangfight between
Takahashi's refurbished clan and the
evil ones is interrupted by the cops.
The head inspector is an old friend of
Takahashi. Takahashi subsequently
stops dragging his feet and finally
asks Izumi to marry him. But their
marriage is broken up by villainous
gangsters who chastise Takahashi for
ignoring Shishido's latest formal fight
challenge. It turns out well-meaning
Koike had hidden the *hatashijo* (challenge) letter so the wedding ceremony
would not be marred by bloodshed.
Incensed, Takahashi heads off to
meet Shishido and fights a beautifully staged duel with him beneath a
bridge and through fields of waving
reeds. The inspector shows up to stop
them. However another senior boss,
with a vested interest in the outcome,
opens fire on the scene, winging the
inspector and mortally wounding
Shishido. Takahashi's sense of fair
play and respect for both Shishido
and the policeman make him boil
over. He goes nuts, foregoing his
usual blunt-edge-of-the-sword tactics
so he actually kills the betraying boss
and his minions. Takahashi's men and
the wedding-garbed Izumi arrive as
the last evildoer bites the dust. The
reunion of Takahashi and Izumi is
genuinely emotional, and it is very
satisfying to see the two finally on
the verge of their unrequited love's
consummation. A well-written, well-
constructed saga with an ebb-and-
flow of action throughout that keeps
you hooked and more than willing to
ignore the usual genre cliches. It is
also especially nice to see Takahashi
and Shishido evenly matched in a
strong film together. #10 of 11 films
* * * 1/2

**NEW A MAN'S CREST – BIRTH
OF A YOUNG BOSS** aka SHIN
OTOKO NO MONSHO – WAKA
OYABUN TANJO 1967 79 min.
DIR. Motomu (Tan) Iida **SCR.**
Hisatoshi Kai **PHOTO COLOR 'SCOPE:**
Izumi Hagiwara **MUSIC:** Seitaro
Omori w/ Hideki Takahashi,
Yoko Yamamoto, Kunie Tanaka,
Kenjiro Ishiyama, Kazuko Tachibana,
Kaku Takashina, Saburo Hiromatsu,
Fujio Suga, Bontaro Miake, Ryoichi

Tamagawa   This starts promisingly enough with an entire new saga beginning, Takahashi working for his adoptive father, a respected teacher who has both political and yakuza enemies. It seems Takahashi's mother was widowed when his real father, a yakuza, was killed in a fight. Takahashi is also in love with Yamamoto, the teacher's daughter. All too soon things go awry when the *sensei* is assassinated. Mourning Takahashi goes on a brief pilgrimage, then returns and is inducted into decent Ishiyama's gang. They turn out to be at odds with evil boss Suga who ultimately attacks their HQ. This interrupts Takahashi's wedding to Yamamoto in a development reminiscent of the last film. Takahashi leaves to thrash the gang in an all too brief sword encounter, finally dispatching Suga and his henchmen. Disappointing. The film seems to have been shot hurriedly, gradually loses steam and becomes more and more formulaic as it lurches predictably to its conclusion. #11 and final in series   * *

A MAN'S CODE aka OTOKO NO OKITE aka CODE OF A MAN 1968 90 min. **Dir.** Mio Ezaki **Scr.** Iwao Yamazaki/Mio Ezaki **Photo color 'scope:** Shohei Ando **Music:** Hajime Kaburagi **w/** Tetsuya Watari, Tetsuro Tanba, Yoko Nozoe, Ryutaro Tatsumi, Yuji Hori, Mieko Tsubouchi, Masako Ota, Hiroshi Nawa, Asao Koike, Shiro Yanase
A decently-executed but fairly routine, contemporary *ninkyo* programmer, with Tanba going to jail in the 1950s after murderously avenging the killing of one of his clan comrades during festival time. He returns a

decade later to find little sis, Meiko Kaji (appearing under her original name Masako Ota), a grown and feisty teenager smitten with young, sports car-loving Watari. Watari, no-nonsense businessman Hori and good-natured traditionalist boss Tatsumi (and his wife) are about the only ones left in the gang. Nevertheless, slimy rival Koike wants their small slice of the construction business in the area, so he starts the backstabbing. Also Nawa, Koike's cohort, is bent on exploiting financially compromised bar hostess Nozoe, the widow of Tanba's blood brother slain so many years before. Cantankerous mayhem escalates, including Koike and Nawa's torching of our heroes' construction business. Tanba tries avenging the wrongs on his own, but is dispatched. More bloodshed finally erupts, with Watari, Tatsumi and Hori decimating the villains. One interesting development: the final fight occurs at a construction site and on a nearby bridge, and Nozoe is the one to kill Nawa, running him over with her car! At the end, the police never appear, and there are surprisingly no consequences for the violence. At the denouement, Tatsumi and family trek to the airport to see off Watari who is leaving for a new opportunity elsewhere. * * 1/2

A MAN'S WORLD aka OTOKO NO SEKAI aka WORLD OF MEN 1971 82 min. **Dir.** Yasuharu Hasebe **Scr.** Ryuzo Nakanishi **Photo color 'scope:** Yoshihiro Yamazaki **Music:** Hajime Kaburagi   **w/** Yujiro Ishihara, Joe Shishido, Ryohei Uchida, Kenji Sugawara, Tamio Kawaji, Tsuneya Oki, Yuji Kodaka, Gen Mitamura, Hideji Otaki,

Keiko Torii
Ishihara returns from Canada after
the murder of his girlfriend by
Uchida. Sugawara gives him a hand
in unearthing information on Otaki,
a yachting club president who has
embezzled a huge amount of money.
Otaki, it seems, was also behind the
death of Ishihara's girl.

MAN THEY TRIED TO KILL
aka KIMI WA NERA WARETE IRU
1961 DIR. Motomu (Tan) Iida SCR.
Mio Ezaki/ Yasuharu Hasebe PHOTO
B&W 'SCOPE: Shigeyoshi Mine
MUSIC: Naozumi Yamamoto
w/ Yuji Kodaka, Uyako Hori, Hisako
Tsukuba, Leanne Bartok, Ichiro
Kijima

Man with the Shotgun

MAN WITH THE SHOTGUN
aka SHOTTAGAN NO OTOKO
aka MAN WITH THE HOLLOW-
TIPPED BULLETS   1961 84 min.
DIR. Seijun Suzuki SCR. Toshio
Matsuura/Yoshikazu (Kiichi?) Ishii

PHOTO COLOR 'SCOPE: Shigeyoshi
Mine MUSIC: Masayoshi Ikeda
w/ Hideaki Nitani, Izumi Ashikawa,
Yuji Kodaka, Yoko Minamida, Akio
Tanaka, Eiji Go, Keisuke Noro, Asao
Sano, Jun Hamamura, Hiroshi Kono
What was obviously slated to be just
one more programmer is transformed
by Suzuki's hands into another
instance of transcending the genre.
Nitani is a mysterious stranger with
a shotgun who arrives in a frontier-
like mountain community and creates
havoc with the gangsters who are
exploiting the hard-drinking, nearly
all male workforce. This is very
similar to the kind of story told in
the DRIFTER and WANDERING
GUITARIST series, both with Akira
Kobayashi. But what more often than
not ended up as routine potboiler
material in those quarters, emerges
here as deliciously anarchic and
profanely funny. Suzuki manages
a difficult tightrope act because he
still stays faithful to genre conventions while making the presentation
fresh through abrupt edits, shockingly
sudden violence and his customary ironic juxtapositions. Amusing
setpieces occur in the big saloon and
in the spectacular outdoors, especially
the surreal action-charged climax
on a volcanic beach of black sand
where Nitani is finally victorious over
the idiosyncratic yakuza. Rowdy,
evil tough Kodaka turns out to be
an undercover cop who arrests the
surviving villains at the last minute.
In the penultimate scene, Nitani opts
to continue his drifting, heading for
the horizon and leaving smitten heartthrob Ashikawa behind. At this point
in his career, Suzuki was obviously
still forced to toe the line, as much
of Nikkatsu's early sixties formula

hokum is in evidence. But there is a subtle subversion of the usual sentimentality through his direction of actors as well as his frequent doses of black humor. * * *

MAP OF VIOLENT TOKYO aka TOKYO BORYOKU CHIZU 1962 **DIR.** Isamu Kosugi **SCR.** Motobu Matsumura/Saburo Endo **PHOTO 'SCOPE:** Kumenobu Fujioka **MUSIC:** Taiichiro Kosugi **w/** Kyoji Aoyama, Minako Kazuki, Hitoshi Miyazaki This may be a sequel to TOKYO DANGER MAP.

MARKET OF WOMEN aka YORU O HIRAKU – ONNA NO ICHIBA aka SEX PEDDLERS OF GINZA 1969 84 min. **DIR.** Mio Ezaki **SCR.** Masashige Narusawa **PHOTO COLOR 'SCOPE:** Shinsaku Himeda **MUSIC:** Masaru Sato w/ Akira Kobayashi, Tamio Kawaji, Yoko Yamamoto, Teruko Hasegawa, Yoshi Kato, Ryohei Uchida

Market of Women

Supposedly related in some way to Kobayashi's WOMEN'S POLICE series. Screenwriter Narusawa wrote scores of these kinds of films at Toei for such series as NIGHT and SONG OF THE NIGHT, all dealing with nocturnal nightclub denizens – bargirls, whores, mama-sans and the men who protect and/or exploit them.

MASSACRE GUN aka MINAGOROSHI NO KENJU aka GUNS OF THE MASSACRE 1967 98 min. **DIR.** Yasuharu Hasebe **SCR.** Ryuzo Nakanishi/Takashi Fujii (aka Y. Hasebe) **PHOTO B&W 'SCOPE:** Kazue Nagatsuka **MUSIC:** Naozumi Yamamoto w/ Joe Shishido, Tatsuya Fuji, Hideaki Nitani, Jiro Okazaki, Yoko Yamamoto, Tamaki Sawa, Ryoji Hayama, Takashi Kanda, Shoki Fukae, Kaku Takashina Shishido, Fuji and Okazaki are brothers who run a saloon and are affiliated with a local yakuza clan. After the youngest brother (Okazaki), an unsuccessful musician who had taken up boxing to make money, is humiliated by both the *oyabun* and clan-owned trainer, he becomes an unsuccessful boxer, too. Shishido and Fuji aren't happy with this and leave the clan. Okazaki doesn't want any trouble, he just wants to play music and be with his gal. But Shishido and Fuji start pulling their own protection racket scams, muscling in on the clan's turf. Before too long, Okazaki is beaten up. Smart-aleck psycho-womanizer Fuji ends up pushing his luck and is gunned-down. Shishido then engineers a showdown/ambush with the clan on an unfinished stretch of deserted freeway. Shishido's old pal Nitani regretfully has to side with the clan. Shishido kills everyone

Massacre Gun

except Nitani. The only ones left, they blaze away at each other. Then they are dead, too. The last shot is of Okazaki hysterically running down the road to the scene of the slaughter. This has a more original story than most yakuza pictures but still something doesn't quite click. However, the choreography of action, the bizarre set design and excellent B&W photography make the film visually exciting, and keep it from being just average. Part of a loosely-linked B&W trio that includes BRANDED TO KILL (1967) and MY GUN IS MY PASSPORT (1967), both of which also starred Shishido.   * * *

Meiji Era's Bloody Wind - The Hawk and the Wolf

MEIJI ERA'S BLOODY WIND – THE HAWK AND THE WOLF

aka MEIJI KEPPU ROKU – TAKA TO OKAMI aka EAGLE AND THE WOLF 1968 98 min. DIR. Akinori Matsuo SCR. Akinori Matsuo/Goro Oku PHOTO COLOR 'SCOPE: Kazumi

Iwasa MUSIC: Taiichiro Kosugi w/ Hideki Takahashi, Keiji Takagi, Kayo Matsuo, Hiroko Ogi, Yuji Hori, Miyuki Takakura, Hideaki Nitani, Mizuho Suzuki, Kamatari Fujiwara *Ninkyo* tale set in the late Meiji period.

Melody of Rebellion VHS art and still

MELODY OF REBELLION

aka HAN GYAKU NO MERODII 1970 84 min. DIR. Yukihiro Sawada SCR. Susumu Saji/Michio Sotake PHOTO COLOR 'SCOPE: Yoshihiro Yamazaki MUSIC: Hiroshi Tamaki w/ Yoshio Harada, Meiko Kaji, Tatsuya Fuji, Takeo Chii, Gajiro Sato, Manami Fuji, Fujio Suga, Shoki Fukae, Yoshiro Aoki, Harada is a lone wolf rebel who has gone counterculture outlaw after having his home yakuza gang disbanded at the beginning of the story. He bands together with several other yakuza outcasts, including mavericks Fuji and Chii and some bikers. Kaji is given criminally little to do as Chii's gal. Considering the excellence of Sawada's ATTACK and KANTO SOCIETY OF LEADING MOBSTERS, this should have been better. It has its moments, but one gets the feeling not enough time was spent on the screenplay. * * 1/2

Midnight Virgin aka *Women's Cruel Double Suicide*

MIDNIGHT VIRGIN aka ZANKOKU ONNA JOSHI aka WOMEN'S CRUEL DOUBLE SUICIDE 1970 86 min. **DIR.** Shugoro Nishimura **SCR.** Iwao Yamazaki **PHOTO B&W 'SCOPE:** Shohei Ando **MUSIC:** Riichiro Manabe   w/ Annu Mari, Sanae Obori, Jiro Okazaki, Shinji Takano, Ken Iba, Haruo Tanaka, Hirotaro Sugie, Saburo Hiromatsu, Toshio Sugiyama, Tomoko Aki   A pimp and mobsters try to separate two lesbian call girls, with tragic consequences. The freewheeling Obori, previously straight, is mystified and disturbed by her attraction to indentured whore Mari, but soon realizes she truly loves her. There is a genuinely weird ambience to the proceedings and admirably nuanced performances by the two leading actresses. Still, it stops just short of being truly great. Undoubtedly radical at the time for portraying virtually every male character (except a gay saloonkeeper) as exploitive, cruel and arrogant bastards – something that didn't really happen again until 1972 with Toei's immensely popular FEMALE CONVICT SCORPION series with Meiko Kaji. * * *

Might Rules aka *Early Afternoon Violence*

MIGHT RULES aka HIRUSA
GARI NO BORYOKU aka EARLY
AFTERNOON VIOLENCE 1959
Dɪʀ. Hiroshi Noguchi Sᴄʀ. Ryuta
Akimoto/Kan Hanase Pʜᴏᴛᴏ B&W
'sᴄᴏᴘᴇ: Kazue Nagatsuka Mᴜsɪᴄ:
Naozumi Yamamoto w/ Tamio
Kawaji, Hisako Tsukuba, Joe
Shishido, Michitaro Mizushima,
Mieko Inagaki, Ichiro Sugai, Shoki
Fukae

Mini-Skirt Lynchers

MINI-SKIRT LYNCHERS aka
ZANKOKU ONNA RINCHI aka
CRUELTY OF WOMEN'S LYNCH
LAW 1969 82 min. Dɪʀ. Yuji Tanno
Sᴄʀ. Iwao Yamazaki Pʜᴏᴛᴏ B&W
'sᴄᴏᴘᴇ: Yoshihiro Yamazaki Mᴜsɪᴄ:
Mitsuhiko (Makoto?) Sato
w/ Masako Ota (Meiko Kaji), Teruko
Hasegawa, Jiro Okazaki, Annu Mari,
Tamio Kawaji, Hiroyuki Nagato,
Kiyomi Katena, Eiji Go, Isao Sasaki,
Mari Shiraki   A thoroughly unsa-
vory tale of two rival girl gangs and
their working class stud boyfriends.

Hasegawa's gang is the more decent
while Mari's revels in kidnapping
and torture. Naive, craven outsider
Ota falls in first with Hasegawa, then
Mari. Grief comes to all, with good
guy Okazaki and sadists Go and
Sasaki biting the dust in the excessively violent climax. A pioneering
precursor to Nikkatsu's STRAY CAT
ROCK series as well as the many
brutal, sexy girl gang pictures at Toei
Studios in the early seventies. Also
Meiko Kaji's only film where she
receives top-billing under her original
birth name, Masako Ota.

**A MODERN SCOUNDREL'S
HONOR & HUMANITY** aka
GENDAI AKUTO JINGI aka A
MODERN SCOUNDREL'S
GAMBLING CODE 1965 103 min.
Dɪʀ. Ko Nakahira Sᴄʀ. Motonari
Wakai Pʜᴏᴛᴏ B&W 'sᴄᴏᴘᴇ:
Yoshihiro Yamazaki Mᴜsɪᴄ: Keitaro
Miho   w/ Joe Shishido, Kazuko
Inano, Yoko Yamamoto, Hideaki
Nitani, Akifumi Inoue, Hiroshi
Hijikata, Shoki Fukae   As the title
indicates, the emphasis is on humor.

MY GUN IS MY PASSPORT
aka KORUTO WA ORE NO PAS-
UPOOTO aka MY COLT IS MY
PASSPORT 1967 89 min.
Dɪʀ. Takashi Nomura Sᴄʀ. Nobuo
Yamada/Shuichi Nagahara Pʜᴏᴛᴏ
B&W 'sᴄᴏᴘᴇ: Shigeyoshi Mine
Mᴜsɪᴄ: Harumi Ibe w/ Joe Shishido,
Jerry Fujio, Chitose Kobayashi,
Ryotaro Sugi, Kanjuro Arashi
A great visually imaginative film
about a couple of hitmen, their target,
their getaway and their hiding-out in
a desolate roadside inn on the coast.
Moody and noirish, with a suspense-
ful, heart-pounding finale that

My Gun is My Passport

manages to be both action-packed and surreal. This film plus MAS-SACRE GUN and BRANDED TO KILL, both B&W and from 1967, are a loosely-linked trio. * * * 1/2

MY WHITE SEX BOOK – DEGREE OF CLIMAX aka WATASHI NO SEKKUSU HAKU SHO – ZECCHODO 1976 70 min. **DIR.** Chusei Sone **SCR.** Akane Shiratori **PHOTO COLOR 'SCOPE:** Kenji Hagiwara **MUSIC:** The Cosmos Factory w/ Maria Mitsui, Nobutaka Masutomi, Akiko Seri, Morihei Murakuni, Yuzuru Kamisaka, Yoko Azusa, Shoichi Kuwayama A pink/roman porno with a yakuza character or two.

NAKED VIRGIN aka HADAKA NO SHOJO aka NUDE HOLY WOMAN 1958 82 min. **DIR.** Hiroshi Noguchi **SCR.** Tetsu Sueyama/Yoshihisa Yanagisawa **PHOTO B&W 'SCOPE:** Kazue Nagatsuka **MUSIC:** Hajime Kaburagi w/ Hisako Tsukuba, Michitaro Mizushima, Yuko Minamikaze, Kyoji Aoyama, Joe Shishido As one can tell from the title and sex-bomb star Tsukuba's involve-ment, this was a sleaze noir that was about as suggestive as Japanese stu-dios got in the late 1950s (which was more risque than you would generally find from American films during the same time period).

NEON POLICE aka **NEON KEISATSU** series

TATTOO OF THE JACK aka JAKKU NO IREZUMI 1970 83 min. **DIR.** Kazushige Takeda **SCR.** Atsushi

Yamatoya/Chusei Sone **PHOTO COLOR 'SCOPE:** Kurataro Takamura **MUSIC:** Hajime Kaburagi w/ Akira Kobayashi, Eiji Go, Junko Natsu, Yoshiro Aoki, Rikiya (Ricky) Yasuoka, Kojiro Kusanagi, Annu Mari, Shoki Fukae, Tomoko Aki, Ruriko Ito Kobayashi and Go are comrade troubleshooters for various gangs. When one of their employers (Fukae) is assassinated, they decide to take over the gang at the request of the other members. Blackmail of the villain gang boss (Aoki) results in the death of a girlfriend and Go, events which are ultimately avenged by Kobayashi. #1 of 2 films

WOMEN SMELL OF THE NIGHT aka ONNA WA YORU NO NIOI 1970 82 min. **DIR.** Takashi Nomura **SCR.** Ei Ogawa **PHOTO COLOR 'SCOPE:** Shigeyoshi Mine **MUSIC:** Taiichiro Kosugi w/ Akira Kobayashi, Ryohei Uchida, Noriko Maki, Tsuneya Oki, Hosei Komatsu, Fujio Suga, Gen Mitamura, Masami Maki, Hiroshi Nagashi Kobayashi helps keep female boss Maki's gang from being destroyed by Suga's rival mob. One-time ally Uchida decides to side with the more powerful Suga. How-ever, Uchida remains friendly and eventually informs Kobayashi of a kidnap plot to snatch Maki. Of course in the meantime Maki is falling-in-love with Kobayashi. After a few gangfights, Kobayashi discovers that corrupt politician Komatsu has been manipulating the two mobs' animos-ity, and he kills the pompous bigwig. #2 of 2 films

NIGHTMARE OF FLESH aka NIKUTAI NO AKUMU aka DEVIL

FLESH 1957 85 min. **Dir.** Hiroshi Noguchi **Scr.** Tetsu Sueyama **Photo color 'scope:** Shinsaku Himeda **Music:** Naozumi Yamamoto **w/** Michitaro Mizushima, Hisako Tsukuba, Shiro Osaka, Tadao Sawamoto This seems to have been the first crime film at Nikkatsu shot in anamorphic widescreen. Noting once again the title and Tsukuba's involvement, this is undoubtedly a sleaze noir/yakuza tale.

NIGHT MIST BLUES aka YOGIRI NO BURUUSU 1963 104 min. **Dir.** Takashi Nomura **Scr.** Takeo Kunihiro **Photo color 'scope:** Kurataro Takamura **Music:** Harumi Ibe **w/** Yujiro Ishihara, Ruriko Asaoka, Asao Koike, Kaneko Iwazaki, Kayo Matsuo, Eiji Go, Osamu Takizawa, Tadao Sawamoto, Ryohei Uchida, Misako Watanabe, Goro Mutsumi A *moodo/akushon* (mood/action) love story that has yakuza elements.

NIGHT MIST ON HIGHWAY TWO aka YOGIRI NO DAI-NI KOKUDO 1958 48 min. **Dir.** Toshio Masuda **Scr.** Iwao Yamazaki **Photo B&W:** Kazumi Iwasa **Music:** Tadashi Yoshida **w/** Akira Kobayashi, Minako Katsuki, Masumi Okada, Kiyoko Horikawa From the short running time, it seems safe to assume that this was a shorter, second support feature.

NUDE AND THE GUN aka RAJO TO KENJU aka NAKED LADY AND THE GUN 1957 88 min. **Dir.** Seijun Suzuki **Scr.** Asami Tabe **Photo B&W:** Umeo Matsubayashi **Music:** Rokuro Hara **w/** Michitaro Mizushima, Mari Shiraki, Ichiro Sugai, Noboru Date, Jun Yukioka, Jun Hamamura, Hideaki Nitani, Tatsuo Matsushita, Joe Shishido

Nude and the Gun

The word "nude" in the title is a bit of a misnomer. Either Suzuki or his producers *do* contrive to have the charismatic Shiraki (in her first starring role) spending at least half the movie parading around in her underwear. But that is as far as it goes. The opening is an incredibly funny, surreal dance number with Shiraki a star-spangled, bikini-clad cowgirl shooting up various targets in a nigtclub. Mizushima is a widowed news photographer and Nitani his apprentice cub reporter. Naive Mizushima gets involved with Shiraki, helping her hide from pursuing hoodlums. But, as a result, he is briefly framed for murder when he is discovered with a wheelchair-bound corpse in her pad. It turns out Shiraki is the dope-dealing main squeeze of ruthless heroin smuggler Sugai. Near the end, she is mortally wounded when she

saves Mizushima's life during, first a
frenzied fistfight, then a pitched gun
battle aboard Sugai's freighter
on the high seas. At the climax,
Mizushima and quickly-fading
Shiraki watch from deck as the gloating Sugai outruns the cops in his
power launch. However, Shiraki has
planted a bomb in his briefcase, and
the villain's glee is cut short when
he is blown to smithereens. Suzuki's
next film pairing Mizushima and
Shiraki, UNDERWORLD BEAUTY
(1958), is slightly better (and is also
Suzuki's first scope picture). * * *

NUMBER ONE GUN STREET
aka KENJU GAI ICHI – CHO MO
1959 Dir. Motomu (Tan) Iida
w/ Michitaro Mizushima, Yuko
Minakaze

*Oman, the Foreigner (#3) aka Oman's
Chaotic Flesh*

OMAN, THE FOREIGNER aka
RASHAMEN OMAN series

**OMAN, THE FOREIGNER –
RAIN ON HOLLAND HILL** aka
RASHAMEN OMAN – AME NO
ORANDA SAKA 1972 Dir. Chusei
Sone Scr. Kazuo Nishida w/ Sari
Mei (Sally May), Shusaku Muto,
Miki Hayashi   The first in a
roman porno series featuring a blonde
female gambler at dice and *hana fuda*
games adrift in Japan in the early
1930s. #1 of 3 films

**OMAN, THE FOREIGNER –
SCATTERED EARLY BLOS-
SOMS** aka RASHAMEN OMAN
– HIGAN BANA WA CHITTA 1972
Dir. Chusei Sone Scr. Atsushi
Yamatoya Photo color 'scope:
Teruo Hatanaka w/ Sari Mei (Sara
May), Miki Hayashi   #2 of 3 films

**AMOROUS SIDE OF A
CHIVALROUS WOMAN'S TALE
– OMAN'S CHAOTIC FLESH**
aka TSUYA SETSU JOKYODEN
– OMAN MIDARE HADA 1972
Dir. Katsuhiko Fujii Scr. Kiyomi
Tanaka Photo color 'scope: Kenji
Hagiwara w/ Sari Mei (Sally May),
Akira Takahashi, Miki Hayashi,
Hiroshi Nagashi #3 and final in series

**ONE HUNDRED GAMBLERS
aka BAKUTO HYAKUNIN
series**

ONE HUNDRED GAMBLERS
aka BAKUTO HYAKUNIN 1969
89 min. Dir. Takashi Nomura Scr.
Iwao Yamazaki/Hisatoshi Kai
Photo color 'scope: Shigeyoshi
Mine Music: Saburo Matsuura
w/ Hideki Takahashi, Joe Shishido,
Akira Kobayashi, Tatsuya Fuji,

Hideaki Nitani, Shinjiro Ebara, Kanjuro Arashi, Masako Izumi, Yoko Yamamoto, Toru Abe, Takamaru Sasaki   Powerful boss Arashi turns his territory over to his two subordinates, Sasaki and Abe. Greedy Abe has Sasaki murdered by killer Shishido. Sasaki's son Takahashi is away at the time and is informed of his father's death by boss Kobayashi. Takahashi decides to seek revenge and breaks off his engagement to Izumi since he is consumed by duty. However, he is foiled in his first attempt to kill Abe and is briefly imprisoned. Izumi becomes a geisha. Abe sets his sights on her, but she is rescued by killer Shishido who turns out to be her errant brother (!). Arashi dies and states in his will that Takahashi is to take over. Released Takahashi goes to a gambling convention of one hundred bosses and exposes Abe's crimes. #1 of 2 films

One Hundred Gamblers (#2)

ONE HUNDRED GAMBLERS – CHIVALROUS PATH aka BAKU-TO HYAKUNIN – NINKYODO aka CHIVALROUS PRIDE 1969 89 min. DIR. Takashi Nomura SCR. Iwao Yamazaki PHOTO COLOR 'SCOPE: Shigeyoshi Mine MUSIC: Saburo Matsuura w/ Hideki Takahashi, Meiko Kaji, Joe Shishido, Michitaro Mizushima, Tatsuya Fuji, Yoko Minamida, Tadao Nakamaru, Ryoji Hayama, Kanjuro Arashi, Toru Abe   #2 of 2 films

ONE MILLION DOLLAR SMASH-'N'-GRAB aka HYAKU-MAN DORU O TATAKIDASE 1961 90 min. DIR. Seijun Suzuki SCR. Naoya Ito PHOTO COLOR 'SCOPE: Shigeyoshi Mine MUSIC: Hajime Okumura w/ Koji Wada, Keisuke Noro, Michiko Sawa, Misako Watanabe, Nobuo Kaneko, Daisaburo Hirata, Toru Abe Wada is a boxer involved with the yakuza. Reportedly Suzuki's THE GUYS WHO BET ON ME from 1962, also with Wada, is a loosely-linked sequel to this film.

ORE NO SENAKA NI HIGA ATARO 1963 99 min. DIR. Ko Nakahira SCR. Ko Nakahira/Yasuo Sahara PHOTO COLOR 'SCOPE: Kurataro Takamaura w/ Mitsuo Hamada, Sayuri Yoshinaga, Ryohei Uchida, Yoko Minamida, Naoko Ozawa, Jiichi Kitami, Takaaki Sato A combination yakuza/youth action film with heavy romantic overtones as evidenced by the Hamada/Yoshinaga pairing. These two usually appeared together in sometimes realistic, sometimes sentimental urban romantic melodramas.

OUR BODYGUARD aka ZURARI ORETACHA YOJINBO 1961 76 min. DIR. Akinori Matsuo SCR. Kazuhiko Kasuwagi/Hiroshi Chino PHOTO COLOR 'SCOPE: Shinsaku Himeda MUSIC: Harumi Ibe w/ Hideaki Nitani, Tamio Kawaji, Koji Wada, Masako Izumi, Nobuo Kaneko, Shiro Osaka

Our Blood Won't Allow It

OUR BLOOD WON'T ALLOW IT aka ORETACHI NO CHI GA YURU-SANAI 1964 97 min. DIR. Seijun Suzuki SCR. Tatsuma Takemori PHOTO COLOR 'SCOPE: Shigeyoshi Mine MUSIC: Tadanori Suzuki w/ Akira Kobayashi, Hideki Takahashi, Chieko Matsubara, Chikako Hosokawa, Yuri Hase, Hiroshi Midorigawa, Kaku Takashina, Akifumi Inoue, Eitaro Ozawa, Saburo Hiromatsu Kobayashi is the eldest offspring of a murdered yakuza *oyabun*. His father had elicited an oath from Kobayashi that he not pursue vengeance and that

he abandon the underworld. Needless to say, he does not, but he *does* keep up a respectable front to decieve his hot-headed younger brother (Takahashi). An incredible nocturnal shootout in the hilly rural countryside – looking like a lushly fertile British moor – climaxes things. The last few minutes are devastating as, first the fatally wounded, blood-drenched Kobayashi stumbles through the landscape, muttering thoughts about his brother, then Takahashi searches in vain for his older sibling, finding only his blood-soaked coat. The last shot is of an empty horizon with Takahashi's anguished cries echoing in the early morning. * * *

OUTLAW (BURAI) series, see HOODLUM series

OUTLAW MAP aka MUHO CHI-ZU 1962 DIR. Isamu Kosugi SCR. Kimiyuki Hasegawa PHOTO 'SCOPE: Toshitaro Nakao MUSIC: Taiichiro Kosugi w/ Kyoji Aoyama, Minako Kazuki, Sumiko Minami, Ichiro Kijima, Shoki Fukae

OUTLAWS AND GOLD aka YARO TO OGON 1958 89 min. DIR. Yoichi Ushihara SCR. Ichiro Ikeda PHOTO B&W 'SCOPE: Shigeyoshi Mine MUSIC: Taiichiro Kosugi w/ Hiroyuki Nagato, Hideaki Nitani, Ikuko Kimuro, Ko Nishimura, Shinsuke Ashida, Hiroshi Kondo, Yuji Kodaka, Mari Shiraki

OUTLAW'S GOLD aka OGON NO YARO DOMO aka THE GOLDEN MOB 1967 88 MIN. DIR. Mio Ezaki SCR. Iwao Yamazaki/Mio Ezaki PHOTO COLOR 'SCOPE: Shohei Ando MUSIC: Harumi Ibe w/ Yujiro Ishihara, Joe Shishido, Hideaki Nitani, Misa Hirose, Akemi Mari, Hiroshi Nawa, Tatsuya Fuji, Yoshiko Hara, Isao Tamagawa, Eiji Go

Outlaw's Gold

Ishihara is instructed by his boss to go after the gang who underbid an associate on a big construction job. Insisting he wants to do it alone, Ishihara makes enemies of his partner, cruel Nawa, who tips off the rival gang of the plan. Warned by friend Nitani, Ishihara changes tactics, taking subordinates Go and Tamagawa along but leaving married Nitani behind when they assault the mob's island casino HQ. Hothead rival gangster Fuji is killed in the attack which sends the rival's second-in-command Shishido over the edge on a vengeance quest. Ishihara confronts his own traitorous boss at a ship-launching party with attendant politicians. Suddenly, Go and Tamagawa appear, the latter blowing

the boss away and sparking a huge fight. Tamagawa is knifed to death, and Ishihara and Go escape, forced to go on the run from their own gang as well as Shishido's bunch. When Ishihara learns that pal Nitani and spouse are being victimized by the rival gang boss, Ishihara engages in fierce battle, finally wiping out the head villain as well as crazy killer Shishido. Despite the cast, this is pretty ho-hum stuff. There are a few entertaining action sequences, but more often than not director Ezaki tends to diffuse tension rather than build it. Routine. * * 1/2

OUTLAWS! GO TO HELL! aka YARO! JIGOKU E IKE 1960 DIR. Motomu (Tan) Iida SCR. Taichi Inubuse/Yoshi Yamamura MUSIC: Hajime Kaburagi w/ Yuji Kodaka, Mihoko Inagaki, Tomoo Nagai, Kaku Takashina

OUTLAW WITHOUT A COUNTRY aka YARO NI KOKKYO WA NAI 1965 99 min. DIR. Ko Nakahira SCR. Hajime Takaiwa/Ichiro Miyagawa/ Yoichiro Fukuda PHOTO B&W 'SCOPE: Yoshihiro Yamazaki MUSIC: Harumi Ibe w/ Akira Kobayashi, Yasushi Suzuki, Misa Hirose

PARADISE PRIEST aka GOKU-RAKU BOZU 1971 82 min. DIR. Kazushige Takeda SCR. Ryozo Nakanishi PHOTO COLOR 'SCOPE: Minoru Yokoyama MUSIC: Hiroki Tamaki w/ Joe Shishido, Jiro Okazaki, Tomoko Mayama, Ganosuke Ashiya, Keiko Aikawa, Shoki Fukae, Jun Otani, Hyoe Enoki, Rika Fujie This may be a knock-off of the THE EVIL PRIEST series at

Toei and the HOODLUM PRIEST series at Daiei. But this one, judging from the photos and poster, is much more erotic in flavor and is set in a contemporary, early 1970s milieu.

PASSPORT TO DARKNESS aka ANKOKU NO RYOKEN 1959 89 min. **DIR.** Seijun Suzuki **SCR.** Hajime Takaiwa **PHOTO B&W 'SCOPE:** Kazue Nagatsuka **MUSIC:** Taiichiro Kosugi/Tomikazu Kawabe w/ Ryoji Hayama, Tamaki Sawa, Mari Shiraki, Masumi Okada, Hiroshi Kondo, Shinsuke Ashida, D. G. Waller Trombone-playing bandleader Hayama searches for his missing girlfriend/singer only to have her turn up strangled in his apartment. The police let him stay out of jail but keep a close watch on him. He tracks down a few threads, realizing his murdered sweetheart was somehow involved with a heroin ring. This leads him into progressively more sleazy and bizarre byways, coming up against various gunmen, junkies, transvestite whores and underworld specimens. Suzuki amazingly keeps inter-est through some slow patches by meticulously orchestrating Hayama's gradual descent into an urban hell. The last half hour begins with an ad-dict girl informer being murdered by a subhuman hitman and then the puz-zle pieces finally falling into place, drug dealer Kondo bringing Hayama to the mastermind's rural HQ. Once outside the house, a mysterious man arrives with Hayama's handcuffed bandmate Okada. Hayama initially believes the man is another gangster and clips him, only to discover that he is an undercover cop and Okada is a desperate addict member of the drug gang. Kondo is killed in a shootout

with Hayama, and Okada mortally wounded when he tries to run over the policeman. Reinforcements arrive as Hayama spots the drug kingpin's gay addict lover sneaking into the country home. Hayama and the cops pursue him inside but discover that the mastermind is actually a foreign emissary who can't be touched due to diplomatic immunity. Hands tied, they follow the pair to the airport and are shocked when the tortured addict shoots his foreign lover and master to death on the tarmac. * * *

Peony and Dragon

PEONY AND DRAGON aka BOTAN TO RYU aka THE DRAGON'S CLAW 1970 100 min. **DIR.** Masahiro Makino **SCR.** Saburo Endo/Jiro Yamakami **PHOTO COLOR 'SCOPE:** Minoru Yokoyama/Sei Kitaizumi **MUSIC:** Taiichiro Kosugi w/ Hideki Takahashi, Masako Izumi, Akira Kobayashi, Michitaro Mizushima, Jun Tazaki, Toru Abe, Shiro Yanase A remake of Toei

Studio's TALES OF JAPANESE
CHIVALRY – ATTACK (1967),
which was also directed by Makino.

PERFECT GAME,
see IMPERFECT GAME

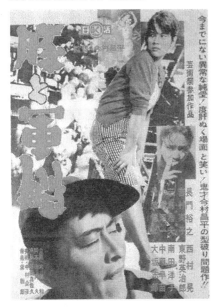

Pigs and Battleships

PIGS AND BATTLESHIPS aka
BUTA TO GUNKAN 1961 108 min.
Dir. Shohei Imamura **Scr.** Hisashi
Yamauchi **Photo B&W 'scope:**
Shinsaku Himeda **Music:** Toshiro
Mayazumi **w/** Hiroyuki Nagato,
Jitsuko Yoshimura, Yoko Minamida,
Shiro Osaka, Sanae Nakahara, Masao
Mishima, Tetsuro Tanba, Shoichi
Ozawa, Eijiro Tono
A superlative, atypical yakuza saga
of Yoshimura, her wannabe gangster
boyfriend Nagato and a plot to sell
pigs on the post-WW2 black market.
Of course, there is Imamura's usual
offbeat dark humor perfectly inte-
grated into his trademark sociology-
lesson-from-hell realism. Yoshimura
and Nagato are stupendous as the

bickering couple imprisoned in their
shantytown, dockside inferno. The
nearby U.S. military base proves
fertile soil for all varieties of crime,
including prostitution, narcotics,
protection rackets, gambling and
black market foodstuffs. There is a
great scene where several gangsters,
including ulcer-plagued tough guy
Tanba, eat some tainted roast pig and
are severely stricken. Tanba, hospitalized from the incident, becomes even
more suicidal after being informed
by subordinate Nagato that big boss
Mishima intends to squeeze him out
of their black market pig business.
The climax where Nagato, beaten
by Mishima's henchmen, grabs a
machine gun and hijacks the truck
convoy of pigs, only to release them
in a porcine stampede in the red light
district is simultaneously hilarious,
scary and sad. Nagato bites the dust

Pigs and Battleships

in the ensuing confrontation with Japanese gangsters and American MPS. He dies face-down in a urinal. The final scene the next morning when hardened, grieving Yoshimura is about to capitulate to becoming a whore, then abruptly does an about-face and bids adieu, walking out of the crime-ridden neighborhood is matter-of-fact and unsentimental, but extremely moving. * * * *

PLEASURE RESORT TROU-BADOR'S SONG – SHINJUKU WOMAN aka SAKARIBA NAGASHI BAO – SHINJUKU NO ONNA 1970 **DIR.** Kazushige Takeda **SCR.** Hideshi (Hidemori?) Yamamura/ Saburo Kuruusu **PHOTO COLOR 'SCOPE:** Kenji Hagiwara **MUSIC:** Hajime Kaburagi w/ Sanae Kitabayashi, Reiko Oshida, Isao Kimura, Tatsuya Fuji, Yokyo Yamamoto, Chigako Miyagi, Keiko (Yoshiko?) Fuji, Manako Fuji, Rika Ohashi, Keiko Nishi, Masao Komatsu Only tangentially a yakuza story dealing with women involved in the exploitive side of the pleasure resort business.

PLUNDERERS OF THE HARBOR aka MINATO NO RYAKU DATSU MONO 1962 **DIR.** Isamu Kosugi **SCR.** Kazuku Uchida **PHOTO 'SCOPE:** Kumenobu Fujioka **MUSIC:** Taiichiro Kosugi w/ Kyoji Aoyama, Minosuke Nakao, Hitoshi Miyazaki, Ryohei Uchida, Minako Kazuki, Akifumi Inoue

PORTRAIT OF A GANG aka GYANGU NO SHOZO 1965 90 min. **DIR.** Takumi Furukawa **SCR.** Takehiro Nakajima/Takumi Furukawa **PHOTO B&W 'SCOPE:**

Saburo Isayama **MUSIC:** Taiichiro Kosugi w/ Hideaki Nitani, Tatsuya Fuji, Kazuko Inano, Tomiko Sayo, Yuji Kodaka, Kaku Takashina, Hiroshi Sugie, Hiroshi Hijikata

POSITION OF SCORCHING HEAT aka SHAKUNETSU NO ISU aka OFFICE OF INCANDES-CENCE 1963 **DIR.** Hiroshi Noguchi **SCR.** Ei Ogawa/Takashi Kanbara **PHOTO 'SCOPE:** Kazue Nagatsuka **MUSIC:** Naozumi Yamamoto w/ Koji Wada, Chieko Matsubara, Minako Kazuki, Satoshi Yamanouchi, Ichiro Sugai, Daisaburo Hirata, Shoki Fukae, Eiji Go, Uyako Hori

POWERFUL SEX BIOGRAPHY – I GIVE YOU DEATH aka SEIGO RETSUDEN – SHINDE MORAIM-ASU 1972 **DIR.** Isao Hayashi **SCR.** Kazuo Nishida **PHOTO COLOR 'SCOPE:** Kurataro Takamura w/ Kazuko Shirakawa, Keiko (Yoshiko?) Aikawa, Fusatomi Hara, Yasushi Suzuki   Judging from the second part of the title – a traditional proclamation of a yakuza before as-sassinating a boss or starting a gang-fight – it seems this is another roman porno/yakuza hybrid.

PRINCE OF WOLVES aka OKAMI NO OJI 1963 103 min. **DIR.** Toshio Masuda **SCR.** Takeshi Tamura/Eitaro Morikawa **PHOTO B&W 'SCOPE:** Yoshio Mamiya **MUSIC:** Harumi Ibe w/ Hideki Takahashi, Ruriko Asaoka, Kenjiro Ishiyama, Yoshi Kato, Tamio Kawaji, Mizuho Suzuki, Mitsuo Yamaguchi, Saburo Hiromatsu, Tatsuya Fuji Director Masuda takes a page out of Kinji Fukasaku's book, creating a gutsy B&W postwar chronicle of poverty giving rise to gangsterism in much the same way Fukasaku did in early sixties WOLVES, PIGS AND PEOLPLE and HIGH NOON FOR GANGSTERS, and later seventies BATTLES W/O HONOR & HUMANITY and GRAVEYARD OF HONOR & HUMANITY. Masuda would later collaborate with Fukasaku on direction of the Japanese footage for TORA! TORA! TORA! Orphan Takahashi grows up in the late fifties/ early sixties, adopted by benevolent boss Ishiyama (who would also play his father in the more lyrical, *ninkyo* yakuza picture A MAN'S CREST). The scene where Ishiyama is stabbed by a killer on a streetcar just after bidding his son Takahashi farewell, then Takahashi running after him when he realizes what has happened, is disturbingly effective. There are many other great scenes with a surplus of on-location ambience and chaotic energy. However, Takahashi seems a bit too gentle and seems just too good to be true in his desire to walk a straight path. He falls in love with crusading reporter Ruriko Asaoka who is busy covering the violent student demonstrations of the era. Tamio Kawaji is extremely good – as is usually the case – as Takahashi's childhood nemesis who has grown up to sadistically relish his role as the bad boss's right-hand man. When another comrade close to Takahashi is murdered, Takahashi goes on the rampage, and Masuda's camera follows him in one continuous tracking shot in broad daylight through the busy hotel until he reaches the craven bosses. We see the dying villains' POV as Takahashi blows them away in the memorably bravura climax. * * * 1/2

Prince of Wolves

PROFIT FROM KILLING aka SATSU RARETE TAMA RUKA 1964 89 min. **DIR.** Tokujiro Yamazaki **SCR.** Ryuzo Nakanishi **PHOTO B&W** **'SCOPE:** Kumenobu Fujioka **MUSIC:** Seitaro Omori **w/** Hideaki Nitani, Isao Tamagawa, Reiko Sassamori,

Yoko Yamamoto, Takamaru Sasaki,
Eiji Go

Profit from Killing

**PUBLIC OSTENTATION OF THE
BEAST** aka YAJU NO YOMI NI
MIETE 1962 DIR. Koreyoshi
Kurahara SCR. Nobuo Yamada
PHOTO 'SCOPE: Yoshio Mamiya
MUSIC: Toshiro Mayuzumi w/ Joe
Shishido, Joji Ai, Izumi Ashikawa,
Daisaburo Hirata, Yoko Minamura,
Noriko Matsumoto, Etsuko Wada

**PUNISHMENT OF A LAWLESS
VILLAIN – SABU** aka BURAI
MUHO NO TO – SABU 1964 102
min. DIR. Takashi Nomura SCR.
Nobuo Yamada PHOTO B&W 'SCOPE:
Kurataro Takamura MUSIC: Harumi
Ibe w/ Akira Kobayashi, Ruriko
Asaoka, Hiroyuki Nagato, Chitose
Kobayashi, Jun Hamamura, Shinsuke
Ashida, Shoki Fukae, Hiroshi Sugie,
Hosei Komatsu
At the end of the Meiji era, when the
samurai is being replaced by the mer-

chant class and western commerce
is opening up the nation, Kobayashi
and slightly retarded brother Nagato
slave as apprentices at a prosperous
artisan's compound.

Punishment of a Lawless Villain - Sabu

Orphaned in their early adolescence,
the two are very close. However,
Kobayashi's arranged marriage with
the merchant's daughter threatens not
only Nagato's frail sense of security
but maid Asaoka who is in love with
Kobayashi. One day Kobayashi is
found by the merchant and foreman
to have a very expensive piece of
design fabric amongst his possessions
– something that was stolen from the
merchant. Kobayashi knows Nagato
had a fondness for the fabric and believes that his brother stashed it there.
But he keeps mum, going to an island
prison for the theft. The whole time
inside he rails against authority and
the heirarchy of convicts, battling the
established gang and building bitter-
ness towards his brother. He attempts

an escape at one point, to no avail. Eventually he is released and returns to the merchant's household. He angrily confronts his sibling Nagato, but Nagato is mystified. Finally, wracked with guilt, Asaoka confesses it was she that planted the fabric, framing Kobayashi so he wouldn't be able to marry the rich daughter. She leaves. Nagato convinces Kobayashi he should go after her, and the two end up together at last with Kobayashi forgiving her transgression. This is no relation to the 2002 film SABU directed by Takashi Miike.   * * *

Pursuer Without Form

PURSUER WITHOUT FORM aka SUGATA NAKI TSUISEKISHA 1962 81 min. DIR. Takumi Furukawa SCR. Ryuta Akimoto PHOTO COLOR 'SCOPE: Saburo Isayama   w/ Hideaki Nitani, Ruriko Asaoka, Eiji Go, Kaku Takashina, Hiroshi Kondo, Nobuo Kaneko

QUICK-DRAW DRIFTER aka NUKIUCHI FURAIBO 1962 94 min. DIR. Isamu Noguchi SCR. Iwao Yamazaki PHOTO COLOR 'SCOPE: Shigeyoshi Mine   w/ Joe Shishido, Chieko Matsubara, Shoki Fukae, Daisaburo Hirata, Ichiro Sugai, Nobuo Kaneko

RAVEN OF THE SEA aka UMI NO GARASU 1963 88 min. DIR. Takumi Furukawa SCR. Kimiyuki Hasegawa PHOTO 'SCOPE: Saburo Isayama MUSIC: Taiichiro Kosugi   w/ Hideaki Nitani, Hideki Takahashi, Masako Izumi, Yuji Kodaka, Sumiko Minami, Shiro Osaka, Asao Sano, Toshio Sugiyama, Daisaburo Hirata

REBEL aka HANGYAKU SHA 1957 92 min. DIR. Takumi Furukawa SCR. Hajime Takaiwa PHOTO B&W: Minoru Yokoyama MUSIC: Masaru Sato   w/ Michitaro Mizushima, Hiroyuki Nagato, Hideko Yamane, Ruriko Asaoka, Hiroshi Nihonyanagi

Red Glass

RED GLASS aka AKAI GURASU
1966 86 min. **DIR.** Ko Nakahira
SCR. Hisatoshi Kai **PHOTO B&W**
'SCOPE: Yoshihiro Yamazaki **MUSIC:**
Shoichi Makino **w/** Tetsuya Watari,
Joji Ai, Tetsuko Kobayashi, Mizuho
Suzuki, Daisaburo Hirata, Keiko
Yuge

Red Handkerchief

RED HANDKERCHIEF aka
AKAI HANKACHI 1964 98 min.
DIR. Toshio Masuda **SCR.** Toshio
Masuda/Ei Ogawa/Iwao (Gan)
Yamazaki **PHOTO COLOR 'SCOPE:**
Shigeyoshi Mine **MUSIC:** Harumi Ibe
w/ Yujiro Ishihara, Ruriko Asaoka,
Hideaki Nitani, Nobuo Kaneko,
Tamio Kawaji, Shinsuke Ashida
1964 was a big year at Nikkatsu
for their so-called mood/action noir
crime/romance melodramas, and
RED HANDKERCHIEF was one
of the biggest hits in this popular
subgenre. Ishihara is a disgraced
ex-police detective, dismissed from
the force after a questionable shooting in the line of duty. He becomes
a construction worker *and* a roving
minstrel – yeah, yeah, I know, but
that was part of Ishihara's charismatic
shtick, and the audiences ate it up.
Ishihara's former boss, cop Kaneko,
comes around, feeling that something
was wrong with the set-up and asks
Ishihara if he wants to unofficially

investigate behind the scenes. It
seems after the shooting, Ishihara's
ex-partner Nitani married the victim's
factory worker daughter (Asaoka),
who coincidentally was the object of
Ishihara's unrequited love. Not only
that, Nitani is now the owner of several department stores. Was he on the
take when he was still on the force?
Kaneko wants Ishihara to find out.
Our hero reluctantly agrees and opens
up a troublesome Pandora's Box of
unpleasant secrets. * * *

Red Harbor

RED HARBOR aka AKAI
HATOBA aka RED QUAY aka
THE LEFT HAND OF JIRO 1958
99 min. **DIR.** Toshio Masuda **SCR.**
Ichiro Ikeda/Toshio Masuda **PHOTO**
B&W 'SCOPE: Shinsaku Himeda
MUSIC: Hajime Kaburagi **w/** Yujiro
Ishihara, Mie Kitahara, Masumi
Okada, Sanae Nakahara, Hideaki
Nitani, Shiro Osaka, Yukiko
Todoroki   Ishihara is a mob killer
dressed in a white suit who hangs out

down at the harbor with other riff-
raff. He has several women, but falls
for the more-straight-arrow Kitahara.
So far the cops have not been able
to pin anything on Ishihara. He is
just too slick. But Kitahara proves
his eventual downfall. The noirish
ambience is effective, but the story is
somewhat slow-moving, and the action scenes are few and far between.
This was remade in color in 1967 by
director Masuda as THE VELVET
HUSTLER with a bit more violence
and a more yakuza slant, this time
with Tetsuya Watari in Ishihara's role.
Many, including this writer, prefer
the remake. It has a charisma that this
version is sorely lacking.   * * 1/2

Retreat Through the Wet Wasteland
still and poster

**RETREAT THROUGH THE WET
WASTELAND** aka NURETA KOYA
O HASHIRE 1973 73 min. DIR.
Yukihiro Sawada SCR. Kazuhiko
Hasegawa PHOTO COLOR 'SCOPE:
Yoshihiro Yamazaki MUSIC: Mio
Tama w/ Yuri Yamashina, Takeo
Chii, Maki Kawamura, Hirokazu
Inoue A notorious pink film tale of
five corrupt police officers who rape,
kill and steal funds from Viet refu-
gees, then frame a teen gang. Compli-
cations arise when a former cop from
their unit escapes from an asylum.
It was controversial upon its initial
release but also critically acclaimed.

RETURN OF THE WOLF aka
KAITTE KITA OKAMI 1966 DIR.
Shugoro Nishimura SCR. Satoshi
Kuramoto/ Mitsugi (Susumu?) Akeda
PHOTO COLOR 'SCOPE: Shinsaku
Himeda MUSIC: Keitaro Miho
w/ Satoshi Yamauchi, Suichi
Kagiyama, Judi Ongu, Ken Sanders,
Eitataro Ozawa

**RISING DRAGON aka
NOBORI RYU series**

**RISING DRAGON'S IRON
FLESH** aka NOBORI RYU
TEKKA HADA aka THE FRIEND-
LY KILLER 1969 90 min.
DIR./SCR. Teruo Ishii PHOTO COLOR
'SCOPE: Sei Kitaizumi MUSIC:
Masao Yagi w/ Hiroko Ogi, Akira
Kobayashi, Tatsuya Fuji, Asao Koike,
Hideki Takahashi, Yoko Yamamoto,
Toru Abe One of popular singing
star Hiroko Ogi's two sword-wielding
yakuza series for Nikkatsu. Here she
plays a boss's daughter who becomes
his successor when he is murdered
at a rival boss's (Abe) instigation.

Kobayashi is a lone wolf who always seems to be around to help her at crucial times. At the end, as he dies, she discovers he was the one hired by Abe to kill her father, and he had been trying to redeem himself ever since. Not bad, but a bit disappointing considering Ishii's later achievement with the third in the series. #1 of 3 films * * 1/2

Rising Dragon's Soft Flesh Exposed (#2)

RISING DRAGON'S SOFT FLESH EXPOSED aka NOBORI RYU YAWA HADA KAICHO aka THE DRAGON TATTOO 1969 85 min. DIR. Masami Kuzuo SCR. Iwao Yamazaki PHOTO COLOR 'SCOPE: Sei Kitaizumi MUSIC: Toshinori Miyazawa w/ Hiroko Ogi, Tatsuya Fuji, Akira Kobayashi, Eiji Go, Tamio Kawaji, Junzaburo Ban, Ryohei Uchida Kuzuo was famed maverick Seijun Suzuki's assistant director on pictures from KANTO WANDERER (1963) through BRANDED TO KILL (1967),

Suzuki's last film at Nikkatsu. This was Kuzuo's first effort as a full-fledged director, and he doesn't seem to have followed it up with any others. There is better than even money that, directing or remaining an assistant, he worked in television in the seventies and eighties. Supposedly Ishii had been hired to direct all three films, but he was also busy with a big picture at Toei Studios, so took a supervisory role, appearing occasionally on set to advise his fledgling assistant Kuzuo on his directorial debut. #2 of 3 films

RISING DRAGON GHOST STORY aka KAIDAN NOBORI RYU aka BLIND WOMAN'S CURSE aka TATTOOED SWORDSWOMAN aka HAUNTED LIFE OF A DRAGON-TATTOOED LASS 1970 85 min. DIR. Teruo Ishii SCR. Teruo Ishii/Chusei Sone PHOTO COLOR 'SCOPE: Sei Kitaizumi MUSIC: Hajime Kaburagi w/ Meiko Kaji, Makoto Sato, Hoki Tokuda, Yoko Takagi, Toru Abe, Ryohei Uchida, Hideo Sunazuka, Yoshi Kato, Yuzo Harumi Kaji takes over Ogi's role (although Kaji is called by a different name). This is an incredibly entertaining tale of a very young female yakuza boss in turn-of-the-century Japan who accidentally blinds the sister (Tokuda) of an opposing clan leader she has just slain during a gangfight in the rain. Although virtually no supernatural events overtly occur, and Ishii sometimes leavens the tone with too much humor, the whole atmosphere of the picture is one of nocturnal spiritual evil looking for an outlet in violent individuals. Ishii keeps the film straddling the border – quite successfully – between

bizarre, surreal horror film and period yakuza tale. The vengeful blind sister comes into town under cover of a traveling horror carnival, and she

Rising Dragon Ghost Story aka Blind Woman's Curse

is aided and abetted by a maniacal hunchback (played by Tatsumi Hijikata, who also appeared in Ishii's HORRORS OF MALFORMED MEN) who has a fetish for dismembered, tattooed female flesh. The blind woman starts plotting, and soon she allies herself with a perverted, sadistic gang boss played by Toru Abe. Sato is a wisecracking lone wolf yakuza who has a crush on Kaji and helps her fight off the villains. The saga climaxes with a beautifully choreographed swordfight between Kaji and Tokuda. A mesmerizing hybrid, and, although not as over-the-top as his most insane pictures, the kind of tale at which Ishii really excels. #3 and final in series
* * * 1/2

ROAR OF THE CITY aka TOKAI NO DOGO 1958 80 min. Dɪʀ. Masahisa Harubara Sᴄʀ. Gen Kobuse Pʜoᴛo B&W 'scope: Yoshio Mamiya Mᴜsɪᴄ: Masayoshi Ikeda w/ Hisako Tsukuba, Kyoji Aoyama, Michitaro Mizushima, Hiroshi Nihonyanagi Kaku Takashina

ROCK BATH LOVE AFFAIR aka IWA FURO NO JOJI 1977 Dɪʀ. Isao Hayashi Sᴄʀ. Shoichi Ikeda Pʜoᴛo ᴄoʟoʀ 'scope: Toshiro Yamazaki Mᴜsɪᴄ: Shin (Nobu?) Takada w/ Naomi Tani, Naozone Oka, Taro Oshiama More yakuza/roman porno shenanigans.

ROUGHNECK aka COARSE VIOLENCE aka ARAKURE 1969 86 min. Dɪʀ. Yasuharu Hasebe Sᴄʀ. Iwao Yamazaki Pʜoᴛo ᴄoʟoʀ 'scope: Muneo Ueda Mᴜsɪᴄ: Hajime Kaburagi w/ Akira Kobayashi, Tatsuya Fuji, Ryoji Hayama, Masako

Izumi, Masahiko Tanimura, Eiji Go, Nijiko Kiyokawa, Jotaro Togami, Isao Tamagawa, Joe Shishido

Roughneck

This starts off with a bumptious comic tone, Kobayashi and accomplices trying to knock over a gambling den, failing, narrowly escaping, then Kobayashi ironically being arrested for not having proper train fare. Kobayashi's pal Fuji is a loser/womanizer who steals from his girlfriends. Fuji's sister Izumi despises him and his yakuza pals. However, Kobayashi is attracted to her. Eventually, Kobayashi, Fuji and pals' lone wolf hijinks go too far. Robbing one extremely greedy clan costs them dearly. All are killed except Kobayashi. Hayama drafts him into his honorable clan's ranks, and they take on the gang's killers. Shishido appears without a single line in a cameo as a hitman for opposing boss Togami. At the end, having dispatched Togami and his henchmen,

Kobayashi strolls leisurely down the street in a black formal kimono. He has finally given-up his lone wolf status and become a comparatively "respectable" member of a clan.
* * *

RUSTY CHAINS aka SABITA KUSARI 1960 94 min. **DIR.** Buichi Saito **SCR.** Ichiro Ikeda/Ryuta Akimoto **PHOTO COLOR 'SCOPE:** Kurataro Takamura **MUSIC:** Taiichiro Kosugi w/ Keiichiro Akagi, Reiko Sassamori, Yukiko Todoroki, Eitaro Ozawa, Yuji Kodaka, Mari Shiraki, Masao Mishima, Shiro Osaka

Rusty Knife

RUSTY KNIFE aka SABITA NAIFU 1958 90 min. **DIR.** Toshio Masuda **SCR.** Shintaro Ishihara/ Toshio Masuda **PHOTO B&W** **'SCOPE:** Kurataro Takamura **MUSIC:** Masaru Sato w/ Yujiro Ishihara, Mie Kitahara, Akira Kobayashi, Mari Shiraki, Shoji Yasui, Joe Shishido, Naoki Sugiura

Ishihara, Kobayashi and Shishido are three *"chinpira"* (yakuza slang for "little pricks") who get into trouble as witnesses to a mob killing of a councilman. Things heat up when Shishido threatens he will testify against the boss responsible. He sends a letter to the DA, but still hopes to get big money blackmailing the boss. He gets pushed into the path of an onrushing train to shut him up. Meanwhile, the DA contacts Ishihara and Kobayashi, who are now working straight jobs in a bar, to try to get them to testify. They won't, and Kobayashi takes hush money from the evil boss, which angers Ishihara when he finds out. Ishihara is also tormented because the whole case is linked to the gang rape and suicide of his ex-girlfriend. A really mixed bag as director Masuda brings a refreshing grit to the look of the film, obviously trying to get away from the standard programmer fare. However, the script and dialogue veer wildly back and forth between credibly hardboiled and laughably cliche-ridden. Yujiro's brother Shintaro co-wrote the screenplay. On the plus side, actresses Kitahara and Shiraki are very strong presences in their roles as the murdered councilman's journalist daughter and Kobayashi's free-spirit girlfriend respectively. * * 1/2

RUSTY PENDANT aka SABITA PENDANTO aka STAINED PENDANT 1967 85 min. **DIR.** Mio Ezaki **SCR.** Iwao Yamazaki/Mio Ezaki **PHOTO COLOR 'SCOPE:** Shohei Ando **MUSIC:** Naozumi Yamamoto w/ Tetsuya Watari, Yoko Yamamoto, Isao Kimura, Seizaburo Kawazu, Akemi Mari More of an action film than a genuine yakuza picture.

Rusty Pendant

SAGA FROM CHICHIBU MOUNTAINS aka CHICHIBU SUI KODEN series

Saga of Chichibu Mountains (#1)

Saga of Chichibu Mountains (#2)

SAGA FROM CHICHIBU MOUNTAINS – ASSASSIN'S SWORD aka CHICHIBU SUI KODEN – HISSATSU KEN 1965 89 min. DIR. Hiroshi Noguchi SCR. Tomoichiro Miyamoto/Takashi Iwasaki PHOTO COLOR 'SCOPE: Toshitaro Nakao MUSIC: Seitaro Omori   w/ Hideki Takahashi, Chieko Matsubara, Hideaki Nitani, Shinsuke Ashida, Hisako (Sumiko?) Minami, Hitoshi Miyazaki, Hiroshi Sugie, Shoki Fukae #1 of 2 films

SAGA FROM CHICHIBU MOUNTAINS – SWORD CUTS THE SHADOWS aka CHICHIBU SUI KODEN – KAGE O KIRU KEN aka LIVING BY THE SWORD 1967 84 min. DIR. Motomu (Tan) Ida SCR.Takashi Iwasaki PHOTO B&W 'SCOPE: Izumi Hagiwara MUSIC: Seitaro Omori w/ Hideki Takahashi, Yoko Yamamoto, Osamu Takizawa, Ryoji Hayama, Michitaro Mizushima, Toru Abe, Daisaburo Hirata, Hiroshi Minami #2 of 2 films

SATAN'S TOWN aka AKUMA NO MACHI 1956 83 min. DIR. Seijun Suzuki SCR. Goro Shiraishi PHOTO B&W: Kazue Nagatsuka MUSIC: Taiichiro Kosugi   w/ Seizaburo Kawazu, Shinsuke Ashida, Ichiro Sugai, Ken Mishima, Shoki Fukae, Azusa Yumi, Mie Tatsuno Suzuki's third film, his first crack at the gangster genre, is a very entertaining yarn with sadistic gang kingpin and all round arch-fiend Sugai escaping from a prison transport then being cozied up to by ambivalent undercover cop Kawazu. Sugai lays low at a posh Chinese-owned casino, plotting a heist with Kawazu, Ashida, et.

al. Some of the bravura *tour de force* visual pieces include one of Kawazu's contacts assassinated in a phone booth then discovered by schoolgirls; Kawazu studying his reflection in the casino swimming pool when Sugai suddenly shoots someone off screen, the victim plummeting into the water so Kawazu's image is obliterated; Kawazu's stop-action daydream of capturing Sugai. As the tale progresses, Sugai becomes more and more ruthless, gratuitously shooting or running people down in the Tokyo streets in his flight from the law. Suzuki even borrows images from WHITE HEAT as Sugai is chased into a natural gas/oil storage plant. Kawazu is finally successful in gunning down Sugai but at the steep price of being riddled with lead himself. SATAN'S TOWN is extremely violent during its second half, with a brutality quotient rare for the time period and even surpassing the then reigning exploitation kings at Shintoho Studios. * * *

Satan's Town

SATSU RUKA YARARE RUKA 1966 DIR. Takashi Nomura SCR. Ryuzo Nakanishi/Takashi Fujii PHOTO COLOR 'SCOPE: Shigeyoshi Mine MUSIC: Harumi Ibe w/ Hideki Takahashi, Naoki Sugiura, Tatsuya

Fuji, Izumi Ashikawa, Hiromi
Hirazuka, Masako Ota, Takeshi Kato

SEA TRAP aka UMI NO WANA
1959 82 min. **DIR.** Motomu (Tan)
Iida **SCR.** Seiji Hoshikawa **PHOTO**
B&W 'SCOPE: Isamu Kakida **MUSIC:**
Naozumi Yamamoto **w/** Michitaro
Mizushima, Joe Shishido, Yuji
Kodaka, Hisako Tsukuba, Sanae
Nakahara, Masumi Okada, Shinsuke
Ashida

SEE THE DREAM WITHIN A
MAN aka OTOKO NARA YUME
O MIRU 1959 89 min. **DIR.** Yoichi
Ushihara **SCR.** Ichiro Ikeda **PHOTO**
COLOR 'SCOPE: Minoru Yokoyama
MUSIC: Masaru Sato **w/** Yujiro
Ishihara, Ryoji Hayama, Osamu
Takizawa, Izumi Ashikawa, Mayumi
Shimizu, Tamio Kawaji
An early contemporary yakuza
action drama.

SEVEN WILD BEASTS aka
SHICHININ NO YAJU aka **THE**
FILTHY SEVEN series

SEVEN WILD BEASTS aka
SHICHININ NO YAJU aka THE
FILTHY SEVEN 1967 92 min.
DIR. Mio Ezaki **SCR.** Iwao Yamazaki/
Mio Ezaki **PHOTO COLOR 'SCOPE:**
Minoru Yokoyama **MUSIC:** Naozumi
Yamamoto **w/** Tetsuro Tanba, Joe
Shishido, Masumi Okada, Chieko
Matsubara, Ryohei Uchida, Annu
Mari, Kaku Takashina
Tanba is an ex-police detective who
had been forced to resign after acci-
dentally killing a gang boss. He is ar-
rested in a gambling raid and coerced
by the cops to help them rescue a
nuclear physicist possessing impor-

tant secrets who is being held captive
in an unidentified embassy. Legally
they have no authority, so everything
is being done in clandestine fashion.
They promise Tanba three million yen
if he will accept. Tanba recruits six
other thieves, conmen and hooligans,
and, utilizing various disguises ala
MISSION: IMPOSSIBLE-style,
they infiltrate the enemy stronghold.
There is a twist ending where the
reward money and atomic secrets are
destroyed. Judging from the tongue-
in-cheek, spy-spoof plot, there seems
to be a humorous tone along with the
violent action. #1 of 2 films

Seven Wild Beasts (#1)

SEVEN WILD BEASTS –
PROCLAMATION OF BLOOD
aka SHICHININ NO YAJU – CHI
NO SENGEN aka RETURN OF
THE FILTHY SEVEN 1967 92
min. **DIR.** Mio Ezaki **SCR.** Mio
Ezaki/Iwao Yamazaki **PHOTO COLOR**
'SCOPE: Shohei Ando **MUSIC:**
Naozumi Yamamoto/Koichi Sakata

w/ Tetsuro Tanba, Joe Shishido, Yoshiro Aoki, Masumi Okada, Asao Koike, Eiji Go, Kaku Takashina, Nakajiro Tomita   Sprung from jail again to rob a yakuza boss, Tanba impersonates the head of police detectives and acts as ringleader of the other six. However, the gang boss is hep to Tanba's game, and the two turn the tables on each other several times. A wild card is introduced at the last minute with one of the boss's henchmen making off with the loot. The "filthy seven" and the boss are left with nothing except irate police. #2 of 2 films

SEX PEDDLERS OF GINZA, see MARKET OF WOMEN

SHOWA ERA LIFE aka SHOWA NO INOCHI aka MAN OF A STORMY ERA 1968 165 min. **DIR.** Toshio Masuda **SCR.** Kaneo Ikegami **PHOTO COLOR 'SCOPE:** Minoru Yokoyama **MUSIC:** Rinichiro Manabe   w/ Yujiro Ishihara, Ruriko Asaoka, Hideki Takahashi, Mie Hama, Ryutaro Tatsumi, Masako Izumi, Tatsuya Fuji, Eiji Okada, Mitsuo Hamada, Sanae Kitabayashi, Koji Nanbara, Katsuo Nakamura, Yoshiro Aoki, Kei Sato, Shogo Shimada, Eijiro Yanagi   As one can tell from the running time and the powerhouse cast, plus top director Masuda, this was one of Nikkatsu's biggest releases of 1968.

SHOWA YAKUZA FAMILY TREE – FACE OF NAGASAKI aka SHOWA YAKUZA KEIZU – NAGASAKI NO KAO aka LINE-AGE OF SHOWA YAKUZA – PROFILE OF NAGASAKI aka SHOWDOWN AT NAGASAKI

1969 94 min. **DIR.** Takashi Nomura **SCR.** Kaneo Ikegami **PHOTO COLOR 'SCOPE:** Shigeyoshi Mine **MUSIC:** Saburo Matsura   w/ Tetsuya Watari, Noboru Ando, Yoshiro Aoki, Kanjuro Arashi, Hiroko Masuda, Tatsuya Fuji Michitaro Mizushima,   Elder boss Arashi welcomes home his son Watari. Soon Arashi dies, and Watari takes over the gang's pop music concert promotion business. It is strange that this was made in 1969 because the pop bands show-cased here on stage are embarassingly bad – sub-par Ventures-meet-the-Lettermen hybrids who stand rooted to the spot as they play their bland renditions. This aspect is downright aggravating since there were other musical combos of both wild and

Showa Yakuza Family Tree - Face of Nagasaki

conservative varieties in other Nikkat-su yakuza and youth pictures at the time that were borderline decent. This does have some interesting touches, such as rival nightclub owner Ando rejecting his colleague Aoki's shoddy, dishonorable treatment of Watari's gang. Watari also occasionally has some kind of dizzy spell where his vision blurs and he sees colored lights. Perhaps because he is suffer-ing from growing up in radioactive Nagasaki (the 2nd city A-bombed by

America after Hiroshima?) It is too bad not much is done with this – it would have been nice, for instance, if Watari had gone into one of these spells while fighting the final duel with Aoki. No such luck. Screenwriter Ikegami penned several great movies, including Eiichi Kudo's original 13 ASSASSINS at Toei Studios. Disappointing, too, in that a team-up of Watari and Ando should have reaped much wilder, stranger fruit. * *

SLEEP OF THE BEAST aka KEMONO NO NEMURI 1960 85 min. **DIR.** Seijun Suzuki **SCR.** Ichiro Ikeda **PHOTO B&W** 'SCOPE: Shigeyoshi Mine **MUSIC:** Hajime Kaburagi   w/ Hiroyuki Nagato, Kazuko Yoshiyuki, Shinsuke Ashida, Kinzo Shin, Yuko Kusunoki, Keisuko Noro   There are no overt traditional yakuza trappings, but this very atmospheric noir focuses on the mystery of a ruthless smuggling gang masquerading as a religious sect. Although his character is not as callous or cynical, Nagato assays a similar role to the one he played in Suzuki's CLANDESTINE ZERO LINE, a no-nonsense investigative reporter intent on getting to the bottom of things, no matter what. Seemingly just a mild-mannered businessman, Ashida disappears from the family home for a few days after returning from abroad. This leads teen daughter Yoshiyuki and her beau Nagato to do some digging on their own when the police discover nothing. Things only get more suspicious when Ashida turns back up with a lame excuse. Before long, Nagato's nosy behavior leads him into jeopardy. There are some great scenes in smoky, urban nightclubs as well as a cool, appropriately jazzy score by

Kaburagi. Suzuki and writer Ikeda delve into the trauma of the comparatively decent Ashida's involvement on not only him and his wife but especially daughter Yoshiyuki. Yoshiyuki's teen character starts the story with the emotions of a child and has to grow quickly into an adult by the time of the downbeat, fiery climax at the religious sect/gang's mansion headquarters. * * *

SO LONG, COMRADE aka ABAYO DACHI KO 1974 95 min. **DIR.** Yukihiro Sawada **SCR.** Fumio Konami **PHOTO COLOR** 'SCOPE: Yoshihiro Yamazaki w/ Yusaku Matsuda, Kenzo Kawaharazaki, Masaaki Okado, Eiji Go

SOMEONE'S MURDER aka KOROSHI TA NO WA DARE TA 1957 91 min. **DIR.** Ko Nakahira **SCR.** Kaneto Shindo **PHOTO B&W:** Shinsaku Himeda **MUSIC:** Akira Ifukube w/ Akira Kobayashi, Ichiro Sugai, Hisako Yamane, Ko Nishimura A gritty troubled youth drama, fueled no doubt by the *taiyozoku* (sun tribe) fever then current.

SONG OF PARTING REGRETS aka SEKIBETSU NO UTA aka SONG OF RELUCTANT FAREWELL 1962 **DIR.** Hiroshi Noguchi **SCR.** Iwao Yamazaki/Yoshio Yamano **PHOTO** 'SCOPE: Kazue Nagatsuka **MUSIC:** Seitaro Omori   w/ Akira Kobayashi, Reiko Sassamori, Mari Shiraki, Nobuo Kaneko, Daisaburo Hirata, Yumi Takano, Shoki Fukae Typical programmer fare with a perfectly innocuous, anemic approach. Just out-of-school Kobayashi falls for sweet Sassamori who just happens to be the daughter of evil yakuza boss Kaneko. It is a familiar yakuza *eiga* plot that has been done much better elsewhere. Unfortunately, this seems to have been aimed at Kobayashi's burgeoning legion of gushing female fans, so punches are pulled and the emphasis is on lightweight tragic romance. Even though Kaneko dies while trying to kill Kobayashi – conveniently shot by one of his own mortally wounded, renegade henchmen, obviously so Kobayashi would not have to sully his hands – Kobayashi nevertheless still departs at the end, leaving the heartbroken Sassamori behind. One of veteran action director Noguchi's blandest films.   * 1/2

SOON AFTER THE KILLING aka KOROSHI O OTTE 1962 **DIR.** Mitsuo Maeda **SCR.** Takumi Furukawa/ Motoshige Wakai **PHOTO 'SCOPE:** Izumi Hagiwara **MUSIC:** Kunio Miyauchi **w/** Yuji Kodaka, Keisuke Yukioka, Sachiko Uesuki, Minako Kazuki, Akifumi Inoue

SPASMS! EVIL EXCHANGE aka MONZETSU! DONDEN GAESHI aka CONVULSIONS! EVIL RETURN GIFT aka PAINFUL BLISS! FINAL TWIST aka EVIL PAYBACK 1977 73 min. **DIR.** Tatsumi Kumashiro **SCR.** Rokuro Kumaya (Kumatani?) **PHOTO COLOR 'SCOPE:** Shinsaku Himeda **w/** Naomi Tani, Jun Aki, Reika Maki, Osamu Tsuruoka, Erina Miyai A reportedly astonishing pink/roman porno yakuza film, helmed by the critically-acclaimed Kumashiro.

STEP ON THE GAS! aka SHINJUKU AUTORO – BUTTO-

BASE 1970 84 min. **DIR.** Toshiya Fujita **SCR.** Shuichi Nagahara/Michio Sotake/Toshiya Fujita **PHOTO COLOR 'SCOPE:** Kenji Hagiwara **MUSIC:** Hiroki Tamaki   **w/** Tetsuya Watari, Yoshio Harada, Meiko Kaji, Mikio Narita, Tsuneya Oki, Aoi Nakajima, Kenji Imai, Chieko Harada Pot dealer Harada welcomes tough guy Watari back to Shinjuku when he is released on parole. Harada asks him to help steal back 30 million yen worth of grass from some vicious hoods. Watari finds old love Kaji working at Harada's bar, and she agrees to help them track the drug thieves. They soon discover that the grass was pilfered by a syndicate headed by Imai and Narita. Meanwhile, the black leather biker gang led by Oki that was supposed to be selling Harada's stuff kidnap Harada's sister (Chieko Harada) and assault her. A battle breaks out between Harada and the pissed-off gang, but Watari intervenes, luring the gang to attack the syndicate's HQ. Kaji is murdered by the syndicate, and the underdogs storm the HQ in earnest. Watari and Harada recover the money reaped from the pot sales, making off with it together in the syndicate helicopter. But fatally wounded Narita continues to shoot at them from the roof, killing the pilot. Watari and Harada are left awkwardly trying to keep the copter in the air since both of them don't know how to land it. Director Fujita freeze-frames them as they zigzag through the sky over a peaceful neighborhood. The first half of this is fairly innocuous, with director Fujita only making halfhearted attempts to integrate suspense into the macho posturing of Watari and Harada and a succession of tension-diffusing, goofy youth-grooving-in-the-streets images. Thankfully something happens at the halfway point, and the film slowly comes more together. Fujita utilizes some simple lighting effects to accentuate a nice love scene between Watari and Kaji and another scene where Watari gets stoned on pot. The final confrontation with Narita's gang, though in cramped, obviously budget-constrained sets, is still effective, and the last scene where Harada and Watari are trying to keep aloft in the copter is deliciously ambiguous, leaving the audience guessing as to whether our counterculture anti-heroes live or die. * * 1/2

Step on the Gas!

THE STORM COMES AND GOES aka ARASHI KITARI SARU 1967 99 min. **DIR.** Toshio Masuda **SCR.** Kaneo Ikegami/Seiji Hoshikawa **PHOTO COLOR 'SCOPE:** Minoru Yokoyama **MUSIC:** Rinichiro Manabe **w/** Yujiro Ishihara, Ruriko Asaoka, Tamaki Sawa, Tatsuya Fuji, Toru Abe, Ryoji Hayama, Kyoko Inoue, Yoshiro Aoki, Hiroyuki Nagato A *ninkyo* yakuza story with what, probably for most squeamish westerners anyway, is a disturbing opening titles sequence. One of the many variations on a yakuza clan's *sakazuki*

(sake cup exchange offering) involves the preparation of a still-alive fish to share as a meal with the other invited clan. The unflinching eye of gorgeous color cinematography zeroes in on the panting, puffing helpless creature as its "blindfolded" then sliced up the middle. The stoic ritual lasts through the entire credits, perhaps a metaphor (?) for the living death of the yakuza hero caught between the-rock-and-a-hard-place that is his chivalrous humanity and his criminal livelihood. There is an atmospheric sword duel between Ishihara and his enemies at the falling-snow climax. * * 1/2

The Storm Comes and Goes

STORM OF BULLETS aka DANKON NO ARASHI 1962 79 min. **DIR.** Takumi Furukawa **SCR.** Ken Sasaki **PHOTO COLOR 'SCOPE:** Shigeyoshi Mine **MUSIC:** Hajime Kaburagi **w/** Joe Shishido, Yuji Kodaka, Reiko Sassamori, Nobuo Kaneko, Shinsuke Ashida

Storm of Bullets

STORY OF A CERTAIN LOVE
aka ARU KOI MONOGATARI
1960 **DIR.** Yoshitsugi Nakajima **SCR.**
Migaku Takemori **PHOTO 'SCOPE:**
Toshitaro Nakao **MUSIC:** Naozumi
Yamamoto w/ Yuji Kodaka, Joji Ai
(Georgie Ai), Shoki Fukae, Mihoko
Inagaki, Minako Kazuki, Hiroshi
Kondo, Kaku Takashina

STORIES OF JAPANESE CHIV-ALRY aka NIHON NINKYODEN series

STORY OF JAPANESE CHIV-ALRY – BLOODBATH CHAL-LENGE aka NIHON NINKYODEN – CHIMATSURI KENKA JO aka BLOODSTAINED CHALLENGE
1966 88 min. **DIR.** Toshio Masuda
SCR. Toshio Matsuura/Toshio Masuda
PHOTO COLOR 'SCOPE: Kenji
Hagiwara **MUSIC:** Harumi Ibe
w/ Hideki Takahashi, Masako Izumi,

Joe Shishido, Yuji Kodaka, Masako
Ota, Tatsuya Fuji, Isao Tamagawa,
Kaku Takashina, Shoki Fukae,
Takashi Kanda, Izumi Ashikawa
#1 of 2 films

Story of Japanese Chivalry (#1)

Story of Japanese Chivalry (#2)

**STORY OF JAPANESE CHIV-
ALRY – FLOWER OF A CHIVAL-
ROUS MAN** aka NIHON NINKY-
ODEN – HANA NO TOSEININ aka
GLORY OF A GAMBLER 1966
79 min. **DIR.** Hiroshi Noguchi **SCR.**
Hisatoshi Kai **PHOTO COLOR 'SCOPE:**
Muneo Ueda **MUSIC:** Hajime
Kaburagi **w/** Hideki Takahashi,
Masako Izumi, Asao Uchida, Tamio
Kawaji, Satoshi Yamauchi, Takamaru
Sasaki, Kokan Katsuura, Shigeyoshi
Fujioka #2 of 2 films

**STRAY CAT ROCK aka NORA
NEKO ROKKU aka WILDCAT
ROCK aka ALLEY CAT ROCK
series**

**STRAY CAT ROCK – WOMAN
BOSS** aka NORA NEKO ROKKU
– ONNA BANCHO aka WILDCAT
ROCK 1970 81 min. **DIR.** Yasuharu
Hasebe **SCR.** Shuichi Nagahara/
Yasuharu Hasebe **PHOTO COLOR
'SCOPE:** Muneo Ueda **MUSIC:**
Kunihiko Suzuki **w/** Akiko Wada,
Meiko Kaji, Koji Wada, Tatsuya Fuji,
Bunsaku Han, Ken Sanders, Tadao
Nakamaru, Yuko Shimazu, Mari
Koiso, Goro Mutsumi
Nikkatsu's premiere delinquent/
bosozoku/sukeban girl gang series, a
yakuza subgenre very much coming
into its own circa 1970. This first
entry is hampered by a convoluted
storyline and what looks like chaotic
production values. Yet this is the film
series that started the ball rolling on
charismatic Kaji's stardom, and she
makes up for a lot of the amateurish
aspects, including rock singer Akiko
Wada's awkward performance. Wada
is a lone wolf, motorcycle-driving
rebel in Shinjuku who helps buck-

skin-clad Kaji's girl gang in a fight
with rival female hoods. Kaji's rebel
gang are a bit reform-minded and
would like to see Shinjuku cleaned-
up. But Kaji's beau (Koji Wada) is
trying to get admitted to a yakuza
gang by fixing a fight featuring his
old friend Sanders. When Sanders
decides to not throw the fight, the
yakuza – known by the somewhat
fascist appellation Black Shirt Corps
– retaliates. Koji Wada is shot and
killed by head hood Mutsumi. Kaji
stabs Mutsumi to death but is fatally
shot, too, with Akiko Wada the only
one left to set things right. Often
exhilarating despite the occasional
amateurishness. #1 of 5 films * * *

Stray Cat Rock - Wild Jumbo (#2)

**STRAY CAT ROCK – WILD
JUMBO** aka NORA NEKO
ROKKU – WAIRUDO JYANBO
1970 84 min. **DIR.** Toshiya Fujita
SCR. Toshiya Fujita/Shuichi Nagahara
PHOTO COLOR 'SCOPE: Shohei Ando
MUSIC: Kiga Hori

Stray Cat Rock (#1)

w/ Meiko Kaji, Tatsuya Fuji, Bunsaku Han, Takeo Chii, Tazuke Natsu, Akiko Wada　Two bands of delinquents attempt to rob funds from a religious cult that are being transported by armored car. A somewhat disjointed mix of heist thriller and goofy "teen fun" antics punctuated by some bravura shock cut sequences as well as some embarassing, suspense-diffusing youth travelogue action. Fujita redeems the picture at the close as the integrated male/female teen gang is cut down by their ruthless pursuers. Especially memorable is Kaji's death scene in a river at the downbeat climax. #2 of 5 films * * 1/2

Stray Cat Rock (#3)

STRAY CAT ROCK – SEX HUNTER aka NORA NEKO ROKKU – SEKKUSU HANTAA
1970 85 min. DIR. Yasuharu Hasebe SCR. Atsushi Yamatoya/Takashi Fujii (aka Hasebe) PHOTO COLOR 'SCOPE: Muneo Ueda MUSIC: Hajime

Kaburagi w/ Meiko Kaji, Tatsuya Fuji, Rikiya Yasuoka, Jiro Okazaki, Mie Hanabusa, Nobuko Aoki　Mixed-race Yasuoka tries to free his sister from a gang involved with white slavery as well as attacks on teenagers of Japanese/African-American ancestry. Fuji is the head villain, The Baron. Kaji is his whip-wielding mistress and a gang leader in her own right. Kaji falls for Yasuoka, and things get complicated. Kaji is also infuriated when Fuji attempts to pimp her galpals to visiting foreign gamblers at a posh party. Her social conscience awakened, she and her girls side with Yasuoka in a tide of escalating violence and reprisals. The film builds steadily with several great action setpieces to a bloody, tragic ending – Yasuoka and Fuji shooting each other to death in the tower of a deserted landing strip. Only mournful Kaji is left alive. BAD GIRL MAKO (1971) dealt with some similar story elements and is a partial remake. Co-scenarist Yamatoya also co-wrote BRANDED TO KILL as well as many of Koji Wakamatsu's wild late sixties/early seventies masterpieces. Director Hasebe co-wrote the script under the name Takashi Fujii (his screenwriting pseudonym).
* * * 1/2 #3 of 5 films

STRAY CAT ROCK – MACHINE ANIMAL aka NORA NEKO ROKKU – MASHIN ANIMARU
1970 82 min. DIR. Yasuharu Hasebe SCR. Ryuzo Nakanishi PHOTO COLOR 'SCOPE: Yoshihiro Yamazaki MUSIC: Akihiko Takashima w/ Meiko Kaji, Tatsuya Fuji, Jiro Okazaki, Bunjaku Han, Eiji Go, Noriko Kurosawa Girl gang leader Kaji is pursued after stealing 500 LSD doses from the bad

guys, one of whom is a U.S. Army deserter from Vietnam. #4 of 5 films

Stray Cat Rock (#4)

Stray Cat Rock (#5)

STRAY CAT ROCK – VIOLENT SHOWDOWN '71 aka NORA NEKO ROKKU – BOSO SHUDAN

'71 aka BEAT '71 1971 87 min. **DIR.** Toshiya Fujita **SCR.** Shuichi Nagahara/Tatsuya Asai **PHOTO COLOR 'SCOPE:** Kenji Hagiwara **MUSIC:** Hiroki Tamaki **w/** Yoshio Harada, Meiko Kaji, Tatsuya Fuji, Bunjaku Han, Michiko Tsukasa, Tasuke Natsu, Eiji Go, Takeo Chii In a small conservative town, a band of young hippie hoods led by Harada attempt to get back one of their own who has been kidnapped by his rich father. He finally returns to his counterculture gang and rejoins his girl Kaji. But both are killed in the crossfire between his gang and his dad's henchmen. Bad scene! This has a reputation in some circles as being the best of the series, but I think SEX HUNTER is just a bit better. #5 and final in series   * * *

SUNSET HILL aka YUHI NO OKA 1964 88 min. **DIR.** Akinori Matsuo **SCR.** Iwao Yamazaki/Takeo Kunihiro **PHOTO COLOR 'SCOPE:** Izumi Hagiwara **MUSIC:** Masayoshi Ikeno **w/** Yujiro Ishihara, Ruriko Asaoka, Ichiro Nakatani, Koji Wada, Shoki Fukae, Akira Nagoya, Akifumi Inoue, Chigako Hosokawa Once more a specimen of the *moodo akushon* (atmospheric noir action) subgenre, this outing a yakuza love story between Asaoka and the late Ishihara (the Astaire/ Rogers of Nikkatsu's romantic action films). An initially mesmerizing, atmosphere-drenched, gorgeous color noir with Ishihara having to take it on the lam to Hokkaido after having an affair with imprisoned mobster buddy Nakatani's girl Asaoka. The first half hour is particularly impressive with Matsuo skillfully exploring Ishihara's inner torment and rampant paranoia with inspired visuals. He soon starts to be conflicted with feelings for his paramour's twin sister (also played by Asaoka). The film falters a bit in the middle with Ishihara biding his time waiting for his true love to join him. Meanwhile he hooks up with minstrel Wada and ne'er-do-well Noro in gambling, then personally takes on local yakuza Fukae in a high-stakes game. He wins a huge sum then thrashes Fukae's boss when they try to cheat him to win back the dough. Noro is subsequently murdered.

Take Aim at the Police Van

fires again but has aimed at and killed ex-flame Asaoka who has followed to watch the pyrotechnics. It seems she had set Nakatani up for hitman Inoue. As you would expect, this messes up Ishihara's peace of mind even more, and he bids adieu next day to the innocent sister on a sunset dappled coastline, realizing the situation is too charged with bad memories to ever work out. * * *

TAKE AIM AT THE POLICE VAN
aka SONO GOSOSHA O NERAE
1960 79 min. DIR. Seijun Suzuki
SCR. Shinichi Sekizawa PHOTO
B&W 'SCOPE: Shigeyoshi Mine
MUSIC: Tomikazu Kawabe
w/ Michitaro Mizushima, Misako Watanabe, Shoichi Ozawa, Shinsuke Ashida, Mari Shiraki, Toru Abe, Ryohei Uchida, Hiroshi Nagashi, Akira Hisamatsu, Saburo Hiromatsu
When cop Mizushima has his prison transport bus waylaid and two mobster passengers picked off by a sharp-

Sunset Hill

Original lover Asaoka shows up just as Ishihara realizes he is really in love with her more innocent twin. She reveals that Nakatani is out of the slammer and bent on revenge. Ishihara goes to have a nocturnal showdown with him at a deserted racetrack. But shot and now dying gunman Inoue has beat him to it, fatally wounding Nakatani. Nakatani

shooter, he takes the undercover job of tracking the guilty parties. Soon he is on the trail of boss Abe's gang. He also runs into stripper Shiraki, conman Ozawa, and Watanabe, the daughter of ailing, retired gang boss Ashida, along the corpse-strewn way. Victims drop like flies, including one prostitute killed with a bow and arrow. Suzuki creates a nightmarish gauntlet for Mizushima of footchases, red herrings, merciless beatings and near-miss shootings in a variety of suburban and rural/seacoast locales. Finally, Mizushima and Watanabe are snatched and placed bound in the cab of an oil tanker. Abe and gum-chewing sharpshooter Uchida set the tanker coasting down a sloping dirt road, the back nozzle open so it gushes gasoline behind it. Once it is ahead a few thousand yards, the gangster pair gleefully light the gas trail. Suzuki generates credible suspense as our hero and heroine have to outrun the pursuing flames. Watanabe manages to singe off her bonds with a cigarette lighter, then unties Mizushima who promptly jumps out and shuts off the gas nozzle. The truck continues to roll until it is out of range of the tongue of flame. When Abe realizes the tanker has not blown, he halts his gang's private bus, and cold-blooded Uchida quickly dispatches the panicking Shiraki and Ozawa when they make a run for it. A hail of bullets erupts, with Mizushima in turn killing Uchida and Abe. Mizushima and Watanabe then close in on the real bigwigs at a local railyard, igniting yet another pitched gunfight. Sickly dad Ashida is revealed as Mr. Big, and powerless daughter Watanabe is horrified as she witnesses his demise by speeding locomotove. * * *

TALES OF CHIVALRY aka YUKYODEN aka YAKUZA TALES series

TALE OF KANTO CHIVALRY aka KANTO YUKYODEN aka TALE OF KANTO YAKUZA 1963 100 min. DIR. Akinori Matsuo SCR. Iwao Yamazaki/Masako Fujizaki PHOTO COLOR 'SCOPE: Kazumi Iwasa MUSIC: Hajime Kaburagi w/ Akira Kobayashi, Joe Shishido, Chieko Matsubara, Hideo Murata, Midori Satsuki, Shinsuke Ashida, Masao Mishima, Daisaburo Hirata, Koji Wada, Shiro Osaka #1 of 3 films

TALE OF TOKAI CHIVALRY aka TOKAI YUKYODEN aka TALE OF TOKAI YAKUZA 1964 85 min. DIR. Motomu (Tan) Ida SCR. Iwao Yamazaki/Masako Fujizaki PHOTO COLOR 'SCOPE: Izumi Hagiwara MUSIC: Hajime Kaburagi w/ Akira Kobayashi, Joe Shishido, Chieko Matsubara, Hideo Murata, Saburo Kitajima, Shiro Osaka, Hiroshi Nihonyanagi, Kazuko Yoshiyuki, Midori Satsuki, Akira Oizumi #2 of 3 films

NEW CHIVALRY STORY aka SHIN YUKYODEN aka NEW TALE OF YAKUZA 1966 85 min. DIR. Buichi Saito SCR. Hisatoshi Kai PHOTO COLOR 'SCOPE: Yoshihiro Yamazaki MUSIC: Taiichiro Kosugi w/ Akira Kobayashi, Hideki Takahashi, Michiko Saga, Kotohide (Tokihide?) Hatsui, Takashi Kanda, Nakajiro Tomita, Kaku Takashina, Keisuke Noro, Hiroshi Kondo While the first two pictures are more serious action dramas, this entry is basically a *ninkyo* action/comedy. Kobayashi and Takahashi are dim-

Tale of Kanto Chivalry (#1)

witted roughneck comrades who occasionally clash while competing for the attentions of geisha madam Saga. At the finale, they join forces to wipe out the evil gang and save their own adopted clan. #3 and last of series * * 1/2

TALE OF THE LAST JAPANESE YAKUZA aka NIHON ZAN KYO-DEN aka JAPANESE GAMBLER'S CODE aka TALE OF THE LAST CHIVALROUS JAPANESE MAN 1969 95 min. DIR. Masahiro Makino SCR. Masahiro Makino/Toshio Nagata PHOTO COLOR 'SCOPE: Minoru Yokoyama MUSIC: Taiichiro Kosugi w/ Hideki Takahashi, Yoko Minamida, Tamio Kawaji, Meiko Kaji, Hiroyuki Nagato, Michitaro Mizushima, Masahiko Tsugawa, Fujio Suga, Shoki Fukae, Masao Mishima Set at the turn of the 20th century, Mizushima is the boss of a clan made up of Tsugawa, Kawaji, Nagato and Go who deal in lumber. He is killed in an accident engineered by bad boss Fukae. Ne'er-do-well drifter Takahashi returns to the fold upon hearing of Mizushima's demise and becomes acting *oyabun* for his widow Minamida. Tsugawa is in love with prostitute Kaji, is murdered after trying to run away with her, and she is then shipped off to Hokkaido by the villain's gang. Formerly known as Masako Ota, this was Kaji's first film under her new name. Director Makino had christened her with her new moniker in honor of Nikkatsu grooming her for stardom, but her part is unfortunaely very small. After Tsugawa's death, sushi retaurant owner Nagato perishes while trying to avenge him. This finally inspires Takahashi, Kawaji and Go to strategically work out an attack plan on Fukae's HQ during festival firewoorks and a rambunctious parade. This gives them cover to enter the police-protected, riverfront gang house. Takahashi and comrades slay the evildoers, including outside manipulator Suga. Director Makino spins this *ninkyo eiga* with a bit more intensity than some of his Toei efforts. It easily matches up to the best of the TALES OF THE LAST SHOWA YAKUZA and TALES OF JAPANESE CHIVALRY series. There is also a lyricism and a sense of the performers really getting inside their characters. Leads Takahashi, Nagato and cameo Ban in particular should all be lauded for exceptional performances without the histrionics that sometimes mar *ninkyo* sagas. The production design is well above average and the tattoo work is also particularly fine, showing a detail not often seen to this degree in yakuza films. * * * 1/2

TATTOOED LIFE aka IREZUMI ICHIDAI aka ONE GENERATION OF TATTOOS aka A LIFE OF TATTOO 1965 87 min. DIR. Seijun Suzuki SCR. Kinya Naoi/Yoshi Hattori PHOTO COLOR 'SCOPE: Kurataro Takamura MUSIC: Masayoshi Ikeda w/ Hideki Takahashi, Masako Izumi, Hiroko Ito, Akira Yamanouchi, Motoshi Hana, Yuji Kodaka, Kayo Matsuo, Hosei Komatsu, Seizaburo Kawazu, Kaku Takashina   In 1920s Japan, Takahashi kills a rival yakuza clan leader, then is forced to flee to a rural mining community with his sensitive, artistic younger brother. Wildly energetic with director Suzuki's surreal sense of visual humor. The climactic showdown is borderline *kabuki*, with a startlingly beautiful use of theatricalized lighting and effects (it takes place during a violent thunderstorm).

Tattooed Life

Suzuki's use of color rivals that of Hitchcock, Sirk and Bava. As the reader of this book has undoubtedly already noted, TATTOOED LIFE star Takahashi also appeared in many other Nikkatsu *ninkyo* yakuza and action pictures, foremost among them the series, A MAN'S CREST. Suzuki received one of his most serious warnings from the top Nikkatsu boss about his unorthodox visuals at the climax. It would not be the last. With each movie after this, Suzuki received more dire warnings to stop his flamboyant visuals and cutting.
* * *

TEENAGE TRAP aka JUDAI NO WANA 1957 87 min. Dɪʀ. Hiroshi Noguchi Scʀ. Iwao Yamazaki Pʜᴏᴛᴏ B&W: Kazue Nagatsuka

Mᴜsɪᴄ: Hajime Kaburagi w/ Hiroyuki Nagato, Shiro Osaka, Misako Watanabe, Minako Katsuki, Tadao Sawamoto

TEENAGE WOLF aka JUDAI NO OKAMI 1960 54 min. Dɪʀ. Mitsuo Wakasugi Scʀ. Genichi Hara Pʜᴏᴛᴏ B&W 'sᴄᴏᴘᴇ: Kan Inoue Mᴜsɪᴄ: Taiichiro Kosugi w/ Kyoji Aoyama, Kazuko Yoshiyuki, Toshio Sugiyama

Territorial Dispute aka Retaliation

TERRITORIAL DISPUTE aka SHIMA WA MORATTA aka TURF WAR aka RETALIATION 1968 94 min. Dɪʀ. Yasuharu Hasebe Scʀ. Yoshihiro Ishimatsu/Reiji Kubota Pʜᴏᴛᴏ ᴄᴏʟᴏʀ 'sᴄᴏᴘᴇ: Muneo Ueda Mᴜsɪᴄ: Hajime Kaburagi w/ Akira Kobayashi, Joe Shishido,

Hideaki Nitani, Tamio Kawaji, Tatsuya Fuji, Jotaro Togami, Ryoji Hayama, Masako Ota (aka Meiko Kaji), Eiji Go, Jiro Okazaki
Director Hasebe's straightforward, kinetic energy and a great cast help to balance out a ho-hum script (surprising considering the exceptional Ishimatsu's involvement), the occasionally sloppy cinematography and what looks like an even more hurried shooting schedule than usual. Kaji makes a keen impression (while still performing under her original name) as Kobayashi's feisty, doomed teen girlfriend. Hasebe takes on a kind of eavesdropping POV for most camera set-ups throughout, something that is unique and marginally effective. An entertaining tale of an all-too-familiar gang turf war with a bizarre, hallucinatory and violent ending in overexposed slow motion. * * *

TETSU'S SHOTGUN aka NIREN-JU NO TETSU 1959 85 min. **DIR.** Yutaka Abe **SCR.** Yasunori Kawauchi/ Ryuta Akimoto **PHOTO B&W 'SCOPE:** Kazumi Iwasa **MUSIC:** Seitaro Omori w/ Akira Kobayashi, Yoko Minamida, Tadao Sawamoto, Uyako Hori, Masumi Okada

THEATER OF LIFE aka JINSEI GEKIJO 1964 105 min. **DIR.** Toshio Masuda **SCR.** Goro Tanada **PHOTO COLOR 'SCOPE:** Yoshio Mamiya **MUSIC:** Harumi Ibe w/ Hideki Takahashi, Joe Shishido, Yoshie Mizutani, Chieko Matsubara, Osamu Takizawa, Tetsu Shimamura, Daisaburo Hirata, Yumi Takano, Yoshi Kato, Jun Hamamura
Unlike several other concurrent adaptations of THEATER OF LIFE at Toei Studios, this adaptation deals almost entirely with the young character played here by a charismatic Takahashi (he is played by Hiroki Matsukata in the Toei films, where he has comparatively little screen time). Also Hisha Kaku, played by Koji Tsuruta in the Toei pictures, doesn't even enter this scenario. The one overlapping character, boisterous hard luck yakuza boss Kira Tsune, portrayed by the always engaging Joe Shishido, is a relatively minor role. Director Masuda and writer Tanada construct the narrative in a very wistful, elegiac way, engendering an achingly beautiful paen to lost youth and ideals. Takahashi is brought up by his grandafather Takizawa who is a bigger-than-life character in their small village. Takizawa has a strange affinity for a huge tree in the backyard and this fixation communicates something of his struggle with powers greater than himself, not to mention his own mortality and the idea of eternity. Takahashi becomes a student and, hanging out with politically ambitious comrade Hirata, is soon sucked into one of the many radical factions espousing nationalist sentiment. There is a subtle reference to the nature of such radical fervor when Takahashi loses his virginity to lovesick geisha Mizutani, and almost immediately suffers a noticeable decrease in enthusiasm for the nationalist cause. At the climax, Shishido is released from prison and visits his mentor Takizawa, only to find the old man bitter, lonely and unfulfilled. Shishido is forced to leave briefly to finish an old, ongoing feud with other local yakuza. When he returns later that night, he finds the old man has shot himself (something which generally happens within the first ten minutes

of other versions). Takahashi returns home to deal with the situation and reunite with older comrade Shishido. It is quite obvious more time and money was spent on this production than many other Nikkatsu films at the time, and it shows in the obvious care and subtlety in Masuda's direction and Tanada's script. Also Mamiya's glorious color scope compositions are resoundingly exquisite without resorting to mere pictorialism.
* * * 1/2

Theater of Life

THIRTEEN TIMES A LOSER aka SHOGAI KYOKATSU – ZENKA JUSANPAN aka THREAT OF INJURY – EX-CONVICT'S THIR-TEEN OFFENSES aka EXTOR-TION – THIRTEEN CONVIC-TIONS 1969 93 min. **DIR.** Akinori Matsuo **SCR.** Iwao Yamazaki/Kazuo Nishida **PHOTO COLOR 'SCOPE:** Kazumi Iwasa **MUSIC:** Harumi Ibe w/ Joe Shishido, Isamu Nagato, Tetsuro Tanba, Jiro Okazaki, Kyoko Mine, Toshiaki Minami, Shoki Fukae, Toru Abe After making love to his girl, Shishido makes a beeline for a mod op art style nightclub where he stabs a rival villain boss (Abe) in broad daylight. Abe survives, and Shishido heads off to stir where he becomes cellmates with Tanba, Okazaki, Fukae and the comical Minami. Shishido bonds with convict Nagato when Nagato saves him in a prison con-struction mishap. Shishido's foster father boss is also murdered while he is serving his sentence. Time passes and Minami gets out. He looks up Okazaki who has gotten a job at the club where the now one-armed Abe frequents. Soon after, Shishido is released, too, and he goes to visit his surrogate mom, the boss's widow. He also discovers his ex-girlfriend has become Abe's mistress. He is almost killed when he goes to visit her but thrashes the would-be assas-sin. Back at his old pad above a sushi restaurant, lonely, teary-eyed Shishido burns a photo of his former sweetheart. When Fukae gets out of stir, he starts a fight at Abe's club but before long ends up working for the evil boss. Complications ensue when Shishido, Nagato, Okazaki and his girl try to steal some plans from Abe's office. Shishido and Nagato have a dramatic one-on-one dice game downstairs to distract the nightclub mobsters while Okazaki and girlfriend try to break into the upstairs safe. Unfortunately, they are caught and tortured, with Abe finally stabbing to death the defiant woman. He then offs Okazaki, too. When Shishido goes to negotiate their release, he is shocked and enraged

Thirteen Times a Loser

to find them dead. At this point, old comrade Fukae has had enough of the sadistic Abe and joins Shishido by turning his gun on his craven *oyabun*. Nagato arrives in the nick of time just as another henchman is about to turn the tables back again. Shishido coerces Abe to give up the documents that will benefit his dead boss's widow and son. Things look like they are taking a turn for the better until the deplorable Abe has the widow and son assassinated. This spurs Shishido, Nagato and Minami to bust in on a big dinner being given in honor of Abe. At this point, Tanba reappears in the saga as one of the banquet's guests-of-honor. Much to Abe's chagrin, he throws his support to Shishido and pals in the ensuing, grandly epic ballroom knifefight. Shishido and Nagato survive their decimation of Abe and his mob but are headed back to prison as the end title unspools. Director Matsuo fashions a very good *ninkyo/jitsuroku* hybrid with lead Shishido his usual exceptional self, striking an expert balance between a world-weary, sensitive tough guy and a hardened gangster persona. * * * 1/2

THREE DRAGON TATTOOS aka MITTSU NO RYU NO IREZUMI 1961 DIR. Hiroshi Noguchi SCR. Seiji Hoshikawa PHOTO 'SCOPE: Kazue Nagatsuka MUSIC: Masayoshi Ikeda w/ Joe Shishido, Reiko Sassamori, Ryoji Hayama, Mari Shiraki, Hiroshi Nihonyanagi, Ichiro Sugai, Shoki Fukae

THREE SECONDS BEFORE THE EXPLOSION aka BAKUHA 3-BYO MAE 1967 84 min. DIR. Motomu (Tan) Ida SCR. Shuichi

Nakahara PHOTO COLOR 'SCOPE: Izumi Hagiwara MUSIC: Seitaro Omori w/ Akira Kobayashi, Hideki Takahashi, Ryoji Hayama, Asao Uchida, Ruriko Ito, Hiroshi Nawa A by-the-numbers spy/gangsters action saga of former hood-turned-government agent Kobayashi trying to keep jewels stolen during WW2 out of the hands of both the yakuza and a Nazi war criminal. * * 1/2

THREE SHE-CATS aka SANBIKI NO MESU NEKO 1966 79 min. DIR. Motomu (Tan) Iida SCR. Iwao Yamazaki PHOTO B&W 'SCOPE: Kenji Hagiwara MUSIC: Seitaro Omori w/ Yumiko Nogawa, Ryoko (Kimiko?) Minakami, Tatsuya Fuji, Eiji Go, Machiko Yashiro

Three Stray Dogs

THREE STRAY DOGS aka SANBIKI NO NORA INU 1965 86 min. DIR. Yoichi Ushihara SCR. Iwao Yamazaki PHOTO B&W 'SCOPE: Shigeyoshi Mine MUSIC: Taiichiro

Kosugi w/ Akira Kobayashi, Joe Shishido, Koji Wada, Satoko Hamagawa, Keiko Yuge, Jun Tatara, Nakajiro Tomita, Kaku Takashina, Eiji Go, Yuji Kodaka Three of Nikkatsu's young male superstars headline in this action-packed contemporary crime opus.

THREE VILLAINS aka SANBIKI NO AKUTO 1969 83 ymin. **Dir.** Akinori Matsuo **Scr.** Seiji Hoshikawa **Photo color 'scope:** Kazumi Iwasa **Music:** Masayoshi Ikeda w/ Akira Kobayashi, Hideki Takahashi, Yoshiko Machida, Kayo Matsuo, Kunie Tanaka, Shokii Fukae, Chieko Naniwa, Hiroshi Kondo

Three Villains

Two lone wolf yakuza (Takahashi and Tanaka) rob a gambling den, then split up when pursued by the angry gang. They eventually meet again at Tanaka's mother's rural farmhouse. By then, one-eyed Kobayashi has wrangled his way into the scenario, intending to get a split of the proceeds (since he had helped them get away). Although there is some dissension amongst the three, they eventually close ranks to fend off their stubborn, relentless pursuers. Unhappily, Tanaka's mother (Naniwa) is killed in the process. There are also love interests (Machida and Matsuo) and some humor along the way. An admirably different approach to the formulaic *ninkyo* yakuza programmer, filmed largely in sweltering summer countryside locations. * * *

THREE WOMEN – NIGHT BUTTERFLIES aka SANNIN NO ONNA – YORU NO CHO 1971 89 min. **Dir.** Mitsumasa Saito **Scr.** Norio Miyashita/Saburo Kuruusu **Photo color 'scope:** Kenji Hagiwara **Music:** Hajime Kaburagi w/ Chieko Matsubara, Meiko Kaji, Yoko Yamamoto, Hideaki Nitani, Tatsuya Fuji, Tamio Kawaji

TIGER AND CUB STRATEGY aka TORA NO KO SAKUSEN 1963 97 min. **Dir.** Kan Hanase **Scr.** Hisatoshi Kai **Photo B&W 'scope:** Toshitaro Nakao **Music:** Masayoshi Ikeda w/ Joe Shishido, Yuji Kodaka, Reiko Sassamori, Akazu Yamada, Kichijiro Ueda, Toru Abe, Eiji Go, Shoki Fukae, Naomi Hoshi Humorous gangster/heist action.

TOKYO DANGER MAP aka TOKYO KIKEN CHIZU 1961 **Dir.** Isamu Kosugi **Scr.** Kimiyuki Hasegawa/Tatsuo Miyata **Photo 'scope:** Umeo Matsuhashi **Music:** Taiichiro Kosugi w/ Kyoji Aoyama, Ryohei Uchida, Minako Kazuki, Ichiro Sugai

TOKYO DAUGHTER aka
TOKYO DODONPA MUSUME
DIR. Motomu (Tan) Iida **SCR.**
Motomu Iida/Fumi Takahashi
PHOTO 'SCOPE: Yasuichiro Yamazaki
w/ Tadao Sawamoto, Minako Kazuki

**TOKYO DRIFTER aka TOKYO
NAGAREMONO series**

TOKYO DRIFTER aka TOKYO
NAGAREMONO 1966 83 min.
DIR. Seijun Suzuki **SCR.** Yasunori
Kawauchi **PHOTO COLOR 'SCOPE:**
Shigeyoshi Mine **MUSIC:** Hajime
Kaburagi **w/** Tetsuya Watari,
Chieko Matsubara, Hideaki Nitani,
Tamio Kawaji, Ryuji Kita, Hiroshi
Minami, Eiji Go, Isao Tamagawa,

Tokyo Drifter (#1)

According to Japanese film critic,
Tadao Sato, this is Suzuki's "most
remarkable film...for its flamboyant
use of color and its comical, eccentric
tempo practically turn it into a pop art
display...based on a popular song of

the same title..." relates the adventures of "...a modern yakuza (Watari)
who is sent wandering in the provinces because of a dispute within in his
gang... resembles flashes of transient
beauty and humor upon the screen of
a revolving lantern." Everything Sato
says is true, although this writer finds
Suzuki's most remarkable films to
be EVERYTHING GOES WRONG,
YOUTH OF THE BEAST, GATE
OF FLESH and BRANDED TO
KILL. Watari gets beat up in a very
high-contrast, amber-tinted pre-titles
sequence to prove to an opposition
gang that he and his boss (Kita) have
gone straight. Which, in fact, they
have. Watari's attachment to Kita is
very much of the father/son type, and
he will do just about anything to help
his *oyabun* out of a jam. Kita owes
interest on a loan to a comparatively
honest landlord. However, that other
gang muscles in, trying to take over
the loan. The bad guys are headquartered in the backroom of a mod
nightmare of a nightclub with glass
floors called the Manhole, and, if you
think its design is a bit minimal, wait
till you see the other club where Watari's lonelyheart, off-again-on-again
girlfriend (Matsubara) sings. Bathed
in yellow light, it looks more like
one's abstract impression of a nightclub in a dream – there are no walls,
only a couple of tables and chairs, a
staircase that leads to nowhere and a
huge gold donut shape structure that
is some sort of sculpture. Suzuki was
getting increasing pressure to play it
visually straight from the big boys
upstairs, and he slashed the budget
even more than necessary to keep
them happy. As a function of that, he
and his longtime collaborator, set de-
signer Takeo Kimura, improvised sets

out of virtually nothing, using vast areas of shadow and colored light to achieve the illusion of interiors. They used standing sets as well, such as the western saloon where Watari has gone to hide out. Run by a friend of Kita's (Minami), it serves as backdrop to a ridiculous brawl punctuated by a shootout with Kawaji, one of Watari's pursuers. The bizarre, cavalier attutude Suzuki implements at the end, when we once again find ourselves in the club of yellow light, Watari confronting his pursuers as well as the betraying Kita, would be annoying if it was not choreographed so well. The performers' rhythms as they jump and roll around, leaping for tossed guns, hiding behind ludicrously skinny columns are complimented by a dazzling editing job – there is no fat here only the lean, mean hungry skeleton of essential cinematic bones. After the last villain has been dispatched, Watari, in incongruous angelic white suit, Matsubara in his arms, casually turns his head to watch father-figure Kita break a glass and suicidally stab himself in the wrist. A geyser of blood festoons the white and yellow color scheme. Watari bids Matsubara adieu and walks out into the Tokyo nightclubbing night.
#1 of 2 films   * * * 1/2

TOKYO DRIFTER – LOVE THE COLOR OF THE CRIMSON SEA
aka TOKYO NAGAREMONO – UMI HA MAKKA NA KOI NO IRO 1966 73 min. DIR. Kenjiro Morinaga SCR. Kagenori Ono/Daigo Myo PHOTO COLOR 'SCOPE: Kazue Nagatsuka MUSIC: Hajime Kaburagi w/ Tetsuya Watari, Teruo Yoshida, Chieko Matsubara, Ryotaro Sugi, Sanae Nakahara, Kazuko Hashi,

Nobuo Kaneko, Hiroshi Kondo, Arihiro Fujimura
Morinaga directed a few Nikkatsu action films, but he primarily supervised moody romances and *seishun* (young people) films. You can tell, despite the occasional bit of languid, well-choreographed action, that that is the direction the studio decided to go with the sequel – the *moodo akushon* (moody, atmospheric action) film, an entire subgenre that was pretty much the exclusive province of Nikkatsu.

Tokyo Drifter (#2)

The accent is on the romantic life of Tetsu (Watari), the drifter, and the girls he loves but can never quite bring himself to settle down with. To make matters even more atmospheric, our story is set in a picturesque harbor town. Yoshida is Watari's double-crossing rival who pays in the end with his life. Fairly superficial, but the tone isn't particularly light; in fact, it is downright melancholic, which is the picture's salvation. The emphasis on Watari never being able to escape his criminal life despite his tender side, the downbeat undercurrent of cynical gang activity amidst the sunset-dappled waves, actually makes this an entertaining sequel. However, Suzuki's irreverent surrealism is replaced by Morinaga's Monet-like impressionism. #2 of 2 films   * * *

TOKYO KNIGHTS aka TOKYO NAITO or TOKYO KISHITAI 1961 81 min. DIR. Seijun Suzuki SCR. Iwao Yamazaki PHOTO COLOR 'SCOPE: Kazue Nagatsuka MUSIC: Seitaro Omori   w/ Koji Wada, Mayumi Shimizu, Yoko Minamida, Nobuo Kaneko   Reportedly Suzuki got in an early bit of trouble with Nikkatsu bigwigs for trying to turn a potboiler gangster script about a young guy having to take over his father's yakuza gang into a comedy. They made him change it back, and supposedly no one, including star Wada, was happy with the result.

TOKYO STREETFIGHTING aka TOKYO SHIGAI SEN aka TOKYO AFTERMATH OF WAR 1967 89 min. DIR. Shugoro Nishimura SCR. Ei Ogawa PHOTO COLOR 'SCOPE: Kenji Hagiwara MUSIC: Hajime Kaburagi   w/ Tetsuya Watari, Joe Shishido, Chieko Matsubara, Tatsuya Fuji, Asao Koike, Takamaru Sasaki, Shoki Fukae, Keiko Yuge   Watari is a soldier coming home to Tokyo immediately post-WW2. Many people are scrambling to make a living in the rubble. He hangs out with a bunch of *tekiya* (street peddlers) who are being terrorized by Korean gangsters led by Koike. In fact, the film starts

in a bombed-out basement in a scene reminiscent of GATE OF FLESH, with several whores haggling over getting paid. Too bad that they are arguing with the wrong guy – Asao Koike playing the sadistic, fashion-plate yakuza boss. He shoots the main troublemaker to death to settle things. The other whores are terrified and put instantly in their place. When the cops investigate, it is obvious that terror runs through every single person in the area, whore or not. When the cops question Koike and his thugs, the regular folks are visibly quaking. All except for Watari who is not intimidated in the least. This leads to him being stoned-with-bricks by the bad guys as soon he is alone.

Tokyo Streetfighting

Pretty soon it is all-out war. At the end, Watari leads the gang of *tekiya* against the yakuza mob. Climax and turnaround comes when he captures a huge heavy machine gun the villains had set up on the second floor of a skeletal ruin of a building. An intriguing footnote re., the GATE OF FLESH reference: Nishimura, himself, went on to direct a roman porno remake for Nikkatsu in 1977. * * 1/2

TORRENT OF LIFE aka GEKI RYU NI IKIRU OTOKO series

TORRENT OF LIFE aka GEKI RYU NI IKIRU OTOKO 1962 84 min. DIR. Takashi Nomura SCR. Iwao Yamazaki/ Kenji Yoshida PHOTO COLOR 'SCOPE: Minoru Yokoyama MUSIC: Seitaro Omori w/ Hideki Takahashi, Hideaki Nitani, Sayuri Yoshinaga, Reiko Sassamori, Mari Shiraki Takahashi is a trumpet player trying to find work in various mobster-owned nightclubs. Yoshinaga is the straight-arrow girl who loves him, and he ends up pulling some raw deals on her to dissuade her from the affection. You know, cliches like "being cruel to be kind"? Which, sadly, is what this film is chockfull of. It doesn't really seem to know what it wants to be. A *seishun* (young people) movie? A yakuza picture? A policier? (Nitani is a cop trying to keep the nightclubs on the up-and-up). There are ways of melding genres together with style, strong characters and action choreographed to build and peak at certain points. Which, again, is not what happens here. Disappointing because, not only are there nice moments, but Nomura's later pictures (especially his yakuza *eiga*) often turned out exceptionally well. #1 of 3 films * *

MAN OF THE NIGHT MIST aka KIRI NO YORU NO OTOKO 1962 86 min. DIR. Akinori Matsuo SCR.

Seiji Hoshikawa PHOTO COLOR 'SCOPE: Izumi Hagiwara MUSIC: Masayoshi Ikeda w/ Hideki Takahashi, Eitaro Ozawa, Sayuri Yoshinaga, Asao Koike, Toru Abe, Daisaburo Hirata #2 of 3 films

A MAN WITH STARS IN HIS EYES aka HOSHI NO HITOMI O MOTSU OTOKO 1962 DIR. Katsumi Nishikawa SCR. Seiji Hoshikawa PHOTO COLOR 'SCOPE: Kazumi Iwasa MUSIC: Masayoshi Ikeda w/ Hideki Takahashi, Sayuri Yoshinaga, Satoshi Yamanouchi, Midori Tashiro, Kazuko Yoshiyuki, Nakajiro Tomita, Zeko Nakamura #3 and final in series

Traces of Lead

TRACES OF LEAD aka NAMARI O BUCHI KOME 1962 83 min. DIR. Buichi Saito SCR. Hisatoshi Kai PHOTO COLOR 'SCOPE: Kazumi Iwasa MUSIC: Taiichiro Kosugi w/ Joe Shishido, Nobuo Kaneko, Ryohei Uchida, Sanae Nakahara, Shoki Fukae, Hiroshi Sugie

TRAMPLED INNOCENCE aka
DORO DAREKE NO JUNJO 1963
90 min. **DIR.** Ko Nakahira **SCR.**
Ataru Baba **PHOTO COLOR 'SCOPE:**
Yoshihiro Yamazaki **MUSIC:** Toshio
Mayuzumi **w/** Mitsuo Hamada,
Sayuri Yoshinaga, Masako Izumi,
Osamu Takizawa, Asao Koike
A delinquent, budding yakuza has a
clash of sensibilities with his good
girlfriend in this gritty tearjerker.

TWELVE NOON, TOKYO aka
TOKYO GOZEN-REIJI 1962
DIR. Isamu Kosugi **SCR.** Kimiyuki
Hasegawa/Tatsuo Miyata **PHOTO**
'SCOPE: Kumenobu Fujioka
MUSIC: Taiichiro Kosugi **w/** Kyoji
Aoyama, Hitoshi Miyazaki, Ryohei
Uchida, Yoko Mihara, Eiji Go, Uyako
Hori, Sumiko Minami, Ichiro Kijima

Underworld Beauty, American DVD art

UNDERWORLD BEAUTY aka
ANKOKUGAI NO BIJO 1958
87 min. **DIR.** Seijun Suzuki **SCR.**

Susumu Saji **PHOTO B&W 'SCOPE:**
Toshitaro Nakao **MUSIC:** Naozumi
Yamamoto **w/** Michitaro Mizushima,
Mari Shiraki, Shinsuke Ashida,
Hiroshi Kondo, Toru Abe, Hideaki
Nitani   A riproaring, action-packed
thriller filled with Suzuki's already
recognizably perverse sense of visual
humor. Black-clad lone wolf
Mizushima links up with former
cohorts, crippled foodstall owner Abe
and gang boss Ashida, to sell some
stolen diamonds to an American bigshot. But unluckily they are held up at
their rooftop rendezvous.

Underworld Beauty frame grabs

Rather than give up the loot, hothead
Abe swallows the stones then jumps
off the roof! Mizushima, greedy
wimp artist Kondo, kingpin Ashida
and strong-arm Takashina lie in wait
across the street from the hospital
morgue. Free spirit Shiraki, Abe's little sister (she is also Kondo's model/
girlfriend), arrives just as Abe's
corpse is delivered. She is angry at
everyone and chases all away except
for Kondo. When she runs out to
drown her sorrows with a carousing American sailor, Kondo uses the
opportunity to retrieve the diamonds
by cutting open dead Abe's stomach.
It is not long before the others realize

Kondo has the stones. Mizushima is the first to challenge him in Kondo's mannequin factory loft. But Ashida and goons show up soon after. Fortunately Shiraki has secreted the gems in a mannequin's breast. Too bad the dummy is removed by workers during the stalemate to be taken to a customer. Mizushima, Shiraki and Kondo have to stand by quietly lest they tip their hand to Ashida. Mizushima tracks the dummy ahead of Kondo but is forced to bring in the loot when Ashida grabs Shiraki as hostage, caging her in a steam room in his turkish bath/ nightclub HQ. Mizushima comes to the rescue, Kondo is shot down and a frenzied battle ensues. Mizushima and Shiraki become trapped in the cellar with one of the steam boilers leaking from bulletholes. The pair try to dig up and out through the coal shute, but only Shiraki escapes with Mizushima cornered by Ashida. Finally detective Nitani and fellow cops bust in to discover the now wounded Mizushima still alive. In the final scene, Shiraki keeps Mizushima company while he recuperates in his open air hospital room. This was Suzuki's first scope film, and he utilizes both real Tokyo locations as well as the studio lot to full advantage in beautifully fluid black-&-white widescreen compositions. A kinetic spark is ignited from the first frame, and Suzuki achieves an incredible balancing act between the comic book scenario and realistic emotions. The entire cast is perfect with Shiraki emerging as an indelibly charismatic, anarchic presence everytime she appears. Mizushima is the ideal tough but worldweary noir anti-hero. Suzuki as well as many Japanese critics claim that he didn't

make any really decent pictures until 1963. Going by the many films viewed for this book from Suzuki's early 1956 – 1962 period, most of the director's fans would object to this point of view. Here especially in UNDERWORLD BEAUTY, Suzuki was already operating on all four cylinders, tackling with hardboiled noir action territory with ease, refusing to let his stories stand still, his characters stagnate or his audience become bored. * * * 1/2

Underworld's Peaceful Man

UNDERWORLD'S PEACEFUL MAN or QUIET UNDERWORLD MAN aka ANKOKU GAI NO SHIZU KANA OTOKO 1961 82 min. **Dir.** Toshio Masuda **Scr.** Mio Ezaki/Ryuzo Nakanishi **Photo color 'scope:** Shinsaku Himeda **Music:** Harumi Ibe **w/** Hideaki Nitani, Masako Izumi, Mari Shiraki, Ichiro Kijima, Akifumi Inoue, Shinsuke Ashida

**UNFOLDING NIGHT OF
DREAMS** aka YUME WA YORU
HIRAKU 1967 81 min. **DIR.** Hiroshi
Noguchi **SCR.** Akira Saiga/Akira
Nakano **PHOTO 'SCOPE:** Muneo Ueda
MUSIC: Yasushi Miyagawa
w/ Hideki Takahashi, Mari Sono,
Tetsuya Watari, Yoko Yamamoto

The Velvet Hustler

THE VELVET HUSTLER aka
KURENAI NO NAGARE HOSHI
aka THE CRIMSON SHOOTING
STAR aka BLOOD OF THE FALL-
ING STAR aka THE WHISTLING
KILLER aka LIKE A SHOOTING
STAR 1967 97 min. **DIR.** Toshio
Masuda **SCR.** Kaneo Ikegami/Toshio
Masuda **PHOTO COLOR 'SCOPE:**
Kurataro Takamura **MUSIC:** Hajime
Kaburagi w/ Tetsuya Watari, Ruriko
Asaoka, Joe Shishido, Kayo Matsuo,
Tatsuya Fuji, Chiyo Okumura,
Ryotaro Sugi, Shoki Fukae
A languid tale of a young amoral hit-
man who likes to sit in a rocking chair
on the end of a concrete harbor jetty

when he is not offing rival mobsters
or boffing babes. Fuji, usually typecast as a delinquent or young yakuza,
does a most unusual turn as a cop,
while Shishido portrays a smooth,
mustachioed backstabber. Speaking
of backstabbing, it is one of Watari's
more straitlaced girlfriends (Asaoka)
who ends up turning him in.
A superior remake of the black-and-
white RED HARBOR also directed
by Masuda which starred Yujiro
Ishihara in the lead. * * * 1/2

**VERMILLION SWORD
SCABBARD CODE** aka
SHUZAYA JINGI series

**VERMILLION SWORD –
SCABBARD CODE SWORD
AMIDST THE SWIRLING
CHERRY BLOSSOMS** aka
SHUZAYA JINGI – TEKKA
MIDARE ZAKURA aka STORM
OF VIOLENCE 1969 93 min. **DIR.**
Buichi Saito **SCR.** Takeshi Aoyama
PHOTO COLOR 'SCOPE: Kenji
Hagiwara **MUSIC:** Taiichiro Kosugi
w/ Hiroko Ogi, Meiko Kaji, Tatsuya
Fuji, Kanjuro Arashi, Jiro Okazaki,
Ryohei Uchida, Kunie Tanaka, Toru
Abe   Actress Ogi, like Meiko Kaji,
became a popular singing star in the
latter sixties. She also sang theme
songs for films (even one of the
CRIMSON BAT films – TRAPPED,
THE CRIMSON BAT!) In addition
to appearing in quite a few films
for Nikkatsu as a sword-wielding
heroine (such as the first two RISING
DRAGON films and THE BOSS'S
WIFE, she also performed in more
traditional roles in various yakuza
(such as ATTACK) and *seishun*
(young people) films, virtually all

between 1969-1971. Director Saito later went on to direct the 4th film in the LONE WOLF AND CUB series in the early 1970s, BABY CART IN PERIL. #1 of 2 films

Vermillion Sword Scabbard Code (#1)

Vermillion Sword Scabbard Code (#2)

VERMILLION SWORD SCAB-BARD CODE – TAKE A LIFE aka SHUZAYA JINGI – O INOCHI CHODAI aka GO TO HELL! 1969 94 min. DIR. Buichi Saito SCR. Takeshi Aoyama PHOTO COLOR 'SCOPE: Kenji Hagiwara MUSIC: Taiichiro Kosugi w/ Hiroko Ogi, Ryo Ikebe, Tatsuya Fuji, Yoko Yamamoto, Jiro Okazaki #2 of 2 films

VIOLENCE aka BORYOKU 1962 79 min. DIR. Isamu Kosugi SCR. Matsumura/ Saburo Endo PHOTO B&W 'SCOPE: Umeo Matsuhashi MUSIC: Taiichiro Kosugi w/ Kyoji Aoyama, Akifumi Inoue, Ichiro Sugai, Mayumi Shimizu

Violent Gambler - Flower-Covered Path to Hell

VIOLENT GAMBLER – FLOWER-COVERED PATH TO HELL aka KENKA BAKUTO – JIGOKU NO HANAMICHI aka CONFLICT aka FIGHTING GAMBLER 1969 DIR. Akinori

Matsuo **SCR.** Ei Ogawa/Tatsuhiko
Kamoi **PHOTO COLOR 'SCOPE:**
Kazumi Iwasa **MUSIC:** Hajime
Kaburagi **w/** Akira Kobayashi,
Hideki Takahashi, Yumiko Nogawa,
Bontaro Miake, Masako Izumi,
Tatsuya Fuji, Isamu Nagato, Jiro
Okazaki, Shoki Fukae
Kobayashi hates his long-lost father
for abandoning him as a child. When
he encounters the parent on his
travels, he realizes that he still has
affection for his old man and, not
revealing his identity, helps him when
he gets in a jam.

VIOLENT GANG OVERCOME
aka BORYOKUDAN NORIKOMU
aka THE GALLANT RAID aka
THE KILLER 1971 **DIR.** Mio Ezaki
SCR. Ryuzo Nakanishi/Yoshi Yokota
PHOTO COLOR 'SCOPE: Akikazu Sakata
w/ Akira Kobayashi, Toru Abe,
Meiko Kaji, Michitaro Mizushima,
Rinichi Yamamoto, Eiji Go, Shoki
Fukae Lone wolf Kobayashi upsets
a top gang led by Abe when he comes
to the aid of rival boss Mizushima – a
man who saved his life. Mizushima
is murdered by Abe's men, and
Kobayashi, in turn, stabs Abe to
death. Amongst the last "straight"
yakuza films made at Nikkatsu before
the studio's switch-over to *pinku eiga.*

VIOLENT SILENCER aka
SHIZUKANARU BORYOKU 1963
87 min. **DIR.** Isamu Noguchi **SCR.**
Saburo Endo **w/** Ryohei Uchida,
Mari Shiraki, Kenjiro Ishiyama,
Shoki Fukae, Ichiro Sugai

VIRGIN BLUES aka BAAJIN
BURUUSU 1975 **DIR.** Toshiya
Fujita **SCR.** Eiichi Uchida
w/ Kumiko Akiyoshi, Hiroyuki

Nagato More *pinku eiga* within a
yakuza milieu.

Voice Without a Shadow

VOICE WITHOUT A SHADOW
aka KAGENAKI OE 1958 99 in.
DIR. Seijun Suzuki **SCR.** Ryuta
Akimoto/ Susumu Saji **PHOTO B&W**
'SCOPE: Kazue Nagatsuka **MUSIC:**
Hikaru Hayashi **w/** Yoko Minamida,
Hideaki Nitani, Joe Shishido, Nobuo
Kaneko, Shinsuke Ashida, Keisuke
Nore A mystery thriller with
Minamida a part-time switchboard
operator who hears the voice of a
killer and later realizes it is one of
her husband's mahjong partners, lone
wolf yakuza gambler Shishido. He is
at his best, mercilessly flirting with
her and constantly showing up at her
side out of nowhere. He is about to
drive her nuts when he turns up murdered, too. Her salaryman husband
is fingered by the cops. Regrettably,
the narrative then virtually deserts
Minamida's point of view for reporter
Nitani, who believes they have got
the wrong man. He goes after the

most logical suspect, another mah-jong player, small time gang boss Ashida. However, by the end, we learn it was the only remaining member of the gambling quartet, weasly shopkeeper Kaneko who had salivated over Shishido's big satchel of cash and had whacked him for it. Based on a mystery novel by popular genre writer Seicho Matsumoto. Suzuki gets points for trying to take a different approach. Not great all the way through, but always watchable. * * 1/2

WANDERER'S GOSSIP aka SON NO FURAIBO 1964 **DIR.** Hiroshi Noguchi **SCR.** Seiji Hosokawa/Shiro Ishimori **PHOTO 'SCOPE:** Isamu Kakida **MUSIC:** Tomokazu Kawabe w/ Hideaki Nitani, Daisaburo Hirata, Tadao Sawamoto, Reiko Sassamori

THE WANDERING GUITARIST aka WATARIDORI aka WANDERER aka BIRD-OF-PASSAGE series

THE WANDERING GUITARIST aka GITAA O MOTTA WATARI-DORI 1959 77 min. **DIR.** Buichi Saito **SCR.** Iwao Yamazaki/ Kenzaburo Hara **PHOTO COLOR 'SCOPE:** Kurataro Takamura **MUSIC:** Taiichiro Kosugi w/ Akira Kobayashi, Ruriko Asaoka, Sanae Nakahara, Misako Watanabe, Joe Shishido, Nobuo Kaneko, Mari Shiraki, Hiroshi Nihonyanagi, Kyoji Aoyama A very popular film series about an ex-cop turned wandering guitar player and his adventures after being wrongly dismissed from the force. He drifts from one part of the country to another with his trusty

guitar (and revolver), fighting crime and romancing beautiful girls. Here in this first entry, he discovers his gal's father is head of the narcotics gang he is after. #1 of 9 films

Wandering Guitarist (#2)

GUITARIST AND THE RANCH-ER aka KUCHIBUE GA NAGAR-ERU MINATO MACHI 1960 84 min. **DIR.** Buichi Saito **SCR.** Toshio Matsuura **PHOTO COLOR 'SCOPE:** Kurataro Takamura **MUSIC:** Taiichiro Kosugi w/ Akira Kobayashi, Joe Shishido, Ruriko Asaoka, Misako Watanabe, Akira Yamanouchi, Mari Shiraki, Hiroshi Kondo #2 of 9 films

WHEN DOES THE MIGRATING BIRD RETURN? aka WATARI-DORI ITSU MATA KAERU aka RETURN OF THE VAGABOND 1960 79 min. **DIR.** Buichi Saito **SCR.** Iwao Yamazaki/Hisao Ogawa **PHOTO COLOR 'SCOPE:** Kurataro Takamura **MUSIC:** Taiichiro Kosugi w/ Akira

Kobayashi, Ruriko Asaoka, Joe
Shishido, Tamio Kawaji, Sanae
Nakahara, Yoko Minamida, Nobuo
Kaneko, Ryohei Uchida, Kaku
Takashina, Yuko Kusunoki #3 of 9

**WANDERER IN THE RED
SUNSET** aka AKAI YUHI NO
WATARIDORI aka RAMBLER IN
THE SUNSET 1960 79 min. **DIR.**
Buichi Saito **SCR.** Iwao Yamazaki/
Hisao Ogawa **PHOTO COLOR 'SCOPE:**
Kurataro Takamura **MUSIC:**
Taiichiro Kosugi w/ Akira
Kobayashi, Ruriko Asaoka, Joe
Shishido, Mari Shiraki, Yuko
Kusunoki, Shoki Fukae, Hiroshi
Kondo, Shiro Osaka #4 of 9 films

**WANDERER ON THE WIDE
PLAINS** aka DAISOGEN NO
WATARIDORI aka RIDER WITH
A GUITAR 1960 83 min.
DIR. Buichi Saito **SCR.** Iwao
Yamazaki **PHOTO COLOR 'SCOPE:**
Kurataro Takamura **MUSIC:**
Taiichiro Kosugi w/ Akira
Kobayashi, Joe Shishido, Ruriko
Asaoka, Yoko Minamida, Mari
Shiraki, Nobuo Kaneko, Goro
Mutsumi #5 of 9 films

**RAMBLER UNDER THE
SOUTHERN CROSS** aka HATO
O KOERU WATARIDORI 1961
79 min. **DIR.** Buichi Saito **SCR.** Iwao
Yamazaki **PHOTO COLOR 'SCOPE:**
Kurataro Takamura **MUSIC:**
Taiichiro Kosugi w/ Akira
Kobayashi, Ruriko Asaoka, Joe
Shishido, Mari Shiraki, Nobuo
Kaneko, Yuji Kodaka, Arihiro
Fujimura #6 of 9 films

RAMBLING IN THE SEA aka O
ONA BARA O YUKU WATARI-

DORI 1961 79 min. **DIR.** Buichi
Saito **SCR.** Iwao Yamazaki **PHOTO
COLOR 'SCOPE:** Kurataro Takamura
MUSIC: Taiichiro Kosugi
w/ Akira Kobayashi, Ruriko Asaoka,
Arihiro Fujimura, Shinsuke Ashida,
Mari Shiraki, Yoko Kusunoki, Goro
Mutsumi #7 of 9 films

**JOURNEY FROM THE NORTH –
WANDERER RETURNS TO THE
NORTH** aka HOKKI KO YORI
– WATARIDORI KITA HE KAERU
1962 79 min. **DIR.** Buichi Saito
SCR. Iwao Yamazaki **PHOTO COLOR
'SCOPE:** Kurataro Takamura
MUSIC: Taiichiro Kosugi w/ Akira
Kobayashi, Ruriko Asaoka, Eiji Go,
Mari Shiraki, Hiroshi Kondo, Ryohei
Uchida #8 of 9 films

WANDERER RETURNS HOME
aka WATARIDORI KOKYO HE
KAERU 1962 83 min. **DIR.** Yoichi
Ushihara **SCR.** Kikuma Shimoizaka
PHOTO COLOR 'SCOPE: Saburo
Isayama **MUSIC:** Seitaro Omori
w/ Akira Kobayashi, Koji Wada,
Yoko Minamida, Reiko Sassamori,
Ryoji Hayama, Daisaburo Hirata, Yuji
Kodaka, Toru Abe, Kayo Matsuo
#9 and final in series

**WANDERING GUN – JAIL-
BREAK BLUES** aka KENJU
MUSHUKU – DATSU GOKU
NO BURUUSU 1965 79 min.
DIR. Kenjiro Morinaga **SCR.** Seiji
Hoshikawa/Shiro Ishimori **PHOTO
B&W 'SCOPE:** Umeo Matsuhashi
MUSIC: Chumei Watanabe
w/ Tetsuya Watari, Tatsuya Fuji,
Chieko Matsubara, Asao Koike,
Eiji Go, Ichiro Sugai, Hiroshi
Nihonyanagi   Watari, overseeing

boss Sugai's construction interests and Fuji, opening a nightclub under Sugai's patronage, are close friends from childhood. Things begin to go wrong when Watari's attempted peace overtures to a rival boss result in embittered, craven Sugai personally supervising a contract hit on his old enemy. He sets Fuji up to take the fall, which Fuji does with grace and good spirits as a debt to his boss who helped in his good fortune. However, Fuji later discovers while in stir that Sugai has raped his girl in his old office at the club. This and other transgressions lead to Fuji escaping prison with Watari's help to kill Sugai and do battle with his gang. Sugai and Fuji as well as many henchmen perish. Watari and girl Matsubara are outraged that big boss Nihonyanagi has brought his cronies to watch the carnage from the sidelines, behaving as if it was a sporting event. This starts very well as a standard, somewhat noirish yakuza picture but peters out midway through with what seems underdeveloped characters and scenario. The action at the climax is nicely staged, but one is left curiously unmoved.   * * 1/2

WANDERING SONG aka HORO NO UTA 1966 **DIR.** Takashi Nomura **SCR.** Iwao Yamazaki/Akira Nakano/Takashi Nomura **PHOTO** 'SCOPE: Shinsaku Himeda **MUSIC:** Harumi Ibe **w/** Akira Kobayashi, Misa Hirose, Chikako Hosokawa, Shoki Fukae, Minako Kazuki, Kaku Takashina This seems to be a borderline yakuza romance.

THE WARPED ONES aka KYONETSU NO KISETSU aka SEASON OF CRAZY HEAT aka

THE WEIRD LOVEMAKERS 1960 75 min. **DIR.** Koreyoshi Kurahara **SCR.** Nobuo Yamada **PHOTO B&W** 'SCOPE: Yoshio Mamiya **MUSIC:** Toshiro Mayuzumi

The Warped Ones

w/ Tamio Kawaji, Yuko Chiyo, Eiji Go, Hiroyuki Nagato, Noriko Matsumoto, Shoki Fukae An over-the-top *taiyozoku* (sun tribe) romp with delinquent trio Kawaji, Go, and Matsumoto victimizing straight young couple, Chiyo and Nagato. The three have zeroed in on them due to a previous run-in with straight-arrow reporter Nagato. Go and Matsumoto eventually become a lawless couple on their own, with Go joining a threadbare yakuza gang. Angry hedonist Kawaji, however, becomes obsessed with Chiyo, whom he has gotten pregnant. She is simultaneously repulsed and attracted to him, and the two have several psychodrama encounters in Kawaji's fave hangout, a jazz-oriented coffee house. Chiyo

stays with mild-mannered, cuckolded
Nagato. Before the film is over, she
has tried to kill party monster
Kawaji by flooding her windows-
closed apartment with gas where the
egotistic boor is drunkenly snoozing.
Too bad for everyone he wakes up
from the ensuing violent coughing spell and survives. Kawaji soon
learns old pal Go has been mortally
wounded after foolishly betraying
his yakuza brethern. The climax then
sees a weird stalemate where Kawaji
and Nagato both accompany Chiyo to
an abortion clinic. Maverick director
Kurahara, who had also manned other
youth pictures at Nikkatsu and was
obviously influenced by some of the
British black-and-white "angry young
man" pictures of the era, delivers
a film that is, by turns, equal parts
groundbreaking, exhilarating and annoyingly pretentious. Kawaji, too, is
alternately brilliant and self-indulgent
in his portrayal of the gonzo, amoral
lone wolf. One or two critics have
speculated that Kawaji is playing
the same Attention Deficit Disorder
character in the later Kurahara effort,
BLACK SUN. This is a good film,
but Kurahara's relatively unknown,
underrated GLASS JOHNNY–
LOOKS LIKE A BEAST is even
better. Originally released in the USA
by Radley Metzger's Audubon Films.
* * *

WATERFRONT GAMBLER aka
HATOBA NO TOBAKUSHI aka
GAMBLERS OF THE WHARF 1963
94 min. **DIR.** Tokujiro Yamazaki
SCR. Masahiro Daikuhara/Iwao
Yamazaki **PHOTO COLOR 'SCOPE:**
Kenji Hagiwara Music: Seitaro
Omori **w/** Akira Kobayashi, Mari
Shiraki, Fushiko Osuga, Yuji Kodaka,

Kinzo Shin, Toru Abe, Shoki Fukae

Waterfront Gambler

WATERFRONT OUTLAW
aka HATOBA NO MUHO MONO
1959 91 min. **DIR.** Buichi Saito
SCR. Toshio Matsuura **PHOTO COLOR**
'SCOPE: Kurataro Takamura **MUSIC:**
Taiichiro Kosugi **w/** Akira
Kobayashi, Ruriko Asaoka, Sanae
Nakahara, Masumi Okada

WHERE THE HORIZON MEETS
THE SUN aka TAIYO UMI O
SOMERU TOKI 1961 89 min.
DIR. Toshio Masuda **SCR.** Nobuo
Yamada **PHOTO COLOR 'SCOPE:**
Shinsaku Himeda **MUSIC:** Harumi
Ibe **w/** Akira Kobayashi, Shinsuke
Ashida, Ruriko Asaoka, Eiji Go, Mari
Shiraki, Midori Tashiro   Kobayashi
is appointed second officer on a ship
that travels between Japan and Brazil.
When he is beaten up by hoods in a
bar fight, his old pal Go takes him
home to recuperate. Going through

a tough time with a huge debt to gangsters, Go decides to take Kobayashi's seaman's passport to escape his troubles. Kobayashi finds out, sympathizes with Go and is going to let him abscond when the yakuza intervene. Go's girl ends up tortured by the hoods. There are also plenty of cliffhanger situations until Kobayashi enlists his new shipmates to rout the yakuza.

WHO IS GETTING REVENGE? aka FUKUSHU WA DARE GA YARU 1957 92 min. **Dir.** Hiroshi Noguchi **Scr.** Yoshihisa Aoki/ Atsundo Kubota **Photo B&W:** Umeo Matsubayashi **Music:** Rokuro Hara **w/** Michitaro Mizushima, Tatsuya Mihashi, Sachiko Hidari, Hisako Tsukuba, Kotaro Bando

THE WIND BLOWS TOMOR-ROW INTO THE NEXT DAY aka ASHITA WA ASHITA NO KAZE GA FUKU aka TOMORROW'S WIND 1958 115 min. **Dir.** Umeji Inoue **Scr.** Umeji Inoue/Toshio Matsuura/ Ichiro Ikeda **Photo color 'scope:** Kazumi Iwasa **Music:** Seitaro Omori **w/** Yujiro Ishihara, Mie Kitahara, Ruriko Asaoka, Michiko Hamamura, Kyoji Aoyama, Shiro Osaka

THE WIND-OF-YOUTH GROUP CROSSES THE MOUNTAIN PASS aka TOGE O WATARU WAKAI KAZE 1961 85 min. **Dir.** Seijun Suzuki **Scr.** Ichiro Ikeda/Fumi Takahashi/Yoshihiko Morimoto **Photo color 'scope:** Saburo Isayama **Music:** Seitaro Omori **w/** Koji Wada, Mayumi Shimizu, Nobuo Kaneko, Shin Morikawa, Arihiro Fujimura, Hideko Kariya   Wada is a vacationing

student who tries his hand at selling goods in a mountain village during summer festival. He encounters numerous *tekiya*, including tough guy Kaneko, as well as a traveling theatrical group who put on magic and music shows. Everything is fairly innocuous, but director Suzuki utilizes the sumptuous rural locations in such an intoxicating way, seamlessly integrating village life, boisterous festival shenanigans, bigger-than-life merchants, theatre pageants and, of course, the evil neighborhood yakuza gang, that we are sucked into the contrived innocent adventure/romance of it all before we even realize it.
* * 1/2

Witness to a Killing

WITNESS TO A KILLING aka SHI NI ZAMA O MIRU aka WATCHING THE SPECTACLE OF DEATH 1964 79 min. **Dir.** Takumi Furukawa **Scr.** Ryuzo Nakanishi **Photo B&W 'scope:** Saburo Isayama **Music:** Hajime

Kaburagi   w/ Hideaki Nitani,
Reiko Sassamori, Akira Yamanouchi,
Hiroshi Sugie, Kaku Takashina

WOLF OF BLUES TOWN aka
AOI MACHI NO OKAMI 1962
80 min. **DIR.** Takumi Furukawa
SCR. Ei Ogawa **PHOTO COLOR 'SCOPE:**
Saburo Isayama **MUSIC:** Masaru
Sato   w/ Hideaki Nitani, Izumi
Ashikawa, Hiroshi Nihonyanagi,
Arihiko Fujimura, Hiroshi Sugie,
Nitani is a G-man battling mobsters.

**WOLVES OF NUMBER ZERO
STREET** aka ZERO BANGAI NO
OKAMI 1959 87 min. **DIR.** Hiroshi
Noguchi **SCR.** Isao Yamazaki **PHOTO
B&W 'SCOPE:** Kazue Nagatsuka
MUSIC: Naozumi Yamamoto
w/ Hideaki Nitani, Yuji Kodaka,
Misako Watanabe, Hisako Tsukuba,
Joe Shishido, Kaku Takashina, Ichiro
Sugai

Wolves of Number Zero Street

WOLVES OF THE NIGHT aka
YORU NO OKAMI 1958 88 min.
DIR. Yoichi Ushihara **SCR.** Keiichi
Abe **PHOTO B&W 'SCOPE:** Saburo
Isayama **MUSIC:** Taiichiro Kosugi
w/ Ryoji Hayama, Nobuo Kaneko,
Izumi Ashikawa, Mari Shiraki

WOMEN'S POLICE aka ONNA
NO KEISATSU series

WOMEN'S POLICE aka ONNA
NO KEISATSU 1969 82 min.
DIR. Mio Ezaki **SCR.** Ryuzo
Nakanishi **PHOTO COLOR 'SCOPE:**
Minoru Yokoyama **MUSIC:** Makoto
Sato   w/ Akira Kobayashi, Yuji
Kodaka, Yukiyo Toake, Noriko Maki,
Asao Uchida, Tatsuya Fuji, Kyoko
Maki, Masako Ota (Meiko Kaji),
Mina Aoe, Ichiro Kijima

Women's Police (#1)

Kobayashi is a professional trouble-
shooter/bodyguard who looks out
for the hostesses who work in Ginza

nightclubs and bars. Toake, a former hostess, comes to him for help when her husband, one of his old school chums, is murdered. Investigating, he uncovers a whole hornets nest of corruption, hypocrisy and depravity. An occasionally fascinating, but just as often static, look into the world of late sixties hostess bars. In some ways this is more of a detective murder mystery than a true yakuza film, although it does largely take place in the underground yakuza subculture of bars and nightclubs and has its share of gangster characters. There is a candy-colored neon ambience throughout that compensates a bit for the slow patches. But there is still not much that happens until the last half hour when Kobayashi's pal Kodaka is murdered by villain Uchida's flunkies. Notable also for featuring Meiko Kaji in one of her last supporting roles billed under her original name, Masako Ota.   #1 of 4 films   * * 1/2

WOMEN'S POLICE 2 aka ZOKU ONNA NO KEISATSU 1969 83 min. **DIR.** Mio Ezaki **SCR.** Ryuzo Nakanishi **PHOTO COLOR 'SCOPE:** Minoru Yokoyama **MUSIC:** Makoto Sato **w/** Akira Kobayashi, Tatsuya Fuji, Akiko Koyama, Rumi Koyama, Mitsuko Oka, Eiji Go, Jotaro Togami, Keiko Nishi, Shiro Yanase, Kaku Takashina, Hirotaro Sugie
The head hostess of a rival club (Akiko Koyama) and an old friend (Fuji) jar Kobayashi's memory of a double suicide five years before. Hostess Koyama turns out to be the dupe of a nefarious yakuza gang who have been bootlegging liquor as well as trying to steal Kobayashi's club's girls. The gang is being shielded by a corrupt public prosecutor who had

also ruled the mysterious deaths of hostess Koyama's sister (Oka) and Rumi Koyama's brother a suicide pact. Kobayashi and Go become embroiled in a feud when they try to help hostess Koyama and a Korean businessman open up a new club. Go is burned to death in an arson attempt. There is supposedly some graphically bloody proceedings as Kobayashi assaults the gang – the boss is electrocuted by neon sign and the prosecutor gored by a metal pole. #2 of 4 films

WOMEN'S POLICE – APPOINTMENT WITH DANGER aka ONNA NO KEISATSU – KOKUSAI SEN MACHI AI SHITSU 1970 84 min. **DIR.** Yuji Tanno **SCR.** Ryuzo Nakanishi/Michio Sato **PHOTO COLOR 'SCOPE:** Yoshihiro Yamazaki **MUSIC:** Taiichiro Kosugi **w/** Akira Kobayashi, Hiroyuki Nagato, Jiro Okazaki, Mina Aoe
Kobayashi investigates when he finds a bar hostess friend of his was kidnapped, forcibly addicted to drugs, then sold as a prostitute in Singapore. He discovers import/exporter Kaga is a notorious white slaver and rescues girlfriend Tobe just as she is about to be injected with narcotics. #3 of 4 films

WOMEN'S POLICE – SWIRLING BUTTERFLIES aka ONNA NO KEISATSU – MIDARE CHO 1970 86 min. **DIR.** Keiichi Ozawa **SCR.** Ryuzo Nakanishi **PHOTO COLOR 'SCOPE:** Minoru Yokoyama **MUSIC:** Hajime Kaburagi **w/** Akira Kobayashi, Mina Aoe, Kumi Mizuno, Ryohei Uchida, Asao Uchida, Eiji Go,
Kobayashi and Mizuno are duped into helping gang boss Asao Uchida recruit beautiful women. They aren't

aware that Uchida is using them as bribes for rich foreigners, hoping lucrative investment opportunities will result. Kobayashi is wounded by the gang when he begins to make inquiries. He follows this up with a raid on the boss's mansion, managing to rescue several of the girls. Things come to a boil when Kobayashi and Go crash a shipboard party for the foreign guests with the battle finally joined by informed police. (See also Kobayashi's MARKET OF WOMEN which has some connection to this series) #4 and final in series

Women's Prison

WOMEN'S PRISON aka ONNA KEIMUSHYO 1978 70 min. **DIR.** Nobuaki Shirai **SCR.** Minoru Katsura **PHOTO COLOR 'SCOPE:** Kurataro Takamura w/ Toru Ibuki, Erina Myai, Natsuko Yashiro, Etsuko Ashikawa Pink women's prison film.

WOMEN OF THE NIGHT aka **YORU NO MESU** series

WOMEN OF THE NIGHT – BUTTERFLY FLOWER aka YORU NO MESU – HANA NO CHO 1969 83 min. **DIR.** Katsumi Nishikawa **SCR.** Akira Saiga (?)/ Ryuzo Nakanishi w/ Yumiko Nogawa, Shinichi Mori, Ryotaro Sugi, Masako Ota (pka Meiko Kaji) Nogawa plays a bar madam responsible for the slightly younger girls in her employ. Popular singer Shinichi Mori has a small recurring role in the series as a nocturnal, strolling Ginza minstrel (at least that is all he does in #3). Also, according to a very short description in Uni-Japan Film Monthly, these three pictures are based on ideas from Mori's songs. It should be noted that singer Mori also had a similar recurring small role in Toei Studios' longer-lived SONG OF THE NIGHT series. #1 of 3 films

WOMEN OF THE NIGHT – WOMAN OF SENIORITY aka YORU NO MESU – TOSHI UE NO ONNA aka THE OLDER WOMAN 1969 88 min. **DIR.** Katsumi Nishikawa **SCR.** Shizuo Taba **PHOTO COLOR 'SCOPE:** Junnosuke Oguri **MUSIC:** Masayoshi Ikeda w/ Yumiko Nogawa, Hideki Takahashi, Masako Izumi, Osami Nabe, Shinichi Mori, Masako Ota (pka Meiko Kaji), Hirotaro Sugie, Tomiko Ishii #2 of 3 films

WOMEN OF THE NIGHT – LIFE OF A FLOWER aka YORU NO MESU – HANA NO INOCHI 1969 91 min. **DIR.** Kenjiro Morinaga **SCR.** Kikuma Shimoizaka **PHOTO COLOR 'SCOPE:** Umeo Matsubayashi **MUSIC:** Masayoshi Ikeda w/ Yumiko Nogawa, Koji Nanbara, Jiro Okazaki, Tamio Kawaji, Osami Nabe, Shinichi

Mori Nogawa runs into trouble with one of her girls using drugs, then disappearing.

Women of the Night (#3)

Although there is not a yakuza plot, virtually all the male characters (except for singer Mori) are yakuza. Nogawa is friendly with bosses as well as *dai kanbu* (leading mobsters) such as Nanbara. Initially, Nogawa is somewhat smitten by Nanbara, but there is something about him that strikes her as odd. It develops that he is a barely-in-control closet sadist who has a couple of missing hostesses drugged and tied-up in his private torture chamber! When Nogawa discovers this, she enlists the aid of some of her younger male friends, and they raid Nanbara's decadent abode. He ends up getting killed in the ensuing action. The print viewed was cut by ten or fifteen minutes as well as panned-and-scanned, so who knows how much extra insanity ended up on the TV station's cutting room floor. As it is, this is one of the strangest Japanese films in this book for unexpected twists coming out-of-left-field. One wonders if the first two entries have a similar "weirdness" quotient. Let us hope so! #3 and final of series * * *

WORLDLY COMRADES or COMRADE SHOWOFFS or SOPHISTICATED PARTNERS aka AITSU series

FEARLESS COMRADES aka FUTEKI NA AITSU 1966 87 min. DIR. Shugoro Nishimura SCR. Hisatoshi Kai/Shiro Ishimori PHOTO COLOR 'SCOPE: Minoru Yokoyama MUSIC: Hajime Kaburagi w/ Akira Kobayashi, Ichiro Nakatani, Tatsuya Fuji, Izumi Ashikawa, Bonta Tokyo Judging from photo stills, handsome Kobayashi and goofy Tokyo appear to be troubleshooters in the netherworld of yakuza intrigue. The emphasis is tongue-in-cheek. #1 of 4 films

THE MAN WITH NINE LIVES aka FUJIMI NA AITSU 1967 87 min. DIR. Buichi Saito SCR. Hisatoshi Kai/Shiro Ishimori PHOTO COLOR 'SCOPE: Yoshihiro Yamazaki MUSIC: Taiichiro Kosugi w/ Akira Kobayashi, Ruriko Asaoka, Hideaki Nitani, Bonta Tokyo #2 of 4 films

TRUE LIFE OF WORLDLY COMRADES aka INOCHI SHIRAZU NO AITSU 1967 91 min. DIR. Akinori Matsuo SCR. Hisatoshi Kai PHOTO COLOR 'SCOPE: Kazumi Iwasa MUSIC: Hidehiko Arashino w/ Akira Kobayashi, Tatsuya Fuji, Ryohei Uchida, Bonta Tokyo #3 of 4 films

EXPLOSIVE MAN AND COMRADES aka BAKUDAN OTOKO TO IWARERU AITSU aka THE SINGING GUNMAN 1967 91 min. **DIR.** Yasuharu Hasebe **SCR.** Kikuma Shimoizaka/ Takashi Fujii **PHOTO COLOR 'SCOPE:** Yoshihiro Yamazaki **MUSIC:** Hajime Kaburagi **w/** Akira Kobayashi, Ko Nishimura, Masayo Banri, Yoshiro Aoki, Tatsuya Fuji, Ryohei Uchida, Jiro Okazaki #4 and last of the series

Wounded Beast

WOUNDED BEAST aka KIZU TSUKERU YAJU 1959 85 min. **DIR.** Hiroshi Noguchi **SCR.** Hajime Takaiwa/Kei Kumai **PHOTO B&W 'SCOPE:** Kazue Nagatsuka **MUSIC:** Teizo Matsumura **w/** Hideaki Nitani, Hisako Tsukuba, Yoko Minamida, Michitaro Mizushima, Tamio Kawaji, Joe Shishido, Hiroshi Kondo

YAKUZA BEASTS aka YAKUZA HIJOSHI series

Yakuza Beasts (#1)

YAKUZA BEASTS – PRISON BROTHERS aka YAKUZA HIJOSHI – MUSHYO KYODAI aka PENITENTIARY BROTHERS 1969 83 min. **DIR.** Akinori Matsuo **STORY:** Noboru Ando **SCR.** Ryuzo Nakanishi **PHOTO COLOR 'SCOPE:** Nobuo Hoshi **MUSIC:** Hajime Kaburagi **w/** Noboru Ando, Tetsuro Tanba, Tamio Kawaji, Hiroyuki Nagato, Toru Abe, Chiyoko Honma, Yoshiko Machida, Daijiro Natsukawa, Matasaburo Tanba, Shiro

Osaka Ando gets released from prison and is met by younger sidekick Kawaji. Almost immediately Ando is attacked by rival gangsters afraid that he will upset the applecart of their neighborhood monopolies. It turns out comrade Nagato, son of senior godfather Natsukawa, has married the daughter of evil boss Abe. Initially this does not prove a problem. But once Abe starts to muscle in, using third party killer Matasaburo Tanba to kill off Kawaji and finally Natsukawa, Abe's daughter commits suicide. Former prison comrade Tetsuro Tanba, intent on remaining neutral, has to finally side with Ando when Abe goes too far over the line. Ando and Nagato attack Abe's HQ and are joined by Tetsuro Tanba midway through. All bite the dust except for Ando, with Nagato stabbed in the back while holding his wife's gassed corpse and bullet-riddled Tanba expiring in Ando's arms. Fairly routine for the most part, but exceptional director Matsuo does his best to keep things visually and dramatically stimulating. #1 of 3 films * * *

YAKUZA BEASTS – LOYALTY OFFERING OF BLOOD aka YAKUZA HIJOSHI – CHI NO SAKAZUKI aka FILL THE CUP WITH BLOOD 1969 86 min. **Dir.** Yorio (Sunao?) Nakagawa **Scr.** Ryuzo Nakanishi **Photo color 'scope:** Yoshio Wakino **Music:** Hideo Ozawa w/ Noboru Ando, Ryohei Uchida, Isao Kimura, Michiko Saga, Ryunosuke Tsukigata, Hiroshi Kondo, Fujio Suga, Michitaro Mizushima
A fairly innocuous programmer of lone wolf Ando taken under the wing of decent boss Tsukigata in immediate postwar Japan. A decade or so later, unscrupulous boss Suga starts muscling in on Tsukigata and other gangs' territories. He ultimately forces Tsukigata to disband his gang and go into retirement. Underboss Kimura, indie businessman Uchida and Tsukigata are all soon assassinated, prompting Ando – who has been in prison for the middle third of the saga – to go on a massive revenge binge at the climax. He brings his sword to wipe out Suga and other evil yakuza who are having a funeral for their fallen comrade, killer Kondo. This final swordfight is actually pretty spectacular but, despite the truly amazing location work, is unevenly staged. Also Hideo Ozawa's music score, although sporting the occasional bizarre flourish is, for the most part, dismally omnipresent and old-fashioned. It is nice to see elderly Tsukigata, a huge *chanbara* star in the silent era and a veteran of many samurai films from the fifties, in one of his last roles. Likewise stalwart hardboiled star Uchida and criminally underrated Kimura (star of numerous prestige pictures in the fifties) are definite assets to the scenario. Unfortunately, Michiko Saga – another star of fifties and early sixties period films – and Mizushima are given nothing to do, their parts amounting to little more than cameos. #2 of 3 films * * 1/2

YAKUZA BEASTS – BLOOD SETTLEMENT aka YAKUZA HIJOSHI – CHI NO KECHAKU 1970 89 min. **Dir.** Ryo Hagiwara **Scr.** Dan Yoshitera **Photo color 'scope:** Nobuo Hoshi **Music:** Hideo Ozawa w/ Noboru Ando, Ryutaro Otomo, Michiko Saga, Juzaburo Akechi,

Ryohei Uchida, Ryosuke Kagawa
An entertaining, but strictly routine
programmer with Ando trying to act
as a stabilizing force against the underhanded yakuza in his district.

Yakuza Beasts (#3)

Ultimately, he once again must go on
a vengeance quest after several of his
brethren, including elder boss
Kagawa, are murdered. Uchida
shines as always, this time as a
contract hitman who is betrayed and
dispatched by his employer after he
has supposedly killed Ando (actually
only grazing him). Ando goes on the
attack on the town's rural outskirts,
and there is great use of a bridge and
grassy hills in this bloodbath finale.
He is also joined by lone wolf Otomo
(another huge *chanbara* star from the
fifties) in wiping out the bad boss's
minions. This climactic fight is very
well-staged, undoubtedly due to
veteran director Hagiwara's expertise
in the samurai genre from the 1930s
onwards. That said, there really isn't

any kind of existential noirish context
here – everything is approached in
a decidedly good-vs.-evil, black
and white vein. It could be that
this simplistic, old-fashioned style
stems from the influence of director
Hagiwara and co-star Otomo. Also
Otomo's swordfighting at the climax
is so over-the-top and gleeful, one
gets the uncomfortable feeling of an
unintentional psychopathic subtext.
Once more actress Saga is underused,
given not much more to do than in
the previous picture.   #3 and final in
series   * * 1/2

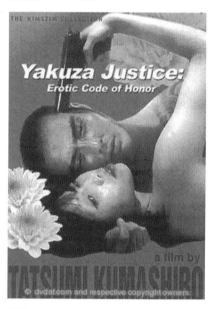

Yakuza Justice - Erotic Code of Honor

**YAKUZA JUSTICE – EROTIC
CODE OF HONOR** aka YAKUZA
GODDESS OF MERCY – WOM-
AN'S HONOR AND HUMANITY
aka YAKUZA KANNON – JO ME
JINGI aka WOMAN'S GAMBLING
CODE 1973 Dir. Tatsumi Kumashiro
Scr. Yoso Tanaka w/ Jiro Okazaki,
Nozomi Yasuda Famous, critically
acclaimed master of the pink/roman

Yakuza Native Ground (#1)

porno genre creates a hybrid sub-genre specimen with a yakuza story.

YAKUZA NATIVE GROUND aka YAKUZA BANGAICHI aka YAKUZA HOME TURF series

YAKUZA NATIVE GROUND aka YAKUZA BANGAICHI aka YAKUZA HOME TURF aka THE LONE REBEL 1969 86 min. DIR. Shugoro Nishimura SCR. Shuichi Nagahara/Tatsuya Asai PHOTO COLOR 'SCOPE: Shohei Ando MUSIC: Rinichiro Manabe w/ Tetsuro Tanba, Kei Sato, Yoko Yamamoto, Akio Hasegawa, Jiro Okazaki, Eiji Go, Kinuko Obata, Eijiro Yanagi, Shoki Fukae, Shiro Yanase
An extremely fast-moving, entertaining example of just exactly what a *gendai* (modern) or *jitsuroku* (true account) yakuza movie should be. Tanba starts out the story as a cynical, almost unprincipled boss recruiting the dregs of the city's hooligans to make up his gang. Soon he reaps the financial rewards. But he gradually pays for his profits by being ostracized by the more ethical yakuza, including his best friend Sato (whom he runs into after many years). Yamamoto is Tanba's sister and is in-love with Hasegawa, a hotheaded, idealistic lieutenant in Sato's gang (Hasegawa seemed to specialize in these roles for a couple of years). Of course, Hasegawa hates Tanba and all he stands for, and Tanba doesn't approve of his sister's choice or her public defiance of him. What makes matters come to a head is a total psychotic jerk who happens to be one of the main men of Tanba's mob. The guy loves to rape women, cause pain and kill people. Not the kind of person you would want to run into in a dark alley. The feud erupts and full-scale nocturnal battles result. Tanba, though not admitting it, begins to regret his actions. Hasegawa is killed by the psycho, and later the psycho is dispatched by one of Sato's cohorts. Sister Yamamoto commits suicide. Sato attempts to kill Tanba. Tanba is vexed to the point of frenzy by his sister's death but still harbors deep feeling for his old friend. So, he does everything he can to avoid injuring him in their duel. Alas, in disarming him, Sato is run through by his own sword. As he dies, Sato tells Tanba he is being exploited and betrayed by the big shots he has fallen in with. Tanba realizes that his desire to be accepted into the heady atmosphere of senior yakuza bosses has warped his vision and destroyed his life as well as the lives of those around him. Grabbing a sword, he heads over to the geisha house/restaurant where the bigwigs congregate and massacres them all before he, himself, is cut down in a literal bath of crimson. Once again, a great effort from underrated director Nishimura. #1 of 2 films * * * 1/2

Yakuza Native Ground (#2)

YAKUZA NATIVE GROUND – KILLING FODDER aka YAKUZA BANGAICHI – MASSATSU aka

SHOWDOWN IN BLOOD 1969
84 min. **DIR.** Kan Hanase **SCR.** Iwao
Yamazaki/Kazuo Nishida **PHOTO
COLOR 'SCOPE:** Izumi Hagiwara
MUSIC: Harumi Ibe w/ Tetsuro
Tanba, Tetsuya Watari, Mitsuko Oka,
Tadao Nakamaru, Ryoji Hayama,
Miyuki Takakura   A fast-moving,
unpretentious and a somewhat more
interesting variation on a standard
yakuza *eiga* plot. Watari attempts
revenge after his senior blood
brothers are ambushed by a rival
gang. He does not succeed, though,
and barely escapes. Boss Tanba is
released from prison and has to deal
with the machinations of two elderly
allied bosses who are bent on turning
Tanba's underbosses Nakamaru and
Hayama against him. Constantly
shifting loyalties and repeated assassination attempts follow. And Tanba
and his underbosses, while not nearly
as dishonorable or dishonest as their
opposition, are still not above torturing one of their enemies with a blowtorch! Nakamaru and Hayama are
also constantly being tested on just
how far they will go to subvert their
principles and loyalties. Once they
both draw the line, they pay for it
with their lives. At the climax, Tanba
and Watari attack a rural *sakazuki*
ceremony where the elderly bosses
are cementing their ties. Director
Hanase stages the fight quite well,
building it into a crescendo inside the
building, then spilling the mayhem
outside with a chase through a ter-
raced garden, the riverside banks
and finally into a concrete aqueduct
where everyone perishes in a golden
sunset massacre. #2 of 2 films
* * *

YAKUZA'S PROFILE aka YAKU-
ZA NO YOKO KAO aka PROFILE
OF A BOSS'S SON 1970 95 min.
DIR. Keiichi Ozawa **SCR.** Ryuzo
Nakanishi **PHOTO COLOR 'SCOPE:**
Kurataro Takamura **MUSIC:**
Rinichiro Manabe w/ Tetsuya
Watari, Joe Shishido, Ryohei Uchida,
Mitsuko Oka, Yoshiko Kayama,
Yoshiro Aoki, Eiji Go, Takehiro
Nakamura, Tsuneya Oki, Reiko Aso
Watari returns from a sojourn at sea
on a cargo ship – which had been
preceded by a short jail term – to
find his dad's gang is still undergoing
hostilities with a rival mob. Watari
is betrayed by a seemingly neutral
boss, then by lone wolf Uchida who
had saved his life. He kills Uchida
in a knifefight, then subsequently his
father is murdered. Aided by seaman friend Shishido, he takes on the
villainous gang. The last scene finds
Watari leaving tearful love interest
Kayama on the pier as he departs to
sea. This is an atmospheric, romantic
saga set on the waterfront similar to
the mood action yakuza films Nikkatsu released with Yujiro Ishihara. But
there are many slow moments that
suck the momentum out of the narrative. It is perversely interesting that
Watari gets involved with Kayama
who coincidentally turns out to be the
estranged mate of Uchida, the ethical killer slotted to dispatch Watari.
But there are elements that diffuse
that tension, including a strange
climax with Watari, Shishido and the
sunglasses-wearing, crippled Aoki
attacking the bad guy HQ, dispatching a few villains but oddly leaving
the two beaten evil bosses alive. Also
bizarre is the overtly homo-erotic
overtones of Watari deciding to leave
the weeping Kayama dockside to

ship out again with carousing buddy, captain Shishido. * * 1/2

YAKUZA'S SONG aka YAKUZA NO UTA 1960 87 min. DIR. Toshio Masuda SCR. Nobuo Yamada PHOTO COLOR 'SCOPE: Kumenobu Fujioka MUSIC: Toshiro Mayuzumi w/ Akira Kobayashi, Nobuo Kaneko, Hideaki Nitani, Izumi Ashikawa, Yoko Minamida, Koji Wada, Taketoshi Naito Kobayashi is a lone wolf out to track his girlfriend's murderer. He has fashioned the bullet that killed her into a pendant he keeps hanging around his neck. Befriending violent young Wada, drunken doctor Kaneko and his daughter Ashikawa, he is hired as a pianist/singer at a club owned by ganglord Naito. Before long, Kobayashi's old pal Nitani, an illegal arms broker for Naito, turns up. Nitani has got a one-armed brother who is tortured by schizo feelings of resentment and inadequacy. In other words, he is sensitive enough to have a decent girlfriend but sick enough to enjoy killing people (!). When he realizes who Kobayashi is looking for, he starts surreptitiously trying to assassinate him. But each attempt ends in failure. Eventually, Kobayashi's snooping around results in a nightclub shootout between Naito's gang and Kobayashi and Wada. Most of the gang is wiped out and the club burned. The one-armed brother's paranoia in full flower, he stabs his girlfriend to death then gives Wada a merciless beating. He challenges Kobayashi to a showdown at the burnt-out husk of a club. Nitani appears, too, but is inadvertently killed. Kobayashi and the one-armed maniac reach a stalemate when Wada abruptly – and conveniently – shows

up to blow the psychopath away. Despite the convoluted narrative, the film is notable for a downbeat storyline and credible cast of characters, something that was harder to do at early sixties Nikkatsu – or any of the formula-obsessed Japanese studios for that matter – than later in the decade. Masuda was becoming one of Nikkatsu's major directors, and his talent for rich narratives is in evidence. That said, there is still something here that doesn't quite gel. Perhaps it is the occasional maudlin sentiment as well as the cardboard thin virtue and inhumanly heroic perfection of Kobayashi who emerges as one of the scenario's least-developed characters. * * 1/2

YAKUZA TEACHER aka YAKUZA SENSEI aka THE REFORMER 1960 106 min. DIR. Akinori Matsuo SCR. Akinori Matsuo/Nobuo Yamada PHOTO COLOR 'SCOPE: Kumenobu Fujioka MUSIC: Toshiro Mayuzumi w/ Yujiro Ishihara, Mie Kitahara, Jukichi Ueno, Tanie Kitabayashi Ishihara returns to work as a counsellor at the private reform school where he spent his youth. He is discouraged at his inability to make a difference, but the head of the school prevails upon him to stick it out. Midway through the saga, a vicious new boy is admitted and, at one point, ends up attacking Kitahara. Soon after a hoodlum comes to spring the boy, and Ishihara is beaten trying to prevent it. In the fall, the staff learns that an airfield is to be built on their site, and the school will close. Trying to prevent this, the head of the school is accidentally killed. The boys and the staff are transferred. Ishihara, who has a questionable past and no teaching credential, is left jobless. He remains upbeat, telling the boys that he will work towards getting a place for all of them once they are released.

YAKUZA WANDERER – VILLAINOUS LIVELIHOOD
aka YAKUZA WATARIDORI – AKUTO KAGYO aka LONER'S JUNCTION aka MISDEED IS MY BUSINESS 1969 83 min. **DIR.** Mio Ezaki **SCR.** Iwao Yamazaki **PHOTO COLOR 'SCOPE:** Minoru Yokoyama **MUSIC:** Masahiko Sato
w/ Akira Kobayashi, Tetsuya Watari, Joe Shishido, Eiji Go, Kazuko Maki, Kayako Sono, Masahiko Tanimura, Nijiko Kiyokawa, Kaku Takashina
A humorous yakuza action melodrama with gangsters, drugs and that old comedy-standby, white slavery.

A YOUNG MAN'S STRONG-HOLD
aka WAKAMONO NO TORIDE 1970 89 min. **DIR.** Toshiya Fujita **SCR.** Toshiya Fujita/ Saburo Kuruusu **PHOTO COLOR 'SCOPE:** Kenji Hagiwara **MUSIC:** Hiroki Teruaki/Jiro Iragashi
w/ Takeo Chii, Renji Ishibashi, Yoko Minamida, Chieko Matsubara, Shinjiro Ebara, Meiko Kaji
Reformed delinquent Chii becomes a private tutor to the troubled Ishibashi, trying to give him benefit of his experience. Ishibashi also has a stepsister (Matsubara) attracted to Chii and a stepbrother (Ebara) engaged to Kaji who is involved in fight promoting. To complicate matters, local councilmen and ambitious teachers attempt to use the troubles at the school for their own ends. A subplot involves Ebara disgraced when found guilty of fixng fights. Ishibashi assaults one of the assemblymen and is shipped off

to reform school with Chii and Matsubara hopeful for his eventual reform.

THE YOUNG, THE BAD AND THE STRANGE
aka WAKA KUTE, WARU KUTE, SUGOI KOI TSURA 1962 86 min. **DIR.** Ko Nakahira **SCR.** Ichiro Ikeda **PHOTO COLOR 'SCOPE:** Shinsaku Himeda **MUSIC:** Toshiro Mayuzumi
w/ Hideki Takahashi, Koji Wada, Masako Izumi, Mayumi Shimizu
More *taiyozoku* (sun tribe) + yakuza style craziness? Seemingly so.

The Young, The Bad and The Strange poster and still

YOUR LIFE aka ANATA NO INOCHI aka YOU ARE MY LIFE 1966 82 min. DIR. Buichi Saito SCR. Yasunari Kawauchi PHOTO COLOR 'SCOPE: Kenji Hagiwara MUSIC: Taiichiro Kosugi w/ Tetsuya Watari, Joe Shishido, Chieko Matsubara, Kei Sato Watari is a nightclub entrepeneur, a fellow with a business of hiring singers and dancers for clubs and cabarets. He is framed for a crime committed by his boss and is sent to prison for a short stay. Upon his release, he sees that the singer/dancer-hiring business has been completely monopolized by a ruthless gang boss. Since all the talent he had formerly worked with and treated well is death-ly afraid of the mobster, Watari can't make any headway at starting things up again. Strangely, it is the gang-ster's bodyguard who gives Watari a tip about a job. Watari saves Matsub-ara from some hooligans and, shortly thereafter, she debuts a singing group which is a huge success on the club circuit. Tragically, Matsubara is found to have leukemia. Watari, still occu-pied with fighting the yakuza, decides to help Matsubara make the trip to see her mother who is living in Hawaii. By the climax, Watari has managed to put her on a plane to fulfill her last wish. A *moodo/akushon* yakuza pic-ture with heavy emphasis on poignant *seishun* romance.

YOUTH OF THE BEAST aka YAJU NO SEISHUN 1963 92 min. DIR. Seijun Suzuki SCR. Ichiro Ikeda/Tadaki Yamazaki PHOTO COLOR 'SCOPE: Kazue Nagatsuka MUSIC: Hajime Okumura w/ Joe Shishido, Ichiro Kijima, Misako Watanabe, Tamio Kawaji, Shoji

Kobayashi, Nobuo Kaneko, Mizuho Suzuki, Hideaki Esumi, Minako Kagawa, Shiro Yanase, Eiji Go, Daisaburo Hirata   One of Suzuki's absolute wildest. It begins in a similar vein to Fritz Lang's THE BIG HEAT with a prominent cop who may be on the take supposedly committing suicide. But Suzuki and his writers supply additional sordidness here by making it a death pact with the lawman's whore mistress. We then witness maniac tough guy Shishido swaggering through squalid streets, surreal nightclubs, campy early-sixties apartments beating-the-shit out of anyone who gives him any lip. He infiltrates two gangs and starts the old YOJINBO/Man with No Name-game of playing one bunch of outlaws off against another. About midway through, it is discovered he is an undercover cop investigating his col-league's death, and guys start tying him upside down to chandeliers and sticking sharp things under his finger-nails. This has many odd interludes including a gangster boss's addict mistress hallucinating a hoodlum skipping playfully away from her with her packet of dope – something that causes her to fall off a stairway landing; Shishido reporting-in to a police substation that is disguised as a knitting school; Shishido using a can of hairspray as improvised blowtorch to torture info out of a movie theater manager on the gang's payroll, etc.,. There is much wild and wooly action choreographed in a riot of carefully selected color and boisterous humor. And it is graced with a downbeat, deliciously ambiguous ending involv-ing Shishido, the suicided cop's wife and villain Kawaji   * * * *

Youth of the Beast

NIKKATSU

PINKU EIGA/ ROMAN PORN YAKUZA HYBRIDS 1972-1980

(TITLES NOT MENTIONED IN THE MAIN NIKKATSU STUDIOS LISTINGS)

CRUEL HIGH SCHOOL GIRL – SEX LYNCHING aka ZANKOKU JOKYO – SEI RINCHI 1975 DIR. Isao Hayashi w/ Naomi Tani, Terumi Azuma

DELINQUENT GIRL – STRAY CAT IN HEAT aka FURYO SHO-JO – NORA NEKO NO SEISHUN 1973 DIR. Chusei Sone w/ Yuko Katagiri,Setsuko Ohyama A girl works for the yakuza as a whore.

FROM THE BACK OR FROM THE FRONT aka USHIRO KARA MAE KARA 1980 DIR. Koyu Ohara w/ Yoko Hatanaka, Yuki Kazamatsuri A delinquent girl tale – with an admirably subtle title – starring well-known-in-Japan pop singer Hatanaka.

GIRL BOSS DETECTIVE – DIRTY MARY aka SUKEBAN DEKA – DIRTI MAARI 1973 DIR. Yasuharu Hasebe w/ Hitomi Azusa, Yuri Yamashina, Junko Miyashita Director Hasebe was a huge fan of director Don Siegel and may have done this as a gender reversal tribute to Siegel's influential Clint Eastwood vehicle, DIRTY HARRY.

GIRL BOSS MAFIA aka SUKEBAN MAFIA series

GIRL BOSS MAFIA aka SUKEBAN MAFIA 1980 DIR. Toshiharu Ikeda w/ Asako Kurayoshi, Yuko Osaki #1 of 2 films

Girl Boss Mafia (#1)

GIRL BOSS MAFIA - DIRTY INSULT aka SUKEBAN MAFIA – CHIYOKU 1980 DIR. Nobuyuki Saito w/ Asako Kurayoshi, Yukiko Mizuki #2 of 2 films

GIRL BOSS SEX VIOLENCE aka SUKEBAN SEKKUSUU BORY-OKU 1973 DIR. Nobuaki Shirai w/ Yuko Katagiri, Masumi Yun, Erina Miyai

LOVE AFFAIR IN PURGATORY aka SAIHATE NO JOJI 1973 DIR. Keiichi Ozawa w/ Maki Kawamura, Keizo Kanie A widow has an affair with a gangster.

ORYU'S PASSION – BONDAGE SKIN aka ORYU JOEN – SHIBARI HADA 1975 DIR. Katsuhiko Fujii w/ Naomi Tani, Terumi Azuma The yakuza rampage in 1920s Osaka.

ROPE aka NAWA series

ROPE HELL aka NAWA JIGOKU 1978 DIR. Koyu Ohara w/ Naomi Tani, Nami Aoki The first of two films with Tani as a tattooed female gambler subjected to S&M abuse from an opposition gang. #1 of 2 films

ROPE AND SKIN aka NAWA TO HADA 1979 DIR. Shugoro Nishimura w/ Naomi Tani, Junko Miyashita, Yuri Yamashina #2 of 2 films

Rope and Skin

SEX CRIME COAST – PIRANHA SCHOOL aka NIKUTAI HANZAI KAIGAN – PIRANHA NO MURE 1973 DIR. Shugoro Nishimura w/ Hitomi Kozue, Masumi Jun

A male gang and female gang carouse at a beach resort, then erupt into violence.

SEX HUNTER – WET TARGET aka SEKKUSU HANTAA – NURE-TA BYOTEKI 1972 DIR. Yukihiro Sawada w/ Joji Sawada, Hiroko Isayama Pinky violence supposedly with motifs plucked from some of the scripts director Sawada helped to write for the STRAY CAT ROCK film series.

TRUE STORY OF A DELIN-QUENT GIRL aka JITSUROKU FURYO SHOJO – KAN 1977 DIR. Toshiya Fujita w/ Tayori Hinatsu, Yuya Uchida Male rock star Yuya Uchida broke into films in the mid-1970s and became a fixture in violent and transgressive independent productions. Reportedly this film is based on the autobiography of real life delinquent, Mako Minato.

True Story of Sex and Violence in a Girls' High School - Ranking Boss

TRUE STORY OF SEX AND
VIOLENCE IN A GIRLS' HIGH
SCHOOL – RANKING BOSS aka
BANKAKU – JOSHI KOKOSEI NO
SEKKUSU TO BORYOKU NO JIT-
TAI 1973 Dir. Koretsugu Kurahara
w/ Hitomi Kozue, Naomi Oka
Unofficial, loose prequel to KANTO
SEX CORPS (see main Nikkatsu
yakuza listings).

True Story of a Woman in Jail (#1)

TRUE STORY OF A WOMAN IN
JAIL aka JITSUROKU ONNA
KANBETSUCHO series

TRUE STORY OF A WOMAN IN
JAIL – SEX HELL aka
JITSUROKU ONNA KANBETSU –
SHO SEI-JIGOKU 1975 Dir. Koyu
Ohara w/ Hitomi Kozue, Meika Seri
First in a trilogy. #1 of 3 films

TRUE STORY OF A WOMAN IN
JAIL CONTINUES aka ZOKU
JITSUROKU ONNA KANBETSU-
CHO 1975 Dir. Koyu Ohara
w/ Hitomi Kozue, Mihoko Arikawa
#2 of 3 films

NEW TRUE STORY OF A
WOMAN IN JAIL –
CONDEMNED TO HELL aka
SHIN JITSUROKU ONNA
KANBETSUCHO – RENGOKU
1976 Dir. Koyu Ohara w/ Hitomi
Kozue, Yuri Yamashina #3 of 3
films

WHITE FEMALE CAT –
ECSTASY AT HIGH NOON aka
SHIROI MESU NEKO – MAHIRU
NO EKKUSTAASI 1975 Dir.
Koyu Ohara w/ Hitomi Kozue, Rie
Tachibana A biker gang girl rocks,
acting out with sex and crime

True Story of a Woman in Jail - Sex Hell

DAIEI STUDIOS

Gambler's Life - Unstoppable Bloodbath

INTRODUCTION

As mentioned in the Nikkatsu Studios introduction, Daiei founder and head Masaichi Nagata had previously been employed by Nikkatsu. There were varying rumors why he left, ranging from Nagata's alleged dissatisfacton with Nikkatsu for arbitrarily firing scores of employees to Nikkatsu's accusations that Nagata had been bribed by rival Shochiku Studios to sabotage Nikkatsu productions. Whatever the case, there were not any complaints from Nagata's quarter when Nikkatsu's filmmaking capability was basically subverted when Nagata's 1942 counterproposal was accepted by the government to merge existing filmmaking concerns into four companies.

In the ensuing postwar years, Daiei head Nagata was often vilified as being a philistine, primarily for his failure to recognize the artistic achievement or worldwide success potential of RASHOMON, one of Akira Kurosawa's rare efforts with the company. To be fair to Nagata, whatever his faults – which were many – he still was the man responsible for greenlighting Kenji Mizoguchi's final great projects and giving groundbreaking directors such as Kon Ichikawa and Yasuzo Masumura a generous amount of artistic freedom.

Nagata also promoted the period samurai and *jidai-geki* film like no other studio, not even Toei. Daiei's period films, although often falling into formulaic scenarios, retained a high degree of intelligence, an exceptional beauty of form and drew from an amazing stable of directors that included such talents as veterans Daisuke Ito, Kazuo Mori, Teinosuke Kinugasa and Kimiyoshi Yasuda as well as first class newcomers Kenji Misumi, Kazuo Ikehiro, Tokuzo Tanaka and Akira Inoue. Nagata was also responsible for helping to promote the careers of a number of great performers, amongst them the legendary Shintaro Katsu, Raizo Ichikawa and Ayako Wakao

In the early fifties, many of Daiei's period films such as Kurosawa's RASHOMON (1950), Kozaburo Yoshimura's TALE OF GENJI (GENJI MONOGATARI, 1951), Mizoguchi's UGETSU (1953) and Teinosuke Kinugasa's GATE OF HELL (JIGOKU MON, 1953) were huge hits on the international festival circuit.

Daiei's sixties output featured a large percentage of consistently high quality genre pieces, a parade of brilliant "outlaw" cinema, frequently set in-period – samurai films (including the ZATOICHI/BLIND SWORDSMAN, KYOSHIRO NEMURI/ SLEEPY EYES OF DEATH AKA SON OF THE BLACK MASS and NINJA/SHINOBI NO MONO series), *ninkyo* yakuza, *kaidans* – amazing pictures that delivered on thrills but possessed a high degree of taste and intelligence.

Starting in the late sixties, Daiei coincidentally fell on hard times much the same as their former rivals, Nikkatsu. In 1971, they, too, were forced to shut down general production. Masaichi Nagata still produced a few high profile films in the ensuing decade, but for all intents and purposes, the heyday of Daiei's golden age was over.

Period and Prestige...

DAIEI Studios

ACROSS DARKNESS aka YAMI
O YOKOGIRE 1959 103 min. **DIR.**
Yasuzo Masumura **SCR.** Yasuzo
Masumura/Ryuzo Kikushima
PHOTO COLOR 'SCOPE: Hiroshi
Murai **w/** Hiroshi Kawaguchi, Sô
Yamamura, Junko Kano, Osamu
Takizawa, Hideo Takamatsu

Across Darkness

BADGE OF THE DEVIL aka
AKUMA KARA NO KUNSHO
1967 **DIR.** Mitsuo Murayama **SCR.**
Kimiyuki Hasegawa **PHOTO B&W**
'SCOPE: Hiroshi Ishida **MUSIC:**
Seitaro Omori **w/** Jiro Tamiya,
Kyoko Enami, Eiko Azusa, Yuko
Hamada, Mike Daneen, Koji
Fujiyama, Toru Abe This may be
more of an action/suspense mystery

thriller.

BADGE OF THE NIGHT aka
YORU NO KUNSHO 1965
86 min. **DIR.** Tetsutaro Murano
SCR. Giichi Fujimoto/Kikuma
Shimoizaka **PHOTO 'SCOPE:**
Yoshihisa Nakagawa **MUSIC:** Tadashi
Yamauchi **w/** Jiro Tamiya, Shigeru
Amachi, Misako Watanabe, Mikio
Narita, Chizuru Hayashi, Junichiro
Yamashita, Fujio Suga

BAD REPUTATION aka
AKUMYO series

BAD REPUTATION aka
AKUMYO aka TOUGH GUY
1961 94 min. **DIR.** Tokuzo Tanaka
SCR. Yoshikata Yoda **PHOTO COLOR**
'SCOPE: Kazuo Miyagawa **MUSIC:**
Akira Ifukube **w/** Shintaro Katsu,
Jiro Tamiya, Tamao Nakamura,
Yoshie Mizutani, Michiko Ai, Yasuko
Nakata, Chieko Naniwa, Mayumi
Kurata, Fujio Suga
Katsu is a young, rowdy but decent
roughneck engaged in various "endeavors" after the war, paired with his
best buddy, matinee-idol handsome
Tamiya and frequently a girlfriend.
They are usually involved with *tekiya*
(street-peddling contingent of yakuza)
selling black market items. He and his
pals often rub up against violent and
unprincipled yakuza opposition.
Although there is drama (or melodrama) in the BAD REPUTATION films,
the tone is often lighthearted with
much boisterous humor punctuating
events. Scenarist Yoda wasn't a run-
of-the-mill screenwriter – he is best
known for his script collaborations
with the late, great Kenji Mizoguchi.
Consequently, though his stories are

full of well-drawn characters and pungent dialogue, there is not alot of the bloody violence one finds in most yakuza films. The violence that does exist in the series is more often of the barroom brawl/back alley fisticuffs variety than the sword/knife/gun action usually seen. #1 of 16 films * * *

ANOTHER BAD REPUTATION STORY aka ZOKU AKUMYO 1961 93 min. DIR. Tokuzo Tanaka SCR. Yoshikata Yoda PHOTO COLOR 'SCOPE: Kazuo Miyagawa MUSIC: Hajime Kaburagi w/ Shintaro Katsu, Jiro Tamiya, Tamao Nakamura, Yoshie Mizutani #2 of 16 films * * *

Bad Reputation (#3) aka New Bad Reputation

A NEW BAD REPUTATION STORY aka SHIN AKUMYO 1962 99 min. DIR. Kazuo Mori SCR. Yoshikata Yoda PHOTO COLOR 'SCOPE: Hiroshi Imai MUSIC: Ichiro

Saito w/ Shintaro Katsu, Jiro Tamiya, Tamao Nakamura, Masayo Banri, Yuko Hamada, Reiko Fujiwara, Fujio Suga Since Tamiya's character was killed in the preceding opus, he begins portraying the character's twin brother here (which continues until near the end of the series). #3 of 16 films * * 1/2

Bad Reputation (#4) aka Another New Bad Reputation Story

ANOTHER NEW BAD REPUTA-TION STORY aka ZOKU – SHIN AKUMYO 1962 99 min. DIR. Tokuzo Tanaka SCR. Yoshikata Yoda PHOTO COLOR 'SCOPE: Senkichiro Takeda MUSIC: Hajime Kaburagi w/ Shintaro Katsu, Jiro Tamiya, Reiko Fujiwara, Mieko Kondo, Yoshie Mizutani, Michiko Ai, Chocho Miyako #4 of 16 films * * 1/2

BAD REPUTATION OF THE BIG THREE aka DAISAN NO AKUMYO 1963 89 min. DIR. Tokuzo Tanaka SCR. Yoshikata Yoda

PHOTO COLOR 'SCOPE: Kazuo Miyagawa **MUSIC:** Hajime Kaburagi w/ Shintaro Katsu, Jiro Tamiya, Hiroyuki Nagato, Reiko Fujiwara, Yumeji Tsukioka   #5 of 16 films

Bad Reputation (#5) aka Bad Reputation of the Big Three

BAD REPUTATION MARKET-PLACE aka AKUMYO ICHIBA 1963 89 min. **DIR.** Kazuo Mori **SCR.** Yoshikata Yoda **PHOTO COLOR 'SCOPE:** Hiroshi Imai w/ Shintaro Katsu, Jiro Tamiya, Michiko Saga, Minoru Shiraki, Kyoko Enami, Reiko Fujiwara, Ganosuke Ashiya, Kogen Ashiya, Makoto Fujita, Haruo Tanaka, Ryuzo Shimada   #6 of 16 films

BAD REPUTATION HARBOR aka AKUMYO HATOBA 1963 92 min. **DIR.** Kazuo Mori **SCR.** Yoshikata Yoda **PHOTO COLOR 'SCOPE:** Shozo Honda **MUSIC:** Ichiro Saito w/ Shintaro Katsu, Jiro Tamiya, Eiko Taki, Makoto Fujita,

Reiko Fujiwara, Keiko Yumi, Hiroshi Mizuhara, Michi Aoyama, Nijiko Kiyokawa, Saburo Date #7 of 16 films

NUMBER ONE BAD REPUTA-TION aka AKUMYO ICHIBAN 1963 91 min. **DIR.** Tokuzo Tanaka **SCR.** Yoshikata Yoda **PHOTO COLOR 'SCOPE:** Senkichiro Takeda **MUSIC:** Hajime Kaburagi w/ Shintaro Katsu, Jiro Tamiya, Kyoko Enami, Reiko Fujiwara, Keiko Yukishiro, Taro Marui, Toru Abe, Hiroshi Nawa, Tatsuo Endo #8 of 16 films

BAD REPUTATION – THE BIG DRUM aka AKUMYO DAIKO 1964 85 min. **DIR.** Kazuo Mori **SCR.** Yoshikata Yoda **PHOTO COLOR 'SCOPE:** Hiroshi Imai **MUSIC:** Ichiro Saito w/ Shintaro Katsu, Jiro Tamiya, Yukiji Asaoka, Yuko Hamada, Kazuko Wakamatsu, Ganosuke Ashiya, Kogen Ashiya, Bontaro Miake #9 of 16 films

FLAG OF BAD REPUTATION aka AKUMYO NOBORI aka NOTORIOUS MEN STRIKE AGAIN 1965 81 min. **DIR.** Tokuzo Tanaka **SCR.** Yoshikata Yoda **PHOTO COLOR 'SCOPE:** Kazuo Miyagawa **MUSIC:** Hajime Kaburagi w/ Shintaro Katsu, Jiro Tamiya, Kei Sato, Yoshie Mizutani, Chocho Miyako, Ryuzo Shimada, Jotaro Senba, Asao Uchida #10 of 16 films

BAD REPUTATION – INVINCIBLE aka AKUMYO MUTEKI 1965 83 min. **DIR.** Tokuzo Tanaka **SCR.** Yoshikata Yoda **PHOTO COLOR 'SCOPE:** Kazuo Miyagawa **MUSIC:** Hajime Kaburagi w/ Shintaro Katsu, Jiro Tamiya,

Kaoru Yachigusa, Shiho Fujimura, Takuya Fujioka, Jotaro Senba, Koichi Mizuhara, Tokubei Hanazawa #11 of 16 films * * 1/2

BAD REPUTATION – CHERRY BLOSSOMS aka AKUMYO SAKURA 1966 85 min. Dir. Tokuzo Tanaka Scr. Yoshikata Yoda Photo color 'scope: Kazuo Miyagawa Music: Hajime Kaburagi w/ Shintaro Katsu, Jiro Tamiya, Etsuko Ichihara, Takuya Fujioka, Sadako Sawamura, Fujio Suga, Jun Tatara #12 of 16 films * * 1/2

LIFE OF BAD REPUTATION aka AKUMYO ICHIDAI 1967 84 min. Dir. Kimiyoshi Yasuda Scr. Yoshikata Yoda Photo color 'scope: Chishi Makiura Music: Hajime Kaburagi w/ Shintaro Katsu, Jiro Tamiya, Mitsuko Mori, Asao Koike, Isamu Nagato, Mikiko Tsubouchi, Yuko Hamada, Yuzo Hayakawa, Asao Koike, Kichijiro Ueda #13 of 16 films * * 1/2

EIGHTEEN BAD REPUTATIONS aka AKUMYO JUHACHIBAN aka NOTORIOUS MEN RETURN 1968 86 min. Dir. Kazuo Mori Scr. Yoshikata Yoda Photo color 'scope: Hiroshi Imai Music: Hajime Kaburagi w/ Shintaro Katsu, Jiro Tamiya, Michiyo Yasuda, Mitsuko Mori, Ko Nishimura, Makoto Fujita, Ryunosuke Kanada, Saburo Date Co-star Tamiya's last entry in the series. Strange, since there was still one more Daiei-produced BAD REPU-TATION film to come, and Tamiya was still under contract to the studio. Friction with co-star Katsu? #14 of 16 films

BAD REPUTATION – SHOW-DOWN OF THE BEST aka AKUMYO ICHIBAN SHOBU 1969 95 min. Dir. Masahiro Makino Scr. Ichiro Miyagawa/Masahiro Makino Photo color 'scope: Hiroshi Imai Music: Hajime Kaburagi w/ Shintaro Katsu, Kyoko Enami, Michiyo Yasuda, Takahiro Tamura, Masahiko Tsugawa, Seizaburo Kawazu, Michitaro Mizushima, Nobuo Kaneko, Mayumi Ogawa, Asao Uchida, Kenjiro Ishiyama, Ryutaro Gomi

Bad Reputation (#15) aka Showdown of the Best

The last installment of the series at Daiei. Several of the studio's other big stars: Enami, Yasuda (since 1980 or so she has been using her married name, Okusu), Tamura are on hand for farewell festivities. Director Makino, who had been helming productions at Toei all through the sixties, directed several films at both Daiei and Nikkatsu during those studios' final days (1970 – '71). Along with Toei's Kosaku Yamashita, Tai Kato and Shigehiro Ozawa, Makino was regarded as one of the masters of the *ninkyo* (chivalrous)-type yakuza picture. You would think that this film would be better considering his involvement. However, the action sequences are too short and few and far between; even the usual trademark battle royale that climaxes *ninkyo* films is given short shrift. Perhaps Katsu and Makino were trying to do something a little different. However, the whole film seems hurried, lackluster, everyone-just-going-through-the-motions. Luckily, the cast is probably one of the best to grace any entry in the series so things even out. #15 of 16 films * * 1/2

BAD REPUTATION – TURF WARS aka AKUMYO NAWA-BARI ARASHI aka NOTORIOUS DRAGON 1974 104 min. **DIR.** Yasuzo Masumura **SCR.** Yoshikata Yoda **PHOTO COLOR 'SCOPE:** Kazuo Miyagawa **MUSIC:** Isao Tomita w/ Shintaro Katsu, Kinya Kitaoji, Yukiyo Toake, Haruko Sugimura, Shuji Otaki, Joji Ai, Ganjiro Nakamura, Kiwako Taichi, Hiroko Isayama, Ichiro Zaitsu, Kenji Imai Katsu Productions and Masumura (formerly a Daiei director) resurrected the series at Toho for the 16th and final entry. It is basically a remake of the first two films linked together, with Kitaoji stepping into Tamiya's role. The time frame is just before WW2, the period of imperialist military actions in Manchuria. Katsu was already at Toho producing the LONE WOLF AND CUB series with his brother, Tomisaburo Wakayama (1972 – '74); starring-in and pro-

ducing the three RAZOR HANZO (GOYO KIBA) films (1972 – '74); and starring-in/producing three more ZATOICHI pictures, In addition, there was the Katsu-produced revival of the HOODLUM SOLDIER series, HOODLUM SOLDIER – FIRING LINE (1972), also with Masumura directing. This is one of the best BAD REPUTATION films. #16 and last of series   * * *

Band of Pure-Hearted Hoodlums

BAND OF PURE-HEARTED HOODLUMS aka GURENTAI JUNJO HA 1963 DIR. Yasuzo Masumura SCR. Yasuzo Masumura/ Mitsuro Kodaki PHOTO B&W 'SCOPE: Setsuo Kobayashi MUSIC: Sei Ikeno w/ Kojiro Hongo, Jun Fujimaki, Jotaro Senba, Karo Otsuji, Eriko Sanjo, Ganjiro Nakamura, Zeko Nakamura, Osamu Ogawa, Keiko Yuge, Yuko Hamada

BEAST'S WOUNDS aka KIZU TSU ITA YAJU 1960 DIR. Taro Yuge SCR. Kikuma Shimoizaka PHOTO 'SCOPE: Hiroshi Ishida MUSIC: Tetsuo Tsukahara w/ Jun Negami, Akihiko Katayama, Hiroko Miki

Bitches' Escape

BITCHES' ESCAPE aka MESU INU DASSO 1965 DIR. Taro Yuge Scr. Kazuo Funabashi PHOTO B&W 'SCOPE: Setsuo Kobayashi MUSIC: Sei Ikeno w/ Miwa Takada, Mikiko Tsubouchi, Eiko Taki,

Masayo Banri, Mikio Narita, Masako Myojo Judging from the photos and poster, there is a good chance this is either a saga of female convicts on the lam or a tale of oppressed prostitutes escaping from their gangster pimps. It does feature quite a few of Daiei's leading ladies of the time.

BLACKNESS aka KURO series

Black Test Car

BLACK TEST CAR aka KURO NO TESUTO KAA 1962 95 min. DIR. Yasuzo Masumura SCR. Kazuo Funabashi/Yoshihiro Ishimatsu PHOTO B&W 'SCOPE: Yoshihisa Nakagawa w/ Jiro Tamiya, Eiji Funakoshi, Junko Kano, Ichiro Sugai, Hideo Takamatsu The first in a series dealing with business espionage and murder – one of the many provinces of the modern yakuza. There are few overt yakuza references in most of the pictures, but the organized crime on display is certainly gangster territory. The tone is noirish, the scenarios a hybrid of suspense thriller and mystery. In this first outing, an auto firm suffers sabotage in their test car division for new models. Masumura's treatment, bordering on deconstruction, eschews cliches for concise economic visuals and his customary dry, ironic humor. Recognized by critics for his more serious "art" films, Masumura was no cultural snob and made many genre films – nearly all of them anarchic, fast-moving and witty. This first entry is gutwrenching, with a snowballing cascade of double-crosses, auto executives betraying each other at the slightest hint of getting ahead. The ending is particularly powerful. Although Masumura apparently had an axe to grind aesthetically with fellow Daiei cinema maestro, Kon Ichikawa, who also made genre films, their visual style, sense of humor and outlook often dovetails. #1 of 11 films * * * 1/2

Black Statement Book (#2)

BLACK STATEMENT BOOK aka KURO NO HOKOKUSHO 1963 94 min. **DIR.** Yasuzo Masumura **SCR.** Yoshihiro Ishimatsu **PHOTO B&W 'SCOPE:** Yoshihisa Nakagawa **MUSIC:** Sei Ikeno w/ Ken Utsui, Junko Kano, Hideo Takamatsu, Bontaro Miake, Mieko Kondo, Keiko Yuge, Eitaro Ozawa #2 of 11 films

Black Money (#3)

BLACK MONEY aka KURO NO SATSUTABA 1963 **DIR.** Mitsuo Murayama **SCR.** Hajime Takaiwa **PHOTO B&W 'SCOPE:** Nobuo Munekawa w/ Keizo Kawazaki, Eriko Sanjo, Kazuko Miyagawa, Hideo Takamatsu, Reiko Fujiwara, Shiro Otsuji, Ko Sugita #3 of 11 films

BLACK DEAD BALL aka KURO NO SHIKYU 1963 **DIR.** Harumi Mizuho **SCR.** Kozo Taguchi **PHOTO B&W 'SCOPE:** Yoshihisa Nakagawa w/ Ken Utsui, Yukiko Fuji, Isao Kuraishi, Mieko Kondo,

Yoshiro Kitahara, Akitake Kono, Ichiro Sugai #4 of 11 films

BLACK TRADEMARK aka KURO NO SHOHYO 1963 Dir. Taro Yuge Scr. Kimiyuki Hasegawa Photo B&W 'scope: Hiroshi Ishida w/ Ken Utsui, Yukiko Fuji, Hideo Takamatsu, Kyoko Enami, Jun Hamamura #5 of 11 films

BLACK PARKING LOT aka KURO NO CHUSHA JO aka LIPS OF RUIN 1963 85 min. Dir. Taro Yuge Scr. Seiji Hoshikawa Photo B&W 'scope: Hiroshi Ishida Music: Sei Ikeno w/ Jiro Tamiya, Yukiko Fuji, Bontaro Miake, Yasuko Nakada, Takashi Nakamura, Jotaro Senba, Eitaro Ozawa   Tamiya is a reformed, educated gangster who becomes partners with the manager of a pharmaceutical company about to put a wonder drug on the market. When Tamiya refuses to merge with the pharmaceutical corporation, his interests are taken over by a ruthless entrepeneur. Tamiya's mentor dies shortly thereafter under mysterious circumstances.Tamiya then enlists the help of a female investigative reporter to find the truth. The company's new unscupulous owner puts the drug on the market without testing it, and Tamiya forces him to temporarily withdraw it from circulation. Between a rock and a hard place, Tamiya is eventually forced to join hands with a rival pharmaceutical company run by a cold-hearted woman. #6 of 11 films

BLACK SPEEDING aka KURO NO BAKUSO aka BLACK RIDERS 1964 89 min. Dir. Sokichi

Tomimoto Scr. Kazuo Funabashi Photo B&W 'scope: Yoshihisa Nakagawa Music: Sei Ikeno w/ Jiro Tamiya, Noriko Fujita, Jun Fujimaki, Akira Natsuki, Eiko Taki, Jotaro Senba, Shiro Otsuji Director Tomimoto specialized in mystery films for Daiei. Unfortunately, I have yet to see any of his pictures. #7 of 11 films

BLACK CHALLENGER aka KURO NO CHOSENSHA 1964 Dir. Mitsuo Murayama Scr. Toshio Matsuura/Yoshihiro Ishimatsu w/ Jiro Tamiya, Mikiko Tsubouchi, Naoko Kubo, Reiko Fujiwara, Ryuzo Shimada #8 of 11 films

BLACK WEAPON aka KURO NO KYOKI 1964 82 min. Dir. Akira Inoue Scr. Kazuo Funabashi/ Michio Kotaki Photo B&W 'scope: Fujio Morita Music: Yoshiaki Otsuka w/ Jiro Tamiya, Reiko Fujiwara, Nobuo Kaneko, Ryuzo Shimada #9 of 11 films

BLACK TRUMP CARD aka KURO NO KIRI FUDA 1964 88 min. Dir. Umeji Inoue Scr. Kimiyuki Hasegawa Photo B&W 'scope: Toru Watanabe Music: Yoshitaka Akimitsu w/ Jiro Tamiya, Ken Utsui, Junichiro Yamashita, Kyosuke Machida, Masayo Banri, #10 of 11 films

Black Trump Card (#10)

Black Trump Card (#10)

BLACK MARK SUPER EXPRESS

aka KURO NO CHOTOKKYU aka
SUPER EXPRESS 1964 93 min.
DIR. Yasuzo Masumura SCR. Yoshio
Shirasaka/Yasuzo Masumura PHOTO
B&W 'SCOPE: Setsuo Kobayashi
MUSIC: Tadashi Yamanouchi

w/ Jiro Tamiya, Yukiko Fuji, Eiji
Funakoshi, Daisuke Kato, Jotaro
Senba, Tatsuya Ishiguro, Fujio
Harumoto, Yuzo Hayakawa

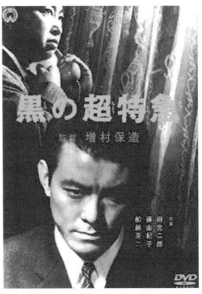

*Blackness (#11) aka Black Mark Super
Express Japanese DVD art*

Tamiya is a real-estate agent tricked
by a development company into
purchasing a vast holding of farmers'
land, supposedly for an auto plant
but, in reality, for resale at a huge
profit to the government for their
express train. Tamiya attempts to
extract "quiet" money from Funakoshi, head of the corporation, but
is turned down. Next he tries to use
Funakoshi's mistress Fuji as leverage. Kato, Funakoshi's enforcer subsequently strangles Fuji when she,
too, requests "financial assistance."
Incredibly enough, it transpires
the prudent Tamiya had had a tape
recorder going in her apartment, and
thus her murder had been preserved
for posterity. He turns it over to the
police so they can arrest Funakoshi
and Kato, and returns to his home-

town, regretting his greed that helped cause Fuji's death. Threadbare on the budget end, but remains a trenchant business espionage thriller from Masumura, employing all his concise, sharp observations of deception and the nasty games even comparatively decent people get caught up in when they smell the scent of easy money. #11 and final in series * * *

BLACK TEMPTATION aka KUROI YUWAKU 1965 84 min. **DIR.** Umeji Inoue **SCR.** Umeji Inoue/ Taguchi Kozo **PHOTO 'SCOPE:** Toru Watanabe **MUSIC:** Harumi Ibe w/ Jiro Tamiya, Kyoko Enami, Machiko Hasegawa, Sanae Nakahara, Yoshio Kitahara, Yuka Konno, Fujio Murakami, Manabu Morita, Bontaro Miake Despite the title, this is not listed in the Japanese film reference books as being part of the previous BLACK-NESS series.

THE BOGUS POLICEMAN aka NISE KEIJI 1967 **DIR.** Satsuo Yamamoto **SCR.** Hajime Takaiwa **PHOTO B&W 'SCOPE:** Setsuo Kobayashi **MUSIC:** Masanobu Higurashi w/ Shintaro Katsu, Michiko Sugata, Yunosuke Ito, Daisuke Kato   Katsu is a cop dismissed from the force after his gun is stolen while he rescues a boy from drowning. The gun is later used in a murder. Soon after, Katsu comes to the aid of a woman being attacked by hoodlums. He gets in deeper trouble when she is injured and one of her kindergarten students is kidnapped by the gangsters. Katsu then really goes on the rampage, impersonating a cop to track the hoods and get the

boy back. He inadvertently uncovers political corruption while doing this, but gains the respect of the girl. However, he faces jailtime for his legal indiscretions.

BOSS OF HADES aka MEIDO NO KAOYAKU 1957 **DIR.** Mitsuo Murayama **SCR.** Hajime Takaiwa **PHOTO:** Kazuo Miyagawa **MUSIC:** Tokujiro Kubo w/ Koji Tsuruta, Yasuko Kawagami, Osamu Murayama, Ikuko Mori, Satoko Minami, Hideo Takamatsu

BROKEN PROMISSORY NOTE aka YABURE SHOMON 1966 **DIR.** Shigeo Tanaka **SCR.** Ryozo Kasahara **PHOTO 'SCOPE:** Michio Takahashi **MUSIC:** Kazuo Kitamura w/ Kojiro Hongo, Michiko Sugata, Hizuru Takachiho, Mikio Narita, Jotaro Senba, Bontaro Miake

A CERTAIN KILLER aka ARU KOROSHI YA aka TO BE A HITMAN series

A CERTAIN KILLER aka ARU KOROSHI YA aka TO BE A HITMAN 1967 82 min. **DIR.** Kazuo Mori **SCR.** Yasuzo Masumura/ Yoshihiro Ishimatsu **PHOTO COLOR 'SCOPE:** Kazuo Miyagawa **MUSIC:** Hajime Kaburagi w/ Raizo Ichikawa, Mikio Narita, Yumiko Nogawa, Asao Koike, Yukiko Kobayashi   Ichikawa plays a stoic WW2 kamikaze veteran turned existentialist hitman working on the fringes of two different yakuza clans. He gets involved in a strange triangle with a backstabbing whore (Nogawa) and a weak-willed opportunist

(Narita), ends up turning the tables on them and everyone else. Poisonously witty dialogue adds to the proceedings. #1 of 2 films * * * 1/2

A Certain Killer (#2) - Killer's Key

A KILLER'S KEY aka ARU KOROSHI YA NO KAGI aka KEY TO BEING A HITMAN 1967 79 min. **DIR.** Kazuo Mori **SCR.** Mitsuro Kodaki **PHOTO COLOR** 'SCOPE: Kazuo Miyagawa **MUSIC:** Hajime Kaburagi w/ Raizo Ichikawa, Ichiro Nakatani, Ko Nishimura, Tomomi Sato, Isao Yamagata, Yoshio Kaneuchi, Asao Uchida, Saburo Date
Ichikawa is hired to assassinate the boss of a large firm at a public reception and manages the deed with a poison needle to the base of the skull. Soon after, he develops numerous liabilities with betraying employers and pursuing law enforcement. A good suspense thriller but lacking the venomously twisted character inter-action screenwriters Masumura and

Ishimatsu brought to the first picture. #2 of 2 films * * *

THE DARING NUN aka AMA KUZURE 1968 83 min. **DIR.** Kazuo Ikehiro **SCR.** Kazuo Funabashi/ Tetsuo Yoshida **PHOTO B&W** 'SCOPE: Senkichiro Takeda **MUSIC:** Takeo Watanabe w/ Michiyo Yasuda, Kayo Mikimoto, Ichiro Nakatani, Shigako Shimegi, Naomi Kobayashi
A liberal nun (Yasuda) believes that the cloistered religious know little about the real world, and she makes a habit of going to explore life outside her convent. She soon saves a young woman (Mikimoto) from the clutches of a gangster named Goro (Nakatani). While out on one of her trips, a fresh man makes a pass and is rejected. He reports Yasuda to her mother superior who, it transpires, is also of a liberal persuasion. The mother superior does nothing to reprimand Yasuda. Goro soon makes waves about getting Mikimoto back from the nunnery. Yasuda agrees to go to bed with Goro if he'll give up on retaking Mikimoto. Before he can make any real moves, one of his many female victims stabs him and he dies.

DOG aka INU series

HOMELESS DOG aka YADO-NASHI INU aka GUTTER DOG aka I STAND ALONE 1964 91 min. **DIR.** Tokuzo Tanaka **SCR.** Giichi Fujimoto **PHOTO B&W** 'SCOPE: Senkichiro Takeda **MUSIC:** Tetsuo Tsukahara w/ Jiro Tamiya, Shigeru Amachi, Kyoko Enami, Mikio Narita, Sumiko Sakamoto, Michitaro Mizushima, Ryuzo Shimada

A yakuza action series about a lone wolf gunman featuring popular BAD REPUTATION co-star, Tamiya. Unlike many yakuza series, Tamiya actually portrays the same character in every movie. In the first outing, he seems to be a bit green in the ways of gangdom, falling-in-love with a woman caught between two rival mobs. His interference helps the Numano Group, and, in thanks, they offer him a job. When he discovers the rival Daiko Group are the men responsible for tearing down his mother's cemetery to build a golf course, he accepts. Before long, he realizes the Numano gang, too, are nothing but vicious hoods, and he leaves to search for his girl. When he finds her, he discovers that because her brother belongs to the Daiko gang, she is trapped. Helping her to escape results in her brother's death. The Daiko men want the girl back and agree to a one-on-one duel with Tamiya. When they show up with the whole gang, Tamiya is left with no choice but to open fire. Miraculously, he survives, having dispatched his enemies. However, he is arrested by the police and is led away as his distraught lover weeps. From the above synopsis (paraphrased from one in a Pacific Film Archives catalogue), you might think this was a fairly serious scenario. I don't know about this initial entry, but the later films in the series – at least starting with RAMPAGING DOG are fairly lightweight in tone. There is a bit of drama, but alot more humor accompanies the action.   #1 of 9 films

Dog (#2) aka **Fighting Dog**

FIGHTING DOG aka KENKA INU aka VIOLENT DOG 1964 89 min. **DIR.** Mitsuo Murayama **SCR.** Giichi Fujimoto **PHOTO B&W** 'SCOPE: Kimio Watanabe **MUSIC:** Keiji Tsuchihashi w/ Jiro Tamiya, Yuko Hamada, Katsuo Uno, Sumiko Sakamoto, Junichiro Yamashita, Ryoichi Tamagawa, Tatsuo Endo, Mikio Narita, Manabu Morita, Jotaro Senba   #2 of 9 films

ROGUE DOG aka GOROTSUKI INU aka RUFFIAN DOG aka A DEDICATED GUNMAN 1965 88 min. **DIR.** Tetsutaro Murano **SCR.** Giichi Fujimoto **PHOTO COLOR** 'SCOPE: Setsuo Kobayashi **MUSIC:** Tadashi Yamauchi w/ Jiro Tamiya, Shigeru Amachi, Kyoko Enami, Jun Negami, Yoshie Mizutani, Mikio Narita   Tamiya, overhearing some mobsters discussing their having to hide out due to a policeman's murder, encounters a rich, beautiful widow. It turns out this widow isn't all she appears to be. However, she claims she is in fear for her life – her husband was supposedly killed by the very same gangsters on whom Tamiya had eavesdropped. Having made some very substantial loans to the hoodlums, he had been eliminated in lieu of repayment. The widow implores Tamiya to murder the three top men, all notorious loan sharks and blackmailers of corporations. When a cop approaches Tamiya and asks him basically the same thing, his curiosity gets the better of him. Before he knows it, he is framed for another mob chieftain's murder. Eventually everything is sorted out when the police attack the gang's HQ. And Tamiya discovers the real power behind the mob is the widow. #3 of 9 films

RAMPAGING DOG aka ABARE INU 1965 92 min. **DIR.** Kazuo Mori **SCR.** Giichi Fujimoto **PHOTO COLOR 'SCOPE:** Hiroshi Imai **MUSIC:** Mitsuru Furutani **w/** Jiro Tamiya, Mitsuko Kusabue, Katsuko Kanai, Sumiko Sakamoto, Chocho Miyako, Shiro Osaka, Fujio Suga, Jiro Takagi, Ryuzo Shimada, Kogen Ashiya An occasionally amusing trifle with Tamiya trying to find out why a lone wolf gunman he had befriended at a flophouse was murdered. He hooks up with the dead man's gal, a dancer/singer at a shady nightclub. She is a total innocent considering the milieu she works in. She is also quite a dancer, ala Cyd Charisse, with some enormously entertaining, unintentionally campy musical numbers thrown into the mix. That and a shooting contest between the one-armed proprietor and Tamiya in the deserted bar are the only things that keep this from being a total washout. Tamiya is depicted as such an impossibly skillful crackshot as well as such a nice guy, it gets a bit tiresome. Tamiya just shoots the guns out of his enemies' hands (!) – a charmingly naive and totally hokey visual conceit that went out of style here in the U.S. sometime in the late 1940s with Saturday cowboy matinees. #4 of 9 films * *

GUN DOG aka TEPPO INU 1965 83 min. **DIR.** Tetsutaro Murano **SCR.** Giichi Fujimoto **PHOTO COLOR 'SCOPE:** Setsuo Kobayashi **MUSIC:** Shunsuke Kikuchi **w/** Jiro Tamiya, Shigeru Amachi, Shoichi Ozawa, Junichiro Yamashita, Sumiko Sakamoto, Tanie Kitabayashi, Michiko Sugata, Toru Abe, Yuzo Hayakawa Tamiya tries to help find a fellow lone wolf on the outs with local mob chief Abe. About midway through, the fellow is killed, and Tamiya concentrates on trying to help the man's sweet sister. Abe and cohorts try to frame Tamiya for another killing. While still fairly light in tone, this film has a much better balance in the action, drama and comedy departments. The humor is actually somewhat funny. Tamiya once more demonstrates his fantastic shooting ability, and Amachi is cast against type as a rumpled, scruffy police detective (I wonder if the creators of "Columbo" ever saw this?) who keeps turning up in the most unlikely places. Some great location work and the pacing keep interest from flagging. #5 of 9 films * * 1/2

RETURN OF GUN DOG aka
ZOKU TEPPO INU 1966 DIR.
Mitsuo Murayama SCR. Giichi
Fujimoto PHOTO COLOR 'SCOPE:
Hiroshi Ishida MUSIC: Seitaro Omori
w/ Jiro Tamiya, Shigeru Amachi,
Sumiko Sakamoto, Naoko Kubo,
Seizaburo Kawazu, Jotaro Senba,
Mayumi Nagisa, Yaeko Wakamizu,
Hiroshi Tachihara   This starts right
off with slambang action in a car
chase and mob-hijacking of another
gang's illicit jade shipment on a deserted stretch of highway. A gunfight
is broken up by intrepid, grizzled
police detective Amachi (reprising his
Colombo-esque role from the previous entry)who promptly gets winged.
He wears a sling for the rest of the
story. Anti-hero lone wolf Tamiya
becomes inadvertently involved when
he develops a crush on the daughter
(Kubo) of mob boss Kawazu. Soon,
Tamiya is sucked in as a bodyguard
for the gang but is almost immediately alienated by their sordid antics.
He splits, accompanied by Kawazu's
secretary Nagisa, and ends up sleeping on her couch – only to awake the
next morning to find her strangled in
her bath. Despite some gritty violence
and torture – the weaker, younger
mob gets pummeled into submis-
sion, then co-opted – this still has
the series' requisite humor courtesy
of Tamiya's sidekicks, most notably
pleasingly plump sex kitten
Sakamoto. Tamiya aids Amachi in
tracking Nagisa's killer, all culminating in a chaotic warehouse shootout
where boss's daughter Kubo accidentally bites the dust. Her loyalties having swung back-and-forth throughout
the picture, she had been trying to
reach Tamiya's side.   #6 of 9 films
* * 1/2

STRAY DOG aka NORA INU
1966 85 min. DIR. Dir. Yoshio Inoue
SCR. Giichi Fujimoto PHOTO COLOR
'SCOPE: Yoshihisa Nakagawa
MUSIC: Tadashi Yamauchi w/ Jiro
Tamiya, Mikio Narita, Sumiko
Sakamoto, Hisako Tamura, Machiko
Hasegawa, Tamotsu Hayakawa,
Takuya Fujioka, Reiko Kasahara
Despite the title, this is not a remake
of the Kurosawa cop/crime film from
1949. Once again the series delivers
an amusing but trivial exercise, clearly designed for the very young adolescent boys in the audience. Tamiya
is his usual lovable, devil-may-care
self trying to work with police detectives and reporters by hustling and
hoodwinking a gang that operates a
crooked casino. This becomes a bit
more interesting when lone wolf gunman Narita is onscreen, someone who
is being hunted by the gang as well as
the cops. Unfortunately, the standard
sentimental contrivance of giving
Narita an innocent sister injured
and recuperating in hospital from a
hit-and-run grates on the nerves. As
usual, there is the customary imaginative production design from Daiei on
a meager budget and some occasionally diverting action setpieces. #7 of
9 films * *

QUICK-DRAW DOG aka
HAYAUCHI INU aka RUNNING
DOG 1967 84 min. DIR. Tetsutaro
Murano SCR. Giichi Fujimoto
PHOTO COLOR 'SCOPE: Akira Uehara
MUSIC: Tadashi Yamauchi w/ Jiro
Tamiya, Shigeru Amachi, Kyoko
Enami, Sumiko Sakamoto, Ichiro
Zaitsu, Mikio Narita, Takuya Fujioka,
Shoichi Ozawa, Saburo Date
From several names in the cast

Dog (#8) *aka* ***Quick Draw Dog***

(Fujioka, Zaitsu, Ozawa), the viewer might deduce that this entry has a bit more humor than usual. And they would be right. Although this still falls short of the pop art classic status of say something like Kihachi Okamoto's AGE OF ASSASSINS, Yasuharu Hasebe's BLACK TIGHT KILLERS or any of Seijun Suzuki's early sixties pictures, director Murano brings a significantly more imaginative, over-the-top imagination to this entry than the other DOG films. There is alot of authentic nightclub youth ambience with some anonymous, but still credible rock 'n' roll music – as opposed to the stodgy imitation R&B swing that usually passes for contempo music in this series. Lone wolf crack shot Tamiya seems to actually be earning his living here as a roving minstrel. Taking a cue from Akira Kobayashi in many of his very early Nikkatsu action films, Tamiya is never without his acoustic guitar or his silly fellow guitarist sidekick Fujioka when out at the clubs. Director Murano takes much of the comic book tone of the series to its logical absurdist extremes, such as plastering Tamiya's apartment walls with a plethora of oversized pictures of revolvers, automatics and handguns (making him look like a certifiable gun nut) and giving the weird secret, neo-fascist society allied to the evil yakuza an all-red color motif that sears the eyeballs. There is a great long shot of their crimson building HQ situated amidst a crowd of greyish, nondescript structures that totally relegates this to live action manga territory. There is also a standout performance from Enami as the drug addict mistress of gang boss Narita. She also happens to be the long lost sister

of a nice young girl Tamiya has just met. A great scene unfolds where the cruel Narita holds out on the drugs to torment Enami, a sequence that almost seems as if it is from another wilder, more adult series. Unfortunately, Enami gets murdered halfway through while meeting Tamiya in a ghetto neighborhood playground. Charismatic Amachi also returns as the Columbo-like police detective (coincidence? or were the creators of the "Columbo" television series Japanese genre film aficionados?). Also Zaitsu, providing broad comic relief as Tamiya's gay neighbor, is revealed at the climax to be a secret government agent investigating Narita's narcotics traffic! If only the ending had a bit more punch, this could have been a little masterpiece. #8 of 9 films
* * *

DOG SHOWDOWN aka SHOBU INU aka SILENT GUN 1967 86 min. **DIR.** Yoshio Inoue **SCR.** Giichi Fujimoto **PHOTO COLOR 'SCOPE:** Nobuo Munekawa **MUSIC:** Tadashi Yamauchi **w/** Jiro Tamiya, Shigeru Amachi, Yuko Hamada, Sumiko Sakamoto, Takuya Fujioka, Michiko Sugata, Masako Myojo This last entry features intrigue and mayhem involving a newfangled smokeless, silent gun supposedly invented by the Nazis during World War 2. Tamiya, a ruthless yakuza gang and cop Amachi try to track down the killer who has it in his possession. Much ado about nothing with only a few mildly diverting sequences. #9 of 9 films   * *

A DROP OF GREASE aka ABURA NO SHITATARI 1966

Dir. Tokuzo Tanaka Scr. Susumu
Takahisa Photo 'scope: Toshihisa
Nakagawa Music: Sei Ikeno
w/ Jiro Tamiya, Naoko Kubo, Mikio
Narita, Nobuo Kaneko, Mizuho
Suzuki, Manami Fuji, Fujio Suga,
Manabu Morita

**DUEL IN THE FOREIGNERS'
CEMETERY** aka GAIJIN
BOCHI NO KETTO 1964 Dir.
Kimiyoshi Yasuda Scr. Shozaburo
Asai Photo 'scope: Shozo Honda
Music: Ichiro Saito w/ Kojiro
Hongo, Jun Fujimaki, Tomisaburo
Wakayama (pka Kenzaburo Jo),
Shiho Fujimura, Ryutaro Gomi,
Saburo Date, Yoshio Inaba, Ikuko
Mori

**DYNAMITE DOCTOR aka
YOIDORE HAKASE aka
DRUNKEN DOCTOR series**

DYNAMITE DOCTOR aka
YOIDORE HAKASE aka DRUNK-
EN DOCTOR 1966 82 min. Dir.
Kenji Misumi Scr. Kaneto Shindo
Photo color 'scope: Fujio Morita
Music: Taichiro Kosugi
w/ Shintaro Katsu. Kyoko Enami,
Eijiro Tono, Jun Hamamura, Chocho
Miyako
A series about a wild drunken doctor
partial to gambling. Not real yakuza
films per se, but containing yakuza
elements and characters. #1 of 3
films

DYNAMITE DOCTOR RETURNS
aka ZOKU YOIDORE HAKASE
aka RETURN OF THE DRUNKEN
DOCTOR 1966 84 min. Dir.
Akira Inoue Scr. Kaneto Shindo
Photo color 'scope Chishi Makiura

Music: Makoto Furuya/The Fresh-
men w/ Shintaro Katsu, Michiko
Sugata, Masumi Harukawa, Nijiko
Kiyokawa, Ichiro Araki, Takashi
Kanda #2 of 3 films

DRUNKEN HARBOR aka
YOIDORE HATOBA 1966 84
min. Dir. Akira Inoue Scr. Kaneto
Shindo Photo color 'scope:
Yasukazu Takemura Music:
Yoshiaki Otsuka w/ Shintaro Katsu,
Miwa Takada, Kaneko Iwazaki,
Michiyo Yokoyama, Eitaro Ozawa,
Takuya Fujioka, Tatsuo Endo
Brawling, inebriated doctor
Katsu continues his antics in the
slums of the waterfront, treating shantytown folk as well as trying to keep
the peace between two yakuza gangs.
Fujioka, head of the more urban
gun-toting mob, and Endo, boss of
the more traditional sword-swinging
bunch, are funny but mug shamelessly in their many confrontations.
Screenwriter Shindo manages to include some pungent social comment
into the wacky proceedings but, that
said, this still isn't much more than a
programmer vehicle for the always
mesmerizing, over-the-top Katsu.
Iwazaki is Katsu's earthy, cafe-
managing mistress and young Takada
his straitlaced nurse. Ozawa is the
cynical local police captain perfectly
willing to let doctor Katsu do all
the dirty work to keep peace in their
lawless neighborhood. Katsu actually manages to get the two gangs to
donate money and services to build
him a clinic, but his peacekeeping efforts backfire when the gangsters start
resenting his influence on their turf.
Things culminate with Katsu
hosing the two rambunctious gangs
down with a paint spray gun in the

anarchic, but contrived climax. #3 and final in series   * * 1/2

EASY MONEY aka ABUKU ZENI 1970 82 min. **DIR.** Kazuo Mori **SCR.** Seiji Hoshikawa **PHOTO COLOR** **'SCOPE:** Fujio Morita **MUSIC:** Seitaro Omori **w/** Shintaro Katsu, Yumiko Nogawa, Shigeru Amachi, Takuya Fujioka, Joji Takagi, Kumi Mizuno, Osamu Sakai, Mikio Narita, Ryutaro Gomi An action-comedy about three men who try to bilk money out of gambling dens.

ESCAPE MAN aka DATSU GOKU SHA aka THE PRISON-BREAKER aka THE BREAKOUT 1967 89 min. **DIR.** Kazuo Ikehiro **SCR.** Hajime Takaiwa **PHOTO 'SCOPE:** Akira Uehara **MUSIC:** Takeo Watanabe **w/** Tetsuro Tanba, Jun Fujimaki, Takashi Nakamura, Mayumi Nagisa, Yoshi Kato, Nobuo Kaneko, Machiko Hasegawa, Kyosuke Machida

FANGS OF VENGEANCE aka FUKUSHU NO KIBA 1965 92 min. **DIR.** Umeji Inoue **SCR.** Umeji Inoue/ Kozo Taguchi **PHOTO 'SCOPE:** Tetsu Watanabe **MUSIC:** Harumi Ibe **w/** Jiro Tamiya, Akiko Koyama, Eiko Taki, Taro Marui, Fujio Murakami, Osamu Ogawa

FORTY-EIGHT HOURS TO KILL aka SHUTSU GOKU YOJUHACHI JIKAN aka FORTY-EIGHT HOURS TO ESCAPE 1969 79 min. **DIR.** Kazuo Mori **SCR.** Tetsuro Yoshida **PHOTO COLOR 'SCOPE:** Kazuo Miyagawa **MUSIC:** Sei Ikeno **w/** Ryunosuke Minegishi, Michiyo Yasuda, Kikko Matsuoka, Akio

Hasegawa, Rokko Toura, Fujio Suga A discharged cop tries to clear himself of false charges and association with gangsters.

Forty-Eight Hours to Kill

FRIENDSHIP ON BULLETHOLE STREET aka DANKON GAI NO YUJO 1960 **DIR.** Mitsuo Murayama **PHOTO 'SCOPE:** Kimio Watanabe **MUSIC:** Kuranosuke Hamaguchi w/ Koichi Ose, Gen Mitamura, Kyoko Enami, Bontaro Miake

GAMBLER'S LIFE – UNSTOP-PABLE BLOODBATH aka BAKUTO ICHIDAI – CHIMATSU-RI FUDO aka SWORN BROTH-ERS 1969 90 min. **DIR.** Kimiyoshi Yasuda **SCR.** Koji Takada **PHOTO COLOR 'SCOPE:** Hiroshi Imai **MUSIC:** Hajime Kaburagi **w/** Raizo Ichikawa, Jushiro Konoe, Mitsuyo Ryui, Machiko Hasegawa, Ryunosuke Kanada, Kenjiro Ishiyama, Nakajiro Tomita, Mitsuko Tanaka, Tatsuo Endo   One of Raizo Ichikawa's last two films – he made only two in 1969 – the other being his final outing as the renegade halfbreed samurai Kyoshiro Nemuri in the mindblowing CASTLE MENAGERIE (NEMURI KYOSHIRO AKUJO-GARI). He died in July of that year. According to Kazuo Ikehiro, director of four of the YOUNG BOSS series, Ichikawa became too ill near the end of shooting GAMBLER'S LIFE, and director Yasuda had to use a stunt double in one or two of the swordfight scenes. I was surprised to hear this as it genuinely looks like Ichikawa all the way through. This is one of the most violent, bleakly beautiful and pared-to-the-bone *ninkyo eiga* made at Daiei. It appears very Toei-studios-influenced, and, in fact, has a loaned-out Toei screenwriter, Takada, as scenarist. Ichikawa also played a yakuza boss in Daiei's eight film YOUNG BOSS (1965 – '67) series. Ichikawa's haggard, suffering appearance due to his illness gives added credibility to his role as a tormented man facing sudden death. * * * 1/2

GAMES aka ASOBI aka PLAY 1971 90 min. **DIR.** Yasuzo Masumura **SCR.** Masayoshi Imako/Masahiro Ito **PHOTO COLOR 'SCOPE:** Setsuo Kobayashi **MUSIC:** Takeo Watanabe **w/** Keiko Sekine, Asao Uchida, Tokuko Kageyama, Akemi Negishi A sexual-awakening *seishun* (youth)/sun tribe picture with some yakuza characters.

G-MEN OF THE SEA – PACIFIC OCEAN BODYGUARDS 1967 87 min. **DIR.** Shigeo Tanaka **SCR.** Kimiyuki Hasegawa **PHOTO 'SCOPE:** Yoshihisa Nakagawa **MUSIC:** Kazuo Kitamura **w/** Ken Utsui, Kojiro Hongo, Mikio Narita, Jun Fujimaki, Kyoko Enami, Michiko Sugata, Kyosuke Machida, Tatsuo Endo

THE GREAT VILLAINS aka DAI AKUTO aka EVIL TRIO 1968 93 min. **DIR.** Yasuzo Masumura

SCR. Yasuzo Masumura/Yoshhiro Ishimatsu **PHOTO B&W 'SCOPE:** Setsuo Kobayashi **MUSIC:** Tadashi Yamauchi **w/** Jiro Tamiya, Kei Sato, Mako Midori, Asao Uchida, Tsutomu Kuraishi, Kazuo Kitamura, Yuzo Hayakawa, Yuji Moriama
Midori is a pupil enrolled in a western dressmaking school, Tamiya is a corrupt lawyer and Sato a sleazy yakuza who become unlikely and uneasy allies in a blackmail scheme. It involves setting up a popular singer by drugging drinks then snapping staged-to-look-real photos. Complications and thorny relations cause the plan to evolve in a homicidal direction. Another of Masumura's intricate labyrinths of a put-upon female turning the tables on those who would exploit her.

The Great Villains
aka The Evil Trio

GUN'S BLOODY MIRE aka DORO DARAKE NO KENJU 1961 **DIR./SCR.** Keigo Kimura **PHOTO**

Hitwoman - Bitch

B&W 'SCOPE: Hiroshi Imai MUSIC: Tadashi Yoshida w/ Jun Fujimaki, Hideo Takamatsu, Yuko Hamada, Mariko Ogasawara

Gun's Bloody Mire

HIDING-PLACE IN THE STORM aka ANABA ARASHI 1971 DIR. Akikazu Ota Scr. Fumi Takahashi w/ Eiko Yatsunami

HIGH SCHOOL OUTCASTS aka KOKO SASURAIHA 1971 86 min. DIR./SCR. Azuma Morisaki PHOTO COLOR 'SCOPE: Kenichi Yoshikawa MUSIC: Tomohiro Koyama w/ Kensaku Morita, Hideko Takehara, Takashi Kanda, Norihiko Yamamoto, Chishu Ryu Morita is an orphaned delinquent who is released from reform school and goes to a beach community on the eastern coast to attend high school. He soon becomes friends with fisherman/student Yamamoto. Both outcast boys become lovers to Takehara whose father is on the school board. The three become inseparable and are increasingly involved in protests such as book-burning and occupying the school's radio station. This results in flight from the police and finding refuge in an old boat. But Takehara's father soon arrives with the cops, intent on arresting the boys on a kidnapping charge. A conflagration subsequently ensues, and Takehara commits suicide.

HITWOMAN – BITCH aka ONNA KOROSHI YA – MESU INU aka THE ART OF ASSASSINA-TION 1969 82 min. DIR. Yoshio Inoue SCR. Mitsuro Otaki PHOTO COLOR 'SCOPE: Yoshihisa Nakagawa MUSIC: Hajime Kaburagi w/ Kyoko Enami, Miyoko Akaza, Koji Nanbara, Kenjiro Ishiyama, Yuki Meguro, Reiko Kasahara, Masao Mishima, Masaya Takahashi, Yukari Yoneyama More entertaining and watchable than it has any right to be since the story is the usual programmer stuff. Enami lends her stoic hardboiled charisma to the role of an expert hitwoman doublecrossed by her employers and left for dead only to come back to track them down with a vengeance. One of her girlfriends, vapid model Akaza, turns out to be mistress of one of the bosses. At the climax, Enami sneaks under the very noses of the cops to strike down top bigshot Mishima, then disappear, slipping through their fingers. * * *

HOODLUM SOLDIER aka HEITAI YAKUZA series

HOODLUM SOLDIER aka HEITAI YAKUZA 1965 103 min. DIR. Yasuzo Masumura SCR. Ryuzo

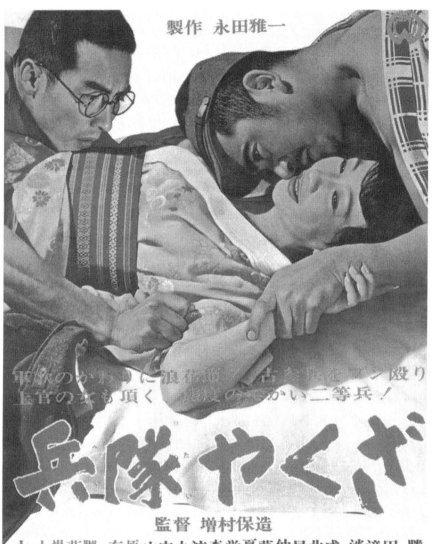

Hoodlum Soldier (#1)

Kikushima **PHOTO B&W 'SCOPE:** Setsuo Kobayashi **MUSIC:** Naozumi Yamamoto **w/** Shintaro Katsu, Takahiro Tamura, Mikio Narita, Eiko Taki, Keiko Awaji   A justly famous anti-war epic from the sixties about a yakuza gambler (Katsu) drafted into the Japanese army in the pre-WW2 Manchurian conflict. He makes friends with another outcast, a pacifist intellectual (Takahiro Tamura). Exuberantly kinetic, irreverent, funny, violent and perverse. This showcases, even more than Masaki Kobayashi's THE HUMAN CONDITION (NINGEN NO JOKEN) trilogy or Toho's DESPERADO OUTPOST (DOKURITSU GURENTAI) series, the full-scope of the Japanese military's sadistic discipline. The corporals beat the privates, and the sergeants beat the corporals and privates (!) on a daily, sometimes hourly basis. Everyone of lower rank is continually being slapped, punched, tripped, pushed, pummeled and otherwise brutalized for the slightest infraction – Katsu sneezing in the face of his superior is a hilarious example. One of the things that makes the film so funny, besides one's incredulity that such military behavior could exist, is that Katsu's character often hits back. Katsu and Tamura finally desert at the end of this first saga, stealing their troop train's locomotive. #1 of 9 films * * * *

RETURN OF THE HOODLUM SOLDIER aka ZOKU HEITAI YAKUZA aka PRIVATE AND THE C.O. 1965 92 min. **DIR.** Tokuzo Tanaka **SCR.** Kazuo Funabashi **PHOTO B&W 'SCOPE:** Senkichiro Takeda **MUSIC:** Taiichiro Kosugi **w/** Shintaro Katsu, Takahiro Tamura,

Akiko Koyama, Yoshie Mizutani, Ryutaro Gomi, Fujio Suga   The locomotive the boys stole at the end of the first film derails, and the two are captured by their own troops. They are put in hospital to heal their wounds, and Katsu develops a crush on caring nurse Koyama. Once Katsu and Tamura are better, they are thrown right back into the front lines. Katsu becomes the gofer for a decent officer who is in love with prostitute Mizutani. Katsu and Tamura are also instrumental in saving civilians when they stand up to another brutal officer who wants to massacre an entire village. Katsu's superior ends up backing up the pair and is later clandestinely murdered in combat for his humane act. This and other constant conflicts with the sadistic regimen of the Japanese army cause Katsu and Tamura to finally desert again. This time they rescue old friend, newly-arrived frontline nurse Koyama as she is about to be raped and take her with them. #2 of 9 films * * *

NEW HOODLUM SOLDIER aka SHIN HEITAI YAKUZA aka HOODLUM SOLDIER DESERTS AGAIN 1966 86 min. **DIR.** Tokuzo Tanaka **SCR.** Kazuo Funabashi **PHOTO B&W 'SCOPE:** Yoshihisa Nakagawa **MUSIC:** Hajime Kaburagi **w/** Shintaro Katsu, Takahiro Tamura, Michiko Saga, Tatsuo Endo, Mikio Narita, Takuya Fujioka, Ryoichi Tamagawa, Takashi Kanda, Bontaro Miake, Fujio Murakami #3 of 9 films   * * *

HOODLUM SOLDIER'S ESCAPE aka HEITAI YAKUZA DATSU GOKU 1966 86 min. **DIR.** Kazuo Mori **SCR.** Kazuo Funabashi **PHOTO**

B&W 'SCOPE: Hiroshi Imai
MUSIC: Tetsuo Tsukahara
w/ Shintaro Katsu, Takahiro Tamura, Mayumi Ogawa, Kunie Tanaka, Ichiro Nakatani, Ryutaro Gomi, Ryuzo Shimada, Manabu Morita The first third of this entry finds our mismatched comrades once again captured and incarcerated in a military prison for their repeated desertions. At this point in the series, credibility was being strained to the breaking point. Although there are many gritty touches and open criticism of the sadistic brutality of the Japanese military throughout each film, the fact that Katsu and Tamura's characters have continued to elude a firing squad reaches absurd new heights. The boys escape from jail, then hook up with another battalion after helping refugees along the way, including whore Ogawa. In the process, they also avenge the death of their pal Tanaka, who had been murdered by a larcenous superior officer for the stolen gems in his possession. #4 of 9 films   * * *

HOODLUM SOLDIER'S FLIGHT TO FREEDOM aka HEITAI YAKUZA DAI DASSO 1966 88 min. **DIR.** Tokuzo Tanaka **SCR.** Kazuo Funabashi **PHOTO B&W 'SCOPE:** Senkichiro Takeda **MUSIC:** Hajime Kaburagi **w/** Shintaro Katsu, Takahiro Tamura, Michiyo Yasuda, Mikio Narita, Yuji Minabe, Gan-osuke Ashiya, Kogen Ashiya, Jotaro Senba, Ryutaro Gomi, Asao Uchida   Katsu and Tamura meet Japanese national Yasuda, a roving minstrel entertainer traveling with a partner. They become her protector when their fellow soldiers cast lecherous designs on her, then,

midway through, Katsu helps the two entertainers escape on a refugee train. In the last third of the tale, the two comrades assume the identities of officers after the rest of their brigade is massacred. Once they join another battalion, they encounter embittered

Hoodlum Soldier (#5)

soldier Narita who is intent on sowing seeds of mutiny when they embark on a mission with a small squad. Before the saga ends, Katsu, Tamura and Narita have bonded, but Narita and the rest of the men are killed when they run into a heavy concentration of Chinese soldiers. Once more the two friends are left to wander. #5 of 9 films * * *

HEITAI YAKUZA – ORE NI MAKASERO 1967 89 min. **DIR.** Tokuzo Tanaka **SCR.** Hajime Takaiwa **PHOTO B&W 'SCOPE:** Nobuo Munekawa **MUSIC:** Hajime Kaburagi **w/** Shintaro Katsu, Takahiro Tamura, Ryohei Uchida, Fumio Watanabe, Fujio Suga, Machiko Hasegawa, Mayumi Nagisa #6 of 9 films

HOODLUM SOLDIER – KILLING SPREE aka HEITAI YAKUZA – NAGURIKOMI aka HOODLUM FLAG-BEARER 1967 89 min. **DIR.** Tokuzo Tanaka **SCR.** Ryozo Kasahara/Masatoshi Tojo (Higashijo?) **PHOTO B&W 'SCOPE:** Senkichiro Takeda **MUSIC:** Hajime Kaburagi **w/** Shintaro Katsu, Takahiro Tamura, Yumiko Nogawa, Kaneko Iwasaki, Toshiyuki Hosokawa, Toru Abe, Hosei Komatsu, Taro Marui, Kayo Mikimoto, Yoshio Inaba #7 of 9 films

HOODLUM SOLDIER – LOOTING AND PILLAGING aka HEITAI YAKUZA – GODATSU aka HOODLUM SOLDIER AND $100,000 1968 80 min. **DIR.** Tokuzo Tanaka **SCR.** Kazuo Funabashi/Tetsuro Yoshida **PHOTO B&W 'SCOPE:** Fujio Morita **MUSIC:**

Hajime Kaburagi **w/** Shintaro Katsu, Takahiro Tamura, Tomomi Sato, Isao Natsuyagi, Yoshio Kaneuchi Katsu is saddled with a babe in swaddling clothes behind enemy lines. Despite the potential for unwelcome sentimentality, director Tanaka keeps the narrative gritty and action-packed, and the humor fresh. Loan-out star from Shochiku, the charismatic Tomomi Sato, is a tough female Chinese officer Katsu falls for. #8 of 9 films (last entry at DAIEI) * * * 1/2

Hoodlum Soldier (#8)

NEW HOODLUM SOLDIER STORY – FIRING LINE aka SHIN HEITAI YAKUZA – KASEN 1972 92 min. **DIR.** Yasuzo Masumura *(see Toho Studios section – released by Toho)*

The Hot Little Gitrl aka *The Electric Jellyfish*

THE HOT LITTLE GIRL aka SHIBIRE KURAGE aka THE ELECTRIC JELLYFISH 1970 92 min. **DIR.** Yasuzo Masumura **SCR.** Yasuzo Masumura/Yoshihiro Ishimatsu **PHOTO COLOR 'SCOPE:** Setsuo Kobayashi **MUSIC:** Tadashi Yamauchi **w/** Mari Atsumi, Yusuke Kawazu, Ryo Tamura, Ryoichi Tamagawa, Asao Uchida
More of a sex melodrama than an actual yakuza film, but it has yakuza elements. Atsumi is a popular model appearing regularly in Sunday supplements and weekly magazines. But she has a drunken leech for a father (Tamagawa) who is constantly draining her resources and emotions. Her business manager boyfriend (Kawazu) requests that Atsumi bed down a powerful Americann businessman who owns a chain of department stores. If she does, Kawazu has been promised a huge order. Atsumi vacillates, but gives in, much to her distaste. Simultaneously, Tamagawa falls into a trap with yakuza thugs who claim he must pay them a million yen. Daughter Atsumi refuses, and daddy goes to Kawazu. Afraid of becoming involved with the gangsters himself, Kawazu refuses to have anything more to do with either pops or offspring. Atsumi is bitter at this cavalier treatment. Surprisingly, she finds a sympathetic friend in one of the hoods (Tamura) who also has a no-good father. They put their heads together and devise a plan to blackmail Kawazu's company. Upon receipt of the funds, Atsumi decides her father can fend for himself for once and turns the full amount over to Tamura, telling him to go straight. Despite director Masumura co-writing the screenplay with accomplished, frequent writing partner Ishimatsu, the film does not really ever take off into the heady heights of VIXEN or YAKUZA MASTERPIECE, two other Masumura efforts made around the same time period. That said, it remains a decent, tight little film, although with few of Masumura's usually rigorous editing rhythms. Atsumi is great in the title role, a follow-up of sorts to her previous outing with Masumura, PLAY IT COOL. * * *

INVITATION TO JAIL aka KANGOKU E NO SHOTAI 1967 88 min. **DIR.** Akira Inoue **SCR.** Kazuo Funabashi **PHOTO B&W 'SCOPE:** Akira Uehara **MUSIC:** Takeo Watanabe **w/** Jiro Tamiya, Yoko Nogiwa, Annu Mari, Akitake Kono, Yuzo Hayakawa, Fumio Watanabe, Mayumi Nagisa, Reiko Kasahara

Invitation to Jail

milieu, this first entry has more of the mod pop flavor of Nikkatsu Studios' STRAY CAT ROCK series and Toei Studios' DELINQUENT GIRL BOSS films, and it pre-dates them.

Kanto Woman Yakuza (#1)

KANTO WOMAN YAKUZA aka KANTO ONNA YAKUZA series

KANTO WOMAN YAKUZA
aka KANTO ONNA YAKUZA
aka DUEL AT THE QUAY 1968
74 min. **DIR.** Akira Inoue **SCR.** Giichi Fujimoto **PHOTO B&W 'SCOPE:** Chishi Makiura **MUSIC:** Takeo Watanabe **w/** Michiyo Yasuda, Mayumi Nagisa, Mako Sanjo, Toshiyuki Hosokawa, Ken Ishiyama, Fumio Watanabe, Osamu Ogawa, Akane Kawazaki
This series was seemingly initiated, so Daiei could have their own "fighting woman" yakuza heroine as opposed to their WOMAN GAMBLING EXPERT series where the heroine usually did nothing but gamble while the males did the nasty, violent stuff. While the second, third and last films were cast in a serious, *ninkyo* (though still contemporary)

A short and sweet, anarchic, deliciously exhilarating urban tall tale with the kind of kinetic visual energy found in much of Britain's early sixties angry young cinema. Director Inoue, choosing from the beautifully composed, high contrast black & white pallette of Chishi Makiura's cinematography, has cut together a vibrantly dynamic picture. When the performances of the young charismatic cast, especially Yasuda and Nagisa, gel, the film transcends into a genuine *tour de force*. Because of the picture's obvious programmer status though, the scenario often slumps in and out of by-the-numbers plot progression. Yasuda, Nagisa and Sanjo make up a jazzy folk trio that sing at a local nightclub. They soon begin running afoul of cruel macho gang boss Watanabe and his cronies. Some of the boys try to rape Nagisa and Sanjo, and Yasuda kicks their asses, aided by her faithful acoustic guitar (with a springloaded knife!) When one of the girls' comrades, young tough guy Hosokawa, is coerced into helping Watanabe's gang track down Yasuda's fugitive brother who had supposedly betrayed them, near tragedy results. There is no particular emotional punch to the proceedings, but the film is, at times, so stunning in its capturing of the lower class, slum milieu and the youthful spirit of the girls, you end up not minding. #1 of 4 films * * * 1/2

Kanto Woman Scoundrel (#2)

KANTO WOMAN SCOUNDREL
aka KANTO ONNA GOKUDO
aka BADGE OF GUTS 1969
87 min. **Dir.** Kazuo Mori
Scr. Kazuo Imaoka **Photo** B&W
'**scope:** Senkichiro Takeda **Music:**
Ichiro Saito **w/** Michiyo Yasuda,

Fumio Watanabe, Hosei Komatsu, Chigako Miyagi, Rokko Toura, Jotaro Senba, Ryutaro Gomi
An extremely satisfying, stunningly photographed followup to the initial film, but in a more *ninkyo* style. Yasuda tries in vain to save her decent *tekiya* boss father from a sword-slashing assassin and receives a nasty scar on her back for her trouble. She makes a go of running the marketplace where many other honest merchants hawk their wares only to have a gang shepherded by evil triumvirate Watanabe, Komatsu and Toura horn in. Soon, formerly loyal comrades like her father's second-in-command Senba are capitulating to the villains. Director Mori skillfully integrates narrative build-ups with suspenseful action setpieces, while Yasuda establishes credibility with her fighting skills. Of course, by the end of the film Yasuda is finally driven to kill ruthless boss Watanabe. #2 of 4 films * * *

Kanto Woman's Bad Reputation (#3)

KANTO WOMAN'S BAD REPUTATION aka KANTO ONNA AKUMYO aka THE LONE AVENGER 1969 83 min.

DIR. Kazuo Mori SCR. Koji Takada PHOTO COLOR 'SCOPE: Fujio Morita MUSIC: Hajime Kaburagi w/ Michiyo Yasuda, Shintaro Katsu, Ko Nishimura, Yoshie Mizutani, Takashi Shimura, Kayo Mikimoto, Shigeru Tsuyuguchi, Ryutaro Gomi, Fujio Suga   Yasuda is the boss of her own group. When she is left with a baby belonging to a desperate couple being pursued by evil mobsters, she journies to see boss Shimura, the child's grandfather. Shimura is having troubles of his own with craven Suga, and he is soon assassinated. Yasuda becomes embroiled in the insanity. Katsu has a small part as a lone wolf who steps into help Yasuda on several dire occasions. Tsuyuguchi is Yasuda's chivalrous, bad guy rival. It is too bad that this is not better. Considering the cast and director, it should have been more than just another decent, if undistinguished program picture. There are some nice moments, but a bit more action would have helped. As it stands, the picture doesn't really come to life until the swordfight climax.   #3 of 4 films
* * 1/2

KANTO WOMAN'S BAD TEMPER aka KANTO ONNA DOKONJO aka JUSTICE AND FURY 1969 79 min.

DIR. Akira Inoue SCR. Koji Takada PHOTO COLOR 'SCOPE: Fujio Morita MUSIC: Takeo Watanabe w/ Michiyo Yasuda, Teruo Yoshida, Ichiro Nakatani, Asao Koike   Yasuda travels south into sunny climes, convening with other bosses. When a duly elected new underboss is assassinated right in front of Yasuda and her friend Yoshida, Yoshida catches the attacker, dispatching him, only to be arrested and sent to prison. Subsequently boss Nakatani has the wool pulled over his eyes by evil Koike, the unscrupulous behind-the-scenes mover. Yasuda has her hands full dealing with Koike and his shenanigans. Although a step back in the right direction after the last lackluster entry, there is still not too much memorable stuff here until Koike engineers a nocturnal hit on both Nakatani and newly-freed Yoshida as they flee on foot together through deserted, rain-drenched back alleys. Nakatani tries to valiantly fight back only to be finally fatally stabbed, gushing blood all over Koike's windshield which is soon cleaned by wipers and the pelting storm. Yasuda picks up the gauntlet next day when she attacks Koike's gang, finally stabbing him to death in broad daylight on an outside staircase, then being led away by the police.   #4 and last of the series   * * *

Kanto Woman's Bad Temper (#4)

KILL BEFORE BEING KILLED aka YARARERU MAE NI YARE 1964

DIR. Taro Yuge SCR. Kimiyuki Hasegawa PHOTO COLOR 'SCOPE: Hiroshi Ishida MUSIC: Harumi Ibe w/ Ken Utsui, Jun Fujimaki, Kenji

The Last Loyalty Offering

Sugawara, Kyoko Enami, Yuriko
Fuji, Hideo Takamatsu, Mikio Narita,
Hikaru Hoshi, Michiko Watanabe

Kill Before Being Killed

KILL THE KILLERS aka
KOROSHI YA O BARASE aka
ASSASSIN'S DESTRUCTION
1969 87 min. **DIR.** Kazuo Ikehiro

SCR. Yoshihiro Ishimatsu **PHOTO
COLOR 'SCOPE:** Kazuo Miyagawa
MUSIC: Takeo Watanabe
w/ Ryunosuke Minegishi, Hiroko
Masuda, Fumio Watanabe, Osamu
Sakai, Akitake Kono, Fujio Suga,
Ryutaro Gomi, Natsuko Oka, Koichi
Mizuhara, Yusaku Terashima
A yakuza gang hires a hitman to get
rid of their boss.

**THE LAST LOYALTY
OFFERING** aka ZANKYO NO
SAKAZUKI aka THE LAST
GALLANTRY 1967 85 min.
DIR. Tokuzo Tanaka **SCR.** Yoshihiro
Ishimatsu **PHOTO COLOR 'SCOPE:**
Kimio (Tadashi?) Watanabe **MUSIC:**
Takeo Watanabe **w/** Jiro Tamiya,
Yuko Hamada, Asao Koike, Yusuke
Kawazu, Fujio Suga, Nobuo Kaneko

LAW OF THE GUN aka KENJU
NO OKITE 1960 **DIR.** Mitsuo
Murayama **SCR.** Hitoshi Sagara
PHOTO 'SCOPE: Tomohiro Makino
MUSIC: Tokajiro Okubo **w/** Teru
Tomoda, Jun Negami, Hideo
Takamatsu, Yuko Hamada, Sachiko
Hidari, Bontaro Miake

A LIFE OF BAD TEMPER aka
DOKONJO ICHIDAI aka
NOTHING BUT GUTS! 1963
84 min. **DIR.** Kazuo Ikehiro **SCR.**
Masayasu Matsumura/Tetsuro
Yoshida **PHOTO B&W 'SCOPE:**
Shozo Honda **MUSIC:** Hajime
Kaburagi **w/** Shintaro Katsu, Hizuru
Takachiho, Machiko Hasegawa,
Meicho Soganoya, Tatsuo Endo,
Yasushi Sugita, Tokio Oki
Set in Osaka during the late Meiji
era, Katsu plays a well-meaning, but
not particularly bright tough guy who
can't seem to get out of his own way.

He is continually exploited until he meets Boss Hashimoto, an *oyabun* who comes to respect Katsu's courage and tenacity and Otami, a woman who seduces him. Lametably, Otami is married to Hashimoto's ruthless, sadistic archrival Otakichi. Hashimoto just barely settles things by having Katsu cut off his pinkie. Then Katsu and Otami – now divorced from Otakichi – are declared a couple and exiled. They wander, with Katsu taking all manner of jobs from rickshaw man to priest. Eventually, of course, Katsu redeems himself, defeating Otakichi in a protracted brawl and thereby saving Hashimoto's rail yard (on the verge of seizure by Otakichi).

The Lowest Man

THE LOWEST MAN aka FUTEKI NA OTOKO aka FEARLESS MAN 1958 81 min. **Dir.** Yasuzo Masumura **Scr.** Kaneto Shindo **Photo B&W 'scope:** Hiroshi Murai w/ Hiroshi Kawaguchi, Hitomi Nozoe, Tomoo Nagai, Eiji Funakoshi, Yasuko Kawakami Kawaguchi, in a role that could almost pass for a continuation of his PUNISHMENT ROOM persona, is caught between two father figures: a cop (Funakoshi) and a yakuza boss. Director Masumura and writer Shindo show Kawaguchi's callous nature from the get-go as he joins with his fellow delinquent brethern in throwing an unconscious man off a railroad bridge into the path of an oncoming train, doing the bidding of their adult gang boss. Shortly after the titles, perpetually drunk Kawaguchi lures naive, just-in-from-the-styx Nozoe to his ramshackle room over a bar, then rapes her. Despite flashbacks showing the disintegration of Kawaguchi's family and his resulting virtual orphan status, Masumura remains remarkably objective in treatment of Kawaguchi's character, skillfully balancing between revulsion and compassion. Midway through the film, Nozoe, since recruited as a bar girl, pretends to willingly go home with Kawaguchi for a night of passion only to stab him, then kick and berate him once he is down. Kawaguchi recovers, but he gradually becomes estranged from his fellow gang members when cop Funakoshi is murdered. He develops an obsession for Nozoe which eventually leads to a violent confrontation with his former gang boss. When the fight ends in his fatally shooting the boss, he goes on the run, pursued by both the cops and the boss's right hand man. Unable to stay away from Nozoe, he is shot repeatedly by the vengeful yakuza when he returns to her building. Both the severely wounded Kawaguchi and his assailant are hauled away by the police. Sobbing Nozoe, at last strangely moved by Kawaguchi's fate, clings to him as he is carted away on a stretcher. A riveting, angry film for the time period and further proof that Masumura should be ranked in the pantheon of postwar Japanese directors.   * * * 1/2

A MAN BLOWN BY THE WIND
aka KARAKKAZE YARO aka
AFRAID TO DIE aka TOUGH
GUY 1960 96 min. DIR. Yasuzo
Masumura SCR. Ryuzo Kikushima/
Hideo Ando PHOTO COLOR 'SCOPE:
Hiroshi Murai MUSIC: Tetsuo
Tsukahara w/ Yukio Mishima,
Ayako Wakao, Eiji Funakoshi,
Takashi Shimura, Yoshie Mizutani,
Jun Negami, Keizo Kawasaki,
Reisaburo Yamamoto, Ken Mitsuda
Famous writer Mishima in an explo-
ration of one hoodlum's self-destruc-
tive macho ethos. Mishima portrays
Takeo, a yakuza just released from
prison who is marked for death by his
former gang. He manages to elude
being murdered by returning home
to his uncle's (Shimura in full body
tattoos!) shop. He falls in love with
Yoshie (Wakao), an employee there.

A Man Blown by the Wind
aka Afraid to Die

Since he is still involved in the
yakuza, drawing an assignment to kill
boss Sagara, things eventually spiral
out of control. With his uncle dead
and the now pregnant Yoshie refusing
an abortion, he decides to go straight.
But Yoshie's brother is kidnapped as
a way of getting to him. A friend rescues the brother and once more things
start to look hopeful. But Takeo goes
out to buy baby clothes and is shot
in the back by the asthmatic assassin
who missed the first time. On one
level this is a bizarre novelty, one of
the rare feature films starring famous
maverick novelist Mishima. He
also co-starred with Shintaro Katsu
and Tatsuya Nakadai in director
Hideo Gosha's samurai masterpiece,
HITOKIRI (TENCHU) and had a
cameo in Kinji Fukasaku's version
of BLACK LIZARD. But this is also
a successful, consistently involving and well-written yakuza picture,
aided immeasurably by Masumura's
determinedly trenchant, unsentimental direction. * * *

MUDCAT OF GINZA aka GINZA
NO DORO NEKO 1960
DIR. Yoshio Inoue SCR. Kikuma
Shimoizaka PHOTO B&W 'SCOPE:
Setsuo Kobayashi MUSIC: Sei Ikeno
w/ Keiko Yuge, Jun Fujimaki, Tazuko
Niki, Kazuko Miyagawa, Kyoko
Enami, Ichizo Itami

NEW THEATER OF LIFE aka
SHIN JINSEI GEKIJO 1961 DIR.
Taro Yuge SCR. Kazuo Funabashi
PHOTO COLOR 'SCOPE: Hiroshi Ishida
MUSIC: Sei Ikeno w/ Jun Fujimaki,
Junko Kano, Hiroshi Kawaguchi,
Mariko Miho, Hideo Murota, Kyoko
Enami, Bontaro Miake, Jerri Fujio,
Yoko Uraji

恋と義理と二本を張って、泣いて笑ってさまよい歩くお転婆娘銀座のどら猫

Mudcat of Ginza

NIGHT OF DOOM aka YORU O SAGASE 1959 DIR. Shue Matsubayashi SCR. Ichiro Ikeda w/ Koji Tsuruta, Yumi Shirakawa

NINJA IN A BUSINESS SUIT aka SEBIRO NO NINJA 1963 88 min.

DIR. Taro Yuge SCR. Gen Edogawa/ Yoshio Shiasaka PHOTO B&W 'SCOPE: Hiroshi Ishida MUSIC: Sei Ikeno w/ Jiro Tamiya, Eiko Taki, Yunosuke Ito, Hideo Talamatsu

NOISY DYNAMITE aka DAINOMAITO DONDON aka DYNAMITE BANG! BANG! 1978 142 min. DIR. Kihachi Okamoto SCR. Masando Ide PHOTO COLOR 'SCOPE: Hiroshi Murai MUSIC: Masaru Sato w/ Bunta Sugawara, Kinya Kitaoji, Kanjuro Arashi, Yoshiko Miyashita, Shin Kishida, Nobuo Kaneko, Frankie Sakai A tongue-in-cheek film involving two rural yakuza clans in post-WW2 times who form baseball teams to resolve their differences. The film seems to go on a bit long, but the cast – especially Sugawara and Sakai who are great together – pull off the humor without getting too silly. In fact, the humor gets noticeably dark by the last half hour when the gangs' baseball game evolves into bloody confrontations, becoming absurdly ultra-violent. A nice return to form for director Okamoto who also manages to integrate some genuine pathos between Kitaoji and Miyashita. A Toei/Daiei co-production. * * *

NUMBER ONE CRIMINAL OPERATION aka HANZAI SAKUSEN NANBA WAN 1963 94 min. DIR. Umeji Inoue SCR. Hajime Takaiwa PHOTO COLOR 'SCOPE: Tetsu Watanabe MUSIC: Harumi Ibe w/ Jiro Tamiya, Kojiro Hongo, Jun Fujimaki, Kyosuke Machida, Eiko Taki, Kyoko Enami, Jun Negami, Yoshiro Kitahara, Mitsuko Hanai

Number One Criminal Operation

NUMBER SIX CRIME TERRI-TORY aka HANZAI ROKUGO CHI 1960 **DIR.** Mitsuo Murayama **SCR.** Keiichi Abe **PHOTO COLOR 'SCOPE:** Hiroshi Murai **MUSIC:** Kuranosuke Hamaguchi **w/** Hideo

Takamatsu,Tazuko Niki, Keiji Noguchi, Kazuko Wakamatsu, Hiromi Ichida, Bontaro Miake

OCEAN FLOOR CRIME #1 aka KAITEI HANZAI #1 1964 **DIR.** Shigeo Tanaka **SCR.** Kikuma Shimoizaka **PHOTO 'SCOPE:** Michio Takahashi **MUSIC:** Chuji Kinoshita **w/** Ken Utsui, Kyoko Enami, Yukiko Fuji, Jotaro Senba, Bontaro Miake, Akitake Kono, Mayumi Kurata, Eitaro Ozawa

Ocean Floor Crime Number One

ONE MAN BOSS aka OTOKO IPPIKI GAKI TAISHO 1971 80 min. **PROD.** Shintaro Katsu **DIR./SCR.** Tetsutaro Murano **PHOTO COLOR 'SCOPE:** Yasuhiro Yoshioka **MUSIC:** Hiroshi Tsutsui **w/** Osamu Sakai, Yoshihiko Aoyama, Tomoko Kinoshita, Masumi Harukawa, Goro Marudan, Shintaro Katsu A crazy gangster/youth comedy. Director Murano had previously turned out a couple of the better entries in Jiro Tamiya's DOG (INU) series. (A KATSU Production released by DAIEI)

ORDER OF YAKUZA aka YAKUZA NO KUNSHO aka MEDALS FOR GANGSTERS 1963 **DIR.** Umeji Inoue **SCR.** Toshio

Matsuura/Umeji Inoue **PHOTO COLOR 'SCOPE:** Tetsu Watanabe **MUSIC:** Hajime Kaburagi w/ Jiro Tamiya, Jun Fujimaki, Kojiro Hongo, Masayo Banri, Kenji Sugawara, Toru Abe, Takamaru Sasaki

Order of Yakuza

Set in post-war Tokai, a band of ruthless freebooters try to steamroller over the local gang who already control the black market. As it turns out the new bunch make the established mob look good. Order is maintained when the police join the embattled yakuza in fighting off the interlopers. The various *tekiya* market owners contribute to the "good" gang's court costs.

OUTLAW ISLAND aka MUHO MONO NO SHIMA 1956 **DIR.** Hiroshi Edogawa **SCR.** Masando Ide **PHOTO B&W:** Kimio Watanabe **MUSIC:** Mitsuo Kato w/ Koji Tsuruta, Yataro Kurokawa, Kyoko Aoyama, Daisuke Kato, Bontaro Miake, Bokuzen Hidari

PICKPOCKET aka SURI 1965 **DIR.** Taro Yuge **SCR.** Fuji Yahiro **PHOTO 'SCOPE:** Nobuo Munekawa **MUSIC:** Sei Ikeno w/ Kojiro Hongo, Miwa Takada, Naoko Kubo, Asao Uchida, Mikio Narita

Play It Cool aka **The Electric Medusa**

PLAY IT COOL aka DENKI KURAGE aka THE ELECTRIC MEDUSA 1970 92 min. **DIR.** Yasuzo Masumura **SCR.** Yasuzo Masumura/Yoshihiro Ishimatsu **PHOTO COLOR 'SCOPE:** Setsuo Kobayashi **MUSIC:** Hikaru Hayashi w/ Mari Atsumi, Yusuke Kawazu, Akemi Negishi, Ko Nishimura, Sanae Nakahara, Ryoichi Tamagawa, Tomoo Nagai   An exploitation sex drama just this side of pink *eiga* with yakuza elements. Maestro Masumura integrates these factors seamlessly into a transcendental, modern urban odyssey. Atsumi plays a beautiful young woman born out of wedlock. She supports herself with dressmaking. Her mom Negishi knows that many of the guests where she and Atsumi stay don't like her and only tolerate their presence because Negishi is friends with the owner Nakahara. One night Negishi discovers that the drunken good-for-nothing she helps to support, Tamagawa, has raped Atsumi. So she kills him. Her mother now in prison, Atsumi becomes a bar hostess but is nearly shanghaied by gangsters. Rescued by Kawazu, she goes to work in the club he manages. She proves a huge success amongst all the men (who are constantly on the make). But she demands that they play poker with her first. The stakes are high – a giant pot of money for her if she wins (which she usually does); or to bed with them if she loses. In the back of her mind, she hopes Kawazu will marry her. However, he knows his boss, the owner Nishimura, is in-love with Atsumi and desires her to be his mistress. She sees Kawazu's attitude and decides on giving into Nishimura. Suddenly, he dies of a heart attack. Kawazu makes Atsumi pregnant so she can claim Nishimura's fortune, pretending the child was his. Atsumi was Daiei's resident sex star as they inched closer and closer to the financial meltdown that would eventually close the studio at the end of 1971. Masumura also filmed THE HOT LITTLE GIRL with Atsumi the same year (1970). There was also a sequel to PLAY IT COOL with Atsumi but not directed by Masumura. * * *

PRETEND AUTHORITY aka GONTAKURE 1966 **DIR.** Tetsutaro Murano **SCR.** Kinya Naoi/ Yoshi Hattori **PHOTO 'SCOPE:** Akira Uehara **MUSIC:** Takeo Yamashita w/ Ken Utsui, Kazuko Yoshiyuki, Mari Sotome, Masako Myojo, Osamu Sakai, Tanie Kitabayashi, Masumi Harukawa, Taro Marui, Asao Uchida   Utsui goes up against violent delinquent gang members.

Prison Break

frame grab and poster for **Punishment Room**

PRISON BREAK aka MUSHYO YABURI aka THE BREAK-OUT 1969 86 min. **DIR.** Kazuo Ikehiro **SCR.** Hajime Takaiwa **PHOTO COLOR 'SCOPE:** Hiroshi Imai **MUSIC:** Hajime Kaburagi **w/** Hiroki Matsukata, Takahiro Tamura, Shiho Fujimura, Naoko Kubo, Rinichi Yamamoto, Asao Uchida

A set-in-1920s *ninkyo* film. After a roving camera *tour-de-force* of an *oyabun* assassination/knifefight courtesy of Matsukata, he hides at his geisha girlfriend (Kubo)'s pad. The house boss and flunkies find out and are going to sell him down the river so he jumps into their midst and slaughters the whole bunch. Regrettably, Kubo is fatally shot. He ends up in prison for a short while, breaks out and you can guess the rest. Very good all the way around – pacing, atmosphere, acting and fight choreography – despite its predictability. There is a great moonlit knife/swordfight climax in an abandoned shed/vacant lot. Lead actor Matsukata's Daiei films were the result of the studio attempting to fill the enormous gulf created by the untimely death of their most popular star, Raizo Ichikawa, movies apparently already written, originally tailored for the late actor. Matsukata, loaned-out temporarily from Toei (he continued his Toei career after Daiei's bankruptcy in 1971) took over three of Ichikawa's series roles: YOUNG BOSS in SECOND GENERATION YOUNG BOSS (1969); Kyoshiro Nemuri in FULL MOON SWORDS-MAN (NEMURI KYOSHIRO ENGETSU SAPPO) and FYLFOT SWORDPLAY (NEMURI KYOSHI-RO MANJI GIRI) (both 1969); and a ninja assassin in MISSION: IRON CASTLE (SHINOBI NO SHU)

(1970). He also filled-in on several one-shot yakuza pictures: PRISON BREAK, WANDERING FUGITIVE SWORD (1970) and SURVIVOR OF THE MASSACRE (1971). * * *

PRISON RELEASE LOYALTY OFFERING aka SHUTSU GOKU NO SAKAZUKI 1966 **DIR.** Umeji Inoue **SCR.** Umeji Inoue/Susumu Takahisa **PHOTO 'SCOPE:** Nobuo Munekawa **MUSIC:** Hajime Kaburagi **w/** Jiro Tamiya, Mikio Narita, Naoko Kubo, Nobuo Kaneko, Joji Ai, Jotaro Senba, Yoshiro Kitahara

PUNISHMENT ROOM aka SHOKEI NO HEYA 1956 96 min. **DIR.** Kon Ichikawa **ORIG. STORY:** Shintaro Ishihara **SCR.** Natto Wada/Keiji Hasebe **PHOTO B&W:** Yoshihisa Nakagawa **w/** Hiroshi Kawaguchi, Ayako Wakao, Seiji Miyaguchi, Keizo Kawasaki, Takashi Kodaka   Nothing less than a phenomenal, astonishing and pioneering film. This spectacle of an angry, ego-driven youth tormented by his own emotional impotence, low self-esteem and resentment towards his parents, in retrospect, seems immensely influential on pictures that came after – from Oshima's CRUEL STORY OF YOUTH (1960) and Suzuki's EVERYTHING GOES WRONG (1960) to Fukasaku's WOLVES, PIGS AND PEOPLE (1964) and GRAVEYARD OF HONOR (1975) to even Imamura's VENGEANCE IS MINE (1979). Kawaguchi, intelligent, but hating the idea of becoming "tamed" (or grown up), rebels against everyone – his ulcer-ridden bank teller dad (Miyaguchi), longsuffering mom, his teachers, his best friends when they decide to take school seriously, and the girl he fancies (Wakao). His treatment of Wakao really sets him apart, slipping her a mickey finn on grad night, then raping her. Even when she falls for him, he is nothing short of abusive, freely admitting he can't feel love or anything else. When his buddies put on one of their lucrative semi-annual dance parties, he tips off a rival youth gang of budding hoodlums, informing them when the take is departing. At the climax, he shows up at their hangout in a bar backroom, only to demand not just his cut but the whole bundle. Even when the brutal kids give him an out, he refuses to take it, plunging headfirst into a brutal beating. Ironically, former heartthrob Wakao arrives with her cousin who is a member of the gang. Initially wishing only to get an apology from him, she is enraged when he continues to taunt and laugh at her. She and the boys continue the thrashing until Wakao accidentally stabs him. Everyone runs, leaving bleeding and temporarily blinded Kawaguchi to crawl from the bar into the alley, still defiant and proclaiming he "refuses to die." Original story writer Shintaro Ishihara, brother of Nikkatsu Studios star Yujiro, had already written several other "sun tribe" (*taiyozoku*) bestsellers about angry, directionless youths propelled by self-will, self-gratification and self-destruction. Two, SEASONS IN THE SUN and CRAZED FRUIT, had already been made at Nikkatsu. Parents' groups, teachers and politicians had been grumbling about them, but PUNISHMENT ROOM was the straw that broke the camel's back, causing all the studios to put a temporary moratorium on any more "sun tribe"

pictures. The moratorium didn't last. A popular genre, by 1958 more were being cranked out by all the studios. Ironically, writer Ishihara is now a prominent, conservative member of the Japanese government. * * * *

RED SIGNAL aka SHINGO WA AKAI DA 1957 **DIR.** Minoru Watanabe **SCR.** Tetsuro Yoshida **PHOTO:** Yukimasa Makita **MUSIC:** Ban Takahashi **w/** Shintaro Katsu, Sumire Harukaze, Naritoshi Hayashi, Kazuko Wakamatsu

SCHOOL OF CRIME aka HANZAI KYOSHITSU aka CRIME CLASSROOM 1964 **Dir.** Harumi Mizuho **SCR.** Kimiyuki Hasegawa/ Kozo Taguchi **PHOTO 'SCOPE:** Hiroshi Ishida **MUSIC:** Hajime Okumura **w/** Ken Utsui, Jun Fujimaki, Yukiko Fuji, Mikio Narita, Noriko Hotaka, Yoshihiko Aoyama, Eriko Sanjo, Reisaburo Yamamoto

School of Crime

SECRET FEMALE INVESTIGATOR – WAGER ON LIPS aka ONNA HIMITSU CHOSAIN – KUCHIBIRU NI KAKERO aka GAMBLING ON THE EDGE aka TIGHTROPE WALKERS 1970 82 min. **DIR.** Mitsuo Murayama **SCR.** Kimiyuki Hasegawa **PHOTO COLOR 'SCOPE:** Kimio Watanabe

MUSIC: Seitaro Omori   w/ Kyoko Enami, Jun Fujimaki, Mikio Narita, Akio Hasegawa, Miyoko Akaza, Minoru Chiaki, Takashi Kanda A borderline yakuza/industrial spy opus with Enami as a super-sexy operative.

SHINJUKU NATIVE GROUND aka SHINJUKU BANGAICHI - YANGU PAUU aka THE CHASE 1969   84 min.   **DIR.** Michihiko Obimori **SCR.** Fumi Takahashi **PHOTO B&W 'SCOPE:** Yoshihisa Nakagawa w/ Ryunosuke Minegishi, Choichiro Kawarazaki, Mari Atsumi, Junko Natsu A sensational sexploitive *seishun* (youth) picture with yakuza elements.

Shinjuku Native Ground

A SHOT RENDS THE DARK-NESS aka YAMI O SAKU IPPA-TSU aka TRIGGER-HAPPY 1968 83 min.   **DIR.** Tetsutaro Murano **SCR.** Ryuzo Kikushima **PHOTO COLOR 'SCOPE:** Akira Uehara **MUSIC:** Takeo

Yamashita w/ Ryunosuke Minegishi, Makoto Sato, Shigeru Tsuyuguchi, Etsushi Takahashi, Takeshi Kato, Yuko Hamada, Miyoko Akaza, Reiko Kasahara   A diligent police detective brings a kidnapper to justice after a chase through the yakuza underworld.

A Shot Rends the Darkness

SHOWA WOMAN'S HONOR AND HUMANITY aka SHOWA ONNA JINGI aka THE WOMAN KILLER 1969 78 min. **DIR.** Taro Yuge **SCR.** Kimiyuki Hasegawa/ Kozo Taguchi **PHOTO COLOR 'SCOPE:** Kimio Watanabe **MUSIC:** Sei Ikeno w/ Kyoko Enami, Yusuke Kawazu, Kenji Sugawara, Mikio Narita, Mari Atsumi, Kazuo Kitamura, Kikko Matsuoka, Rokko Toura, Asao Koike, Kazuo Mori   Enami stars as a woman trying to find the murderer of her lover, a man belonging to the Horikawa gang. Probably more violent as far as Enami's character's participation than her WOMAN

GAMBLING EXPERT roles. According to one source, this was supposed to be the first of a series with Enami as an underworld detective. But to my knowledge no more were forthcoming.

Showa Woman's Honor & Humanity

SHOWDOWN AT NIGHT'S END aka SHOBU WA YORU TSUKERO aka ANTICIPATED NIGHT SHOWDOWN 1964 **DIR.** Akira Inoue **SCR.** Kazuo Funabashi **PHOTO 'SCOPE:** Fujio Morita **MUSIC:** Kunihiko Murai **w/** Jiro Tamiya, Naoko Kubo, Yusuke Kawazu, Eitaro Ozawa, Hiroko Nakagawa, Saburo Date, Fujio Suga, Ikuko Mori
Possibly more in a noirish mystery/suspense vein with hero Tamiya in turtleneck, long black leather coat, black leather hat and a cane sword. He is up against villainy and murder on the waterfront.

SNAPPING TURTLE GIRL GANG BOSS aka SUPPON ONNA BANCHO aka LIVE AND LEARN 1971 83 min. **DIR.** Taro Yuge **SCR.** Fumi Takahashi **PHOTO COLOR 'SCOPE:** Akira Uehara **MUSIC:** Sei Ikeno **w/** Eiko Yatsunami, Kichijiro Ueda, Junzaburo Ban, Ryohiko Aoyama, Reiko Kasahara, Michiko Kogano, Etsuko Kawachi, Bokuzen Hidari, Akira Oizumi   A girl called Snapping Turtle (!) comes to Shinjuku looking for the man who stole her 100,000 yen. Daiei's take on the *sukeban* (Girl Boss) subgenre then currently in vogue at Toei and Nikkatsu. The Daiei films are much harder to track down and document, possibly because of their shamelessly uninspired, derivative nature. There were several others, most starring Yatsunami.

SPARKS aka HIBANA 1957 **DIR.** Teinosuke Kinugasa **SCR.** Teinosuke Kinugasa/Jun Sagara **w/** Koji Tsuruta, Jun Negami, Fujiko Yamamoto

STORY OF A BAD TEMPER aka **DOKONJO MONOGATARI** series

STORY OF A BAD TEMPER – IMPUDENT FELLOW aka DOKONJO MONOGATARI – ZUBUTOI YATSU 1964 85 min. **DIR.** Kazuo Mori **SCR.** Ryuji Shiina **PHOTO COLOR 'SCOPE:** Hiroshi Imai **MUSIC:** Seitaro Omori **w/** Shintaro Katsu, Yukiji Asaoka, Miwa Takada, Eijiro Tono #1 of 2 films

Story of a Bad Temper - The Money Dance (#2)

STORY OF A BAD TEMPER – THE MONEY DANCE aka DOKONJO MONOGATARI – ZENI NO ODORI 1964 90 min. **DIR.** Kon Ichikawa **SCR.** Christie (Kon Ichikawa) **PHOTO COLOR 'SCOPE:** Kazuo Miyagawa **MUSIC:** Hajime Hana **w/** Shintaro Katsu, Chiemi Eri, Jun Hamamura, Eiji Funakoshi A satirical crime thriller with Katsu as a self-righteous crime-hating taxi driver who discovers his new employers (Funakoshi, Hamamura, et. al.) – supposedly dogooder crusaders out to stamp out blackmailers and drug dealers – are actually just scheming, homicidal gangsters. He turns the tables on them and their smuggling partners in crime, something which results in much darkly humorous, homicidal mayhem. Singing star Eri does one of her rare bits of film acting (she also made several period musicals at Toei with Hibari Misora) and is a perfect foil for Katsu. Their scenes are a joy to watch. Eri has an easygoing, yet hard-edged intensity that could have well-proved daunting to any other Japanese leading man not possessing Katsu's manic, blustery stature. Too bad it is so hard to see. #2 of 2 films   * * *

STUDENT GAMBLING CODE aka GAKUSEI JINGI aka STUDENT HONOR AND HUMANITY 1965 **DIR.** Mitsuo Murayama

SCR. Kinya Naoi/ Komori Maki **PHOTO 'SCOPE:** Tetsu Watanabe **MUSIC:** Seitaro Omori **w/** Kojiro Hongo, Kyoko Enami, Ryohei Uchida, Mikio Narita, Bontaro Miake

SURVIVOR OF THE MASSACRE aka MINAGOROSHI NO SUKYATTO 1971 80 min. **DIR.** Kazuo Mori **SCR.** Hajime Takaiwa/Kanji Yasumoto **PHOTO COLOR 'SCOPE:** Hiroshi Imai **MUSIC:** Shunsuke Kikuchi **w/** Hiroki Matsukata, Ryunosuke Minegishi, Mikio Narita, Mari Tanaka, Reiko Kasahara, Yoko Minamikawa In the mod-1960s, young, wavy-haired Matsukata returns from the U.S. after studying to be a cameraman and is caught in the middle of a gang war. He develops a strange love/hate friendship with sniper/hitman (Minegishi) who smokes a pipe, dresses in cowboy hat, sunglasses and buckskin fringe jacket (!) – and may be the man who killed his father. Weirdly contrived, but good.   * * *

Survivor of the Massacre

Tale of Dark Ocean Chivalry - With the Courage of Desperation

**TALE OF DARK OCEAN CHIV-
ALRY – WITH THE COURAGE
OF DESPERATION** aka GENKAI
YUKYODEN – YABURE KABURE
aka THE BORN FIGHTER 1970
101 min. Dir. Masahiro Makino
Scr. Kazuo Kasahara Photo color
'scope: Chishi Makiura Music:
Masao Yagi w/ Shintaro Katsu,
Michiyo Yasuda (now Okusu),
Machiko Kyo, Masahiko Tsugawa,
Hiroki Matsukata, Michitaro
Mizushima, Bin Amatsu, Shin
Kishida, Rinichi Yamamoto
Ninkyo yakuza film masters, director
Makino, writer Kasahara and com-
poser Yagi, were loaned-out from
Toei for this Daiei film. Too bad it is
not better. Katsu portrays a true-life
yakuza leader who supposedly fought
for fishermen/coal haulers' rights in
turn-of-the-century Japan while living
in the pleasure quarter. The love of
his life commits suicide in the street

while he is leading decent folk/rab-
ble to victory in a sword/gun battle
down the block. The last shot is of the
illustrious fellow's statue overlooking a bridge and river beside a city
(Fukuoka? Osaka?). This is a remake
of JAPAN'S MOST CHIVALROUS,
a film that director Makino and writer
Kasahara did at Toei Studios a couple
of years before (which was much
better). NOTE: There was a quasi-
political, rabidly rightist organization
in 1880s Japan called the Dark Ocean
Society (Genyosha) with roots almost
exclusively in the yakuza and ex-
samurai of Fukuoka. Its founder, Mitsuru Toyama, was revered as a kind
of Robin Hood of the slums and was
also feared for his fascist strong-arm
tactics against any opposition. However, the look of this film seems more
like 1900 than the 1880s, and Katsu's
character is not called Toyama.
* * *

TERRITORY OF THE NIGHT
aka YORU NO NAWABARI aka
RULE OVER NIGHT 1967 84 min.
Dir. Tetsutaro Murano Scr. Yoshio
Shirasaka Photo color 'scope:
Akira Uehara Music: Takeo
Yamashita w/ Jiro Tamiya, Shinjiro
Ebara, Hitomi Nozoe, Kikko
Matsuoka, Mikio Narita, Naoko
Kubo, Fujio Suga, Asao Uchida,
Takamaru Sasaki, Reiko Kasahara

THREE BOSSES aka SANNIN
NO KAOYAKU aka THE LAST
BETRAYAL 1960 Dir. Umeji Inoue
Scr. Ryosuke Saito/Toshiro Serizawa/
Umeji Inoue Photo color 'scope:
Setsuo Kobayashi Music:
Tomokazu Kawabe w/ Kazuo
Hasegawa, Hiroshi Kawaguchi,
Machiko Kyo, Shintaro Katsu, Kenji

Sugawara, Hitomi Nozoe, Hiromi Ichida   Naive, lovesick yakuza boss Hasegawa is led down the primrose path with red herrings until he realizes that the two who betrayed him are his gal Kyo and his best friend/ young underboss Kawaguchi (who is her secret lover). This turns out to be one of director Inoue's more successful crime films, with a noirish, claustrophobic atmosphere of rainsoaked streets and seductive betrayers – a quality that is too often missing in his other films. Many of his other efforts are entertaining but fairly standard programmers. Katsu is fine as a friend who helps Hasegawa while he is on the run. But Kyo and Kawaguchi are especially good as the two amoral, secretive lovers planning Hasegawa's overthrow. The film's only liability: Hasegawa does register the proper neurotic paranoia in his role of a man framed by friends and hunted by the police, but he never really communicates the toughness that is a prerequisite for a gang boss. * * *

THREE BROTHERS' DUEL aka SAN KYODAI NO KETTO aka THREE BROTHERS AND THE UNDERWORLD 1960 83 min. **Dir.** Shigeo Tanaka **Scr.** Katsuya Suzaki/Ko Suzumura **Photo 'scope:** Michio Takahashi **Music:** Noboru Nihiyama   w/ Kazuo Hasegawa, Hiroshi Kawaguchi, Junko Kano, Jun Fujimaki, Keiko Yuge

THIRD GENERATION'S LOYALTY OFFERING aka SANDAI NO SAKAZUKI 1962 87 min. **Dir.** Kazuo Mori **Scr.** Tetsuro Yoshida **Photo color 'scope:** Shozo Honda **Music:** Ichiro Saito w/ Shintaro Katsu, Akiko Koyama,

Yoshie Mizutani, Chitose Mashiro, Matasaburo Tanba, Gen Mitamura, Ariko Mori

Third Generation's Loyalty Offering

Mori previously made another version of this in 1943, also for Daiei, with Chiezo Kataoka. This straddles the border between an in-period *matatabi* and a *ninkyo* yakuza film. The story begins in the 1870s just after the Meiji Restoration has taken place. The story illustrates the change in traditions of Japanese society in general and yakuza life in particular – progress from an insulated feudal society to a more modern westernized one. Of course, the yakuza clans were tradition-bound for many decades right into the 20th century. Feudal hierarchy and ideals are still largely in place, even today. They may have cut their samurai hairstyle, discarded their straw travel hats and stopped carrying swords in public – all transitions we see in this film – but in many other respects the yakuza have changed very little. The story relates Katsu's struggles during this early transitional period. It is too bad that there is not more action as the film seems to be a bit static and talky. * * 1/2

Tokyo Crime Map

TOKYO CRIME MAP aka TOKYO HANZAI CHIZU aka MAP OF MURDER 1956 86 min. **Dir.** Mitsuo Murayama **Scr.** Kaneo Ikegami **Photo B&W:** Yoshihisa Nakagawa **Music:** Tetsuo Tsukahara w/ Kenji Sugawara, Eiji Funakoshi, Hideo Takamatsu, Takashi Shimura, Hiroko Yajima, Mieko Kondo, Toyomi Karita

TOKYO GAMBLER aka TOKYO BAKUTO 1967 82 min. **Dir.** Kimiyoshi Yasuda **Scr.** Kazuo Funabashi **Photo color 'scope:** Yasukazu Takemura **Music:** Taiichiro Kosugi w/ Jiro Tamiya, Shigeru Amachi, Shiho Fujimura, Masumi Harukawa, Michio Minami

Tokyo Gambler

TOKYO GUARDSMEN series

TOKYO BODYGUARDS aka ZA GAADOMAN – TOKYO YOJINBO 1965 85 min. **Dir.** Akira Inoue **Scr.**

Kimiyuki Hasegawa PHOTO B&W
'SCOPE: Kimio Watanabe w/ Ken
Utsui, Jun Fujimaki, Kyoko Enami,
Naoko Kubo   Two films that are
spinoffs from the popular sixties
Japanese TV show "The Guardsmen,"
about undercover security forces
against organized crime. #1 of 2

Tokyo Ninja Force aka Guardsmen (#2)

TOKYO NINJA FORCE aka ZA
GAADOMAN – TOKYO NINJA
BUTAI 1965 DIR. Taro Yuge SCR.
Kimiyuki Hasegawa PHOTO B&W
'SCOPE: Nobuo Munekawa w/ Ken
Utsui, Jun Fujimaki, Mikio Narita,
Machiko Hasegawa #2 of 2

TRUMP CARD OF REVENGE
aka FUKUSHU NO KIRI FUDA
1966 DIR. Harumi Mizuho SCR.
Toshio Matsuura PHOTO B&W
'SCOPE: Toru Watanabe w/ Jiro
Tamiya, Kyoko Enami. Kyosuke
Machida, Machiko Hasegawa
Humorous elements pepper this
vehicle for Tamiya, most revolving
around the various disguises he assumes.

Underworld's Number One

**UNDERWORLD'S NUMBER
ONE** aka ANKOKU GAI #1
1963 DIR. Shigeo Tanaka SCR.
Toshio Matsuura PHOTO COLOR
'SCOPE: Michio Takahashi MUSIC:
Chuji Kinoshita w/ Ken Utsui,

Vixen

Kyoko Enami, Eiko Taki, Jun Fujimaki, Hideo Takamatsu, Yuzo Hayakawa

USELESS CREATURE – FIGHTING MAN'S LIFE aka DODE KAI YATSU – KENKA YA ICHIDAI aka SOFT-BOILED GORO 1970 87 min. **DIR.** Kazuo Ikehiro **SCR.** Yoshihiro Ishimatsu **PHOTO COLOR 'SCOPE:** Fujio Morita **MUSIC:** Takeo Watanabe **w/** Shintaro Katsu, Akira Yamanouchi, Ko Nishimura, Yumiko Fujita, Shingo Ibuki, Akane Kawazaki, Natsuko Oka, Ichiro Yamamoto, Tokio Oki
This has its moments but is basically disappointing considering Ikehiro, Ishimatsu and Katsu's involvement. Boisterous lone-wolf tough Katsu is idolized by a strange DODES KA DEN-type junkyard community about to be evicted because of a ruthless conglomerate's plan for a building complex. Amidst his other schemes and scams, Katsu also tries to save the junkyard folks. When his various machinations and extortions fail, he resorts to violence. He ends up being cut down by the cops when he fires into their midst. Katsu's rival, bigwig Yamanouchi, is not really that bad a guy and is sorry to see Katsu bite the dust. This seems a bit overly-sentimental at times. Then again the version I saw was an atrociously panned-and-scanned, butchered, commercial-interrupted mess recorded off of Japanese TV broadcast sometime in the late 1980s, so maybe it deserves another 1/2 notch up in my rating. * * 1/2

USELESS HANDCUFFS aka TEJO MUYO aka HANDCUFFS 1969 89 min. **DIR.** Tokuzo Tanaka

SCR. Ichiro Ikeda **PHOTO COLOR 'SCOPE:** Chishi Makiura **MUSIC:** Taiichiro Kosugi **w/** Shintaro Katsu, Makoto Fujita, Shiho Fujimura, Tomomi Sato, Machiko Hasgawa, Mikio Narita, Mayumi Nagisa, Hideko Yoshide, Osamu Ogawa
An entertaining, though pretty forgettable action comedy about master safecracker Katsu who can break into any safe, out of any handcuffs, etc.,. through his knowledge coupled with manual dexterity. Sato is one pretty, sexy doublecrosser here. * * 1/2

VIXEN aka JOTAI aka A WOMAN'S BODY 1969 95 min. **DIR.** Yasuzo Masumura **SCR.** Ichiro Ikeda/Yasuzo Masumura **PHOTO COLOR 'SCOPE:** Setsuo Kobayashi **MUSIC:** Hikaru Hayashi **w/** Ruriko Asaoka, Eiji Okada, Eiko Azusa, Kyoko Kishida, Takao Ito, Yusuke Kawazu, Eitaro Ozawa
Asaoka tries to extort money from the chancellor of a large university that is being plagued with violent student demonstrations. The chancellor's son had raped her, and she wants compensation. The chancellor's other son Okada takes money out of an account in which the college deposits student bribe money. Asaoka, of course, ends up boldly seducing Okada, and he falls in-love with her. Her old boyfriend (Kawazu), who is a gangster, tries to blackmail Okada about the source of Asaoka's payment, the unauthorized withdrawal made by Okada from an illicit account. Okada ends up killing him. He confesses to the police and, after many days of questioning, is released. He then requests a divorce from wife Kishida and subsequently opens

a bar with Asaoka. Okada's sister comes to visit with her fiancee (Ito). When Ito rescues Asaoka from a drunken customer, she falls for him and begins to pursue him as she did Okada. Okada is so enraged he nearly strangles her, not merely jealous but protective of his sister's happiness. Asaoka swears not to see Ito again. But she is lying. She goes for a drive with Ito, crashes the car, and Ito is seriously injured. Okada's sister tries to kill Asaoka at the hospital. Okada threatens her. Asaoka is drinking heavily and Okada, finally having had enough, splits. Later Asaoka accidentally dislodges the gas hose from the water heater as she climbs into her bath. Another astonishing example of Masumura transforming seemingly potboiler material into an unpretentious, uncompromising work of art. It also, probably more than any other of the director's films, shows his ability to bring out the full potential of his performers. Although Asaoka has demonstrated her range in a few of Nikkatsu's "mood/action" noirs with Yujiro Ishihara as well as her surprising turn in Hideo Gosha's samurai masterpiece, GOYOKIN, nothing really prepares one for her performance here. She is truly a volcano of anarchic charisma. Her character is a total sociopath with the emotional maturity of a 12-year-old. At the same time, Masumura shows her in private, deliriously overcome with a childlike exuberance and joy as she – clad either in her underwear or the latest mod fashion – dances uninhibitedly around her bedroom or living room. These dances are amazing – simultaneously exhilarating, funny, sad and moving. A strange film, in some ways similar to Masumura's HOT LITTLE GIRL and PLAY IT COOL with Mari Atsumi. Although not a pure yakuza film, it does have quite a few of the genre's elements and, more importantly, it truly gets inside the sociopathic soul that serves as fertile ground for the ever-burgeoning yakuza ranks. * * * 1/2

WANDERER IN A BUSINESS SUIT aka SEBIRO SUGATA NO WATARIDORI 1961 DIR. Kunihiko Sunami PHOTO 'SCOPE: Tetsu Watanabe MUSIC: Harumi Ibe w/ Koichi Ose, Mitsuo Sagawa, Hiroko (Yuko?) Miki

WANDERER'S STORY – CHECKMATE aka FURAI MONOGATARI – ABARE HISHA 1960 DIR./SCR. Kunio Watanabe PHOTO 'SCOPE: Takashi Watanabe MUSIC: Eiichi Yamada w/ Kazuo Hasegawa, Kojiro Hongo, Tazuko Niki, Katsuhiko Kobayashi, Jun Negami, Tamao Nakamura, Keiko Yuge, Misako Uji, Isuzu Yamada There is a chance, judging from the director and star, that this might not be a contemporary yakuza story but a *matatabi* tale set "in-period."

WANDERING FUGITIVE SWORD aka KYOJO NAGARE DOSU aka THE ANGRY SWORD 1970 83 min. DIR. Kenji Misumi SCR. Kinya Naoi PHOTO COLOR 'SCOPE: Senkichiro Takeda MUSIC: Taiichiro Kosugi w/ Hiroki Matsukata, Yusuke Kawazu, Kenjiro Ishiyama, Isaori Maki, Mitsuko Nakata, Akane Kawazaki, Rokko Toura Misumi is one of the all-time great directors. So, it is with some disappointment I cannot report this is an unqualified masterpiece.

Another set in pre-war period (1920s –'30s) *ninkyo* tale with Matsukata as an itinerant lone wolf coming to the rescue of a girl trying to escape prostitution and having the whole yakuza world fall in on him. More setbound than most of either Misumi's or Daiei's other films. It *does* have a particularly vigorous swordfight showdown at the climax, though. This is one of the several Daiei films originally written for the late Raizo Ichikawa but featuring the drafted-from-Toei Studios-in-an-emergency Matsukata instead. * * 1/2

Wandering Fugitive Sword

WAY OUT, WAY IN aka KOKOSEI BANCHO aka HIGH SCHOOL BOSS 1970 84 min. **DIR.** Michihiko Obimori **SCR.** Katsuya Suzaki **PHOTO COLOR 'SCOPE:** Yoshihisa Nakagawa **MUSIC:** Harumi Ibe **w/** Yoko Namikawa, Saburo Shinoda, Ichiro Ogura, Kozaburo Onogawa, Eiko Yatsunami, Ayako Naruse Priviliged high school day

students and poorer night students interact and begin a feud, fueled by sexual insults and harassment. Nighttime Onogawa and dayboy Shinoda fix on a motorcycle race as a way of deciding the winner of their peculiar gang war. More pseudo-*sukeban/bosozoku* hijinks.

WICKED NUN aka AKUMYO AMA aka NUN'S BAD REPUTATION 1971 **DIR.** Shigeo Tanaka **SCR.** Fumi Takahashi **PHOTO COLOR 'SCOPE:** Kyuji Yokote **MUSIC:** Kazuo Kitamura **w/** Eiko Yatsunami, Mieko Komine, Kaoru Sono, Hiroko Sakurai, Bontaro Miake A sexploitive female yakuza picture with sizzling Yatsunami in the lead role. When I first saw the poster for this film, I was sure it was one of Toei's brazenly ribald girl gang pictures – until I saw Daiei's logo in the corner!

Wicked Nun

WIND GOD, THUNDER GOD aka FUJIN RAIJIN 1963 **DIR.** Mitsuo

Murayama Scr. Toshio Matsuura/
Keigo Takaoka Photo B&W 'scope:
Kimio Watanabe Music: Hajime
Okumura w/ Kojiro Hongo, Jun
Fujimaki, Hideo Takamatsu, Eiko
Taki A *ninkyo* yakuza tale in a
contemporary time frame.

Wind God, Thunder God

WIND VELOCITY 75 METERS
aka FUSOKU SHICHI-JUGO
METORU 1963 Dir. Shigeo
Tanaka Scr. Hajime Takaiwa/Kozo
Taguchi Photo B&W 'scope:
Michio Takahashi w/ Jiro Tamiya,
Ken Utsui, Junko Kano, Yuzo
Horikawa, Hideo Takamatsu
A cop and a big business saboteur
do battle during a violent typhoon.
There are some organized crime
elements here, but this is really more
of a noirish action thriller. * * 1/2

Wind Velocity 75 Meters

WOLF'S UNIFORM aka SEI-
FUKU NO OKAMI 1964 Dir.
Taro Yuge w/ Mikio Narita,
Michiko Sugata

WOMAN BOSS aka ONNA
KUMICHO aka THE GEISHA
FIREFIGHTER 1970 82 min.
Dir. Masahiro Makino Scr. Ichiro
Miyagawa/Masahiro Makino Photo
color 'scope: Yoshihisa Nakagawa
Music: Hajime Kaburagi w/ Kyoko

Enami, Mikio Narita, Makoto Sato, Nobuo Kaneko, Kumi Mizuno, Masahiko Tsugawa, Michitaro Mizushima, Isuzu Yamada, Shuji Sano, Junzaburo Ban, Frankie Sakai One of Makino's few sorties helping out at Daiei in their final releases before the studio's bankruptcy in 1971, with a pretty amazing cast. This may be an early treatment of a scenario that was later filmed by Makino as Junko Fuji's final film, the Toei-produced CHERRY BLOSSOM FIRE GANG (KANTO HIZAKURA IKKA) in 1972.

Woman Boss

WOMAN GAMBLING EXPERT aka ONNA TOBAKUSHI aka WOMAN YAKUZA series

GAMBLING WOMAN aka ONNA NO TOBA 1966 DIR. Shigeo Tanaka   Scr. Kinya Naoi/ Yoshi Hattori   PHOTO COLOR 'SCOPE: Setsuo Kobayashi   MUSIC: Sei Ikeno

w/ Kyoko Enami, Yusuke Kawazu, Fumio Watanabe, Koichi Mizuhara, Osamu Sakai, Bontaro Miake, Hiroshi Minami, Akira Natsuki, Koji Fujiyama   Contrary to my original expectations on hearing of this series, this is not set in the pre-WW2 1920s period but in a contempo sixties time slot. Too bad, because I feel that the whole "noble woman outlaw" premise suffers in a modern milieu. Even though Toei Studios' RED PEONY GAMBLER series started a year or two later and definitely copped some imagery from the Daiei series, their depiction of period atmosphere and a just, "honest" woman outlaw on her own in a cruel environment is much more on the mark. Charismatic Kyoko Enami doesn't always play the same character from film to film in the series which also gets a bit confusing. That said, there is still something about this series that I like. Although quite a few of the entries are fairly routine potboilers, there are also several films that achieve a low key intensity from their very matter-of-fact, flat depiction of the often mundane environment of the yakuza gambling world and a woman's place in it. This first movie sets the template for many of those following. Though talky, it is straightforward and is presented with a zenlike, spartan simplicity that often recalls the joys of Kenji Misumi's directorial style. Composer Sei Ikeno's trademark lush, dreamlike score and orchestration emphasize this. Small restaurant owner Enami's father is accused of cheating, shoots himself, then Enami and her rebellious teen brother must deal with the fallout. She gradually learns that her father's accuser, yakuza underboss and exotic strip club owner, Watanabe, may have set her father up. As the film progresses, the onion layers are gradually peeled away, her conventional romance with a straight-arrow architect is sabotaged, and Enami verifies what she always thought about craven Watanabe. She takes an intense training course from her father's younger protege, Kawazu, becomes a *hana fuda* card expert and sets up Watanabe the same way he had set up her father. In the end, exposed to his fellow bosses as a deceiving scoundrel, Watanabe is disgraced and shoots himself off-screen. #1 of 17 films * * *

Woman Gambling Expert (#2)

WOMAN GAMBLING EXPERT
aka ONNA TOBAKUSHI 1967
85 min. **DIR.** Taro Yuge **SCR.** Toshio Matsuura **PHOTO COLOR 'SCOPE:** Nobuo Munekawa **MUSIC:** Sei Ikeno w/ Kyoko Enami, Koeda Kawaguchi, Kojiro Hongo, Yoshi Kato, Asao Uchida, Ryohei Uchida, Yuzo

Hayakawa, Tadashi Nakamura, Koichi Mizuhara   Enami is an expert *hana fuda* card dealer, pianist *and* part-time model working at a nightclub located downstairs from her beau Hongo's photography studio. Boss Uchida, though friendly on the outside, begins devising plans to subvert Enami as a gambler and seduce her into being his mistress. He uses female teenage gambler wannabe Kawaguchi's jealousy of Enami to throw a monkeywrench into Enami and Hongo's love affair. Hongo is something of a straight arrow square anyway, so he has little affection for Enami's card game expertise. When Kawaguchi flaunts her body at him, simultaneously trying to seduce him and secure a modeling job, Hongo soon succumbs. Despite the fact that pudgy Kawaguchi's annoyingly unattractive personality and appearance make it hard to believe Hongo would reject graceful, gorgeous Enami in favor of her, this actually works to the story's advantage. Hongo's character, regardless of his talent as a photographer, is supposed to be a rather prosaic young man who wants to be with a woman he can control. And the seemingly traditional, yet very independent-minded Enami certainly does not fit the bill. In a plot convention from the first film, Uchida orchestrates Enami's gambler father Kato to come out of retirement to play a big game then, after a police raid, coerces the old man into committing suicide. When Enami and her fellow gambler friend discover Uchida's dirty work, they engineer a plan to kill the villain. Enami pretends a mutual attraction, but is foiled by Uchida when she tries to stab him as they make love. Luckily for

Enami her pal is waiting in the wings and promptly skewers Uchida in the back while still straddling the prone Enami. Enami and cohort leave the hotel, but the dying Uchida phones his men, telling them to search for the pair. Unawares they are in danger, Enami and comrade go their separate ways. Enami leaves town on a train, but her friend, traversing back alleys to keep a low profile, is waylaid by Uchida's men and stabbed to death in broad daylight. Although there is little action and seemingly not much happens, this entry remains strangely memorable with many low-key, well-acted scenes. It is matter-of-fact and unpretentious, with a comparatively fresh story compared to the more formulaic scenarios that soon became commonplace in the series. Composer Sei Ikeno also delivers his customarily lush atmospherics in the music score, sonically mapping the subconscious undercurrents of the characters. #2 of 17 films * * *

WOMAN GAMBLING STORM

aka ONNA TOBA ARASHI aka THE SISTER GAMBLERS 1967 DIR. Taro Yuge SCR. Kimiyuki Hasegawa PHOTO COLOR 'SCOPE: Tetsu Watanabe MUSIC: Hajime Kaburagi w/ Kyoko Enami, Mikio Narita, Yoshi Kato, Hizuru Takachiho, Asao Koike, Kyosuke Machida, Jotaro Senba Enami, who runs a tiny, hole-in-the-wall record store, is secretly enamored of throwing dice. She has become a bit of an expert, winning money from patrons at local bars. Lone wolf yakuza Narita spots her and introduces her to the illicit thrills of yakuza gambling dens. She wins big in her first game. But her father Kato – who is a former

gambler – is outraged and takes the money, barges back into the secret gambling parlor and proves to the unawares patrons that the host gang is cheating them. He is beaten to a pulp on his way home and soon dies in the hospital. Narita gets together with Enami after the cremation and is genuinely contrite, not knowing that his bringing her to the game would cause such tragedy. However, he reveals to her that the dice she was using at the local bars *were* rigged, something that he thought she knew. It turns out that the dice belonged to her reformed father, and that his indignation and shame were exacerbated because of this. Narita ends up schooling Enami obsessively in honest gambling, both dice-throwing and card-dealing, and the pair go traveling to various towns, making Enami's reputation. Narita's ex-girlfriend enters the picture and is soon causing trouble. Two thirds of the way through the saga, the film abruptly shifts into Toei Studios' style *ninkyo* territory with evil boss Machida (soon to become a fixture in Toei yakuza pictures) attempting to kill Enami and Narita at the fog-shrouded climax with his sword-wielding henchmen. Narita grabs a sword and slaughters many of the villains, a couple of them in incongruously gory detail. Right before the confrontation ends, Narita's ex steps in front of a blade to shield her nemesis Enami and is mortally wounded. The villains repulsed, she dies in Narita's arms as Enami looks on. Once again, an original scenario but director Yuge's execution is fairly humdrum and the threadbare production seems rushed. #3 of 17 films * * 1/2

**THREE WOMEN GAMBLING
EXPERTS** aka SANBIKI NO
ONNA TOBAKUSHI aka THOR-
OUGHBRED WOMEN GAM-
BLERS 1967 88 min. DIR. Shigeo
Tanaka SCR. Kikuma Shimoizaka
PHOTO COLOR 'SCOPE: Yoshihisa
Nakagawa MUSIC: Hajime Kaburagi
w/ Kyoko Enami, Michiyo Yasuda,
Mako Sanjo, Akio Hasegawa,
Bontaro Miake, Ryutaro Gomi

Three Women Gambling Expeerts

Like its predecessors, this fourth
entry, although already starting to
show the monotony of the formula,
has many small pleasures scattered
throughout to compensate. Traditionalist Enami and younger, swinging
sixties kid sister Yasuda come from a
"respectable" yakuza household and
are devoted to their ailing father. Both
are also acquainted with third girl
gambler Sanjo, a notorious, unscrupulous cheat married to their estranged
hothead of a brother. What nobody
else realizes is that Sanjo is two-timing her hubby with a slick, equally-
underhanded yakuza. The pair are
plotting to usurp Enami's favored
role as card dealer for yakuza gang
boss Gomi's games. One particularly
disturbing sequence has Sanjo's oily
beau running down the limping father
in the driving rain, with the mortally-
wounded patriarch then lying in a
squalid alley where he is not found
until hours later. It is these kinds of
understated horrors in Shimoizaka's
script as well as some stretches of
dialogue chronicling nakedly brutal
betrayals of personal trust that help to
elevate the film out of simple programmer status. This, despite the fact
that there is a certain conservative
bias informing the saga that little sis
Yasuda's love of a mod lifestyle is
synonymous with fuzzy thinking and
naïve superficiality. Yasuda is depicted as just as intelligent, honest and
fearless as her very traditional elder
sibling Enami, but she is also painted
as hopelessly naïve and hot-tempered,
ready to believe Sanjo's evil rumors
about Enami without checking her
facts. Inevitably, Sanjo and partner
are exposed in the end before Gomi's
gang as the ignoble skunks they are,
with Enami, Yasuda and even their
finally contrite brother reuniting to
defeat the threat to their family. #4 of
17 films * * *

**KANTO WOMAN GAMBLING
EXPERT** aka KANTO ONNA
TOBAKUSHI aka THE WOMAN
CHAMPION 1968 86 min.
DIR. Yoshio Inoue SCR. Kimiyuki
Hasegawa PHOTO COLOR 'SCOPE:
Yoshihisa Nakagawa MUSIC: Hajime
Kaburagi w/ Kyoko Enami,
Yunosuke Ito, Kunie Tanaka,

Taketoshi Naito, Takashi Shimura, Takao Ito, Michiko Sugata, Koichi Mizuhara, Hikaru Hoshi   #5 of 17 films

WOMAN GAMBLING EXPERT OVERCOMING ADVERSITY aka ONNA TOBAKUSHI NORIKOMU aka THE GEISHA GAMBLER 1968   87 min.   **DIR** Shigeo Tanaka **SCR** Kimiyuki Hasegawa **PHOTO COLOR 'SCOPE:** Yoshihisa Nakagawa **MUSIC:** Hajime Kaburagi w/ Kyoko Enami, Michiyo Yasuda, Machiko Hasegawa, Chieko Naniwa, Mako Sanjo, Mitsuko Mito, Yuzo Hayakawa, Yusuke Takita
Dignified, traditional dice expert Enami is humiliated when a gambling den boss replaces her with his vulgar stripper mistress Sanjo. Complications ensue when Enami's little sister Yasuda starts getting into trouble with a lecherous young yakuza in the boss's employ. But things really go downhill when the mother of the two siblings unexpectedly dies. Enami tearfully vows to leave the gambling world and concentrate on her geisha performances in a theatrical troupe. Sister Yasuda – already fronting a pop group! – backs her up on shamisen. At the close, Enami decides to go back to the dice to help out her gambling mentor as well as her hard-boiled, elder patroness, both of whom are in hock to the villain. When she wins the match against Sanjo, her patroness is elated, but her mentor is stabbed to death by three hoodlums out back. Unlike other female yakuza series from around this time, Enami exacts no reprisals nor embarks on any vendetta. Probably just like what would happen in real life. Enami and Yasuda are very good as always,

and the story concentrates more on character and moral dilemnas. There is virtually no fighting; the action film fan is forewarned.   #6 of 17 films
* * 1/2

WOMAN GAMBLING EXPERT – GAMBLING DEN TORN APART aka ONNA TOBAKUSHI – TEKKABA YABURI aka THE WOMAN DICER 1968   88 min. **DIR** Yoshio Inoue **SCR** Kimiyuki Hasegawa **PHOTO COLOR 'SCOPE:** Yoshihisa Nakagawa **MUSIC:** Hajime Kaburagi w/ Kyoko Enami, Ryutaro Otomo, Mikio Narita, Wasako Hara, Goro Mutsumi, Reiko Oshida, Koichi Mizuhara, Taketoshi Naito, Jotaro Senba   Burnt-out Enami and perpetual sunglasses-wearing Hara go from gambling den to gambling den exposing various dice and card cheat schemes. Smooth operator Narita hires them to stay on at his den of iniquity which also includes a labyrinthine brothel. Enami starts dice-throwing for the gang but is soon on the outs when she balks at their shady ways. In a somewhat similar pattern to the previous film, she gets humiliated and decides to go into the legitimate massage/acupuncture business (!). Hara wastes no time and enlists ex-whore/teen waif Oshida (later of Toei Studio's DE- ﹅ LINQUENT GIRL BOSS series) to take Enami's place as her protege. In the last third of the film, Enami returns to the gaming tables as a favor to decent boss Otomo and inevitably runs up against sleazy, sociopathic Narita and underhanded Hara. Enami enlists Hara's dissolute gambler ex-husband in a plan to expose Hara's cheating sleight of hand. This causes Hara to vengefully try to stab her

ex, something which ironically ends with her own poignant demise. Well-written but often static and extremely short on action. #7 of 17 films
* * 1/2

WOMAN GAMBLING EXPERT – CONVENT GAMBLING MATCH aka ONNA TOBAKUSHI AMADERA KAICHO aka WOMAN GAMBLER AND THE NUN 1968 84 min. **DIR.** Shigeo Tanaka **SCR.** Hajime Takaiwa **PHOTO COLOR 'SCOPE:** Yoshihisa Nakagawa **MUSIC:** Hajime Kaburagi **w/** Kyoko Enami, Yusuke Kawazu, Mako Sanjo, Takashi Shimura, Shiro Osaka, Yuzo Hayakawa, Koichi Mizuhara, Jotaro Senba, Toshitaro Kitashiro   Enami travels with ne'er-do-well father Osaka as he deals cards in various gambling dens. Slimy boss Kitashiro's gang take offense at Enami's potential suitor, so hoodlum Senba runs Osaka, Enami and boyfriend's car off the road. Enami is briefly hospitalized and her male friend killed. Osaka then gets busted with an inept friend for cheating when slut Sanjo blows the whistle on him during a game. Kitashiro agrees to not severely punish Osaka if he continues to cheat but for the gang's benefit, as well as enlist daughter Enami as his protege. Things go from bad to worse when Osaka tries to help out in a gangfight in the den's offices. He goes to jail after severely stabbing his old friend Kawazu, who has accused Kitashiro of cheating. This seems poised to be a bit more potent than the previous entries when slutty Sanjo rebels against Kitashiro trying to stab him, but she is blindsided by a floor trapdoor. Underboss Senba heads down to the cellar and proceeeds to

tear off her clothes, then rape her! This scene is actually a little shocking considering when it was filmed and how little of this kind of thing can be found in the rest of the series. Even though the nudity is brief, Daiei really didn't go in for such borderline explicit shenanigans until 1969 when competition for titillating cinema became fierce amongst the studios. Regrettably, the story deflates from there on in as Enami hooks up with her just-released dad Osaka on her town-to-town pilgrimage of dealing cards. Osaka is subsequently murdered by Kitashiro's bunch in the picaresque coastal village where Enami is staying. She runs into friendly lone wolf Kawazu again as well as family friend Takashi Shimura (who is given little to do here aside from being his type-cast benevolent self). Underboss Senba has left the gang and is now living with Sanjo who has become a Buddhist nun! However, Sanjo and Senba are still up to their old tricks running crooked *hana fuda* games. Senba is murdered by his former comrades, and Kitashiro forces Sanjo to engage in a crooked one-on-one game with Enami. Kawazu and Enami spot Sanjo's cheating, Kawazu battles Kitashiro's bunch and defeats them. Like many entries in the series, intriguing situations are set up but quite often not followed through to their fullest potential. Pretty lackluster considering the excitement quotient of similar films at Toei and Nikkatsu in the same time frame. #8 of 17 films * * 1/2

WOMAN GAMBLING EXPERT – SEVERED RELATIONS aka ONNA TOBAKUSHI – ZETSU ENJO aka CHAMPION WOMAN

GAMBLER 1968 87 min. **DIR.** Shigeo Tanaka **SCR.** Kimiyuki Hasegawa **PHOTO COLOR 'SCOPE:** Izumi Kitazaki **MUSIC:** Hajime Kaburagi **w/** Kyoko Enami, Shogo Shimada, Mikio Narita, Machiko Hasegawa, Kenjiro Ishiyama, Minako Saijo, Tadasu Hiraizumi, Toru Abe, Koichi Mizuhara This initially seems to be more of the same from pedestrian director Tanaka and static writer Hasegawa. But it gets better and better as it goes along. Enami is schooled in the fine art of dice-throwing by elderly mentor Shimada and eventually starts to preside over games for bad gang boss Abe after his regular female gambler (Machiko Hasegawa) is caught cheating. Already jealous of Enami, even though Hasegawwa manages her own bar, the insecure Hasegawa plunges into a black pit of hatred towards our mild-mannered heroine. To make matters worse, Hasegawa's beau Narita – though Enami's rival as champion dice-thrower – holds Enami in high esteem for her integrity and skill. This entry actually gets pretty good when it decides to focus on tormented Hasegawa's machinations and gradual softening towards Enami as she fights her inner demons. Things come to a head when Shimada forces boss Abe to return stolen documents, something which culminates in Shimada's murder. The climax has Abe and right hand man shot-to-death by an anonymous, disgruntled gambling den employee. However, Abe had already set the wheels in motion to kill Enami, too. However, the designated hit team decide to take Enami out right in front of Hasegawa's club. Coincidentally, Hasegawa just happens to be outside smoking when she spots the bad guys poised to throw a knife in Enami's back. She impulsively dives in the way to shield her nemesis and receives the dagger between her own shoulder blades as reward. The thing that is truly great about this scene is that Enami is distracted by the wind and by the taxi that has stopped for her, and she does not even notice that her mortal enemy has just saved her life by sacrificing her own. It is a nice surprise to see Daiei veteran actress Hasegawa get to flex her acting prowess, something she did not get to do too often in the countless supporting roles she assayed in Daiei's samurai and yakuza programmers. #9 of 17 films   * * *

WOMAN GAMBLING EXPERT – RAISING THE INNER SANCTUM'S CURTAIN aka ONNA TOBAKUSHI – OKU NO INKAICHO aka WOMAN GAMBLER'S REVENGE 1968 83 min. **DIR.** Yoshio Inoue **SCR.** Yoshihiro Ishimatsu **PHOTO COLOR 'SCOPE:** Yoshihisa Nakagawa **MUSIC:** Hajime Kaburagi **w/** Kyoko Enami, Junzaburo Ban, Kunie Tanaka, Bontaro Miake, Reiko Kasahara, Koji Fujiyama, Taketoshi Naito, Ryuji Kiba   Enami leaves her knife-throwing stage act and her adoptive family (that includes Miake and Tanaka, both of whom are completely wasted in their roles) to go back to gambling. She hooks up with estranged father figure/gambling expert Ban, who schools her further in dice and cards. At the end she is pitted against him in a big game presided over by villainous boss Naito. Ban sacrifices himself, getting in the way of Naito's blade when the bad

guy tries to kill Enami. A pretty disappointing by-the-numbers programmer, especially when you consider
excellent screenwriter Ishimatsu (who
collaborated on countless great films
with Fukasaku, Masumura, Junya
Sato and Kazuo Ikehiro) penned the
script. #10 of 17 films * * 1/2

**WOMAN GAMBLING EXPERT –
CROOKED DICE CUP** aka
MELTING POT OF CORRUP-
TION aka ONNA TOBAKUSHI
– MIDARE TSUBO aka WOMAN
GAMBLER'S SUPPLICATION
1968 83 min. **DIR.** Shigeo Tanaka
SCR. Hajime Takaiwa **PHOTO COLOR**
'SCOPE: Yoshihisa Nakagawa **MUSIC:**
Hajime Kaburagi **w/** Kyoko Enami,
Michiyo Yasuda, Chieko Naniwa,
Machiko Hasegawa, Yusuke Kawazu,
Tatsuo Terashima, Eijiro Yanagi,
Isamu Nagato, Utako Kyo, Hosei
Komatsu A surprisingly good entry
with tradition-bound Enami at odds
with her mod, gambling younger
sister Yasuda who is being manipulated by slick gambling boss/pimp
Komatsu. There is a great tapestry
of characters here with Hasegawa
as a degenerate gambler nun who
becomes Komatsu's mistress, Naniwa
as Enami and Yasuda's tough-talking,
restuarant-owning gambler mom,
Kawazu as a lone wolf yakuza who
dies trying to save Enami in a knifefight and Nagato as a gambler-for-hire
who becomes chivalrous, slashing-to-
death his boss Komatsu when the villain tries to assassinate Enami at the
final big game. Also of note: Enami
gets to actually fight a bit with a knife
in a mid-story action sequence, a very
welcome development. #11 of 17
films * * *

**WOMAN GAMBLING EXPERT –
TAINTED DICE** aka ONNA
TOBAKUSHI – SAIKORO GESHO
aka TWO ENEMY WOMEN
GAMBLERS 1969 83 min.
DIR. Yoshio Inoue **SCR.** Yoshihiro
Ishimatsu/ Yoshio Inoue **PHOTO**
COLOR 'SCOPE: Yoshihisa Nakagawa
MUSIC: Hajime Kaburagi
w/ Kyoko Enami, Naoko Kubo,
Shigeru Tsuyuguchi, Shiro Osaka,
Mikio Narita, Yoshihiko Aoyama,
Reiko Kasahara, Koichi Uenoyama,
Ryuji Kita, Asao Uchida, Toshitaro
Kitashiro #12 of 17 films

Woman Gambling Expert (#13)

**WOMAN GAMBLING EXPERT
– TEN GAMES** aka ONNA
TOBAKUSHI – JUBAN SHOBU
aka WOMAN GAMBLER'S TRAP
1969 84 min. **DIR.** Shigeo Tanaka
SCR. Hajime Takaiwa **PHOTO COLOR**
'SCOPE: Yoshihisa Nakagawa
MUSIC: Hajime Kaburagi **w/** Kyoko
Enami, Ryunosuke Minegishi, Eiji
Funakoshi, Fumio Watanabe, Junko

Natsu, Shiro Osaka, Hosei Komatsu, Hizuru Takachiho, Yasuko Matsui, Bontaro Miake   A so-so story of gambling woman Enami turned away from a certain yakuza gang after the death of their boss, who had been one of her best friends. All kinds of intrigue develop involving her being kidnapped. She puts up shamelessly weak resistance. Toei Studios' RED PEONY Oryu (Junko Fuji) would have either slashed, shot or at least judo-thrown a few of her attackers before succumbing. A cool-looking guy in black leather (Minegishi) rescues her, but she ends up getting pushed by one of the bad guys and hitting her head on a crate. She develops a concussion (!) and starts to experience eye trouble. A woman eye doctor (will this make up for some of the other sexist stuff here?) predicts possible blindness. Whoops! No more dice-throwing or flower card games. But, after a couple days of anxiety, lo and behold another doctor, a *male* eye doctor – and an alcoholic gambler (oh, well, sexism returns) – sets her right in time for the big game. The actual gambling den scenes/games are quite well done and very atmospheric, but I was otherwise disappointed when Enami did not even raise a finger in the climactic massacre, letting cool black leather stud Minegishi do the dirty work. Oh well, another uneven entry in this uneven series. #13 of 17 films   * *

WOMAN GAMBLING EXPERT – ODD /EVEN GAMBLING TRIP aka ONNA TOBAKUSHI – CHO-HAN TABI aka WOMAN GAMBLER'S SAPPHIRE 1969 84 min. Dir. Yoshio Inoue Scr. Takehiko Sakai Photo color

'scope: Setsuo Kobayashi Music: Hajime Kaburagi w/ Kyoko Enami, Naoko Kubo, Makoto Sato, Jun Fujimaki, Asao Uchida, Mizuho Suzuki, Teruko Yamagishi, Shozaburo Sato, Toshitaro Kitashiro Unhappily, this is not much beyond the previous film's standard programmer scenario. Here Enami's obviously a neophyte being schooled in the art of dice-throwing by mentor Sato after his elderly master gambler father dies. They are up against an evil gambling gang led by Suzuki who has got a rigged lighting system to signal his dice champion and insure his continued victories. It is pretty much potboiler territory all the way, with Sato developing the same debilitating brain ailment that killed his dad before being murdered by Suzuki's bunch after he discovers their cheating secrets.

Woman Gambling Expert (#14)

This does have some nice *grand guignol* bloodletting in a couple of unexpected sequences. Sad to report that despite Enami's character's tenacious efforts to hone her gambling skills, she portrays the usual yakuza *eiga* shrinking-violet woman's role, only once warding off a knife attack with her parasol. Otherwise she is helpless in the face of macho violence. Perhaps the filmmakers were trying to get across a more realistic portrait of a woman in the gambling underworld. If so, they could have taken a cue from Yumiko Nogawa's CAT GIRL GAMBLING trio of films at Nikkatsu – movies that weren't the tall tale legends of Toei's RED PEONY GAMBLER series, but nevertheless featured a realistic woman willing to defend herself and fight if she had to. #14 of 17 films   * * 1/2

WOMAN GAMBLING EXPERT – TRUMP FLOWER CARD aka ONNA TOBAKUSHI – HANA NO KIRI FUDA aka WOMAN GAMBLER'S TRUMP CARD 1969 86 min. **DIR.** Yoshio Inoue **SCR.** Yoshihiro Ishimatsu **PHOTO COLOR 'SCOPE:** Yoshihisa Nakagawa w/ Kyoko Enami, Shigeru Amachi, Masahiko Tsugawa, Mikio Narita, Mieko Inagaki, Eiji Funakoshi, Takamaru Sasaki, Fujio Suga, Yuzo Hayakawa, Osamu Ogawa #15 of 17 films

WOMAN GAMBLING EXPERT – STAKES OF A GAME OF CHANCE aka ONNA TOBAKUSHI – TSUBO KURABE aka WOMAN GAMBLER'S CHALLENGE aka COMPARING THE DICE CUPS 1970 87 min. **DIR.** Yoshio Inoue **SCR.** Hajime Takaiwa/ Yoshio Inoue **PHOTO COLOR 'SCOPE:** Setsuo Kobayashi **MUSIC:** Hajime

Kaburagi   **w/** Kyoko Enami, Akihiro Maruyama, Mikio Narita, Tomoko Mayama, Ken Nakahara, Masaya Takahashi, Ryuji Kita *Tsubo* means pot, and I surmise that they are using it the same way Americans do when talking about card games stakes as "throwing money in the pot." It can also be slang for the dice cup. Akihiro Maruyama is the same female impersonator/actor who portrayed the lead villainess in Kinji Fukasaku's BLACK LIZARD (KUROTO KAGE) (1969) and BLACK ROSE MANSION (KURO BARA NO YAKATA) (1969). She remains true to charismatic form, although the role is fairly thankless, with Maruyama appearing as Enami's rival in the climactic dice games. This is actually one of the best entries in the series with Enami and her father being tossed into the drink in the first frames, left for dead by a gambling gang after her father is caught cheating. Dad does not survive, but she does, heading to the snowy north by train. Before long, she runs into former gambling nemesis Narita, the lover of her bar madam employer Mayama. There is some great story background revealed in flashback, with Narita the childhood friend of the one-eyed villain boss. As a kid, Narita had accidentally whipped his fishing line hook into his young pal's eye, thus forever bonding them in a strange, masochistic web of guilt/ obligation. When Enami exposes the boss as engineering a cheating system of magnets in the final big game, mortified Narita whips out a knife and commits impromptu *hara-kiri*! Despite some border-

Woman Gambling Expert (#17)

line absurd plot developments, this remains a bleak and mournfully melancholic saga. #16 of 17 films * * *

NEW WOMAN GAMBLING EXPERT – CONSEQUENCES OF FLESH GONE ASTRAY aka SHIN ONNA TOBAKUSHI – TSUBO GURE HADA aka WOMAN GAMBLER'S IRON RULE aka FLESH TURNS THE DICE CUP 1971 79 min. DIR. Kenji Misumi SCR. Hajime Takaiwa PHOTO COLOR 'SCOPE: Toshio Kajiya MUSIC: Hajime Kaburagi w/ Kyoko Enami, Michiyo Yasuda, Kojiro Hongo, Fumio Watanabe, Akane Kawazaki, Shingo Ibuki, Saburo Date It looks like they either brought in top director Misumi to try to enliven the series or, knowing it was the swan song, wanted to give Enami a nice send-off. Lamentably, Daiei proved to be on the verge of financial collapse at this point. Misumi brings a refreshingly straightforward approach and action dynamic to the series that it had sorely needed for a while. Its short running time also helps things move along at a brisk pace. When the climax comes with evil boss Watanabe suddenly shooting the elder "good" boss right in front of everybody during a gambling match, it is a nice shock. Both Enami with her hairpin knife and rebellious Yasuda with her sword get to do quite a bit of fighting in the ensuing melee dispatching villains, a welcome change to the lack of female swordplay in the vast majority of the series entries. But even director Misumi cannot do much about the programmer material, the same tired plot formula that had been followed

in most of the films. Better than much of the rest of the series, but the magical quality often achieved in Toei, and even Nikkatsu, yakuza pictures, just never seemed to gel here in this series. #17 and final in series * * *

YAKUZA MASTERPIECE aka YAKUZA ZESSHO aka A FINE YAKUZA SONG aka THE FINAL PAYOFF 1970 92 min. DIR. Yasuzo Masumura SCR. Ichiro Ikeda PHOTO COLOR 'SCOPE: Setsuo Kobayashi MUSIC: Hikaru Hayashi w/ Shintaro Katsu, Naoko Otani, Masakazu Tamura, Yusuke Kawazu, Kiwako Taichi, Yoshi Kato, Asao Uchida   Nothing short of brilliant. Katsu plays a brutal yakuza tough who only has a soft spot for his sister Otani whom he smothers with gifts and keeps locked-up at night. Ironically enough, he treats every other woman like trash, including his girlfriend. Knockdown, drag-out fights are commonplace and, when Katsu responds to his girl's jealousy over his buying his sister a new dress, he throws her down on the floor and rapes her right in front of Otani. Otani finally explodes and demands him to stop. He does, and the now ex-girlfriend splits. Meanwhile, Katsu's boss Uchida has given him a contract to fulfill. He makes a stab at it at the Turkish bath his prospective victim frequents, but circumstances are not fortuitous. Instead he gets into an incredibly savage fight in his favorite bar. Not only does he not stop when the cops arrive, but he beats the hell out of them, too. All of which lands him in jail for a few months. His sister Otani, already trying to come into sexual flower, is finally granted some freedom and starts seeing the son (Tamura) of a couple who were friends with her dead mother. The father (Kato) of the boy had been hounding Katsu for months, attempting to get permission for marriage, to no avail. When she is finally on her own and agrees to go out with the boy, the father dies. Katsu has been kept posted in prison by one of his flunkies and puts the kibosh on the relationship as soon as he is out.

Yakuza Masterpiece

However, Otani and Tamura will not take no for an answer and come to talk to him face-to-face. When he still says no, drawing a knife, Otani feigns breaking-up with beau Tamura. Once he has left in a huff, she explains to Katsu, without any animosity, that he stands in the way of her happiness, and she must kill him. Which she promptly tries to do with his knife. After several futile lunges on her part, Katsu sadly disarms her and leaves. Seeing Tamura waiting down the street, Katsu tells him to go back to her, that he will not come between them. He then goes to the Turkish bath to fulfill his hit contract. He calmly plugs his victim, emptying the gun into the guy's nude flesh. Suddenly, the dead guy's bodyguards rush in (two guys who have repeatedly been beaten senseless by Katsu in the past), and they empty their guns into Katsu. He lies quietly dying on the tile floor. Mindblowing.
* * * *

YOU AND I aka KISAMA TO ORE 1966 DIR. Taro Yuge w/ Jiro Tamiya, Mikio Narita, Machiko Hasegawa, Ko Sugita

YOUNG BOSS aka WAKA OYABUN series

Young Boss (#1)

YOUNG BOSS aka WAKA OYABUN aka YOUNG BOSS TAKESHI 1965 86 min.

DIR. Kazuo Ikehiro SCR. Hajime Takaiwa/Shozaburo Asai PHOTO COLOR 'SCOPE: Senkichiro Takeda MUSIC: Taiichiro Kosugi w/ Raizo Ichikawa, Yukiji Asaoka, Shiho Fujimura, Kei Sato, Mikio Narita, Haruo Minami, Junichiro Yamashita, Tatsuya Ishiguro, Koichi Mizuhara, Saburo Date
One of Ichikawa's four film series at Daiei. His most popular and justly famous is the surreal, perverse, violent and sometimes macabre twelve film KYOSHIRO NEMURI – SON OF THE BLACK MASS aka SLEEPY EYES OF DEATH samurai series. He also did a five film WW2 spy series NAKANO SPY SCHOOL (RIKU GUN NAKANO GAKU) and an eight film ninja series NINJA – BAND OF ASSASSINS (SHINOBI NO MONO). This first YOUNG BOSS is quite beautifully done, set in the late Meiji era (just pre-1910, it seems), and the acting is good. However, Ichikawa seems a bit indifferent in his portrayal - the character, a young fellow just discharged from the navy upon the murder of his father, an *oyabun*/yakuza clan leader, seems a bit too good to be true, showing wisdom and virtually no faults for someone his age. Ichikawa is Nanjo, the same character in all eight films of the series. The concept and feel is somewhat similar to the equally good, but largely unavailable A MAN'S CREST series from Nikkatsu studios (1963 –'67) with Hideki Takahashi. Takahashi had also played a young man taking over a yakuza clan upon his *oyabun* father's murder. Conflicts in this story revolve around dealing with the father's death and trying to keep a tight rein on his fellow clan brothers who are chomping at the bit

to annihilate the opposing gang boss they believe to be the guilty party. Kei Sato, sleazy, sadistic head of another third clan, exploits this rivalry and encourages the belief that the obvious party is responsible. As it turns out, Ichikawa's prudence is rewarded for it is Sato who had hired the killer. #1 of 8 films   * * *

YOUNG BOSS – PRISON RELEASE aka WAKA OYABUN – SHUTSU GOKU 1965 87 min. DIR. Kazuo Ikehiro SCR. Shozaburo Asai/ Kichinosuke Shinohara (Sasahara?) PHOTO COLOR 'SCOPE: Shozo Honda MUSIC: Hajime Kaburagi w/ Raizo Ichikawa, Yukiji Asaoka,Jotaro Senba, Mikiko Tsubouchi, Aichi Yamada, Asao Uchida, Koichi Mizuhara, Takashi Kanda, Saburo Date, Tatsuya Ishiguro
Ichikawa/Nanjo is released from prison a short time after killing Sato (the villain from the first film). Apparently his release and that of a handful of other inmates, is consequence of an amnesty to commemorate the end of the Taisho era and the birth of the Showa era. It appears – at least if you can judge from several other yakuza pictures (including Hideo Gosha's THE WOLVES) – that the government had a pre-WW2 tradition of granting general amnesties to many prisoners, political or not, at the start of a new era (an "era" corresponds to the reign of an Emperor climaxing in his death). Since Ichikawa's unannounced discharge is way ahead of schedule, no one is at the prison gate to greet him. As he drifts back into his hometown, he notices signs of another clan making various people's lives miserable. Before long, he has pulled his loosely-knit gang back into

tight cohesion, and finds himself in conflict with this rival clan, a bunch manipulated by powerful industrialist Uchida. Military affiliation is the buffer that villain Uchida uses to mask many criminal enterprises. Coincidentally, Ichikawa's old flame (Asaoka) is now this man's mistress. She had assumed Ichikawa would be old and grey by the time he got out. She is most upset to see that her judgement was faulty. Though she is happy to see Ichikawa and obviously still in-love with him, Ichikawa spurns her. He is not so much jealous as disgusted that she would lower her sights to such an avaricious creature as Uchida. Unbeknownst to Ichikawa, she delivers a huge cache of cash to a mediating elder with the instruction it go to Ichikawa's nearly-bankrupt clan, but as an anonymous donation.

Young Boss (#2)

Also by coincidence, Ichikawa's military/naval buddies – his closest comrades up until the time he was discharged from active duty – are plotting to assassinate the industrial-

ist. They feel he is draining Japan's lifeblood as well as dishonoring the military by his greedy, unscrupulous imperialism. Ichikawa, however, after destroying the rival clan, does it for them – in the white full-dress of his reserve naval uniform yet. He is a rare bird, indeed, in that at least two-thirds of the real-life yakuza from this time period were supporting the machinations of many identically-inclined right-wing imperialists! #2 of 8 films   * * *

YOUNG BOSS – INVITATION TO FIGHT aka WAKA OYABUN – KENKA JO 1966 83 min. Dir. Kazuo Ikehiro Scr. Hajime Takaiwa Photo color 'scope: Fujio Morita Music: Ichiro Saito w/ Raizo Ichikawa, Miwa Takada, Kyoko Enami, Akiko Koyama, Ryuji Kita, Taketoshi Naito, Rokko Toura, Masao Mishima, Ryuzo Shimada, Ryosuke Kagawa   This begins, strangely enough, with Ichikawa on a clandestine undercover mission into Manchuria to rescue a political prisoner (Enami) being held by the Chinese. Upon their return, Ichikawa delivers her to Mishima, a benevolent government official. Mishima is also informal *sensei* to a group of fanatical young soldiers led by Toura. This all leads to a reintroduction to elder *oyabun* Kita, a decent boss and friend to Ichikawa's late father. Kita arranges a formal introduction for Ichikawa to all the *oyabuns* in town at a casual mid-afternoon get-together at chief boss Kagawa's. All are extremely impressed by Ichikawa except the one boss nearest him in age. This boss (Naito) is also the only one who affects western style-clothing. He is clad in a suit-and-tie and displays the fetish of a deck of western playing cards perpetually being shuffled in his nervous hands. He makes some very rude comments about Ichikawa. When Ichikawa replies to his nastiness with some words of wisdom, he leaves in a huff. This "western-style" boss is in the service of a rich politician, and between them they are concocting various imperialist deals, primary of which is control of the burgeoning opium trade in Japan. Toura and his men are led to believe their mentor Mishima is responsible for much of the opium problem and is, in fact, betraying them behind their backs. Too bad Toura's cronies are such gullible hotheads because they waylay Mishima outside his home one morning and murder him. Ichikawa, upon hearing the news, dons his naval reserve uniform and heads for military headquarters. He confronts Toura and his men, berating them for their idiocy. Toura, who had not been aware ahead of time that Gomi et. al. were actually going to do away with Mishima, nevertheless attempts to save face. To no avail. Ichikawa's righteousness is withering. Gomi, outraged at Ichikawa's nerve, nearly draws his sword, but the shamed Toura slaps him down. Ichikawa departs, knowing that the conscientious Toura will be his own harshest judge. Ichikawa and his clan also become involved with the brother/sister team that run the local newspaper, paying a visit to their office when an editorial appears lambasting all yakuza. The brother is an angry intellectual weakling, indignant and judgmental due to a humiliating experience being tormented by the villain's clan. Sis (Takada), though, senses Ichikawa is

a decent sort, and she suddenly gets to see proof of this when hoodlums attack the office. Ichikawa repels the invaders. Later on, the bad guys mistake Kita's rickshaw for Ichikawa's as the elder boss leaves the geisha house that they had both been visiting. When the assassins realize their error, they continue anyway, chasing the wounded and valiantly struggling Kita. They dispatch him in a filthy back alley storm drain under a flurry of falling snow. Ichikawa reaches his breaking point. He challenges the villain clan to a fight and ambushes them in a waterfront grain warehouse just past midnight. This is one of the most exciting sword battles in the first few films of the series and, of course, Ichikawa is the victor. As he afterwards walks along the wave-drenched pier in the freezing, swirling snow, he hurls his bloody sword into the sea. #3 of 8   * * *

Young Boss (#4)

YOUNG BOSS – OVERCOMING ADVERSITY aka WAKA OYABUN – NORIKOMU 1966 83 min. DIR. Akira Inoue SCR. Shozaburo Asai PHOTO COLOR 'SCOPE: Hiroshi Imai MUSIC: Taiichiro Kosugi w/ Raizo Ichikawa, Kojiro Hongo, Shiho Fujimura, Kayo Matsuo, Masao Mishima, Tatsuo Endo, Tokio Oki, Goro Tarumi, Shinobu Araki, Toshitaro Kitashiro An extremely intriguing look at yakuza interaction with various elements of the Japanese military pre-WW2. If this series is to be believed – as many of its films deal with this idea to some degree – the brutal, fascist secret police known as the *kempeitai* were not only often in bed with ultra-right wing yakuza gangs but also engaged in sometimes violent clashes with more idealistic, humane factions in the military such as the navy. I don't know enough about Japanese military history to know if this is based on actual fact or is only a fictional invention fueled by a writer's speculation. My intuition is that it is a distinct probability it is true. When independent young boss Ichikawa travels to visit friends in another village, he and friend Hongo witness the *kempeitai's* pursuit of an alleged deserter even after the man has jumped off their train. Once in the village, Hongo joins up with an evil clan in cahoots with the *kempetai* involving theft and profiteering. Ichikawa's friend, an elderly boss, is beaten to death by the secret police soon after, and Ichikawa helps the deceased man's daughter Fujimura keep their benevolent gang from disintegrating into vengeful chaos. Before long, Ichikawa finds himself at odds with the *kempeitai* and villainous yakuza. His old buddy Hongo even tries to kill him in the forest. Ichikawa thwarts the attempt and ends up rescuing Hongo from his own gang when they beat Hongo for failing to kill him. Hongo and his girlfriend, the always charismatic Matsuo, attempt to leave town in a rainstorm, but Hongo is severely wounded when they are attacked. Ichikawa and Fujimura shelter the supposed deserter from the film's beginning when he shows up but are surprised to learn from him that he is really being pursued because he witnessed the military police kill a wealthy grain merchant who wouldn't play ball with the yakuza gang. Ichikawa enlists the help of some of his naval officer friends. He manages to wipe out the evil gang in a big swordfight. But he still must contend with the *kempeitai* who want him dead. There is a great scene where Ichikawa fights the second-in-command officer, wins, then strips the man of his rank. Two other officers attempt to then run Ichikawa down with a motorcycle and sidecar but miss and crash into a wall, perishing in flames. There is a standoff at the conclusion with Ichikawa and naval buddies facing off the secret police. Both Ichikawa and the head of the local *kempeitai* are arrested. Ichikawa's girlfriend Fujimura watches as he is driven away. A nicely realistic account without any sugarcoating or concessions to a neat wrapup to satisfy the suits in the studio's head office. #4 of 8 films * * *

YOUNG BOSS – RICKSHAW MAN RAMPAGE aka WAKA OYABUN – ABARE HISHA aka VIOLENT CHECKMATE 1966 84 min. DIR. Shigeo Tanaka

SCR. Hajime Takaiwa PHOTO COLOR 'SCOPE: Michio Takahashi MUSIC: Kazuo Kitamura w/ Raizo Ichikawa, Michiko Saga, Jun Fujimaki, Akira Natsuki, Bontaro Miake, Yoshihiko Aoyama, Hiroshi Nihonyanagi, Saburo Ishiguro, Ryuji Kita Ichikawa pays a visit to a coastal village and a retired boss who now runs a rickshaw franchise with his son and young comrades. It also happens to be a town where Ichikawa had won a swordfight, mortally wounding the elder boss of a rival clan. Michiko Saga is the madam of a geisha teahouse who falls for Ichikawa. Hayashi and Fujimaki are former naval officer comrades of Ichikawa who are passing through town. Hayashi is a loyal pal, but Fujimaki is intolerant of all yakuza and has no love lost for Ichikawa. There is an exciting fight nearly halfway through where the bad guys stage an afternoon ambush of Ichikawa in the teahouse. It is particularly well-choreographed with Ichikawa defending himself first with fists, then graduating to a sword thrown to him by Saga. Eventually, Fujimaki is set up and blackmailed by a yakuza whore, and the benevolent retired boss is murdered because he overheard the extortion scheme. Fujimaki is held captive by the evil gang who are in league with corrupt politicians. Ichikawa shows up on a vengeance mission, as well as to free Fujimaki. The resultant swordfight is very well-staged and very convincing. Saga ends up saving Ichikawa's life by stabbing an attacker and gets killed for her trouble. #5 of 8 films * * 1/2

EXTERMINATE THE YOUNG BOSS! aka WAKA OYABUN O

KESE 1967 80 min. DIR. Chuzo Nakanishi SCR. Shozaburo Asai PHOTO COLOR 'SCOPE: Hiroshi Imai MUSIC: Takeo Watanabe w/ Raizo Ichikawa, Shiho Fujimura, Michiyo Kogure, Toru Abe, Ryutaro Gomi, Takamaru Sasaki, Jotaro Senba This was assistant director Nakanishi's first full-fledged directorial effort, to my knowledge. There are some nice moments, but there really is not much to hang your hat on. Ichikawa is released from jail and is met by an elderly *oyabun* who is promptly murdered on their train. Ichikawa narrowly misses catching the killer and only has a left-behind knife scabbard to go on for evidence. The edge of it is emblazoned with half of an engraving of a bat. So, if he manages to find a knife with the other half of the bat on its hilt, he will know the killer. He journeys to the elderly boss's hometown and stays under an assumed name with a decent gang who run a sushi restaurant and gambling den. However, evil boss Toru Abe has it in for them. Not much happens until the last ten minutes when the picture once again comes alive, Ichikawa singlehandedly battling Abe's gang – including Gomi, the boss's killer – in a harbor fuel depot at night. The fight is protracted into a nicely done action setpiece but does not generate much suspense. Ichikawa does manage to kill everyone, saving Abe for last. Cornered by Abe's gunfire, Ichikawa spills kerosene over a rail car, sets it aflame, then releases the brake and sends it careening towards the villain. Abe is simultaneously crushed and incinerated in one of the more gruesome death scenes in the series. As Ichikawa departs, rescued hostage

Fujimura professes her love. Ichikawa petulantly reveals his true identity, explains how he cannot be tied down and splits. #6 of 8 films * * 1/2

YOUNG BOSS, FUGITIVE aka WAKA OYABUN – KYOJOTABI 1967 84 min. **Dir.** Kazuo Mori **Scr.** Hajime Takaiwa **Photo color** **'scope:** Hiroshi Imai **Music:** Hajime Kaburagi **w/** Raizo Ichikawa, Kyoko Enami, Jun Fujimaki, Fumio Watanabe, Yoshi Kato, Ryuzo Shimada, Yoko Hayama, Ryutaro Gomi Once more Ichikawa finds himself in a coastal town, this time staying with Kato, an old, sake-drinking priest. One of the most interesting developments has a nurse (Hayama) Ichikawa is sweet on realize who he is and that he was her brother's commanding training officer in the navy. In a flashback, we see a particularly grueling summer exercise where her sibling is feverishly ill. At first, Ichikawa believes the fellow is shirking then, when he sees the boy is truly sick, he excuses him, writes him a note and instructs him to walk back to base. On his return, the young recruit loses the note and dies of a seizure while frantically searching for it. This memory cools any possible ardor between the two. The other female lead, the great Kyoko Enami, is a feisty construction worker supervisor, a strong woman's role all too rare in most *ninkyo* yakuza films which are usually populated with shrinking-violet female characters. Eventually, Ichikawa is forced to go up against boss Watanabe and his gang when they continue to harass him as well as assorted townfolk. He also must fight a former military nemesis-turned-friend-turned-nemesis-again during the climactic swordfight in a ship graveyard. This sequence ultimately falls short, despite the atmospheric imagery of burning and smoldering ship wreckage on the beach, because the swordfight itself is so decidedly lackluster and low energy. In fact, the previous film EXTERMINATE THE YOUNG BOSS had a much more exciting closing action sequence despite its weaker story. This entry is also disappointing when one considers the usually great director Mori's involvement. #7 of 8 films * * 1/2

Young Boss (#8)

YOUNG BOSS – LEADER'S FLESH aka WAKA OYABUN – SEN RYO HADA aka TORPEDO X 1967 83 min. **Dir.** Kazuo Ikehiro **Scr.** Kinya Naoi **Photo color** **'scope:** Senkichiro Takeda **Music:** Takeo Watanabe **w/** Raizo Ichikawa, Shiho Fujimura, Isamu Nagato, Naoko Kubo, Jun Fujimaki, Eijiro Tono, Sumiko Sakamoto, Ichiro Zaitsu, Masao Mishima

Ichikawa is wounded by the guns of a would-be assassin when he stops to help a man feigning illness on a mist-shrouded path. He takes refuge in a traveling theatre group headed by wisecracking, judo proficient magician Nagato. The troupe is being persecuted by a gang led by Tono. However, decent boss Tono is not aware of all the machinations or that a couple of his gang were the ones to target Ichikawa whom he considers a friend. Ichikawa runs into naval officer pal Fujimaki who is in the coastal town with the navy to test a new kind of torpedo. But another betraying naval man, as well as wealthy fanatic Mishima, *dojo* head Gomi and boss Tono's right hand man are intent on sabotaging the weapon and stealing the plans. Ichikawa becomes gradually more involved when he finds himself first on the scene after a saboteur's explosion. The *kempeitai* (once again, the military secret police) and Mishima's fascist bunch go after him. When boss Tono commits suicide, daughter Fujimura is left to head the clan. Subsequently, Tono's wayward son has to go into hiding when it is learned he knows the saboteur's identity. Despite the labyrinthine, sometimes convoluted plot, this is a nice return to form for the series with director Ikehiro certainly largely responsible. One gets the feeling of life going on beyond the camera frame with excellent atmosphere as well as realistic sonic ambience. There is also a momentum and vitality all the way through that is not always in evidence in films # 6 and 7. Ikehiro and writer Naoi create an unstable environment with well-researched political background for lead actor Ichikawa where no one is necessarily who they seem

to be and all factions are riddled with betrayers. The action choreography, particularly Ichikawa's raid on villain Mishima's *dojo* and subsequent pursuit along a rocky coastline, is exciting and imaginatively staged, unlike standard swordfight climaxes in many *ninkyo* yakuza pictures. #8 of 9   * * *

SECOND GENERATION YOUNG BOSS aka NIDAIME WAKA OYABUN aka THE YOUNG BOSS 1969 87 min. **DIR.** Kimiyoshi Yasuda **SCR.** Tetsuro Yoshida **PHOTO COLOR 'SCOPE:** Fujio Morita **MUSIC:** Taiichiro Kosugi **w/** Hiroki Matsukata, Ko Nishimura, Rinichi Yamamoto, Yoko Nanbikawa It is debatable that this should actually be considered part of the series. Since Ichikawa's death in July, 1969, Daiei scrambled to fill the void, drafting freelance Matsukata – son of famed *chanbara* actor Jushiro Konoe, and a rising star who mainly appeared in Toei Studios' samurai and yakuza films in the sixties and seventies – to appear in the remaining films that had been earmarked for Ichikawa. This entry is actually a remake of films # 1 and 2 of the YOUNG BOSS series, and director Yasuda does a commendable job of compressing the story down into a fast-moving, atmospheric 87 minutes. #9 and final in series   * * *

ZERO ESCAPE VISIBILITY aka SHIKAI ZERO NO DASSHUTSU 1963 **DIR.** Tetsutaro Murano **SCR.** Hideo Ando **PHOTO 'SCOPE:** Kimio Watanabe **MUSIC:** Tadashi Yamauchi **w/** Kojiro Hongo, Eriko Sanjo, Setsuko Tanaka

SHOCHIKU STUDIOS

Black Curtain

INTRODUCTION

Shochiku, founded circa 1920 by two entrepeneurs, Matsujiro Shirai and Takejiro Otani, who had previously held Shochiku has a theatrical company featuring *kabuki, shimpa* and other traditional forms of Japanese stageplay, was at first overly swayed by American films and methods. This excessive early reliance on western influences and a habit of throwing money at a problem to solve it, caused significant setbacks. But by 1921, Shochiku was starting to find its voice, a style that successfully integrated American styles and narrative forms with Japanese stagecraft and stories.

Despite their highly-publicized feuds with rivals Toho and Nikkatsu in the 1930s, Shochiku remained a wealthy company from the outset, and they continued to reap box office rewards well into Japan's march towards militarism and war. Post-war, Shochiku seemed to have an easier time of it with the labor unions. Not only did they take a more conciliatory attitude, company head Shiro Kido and his management already held a record of trying to keep their employees comparatively happy. Of course, this was done less out of altruism and more out of just plain good business sense, knowing that less friction in the workplace would keep films in production and a healthier work attitude that would be reflected in the final product.

Shochiku solidified their reputation for the "home" drama during the fifties with pantheon directors such as Yasujiro Ozu and Keisuke Kinoshita, films specializing in the pathos, romance and humor of everyday life in contemporary families. Shochiku also turned out comedies and musicals like clockwork.

But, along with Daiei, Toei and Toho, they created scores and scores of period *jidai-geki*. Many were exceptional. As the sixties began, Shochiku's samurai pictures, largely through the pioneering efforts of directors like Hideo Gosha with THREE OUTLAW SAMURAI and SWORD OF THE BEAST, Masahiro Shinoda with AS-SASSINATION and SAMURAI SPY and Kazuo Inoue with ESCAPE FROM HELL (MUSHUKUNIN-BETSUCHO aka WANDERERS' BLACK LIST, 1963), began to sport a gritty, hardboiled sensibility that retained sensitivity towards genuine emotion while jettisoning anything that could pass for sentimentality. This welcome development mirrored similar period pictures being made by Eiichi Kudo, Tai Kato and Tadashi Imai at Toei, Kenji Misumi at Daiei and Kihachi Okamoto at Toho. Shochiku made a small but impressive number of *kaidans*, too, including Kazuo Hase's superior CURSE OF THE BLOOD (KAIDAN ZANKOKU MONOGATARI, 1968). Shochiku also composed crime films – mystery as well as yakuza. Unfortunately, these crime and yakuza genre efforts are, as a rule, harder to see even on Japanese cable television than even the rarest of Shintoho Studio's 1950s thrillers. A real shame.

Of course, Shochiku – despite company head Shiro Kido's misgivings – was responsible as well for one of the most prodigious outpourings of daring *nouvelle vague* (or new wave) cinema from Japan in the early sixties, most prominently seen in the work of Nagisa Oshima, Masahiro Shinoda and Yoshishige Yoshida.

Shochiku was another studio that survived the catastrophic box office down-turn in the late sixties and throughout the seventies. Although they had diversified their holdings which helped immeasurably, it was not to the same extent as Toho and Toei. But Shochiku was also lucky enough to have one particular director churning out very popular films throughout the seventies and eighties. Yoji Yamada brought a constantly reliable source of revenue into the company coffers thanks to not only his incredibly long-running TORA-SAN (OTOKO WA TSURAI YO aka IT'S TOUGH TO BE A MAN, 1969-1995) series but his other occasional one-off wistful comedy-dramas. One of his most recent ef-forts is the exceptionally fine character study, THE TWILIGHT SAMURAI (2002).

The Artistic Crime Film...

SHOCHIKU Studios

BATTLE STREET aka KETTO GAI aka FIGHT STREET 1959 **Dir.** Manao Horiuchi **w/** Minoru Oki, Hizuru Takachiho

BLACK CURTAIN aka KURO-MAKU aka WIREPULLER 1966 **Dir.** Satoru (Go) Kobayashi **Scr.** Kazuo Horie **Photo B&W** 'scope: Takeo Kurata **w/** Shigeru Amachi, Yumiko Nogawa, Keiji Takamiya, Kyoko Ogimachi, Tonpei Hidari An adult-oriented yakuza feature about those high-powered corrupt men behind the scenes who pull the strings and manipulate the government. Shintoho-veteran Kobayashi (no relation to Masaki) was an early indie pink film pioneer.

Blackmail is My Life

BLACKMAIL IS MY LIFE aka KYOKATSU KOSO WA GA JINSEI aka BLACKMAIL IS MY BUSINESS 1968, 90 min. **Dir.** Kinji Fukasaku **Scr.** Fumio Konami/Kibu Nagata/ Hiro Matsuda **Photo color** 'scope: Yoshikazu (Keishi?) Maruyama **Music:** Hajime Kaburagi **w/** Hiroki Matsukata, Tomomi Sato, Tetsuro Tanba, Shigeru Amachi, Yoko Mihara, Hideo Murota, Akira Maki, Kenjiro Ishiyama, Keijiro Morokado A pungent, extremely entertaining, tale of hedonistic, amoral blackmailer Matsukata, who, with his partners Sato and Murota, target various well-to-do businessmen for various indiscretions. Up-from-the-slums Matsukata will do just about anything short of murder to keep his freewheeling lifestyle intact. Things start to unravel when he crosses paths with a political boss (Tanba) who is particularly intolerant of his under-handed scams. After much violence and brutality, Matsukata thinks himself on the other side of his aggravations, only to be anti-climactically stabbed-to-death while crossing the street one afternoon on a busy thoroughfare. Another one of director Fukasaku's unflinchingly honest portraits of the multi-faceted all-too-human, soft white underbelly of the Japanese under-world. This was a rare such effort for Shochiku as Fukasaku did most of his yakuza films for Toei. * * *

BLACK RIVER aka KUROI KAWA 1957, 114 min. **Dir.** Masaki Kobayashi **Scr.** Zenzo Matsuyama **Photo B&W:** Yuharu Atsuta **Music:** Chuji Kinoshita **w/** Fumio Watanabe, Tatsuya Nakadai, Ineko Arima, Keiko Awaji, Asao Sano, Seiji Miyaguchi, Eijiro Tono

Director Kobayashi tackles contemporary yakuza subject matter for the only time in his career in this exposé of the seedy districts that sprouted up around U.S. military bases in Japan. Actor Nakadai also makes his debut as a leading man, portraying a cruel, ne'er-do-well gangster who forces poor intellectual Watanabe's girl (Arima) into prostitution. There are also many human interest vignettes with other denizens of the slum. The emotionally-charged climax has Watanabe screw up his courage to finally challenge Nakadai in one of his bar haunts. However, the outcome is a stalemate.

Black River

The drunken Nakadai is finally lured out by the despairingly calculating Arima, and they walk down the darkened main boulevard that leads into the military base. Army trucks are continually racing in-and-out at breakneck speed. Arima waits till she sees one coming, then lustily kissing the all-too-eager Nakadai, gives him a

fatal shove under the massive wheels as the truck whizzes by. Ironically, other leading man Watanabe went on to become a much-in-demand villain in countless Toei late sixties/early seventies yakuza *eiga*. * * *

Blind Woman - Flower and Fangs

BLIND WOMAN – FLOWER AND FANGS aka ONNA MEKU-RA – HANA TO KIBA aka FANGS OF A FEMALE 1968 90 min. Dɪʀ. Hirokazu Ichimura Sᴄʀ. Yoshi Hattori Pʜᴏᴛᴏ ᴄᴏʟᴏʀ 'sᴄᴏᴘᴇ: Masao Kosugi Mᴜsɪᴄ: Takeo Watanabe w/ Chizuko Arai, Koreharu Hisatomi, Isao Yamagata, Ken Sanders, Ryohei Uchida, Yuki Shima, Shunji Imai, Keijiro Morokado, Rokko Toura
A blind *femme fatale* anti-heroine struts her stuff in what looked like the start of a film series (it says #1 – or first episode – on the poster), but it must have done lukewarm business at the box office; no more were forthcoming.

BRACELET OF NIGHT PATHS
aka SENJI NO YORU series

BRACELET OF NIGHT PATHS
aka SENJI NO YORU 1968 **DIR.**
Umeji Inoue **SCR.** Toshio Fujinami
PHOTO 'SCOPE: Chitora Ogoe **MUSIC:**
Kenjiro Hirose **w/** Akira Kurizuka,
Yuki Makino, Katsuhiko Kobayashi,
Yukiji Asaoka, Fumio Watanabe,
Shunji Imai, Noboru Nakata, Keijiro
Morokado   Kurizuka is a hitman in
this trilogy. #1 of 3

KILLER IN THE NIGHT MIST
aka KIRI NI MUSEBU YORU 1968
91 min.   **DIR.** Meijiro Umezu
w/ Akira Kurizuka, Miwa Takada,
Ryohei Uchida, Satoshi Yamanouchi
A hitman returns to Japan after a long
sojourne.   #2 of 3

RED MIST aka KIRI NO BARA-
DO 1969 82 min. **DIR.** Meijiro
Umezu **SCR.** Kimiyuki Hasegawa
PHOTO 'SCOPE: Kasui Hamajima
MUSIC: Chuya Inoue   **w/** Akira
Kurizuka, Tomomi Sato, Teruo
Yoshida, Hosei Komatsu, Yukiji
Asaoka, Keijiro Morokado, Hideo
Sunazuka   Gangster Kurizuka tries
to help a former colleague flee to
Brazil. #3 and final in series

CASH CALLS HELL aka
GOHIKI NO SHINSHI aka FIVE
GENTLEMEN 1966 93 min. **DIR.**
Hideo Gosha **Scr.** Yasuko Ono/Hideo
Gosha **PHOTO B&W 'SCOPE:** Tadashi
Sakai **MUSIC:** Masaru Sato
w/ Tatsuya Nakadai, Miyuki Kuwano,
Mikijiro Hira, Kunie Tanaka, Ichiro
Nakatani, Eisei Amamoto, Hisashi
Igawa   Nakadai is a normal guy
who is involved in a fatal car ac-
cident. Abruptly, he is sucked into

a nightmare world, losing his job
and fiancee, then thrown into jail for
two years because he can't pay the
victim's wife her compensation (her
husband and child had died). Hira is a
warped, crippled criminal mastermind
who had been involved in a robbery
of a yakuza gang with four other men.
He had then been sentenced to jail on
a minor fraud charge, something he
had given into so he could take refuge
until things cooled down. He hires
Nakadai, who is in the process of
being released, to kill his four accomplices so he and his bitchy
waitress girlfriend can keep all the
money for themselves. Nakadai can't
bring himself to kill the first guy, and
suddenly the gangsters that had been
robbed originally turn up and do it for
him. This is pretty bleak but has a bit
too many sentimental contrivances
involving the hit-and-run victim's
widow and little girl. Despite the
downbeat factor – everyone dies –
and the evocative black-and-white
noir images, this is one of maestro
Gosha's good but still lesser films.
* * *

CHALLENGE AT DAWN aka
AKATSUKI NO CHOSEN 1971
DIR. Toshio Masuda **SCR.** Shinobu
Hashimoto/ Ichiro Ikeda/Takeo
Kunihiro **MUSIC:** Takeo Watanabe
w/ Kinnosuke Nakamura, Tetsuya
Watari, Mitsuko Baisho, Tatsuya
Nakadai, Takeshi Wakabayashi,
Shogo Shimada, Ryutaro Tatsumi,
Nana Ozaki, Ichiro Zaitsu, Kei Sato,
Ryohei Uchida (FUJI TV Produc-
tions/Distributed by SHOCHIKU
Studios)

CHASE THAT MAN aka
OITSUMERU 1972 93 min. **DIR.**

Cash Calls Hell, *detail from French DVD box art*

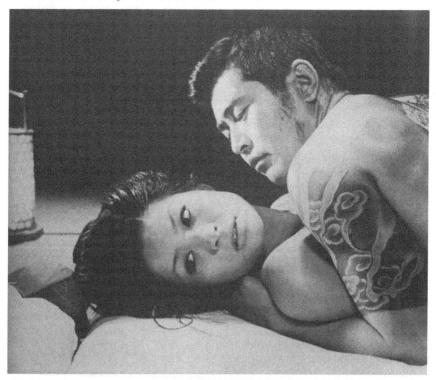

Challenge at Dawn

Toshio Masuda Scr. Tatsuo Nogami
Photo color 'scope: Masao Kosugi
Music: Hajime Kaburagi
w/ Tetsuya Watari, Jiro Tamiya, Kei
Sato, Mitsuko Baisho, Tatsuya Fuji,
Kazuko Yoshiyuki, Etsuko Ikuta,
Mizuho Suzuki
A tale of the intense rivalry between
yakuza bigwig Watari and cop
Tamiya.

Chase that Man

COBRA series

**ATTACK BEFORE BEING
ATTACKED** aka UTARERU MAE
NI UTE 1976 95 min. Dir./Scr.
Umeji Inoue Photo color 'scope:
Masao Kosugi Music: Hajime
Kaburagi w/ Jiro Tamiya, Yoko
Yamamoto, Keiko Matsuzaka, Tadao
Nakamaru, Kumi Taguchi, Eiji
Okada, Janet Hatta, Toru Abe, Isao
Tamagawa, Nobuo Kaneko, Ryohei
Uchida, Asao Koike
Director Umeji Inoue had helmed
some early and mid-sixties *gendai*
yakuza films at Toei as well as scores
of very successful Chinese language
pictures for the Shaw Brothers in
Hong Kong throughout the sixties and
early seventies. So he seems the per-
fect choice to helm these yakuza/kung
fu/policier hybrids. Unfortunately,
these seem to be two of the last films
actor Jiro Tamiya made before his

untimely death by suicide. #1 of 2

**ANGRY COBRA – KILL THE
WITNESS** aka IKARE
COBRA – MOKUGEKISHA O
KESE 1976 Dir./Scr. Umeji Inoue
Photo color' scope: Masao Kosugi
w/ Jiro Tamiya, Yoko Yamamoto,
Fujiko Nara, Tadao Nakamaru, Wu
Pin, Kao Chan, Fumio Watanabe #2
of 2

Angry Cobra - Kill the Witness

**COMEDY – BIG SUDDEN
ATTACK** aka KIGEKI – DAI
GEKI TOTSU aka STRANGE
COMRADES 1969 84 min.
Dir. Yasuyoshi Tanaka   A comedy
about the friendship of a man who
hates being a hood and another who
desperately wants to be one.

COMEDY - THE GREAT BOSS
aka KIGEKI - DAI OYABUN Dir.
Kinya Sakai Scr. Toshio Ashigawa
Photo 'scope: Haruo Ohara Music:

Tadashi Makino   w/ Isamu Nagato, Kanichi Tani, Shinichi Yanagizawa, Michiko Yashima, Hiroshi Nihonyanagi, Bokuzen Hidari

COMEDY – A MAN'S TRIAL OF STRENGTH aka KIGEKI – OTOKO NO UDE DAMESHI 1974 **DIR.** Masaharu (Shoji) Segawa **SCR.** Kei Tasaka/ Shizuo (Motoo?) Nagai **PHOTO COLOR 'SCOPE:** Keishi Maruyama **MUSIC:** Hachiro Aoyama w/ Frankie Sakai, Kiwako Taichi, Etsuko Ichihara, Masumi Harukawa, Ruriko Ikejima, Ryoichi Tamagawa, Yasushi Suzuki

COURAGE FIRST aka DOKYO ICHIBAN aka SHOW YOUR PLUCK 1970 90 min. **DIR./SCR.** Umeji Inoue **PHOTO COLOR 'SCOPE:** Hiroyuki Nagaoka **MUSIC:** Seitaro Omori   w/ Ichiro Zaitsu, Mariko Okada, Junzaburo Ban, Shinji Maki, Toru Yuri   A comedy about a timid guy mistaken for a gangster.

Cruel Story of Youth

CRUEL STORY OF YOUTH aka SEISHUN ZANKOKU MONO-GATARI aka NAKED YOUTH – STORY OF CRUELTY 1960 96 min. **DIR./SCR.** Nagisa Oshima **PHOTO COLOR 'SCOPE:** Takashi Kawamata **MUSIC:** Rinichiro Manabe w/ Miyuki Kuwano, Yusuke Kawazu, Yoshiko Kuga, Fumio Watanabe, Kei Sato, Shin Morikawa, Jun Hamamura
Only tangentially a yakuza film in that it deals with teens extorting money, and has many similar story elements to various juvenile delinquent films such as BAD GIRL MAKO and the STRAY CAT ROCK series as well as the mid-1950s cycle of *taiyozoku* pictures. However, the execution is a bit different in that this is not really a genre film. Unflinching, truthful and generally without any proselytizing or pretentions. A couple set up lecherous men, then intimidate them for money. Kuwano is the bait, then suddenly Kawazu appears as the upset boyfriend demanding satisfaction. The other kids they hang with are into similar hustles, and no one is very happy. Kawazu and Kuwano make love constantly and their passion results in an abortion as well as recriminations and physical abuse. The haunted couple, stumbling through a continual series of incred-ible wide screen compositions out of seemingly cramped urban landscapes, remain strangely sympathetic despite their behavior, and there is a despond-ent, open-ended finale. * * * *

CRUEL TATTOO aka **IREZUMI MUZAN series**

CRUEL TATTOO aka IREZUMI MUZAN aka TATTOOED TEMPTRESS 1968

Cruel Tattoo (#1)   *stills from* **Cruel Tattoo (#1)**

Shinjuku Bred *aka* **Cruel Tattoo (#3)**

89 min. **DIR.** Hideo Sekigawa **SCR.**
Kikuma Shimoizaka/ Toru Ichijo
PHOTO COLOR 'SCOPE: Masao Kosugi
MUSIC: Masao Yagi **w/** Chizuko Arai,
Toru Abe, Yusuke Kawazu, Kikko
Matsuoka, Eiji Okada, Chikako
Miyagi, Yuko Minamikaze
(Nankaze?), Eizo Kitamura,
Masatoshi Okabe   An obsessive
love maze finds bar woman Arai
acquiescing to her elder, fetishistic
patron Abe's penchant for tattooed
wenches, getting an elaborate flying
angel etched on her back. There is
also a young tattooed yakuza
(Kawazu) who desires Arai and, once
they consummate their lust, Arai
realizes it is him she truly loves. To
complicate matters even further, a
young girl (Matsuoka) is also in love
with Arai and gets tattooed to please
her. Ironically, once tattooed,
Matsuoka also falls prey to the preda-
tory Abe. Before things wrap up,
Kawazu runs away with the tattooist's
wife then, realizing his mistake, returns to kill Abe and reunite with his
true love Arai. Their sordid lifestyle
is too much for them, though, so they
end things in a double suicide. The
epilogue relates how Arai's beautiful
tattooed skin now hangs in a medical
museum! #1 of 3 films

**NEW CRUEL TATTOO STORY
– CODE OF THE SWORD** aka
SHIN IREZUMI MUZAN – TEKKA
NO JINGI aka DEVIL IN MY
FLESH aka GAMBLING CODE
SWORD aka IRON HONOR &
HUMANITY 1968 88 min. **DIR.**
Hideo Sekigawa **SCR.** Kikuma
Shimoizaka/Takayuki Kase **PHOTO**
COLOR 'SCOPE: Masao Kosugi
MUSIC: Kanyo (Tomiyo?) Ogawa
w/ Chizuko Arai, Eiji Okada,

Keisuke Sonoi, Kikko Matsuoka, Isao
Natsuyagi, Chieko Naniwa, Haruo
Tanaka, Mina Aoe, Hiroyuki Katsube
#2 of 3 films

SHINJUKU BRED aka SHINJUKU
SODACHI 1969 **DIR.** Kazuo Hase
SCR. Masashige Narusawa **PHOTO**
COLOR 'SCOPE: Keishi Maruyama
w/ Chizuko Arai, Kikko Matsuoka,
Yusuke Kawazu, Hideo Oki, Nobuo
Kaneko, Yoko Tsuyama   #3 of 3
films

**DOUBLE SUICIDE – JAPANESE
SUMMER** aka MURI SHINJU
– NIHON NO NATSU 1967 **DIR.**
Nagisa Oshima **SCR.** Nagisa Oshima/
Mamoru Sasaki/Takeshi Tamura
PHOTO B&W' SCOPE: Tasuhiro
Yoshioka **MUSIC:** Hikaru Hayashi
w/ Kei Sato, Keiko Sakurai, Rokko
Toura, Masakazu Tamura, Hosei
Komatsu   A dark comedy with
Oshima satirizing the staple of tragic
Japanese romantic dramas, the love
suicide. He updates it to the contempo
sixties with an alienated and apathetic
Sato and Sakurai finding each other.
Sato is not "in-love" with Sakurai,
he is merely looking for a woman
to kill him. Sakurai is not "in-love"
but "in-lust." They get mired in the
battles of two warring yakuza mobs.
Near the end, a glasses-wearing
American youth, apparently representing then-in-the-news University
of Texas sniper, Charles Whitman (?),
makes an appearance, and he takes
on the police along with the criminals. Previous to being cut down by
the cops, Sato and Sakurai abruptly
kill themselves. Despite the promising synopsis, Oshima's approach is
not straightforward as in CRUEL

STORY OF YOUTH or even THE SUN'S BURIAL. Instead, the film is pretentiously Brechtian in an overly didactic way, blunting impact and overstaying its welcome. There are occasional moments of sharp humor or striking imagery but, overall, these are outnumbered four-to-one. Disappointing. * * 1/2

Double Suicide - Japanese Summer

Eighteen Toughs Stir Up a Storm

EIGHTEEN TOUGHS STIR UP A STORM aka ARASHI O YOBU JUHACHININ aka EIGHTEEN TOUGHS 1963 108 min. DIR./SCR.

Yoshishige Yoshida   PHOTO **B&W** '**SCOPE:** Toichiro Narushima   **MUSIC:** Hikaru Hayashi
w/ Tamotsu Hayakawa, Yoshiko Kayama, Katsuyoshi Nishimura, Eiji (Hideji) Matsui, Takeshi Iwamoto
An early, more narratively linear film from underground director Yoshida while he was apprenticing at Shochiku. He went on to direct the avant-garde EROS PLUS MASSACRE (1969) and COUP D'ETAT aka MARTIAL LAW (KAIGENREI) (1973). Hayakawa is a maverick boilermaker working in a shipyard in a small coastal town not too far from Hiroshima. Broke, he finds himself in charge of a barracks full of eighteen itinerant, borderline delinquent teenage boys from Osaka who have been hired as extra workers at the unionized yard. He initially despises them as they remind him of his own youth. Complications ensue as the months tick by, including the rape of his girlfriend (who he finally marries) and the stabbing of a yakuza by one shy boy who was ganged-up on by the hoods. Director Yoshida eschews sentimentality, telling a great, unpretentious story, in the final analysis moving the viewer. * * * 1/2

Escape from Japan

ESCAPE FROM JAPAN aka
NIHON DASSHUTSU 1964 96 min.
DIR./SCR. Yoshishige Yoshida PHOTO
COLOR 'SCOPE: Toichiro Narushima
MUSIC: Toru Takemitsu/Masao Yagi
w/ Yasushi Suzuki, Miyuki Kuwano,
Kyosuke Machida, Ryohei Uchida,
Sumiko Sakamoto, Etsuko Ichihara
A naive roadie (Suzuki) to a jazz band
teams up with his gangster drug addict mentor (Machida), a murderous
ex-bicycle racer (Uchida) and a bathhouse girl (Kuwano) to burglarize her
boss's safe. A cop gets killed by
Uchida, and later Suzuki kills Uchida
for raping Kuwano. Suzuki and
Kuwano try to escape together but are
continually stymied by a succession
of nightmarish events. The simple-
minded Suzuki cannot handle the
pressure and constantly bursts into
hysterics (which is difficult to watch).
Kuwano starts to care for him as she
realizes he is as alienated as she is,
but he constantly misinterprets her
attempts to arrange for him to escape
Japan as her trying to get rid of him.
The climax occurs amidst celebra-
tions of the opening of the Tokyo
Olympics. Reportedly final scenes
of the dysfunctional hero's disintegration into madness in prison were
removed by the studio, and Yoshida
left Shochiku as a result. A disturbing
movie with perhaps actress Kuwano's
best performance (equal to her turn in
CRUEL STORY OF YOUTH). * * *

FACE OF THE DICE aka KAO
O DAISE 1966 DIR. Noriaki Yuasa
SCR. Noriaki Yuasa/Kyuzo
Kobayashi/Akira Hayashi PHOTO
'SCOPE: Mamoru Morita MUSIC:
Jun Suzuki w/ Keiji Takagi, Mayumi
Shimizu, Chizuko Arai, Kikko
Matsuoka, Bunta Sugawara

Face of the Dice

FAREWELL TEARS aka NAMIDA
SAYONARA O 1965 DIR. Yoichi
Maeda SCR. Nobuhiko Mitsuse
(Mitsurai?) PHOTO 'SCOPE: Hiroshi
Takemura MUSIC: Hirooka Ogawa
w/ Yukio Hashi, Yoshiko Kayama,
Kamatari Fujiwara, Chieko Baisho,
Tatsuya Ishiguro

Farewell to the Code

FAREWELL TO THE CODE aka
SARABA OKITE aka LAW OF

THE OUTLAW 1971 90 min.
DIR. Toshio Masuda **SCR.** Tatsuhiko
Kamoi **PHOTO COLOR 'SCOPE:**
Mitsushi Kaneuma **MUSIC:** Harumi
Ibe **w/** Tetsuya Watari, Shima
Iwashita, Bunsaku Han, Yoshiro
Aoki, Shinsuke Ashida, Takashi
Fujiki, Shoki Fukae, Shiro Yanase,
Noboru Nakata, Toshio Masuda
Watari's director Masuda, from the
first of the Nikkatsu series HOOD-
LUM, and the screenwriter Kamoi,
who had written one of Watari's best
Nikkatsu efforts, KANTO SOCIETY
OF LEADING MOBSTERS, teamed
up for this. It is also Watari's first picture after leaving his nearly bankrupt
parent studio. He plays a retired hood
laying low as a flower-seller who
becomes inadvertently exposed to his
former evil comrades when he saves
the exquisite, tormented Han from
suicide. Watari and Han fall in love,
but happiness is not to be. Not only
does Han's father, Ashida, enter the
picture wanting to commit her to the
nuthouse, Watari's vengeance-mind-
ed mob friends, led by boss Fukae,
capture and torture him. When Watari
tries to reach his fatally wounded
pal Aoki during a wild gun battle at
the climax, he perishes in a hail of
bullets.

**FEMALE MASSEUR GUERRILA
– GREAT ATTACK** aka ONSEN
GERIRA – DAI SHOGEKI 1968 90
min. **DIR.** Hirokazu Ichimura **PHOTO
COLOR 'SCOPE:** Masao Kosugi
MUSIC: Hiroku Ogawa **w/** Osami
Nabe, Hiroshi Inuzuka, Yoshiko
Kayama From the cast and title, this
seems slanted towards the comic.

***FLAME AT THE PIER, see TEARS
ON THE LION'S MANE***

FIGHTERS ON FIRE aka
NIPPON GERIRA JIDAI aka AGE
OF JAPANESE GUERILLAS 1968
89 min. **DIR.** Yusuke Watanabe
A girl is tormented by her love of a
hoodlum and her friendship with a
smuggler. This may be a comedy.

**FLOWER AND DRAGON –
STORY OF YOUTH/STORY OF
LOVE /STORY OF THE ANGRY
WAVES** aka HANA TO RYU –
SEIUN HEN/AIZO HEN/ DOTO
HEN 1973 165 min. **DIR.** Tai Kato
SCR. Tai Kato/Teruhiko Mimura/
Yoshitaro Nomura **PHOTO COLOR
'SCOPE:** Keishi Maruyama
MUSIC: Hajime Kaburagi **w/** Tetsuya
Watari, Jiro Tamiya, Muga Takewaki,
Yoshiko Kayama, Mitsuko Baisho,
Koji Ishizaka, Rinichi Yamamoto,
Chishu Ryu, Kei Sato One of the
best and probably the most complete
of all the versions of this oft-filmed
tale. The only time, if I'm not
mistaken, that the entire novel with
its twenty-five year time span was
faithfully lensed. Some of the other
adaptations – especially FLOWER
AND DRAGON (Dir. Masahiro
Makino, 1969) linked with second
part RISING DRAGON (Dir. Kosaku
Yamashita, 1970) (see the TALES
OF JAPANESE CHIVALRY series
under the Toey Studios section) - are
significantly different. But this "epic"
gives you the idea what Kato could
have done with twice the budget
and shooting schedule on his Toei
yakuza pictures (particularly the RED
PEONY GAMBLER films – which,
nevertheless, remain quite good).
This is fast-moving, considering the
running time. It also works on the
level of family saga and love story as

well as that of a *ninkyo* yakuza film. Everyone in the cast is excellent, particularly Ryu as Watari's drunken father, Baisho as the sensual, lonely card dealer and Takewaki as Watari's son (who does not appear until the last half of the film). The subplot of Takewaki's geisha sweetheart being shanghaied to work as a whore for the military in the Phillipines is especially gutwrenching as is his interlude at her grave in a ramshackle cemetery in Manila. Set against a spectacularly painted sunset backdrop, this concluding scene is very poignant and is made even more poetic and transcendental by what is probably Hajime Kaburagi's best score. An almost as affecting version of the story is that of the above-mentioned TALES OF JAPANESE CHIVALRY series entries with Ken Takakura and Junko Fuji. * * * 1/2

FROM THE KAWACHI WIND – BEATING DRUM aka KAWACHI NO KAZE YORI – ABARE DAIKO 1963 **DIR.** Tatsuo Sakai **SCR.** Motonari Wakai/Kazuo Hase **PHOTO** B&W **'SCOPE:** Shigetsuka Sekine **MUSIC:** Seiichi Suzuki **w/** Tatsuo Terashima, Miyuki Kuwano, Mitsuko Sakai, Eitaro Shindo, Bunta Sugawara, Juzaburo Akechi

GAMBLER'S LUCK aka UN GA YOKE RYA **DIR.** Yoji Yamada

GIRLS BEHIND BARS aka OINARU AI NO KANATANI 1960 **DIR.** Tetsuo Ono **SCR.** Yoshio Tomita/ Yoshiro Ashizawa **PHOTO 'SCOPE:** Haruji (Seiji) Inoue **MUSIC:** Hachio Nakamura **w/** Fumio Watanabe, Miyuki Kuwano, Hizuru Takachiho, Hisao Toake, Yusuke Kawazu

From the Kawachi Wind - Beating Drum

GOOD-FOR-NOTHING aka ROKU DENASHI 1960 88 min. **DIR./SCR.** Yoshishige Yoshida **PHOTO** B&W **'SCOPE:** Toichiro Narushima **MUSIC:** Chuji Kinoshita **w/** Masahiko Tsugawa, Hizuru Takachiho, Yusuke Kawazu, Junichiro Yamashita,

Yosuke Hayashi, Masao Mishima, Shoji Yasui, Fumio Watanabe Avant-garde filmmaker Yoshida's first film. It relates the story of three college buddies who harass one of their father's secretaries (Takachiho) who carries a large amount of money for dad's company. Impoverished Tsugawa is attracted to her, though she initially despises him. Eventually, the two go to bed, but Tsugawa is so full of self-loathing at his leeching off the rich, phony nihilist of the group – the son (Kawazu) of the business owner – and his desire to not be tied down, the relationship disintegrates.

Good-For-Nothing

He and one other poor boy, who is a no good hood and desperate for cash, decide to rob her for real. Conflicted Tsugawa surprises everyone when he does an about-face. Mortally wounded, he runs over his fleeing buddy, retrieves the gal's handbag and returns it, only to have her show him it was filled with newsprint. The

back-and-forth of defensive pride between Tsugawa and Takachiho is skillfully orchestrated as an ever-escalating game of self-destructive one-upmanship, much of it egged on by the venal values of Tsugawa's and Takachiho's friends. This fits into the *taiyozoku* subgenre, with an ending reminiscent of BREATHLESS, but minus the silly humor. * * * 1/2

THE GREAT TURNABOUT aka SOKKURI DAI GYAKUTEN 1967 **DIR.** Michiyoshi Doi **SCR.** Azuma Morizaki/Kuzo Kobayashi **PHOTO COLOR 'SCOPE:** Masayuki Kato **MUSIC:** Kenjiro Hirose **w/** Isamu Nagato, Chiharu Kuri, Jerri Fujio Nagato is featured in a dual role in this gangster action comedy.

THE GREAT VILLAIN'S STRATEGY aka DAI AKUTO SAKUSEN 1966 **DIR./SCR.** Teruo Ishii **PHOTO COLOR 'SCOPE:** Shizuo Hirase **MUSIC:** Masao Yagi **w/** Joe Shishido, Teruo Yoshida, Hideo Taka, Kyosuke Machida, Kanjuro Arashi, Mayumi Shimizu, Antonio Koga, Toru Abe, Kunie Tanaka, Yoko Mihara This has more of a comic tone than Ishii's other yakuza crime pictures at Shochiku. With Joe Shishido's involvement, it seems to be patterned along the lines of some of Shishido's more tongue-in-cheek crime films at Nikkatsu. This remains one of Shishido and Ishii's less memorable efforts, descending into feather-brained, disorganized hijinks outside a snowy mountain resort by the end. A bit reminscent of similar cult director Jess Franco at his most mediocre. * *

HIGH-RANKING YAKUZA aka
SEIUN YAKUZA series

High-Ranking Yakuza (#1)

HIGH-RANKING YAKUZA aka
SEIUN YAKUZA 1965 Dɪʀ. Meijiro
Umezu Sᴄʀ. Ichiro Ikeda Pʜᴏᴛᴏ
ᴄᴏʟᴏʀ 'sᴄᴏᴘᴇ: Masayuki Kato
Mᴜsɪᴄ: Rinichiro Manabe w/ Muga
Takewaki, Taketoshi Naito, Yukiko
Murase, Ryunosuke Tsukigata, Bunta
Sugawara, Tetsuro Tanba, Akemi
Mari, Ryohei Uchida, Kenjiro
Ishiyama #1 of 2 films

**HIGH-RANKING YAKUZA
RETURNS – A MAN'S RAGE** aka
ZOKU SEIUN YAKUZA – IKARI
NO OTOKO 1965 Dɪʀ. Kazuo Hase
Sᴄʀ. Ichiro Ikeda Pʜᴏᴛᴏ ᴄᴏʟᴏʀ
'sᴄᴏᴘᴇ: Masao Kosugi Mᴜsɪᴄ:
Yoshioki Ogawa w/ Muga
Takewaki, Bunta Sugawara, Asao
Matsumoto, Yoshiko Aoyama, Kenji
Sugawara, Hiroshi Nihonyanagi,
Minoru Oki, Ryohei Uchida, Kanjuro

Arashi, Hiroyuki Nagato #2 of 2
films

HISTORY OF A MAN'S FACE aka
OTOKO NO KAO WA RIREKISHO
aka BY A MAN'S FACE YOU
SHALL KNOW HIM 1966 89 min.
Dɪʀ. Tai Kato Sᴄʀ. Tai Kato/Seiji
Hoshikawa Pʜᴏᴛᴏ ᴄᴏʟᴏʀ 'sᴄᴏᴘᴇ:
Tetsuo Takaba Mᴜsɪᴄ: Mitsuru
Hayashi w/ Noboru Ando, Ichiro
Nakatani, Sanae Nakahara, Ryohei
Uchida, Kanjuro Arashi, Ichizo Itami,
Akemi Mari, Torahiko Hamada,
Masao Mishima, Tomiko Ishii, Haruo
Tanaka, Bunta Sugawara

History of a Man's Face

An intense, pared-to-the-bone
melodrama of a doctor (Ando) in
an outlying rural community being
confronted with a person from his
past. A shooting victim is brought
into Ando's small clinic, and he
recognizes the fellow (Nakatani) as
a gangster who had run off with his
nurse/lover. Nakatani and the woman
are now married with a little child.
Ando goes into a flashback reverie as
Nakatani is prepped for the operation. Ando's feelings are confused,
divided between friendship and

High-Ranking Yakuza (#2)

loathing. Despite his rough and often cruel demeanor, Nakatani was the only comparatively "decent" person strong enough to help Ando fight and ultimately destroy the evil Korean gang that ruled over the small town in post-WW2 times. Korean himself, Nakatani had also served under Ando during the war and knew him to be a just and honorable person. The gang, led by bitterly resentful Uchida, was always able to either scare or pull the wool over the eyes of the police in the community. Since it was immediately post-WW2, the police force stationed in the village were very reluctant to take action since the mob was made up of Korean immigrants. Previously discriminated against, Koreans and other foreigners had come under the protective umbrella of the U.S. Occupation Forces. After the final massacre, Nakatani had run off with the doctor's nurse Nakahara, leaving him to face arrest and apparently a brief jail term by himself. This has some very intense performances and truly grueling action scenes, something not always that common in Shochiku crime films. One of director Kato's only *gendai* yakuza pictures. It was – and still is – considered a controversial film in Japan. Some critics and politicians felt that it had a politically incorrect tone due to its seemingly Japanese vs. Korean storyline. One of Kato's points, however, is how only truly honorable, decent people are capable of transcending ethnic divisions and stereotypes. * * * 1/2

HOTSPRINGS HOTSHOTS aka DAI SHO GEKI 1968 90 min. **DIR.** Hirokazu Ichimura   Two mobster wannabes cause havoc at a hotsprings resort in this action comedy.

IF YOU WERE YOUNG – RAGE aka KIMI GA WAKAMONO NARA aka RAGE aka OUR DEAR BUDDIES 1970 89 min. **DIR.** Kinji Fukasaku **SCR.** Takehiro Nakajima/ Koji Matsumoto/Kinji Fukasaku **PHOTO COLOR 'SCOPE:** Takamoto Ezure **Music:** Taku Izumi w/ Tetsuo Ishidate, Gin Maeda, Choichiro Kawarazaki, Ryunosuke Minegishi, Hideki Hayashi, Michie Terada, Michiko Araki   Five poor young men lose their jobs when their factory goes bankrupt. Banding together, they idealistically decide to try to start their own freight company. Working at various jobs, their collective savings start to accumulate. Then disaster strikes. Minegishi is killed while participating in a strike, and Kawarazaki is arrested after joining gang associates in a robbery. Disillusioned, Hayashi abandons his comrades to marry a bar hostess. Eventually the only two remaining, Ishidate and Maeda, are able to purchase their dump truck. More complications set in when they are visited by Kawarazaki's mom Araki and sister Terada who have come to Tokyo to see Kawarazaki in jail. Both boys fall for Terada. Soon Kawarazaki escapes, kills a cop and convinces Maeda and sister Terada to drive him in the truck to his hometown. They acquiesce, but he expires from his wounds. Maeda is so overcome, he gets out and sends the truck careening over a cliff. Ishidate and Maeda struggle to optimistically look to the future. Director Fukasaku exhibits the same brand of ferocious vitality in this saga of disaffected youth, economic class barriers and small time crime that is also found in his 1970s Toei yakuza pictures such as the BATTLES WITHOUT HONOR & HUMANITY series. * * *

JAPAN'S ZERO ZONE – NIGHT WATCH aka NIHON ZERO CHITAI – YORU O NERAE 1966 90 min. **DIR./SCR.** Teruo Ishii **PHOTO COLOR 'SCOPE:** Shizuo Hirase **MUSIC:** Masao Yagi w/ Teruo Yoshida, Muga Takewaki, Yoshiko Kayama, Yoko Mihara, Naoki Sugiura, Kanjuro Arashi, Kyosuke Machida, Mayumi Shimizu, Takashi Fujiki, Kunie Tanaka   The first ten minutes of this is such a visual *tour-de-force*, I began to think just maybe this was going to prove to be director Ishii's BRANDED TO KILL. Alas, it was not to be. Ishii was either unwilling, unable or too lazy to sustain the kinetic energy and invention.

Japan's Zero Zone - Night Watch

Initially, Ishii takes us on a break-neck, stream-of-consciousness tour of nocturnal big city Japan – the neon, nightclubs and sexy night women. Once it settles into a loose narrative, the story strays episodically all over the place. But the film is ultimately no more than a pot-boiler. In many ways (and as the title indicates) it is a throwback to

Ishii's LINE (aka ZONE), forays into the noirish demi-monde of sleaze and crime he pioneered at Shintoho Studios in the late 1950s. Lone wolf Takewaki – who we discover at the close is an undercover cop – runs into old acquaintance Yoshida while investigating a case. Before long, the pair is reminiscing over drinks about their post-war meeting spurred by ex-soldier Takewaki searching out his sister who happened to be Yoshida's sweetheart. These flashbacks make up the middle third of the saga. There are more memories of Yoshida trying to pry his girl away from a geisha racket run by yakuza, then the girl seeing him off when he is conscripted into the military. This farewell where she follows as he marches off to war is another brief, visually-stunning and emotionally-affecting sequence that shows what the film could have been had Ishii taken a little more time and effort. During the final third, Takewaki witnesses the yakuza boss he is investigating torturing mistress Mihara by teasingly withholding her heroin – another dynamic, short-lived setpiece. Suddenly, our hero finds the tables turned, and he is exposed as a cop, then subsequently tortured with electric shock to reveal what he knows. Although some of this is intriguingly staged, it becomes increasingly contrived and corny when Yoshida comes to his rescue. A not particularly well-staged shootout climaxes things in the gang's basement, with police reinforcements finally arriving to wrap things up, and all baddies tidily terminated. Machida is a standout as the evil boss's right-hand man. Ishii seems to have been just too indifferent to sustain a consistent tone through the entire film.

Then again, maybe studio bigwigs rained on his parade. The result is frustrating. In light of the cumulative fifteen or twenty minutes of bravura filmmaking on display throughout, side-by-side with inappropriate comic relief, hackneyed dialogue and manufactured, Saturday matinee-style thrills, the viewer familiar with Ishii's best work cannot help but see this as a missed opportunity. Intermittently entertaining. * * 1/2

Joe's Whisper aka Whispering Joe

JOE'S WHISPER aka SASAYAKI NO JO aka WHISPERING JOE 1967 **DIR/ SCR/ PHOTO/MUSIC:** Koichi Saito   **w/** Jin Nakayama, Reiko Asabu, Manami Fuji, Ko Nishimura, An offbeat hitman tale, and one of director Saito's first films.

KILLERS ON PARADE, see MY FACE RED IN THE SUNSET

THE LAST TRUMP CARD aka SAIGO NO KIRI FUDA 1960

DIR. Yoshitaro Nomura   **SCR.** Shinobu Hashimoto **PHOTO COLOR** '**SCOPE:** Takashi Kawamata **w/** Keiji Sada, Miyuki Kuwano, Keiko Hibino, Yoshi Kato, Seiji Miyaguchi

The Last Trump Card

Leading man Keiji Sada was one of the big box office draws at Shochiku and was in several of director Ozu's

Blood and the Law (#1)

Escape and the Law (#3)

"home" dramas. Like Daiei star Raizo Ichikawa and Nikkatsu's Keiichiro Akagi, he died relatively young and unexpectedly (he was only 37). He also appeared in Yoshishige Yoshida's subversive melodrama, DRY BLOOD (1960) about the exploitation by the media of an unstable suicidal man, Kazuo Hase's downbeat in-period yakuza tale, ES-CAPE FROM HELL and Hiromichi Horikawa's crime/mystery film at Toho Studios, BRAND OF EVIL (1964).

LAW aka OKITE aka CODE series

BLOOD AND THE LAW aka CHI TO OKITE 1965 DIR./SCR. Noriaki Yuasa PHOTO B&W 'SCOPE: Miyao Okada MUSIC: Terukuni Takamori w/ Noboru Ando, Tetsuro Tanba, Bunta Sugawara, Keiji Takagi, Miho Shiro, Shigekatsu Kanazawa, Kimihei Tsuzaki, Takeshi Oki, Kenzo Kawabe, Hiroshi Fujioka   Ando's initial yakuza film series. He labored at his first studio, Shochiku, to only minor success before leaving and going onto true stardom at Toei Studios. These films were awfully early in Ando's career – a novice actor and former yakuza given immense notoriety by his newspaper-serialized bio upon his release from prison (for more on Ando, see the entries for TRUE ACCOUNT OF THE ANDO GANG series in the Toei Studios section). It is strange that Ando was signed up by Shochiku, a studio not particularly enamored of the yakuza genre. #1 of 5 films

LAW OF THE WILD aka YASAGURE NO OKITE 1965 DIR./SCR. Noriaki Yuasa PHOTO B&W 'SCOPE: Miyao Okada MUSIC: Mitsuhiko Sato w/ Noboru Ando, Keiji Takagi, Rika Fujie, Emi Shindo, Mariko Taki, Kimihei Tsuzaki, Ryuji Kita, Harumi Matsukaze, Kenzo Kawabe, Mutsuko Sakura, Hiroshi Fujioka   #2 of 5 films

ESCAPE AND THE LAW aka TOBO TO OKITE aka PIER WITHOUT PITY 1965 DIR./SCR. Noriaki Yuasa PHOTO B&W 'SCOPE: Mamoru Morita MUSIC: Hiroji Hayakawa   w/ Noboru Ando, Michitaro Mizushima, Teruko Ichikawa, Keiji Takagi, Mayumi Shimizu, Bunta Sugawara, Ichiro Izawa, Kenzo Kawabe, Kimihei Tsuzaki, Takeshi Oki   #3 of 5 films

NOSTALGIA AND THE LAW aka BOKYO TO OKITE aka BETRAY-ERS OUT 1966 DIR. Yoshitaro Nomura SCR. Masando Ide PHOTO B&W 'SCOPE: Takashi Kawamata MUSIC: Rinichiro Manabe w/ Noboru Ando, Muga Takewaki, Yuko Kusunoki, Kiyoshi Atsumi, Torahiko Hamada, Hideo Sunazuka, Mitsuko Nakamura An uneven take on Ando's involve-ment with a ragtag bunch he socializ-es with on the impoverished water-front after his release from prison. It is surprising that this isn't better as writer Ide contributed to several Akira Kurosawa films, and Nomura is a talented director. Things start out promisingly with Ando leaving the penitentiary and then discovering that his ex-girl is shacked up with a sleazy, cruel gang boss, elements that mirror many similar sequences in French crime films such as Melville's SECOND BREATH and RED CIRCLE. Economic, starkly noirish compositions give way to some gritty, near documentary style footage of young hood Takewaki and his pals in real waterfront locations. But the film becomes bogged down when Ando starts hobnobbing with Takewaki and the denizens of a rickety harbor restaurant. Some of these sequences go on forever and fail to ring true. Ando and cronies decide to rob the sleazy gang boss's gold smuggling operation, but things go awry when goofy turncoat Atsumi (TORA-SAN star) spills the beans when tortured by the bad guys. Predictable deaths occur with the police close behind. Takewaki is one step ahead of Ando in the vengeance department and gets ventilated by the boss's bodyguard for his trouble. Ando arrives, dispatches the bodyguard and boss in full view of his shocked ex-girlfriend. This last sequence where Ando escapes, driving away with the dying Takewaki, only to be caught by the police at dawn redeems the film back in the direction of the promising opening minutes. #4 of 5 films * * 1/2

FIRE AND THE LAW aka HONOO TO OKITE 1966 **DIR.** Umeji Inoue **SCR.** Umeji Inoue/ Akira Tachibana **PHOTO** B&W '**SCOPE:** Takashi Kawamata **MUSIC:** Kenjiro Hirose **w/** Noboru Ando, Hizuru Takachiho, Mitsuko Nakamura, Shinichi Yanagisawa, Kenji Sugawara, Bunta Sugawara, Toru Abe, Juzaburo Akechi, Chiaki Tsukioka, Akitake Kono #5 and final in series

Fire and the Law (#5)

Nostalgia and the Law (#4)

The Left-Handed Sniper - Tokyo Bay

THE LEFT-HANDED SNIPER – TOKYO BAY aka HIDARIKI KI NO SOGEKISHA – TOKYO WAN

aka THE LEFT HAND OF JIRO 1962 83 min. DIR. Yoshitaro Nomura SCR. Zenzo Matsuyama/Shosuke Taga PHOTO B&W 'SCOPE: Takashi Kawamata MUSIC: Yasushi Akutagawa w/ Ko Nishimura, Isao Tamagawa, Toshio Hosokawa, Kei Sato, Jiro Ishizaki, Hiromi Sasaki, Kyoko Aoi, Koji Mitsui, Masao Oda Nishimura is a cop investigating sniper murders in the narcotics trade along with a fellow inspector (Hosokawa). He discovers an old comrade, the left-handed Tamagawa, who had saved his life during the war, is the hired killer for the gang. This is a beautifully done police procedural trawling through Tokyo back alleys and the grimy waterfront that becomes an uncompromisingly downbeat noir thriller of intertwined destinies during the second half. The contrast between the two men's home lives, cop Nishimura with a dissatis-fied wife and killer Tamagawa with a happy, devoted spouse, is perversely memorable. Likewise, the incredibly brutal fight between Nishimura and Tamagawa, both handcuffed together, on a speeding train is a certifiable hair-raiser. When Tamagawa falls out of the train, dragging furiously along the ground while still cuffed to the suffering Nishimura – who is trying in vain to hang on – the effect is devastating. Both of their corpses are found hanging from a railroad trestle bridge a few hours later, silhouetted against the dawn. Nishimura's wife, agonizing over her last treatment of him, and his young detective friend watching as the bodies are lowered, adds to the poignance. * * * 1/2

LIFE OF A CHIVALROUS WOMAN aka JOKYO ICHIDAI

aka THE UNDEFEATED WOMAN 1958 DIR. Seiichiro Uchikawa w/ Nijiko Kiyokawa, Miki Mori From the title and also photos in a Kinema Junpo back issue, this seems to be an early *ninkyo* yakuza film with a female protagonist.

LOVE OF A BAD WOMAN aka **KAWAI AKUJO** series

LOVE OF A BAD WOMAN aka KAWAI AKUJO 1971 DIR./SCR. Umeji Inoue PHOTO COLOR 'SCOPE: Masao Kosugi MUSIC: Kenjiro Hirose w/ Bunsaku Han, Tadao Nakamaru, Yusuke Takita Etsuko Ikuta #1 of 2

Love of a Bad Woman (#1)

LOVE OF A BAD WOMAN – KISS BEFORE THE KILLING 1972 DIR./SCR. Umeji Inoue PHOTO COLOR 'SCOPE: Yoshi Maruyama MUSIC: Kenjiro Hirose w/ Bunsaku Han, Hiroshi Moritsugi, Arihiro Fujimura, Miyoko Akaza, Ichiro Zaitsu, Frankie Sakai #2 of 2

My Face Red in the Sunset aka *Killers on Parade*
poster and still

Pale Flower

MAN aka OTOKO series

SOUL OF A MAN aka OTOKO
NO KON aka MAN'S SPIRIT
1966 **DIR.** Meijiro Umezu **SCR.** Seiji
Hoshikawa **PHOTO 'SCOPE:**
Masayuki Kato **MUSIC:** Shosuke
Ichikawa   **w/** Muga Takewaki,
Yoshiko Kayama, Kumiko Kishi,
Seizaburo Kawazu, Ryohei
Uchida, Takashi Fujiki, Tetsuro
Tanba, Yoshiko Sano, Joji Ai, Bunta
Sugawara #1 of 2 films

MAN'S HOT BLOOD aka ATSUI
CHI NO OTOKO 1966 **DIR.** Meijiro
Umezu **SCR.** Seiji Hoshikawa **PHOTO**
'SCOPE: Masayuki Kato **MUSIC:**
Shosuke Ichikawa   **w/** Muga
Takewaki, Isao Kimura, Ryohei
Uchida, Yoshi Kato, Yoshiko
Kayama, Koji Nanbara, Chizuko
Arai #2 of 2 films

A MAN'S SHADOW aka OTOKO
NO KAGE 1964 **DIR.** Yoshikazu
(Giichi?) Otsuki **SCR.** Yoshikazu
Otsuki/Tsutomu Kumagaya/Hisatoshi
Kai **PHOTO 'SCOPE:** Haruo Ohara
MUSIC: Chuji Kinoshita **w/** Keisuke
Sono, Miyuki Kuwano, Yoshi Kato,
Muga Takewaki, Teruo Yoshida,
Tatsuo Masumura, Tatsuo Hasegawa

MAN'S STORM aka OTOKO NO
ARASHI aka A MAN'S ANGER
1963 **DIR.** Nobuo Nakagawa **SCR.**
Toshio Matsuura **PHOTO 'SCOPE:**
Shiro Miyanishi **MUSIC:** Hideo
Ozawa   **w/** Hideo Murata, Kyoko
Aoyama, Tomi Yamamoto, Shingo
Kiyokawa, Jushiro Kobayashi

MELODY OF CRIME aka
HANZAI NO MERODII 1964

DIR. Umeji Inoue **SCR.** Hajime
Takaiwa/Umeji Inoue **PHOTO**
'SCOPE: Shizuo Hirase **MUSIC:**
Kenjiro Hirose **w/** Kyosuke
Machida, Teruo Yoshida, Haruko
Wanibuchi, Miyuki Kuwano, Naoko
Kubo, Tatsuo Terashima

MY FACE RED IN THE SUNSET
aka YUHI NI AKAI ORE NO KAO
aka KILLERS ON PARADE 1961
82 min. **DIR.** Masahiro Shinoda **SCR.**
Shuji Terayama **PHOTO COLOR**
'SCOPE: Masao Kosugi **MUSIC:**
Naozumi Yamamoto **w/** Yusuke
Kawazu, Shima Iwashita, Kayako
Honoo, Ryohei Uchida, Fumio
Watanabe, Kazue Kozaka   A young,
inexperienced gunman (Kawazu)
falls-in-love with his assignment, a
journalist (Iwashita) writing exposés
on yakuza-affiliated building contrac-
tors. Black humor figures in the equation when the professional hitmen
following Kawazu as back-up, inadvertently start knocking off the wrong
people. The career killers' tempers
are as hair-trigger as their guns since
they are also envious of Kawazu's
shooting prowess. In Audie Bock's
book, JAPANESE FILM DIREC-
TORS, she quotes Shinoda as saying
that he is convinced MY FACE... did
poorly due to its "eccentricity." Like
Shinoda's TEARS ON THE LION'S
MANE, this is yet another great film
that Shochiku, for some arbitrary
reason or another, has yet to make
available on video. It has been spo-
radically available streaming online
in the USA as of mid-2012 through
the Criterion section on the Hulu-Plus
video site. After finally viewing it,
the above plot description does not do
the film justice. Although occasionally disjointed and static, more often

than not Shinoda keeps the startling, stylized images flowing at breakneck speed. A colorful pop art masterpiece, and it seems a reasonable assumption that other adventurous directors saw this and were influenced or, at least, inspired by it. While watching this, Suzuki's TOKYO DRIFTER, BRANDED TO KILL and THE GUYS WHO BET ON ME, Yasuharu Hasebe's BLACK TIGHT KILLERS and Kihachi Okamoto's non-yakuza spy spoof AGE OF ASSASSINS came to mind. * * * 1/2

ONNA GIRAI 1964 95 min. **DIR.** Hirokazu Ichimura **PHOTO 'SCOPE:** Masao Kosugi **w/** Teruo Yoshida, Chieko Baisho, Norihei Miki

OSAKA TOUGH aka OSAKA YARO 1961 **DIR.** Tatsuo Ohsone **SCR.** Obu Motoyama **PHOTO 'SCOPE:** Hideo Ishimoto **MUSIC:** Mitsuo Kato **w/** Minoru Oki, Junzaburo Ban, Yuriko Yamada, Chieko Naniwa, Meicho Soganoya, Tatsuo Endo, Hiroshi Nawa

PALE FLOWER aka KAWAITA HANA 1963 **DIR.** Masahiro Shinoda **ORIG. STORY:** Shintaro Ishihara **SCR.** Ataru Baba/ Masahiro Shinoda **PHOTO B&W 'SCOPE:** Masao Kosugi **MUSIC:** Toru Takemitsu **w/** Ryo Ikebe, Mariko Kaga, Takashi Fujiki, Chisako Hara, Koji Nakahara, Shinichiro Mikami, Naoki Sugiura, Eijiro Tono   A great, profoundly realized film on the existential lives of a middle-aged lone wolf yakuza hitman and a spoiled, thrill-seeking rich girl. Their platonic relationship fuels a neurotic, almost masochistic spiritual hunger already present in both of them. Their mutual bankrupt-

cy of emotion, their inability to feel anything genuine, leads them from progressively higher risk card games to increasingly more dangerous past-times. When appointed by his boss to make a hit to avenge a rival clan's murderous indiscretion, Ikebe takes the girl with him to a crowded restaurant to witness the act. As religious music plays in the background, he stabs the man, all the time staring into the raptly attentive eyes of the girl on the other side of the balcony. Later, while in prison, Ikebe discovers from a fellow inmate that the girl – since turned into an addict by a junkie killer (Fujiki) who also used to frequent the games – has OD'ed. Shinoda has made several excellent films, but this is his most visually stunning. It is also probably his most economic and pared to the bone. * * * *

The Perennial Weed

THE PERENNIAL WEED aka SHOWA KARESUSUKI 1975 87 min. **DIR.** Yoshitaro Nomura **SCR.**

Kaneto Shindo **PHOTO COLOR 'SCOPE:**
Takashi Kawamata **MUSIC:** Mitsuaki
Kanno   w/ Hideki Takahashi,
Kumiko Akiyoshi, Shino Ikenami,
Hiroko Isayama, Mizuho Suzuki,
Yoshio Inaba   Cop Takahashi is
thrown into turmoil when his younger
sister falls for an upstart gangster.

**PORT OF VIOLENCE – TIGER
AND WOLF** aka BORYOKU
NO MINATO – TORA TO OKAMI
1965 **DIR.** Michiyoshi Doi **SCR.**
Onobu Motoyama/Yuhiro Matsumura
PHOTO 'SCOPE: Shigeki Honda
MUSIC: Yoshioki (Kanyo?) Ogawa
w/ Tetsuro Tanba, Ryohei Uchida, Ko
Nishimura, Toshiya Wazaki, Kinuko
Obata, Tatsuo Endo, Shinsuke
Mikimoto

*Pursuit of Murder - Shinjuku's 25th
Hour*

**PURSUIT OF MURDER –
SHINJUKU'S 25TH HOUR** aka
KOROSU MADE OE – SHINJUKU

25 JI aka SHINJUKU AFTER
DARK 1969 90 min. **DIR.** Kazuo
Hase **SCR.** Ichiro Miyagawa/Kazuo
Hase **PHOTO COLOR 'SCOPE:** Keiji
Maruyama **MUSIC:** Hajime Kaburagi
w/ Shigeru Amachi, Makoto Sato,
Yoshiko Kayama, Masako Tomiyama,
Yusuke Kawazu, Eriko Sono,
Chisako Hara   Police detective
Amachi fights against those who
banished him from his job – both
cops and criminals.

REBELLIOUS JOURNEY aka
HAN GYAKU NO TABI 1976 92
min. **DIR.** Yusuke Watanabe **SCR.**
Kibu Nagata **PHOTO COLOR 'SCOPE:**
Masao Kosugi **MUSIC:** Hajime
Kaburagi w/ Yoshio Harada, Yoko
Takahashi, Reiko Aso, Kunie Tanaka

THE ROSE ON HIS ARM aka
TAIYO TO BARA aka THE SUN
AND THE ROSE 1956 **DIR/SCR.**
Keisuke Kinoshita **PHOTO B&W:**
Hiroyuki Kusuda **MUSIC:** Chuji
Kinoshita w/ Katsuo Nakamura,
Sadako Sawamura, Yoshiko Kuga
Young punk Nakamura disregards
his mother's wishes, aspiring to the
unsavory world of the yakuza.
Director Kinoshita's complex, uncompromising and emotionally draining take on the *taiyozoku* (sun tribe)
subgenre that was then in vogue. The
performances are withering. This
rivals other sun tribe pictures such
as Kon Ichikawa's PUNISHMENT
ROOM and Ko Nakahira's CRAZED
FRUIT for featuring the most downbeat climax in mid-1950s Japanese
cinema. Best Foreign Language Film
winner at the Golden Globes in 1957.
* * * 1/2

THE RULING POWER'S AGREEABLE MAN aka TENKA NO KAI DANSHI 1966 DIR. Kazuo Hase SCR. Ichiro Ikeda w/ Muga Takewaki, Yoshiko Kayama

RUSTY FLAMES aka SABITA HONOO 1977 91 min. DIR. Kazuhiko Sadanaga SCR. Kyuzo Kobayashi PHOTO COLOR 'SCOPE: Takashi Kawamata MUSIC: Toru Takemitsu w/ Tetsuro Tanba, Meiko Kaji, Mieko Harada, Mikijiro Hira, Atsuo Nakamura, Hiroshi Fujioka This is more of a suspense thriller than a yakuza film.

Secret Agent 101 - Bodyguard Murder

SECRET AGENT 101 – BODY-GUARD MURDER aka SHINKA 101 – KOROSHI NO YOJINBO 1966 90 min. DIR. Teruo Ishii SCR. Takeo Kunihiro PHOTO COLOR 'SCOPE: Shizuo Hirase MUSIC: Masao Yagi w/ Muga Takewaki, Jitsuko Yoshimura, Teruo Yoshida, Kanjuro Arashi, Minoru Oki, Takashi Fujiki,

Hideo Takamatsu, Bunta Sugawara An intermittently amusing, entertaining tongue-in-cheek timewaster with Bond-type operative Takewaki up against charming yakuza Oki in Hong Kong and Macao locations. At times, when Takewaki is bouncing around town trying to keep his airheaded, Playboy-bunny girlfriend Yoshimura safe, it is a bit reminiscent of Jess Franco's absurd films KISS ME, MONSTER and TWO UNDER-COVER ANGELS with Janine Reynaud and Rosanna Yanni as freelance private eyes, The Red Lips. However, there are none of the goofy, stream-of-consciousness non-sequitors and bizarre visual asides that glut those films. This makes up for it a bit in virtually non-stop action, a good cast and striking locations. Ultimately, though, it is all pretty forgettable. * * 1/2

SHAPE OF THE NIGHT aka YORU NO HENRIN aka THE BEAUTIFUL PEOPLE 1965 109 min. DIR. Noboru Nakamura SCR. Toshihide Gondo PHOTO COLOR 'SCOPE: Toichiro Narushima w/ Miyuki Kuwano, Mikijiro Hira, Bunta Sugawara, Masuyo Iwamoto, Isao Kimura, Keisuke Sonoi A young girl (Kuwano) falls in love with a handsome young fellow (Hira) in a small Tokyo bar. She gives up her virginity when he forces himself on her, thinking it will mean marriage in the near future. But he turns out to be a gangster who forces her into prostitution. He is virtually castrated in a gangfight and, becoming dependent on her, realizes he genuinely loves her. Later, one of her customers falls-in-love with her and tries to persuade her to run away with him. She feels it is impossible, that her life has already been permanently ruined. Unable to run away or continue her sordid life, she stabs Hira to death.

SLAUGHTER IN BROAD DAYLIGHT aka HAKUCHU NO ZANSATSU 1967 DIR. Meijiro Umezu SCR. Seiji Hoshikawa PHOTO 'SCOPE: Masayuki Kato MUSIC: Rinichiro Manabe w/ Noboru Ando, Masakazu Hirai, Yunosuke Ito, Kenjiro Ishiyama, Takashi Inagaki, Toshio Hosokawa, Hideo Sunazuka, Chizuko Arai

Slaughter in Broad Daylight

SONG OF VENGEANCE aka FUKUSHU NO UTA GA KIKOERU aka HEARING THE SONG OF VENGEANCE 1968 90 min. DIR. Yoshihisa Sadanaga/Narayuki (Shigeyuki?) Yamane ORIG. STORY/ SCR. Shintaro Ishihara PHOTO B&W 'SCOPE: Tadashi Sakai/Mitsumori Kanuma MUSIC: Rinichiro Manabe w/ Yoshio Harada, Ryohei Uchida,

Tayo (Tashiro?) Iwamoto, Eijiro Tono, Atsuo Nakamura
The fact that Japanese reference book, Cinema Club '94, gives it a meager * 1/2 rating, and that there are two directors and two cinematographers credited does not bode well. Then again, mainstream Japanese film critics – as mainstream critics everywhere – may not know what they are talking about. It *does* have a great poster. Harada's debut as a leading man. This may not be a yakuza film.

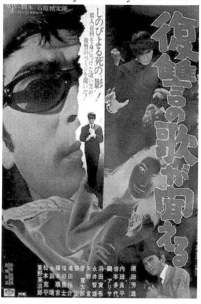

Song of Vengeance

STRAY DOG aka NORA INU 1973 104 min. DIR. Azuma Morizaki SCR. Azuma Morizaki/ Baku Isshiki PHOTO COLOR 'SCOPE: Kenichi Yoshikawa MUSIC: Masaru Sato w/ Tetsuya Watari, Shinsuke Ashida, Keiko Matsuzaka A remake of Kurosawa's 1949 film with Watari in Mifune's part of the cop trying to retrieve his gun from a yakuza killer. Ashida has Takashi Shimura's role of the young cop's detective mentor.

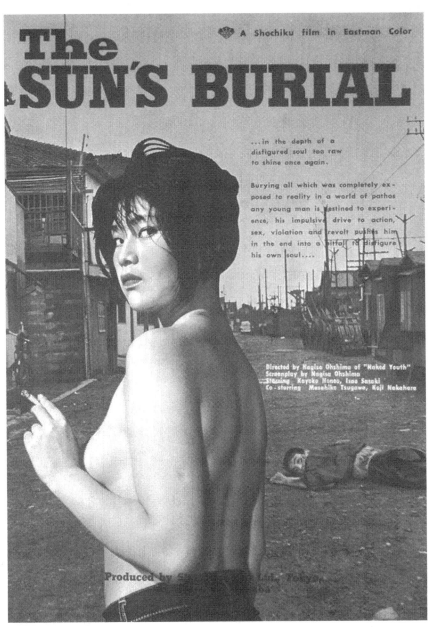

The Sun's Burial

Stray Dog

THE SUN'S BURIAL aka
TAIYO NO HAKABA 1960 87
min. **DIR.** Nagisa Oshima **SCR.**
Nagisa Oshima/Toshiro Oshido
PHOTO COLOR 'SCOPE: Takashi
Kawamata **MUSIC:** Rinichiro
Manabe **w/** Kayoko Hono, Masahiko
Tsugawa, Isao Sasaki, Yusuke
Kawazu, Junzaburo Ban, Fumio
Watanabe   An unrelievedly glum
picture of slum life and the various
young hoodlums, disillusioned old
soldiers, young exploited women
and unwanted children who live in
one particular ghetto. Oshima has
his political agenda all too clearly
stamped on every scene. Whatever
one's political leanings, to the left or
right, or insights on poverty, a diligent
conscience and astute, uncompromising vision does not necessarily a good
movie make. Oshima is definitely
talented, and there are images here
that sear their way into the viewer's
brain, indelibly etched. One is the
fight between Tsugawa and Sasaki on

the railroad tracks. Unfortunately, this
is one of Oshima's more pretentious
films. * * 1/2

SWORD AND FLOWER aka
KEN TO HANA 1972 **DIR.** Toshio
Masuda **SCR.** Kaneo Ikegami **PHOTO
COLOR 'SCOPE:** Masao Kosugi
MUSIC: Rinichiro Manabe **w/** Tetsuya
Watari, Emi Shindo, Masayuki Mori,
Jiro Tamiya, Junko Natsu, Miyoko
Akaza   Another impossible to
see yakuza picture from Shochiku
Studios. Nikkatsu veterans, director
Masuda and actors Watari and Natsu,
and former Daiei Studios leading man
Tamiya team up. Watari *does* appear
a bit more clean-cut than usual on the
rather static-looking poster.

Sword and Flower

**SWORD – FLOWER-STREWN
PATH OF COURAGE** aka DOSU
– DOKYO NO HANAMICHI 1966
DIR. Hiroki Matsuno **SCR.** Hajime
Takaiwa/Makoto Horiuchi/Yoshihisa
Sakurai **PHOTO COLOR 'SCOPE:**

Tomoichi Kuramochi **MUSIC:** Hajime Kaburagi **w/** Isamu Nagato, Toru Abe, Keiji Takagi, Yoshiko Kayama, Bunta Sugawara, Ryunosuke Tsukigata, Masakazu Tamura, Tsutomu Sasaki, Hosei Komatsu

Sword - Flower-Strewn Path of Courage

TALE OF SCARLET LOVE aka MAKKANO KOI NO MONOGA-TARI aka THE SCARLET ROSE

1964 99 min. **DIR.** Umeji Inoue **SCR.** Umeji Inoue/Yoshio Shirasake **PHOTO COLOR 'SCOPE:** Horiyuki Nagaoka **MUSIC:** Toshiro Mayuzumi **w/** Mariko Okada, Teruo Yoshida, Hiromi Sasaki, Minoru Oki, Takashi Fujiki, Jun Negami, Keijiro Morokado   An unusual story of obsessive love with undercover cop Yoshida infiltrating a drug gang by posing as a nightclub piano player. He is smitten with singer Okada, who he discovers is the gang's real boss. When Yoshida is tortured into revealing his true identity, one of his partners is murdered as a result. He resigns and becomes a gangster himself. Once again finding himself Okada's lover, her fickle nature soon makes him realize that he has wasted his life. He kills her, whereupon her henchmen then terminate him.

TATSU IN THE STORM aka ARASHI NI TATSU

1968 **DIR.** Kazuo Hase **SCR.** Umeji Inoue/ Kazuo Hase **w/** Jin Nakayama, Nana Ozaki, Masakazu Tamura, Yumiko Nogawa, Toru Abe, Fumio Watanabe, Kayo Matsuo

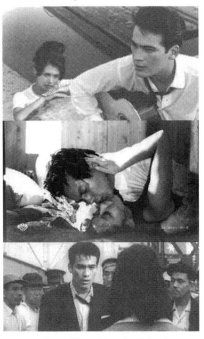

images from **Tears on the Lion's Mane** *aka* **Flame at the Pier**

TEARS ON THE LION'S MANE aka NAMIDA O SHISHI NO TATE-GAMI NI aka FLAME AT THE PIER

1962 97 min. **DIR.** Masahiro Shinoda **SCR.** Shuji Terayama/ Masahiro Shinoda/Ichiro Mizunuma **PHOTO B&W 'SCOPE:** Masao Kosugi **MUSIC:** Toru Takemitsu **w/** Takashi Fujiki, Mariko Kaga, So Yamamura,

Koji Nanbara, Tetsuro Tamba, Kyoko Kishida, Asao Koike, Jun Hamamura, Toshio Hosokawa

Another one of Shinoda's early films before he was "accepted" by the critics. A truly bizarre hybrid of hardboiled noirish yakuza saga, social consciousness message picture and rock musical. It doesn't always click, but the fact that it does work through most of its fast-moving running time is pretty amazing. Try to imagine Elia Kazan casting Elvis Presley in Brando's part in ON THE WATERFRONT, then having his lead character bursting into song a couple of times – yet still retaining the gritty, uncompromising style. Crazy, but Shinoda earns top marks for guts in attempting such inspired madness. Certainly screenwriting collaborator, avant-garde playwright Shuji Terayama, can be credited with encouraging Shinoda's audacious ideas. Interestingly, Shinoda claims he had not yet seen ON THE WATERFRONT or other movies it resembles, such as WEST SIDE STORY, at the time he made the film. Young tough Fujiki, working for crippled, paternal gang boss Nanbara, has his naivete shattered during union struggles and ends up accidentally killing his gal's father. Produced by Shochiku but unfortunately not available on DVD – at least at the moment. * * *

THEATER OF LIFE aka JINSEI GEKIJO 1972 167 min. **Dir.** Tai Kato **Scr.** Tai Kato/Yoshitaro Nomura/Teruhiko Mimura **Photo color 'scope:** Keishi (Yoshimori?) Maruyama **Music:** Hajime Kaburagi w/ Hideki Takahashi, Muga Takewaki, Tetsuya Watari, Jiro Tamiya, Mitsuko Baisho, Hisaya

Morishige, Yoshiko Kayama, Keiko Tsushima, Masahiko Tanimura, Junzaburo Ban

Theater of Life

An amazingly effective low budget hybrid that crosses the intimate with the epic in yet another adaptation of the popular THEATER OF LIFE novel. At times looking a bit like one of his RED PEONY GAMBLER films, albeit with a somewhat more painstaking production design, director Kato revels in the minimal, relating almost the entire narrative in medium shots or tight close-ups. Occasionally it comes across as a bit talky, but there are some rousingly rambunctious, bloody swordfights and brawls to punctuate the quieter moments. Everyone in the cast is a standout, with Takewaki as the young master (usually a more minor role in the Toei versions with Hiroki Matsukata in the part), Tamiya as Kira Tsune and Takahashi as Hisha Kaku. Watari is Takahashi's best friend, consumed by guilt when he sleeps with imprisoned Takahashi's woman Otoyo (Mitsuko Baisho) when he finds her reduced to making a living as a prostitute. Takahashi and Baisho are particularly affecting in their scenes together, igniting a smoldering passion that is more than convincing. All in all, this THEATER OF LIFE version is mesmerizingly evocative of a grueling life on the edge. * * * 1/2

THUS ANOTHER DAY aka KYO MO MATA KAKUTE ARI NAN 1959 73 min. Dir./Scr. Keisuke Kinoshita PHOTO COLOR 'SCOPE: Hiroshi Kusuda MUSIC: Chuji Kinoshita w/ Teiji Takahashi, Yoshiko Kuga, Takahiro Tamura, Kanzaburo Nakamura, Kankuru Nakamura, Rentaro Mikuni, Kazuya Kosaka Basically a "home" drama/ melodrama by humanist Kinoshita depicting a white collar family and a retired militarist who are tormented by the yakuza in a mountain town. The focus is on the beautiful, lonely housewife Kuga who is tiring of her salaryman husband's slavish devotion to his job, especially when they are spending a few summer months with her family in the country out of economic necessity. She befriends a sad middle-aged veteran who is suffering from survivor's guilt, and she is powerless to alleviate his suffering when his stepdaughter dies of typhus and his estranged wife plunges off the deep end, going on a drunken binge at the house of the scummy yakuza boss (Mikuni) for whom she has been working as a housemaid. Kuga is devastated when the veteran gets out his samurai sword from the war and goes on a rampage, killing the boss and his flunkies before expiring from their bullets. When she and her husband and tiny son return to their own home, she has a new appreciation for her family and for the fragility of human relationships. Not a traditional yakuza film by any means, with the gang's presence in the small village serving as a catalyst/symbol for the kind of random violence that can sometimes pop up out of nowhere to destroy the lives of innocent people. Kuga is a powerhouse actress. She appeared in only Shochiku productions, so despite decades of Japanese film viewing, this author is only now discovering her. * * *

TOKYO BAY see LEFT-HANDED SNIPER, THE

Tokyo Wanderer

TOKYO WANDERER aka TOKYO MUSHUKU 1966 Dir./ Scr. Noriaki Yuasa PHOTO 'SCOPE: Tomoya (Yuya?) Sekiguchi MUSIC: Jun Suzuki w/ Keiji Takagi, Yoshiko Hatsuna, Mariko Taki, Chizuko Arai, Kikko Matsuoka

TRAP IN BROAD DAYLIGHT aka MAHIRU NO WANA 1961

DIR./SCR. Mitsuo Yagi **PHOTO**
'SCOPE: Haruo Ohara **MUSIC:** Chuji
Kinoshita   **w/** Isao Sasaki, Shima
Iwashita, Sadako Sawamura, Koji
Nanbara, Keiko Hibino, Shoji Yasui

Trump Card of a Man's Face

**TRUMP CARD OF A MAN'S
FACE** aka OTOKO NO KAO
WA KIRI FUDA 1966   **DIR.**
Masahiro Makino **SCR.** Ichiro
Miyagawa **PHOTO COLOR 'SCOPE:**
Shigeki Honda **MUSIC:** Hiroshi
Ogura   **w/** Noboru Ando, Masuichi
Hirai, Masahiko Tsugawa, Hiroyuki
Nagato, Chiyonosuke Azuma,
Michitaro Mizushima, Ko Nishimura,
Toshiya Wazaki, Yukiko Todoroki
Makino, an old specialist at this type
of picture, helms a *ninkyo* yakuza film
with newcomer, real life ex-yakuza
Ando. As a marketing ploy, Shochiku
titled one of the other 1966 Noboru
Ando films HISTORY OF A MAN'S
FACE, an excellent movie directed by
Tai Kato. The unspoken selling point
behind the phrase "A MAN'S FACE"

is that Ando sported a quite large
real-life scar on one cheek from a
knife fight in his gangster past.

VIOLENT HARBOR aka
BORYOKU NO HATOBA 1957
DIR. Manao Horiuchi **SCR.** Yoshiro
Tomita/ Osamu Takahashi **PHOTO:**
Haruo Ohara **MUSIC:** Chuji
Kinoshita   **w/** Minoru Oki, Hiroko
Sugita, Miyuki Kuwano, Eitaro
Ozawa, Eijiro Tono

**WATCH YOUR HEART,
TAMEGORO** aka YARUZO MITE
ORE TAMEGORO 1971 84 min.
DIR. Yoshitaro Nomura   **w/** Kiyoshi
Atsumi   An easygoing gambler
played by Atsumi (later to gain fame
as Tora-san) gets caught in the cross-
fire of two gangs' warfare.

WILD DETECTIVE aka OUT-
LAW COP aka YASAGURE DEKA
1976 74 min. **DIR.** Yusuke Watanabe
SCR. Yusuke Watanabe/Takeo
Kunihiro **PHOTO COLOR 'SCOPE:**
Keimori (Keishi?) Maruyama
MUSIC: Hajime Kaburagi
w/ Yoshio Harada, Naoko Otani,
Etsushi Takahashi, Takashi Kanda,
Miyako Akaza, Tokubei Hanazawa
DIRTY HARRY and THE FRENCH
CONNECTION had a huge influ-
ence on Japanese yakuza films in
the early-to-mid 1970s, as seen in
Toho Studios' WILD COP duo with
Tetsuya Watari and Kinji Fukasaku's
YAKUZA BURIAL (also with
Watari). Here Shochiku takes a
shot with their resident young, mod
tough guy, Yoshio Harada. Harada is
probably best known by Japanese
movie fans in the West for his roles in
Kazuo Ikehiro's TRAIL OF BLOOD
matatabi trilogy and as the one-

eyed swordsman in Hideo Gosha's
HUNTER IN THE DARK.

Wild Detective aka Outlaw Cop

WORLDLY COMRADES DISAPPEAR IN THE HARBOR
aka KO NI KIETA AITSU 1963
DIR. Hirokazu Ichimura **SCR.**
Yuichiro Yamane/Yoshiaki Tomita
PHOTO 'SCOPE: Masao Kosugi
MUSIC: Hirokoshi Ogawa
w/ Tatsuo Terashima, Haruko
Wanibuchi, Takashi Shimura, Naoko
Kubo, Ryohei Uchida, Eitaro Shindo,
Ichiro Sugai, Bunta Sugawara,
Saburo Kitajima

YORU GAKU ZURETA 1978
93 min. **Dir.** Masaku (Masahisa?)
Sadanaga **SCR.** Masaku (?)
Sadanaga/Kei Tasaka **PHOTO COLOR**
'SCOPE: Takashi Kawamata **MUSIC:**
Masaru Sato w/ Hiroshi Katsuno,
Yoshio Harada, Kaori Momoi, Isao
Natsuyagi, Kazuko Yoshiyuki

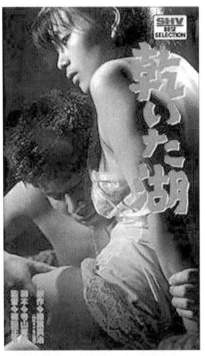

Youth in Fury Japanese VHS artwork

YOUTH IN FURY aka KAWAITA
MIZUUMI aka DRY LAKE 1961
89 min. **DIR.** Masahiro Shinoda
SCR. Shuji Terayama **PHOTO COLOR**
'SCOPE: Masao Kosugi **MUSIC:** Toru
Takemitsu w/ Shinichiro Mikami,
Shima Iwashita, Kayoko Honoo,
Hizuru Takachiho, Yunosuke Ito,
Junichiro Yamahita
No yakuza genre trappings, but an
exuberant, profane saga of jaded
taiyozoku delinquent antics grating
against naive, leftist student activist
ideals. Mikami is a relatively poor
student who takes money from his
older bar hostess mistress. Born out
of wedlock (to a woman in virtually
the same profession), he also dallies
with a hedonistic, wild delinquent
girl (Honoo) who is stuck on him and
whom he eventually gets pregnant.

But he gradually cultivates the mutual affinity he has with individualistic, independent student Iwashita. Her businessman father has just commited suicide, taking the fall for corruption which should be properly placed at the door of the father's right-wing politician crony (Ito). Iwashita sees not only her elder sister's marriage plans destroyed because of this – her fiancé is a spineless twit – what is worse, politician Ito steps into the breach to save the bankrupt mother and two sisters by making the jilted elder sister his mistress! Mikami views all this with a cynical eye. He is almost as cold-hearted as his friend, rich boy Yamashita, who regularly sets up situations to humiliate his "friends," particularly women, who come to him desperate for help with tuition money. Mikami also hangs out with a leftist student council protesting the U.S./Japan Security Treaty, but he grows to despise them, as well as the right-wing hypocrites who seem to care only about money. He is a mess of contradictory sadistic and idealistic impulses, the only student to sport jeans and a black leather jacket and possessed of an OCD fascination with the images of world leaders, swinging the gamut from FDR and Castro to Tojo and Hitler. He gets his ghetto denizen prizefighter pal to beat up Iwashita's sister's ex-boyfriend, and takes Iwashita along to watch. However, the psychotic, brain-damaged ex-fighter goes too far, slashing the man's face with a razor. Despite Iwashita's repulsion, she eventually falls-in-love with Mikami, and they spend an idyllic night together making love, with him reciting verse from his favorite poet, African-American writer Langston Hughes! Mikami's

self-obsession, his desire to constantly expose hypocrisy in the cruelest ways while being guilty of some of the same conduct, ultimately drives the heartbroken Iwashita away from him and into the arms of the student demonstrators who are rallying in the streets. Disgusted with everyone, Mikami decides to take decisive action, making homemade bombs to blow up the Diet (Japanese Parliament). But just as he is leaving his slum flat with his bag of explosives, he is arrested by the cops for instigating the disfigurement of Iwashita's sister's fiancé. A wild, beautifully-written, directed and performed movie that captures the exhilaration, confusion, disappointments, humiliations and violence of growing up in early 1960s urban Japan. It deserves much wider exposure and recognition. * * * 1/2

TOHO STUDIOS

The Wolves

INTRODUCTION

In 1935, Ichizo Kobayashi, a real estate tycoon and founder of the Takarazuka all-girl opera troupe, bought up control of P.C.L. (Photo Chemical Laboratories) and J. O. (Jenkins-Ozawa), two production companies that had already been churning out both feature and advertising films. This enabled the P.C. L. to finally offer enough of a financial incentive to lure away such big directors as Kajiro Yamamoto from Nikkatsu and Mikio Naruse from Shochiku By the following year, boss Kobayashi had also formed a distribution corporation, although his theater holdings were initially deficient compared to industry giants like Shochiku.

Toho subsequently attempted to develop a friendly, mutually beneficial relationship with cash-deficient Nikkatsu, but this served to escalate antagonism towards both companies from the jealous-to-stay-on-top Shochiku. Distribution feuds followed. Financial intimidation, usually from Shochiku in the form of a booking boycott, was aimed at various theater owners who refused to exclusively play one studio's product. Talent raids, at first primarily from Toho, were used as retaliation, and Toho boss Kobayashi managed to lure away such popular actors as Kazuo Hasegawa and Denjiro Okochi and such directors as Sadao Yamanaka and Mansaku Itami. Shortly after jumping the Shochiku ship in 1937, Hasegawa was actually attacked by a razor-wielding yakuza hired by a Shochiku labor boss, and received a scar that would stay with him for the rest of his long career (he retired in 1963 with his 300th film, the classic REVENGE OF A KABUKI ACTOR aka AN ACTOR'S REVENGE directed by Kon Ichikawa at Daiei). The attack backfired, putting the public on Toho's side. Toho's fortunes only improved in the ensuing years as they composed more hit films and acquired more talent looking for greener pastures.

As noted in the Shintoho Studios introduction, Toho enjoyed more than its share of labor difficulties post-WW2. But they also continued to make exceptional films, many by respected veteran filmmakers such as Mikio Naruse, Kajiro Yamamoto, Hiroshi Inagaki and Masahiro Makino as well as such new talent as Akira Kurosawa, Senkichi Taniguchi and Kon Ichikawa. By the mid-fifties they were back on top with such international hits as GODZILLA (GOJIRA, 1954) directed by Ishiro Honda and THE SEVEN SAMURAI (SHICHININ NO SAMURAI, 1956) directed by Kurosawa and such domestic goldmines as Masahiro Makino's *matatabi* series, JIROCHO OF THREE PROVINCES (JIROCHO SAN GOKUSHI, 1952 – 1954).

Although Toho churned out a healthy dose of genre pictures between the mid-fifties and the early eighties, concentrating on the lucrative staple of science-fiction/*kaiju* (giant monster) films, *jidai-geki chanbara* and American-influenced crime films, they had a well-rounded line-up of comedies, youth romances, dramas and war movies as well. They also produced a decent crop of unclassifiable, prestige "art" films during the same period, including critically regarded masterworks by Kurosawa and Masaki Kobayashi. Hit by the same box office slump that had virtually destroyed Daiei and Nikkatsu in the early seventies, Toho, like Toei and Shochiku, survived because of not only their savvy marketing instincts but also from prudent diversification into real estate, television and other enterprises.

Japanese Mainstream...

TOHO Studios

ATOMIC OBAN series

ATOMIC OBAN aka ATOMIKKU
OBAN – SURIMASU WAYO NO
MAKI 1961 **Dir.** Kozo Saeki **Scr.**
Ruisu (Ruihisa?) Yanagisawa **Photo**
'**scope:** Tokuzo Kuroda **Music:**
Taku Izumi w/ Yoshie Mizutani,
Sonomi Nakajima, Masumi
Harukawa, Michiyo Yokoyama,
Kiyoshi Atsumi, Ichiro Nakatani
Action comedy about female *oyabun*,
her cohorts and exploits. #1 of 2

**ATOMIC OBAN – STORY OF A
FEMALE BOSS'S FIGHT** aka
ATOMIKKU OBAN – ONNA
OYABUN TAIKETSU NO MAKI
1961 **Dir.** Kozo Saeki **Scr.** Ruisu
(Ruihisa?) Yanagisawa **Photo**
'**scope:** Tokuzo Kuroda **Music:**
Taku Izumi w/ Yoshie Mizutani,
Sonomi Nakajima, Masumi
Harukawa, Michiyo Yokoyama,
Kiyoshi Atsumi, Ichiro Nakatani
#2 of 2

ATTACK ON THE SUN aka
HAKUCHU NO SHUGEKI aka
ATTACK IN BROAD DAYLIGHT
1970 88 min. **Dir.** Kiyoshi Nishimura **Scr.** Yoshio Shirasaka/Kiyoshi
Nishimura **Photo color** '**scope:**
Tokuzo Kuroda **Music:** Komasa
Hibino w/ Toshio Kurosawa,
Kazuko Takahashi, Mako Midori,
Shin Kishida, Kuniko Ishii, Rex
Houston   A stylishly mod story
of disenfranchised, resentful truck
driver Kurosawa becoming enamored
with go-go dancer Takahashi, then
experiencing intoxicating power
when loaned a gun by his best pal.
This leads to supermarket holdups,
then a confrontation with some rich
young tough guys at a country resort.
After a tussle in the woods which
causes severe wounds to Kurosawa's
epidermis, the gun accidentally
discharges in the ruckus. One of the
boys dies, and Kurosawa kills the
other fleeing youth to conceal his
guilt. His pal gets him out of the area,
and the two are then taken under the
wing of gangster clubowner Kishida
and his woman Midori. Things calm
down for a while with Kurosawa
tending bar at the club and partying
with gal Takahashi. Kurosawa soon
has to help Kishida revolt against fellow yakuza who want to assassinate
their returning-from-jail boss. Working now for the elder boss as well as
Kishida, Kurosawa is soon required
to prove his mettle by killing two of
the betrayers. Kurosawa is shocked
to see Kishida turn up dead himself,
several days later. Allied with his pal
and American teen Houston,
Kurosawa attempts to rob his new
boss but ends up having to kill the
whole gang when things go wrong.
At the close, despondent Takahashi
realizes Kurosawa has to be stopped
and informs on him to the police.
The cops corner Kurosawa and pals
in their car at the marina, something
which escalates into a bloody massacre where nearly everyone perishes,
including the police. Kurosawa escapes with one of his wounded comrades only to collapse and die on a
crowded sidewalk a short while later.

Alternately charming, poetic, visually stunning as well as pretentious and superficial, ATTACK...nevertheless manages to never be boring. In some ways, a bit similar to Italian crime/delinquent film, SEASON OF ASSASSINS directed by Marcello Andrei with Joe Dallesandro (although that film packs considerably more wallop). * * *

Attack on the Sun

BAD BOYS aka FURYO SHONEN 1956 DIR. Senkichi Taniguchi SCR. Ryuzo Kikushima/Hiroshi Nishijima PHOTO: Kazuo Yamada MUSIC: Urando Watanabe w/ Kenji Sugawara, Chishu Ryu, Kyoko Anzai, Kyoko Aoyama, Setsuko Nakata, Akira Kubo, Haruo Tanaka

THE BAD SLEEP WELL aka WARUI YATSU HODO YOKU NEMURU aka ROSE IN THE MUD 1960 151 min.(135 min. outside Japan) DIR. Akira Kurosawa Scr. Shinobu Hashimoto/Hideo Oguni/ Ryuzo Kikushima/Eijiro Hisaita/

Akira Kurosawa PHOTO B&W 'SCOPE: Yuzuru Aizawa MUSIC: Masaru Sato w/ Toshiro Mifune, Masayuki Mori, Kyoko Kagawa, Tatsuya Mihashi, Takashi Shimura, Takeshi Kato, Ko Nishimura, Kamataro Fujiwara, Gen Shimizu, Chishu Ryu A startingly bleak saga of Mifune infiltrating the family of the corrupt big businessman (Mori) who had his father, one of his underlings, murdered. Mifune, having switched identities with friend Kato, worms his way into Mori's household by marrying Mori's crippled daughter (Kagawa) and becoming best friends with his son (Mihashi) – both of whom are decent and do not approve of their father's nefarious connections with the underworld. Ironically, it is Mifune actually falling-in-love with Kagawa which lessens his resolve. Something which Mori ultimately manipulates to also murder Mifune. Grimly uncompromising, although a bit static towards the end. * * * 1/2

BEAST ALLEY aka KEMONO NO MICHI aka BEAST STREET 1965 150 min. DIR. Eizo Sugawa SCR. Eizo Sugawa/Yoshio Shirasaka PHOTO COLOR 'SCOPE: Yasudo Fukuda MUSIC: Toru Takemitsu w/ Junko Ikeuchi, Keiju Kobayashi, Eitaro Ozawa, Ryo Ikebe, Susumu Kurobe, Yunosuke Ito, Tadao Nakamaru I have not seen this, but from what I understand this adaptation of a Seicho Matsumoto mystery story is more of a suspense thriller than gangster film.

BEAST HUNT aka YAJU GARI 1973 83 min. DIR. Eizo Sugawa SCR. Zenzo Matsuyama/Osamu Nishisawa PHOTO COLOR 'SCOPE: Daisaku Kimura MUSIC: Kunihiko

Murai   w/ Hiroshi Fujioka, Junzaburo Ban, Yoshio Inaba, Mayumi Nagisa, Kazuo Kato, Mariko Nakamura   A taut, economical policier-cum-gang-hostage thriller from the man who gave us the original BEAST MUST DIE. A handful of psychopaths kidnaps a wealthy executive and holds him for ransom. Fujioka is the hotheaded police detective assigned to deliver the money in broad daylight on a busy street, an assignment that starts hitting snags from the get-go and results in an exhausting footchase/fight with members of the gang through the city's back alleys. Ban is Fujioka's put-upon senior partner who seems to have a patent on patience. Inaba is another senior cop who misguidedly uses a police dog (!) to track the kidnappers through the streets by himself. He is successful, only to be bludgeoned and left near death. One of the strongest scenes has the one girl gang member sneak in as a nurse and give Inaba a fatal injection since, at that point, he is the only one who can ID members of the gang. However, when Fujioka arrives to visit just minutes later, he finds, to both his and our surprise, the panicking girl killer handcuffed to the now dead Inaba.

Fujioka finally tracks down the gang to a downtown highrise. Knowing that they are cornered, they hang the bag of money and the now dead executive upside down from the top of the building over ever-growing throngs of onlookers. A pitched battle then ensues with Fujioka, Ban et. al. shooting it out on the roof with the gang. There are some moments here that are truly vertigo-inducing with Fujioka, obviously without a protective cable, doing his own stunts over a dozen stories high.

Beast Hunt

The Bad Sleep Well

On the negative side, character development is minimal and, as is all too usual in Japanese action films, the female lead (in this case the always splendid Mayumi Nagisa) is completely wasted. It compares favorably with some of the better Italian crime/cop films being made around the same time. * * *

The Beast Must Die

THE BEAST MUST DIE aka YAJU SHISUBESHI 1959 96 min. **DIR.** Eizo Sugawa **SCR.** Yoshio Shirasaka **PHOTO** B&W 'SCOPE: Fukuzo Koizumi **MUSIC:** Toshio Mayuzumi w/ Tatsuya Nakadai, Hiroshi Koizumi, Makoto Sato, Reiko Dan, Yumi Shirakawa, Eijiro Tono One of the first "lonely hitman" or "lonely killer" tales to really define future forays into this surprisingly prolific sub-genre. This is another one of those borderline films, whether or not to be recognized as yakuza *eiga*. One needs to consider criteria that also take into account visual style and dramatic structural dynamics as

well as the story content – I felt this was one of those genre determinants, despite its lack of the traditional "yakuza-gang organizational elements." Nakadai is a psycho lone wolf college student who doubles as a killer, enjoying the nihilistic intellectual challenge as well as the power he wields in dispensing death. The first scene, Nakadai murdering a police detective on a rainy deserted street, then the tiny toy robot the man had bought for his son stiffly pursuing the getaway car, is packed with unforgettable images. Now in possession of the dead cop's ID, Nakadai poses as the lawman and robs two yakuza of their gambling take. Later, homicide cop Koizumi spots Nakadai in a bar they both frequent when Nakadai cruelly taunts an old flower peddler to dance and sing by offering an outrageous amount of money. Koizumi follows Nakadai out; however he stops short of arresting him. The next day, when Koizumi questions him at a boxing gym, the two actually start to become friends. Soon after, Nakadai runs into his previous yakuza victims, and they give chase. He picks up a gay hustler as cover then steals a car. The pursuit escalates as the hoods track him in their own vehicle. A shootout erupts between the automobiles, with Nakadai abruptly pushing the hustler out of the speeding vehicle to his death to draw fire. Since he has created a diversion, Nakadai is able to massacre the two gangsters. The saga climaxes with Nakadai recruiting a tubercular fellow student to help him rob the school accounting office at closing time. Unfortunately, his pal panics, and they wrap things up by slaughtering everyone. Nakadai then kills his accomplice and dumps the body and their getaway car in the bay. More than ever, the cops are suspicious of Nakadai. They trail him to his girl's pad and briefly question him, but come up with nothing. Our sociopathic anti-hero catches a flight the next day. Detectives Koizumi and Tono lie in wait, but conclude they just do not have enough evidence to stop him. The plane takes off. A devastatingly coldblooded noir thriller from director Sugawa. * * * 1/2

The Beast Must Die - The Mechanic's Revenge

THE BEAST MUST DIE – THE MECHANIC'S REVENGE
aka YAJU SHISUBESHI – FUKUSHU NO MEKANIKKU 1974 86 min. DIR. Eizo Sugawa SCR. Yoshio Shirasaka/Eizo Sugawa/Yasuhiro Kudo PHOTO COLOR 'SCOPE: Daisaku Kobayashi MUSIC: Kunihiko Murai w/ Hiroshi Fujioka, Toshio Kurosawa, Mako Midori, Akemi Mari, Hosei Komatsu, Kunio Murai, Yoshi Kato The director of the original turns out a remake/sequel. The word "Mechanic" in the title is apparently used as it is in American gangster-slang to represent a hitman. Fujioka is a nihilistic, intellectual English literature teacher(!) who does hits for the cruel excitement of the hunt and the kill, not the money. Kurosawa is the intrepid police detective on his trail.

Fujioka, motivated to destroy the decadent corrupt businessmen who hire him, plays executives' wives and business partners off against each other, sowing madness and destruction in his wake. Near the end, he enlists the help of one of his angry, disturbed students. Fujioka is finally ambushed by the police after he sets off a chain reaction massacre amongst gangster businessman Komatsu and his cohorts in the nocturnal countryside. Ruthlessly dark and downbeat, with director Sugawa's trademark economy of narrative and welcome absence of genre hokum. * * *

Big Shots Die at Dawn

BIG SHOTS DIE AT DAWN
aka KAOYAKU AKATSUKI NI SHISU aka BOSS FIGHTS TO THE DEATH AT DAWN 1961 97 min. DIR. Kihachi Okamoto SCR. Ichiro Ikeda/Ei Ogawa PHOTO COLOR 'SCOPE: Yukio Ota MUSIC: Sei Ikeno w/ Yuzo Kayama, Ichiro Nakatani, Yukiko Shimazaki, Kumi Mizuno,

Tadao Nakamaru, Jun Tazaki, Akihiro Hirata   Kayama returns from Alaska to find his dad, the town mayor, assassinated. He immediately goes on the warpath looking for the culprit. His uncle (Yanagi) points him in the direction of the two established yakuza gangs, one headed by Nakamaru, the other by nightclub owner Hirata. To son Kayama's surprise, he discovers his dad had remarried to sexy gal Shimazaki. But he soon learns she is Hirata's woman. There is also a rifle bullet shell with a fingerprint on it in the possession of a corrupt cop who wants to sell it to the highest bidder. Kayama manages to sow suspicion and mistrust among the gangs' ranks, aggravates decent detective Tazaki and wins the grudging friendship of killer Nakatani. The corrupt cop gets murdered and a twisted blackmail victim frames Kayama for a near fatal attack on detective Tazaki. To complicate matters further, a gang war erupts, climaxing in a visually stylish shootout at a deserted amusement park. Kayama has also fallen in love with Mizuno, but it turns out she is his uncle Yanagi's mistress. Killer Nakatani, dying at the park shootout, tells Kayama that it was his uncle who was responsible for his father's death. Kayama goes to Mizuno's pad, finds uncle Yanagi there and confronts him. In a struggle over a pistol, Mizuno accidentally kills Yanagi, and Kayama is later exonerated by detective Tazaki. The film ends on a strangely humorous note with Kayama toasting a picture of his dead dad and making faces imitating his pop's dour expression. BIG SHOTS... is fun, occasionally exhilarating, but overall distressingly inconsequential. In some ways, it is a bit similar to Seijun Suzuki's Nikkatsu action yakuza pictures. But Suzuki's humor is integrated better into his stories and his characters, and is also much more subversive. * * *

BLOOD AND DIAMONDS aka CHI TO DAIYAMONDO 1964 95 min. **Dir.** Jun Fukuda **Scr.** Ei Ogawa/Moriyuki Mado **Photo B &W 'scope:** Shinsuke Ueno **Music:** Shungo Sawada w/ Makoto Sato, Kumi Mizuno, Akira Takarada, Takashi Shimura, Yuki Nakamura, Yosuke Natsuki, Yu Fujiki, Hideo Inuzuka, Jun Tazaki, Tatsuo Endo A downbeat, noirish thriller with Sato's gang ambushed by more established Tazaki's mob when they perpetrate a diamond heist. Takarada is a shadowy undercover operative who utilizes restaurant hostess Mizuno to locate severely wounded Sato and his bunch who are laying low in a warren of ruined concrete bunkers on the city's outskirts. Some of the gang kidnaps teenage Nakagawa in order to extort her surgeon father Shimura's help in patching up ailing Sato. Meanwhile, Tazaki has his feelers out, torturing Chinese fence Endo, hoping to find the wherabouts of Sato and the precious gems. Young police investigator Natsuki has his own dragnet in motion. Doc Shimura tends to Sato, but things become complicated when one of Sato's gang tries a doublecross. Femme fatale Mizuno has also gone the betrayal route, letting Tazaki know the gang's location. There is a great shootout at the end with Tazaki's snipers picking off anyone foolish enough to make a run for it outside the bunker. The whole embattled gang is wiped out, including doublecrosser Mizuno, but the cops arrive in time to save Takarada, Shimura and his daughter, arresting Tazaki's hoods. Despite the routine programmer nature of the story, Fukuda's direction is quite good, drawing in the viewer repeatedly with beautiful black-and-white scope compositions, well-orchestrated action and direction of performers, particularly Sato and Shimura. * * *

BLOSSOM AND THE SWORD aka TALE OF FLOWER OF JAPANESE CHIVALRY aka NIHON KYOKA DEN 1973 147 min. DIR./SCR. Tai Kato PHOTO COLOR 'SCOPE: Hiroshi Murai MUSIC: Hajime Kaburagi w/ Tetsuya Watari, Yoko Maki, Kinya Kitaoji, Go Kato, Miyoko Shibata, Toru Abe, Kin Sugai, Kamatari Fujiwara, Meicho Soganoya, This is one of director Kato's least known later films, and it is also one of his best. A splendid odyssey through a turn-of-the-century Japan in violent upheaval, Kato chooses for the most part to focus on a young, traveling merchant (Maki) and her turbulent destiny. His look at impoverished common people radicalized into action by oppression is much more detailed here than in many of his similar-themed *ninkyo* yakuza at Toei.

His ability to more credibly expose the rightist lockdown on dissent and labor of the era is fascinating, and abetted by the picture's longer running time. Maki's encounter with a radical socialist (Shibata in a grueling revelatory performance) and a lone wolf yakuza killer (Watari) on a train will alter her life forever. Likewise, callow Kitaoji – who has run away with her – throwing her over when his rich parents follow the couple and coerce him back into the fold, throws a monkeywrench into her dreams of happiness. She subsequently almost drowns when she falls off a cliff overlooking the ocean, but is rescued by blustery, dockworker yakuza boss Soganoya. Nursed back to health, she becomes part of the clan, eventually suceeding Soganoya as leader upon his tragic death. Reluctantly becoming involved with violent Watari after Soganoya's demise, she ends up allying herself with him when the police and other corrupt yakuza strongarm and crush the dockworkers attempt to organize labor. Before the tale ends, Watari and Maki become lovers. At the climax, doomed Watari challenges the fascist police and in-cahoots yakuza on a rocky shoreline in one of director Kato's bloodiest, most evocative, skillfully orchestrated fight scenes. Poetic, gutwrenching and, at times, very moving. * * * *

Blossom and the Sword

The Boss

THE BOSS aka KAOYAKU
1971 98 min. PROD./DIR. Shintaro
Katsu SCR. Shintaro Katsu/Ryuzo
Kikushima PHOTO COLOR 'SCOPE:
Chishi Makiura MUSIC: Kunihiko
Murai   w/ Shintaro Katsu,
Tomisaburo Wakayama, Takuya
Fujioka, Tsutomu Yamazaki, Isao
Yamagata, Kiwako Taichi, Junzaburo
Ban, Shuji Otaki, Shoki Fukae, Rie
Yokoyama   As the credits attest, an
"auteur" project featuring not only
the director/co-writer, but also his
real-life brother Wakayama. Katsu
is an unorthodox, insubordinate
cop putting the screws on yakuza
big shots Yamagata and Yamazaki.
Katsu finally punches out his boss
and leaves the force. At the close, he
pushes lone gang boss Yamagata's
car into a deep ditch then proceeds
to bury the arrogant gangster alive
with a bulldozer. One might call this
Katsu's experimental gangster film
as it is loaded with plenty of visually
audacious but too often pretentious,
incoherent images. A shame since it
is photographed by master veteran
Makiura, who shot many of director Kenji Misumi's most visually
stunning pictures. He also was the
cinematographer of choice on many
early ZATOICHI films with Katsu, as
well as several LONE WOLF AND
CUB films (that Katsu produced). I
believe this was the first film Katsu
directed. His visual style had calmed
down a wee bit by the time of his next
directorial assignment, ZATOICHI IN
DESPERATION in 1972. By the time
Katsu's last film as the blind swordsman, called simply ZATOICHI, had
rolled around in 1989, Katsu had
evolved into an exceptionally fine
director. * * 1/2

**BOSS AND THE EXPLOSIVE
DAUGHTER** aka KAOYAKU
TO BAKUDAN MUSUME 1959
DIR. Masunori Kakei SCR. Tokubei
Wakao PHOTO 'SCOPE: Masao Tamai
MUSIC: Hachiro Matsui w/ Tatsuya
Mihashi, Sonomi Nakajima, Ikio
Sawamura, Kamatari Fujiwara, Tadao
Nakamaru   Judging from the title,
probably a gangster comedy.

BULLET HOLES aka DANKON
aka BULLET WOUND 1969
94 min. DIR. Shiro Moritani SCR.
Shuichi Nagahara PHOTO COLOR
'SCOPE: Tadao Saito MUSIC: Toru
Takemitsu w/ Yuzo Kayama, Eiji
Okada, Kei Sato, Kiwako Taichi, Shin
Kishida   A bit of a distant relative
to Kayama's other high-powered
sniper/hitman tales SUN ABOVE,
DEATH BELOW (1968) and TAR-
GET OF ROSES (1972), but this one
is exclusively devoted to counter-
espionage in the wake of Communist-
perpetrated terrorism.

BULLET TERROR aka KYOFU
NO DANKON 1957 87 min.
DIR. Shigeaki Hidaka SCR. Toshio
Matsuura PHOTO B&W: Seiichi
Endo MUSIC: Yoshikazu Mawatari
w/ Akira Takarada, Kyoko Anzai,
Yumi Shirakawa, Seizaburo
Kawazu, Eitaro Ozawa, Jun Tazaki,
Yoshio Tsuchiya   An entertaining
tale of young accountant Takarada
becoming sucked into the three-way
financial machinations of nightclub
owner Ozawa, club manager Kawazu
and traditional-minded yakuza boss
Tazaki. Ozawa's decent daughter
Shirakawa develops a crush on
Takarada, and Tazaki's daughter – the
exotically beautiful Anzai – appears

to exact revenge when it is believed that Takarada killed dad in a clifftop altercation with his gang. However, Tazaki reappears, albeit missing an arm. Kawazu clandestinely plays Tazaki off against his employer Ozawa, fomenting the climactic confrontation. Already moving at a respectable clip, the movie really kicks into high gear during the last third with a windswept, moonlit duel between samurai sword-wielding Tazaki and judo-proficient Takarada, then a grueling fistfight between Takarada and Kawazu in a car teetering on the brink of a cliff. The film ends with Kawazu momentarily getting the better of Takarada, then stealing his car – which has a time bomb planted in it. Kawazu ends up blowing up at the end with Takarada and Shirakawa left on the mountainside unscathed. Old-fashioned but engrossing throughout, with enough gritty nightclub ambience to neutralize the homogenized slickness starting to show up in Toho productions.
* * *

CALL OF THE DEVIL aka AKUMA GA YONDEIRU 1970 **Dir.** Michio Yamamoto **Scr.** Ei Ogawa **Photo color 'scope:** Kazumi Hara **Music:** Riinchiro Manabe **w/** Wakako Sakai (Utako Sakaiwa?), Takashi Fujiki, Toshiaki Nishizawa, Chikara Harada, Hideji Otaki   This may be more of a suspense thriller with yakuza elements. Yamamoto made mostly thrillers and a few horror pictures (the BLOOD (CHI) series aka BLOODTHIRSTY EYES, et. al.)

CAR 33 DOESN'T ANSWER aka 33 GO-SHA OUTOU NOSHI 1955

92 min. **Dir.** Senkichi Taniguchi **Scr.** Ichiro Ikeda/Senkichi Taniguchi **Photo B&W:** Kazuo Yamada **Music:** Yasushi Akutagawa **w/** Ryo Ikebe, Takashi Shimura, Akihiro Hirata, Keiko Kishi, Akemi Negishi, Sonosuke Sawamura, Kichijiro Ueda   A gritty, slice-of-life police procedural following squad car cops Ikebe and senior Shimura on their nocturnal beat on Christmas Eve. There is some great incidental stuff of them rousting rowdy drunks then encountering a catatonic man in a pharmacy whom they learn, after taking him home, has murdered his whole family. The last half of the film finds the pair shanghaied by gangster killer Hirata and his drugdealing henchman Sawamura.

Car 33 Doesn't Answer

Some of the scenes at Sawamura's sleazy pad. where street urchin junkie thieves congregate, are incredibly strong, unusually potent for such mainstream 1950s Japanese fare, especially coming from Toho. There is a scene where a young boy no older than ten shoots up between his toes that would be shocking no matter the time period. Intent on making their getaway, Hirata dresses up in unconscious Shimura's uniform and takes both cops with him as well as his party-loving girlfriend Negishi. They use the squad car to affect the getaway as it will be able to slip through police roadblocks. However, Hirata causes an accident when he presses Ikebe's foot on the accelerator. Hirata and Negishi hightail it on foot into a harbor coal yard. Ikebe pursues them while partner Shimura is finally able to make an emergency call on the radio. Hirata and Negishi ride on an ore conveyor belt in desperate flight, but Negishi slips off, plummeting to a gruesome death with the unflinching camera following her descent. A bone-crunching fight ensues between Ikebe and Hirata on mountains of coal. Finally reinforcements arrive and the hair-raising yuletide eve is over. You could compare this favorably with Akira Kurosawa's Toho pictures at the time. Indeed, Taniguchi was a close comrade of Kurosawa and shows enormous promise here in this, one of his earliest pictures. Too bad that the promise was not borne out. Most of his 1960s films are decidedly routine. * * * *

CITY OF BEASTS aka YAJU TOSHI 1970 86 min. **Dir.** Jun Fukuda **Scr.** Yoshihiro Ishimatsu **Photo color 'scope:** Yuzuru Aizawa

Music: Masaru Sato w/ Toshio Kurosawa, Rentaro Mikuni, Noriko Takahashi, Hosei Komatsu, Yoshiro Aoki, Shuji Otaki Kurosawa is a chemistry student and a loner leaning to the right (if he has ever really cared about politics). He decides to quit his studies when the violently radical student demonstrations occuring interrupt his work once too often. Rich and corrupt businessman Mikuni hires him as his bodyguard and, before long, he is trading shots with Mikuni's mortal yakuza enemies. Despite Mikuni's ruthless attitude towards competition, Kurosawa obviously identifies with him as a similarly alienated loner and even develops a father/son attachment to him before the film's bleak wrap-up. Mikuni ends forcing his daughter into a marriage with the son of a business rival who, using a yakuza gang, is trying to take over Mikuni's business.

City of Beasts

This leads to a chain reaction of escalating disasters as Kurosawa and

Mikuni kidnap the clueless son-in-law, then the son-in-law's father kidnaps Mikuni's daughter. Before the end, Mikuni has been captured himself by the boy's father and mercilessly tortured by gangster Aoki, at the behest of big boss Kita. When Kurosawa and daughter Takahashi get him back, Mikuni's not long for this world. Kurosawa goes on a vengeance quest, succeeds, but dies in the backseat of the getaway car driven by sole survivor Takahashi. Screenwriter Ishimatsu's script is pretty nihilistic but as always his scenarios are straightforward, astute and uncompromisingly subversive in portraying the psychological subtext for social ills caused by an excess of greedy materialism. Director Jun Fukuda's gangster pictures consistently point to a re-evaluation of him as a succinct, perceptive, no-bullshit filmmaker. Fukuda was the other main director of GODZILLA movies after master Ishiro Honda and has occasionally been unjustly disparaged for his contributions to the giant monster genre. * * * 1/2

COMEDY – DEFRAUDING HONOR AND HUMANITY aka KIGEKI – DAMASHI NO JINGI 1974 DIR. Jun Fukuda SCR. Ichikuni (Kazuho?) Kobayashi/ Tsunesaburo Nishikawa/Jun Fukuda/ Shizuo (Yasuo?) Tanami PHOTO COLOR 'SCOPE: Yuzuru Aizawa MUSIC: Chuji Kinoshita w/ Kei Tani, Joro Kishibe, Shoichi Ozawa, Michiyo Yasuda, Kazuko Inano, Michiko Honda, Hisao Toake NOTE: "Kigeki" translates as "Comedy."

COMEDY – THE GREAT THIEF FAMILY – CATCH THE AN-

GEL aka KIGEKI – DOROBO DAI KOZOKU - TENSHI O TORU 1972 DIR. Takashi Tsuboshima SCR. Shizuo Tanami/Ryuzo Nakanishi PHOTO COLOR 'SCOPE: Kozo Okazaki MUSIC: Masaru Sato w/ Miyoshi Ueki, Eiko Yatsunami, Kei Tani, Kiwako Taichi, Makoto Fujita, Miyako Chocho, Junzaburo Ban, Norihei Miki, Ryunosuke Minegishi

COUNTERSTROKE aka HOERO DATSUGOKUSHU 1961 75 min. DIR. Jun Fukuda SCR. Katsuya Suzaki PHOTO B&W 'SCOPE: Shoji Uchiumi MUSIC: Kenjiro Hirose w/ Makoto Sato, Yosuke Natsuki, Yuriko Hoshi, Jun Tazaki, Kumi Mizuno Sato breaks out of jail bent on proving he is innocent of his brother's murder. He enlists the help of reluctant hostess Hoshi, his brother's girl, but Tazaki, Hoshi's boss, tries to dissuade her from helping him. Before long, it is revealed Tazaki's right hand man Natsuki is actually an undercover cop. Sato and Natsuki butt heads about the best way to get evidence that Tazaki was the murderer, but eventually, in predictable fashion, justice is served. * * 1/2

DAI NIPPON SHURI SHUDAN 1969 95 min. DIR. Jun Fukuda SCR. Giichi Fujimoto PHOTO. COLOR 'SCOPE: Yuzuru Aizawa MUSIC: Masaru Sato w/ Kunie Tanaka, Norihei Miki, Keiju Kobayashi, Wakako Sakai Another crime comedy from Toho, who seemed to specialize in comedies after their giant monster/sci-fi genres.

DARK OCEAN DISASTER – TRUE STORY OF CHIVALRY

aka GENKAI NADA – NINKYO GAIDEN 1976 122 min. **DIR.** Juro Kara **SCR.** Juro Kara/ Toshio Ishido **PHOTO COLOR 'SCOPE:** Hiroshi Segawa **MUSIC:** Tao Anpo **w/** Noboru Ando, Joe Shishido, Jinpachi Nezu, Reinori Ri, Hosei Komatsu, Bin Amatsu, Kin Omae, Renji Ishibashi, Juro Kara　Ando and Shishido portray doctors caught up with the mob. Director Kara is famous in Japan for his avant-garde antics in theater and film in the late sixties/early seventies, best known in the West as a cast member of several of director Nagisa Oshima's more radical films such as DIARY OF A SHINJUKU THIEF (1969) as well as the killer in Koji Wakamatsu's disturbingly transgressive masterpiece, VIOLATED ANGELS.

Dark Ocean Disaster-True Story of Chivalry

DUEL IN THE NIGHT MIST aka YOGIRI NO KETTO aka THE FORGOTTEN WATERFRONT 1959 **DIR.** Umeji Inoue **SCR.** Toshio Matsuura/Umeji Inoue **PHOTO**

'SCOPE: Kozo Okazaki **MUSIC:** Seitaro Omori　**w/** Koji Tsuruta, Keiko Awaji, Tatsuya Mihashi, Izumi Yukimura, Masayuki Mori, Tetsuro Tanba, Asao Uchida, Hideo Takamatsu　Lackluster, somewhat pointless saga of lone wolf former trumpet player Tsuruta trying to track the attackers who severely wounded him and left him for dead after a botched, clandestine dollars-for-yen money exchange. Nursed back to health but suffering partial amnesia, he returns to his old haunts, piecing together the puzzle that will lead to gunmen Tanba and Takamatsu and gang leader Mori. Head cop Uchida and undercover man Mihashi monitor his progress along the way. Pretty routine.　* *

DUEL ON THE PRECIPICE aka DANGAI NO KETTO aka KILL THE KILLERS 1961 85 min. **DIR.** Kozo Saeki **SCR.** Fumio Shibano **PHOTO COLOR 'SCOPE:** Kozo Okazaki **MUSIC:** Rinichiro Manabe **w/** Yosuke Natsuki, Tatsuya Mihashi, Kumi Mizuno, Tetsuro Tanba, Keiko Awaji, Akihiro Hirata, Tadao Nakamaru, Tatsuo Endo Natsuki is the only son of a murdered gang boss trying to track down the killer by locating the sole eyewitness, a bar hostess (Mizuno). She is reluctant to help when she realizes the killer (Nakamaru) is an associate of her hoodlum brother (Hirata). However, Natsuki's persuasive charm helps convince her. Also the assistance of friends Tanba and Awaji and undercover cop Mihashi coupled with the eruption of a gang war finally enables Natsuki to get his vengeance. This is strictly programmer material and is, for the most

part, unimaginitively handled by director Saeki. The film does come alive during the last third with almost nonstop, riproaring action. Still, it is all imminently forgettable stuff.
* * 1/2

THE ENTRAPPED GANGSTERS aka TEJO O KAKERO 1959 **DIR.** Shigeaki Hidaka **SCR.** Shigeaki Hidaka/Tokubei Wakao **PHOTO** 'SCOPE: Fukuzo Koizumi **MUSIC:** Sei Ikeno **w/** Makoto Sato, Ryo Ikebe, Akiko Wakabayashi, Fumie Noguchi, Tadao Nakamaru

Extortion

EXTORTION aka KYOKATSU aka BLACKMAIL 1958 **DIR.** Kozo Saeki **w/** Tatsuya Mihashi, Keiko Awaji, Kyoko Kishida, Eitaro Ozawa, Jun Tatara   Director Saeki specialized in comedies but also directed a number of crime films in the fifties and sixties. This realistic, sometimes shocking-for-the-time tale of tough guy extortionist Mihashi stands up well in comparison to many of the American noirs from the same decade. Mihashi is released from prison and reunites with his patron yakuza gang as well as his conman mentor, Ozawa. Soon Mihashi is not only putting the squeeze on businessmen but also hobnobbing with and abusing various sexy barflies from the local crime-ridden nightclub. He enjoys a lusty tryst with the club's resident, two-faced torch singer (Kyoko

Kishida) before hooking up with a more serious woman-about-town (Keiko Awaji) who really loves him. Mihashi's get-rich scam of strong-arming a payoff from a businessman and the man's slippery eel cohort (Jun Tatara) backfires at the climax as he tries to escape. Walking down an empty street, he is fatally shot in the back by two young punks intent on stealing his loot. A bleak crime film and welcome antidote to some of Toho's other corny gangster opuses of the period.   * * *

FAREWELL TO THE GUN – from SONG OF MASSACRE aka KENJU YOSARABA - MINAGOROSHI NO UTA YORI aka GET 'EM ALL 1960 87 min. **DIR.** Eizo Sugawa **SCR.** Shuji Terayama **PHOTO B&W** 'SCOPE: Yukio Ota **MUSIC:** Hachio (Yatai?) Nakamura **w/** Tatsuya Nakadai, Hiroshi Mizuhara, Tetsuro Tanba, Yukiko Shimazaki, Akihiko Hirata, Akemi Kita, Seiji Miyaguchi, Jerry Fujio   Avant-garde writer (later turned director) Terayama scripts Sugawa's worthy followup to the previous year's THE BEAST MUST DIE. Mizuhara is a young delinquent seeking his hoodlum brother's killer. He turns the spotlight on a crew of cutthroat thieves led by Tanba and boxer Nakadai. Staying at Nakadai's gym, he finds a gun in a cigar box and is soon astonished at the newfound power it gives him. He becomes intoxicated with feelings of supremacy when his girl's bullying ex (Fujio) is reduced to a whimpering lump of jelly at the mere sight of the gun in his waistband. Soon, Mizuhara is dispatching the various gang members, initially shooting Tanba at the noisy motorcycle races,

Great Cherry Blossom Crest

then later nervous Miyaguchi and the others. The cops begin to narrow their search for the killer, but Mizuhara confronts the one last hood Nakadai before they can close in. Nakadai reveals a huge cache of money stuffed into the gym's large punching bag, something that precipitates a scuffle between the two, and they end up accidentally shooting each other. Mizuhara's girl Kita leads the cops to the gym but gets no answer at the door. Nakadai and Mizuhara lie dead inside amidst the heaps of cash. A well done, edgy noir thriller with some great touches. One standout scene has a young boy in a vacant lot unexpectedly pluck Mizuhara's pistol from his waistband and then point it at the terrified delinquent. Two passing cops think it is funny, believing the gun is only a toy. Pretty much all along the line director Sugawa and writer Terayama go the extra distance to turn cliches on their head.   * * *

GATE OF YOUTH aka SEISHUN NO MON 1975 188 min. **DIR.** Kirio Urayama **SCR.** Akatsuki Hayasaka/ Kirio Urayama **PHOTO COLOR 'SCOPE:** Hiroshi Murai **MUSIC:** Rinichiro Manabe   **w/** Ken Tanaka, Tatsuya Nakadai, Akira Kobayashi, Sayuri Yoshinaga, Shinobu Otake, Keiko Sekine, Shoichi Ozawa, Susumu Fujita, Takeshi Kato, Choichiro Kawarazaki   Another one of those big-budget sagas based on a popular novel. The closest comparison would be the much more popular THEATER OF LIFE which has been made into many versions. This probably could not be called a yakuza story per se, because of its sprawling nature and many diverse characters, but there are many yakuza elements such

as youthful student hero Tanaka's brother Kobayashi being the boss of a rural yakuza clan up against rival Nakadai. It was remade at Toei in 1981, that version co-directed by Koreyoshi Kurahara and Kinji Fukasaku. * * *

GATE OF YOUTH – SAGA OF INDEPENDENCE aka SEISHUN NO MON – JIRITSU HEN 1977 161 min. **DIR.** Kirio Urayama **SCR.** Kirio Urayama/ Akatsuki Hayasaka **PHOTO COLOR 'SCOPE:** Hiroshi Murai **MUSIC:** Rinichiro Manabe   **w/** Ken Tanaka, Shinobu Otake, Ayumi Ishida, Etsushi Takahashi, Tatsuo Umemiya, Haruna Takase, Akira Kobayashi, Eiji Okada   A sequel relating the last portion of the epic novel.

GREAT CHERRY BLOSSOM CREST, THE aka SAKURA NO DAIMON 1973 89 min. **DIR.** Kenji Misumi **ORIG. STORY:** Tomisaburo Wakayama **SCR.** Yoshihiro Ishimatsu **PHOTO COLOR 'SCOPE:** Fujio Morita **MUSIC:** Kunihiko Murai **w/** Tomisaburo Wakayama, Minoru Oki, Kayo Matsuo   Although relentlessly downbeat and uncompromising, this is a lackluster, somewhat disappointing policier/ yakuza action drama, especially when you consider writer Ishimatsu, director Misumi and star Wakayama (the latter two brought us the best of the LONE WOLF AND CUB films) were at the helm. The insignia/coat-of-arms of the Japanese police force is a cherry blossom crest.   * * 1/2

HALFBREED RIKA aka MIXED RACE CHILD, RIKA aka RICA

aka KONKE TSUJI RIKA aka GI BABY RIKA series

HALFBREED RIKA aka MIXED RACE CHILD, RIKA aka RICA aka KONKE TSUJI RIKA 1972 90 min. **DIR.** Ko Nakahira **SCR.** Kaneto Shindo **PHOTO COLOR 'SCOPE:** Yasukuri Sugita **MUSIC:** Jiro Takemura w/ Rika Aoki, Kazuko Nagaki, Kazuko Imai, Ryohei Uchida, Jun Otomi   Toho's bid to compete with the GIRL BOSS (SUKEBAN) pictures at Toei but with a more prestigious screenwriter and more social relevance. Kaneto Shindo adapts from the original RIKA *manga* with a straightforward freshness of approach that, although occasionally tongue-in-cheek with the tall tale elements, never descends to the lowbrow, dumb humor that often afflicts the middle third of most films of the GIRL BOSS and DELINQUENT GIRL BOSS series. These are extremely low budget with an ambience closer to Nikkatsu's STRAY CAT ROCK movies with Meiko Kaji. There are also none of the surreal, superbly polished and orchestrated setpieces Norifumi Suzuki conjured up for the GIRL BOSS films. However, there are plenty of incredibly outrageous elements that emerge as just as shocking and, because of the rough, episodic quality, even more biting and pertinent as unpretentious social commentary. Also, strangely enough, these films employ the profuse blood-spurting technology utilized in many of the other Toho action series of the time such as LONE WOLF AND CUB and LADY SNOWBLOOD. Rika Aoki is the halfbreed offspring of a country girl mom raped by American GIs several years into the post-war Occupation. The film begains with teenage Rika herself delivering the unwanted baby of an abandoned girlfriend on a beach of volcanic black sand then bringing the stillborn child to the heartless, womanizing yakuza dad. Something which provokes a gangfight that ends with his death and her arrest.

Halfbreed Rika (#1)

Languishing in the paddy wagon, she flashes back on how she was deflowered by her mother's corrupt businessman lover. Once in reform school she does battle wth a tattooed rival, escapes to rejoin her best friend on the outside, avenge a salaryman who has had his business contracts stolen by seducing the young hoodlum thief and cutting off the boy's arm (!) then, after the boy's boss shoots the boy in the back of the head, stabbing the boss in the heart. She also finds time to become a lip-synching, bikini-clad popstar in a gangster nightclub, go back to reform school, escape again, be rescued by a gentle lone wolf who eventually becomes her lover and finally rescue both her girlfriends and bitter rivals when they are shanghaied as sex slaves by evil foreigner Uchida! Not to mention kidnap the man who deflowered her then deliver him to her crazed, homeless, now drug addict mom who promptly stabs him to death! The ultra paucity of production values does occasionally detract from the proceedings. Still astonishing, though, and unworthy of its relatively unknown status in the West. #1 of 3 films * * * *

HALFBREED RIKA – A LONELY RAMBLING TRIP aka RICA 2 aka KONKE TSUJI RIKA – HITORI YUKU SASURAI TABI 1973 83 min. **DIR.** Ko Nakahira **SCR.** Kaneto Shindo **PHOTO COLOR 'SCOPE:** Yasukuri Sugita **MUSIC:** Jiro Takemura w/ Rika Aoki, Ryunosuke Minegishi, Mizuho Suzuki, Yasushi Suzuki, Takashi Fujiki, Kaoru Hama Not quite up to the out-of-left-field lunacy of the first film, though it certainly has its share of outrageous moments. There is a crew of yakuza killers after Rika and her pals, two of them being witness to a merchant ship explosion perpetrated by the gang. Rika's having lunch with one of her on-the-run girlfriends when the waif is abruptly shot in the head through the cafe window in broad daylight, spraying Rika's pretty visage with blood. A couple of other similar abrupt and violent deaths occur

before Rika journeys north to snowy environs where black galpal – also a mod nightclub singer like Rika – is in the jail of the corrupt local police.

Halfbreed Rika 2 aka Rica 2

Too bad that the middle third of the saga is just paint-by-numbers, unusual considering screenwriter Shindo's involvement. There are several other great sequences: Rika running up and over an onrushing car managing simultaneously to kick out its windshield; Rika and Minegishi's escape from the American hippie (!) gangsters' sex slave ship just before the Americans execute not only their rival yakuza but all the whores on board, all the while whistling "Yankee Doodle Dandy" (needless to say there is some virulent anti-American sentiment expressed); the evil Japanese businessman and his sadistic blonde girlfriend gleefully whipping and finally shooting-to-death the corrupt police captain while he writhes on the floor in his underwear; and last but not least the climactic shootout where formerly traditional female yakuza Hama dons a black leather jumpsuit and joins Rika and Minegishi in a shootout with the American gangsters, killing not only them but the businessman and his lingerie-wearing moll. #2 of 3 films * * * 1/2

HALFBREED RIKA – LULLABY OF YOKOHAMA HOODS aka RICA 3 aka KONKE TSUJI RIKA – HAMAGURE KOMORI UTA 1973 85 min. **DIR.** Kimisaburo Yoshimura **SCR.** Kaneto Shindo **PHOTO COLOR 'SCOPE:** Yasukuri Sugita **MUSIC:** Jiro Takemura w/ Rika Aoki, Chojiro Kawarazaki

Halfbreed Rika 3

The least of the three RIKA films with Rika in-and-out of reform school, then allied with lone wolf lover Kawarazaki against the mob who have shanghaied a black Japanese woman's halfbreed daughter for porn. As with the previous films, this has its audacious moments, namely some bizarre bits with Rika and rival inmates sentenced to solitary in the mentally-disturbed wing of the prison. There they encounter a moronic monster man whom they must defeat before once again gaining freedom. Also the climactic battle in the gang's beach bunker HQ where Rika and comrades rescue the half-breed schoolgirl is bursting with kinetic energy and entertaining, despite threadbare production values. Yoshimura was a fairly prestigious director at Daiei Studios in the fifties and sixties, and it is a sign of the precipitous depression in the 1970s Japanese film industry that he was reduced to working on a *manga*-based exploitationer. * * *   #3 and last of series

HE'S THE KILLER aka YATSU GA SATSUJIN-SHA DA 1958 94 min. **DIR.** Kunobu Marubayashi **SCR.** Shinobu Hashimoto **PHOTO B&W 'SCOPE:** Seiichi Endo **MUSIC:** Koji Taku w/ Makoto Sato, Yoshio Tsuchiya, Eisei Amamoto, Keiko Awaji, Tadao Nakamaru, Setsuko Nakata   This starts as a police procedural with homicide detectives Tsuchiya and Nakamaru tracking the killer in a brutal series of unexplained gang slayings. About halfway through, it switches gears to the viewpoint of hood Sato who we learn at the end is an undercover cop. Meanwhile, he has infiltrated into the deepest ranks of a drug gang who are using homicidal addict Amamoto to fulfill contracts on various liabilities. Amamoto gives an astonishingly realistic portrayal of a junkie in the throes of a hellish descent into madness. Screenwriter Hashimoto, who also wrote for master filmmakers Akira Kurosawa and Masaki Kobayashi, supplies some great touches with Sato establishing a genuine rapport and compassion for tormented Amamoto. This could have been much better, though, if director Marubayashi had been more emotionally connected in steering the way. His direction is never less than competent, but also comes across as somewhat indifferent and uninspired. * * *

HOMELESS VAGABONDS aka YADONASHI aka THE HOME-LESS 1974 97 min. **DIR.** Koichi Saito **SCR.** Takehiro Nakajima/ Michio Sotake **PHOTO COLOR 'SCOPE:** Tsuneryu Sakamoto **MUSIC:** Hachiro Aoyama   w/ Ken Takakura, Shintaro Katsu, Meiko Kaji, Noboru Ando, Ichiro Nakatani, Murasaki Fujima, Kenji Imai, Renji Ishibashi With this cast, you would think it could not miss. Well, hate to be the one to tell you, but... In the 1920s – 1930s period, Takakura and Katsu simultaneously leave prison. They have been competing rivals in stir, and Takakura is sick of it. He is an *ippiki okami* (lone wolf). Out on the road, Katsu wants to tag along, kind of like a puppy that doesn't know when it is being snubbed. Takakura has many things getting to him, primary of which is the need to rescue his former girlfriend (Kaji) from a brothel. Of course, by coincidence, Katsu turns up. He and another buddy create a disturbing-the-peace distrac-tion in the street so Takakura and Kaji can slip away. Once they have been on the road for a while and are obvi-ously safe, Takakura takes off on his own. Much to her consternation, Kaji is thrown together with Katsu who keeps getting them in scrapes with his petty crimes. Wandering Takakura runs into Ando. The two have a knife-fight in the forest to resolve an old grudge. Ando nearly dies. Takakura joins company with Katsu and Kaji again, and Katsu ropes Takakura into a seemingly idiotic deep sea treasure salvaging operation involving just the three of them on a deserted coastline. After many futile dives, they finally come up with something, and even Takakura, for once, looks happy. The three are talking and eating lunch in a lean-to on the desolate beach when a car drives up a few hundred yards away. Takakura recognizes men from Ando's clan. He walks towards them. Halfway to the auto, a shot rings out, and Takakura falls. Katsu runs up and is blasted, too. Kaji is left alone. Well, they really *do try* to tell a differ-ent kind of yakuza story. Unhappily, Koichi Saito's direction is much too overly-stylized. Conflicts are diffused, and the action, even when it is violent, is presented in too oblique and glossy a manner. Saito has opted for a mini-malism that is simultaneously lavish confection and empty shell. Actress Kaji mentioned in an interview that director Saito was inspired by French filmmaker Bernard Blier's GOING PLACES and was striving for a simi-lar ambience. The last third of the film also has striking similarities to the last third of another French film, THE ADVENTURERS (LES AVENTU-RIERS, 1967) directed by Robert Enrico from a novel by crime fiction writer, Jose Giovanni. Lino Ventura, Alain Delon and Joanna Shimkus appear as a similar star-crossed trio of talented but misfit losers involved in a deep sea-diving salvage operation, an adventure that does not end well.

The similarity to the Ventura/Delon movie appears to have been more than coincidence: a July 2011 posting of a HOMELESS VAGABONDS' trailer on the French website Wild Grounds – which is devoted to Japanese cinema – confirms this writer's suspicions. Reportedly a flop, the film temporarily hurt all three Japanese stars' careers. * * 1/2

Homeless Vagabonds

HUMAN REVOLUTION aka NINGEN KAKUMEI series

HUMAN REVOLUTION aka NINGEN KAKUMEI 1973 Dir. Toshio Masuda Scr. Shinobu Hashimoto Photo color 'scope: Rokuro Nishigaki Music: Harumi Ibe w/ Tetsuro Tanba, Tatsuya Nakadai, Shinsuke Ashida, Tetsuya Watari   #1 of 2 films

Human Revolution

HUMAN REVOLUTION 2 aka ZOKU NINGEN KAKUMEI 1976 Dir. Toshio Masuda Scr. Shinobu Hashimoto Photo color 'scope: Rokuro Nishigaki Music: Harumi Ibe w/ Tetsuro Tanba, Michiyo Aratama, Tetsuya Watari, Teruhiko Aoi, Shinsuke Ashida, Akio Hasegawa, Yoshio Inaba, Masumi Harukawa, Shin Kishida, Junko Natsu, Yoshiro Aoki, Ichiro Nakatani, Takashi Shimura #2 of 2 films

JAPAN'S #1 YAKUZA MAN aka NIHON ICHI NO YAKUZA OTOKO 1970 Dir. Kengo Furusawa Scr. Yasuo (Nobuo?) Tanami Photo color 'scope: Kiyoshi Hasegawa Music: Naozumi Yamamoto w/ Hitoshi Ueki, Yoko Tsukasa, Makoto Fujita, Yumiko Nogawa, Toru Abe, Hiroshi Nawa, Jun Tatara, Jun Tazaki, Hajime Hana, Kenji Sawada   A spoof of *ninkyo* yakuza pictures with Toho's most popular comic Ueki (of CRAZY CATS fame).

LADY SNOWBLOOD aka SHURA YUKIHIME series

LADY SNOWBLOOD aka SHURA YUKIHIME aka FIGHTING LADY YUKI aka FIGHTING LADY SNOW 1973 97 min. Dir. Toshiya Fujita Scr. Kibu Nagata Photo color 'scope: Masatake Tamura Music: Masaaki Hirao w/ Meiko Kaji, Toshio Kurosawa, Eiji Okada, Ko Nishimura, Masaaki Okado, Sanae Nakahara, Miyako Akaza   A band of conmen/ brigands assaults a young couple out for a walk in the country. The

Lady Snowblood

husband, a schoolteacher – believed to be a government exploiter – is brutally murdered in literal geysers of crimson. The wife barely holds onto her sanity as she is gang-raped then thrown into jail. She gives birth to a baby girl one snowy night with the other inmates tearfully attending. She christens the little tyke Yuki because of the blizzard outside, then expires. Yuki grows into a young girl. An elderly Shinto priest/martial arts master (Nishimura) instructs her mercilessly in the art of sword and killing so when the time comes she can avenge her parents. Yuki blossoms into a beautiful woman (Kaji). Okada, leader of the bandits, is now a respected and wealthy right-wing fanatic helping to raise havoc behind the scenes of the turn-of-the-century Japanese government. Yuki finds each of the men involved in her parents' deaths and slays them. Along the way, a sadistic whore who had been tagging along with the evil men, nearly kills Yuki. A leftist political writer (Kurosawa) joins Yuki in her mission and helps her kill the monstrous bitch. At the climax, he sacrifices himself to pin Okada to the wall so Yuki can run him through. Shot several times, Yuki stumbles away from the mansion and masked ball in progress. She collapses prostrate in the snow and falls asleep. We assume she could never survive. However, when the sun rises, a yellow glow on her face awakens her. She rises and staggers away. #1 of 2 films   * * * 1/2

LADY SNOWBLOOD – LOVE SONG OF VENGEANCE aka SHURA YUKIHIME – URAMI KOI UTA aka WEB OF TREACHERY 1974 89 min. **DIR.** Toshiya Fujita

SCR. Kibu Nagata/Kiyohide Ohara PHOTO COLOR 'SCOPE: Tatsuo Suzuki MUSIC: Kenjiro Hirose   w/ Meiko Kaji, Yoshio Harada, Juzo Itami, Shin Kishida, Koji Nanbara, Kazuko Yoshiyuki, Rinichi Yamamoto

Lady Snowblood 2

Yuki is attacked by police in a cemetery as she visits a loved one's grave. The film opens up with an intoxicatingly delirious tracking shot as Yuki slashes her way down a forest path, dispatching her pestering official pursuers in a rain of blood. In fact, the whole first ten minutes or so of the film is unrelieved carnage, a visceral vicarious stretch of nihilistic thrills that end only when Yuki tires and gives herself up. As she is carted away to jail, a band of caped men ambush her prison wagon and kidnap her to their elegant lair. Classic Toho villain Kishida plays the ringleader of another bunch of fascist/nationalist maniacs who want to shanghai Yuki to use as one of their assassins. To escape their clutches, she will agree to almost anything. They plant her as a maid in the house of another subversive, this time a Marxist writer (Itami). They don't count on her befriending the fellow. Finally, they kidnap him, and Yuki escapes. Horrible torture of the writer follows. Yuki hides out with the writer's estranged brother, a cynical doctor (Harada) who had helped her earlier. He is now living in abject poverty in a ghetto. The writer is released on the edge of the slum. Harada reluctantly tends his brother's wounds only to discover he has been infected with plague virus in a germ warfare experiment to eradicate the ghetto's undesirables (!) Quarantined by Harada, his sibling soon dies. The dead writer's other maid, who was his lover, goes crazy. She assaults the evil detective (Yamamoto) who had interrogated the writer and stabs him in the eye. Even after several of the inspector's colleagues slash at her with their swords, she has to be literally pried off his bleeding face. Having captured Yuki again and locked her in one of the mansion's rooms, the fascists set fire to the ghetto. Yuki escapes and kills all the fascists at the house. She makes a beeline to the smoking ashes of the ruins. Harada has survived the inferno but is near collapse. He draws his sword and insists on accompanying Yuki to attack the remaining fascist ringleaders. All of them are cut down on the grounds of a temple. Kishida is the last to die, and he pumps lead into both Harada and Yuki. Once again the male lead, this time Harada, sacrifices himself, holding onto Kishida even though it means death, so Yuki can approach and stab him. These two films are tall tales. While not being overt yakuza films, they still depict a much more realistic background/ historical perspective on the yakuza/ criminal element behind much of the fascist/nationalist political machine in pre-WW2 Japan than the TALES OF THE LAST SHOWA ERA YAKUZA series or other Toei yakuza films set in the same period. There is also well-researched background into the leftist political anarchist contingent hoping to sabotage the severe right-wing madness of the times. Director Fujita helmed several yakuza and many anarchic juvenile delinquent pictures at Nikkatsu in the 1969-1971 period before the studio changed over almost exclusively to a roman porno output. Kaji appeared in many of his pictures, but asserts that their teaming up here was merely coincidental. Fujita was also a friend, if not protege, of maverick auteur Seijun Suzuki, and later appeared as one of the lead actors (w/ Yoshio Harada) in Suzuki's 1980 experimental ghost story, ZIGEUNERWEISEN. Both LADY SNOW-BLOOD films were adapted from the *manga* series by Kazuo Koike (creator/writer of LONE WOLF & CLUB). #2 of 2 films   * * * 1/2

THE LAST CHALLENGE aka AOI YOGIRI NO CHOSENJO aka CHALLENGE IN THE BLUE NIGHT MIST 1961 84 min. DIR. Kengo Furusawa SCR. Motosada Nishigane PHOTO B&W 'SCOPE: Masaharu Utsumi MUSIC: Kenjiro Hirose w/ Yosuke Natsuki, Kumi Mizuno, Makoto Sato, Yuriko Hoshi, Jun Tazaki, Tadao Nakamaru, Akemi Kita Wayward youth Natsuki works in a benevolent old man's orchard and is in love with Hoshi, the man's daughter. The old man is murdered by an unknown assailant, undoubtedly due to his refusal to sell his orchard to one of two rival gangs. Natsuki goes to see boss Tazaki with the intention of avenging the old man, but glib smoothie Tazaki points him to the rival boss. Natsuki is nearly framed when the other boss is murdered in a crowded nightclub, and he goes through increasingly labyrinthine convolutions trying to figure out just what is going on. He is helped by Sato, one of Tazaki's rowdy, lone wolf subordinates who admires his guts and loner attitude. There is some great interplay between the two when they are psychologically torturing Nakamaru from the rival mob at a deserted, underground shooting range. Mizuno is Natsuki's old prostitute girlfriend who shows up involved with the rival gang, and she ultimately weighs in on his side. Both Sato and Mizuno pay with their lives for helping Natsuki. Furusawa was Toho's prime comedy director, but his forays into the crime and the samurai film genres (as in the later epic DUEL AT FORT EZO) show him equally adept at gutsy action thrillers. His camera placement, direction of actors and action and minimal display of histrionics show him ahead of his time. This film, in particular, is very hard-edged and, though it has a happy ending, it still comes across as an incredibly atmospheric noir thriller. Cinematographer Utsumi's superbly luminous black-and-white scope work also deserves praise here. * * *

MAN AGAINST MAN aka OTOKO TAI OTOKO 1960 90 min. **DIR.** Senkichi Taniguchi **SCR.** Ichiro Ikeda/Ei Ogawa **PHOTO COLOR 'SCOPE:** Rokuro Nishigaki **MUSIC:** Masaru Sato w/ Toshiro Mifune, Ryo Ikebe, Takashi Shimura, Yuzo Kayama, Akihiro Hirata,

Jun Tazaki, Akemi Kita, Yuriko Hoshi, Yumi Shirakawa Noboru Sada, Ikio Sawamura, Tadao Nakamaru

Former wartime comrades (Mifune, Ikebe) meet again years later in the port of Yokohama. Ikebe is running a huge supper nightclub called the Blue Moon with tangential ties to boss Tazaki's yakuza gang, and Mifune is the foreman of old man Shimura's shipping company. Boss Tazaki has it in for Shimura, sabotaging the running of the shipping lines whenever possible. He uses sadistic killer Hirata as his main enforcer. Hirata manipulates his slutty girlfriend Kita into helping steal securities from the shipping concern through Shimura's rowdy, naive son Kayama. Things keep getting worse with Shimura the victim of a hit-and-run by Hirata, then Hirata raping Ikebe's mute wife Hoshi, thus causing her suicide. At odds with each other off and on throughout the film, Mifine and Ikebe join forces at the climax to wipe out the mob. Ikebe is fatally wounded. Although this is entertaining – if for no other reason than the stupendous cast – it is also extremely old-fashioned in execution, pulling its punches all the way down the line except in the sentiment department. * * 1/2

MAN FROM THE EAST aka HIGASHI KARA KITA OTOKO 1961 103 min. **DIR.** Umeji Inoue **SCR.** Katsuya Suzaki/Yoshio Hasuike **PHOTO COLOR 'SCOPE:** Kozo Okazaki **MUSIC:** Hajime Kaburagi w/ Yuzo Kayama, Yuriko Hoshi, Makoto Sato, Shiro Osaka, Jun

Funada, Tatsuo Endo, Toru Abe, Kenji Sahara, Asao Uchida
Kayama is an ex-prizefighter turned wandering street musician after accidentally killing his best pal in the ring. He falls into staying with the remains of a family whose lucrative candy business was destroyed in WW2 chaos. Their land, now surrounded by slums, is desired by gangsters. The local poor are protective of the beautiful Hoshi and family, and resist the gang's attempts to take over. However, Kayama is mysteriously non-violent. When one of the mobsters discovers Kayama's past and tells the slum dwellers that the friend Kayama killed in the ring was Hoshi's brother, they drive him away. When Kayama's other best friend, an itinerant poet, is mortally beaten by the thugs, Kayama returns and finally repels the villains.

THE MAN IN RED aka SHINKU NO OTOKO 1960 88 min. **DIR.** Ishiro Honda **SCR.** Moriyuki Mado **PHOTO COLOR 'SCOPE:** Hajime Koizumi **MUSIC:** Kenjiro Hirose **w/** Makoto Sato, Chisako Hara, Yumi Shirakawa, Akira Kubo, Ikio Sawamura, Sachio Sakai, Ko Nishimura, Ichiro Nakatani
Sato, a student, had taken the rap for his foster father, the president of a construction company who had shot a gangster. Coming out of prison after four years, he finds his old neighborhood rife with yakuza and drug pushers. An old pal warns him to split, but he feels he must first find his old girlfriend. His search leads him into the midst of the narcotics gang, something which nearly gets him killed and does cause the death of his foster father. When Sato arranges for

the gang boss and the entire ring to be rounded up by police, he finally finds his girl. She has undergone changes that make her almost unrecognizable – she is now the crime boss's woman and a desperate, desolate addict. Sounds pretty bleak and downbeat for a Toho action picture. I have always felt Honda had a much deeper side than most of his *kaiju eiga* (giant monster movies) suggest. It would be nice to see his other non-monster films – if they only were available.

The Man in Red

THE MERCILESS BOSS – based on NUMBER ONE MAN aka KAOYAKU MUYO – DANSEI No. 1 Yori 1955 **DIR.** Kajiro Yamamoto **SCR.** Masando Ide **PHOTO B&W:** Kazuo Yamada **MUSIC:** Ikuma Dan **w/** Koji Tsuruta, Toshiro Mifune, Mariko Okada, Shin Tokudaiji
An anemic, virtually toothless tale of friction between dandyish ladies man/ money collector Tsuruta and blustery, small time gang boss/fight promoter Mifune. Much ado about nothing. It is

hard to believe that not only was director Yamamoto Akira Kurosawa's mentor at Toho, but that screenwriter Ide worked on several of Kurosawa's projects. This is not even close to the quality of Yamamoto's next gangster picture, UNDERWORLD, from 1956 – a film that wasn't that great, either. If it wasn't for Tsuruta and Mifune, this would rate only one star. * *

The Merciless Boss

THE MERCILESS TRAP aka NASAKE MUYO NO WANA 1961 82 min. **DIR** Jun Fukuda **SCR** Katsuya Suzaki **PHOTO B&W** **'SCOPE:** Masaharu Utsumi **MUSIC:** Kenjiro Hirose **w/** Makoto Sato, Kumi Mizuno, Akihiro Hirata, Ichiro Nakatani, Kunie Tanaka, Tadao Nakamaru Ex-con trucker Sato is framed for a woman's murder, and call girl Mizuno, who was with him, is threatened with death by killer Tanaka if she tells the truth. Police detective Nakatani thinks Sato is guilty until Sato saves his life. Mizuno finally gets the courage to give Sato his alibi, hooks up with him, then is run over and killed by Tanaka as soon as she leaves. But she had already revealed to Sato that the guilty party behind Tanaka is Sato's boss Hirata. Sato and cop Nakatani converge on the garage, firmly

thrashing Hirata and Tanaka after a vigorous fistfight. A routine story expertly handled by pro Fukuda with maximum suspense, noirish ambience and plenty of action. The film's only liability is that Sato's surfeit of over-the-top energy occasionally spills over into scenery-chewing. * * *

New Hoodlum Soldier - Firing Line (#9 and final in the series started at Daiei Studios)

NEW HOODLUM SOLDIER STORY – FIRING LINE aka SHIN HEITAI YAKUZA – KASEN 1972 92 min. **DIR** Yasuzo Masumura **SCR** Yasuzo Masumura/ Masatoshi Tojo (Higashijo?) **PHOTO COLOR 'SCOPE:** Setsuo Kobayashi **MUSIC:** Kunihiko Murai **w/** Shintaro Katsu, Takahiro Tamura, Michiyo Yasuda, Koichi Ose, Joe Shishido, Shuji Otaki, Kaoru Sakamoto Director of the original movie, Masumura, returns for the last HOODLUM SOLDIER film, a Katsu Production but released through Toho. It is also the only one in color. Masumura nearly matches the excellence of the first film at Daiei, with some incredibly funny as well as disturbingly grueling violent set-pieces. Katsu befriends a Chinese girl (Yasuda) working at the military outpost. Brutal sergeant Shishido has it in for her, but every time he assaults her, he must deal with his nemesis Katsu. The two go through a series of progressively more insane fistfights as the saga progresses, until the end, when they engage in one of the most over-the-top brawls since Sean Connery/Robert Shaw in FROM RUSSIA WITH LOVE and Rod Taylor/William Smith in DARKER THAN AMBER. The fight actually eclipses those other on-screen displays of mayhem, and Katsu's triumph finally culminates in Shishido's death. It is a pity this movie seems to be virtually unseen by anyone in western nations. #9 and last of the series, the others released by DAIEI. (A Katsu Production) * * * 1/2

Procurers of Hell

PROCURERS OF HELL aka JIGOKU NO UTAGE (KYOEN) aka BANQUET IN HELL 1961 94 min. **DIR.** Kihachi Okamoto **SCR.** Ichiro Ikeda/Ei Ogawa **PHOTO B&W** 'SCOPE: Tokuzo Kuroda **MUSIC:**

Masaru Sato **w/** Tatsuya Mihashi, Reiko Dan, Jun Tazaki, Junko Ikeuchi, Kei Sato, Chieko Nakakita, Bin Amatsu Mihashi is a pimp who finds a roll of exposed film. Coincidence of coincidences, it shows his hated former sergeant from WW2 (Tazaki) in compromising poses with his mistress (Dan). As Mihashi discovers, Tazaki is now the president of a huge construction company, and in addition to mistress duties, Dan is also the man's secretary. But according to Dan, Tazaki has just died, and she still wants the film returned. Mihashi's price is her overnight stay. She agrees and gets the film the next morning, unaware that Mihashi has made prints. Upon closer inspection, Mihashi realizes from a dated newspaper visible in the photos that they are too recent and Tazaki can't be dead. It is a trick to cover up his embezzlement of company funds. Mihashi locates Tazaki and finds the avaricious businessmeister with Dan. Now our pimp anti-hero demands half the swindled money for the negatives, prints and his full silence. Tazaki attempts to give Mihashi less, is stymied and is coerced to give in. Dan decides she prefers Mihashi and tries to coax him to murder Tazaki. Mihashi is a bit shocked. He knows he is a sleazy bum, but he draws the line at killing. Nevertheless, Mihashi and Dan escape with the loot, and Tazaki is arrested after all. An ironic denouement has the couple shot-to-death in the street by unknown assailants. A strange cross between noir thriller and very black comedy that is, along with DESPERADO OUTPOST, one of director Okamoto's best early films. The textured, sharp black-and-white cinematography by Kuroda,

Okamoto's camera placement and cutting and Sato's languid, sensual score are all exceptionally fine. The only incongruity is that some of the humor tends to unbalance things a little. (In Toho's 1961 promo booklets, they romanize KYOEN as UTAGE which may be slang for banquet. However in numerous editions of Japan's Cinema Club, it is romanized traditionally as KYOEN). * * *

Resurrection of the Beast

RESURRECTION OF THE BEAST aka YAJU NO FUKKATSU 1969 86 min. **DIR.** Michio Yamamoto **SCR.** Ei Ogawa /Katsu Takesue **PHOTO COLOR 'SCOPE:** Masaharu Utsumi **MUSIC:** Taiichiro Kosugi **w/** Tatsuya Mihashi, Toshio Kurosawa, Yoshiko Mita, Mika Kitagawa, Goro Mutsumi
When his gang is busted on a narcotics rap, Mihashi agrees to take the fall if he is allowed to retire from gangster life after his prison term. Once

he gets out, he establishes a reputable business in a port town and falls-in-love with Mita, a bar madam. But he is inevitably drawn back into the fray when his younger brother Kurosawa and Kitagawa, the boy's pregnant sweetheart, show up on the run from the former gang. Brother Kurosawa, still in the gang and balking at his assignment to kill a man, has gone on the run. Mihashi goes to his former boss, asking him to spare the couple. The boss agrees if Mihashi will take over the contract. Which he does. Upon completion of the killing, he learns his boss has sent the killers after the couple anyway. He finds not only the two young lovers dead, but also a slaughtered ex-convict buddy, and his house in flames. Mihashi then storms his former gang HQ, wiping out everyone, including his former double-crossing boss. A not bad yakuza action thriller that Yamamoto made just prior to his famous cult-film vampire trilogy THE BLOODTHIRSTY DOLL (YUREI YASHIKI NO KYOFU – CHI O SU NINGYO) (1970), BLOODTHIRSTY EYES aka LAKE OF DRACULA (NOROI NO YAKATA – CHI O SU ME) (1971) and THE BLOODTHIRSTY ROSE aka EVIL OF DRACULA (CHI O SU BARA) (1974). * * *

REVOLT AGAINST GLORY aka EIKO E NO HANGYAKU 1970 92 min. **DIR.** Ko Nakahira **ORIG. STORY:** Renzaburo Shibata **SCR.** Ryuzo Nakanishi/Yukio (Norio?) Miyashita **PHOTO COLOR 'SCOPE:** Tokuzo Kuroda **w/** Toshio Kurosawa, Chieko Matsubara, Tatsuya Mihashi, Eiji Okada, Kunie Tanaka, Kazuko Takahashi   A visually stunning. old-fashioned tale with some modern nihilist trappings as Christian boxer Kurosawa drops out of the loop after accidentally killing an opponent in the ring. His hardnosed promoter Mihashi is not happy about the situation, but there is little he can do. Kurosawa treks up to the snowy north to get back to his roots and is welcomed into a mountain community by a rowdy bunch of woodsmen after being left for dead by a gang of sadistic thieves. His rescuer, young girl Takahashi, has a lusty yen for him and is not happy when Kurosawa's devoted girlfriend Matsubara shows up in the chilly environs to find her reluctant beau. Meanwhile, Kurosawa's best new friend Tanaka is murdered by the thieves. Soon after, Kurosawa locates his uncle, mountain man Okada, who lives alone in a secluded log cabin. Okada had been instrumental in helping Kurosawa's father stand up to a local yakuza gang when Kurosawa was just a tyke. In fact, these flashbacks where the yakuza boss is dispatched with a spear are some of the wildest scenes in the film. Despite the hokey premise and attendant cliches, director Nakahira (most famnous for his "sun tribe" film at Nikkatsu, CRAZED FRUIT and his two RIKA pictures) continually pumps up the adrenaline with nearly non-stop two-fisted action and the tempestuous triangle of Kurosawa, Matsubara and Takahashi. Finally, near the end, after they have killed uncle Okada and assaulted his lover Matsubara. Kurosawa defeats the brutal thieves with his bare hands. Right on cue, promoter Mihashi shows up and convinces Kurosawa to come back to fight again. Unbelievably, Kurosawa consents, wins the new bout but once again decides to opt for the simple mountain life in his late uncle's cabin. Matsubara joins him in an idyllic, romantic closing shot. Remarkably refreshing, despite the hackneyed plot, with cinematographer Kuroda supplying some of the most sumptuously gorgeous winter landscapes on film since Hideo Gosha's samurai masterpiece, GOYOKIN. Writer of the original story, Renzaburo Shibata, also penned numerous *chanbara* samurai pictures and novels, including his most famous creation KYOSHIRO NEMURI aka SLEEPY EYES OF DEATH. Twelve films with the late superstar Raizo Ichikawa portraying Nemuri were lensed at Daiei Studios between 1963 – 1969. * * *

Reward for Rebellion

REWARD FOR REBELLION aka HAN GYAKU NO HOSHU   1973 86 min. **DIR.** Yukihiro Sawada **SCR.** Shuichi Nagahara/Kibu Nagata **PHOTO COLOR 'SCOPE:** Mitsushi Kaneuma **MUSIC:** Takeo Watanabe/ Kenjiro Hirose **w/** Yujiro Ishihara, Tetsuya Watari, Haruko Wanibuchi, Mikio Narita, Junko Natsu, Asao Koike, Mieko Takamine, Shoki Fukae Maverick Vietnam combat photographer Watari returns to Japan with a key given to him by a dying American GI to pass on to girlfriend Wanibuchi. It turns out she is involved with evil Narita's drug gang. She is also the ex-girl of Ishihara who had been betrayed and left for dead by Narita several years previous. Ishihara, Watari and Watari's girl friday Natsu team up to put the screws on Narita. Unfortunately, Wanibuchi, who has been forced into virtual slavery by Narita, gets killed in the process. A continuation of the type of moodily noirish, gangster action thrillers director Sawada and actors Ishihara and Watari made at their original studio, Nikkatsu, in the sixties. Entertaining and well-done, but not much more than routine. Ishihara produced. * * 1/2

SHOWDOWN ON PIER #3 aka DAI SAN HATOBA NO KETTO 1960 102 min. **DIR.** Kozo Saeki **SCR.** Fumio Shibano **PHOTO COLOR 'SCOPE:** Kozo Okazaki **MUSIC:** Rinichiro Manabe   **w/** Tatsuya Mihashi, Akira Takarada, Keiko Awaji, Izumi Yukimura, Akemi Kita, Tetsuro Tanba, Seizaburo Kawazu, Akihiro Hirata, Kenji Sahara, Ko Nishimura, Eisei Amamoto
Ex-cop Takarada pretends to go bad and infiltrates Kawazu and Tanba's drug gang in Kobe that smuggle heroin from Hong Kong in golf balls. He funnels information through feisty good girl Yukimura – whose father is a junkie! – to help former rival, cop Mihashi, who has been assigned to the case. Too bad during the final shootout Takarada is fatally wounded, forfeiting his life to prove his worth. Although it does not really amount to much, this is nevertheless a very entertaining noirish action thriller with great pacing of tough gangster action and sumptuous color photography by Okazaki. Despite the contrived

nature of the story, this is actually a pretty well-written and directed picture – certainly one of director Saeki's best – and is refreshingly free of the cornball histrionics sometimes plaguing late fifties/early sixties Toho crime films. Everyone in the cast is great, especially Mihashi, Yukimura and Tanba. Ko Nishimura is phenomenally menacing, having fun with his small part as the soft-spoken heroin supplier to Kawazu's gang. * * *

STAMP OUT THE CHAOS aka DOJI O FUMUNA 1957 (1956?) **DIR.** Shigeaki Hidaka **SCR.** Tokubei Wakao **PHOTO B&W:** Fukuzo Koizumi **MUSIC:** Sei Ikeno **w/** Hiroshi Koizumi, Yasuko Nakata, Ichiro Arishima, Yu Fujiki, Fumie Noguchi

THE SUN ABOVE, DEATH BELOW aka SOGEKI 1968 87 min. **DIR.** Hiromichi Horikawa **SCR.** Shuichi Nagahara **PHOTO COLOR 'SCOPE:** Kiyoshi Hasegawa **MUSIC:** Rinichiro Manabe **w/** Yuzo Kayama, Ruriko Asaoka, Masayuki Mori, Shin Kishida, Takashi Fujiki, Shoichi Ozawa   Pro hitman Kayama is commissioned to make a gold-smuggling gang disappear. Simultaneously, he meets model Asaoka, and they fall in-love with each other. Kayama discovers that the gold smugglers have disbanded on their own. But another killer, Mori, is now after him and his employers. Asaoka wants Kayama to leave the country to go with her to New Guinea to settle down. Kayama, though, knows it is hopeless unless he kills Mori first. Mori finds Kayama's employers and dispatches them, then murders Asaoka. In the final shoot-

clockwise from top left:

The Sun Above, The Death Below

Stamp Out the Chaos

Too Young to Die

ing match, Kayama gets the upper hand and shoots Mori. However, he is left with nothing. At times, a bizarre, often over-stylized tall tale with a couple of very strange psychedelic montages built around Kayama and Asaoka's love scenes. Still, Horikawa's cinematic purple prose is preferable to boring business-as-usual. As far as the cast, Asaoka is, as always, splendid, but Kayama seems somewhat miscast in his schizophrenically tormented, coldblooded role. Mori, veteran of countless "prestige" pictures, is a true maestro of projecting menace in quiet, subtle ways and, with virtually no dialogue, sticks in the mind as a particularly memorable villain. His smiling, at times serenely happy attitude towards his homicidal work conveys an almost spiritual ecstasy in killing. There are a few slow patches, but overall this is a rewarding picture – an effective, starkly economical and downbeat thriller by Akira Kurosawa's former assistant director, Horikawa. * * *

TARGET OF ROSES aka BARA NO HYOTEKI 1972 94 min. **DIR.** Kiyoshi Nishimura **SCR.** Yoshio Shirasaka/Chiho Katsura **PHOTO COLOR 'SCOPE:** Kazumi Hara **w/** Yuzo Kayama, Chen Chen, Eiji Okada   Wealthy fascist industrialist and devotee of Hitler, Okada, enlists the services of long dormant hitman/sniper Kayama in his quest to protect his secret human experiments and to build a private neo-Nazi army. Kayama crosses paths with Chinese nature photographer Chen Chen when he assassinates her German foster father – a man who had accidentally discovered Okada's project and had begun investigating. The two fall

in-love and most of their dialogue together is in awkward English (although Kayama acquits himself surprisingly well, considering). Kayama also has a fascination for outmoded steam locomotives, and their obsolescence and dismantling in the modern age is used as a heavy-handed metaphor for Kayama's thing-of-the-past lone wolf romantic individuality. He ends up trying to foil Okada but is captured in the process, then coerced to kill his girl Chen. He finally ends up turning the tables, causes Interpol to become involved, then tracks Okada into the wilderness. Kayama is ambushed in an idyllic meadow and fatally wounded, but manages to shoot-to-death Okada at the last minute. Plodding through most of its length, as well as convoluted and pretentious, it nevertheless has some genuinely poetic moments, particularly the ending duel between Kayama and Okada where Kayama hallucinates the destruction of locomotive wheels as he expires. * * 1/2

THEATER OF LIFE - STORY OF YOUTH aka JINSEI GEKIJO - SEISHUN HEN 1958 **DIR.** Toshio Sugie **SCR.** Ryuji Shiina **PHOTO B&W 'SCOPE:** Taiichi Shishigura **MUSIC:** Yoshiyuki Kozu **w/** Ryo Ikebe, Mitsuko Kusabue, Takashi Shimura, Hisaya Morishige, Hisako Takibana, Koji Osawa, Eijiro Tono, Kan Yanagiya, Misako Azuka See write-ups in the Toei, Shochiku or Nikkatsu Studios sections for some of the other versions and their story details, although it is really anyone's guess what part of the sprawling epic novel on which director Sugie and writer Shima focused.

TOO YOUNG TO DIE aka
SHINUNIWA MADA HAYAI aka
DIE QUICKLY 1969 82 min. **DIR.**
Kiyoshi Nishimura **SCR.** Yoshihiro
Ishimatsu/Hajime Kodera **PHOTO**
COLOR 'SCOPE: Kazutami (Itami?)
Hara **MUSIC:** Iwao Akune **w/** Toshio
Kurosawa, Mako Midori, Koji
Takahashi, Daisuke Wakamiya, Jin
Nakayama, Kazuya Oguri, Tatsuji
Ebara   Lone psycho hood
Kurosawa stalks into a bar located
along a busy highway then takes
the patrons hostage after shooting
to death a cop questioning customers about a fugitive gangster. Except
for a few moments at the beginning,
where race car driver Takahashi and
girlfriend Midori make love intercut
with Takahashi's flashbacks of earlier
in the day when he narrowly escaped
death in a crash, this whole film takes
place between the walls of the tiny
club. Claustrophobic and intense
almost to the point of being difficult
to watch at times, this delivers across
the board with some great performances and nervewracking suspense.
Nerves-of-steel Takahashi, having
faced many close shaves on the track,
calls cruel psycho Kurosawa's bluff
several times, but it is one of the
abused patrons who finally blows
away Kurosawa at the end. The eccentric, quiet loner building matchstick houses on the bar counter is actually the fugitive gangster sought by
police, and he keeps a low profile, not
wanting to draw attention to himself
until the situation in the bar becomes
so dire, he must act. Finally, he draws
his own concealed pistol to pump
shocked Kurosawa full of lead. More
of a suspense thriller than a yakuza
film, the direction and tone occasionally borders on the pretentious but
manages to successfully walk the
aesthetic tightrope, in part, by moving
at a fast clip and coming in under 90
minutes running time.   * * *

TRAMPLED INNOCENCE aka
DORO DARAKE NO JUNJYO
1977 96 min. **DIR.** Masayoshi
Tomimoto **SCR.** Shiro Ishimori
PHOTO COLOR 'SCOPE: Shohei Ando
MUSIC: Hajime Kaburagi
w/ Momoyoshi Yamaguchi, Ryohei
Uchida, Shiro Osaka, Tomokazu
Miura   This seems to be a remake
of one of those Mitsuo Hamada/
Sayuri Yoshinaga Nikkatsu youth
(*seishun*)/love melodramas but, seem-
ingly this time, with the bad boy's
yakuza association played up.
(Independent film distr. by TOHO)

UNDERWORLD aka ANKOKU
GAI series

Underworld

UNDERWORLD aka ANKOKU
GAI 1956 94 min. **DIR.** Kajiro

Yamamoto **SCR.** Norihei (Tokubei?) Wakao **PHOTO B&W:** Seiichi Endo **MUSIC:** Ikuma Dan w/ Koji Tsuruta, Toshiro Mifune, Takashi Shimura, Hiroshi Koizumi, Shosaku Sugiyama, Kyoko Aoyama, Seiji Miyaguchi, Minosuke Yamada One of the first modern gangster movies done by a major Japanese studio with big box-office stars. Evidently successful as it spawned the loosely-related UNDER-WORLD series at Toho. Still, a very slow-moving and old-fashioned tale of Koji Tsuruta who is the business manager of a nightclub owned by the yakuza. The gang is presided over by Shimura who has heart trouble. Aoyama plays Shimura's daughter, a greedy club hostess and expert gold-digger, who is also Tsuruta's woman. Negishi is a young female doctor who is called in for ailing Shimura. Being a bit innocent, she believes the gang is not that bad. One night she gets drunk at the club, and Tsuruta has to help her out. Jealous Aoyama spots this from afar and jumps to the wrong conclusion. She tells pop Shimura, who is already angry about something else. Henchman Yamada, dying to get rid of Tsuruta and seeing an opportunity, says he will take care of it and runs out with a gun before Shimura can stop him. Cooled down Aoyama warns Tsuruta, and he makes a break from the club only to be cornered by his mob comrades. He takes it on the lam through the streets and is chased into a deserted stadium. Finally, after psyching Tsuruta out, Yamada shoots him and brings him back to the mob HQ. Shimura summons physician Negishi and bids her patch up Tsuruta then makes a drunken pass at her. Suddenly, Negishi realizes how bad these guys are. Unhappily,

Yamamoto's depiction of her revelation is quite hokey. At the conclusion, police inspector Mifune (in what amounts to little more than a cameo) stages a raid on the gang HQ, rescuing Negishi and Tsuruta. Tsuruta subsequently recuperates in a prison hospital bed while the rest of the gang languishes behind bars. Aoyama gets off scot-free and splits with an elderly rich man. The last shot is of the half-finished massage business building that was Tsuruta's brain-child, now forlorn and abandoned. UNDERWORLD is seemingly more influenced by French crime pictures directed by the likes of Jacques Becker than any American movies, with an atmospheric score full of mournful cabaret accordions and harmonicas, and noirish images of newspapers blowing down deserted night streets. But the story is slight, and the characters too innocuous to pull in the viewer. A disappointment considering that director Yamamoto was Akira Kurosawa's mentor at Toho. * * 1/2

UNDERWORLD BOSS aka ANKOKU GAI NO KAOYAKU aka THE BIG BOSS 1959 102 min. **DIR.** Kihachi Okamoto **SCR.** Motosada Nishigame/Shinichi Sekizawa **PHOTO COLOR 'SCOPE:** Asaichi Nagai **MUSIC:** Masaru Sato w/ Koji Tsuruta, Toshiro Mifune, Akira Takarada, Tadao Nakamaru, Yumi Shirakawa, Seizaburo Kawazu, Mitsuko Kusabue, Keiko Yanagawa Tsuruta is a gangster with a younger nightclub singer brother Takarada – a greenhorn to gang ways saddled with driving hitman Sato's getaway car as the film begins. Bad boss Kawazu and second banana Tanba are antsy about his untested loyalty, and soon brother Takarada is in hiding. Tsuruta is also the single father of a crippled son who is stashed at a special school run by Tsuruta's heartthrob. Hirata is the manager of Kawazu's nightspot where Takarada sings and is Tsuruta's best friend. There is a bizarre sequence where Tsuruta and Hirata visit a rural club run by foreign gangsters that features fixed roulette games.

Underworld Boss aka The Big Boss

There are other nice images all through the film such as Tsuruta tying his tie in a mirror with a toy robot in the foreground looking as if it is going to strangle him and a great, too short sequence where passed-out, drunken Tsuruta dreams of pursuing his beloved brother through a spooky swamp and shooting him. When Takarada becomes a more serious security risk, hitman Sato is assigned to watch Tsuruta, a task that creates an evolving chemistry and uneasy

friendship between the two. Near the end, Tsuruta and Takarada are held for gang execution at Kawazu's auto repair garage. Mifune, once again in little more than a cameo, is a put-upon mechanic who finally erupts when the gang is about to kill the pair. Luckily, Sato and Kawazu's mistress also step in at that point to help the two brothers. There is a big shootout, and Kawazu and Tanba flee, only to die in a fiery crash after being pursued by the mortally wounded Tsuruta. UNDERWORLD BOSS is not bad but ultimately nothing more than a potpourri pastiche/melodrama with way too many trivial moments and little impact. These early yakuza pictures by director Okamoto are very uneven, possessing little of the ambience or emotional wallop of his later masterpieces, SWORD OF DOOM, KILL! and RED LION. The often prevalent humor is nowhere near as irreverent or dangerous as Okamoto's cinematic soul brother Seijun Suzuki's Nikkatsu pictures. Curious, as Okamoto's humor in action comedy dramas like DESPERADO OUTPOST and KILL! is on-target. * * 1/2

UNDERWORLD DUEL aka ANKOKU GAI NO TAIKETSU aka THE LAST GUNFIGHT 1960 95 min. **Dir.** Kihachi Okamoto **Scr.** Shinichi Sekizawa **Photo color 'scope:** Kazuo Yamada **Music:** Masaru Sato **w/** Toshiro Mifune, Koji Tsuruta, Seizaburo Kawazu, Yoko Tsukasa, Makoto Sato, Tadao Nakamaru, Eisei Amamoto
A melodramatic tale of special operative Mifune tracking down criminals (led by Kawazu as usual) who have stolen a U.S. weapons shipment.

Underword Duel aka The Last Gunfight

Bar-owner Tsuruta helps Mifune. There is a surfeir of corny humor that would later become typical of the Bond films, and it comes off as dated. Although several of Okamoto's pictures, especially SAMURAI ASSASSIN (1965) and SWORD OF DOOM (1966), are extremely bleak, grim, brutal, he is known much more for action films punctuated with humor. Most of his serio-comic action pictures such as KILL!, AGE OF ASSASSINS, ZATOICHI MEETS YOJINBO and especially the avant-garde HUMAN BULLET are laced with a bitingly edgy, satirical wit. However, the humor here is pretty lightweight and inconsequential.
* * 1/2

UNDERWORLD BULLETS aka ANKOKU GAI NO DANKON aka BLUEPRINT FOR MURDER 1961 73 min. **DIR.** Kihachi Okamoto **SCR.** Shinichi Sekizawa **PHOTO COLOR**

'**SCOPE:** Fukumi Koizumi **MUSIC:** Masaru Sato   w/ Yuzo Kayama, Makoto Sato, Tatsuya Mihashi, Ichiro Nakatani, Kumi Mizuno, Mickey Curtis, Mie Hama, Tadao Nakamaru, Seizaburo Kawazu, Eisei Amamoto There is an outstandingly exhilarating, breakneck chase scene between a car and motorcycle in the opening frames, Okamoto refusing to waste any time or motion, as hero Kayama's brother is finally forced over the edge of a cliff. His car somersaults down the incline, bursting into flames. Whale-hunting teacher Kayama – hey, people, he is good with a harpoon! – gets the news and journeys to the small town where his sibling was to meet friend Nakatani. He comes up against ultra-cool, sunglasses-wearing police inspector Mihashi and black leather-jacketed lone wolf Sato, both of whom prove to be on his side.

Underword Bullets

The seemingly evil boss Kawazu is really only a figurehead with sultry torch singer Hama and brutal gambler Nakamaru the real power behind the scenes. They are in collusion with corrupt town officials, including a seemingly milquetoast, bespectacled politician who proves to be as ruthless as his gangster cronies. It turns out the villains are after a revolutionary car engine and had killed Kayama's brother to keep him from spilling the beans. Sato, Kayama and good girl Mizuno are captured by the gang and nearly killed. They manage to escape but are then engaged in a riproaring shootout with the bad guys when cornered in a construction site. Kayama is wounded in both arms and Sato blinded by blood when his forehead is grazed by a bullet. The boys get so desperate at the climax, they resort to using a nail gun to disable the evil gunmen, only to have cop Mihashi finally arrive in the nick of time to arrest the remaining gangsters. Still a potboiler, but marginally better than director Okamoto's other early yakuza eiga.   * * *

UNDERWORLD EXTERMINA-TION ORDER aka ANKOKU GAI GEKIMETSU MEIREI aka WITNESS KILLED 1962 87 min. **Dir.** Jun Fukuda **Scr.** Ei Ogawa **Photo color 'scope:** Shoji Utsumi **Music:** Shungo Sawada **w/** Tatsuya Mihashi, Makoto Sato, Yuriko Hoshi, Kumi Mizuno, Jun Tazaki, Tadao Nakamaru, Seizaburo Kawazu, Ichiro Nakatani Police detective Mihashi's girl is murdered when she witnesses the late night robbery and killing of three guards transporting the take of a bicycle racetrack. Mihashi goes undercover to find the Italian-made murder gun and its owner. His cred-

ibility swings back-and-forth as he is alternately deemed untrustworthy and then cleared by the two suspect rival gangs. Sato, one of the few hoods he can actually get along with, turns out to be the coldblooded killer. This film pales compared to UNDER-WORLD'S STRATEGY OF AN-NIHILATION which is, along with the later CITY OF BEASTS, the best of director Fukuda's gangster films. There is the occasional *frisson* and evocative image, but not much really happens here. Sato's character is nowhere near as interesting as the bad guys he usually portrays. Mizuno's performance as his nightclub dancer girlfriend is the lone exceptional standout in a cast seemingly content to just go through the motions.   * *

UNDERWORLD FANGS aka ANKOKU GAI NO KIBA aka WEED OF CRIME 1962 90 min. **Dir.** Jun Fukuda **Scr.** Ei Ogawa/ Takashi Tsuboshima **Photo color 'scope:** Shoji Utsumi **Music:** Kenjiro Hirose **w/** Yosuke Natsuki, Tatsuya Mihashi, Makoto Sato, Kumi Mizuno, Mie Hama, Akiko Wakabayashi, Jun Tazaki Sometimes gritty, sometimes silly story of teenagers involved with methedrine-dealing gangsters (Sato et.al.) and the mysterious private eye (Mihashi) out to stop them. Some strange early sixties ambience, especially at the beginning when one of our heroes – the suit-'n-tie-wearing guitarist of a Ventures-type combo – watches a kid go into drug convulsions on a dance floor and die. * * 1/2

GUN AND SWORD

CHRIS D.

**UNDERWORLD'S STRATEGY
OF ANNIHILATION** aka
ANKOKU GAI ZEMETSU
SAKUSEN aka UNDERWORLD'S
KILLING TACTICS 1965 **Dir.** Jun
Fukuda **Scr.** Jun Fukuda/ Yoshihiro
Ishimatsu/Ei Ogawa **Photo color**
'scope: Shinsaku Uno **Music:**
Kenjiro Hirose **w/** Tatsuya Mihashi,
Mie Hama, Makoto Sato, Akihiro
Hirata, Akemi Kita, Sachio Sakai,
Shoji Nakayama, Takamaru Sasaki,
Ryosuke Kagawa
This is a surprisingly uncompromising, very enjoyable gangster melodrama. It certainly cleaves closer to reality than director Okamoto's similar
forays at Toho. Gone is the disjointed
tone of most of Okamoto's early
sixties yakuza films which often com-
bined silly humor and manipulative
melodramatics within the space of a
few minutes. It is also indicative that
director Fukuda's Godzilla pictures
are not a fair barometer of his talent.
The feel here is of an unremitting
bleakness and disassociation from
anything that could be called normal
life. Even the, at first, sympathetic
murdered boss's daughter Hama turns
out to be a venal, shallow girl who
gets drunk in her bar hostess job and
loves to frug and watusi to big band
R&B on the radio. The story concerns
Sato trying to avenge the death of his
boss who is also girlfriend Hama's father. The rival gang's second-in-command Mihashi sows seeds of discon-
tent in his group that metamorphosis
into rebellion. Sato and Mihashi leave
their respective mobs to start their
own. The status quo is threatened
when Sato learns from frightened
Hama that Mihashi not only killed
murder witness Kita but also her
father. Initially vengeful, Sato realizes

he still needs lone wolf Mihashi as
an ally. But even after their gang has
won hard-earned supremacy, and Sato
has finally killed Mihashi, there is no
happy ending. Sato, the new boss, is
murdered by a sniper as he enters his
new office. There are some striking
setpieces: quiet, psychotic Mihashi
(in one of his best performances
this side of a Kurosawa film) cannot
stand loud noises and is driven to
distraction by train whistles after he
murders Sato's boss on board the local express; Hama dancing frantically
with various excited young hoods at
gang HQ as Mihashi does a slow burn
from the racket; Mihashi's murder
of drunken Kita in a deserted canal
while Hama watches; Mihashi and
Sato's final shootout beneath a bridge
where Mihashi becomes suddenly
disoriented by the sound of a speeding bullet train passing overhead.
Even though some of Toho's gangster
films from the period had downbeat
endings, they often also had a somewhat maudlin tone. Here in Fukuda's
film, there is a completely straightforward, unsentimental vibe that is
most welcome. This undoubtedly
has something to do with excellent
screenwriter Ishimatsu's involvement.
This is also, to my knowledge, one of
the earliest yakuza movies (set in a
contemporary time period) to feature
a *sakazuki* ceremony. * * * 1/2

**UNITED CRIES OF ONE HUN-
DRED PEOPLE** aka HYAKU NIN
NO DAIBOKEN aka ADVEN-
TURES OF ONE HUNDRED 1972
95 min. **Dir.** Eizo Sugawa **Scr.**
Hisashi Takabatake **Photo color**
'scope: Kurataro Takamura **Music:**
Naozumi Yamamoto **w/** Go
Wakabayashi, Wakako Sakai, Shin

Kishida, Ryunosuke Minegishi, Shiro Osaka, Kaku Takashina

WILD COP aka GOKKIBURI DEKA aka COCKROACH COP series

WILD COP aka GOKKIBURI DEKA aka COCKROACH COP 1973 83 min. **DIR.** Tsugunobu Kotani **SCR.** Wataru Kenmochi **PHOTO COLOR 'SCOPE:** Mitsushi Kanau **MUSIC:** Takeo Watanabe w/ Tetsuya Watari, Takeo Chii, Masaaki Okado, Mariko Kaga, Kei Nishio, Shoki Fukae, Eiji Go

Wild Cop

A duo of films heavily influenced by the brutal lone wolf cop archetype spawned by the DIRTY HARRY pictures. However, Watari makes Harry look like a flower-child in comparison. Stationed on the edge of a blighted industrial wasteland, detective Watari investigates the murder of a cop at a huge oil refinery yard. It transpires not only yakuza boss Fukae is involved but also Watari's partner

Chii. There are some nervewracking hair's breadth escapes as well as some grueling brutality, with Watari basically executing several gangsters without immediate provocation. At the climax, Watari corners the villain's henchmen in their HQ and destroys the dwelling with an earthmover. Both WILD COP films were produced by actor Yujiro Ishihara's production company. The pair of films are very entertaining, but not for timid viewers. #1 of 2 films   * * *

WILD COP RETURNS aka SA GOKKIBURI aka COCK-ROACH COP RETURNS 1973 83 min. **DIR.** Tsugunobu Kotani **SCR.** Tsugunobu Kotani/Wataru Kenmochi **PHOTO COLOR 'SCOPE:** Mitsushi Kanau **MUSIC:** Takeo Watanabe w/ Tetsuya Watari, Koji Nanbara, Toru Abe, Seizaburo Kawazu, Tetsuro Tanba, Ryunosuke Minegishi, Hitomi Kozoe, Tsuneya Oki, Yoshiro Aoki, Michiko Honda

Wild Cop Returns

An action-packed, trenchantly corrosive thriller with renegade cop Watari investigating murders of persons who have been trying to reveal the gross pollution of oil and chemical plants owned by yakuza boss Abe and evil businessmen Nanbara, Kawazu and Tanba. He also has to go up against homicidal, corrupt colleague Aoki. There are some great setpieces, including Watari's suspenseful escape from a car buried under several dumptrucks' loads of rock. All the villains except Tanba meet violently bloody ends with Kawazu murdered in his bath by Abe's mistress, then Abe and nude mistress shot-to-death on their revolving mirror bed by Watari. Nanbara is blown to smithereens – along with the precious incriminating scientific report on the pollution – when he unsuccessfully tries to throw a vial of nitroglycerine at Watari. There is virtually no character depth nor development, but it doesn't really matter as this is a just-about-perfect live action comic book. #2 of 2 films   * * * 1/2

The Wolves

THE WOLVES aka SHUSSO IWAI aka PRISON RELEASE CELEBRATION 1971 131 min. **DIR.** Hideo Gosha **SCR.** Kei Tasaka/ Hideo Gosha **PHOTO COLOR 'SCOPE:** Kozo Okazaki **MUSIC:** Masaru Sato

w/ Tatsuya Nakadai, Noboru Ando, Kyoko Enami, Isao Natsuyagi, Toshio Kurosawa, Komaki Kurahara, Tetsuro Tanba, Kunie Tanaka
Gosha once again turns out a sumptuous masterpiece with saturated color detail and emotionally wrenching performances. Unlike the almost as great amoral cinema-of-yakuza-cruelty tale VIOLENT STREET that Gosha did for Toei, he obviously has a little more time and money at his disposal here, and it is definitely to the story's advantage. After a knife brawl in a movie theater (it is the late 1920s so they are showing silent film newsreels with live *benshi* narration), Nakadai, Ando and Kurosawa receive long jail terms for murder. But after only four years pass, the Emperor dies and the Taisho era is at an end. In celebration of the new Emperor and the beginning of the Showa era, a general amnesty is declared. The three are released from incarceration. When Nakadai gets out he seems a changed man, sick of the violence and betrayal. He still has a few naive ideals left, and it is only a matter of time before those will be painfully quashed forever. By himself out in a lush field beside the railroad tracks, Nakadai finds a small puppy, and his natural gentleness toward the animal show that he is only in the yakuza because that is all he knows and has no other choice. On the seashore he spies a sad woman (Enami of Daiei Studios' WOMAN GAMBLING EXPERT series) throwing tiny paper cranes into the surf. Their chance meeting is bittersweet. Before long their anonymous tryst turns into a drunken binge at a roadside inn. They escape into sex, but it cannot erase the lonely lives they lead. Enami is a tattoo artist

who doubled once as an assassin –
assisting in the murder of whom we
later learn was Nakadai's boss – and
it is through her we first meet the
silent female duo/hit squad that will
dispatch several liabilities for politician Tanba – liabilities who turn out
to be friends of Nakadai. Originally
Nakadai and Ando were enemies, but
since being released from jail they
strike up a friendship that causes both
gangs, as well as Tanba, trepidation.
There are several other complications,
including a doomed love match between Kurosawa and the dead boss's
daughter Kurahara, that help to bring
to a head the final set of betrayals by
Nakadai's former comrade and new
boss Natsuyagi – betrayals that
climax in a final, hypnotic twenty
minute swirl of intoxicating color,
perverse beauty and bone-splintering
violence, dynamics that suck the
viewer into a whirlpool of voyeuristic
empathy. An amazing film and one of
the all-time masterpieces of the genre.
* * * *

YOUNG WOLF aka WAKAI
OKAMI aka HIDDEN FANGS
1961 83 min. **Dir./Scr.** Hideo Onchi
Photo B&W 'scope: Yuzuru Aizawa
Music: Michio Mamiya w/ Yosuke
Natsuki, Yuriko Hoshi, Kin Sugai,
Kazuo Suzuki, Ko Nishimura

ZENI GEBA 1970 91 min.
Dir. Yoshinari Wada **Scr.** Mitsuro
Kodaki/Hisashi Takabatake **Photo**
color 'scope: Shohei Ando **Music:**
Kenjiro Hirose w/ Juro Kara,
Kensuke Raimon, Takeshi Kato,
Kazuko Inano, Meicho Soganoya,
Mako Midori, Rie Yokoyama, Kinzo
Shin, Shin Kishida, Hiroko Sakurai
A *manga*-based bloodfest about a

totally sociopathic guy who will do
anything – robbery, rape, murder –
in pursuit of riches.

MATATABI (WANDERING GAMBLER) AND PERIOD YAKUZA FILMS

The Lone Stalker

(IMAGE © KADOKAWA PRODUCTIONS)

Appendix 1

INTRODUCTION: MATATABI & PERIOD YAKUZA FILMS

Cold Wind Monjiro
(IMAGE © TOEI)

The *matatabi* and period yakuza film have been staples of Japanese cinema since the early 1920s. Between 1955 – 1965 an incredible number of *matatabi* films were released. The term, when used in talking about Japanese film, refers to a specific subgenre that is peculiar not only to the yakuza film but the samurai film as well. In context of a yakuza or samurai picture, *matatabi* means wanderer or drifter, usually a *ronin* (masterless samurai) who is now a gambler. He can be affiliated with a yakuza clan or not. Usually, if he is the hero of a film, he is an *ippiki okami* (lone wolf) who has been wronged either by his clan or a clan he has stayed with while passing through some village. He wanders from town to town, and his motives for drifting can range from seeking revenge or redress for some past injustice, his flight from an unhappy love affair where he has been spurned due to his *ronin* status, an accident of birth or something as simple – and romantic – as a love for the vagabond life of the road. Quite often, too, the chivalrous *matatabi* will leave a relationship or fail to consummate one, no matter how much in-love he is with the woman, because he knows that he will only bring her grief.

    The *matatabi* occupies a prominent place in Japanese folklore – his character is found in popular fiction (novels and short stories), television dramas, and even popular music where a whole *matatabi* subgenre of folk music exists. There are several actors – Saburo Kitajima, for instance – famous for their roles in yakuza and/or samurai films who still give concerts in *matatabi* costume: short, striped blue cape, skintight sky-blue trousers, flat straw hat, sword and quite often a blade of grass or straw between the teeth. The songs are similar to American folk murder ballads or 1950s – 1960s-era country-western lost-love laments in that they tell a story. The *matatabi* song invariably relates a tale of a romantic ne'er-do-well, a drifting, gambling swordsman, and from his view-point we hear tragic revelations of why he left his home and/or family to wander. Enforced exile, financial ruin, nobly taking the blame for a friend's indiscretion, the death of his wife or loved ones, seeking vengeance for his family's or friend's murder, a vagabond's need to hit the road – the list of motives is endless.

For various political reasons, it was unheard of to place a realistic and authentic yakuza story in a contemporary milieu until the early 1960s and even *jitsuroku* (true account) realism didn't hit the screens until the early 1970s. Modern Japanese gangster films from the 1950s modeled themselves almost exclusively on their American or Euro counterparts. The yakuza brotherhood, the *sakazuki* rituals, the ascendant heirarchy were virtually never shown except in the *matatabi* samurai film. Another case of depicting a relevant truth common in the past to metaphorically illuminate the present. The yakuza clans had been around since the 1700s. Then again, these were tall tales, romantic legends and have about as much relevance to real history as the spaghetti westerns of the sixties and seventies.

Fodder for legends bloom from the wellspring of history. True-life characters such as Chuji Kunisada and Jirocho of Shimizu crop up in various manifestations in throngs of *matatabi* sagas. But historical accuracy was granted the same priority as in American westerns featuring such personages as Jesse James, Billy the Kid, Wyatt Earp and Doc Holliday. The tarnished reputations of villains or dubious heroes were polished up in their transference to celluloid. Likewise fictional characters with such monikers as Chutaro, Cold Wind Monjiro, Ginpei, Tokijiro, Hantaro, Yataro, Asataro, et.al., brandished their *nagadosu* (long swords) and swashbuckled their way onto the big screen.

One other facet of *matatabi* cinema that is somewhat subliminal but should not be overlooked is the depiction of seasonal change in these stories' rural landscapes. Whether it be Fall, Winter, Spring, or Summer is an important aspect of a wandering gambler's tale. The season quite often serves as subtle metaphor or sledgehammer symbol depending upon the quality of the direction.

I had originally hoped to include a listing which would be as complete as possible of *matatabi* and period yakuza pictures in this appendix. But matters of space preclude this luxury. So, I have decided to present a cross-section of what I feel are the most important and most representative of the incredibly broad spectrum of this subgenre. The *matatabi* hero is very relevant as an archetype of the male image in Japanese cinema, as well as folklore, and was instrumental in forging the many variations of the *ippiki okami* (lone wolf) hero/anti-hero in yakuza *eiga*.

Note: *There are several silent era matatabi films listed here. Because of various financial hurdles in converting theaters to sound, the strong union of benshis (the "live" narrators in the theaters showing silent films) and difficulties with the technology, silent films were still being produced in Japan well into the mid-1930s.*

Kill! (1968)
(Image © Toho)

An Incomplete Selection –

MATATABI
(WANDERING GAMBLER)
AND PERIOD YAKUZA
FILMS

AN ACTOR'S REVENGE, see
GOBLIN YUKINOJO

BAMBOO LEAF OMON aka
SASSABUE OMON aka GIRL
WITH THE BAMBOO LEAVES
1969 76 min. **DIR.** Tokuzo Tanaka
SCR. Tetsuro Yoshide **PHOTO COLOR**
'SCOPE: Chishi Makiura **MUSIC:**
Hiroaki Watanabe **w/** Michiyo
Yasuda, Ryohei Uchida, Akane
Kawazaki,Fujio Suga, Asao
Uchida, Ryutaro Gomi   Yasuda
plays Omon, a woman using bamboo
leaves as darts/blades to disable and
kill her enemies. (DAIEI Studios)

Bamboo Leaf Omon
(IMAGE © KADOKAWA PRODUCTIONS)

BLIND MONK SWORDSMAN aka
AKU BOZU KYOKAKUDEN aka
CHIVALROUS STORY OF A BAD
MONK 1962 **DIR.** Hideaki Onishi
w/ Jushiro Konoe, Chiyonosuke
Azuma, Haruo Tanaka, Shinobu
Chihara, Masao Mishima
The prototype for the later two yakuza priest series with Shintaro Katsu
and Tomisaburo Wakayama? Apparently so. And the blind swordsman
motif seems to have been concurrent
with Daiei's first ZATOICHI production, also from 1962. (TOEI Studios)

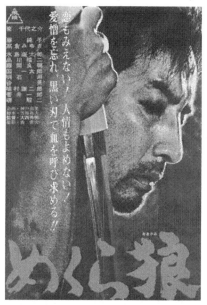

Blind Wolf (IMAGE © TOEI)

BLIND WOLF aka MEKURA
OKAMI 1963 83 min. **DIR.**
Hideaki Onishi **SCR.** Kazuo
Kasahara **PHOTO B&W** 'SCOPE:
Tsuneji Mori **MUSIC:** Toshiaki
Tsushima w/ Chiyonosuke Azuma,
Junko Fuji, Miyuki Takakura,
Michitaro Mizushima, Ryuzo
Shinagawa, Ichiro Sugai   After the
success of the first two Zatoichi blind

swordsman films at Daiei, Toei try to hit paydirt with another outcast blind hero up against evil yakuza. (TOEI)

The Bloody Shuriken
(IMAGE © KADOKAWA PRODUCTIONS)

THE BLOODY SHURIKEN aka AKAI SHURIKEN aka THE RED SHURIKEN 1965 87 min. **DIR.** Tokuzo Tanaka **SCR.** Hajime Takaiwa/Tatsuo Nogami **PHOTO COLOR 'SCOPE:** Kazuo Miyagawa **MUSIC:** Tetsuo Tsukahara **w/** Raizo Ichikawa, Koji Nanbara, Masumi Harukawa, Chitose Kobayashi, Fujio Suga, Yoshio Yoshida, Isao Yamagata This is not exactly a period yakuza film but the closest you could come to a category. Ichikawa is a leather-clad thief with sword prowess but given to throwing *shurikens* (ninja darts). He is after a cache of gold, along with a whole village of thieves, including the local yakuza clan and roving itinerant cutthroats. One of the most brutal villains is Nanbara whom Ichikawa engages in a stupendous duel at the

climax. This is much spaghetti western ambience – the village looks as if it is perched on the edge of a parched desert, and there are hitching posts for horses in front of every inn/saloon. Action-packed and rewardingly strange. * * * (DAIEI Studios)

BOHACHI BUSHIDO series

BOHACHI BUSHIDO – HISTORICAL PORNO STORY
aka BOHACHI SAMURAI CODE aka BOHACHI BUSHIDO – PORUNO JIDAI-GEKI aka CLAN OF THE FORGOTTEN EIGHT 1973 **DIR.** Teruo Ishii **SCR.** Susumu Saji **PHOTO COLOR 'SCOPE:** Juhei Suzuki **MUSIC:** Hajime Kaburagi **w/** Tetsuro Tanba, Goro Ibuki, Tatsuo Endo, Ruriko Ikejima, Yuriko Hishimi, Rina Ichinose, Ryohei Uchida, Shoki Fukae   A demented, over-the-top adaptation from Kazuo Koike's *manga* about a privileged yakuza clan in charge of recruiting women for prostitution in old Edo's pleasure quarter. Koike's *mangas* of LONE WOLF AND CUB, LADY SNOWBLOOD and especially RAZOR HANZO had already catalogued numerous, imaginatively psychotic tableaus of *grand guignol* violence and aberrant sexuality. *Enfant terrible* Teruo Ishii, already a veteran of a series of period erotic/grotesque films for Toei with such titles as HELL'S TATTOOERS, SHOGUN'S JOY OF TORTURE, ORGIES OF EDO and YAKUZA PUNISHMENT – LYNCH LAW! was a perfect match for this unapologetically decadent, phantasmagorical display of softcore samurai sadism. Despite the absurdly exploitative treatment and blatant

Bohachi Bushido (#1)   (IMAGE © TOEI)

misanthropy (some might narrow it down and call it misogyny, but both genders are severely abused here), Ishii's film is a fascinating, brilliant and amoral travelgue through an ancient subculture obsessed with cruel, violent death and cruel, violent sex. Tanba is a standout as an almost superhuman swordsman employed by the clan to safeguard their sex slave business from the Shogunate and rival gangs. When he goes into action, blood sprays, heads and limbs fly. Tatsuo Endo is the degenerate old powermonger behind the yakuza clan, a near demonic elder with metal teeth. Irredeemably trashy but mesmerizing entertainment. #1 of 2 films * * * (TOEI Studios)

BOHACHI BUSHIDO – THE VILLAIN aka BOHACHI BUSHIDO – SA BURAI 1974 **Dir.** Takashi Harada **Scr.** Sadao Nakajima/Takeo Kaneko **Photo color 'scope:** Shigeru Akatsuka w/ Goro Ibuki, Reiko Ike, Bin Amatsu, Kenji Musumoto, Takuzo Kawatani Young up-and-coming star Ibuki takes over Tanba's role. #2 of 2 films (TOEI Studios)

CHUJI MAKES A NAME FOR HIMSELF aka CHUJI URIDASU 1935 **Dir.** Mansaku Itami **Music:** (SILENT?) w/ Asataro Ichikawa, Ryunosuke Tsukigata, Keiko Takatsu (NIIOKI Studios)

CHUJI'S TRAVEL DIARY aka **CHUJI TABI NIKKI series**

CHUJI'S TRAVEL DIARY – STORY OF KOSHU'S KILLER aka CHUJI TABI NIKKI – KOSHU SATSUJIN HEN aka SWASH-BUCKLING IN KOFU 1927 **Dir.** Daisuke Ito (SILENT) w/ Denjiro Okochi, Haruko Sawamura #1 of 3 films (NIKKATSU Studios)

CHUJI'S TRAVEL DIARY – STORY OF BLOODY SHINSHU aka CHUJI TABI NIKKI – SHIN-SHU KESSHO HEN aka BLOODY LAUGH IN SHINSHU 1927 **Dir.** Daisuke Ito (SILENT) w/ Denjiro Okochi, Hideo Nakamura #2 of 3 films (NIKKATSU Studios)

CHUJI'S TRAVEL DIARY – THE OFFICIAL STORY aka CHUJI TABI NIKKI – GOYO HEN aka CHUJI'S ARREST 1927 **Dir.** Daisuke Ito (SILENT) w/ Denjiro Okochi, Naoe Fushimi #3 and last of series (NIKKATSU Studios)

CHUJI'S TRAVELS aka KUNISADA CHUJI aka CHUJI KUNISADA aka 1935 **Dir.** Sadao Yamanaka (SILENT?) w/ Denjiro Okochi (NIKKATSU Studios)

CHUTARO OF BANBA – LONG-SOUGHT MOTHER aka BANBA NO CHUTARO – MABUTA NO HAHA 1931 72 min. **Orig. story:** Shin Hasegawa **Dir./Scr.** Hiroshi Inagaki **Photo B&W:** Hideo Ishimoto **Music:**(SILENT) w/ Chiezo Kataoka, Isuzu Yamada, Shinpachiro Asaka, Misako Tokiwa, Michisaburo Segawa
One of the first of several film versions of author Hasegawa's famous *matatabi* tale. Kataoka is a young man brought up by foster parents who is determined to find the birth mother

he never knew. He is a *matatabi* wandering the country, financing his travels with money he sometimes wins gambling. In some of the later versions, the first part of the title – CHUTARO OF BANBA – was eliminated, leaving the LONG-SOUGHT MOTHER by itself. This Inagaki interpretation was almost certainly silent (that would help make sense out of why I have not been able to find a music score credit). Most Japanese films were without sound until 1935-'36. (CHIEZO Productions)

CHUTARO OF BANBA – LONG-SOUGHT MOTHER aka BANBA NO CHUTARO – MABUTA NO HAHA 1955 86 min. **ORIG. STORY:** Shin Hasegawa **DIR.** Nobuo Nakagawa **SCR.** Shintaro Mimura **PHOTO B&W:** Kato Okado **MUSIC:** Yasuji Kiyose **w/** Tomisaburo Wakayama, Isuzu Yamada, Hisaya Morishige, Koji Mitsui, Yoko Katsuki   Nakagawa, who later directed the incredible GHOST OF YOTSUYA (1959), HELL (JIGOKU) (1961) and two-out-of-three of the QUICK-DRAW OKATSU (1969) trio, takes a stab at the classic saga. One of Wakayama's first high-profile starring roles. Director Nakagawa was a natural born director; his instinctive shot compositions and use of location landscapes as well as sets flow naturally onto the screen and are always a pleasure to watch. One of the unsung masters of unpretentious storytelling. (SHINTOHO Studios)

COLD-WIND MONJIRO aka KOGARASHI MONJIRO series

Cold Wind Monjiro (IMAGE © TOEI)

COLD WIND MONJIRO aka KOGARASHI MONJIRO 1972 91 min. **DIR.** Sadao Nakajima

ORIG. STORY: Saho Sasazawa SCR.
Takayuki Yamada/Sadao Nakajima
PHOTO COLOR 'SCOPE: Motoya Washio
MUSIC: Chuji Kinoshita w/ Bunta
Sugawara, Kyoko Enami, Goro Ibuki,
Tsunehiko Watase, Asao Koike,
Rinichi Yamamoto, Takuzo Kawatani
Matatabi Monjiro (Sugawara), lives
with his girlfriend (Enami) in a hut
on a cliff overlooking the ocean. She
is terminally depressed (through no
fault of his) and ends up committing
suicide by leaping from the precipice
into the sea. Several of Monjiro's
buddies (Yamamoto, Ibuki, et.al.)
are true cutthroats and would like to
cut his to get the bounty. In any case,
before they can lay a trap for him, the
neighboring volcano erupts. Monjiro
ends up in a boat with these killers as
they escape by sea. There is a great
scene near the end where Monjiro is
attempting to rescue a woman held
by villain Koike. He spits the piece of
straw in his mouth like a dart, blind-
ing Koike in one eye. #1 of 2 films
* * * (TOEI Studios)

**COLD WIND MONJIRO – NONE
OF MY BUSINESS** aka KOGAR-
ASHI MONJIRO – KAKAWARI
GOZANSEN 1972 90 min.
DIR. Sadao Nakajima ORIG. STORY:
Saho Sasazawa SCR. Tatsuo
Nogami PHOTO COLOR 'SCOPE:
Motoya Washio MUSIC: Toshiaki
Tsushima w/ Bunta Sugawara,
Etsuko Ichihara, Kunie Tanaka, Mi-
noru Oki, Rinichi Yamamoto,
Kyosuke Machida, Hiroshi Nawa #2
of 2 films (TOEI Studios)

Cold Wind Monjiro (#2) (IMAGE © TOEI)

CRIMSON BAT aka **MEKURA
NO OICHI** aka **BLIND OICHI**
series

**CRIMSON BAT, BLIND
SWORDSWOMAN** aka STORY
OF BLIND OICHI – WANDERING
RED BIRD aka MEKURA NO

Crimson Bat, Blind Swordswoman (#1)   (IMAGE © SHOCHIKU)

OICHI MONOGATARI – MAKKA-
NA NAGARE DORI 1969 88 min.
DIR. Sadatsugu (Teiji) Matsuda SCR.
Hajime Takaiwa/Ichiro Miyagawa/
Ikuro Suzuki PHOTO COLOR 'SCOPE:
Shintaro Kawasaki MUSIC: Hajime
Kaburagi w/ Yoko Matsuyama,
Chizuko Arai, Isamu Nagato, Bin
Amatsu, Jun Tatara
Matsuyama is Oichi, abandoned as a
child by her mother during a rainstorm and blinded when a tree beside
her is struck by lightning. Adopted by
kindly neighbor Kono, she grows into
young adulthood without incident.
But one day Kono is killed by Devil
Denzo (Amatsu) and his henchmen,
and Oichi is on the verge of being dispatched herself when rescued by wandering samurai Nagato. Nagato trains
her in swordfighting. The two fall-
in-love, but Nagato believes himself
unworthy and leaves without saying
goodbye. Soon after, Oichi rescues
old crook Tatara, a former comrade
of foster dad Kono, who is also being
hunted by Denzo. It seems Denzo
is now respectable and is looking to
eradicate his former crime partners so
there will be no chance of exposure.
Tatara's daughter is indentured as a
whore in a brothel that turns out to be
run by Oichi's long-lost mom. Oichi
wins funds at a local gambling den to
pay off Tatara's daughter's debt, but
Denzo gets back to the brothel first,
killing Tatara and the girl. Oichi is
convinced her guilt-wracked mother
knows who killed them. Nagato appears, explaining that it was Denzo
who murdered the pair and that he is
scheduled to fight Denzo in a nearby
clearing. Oichi asks to go in his place,
and he agrees. She shows up on the
windy plain and, within minutes of
ferocious battle, has slain Denzo.

Nagato watches Oichi's lonely figure
disappear into the distance. Despite
the storyline, this first entry in the
series emerges as less sentimental
in tone than # 3 and 4. However,
compared to the next three, there is
also less fighting here, not as much
location work with more exterior
scenes shot on a soundstage. Director Matsuda was a prominent director
of *jidai-geki* films, including many
matatabi opuses, at Toei Studios during the fifties and sixties and seems
to have been loaned out here for the
first pair of CRIMSON BAT sagas.
Obviously inspired by Daiei Studios'
phenomenally popular ZATOICHI
films, CRIMSON BAT was also a
TV show at the time with episodes
directed by the likes of such experts
as Kazuo Ikehiro and Teruo Ishii. But
I have little additional information on
those productions. All four of these
films are rare. The versions discussed
here are the dubbed-in-English ones
with the dubbing sounding as if it was
done by the same folks who dubbed
many kung-fu pictures. Fortunately
none of these films sink to the level of
dubbing incoherence found in some
sixties and seventies Hong Kong
productions. #1 of 4 films   * * *
(SHOCHIKU Studios)

TRAPPED, THE CRIMSON BAT!
aka MEKURA NO OICHI – JIG-
OKU HADA aka BLIND OICHI
– HELL FLESH 1969 87 min. DIR.
Sadatsugu (Teiji) Matsuda SCR.
Hiro Matsuda/Ikuro Suzuki PHOTO
COLOR 'SCOPE: Shintaro Kawasaki
MUSIC: Hajime Kaburagi w/ Yoko
Matsuyama, Yasunori Irikawa, Kikko
Matsuoka, Jushiro Konoe, Toru Abe,
Ryoichi Tamagawa, Tadao Nakamaru,
Hiroko Ogi

My favorite of the series with several bravura action setpieces, as well as being the most convincing tall tale in character and tone. The pre-title sequence has Oichi, now a seasoned bounty hunter, tangling with an outlaw *ronin* (Nakamaru in a cameo) with a price on his head. After an exciting fight, Oichi kills him and collects the money. There is another female bounty hunter/gambler in the area played by Matsuoka, a sadistic villainess with a whip woven from human hair "from the heads of men who broke women's hearts!" Not a bad sentiment, but otherwise Matsuoka is as wicked as they come. She and Oichi are constantly at odds. Matsuoka also likes to throw poisonous snakes at her opponents when she is losing a fight and leaves Oichi near death from a venomous bite. A young farmer finds her and nurses her back to health. They soon fall in love and actually get married. But local cruel yakuza boss Abe, who is also Matsuoka's brother, is exploiting the farmers. He tries to trick Oichi into killing decent *ronin* Konoe, the farmers' protector. Oichi, however, sees through the subterfuge and leaves her husband to battle with Abe, Matsuoka and their gang. What follows is the most excitingly-choreographed swordfight in the series with Oichi overcoming whipweilding Matsuoka, Abe and various swordsmen. In the last third of the protracted massacre, the lighting abruptly changes. The early morning sun is blotted out as a deep dark blue envelopes everyone. Oichi slashes and tears in slow motion, red spurting in surreal geysers. Then there is a freeze-frame and "The End." Also of note is the excellent traditional score

by the virtually unknown-in-the-U.S. Hajime Kaburagi with the eerie echoing of *shamisens* and *biwas*. #2 of 4 films * * * 1/2 (SHOCHIKU Studios)

Trapped, The Crimson Bat! (#2)
(IMAGE © SHOCHIKU)

WATCH OUT, CRIMSON BAT! aka BLIND OICHI – SWIRLING TRAVEL HATS aka MEKURA NO OICHI – MIDARE GASA 1969 87 min. DIR. Hirokazu Ichimura SCR. Kinya Naoi/Kei Hattori PHOTO COLOR 'SCOPE: Masao Kosugi MUSIC: Takeo Watanabe w/ Yoko Matsuyama, Goro Ibuki, Asahi Kurizuka, Kiyoko Inoue, Jun Hamamura, Rokko Toura, Yoichi Numata   Oichi becomes involved with a couple of scruffy orphans and a *ronin* (Ibuki) trying to recover a scroll of a secret recipe for a newly-invented gunpowder. She falls-in-love with Ibuki, but he is engaged to marry the gunpowder inventor's daughter. Both the inventor and daughter are being held hostage by a clan greedy for the secret formula. Disillusioned Oichi splits only to return when she hears that her beloved has also been captured. She is aided by Kurizuka, a swordsman hired by the clan, who has an attack of conscience. A hokey plot made palatable by Ichimura's non-stop action pyrotechnics. #3 of 4 films * * 1/2 (SHOCHIKU)

Watch Out, Crimson Bat! (#3)
(IMAGE © SHOCHIKU)

CRIMSON BAT – OICHI! WANTED DEAD OR ALIVE aka MEKURA NO OICHI – INOCHI MORAIMASU 1970 86 min. DIR. Hirokazu Ichimura SCR. Koji Takada PHOTO COLOR 'SCOPE: Masao Kosugi MUSIC: Takeo Watanabe w/ Yoko Matsuyama, Yuki Meguro, Tetsuro Tanba, Meicho Soganoya, Reiko Oshida, Jun Tazaki

Oichi is pursued by three desperate bounty hunters: a giant ex-priest, a sickle-and-chain weapons master and an ex-doctor (Meguro). A yakuza boss

(Tazaki) is in league with the local magistrate in trying to drive out the inhabitants of a fishing village so they can construct a lucrative new port. Soganoya, the village elder, and daughter Oshida lead the opposition in town.

Crimson Bat - Oichi! Wanted Dead or Alive (#4) (IMAGE © SHOCHIKU)

Of course, Oichi becomes involved. Before long Meguro, a disenchanted idealist, is moved by Oichi's virtue and strength and turns the tables on his two fellow bounty hunters. Oichi and Meguro then fight the yakuza gang on the town's behalf. At the last minute they are aided by boss Tazaki's *yojinbo* Tanba – who actually turns out to be a government spy bent on rooting out corruption. This is probably the corniest of all four films with the lamest plot contrivances. Still, there is plenty of action, and the film manages to remain entertaining. #4 and final in series * * 1/2 (SHOCHIKU Studios)

Death Shadows (IMAGE © SHOCHIKU)

DEATH SHADOWS aka JITTE-MAI 1986 116 min. **DIR.** Hideo Gosha **ORIG. STORY**: Hideo Gosha/Kotaro Mori **SCR.** Motomu Furuta **PHOTO COLOR PANAVISION**: Fujio Morita **MUSIC**: Masaru Sato w/ Mariko Ishihara, Mari Natsuki, Takuzo Kawatani, Tsunehiko Watase, Naoto Takenaka, Takeo Chii, Eitaro Ozawa, Kiminori Sera   Three thieves are given the choice between execution and working as a secret enforcement, sometimes assassination squad for a corrupt government official (Watase). To keep them in line and to symbolically silence them from ever divulging their function, their vocal cords are cut. One of the thieves (Kawatani) meets and marries a beautiful woman. His courtship and marriage to her has come in a lull in his work as a Death Shadow. A daughter is born, and she is ten or eleven years old when he is called away to constant service as an assassin. He is given no choice by Watase, except to desert them. Many years

later, his wife dead, he runs into his grown-up daughter (Ishihara). She turns out to be trying to foil some dastardly villains herself. At first, she is openly hostile to her returned dad. But when he appears with his Shadow cohorts to rescue her from the evil gang boss, her heart softens. Kawatani snags her from her place hanging above a vat of boiling oil, but is fatally wounded in the process. So, too, are the other Shadows as well as the gang boss. Evil Mari Natsuki, in a most enjoyable performance, takes over the gang (the boss had been her lover). Subsequently Watase recruits Ishihara to replace her father as a spy/killer (although she escapes having her larynx cut). Soon everyone is after a silken kimono cord that has a secret document inside. Another entertaining performance comes from Naoto Takenaka as an over-the-top, psychotic/sex maniac policeman. Much intrigue, swordfights, martial arts, blackmail, tall-tale characters, all involved in the Japanese underworld – yakuza gangs and their vendettas, feuds and coalition arrangements with a corrupt government. Entertaining, but the dubbing on the American version is some of the worst that I have ever heard. The Japanese version works far better with the original voices. Ishihara is the one weak link in the cast; she just does not have the kind of forceful personality or charisma one expects in this kind of genre film. Gosha seems to have been experimenting with a controlled shooting atmosphere since many of the exteriors, daytime/nighttime, were filmed on the stylized sets of a soundstage. * * * (SHOCHIKU Studios)

Escape from Hell (IMAGE © SHOCHIKU)

ESCAPE FROM HELL aka MUSHUKUNIN-BETSUCHO aka WANDERERS' BLACK LIST 1963 **DIR.** Kazuo Hase **SCR.** Hideo Oguni **PHOTO B&W 'SCOPE:** Hiroshi Dowaki **MUSIC:** Masayoshi Ikeda w/ Keiji Sada, Rentaro Mikuni, Mariko Okada, Takahiro Tamura, Ko Nishimura, Junzaburo Ban, Kiyoshi Atsumi   A disgracefully obscure hardboiled masterpiece about a large cortege of prisoners – yakuza criminals, wayward *ronin* and dissidents – being escorted by government samurai through the wilderness. The caravan is broken up by a nightmarish escape attempt that ends in a massive swordfighting melee and massacre. Screenwriter Oguni is a co-writer for some of Akira Kurosawa's greatest works, including SEVEN SAMURAI, THRONE OF BLOOD, THE HIDDEN FORTRESS, THE BAD SLEEP WELL and SANJURO. * * * 1/2 (SHOCHIKU Studios)

ETERNAL KILLER WOMAN aka ONNA SHIKAKU MANJI 1969 **DIR.** Kosaku Yamashita **SCR.** Norifumi Suzuki/Sadao Nakajima/ Michio Fukao w/ Junko Miyazono, Makoto Sato, Masumi Tachibana, Rokko Toura, Yoichi Numata, Toru Abe (TOEI Studios)

Eternal Killer Woman (IMAGE © TOEI)

Flames of Blood (IMAGE © TOHO)

FLAMES OF BLOOD aka HONOO NO GOTOKU 1981 147 min. (TV version approx. 132 min.) **DIR./SCR.** Tai Kato **PHOTO COLOR 'SCOPE VISTAVISION:** Keiji Maruyama **MUSIC:** Hajime Kaburagi w/ Bunta Sugawara, Mitsuko Baisho, Tomisaburo Wakayama, Makoto Sato, Hiroko Sakuramachi, Goro Ibuki, Tetsuro Tanba, Kokichi Takada, Makoto Fujita, Ryutaro Otomo   Sugawara plays a somewhat dim *matatabi* who, on his wanderings, falls-in-love with Orin (Baisho) a blind itinerant, *shamisen* player (I don't know if it is coincidence or tradition, but most female blind *shamisen* players in Japanese literature and film are called Orin). Once they have settled down after a couple of near-death experiences on the road, Sugawara gets into trouble for stupidly building a gambling den in another clan's territory. Orin is accidentally killed, and Sugawara goes on a vengeance quest. However, he gets sidetracked before achieving his goal by a group of yakuza elders led by Wakayama. Time passes and as the second half of the film unspools, the notorious Shinsengumi (Assassin's Group) begins their operations in Kyoto and Edo. The Shinsengumi killed scores of officials and reformers (both just and unjust) and have been featured prominently in dozens of Japanese films and books. They were the perfect example of an initially idealistic band of courageous swordsmen becoming corrupted from within and without by temptations of wealth, power, privilege, an unquenchable thirst for blood and their own inability to adapt their principles to unfolding, ever-changing reality. Sugawara becomes friendly with Sato, one of the commanders and a comparatively decent member of the group. A young samurai in the Shinsengumi tries to keep his fiancee safe from harm but is powerless against his asinine, sex-crazed superior who desires the girl. They run away but are killed outside town. Sugawara, their godfather, attempts revenge but is once again sidetracked when the dramatic destruction of the Shinsengumi occurs. At the very end, amongst fiery ruins of his gang's headquarters – part of the city has

been torched – Sugawara stares into a well. The ghost of Orin appears, a gentle, benevolent spirit to help him transcend the insanity surrounding him. The scenario is quite good and constantly involving. But Sugawara, who I usually consider stupendous, overacts in several stretches creating a slight annoyance factor. Undoubtedly he was reaching for the essence of a character with decent and noble impulses who is, nevertheless, somewhat deficient in intellect. Toshiro Mifune, too, has been guilty of similar excesses in films such as Okamoto's RED LION (1969) and Inagaki's RICKSHAW MAN (1958), both cases – as here – of strong directors reluctant to rein in excellent actors because of either temperament or fear of frustrating the creative process. Other liabilities in production: many scenes photographed by cinematographer Maruyama look flat and poorly lit, as if filmed in a hurry for television. Also the prodigious, usually excellent Kaburagi contributes what has to be one of the worst scores of his career – self-indulgent electric guitar noodling supported by a lackluster rhythm section – more evidence of the dreaded TV influence. A shame because this film had the ingredients of a masterpiece. As it is, it is just a good film with mediocre spots. * * * (DAIWA SHINSHA Productions; released by TOHO Studios)

THE GAMBLING SAMURAI aka KUNISADA CHUJI aka CHUJI KUNISADA 1960 101 min. DIR. Senkichi Taniguchi SCR. Kaneto Shindo PHOTO COLOR 'SCOPE: Rokuro Nishigaki MUSIC: Masaru Sato w/ Toshiro Mifune, Michiyo

Aratama, Eijiro Tono, Daisuke Kato, Yosuke Natsuki, Hisashi Fujiki, Tetsuro Tanba   This is the only film I have seen about Chuji, the famous Robin Hood yakuza boss of Japanese legend. There have been many versions. He also shows up as a supporting character in many other films. It is too bad this one is not better, especially when you consider that Shindo wrote the scenario. What should have been excellent is merely decent. Mifune as Chuji returns to his hometown from several years gambling on the road with his pals. He finds his parents dead, his house in tattered ruins, and his sister insane from being raped by the local magistrate. Benevolent uncle Tono is now the village constable, caught between a rock-and-a-hard-place since his nephew Chuji is a wanted man. It is no surprise that Chuji gets his revenge on the government evildoers in town before the final frame unspools.
* * 1/2 (TOHO Studios)

The Gambling Samurai (IMAGE © TOHO)

GOBLIN SABER aka TENGU TO aka BLOOD END 1969 DIR. Satsuo Yamamoto SCR. Hajime Takaiwa/ Shun Inagaki PHOTO COLOR 'SCOPE:

Chishi Makiura MUSIC: Sei Ikeno w/ Tatsuya Nakadai, Go Kato, Ayako Wakao, Yukiyo Toake, Kichiemon Nakamura   In a role similar to the one he played in Kihachi Okamoto's KILL!, Nakadai is a disillusioned former samurai who has turned to the rootless, *matatabi* yakuza lifestyle. But he is still involved tangentially with his former clan and the Shinsengumi-type political assassins group called Tengu-To. Prodigious bloodshed and tragedy follow in his wake. Unlike Okamoto's equally fine film, this has little humor and has the overpowering feeling of one lone wolf caught up in a struggle against the insanity of the period, much like Yamamoto's earlier, better known first two installments in the NINJA, BAND OF ASSASSINS series with Raizo Ichikawa.   * * * 1/2 (DAIEI Studios)

Goblin Saber aka Blood End
(IMAGE © KADOKAWA PRODUCTIONS)

GOBLIN YUKINOJO or GOBLIN
LADY YUKI aka YUKINOJO
HENGE (SOSHO HEN) 1935
98 min. **DIR.** Teinosuke Kinugasa
SCR. Teinosuke Kinugasa/Daisuke Ito
PHOTO B &W: Kimihira Sugiyama
w/ Kazuo Hasegawa (under his
original name Chojiro Hayashi),
Tokusaburo Arashi, Kensaku Hara
(SHOCHIKU Studios)

GOBLIN YUKINOJO or GOBLIN
LADY YUKI aka YUKINOJO
HENGE 1959 85 min.
DIR. Masahiro Makino **SCR.** Heigo
Suzuki **PHOTO COLOR 'SCOPE:**
Shigeto Miki **MUSIC:** Seiichi Suzuki
w/ Hashizo Okawa, Chikage
Awashima, Keiko Okawa, Eitaro
Shindo (TOEI Studios)

Goblin Yukinojo aka An Actor's Revenge
(IMAGES © KADOKAWA PRODUCTIONS)

GOBLIN YUKINOJO or GOBLIN
LADY YUKI aka YUKINOJO
HENGE aka AN ACTOR'S RE-
VENGE aka **REVENGE OF A
KABUKI ACTOR** 1963 113 min.
DIR. Kon Ichikawa **SCR.** Natto Wada
PHOTO COLOR 'SCOPE: Setsuo

Kobayashi **MUSIC:** Masao Yagi
w/ Kazuo Hasegawa, Fujiko
Yamamoto, Ayako Wakao, Ganjiro
Nakamura, Eiji Funakoshi, Saburo
Date, Raizo Ichikawa, Shintaro Katsu
A beautiful period melodrama
featuring Hasegawa in a dual role
to commemorate his 300th film. He
plays Yukinojo, the *onnagata* (female
impersonator) kabuki actor seeking revenge on the evil Nakamura
who is responsible for his parents'
bankruptcy and subsequent suicides.
He also plays a good-hearted burglar
who helps Yukinojo. Everyone in the
cast is excellent, especially Fujiko
Yamamoto (probably her best role)
as a tough, sensual, wisecracking
pickpocket in love with the burglar,
and Ayako Wakao as Nakamura's
innocent, beautiful daughter who
falls-in-love with Yukinojo. One of
the main story components is
Yukinojo, at first, objectifying Wakao
as a tool for his revenge, then gradually falling-in-love, himself. Saburo
Date, usually relegated to Daiei's bit
parts, excels in a substantial supporting role as one of Nakamura's
venal associates. Ichikawa and Katsu,
Daiei's two biggest male stars, appear
in cameos. Setbound, but, much like
Toho Studios' KWAIDAN (1964)
which was directed by Masaki
Kobayashi, this is an attribute rather
than a liability as Ichikawa uses all
kinds of imaginative lighting set-ups,
color compositions and art direction to create nearly avant-garde
effects. Not specifically a yakuza
story, but has all the elements of the
period yakuza saga – the evil corrupt
merchants, whores and honorable and
dishonorable thieves/ne'er-do-wells
who form the core characters of the
genre. * * * 1/2 (DAIEI Studios)

THE GREAT DUEL aka OGEN-KA 1964 93 min. Dɪʀ. Kosaku Yamashita Scʀ. Akira Murao/ Norifumi Suzuki/Sadao Nakajima Mᴜsɪc: Chuji Kinoshita w/ Hashizo Okawa, Tetsuro Tanba, Yukiyo Toake, Yoshi Kato, Nobuo Kaneko, Ko Nishimura, Choichiro Kawarazaki, Wakabe Irie, Tatsuo Endo
A surprisingly good, gritty tale of insecure young man Okawa swearing allegiance to his sweetheart Toake's father (Kato), a decent yakuza boss, then going off to wander for a couple of years after a gangfight. When he returns with his fighting skills honed and a new sense of self-worth, he finds his gal shacked up with his old friend who is now the village constable. Boss Kato is embittered and disillusioned, and sleazy bosses Kaneko and Endo are gradually usurping control of the town with the help of ruthlessly bloodthirsty *yojinbo* Tanba. At one point, Tanba engineers the kidnapping of Toake, something which sparks his own tortured memories of how his wife was gangraped. Tanba had killed her assailants then slit her throat since she had been sullied by the flesh of other men. This pride and inflexibility had driven him from respectable samurai life into a world of crime and hiring out his sword for easy money. To his initial disgust and chagrin, he gradually begins to identify with Okawa's plight and, during the long, extremely bloody gangfight climax in the village, he helps Okawa wipe out Kaneko, Endo and their men. At the close, when Okawa turns on him, Tanba welcomes the swordthrust to his abdomen with open, grateful arms. The village is once again peaceful. But even with both Toake's father and her consta-ble beau dead, Okawa still cannot reconcile his feelings of revulsion that Toake has been with another man and, stealing one last glance at her before he leaves, he sets off to wander. The regressive sexual politics of the "heroic" male characters are distressing to say the least, but are unhappily true for the story's time period. So, for the viewer, getting beyond that boneheadedness is essential and, in fact, adds to the tragedy of Ozawa and Tanba, the truly fucked-up-from-birth protagonists. Although not quite as great as director Yamashita's other *matatabi* masterpiece, YATAPPE OF SEKI, from around the same time, this still does not deserve its nearly forgotten, underrated status.   * * * 1/2 (TOEI Studios)

The Great Duel (ɪᴍᴀɢᴇ © Toᴇɪ)

HELL'S TATTOOERS aka TOKU-GAWA IREZUMI SHI – SEME JIGOKU akaTOKUGAWA TATTOO STORY – HELL TORTURE aka INFERNO OF TORTURE 1969 90

Hell's Tattooers aka *Inferno of Torture* (IMAGE © TOEI)

min. **DIR.** Teruo Ishii **SCR.** Teruo
Ishii/Masahiro Kakefuda **PHOTO**
COLOR 'SCOPE: Motoya Washio
MUSIC: Masao Yagi **w/** Teruo
Yoshida, Yukie Kagawa, Mieko
Fujimoto, Masumi Tachibana,Haruo
Tanaka, Asao Koike, Reiichi
Hatanaka, Eiji Wakasugi, Junko
Maki, Kamiko Katayama
Two rival tattoo artists, one decent,
one depraved, in love with the same
girl, compete in a corrupt, sadistic
nobleman's tattoo contest against the
backdrop of an illicit trade in tattooed
women sold to degenerate western
merchants. One of the sextette of
"erotic/grotesque" horror action films,
usually set in period that Ishii made
at Toei in the late 1960s. Two of the
other films, LOVE AND CRIME and
YAKUZA PUNISHMENT – LYNCH
LAW also had yakuza story elements
(see the main Toei Studios section
elsewhere in the book). Salaciously
entertaining and deliriously phantasmagorical.   * * *   (TOEI Studios)

HOODLUM PRIEST aka
YAKUZA BOZU series

HOODLUM PRIEST aka
YAKUZA BOZU 1967 84 min.
DIR. Kimiyoshi Yasuda **SCR.** Hajime
Takaiwa **PHOTO COLOR 'SCOPE:**
Fujio Morita **MUSIC:** Yukiaki Sone
w/ Shintaro Katsu, Mayumi Ogawa,
Mikio Narita, Jun Tatara, Naoko
Kubo, Hosei Komatsu   Daiei's
two-film series about a wandering,
gambler priest proficient in judo
and swordplay set in the mid-19th
century. For a similar film series, see
SCOUNDREL PRIEST (GOKUAKU
BOZU) from Toei with Katsu's
brother Tomisaburo Wakayama set at

the turn-of-the-century (see the regular yakuza film listings). Surprisingly
the Toei series is somewhat better
with a more involved choreography
of the action. #1 of 2 films   * * 1/2
(DAIEI Studios)

Hoodlum Priest (#1)
(IMAGE © KADOKAWA PRODUCTIONS)

PRIEST AND THE GOLD MINT
aka ZOKU YAKUZA BOZU aka
RETURN OF THE HOODLUM
PRIEST 1968 80 min. **DIR.**
Kazuo Ikehiro **SCR.** Ryozo
Kasahara/Hisashi Sugiura **PHOTO**
COLOR 'SCOPE: Fujio Morita (I have
also seen Senkichiro Takeda credited
as cinematographer for this entry)
MUSIC: Takeo Watanabe **w/** Shintaro
Katsu, Yukiji Asaoka, Kayo Matsuo,
Taketoshi Naito, Osamu Okawa,
Sonosuke Sawamura, Tatsuo Endo
#2 of 2 films   * * 1/2   (DAIEI
Studios)

Hunter in the Dark (IMAGE © SHOCHIKU)

HUNTER IN THE DARK aka
YAMI NO KARIUDO 1979
137 min. **DIR.** Hideo Gosha **FROM
THE NOVEL BY** Shotaro Ikenami
SCR. Naoto Kitazawa/Takeshi Endo
PHOTO COLOR 'SCOPE: Tadashi Sakai
MUSIC: Masaru Sato **W/** Tatsuya
Nakadai, Yoshio Harada, Ayumi
Ishida, Shinichi "Sonny" Chiba,
Keiko Kishi, Tetsuro Tanba, Tatsuo
Umemiya, Kayo Matsuo, Isao
Natsuyagi, Eijiro Tono, Hideo
Murota, Makoto Fujita, Mikio Narita,
Yoshi Kato, Hajime Hana
An all-star cast in a saga of a chival-
rous, fairly ethical, yet by no means
saintly, yakuza boss Gomyo
(Nakadai) who tries to save the life
of his loyal, amnesiac, one-eyed
bodyguard Tanigawa (Harada).
Tanigawa is actually Heizaburo, a
high-born samurai being victimized
by Samon Shimogumi (Chiba), head
of Edo's secret police and prime minister Tanuma (Tanba), who are trying
to steal Ezo, a huge tract of unspoiled
land that represents Heizaburo's title
and inheritance. In flashback, we
learn that Heizaburo had been blinded
in one eye when he had tried to kill
Shimogumi, but had instead accidentally assassinated his own father
(Kato). Subsequently burned-out
of his rural hiding place and tossed
over a cliff by Shimogumi's men,
he loses his memory. It turns out his
traumatized wife (Ishida), believing
him dead, had tried to kill herself
but was saved by Gomyo. Weak and
frightened, she had allowed herself
to be taken under Gomyo's wing and
had become his lover. Although a
criminal, Gomyo loves the woman so
much and values Heizaburo/
Tanigawa's loyalty (Heizaburo/
Tanigawa having saved his life)
to the point he ends up sacrificing
himself and his gang to reunite them
– as it turns out, in vain. * * * *
(SHOCHIKU Studios)

Inn of Evil (IMAGE © TOHO)

INN OF EVIL aka INOCHI BO NI FURO aka WE GIVE OUR LIVES FOR NOTHING 1971 124 min. **Dir.** Masaki Kobayashi **Scr.** Tomoe Ryu (aka Kyoko Miyazaki) **Photo B&W 'scope:** Kozo Okazaki **Music:** Toru Takemitsu **w/** Tatsuya Nakadai, Shintaro Katsuo, Kei Sato, Komaki Kurihara, Kanemon Nakamura, Shigeru Koyama, Ichiro Nakatani, Shin Kishia, Yosuke Kondo, Shun Makita, Wakako Sakai
Two new samurai police inspectors (Koyama, Nakatani) in a notorious district of Edo are looking for new ways to bring down a den of thieves and smugglers living in a ramshackle inn on a small island mid-river. Nakadai is supposedly one of the most ruthless of the cutthroats, rumored to have murdered his much-loved, long-lost mother upon running into her again and finding her a degraded prostitute. Nakamura is the philosophical inn owner and gang leader. Kurihara is Nakamura's teen daughter, wise-beyond her-years and secretly-in-love with Nakadai. Katsu is a perpetually drunken stranger who the gang first believes may be a spy. But it turns out he is just a man who had left his wife and daughter to make his fortune, only to find them dead when he had returned several years later. One night, a pathetic, beaten young man stumbles into the inn. At first, everyone mocks him. Then, after telling his story of wanting to ransom his beloved who had been sold to a house of prostitution, the gang begins to empathize. Several of them, including Sato and Kishida, relate to the desperate youth's impoverished state and the seemingly random cruelty of fate that has singled the innocent couple out

for destruction. They decide to go through with a dangerous smuggling scheme they suspect is a trap set up by cop Koyama and a two-faced local merchant. Things go downhill from there for the bunch as they go on their mission but are ambushed. Later, the samurai police stage a massive raid on the inn, but the young man, aided by mortally-wounded Nakadai, escapes with money that a drunken Katsu had given him. The next day, melancholic Kurihara watches from a distance as the young man and his ransomed bride return to pay silent homage to the strangers who died for them. An entertaining, well-acted and atmospheric tale. But unlike many of Kobayashi's other films, it is curiously unmoving. It has none of the rigorous relentlessness of Kobayashi's earlier HARA KIRI or SAMURAI REBELLION, nor the audacious, haunting visual poetry of his KWAIDAN. It resembles any one of a number of other good, but not great period pictures Toho Studios made in the late sixties and early seventies. One can only guess that with the shooting schedule shorter, Kobayashi did not have as much control as usual, and perhaps he needed the money.
* * * (TOHO Studios)

ISHIMATSU OF THE FOREST aka MORI NO ISHIMATSU 1949 97 min. **Dir.** Kozaburo Yoshimura **Scr.** Kaneto Shindo **Photo B&W:** Toshio Ubukata **Music:** Hiroshi Yoshisawa **w/** Susumu Fujita, Takashi Shimura, Yukiko Todoroki, Choko Iida, Chishu Ryu, Kyoko Asagiri   Director Yoshimura paints an interesting picture of the famous Ishimatsu character, one of legendary Boss Jirocho's proteges, making him a genius of shameless self-promotion, an inventor of his own legend. This has the reputation of being an excellent film. (SHOCHIKU Studios)

ISHIMATSU OF THE FOREST
aka MORI NO ISHIMATSU 1960
83 min. DIR. Tadashi Sawashima
SCR. Wataru (Kazuyoshi?) Takazawa
PHOTO COLOR 'SCOPE: Takeo Ito
MUSIC: Masao Yoneyama
w/ Hibari Misora, Tomisaburo Wakayama, Denjiro Okochi, Kotaro Satomi, Yoshio Yoshida, Koinosuke Onoe, Kunio Kaga
An extremely uneven melange of the popular legendary hero (played by Misora in male drag), *chanbara*, low comedy, vulgar musical interruptions and manipulative sentimentality. I feel schizophrenic about this film due to the fact Sawashima is a very good director and many times makes the disparate elements coalesce here where another lesser director could not. Still, that does not change the fact there are some extremely annoying bits side-by-side with the tolerable and the just plain wonderful. The late Misora is a revered icon in Japan, someone who is looked upon with almost sacred reverence. Although one can certainly acknowledge her great talent, one cannot ignore her lack of taste in some respects. The vulgarity may be Toei's fault, but one would assume a superstar of Misora's status – even in Japan where many feudal labor practices were/are still in force – would have the clout to change some of the more insipid bits. Especially when working with otherwise discriminating filmmakers such as Sawashima and Eiichi Kudo. It is hard to believe that such talented directors were unaware of the

occasional crassness. If you can suppress your aesthetic sense and better instincts every ten or fifteen minutes, there is much to be enjoyed here between the more florid moments.
* * 1/2 (TOEI Studios)

JIROCHO FILMS AND FILM SERIES

Jirocho is probably one of the most famous characters in Japanese film originating from song and legend – Jirocho is a "benevolent" yakuza boss from the late 19th century and was the subject of numerous successful film series during the fifties and early sixties. The key word here is "benevolent." From what I have read, there were very, very few "benevolent" yakuza bosses anywhere at anytime. However, as in England's Robin Hood legend, as well as countless tall tales about heroes and rogues from America's Old West, that does not really matter. What we are talking about here is the romantic tall tale writ large.

JIROCHO ON MT. FUJI aka JIROCHO FUJI series

JIROCHO ON MT. FUJI aka
JIROCHO FUJI 1959 103 min.
DIR. Kazuo Mori SCR. Fuji Yahiro
PHOTO COLOR 'SCOPE: Shozo Honda
MUSIC: Ichiro Saito w/ Kazuo Hasegawa, Raizo Ichikawa, Machiko Kyo, Ayako Wakao, Shintaro Katsu, Fujiko Yamamoto, Yataro Kurokawa, Jun Negami, Eiji Funakoshi, Joji Tsurumi, Kojiro Hongo, Mieko Kondo, Yoko Uraji, Tamao Nakamura
Hasegawa plays the legendary boss Jirocho. This particular tale relates

Jirocho's flight from police for helping various men under him avenge wrongdoing. Obviously from the cast, this was one of Daiei's big guns at the box office that year. It is inconsequential and occasionally silly, with too much humor. However, unlike Makino's ill-advised but immensely popular Jirocho series at Toei in the early sixties with Kinnosuke Nakamura and, subsequently, Koji Tsuruta, these two films are actually somewhat amusing, largely thanks to a pre-Zatoichi Shintaro Katsu as the one-eyed lone wolf, Ishimatsu. His comic timing as well as the timing and performances of the rest of the cast, director Mori's pacing and writer Yahiro's deliciously old-fashioned scenario, make for mindless, but entertaining escapist fare. Superior to most of the other Jirocho films being made at the time. #1 of 2 films
* * 1/2 (DAIEI Studios)

JIROCHO, THE CHIVALROUS
aka ZOKU JIROCHO FUJI aka RETURN OF JIROCHO ON MT. FUJI 1960 108 min. **DIR.** Kazuo Mori **SCR.** Fuji Yahiro **PHOTO COLOR** 'SCOPE: Yukimasa Makita **MUSIC:** Hiroki Ogawa w/ Kazuo Hasegawa, Raizo Ichikawa, Shintaro Katsu, Kojiro Hongo, Masaya Tsukida, Jun Negami, Tamao Nakamura, Yutaka Nakamura, Joji Tsurumi, Naritoshi Hayashi   A sequel to the above with young man Shichi (Hongo) trying to join Jirocho's clan. Also Jirocho's friend, Ishimatsu (Katsu) is murdered, something unusual since Ishimatsu is one of those immortal characters. Anyway, complications arise between bosses with a magistrate intervening to negotiate peace. There is one boss, Yuzo, who is Jirocho's mortal enemy. He plots secretly with someone called the Black Dragon and a blind samurai Senpachi to kill Jirocho. #2 of 2 films
* * 1/2 (DAIEI Studios)

Jirocho on Mount Fuji
(IMAGE © KADOKAWA PRODUCTIONS)

Jirocho, The Chivalrous (#2)
(IMAGE © KADOKAWA PRODUCTIONS)

BLOODY ACCOUNT OF JIROCHO aka JIROCHO KESSHO KI series

BLOODY ACCOUNT OF JIROCHO – DUEL AT AKIBA aka JIROCHO KESSHO KI – AKIBA NO TAIKETSU 1960 76 min. **DIR.** Eiichi Kudo **SCR.** Michihei Muramatsu **PHOTO COLOR 'SCOPE:** Eiji (Hideji?) Mori **MUSIC:** Ban Takahashi w/ Yataro Kurokawa, Ryuji Shinagawa, Shinobu Chihara, Sentaro Fushimi, Kusuo Abe   When I had initially become aware of this quartet, I had hoped that they would possess the more realistic quality of Kudo's later *jidai-geki* masterpieces, THIRTEEN ASSASSINS, THE GREAT KILL- ING and ELEVEN SAMURAI. But it was too early in his career for that. These still work surprisingly well and are significantly less hokey, silly and sentimental than director Makino's Jirocho films. #1 of 4 films * * 1/2 (TOEI Studios)

BLOODY ACCOUNT OF JIROCHO – MASSACRE JOUR- NEY or JOURNEY TO ATTACK aka JIROCHO KESSHO KI – NA- GURIKOMI DOCHU 1960 75 min. **DIR.** Eiichi Kudo **SCR.** Michihei Muramatsu **PHOTO COLOR 'SCOPE:** Eiji (Hideji?) Mori **MUSIC:** Ban Takahashi w/ Yataro Kurokawa, Ryuji Shinagawa, Hiromi Hanazono, Sentaro Fushimi, Kyonosuke Nango #2 of 4 films (TOEI Studios)

BLOODY ACCOUNT OF JIROCHO – DUEL OF FUJIMI PASS aka JIROCHO KESSHO KI – FUJIMI TOGE NO TAIKETSU 1960 83 min. **DIR.** Eiichi Kudo

SCR. Michihei Muramatsu **PHOTO COLOR 'SCOPE:** Motoya Washio **MUSIC:** Ban Takahashi w/ Yataro Kurokawa, Ryuji Shinagawa, Shinobu Chihara, Jushiro Konoe, Kotaro Bando #3 of 4 films (TOEI Studios)

BLOODY ACCOUNT OF JIROCHO – ATTACK AT KOJIN MOUNTAIN or ATTACK AT KITCHEN – GOD MOUN- TAIN aka JIROCHO KESSHO KI – NAGURIKOMI KOJIN YAMA 1960 84 min. **DIR.** Eiichi Kudo **SCR.** Michihei Muramatsu **PHOTO COLOR 'SCOPE:** Motoya Washio **MUSIC:** Ban Takahashi w/ Yataro Kurokawa, Tomisaburo Wakayama, Kyoko Aoyama, Kusuo Abe, Kichiya Bando #4 and final in series (TOEI Studios)

JIROCHO OF THREE PROV- INCES aka JIROCHO SAN GOKUSHI (TOHO) series

Jirocho of Three Provinces (#2) (IMAGE © TOHO)

JIROCHO OF THREE PROV- INCES – JIROCHO MAKES A NAME FOR HIMSELF aka JIROCHO SAN GOKUSHI – JIROCHO URIDASU 1952 82 min. Dir. Masahiro Makino **SCR.** Toshio

Matsuura **Photo B&W:** Kazuo Yamada **Music:** Seiichi Suzuki w/ Akio Kobori, Setsuko Wakayama, Jun Tazaki, Kenji Mori, Seizaburo Kawazu, Haruo Tanaka The popular series from the fifties with Kobori as Jirocho. A rare bird in that it was a huge success with the critics as well as the general movie-going public. I have not seen any of them. Hopefully they are better than Makino's silly, very dated approach to Jirocho at Toei in the early sixties. #1 of 9 films (TOHO Studios)

JIROCHO OF THREE PROVINCES – EARLY TRAVELS aka JIROCHO SAN GOKUSHI – JIROCHO HATSU TABI 1953 83 min. **Dir.** Masahiro Makino **Scr.** Toshio Matsuura **Photo B&W:** Kazuo Yamada **Music:** Seiichi Suzuki w/ Akio Kobori, Setsuko Wakayama, Seizaburo Kawazu, Jun Tazaki, Kenji Mori, Haruo Tanaka, Kazuo Ishii, Hisaya Morishige #2 of 9 films (TOHO Studios)

JIROCHO OF THREE PROVINCES – JIROCHO AND ISHIMATSU aka JIROCHO SAN GOKUSHI – JIROCHO TO ISHIMATSU 1953 87 min. **Dir.** Masahiro Makino **Scr.** Toshio Matsuura **Photo B&W:** Kazuo Yamada **Music:** Seiichi Suzuki w/ Akio Kobori, Hisaya Morishige, Setsuko Wakayama, Seizaburo Kawazu, Jun Tazaki #3 of 9 films (TOHO Studios)

JIROCHO OF THREE PROVINCES – FULL-HOUSE AT PORT SHIMIZU aka JIROCHO SAN GOKUSHI – SEZOROI SHIMIZU MINATO 1953 80 min. **Dir.**

Masahiro Makino **Scr.** Toshio Matsuura **Photo B&W:** Kazuo Yamada **Music:** Seiichi Suzuki w/ Akio Kobori, Hisaya Morishige, Jun Tazaki, Seizaburo Kawazu, Hiroshi Koizumi, Kenji Mori, Haruo Tanaka, Daisuke Kato #4 of 9 films (TOHO Studios)

JIROCHO OF THREE PROVINCES – ATTACK ON KOSHU ROAD aka JIROCHO SAN GOKUSHI – NAGURIKOMI KOSHUJI 1953 78 min. **Dir.** Masahiro Makino **Scr.** Toshio Matsuura **Photo B&W:** Tadashi Iimura **Music:** Seiichi Suzuki w/ Akio Kobori, Seizaburo Kawazu, Hisaya Morishige, Jun Tazaki #5 of 9 films (TOHO Studios)

JIROCHO OF THREE PROVINCES – WANDERING TRAVELS OF JIROCHO'S CLAN aka JIROCHO SAN GOKUSHI – TABI GARASU JIROCHO IKKA 1953 104 min. **Dir.** Masahiro Makino **Scr.** Toshio Matsuura **Photo B&W:** Tadashi Iimura **Music:** Seiichi Suzuki w/ Akio Kobori, Asami Kuji, Hisaya Morishige, Setsuko Wakayama, Hiroyuki Nagato, Seizaburo Kawazu #6 of 9 films (TOHO Studios)

JIROCHO OF THREE PROVINCES – FIRST CELEBRATION AT PORT SHIMIZU aka JIROCHO SAN GOKUSHI – HATSU IWAI SHIMIZU MINATO 1954 87 min. **Dir.** Masahiro Makino **Scr.** Toshio Matsuura **Photo B&W:** Tadashi Iimura **Music:** Seiichi Suzuki w/ Akio Kobori, Asami Kuji, Hisaya Morishige, Seizaburo Kawazu #7 of 9 films (TOHO Studios)

**JIROCHO OF THREE PROV-
INCES – LONE THUNDER ON
COAST HIGHWAY** aka JIRO-
CHO SAN GOKUSHI – KAIDO
ICHI NO ABARENBO 1954 103
min. DIR. Masahiro Makino SCR.
Saneakira Ogawa/Toshiya Tsukahara
PHOTO B&W: Tadashi Iimura
MUSIC: Seiichi Suzuki w/ Akio
Kobori, Hisaya Morishige, Kyoko
Aoyama, Michitaro Mizushima,
Takashi Shimura, Seizaburo Kawazu
#8 of 9 films (TOHO Studios)

**JIROCHO OF THREE PROV-
INCES – KOJIN MOUNTAIN
– PREQUEL** aka JIROCHO SAN
GOKUSHI – KOJIN YAMA – ZEN
BEN 1954 82 min. DIR. Masahiro
Makino SCR. Shinobu Hashimoto
PHOTO B&W: Kazuo Yamada
MUSIC: Seiichi Suzuki
w/ Akio Kobori, Seizaburo Kawazu,
Jun Tazaki, Masao Wakahara, Mariko
Okada #9 and last of the series
(TOHO Studios)

**JIROCHO OF THREE PROV-
INCES** aka **JIROCHO SAN
GOKUSHI (TOEI) series**

**JIROCHO OF THREE PROV-
INCES – PART ONE** aka
JIROCHO SAN GOKUSHI – DAI
ICHI BU aka KINGDOM OF
JIROCHO 1963 102 min. DIR.
Masahiro Makino SCR. Masahiro
Makino/Tetsuya Yamauchi PHOTO
COLOR 'SCOPE: Shigeto Miki MUSIC:
Seiichi Suzuki w/ Koji Tsuruta,
Yoshiko Sakuma, Hiroki Matsukata,
Shingo Yamashiro, Minoru Oki,
Haruo Tanaka, Masahiko Tsugawa,
Junko Fuji, Makoto Fujita

What with the cast and the subject
matter, I had high hopes for this. But
I was severely disappointed. This is a
loose remake/reworking of Makino's
Jirocho series at Toho Studios from
the mid-fifties. That series was highly
regarded in many critics' circles. But
if it was anything like this, it is a
mystery why. The approach is tongue-
in-cheek light comedy with, at least
in the first installment, a paucity of
action sequences. This epitomizes
everything that I find mediocre and
empty-headed in Toei's late fifties/
early sixties period films – glossy,
cornball entertainments with a
potpourri of story elements and *faux*
emotions. Unfortunately, the comedy
bits are shrill and annoying #1 of 4
films * 1/2 (TOEI Studios)

**JIROCHO OF THREE PROV-
INCES – PART TWO** aka
JIROCHO SAN GOKUSHI – DAI NI
BU aka KINGDOM OF JIROCHO –
PART 2 1963 89 min. DIR. Masahiro
Makino SCR. Masahiro Makino/
Tetsuya Yamauchi PHOTO COLOR
'SCOPE: Shigeto Miki MUSIC: Seiichi
Suzuki w/ Koji Tsuruta, Yoshiko
Sakuma, Shingo Yamashiro,
Hiroyuki Nagato, Satomi Oka,
Masahiko Tsugawa, Hiroki
Matsukata, Jushiro Konoe #2
of 4 films (TOEI Studios)

**JIROCHO OF THREE PROV-
INCES – PART THREE** aka
JIROCHO SAN GOKUSHI – DAI
SAN BU aka KINGDOM OF
JIROCHO – PART 3 1964 94 min.
DIR. Masahiro Makino SCR.
Masahiro Makino/Tetsuya Yamauchi
PHOTO COLOR 'SCOPE: Shigeto Miki
MUSIC: Seiichi Suzuki w/ Koji
Tsuruta, Yoshiko Sakuma, Satomi

Oka, Hiroyuki Nagato, Tatsuo Endo, Masahiko Tsugawa   #3 of 4 films (TOEI Studios)

Jirocho of Three Provinces - Attack on Koshu Road (#4) (IMAGE © TOEI)

JIROCHO OF THREE PROVINCES – ATTACK ON KOSHU ROAD or KOSHU ROAD MASSACRE aka JIROCHO SAN GOKUSHI – KOSHUJI NAGURIKOMI 1965 90 min. **DIR.** Masahiro Makino **SCR.** Masahiro Makino/ Tetsuya Yamauchi **PHOTO COLOR 'SCOPE:** Nagaki Yamagishi **MUSIC:** Shunsuke Kikuchi w/ Koji Tsuruta, Minoru Oki, Shingo Yamashiro, Hiroyuki Nagato, Junko Fuji, Yoshiko Sakuma A remake of the film below, which was released only two years previous? #4 and final in series (TOEI Studios)

JIROCHO AND FIGHTING MEN – ATTACK ON KOSHU ROAD aka JIROCHO TO KOTENGU – NAGURIKOMI KOSHUJI 1962 86 min. **DIR.** Masahiro Makino **SCR.** Masahiro Makino/Shin Dezaki **PHOTO COLOR 'SCOPE:** Sadatsugu Yoshida   w/ Kinnosuke Nakamura, Kinya Kitaoji, Tetsuko Kobayashi, Michitaro Mizushima, Jerry Fujio Once again, I had had high hopes for these both from print ads in the then current editions of film journal Kinema Junpo and film stills, but this is nothing but a potluck stew of audience-pleasing elements. There is plenty of cornball humor and sentiment within young Jirocho's (Nakamura) gang as well as clumsily inserted romance courtesy of lone wolf Kitaoji. Contrived and boring, with the action all too rare. Actually, this should probably be considered as part of the DAYS OF YOUNG JIROCHO series on the next page (even though no Japanese reference books I have seen have made the connection).

* 1/2 (TOEI Studios)
DAYS OF YOUNG JIROCHO aka
WAKA KI HI NO JIROCHO (3rd
TOEI series)

**DAYS OF YOUNG JIROCHO
– BOSS OF TOKAI** aka WAKA
KI HI NO JIROCHO – TOKAI NO
KAOYAKU 1960 88 min. **DIR.**
Masahiro Makino **SCR.** Kazuo
Kasahara/Ryunosuke Kono **PHOTO
COLOR 'SCOPE:** Makoto Tsuboi
MUSIC: Seiichi Suzuki
w/ Kinnosuke Nakamura, Satomi
Oka, Keiko Okawa, Denjiro Okochi,
Ryunosuke Tsukigata, Chiyonosuke
Azuma   From all accounts, this
was touted as close to recovering the
vitality of Makino's silent *chanbara*
as well as his Toho Jirocho series
(1952 –'54). Nakamura plays a young
Jirocho before he became a respected
(and feared?) boss, an aspect of the
character not seen that often before
this series. However, there seems a
great deal of ill-conceived humor and
sentiment in the series, something that
totally ruined the related feature by
Makino, JIROCHO AND FIGHTING
MEN (see above). Be forewarned. #1
of 3 films * * (TOEI Studios)

**DAYS OF YOUNG JIROCHO –
THE YOUNG BOSS ALONE IN
TOKAI** aka WAKA KI HI NO JI-
ROCHO – TOKAI ICHI NO WAKA
OYABUN 1961 94 min. **DIR.**
Masahiro Makino **SCR.** Ryunosuke
Kono **PHOTO COLOR 'SCOPE:** Makoto
Tsuboi **MUSIC:** Ryoichi Hattori
w/ Kinnosuke Nakamura, Michitaro
Mizushima, Satomi Oka, Jerry Fujio,
Noriko Kitaizawa, Nobuko Chihara
Although part of the series, this
installment does not have the series
name on the posters and promo mate-
rials. #2 of 3 films (TOEI Studios)

**DAYS OF YOUNG JIROCHO –
WHIRLWIND OF THE TOKAI
HIGHWAY** aka WAKA KI HI
NO JIROCHO – TOKAIDO NO
TSUMUJI KAZE 1962 89 min.
DIR. Masahiro Makino **SCR.**
Ryunosuke Kono **PHOTO COLOR
'SCOPE:** Makoto Tsuboi **MUSIC:**
Ryoichi Hattori   w/ Kinnosuke
Nakamura, Kiyoshi Atsumi,
Michitaro Mizushima, Satomi Oka,
Minoru Chiaki, Jerry Fujio #3 and
final in series (TOEI Studios)

KILL! aka KIRU aka CUT 1968
115 min. **DIR.** Kihachi Okamoto
SCR. Kihachi Okamoto/Akira
Murao **PHOTO B&W 'SCOPE:**
Rokuro Nishigaki **MUSIC:** Masaru
Sato w/ Tatsuya Nakadai, Etsushi
Takahashi, Yuriko Hoshi, Atsuo
Nakamura, Shigeru Kamiyama, Eijiro
Tono, Tadao Nakamaru, Shin Kishida,
Yoshio Tsuchiya, Akira Kubo

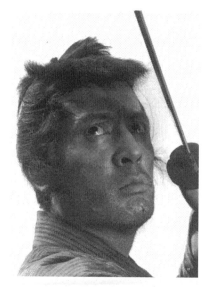

Kill! (IMAGE © TOHO)

敵か味方か凄い奴二人\
血しぶきあげて悪が飛ぶ

Kill! (IMAGE © TOHO)

An immensely entertaining saga of a dispossessed samurai-turned-*matatabi* (Nakadai) wandering into a wind-swept ghost town (the result of a war between samurai and a yakuza gang). He encounters bumpkin swordsman/samurai-wannabe Takahashi, and the two become wary friends, tied together by their impoverished, starving status. The tension and humor is generated by Nakadai's worldy knowledge and contempt for his former, hypocritical samurai comrades and Takahashi's naive belief that becoming a clan samurai is the answer to all his problems. The ending finds the bandaged, sheepishly heroic Nakadai trying to slink off in the rain unnoticed. When he is joined by Takahashi (who has come around to Nakadai's way of thinking), a band of grateful, liberated whores in tow, as well as a beautiful noblewoman who loves Nakadai, the effect is both funny and genuinely moving with-

out any false sentimentality. Greatly enhanced by one of Sato's best scores – an electric guitar-heavy melange certainly reflecting as much spaghetti western ambience as then-current pop sensibility. It is also fascinating to note that, despite Okamoto's apparent ignorance of the genre, there is a syn-chronistic similarity in tone, attitude and style of integrating humor with gritty action that is the Eastern cousin of such Sergio Corbucci Italian west-ern masterpieces as COMPANEROS and THE MERCENARY. * * * * (TOHO Studios)

LADY YAKUZA, FLOWER OF GREAT EDO aka HANA NO O EDO NO YAKUZA HIME 1961 **DIR.** Eiichi Kudo **SCR.** Koji Takada/ Naoji Mizuto **PHOTO COLOR 'SCOPE:** Takeo Ito **MUSIC:** Masao Yoneyama w/ Hibari Misora, Kotaro Satomi, Noriko Kitaizawa, Shoji Yasui, Kunio Kaga, Kusuo Abe   An alternately enjoyable/annoying period yakuza/ *matatabi* adventure/musical. Kudo is great with the action-direction and the general ambience of the period recreation. My one big problem is the same problem I always have with these *jidai-geki* musicals: instead of using period/ethnically-Japanese instruments such as biwas, shamisens, flutes, etc., the main influences for the production numbers are Western pop music/big band instrumentation/ arrangements. I don't know about Japanese audiences, but for me it creates an incredibly jarring, vulgar effect that puts me off all the good qualities of the film – which there are admittedly many. Of course, the storyline and production are all geared towards one thing and one thing only: entertainment. So why

Legend of the Poisonous Seductress (#1) (IMAGE © TOEI)

should I expect high art when the producers were, at that time, melding various saleable elements into one big potluck cinematic stew to attract as many age groups in the audience as possible? These *jidai-geki* musicals, especially Misora's, were very popular for a number of years. Luckily as the sixties progressed, the hackneyed, formula-production numbers and inferior music went out-of-fashion. Also, to make matters worse, the print I saw of this particular film was panned-and-scanned off Japanese TV with at least ten minutes missing.
* *   (TOEI Studios)

LEGEND OF THE POISONOUS SEDUCTRESS aka POISON-OUS STORY OF A BEAUTIFUL WITCH aka YOEN DOKUFU DEN aka QUICK-DRAW OKATSU series

LEGEND OF THE POISONOUS SEDUCTRESS – FEMALE DEMON OHYAKU aka POISONOUS STORY OF A BEAUTIFUL WITCH – ONE HUNDRED PRAYERS OF THE DEMONESS aka OYAKU OF HANNAYA aka YOEN DOKUFUDEN – HANNYA NO OYAKU 1968 90 min. **DIR.** Yoshihiro Ishikawa **SCR.** Koji Takada **PHOTO** B&W 'SCOPE: Nagaki Yamagishi **MUSIC:** Toshiaki Tsuhima   **w/** Junko Miyazono, Tomisaburo Wakayama, Koji Nanbara, Teiji Takano, Hosei Komatsu, Kunio Murai   This series is similar to Daiei Studios' rarely seen WOMAN SAZEN (ONNA SAZEN) (1968) with Michiyo Yasuda. Miyazono portrays a different character in each, a succession of orphaned

young women whose families have been slaughtered or have otherwise perished. She transforms herself into a vengeance-bent wanderer up against all manner of degenerate lords, depraved yakuza bosses, etc.,. The director of this first installment, Ishikawa, was a colleague of director Nobuo Nakagawa (who directed numbers 2 and 3 of the trilogy) at Shintoho Studios in the fifties and served as Nakagawa's assistant director on many of his classic films from that period. In case the reader does not realize, the terms "poisonous" and "witch" used in the series' title are meant to be ironic, viewing Okatsu (named Oyaku here in the first installment) through the eyes of the villains. As a child, Oyaku (Miyazono) survives her mother's suicidal leap into the river but bares a nasty scar on her back. Once an adult, we find her making a living as a con artist and tightrope walker (!). She gets in trouble when she repulses the advances of randy local lord Nanbara. Lone wolf ronin Murai helps her and soon they are lovers. Both get sucked into a scheme by disenfranchised lord Wakayama to steal a cache of gold being transported in the country. However, Wakayama's allies are friends of Nanbara, and they betray the couple after the gold is safely back at the hideout. There is a gory sword battle, Oyaku and wounded Murai are captured, and Nanbara proceeds to persecute both in his torture chamber. Oyaku is strung up by her hair, unhappily the only thing holding the guillotine blade poised over Murai's neck. Eventually, Murai is decapitated, and traumatized Oyaku is shipped off to a prison mine on a remote island. There she is repeatedly accosted by inmates but ferociously manages to hold her own. Soon she concocts a scheme with her former inmate nemesis to escape. She seduces the lesbian tattoo artist who is mistress of jailer Komatsu, getting a hideous demon tattooed on her back. On the night of a violent thunderstorm, Oyaku sets the two against each other, engineering both their demise in a startlingly grue-some, *grand guignol* setpiece. Finally, managing to escape, she infiltrates Nanbara's stronghold, subdues him and subjects him to the same torture he had inflicted on Oyaku and Murai. This first entry is very entertaining and constantly surprising in its hard-edged brutality. It is a real shame director Ishikawa did not direct more films at Toei as he was, like mentor Nakagawa, an expert practitioner of in-period, *ero-guro grand guignol*. #1 of 3 films   * * *   (TOEI Studios)

LEGEND OF THE POISONOUS SEDUCTRESS – QUICK-DRAW OKATSU aka POISONOUS STO-RY OF A BEAUTIFUL WITCH – OKATSU, THE KILLER aka YOEN DOKUFUDEN – HITOKIRI OKATSU 1969 89 min. **DIR.** Nobuo Nakagawa **SCR.** Koji Takada **PHOTO COLOR 'SCOPE:** Masahiko Iimura **MUSIC:** Tomokazu Kawabe w/ Junko Miyazono, Ko Nishimura, Tomisaburo Wakayama, Reiko Oshida, Yukie Kagawa, Kenji Imai, Masaomi Kondo, Yuriko Mishima, Harumi Sone, Nakajiro Tomita Director Nakagawa is, of course, the same Nakagawa who helmed GHOST OF YOTSUYA (1959) and HELL (aka JIGOKU, 1960), as well as many other classic *kaidan* and *chanbara* at Shintoho in the fifties and Toei

in the sixties. This second entry is a rivetingly visceral, action-packed *chanbara* with some often shocking violence and *grand guignol* imagery.

Legend of the Poisonous Seductress (#2)
(IMAGE © TOEI)

Imai is a depraved, sadistic lord oppressing the populace who decides to kidnap and torture feisty Okatsu (Miyazono) when she sticks her nose into his business, namely trying to save her foolish brother who has gotten himself into trouble with the lord. Okatsu's father Nishimura is the respected sword master of the local *dojo* and one of the few samurai revered by the peasants. When he offers to trade himself as hostage in exchange for Okatsu's freedom, he is mercilessly tortured, blinded in one eye then slaughtered in front of his enraged daughter. She breaks loose, secures a sword and starts swinging, decimating many men before being subdued by her father's turncoat second-in-command. She is then sold into prostitution through ragamuffin yakuza Sone, and director Nakagawa uses the brothel to stage an arresting setpiece, using interiors as well as expertly choreographed long shots of the building exterior, the windows and doors thrown wide in the nocturnal summer heat, to depict the bawdy, then chaotically violent action. Okatsu fights her way to freedom, first turning the madam and the madam's randy paramour Sone against each other, then slashing her way through several yakuza henchmen. Not only does she free herself but also her dead brother's sweetheart Kagawa and all the whores. Through the rest of the film she is often abetted by mysterious teenage swordswoman Oshida. During the last third, Okatsu's status as a notorious fugitive attracts the attention of bounty hunter Wakayama (guest-starring as the character he portrays in his BOUNTY HUNTER (SHOKIN KASEGI) films). Wakayama captures her but, before long, is won over to let her complete her bloody vendetta against

lord Imai and her father's betrayer. #2 of 3 films * * * 1/2 (TOEI Studios)

Legend of the Poisonous Seductress (#3)
(IMAGE © TOEI)

LEGEND OF THE POISONOUS SEDUCTRESS – OKATSU, THE FUGITIVE aka POISONOUS STORY OF A BEAUTIFUL WITCH – OKATSU, THE FUGITIVE aka YOEN DOKUFUDEN – OKATSU KYOJOTABI aka VENDETTA OF A SAMURAI GIRL 1969 84 min. DIR. Nobuo Nakagawa SCR. Koji Takada/Hideaki Yamamoto PHOTO COLOR 'SCOPE: Yoshikazu (Giichi) Yamazawa MUSIC: Tomokazu Kawabe w/ Junko Miyazono, Tatsuo Umemiya, Yataro Kitagami, Toru Abe, Reiko Oshida, Yoichi Numata, Hiroshi Nawa, Akitake Kono As already mentioned, each entry in this series is a separate story unto itself with Miyazono a different character in each installment. This final film is a similar story to the second and almost a variation on a theme. Okatsu's father and mother are captured and tortured by the local lord who is in league with avaricious gang boss Abe and cruelty freak, *yojinbo* Numata. When Okatsu tries to rescue her parents, things dissolve into chaos in the lord's subterranean torture lair. She cuts a swath through many villains. When things look bleak for the bad guys, they fatally slash Okatsu's father, who then crawls to his wife's cell to help her commit suicide with a hairpin to the throat. He then finishes himself off in similar fashion before Okatsu's horrified eyes. The lord Abe and *yojinbo* Numata make way for Okatsu's supposedly decent sword teacher Nawa, who promptly disarms her and knocks her unconscious. Eventually, Okatsu escapes with help from former platonic beau Kitagami, who it turns out is motivated by self-interest, hoping she will lead him to an important document belonging to her dead father. Before the tale ends, Okatsu has enlisted the help of local teacher and expert swordsman Umemiya who runs an orphanage at an abandoned temple. Although there is plenty of action all the way through the tale, with a decidedly macabre finale where Okatsu very brutally and cruelly finishes off the evil lord and his mistress as they flail helplessly in a murky bottomless pool, this does not quite reach the heights of the previous entry. However, it should be noted that Miyazono acquits herself very well as an action heroine and deserves to have enjoyed more success as a leading lady instead of being relegated to her countless thankless supporting roles in late sixties, early seventies Toei fare. Nakagawa, draw-

ing on his period horror experience, supplies an arsenal of hellishly grotesque imagery in both of his entries to punctuate Okatsu's descent into the infernal netherworld of sadistic macho violence. #3 and final in series * * * (TOEI Studios)

THE LONE STALKER aka HITORI OKAMI aka ONE WOLF or LONE WOLF 1968 83 min. **DIR.** Kazuo Ikehiro **SCR.** Kinya Naoi **PHOTO COLOR 'SCOPE:** Hiroshi Imai **MUSIC:** Takeo Watanabe w/ Raizo Ichikawa, Isamu Nagato, Mayumi Ogawa, Asao Koike, Akio Hasegawa, Kaneko Iwazaki, Ryutaro Gomi, Asao Uchida   An excellent example of the *matatabi* film. It ranks up there with the KYOSHIRO NEMURI, SON OF BLACK MASS aka SLEEPY EYES OF DEATH) (1963 –'69) and NINJA, BAND OF ASSASSINS (1962 –'66) series as one of actor Ichikawa's all-time best efforts. Per usual, director Ikehiro displays a surfeit of youthful, kinetic energy that is applied equally to direction of actors, camera movement and editing. Beautiful photography by Imai captures beautiful exteriors in different seasons, and there is classic storytelling with flashback vignettes within flashbacks that is reminiscent of a cross between early Sergio Leone and Randolph Scott-era Budd Boetticher. Economic, pared-to-the-bone, but still full of passionate emotion. The beautiful images of nature are not an end in themselves but a moving backdrop of contrast to one chivalrous individual's descent from naive-young-man-in-love to tragic-vengeance-bent-wanderer. A descent precipitated by the subtlest of class barriers and a father/mother steadfast in determining who will be their daughter's husband. Fascinating that the spaghetti western ambience is a definite result of Ikehiro's taste for Italian cinema. Asked about this in an interview, he asserted that films such as DJANGO (as well as the Bond films) had a definite influence on his action movies in the mid-to-late sixties. * * * * (DAIEI Studios)

LONE WANDERER aka MUSHUKU MONO 1964 88 min. DIR. Kenji Misumi SCR. Seiji Hoshikawa PHOTO COLOR 'SCOPE: Chishi Makiura MUSIC: Sei Ikeno w/ Raizo Ichikawa, Jun Fujimaki, Eiko Taki, Sonosuke Sawamura, Mikiko Tsubouchi, Kenjiro Ishiyama, Koichi Mizuhara An audacious and gutsy piece for the period (as far as Daiei Studios goes), with a truly sweltering atmosphere of rural summer along the seacoast. Ichikawa and Fujimaki are *matatabi* rivals forced to work together under an uneasy truce. Ichikawa carries a red sword scabbard that was taken from a samurai that his sociopathic father murdered, and it acts as a visual catalyst for some delirious flashbacks. Ichikawa finally confronts his yakuza *oyabun* parent (Ishiyama) at the climax, fighting a duel to the death on a rocky ocean shore. Misumi also used cinematographer Makiura on the four out of six LONE WOLF AND CUB films (1972 –'73) that he directed, and one cannot help but notice that this is a striking dry-run precursor to the visual brilliance of that series. * * * (DAIEI Studios)

Lone Wanderer (IMAGE © KADOKAWA)

LONG-SOUGHT MOTHER aka MABUTA NO HAHA 1938 84 min. DIR. Katsuhiko Kondo ORIG. STORY: Shin Hasegawa SCR. Makoto Takei PHOTO B&W: Takeo Ito MUSIC: Nobuhiro (Shinhiro?) Matsudaira w/ Kazuo Hasegawa,

Nobuko Satsuki, Noboru Kiritachi, Jushiro Kobayashi, Akira Kishii (TOHO Studios)

LONG-SOUGHT MOTHER aka MABUTA NO HAHA 1962 97 min. **DIR./SCR.** Tai Kato **ORIG. STORY:** Shin Hasegawa **PHOTO COLOR 'SCOPE:** Makoto Tsuboi **w/** Kinnosuke Nakamura, Hiroki Matsukata, Keiko Okawa, Hitomi Nakahara, Chieko Naniwa, Shizue Natsukawa, Michiyo Kogure, Sadako Sawamura, Juro Hoshi, Isao Yamagata   A critically-acclaimed version of yet another story penned by Shin Hasegawa that has been remade many times. Kato reportedly took this project on at the spur of the moment with a truly breakneck schedule. Rather than skimp on coverage, he spent a small bit of time on intensive rehearsal of his cast, then photographed many scenes with long takes and a roving camera – as well as an expertly-super-vised second-unit – to minimize the need for cutting later. A daring *tour-de-force* in many respects – especially if looked at in comparison to many other similar Toei pictures from the early sixties. Although having many of the stock tearjerking elements of a somewhat maudlin scenario, Kato resorts as little as possible to senti-mental cliches. This has a similar, not quite as intense emotional impact to director Kosaku Yamashita's YAT-APPE OF SEKI from the very next year (1963).   * * *   (TOEI Studios)

LONG SWORDS OF THE LOYAL FORTY-SEVEN aka NAGADOSU CHUSHINGURA 1962 97 min. **DIR.** Kunio Watanabe **SCR.** Fuji Yahiro/Kunio Watanabe **PHOTO COLOR 'SCOPE:** Takashi Watanabe

MUSIC: Kuhiro Fukunaga   **w/** Raizo Ichikawa, Ken Utsui, Katsuhiko Kobayashi, Shiho Fujimura, Shintaro Katsu, Kojiro Hongo, Keiko Awaji, Michiko Ai, Shogo Shimada, Hiroshi Nawa, Shigeru Amachi   A *matatabi* version of the CHUSHINGURA saga and an all-star period yakuza romp *ala* some similar all-star bashes being shot at Toei Studios during the same time period. Utsui is a young *oyabun* who saves a child in the path of a maniacal *daimyo* (Nawa)'s horse. He gets whipped for his trouble, then a death sentence. Ichkawa, Utsui's second-in-command, is gone on a trip and returns after Utsui's execution.

Long Swords of the Loyal 47
(IMAGE © KADOKAWA PRODUCTIONS)

With his men, he immediately makes pilgrimages to various yakuza clans in the nearby provinces, hoping to achieve solidarity and get help to overthrow the government nutcase. But, as one might expect, assistance is not forthcoming. Luckily it is the mid-1860s and sympathy for the Shogunate's appointees is at an all-time low. Anti-Shogunate troops are also making huge inroads in winning battles. Finally, Ichikawa musters enough forces to attack Nawa's stronghold. They manage to completely wipe out all of his soldiers. Anti-Shogunate fighters (led by Hongo) arrive just as the battle ends, and they praise Ichikawa's men for doing the job they meant to do. Entertaining, despite the occasional hokum and obvious gimmicks. Surprisingly enough, considering reputedly conservative Watanabe at the helm, the film is full of strong women's roles, particularly Ichikawa's worldly ally who even judo throws a couple of Nawa's men and holds more at bay with a flintlock pistol. * * * (DAIEI Studios)

MOON WANDERER aka TSUKI NO WATARIDORI 1951 83 min. **Dir./Scr.** Teinosuke Kinugasa **Orig. story:** Shin Hasegawa **Photo B&W:** Kimihei Sugiyama **Music:** Goro Nishi **w/** Kazuo Hasegawa, Nobuko Otowa, Yataro Kurokawa, Ryosuke Kagawa, Kunitaro Sawamura (DAIEI Studios)

MORNING MIST ROAD aka ASAGIRI KAIDO 1961 83 min. **Dir.** Tai Kato **Scr.** Heigo Suzuki **B&W 'scope:** Motoya Washio **Music:** Ban Takahashi **w/** Koji Takada, Michiyo Kogure, Keiko Ogimachi, Noriko Kitamura, Shingo Yamashiro, Ryuzaburo Nakamura, Kotaro Bando   If ever there was proof that Tai Kato was a great director, this is it, with the assertive hands-on filmmaker using his rigorously modern visual style and skill with ac-

tors to triumph over a totally routine *matatabi* story. Indeed, star Takada had assayed a number of moderately popular roles all through the 1950s in a variety of wandering gambler pot-boilers, usually punctuated with song, at various studios, including Shochiku and Toei. But his charisma was negligible. Not surprisingly, Kato extracts previously unexplored depths in the actor's persona. Likewise, actress Kogure (who was an accomplished performer), portraying a restaurant manager with a tragic past, delivers one of her finest performances. Wanted fugitive, *matatabi* Takada, returns to his fishing village after many years, having to deal with his sister (Kitamura), his lost love (Ogimachi, now wed to ineffectual Nakamura), conflicted new friend Kogure (who falls in love with him by the end, to sad result) and the out-of-control yakuza gang victimizing the people. All through this he knows a samurai cop (Bando) is hard on his trail. Although Suzuki's script occasionally falls into hackneyed formula and Takahashi's decent score frequently is old-fashioned, Kato's direction and Washio's beautiful B&W scope have the power to make one think they are watching a film shot in the late 1960s, rather than the beginning of the decade. * * * (TOEI Studios)

A QUICK AND CHIVALROUS RAVEN aka NINKYO KISO GARASU 1965 89 min. **Dir.** Eiichi Kudo **Scr.** Yoshitake Hisa **Photo color 'scope:** Shin Furuya **Music:** Seiichi Suzuki **w/** Hashizo Okawa, Satomi Oka, Ryohei Uchida, Ryutaro Otomo, Bin Amatsu, Sentaro Fushimi   Although accomplished director Kudo tries mightily, keeping sentiment to a minimum, there is not much he can do with this by-the-numbers tale of naive, respected samurai clan member Okawa turning into an embittered but chivalrous *matatabi* after being framed for theft by evil lord Endo and gang boss Amatsu. Lo and behold, they are also trying to victimize geisha Oka who Okawa becomes obsessed with saving. Otomo and Uchida are irreverent, rulebreaking undercover police agents who try to help Okawa along the way. Unfortunately, most of the story is just treading water until the well-choreographed big gang swordfight at the climax. * * 1/2 (TOEI Studios)

Quick-Draw Raven (IMAGE © KADOKAWA)

QUICK-DRAW RAVEN aka NUKI UCHI GARASU 1962 DIR. Bin Kado SCR. Teinosuke Kinugasa/Minoru Inuzuka PHOTO B&W 'SCOPE: Shozo Honda MUSIC: Ban Takahashi w/ Tomisaburo Wakayama (pka Kenzaburo Jo), Shigeru Amachi,

Junichiro Narita, Ryuzo Shimada, Mieko Kondo, Chitose Maki (DAIEI Studios)

RAT KID JIROKICHI aka NEZUMI KOSO JIROKICHI 1933 DIR. /SCR. Sadao Yamanaka PHOTO B&W: Seitaro Yoshida MUSIC: (SILENT) w/ Denjiro Okochi, Chiyoko Ogura (NIKKATSU Studios)

RAT KID JIROKICHI aka NEZUMI KOSO JIROKICHI 1965 76 min. DIR. Kenji Misumi SCR. Kaneto Shindo PHOTO COLOR 'SCOPE: Chishi Makiura MUSIC: Hajime Kaburagi w/ Yoichi Hayashi, Michiko Sugata, Machiko Hasegawa, Shiho Fujimura, Masako Myojo, Fujio Suga, Takashi Kanda, Takao Ito, Jotaro Senba, Tatsuo Endo One of many versions of the saga of famous thief, Rat Kid Jirokichi, notorious denizen of the Edo underworld. (DAIEI Studios)

RAT KID'S JOURNEY aka NEZUMI KOSO TABI MAKURA 1931 DIR./SCR. Daisuke Ito (SILENT) w/ Denjiro Okochi, Ryuzaburo Mitsuoka (NIKKATSU Studios)

SAMURAI GAMBLER aka BAKUTO ZAMURAI 1964 93 min. DIR. Kazuo Mori SCR. Hajime Takaiwa/Atsushi Takeda PHOTO B&W 'SCOPE: Hiroshi Imai MUSIC: Tetsuo Tsukahara w/ Raizo Ichikawa, Kojiro Hongo, Mikiko Tsubouchi, Shinsuke Ashida, Takao Ito, Kenjiro Uemura Ichikawa and Hongo are pals in boss Kagawa's clan who have to watch as their leader is carted off to the hoosegow by a corrupt magistrate.

The official proposes he will release Kagawa if Ichikawa and Hongo deliver a rival boss. The pair do snare the enemy yakuza, but the magistrate reneges on his deal, then bids his men kill Ichikawa, Hongo and the rest of Kagawa's gang. The boys flee and, for a while, Ichikawa works for a benevolent money changer in a port town that is rife with greedy foreign traders. When Hongo shows up, the two comrades run afoul of one particularly nasty foreigner and are jailed. Soon afterwards, Ichikawa and Hongo are recruited by middle-aged samurai Ashida into his band of Shinsengumi-like political assassins. Despite the two friends believing in Ashida and his cause, they depart after generating friction with Ashida's arrogant, bullying partner. The two young men decide to rob the rich foreigner that previously got them in trouble and then donate their take to Ashida to help fund his movement. Re-enter the corrupt magistrate who is abusing the local people. When Hongo loses his temper, killing the cruel official, he flees to Ashida's headquarters. But, to Ichikawa's chagrin inside, Ashida refuses to open the door for Hongo, and police sharpshooters corner him outside, mowing him down. This final craven act of political expediency opens a permanent rift between angry Ichikawa and Ashida. Ichikawa splits, but Ashida realizes he cannot leave bitter Ichikawa alive and sends his swordsmen after him. Cornered several blocks away, Ichikawa fights off his attackers, killing all except for the one young swordsman who had befriended him. He stumbles off, severely wounded. This is a great, cynical story depicting multi-layers of

duplicity coming from both obvious and unexpected quarters. There is also Mori's usual assured direction, Ichikawa et .al. giving white-hot performances. However, somehow it all just does not quite come completely together. It is unclear if the film's shooting schedule was too hurried or if perhaps there were other problems, but the film remains curiously unmoving. It is too bad, because this had the potential of four-star status in the league of Tai Kato's non-yakuza CRUEL STORY OF THE SHOGUNATE'S DOWNFALL (BAKUMATSU ZANKOKU MONOGATARI) if only a little more time had been spent on the script, schedule and planning. * * * (DAIEI Studios)

Samurai Gambler (IMAGE © KADOKAWA)

SAMURAI WOLF aka KIBA OKAMINOSUKE series

SAMURAI WOLF aka KIBA OKAMINOSUKE 1966 74 min.

DIR. Hideo Gosha SCR. Kei Tasaka
PHOTO B&W 'SCOPE: Sadatsugu
Yoshida MUSIC: Toshiaki Tsushima
w/ Isao Natsuyagi, Ryohei Uchida,
Junko Miyazono, Tatsuo Endo,
Misako Tominaga, Junkichi Orimoto,
Yoshiro Aoki

Samurai Wolf (#1) (IMAGE © TOEI)

An exhilarating straightforward,
action-packed, poignant and unpretentious saga of scruffy drifter and
expert swordsman Kiba Okaminosuke
(Natsuyagi). He becomes involved
with courier service boss, blind
Miyazono and her attempt to keep her
business out of the hands of yakuza
gutter rats led by Endo. Uchida is the
bitter, cold-blooded samurai-for-hire
who not only has it in for Natsuyagi
but turns out to be Miyazono's long
lost spouse. Everyone in the cast is
stupendous, especially Natsuyagi and
Uchida. Gosha blends a down-in-the-
dirt realism with a spaghetti western-
style tall tale ambience and some of
the most blistering cinematic swordfights you will ever see. Amazing

and on par with Gosha's other early
masterpieces, THREE OUTLAW
SAMURAI and SWORD OF THE
BEAST.   #1 of 2   * * * *
(TOEI Studios)

SAMURAI WOLF – HELL CUT
aka KIBA OKAMINOSUKE –
JIGOKU GIRI 1967 72 min.
DIR. Hideo Gosha SCR. Norifumi
Suzuki/Yasuko Ono/Kei Tasaka
PHOTO B&W 'SCOPE: Sadatsugu
Yoshida MUSIC: Toshiaki Tsushima
w/ Isao Natsuyagi, Ko Nishimura,
Ineko Arima, Ichiro Nakatani, Bin
Amatsu An exceptionally grueling
follow-up to the first film, with
Gosha delving a bit more into Kiba's
(Natsuyagi) background. When
Kiba helps a contingent of samurai
police with his sword prowess fight
off a gang trying to assassinate their
prisoners (Nishimura et. al.), he gets
offered the job of helping guard
them overnight at a rain-drenched
temple. Since Kiba champions the
underdog (and since Nishimura also
resembles his long-dead father who
was murdered by samurai), he leaves
Nishimura with some scissors to help
him escape. This fateful act creates a
snowball of violence that grows ever-
larger and more wildly dangerous as
the saga progresses. It turns out ruthless Nishimura knows about a gang
of illegal gold-miners working an
abandoned Shogunate mine, and their
boss (Amatsu) and his sociopathic
gang are out to kill Nishimura before
he can spill the beans. As scores
are left dead, Kiba gets sucked into
the struggle when he realizes gold-
mining boss Amatsu's daughter is
the sweet, mentally deficient woman
he had rescued from samurai sword
students in the opening scene.

Samurai Wolf - Hell Cut (#2) (IMAGE © TOEI)

Gosha has seemingly even less money and access to locations than in the first low budget entry, but he makes the most of his starkly barren locations. Similarly, cinematographer Yoshida delivers more crisp and beautiful black-and white scope compositions, quite possibly some of the finest in his long career at Toei. Relentlessly gutsy and exciting, the viewer is left spent and wrung dry by the nerve-wracking climax. Highly recommended. * * * * #2 of 2 (TOEI Studios)

Scar Yosaburo (IMAGE © KADOKAWA)

SCAR YOSABURO aka KIRARE YOSABURO 1960 94 min. **Dir./Scr.** Daisuke Ito **Photo color 'scope:** Kazuo Miyagawa **Music:** Ichiro Saito **w/** Raizo Ichikawa, Keiko Awaji, Manami Fuji, Tamao Nakamura, Reiko Fujiwara, Jun Tatara, Eitaro Ozawa, Ryosuke Kagawa   Yosaburo (Ichikawa), an actor in a theater troupe, falls in love with the mistress (Awaji) of a yakuza boss. One stormy night they are caught trying to run away. The gangsters hang Yosaburo by his wrists and take turns cutting him all over, a process which leaves him with scars on face and body. He is left for dead,

but is found by another theater troupe traveling along the river. A young actress (Nakamura) takes him under her wing. However, it is not long before she betrays Yosaburo in a fit of hysterics while being threatened by a bunch of yakuza. Yosaburo, who is standing right there and can't believe his ears, draws a sword and angrily cuts down his enemies. During the extremely exciting swordfight, Yosaburo holds his own and attempts to get a clear path for his blade to kill traitor Nakamura. Just as he is about to flee outside, he stabs the form behind a curtain and Nakamura screams, falling dead. Yosaburo continues to wander, enlisting the help of Tatara, a thief with a bat tattooed on his face. Soon he realizes true love with Fuji, his estranged stepsister, a very young noblewoman being victimized by villains. They escape together with both police and gang in hot pursuit. In the misty moonlight, they find refuge in a shack on the river shore. Yosaburo knows it is hopeless if she sticks with him. Wishing to spare her probable execution when found, he ties her up to make it look like she has been kidnapped by him. He does not know it, but she has hidden a razor in her kimono. She manages to slip it out and cut her bonds. Pledging her undying love, she impetuously plunges the blade into her jugular before the startled, departing Yosaburo can make the leap across the room. He lifts her lifeless form into his arms and begins to walk into the water. The moon hangs high above them and the muffled cries of the approaching pursuers can be heard closing in. An extremely romantic and beautiful tale – once more from kabuki origins – about an unsung hero, not

perfect, but someone who believes
in romantic love, and his travails just
trying to find a comparatively small
bit of peace in an evil, chaotic world.
Ichikawa is perfect as Yosaburo, and
this is one of his best films (out of
many excellent pictures). Master filmmaker Ito also turns out one of his
finest achievements from the fifties;
he manages to mix genres, treading
the narrow path between love story
and *chanbara* , keeping his balance
without overemphasizing either side.
* * * 1/2   (DAIEI Studios)

Seven Miles to Nakayama
(IMAGE © KADOKAWA PRODUCTIONS)

SEVEN MILES TO NAKAYAMA
aka NAKAYAMA SHICHI RI aka
THE ONE AND ONLY GIRL I
EVER LOVED aka IN A RING OF
MOUNTAINS 1962 86 min. **DIR.**
Kazuo Ikehiro **ORIG. STORY:** Shin
Hasegawa **SCR.** Ikuo Uno/Masaharu
Matsumura **PHOTO B&W 'SCOPE:**
Senkichiro Takeda **MUSIC:** Tetsuo
Tsukahara   w/ Raizo Ichikawa,

Tamao Nakamura, Koichi Ose, Ko
Sugita, Nakajiro Tomita, Sonosuke
Sawamura, Eijiro Tono, Hisako
Takibana, Saburo Date   Ichikawa is
a worker in a yakuza clan's lumberyard. One night he flees a gambling
den being raided by corrupt police.
To appear inconspicuous, he falls
in step next to a beautiful woman
(Nakamura) strolling home. She goes
along with the ruse when the cops run
by. They fall-in-love and get married.
She keeps her job as a waitress in the
local inn but ends up getting raped
by the evil magistrate. Unable to live
with the "shame," she immediately
kills herself. Ichikawa avenges her by
killing the official. Then, inconsolable, he takes to the road to wander.
A couple of years later, he comes out
of a gambling den and sees a woman
faint after being harassed by local
hooligans. When he helps her up,
he is stunned to see a dead ringer of
his late wife. He helps the girl (also
played by Nakamura) back to her
house and puts her to bed. It turns out
that she has no twins, not even any
sisters. He is mystified. Just then her
husband (Ose) arrives home, an immature fellow Ichikawa had sat next
to in the gambling hall. The man had
lost all of his money, and the yakuza
clan had insisted on obtaining his
wife in lieu of payment on his losses.
Ichikawa helps them escape the clan.
On the run, Nakamura eventually
falls-in-love with Ichikawa. He makes
it plain that he is still in-love with his
dead wife, not her. Nevertheless, friction develops between the husband
and Ichikawa. The villains catch
up to them, and, in a set-piece very
similar to the climax of Ichikawa's
TOKIJIRO KUTSUKAKE, Ichikawa
dispatches all the bad guys with nary

a scratch. He then goes on his way, leaving the couple to sort out their life. * * * (DAIEI Studios)

SLEEPING WITH A LONG SWORD aka DAKINE NO NAGADOSU 1932 **DIR.** Sadao Yamanaka (SILENT) **w/** Kanjuro Arashi, Tsukishi Matsuura (KANJURO Productions)

THE SPIDER TATTOO aka IREZUMI aka TATTOO 1966 85 min. **DIR.** Yasuzo Masumura **ORIG. STORY:** Junichiro Tanizaki **SCR.** Kaneto Shindo **PHOTO COLOR 'SCOPE:** Kazuo Miyagawa **MUSIC:** Hajime Kaburagi **w/** Ayako Wakao, Akio Hasegawa, Kei Sato, Gaku (Jun?) Yamamoto, Fujio Suga, Reiko Fujiwara, Asao Uchida

The Spider Tattoo (IMAGE © KADOKAWA)

An erotic thriller loosely-derived from the Tanizaki tale of the same name. An eloping couple are aided by a husband and wife who own an inn/gambling den. But the young lovers are betrayed - the girl Otsuya (Wakao) is sold into prostitution and her beau Shinsuke (Hasegawa) is carted away by an assassin to be murdered. Shinsuke turns the tables, slaying his captor and then going into hiding. But Otsuya is totally disillusioned. Her dreams and ideals destroyed, and not yet knowing that Shinsuke has escaped, she is transformed into a sexually voracious and vindictive destroyer of nearly every male that falls into her bed. A famous tattoo artist has gotten the brothel owner to let him create his masterpiece on Otsuya's gorgeous back. Otsuya later claims that the rendering of a black widow spider with a woman's head on her luscious epidermis is to blame for her drastic change from sweet young girl to murderess. Shinsuke reveals himself to Otsuya, and she promises to hide him. However, she has also promised yakuza Gonji, the gambling den owner, that she would marry him once he has killed his wife. When Otsuya backpedals on Gonji, refusing to go through with the union, he becomes abusive, and Shinsuke slays him to protect her. Tokubei, the brothel owner and Otsuya plan to blackmail lecherous Lord Serizawa (Sato), but the scheme backfires. Tokubei is seriously wounded by Serizawa. Once they have escaped, Otsuya decides to finish off Tokubei, and Shinsuke is forced to help. Shinsuke is tortured by Otsuya's changed character. Serizawa pursues her, and she ends up falling-in-love with the lord, much to Shinsuke's jealous consternation. When Shinsuke tries to kill her, she manages to deflect the blade and stab him instead. The tattoo artist Sekichi, who has witnessed these depraved events from the sidelines, asks Otsuya to show him her tattoo one last time before she returns to Serizawa. He then drives a knife into the tattoo, killing her, then kills himself. Masumura shows the corruption and degradation of women when exploited by men, revealing a transformation that must grow from the seeds (anger, resentment, revenge, etc.) already potentially within, but that these could not be cultivated without the fertile soil of a decadent, exploitive, hypocritical and cruel society. * * *   (DAIEI Studios)

TALES OF SURUGA YAKUZA aka SURUGA YUKYODEN aka SURUGA CHVALRY series

Tales of Suruga Yakuza - Gambling Storm (#1) (IMAGE © KADOKAWA)

TALES OF SURUGA YAKUZA – GAMBLING STORM aka SURUGA YUKYODEN – TOBA ARASHI aka STORY OF SURUGA CHIVALRY 1964 90 min. DIR. Kazuo Mori ORIG, STORY: Kan Shimozawa SCR. Kaneto Shindo PHOTO COLOR 'SCOPE: Hiroshi Imai MUSIC: Tetsuo Tsukahara w/ Shintaro Katsu, Shiho Fujimura, Michiko Saga, Shigeru Amachi, Eitaro Shindo   Yet another

take on the Jirocho mythos as Katsu portrays the legendary boss as a precocious, wandering young gambler getting into scrapes and living on the road by his wits with his cowardly nervous wreck of a friend.

Tales of Suruga Yakuza - Gambling Storm (#1) (IMAGE © KADOKAWA)

Over the course of the three films, Katsu's Jirocho gradually evolves into a respected, fairly benevolent yakuza boss. Although the trilogy is definitely in the tongue-in-cheek mold of many other Jirocho films, the humor here is much more natural and balanced, stemming from the genuine personalities of the characters. Unlike the often clumsily inserted comedy, formulaic subplots and manipulative sentimentality employed in many of Toei's Jirocho films (particularly those directed by Masahiro Makino), director Mori and screenwriter Shindo integrate all elements in effortless fashion without anything ever feeling forced or contrived. This is not an especially trailblazing, pyrotechnic action film. But Mori and Shindo's work, coupled with Imai's beautiful cinematography and the imaginative use of Daiei's familiar rural locations, as well as Katsu's performance, helps this first entry often attain a poetic, wistful quality and a simultaneously charming bawdiness that is all too missing in more recent Japanese period films. #1 of 3 films   * * * (DAIEI Studios)

TALES OF SURUGA YAKUZA – BROKEN SWORDS aka SURUGA YUKYODEN – YABURE TEKKA 1964 **Dir.** Tokuzo Tanaka **Orig. Story:** Kan Shimozawa **Scr.** Hajime Takaiwa **Photo color 'scope:** Kazuo Miyagawa **Music:** Akira Ifukube   **w/** Shintaro Katsu, Kazuko Fujiyoshi, Hiroshi Mizuhara, Karo Otsuji, Ryutaro Gomi, Reisaburo Yamamoto   Somewhat uneven, with this entry a bit more obvious in the comedy department. A few scenes, including one where Katsu's character ends up briefly in

prison, emerge as borderline silly. But there is a particularly great swordfight near the end where Katsu and cronies attack the rival villainous yakuza clan to rescue their ailing, elderly boss. The action choreography, cinematography and editing of this sequence is quite brilliant, treading a difficult tightrope act between genuinely goofy antics and exhilirating, bloody violence. #2 of 3 films   * * 1/2 (DAIEI Studios)

TALES OF SURUGA YAKUZA – COURAGEOUS RAVEN aka SURUGA YUKYODEN – DOKYO GARASU 1965 80 min. **Dir.** Kazuo Mori **Orig. Story:** Kan Shimozawa **Scr.** Ryuzo Kasahara **Photo color 'scope:** Hiroshi Imai **Music:** Seitaro Omori   **w/** Shintaro Katsu, Miyuki Kuwano, Asao Koike, Kazuko Fujiyoshi, Shoichi Ozawa #3 and last of series   * * 1/2 (DAIEI Studios)

TENPO ERA RIVER STORY – YUGAKU OHARA aka TENPO SUI KO DEN – OHARA YUGAKU 1976 147 min. **Dir.** Satsuo Yamamoto **Scr.** Hisashi Yamauchi **Photo color 'scope:** Setsuo Kobayashi **Music:** Tadashi Yamauchi   **w/** Mikijiro Hira, Ruriko Asaoka, Yoshiko Kayama, Shinobu Otake, Etsushi Takahashi, Hajime Hana, Osamu Takizawa This is the story of Yugaku Ohara, a peaceful, idealistic samurai who supposedly actually existed. He was instrumental in teaching farmers new, revolutionary rice-planting methods to make their harvests more productive. This did not sit well with the local yakuza clan and provincial government (who, at least here in the film, are in collusion). Hira and Asaoka are their usual excellent selves. Also of note, the underrated Takahashi is great as a tubercular hired ronin. Yamamoto also treated this subject matter in the 16th Zatoichi film, ZATOICHI, THE OUTLAW (1967) with Mizuho Suzuki playing Ohara. * * * (DAIEI Studios)

TOKAI HIGHWAY FULL-HOUSE aka SEZOROI TOKAIDO 1963 75 min. Dir. Sadatsugu (Teiji) Matsuda Scr. Hajime Takaiwa Photo color 'scope: Shintaro Kawazaki w/ Chiezo Kataoka, Utaemon Ichikawa, Kotaro Satomi, Hashizo Okawa, Kinnosuke Nakamura, Hibari Misora, Naoko Kubo, Kinya Kitaoji, Hiroki Matsukata, Chiyonosuke Azuma, Kokichi Takada, Kunio Kaga, Isao Yamagata, Satomi Oka, Hiroko Sakuramachi, Jushiro Konoe
One of several all-star period yakuza blow-outs Toei Studios made in the early sixties. Okawa plays a young *oyabun* married to Misora. They are happy as can be with a new baby just arrived. Older *oyabun* Kataoka is more or less godfather to the child. Something goes wrong, and Okawa ends up challenged to a gangfight by evil *oyabun* Yamagata. During the combat – which features some pretty amazing swordplay – Yamagata employs riflemen to cut down Okawa. A couple of Okawa's reinforcements spot the unfair gunplay, then root out and slash the sharpshooters. Okawa dies in his men's arms, and the stage is set for a massive build-up of woe and angst that will fuel a vendetta. Kataoka, Nakamura, et. al. end up attacking Yamagata's clan stronghold

and wiping out the villainy. Corny as hell, but enormously entertaining. * * * (TOEI Studios)

TOKIJIRO KUTSUKAKE aka KUTSUKAKE TOKIJIRO 1929 63 min. Dir. Kiichiro Tsuji Orig. story: Shin Hasegawa Scr. Satoshi Kisaragi Photo B&W: Yasushi Tanimoto (SILENT) w/ Denjiro Okochi, Yoneko Sakai (NIKKATSU Studios)

TOKIJIRO KUTSUKAKE aka KUTSUKAKE TOKIJIRO 1961 86 min. Dir. Kazuo Ikehiro Orig. story: Shin Hasegawa Scr. Masao Ueno Photo color 'scope: Kazuo Miyagawa Music: Ichiro Saito w/ Raizo Ichikawa, Michiyo Aratama, Ryuzo Shimada, Fujio Suga, Takashi Shimura, Haruko Sugimura
Shimada is a man in trouble with a yakuza clan. Just before dawn, the boss (Suga) and his men are on their way to kill him. Tokijiro (Ichikawa) arrives there first, after Shimada has sent his wife (Aratama) and small son away. Tokijiro challenges him to a fight and wounds him in the arm. He then declares that he is satisfied and wishes Shimada good luck in his escape. Shimada takes off running, but within a mile runs right into his enemies. He puts up a valiant fight but is slain. Tokijiro arrives as the man breathes his last and angrily confronts the boss. The clan then descends on him. Using the blunt edge of his sword, Tokijiro manages to cripple many of the men. Later he helps widow Aratama and the boy journey to another town. The evil boss still wishes revenge on both Tokijiro and Aratama, fearing retaliatory revenge vendettas down the line. To make

ends meet, Tokijiro and the widow stroll through the street playing *shamisen* and singing for coins. The boss of the town (Shimura) takes a liking to Tokijiro and helps him when he is beset by some of Suga's advance men. But Suga challenges Shimura to a gangfight for his interference. He uses another boss friend who runs a corrupt gambling den outside town to help. Tokijiro, feeling indebted to Shimura, goes with Shimura's clan to fight. This battle in the moonlight on the wooded grounds of a deserted temple is very well-choreographed and the most exciting sequence in the film. Also, sound effects of swishing swords and ripping flesh are used, something not occurring in most samurai/yakuza films till mid-1963. Once the tide has turned in the fight, both Tokijiro and Shimura realize that Suga and his men have not shown up, just the other boss's men. Tokijiro immediately realizes Aratama and son are in danger and races back to their inn. Sure enough, Suga and his men have arrived. Aratama lies dying on the floor. Suga's *yojinbo* had struck her in the stomach. Already experiencing a difficult pregnancy, her body cannot take it. She expires in Tokijiro's arms. Tokijiro tricks the villains, gets the boy back, then lures the whole gang outside into the morning fog. Using various ploys inside the next-door stable, he manages to kill all the men, then finally cuts off Suga's arms, slaying him. He returns the little boy to his grandparents and leaves to again take up his wandering. One thing that is very noticeable here, compared to Ikehiro's later *matatabi* films – such as LONE STALKER and even SEVEN MILES TO NAKAYAMA – is there is no real depth to

Tokijiro/Ichikawa's character. He is a superficial, happy-go-lucky fellow without any angst or regrets. Another thing that mars this otherwise good film is just a bit too much heavenly choral singing over sentimental montages. It definitely dates the picture. * * * (DAIEI Studios)

Tokijiro Kutsukake - Lone Yakuza
(IMAGE © TOEI)

TOKIJIRO KUTSUKAKE – LONE YAKUZA aka KUTSUKAKE TOKIJIRO – YUKYO IPPIKI 1966 91 min. **DIR.** Tai Kato **ORIG. STORY:** Shin Hasegawa **SCR.** Masahiro Kakefuda/Takayuki Suzuki **PHOTO COLOR 'SCOPE:** Shin Furuya **MUSIC:** Ichiro Saito **w/** Kinnosuke Nakamura, Junko Ikeuchi, Chiyonosuke Azuma, Kiyoshi Atsumi, Nijiko Kiyokawa, Yoko Mihara   A much deeper version of the oft-filmed saga and more entertaining because of it. Nakamura is a wandering gambler quick with his sword, and he is presented with all too many opportunities to use it. The first duel mere minutes into the film on a bright river shore is a *tour de force* of editing and carefully framed shots. Other outlaws with a grudge attack and are lustily, gorily dispatched with much blood spraying. Next we see Tokijiro (Nakamura) lying lazily

on the floor of a geisha house, surrounded by partying people who have
been forced inside by a rainstorm. But
he is moody, reflective, flashing back
on the carnage he had perpetrated
that afternoon. Soon he is caught in
another gangfight in service to an
oyabun. He ends up killing Azuma,
the husband of Ikeuchi, and from then
on he feels acutely responsible for
her and her small son. Kato unspools
his customarily unpretentious narrative in intimate character details and
standard genre elements that coalesce
into a whole that transcends the usual
genre cliches. It is regrettable that
not a single one of Kato's films are
legimately available in America on
subtitled DVD. * * * 1/2 (TOEI
Studios)

Torn Parasol (IMAGE © KADOKAWA)

TORN PARASOL aka YABURE
GASA CHO AN 1963 96 min. Dir.
Kazuo Mori Scr. Minoru Inuzuka/
Hisakazu Tsuji Photo B&W
'scope: Hiroshi Imai Music: Hajime

Kaburagi w/ Shintaro Katsu, Shiho
Fujimura, Kimiko Fukuda, Masayo
Banri, Ganjiro Nakamura, Shigeru
Amachi (DAIEI Studios)

**TRAIL OF BLOOD aka MUSH-
UKUNIN MIKOGAMI NO
JOKICHI aka JOKICHI OF
MIKOGAMI, WANDERING MAN
series**

Trail of Blood (#1) (IMAGE © TOHO)

**JOKICHI MIKOGAMI,
WANDERER – PULLING THE
FANGS THAT RIP AND TEAR**
aka MUSHUKUNIN MIKOGAMI
NO JOKICHI – KIBA WA HIKI
RETSU ITA aka TRAIL OF
BLOOD #1 1972 88 min. Dir.
Kazuo Ikehiro Orig. story: Saho
Sasazawa Scr. Kazuo Ikehiro/
Yoshihiro Ishimatsu Photo
color 'scope: Kazuo Miyagawa
Music: Takeo Watanabe w/ Yoshio
Harada, Atsuo Nakamura, Ryunosuke
Minegishi, Sanae Kitabayashi, Kayo
Matsuo, Ryohei Uchida   The origi-
nal source material for this trilogy
was written by Sasazawa, the same
man responsible for creating COLD
WIND MONJIRO. This likewise con-
cerns a *matatabi*, Jokichi Mikogami
(Harada). But unlike free spirit drifter
Monjiro, Harada's *matatabi* briefly
settles down, marrying an inn owner

and fathering a son, attempting to go straight and renouncing his sword until his family is murdered by cruel yakuza. Possessing much spaghetti western ambience as well as Toho Studios' heavy 1970s bloodletting quotient, director Ikehiro toughens up the *matatabi* mythos, debunking the reputation of legendary Robin Hood-like boss Chuji Kunisada, here presented as a dubious entity whose men may be partially responsible for the deaths of Harada's family. These three films also proved to be Ikehiro's big-screen swan song (until the 1980s when he directed one more non-genre film). He also went on to direct a lot of episodic television and TV movies as did his contemporaries. Ikehiro was one of Daiei's best directors, and the cast of each of these pictures is full of excellent performers. Harada had come up from the ranks of suave, swaggering outlaws in Shochiku and Nikkatsu studios yakuza and juvenile delinquent movies and went on to become a huge star in the later 1970s and into the 1980s. He is probably best known in America as the one-eyed, amnesiac swordsman Tanigawa in HUNTER IN THE DARK (1979) directed by Hideo Gosha. TRAIL OF BLOOD co-star, Atsuo Nakamura, went on to portray COLD-WIND MONJIRO on Japanese television. #1 of 3 films * * * (TOHO Studios)

JOKICHI MIKOGAMI, WANDERER – DRIFTING IN THE RIVER WIND aka MUSH-UKUNIN MIKOGAMI NO JOK-ICHI – KAWA KAZE NI KAKO WA NAGARE TA aka TRAIL OF BLOOD #2 – FEARLESS AVENG-ER 1972 80 min. DIR. Kazuo Ikehiro ORIG. STORY: Saho Sasazawa SCR.

Kazuo Ikehiro/Yoshihiro Ishimatsu PHOTO COLOR 'SCOPE: Kazuo Miyagawa MUSIC: Takeo Watanabe w/ Yoshio Harada, Ryohei Uchida, Asao Uchida, Atsuo Nakamura, Toshitaro Nakao, Yoshi Kato Harada as Mikogami continues his vengeance quest which brings him to a yakuza boss convention/gambling game in another village. He announces his intention to kill the evil one in question who had been largely responsible for his wife and son's death, and is quickly overcome. But not before killing a couple of the home gang. The subordinates are going to kill Harada when stopped by the big elder boss (Asao Uchida) who instructs them to throw him in the river instead. Luckily, an elderly couple who make their living from fishing dredge him out before he can drown. Ambivalent acquaintance, one-eyed Nakamura, greets him in the morning, making a few ironic comments before departing. Local boss Nakao, impressed by Harada's guts, hires him to transport boss Asao Uchida's daughter back to her hometown. The brief sequence where he shepherds her home, only to inadvertently get her killed when some vengeful *matatabi* attack him, is the best part of the film. As coldbloodedly nihilistic and vengefully bloodthirsty as he is, his honor and duty is still intact. After burying her, he travels to the hometown and informs her father of her unfortunate demise. Uchida's underlings want Harada dead but Uchida, fighting his own anger, allows Harada to leave. Shortly after, Harada encounters yakuza led by boss Toru Abe. Allied with Harada's hated quarry, Abe hires him to help in a gangfight, unaware of Harada's

Jokichi Mikogami, Wanderer (#1) *aka* ***Trail of Blood*** (IMAGE © TOHO)

identity. Once at the riverbanks show-down, Harada flipflops and helps the other side led by elderly boss Yoshi Kato. Soon Harada's nemesis shows up. Before the dust settles, Harada has expunged his enemy as well as Abe and most of the villain's gang. Unfortunately, after the excellent middle third chronicling the tragic trip with Boss Uchida's daughter, this last quarter of the movie emerges as strangely anticlimactic. #2 of 3 films * * * (TOHO Studios)

JOKICHI MIKOGAMI, WANDERER – JUMPING AT THE FLASH OF GOLD aka MUSHUKUNIN MIKOGAMI NO JOKICHI – KOKAI NI SENKO GA HINDA aka TRAIL OF BLOOD – SLAUGHTER IN THE SNOW

1973 83 min. DIR. Kazuo Ikehiro ORIG. STORY: Saho Sasazawa SCR. Shuichi Nagahara/Kazuo Ikehiro PHOTO COLOR 'SCOPE: Kozo Okazaki MUSIC: Takeo Watanabe w/ Yoshio Harada, Isao Natsuyagi, Michiyo Yasuda, Renji Ishibashi
Harada encounters *shamisen* play-ing Yasuda and tubercular, knife-throwing Natsuyagi. Underrated Natsuyagi, known predominantly for roles in such Hideo Gosha-directed films as SAMURAI WOLF 1 & 2, THE WOLVES, GOYOKIN, etc., is very good. Drifter Natsuyagi is in love with a yakuza boss's mistress who basically uses him, then discards him as soon as she no longer needs him. Once minstrel Yasuda has been saved then ignored by ambivalent Harada, she becomes obsessed and follows both Harada and Natsuyagi, who have formed an uneasy alliance, on their travels. At the close, Harada finally gets to wipe out the remaining

villains, Yasuda is mortally wounded and then, when all the carnage is over, Harada and Natsuyagi engage in a duel to the death. If anything, Harada has become more coldblooded and ruthless as the trilogy has progress-ed, and finally dispatches ailing Natsuyagi with little hesitation. He only pays heed to loyal Yasuda after she has bled to death on the sidelines while watching the two fight. Be-grudgingly he picks up her body to carry it away. This final TRAIL OF BLOOD installment is an original, strange but curiously unaffecting cli-max to the trilogy but does have some great acting from this powerhouse trio. Overall, it is a worthwhile effort for it's unsentimental treatment of traditional *matatabi* story elements. #3 and final in series * * * (TOHO Studios)

TWO BODYGUARDS aka NIHIKI NO YOJINBO series

TWO BODYGUARDS aka NIHIKI NO YOJINBO 1968

81 min. DIR. Kenji Misumi SCR. Hideo Ando/Hisashi Sugiura PHOTO COLOR 'SCOPE: Hiroshi Imai MUSIC: Taiichiro Kosugi w/ Kojiro Hongo, Isamu Nagato, Miwa Takada, Miyoko Akaza, Toru Abe, Machiko Hasegawa, Ryutaro Gomi
The first of two films with much fighting but also whimsical humor concerning two *matatabi* gamblers and their love/hate friendship. This is yet another version of YATAPPE OF SEKI. It was originally prepared by director Misumi with Raizo Ichikawa, but then aborted when Ichikawa was too ill with terminal cancer to continue. It was restarted with Hongo

taking over. Unfortunately, it does not reach its full potential, especially considering Misumi's involvement. Screenwriters Ando and Sugiura change some story elements which end up affecting the saga's impact (for a rundown on plot, etc., see the write-up in this section of Toei's YATAPPE OF SEKI).

Two Bodyguards (IMAGE © KADOKAWA)

Misumi seems intent on leaching out the more sentimental aspects of the story, but goes a bit too far in the opposite direction. Despite the good performances of Nagato (the spear-carrying swordsman from Gosha's THREE OUTLAW SAMURAI), Takada and the underrated Hongo as Yatappe, elements fail to coa-lesce. The viewer gets the feeling that Misumi's heart was not in the proceedings, although I imagine the death of original star Ichikawa could have had a profoundly chilling affect on the production. Nagato's character, too, is spared at the climax (unlike in

the other versions), probably to make room for a sequel, and this blunting of the story's tragedy further mutes the expressive force of the narrative. Then again, I have not seen the sequel, and perhaps both films are more effective if viewed as two parts of a whole. * * 1/2 #1 of 2 films (DAIEI Studios)

FUGITIVE BODYGUARD aka YOJINBO KYOJOTABI aka THE BODYGUARD'S REVENGE 1969 82 min. **DIR.** Akira Inoue **SCR.** Hisashi Sugiura **PHOTO COLOR** **'SCOPE:** Senkichiro Takeda **MUSIC:** Takeo Watanabe   w/ Kojiro Hongo, Isamu Nagato, Akane Kawazaki. Machiko Hasegawa, Ryutaro Gomi #2 and last of the series (DAIEI Studios)

WANDERER OF 1001 NIGHTS aka MATATABI SENICHI YA aka JOURNEY OF 1001 NIGHTS 1936 **DIR.** Hiroshi Inagaki w/ Kanemon Nakamura, Sadako Sawamura (NIKKATSU Studios)

The Wanderers (IMAGE © ATG/TOHO)

THE WANDERERS aka MATA-TABI 1973 96 min. **DIR.** Kon Ichikawa **SCR.** Shuntaro Tanikawa/ Kon Ichikawa **PHOTO COLOR:** Setsuo Kobayashi **MUSIC:** Kuri Shitei/Yukio Asami   w/ Kenichi Hagiwara, Isao

Bito, Ichiro Ogura, Reiko Inoue Director Ichikawa's debunking of the chivalrous *matatabi* myth. Showcasing three shallow, hypocritically callow youths who idolize the yakuza idyll, but constantly betray their own code, any conception of common sense and notion of human decency. One of them, at the behest of a boss he is obligated to, kills his estranged, drunken father, then lies down and weeps beside his body all night long. Later on this same young man sells his devoted girlfriend – who has killed her farmer husband to be with him – into prostitution. However, one wonders how much a victim she really is as it seems to be her idea! The young fellow weeps inconsolably as he takes his leave. By the end of the film, one of them dies from gangrene. The other two are walking down a deserted trail when they get into a fight over the finer points of *jingi* (the gambler's code). One of them runs away. While he is gone, the other fellow trips and rolls down a steep hillside. Just before reaching the bottom, he strikes his head on a rock and is killed. The other returns to the trail and is mystified as to where his comrade has gone. End. Even though it takes place in the mid-19th century, Ichikawa called this his version of EASY RIDER. Despite the very realistic depiction of what *matatabi* were probably like – too miserably cold and hungry to worry about chivalrous behavior – the viewer should note that many yakuza films – especially *matatabi* and other "in-period" yakuza pictures – showed their heroes and sympathetic protagonists as being a rare breed, if not outright exceptions. The ZATOICHI series often depicted Ichi as the only decent, *jingi*

-bound yakuza for miles; when other "good" or "humane" yakuza characters (or even rarer, a decent clan) appear, they are always shown as being a tiny percentage of what is, at best, a morally ambivalent whole, at worst, a ruthless, murderously cruel entity. So, though many times the romantic outlaw myth seems to blindly dominate the yakuza/period-yakuza genre, the fact that such lone wolf period-heroes as Chuji, Jirocho, Yataro, Ginpei, etc., achieve exalted status is due to the enormous proliferation of villains that signifies the lifestyle's majority. In other words, the reason they are heroes to begin with is because they are so rare. If the majority of the outlaw population, even in romantic tall tales, were truly bound by chivalrous principles, by *jingi*, then where would the overwhelming odds against our heroes come from? The *goyo* or police, of course, but not in a way that would make the conflicts philosophically intriguing. The fact that our heroes/anti-heroes are often tied to amoral or immoral comrades through past deeds, blood ties, or mere friendship create the moral tension, the contradictions of humanity and duty that so frequently drive these stories. Just some rhetorical questions as to if a debunking of the myth was really all that necessary. Then again, if you were working in the film and TV industry in Japan during the 1950s-1960s, it was probably very easy to become sick-to-death of the enormous proliferation of formulaic *matatabi* stories being told on big and small screens alike. Despite my questions, this is an excellent, very entertaining, brilliant, sad, bleakly hilarious film that manages to keep the characters sympathetic even as they do reprehensible things. NOTE: As with most ATG-funded productions, this was shot in 1:33 Academy standard aspect ratio. * * * * (ATG Productions, distributed by TOHO)

Wanderers - Three Yakuza Japanese *VHS cover artwork* (IMAGE © TOEI)

WANDERERS – THREE YAKUZA aka MATATABI – SANNIN YA-KUZA aka THREE WANDERING YAKUZA 1965 120 min. **DIR.** Tadashi Sawashima **SCR.** Kazuo Kasahara ("Fall Chapter"); **SCR.** Sadao Nakajima ("Winter Chapter"); **SCR.** Tatsuo Nogami ("Spring Chapter") **PHOTO COLOR 'SCOPE:** Shin Furuya **MUSIC:** Masaru Sato "Fall:" **w/** Tatsuya Nakadai, Hiroko Sakuramachi, Kunie Tanaka, Asao Uchida; "Winter:" **w/** Hiroki Matsukata, Junko Fuji, Takashi Shimura; "Spring:" **w/** Kinnosuke Nakamura, Wakaba Irie, Shinjiro Ebara, Takeshi Kato

A cinematic anthology that starts in promising fashion with the excellent first tale, the poetic, dynamic "Fall" starring wandering Nakadai as a fugitive drifter who attempts to help put-upon working girl Sakuramachi. Things waver a notch but remain on a fairly even keel with the second story, "Winter," as snowbound wanderer Matsukata is stranded at the forest home of Fuji and her dad Shimura. Unfortunately, the last tale, the slightly humorous "Spring" starring Nakamura as a timid *matatabi* wan-nabe forced to prove his mettle when confronted with a violently abusive samurai in a country village, is a bit of a misfire. It emerges as an okay but forgettable conclusion to the trilogy with the more worthwhile tall tales having come before. * * * (TOEI Studios)

Wind, Women and Ravens (IMAGE © TOEI)

WIND, WOMEN AND RAVENS aka KAZE TO ONNA TO TABI GARASU aka WIND, WOMEN AND WANDERERS 1958 91 min. **DIR.** Tai Kato **SCR.** Masashige Narusawa **PHOTO B&W 'SCOPE:** Makoto Tsuboi **MUSIC:** Chuji Kinoshita **w/** Kinnosuke Nakamura, Rentaro Mikuni, Satomi Oka, Yumiko Hasegawa. Nakamura is a self-centered young *matatabi* who encounters cowardly thief Mikuni on his trek through the forest. They accidentally come into possession of

Women's Prison *aka Secrets of a Women's Prison (#1)* (IMAGE © KADOKAWA PRODUCTIONS)

a village procession's tax box after the couriers are scared off by the cantankerous duo's impromptu quarrel with swords on the road. The two form an uneasy alliance frequently punctuated with violence, but are captured by the villagers. Wounded Nakamura and glib, basically decent Mikuni talk their way into the villagers' good graces until an evil yakuza clan appears, a gang who is on all-too-friendly terms with the boys. The uneasy comrades are alternately torn between their more decent impulses towards the kind townspeople and their survival instincts. Violence erupts again, both between themselves and against the yakuza clan before the two rise to their better natures. However, once the villains are vanquished, too many bitter words have been said. Nakamura leaves to wander while Mikuni opts to stay in the village. Along with Akira Kurosawa at Toho, much lesser known Tai Kato was one of the few genre directors in the late fifties and early sixties attempting to present more realistic period pictures with intelligence and integrity, and this, his first really critically acclaimed film, is a prime example. * * * (TOEI Studios)

WOMEN'S PRISON aka HIROKU ONNA RO aka SECRETS OF A WOMEN'S PRISON series

SECRETS OF A WOMEN'S PRISON aka HIROKU ONNA RO aka WOMEN'S PRISON 1968 76 min. **DIR.** Akira Inoue **SCR.** Shozaburo Asai **PHOTO B&W** **'SCOPE:** Yasukazu Takemura **MUSIC:** Takeo Watanabe **w/** Michiyo

Yasuda, Sanae Nakahara, Mayumi Nagisa, Shigako Shimegi An infamous "cinema-of-cruelty" piece that was reportedly quite popular and controversial upon its initial release. Looking at it now, one wonders what all the fuss was about. Unlike Teruo Ishii's JOYS OF TORTURE (1968), ORGIES OF EDO (1968) and several others, which even now still retain the capacity to shock, most of this series seems pretty tame today. A decent young woman (Yasuda) is unjustly sent to prison in 1860s Japan, and we get to see the dark underbelly of fellow prisoners' cruelty and the torture from the guards and wardens. Each film has different characters so the series aspect comes in the time period – 1860 to 1880 – and the spectacle of women criminals in jeopardy/torture. Daiei's directors were a little too genteel and tasteful, in spite of themselves. On the plus side, Daiei's "cruelty" films generally sport a more solid narrative structure as well as better performances by the leads. All of the films are decent, ranging from good to excellent, but none are very transgressive or disturbing. #1 of 6 films * * * (DAIEI Studios)

WOMEN'S CELL aka ZOKU HIROKU ONNA RO aka MORE SECRETS OF A WOMEN'S PRISON 1968 84 min. **DIR.** Kimiyoshi Yasuda **SCR.** Shozaburo Asai **PHOTO B&W 'SCOPE:** Chishi Makiura **MUSIC:** Takeo Watanabe **w/** Michiyo Yasuda, Sanae Nakahara, Machiko Hasegawa, Rokko Toura, Kayo Mikimoto More of the same, occasionally evocative and atmospheric, with superlative acting as usual. But not much happens. Toura is the evil, sadistic warden (the kind of part this worthy, but too-often-typecast actor can play in his sleep). Yasuda and her mates finally have enough and take over the compound at the climax, kidnapping Toura and his corrupt guards, then delivering them to the magistrate. However, all must still suffer the consequences of their actions, especially ringleader Yasuda. Leaving the prison under guard – presumably for execution – she is strangely joyful, transcending the situation and at last knowing she has done all that she could to remedy the appalling conditions. #2 of 6 films   * * 1/2   (DAIEI Studios)

Women's Cell (#2) (IMAGE © KADOKAWA)

THE YOSHIWARA STORY aka HIROKU ONNA GURA aka SECRETS OF WOMEN'S QUARTERS or SECRETS OF A PLEASURE QUARTER BROTHEL 1968 78 min. **DIR.** Kazuo Mori **SCR.** Shozaburo Asai **PHOTO B&W** 'SCOPE: Senkichiro Takeda **MUSIC:**

Hajime Kaburagi   w/ Michiyo Yasuda, Masakazu Tamura, Machiko Hasegawa, Kayo Mikimoto, Yuko Hamada, Hosei Komatsu, Ichiro Sugai   This is the best of the series, with director Mori exhibiting his usual skill, taste, sensitivity and subtlety. It is also the most unassuming and throwaway on the surface. Yasuda is a geisha who has been forced into prostitution with Tamura as a young, unscrupulous yakuza who simultaneously emerges as her tormentor, exploiter and protector. #3 of 6 films   * * * 1/2   (DAIEI Studios)

The Yoshiwara Story (#3) (IMAGE © KADOKAWA)

SECRETS OF A WOMEN'S TEMPLE aka HIROKU ONNA DERA 1969 79 min. **DIR.** Tokuzo Tanaka **SCR.** Shozaburo Asai **PHOTO B&W** 'SCOPE: Chishi Makiura **MUSIC:** Hajime Kaburagi w/ Michiyo Yasuda, Sanae Nakahara, Shigako Shimegi, Machiko Hasegawa

One of the most interesting stories of the series involving corruption and institutionalized cruelty inside a Buddhist convent, but at the same time it comes off as somewhat artificial and uninvolving, a film where everyone just seems to be going through the motions. #4 of 6 films * * 1/2 (DAIEI Studios)

Secrets of a Women's Temple (#4)
(IMAGE © KADOKAWA)

ISLAND OF HORRORS aka ONNA RO HIZU aka DECAPITATION ISLAND 1970 82 min. DIR. Toshiaki Kunihara SCR. Shozaburo Asai PHOTO COLOR 'SCOPE: Senkichiro Takeda MUSIC: Hajime Kaburagi   w/ Masakazu Tamura, Maya Kitajima, Reiko Kasahara, Hiroko Sakurai, Hiroshi Kondo   With a change to color and comparatively new directors, the series gets a little wilder. Daiei was undergoing terrible financial problems. Most of their stars were not doing as many films, apparently because there just wasn't the money to pay such star salaries as often. So for the last two films in the series newer, lesser known performers (Tamura is the sole exception) took the lion's share of roles. Director Kunihara here and Ota, helmer of the next film, had been assistant directors until as recently as 1969; both had also been Daiei screenwriters throughout the 1960s, and they went on to direct a lot of televsion in the 1970s, including episodes of the long-running ZATOICHI TV show. This particular installment chronicles an evil island women's prison of tortures. Tamura is a dispossessed samurai-turned-ronin now stuck with occasionally transporting female prisoners to the island. He delivers the latest inmates, feisty Kitajima and opium addict Kasahara. This is typical programmer fare with few surprises, but still very well done, especially considering the claustrophobic set and budget limitations. By the end, the whole corrupt establishment is collapsing in on itself, and the girls revolt with the help of the ambivalent, doomed Tamura. There is a nicely choreographed extended swordfight between Tamura and the rest of the samurai guards at the climax. Very watchable and fulfilling as unpretentious thriller. #5 of 6 films * * * (DAIEI Studios)

WOMEN'S PRISON FOR TORTURE aka HIROKU – NAGASAKI ONNA RO aka SECRETS – NAGASAKI WOMEN'S PRISON 1971 85 min. DIR. Akikazu Ota SCR. Hajime Takaiwa PHOTO COLOR 'SCOPE: Hiroshi Imai MUSIC: Hajime Kaburagi   w/ Akane Kawazaki, Tomoko Mayama, Rie Yokoyama, Hinako Yamaguchi, Yoshiko Hara

Island of Horrors aka Women's Prison (#5) (IMAGE © KADOKAWA PRODUCTIONS)

Women's Prison for Torture (#6)
(IMAGE © KADOKAWA)

The last in the series and another fairly worthwhile entry, though occasionally some of the talkier stretches go on a bit long. Kawazaki is a half-breed Euro-Japanese persecuted for

obvious mixed heritage (she has got a mane of red hair) and framed for the murder of her employer (he had been found with her jeweled, European dagger in his back). But it turns out it was her co-worker and lover. By the end, she escapes with another prisoner, the previously-hardhearted villainess (who decides to help her clear her name since she knows the truth). Too bad that the guilty man resists strenuously, pulling Kawazaki's defender into a knifefight to the death. Kawazaki finally has to stab the man before he finishes off her friend. Both die, Kawazaki is recaptured and then quickly crucified. #6 and last of series * * * (DAIEI Studios)

YATAPPE OF SEKI aka SEKI NO YATAPPE 1935 DIR. Hiroshi Inagaki ORIG. STORY: Shin Hasegawa MUSIC: (SILENT) w/ Denjiro Okochi, Fujiko Fukami (NIKKATSU)

YATAPPE OF SEKI aka SEKI NO YATAPPE aka YAKUZA OF SEKI 1963 84 min. DIR. Kosaku Yamashita ORIG. STORY: Shin Hasegawa SCR. Masamoto Naruzawa PHOTO COLOR 'SCOPE: Shin Furuya MUSIC: Chuji Kinoshita w/ Kinnosuke Nakamura, Yukiyo Toake, Isao Kimura, Kaneko Iwazaki, Ryunosuke Tsukigata, Shiro Osaka, Toru Abe, Sonosuke Sawamura One of the most filmed *matatabi* tales after the Jirocho and Chuji legends. But this is regarded by most Japanese film critics as the finest interpretation. It certainly is exceptional. A moving, emotion-wringing film that takes a story filled with sentiment and manages to tell it in as non-manipulative, austere and simple a way as possible. Which makes the poignance and sacrifice in the film all the more effective. Nakamura is a young, free-spirited *matatabi* who saves a young girl from drowning. Her father (Osaka) picks his pocket, and by the time Nakamura realizes it, the man and child are down the road. He goes searching and soon finds the father. But dad has given the fat wallet to his little girl to carry with her on her way to the next nearby village. She is to move in with her grandmother, aunt and uncle. Nakamura, though, has found the introductory letter which the child has dropped in the road. The father is beside himself with concern that his mother, brother and sister won't believe that the little girl is really his daughter without the letter. Nakamura gets so angry he draws his sword to scare the man. However, they are being watched by third party Kimura, another *matatabi*, sent by a yakuza clan after the errant Osaka. He quickly draws his blade and slashes Osaka from behind, then leaves. Nakamura is horrified; he had never intended to slay the man. As Osaka dies, he begs Nakamura to go after the little girl and shepherd her to his mother's house. Nakamura reluctantly acquiesces. When he catches up with the child she no longer has the money. She had given it to Kimura. Nakamura takes the girl to her grandmother's and explains the strange circumstances. The grandmother, aunt, and uncle are initially suspicious and remain incredulous until it is almost too late. But a song the girl sings convinces them she truly is the late Osaka's progeny. Nakamura promises to return with some money to help bring her up. Shortly thereafter he goes into a gam-

bling den to raise the funds and runs into Kimura. To his astonishment, Kimura returns the money to him. Nakamura rewards him with a gold coin from the wallet, and their friendship is sealed. He returns to the little girl's new home and watches from behind some purple tulips as the girl's aunt sings with her in the garden. Not wishing to draw attention to his good deed, he picks a flower, places it so it is protruding from his wallet and leaves the package on a prominent windowsill. The grandmother finds it a few moments later, but Nakamura has already disappeared. When next we see Nakamura, it is ten years later, and his shaved pate and topknot is now grown in with bushy hair. A long scar runs down the length of one cheek. He is obviously now an older man scarred by a wandering gambler's life. He drinks with abandon but is sober and steady as a rock. Suddenly, a man from a yakuza clan he is obligated to appears out of a fierce rainstorm, begging him to come and fight in their battle against a rival clan's boss. He agrees with relish, and approaches the skirmish with bloodthirsty enthusiasm. However, after minutes of combat, he encounters Kimura from the opposing side. They frantically exchange info as they pretend to continue fighting. It transpires Kimura is trying to help Nakamura's old boss and friend (Tsukigata) escape from the unscrupulous Toru Abe and his gang. Nakamura switches sides, an act which will prove to have dire consequences by the film's end. Nakamura, Tsukigata and Kimura escape. Eventually Kimura discovers that Osaka's child has grown up into a beautiful young woman (Toake). He goes to their household, claiming to be the man who had saved her life and left the money. The grandmother, aunt and uncle have their doubts but are more or less convinced Kimura is the real thing. When Toake excitedly enters, overjoyed to once again see her benefactor, she is visibly crestfallen when she spots Kimura. Nakamura discovers Kimura's act and sends a message that he meet him in a nearby grove. Kimura refuses to stop the subterfuge. Nakamura still has affection for Kimura, but asserts they must fight if Kimura continues his deceit.

Yatappe of Seki aka Yakuza of Seki
(IMAGE © TOEI)

Thus Nakamura ends up slaying one of his only friends. He returns to Toake's house, staying outside the garden. Toake sees him, and their gazes lock for several silent minutes in one of the most moving segments of the film. It is obvious there is an intense bond of love between them. But Nakamura, chivalrous and selfless, realizing he will only bring the

girl grief, turns and walks away. He hides beneath a bridge as she pursues him, calling his name. Once she is gone, he goes out to meet Abe and the remaining dozen or so of the villain's gang who are waiting down the road for a fight. Though Nakamura has been portrayed as a proficient swordsman, the film is based enough in reality to suggest he may, in fact, meet his death. The end titles appear just before he reaches his rendezvous with Fate. * * * * (TOEI Studios)

YATARO'S TRAVEL HAT – PREQUEL STORY aka YATARO GASA – ZENKO HEN 1952 159 min. **Dir.** Masahiro Makino **Orig. story:** Kan Shimozawa **Scr.** Toshio Matsuura **Photo B&W:** Yoshitomi Hirano **Music:** Seiichi Suzuki w/ Koji Tsuruta, Keiko Kishi, Seizaburo Kawazu, Kokichi Takada, Daisuke Kato, Michiyo Kogure, Rentaro Mikuni (SHINTOHO)

Yataro's Travel Hat (1957)
(IMAGE © KADOKAWA)

YATARO'S TRAVEL HAT aka
YATARO GASA 1957 94 min.
DIR. Kazuo Mori ORIG. STORY: Kan
Shimozawa SCR. Fuji Yahiro
PHOTO COLOR: Shozo Honda MUSIC:
Ichiro Saito w/ Raizo Ichikawa,
Michiyo Kogure, Eijiro Yanagi, Yoko
Uraji, Hiroko Yashima, Tatsuya
Ishiguro, Ryosuke Kagawa
Ichikawa is the roving gambler Yataro
who becomes smitten with a benevolent village boss's daughter. However,
he is a wandering spirit and unable
to stand still for long. He learns
sometime later, when he spots the
girl's prized hairpin up for grabs in a
dice game, that she is in trouble and
returns to the town to discover her
father has been murdered by bosses
Yanagi's and Kagawa's psychotic
yojinbo Ishiguro. Although missing
the existentual angst that was starting
to occur more and more in *matatabi*
movies as the sixties progressed,
director Mori does keep the offbeat,
unnerving elements percolating,
weaving a skilled, unpretentious
narrative without the by-the-numbers
feel of Makino's 1960 Toei version.
I have not seen other than these two
versions, but one of the more intriguing characters, female star Kogure's
morally compromised dice dealer,
seems grafted onto the scenario to not
only give the actress a showcase but
to add a poignant counterbalance to
the utterly one-dimensional sweetness
of Yataro's true love, the dead boss's
daughter. Likewise Ishiguro's psychopathic killer is a welcome creation,
a harbinger of unpredictable deadly
menace sorely lacking in Makino's
1960 version. * * * (DAIEI
Studios)

YATARO'S TRAVEL HAT aka
YATARO GASA 1960 96 min. DIR.
Masahiro Makino SCR. Mitsumasa
Kanze/Michihei Muramatsu PHOTO
B&W 'SCOPE: Shigeto Miki MUSIC:
Seiichi Suzuki w/ Kinnosuke
Nakamura, Denjiro Okochi, Satomi
Oka, Chiyonosuke Azuma, Sumiko
Hidaka, Susumu Fujita, Minoru
Chiaki, Haruo Tanaka A great cast
is not given much to do in this version of the oft-filmed tale. Nakamura
is a natural for the carefree *matatabi*
– it was one of his specialties at Toei
Studios in the fifties and early sixties
– but, as in the Ichikawa version directed by Mori, there is little realism
or character development. Veteran
chanbara star Okochi is the decent
boss murdered by rival Fujita (star of
Kurosawa's SANSHIRO SUGATA).
Oka is adequate as the daughter men-
aced by the bad clan after her father's
demise, but there is not much to work
with in the character as written.

Yataro's Travel Hat (1960)
(IMAGE © TOEI)

One advantage this does have over Mori's Daiei version (which is otherwise the better film) is its stunning black-and-white scope compositions. However, although the swordplay is well-choreographed, the film still comes across as routine and even more old-fashioned than its predecessor. Makino was a talented, although uneven director, responsible for as many mediocre efforts as exceptional ones. * * (TOEI Studios)

Yojinbo (IMAGE © TOHO)

YOJINBO aka THE BODYGUARD 1961 104 min. **DIR.** Akira Kurosawa **SCR.** Ryuzo Kikushima/ Akira Kurosawa **PHOTO B&W 'SCOPE:** Kazuo Miyagawa **MUSIC:** Masaru Sato **w/** Toshiro Mifune, Eijiro Tono, Seizaburo Kawazu, Tatsuya Nakadai, Isuzu Yamada, Daisuke Kato, Yoko Tsukasa, Takashi Shimura, Kamatari Fujiwara, Atsushi Watanabe, Ikio Sawamura, Ko Nishimura, Yoshio Tsuchiya,

Susumu Fujita, Yosuke Natsuki One of Kurosawa's lighter pictures. Sardonic gallows humor permeates a near-perfect adventure film with real, human characters. The maestro, himself, refers to it as a comedy. Mifune plays Sanjuro, a shiftless, wandering *ronin* who happens onto a starving village beset by a yakuza gang war between two rival gambling clans. To make money as well as amuse himself (and perhaps as a third low priority consideration, do the village some good), he plays them off against each other and nearly gets killed in the process. Nakadai does a memorable star turn in a comparatively small role as the younger, dandy brother of one of the bosses. He proves to be one of Sanjuro's most dangerous adversaries – he is not only smart but also an expert shot with the only gun (a pistol) in town. Sergio Leone did an unauthorized remake, the almost-as-good spaghetti western, A FISTFUL OF DOLLARS (1964) with Clint Eastwood (which in some sequences is nearly shot-for-shot). But Kurosawa got the idea from Dashiell Hammet's tough-as-nails 1929 crime novel, *Red Harvest*, about a nameless, hard-drinking operative in the midst of a gang war in a small, northwestern industrial town. When YOJINBO was remade again in 1996 by Walter Hill as the Bruce Willis vehicle, LAST MAN STANDING, the action was returned to its original late 1920s time period and American location. In the process, it became basically a film of *Red Harvest*. Which would have been okay if the Hammet novel was credited as the other source besides YOJINBO on LAST MAN STANDING's titles. But it wasn't. What was okay for Kurosawa who got an idea from an American crime novel set in the 1920s, transposing it to the samurai/period-yakuza genre in mid-19th century rural Japan, is not okay for an American film which returns the story to its original time period and locale, then gives not a mention to the prototype Hammet novel in the credits and/or advertising, sleazing around it by crediting the Kurosawa/Kikushima screenplay. But why should I be surprised when people in the film industry do such things? The Coen Brothers expertly mixed and matched elements from Hammett's novels *Red Harvest* and *The Glass Key* for their 1990 classic, MILLER'S CROSSING. In any case, Kurosawa's YOJINBO is a masterpiece. * * * * (TOHO Studios)

ZATOICHI aka BLIND MASSEUR ICHI aka THE BLIND SWORDSMAN series

Tale of Zatoichi (#1)
(IMAGE © KADOKAWA)

TALE OF ZATOICHI aka ZATO-ICHI MONOGATARI aka **LIFE AND OPINION OF MASSEUR ICHI** aka THE STORY OF BLIND MASSEUR ICHI aka 1962 96 min. **DIR.** Kenji Misumi **ORIG. STORY:** Kan Shimozawa **SCR.** Minoru Inuzuka **PHOTO B&W 'SCOPE:** Chishi Makiura **MUSIC:** Akira Ifukube **w/** Shintaro Katsu, Shigeru Amachi, Masayo Banri, Ryuzo Shimada, Eijiro Yanagi, Gen Mitamura, Michio Minami, Toshiro Chiba, Eigoro Onoe, Yoshido Yamaji Although there are numerous injustices in the pathetic history of Japanese genre films distribution in America, none is more astounding than the, until recently, near-anonymity of Japanese superstar Shintaro Katsu. Katsu is one of those actors in company as disparate as Charlie Chaplin, James Dean, Robert Mitchum, Orson Welles, et. al., a mega entity of the cinema whose stature and talent has achieved mythic proportions. In the character of Zatoichi – the wandering blind masseur/gambler/master swordsman – Katsu, in collaboration with writer Kan Shimozawa, gave birth to a character as original as Chaplin's "Little Tramp" or Clint Eastwood's "Man With No Name." Astonishingly enough, when you consider that Katsu as well as the Zatoichi character were, until the turn of the millenium, virtually unknown in the U.S. (except Hawaii where television still airs the subtitled films and reruns of the TV shows), the Zatoichi films were the most popular money-makers in domestic Japan during the 1960s. They surpassed the much-more-familiar-to-Americans Godzilla movies. Shochiku Studios' bittersweet TORA-SAN comedy series (aka IT'S

HARD TO BE A MAN) about a wandering *tekiya* (traveling salesman) finally usurped the honor of most lucrative, longest-running Japanese film series in the 1980s. Zatoichi proved popular not only because of the spectacular swordsmanship coming from an unexpected quarter but also the philosophical wisecracks popping out of the mouth of the smart-aleck hero. This tightrope act of humor, drama and exhilaratingly choreographed violence kept the series in favor for over a decade. Ichi roamed the back roads of Japan in the 1840s, a decade which saw the nearly 400 year-old rule of the Tokugawa Shogunate finally start to crumble. This was an era of dramatic change where the idea of a caste system was being challenged, where starving farmers were finally revolting against centuries of brutally unfair taxes and oppression. Ichi is a mass of contradictions – a yakuza gambler, he is scrupulously on the up-and-up with honest, common people but proves a ruthless conman trickster with anyone attempting to deceive or cheat him. An expert masseur and acupuncturist, he is also the most skilled swordsman in Japan. Despite being at the bottom of the ladder of a still-in-place caste system, Ichi has opportunities to make good, settle down and even marry. But either because of his own choice or the stormy weather of circumstance, his fate is to wander. In this initial outing, Ichi cons his way into staying at a rural yakuza clan's HQ. The two-faced boss (Yanagi) who knows Ichi's reputation, lays it on thick with hospitality, hoping Ichi will fight on their side in an upcoming battle against a rival clan from a nearby village. A waitress (Banri) in the next-door restaurant –

who has a scoundrel rat of a brother belonging to the clan – gradually falls-in-love with Ichi for his sweetness, chivalry and courage in the face of cruel, dishonorable behaviour. Ichi also develops an infatuation with her but keeps his distance, knowing from previous experience and his own wanderlust nature that he will only bring her grief. While fishing, Ichi meets a lonely, honorable and slowly dying tubercular samurai (Amachi) who turns out to be the rival clan's hired killer. The two become friends, and it is only through a series of accidents and gang manipulations that the two do, indeed, end up crossing swords. Ichi initially believes he will be taking unfair advantage because of Amachi's health and refuses. Amachi, dreading a quiet death in bed, convinces Ichi he would rather die on his feet with his sword in his hand, Ichi reluctantly acquiesces to his dying friend's request. #1 of 26 films
* * * *   (DAIEI Studios)

RETURN OF MASSEUR ICHI aka ZOKU ZATOICHI MONOGA-TARI aka TALE OF ZATOICHI CONTINUES 1962 72 min. **Dir.** Kazuo Mori **Orig. story:** Kan Shimozawa **Scr.** Minoru Inuzuka **Photo B&W 'scope:** Shozo Honda **Music:** Ichiro Saito   w/ Shintaro Katsu, Tomisaburo Wakayama (pka Kenzaburo Jo), Yoshie Mizutani, Masayo Banri, Yutaka Nakamura, Eijiro Yanagi, Sonosuke Sawamura, Yoshido Yamaji   Ichi runs into his estranged one-armed brother (played by real-life brother Wakayama under the pseudonym he used in Daiei films, Kenzaburo Jo; he was under contract to Toei in the 1960s). Wakayama had been responsible for stealing Ochiyo,

Life and Opinion of Masseur Ichi aka *Tale of Zatoichi* (#1)

the love of Ichi's life. Ichi is being pursued by bounty hunters sent by the yakuza boss (Yanagi) from the first film. Wakayama actually saves Ichi at one point totally unbeknownst to Ichi (he is sleeping). Before the tale ends, Wakayama dies in Ichi's arms, both of them reconciled, and Ichi leaves his hideout to confront the clan and avenge his brother's death. Mizutani plays a good-hearted whore who is a dead ringer for the now deceased Ochiyo, and Banri reprises her role from the first entry in what amounts to little more than a cameo. Where the action/swordplay was pretty much saved for the climax in the first film, action permeates this first sequel. With the short 72 minute running time, this emerges as one of the most fast-moving entries in the series. #2 of 26 films * * * * (DAIEI Studios)

MASSEUR ICHI ENTERS AGAIN aka SHIN ZATOICHI MONOGA- TARI aka NEW TALE OF ZATO- ICHI 1963 91 min. DIR. Tokuzo Tanaka ORIG. STORY: Kan Shimozawa SCR. Minoru Inuzuka/ Kikuo Umebayashi PHOTO COLOR 'SCOPE: Chishi Makiura MUSIC: Akira Ifukube w/ Shintaro Katsu, Mikiko Tsubouchi, Seizaburo Kawazu, Fujio Suga   Ichi visits his sword teacher (Kawazu) only to find him an embittered man. When Ichi and the teacher's sister (Tsubouchi) plan to marry, Ichi vowing to give up gambling and his sword, the teacher explodes. He insults Ichi, barring him from their house. Subsequently, Ichi discovers that not only is his teacher corrupt, but also responsible for sev- eral murders. He confronts his former mentor and, since the series contin-

ues, you can guess the outcome. This was the first entry shot in color. Still, a slight comedown from the previous two films, mainly due to the climactic swordplay occuring in an obviously setbound forest clearing. #3 of 26 films * * *   (DAIEI Studios)

Masseur Ichi Enters Again aka New Tale of Zatoichi (#3) (IMAGE © KADOKAWA)

ZATOICHI, THE FUGITIVE aka ZATOICHI KYOJOTABI 1963 86 min. DIR. Tokuzo Tanaka ORIG. STORY: Kan Shimozawa SCR. Minoru Inuzuka/Seiji Hoshikawa PHOTO COLOR 'SCOPE: Chishi Makiura MUSIC: Akira Ifukube w/ Shintaro Katsu, Masayo Banri, Miwa Takada, Junichiro Narita, Toru Abe, Toshitaro Kitashiro, Hiroshi Nawa, Katsuhiko Kobayashi   One of the best in the series with a very moving opening title sequence – just Ichi walking down a rural path in the oppressive, sweltering heat of summer, but with one of Akira Ifukube's most-heart- rending scores underneath. There is a very funny scene early on where Ichi tries his hand at sumo wrestling, beating all the opposition at the village festival and winning first prize. While eating his lunch on a placid, deserted riverbank, Ichi is attacked by a lone yakuza seeking the bounty on his head. Ichi attempts to warn the fellow off, but becomes angry when the man insults him. Abruptly, the attacker is expiring from wounds that Ichi has inflicted. The fellow calls out for his mother, Ichi finds out his name, and once more is caught up in a feeling of obligation to someone who has died at his hand. Ichi travels to the nearby village and notifies the elderly woman who is housekeeper for the local yakuza clan. At first enraged, she soon calms down, realizing that her no-good son was bound to come to such an end. Ichi stays for the burial and is in the process of leaving when he is confronted by the dead man's craven boss (Abe) and henchmen. The old lady begs them to let Ichi go. The young boss of the other clan (Narita) steps in to avert bloodshed. Abe, who wants to fully take over the territory he shares with Narita, begins a series of subterfuges to trap the inexperienced and frightened younger man in a losing situation. Abe also quadruples the bounty on Ichi's head. Meanwhile, Ichi is staying at an inn run by the older ex-boss who had lost his territory to Narita's deceased father. Takada is his beautiful daughter in-love with Narita. Banri once again reprises her role from the first two films. However, she is now somewhat of a fallen woman, having been jilted by her former suitor. She is hooked up with a surly, drunken *ronin* (Kitashiro) who has been summoned by Takada's father as *yojinbo*/hired killer to use as muscle against Narita.

Abe has soon co-opted the unprincipled man's services. Banri initially avoids Ichi, ashamed at how low she has sunk. However, Ichi refuses to judge her or believe she has become a bad person. The scene near the end where Banri attempts to keep her cruel lover from fighting Ichi and is, as a result, killed herself, is one of the most chilling sequences in any of the Zatoichi films. Takada relating to Ichi what she has just witnessed befall Banri outside causes Ichi to erupt, throwing caution to the winds. He bursts from his ruined house hiding place to slaughter nearly the enture clan, including Abe. The penultimate duel between Kitashiro and Ichi is one of the most nervewracking in the series and is given additional emotional weight by the fact Ichi loved Banri and Kitashiro is insanely jealous of their "pure" love. #4 of 26 films * * * * (DAIEI Studios)

Zatoichi (#5) (IMAGE © KADOKAWA)

ZATOICHI AND THE SCOUNDRELS aka ZATOICHI KENKA TABI aka BLIND MASSEUR ICHI'S VIOLENT

JOURNEY aka ZATOICHI ON THE ROAD 1963 87 min. **DIR.** Kimiyoshi Yasuda **ORIG. STORY:** Kan Shimozawa **SCR.** Minoru Inuzuka **PHOTO COLOR 'SCOPE:** Shozo Honda **MUSIC:** Akira Ifukube w/ Shintaro Katsu, Shiho Fujimura, Ryuzo Shimada, Reiko Fujiwara, Matasaburo Tanba
Ichi's services are fought over, all the while he is trying to escort a kidnapped woman (Fujimura) safely back to her family. The film has a sturdy framework and is entertaining despite establishing pretty much what, at times, became the formulaic blueprint for some of the lesser blind swordsman films. However, it must be remembered that even lesser Zatoichi films are usually superior to many other period genre films of the time. #5 of 26 films * * * (DAIEI Studios)

very rare bare bones English language poster for Zatoichi (#5)
(IMAGE © KADOKAWA PRODUCTIONS)

Zatoichi and the Chest of Gold (#6)
(IMAGE © KADOKAWA)

ZATOICHI AND THE CHEST OF GOLD aka ZATOICHI SEN-RYO KUBI aka 100 GOLD COINS ON BLIND MASSEUR ICHI'S HEAD 1964 82 min. **DIR.** Kazuo Ikehiro **ORIG. STORY:** Kan Shimozawa **SCR.** Shozaburo Asai/Akikazu Ota **PHOTO COLOR 'SCOPE:** Kazuo Miyagawa **MUSIC:** Ichiro Saito w/ Shintaro Katsu, Tomisaburo Wakayama (pka Kenzaburo Jo), Mikiko Tsubouchi, Machiko Hasegawa, Shogo Shimada, Saburo Date, Tatsuya Ishiguro, Toshitaro Kitashiro Ichi tries to retrive a chest of gold – representing a poor village's taxes – from corrupt officials and their cutthroat samurai. Shimada portrays famous yakuza Robin Hood, Chuji Kunisada, and Wakayama plays an evil, scarred, whip-wielding swordsman with sadistic glee. There is a grueling climactic duel between him and Ichi that is yet another of the many highlights in the series. Young Ikehiro once again demonstrates he was one of Daiei's most promising up-and-coming directors. #6 of 26 films * * * 1/2 (DAIEI Studios)

Zatoichi's Flashing Sword (#7)
(IMAGE © KADOKAWA PRODUCTIONS)

ZATOICHI'S FLASHING SWORD aka ZATOICHI ABARE DAKO aka BLIND MASSEUR ICHI'S RAGING KITE 1964 82

min. DIR. Kazuo Ikehiro ORIG. STORY: Kan Shimozawa SCR. Minoru Inuzuka PHOTO COLOR 'SCOPE: Yoshikazu Takemura MUSIC: Sei Ikeno w/ Shintaro Katsu, Naoko Kubo, Mayumi Nagisa, Tatsuo Endo Ichi tries to help an honorable clan against Endo's evil gang intent on stealing the river-crossing rights of the village. Kubo and Nagisa are daughters of the ethical boss. When the evil clan triumphs, wiping out the good guys, Ichi goes on a rampage. This final swordfight takes place beneath a sky of colorful fireworks, and we see the dissipating red and green glow on the faces of the fighting, dying men. Unfortunately the final massacre, though filled with nice visual touches, comes off as a bit threadbare.

Director Ikehiro was obviously hampered by a meager budget and hurried shooting schedule. #7 of 26 films * * 1/2 (DAIEI Studios)

FIGHT, ZATOICHI, FIGHT
aka ZATOICHI KESSHO TABI aka BLIND MASSEUR ICHI'S BLOODY JOURNEY 1964 87 min. DIR. Kenji Misumi ORIG. STORY: Kan Shimozawa SCR. Seiji Hoshikawa/Tetsuro Yoshida/ Masaharu Matsumura PHOTO COLOR 'SCOPE: Chishi Makiura MUSIC: Akira Ifukube w/ Shintaro Katsu, Hizuru Takachiho, Nobuo Kaneko, Yoshi Kato, Toshitaro Kitashiro, Tatsuya Ishiguro, Saburo Date Ichi gets saddled having to transport a baby safely to its nearest kin. This could have been phony/sentimental, but once again director Misumi demonstrates his much underrated talent for sparse, straightforward storytelling with a surfeit of visual poetry and no trace of vulgarity. #8 of 26 films * * * (DAIEI Studios)

ADVENTURES OF A BLIND MAN aka ZATOICHI SEKISHO YABURI aka BLIND MASSEUR ICHI BREAKS THROUGH THE CHECKPOINT 1964 86 min. DIR. Kimiyoshi Yasuda ORIG. STORY: Kan Shimozawa SCR. Shozaburo Asai PHOTO COLOR 'SCOPE: Shozo Honda MUSIC: Taiichiro Kosugi w/ Shintaro Katsu, Eiko Taki, Miwa Takada, Mikijiro Hira, Kenjiro Ueda Ichi takes a message to a waitress (Taki) at a local inn from her fugitive beau only to get embroiled in another evil yakuza clan's nefarious plot. Takada is the daughter of a boss who has been murdered and her brother soon meets the same fate.

Hira (veteran star of such excellent films as Hideo Gosha's THREE OUTLAW SAMURAI and SWORD OF THE BEAST) is the hired outlaw *ronin* Ichi must fight in the climactic struggle. Unfortunately, considering the expertise of both Katsu and Hira in *chanbara* roles, their duel is not milked for its full potential. #9 of 26 films * * 1/2 (DAIEI Studios)

ZATOICHI'S REVENGE aka ZATOICHI NIDAN GIRI aka BLIND MASSEUR ICHI'S DOUBLE-CUT SWORD STYLE 1965 83 min. DIR. Akira Inoue ORIG. STORY: Kan Shimozawa SCR. Minoru Inuzuka PHOTO COLOR 'SCOPE: Fujio Morita MUSIC: Akira Ifukube w/ Shintaro Katsu, Mikiko Tsubouchi, Norihei Miki, Takeshi Kato, Fujio Harumoto, Mayumi Kurata, Yukiko Kobayashi, Saburo Date
Ichi finds that his masseur teacher has been murdered. He goes on a vengeance quest to find the guilty party – another outlaw *ronin* employed by ruthless yakuza, this time played by Takeshi Kato. #10 of 26 films * * 1/2 (DAIEI Studios)

ZATOICHI AND THE DOOMED MAN aka ZATOICHI SAKATE GIRI aka BLIND MASSEUR ICHI'S REVERSE SWORDSTYLE 1965 77 min. DIR. Kazuo Mori ORIG. STORY: Kan Shimozawa SCR. Shozaburo Asai PHOTO COLOR 'SCOPE: Hiroshi Imai MUSIC: Seitaro Omori w/ Shintaro Katsu, Eiko Taki, Kenjiro Ishiyama, Hiromi Fujiyama, Ryuzo Shimada
A disappointing entry with too much comic relief from a thief (Fujiyama) who likes to impersonate Shinto priests. He ends up in hot water after trying to impersonate his pal/traveling companion Zatoichi. Fujiyama was a noted comic film actor in mid-to-late-sixties Japan, appearing in supporting "sidekick" roles in many of Toei Studios' *ninkyo* yakuza films. #11 of 26 films * * (DAIEI Studios)

ZATOICHI AND THE CHESS EXPERT aka ZATOICHI JIGOKU TABI aka BLIND MASSEUR ICHI'S TRIP TO HELL 1965 87 min. DIR. Kenji Misumi ORIG. STORY: Kan Shimozawa SCR. Daisuke Ito PHOTO COLOR 'SCOPE: Chishi Makiura MUSIC: Akira Ifukube w/ Shintaro Katsu, Mikio Narita, Chizu Hayashi, Kaneko Iwasaki, Taro Marui The series gets great again with this entry penned by master Daisuke Ito. Ichi befriends a lone wolf samurai (Narita in one of his best roles) who not only turns out to be an expert chess player, but a paranoid psychotic to boot. Ichi also falls in with the wife and child of a man he had killed in a grudge fight. The wife, at first intent on revenge – she is acting as advance scout for her husband's murderous *matatabi* pals – does a turnabout when Ichi braves killers from another yakuza gang and other stacked odds to bring back tetanus medicine from a neighboring village for her injured daughter. Misumi expertly paces the story's subplots to sustain the suspense of the battle of wits between Ichi and Narita. #12 of 26 films * * * 1/2 (DAIEI Studios)

THE BLIND SWORDSMAN'S VENGEANCE aka ZATOICHI NO UTA GA KIKOERU aka BLIND MASSEUR ICHI'S SONG OF VENGEANCE 1966 83 min.

Zatoichi and the Chess Expert (#12) (IMAGE © KADOKAWA PRODUCTIONS)

Dir. Tokuzo Tanaka **Orig. story:**
Kan Shimozawa **Scr.** Hajime Takaiwa **Photo color 'scope:** Kazuo
Miyagawa **Music:** Akira Ifukube
w/ Shintaro Katsu, Shigeru Amachi,
Kei Sato, Mayumi Ogawa, Jun
Hamamura, Mitsuko Yoshikawa
This has the customary plot of a
village threatened by an evil yakuza
clan, but with a few welcome twists
to make up for the lack of originality. Ichi tries to lay aside his sword
several times when he is shamed
by a condescending, self-righteous,
wandering blind *biwa* player. He also
becomes involved with a beautiful
but drunken and despairing whore
(Ogawa) in-love with the desperate
ronin (Amachi) hired by yakuza boss
Sato to kill Ichi. The climax takes
place on a bridge where the yakuza
gang approaches from both ends beating giant festival drums in an attempt
to disorient Ichi. #13 of 26 films
* * * (DAIEI Studios)

ZATOICHI'S PILGRIMAGE aka
ZATOICHI UMI O WATARU aka
BLIND MASSEUR ICHI'S TRIP
ACROSS THE SEA 1966 82 min.
Dir. Kazuo Ikehiro **Orig. story:**
Kan Shimozawa **Scr.** Kaneto Shindo
Photo color 'scope: Senkichiro
Takeda **Music:** Ichiro Saito
w/ Shintaro Katsu, Michiyo Yasuda,
Isao Yamagata, Masao Mishima,
Ryutaro Gomi, Hisashi Igawa, Kunie
Tanaka Another very good entry
this time written by Shindo (ONI-BA-
BA, KURONEKO, et.al). Ichi decides
to make a pilgrimage to a temple for
each man he has killed – about 87 or
so in all. Crossing a remote bridge
in the lush wilderness, he is attacked
and slays the man. The man's horse
follows Ichi for a while and, when

Ichi makes a wrong turn, the horse
corrects him and takes the lead. The
horse stops at its owner's house, and
the dead man's sister (Yasuda) comes
out to greet Ichi. Ichi being the honest, contrite fool that he is, explains
to her what happened. Losing her
temper, Yasuda impulsively runs
to a closet, grabs a short sword and
slashes Ichi's shoulder. Seeing Ichi
all bloody, silently suffering and not
responding to her attack, she regains
her senses and nurses Ichi's wound.
He gets a fever and consequently
stays a few days. Unfortunately, her
brother's cohorts, a mountain bandit
clan, discovers Ichi's presence and
culpability in their comrade's death.
They make things decidedly unpleasant. A wild and woolly climactic
showdown features Ichi performing
uncanny dodging of arrows. My only
complaint is that actress Yasuda never
picks up a sword again. She was a
huge star at Daiei in the mid-to-late
sixties and was known primarily for
her action roles as a sword-weilding
heroine in various yakuza and samurai *chanbara* pictures (the KANTO
WOMAN YAKUZA and WOMAN
SAZEN series especially). But then
again that is one area in which the
Zatoichi films were strangely conservative – while other yakuza and
chanbara films/series in the sixties
and early seventies would quite often
spotlight a swordswoman, none ever
appeared in any of the Blind Swordsman opuses. The film ends with a bit
of an echo from HIGH NOON where
Ichi tries to get help from the village
where he has been staying, people
who all hate the bullying bandit clan,
but remain barricaded behind their
doors, silently listening to Ichi's
knocking, not emerging till Ichi has

been almost killed but has decimated the clan. One brave young soul makes an effort to help Ichi but is killed for his trouble. Reportedly the script was full of even more original ideas than the finished film. Director Ikehiro explained in an interview that the big production boss called him and screenwriter Shindo on the carpet after reading the first draft, explaining that it was good, but that it was way too unorthodox for what was Daiei Studios' main income franchise. So they had to rewrite it a bit in a more conventional direction while still trying to take a somewhat different approach. This is another of the prime reasons star Katsu formed his own production company, to forego the dictates of studio brass. #14 of 26 films   * * * 1/2   (DAIEI Studios)

The Blind Swordsman's Cane Sword #15) (IMAGE © KADOKAWA)

THE BLIND SWORDSMAN'S CANE SWORD aka ZATOICHI TEKKA TABI aka BLIND

MASSEUR ICHI'S SWORD TRIP 1967 93 min. **DIR.** Kimiyoshi Yasuda **ORIG. STORY:** Kan Shimozawa **SCR.** Ryozo Kasahara **PHOTO COLOR 'SCOPE:** Senkichiro Takeda **MUSIC:** Ichiro Saito   w/ Shintaro Katsu, Shiho Fujimura, Eijiro Tono, Makoto Fujita, Masumi Harukawa, Tatsuo Endo   While Ichi gets his broken sword repaired, the swordmaker (Tono), unbeknownst to Ichi, gives him the most coveted sword in the land as a loner – a yakuza boss (Endo) and his henchmen have already tried to steal it. Anyway, it doesn't do the swordmaker much good because he still ends up dead. Ichi discovers what has happened and seeks vengeance as well as freedom for numerous village women enslaved by Endo as prostitutes. Not bad, but once again there is too much comic relief. #15 of 26 films   * * * (DAIEI Studios)

Zatoichi, The Outlaw (#16) (IMAGE © TOHO)

ZATOICHI, THE OUTLAW aka
ZATOICHI RO YABURI aka
BLIND MASSEUR ICHI – THE
BREAK OUT aka ZATOICHI'S
RESCUE 1967 95 min. DIR. Satsuo
Yamamoto ORIG. STORY: Kan
Shimozawa SCR. Takehiro Nakajima/
Koji Matsumoto/Kiyokata Saruwaka
PHOTO COLOR 'SCOPE: Kazuo
Miyagawa MUSIC: Sei Ikeno
w/ Shintaro Katsu, Rentaro Mikuni,
Yuko Hamada, Kenjiro Ishiyama,
Mizuho Suzuki, Kayo Mikimoto, Ko
Nishimura, Toshiyuki Hosokawa,
Takuya Fujioka, Tatsuo Endo
Ichi ends up misjudging character,
supporting a seemingly honest yakuza
boss (Mikuni) who turns out to be
corrupt and a betrayer of the common
people. As soon as Ichi has left town,
Mikuni takes over as village mag-
istrate/constable and persecutes the
farmers mercilessly. Ichi returns after
hearing of the village's misery from
a girl (Mikimoto) who has been sold
into prostitution. This has one of the
most exciting and moving climaxes
as Ichi beheads his formerly trusted
friend and mentor Mikuni then, badly
wounded, is carried by the villagers to
catch up to a police caravan transporting the non-violent samurai leader
(Suzuki) of the farmers to execution.
Zatoichi stories are always told from
the viewpoint of the downtrodden and
oppressed, but this entry has probably the most extreme political tone
of the whole series with the radically leftist master/auteur Yamamoto
(NINJA BAND OF ASSASSINS,
THE GREAT WHITE TOWER, etc.,)
directing. Yamamoto later directed
a *jidai-geki chanbara* about the
real-life swordless samurai/farm-
ers' advocate Yugaku Ohara in 1976
with Mikijiro Hira called TENPO

ERA RIVER STORY – YUGAKU
OHARA. OUTLAW was also Katsu's
first stint at producing – he formed
Katsu Productions with this one,
later to turn out the six excellent
LONE WOLF AND CUB features
(1972 – '74) with his real-life brother
Tomisaburo Wakayama. Interestingly enough, the Zatoichi pictures
that Katsu produced are much more
challenging and entertaining (with a
couple of exceptions) than the straight
"middle-period Zatoichi" Daiei Studios productions. Even though this
film was released by Daiei, Toho now
have the rights. OUTLAW also marks
the first time Katsu sings a theme
song (voiceover during an atmospheric montage of Ichi's wanderings
midway through). #16 of 26 films
* * * * (A KATSU Production
originally released by DAIEI Studios;
rights now with TOHO)

ZATOICHI CHALLENGED aka
ZATOICHI CHI KEMURI KAIDO
aka BLIND MASSEUR ICHI'S
BLOOD-SPRAYED PATH or BLIND
MASSEUR ICHI'S BLOODY PATH
1967 86 min. DIR. Kenji Misumi
ORIG. STORY: Kan Shimozawa SCR.
Ryozo Kasahara PHOTO COLOR
'SCOPE: Chishi Makiura MUSIC:
Akira Ifukube w/ Shintaro Katsu,
Jushiro Konoe, Miwa Takada, Asao
Koike, Mikiko Tsubouchi, Eitaro
Ozawa, Yukiji Asaoka, Jotaro Senba
Ichi once more has a young child in
his charge, this time a boy around six
or seven years old after his mother
dies of an illness. Ichi must take
the boy to join up with his father, a
talented artist shanghaied by a corrupt
official (Ozawa) and a yakuza boss
(Koike) to do erotic renderings on
ceramic vases/dishes. That kind of

thing was considered pornography at the time and was punishable by death. Swordsman Konoe is a Shogunate agent sent by the government to dispatch all the guilty parties, including the coerced artist. Ichi intervenes, having had an earlier friendly relationship with Konoe. However, Konoe is resolute, and the pair cross swords in the falling-snow-dusk in what is unquestionably one of the best-choreographed one-on-one duels in the series. #17 of 26 films * * * (DAIEI Studios)

Zatoichi Challenged (#17)
(IMAGE © KADOKAWA)

BLIND SWORDSMAN AND THE FUGITIVES aka ZATOICHI HATASHIJO aka BLIND MASSEUR ICHI'S FIGHT CHALLENGE 1968 82 min. **DIR.** Kimiyoshi Yasuda **ORIG. STORY:** Kan Shimozawa **SCR.** Kinya Naoi **PHOTO COLOR 'SCOPE:** Kazuo Miyagawa **MUSIC:** Seitaro Omori **w/** Shintaro Katsu, Takashi Shimura, Kyosuke Machida, Kayo

Mikimoto, Yumiko Nogawa, Akifumi Inoue, Hosei Komatsu, Jotaro Senba Ichi comes to a village being terrorized by sadistic bandit killers hired by the local yakuza. Machida is the wayward son of the benevolent local doctor (Shimura) and brother to the beautiful Mikimoto. He is also the leader of the brigands. The always-excellent Nogawa (of Suzuki's GATE OF FLESH and STORY OF A PROSTITUTE) is the misguided thief apprentice to the bunch. Ichi manages to steer her onto the straight-and-narrow by scaring her out-of-her-wits. Once again great atmosphere, cast, incredible cinematography by the master Miyagawa and excellent choreography of action/ fighting. #18 of 26 films * * * 1/2 (DAIEI Studios)

Blind Swordsman and the Fugitives (#18) (IMAGE © KADOKAWA)

THE BLIND SWORDSMAN SAMARITAN aka ZATOICHI KENKA DAIKO aka BLIND MASSEUR ICHI & THE BATTLE

DRUM 1968 82 min. Dir. Kenji Misumi Orig. story: Kan Shimozawa Scr. Hisashi Sugiura/ Tetsuro Yoshida/Kiyokata Saruwaka Photo color 'scope: Fujio Morita Music: Sei Ikeno w/ Shintaro Katsu, Yoshiko Mita, Makoto Sato, Ko Nishimura, Takuya Fujioka, Rokko Toura, Chocho Miyako
Ichi is along for the ride when his host gang goes to settle a score with a young gambler who has a delinquent debt. He ends up being the one to kill the fellow just before the man's sister (Mita) returns with the money. The gang wants to take her as interest – it turns out the corrupt local magistrate has had his eye on her for some time – but Ichi and his bumbling *matatabi* pal (the comic Fujioka) step in. Once again Ichi feels obligated to give safe passage to someone who, initially, wants him dead to avenge a loved-one's demise. Sato is an unscrupulous, lust-driven *ronin* out to get Mita for himself, and he throws a monkeywrench into Ichi and Mita's escape plans. An extremely entertaining entry, although the story is not particularly original. As is more often the case than not, director Misumi pulls excellence out of his hat. Genuinely funny humor, great swordfights that are astoundingly photographed and Misumi's tasteful and subtle poetic sensibility regarding nature and everything else. Also of note, an exceptional score by the underrated and comparatively unknown Ikeno. #19 of 26 films * * * 1/2 (DAIEI Studios)

ZATOICHI MEETS YOJINBO
aka ZATOICHI TO YOJINBO aka BLIND MASSEUR ICHI AND THE BODYGUARD 1970 116 min. Dir.

Kihachi Okamoto Orig. story: Kan Shimozawa Scr. Kihachi Okamoto/ Tetsuro Yoshida Photo color 'scope: Kazuo Miyagawa Music: Akira Ifukube w/ Shintaro Katsu, Toshiro Mifune, Ayako Wakao, Kanjuro Arashi, Osamu Takizawa, Shin Kishida The title says it all with Ichi and Sanjuro (Mifune) alternately teaming-up, fighting, teaming-up again amidst internecine warfare amongst a craven merchant father (Takizawa) and his greedy, errant sons: one, a yakuza boss who has hired Sanjuro as *yojinbo*, the other an employee of the Edo gold mint who is embezzling the yellow stuff. Wakao is the beautiful whore in-love with Sanjuro; veteran *chanbara* star Arashi is the former village headman reluctantly assisting Takizawa; and Kishida is the sinister Shogunate agent sent to check up on Sanjuro. Mifune it turns out is also, however reluctantly, a government spy. The climax is a variation on THE TREASURE OF SIERRA MADRE's ending. *Chanbara* expert director Okamoto (KILL!, SWORD OF DOOM) reportedly had trouble with mega-stars Katsu and Mifune in regards to deciding who would win the final sword duel. See the result for yourself. But, let's put it this way: it is not unexpected. #20 of 26 films * * * 1/2 (A KATSU Production released by DAIEI Studios; rights now: TOHO)

ZATOICHI'S FESTIVAL OF FIRE
aka ZATOICHI ABARE HIMATSURI aka BLIND MASSEUR ICHI'S FIRE FESTIVAL RAMPAGE 1970 95 min. Dir. Kenji Misumi Orig. story: Kan Shimozawa Scr. Shintaro Katsu/Ryuji (Takashi?) Yamada Photo color 'scope:

Zatoichi Meets Yojinbo (#20) (IMAGE © TOHO)

Kazuo Miyagawa **MUSIC:** Isao Tomita w/ Shintaro Katsu, Tatsuya Nakadai, Masayuki Mori, Reiko Ohara, Ko Nishimura, Peter, Kunie Tanaka One of the top three best Zatoichi films with much action, humor, pathos and Misumi's visual poetry. Mori plays a contemptible blind yakuza boss-of-bosses who devises one of the most sadian death traps Ichi has ever had to wrangle-out-of. Nakadai is the tormented, obsessed former Hatamoto samurai (the Hatamoto were the Shogun's top-ranking squad of samurai) who has murdered his promiscuous wife. He is out to get Ichi, believing Ichi had also slept with her. Ohara is the beautiful daughter of underboss Nishimura who is first sent to trap Ichi but ends up falling-in-love with him. And Peter is the sexually ambivalent teenage pimp son of another underboss who wishes Ichi to "show him how to be a man." #21 of 26 films * * * * (A KATSU Production released by DAIEI Studios; rights now: TOHO)

THE BLIND SWORDSMAN MEETS HIS EQUAL aka SHIN ZATOICHI YABURE! TOJIN KEN! aka NEW BLIND MASSEUR ICHI – BREAK THE CHINESE SWORD! aka ZATOICHI MEETS THE ONE-ARMED SWORDSMAN 1971 95 min. **DIR.** Kimiyoshi Yasuda **ORIG. STORY:** Kan Shimozawa **SCR.** Kimiyoshi Yasuda/Ryuji (Takashi?) Yamada **PHOTO COLOR 'SCOPE:** Chishi Makiura **MUSIC:** Isao Tomita w/ Shintaro Katsu, Wang Yu (pka Jimmy Wang Yu), Koji Nanbara, Yuko Hamaki, Michie Terada, Toru Abe, Takamaru Sasaki Chinese veteran of countless Hong Kong

martial arts films, Jimmy Wang Yu, had his own much shorter-lived series about a peculiar swordsman; his handicap? One arm. He also starred in a one-armed kung fu boxer series. There are different stories about this, but it seems to have been, despite being executive-produced by Katsu for Daiei, a Japanese/Hong Kong co-production. It is also the only one of the series to not see a video release in Japan until the turn of the millenium. One-armed swordsman Wang Yu is traveling in Japan, but unable to speak the language. He is appalled and goaded to action when not only a Chinese couple he has met, but a number of common Japanese travelers, are slain by arrogant samurai. The Chinese couple's son survives and is helped by Ichi, something that Wang Yu initially misinterprets. Soon Ichi, the boy and Wang Yu are traveling together as fugitives, but communication proves difficult due to the language barrier. Before long, Ichi becomes separated from them by accident and Wang Yu is led to believe by an unfortunate coincidence that Ichi has slain their farmer benefactors who have sheltered them - a bit of an illogical conclusion and one of the contrived devices to get Wang Yu and Ichi to turn against each other. Soon Wang Yu and the boy find shelter at a monastery with Wang Yu's old comrade, a Buddhist priest who is also an expert martial-arts pole-fighter (Nanbara). But Nanbara turns out to be a greedy, untrustworthy friend, more interested in the bounty on Wang Yu and Ichi's heads and eager to foster dissension between the two. Things end with Ichi and Wang Yu decimating the corrupt samurai as well as Nanbara, then turning their swords on each other. It has been asserted by different sources to have a slightly different ending in the Chinese release – one source maintains both Wang Yu and Katsu wound each other in the climactic duel but both survive; another source maintains that Wang Yu kills Ichi! Wang Yu dies in the Japanese release. It is too bad that the script is not particularly well-written. Though this entry is good, it is not particularly memorable. Considering the legendary iconography that Katsu and Wang Yu represent, this should have been a masterpiece. But it just isn't. #22 of 26 films   * * * (A KATSU Production released theatrically at the time by DAIEI Studios; rights now: TOHO)

ZATOICHI AT LARGE   aka ZATOICHI GOYOTABI   aka BLIND MASSEUR ICHI'S JOURNEY OF OBLIGATION 1972 90 min. DIR. Kazuo Mori ORIG. STORY: Kan Shimozawa SCR. Kinya Naoi PHOTO COLOR 'SCOPE: Fujio Morita MUSIC: Kunihiko Murai/Osamu Sakai w/ Shintaro Katsu, Rentaro Mikuni, Hisaya Morishige, Etsushi Takahashi, Naoko Otani, Shoki Fukae

Ichi comes across a dying pregnant woman in an overgrown field and, with much reluctant trepidation, delivers her baby. Her other child, a five or six year old boy, is watching from a short distance. He believes Ichi is hurting his mother and is under the impression through most of the rest of the saga that Ichi killed her. Though there are wanted posters all over the area, Ichi braves being seen in the nearby village to try to find someone to care for the newborn tyke. The village is preparing for a festival and the various performers and vendors are

being put through the hoops by the greedy local yakuza boss (Mikuni). The local constable – an honest man (Morishige) stands up to Mikuni and gang but to no avail until Ichi intervenes. Morishige also has a disrespectful son who is a budding yakuza. It takes his father being murdered for the unruly teenager to come to his senses. Takahashi is a hired *ronin* who goes up against Ichi as he leaves town at the denouement. #23 of 26 films   * * *   (A KATSU Production released by TOHO)

Zatoichi in Desperation (#24)
(IMAGE © TOHO)

ZATOICHI IN DESPERATION aka SHIN ZATOICHI MONOGA-TARI – ORETA TSUE aka NEW BLIND MASSEUR ICHI STORY – BROKEN CANE 1972 92 min. DIR. Shintaro Katsu ORIG. STORY: Kan Shimozawa SCR. Minoru Inuzuka PHOTO COLOR 'SCOPE: Fujio Morita MUSIC: Kunihiko Murai/ Mitsuo Miyamoto w/ Shintaro Katsu, Kiwako Taichi, Katsuo

Nakamura, Kyoko Yoshizawa, Asao Koike, Joji Takagi, Masumi Harukawa, Hideji Otaki   Ichi passes an elderly female *shamisen* player on a rickety footbridge. The woman slips between the ties and is suddenly holding on for dear life. She begs Ichi to take her *shamisen* to her daughter in a nearby village, then falls to her death in the river below. Ichi feels somehow responsible and picks up the *shamisen*. The daughter is a prostitute in the village brothel. Ichi develops his usual adversary relationship with the town's exploitive yakuza gang, and, before the story is over, has all of his fingers brutally smashed. He has to tie his sword to his hand to cut the evildoers to ribbons. This film also shows Ichi actually making love to a whore, something alluded to in other earlier films but never shown. This was Katsu's directorial debut. Though skilled with actors and narrative, he occasionally utilizes self-consciously unusual camera angles. However, he more than makes up for this first-time-out self-indulgence by delivering, without question, what is the most downbeat, bleak and realistic entry in the series. There is a very-faithful-to-the-time-and-place ambience along with several truly disturbing scenes, chief amongst them cruel yakuza toughs killing a little boy who has been throwing stones at them and, later, masturbating (!) a severely retarded teenager on the beach. #24 of 26 films   * * *   (A KATSU Production released by TOHO)

ZATOICHI'S CONSPIRACY
aka SHIN ZATOICHI MONOGA-TARI – KASAMA NO CHIMAT-SURI aka NEW BLIND MASSEUR ICHI STORY – BLOODBATH AT

KASAMA   1973   88 min.   **Dir.** Kimiyoshi Yasuda   **Orig. story:** Kan Shimozawa   **Scr.** Yoshiko Hattori   **Photo color 'scope:** Chishi Makiura   **Music:** Akira Ifukube

***Zatoichi's Conspiracy** (#25)*
(IMAGE © TOHO)

w/ Shintaro Katsu, Yukiyo Toake, Kei Sato, Eiji Okada, Takashi Shimura, Rie Yokoyama   Ichi journeys back to his hometown of Kasama only to find his old house on the edge of the village a dilapidated shack. A homeless pack of rebellious teenage derelicts take shelter there. Ichi becomes involved with them as well as running up against the usual evil yakuza leader (Sato). An okay but disappointing end to the original series of films. It was the last Zatoichi picture until 1989. After this, Katsu took the character to a very successful run on television. Most of the TV episodes are extremely low budget. Fortunately, though, Katsu, as the guiding light of the TV series, kept a tight rein. He made sure that the writing, directing and acting were all top-notch. He utilized many of the directors who helmed the films – Kenji Misumi, Kazuo Mori, Kimiyoshi Yasuda, Akira Inoue, et. al. as well as newer talent such as Akikazu Ota and Toshiaki Kunihara (former screenwriters and assistant directors at Daiei). There were the occasional clinkers but, by and large, the TV show was a more than honorable extension of the film series, often dealing with stories too introspective, too character-driven and small-in-scope to have been done on the big screen. #25 of 26 films * * 1/2 (A KATSU Production released by TOHO)

ZATOICHI 1989 116 min. **Dir.** Shintaro Katsu **Scr.** Shintaro Katsu/Tsutomu Nakamura/Tatsumi Ichiyama **PHOTO COLOR PANAVISION:** Mutsuo Naganuma **Music:** Takayuki Watanabe w/ Shintaro Katsu, Ken Ogata, Yomiko Higuchi, Yuya Uchida, Takeo Okumura, Norihei Miki   The most spectacular, most poignant and poetic of the whole blind swordsman film series. A genuine masterpiece, with Katsu's directorial style maturing into the realm of Gosha and Misumi. Much better, in this writer's opinion, than the last couple of Kurosawa-helmed period/samurai films, and it deserves to have been released in theaters worldwide. All this with Katsu an extremely spry 57 years old. There are standout performances from Uchida as one of the deliciously slimy yakuza bosses; Okumura (Katsu's son) as the scarred young upstart boss who wipes out all opposition and has put a bounty on Ichi's head; Ogata as the artist/master swordsman who is Ichi's inwardly tortured, impoverished friend who will become conflicted by the bounty on Ichi's head; Miki as one of Ichi's oldest comrades who lives in a house on a windswept beach. Higuchi also excels as a female boss, the only gang-affiliated yakuza in the story with any integrity. The scene where Ichi makes love to her in a hotsprings with the moonlight shifting beneath moving clouds is tender, yet erotic. #26 and final in the series * * * * (A KATSU Production released by SHOCHIKU)

NOTE: In this 1989 ZATOICHI (and the swan song of Katsu as the blind masseur), a stuntman was killed during a swordfight. Too make matters worse, Katsu's son Takeo Okumura (aka Ryutaro Gan) was the one who accidentally struck the fatal blow. Although negligence was found, Katsu and son seemed to have not suffered any serious consequences. Katsu died of throat cancer in 1997. He had had his share of troubles in the last decade of his life, what with his cocaine bust in Hawaii in the early 1990s (which reportedly sabotaged getting the role of the old yakuza boss in Ridley Scott's BLACK RAIN, which then went to his brother) and the death of said beloved sibling, Tomisaburo Wakayama, from heart failure brought on by diabetes in 1992. Katsu, despite his monumental ego and difficult ways (particularly if you were a director working with him), was a true giant of Japanese genre film and deserves recognition as such for not only the pleasure he has brought to millions, but for his steadfast tradition of taste, aesthetic purity and soul-baring in all of his films.

APPENDIX 2
ATG (ART THEATRE GUILD)
INDEPENDENTS (INCLUDING PINK FILMS)

Japan's Evil Spirits

Appendix 2

INTRODUCTION: ATG (ART THEATRE GUILD), INDEPENDENTS (INCLUDING PINKU EIGA AND ROMAN PORN)

Blood and Flesh

For all intents and purposes, independent film productions in Japan between 1940 – 1960 were largely non-existent, unless you were engaged in making extremely low-budget, so-called "adults only" features. Even these "adults only" movies, which came to be known as *pinku eiga* (pink films), barely existed before mid-century. The most-financially-strapped major studio, Shintoho, started to produce some fairly tame examples of adult-oriented movies in the mid-1950s; in other words, genre pictures (mostly crime, adventure or horror) that emphasized scantily-clad heroines in jeopardy. Executive producer (and rumored former carnival huckster) Mitsugu Okura ushered in this trend when he took over control of the company, trying to rescue it from declining revenue and the threat of insolvency. Some fleeting glimpses of nudity began to appear, and other major studios such as Toho, Daiei and especially Toei and Nikkatsu followed suit, to varying economic rewards. Shochiku produced adult films, as well, but under the subsidiary/pseudonym Tokatsu.

When Shintoho went bankrupt in 1961 and lost their status as one of the major players in production and exhibition, its holdings were sold off. Producer Okura started his own small company called, modestly enough, Okura Eiga. They continued making genre films, once again mostly crime and horror, but with much lower budgets, much more exposed female flesh and largely unknown talent. Other companies sprouted, all of them one step ahead of censorship laws. The entrepreneur who bought the rights to Shintoho's name started to once again release product under that moniker.

Although all of the major studios adopted the anamorphic CinemaScope aspect ratio in 1958, the process was not constantly in use by the small pink film companies. Some used it, some did not. Likewise, color film stock and processing (not to mention duplicating color prints for distribution) was often out of range of these small businesses' budgets. Most of their films in the early 1960s were shot in black-and-white. But by 1965 –'66, due to strong competition, many of the companies had no choice and, at the very least, released films in what came to be called "part-color," literally meaning that a few sequences (especially the climax) would appear in color (thus the split B&W/color credit on a select number of the few cinematography credits you will find in the following listings). Sometimes the color appellation meant full color, and sometimes it just meant tinted stock.

Due to the often fly-by-night nature of these miniscule companies, many of their productions from the 1960s are irretrievably lost, having been junked once their distribution release and re-release schedule was met. Their shelf-life expired, they disappeared down the chutes into the dustbins of time. Some of these companies were not particularly long-lived themselves, and profits went into the pockets of the one or two company owners. Media exploitation of product through VHS and Beta videocassettes, not to mention DVD and Blu-Ray, was not even on the horizon, and sales to television, due to the subject matter, was out of the question.

ATG (or the Art Theatre Guild) began distributing "arthouse" movies in Japan in 1961, beginning with the Polish MOTHER JOAN OF THE ANGELS (MATKA JOANNA OD ANIOLOW), then continuing with a few avant-garde style Japanese features in the mid-1960s. They did not enter into actual production until 1967, when they co-produced Shohei Imamura's semi-documentary, A MAN VANISHES (NINGEN JOHATSU). Helped to some degree by Japanese government culture grants, ATG continued to produce/co-produce a number of prestigious, critically-acclaimed pictures – "difficult" fare that was sometimes picked up later – if the movie had "legs" – for distribution by the majors, especially Toho.

ATG made it possible for such films as Kihachi Okamoto's savagely surrealist WW2 satire, THE HUMAN BULLET (NIKUDAN, 1968), Nagisa Oshima's DEATH BY HANGING (KOU SHIKEI, 1968), BOY (SHONEN, 1969), THE CEREMONY (GISHIKI, 1971), Akio Jissoji's THIS TRANSIENT LIFE (MUJO, 1970), Yoshishige Yoshida's HEROIC PURGATORY (RENGOKU EROIKA, 1970), Toshio Matsumoto's FUNERAL PARADE OF ROSES (BARA NO SORETSU, 1969), Koji Wakamatsu's brutal dismantling of violent radical politics, ECSTASY OF THE ANGELS (TENSHI NO KOKOTSU, 1972), and Kon Ichikawa's excellent tragi-comic deconstruction of the in-period *matatabi* yakuza subgenre, THE WANDERERS (MATATABI, 1973) – to name only a few – to exist. ATG ceased all production and most distribution in 1985.

ATG/INDEPENDENTS/ PINKU EIGA

Ancient-Looking Priest's 48 Killings

ANCIENT-LOOKING PRIEST'S 48 KILLINGS aka KOSHUKU BOZU YON-JU HACHI TE KIRI 1969 **Dir.** Kaoru Umezawa (pka Kaoru Higashimoto) **w/** Teruo Sakamaki, Miki Hayashi, Setsu Shimizu, Kazuko Shirakawa A pink film spoof of the ZATOICHI, BLIND SWORDSMAN films. (UEMATSU PRO/NICHIEI)

ATOMIC WAR aka GENSHI RYOKU SENSO 1977 **Dir.** Kazuo Kuroki **Scr.** Tatsuhiko Kamoi **w/** Yoshio Harada, Sayoko Yamaguchi, Jun Fufuki, Eiji Okada, Kei Sato (ATG)

BENTEN Series

DESPECIABLE MAN-KILLING BENTEN aka OTOKO GOROSHI

GOKUAKU BENTEN 1969 **Dir.** Mamoru Watanabe **Scr.** Atsushi Yamatoya   **w/** Tamaki Katori A pair of totally under-the-radar pink, in-period *ninkyo* yakuza films supposedly inspired by Junko Fuji's RED PEONY GAMBLER Oryu character. Credits include the atypical participation of the supremely imaginative writer Yamatoya, a man whose taste usually ran to more surrealist-cum-contemporary crime sex sagas such as BRANDED TO KILL, STRAY CAT ROCK – SEX HUNTER and his own self-directed INFLATABLE SEX DOLL OF THE WASTELANDS. Many thanks to writer Jasper Sharp for pointing these Benten films out in his detailed chronicle of Japan's sex film history, *Behind the Pink Curtain*. Note: It seems that despite the second movie below sharing most of the same credits, as well as a continuing storyline, the sequel was produced by a different company. (NIHON GEIJUTSU KYOKAI)

WOMAN HELL SONG – BAMBOO FLUTE BENTEN aka ONNA JIGOKU UTA – SHAKUHACHI BENTEN 1970 **Dir.** Mamoru Watanabe **Scr.** Atsushi Yamatoya **w/** Tamaki Katori, Noriko Tatsumi, Rima Aoyama (KANTO EIHAI)

BLOOD AND FLESH aka CHI TO NIKU 1965 **Dir.** Kinnosuke Fukada **Scr.** Moto Yatsuka **Photo B&W** (**'scope?**): Hiroshi Matsui **w/** Keiko Kayama, Kazumitsu Okura, Hiroko Shima, Ichiro Kojima (ROPPO Eiga)

BLOOD IS REDDER THAN THE SUN aka CHI WA TAIYO YORI AKAI aka THE SUN IS REDDER

THAN BLOOD 1966 80 min.
DIR. Koji Wakamatsu **SCR.** Yoshiaki
Otani **PHOTO B&W/COLOR 'SCOPE:**
Hideo Ito   w/ Kazuhiko Otsuka,
Tamami Wakahara, Kikio Terajima
According to Jasper Sharp, writing
in his *Behind the Pink Curtain* book,
this was "...Wakamatsu's answer to
Nikkatsu's earlier sun tribe movies..."
and was also raved about by no less a
personage than filmmaker/playwright
Shuji Terayama. (WAKAMATSU
Productions)

**BLUE ASSAULT – ACCOUNT OF
AN ABNORMAL EXPERIENCE**
aka 1967 67 min. **DIR.** Takae Shindo
w/ Yukari Ejima, Takahiro Ohira,
Nami Kawamura   A young rural
woman is rescued by a Tokyo man
from gang rape by some hometown
lowlifes. When the seemingly sensitive rescuer returns to Tokyo, the
woman follows him to try to better
her situation only to go from the frying pan into the fire. Her rescuer ends
up drugging her and offering her to
clients, and she soon discovers he is
really a yakuza pimp behind many
other similar incidents. (KOKUEI)

BONELESS aka HONENUKI aka
MUTILATION 1967 72 min. **DIR.**
Seiichi Fukuda   w/ Mari Nagisa,
Kaoru Miya, Masao Shirakawa,
Noriko Chigetsu   A married woman
has a tryst with an old boyfriend who
has blown back into town, and she
is then blackmailed by gangsters to
work as a prostitute for them. Things
get complicated when one of her
clients ends up being a *gaijin* who has
business dealings with her husband.
(ROPPO Eiga; distributed by Harry
Novak's Boxoffice International in
the USA)

Bullet Aesthetics

BULLET AESTHETICS aka
TEPPO DAMA NO BIGAKU 1972
100 min. **DIR.** Sadao Nakajima
SCR. Tatsuo Nogami **PHOTO COLOR**
('SCOPE?): Umeo Masuda **MUSIC:**
Ichiro Araki/Zuno Keisatsu
w/ Tsunehiko Watase, Miki
Sugimoto, Mitsuru Mori, Asao
Koike, Jon Midorigawa
The usually very commercial director
Nakajima does a film that is seeming-
ly off-kilter enough to be produced by
ATG (Art Theatre Guild). The second
name credited under the music score,
Zuno Keisatsu, I suppose is a joke as
it means "Head of Police." (ATG)

**CODE OF THE CRIMINAL
WOMAN** aka ONNA HAN NO
OKITE 1963 **DIR.** Satoru
(Go) Kobayashi **SCR.** Shokei
Machida **PHOTO 'SCOPE:** Yoshio
Wakino Music: Hisao Ninomiya
w/ Shiro Enami, Kinuko Ohara,
Shizuko Terakado (NIHON SHIN-
EMA FYURUUMU EIGA or A
JAPAN CINEMA FILM MOVIE)

Ecstasy of Wickedness aka *Evil Agony*

ECSTASY OF WICKEDNESS
aka AKU NO MODAE aka EVIL
AGONY 1964 67 min. DIR. Koji
Wakamatsu SCR. Michio Yoshioka
PHOTO B&W ('SCOPE?): Kaizo
Akiyama w/ Yasuko Matsui, Tamaki
Katori, Mikio Tershima, Akio
Shiakawa (NIHON Cinema)

**THE DEVIL DWELLS IN A
WOMAN'S VALLEY** aka
1972 **Dir.** Giichi Nishihara (pka
Shiro Sekiya)

FLESH MARKET aka NIKUTAI
ICHIBA 1962 49 min. (**only 21 min.
survive**) DIR. Satoru (Go) Kobayashi
w/ Tamaki Katori, Hiroshi Asami,
Shiro Enami A teenage girl investigates the mysterious death of her
sister in Tokyo's *gaijin* club district,
Roppongi, and falls into the clutches
of a gang. One of the earliest examples of the more daring pink film,
directed by Shintoho veteran
Kobayashi. (OKURA Eiga)

FEMALE SACRIFICE aka
MARU HADAKA – JORO IKENIE
1977 63 min. Dir. Mamoru
Watanabe w/ Kyoko Aizome (pka
Kyoko Aoyama), Riko Izumi, Jiro
Kokubo A set-in-period saga of hell-
ish conditions in the old Yoshiwara
prostitution district. (SHINTOHO)

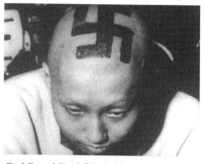

God Speed You! Black Emperor

**GOD SPEED YOU! BLACK EM-
PEROR** aka BURAKKU EN-
PERAA – GODDO SUPIIDO YUU!
1978 91 min. DIR. Mitsuo Yan-
agimachi PHOTO B&W: Kasutoshi
Iwanaga/Yoshifumi Yokoyama/Kimio
Tsukamoto/Makoto Sugiura/Taro
Akashi w/ Burakku Enperaa (Black
Emperor) *Bosozuku* (violent tribe)
quasi-documentary about a famed
biker/apprentice hood from mid-
1970s Japan.

**GROTESQUE PERVERTED
SLAUGHTER** aka BIZARRE
MODERN SEX CRIME aka
GENDAI RYOKI SEI HANZAI
1976 DIR. Giichi Nishihara
w/ Keiko Sugi, Kiyoshi Nakayama,
Yuri Izumi
Director Nishihara originally started
out in the legitimate film business,
toiling away post-WW2 at studios
like Daiei and Shochiku as both an
actor and assistant director. But in the
1960s, he struck out on his own into

the burgeoning pink film market, soon becoming known as an "out-there" director with financial ties to real yakuza. He has a reputation as something of an *ero/guro* sub-genius who shot some of the sickest scenarios ever to emerge from *pinku eiga*. He was also married to actress Izumi. The plot here owes as much to the splatter horror genre as *pinku* and yakuza *eiga*. A man's mistress hires some yakuza to kill her lover's wife. The wife barely survives a brutal rape from the hoods, then turns the tables on the mistress, struggling with her, eventually killing her and dismembering her. She and her chastened husband then have savage sex while the mistress' body parts decompose under their bed! Wow. (AOI Eiga/SHINTOHO)

HIGH SCHOOL GIRL GUERRILLA aka JOGAKUSEI GERIRA 1969 73 min. DIR. Masao Adachi w/ Eri Ashikawa, Kenji Fukuma, Sachiko Ichiji   Director Adachi was a real-life Japan Red Army member as well as an artistic collaborator with filmmakers Koji Wakamatsu and Nagisa Oshima. This picture was reportedly made concurrently with Wakamatsu's own VIOLENT VIRGIN. It makes a fascinating demarcation point between the violent but politically tamer examples of the *sukeban* genre such as Toei Studios' DELINQUENT GIRL BOSS, Nikkatsu's STRAY CAT ROCK series and Toei's later more subversive, bestial GIRL BOSS and TERRIFYING GIRLS' HIGH SCHOOL movies. But whereas the latter series may have been more unrestrained – and perhaps even influenced by filmmakers such as Wakamatsu, Adachi and Atsushi Yamatoya (Yamatoya *did* help script

STRAY CAT ROCK – SEX HUNTER and RANKING BOSS ROCK), it also should be noted that even the most excessive of these early-to-mid 1970s mainstream *sukeban* films were more in the province of tall tales or *manga*-style fantasies, while a much, much lower-budgeted film like Adachi's is in an almost neo-realist vein and is, in fact, intent on demythologizing revolutionary politics and the romanticized image of the teen rebel. Of course, doing so all under the guise of a sex film! (WAKAMATSU Productions)

Hot Night

HOT NIGHT aka ATSUI YORU 1965 Dir. Susumu Okano w/ Yosuke Hayashi (TOKYO HOEI)

INFLATABLE SEX DOLL OF THE WASTELANDS aka KOYA NO DAACHII WAIFU aka DUTCH WIFE IN THE WILDERNESS aka HORROR DOLL 1967 85 min. DIR./ SCR. Atsushi Yamatoya PHOTO B&W 'SCOPE: Hajime Kai MUSIC: Yosuke

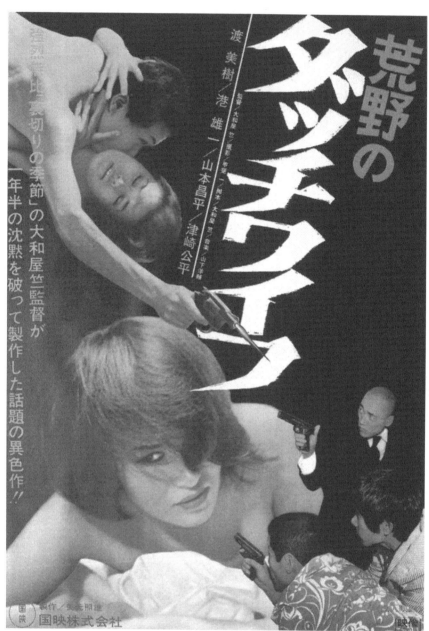

Inflatable Sex Doll of the Wastelands

Yamashita **w/** Yuichi Minato, Shôhei Yamamoto, Akaji Maro, Mari Nagisa, Noriko Tatsumi, Misa Watari, Taka Okubo   An unsavory private detective is hired to find a woman who has apparently been murdered by a gang in a snuff film. It turns out the woman is not dead, and he gets sucked into a torrid affair with her that leaves him questioning his sense of reality. Director Yamatoya also co-wrote the screenplay for Suzuki's masterpiece, BRANDED TO KILL, and this seems to be in the same surreal visual realm. (KOKUEI)

JAPAN'S EVIL SPIRITS
aka NIHON NO AKU RYO 1970 96 min. **DIR.** Kazuo Kuroki **SCR.** Yoshiyuki Fukuda/Kazumi Takahashi **PHOTO B&W:** Yasuhiro Hotta **MUSIC:** Nobuyasu Okabayashi/Yoshio Hatakawa   **w/** Kei Sato, Yosuke Natsuki, Tatsuo Takahashi, Fumio Watanabe, Akio Hayashi, Masahiko Naruse, Tatsumi Hijikata,Haruhiko Okamura, Eiko Horie, Akemi Nara, Nobuyasu Okabayashi
A yakuza bodyguard and a police officer/ex-student activist look so much alike, they decide to switch their positions. (ATG Productions)

LEAD TOMBSTONE aka NAMARI NO BOHYO aka TOMBSTONE DIALECT 1964 85 min. **DIR.** Koji Wakamatsu **w/** Kahoru Tashiro, Yoko Tsukui, Masayoshi Nogami, Mikio Terajima Wakamatsu had already shown promise as a perversely intuitive visual stylist and natural born storyteller from his earliest efforts. He tracks the progress of a young sociopathic rake who had, immediately post-WW2, rescued his country farmer mother

from rape by stabbing the offending American soldier in the back with a pitchfork. Once grown, the boy continues his violent life as a hoodlum on the run, repaying an outlaw couple who have sheltered him by raping the wife then, at his gang boss's behest, murdering the husband. He is also not above strangling a girl in her bathtub for kicks. The one spot of normalcy in his life is his shopgirl lover, an innocent who, once she discovers his other life, confronts his boss. It is something that proves fatal, as the boss then orders the boy to kill her. Shooting her on a rocky cliff overlooking the beach, he is immediately remorseful, but when he bends over to caress her face, another shot rings out from an unseen gunman, and he drops dead at her side. (KOKUEI)
* * *

Lone Woman

LONE WOMAN aka ONNA NO IPPATSU 1965? 1966? **DIR.** Kiyoshi Komori   **w/** Keiko Tachibana, Shinobu Ayakawa   (KPC Productions/SHINTOHO)

LOOSE WOMEN aka MUKIDO JOSEI 1967 76 min. **DIR.** Jiro Matsubara **SCR.** Oniroku Dan **PHOTO COLOR:** Tomoji Asano **w/** Rie Taki, Tadashi Tanemura, Miki Hayashi, Michiyo Mori, Koji Satomi, Yukari Yamabuki   Newlyweds arrive in the big city from their rural hometown, only to be victimized by gangsters, and the wife is raped. (OKURA Eiga)

Loose Women

LUSTY WOMAN'S MISTAKES aka JOYOKU ONNA NO AYAMACHI aka GIRL AND THE GANGSTERS aka FAULT OF A LUSTFUL WOMAN 1968 68 min. **DIR.** Takae Shindo **w/** Mari Ibuki, Tatsuya Yoshida (OKURA Eiga)

Naked Bullet aka Man-Murder, Woman Murder- Soft Fugitive Flesh

NAKED BULLET aka HADAKA NO JUDAN aka OTOKO GOROSHI ONNA GOROSHI - YAWA HADA MUSHUKU 1969 72 min. **DIR.** Koji Wakamatsu **SCR.** Izuru Deguchi **PHOTO B&W/ COLOR 'SCOPE:** Hideo Ito **w/** Ken Yoshizawa, Miki Hayashi, Eri Ashikawa   Two gangs are exchanging cash for heroin when robbed in a shootout. The three thieves take the moll (Hayashi) of the gang boss hostage and flee. To make matters more contentious, the moll had hidden the heroin beforehand, replacing it with flour. One of the three lone wolves (Yoshikawa) wants the money and the girl for himself. We see early on – in a grueling color flashback – that Yoshizawa had been through a similar situation five years before, having run away with another girlfriend of the same boss. Once caught, he and the girl were brutally punished in an abandoned warehouse. His traumatized paramour had run off to become a drug-addicted whore. This time, Yoshizawa is more concerned with the loot than the woman, and taking the moll is icing on the cake. Too bad for Yoshizawa, this woman is a shrewd manipulator. As she and Yoshizawa flee from the city to a rural hotsprings resort, they are pursued

by both the boss's hitmen and the two friends Yoshizawa has betrayed. This is a finely honed, suspenseful, erotic gem, well-acted by all, with a quirky, piercing twist in the very last scene. Note: I ran across a poster for NAKED BULLET with the same Japanese umbrella title (OTOKO GOROSHI ONNA GOROSHI). However, the second part of the title is not HADAKA NO JUDAN (translated as NAKED BULLET) but YAWA HADA MUSHUKU (translated here as SOFT FUGITIVE FLESH). Some pink films were retitled for re-release, which may be the case here.
* * * 1/2   (AOI Eiga/ WAKAMATSU Productions)

Rina Hoshi (AOI Eiga)

Outlaw and the Adultress

Naked Bullet aka Man-Murder, Woman Murder- Soft Fugitive Flesh

OUTLAW AND THE ADULTRESS aka YARO TO JOFU 1969 Dir. Hajime (Gen) Sasaki Scr. Bun Tachibana Photo color ('scope?): Seiji Ikeda w/ Setsu Shimizu, Kazuko Shirakawa, Mayumi Togawa,

Resurrection of the Golden Wolf

RESURRECTION OF THE GOLDEN WOLF aka YOME-GAERU KINRO 1975 131 min. Dir. Toru Murakawa Scr. Shuichi Nagahara Photo color 'scope: Seizo Sengen w/ Yusaku Matsuda, Jun Fubuki, Shinichi "Sonny" Chiba, Mikio Narita, Asao Koike
Matsuda is a ruthless anti-hero bent on wresting control of a corporation from the mob. (KADOKAWA Productions)

Resurrection of the Golden Wolf

Secret Whore

SECRET WHORE aka HIMITSU SHO 1969 DIR. Yasuhiko Saga SCR. Masayoshi Ikeda w/ Noriko Tatsumi, John Mahara (NIHON CINEMA)

SEX PROHIBITION IN JAPAN – TRADE IN WOMEN aka NIHON GOKINSEI – NYONIN BAIBAI aka PROHIBITED IN JAPAN – FEMALE TRAFFICKING 1977 60 min. DIR. Koji Wakamatsu w/ Mimi Sawaki (SHINTOHO)

SEXY FEMALE BEAST aka SEKKUUSU NO ONNA KEDA-MONO 1968 DIR. Kinya Ogawa w/ Akemi Nijo, Kaoru Nakahara (OKURA Eiga)

Rival Female Yakuza - 28 Passions

RIVAL FEMALE YAKUZA – 28 PASSIONS aka KYO ONNA GOKUDO – SHIKIDO NIJU-HACHI-NIN SHU 1969 DIR. Yuki Takeda w/ Rumi Tama, Miki Hayashi, Noriko Tatsumi, Kaoru Miya (ROPPO Eiga)

Sexy Female Beast

Shinjuku Mad

SHINJUKU MAD aka SHINJUKU
MADDO 1970 66 min. **DIR.** Koji
Wakamatsu **w/** Toshiyuki Tanigawa,
Ryushiro Yoshimura
Dissatisfied with the official story and
the fact that the police have decided
to drop the case, a middle-aged man
comes from a rural town to Tokyo's
Shinjuku district to investigate his
son's murder. He finally encounters
the youth gang responsible, a kind
of hedonistic, anarchic *bosozoku*
bunch hiding behind cries of revolution for its own sake to excuse their
animalistic behavior and do-anything-

for-a-kick lifestyle. (WAKAMATSU
Productions) * * *

Soft Drizzling Rain

SOFT DRIZZLING RAIN aka
YAWA HADA SHIGURE 1967 **DIR.**
Ryo Hida **SCR.** Oniroku Dan **PHOTO**
COLOR ('SCOPE?): Noboru (Minoru?)
Funabashi **w/** Miki Hayashi
(YAMABE Productions)

SPECIAL aka SUUPESHURU
1967 **DIR.** Koji Seki **PHOTO B&W/**
COLOR: Yuji Go **w/** Shin Nanaoka,
Naomi Tani, Akihiko Kanbara, Koji
Satomi, Noriko Tatsumi
A black market *tekiya* and his girl-
friend arrive in a hot springs resort,
hoping to fleece the local citizens, but
they get the tables turned on them.
(SHIN NIHON Eiga/KOKUEI)

TREMBLING WHITE BREASTS
aka SHIROI CHIBUSA NO SEN-
RITSU 1970 71 min. **DIR.** Kinya
Ogawa **w/** Noriko Tatsumi
(MILLION Film)

Trembling White Breasts

TRUE ACCOUNT OF A TAMAGO PORTER – KILLING SPREE AT METROPOLITAN POLICE HQ aka JITSUROKU TAMAGO UMPANNIN – KEISHICHO NA-GURIKOMI 1976 68 min. DIR./ PHOTO.: Kaneto Hijikata SCR. Yojiro Nagashima MUSIC: Minokuni Yasushi w/ Yoichi (Hirokazu?) Iijina, Osamu Mihashi, Oshi (Yushi?) Watanabe, Mariko Yamaguchi Oddball indie film (shot in 16mm) apparently giving a realistic account of a true-life event.

VIOLENCE WITHOUT REASON aka GENDAI SEI HANZAI ZEK-KYO HEN – RIYUNAKI BOKO aka MODERN SEX CRIMES – FIERCE SCREAMS, GRATUITOUS VIOLENCE 1969 72 min. DIR. Koji Wakamatsu w/ Hiroshi Muraoka, Kazuya Jo, Toshimasa Sakaguchi Three slacker students, overcome with boredom (they constantly listen to a 45 of Ken Takakura singing the theme song for the ABSHIRI PRIS-ON series!) and frustration, decide to go on a rampage. They sexually abuse a couple on a lonely beach, then rape one of their own female friends from high school, claiming her to be haughty. Their own lack of spine, their defeatism and delusional, misogynist ideas about the opposite gender spur their conviction that taking sex whenever they want it seems to be the only power they have in the world. They track down a nude model whom they idolize and are stunned when she is nice to them, inviting them in for a drink. They get up the nerve to tell her they all really want to sleep with her and are once more astonished when she happily agrees. But midway through their escapades, a couple of her yakuza boyfriends enter, thrash the students and send them packing. As the next few days tick by, two of the boys commit suicide (both off-screen). Wakamatsu's most effective use of deadpan humor comes when two police detectives ask the surviving, glasses-wearing nebbish if they can have permission to report that the boys killed themselves because of the insane pressures of an overly-capitalist society! Going home, the dejected boy is jostled by a fleeing thief, who drops his gun. The boy picks it up just as a pursuing cop rounds the corner. The boy refuses to drop the revolver when the cop orders him to, instead cocking the trigger, and both die as they fire at each other. End. * * 1/2 (WAKAMATSU Productions)

Violent Virgin

VIOLENT VIRGIN aka SHOJO GEBA GEBA 1969 67 min. Dir. Koji Wakamatsu Scr. Izuru Deguchi w/ Eri Ashikawa, Toshiyuki Tanigawa   A stark, feverish nightmare as two lovers are driven into the barren countryside by partying yakuza and tormented. The woman of the pair had been the boss's lover and had dared to be unfaithful. For this unpardonable sin, she is crucified while her terrified beau is thrown in a tent at the foot of the cross and forced to have sex with various whores/gun molls. Finally seizing an opportunity,

he strangles one of them, takes her slip as clothing since he is nude and slips under the back tentflap to make his escape down an obscured gulley. By the time his hoodlum captors realize he is gone, he is nearly a mile away, asleep from exhaustion and having bad dreams about his situation. Soon after he awakens, he manages to return and somehow destroy his tormentors but his girl has already been fatally wounded from afar by a highpowered rifle set up by the jealous, cuckolded boss. Wakamatsu uses gritty black and white cinematography punctuated in the last third of the film with both full color and tinted sequences to slam home the nihilistic narrative's full surrealistic impact.
* * * 1/2 (WAKAMATSU Productions)

Violent Virgin

Yakuza Geisha

YAKUZA GEISHA 1965 Dir. Kyoko Ogimachi w/ Miharu Shima, Kaoru Miya, Yoko Saegusa (CENTURY Eiga-sha)

Chris D. is also author of the novels *NO EVIL STAR, MOTHER'S WORRY, SHALLOW WATER* and the collection *DRAGON WHEEL SPLENDOR AND OTHER LOVE STORIES OF VIOLENCE AND DREAD*, all from Poison Fang Books. His anthology *A MINUTE TO PRAY, A SECOND TO DIE*, a 500 page collection of selected short stories, excerpts from novels and scores of dream journal entries, as well as all of his poetry and song lyrics, was published in December 2009. His non-fiction *OUTLAW MASTERS OF JAPANESE FILM* was published by IB Tauris (distributed by Palgrave Macmillan in the USA) in 2005.

He saw release of his first feature film as director, *I PASS FOR HUMAN*, in 2004 (and its DVD release in 2006), and worked as a programmer at The American Cinematheque in Hollywood, California from 1999-2009.

Chris D. is also known as the singer/songwriter of the bands The Flesh Eaters, Divine Horsemen and Stone by Stone. He was an A&R rep and in-house producer at Slash Records/Ruby Records from 1980-1984.

Upcoming books include the novels *VOLCANO GIRLS, TIGHTROPE ON FIRE* and *TATTOOED BLOOD*, from Poison Fang Books.

INDEX
of Most Well-Known Films
and Films Receiving * * * 1/2 or * * * * Rating

Selected Bibliography

Anderson, Joseph L. & Richie, Donald, **The Japanese Film – Art and Industry** (Expanded Edition), Princeton, NJ, Princeton University Press, 1982

Bock, Audie, **Japanese Film Directors**, Tokyo/New York, Kodansha International, 1978, 1988

Desser, David, **Eros Plus Massacre – An Introduction to Japanese New Wave Cinema**, Bloomington, Indiana, Indiana University Press, 1988

Fukasaku, Kinji & Yamane, Sadao, **Eiga Kantoku Fukasaku Kinji**, Tokyo, Waizu Shuppan, 2003

Galbraith IV, Stuart, **The Emperor and the Wolf**, New York, Faber & Faber, 2002

Galloway, Patrick, **Warring Clans, Flashing Blades: A Samurai Film Companion**, Stone Bridge Press, , 2009

Hunter, Jack, **Eros in Hell – Sex, Blood and Madness in Japanese Cinema**, (Creation Cinema Collection, Vol. 9), London, Creation Books International, 1998

Ishii, Teruo & Fukuma, Kenji, **Ishii Teruo Eiga Oni**, Tokyo, Waizu Shuppan, 1992

Kato, Tai & Kato, Sakae, **Kato Tai Eiga Bana**, Tokyo, Waizu Shuppan, 1996

Nachi, Shiro & Shigeto, Toshiyuki, **Yokashi Okura Shintoho**, Tokyo, Waizu Shuppan, 2001

Nozawa, Kazuma, **Nikkatsu 1954 – 1971**, Tokyo, Waizu Shuppan, 2000

Sato, Tadao, **Currents In Japanese Cinema**, (translated by Gregory Barrett), New York, Kodansha International, 1987

Schilling, Mark, **No Borders, No Limits: Nikkatsu Action Cinema**, London, Fab Press, 2007

Sharp, Jasper, **Behind the Pink Curtain: The Complete History of Japanese Sex Cinema**, London, Fab Press, 2008

Shindo, Kaneto & Sato, Tadao & Miyamoto, Haruo & Hachimori, Minoru, **Nihon Eiga 100 Nen – Miso No Collection**, Tokyo, Asahi Graph, 1995

Silver, Alain, **The Samurai Film**, Woodstock, NY, Overlook Press, 1977

Sugisaku, Jtaro & Uechi, Takeshi, **Jinginaki Tatakai**, Tokyo, Tokuma, 1998

Sugisaku, Jtaro & Uechi, Takeshi, **Pinky Violence – Toei's Bad Girl Films**, Tokyo, Tokuma, 1999

Suzuki, Kensuke, **Jigoku de YoiHai Nakagawa Nobuo – Kaidan-Kyofu Eiga**, Tokyo, Waizu Shuppan, 2000

Tayama, Rikiya, **Gendai Nihon Eiga No Kantokutachi**, Tokyo, Shakai Shisosha, 1991

Ueno, Koshi, **Suzuki Seijun – Zen Eiga**, Tokyo, 1986

Yamada, Seiji, **Legend Of Mitsugu Okura and Japanese Horror Film**, Tokyo, Movie Treasures, 1997

Yamane, Sadao et. al., **Kihachi – Fubito No Aru Chizan – Okamoto Kihachi Eiga Kantoku**, Tokyo, Toho, 1992

The life of recovering addict and Namvet Milo unravels when ex-CIA friend Dave goes off the deep end. Not only is Dave the heist man whacking NYC drug dealers, he's also hatching a scheme to plunder mob boss Nunzio's art treasures pilfered in WWII. Complicating matters, Yuen, an ex-Viet Cong with a grudge against Milo and Dave, arrives in New York.

"A healthy authorial sense of curiosity and generosity lends weight to No Evil Star's intersecting lives, where Chris D. ably traces out the contours of human torment in a manner recalling American films of the 1970s."
– Grace Krilanovich, author of THE ORANGE EATS CREEPS

AVAILABLE NOW FROM POISON FANG BOOKS

In Chris D.'s title novella, brilliant, alcoholic Anne, unable to succeed in downtown L.A.'s arts community, helps a Japanese-American girl escape forced prostitution, only to ignite a string of violent deaths. In "The Glider," a British policewoman falls in-love with a serial killer near the white cliffs of Dover; plus five more twisted love tales.

"...seems to shimmer with menace... with DRAGON WHEEL SPLENDOR, the great Chris D should finally find the audience he deserves...a book that can kill the voices in your head - or make you love them."
– Jerry Stahl, author of PLAINCLOTHES NAKED, PAINKILLERS and PERMANENT MIDNIGHT

DRAGON WHEEL SPLENDOR
and Other Love Stories of Violence and Dread
by Chris D.

"...shimmers with menace...the great Chris D. should finally find the audience he deserves..."
-- Jerry Stahl

The year is 1987, and outlaw Ray Diamond's mother is the queenpin of crime in Mystic, GA. After his Navy discharge, Ray knocks over a mob-connected El Paso liquor store, not counting on Eli, the owner's psycho son, dogging his trail. Back home in Mystic, Ray's girl, Connie Eustace, resorts to stripping at Mama Lorna's club to make ends meet. Witness to a murder by the local sheriff, she goes on a drug-and-drink bender, jumping from the frying pain into the fire.

"...a crazy dive into a universe populated largely by monsters...a classic update of the Gold Medal/Lion Library loser noir tradition. Great work..."
– Byron Coley, writer for WIRE magazine, author of C'EST LA GUERRE: EARLY WRITINGS 1978-1983

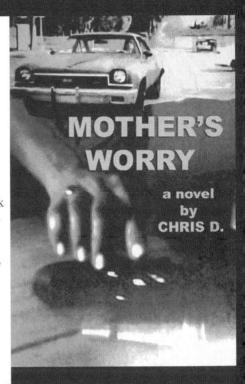

MOTHER'S WORRY

a novel by CHRIS D.

FROM POISON FANG BOOKS AVAILABLE NOW

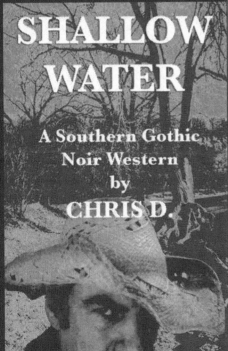

SHALLOW WATER

A Southern Gothic Noir Western by CHRIS D.

Post-Civil War, bitter rebel veteran and bounty hunter, Santo Brady, drifts through the Deep South. When he rescues halfbreed Indian prostitute, Lucy Damien, from one backwater town, he has the whole world fall in on his head. They embark on a freight-train-hopping odyssey to New Orleans, unaware that Lucy's rich white father and homicidal brother are tracking them. A tragic tall tale plunging head-first into a wild heart of darkness.

"One sinister serpent of a story, an old Republic Pictures western serial scripted by James M. Cain and reimagined by Sam Peckinpah. I loved it."
– Eddie Muller, author of THE DISTANCE and SHADOW BOXER

Two New Novels from Chris D.
Available October 2013

Half-sisters, schoolteacher Mona and junkie punk rocker Terri, are uneasy roommates while taking care of their sick mother. When their boyfriends, cop Johnny Cullen and killer Merle Chambers, clash due to labor struggles in their small town of Devil's River, the two women are pulled into the fray. To make matters worse, jealous female sheriff, Billie Travers, decides Mona is intruding on her faltering love affair, and quiet small town life amps up into an apocalyptic nightmare of uncontrollable violence and destruction.

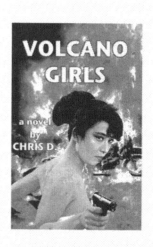

Corrupt female police detective, Frankie Powers, is treading water in her small desert hometown of Sweet Home, California. Burned-out and emotionally numb after losing her husband and child in a mysterious fire ten years before, her conscience is reawakened when her affair with a Bakersfield narc brings new facts to light. Frankie's mob boss uncle, Jack Richman, has been kidnapping under-age girls for his Vegas prostitution syndicate; he's also been victimizing his own teen daughters, Frankie's twin bad girl cousins, Valerie and Vanessa. Soon Frankie finds herself singlehandedly fighting tooth-and-nail against not only wicked uncle Jack but also his dominatrix wife, Marilyn and their degenerate hitman, Cal Nero. Can a lone shewolf survive against the bloodthirsty pack?

from Poison Fang Books

Made in the USA
San Bernardino, CA
15 November 2018